BRITISH WRITERS

BRITISH WRITERS

GEORGE STADE

SARAH HANNAH GOLDSTEIN

Editors

SUPPLEMENT V

CHARLES SCRIBNER'S SONS

NEW YORK

Charles Scribner's Sons
1633 Broadway, 7th floor
New York, New York 10019

Library of Congress Cataloging-in-Publication Data
British writers: Supplement V / George Stade and Sarah Hannah Goldstein, editors.
   p.   cm.
Includes bibliographical references and cumulative index.
ISBN 0-684-19593-3 (alk. paper: full set).—ISBN 0-684-80615-0 (alk. paper)
1. English literature—History and criticism.   2. English literature—Bio-bibliography.
2. Authors, English—Biography.   I. Stade, George.   II. Goldstein, Sarah Hannah.
PR85.B688, Suppl. 5
820.9—dc20
[B]   95-38155
                                                                      CIP

3 5 7 9 11 13 15 17 19 20 18 16 14 12 10 8 6 4 2

Printed in the United States of America

The paper used in this publication meets the requirements of ANSI/NISO Z39.48-1992 (Permanence of Paper).

Acknowledgments

Acknowledgment is gratefully made to those publishers and
individuals who permitted the use of the following materials in copyright:

EAVAN BOLAND   From *An Origin Like Water: Collected Poems 1967–1987*. Copyright © 1996 by Eavan Boland. Excerpt from "That the Science of Cartography is Limited" in *In A Time of Violence*. Copyright © 1994 by Eavan Boland. Excerpt from *Object Lessons: The Life of the Woman and the Poet in Our Time*. Copyright © 1995 by Eavan Boland. Excerpt from *Outside History: Selected Poems 1980–1990* by Eavan Boland. Copyright © 1990 by Eavan Boland. Used by permission of W. W. Norton & Company, Inc. and of Carcanet Press Limited.

ANITA DESAI   From "Against the Current: An Interview with Anita Desai" by Corinne Demas Bliss reprinted from *The Massachusetts Review*, copyright © 1988 The Massachusetts Review Inc. From *Interview with Writers of the Post-Colonial World*, eds. Feroza Jussawalla & Reed Way Dasenrock (1992). Used by permission of the publisher, the University Press of Mississippi.

RODDY DOYLE   Excerpt from *Paddy Clarke Ha Ha Ha*. Copyright © 1993 by Roddy Doyle. Published in Great Britain by Martin Secker & Warburg. From *The Snapper*. Copyright © 1990 by Roddy Doyle. Published in Great Britain by Martin Secker & Warburg. From *The Van*. Copyright © 1991 by Roddy Doyle. Published in Great Britain by Martin Secker & Warburg. From *The Woman Who Walked Into Doors*. Copyright © 1996 by Roddy Doyle. Published in Great Britain by Jonathan Cape. Excerpts from "Brownbread," "War," "Introduction," in *Brownbread and War*. Copyright © 1992 by Roddy Doyle. Published in Great Britain by Martin Secker & Warburg. Used by permission of Viking Penguin, a division of Penguin Putnam Inc. and Random House UK Ltd. From *The Commitments*. Copyright © 1987 by Roddy Doyle. Used by permission of Vintage Books, a division of Random House, Inc. and Random House UK Ltd.

PENELOPE FITZGERALD   From *Contemporary Authors Autobiography Series*, vol. 10, 1989. Copyright © Gale Research, Inc. Used by permission of The Gale Group.

TONY HARRISON   Excerpts from "Thomas Campy and the Copernican System" and "On Not Being Milton," in *Selected Poems*. Copyright © 1987 by Tony Harrison. Reprinted by permission of Random House, Inc. and Penguin Books Ltd.

GEOFFREY HILL   From *New and Collected Poems 1952–1992*. Copyright © 1994 by Geoffrey Hill. From *Canaan*. Copyright © 1996 by Geoffrey Hill. Used by permission of Houghton Mifflin Co. and Penguin Books Ltd. All rights reserved. From "Kermvoran" and "Tenebrae" from *Poems of Paul Celan*, translated by Michael Hamburger. Copyright © 1995 by Michael Hamburger. Used by permission of Pearsea Books, Inc. and Anvil Poetry Press. German version from *Die Niemandsrose*, © S. Fischer Verlag, Frankfurt am Main, 1963. Excerpts from "Blessed Arc" in *Basic Verities* by Charles Peguy, translated by Anne and Julian Green. Copyright © 1943 by Pantheon Books, Inc. Used by permission of Pantheon Books, a division of Random House, Inc. and Taylor & Francis Books Ltd.

ELIZABETH JENNINGS   From *Collected Poems*, published by Carcanet. From *The Secret Brother*, published by Macmillan. From an autobiographical ms. in Special Collections at the University of Delaware Library, Newark, Del. Used by permission of David Higham Associates. From "Bag Lady of the Sonnets" by Candida Crew in *The Times Saturday Review*, 23 November 1991, © Times Newspapers Ltd. Used by permission.

RUTH PRAWER JHABVALA   From "Disinheritance" first published in *Blackwood's* magazine, © Ruth Prawer Jhabvala, by permission of Harriet Wasserman Literary Agency Inc. From *Out of India: Selected Stories*. Copyright © 1976, 1986 by Ruth Prawer Jhabvala. Used by permission of William Morrow & Co., Inc. and John Murray (publishers) Ltd.

JAMES KELMAN   From *How Late it Was, How Late*. Copyright © 1994 by James Kelman. Used by permission of W.W. Norton & Co., Inc. and Random House UK Ltd. "Interview with James Kelman" by Kirsty McNeill in *Chapman*, 56, Summer 1989, 1-9, used by permission. "James Kelman Interviewed" used by kind permission of Polygon on behalf of Duncan McLean. First published in *Nothing Is Altogether Trivial* (1995), ed. by Murdo Macdonald.

MEDBH MCGUCKIAN   From *The Flower Master* and *Venus and the Rain* used by kind permission of the author and Gallery Press. From *Shelmalier, Marconi's Cottage, On Ballycastle Beach*, and *Captain Lavender* used by kind permission of the author, Gallery Press, and Wake Forest University Press. From "Comhra: Medbh McGuckian and Naula Ni Dhomnaill" by Laura O'Connor used by permission of the Southern Review.

A. A. MILNE   From *Winnie-the-Pooh* by A. A. Milne, illustrated by E. H. Shepard. Copyright 1926 by E. P. Dutton, renewed © 1954 by A. A. Milne. From *The House at Pooh Corner* by A. A. Milne, illustrated by E. H. Shepard. Copyright 1928 by E. P.

ACKNOWLEDGMENTS

Dutton, renewed © 1956 by A. A. Milne. "Disobedience," "Market Square," "Spring Morning," "Vespers" by A. A. Milne from *When We Were Very Young* by A. A. Milne, illustrated by E. H. Shepard. Copyright 1924 by E. P. Dutton, renewed © 1952 by A. A. Milne. "Busy," "Cherry Stones," "The End," "The Friend," "Solitude" by A. A. Milne from *Now We Are Six* by A. A. Milne, illustrated by E. H. Shepard. Copyright 1927 by E. P. Dutton, renewed © 1955 by A. A. Milne. All titles © A. A. Milne by the Berne Convention. Used by permission of Dutton's Children's Books, a division of Penguin Putnam Inc. and Methuen, an imprint of Egmont Children's Books Ltd., London.

RICHARD MURPHY From "Why Has Narrative Poetry Failed." Copyright © 1951 by Richard Murphy. From *The Mirror Wall*. Copyright © 1989 by Richard Murphy. From *The Price of Stone*. Copyright © 1985 by Richard Murphy. From "The Pleasure Ground." Copyright © 1964 by Richard Murphy. From "The God Who Eats Corn." Copyright © 1968 by Richard Murphy. Used by permission of Gillon Aitken Associates Ltd.

EDNA O'BRIEN From *The Country Girls Trilogy and Epilogue*. Copyright © 1986 by Edna O'Brien. From *Down By The River*. Copyright © 1996 by Edna O'Brien. From *House of Splendid Isolation*. Copyright © 1994 by Edna O'Brien. Used by permission of Farrar, Strauss & Giraux, Inc. From "Remorse for Intemperate Speech" excerpted with permission of Simon & Schuster, Inc. and A. P. Watt Ltd. on behalf of Michael B. Yeats from *The Poems of W. B. Yeats: A New Edition*, ed. by Richard J. Finneran. Copyright 1993 by Macmillan Publishing Co.; copyright renewed © 1961 by Bertha Georgia Yeats.

BEN OKRI From *The Famished Road*. Copyright © 1991 by Ben Okri. A Nan A. Talese Book. reprinted by permission of Doubleday, a division of Bantam Doubleday Dell Publishing Group, Inc. Used by permission of Doubleday, a division of Random House, Inc. From *Stars of the New Curfew*. Copyright © 1988 by Ben Okri. Used by permission of Viking Penguin, a division of Penguin Putnam Inc. From *An African Elegy* Published in Great Britain by J. Cape. Reprinted by permission of Random House UK Ltd. From *Incidents at the Shrine*. Published in Great Britain by J. Cape. Reprinted by permission of Random House UK Ltd. From "Azaro and the Spirits" from the *Washington Post*, October 3, 1993. Copyright © K. Anthony Appiah. By permission of the author. From the article "Fantasies Born in the Ghetto," by Nicholas Shakespeare from *The Times*, 24 July, 1986. Copyright © Times Newspapers Limited, London 1986. From "CA Interview" by Jean Ross from *Contemporary Authors Autobiography Series*, vol. 138, 1993. Copyright © 1993 by Gale Research, Inc.

WILL SELF From *The Quantity Theory of Insanity* and *My Idea of Fun*. Used by permission of Grove/Atlantic Inc. and Bloomsbury Publishing.

ALAN SILLITOE From *Saturday Night and Sunday Morning*. Copyright © 1958 by Alan Sillitoe. Used by permission of Alfred A. Knopf, Inc., and HarperCollins Publishers.

GRAHAM SWIFT From *Learning to Swim and Other Stories* and from *Waterland*. Used by permission of A. P. Watt Ltd. on behalf of the author.

Editorial and Production Staff

Contents

Introduction

The twenty-five articles in *British Writers, Supplement V* survey writers who for one reason or another are not represented in either the initial seven volumes of *British Writers* (1979–1984) or in supplements I (1987), II (1992), III (1996), or IV (1997). In Supplement V, as in its immediate predecessor, all but a couple of the writers came of age following World War II; they are not only moderns, but contemporaries, their careers still evolving.

From its inception, *British Writers* was designed as a companion to the ongoing *American Writers* (1974–). These two sets were followed by *Ancient Writers: Greece and Rome* (2 vols., 1982), by *European Writers* (14 vols., 1983–1991) and its three-volume redaction, *European Writers* (1992), by *Latin American Writers* (3 vols., 1989), and by *African Writers* (2 vols., 1996). These volumes constitute, so far, the Scribner World Literature series. And they are allied to works such as *Science Fiction Writers* (1982), *Supernatural Fiction Writers* (2 vols., 1985), *William Shakespeare: His World, His Work, His Influence* (3 vols., 1985), *Writers for Children* (1988), *The Books of the Bible* (1989), *Modern American Women Writers* (1991), *African-American Writers* (1991), and *American Nature Writers* (2 vols., 1996).

Each article in *British Writers, Supplement V* is devoted to a single writer; each is at least twelve thousand words long. Each article presents an account of the writer's works, life, and relations to his or her time, place, and literary context. But from article to article the emphasis varies, just as from writer to writer the relative interest of the life, the reading, the situation varies. Whatever the relative emphasis, the works come first; other matters are taken up to the extent that they form or inform the works.

In style and scope, the articles are expressly written for that mythical but inspiring figure, the general reader, rather than for the specialist. They are written, that is, for high school, college, and graduate students, as well as for their teachers; for librarians and editors; for reviewers, scholars, and critics; for literary browsers; for anyone who wants to repair an erosion or gap in his or her reservoir of knowledge. The article that can at once inform the general reader and stimulate the specialist will have achieved its goal.

Above all, and in consultation with librarians, the editors asked themselves whether a writer under consideration for inclusion was someone that English-speaking readers were likely to look up—upon publication of Supplement V or twenty years later. The editors therefore took into account a shift in reader interest and critical activity and classroom attention that has not yet worked itself out. That shift, which is often thought of as a process of decanonization, includes a weakening of the distinction between popular literature and the other kind, whatever we call it. Thus earlier supplements include articles on such "popular" writers as Agatha Christie, John le Carré, Bram Stoker, H. Rider Haggard, Dorothy L. Sayers, Daphne du Maurier, Eric Ambler, and P. D. James. Thus Supplement V includes articles on Patricia Highsmith and J. G. Ballard.

In accordance with a practice that evolved early in the series, not all the writers represented in Supplement V are "British" in one or another restricted sense of the word. Anita Desai, for example, was born in Mussoorie, India; Patricia Highsmith was born in the United States; Eavan Boland, Medbh McGuckian, and Thomas Kinsella are very much Irish. But their relation to British literary culture was continuous and formative, if sometimes adversarial; their work shows up most vividly for what it is against the background of that British literary culture it enlarges or contests. In any case, the editors felt that readers would want to look up Desai and Boland, for example, but could not do so elsewhere in articles like the ones that make up this volume. This last justification, however, could apply to all the articles in this volume: they are all about writers who are well worth looking up.

GEORGE STADE
SARAH HANNAH GOLDSTEIN

Chronology

1901–1910   Reign of King Edward VII

1901   William McKinley assassinated; Theodore Roosevelt succeeds to the presidency

First transatlantic wireless telegraph signal transmitted

Chekhov's *Three Sisters*

Freud's *Psychopathology of Everyday Life*

Rudyard Kipling's *Kim*

Thomas Mann's *Buddenbrooks*

Potter's *The Tale of Peter Rabbit*

Shaw's *Captain Brassbound's Conversion*

August Strindberg's *The Dance of Death*

1902   Barrie's *The Admirable Crichton*

Arnold Bennett's *Anna of the Five Towns*

Cézanne's *Le Lac d'Annecy*

Conrad's *Heart of Darkness*

Henry James's *The Wings of the Dove*

William James's *The Varieties of Religious Experience*

Kipling's *Just So Stories*

Maugham's *Mrs. Craddock*

Christina Stead born

Stevie Smith born

Times Literary Supplement begins publishing

1903   At its London congress the Russian Social Democratic Party divides into Mensheviks, led by Plekhanov, and Bolsheviks, led by Lenin

The treaty of Panama places the Canal Zone in U.S. hands for a nominal rent

Motor cars regulated in Britain to a 20-mile-per-hour limit

The Wright brothers make a successful flight in the United States

Burlington magazine founded

Samuel Butler's *The Way of All Flesh* published posthumously

Cyril Connolly born

George Gissing's *The Private Papers of Henry Ryecroft*

Thomas Hardy's *The Dynasts*

Henry James's *The Ambassadors*

Alan Paton born

Shaw's *Man and Superman*

Synge's *Riders to the Sea* produced in Dublin

Yeats's *In the Seven Woods* and *On Baile's Strand*

1904   Roosevelt elected president of the United States

Russo-Japanese war (1904–1905)

Construction of the Panama Canal begins

The ultraviolet lamp invented

The engineering firm of Rolls-Royce founded

Barrie's *Peter Pan* first performed

Cecil Day Lewis born

Chekhov's *The Cherry Orchard*

Conrad's *Nostromo*

Henry James's *The Golden Bowl*

Kipling's *Traffics and Discoveries*

Georges Rouault's *Head of a Tragic Clown*

G. M. Trevelyan's *England Under the Stuarts*

Puccini's *Madame Butterfly*

First Shaw-Granville Barker season at the Royal Court Theatre

The Abbey Theatre founded in Dublin

1905   Russian sailors on the battleship *Potemkin* mutiny

After riots and a general strike the czar concedes to demands by the Duma for legislative powers, a wider franchise, and civil liberties

Albert Einstein publishes his first theory of relativity

The Austin Motor Company founded

Bennett's *Tales of the Five Towns*

Claude Debussy's *La Mer*

E. M. Forster's *Where Angels Fear to Tread*

Henry Green born

Richard Strauss's *Salome*

H. G. Wells's *Kipps*

Oscar Wilde's *De Profundis*

CHRONOLOGY

1906 Liberals win a landslide victory in the British general election
The Trades Disputes Act legitimizes peaceful picketing in Britain
Captain Dreyfus rehabilitated in France
J. J. Thomson begins research on gamma rays
The U.S. Pure Food and Drug Act passed
Churchill's *Lord Randolph Churchill*
William Empson born
Galsworthy's *The Man of Property*
Kipling's *Puck of Pook's Hill*
Shaw's *The Doctor's Dilemma*
Yeats's *Poems 1899–1905*

1907 Exhibition of cubist paintings in Paris
Henry Adams' *The Education of Henry Adams*
Henri Bergson's *Creative Evolution*
Conrad's *The Secret Agent*
Daphne du Maurier born
Forster's *The Longest Journey*
Christopher Fry born
André Gide's *La Porte étroite*
Shaw's *John Bull's Other Island* and *Major Barbara*
Synge's *The Playboy of the Western World*
Trevelyan's *Garibaldi's Defence of the Roman Republic*

1908 Herbert Asquith becomes prime minister
David Lloyd George becomes chancellor of the exchequer
William Howard Taft elected president of the United States
The Young Turks seize power in Istanbul
Henry Ford's Model T car produced
Bennett's *The Old Wives' Tale*
Pierre Bonnard's *Nude Against the Light*
Georges Braque's *House at L'Estaque*
Chesterton's *The Man Who Was Thursday*
Jacob Epstein's *Figures* erected in London
Forster's *A Room with a View*
Anatole France's *L'Ile des Pingouins*
Henri Matisse's *Bonheur de Vivre*
Elgar's First Symphony
Ford Madox Ford founds the *English Review*

1909 The Young Turks depose Sultan Abdul Hamid
The Anglo-Persian Oil Company formed
Louis Bleriot crosses the English Channel from France by monoplane
Admiral Robert Peary reaches the North Pole
Freud lectures at Clark University (Worcester, Mass.) on psychoanalysis
Serge Diaghilev's Ballets Russes opens in Paris
Galsworthy's *Strife*
Hardy's *Time's Laughingstocks*
Eric Ambler born
Malcolm Lowry born
Claude Monet's *Water Lilies*
Stephen Spender born
Trevelyan's *Garibaldi and the Thousand*
Wells's *Tono-Bungay* first published (book form, 1909)

1910–1936 Reign of King George V

1910 The Liberals win the British general election
Marie Curie's *Treatise on Radiography*
Arthur Evans excavates Knossos
Edouard Manet and the first post-impressionist exhibition in London
Filippo Marinetti publishes "Manifesto of the Futurist Painters"
Norman Angell's *The Great Illusion*
Bennett's *Clayhanger*
Forster's *Howards End*
Galsworthy's *Justice* and *The Silver Box*
Kipling's *Rewards and Fairies*
Rimsky-Korsakov's *Le Coq d'or*
Stravinsky's *The Firebird*
Vaughan Williams' *A Sea Symphony*
Wells's *The History of Mr. Polly*
Wells's *The New Machiavelli* first published (in book form, 1911)

1911 Lloyd George introduces National Health Insurance Bill
Suffragette riots in Whitehall
Roald Amundsen reaches the South Pole
Bennett's *The Card*
Chagall's *Self Portrait with Seven Fingers*
Conrad's *Under Western Eyes*
D. H. Lawrence's *The White Peacock*
Katherine Mansfield's *In a German Pension*
Edward Marsh edits *Georgian Poetry*
George Moore's *Hail and Farewell* (1911–1914)
Flann O'Brien born
Strauss's *Der Rosenkavalier*
Stravinsky's *Petrouchka*

Trevelyan's *Garibaldi and the Making of Italy*

Wells's *The New Machiavelli*

Mahler's *Das Lied von der Erde*

1912 Woodrow Wilson elected president of the United States

SS *Titanic* sinks on its maiden voyage

Five million Americans go to the movies daily; London has four hundred movie theaters

Second post-impressionist exhibition in London

Bennett's and Edward Knoblock's *Milestones*

Constantin Brancusi's *Maiastra*

Wassily Kandinsky's *Black Lines*

D. H. Lawrence's *The Trespasser*

1913 Second Balkan War begins

Henry Ford pioneers factory assembly technique through conveyor belts

Epstein's *Tomb of Oscar Wilde*

New York Armory Show introduces modern art to the world

Alain Fournier's *Le Grand Meaulnes*

Freud's *Totem and Tabu*

D. H. Lawrence's *Sons and Lovers*

Mann's *Death in Venice*

Proust's *Du côté de chez Swann* (first volume of *A la recherche du temps perdu,* 1913–1922)

Barbara Pym born

Ravel's *Daphnis and Chloé*

1914 The Panama Canal opens (formal dedication on 12 July 1920)

Irish Home Rule Bill passed in the House of Commons

Archduke Franz Ferdinand assassinated at Sarajevo

World War I begins

Battles of the Marne, Masurian Lakes, and Falkland Islands

Joyce's *Dubliners*

Shaw's *Pygmalion* and *Androcles and the Lion*

Yeats's *Responsibilities*

Wyndham Lewis publishes *Blast* magazine and *The Vorticist Manifesto*

1915 The Dardanelles campaign begins

Britain and Germany begin naval and submarine blockades

The *Lusitania* is sunk

Hugo Junkers manufactures the first fighter aircraft

Poison gas used for the first time

First Zeppelin raid in London

Brooke's *1914: Five Sonnets*

Norman Douglas' *Old Calabria*

D. W. Griffith's *The Birth of a Nation*

Gustav Holst's *The Planets*

D. H. Lawrence's *The Rainbow*

Wyndham Lewis's *The Crowd*

Maugham's *Of Human Bondage*

Pablo Picasso's *Harlequin*

Sibelius' Fifth Symphony

1916 Evacuation of Gallipoli and the Dardanelles

Battles of the Somme, Jutland, and Verdun

Britain introduces conscription

The Easter Rebellion in Dublin

Asquith resigns and David Lloyd George becomes prime minister

The Sykes-Picot agreement on the partition of Turkey

First military tanks used

Wilson reelected president of the United States

Henri Barbusse's *Le Feu*

Griffith's *Intolerance*

Penelope Fitzgerald born

Roald Dahl born

Joyce's *Portrait of the Artist as a Young Man*

Jung's *Psychology of the Unconscious*

Moore's *The Brook Kerith*

Edith Sitwell edits *Wheels* (1916–1921)

Wells's *Mr. Britling Sees It Through*

1917 United States enters World War I

Czar Nicholas II abdicates

The Balfour Declaration on a Jewish national home in Palestine

The Bolshevik Revolution

Georges Clemenceau elected prime minister of France

Lenin appointed chief commissar; Trotsky appointed minister of foreign affairs

Conrad's *The Shadow-Line*

Douglas' *South Wind*

Eliot's *Prufrock and Other Observations*

Modigliani's *Nude with Necklace*

Sassoon's *The Old Huntsman*

Prokofiev's *Classical Symphony*

Yeats's *The Wild Swans at Coole*

CHRONOLOGY

1918   Wilson puts forward Fourteen Points for World Peace

Central Powers and Russia sign the Treaty of Brest-Litovsk

Execution of Czar Nicholas II and his family

Kaiser Wilhelm II abdicates

The Armistice signed

Women granted the vote at age thirty in Britain

Rupert Brooke's *Collected Poems*

Gerard Manley Hopkins' *Poems*

Joyce's *Exiles*

Wyndham Lewis' *Tarr*

Sassoon's *Counter-Attack*

Oswald Spengler's *The Decline of the West*

Strachey's *Eminent Victorians*

Béla Bartók's *Bluebeard's Castle*

Charlie Chaplin's *Shoulder Arms*

1919   The Versailles Peace Treaty signed

J. W. Alcock and A. W. Brown make first transatlantic flight

Ross Smith flies from London to Australia

National Socialist party founded in Germany

Benito Mussolini founds the Fascist party in Italy

Sinn Fein Congress adopts declaration of independence in Dublin

Eamon De Valera elected president of Sinn Fein party

Communist Third International founded

Lady Astor elected first woman Member of Parliament

Prohibition in the United States

John Maynard Keynes's *The Economic Consequences of the Peace*

Eliot's *Poems*

Maugham's *The Moon and Sixpence*

Shaw's *Heartbreak House*

The Bauhaus school of design; building, and crafts founded by Walter Gropius

Amedeo Modigliani's *Self-Portrait*

1920   The League of Nations established

Warren G. Harding elected president of the United States

Senate votes against joining the League and rejects the Treaty of Versailles

The Nineteenth Amendment gives women the right to vote in the United States

White Russian forces of Denikin and Kolchak defeated by the Bolsheviks

P. D. James born

Karel Čapek's *R.U.R.*

Galsworthy's *In Chancery* and *The Skin Game*

Sinclair Lewis' *Main Street*

Katherine Mansfield's *Bliss*

Matisse's *Odalisques* (1920–1925)

Ezra Pound's *Hugh Selwyn Mauberly*

Paul Valéry's *Le Cimetière Marin*

Yeats's *Michael Robartes and the Dancer*

1921   Britain signs peace with Ireland

First medium-wave radio broadcast in the United States

The British Broadcasting Corporation founded

Braque's *Still Life with Guitar*

Chaplin's *The Kid*

Aldous Huxley's *Crome Yellow*

Paul Klee's *The Fish*

Brian Harris born

Patricia Highsmith born

D. H. Lawrence's *Women in Love*

John McTaggart's *The Nature of Existence* (vol. 1)

George Moore's *Héloïse and Abélard*

Eugene O'Neill's *The Emperor Jones*

Luigi Pirandello's *Six Characters in Search of an Author*

Shaw's *Back to Methuselah*

Strachey's *Queen Victoria*

1922   Lloyd George's Coalition government succeeded by Bonar Law's Conservative government

Benito Mussolini marches on Rome and forms a government

William Cosgrave elected president of the Irish Free State

The BBC begins broadcasting in London

Lord Carnarvon and Howard Carter discover Tutankhamen's tomb

The PEN club founded in London

The *Criterion* founded with T. S. Eliot as editor

Kingsley Amis born

Eliot's *The Waste Land*

A. E. Housman's *Last Poems*

Joyce's *Ulysses*

D. H. Lawrence's *Aaron's Rod* and *England, My England*

Sinclair Lewis' *Babbitt*

O'Neill's *Anna Christie*
Pirandello's *Henry IV*
Edith Sitwell's *Façade*
Virginia Woolf's *Jacob's Room*
Yeats's *The Trembling of the Veil*

1923 The Union of Soviet Socialist Republics established
French and Belgian troops occupy the Ruhr in consequence of Germany's failure to pay reparations
Mustafa Kemal (Ataturk) proclaims Turkey a republic and is elected president
Warren G. Harding dies; Calvin Coolidge becomes president
Stanley Baldwin succeeds Bonar Law as prime minister
Adolf Hitler's attempted coup in Munich fails
Time magazine begins publishing
E. N. da C. Andrade's *The Structure of the Atom*
Brendan Behan born
Christine Brooke-Rose born
Bennett's *Riceyman Steps*
Churchill's *The World Crisis* (1923–1927)
J. E. Flecker's *Hassan* produced
Nadine Gordimer born
Paul Klee's *Magic Theatre*
D. H. Lawrence's *Kangaroo*
Rainer Maria Rilke's *Duino Elegies* and *Sonnets to Orpheus*
Sibelius' Sixth Symphony
Picasso's *Seated Woman*
William Walton's *Façade*

1924 Ramsay MacDonald forms first Labour government, loses general election, and is succeeded by Stanley Baldwin
Calvin Coolidge elected president of the United States
Noël Coward's *The Vortex*
Forster's *A Passage to India*
Mann's *The Magic Mountain*
Shaw's *St. Joan*

1925 Reza Khan becomes shah of Iran
First surrealist exhibition held in Paris
Alban Berg's *Wozzeck*
Chaplin's *The Gold Rush*
John Dos Passos' *Manhattan Transfer*
Theodore Dreiser's *An American Tragedy*
Sergei Eisenstein's *Battleship Potemkin*
F. Scott Fitzgerald's *The Great Gatsby*
André Gide's *Les Faux Monnayeurs*

Hardy's *Human Shows and Far Phantasies*
Aldous Huxley's *Those Barren Leaves*
Kafka's *The Trial*
Sean O'Casey's *Juno and the Paycock*
Virginia Woolf's *Mrs. Dalloway* and *The Common Reader*
Brancusi's *Bird in Space*
Shostakovich's First Symphony
Sibelius' *Tapiola*
Elizabeth Jennings born

1926 Ford's *A Man Could Stand Up*
Gide's *Si le grain ne meurt*
Hemingway's *The Sun also Rises*
Kafka's *The Castle*
D. H. Lawrence's *The Plumed Serpent*
T. E. Lawrence's *Seven Pillars of Wisdom* privately circulated
Maugham's *The Casuarina Tree*
O'Casey's *The Plough and the Stars*
Puccini's *Turandot*
John Berger born

1927 General Chiang Kai-shek becomes prime minister in China
Trotsky expelled by the Communist Party as a deviationist; Stalin becomes leader of the party and dictator of the Soviet Union
Charles Lindbergh flies from New York to Paris
Ruth Prawer Jhabvala born
Richard Murphy born
J. W. Dunne's *An Experiment with Time*
Freud's *Autobiography* translated into English
Albert Giacometti's *Observing Head*
Ernest Hemingway's *Men Without Women*
Fritz Lang's *Metropolis*
Wyndham Lewis' *Time and Western Man*
F. W. Murnau's *Sunrise*
Proust's *Le Temps retrouvé* posthumously published
Stravinsky's *Oedipus Rex*
Virginia Woolf's *To the Lighthouse*

1928 The Kellogg-Briand Pact, outlawing war and providing for peaceful settlement of disputes, signed in Paris by sixty-two nations, including the Soviet Union
Herbert Hoover elected president of the United States
Women's suffrage granted at age twenty-one in Britain

Alexander Fleming discovers penicillin
Anita Brookner born
Thomas Kinsella born
Alan Sillitoe born
William Trevor born
Bertolt Brecht and Kurt Weill's *The Three-Penny Opera*
Eisenstein's *October*
Aldous Huxley's *Point Counter Point*
Christopher Isherwood's *All the Conspirators*
D. H. Lawrence's *Lady Chatterley's Lover*
Wyndham Lewis' *The Childermass*
Matisse's *Seated Odalisque*
Munch's *Girl on a Sofa*
Shaw's *Intelligent Woman's Guide to Socialism*
Virginia Woolf's *Orlando*
Yeats's *The Tower*

1929   The Labour party wins British general election
Trotsky expelled from the Soviet Union
Museum of Modern Art opens in New York
Collapse of U.S. stock exchange begins world economic crisis
Brian Friel born
Thom Gunn born
Robert Bridges' *The Testament of Beauty*
William Faulkner's *The Sound and the Fury*
Robert Graves's *Goodbye to All That*
Hemingway's *A Farewell to Arms*
Ernst Junger's *The Storm of Steel*
Hugo von Hoffmansthal's *Poems*
Henry Moore's *Reclining Figure*
J. B. Priestley's *The Good Companions*
Erich Maria Remarque's *All Quiet on the Western Front*
Shaw's *The Applecart*
R. C. Sheriff's *Journey's End*
Edith Sitwell's *Gold Coast Customs*
Thomas Wolfe's *Look Homeward, Angel*
Virginia Woolf's *A Room of One's Own*
Yeats's *The Winding Stair*
Second surrealist manifesto; Salvador Dali joins the surrealists
Epstein's *Night and Day*
Mondrian's *Composition with Yellow Blue*

1930   Allied occupation of the Rhineland ends
Mohandas Gandhi opens civil disobedience campaign in India

The *Daily Worker,* journal of the British Communist party, begins publishing
J. W. Reppe makes artificial fabrics from an acetylene base
J. G. Ballard born
John Arden born
W. H. Auden's *Poems*
Coward's *Private Lives*
Eliot's *Ash Wednesday*
Wyndham Lewis' *The Apes of God*
Maugham's *Cakes and Ale*
Ezra Pound's *XXX Cantos*
Evelyn Waugh's *Vile Bodies*

1931   The failure of the Credit Anstalt in Austria starts a financial collapse in Central Europe
Britain abandons the gold standard; the pound falls by twenty-five percent
Mutiny in the Royal Navy at Invergordon over pay cuts
Ramsay MacDonald resigns, splits the Cabinet, and is expelled by the Labour party; in the general election the National Government wins by a majority of five hundred seats
The Statute of Westminster defines dominion status
Ninette de Valois founds the Vic-Wells Ballet (eventually the Royal Ballet)
Coward's *Cavalcade*
Dali's *The Persistence of Memory*
John le Carré born
Fay Weldon born
O'Neill's *Mourning Becomes Electra*
Anthony Powell's *Afternoon Men*
Antoine de Saint-Exupéry's *Vol de nuit*
William Walton's *Belshazzar's Feast*
Virginia Woolf's *The Waves*

1932   Franklin D. Roosevelt elected president of the United States
Paul von Hindenburg elected president of Germany; Franz von Papen elected chancellor
Sir Oswald Mosley founds British Union of Fascists
The BBC takes over development of television from J. L. Baird's company
Basic English of 850 words designed as a prospective international language
The Folger Library opens in Washington, D.C.

CHRONOLOGY

The Shakespeare Memorial Theatre opens in Stratford-upon-Avon
Geoffrey Hill born
Edna O'Brien born
Faulkner's *Light in August*
Aldous Huxley's *Brave New World*
F. R. Leavis' *New Bearings in English Poetry*
Boris Pasternak's *Second Birth*
Ravel's *Concerto for Left Hand*
Rouault's *Christ Mocked by Soldiers*
Waugh's *Black Mischief*
Yeats's *Words for Music Perhaps*

1933   Roosevelt inaugurates the New Deal
Hitler becomes chancellor of Germany
The Reichstag set on fire
Hitler suspends civil liberties and freedom of the press; German trade unions suppressed
George Balanchine and Lincoln Kirstein found the School of American Ballet
Joe Orton born
Lowry's *Ultramarine*
André Malraux's *La Condition humaine*
Orwell's *Down and Out in Paris and London*
Gertrude Stein's *The Autobiography of Alice B. Toklas*

1934   The League Disarmament Conference ends in failure
The Soviet Union admitted to the League
Hitler becomes Führer
Civil war in Austria; Engelbert Dollfuss assassinated in attempted Nazi coup
Frédéric Joliot and Irene Joliot-Curie discover artificial (induced) radioactivity
Einstein's *My Philosophy*
Fitzgerald's *Tender Is the Night*
Graves's *I, Claudius* and *Claudius the God*
Toynbee's *A Study of History* begins publication (1934–1954)
Waugh's *A Handful of Dust*

1935   Grigori Zinoviev and other Soviet leaders convicted of treason
Stanley Baldwin becomes prime minister in National Government; National Government wins general election in Britain
Italy invades Abyssinia
Germany repudiates disarmament clauses of Treaty of Versailles
Germany reintroduces compulsory military service and outlaws the Jews

Robert Watson-Watt builds first practical radar equipment
Thomas Keneally born
David Lodge born
D. M. Thomas born
Karl Jaspers' *Suffering and Existence*
Ivy Compton-Burnett's *A House and Its Head*
Eliot's *Murder in the Cathedral*
Barbara Hepworth's *Three Forms*
George Gershwin's *Porgy and Bess*
Graham Greene's *England Made Me*
Isherwood's *Mr. Norris Changes Trains*
Malraux's *Le Temps du mépris*
Yeats's *Dramatis Personae*
Klee's *Child Consecrated to Suffering*
Benedict Nicholson's *White Relief*

1936   Edward VII accedes to the throne in January; abdicates in December

1936–1952   Reign of George VI

1936   German troops occupy the Rhineland
Ninety-nine percent of German electorate vote for Nazi candidates
The Popular Front wins general election in France; Léon Blum becomes prime minister
Roosevelt reelected president of the United States
The Popular Front wins general election in Spain
Spanish Civil War begins
Italian troops occupy Addis Ababa; Abyssinia annexed by Italy
BBC begins television service from Alexandra Palace
A. S. Byatt born
Auden's *Look, Stranger!*
Auden and Isherwood's *The Ascent of F-6*
A. J. Ayer's *Language, Truth and Logic*
Chaplin's *Modern Times*
Greene's *A Gun for Sale*
Aldous Huxley's *Eyeless in Gaza*
Keynes's *General Theory of Employment*
F. R. Leavis' *Revaluation*
Mondrian's *Composition in Red and Blue*
Dylan Thomas' *Twenty-five Poems*
Wells's *The Shape of Things to Come* filmed

1937   Trial of Karl Radek and other Soviet leaders
Neville Chamberlain succeeds Stanley Baldwin as prime minister
China and Japan at war

Frank Whittle designs jet engine
Picasso's *Guernica*
Shostakovich's Fifth Symphony
Magritte's *La Reproduction interdite*
Anita Desai born
Tony Harrison born
Hemingway's *To Have and Have Not*
Malraux's *L'Espoir*
Orwell's *The Road to Wigan Pier*
Priestley's *Time and the Conways*
Virginia Woolf's *The Years*

1938 Trial of Nikolai Bukharin and other Soviet political leaders
Austria occupied by German troops and declared part of the Reich
Hitler states his determination to annex Sudetenland from Czechoslovakia
Britain, France, Germany, and Italy sign the Munich agreement
German troops occupy Sudetenland
Caryl Churchill born
Edward Hulton founds *Picture Post*
Cyril Connolly's *Enemies of Promise*
du Maurier's *Rebecca*
Faulkner's *The Unvanquished*
Graham Greene's *Brighton Rock*
Hindemith's *Mathis der Maler*
Jean Renoir's *La Grande Illusion*
Jean-Paul Sartre's *La Nausée*
Yeats's *New Poems*
Anthony Asquith's *Pygmalion* and Walt Disney's *Snow White*

1939 German troops occupy Bohemia and Moravia; Czechoslovakia incorporated into Third Reich
Madrid surrenders to General Franco; the Spanish Civil War ends
Italy invades Albania
Spain joins Germany, Italy, and Japan in anti-Comintern Pact
Britain and France pledge support to Poland, Romania, and Greece
The Soviet Union proposes defensive alliance with Britain; British military mission visits Moscow
The Soviet Union and Germany sign non-aggression treaty, secretly providing for partition of Poland between them
Germany invades Poland; Britain, France, and Germany at war
The Soviet Union invades Finland
New York World's Fair opens

Eliot's *The Family Reunion*
Alan Ayckbourn born
Margaret Drabble born
Seamus Heaney born
Isherwood's *Good-bye to Berlin*
Joyce's *Finnegans Wake* (1922–1939)
MacNeice's *Autumn Journal*
Powell's *What's Become of Waring?*

1940 Churchill becomes prime minister
Italy declares war on France, Britain, and Greece
General de Gaulle founds Free French Movement
The Battle of Britain and the bombing of London
Roosevelt reelected president of the United States for third term
Betjeman's *Old Lights for New Chancels*
Angela Carter born
Bruce Chatwin born
Chaplin's *The Great Dictator*
Disney's *Fantasia*
Greene's *The Power and the Glory*
Hemingway's *For Whom the Bell Tolls*
C. P. Snow's *Strangers and Brothers* (retitled *George Passant* in 1970, when entire sequence of ten novels, published 1940–1970, was entitled *Strangers and Brothers*)

1941 German forces occupy Yugoslavia, Greece, and Crete, and invade the Soviet Union
Lend-Lease agreement between the United States and Britain
President Roosevelt and Winston Churchill sign the Atlantic Charter
Japanese forces attack Pearl Harbor; United States declares war on Japan, Germany, Italy; Britain on Japan
Auden's *New Year Letter*
James Burnham's *The Managerial Revolution*
F. Scott Fitzgerald's *The Last Tycoon*
Aldous Huxley's *Grey Eminence*
Shostakovich's Seventh Symphony
Michael Tippett's *A Child of Our Time*
Orson Welles's *Citizen Kane*
Virginia Woolf's *Between the Acts*

1942 Japanese forces capture Singapore, Hong Kong, Bataan, Manila
German forces capture Tobruk
U.S. fleet defeats the Japanese in the Coral Sea, captures Guadalcanal

CHRONOLOGY

Battle of El Alamein
Allied forces land in French North Africa
Atom first split at University of Chicago
William Beveridge's *Social Insurance and Allied Services*
Albert Camus's *L'Étranger*
Joyce Cary's *To Be a Pilgrim*
Edith Sitwell's *Street Songs*
Waugh's *Put Out More Flags*

1943   German forces surrender at Stalingrad
German and Italian forces surrender in North Africa
Italy surrenders to Allies and declares war on Germany
Cairo conference between Roosevelt, Churchill, Chiang Kai-shek
Teheran conference between Roosevelt, Churchill, Stalin
Pat Barker born
Eliot's *Four Quartets*
Henry Moore's *Madonna and Child*
Sartre's *Les Mouches*
Vaughan Williams' Fifth Symphony

1944   Allied forces land in Normandy and southern France
Allied forces enter Rome
Attempted assassination of Hitler fails
Liberation of Paris
U.S. forces land in Philippines
German offensive in the Ardennes halted
Roosevelt reelected president of the United States for fourth term
Education Act passed in Britain
Pay-as-You-Earn income tax introduced
Eavan Boland born
Beveridge's *Full Employment in a Free Society*
Cary's *The Horse's Mouth*
Aldous Huxley's *Time Must Have a Stop*
Maugham's *The Razor's Edge*
Sartre's *Huis Clos*
Edith Sitwell's *Green Song and Other Poems*
Graham Sutherland's *Christ on the Cross*
Trevelyan's *English Social History*

1945   British and Indian forces open offensive in Burma
Yalta conference between Roosevelt, Churchill, Stalin
Mussolini executed by Italian partisans
Roosevelt dies; Harry S. Truman becomes president

Hitler commits suicide; German forces surrender
The Potsdam Peace Conference
The United Nations Charter ratified in San Francisco
The Labour Party wins British general election
Atomic bombs dropped on Hiroshima and Nagasaki
Surrender of Japanese forces ends World War II
Trial of Nazi war criminals opens at Nuremberg
All-India Congress demands British withdrawal from India
De Gaulle elected president of French Provisional Government; resigns the next year
Betjeman's *New Bats in Old Belfries*
Britten's *Peter Grimes*
Orwell's *Animal Farm*
Bertrand Russell's *History of Western Philosophy*
Sartre's *The Age of Reason*
Edith Sitwell's *The Song of the Cold*
Waugh's *Brideshead Revisited*

1946   Bills to nationalize railways, coal mines, and the Bank of England passed in Britain
Nuremberg Trials concluded
United Nations General Assembly meets in New York as its permanent headquarters
The Arab Council inaugurated in Britain
Julian Barnes born
James Kelman born
Frederick Ashton's *Symphonic Variations*
Britten's *The Rape of Lucretia*
David Lean's *Great Expectations*
O'Neill's *The Iceman Cometh*
Roberto Rossellini's *Paisà*
Dylan Thomas' *Deaths and Entrances*

1947   President Truman announces program of aid to Greece and Turkey and outlines the "Truman Doctrine"
Independence of India proclaimed; partition between India and Pakistan, and communal strife between Hindus and Muslims follows
General Marshall calls for a European recovery program
First supersonic air flight

xxi

CHRONOLOGY

Britain's first atomic pile at Harwell comes into operation

Edinburgh Festival established

Discovery of the Dead Sea Scrolls in Palestine

Princess Elizabeth marries Philip Mountbatten, duke of Edinburgh

David Hare born

Salman Rushdie born

Auden's *Age of Anxiety*

Camus's *La Peste*

Chaplin's *Monsieur Verdoux*

Lowry's *Under the Volcano*

Priestley's *An Inspector Calls*

Edith Sitwell's *The Shadow of Cain*

Waugh's *Scott-King's Modern Europe*

1948 Gandhi assassinated

Czech Communist Party seizes power

Pan-European movement (1948–1958) begins with the formation of the permanent Organization for European Economic Cooperation (OEEC)

Berlin airlift begins as the Soviet Union halts road and rail traffic to the city

British mandate in Palestine ends; Israeli provisional government formed

Yugoslavia expelled from Soviet bloc

Columbia Records introduces the long-playing record

Truman elected president of the United States for second term

Ian McEwan born

Greene's *The Heart of the Matter*

Aldous Huxley's *Ape and Essence*

Leavis' *The Great Tradition*

Pound's *Cantos*

Priestley's *The Linden Tree*

Waugh's *The Loved One*

1949 North Atlantic Treaty Organization established with headquarters in Brussels

Berlin blockade lifted

German Federal Republic recognized; capital established at Bonn

Konrad Adenauer becomes German chancellor

Mao Tse-tung becomes chairman of the People's Republic of China following Communist victory over the Nationalists

Martin Amis born

Graham Swift born

Simone de Beauvoir's *The Second Sex*

Cary's *A Fearful Joy*

Arthur Miller's *Death of a Salesman*

Orwell's *Nineteen Eighty-four*

1950 Korean War breaks out

Nobel Prize for literature awarded to Bertrand Russell

Medbh McGuckian born

R. H. S. Crossman's *The God That Failed*

T. S. Eliot's *The Cocktail Party*

Fry's *Venus Observed*

Doris Lessing's *The Grass Is Singing*

C. S. Lewis' *The Chronicles of Narnia* (1950–1956)

Wyndham Lewis' *Rude Assignment*

George Orwell's *Shooting an Elephant*

Carol Reed's *The Third Man*

Dylan Thomas' *Twenty-six Poems*

1951 Guy Burgess and Donald Maclean defect from Britain to the Soviet Union

The Conservative party under Winston Churchill wins British general election

The Festival of Britain celebrates both the centenary of the Crystal Palace Exhibition and British postwar recovery

Electric power is produced by atomic energy at Arcon, Idaho

Paul Muldoon born

W. H. Auden's *Nones*

Samuel Beckett's *Molloy* and *Malone Dies*

Benjamin Britten's *Billy Budd*

Greene's *The End of the Affair*

Akira Kurosawa's *Rashomon*

Wyndham Lewis' *Rotting Hill*

Anthony Powell's *A Question of Upbringing* (first volume of *A Dance to the Music of Time*, 1951–1975)

J. D. Salinger's *The Catcher in the Rye*

C. P. Snow's *The Masters*

Igor Stravinsky's *The Rake's Progress*

1952 Reign of Elizabeth II

At Eniwetok Atoll the United States detonates the first hydrogen bomb

The European Coal and Steel Community comes into being

Radiocarbon dating introduced to archaeology

Michael Ventris deciphers Linear B script

Dwight D. Eisenhower elected president of the United States

Beckett's *Waiting for Godot*

Charles Chaplin's *Limelight*

Ernest Hemingway's *The Old Man and the Sea*

Arthur Koestler's *Arrow in the Blue*

F. R. Leavis' *The Common Pursuit*

Lessing's *Martha Quest* (first volume of *The Children of Violence*, 1952–1965)

C. S. Lewis' *Mere Christianity*

Thomas' *Collected Poems*

Evelyn Waugh's *Men at Arms* (first volume of *Sword of Honour*, 1952–1961)

Angus Wilson's *Hemlock and After*

1953 Constitution for a European political community drafted

Julius and Ethel Rosenberg executed for passing U.S. secrets to the Soviet Union

Cease-fire declared in Korea

Edmund Hillary and his Sherpa guide, Tenzing Norkay, scale Mt. Everest

Nobel Prize for literature awarded to Winston Churchill

General Mohammed Naguib proclaims Egypt a republic

Beckett's *Watt*

Joyce Cary's *Except the Lord*

Robert Graves's *Poems 1953*

1954 First atomic submarine, *Nautilus*, is launched by the United States

Dien Bien Phu captured by the Vietminh

Geneva Conference ends French dominion over Indochina

U.S. Supreme Court declares racial segregation in schools unconstitutional

Nasser becomes president of Egypt

Nobel Prize for literature awarded to Ernest Hemingway

Kazuo Ishiguro born

Kingsley Amis' *Lucky Jim*

John Betjeman's *A Few Late Chrysanthemums*

William Golding's *Lord of the Flies*

Christopher Isherwood's *The World in the Evening*

Koestler's *The Invisible Writing*

Iris Murdoch's *Under the Net*

C. P. Snow's *The New Men*

Thomas' *Under Milk Wood* published posthumously

1955 Warsaw Pact signed

West Germany enters NATO as Allied occupation ends

The Conservative party under Anthony Eden wins British general election

Cary's *Not Honour More*

Greene's *The Quiet American*

Philip Larkin's *The Less Deceived*

F. R. Leavis' *D. H. Lawrence, Novelist*

Vladimir Nabokov's *Lolita*

Patrick White's *The Tree of Man*

1956 Nasser's nationalization of the Suez Canal leads to Israeli, British, and French armed intervention

Uprising in Hungary suppressed by Soviet troops

Khrushchev denounces Stalin at Twentieth Communist Party Congress

Eisenhower reelected president of the United States

Anthony Burgess' *Time for a Tiger*

Golding's *Pincher Martin*

Murdoch's *Flight from the Enchanter*

John Osborne's *Look Back in Anger*

Snow's *Homecomings*

Edmund Wilson's *Anglo-Saxon Attitudes*

1957 The Soviet Union launches the first artificial earth satellite, *Sputnik I*

Eden succeeded by Harold Macmillan

Suez Canal reopened

Eisenhower Doctrine formulated

Parliament receives the Wolfenden Report on Homosexuality and Prostitution

Nobel Prize for literature awarded to Albert Camus

Beckett's *Endgame* and *All That Fall*

Lawrence Durrell's *Justine* (first volume of *The Alexandria Quartet*, 1957–1960)

Ted Hughes's *The Hawk in the Rain*

Murdoch's *The Sandcastle*

V. S. Naipaul's *The Mystic Masseur*

Eugene O'Neill's *Long Day's Journey into Night*

Osborne's *The Entertainer*

Muriel Spark's *The Comforters*

White's *Voss*

1958 European Economic Community established

Khrushchev succeeds Bulganin as Soviet premier

Charles de Gaulle becomes head of France's newly constituted Fifth Republic

The United Arab Republic formed by Egypt and Syria

CHRONOLOGY

1964   Tonkin Gulf incident leads to retaliatory strikes by U.S. aircraft against North Vietnam

Greece and Turkey contend for control of Cyprus

Britain grants licenses to drill for oil in the North Sea

The Shakespeare Quatercentenary celebrated

Lyndon Johnson elected president of the United States

The Labour party under Harold Wilson wins British general election

Nobel Prize for literature awarded to Jean-Paul Sartre

Saul Bellow's *Herzog*

Burgess' *Nothing Like the Sun*

Golding's *The Spire*

Isherwood's *A Single Man*

Stanley Kubrick's *Dr. Strangelove*

Larkin's *The Whitsun Weddings*

Naipaul's *An Area of Darkness*

Peter Shaffer's *The Royal Hunt of the Sun*

Snow's *Corridors of Power*

1965   The first U.S. combat forces land in Vietnam

The U.S. spacecraft *Mariner* transmits photographs of Mars

British Petroleum Company finds oil in the North Sea

War breaks out between India and Pakistan

Rhodesia declares its independence

Ontario power failure blacks out the Canadian and U.S. east coasts

Nobel Prize for literature awarded to Mikhail Sholokhov

Robert Lowell's *For the Union Dead*

Norman Mailer's *An American Dream*

Osborne's *Inadmissible Evidence*

Pinter's *The Homecoming*

Spark's *The Mandelbaum Gate*

1966   The Labour party under Harold Wilson wins British general election

The Archbishop of Canterbury visits Pope Paul VI

Florence, Italy, severely damaged by floods

Paris exhibition celebrates Picasso's eighty-fifth birthday

Fowles's *The Magus*

Greene's *The Comedians*

Osborne's *A Patriot for Me*

Paul Scott's *The Jewel in the Crown* (first volume of *The Raj Quartet*, 1966–1975)

White's *The Solid Mandala*

1967   Thurgood Marshall becomes first black U.S. Supreme Court justice

Six-Day War pits Israel against Egypt and Syria

Biafra's secession from Nigeria leads to civil war

Francis Chichester completes solo circumnavigation of the globe

Dr. Christiaan Barnard performs first heart transplant operation, in South Africa

China explodes its first hydrogen bomb

Golding's *The Pyramid*

Hughes's *Wodwo*

Isherwood's *A Meeting by the River*

Naipaul's *The Mimic Men*

Tom Stoppard's *Rosencrantz and Guildenstern Are Dead*

Orson Welles's *Chimes at Midnight*

Angus Wilson's *No Laughing Matter*

1968   Violent student protests erupt in France and West Germany

Warsaw Pact troops occupy Czechoslovakia

Violence in Northern Ireland causes Britain to send in troops

Tet offensive by Communist forces launched against South Vietnam's cities

Theater censorship ended in Britain

Robert Kennedy and Martin Luther King, Jr., assassinated

Richard M. Nixon elected president of the United States

Booker Prize for fiction established

Durrell's *Tunc*

Graves's *Poems 1965–1968*

Osborne's *The Hotel in Amsterdam*

Snow's *The Sleep of Reason*

Solzhenitsyn's *The First Circle* and *Cancer Ward*

Spark's *The Public Image*

1969   Humans set foot on the moon for the first time when astronauts descend to its surface in a landing vehicle from the U.S. spacecraft *Apollo 11*

The Soviet unmanned spacecraft *Venus V* lands on Venus

CHRONOLOGY

Capital punishment abolished in Britain

Colonel Muammar Qaddafi seizes power in Libya

Solzhenitsyn expelled from the Soviet Union

Nobel Prize for literature awarded to Samuel Beckett

Carter's *The Magic Toyshop*

Fowles's *The French Lieutenant's Woman*

Storey's *The Contractor*

1970 Civil war in Nigeria ends with Biafra's surrender

U.S. planes bomb Cambodia

The Conservative party under Edward Heath wins British general election

Nobel Prize for literature awarded to Aleksandr Solzhenitsyn

Durrell's *Nunquam*

Hughes's *Crow*

F. R. Leavis and Q. D. Leavis' *Dickens the Novelist*

Snow's *Last Things*

Spark's *The Driver's Seat*

1971 Communist China given Nationalist China's UN seat

Decimal currency introduced to Britain

Indira Gandhi becomes India's prime minister

Nobel Prize for literature awarded to Heinrich Böll

Edward Bond's *The Pope's Wedding*

Naipaul's *In a Free State*

Pinter's *Old Times*

Spark's *Not to Disturb*

1972 The civil strife of "Bloody Sunday" causes Northern Ireland to come under the direct rule of Westminster

Nixon becomes the first U.S. president to visit Moscow and Beijing

The Watergate break-in precipitates scandal in the United States

Eleven Israeli athletes killed by terrorists at Munich Olympics

Nixon reelected president of the United States

Bond's *Lear*

Snow's *The Malcontents*

Stoppard's *Jumpers*

1973 Britain, Ireland, and Denmark enter European Economic Community

Egypt and Syria attack Israel in the Yom Kippur War

Energy crisis in Britain reduces production to a three-day week

Nobel Prize for literature awarded to Patrick White

Edward Bond's *The Sea*

Greene's *The Honorary Consul*

Lessing's *The Summer Before the Dark*

Murdoch's *The Black Prince*

Peter Shaffer's *Equus*

White's *The Eye of the Storm*

1974 Miners strike in Britain

Greece's military junta overthrown

Emperor Haile Selassie of Ethiopia deposed

President Makarios of Cyprus replaced by military coup

Nixon resigns as U.S. president and is succeeded by Gerald R. Ford

Betjeman's *A Nip in the Air*

Bond's *Bingo*

Durrell's *Monsieur* (first volume of *The Avignon Quintet*, 1974–1985)

Larkin's *The High Windows*

Solzhenitsyn's *The Gulag Archipelago*

Spark's *The Abbess of Crewe*

1975 The U.S. *Apollo* and Soviet *Soyuz* spacecrafts rendezvous in space

The Helsinki Accords on human rights signed

U.S. forces leave Vietnam

King Juan Carlos succeeds Franco as Spain's head of state

Nobel Prize for literature awarded to Eugenio Montale

1976 New U.S. copyright law goes into effect

Israeli commandos free hostages from hijacked plane at Entebbe, Uganda

British and French SST Concordes make first regularly scheduled commercial flights

The United States celebrates its bicentennial

Jimmy Carter elected president of the United States

Byron and Shelley manuscripts discovered in Barclay's Bank, Pall Mall

Hughes's *Seasons' Songs*

Koestler's *The Thirteenth Tribe*

Paul Scott's *Staying On*

Spark's *The Take-over*

White's *A Fringe of Leaves*

CHRONOLOGY

1977   Silver jubilee of Queen Elizabeth II celebrated

Egyptian president Anwar el-Sadat visits Israel

"Gang of Four" expelled from Chinese Communist party

First woman ordained in the U.S. Episcopal church

After twenty-nine years in power, Israel's Labour party is defeated by the Likud party

Fowles's *Daniel Martin*

Hughes's *Gaudete*

1978   Treaty between Israel and Egypt negotiated at Camp David

Pope John Paul I dies a month after his coronation and is succeeded by Karol Cardinal Wojtyla, who takes the name John Paul II

Former Italian premier Aldo Moro murdered by left-wing terrorists

Nobel Prize for literature awarded to Isaac Bashevis Singer

Greene's *The Human Factor*

Hughes's *Cave Birds*

Murdoch's *The Sea, The Sea*

1979   The United States and China establish diplomatic relations

Ayatollah Khomeini takes power in Iran and his supporters hold U.S. embassy staff hostage in Teheran

Rhodesia becomes Zimbabwe

Earl Mountbatten assassinated

The Soviet Union invades Afghanistan

The Conservative party under Margaret Thatcher wins British general election

Nobel Prize for literature awarded to Odysseus Elytis

Golding's *Darkness Visible*

Hughes's *Moortown*

Lessing's *Shikasta* (first volume of *Canopus in Argos, Archives*)

Naipaul's *A Bend in the River*

Spark's *Territorial Rights*

White's *The Twyborn Affair*

1980   Iran-Iraq war begins

Strikes in Gdansk give rise to the Solidarity movement

Mt. St. Helen's erupts in Washington State

British steelworkers strike for the first time since 1926

More than fifty nations boycott Moscow Olympics

Ronald Reagan elected president of the United States

Burgess' *Earthly Powers*

Golding's *Rites of Passage*

Peter Shaffer's *Amadeus*

Storey's *A Prodigal Child*

Angus Wilson's *Setting the World on Fire*

1981   Greece admitted to the European Economic Community

Iran hostage crisis ends with release of U.S. embassy staff

Twelve Labour MPs and nine peers found British Social Democratic party

Socialist party under François Mitterrand wins French general election

Rupert Murdoch buys *The Times* of London

Turkish gunman wounds Pope John Paul II in assassination attempt

U.S. gunman wounds President Reagan in assassination attempt

President Sadat of Egypt assassinated

Nobel Prize for literature awarded to Elias Canetti

Spark's *Loitering with Intent*

1982   Britain drives Argentina's invasion force out of the Falkland Islands

U.S. space shuttle makes first successful trip

Yuri Andropov becomes general secretary of the Central Committee of the Soviet Communist party

Israel invades Lebanon

First artificial heart implanted at Salt Lake City hospital

Bellow's *The Dean's December*

Greene's *Monsignor Quixote*

1983   South Korean airliner with 269 aboard shot down after straying into Soviet airspace

U.S. forces invade Grenada following left-wing coup

Widespread protests erupt over placement of nuclear missiles in Europe

The £1 coin comes into circulation in Britain

Australia wins the America's Cup

Nobel Prize for literature awarded to William Golding

Hughes's *River*

	Murdoch's *The Philosopher's Pupil*
1984	Konstantin Chernenko becomes general secretary of the Central Committee of the Soviet Communist party
	Prime Minister Indira Gandhi of India assassinated by Sikh bodyguards
	Reagan reelected president of the United States
	Toxic gas leak at Bhopal, India, plant kills 2,000
	British miners go on strike
	Irish Republican Army attempts to kill Prime Minister Thatcher with bomb detonated at a Brighton hotel
	World Court holds against U.S. mining of Nicaraguan harbors
	Golding's *The Paper Men*
	Lessing's *The Diary of Jane Somers*
	Spark's *The Only Problem*
1985	United States deploys cruise missiles in Europe
	Mikhail Gorbachev becomes general secretary of the Soviet Communist party following death of Konstantin Chernenko
	Riots break out in Handsworth district (Birmingham) and Brixton
	Republic of Ireland gains consultative role in Northern Ireland
	State of emergency is declared in South Africa
	Nobel Prize for literature awarded to Claude Simon
	A. N. Wilson's *Gentlemen in England*
	Lessing's *The Good Terrorist*
	Murdoch's *The Good Apprentice*
	Fowles's *A Maggot*
1986	U.S. space shuttle *Challenger* explodes
	United States attacks Libya
	Atomic power plant at Chernobyl destroyed in accident
	Corazon Aquino becomes president of the Philippines
	Giotto spacecraft encounters Comet Halley
	Nobel Prize for literature awarded to Wole Soyinka
	Final volume of *Oxford English Dictionary* supplement published
	Amis' *The Old Devils*
	Ishiguro's *An Artist of the Floating World*
	A. N. Wilson's *Love Unknown*
	Powell's *The Fisher King*

1987	Gorbachev begins reform of Communist party of the Soviet Union
	Stock market collapses
	Iran-contra affair reveals that Reagan administration used money from arms sales to Iran to fund Nicaraguan rebels
	Palestinian uprising begins in Israeli-occupied territories
	Nobel Prize for literature awarded to Joseph Brodsky
	Golding's *Close Quarters*
	Burgess' *Little Wilson and Big God*
	Margaret Drabble's *The Radiant Way*
1988	Soviet Union begins withdrawing troops from Afghanistan
	Iranian airliner shot down by U.S. Navy over Persian Gulf
	War between Iran and Iraq ends
	George Bush elected president of the United States
	Pan American flight 103 destroyed over Lockerbie, Scotland
	Nobel Prize for literature awarded to Naguib Mafouz
	Greene's *The Captain and the Enemy*
	Amis' *Difficulties with Girls*
	Rushdie's *Satanic Verses*
1989	Ayatollah Khomeini pronounces death sentence on Salman Rushdie; Great Britain and Iran sever diplomatic relations
	F. W. de Klerk becomes president of South Africa
	Chinese government crushes student demonstration in Tiananmen Square
	Communist regimes are weakened or abolished in Poland, Czechoslovakia, Hungary, East Germany, and Romania
	Lithuania nullifies its inclusion in Soviet Union
	Nobel Prize for literature awarded to José Cela
	Second edition of *Oxford English Dictionary* published
	Drabble's *A Natural Curiosity*
	Murdoch's *The Message to the Planet*
	Amis' *London Fields*
	Ishiguro's *The Remains of the Day*
1990	Communist monopoly ends in Bulgaria
	Riots break out against community charge in England
	First women ordained priests in Church of England

CHRONOLOGY

de Klerk announces end of South African emergency measures and freeing of political prisoners, including Nelson Mandela

East and West Germany united

Iraq invades Kuwait

Margaret Thatcher resigns as prime minister and is succeeded by John Major

Nobel Peace Prize awarded to Mikhail Gorbachev

Nobel Prize for literature awarded to Octavio Paz

Amis' *The Folks that Live on the Hill*

Byatt's *Possession*

Pritchett's *Complete Short Stories*

1991 American-led coalition forces Iraqi withdrawal from Kuwait in Persian Gulf War

Rajiv Gandhi assassinated

Civil war breaks out in Yugoslavia; Croatia and Slovenia declare independence

Bush and Gorbachev sign START agreement to reduce nuclear-weapons arsenals

President Jean-Baptiste Aristide overthrown by military in Haiti

Boris Yeltsin elected president of Russia

Dissolution of the Soviet Union

Nobel Prize for literature awarded to Nadine Gordimer

1992 U.N. Conference on Environment and Development (the "Earth Summit") meets in Rio de Janeiro

Prince and Princess of Wales separate

War in Bosnia-Herzegovina intensifies

Bill Clinton elected president of the United States in three-way race with Bush and independent candidate H. Ross Perot

Nobel Prize for literature awarded to Derek Walcott

1993 Czechoslovakia divides into the Czech Republic and Slovakia;

Playwright Vaclav Havel elected president of the Czech Republic

Britain ratifies Treaty on European Union (the "Maastricht Treaty")

U.S. troops provide humanitarian aid amid famine in Somalia

United States, Canada, and Mexico sign North American Free Trade Agreement

Nobel Prize for literature awarded to Toni Morrison

1994 Nelson Mandela elected president in South Africa's first post-apartheid election

Jean-Baptiste Aristide restored to presidency of Haiti

Clinton health care reforms rejected by Congress

Civil war in Rwanda

Republicans win control of both houses of Congress for first time in forty years

Prime Minister Albert Reynolds of Ireland meets with Gerry Adams, president of Sinn Fein

Nobel Prize for literature awarded to Kenzaburo Öe

Amis' *You Can't Do Both*

Naipaul's *A Way in the World*

1995 Britain and Irish Republican Army engage in diplomatic talks

Barings Bank forced into bankruptcy as a result of a maverick bond trader's losses

United States restores full diplomatic relations with Vietnam

NATO initiates air strikes in Bosnia

Death of Stephen Spender

Israeli Prime Minister Yitzhak Rabin assassinated

Nobel Prize for literature awarded to Seamus Heaney

1996 British government destroys around 100,000 cows suspected of infection with Creutzfeldt-Jakob, or "mad cow," disease

IRA breaks cease-fire; Sein Fein representatives barred from Northern Ireland peace talks

Prince and Princess of Wales divorce

Cease-fire agreement in Chechnia; Russian forces begin to withdraw

Boris Yeltsin reelected president of Russia

Bill Clinton reelected president of the United States

Nobel Prize for literature awarded to Wislawa Szymborska

1997 Diana, Princess of Wales, dies in an automobile accident

Unveiling of first fully cloned adult animal, a sheep named Dolly

xxix

Booker McConnell Prize for fiction awarded to Arundhati Roy

Labour party under Tony Blair wins British general election

Bertie Ahern becomes prime minister of Ireland

Britain cedes Hong Kong to People's Republic of China

NATO expands to include Czech Republic, Hungary, and Poland

1998   United States renews bombing of Bagdad, Iraq

Independent legislature and Parliaments return to Scotland and Wales

Ted Hughes, Symbolist poet and husband of Sylvia Plath, dies

Booker McConnell Prize for fiction awarded to Ian McEwan

Nobel Prize for literature awarded to Jose Saramago

1999   King Hussein of Jordan dies

United Nations responds militarily to Serbian President Slobodan Milosevic's escalation of crisis in Kosovo

List of Contributors

GABRIEL BROWNSTEIN. Lecturer, Writing Program, State University of New York at Stony Brook. **Ben Okri**

ANGUS COCHRAN. Teacher of literature, most recently at Bowdoin College. His research interests lie in British and Irish modernist and postmodernist literature. He has written and spoken on Robert Burns, Virginia Woolf, James Joyce, Ian McEwan, and Irvine Welsh, among others. **James Kelman**

JOSEPH DEVLIN. Assistant Professor of English Literature, Western State College of Colorado. Publications include several essays on Irish writers, J. M. Synge, Somerville and Ross, and Brian O'Nolan (Flann O'Brien). Writing a book, *Irony and Empire: The Irish Satirical Tradition*. **Brian Friel**

LAURA ENGEL. English teacher, the Spence School. Doctoral candidate, Department of English, Columbia University. Dissertation examines the memoirs and portraits of eighteenth-century British actresses. **Edna O'Brien**

BLYTHE FRANK. Freelance writer and graduate student, Columbia University. **Patricia Highsmith**

DAVID HAWKES. Associate Professor of English, Lehigh University. His most recent book is *Ideology*, published by Routledge in 1996. **Roddy Doyle**

ANGELYN HAYS. Writer. Has published essays, biographies, reviews, and poems. Recently finished a screenplay adaptation of the Old English poem *Beowulf*. Currently a contributing editor for an anthology of twentieth-century ballads. **Elizabeth Jennings**

RADHIKA JONES. Doctoral candidate, Department of English, Columbia University. Areas of study focus on nineteenth- and twentieth-century British fiction and postcolonial studies. **Ruth Prawer Jhabvala**

KAREN KARBIENER. Preceptor, Literature Humanities, Columbia University; Instructor of Literature, The Cooper Union. Completing doctoral dissertation in Columbia University's Department of English and Comparative Literature, with focus on Walt Whitman's debt to Coleridge, Wordsworth, Felicia Hemans, and Mary Howitt. Published essays on transatlantic literary influence and music-literary relationships. Currently at work on historical novel about own family's experience in postwar Yugoslavia. **Penelope Fitzgerald**

KENNETH KRAUSS. Associate Professor of Drama, The College of Saint Rose, Albany, New York. Books include *Maxwell Anderson and the New York Stage*, *Private Readings, Public Texts*. Plays include *There's a War Going On!* Working on study of French drama during the German Occupation. **Alan Ayckbourn**

VERA KUTZINSKI. Professor of English, African-American Studies, and American Studies, Yale University. Books include prize-winning *Against the American Grain*, *Sugar's Secrets: Race and the Erotics of Cuban Nationalism*, and translation of Nicolás Guillén's *The Daily Daily*. Sub-editor of the ICLA's *History of Literature in the Caribbean*. Her essays on New World literatures have appeared in numerous books, magazines, and journals. Her current projects include books on contemporary Caribbean fiction and on American modernism. **Wilson Harris**

BENJAMIN LA FARGE. Professor of Literature, Bard College. His article on William Trevor appeared in *British Writers Supplement IV*. **Richard Murphy**

A. MICHAEL MATIN. A professor of English at Warren Wilson College. Has published articles in the *Journal of Modern Literature* and *Studies in the Novel*. His work will appear in the forthcoming Norton Critical Edition of Rudyard Kipling's *Kim*.

He is currently writing a book with the working title *Securing Britain: Invasion-Scare Literature Before the Great War*. He has contributed essays on T. S. Eliot and W. H. Auden to Scribner's *Poets for Students* and the essay on David Lodge to *British Writers, Supplement IV*. **Anita Desai**

GITA MAY. Professor of French and Romance Philology, Columbia University. Has published extensively on French Enlightenment, eighteenth-century aesthetics, the post-revolutionary era, and women writers and artists. Author of *Diderot et Baudelaire, critiques d'art, Madame Roland and the Age of Revolution*, and *Stendhal and the Age of Napoleon*. Publications also include extensive articles on Denis Diderot, George Sand, Rebecca West, and Anita Brookner. Co-editor of *Diderot Studies III*, contributing editor of Diderot's *Oeuvres complètes*, and general editor of the series "The Age of Revolution and Romanticism." **Graham Swift**

TYRUS MILLER. Assistant Professor of English and Comparative Literature, Yale University. Author of *Late Modernism: Politics, Fiction, and the Arts Between the World Wars*, published by University of California Press, 1999. **Geoffrey Hill**

KAREN ODDEN. MacCracken Fellow, New York University. Dissertation entitled *Broken Trains of Thought: The Railway, Trauma and Narrative in the British Novel, 1848–1906*. Publications include essays on popular fiction, Matthew Arnold, and Robert Browning. Short pieces have appeared in women's magazines and *The New York Times*. Her research interests include the history of medicine, psychoanalysis, and law. **Eavan Boland**

SUSANA POWELL. Associate Professor and Deputy Chair of Speech, Communication and Theatre Arts, and Co-Director of the Teaching Center, Borough of Manhattan Community College (City University of New York). Dissertation on Shakespeare's demonic women has led to examination of female icons in the arts and the role they play in shaping women's lives in diverse cultures. Her current research focuses on Kali (India) and Rangda (Indonesia). **Thomas Kinsella**

MARTIN PUCHNER. Assistant Professor of English and Comparative Literature, Columbia University. Lectured and published on modernism, in particular on such figures as Beckett, Pinter, Kafka, and Joyce. Currently preparing a book entitled *Vulgar Mimes: Modernism, Mimesis, and the Æsthetics of Gesture*, which explores the processes by which gesturing actors are transported into modernist texts and theater. Also working on projects on the manifesto, the closet drama, and machine art. **Joe Orton**

MAURA SPIEGEL. Visiting Associate Professor of English and Comparative Literature, Columbia University and Barnard College. She has written on Dickens, the history of the emotions, film, and fashion. Her book, *The Grim Reader*, edited with Richard Tristman, was published by Anchor/Doubleday in 1997. Working on collection of essays on Hollywood movies. **Will Self**

ROBERT SQUILLACE. General Studies Faculty, New York University. Author of *Modernism, Modernity, and Arnold Bennett*, published by Bucknell University Press in 1997. Publications include essays on Bennett, Thomas Hardy, H. G. Wells, and V. S. Pritchett. His fiction has appeared in the journal *Æthlon*. **Tony Harrison**

BRIAN STABLEFORD. Full-time writer; previously lecturer at the University of Reading. His forty-eight novels include *The Empire of Fear* (1988), *Inherit the Earth* (1998) and *Architects of Emortality* (1999), and a few of his many short stories are collected in *Sexual Chemistry: Sardonic Tales of the Genetic Revolution* (1991). His non-fiction books include *Scientific Romance in Britain, 1890–1950* (1985), *Yesterday's Bestsellers* (1998) and *Glorious Perversity: The Decline and Fall of Literary Decadence* (1998). He is also a prolific contributor to reference books on literary history. **J. G. Ballard**

JOHN TUCKER. Professor of English, Nassau Community College, State University of New York; Adjunct Assistant Professor of English and Comparative Literature, Columbia University. Publications include essays on George Eliot and H. Rider Haggard. His fields of study include romanticism and the history of the novel. **Alan Sillitoe**

CLAIR WILLS. Lecturer of English, Queen Mary and Westfield College, University of London. She has written widely on contemporary Irish, English, and American poetry. Her most recent book, *Reading Paul Muldoon*, was published by Bloodaxe Books in 1998. She is editor of the "Contemporary

LIST OF CONTRIBUTORS

Writing" section of the forthcoming *Field Day Anthology of Irish Writing, Volume IV*. **Medbh McGuckian**

LOUISE YELIN. Professor of Literature, Purchase College, State University of New York. Teaches courses in nineteenth- and twentieth-century British literature, feminism, and postcolonial studies. She is the author of *From the Margins of Empire: Christina Stead, Doris Lessing, Nadine Gordimer*, published by Cornell University Press in 1998, which examines the construction of national identity in the work of these authors. Publications include essays on Dickens, Victorian studies, feminism, and postcolonial literature. **Caryl Phillips**

BRITISH WRITERS

ALAN AYCKBOURN

(1939–   )

Kenneth Krauss

BORN ON THE eve of the Second World War, Alan Ayckbourn became the most prolific and popular British playwright of the second half of the twentieth century. He has produced an extraordinarily diverse body of work ranging from television and film scripts to stage works that include comedies, dramas, musicals, children's plays, cabaret, revue sketches, and modernizations of plays by earlier dramatists. For all his success with audiences, however, critics have not always been kind to Ayckbourn. Because he is best known for comedies—both rollicking farces and amusing yet unsettling combinations of laughter and pain—theater reviewers have been quick to categorize him purely as an entertainer. Moreover, his triumphs in the West End and on Broadway have prompted many literary critics to dismiss his plays as commercial pandering to a mainstream audience.

Nevertheless, the public's enthusiasm for Ayckbourn's plays suggests that they are relevant as well as entertaining works. Even on the surface, his broadest comedies reflect an ongoing and intense preoccupation with modern culture, in particular with the institution of marriage. His most madcap scripts, no less than his more serious works, analyze, explore, and find fault with the legal bond connecting husbands and wives. Only rarely, in his more whimsical musicals and children's plays, does a couple manage to live happily ever after. In his solid hits and more experimental forays, he consistently questions even the possibility that matrimony can lead to contentment.

Ayckbourn examines an assortment of other, related, concerns through his drama, including the darker aspects of the family, gender roles as defined by society, the influence of social class on individual behavior, difficulties in communication between individuals, the significance of choice in people's lives, and the conflict between success and happiness. The preponderance of such immediate issues substantiates the claim that, despite his penchant for comedy, Ayckbourn is a very topical and hence serious playwright indeed.

In Ayckbourn's plays significant ideas are accompanied by a sophisticated approach to drama and stagecraft. His inventive storytelling and ingenious sense of staging make the way the story is told just as interesting as the story itself. Time may be bent or stopped, releasing the plot from its usual chronological restrictions. Frequently the setting is so crucial to the play that it becomes as important as the characters: his innovative conceptualizations, such as dividing the stage horizontally or vertically, add new dimensions to the traditionally unified playing space. Allowing actors to determine what their characters will do in particular situations and providing "alternative scenes" that reflect their choices, Ayckbourn opens the plot to different developments and conclusions. Even in his most farcical efforts, the theatricality of his dramaturgy is in itself fascinating to witness.

In short, although his reputation as an effective and prosperous dramatist has led some to cast doubt on his importance, Ayckbourn has clearly achieved far more than mere commercial success and public acclaim. His accomplishments in the theater have been underrated by both his more conservative and radical contemporaries, whose tastes and values differ from those of the general public. Dramatic and literary critics cannot easily decide where to place him. He often is compared to Noël Coward, the great comedic British playwright of the first half of the twentieth century. Blessed with a talent to amuse, both these entertainers also offer a wealth of ingenious staging and social commentary.

Ayckbourn was born in Hampstead, London, on 12 April 1939. His mother, Irene Worley Ayckbourn, wrote romance novels, and his father, Horace Ayckbourn, played violin in the London

1

Symphony. They divorced in 1943. At age seven Alan entered boarding school; in 1947 his mother married Cecil Pye, a bank manager. In 1951 Alan won a scholarship to the prestigious public school Haileybury in Herefordshire. There he joined the drama society, which in 1955 performed in Holland and in 1956 toured North America.

In 1956 Ayckbourn left school and worked with actor-manager Donald Wolfit at the Edinburgh Festival. Ayckbourn then worked as assistant stage manager for a repertory company at Worthing, and the following season joined another repertory company at Leatherhead, Surrey. He next served as assistant manager, actor, and lighting technician at the Scarborough Studio Theatre, directed by Stephen Joseph, who taught drama at Manchester University and had launched his company in 1955 in the local library's concert hall. They performed in a theater-in-the round, with spectators surrounding the stage on all sides, and also toured northern England. Joseph sought out playwrights, and, as he watched Ayckbourn develop, he saw in him a potential dramatist. In 1958 Ayckbourn gave Joseph a script. Shortly after, while touring with the actress Christine Roland, Ayckbourn announced their engagement; they married, and Ayckbourn combined their names into the pseudonym "Roland Allen." His first play, *The Square Cat*, a comedy about a Jekyll-and-Hyde pop star, premiered in 1959. That same year Ayckbourn completed *Love After All*, an Edwardian-style farce, also produced at Scarborough. In 1960 he was drafted but quickly received a medical discharge. "Roland Allen" wrote a Christmas show with singing and dancing titled *Dad's Tale*. The comedy *Standing Room Only*, about overpopulation in the future, opened in 1961.

In 1962 Ayckbourn became a founder of the Victoria Theatre, Stoke-on-Trent, where his next play, *Xmas v. Mastermind*, the first to which he signed his actual name, premiered to terrible notices. He revived *Standing Room Only* and in 1963 offered *Mr. Whatnot*, a comedy using mime. A success at Stoke-on-Trent, *Mr. Whatnot* moved the following summer to London, where it was panned. Ayckbourn's last role on the stage came in William Gibson's *Two for the Seesaw*. Believing *Mr. Whatnot* would succeed in London, he had left the Victoria. Now unemployed, he joined the British Broadcasting Corporation (BBC) as a radio producer.

During this period Ayckbourn and Christine Roland separated, then divorced; thereafter he lived with the actress Heather Stoney, with whom he had toured in *Two for the Seesaw*. He also continued writing scripts for Joseph. One, for the 1964 season, *Meet My Father*, concerned a young woman who breaks off her affair with an older man so she can marry her true love. Retitled *Relatively Speaking*, it opened in 1967 in London, where it became a hit. That year, *The Sparrow*, a dismally comic tale of vengeance among working-class characters, opened at Scarborough. Those who saw in Ayckbourn's *Relatively Speaking* the promise of a comedian now wondered if his hit was an accident.

Stephen Joseph died in 1967, but Ayckbourn remained loyal to Scarborough. His 1969 comedy *How the Other Half Loves* first played there; a year later it traveled to London for a two-year run. He also contributed a sketch, "Countdown," to *Mixed Doubles*, an evening of playlets by other writers, which opened in London in 1969, during which time Ayckbourn also published a children's script, *Ernie's Incredible Illucinations*, which later played in London. In 1970 he left the BBC and assumed Joseph's position at Scarborough. *The Story So Far*, which opened in the summer of 1970 and later started a pre-London tour, fizzled. It was revised in 1972 and again in 1978, when it premiered to mixed reviews. *Time and Time Again*, about a nonconformist with a demanding ego, followed in 1971; *Absurd Person Singular*, concerning six hapless characters over three Christmases, premiered in 1972. Both went to London.

Ayckbourn's best-known work remains *The Norman Conquests*, comprised of three individual plays, *Table Manners, Living Together,* and *Round and Round the Garden*. The plays depict the same characters, and each script takes place during the same period, over a summer weekend. By setting each play in a separate place—one in a dining room, another in the adjacent living room, another in the garden—Ayckbourn discloses the complexity of these misguided people. The cleverness of structure is exceeded by the depth of characterization. The trilogy, which must be seen over three evenings, was performed in Scarborough (1973), in London (1974), on Broadway (1975), and on television (1977), and was greeted with high praise.

This combination of humor and seriousness had already surfaced in *Time and Time Again*, with its intriguing but immature protagonist, and in *Absurd Person Singular*, in which a fed-up housewife, numbed by tranquilizers, attempts suicide while her friends fail to notice. In *Absent Friends* (1974) a group of ordinary people—some married, some friends, some former acquaintances—attend a party, during which they move from normalcy to the verge of madness. A similar unraveling occurs in *Just Between Ourselves* (1976), in which a housewife is undone by her neglectful husband and overbearing mother-in-law.

The hilarious *Bedroom Farce*, first performed in 1975, shows how four different couples survive a Saturday evening fraught with marital discontent. An evening of loosely connected one-act plays, *Confusions* (1974), explores five uncomfortable episodes caused by marital infidelity. And in *Ten Times Table* (1977), what starts as the staging of a historical pageant becomes a present-day political melee between the elite and lower classes.

The premiere of *Ten Times Table* took place in the new Stephen Joseph Theatre-in-the-Round. The bittersweet *Joking Apart* was performed there in 1978, depicting the lives of an unmarried couple and friends over the course of twelve years. For the following season Ayckbourn offered *Sisterly Feelings*, one script containing four possible plays. The flipping of a coin at the end of the first scene determines what scene comes next. That year, Ayckbourn also presented *Taking Steps*, a farce leading through bizarre twists at breakneck speed. In the 1970s Ayckbourn also adapted stage scripts for television, wrote a teleplay for the BBC, contributed book and lyrics to the ill-fated musical *Jeeves* (1975), for which Andrew Lloyd Webber composed the music, and wrote sketches and lyrics for a late-night review, *Men on Women on Men* (1978), with music by Paul Todd.

In the 1980s Ayckbourn expanded his work in musical comedy and children's theater but remained best known for his comedies. *Season's Greetings*, about a dysfunctional gathering over the course of Christmas weekend, opened in 1980. A year later came *Way Upstream*, about an ill-fated shipboard vacation involving two couples. Continuing his experimentation, he began a script consisting entirely of alternative scenes. *Intimate Exchanges* contained eight possible plays, each with two alternative endings; the first, *A Game of Cricket*, was performed in 1982, and in 1983 all eight were performed on successive nights. The following season Ayckbourn introduced *A Chorus of Disapproval*, a comedy involving an amateur troupe producing John Gay's *Beggar's Opera*, and in 1985, *Woman in Mind*, in which the overburdened wife of a vicar chooses fantasy over the

dreary relationships she faces in life. These last two were both produced in London by the National Theatre, which in 1986 offered Ayckbourn a position. Ayckbourn arranged a leave of absence from Scarborough.

At the National, Ayckbourn directed works by other authors and in 1987 his own *A Small Family Business*, a cynical comedy involving a family-run firm that is going broke due to family corruption. Another new script, *Henceforward . . .* , set in a violent future, premiered at Scarborough that year. In 1988 Ayckbourn returned to Scarborough and produced *Man of the Moment*, a satirical look at both the famous and the obscure. The following season he launched *The Revengers' Comedies*, a pair of plays that are to be performed on succeeding evenings. In the style of an episodic novel, the plot follows two characters who avenge themselves on those who nearly destroyed them. Like *Man of the Moment*, the plays articulated Ayckbourn's disgust for the self-seeking 1980s. At the same time, however, he added two notable plays to his body of work for children's theater, *Invisible Friends* (1989) and *This Is Where We Came In* (1990).

Ayckbourn's plays of the 1990s began with *Body Language*, which proceeds from the premise that two women—one a fitness fanatic, the other an overweight hedonist—exchange bodies; the play explores common assumptions about gender. In 1991's *Wildest Dreams*, four people who participate in a role-playing game take in a fifth player, and their lives merge with their roles in the game. The same season witnessed *My Very Own Story*, a children's play about storytellers. A serious comedy, *Time of My Life*, opened in 1992. The dissolution of a family occurs in scenes superimposed upon their last dinner together.

In 1994 Ayckbourn made headlines with his direction of an Australian children's play about AIDS, *Two Weeks with the Queen*. That year, *Communicating Doors* depicted a future in which characters reach into the past and, by helping their predecessors, change their own lives. Ayckbourn also presented two children's plays for Christmas, *The Musical Jigsaw Play*, about a rock group trapped in a board game, and *The Champion of Paribanou*, an *Arabian Nights* fantasy, with touches of *Star Wars*, in which the timid son of a sultan must become a brave warrior. Ayckbourn returned to the musical he wrote with Andrew Lloyd Webber, now retitled *By Jeeves*. *Things We Do For Love*, a bitterly comedic tale of love and deception, opened in London to mixed reviews in 1998.

In many ways, Ayckbourn's life set the stage for his plays' themes and structures. His parents' stormy match and subsequent breakup, his divorce from Christine Roland, and his subsequent happy relationship with a partner with whom he had no legal connection but only bonds of affection suggest that much of his disenchantment with marriage comes from personal experience. Similarly, his middle-class upbringing and longtime residence in the suburbs offers clues to the people and environment he consistently depicts. Because he worked both backstage and onstage during his formative years, his knowledge of the theater is voluminous, extending into technical areas of production with which many playwrights are unfamiliar. Ultimately, Stephen Joseph, from his vantage point as a mentor, director, and producer, was absolutely correct in his estimate of Ayckbourn's potential as a dramatist.

MAJOR PLAYS

ALTHOUGH most of Ayckbourn's plays are in print, the majority appear in acting editions, published by specialized theatrical publishers for groups and companies wishing to perform them. While these editions are easily accessible to theater people, they often are not obtainable in bookstores and libraries. Indeed, some plays are easier to find onstage than in print. Some scripts had not been published by the end of the 1990s, including early plays (by "Roland Allen") and unsuccessful later pieces. This discussion emphasizes Ayckbourn's major plays, which have had successful runs in London and which may be read as well as seen.

Ayckbourn's first plays, produced at Scarborough, and his first West End hit, *Relatively Speaking* (1964), show the promise of a comedic playwright-in-the-making, although these early works are very conventionally composed. However, "Countdown" (1969), the short sketch he contributed to the revue *Mixed Doubles,* blends the conventional with the experimental. Ayckbourn shows us a couple finishing dinner. Although their conversation is sparse, husband and wife share their thoughts with the audience—a litany of spousal complaints, worries, and pet peeves.

"Countdown" anticipates *How the Other Half Loves* (1969), a farce that breaks with realistic staging. Frank Foster, a businessman, and his wife, Fiona, argue about why Fiona came home late the night before. Meanwhile, across town, Bob Phillips, Frank's employee, and his wife, Teresa, argue about where Bob was. To cover his liaison with Fiona, Bob tells Teresa he went out with a fellow employee, William Detweiler, who suspects he has been betrayed by his wife, Mary, who in turn suspects the same thing of him. Later, after Fiona phones Bob, she adapts his story: she tells Frank she was out with Mary Detweiler.

Frank and Teresa feel sympathy for the Detweilers. Each invites the couple to dinner, Frank that very night and Teresa the night after. We observe both disastrous dinners simultaneously. In the second act, Bob and Fiona's story unravels. Frank forgives Fiona. Bob and Teresa make an uneasy truce. The Detweilers are the real victims; with each convinced the other is committing adultery, they barely manage to hold on to their marriage.

The original London production was anchored by Robert Morley, a character actor widely associated with farce. Thus, as spectators enjoyed Morley's reliable performance, they easily accepted the nontraditional staging. Indeed, what critics remembered was not the play's commentary on marriage or its comedy of deception but its innovative dinner-party scene, in which everything appears to happen at once. The compression of the moment and intensification of the humor remain highly original. At the same time, the ending is far from neatly resolved. The Detweilers may never reconcile, Bob and Teresa are only temporarily together, and the peace negotiated by Frank and Fiona is more like a friendship than a marriage.

For all the inventive staging of *How the Other Half Loves,* its characters are the same middle-class Londoners found in most traditional West End fare. However, in *Time and Time Again* (1971), Ayckbourn offers more developed characterizations as he tells the story of Leonard, a working-class-turned-middle-class misfit. After a brilliant degree at university, followed by a teaching job and marriage, Leonard is divorced and now lives aimlessly in a provincial city. Amusing and bright, he has a boyish charm and the sense of responsibility of a ten-year-old. The comedy arises from Leonard's infatuation with Joan, whose fiancé, Peter, Leonard befriends so that he may get closer to her. Ayckbourn's interest in his characters transcends his previous light-comedy formula. There is a sadness in Leonard's adolescent evasiveness and refusal to be accountable for his own actions; he resembles Simon Gray's Butley and other British stage and film antiheroes of the late 1960s and early 1970s. In this play, Ayckbourn modeled his characters on people with whom his Scarborough audiences would have been familiar—people who came from industrial cities or dreary suburbs, people who were down to earth, even banal.

Time and Time Again set the stage for *The Norman Conquests* (1973), which consists of the three separate but related plays *Table Manners, Living Together,* and *Round and Round the Garden,* all of which center around the same events. Over a July weekend, a married couple, Sarah and Reg, come to relieve Reg's sister, Annie, whose mother is confined to bed. This is Annie's first vacation in three years. Sarah believes Annie is going away with Tom, a local veterinarian. But Annie is actually meeting her sister Ruth's husband, Norman, with whom she had a secret fling six months earlier.

As we have seen, each play is set in a different part of the house—*Table Manners* in the dining room, *Living Together* in the living room, and *Round and Round the Garden* outdoors—but covers the same time period between Saturday evening and the following Monday morning. As we move through each play we observe different patterns and significances in relationships between characters. Sarah, in *Table Manners,* seems a terrible prude, but by the close of *Round and Round the Garden* she emerges more sympathetically as a neglected and sexually repressed wife. Similarly Norman, who initially appears to be a charmingly unconventional man, shows by the end of the trilogy that he is an egomaniac obsessed with conquering women. Eventually Annie takes charge. She tells Tom, who finally proposes, that she is not sure she wants to marry him, and she dismisses Norman. In the end, Norman is abandoned by the women he has enticed.

As with *Time and Time Again,* the action in *The Norman Conquests* revolves around a ne'er-do-well protagonist who is charming, manipulative, and frighteningly narcissistic. As the audience engages with the action and the characters over three nights, Norman himself becomes increasingly predictable while the less histrionic characters, who initially appear somewhat flat, emerge as complex and multidimensional. As the spectators' point of view develops, they see past the engaging comedy and into the unsatisfied needs of the people—especially the women—onstage. By the time *The Norman Conquests* played to rave reviews in London and New York, Ayckbourn had gained a reputation not only as a disparager of wedded bliss but also as a champion of its female victims. Despite the trilogy's title, the women characters in these plays manage to emerge from the chaotic weekend with some shred of dignity.

Audiences recognized and identified with these middle-class people trapped in unfulfilled lives. The humor derives largely from the characters' personalities: Norman's constant conniving, Annie's desperate desire for fun, Tom's inability to commit, Reg's ability to ignore everyone, Sarah's veneer of prudishness, and Ruth's tired acceptance of her philandering husband, all appear laughably shortsighted but very familiar. *The Norman Conquests* brings us into the world not of the wealthy upper classes but of ordinary suburbanites.

Ayckbourn had already clarified his advocacy for women in this middle-class context in *Absurd Person Singular* (1972). Set in a suburb, the play takes place in three different kitchens over three Christmases. The first year, Sidney and Jane prepare a party in their well-equipped kitchen. Sidney is nervous, and Jane tries not to panic. First to arrive are Dick and Lottie (who are never seen); they remain in the living room, but other guests flock to the kitchen. Ronald, the bank manager from whom Sidney wants a loan, and his wife, Marion, who has a drinking problem, chat with host and hostess. Sidney and Jane bring in Geoff, a philandering architect, and Eva, his manic-depressive wife. The three husbands chat, with Geoff prodding Ronald to drop his name to a local builder, Ronald voicing his envy of Geoff's ability to sleep around, and Sidney remaining at a loss. When Jane is accidentally locked out and drenched by rain, the party abruptly halts.

One Christmas later, in her chaotic kitchen, Eva takes a handful of sleeping pills. She tries writing a suicide note, and when Geoff arrives, he eventually notices and runs upstairs to phone the hospital. Jane, the first of their holiday visitors, comes in and, seeing Eva with her head in the oven, assumes she is cleaning the stove. Sidney enters and tries to unstop the sink drain. Geoff, unwilling to tell them what Eva has done, comes downstairs, announces he must fetch the doctor, and promises to return. Eva continues looking for ways to take her own life. She attempts to hang herself with clothesline but breaks the light fixture. She attempts to electrocute herself on the fixture's loose wires but cannot. Induced by Marion to share some gin, Eva ends up on the kitchen table singing carols.

Yet another Christmas later, in an expensive kitchen, Ronald makes tea for Marion, who is ill upstairs. As Eva, now recovered, and Geoff, the ceiling of whose latest building has collapsed, enter with holiday greetings, Marion comes downstairs. The four commiserate about their miserable lives. When Sidney and Jane ring the doorbell, the four inside turn off the lights, hoping the couple will leave, but Sidney and Jane come in through the back. They offer gifts and insist on cheering everyone with a game based on musical chairs. The play ends with the six dancing, pretending they are having fun.

The critique of holy, or as Ayckbourn might put it, unholy, matrimony in *Absurd Person Singular* is crystal clear, but the enduring images—Jane dripping with rain; Eva, drunk and drugged, singing carols on the table; Marion in her negligee, adorned with makeup and jewelry, playing Camille—are of wives who suffer as their impatient and negligent husbands look on. Although the dance that closes the play involves all partners, Ayckbourn implies that men, despite their complaints, are the main beneficiaries of marriage and women must bear the heavy matrimonial yoke. The couples' dance of marital bliss is as amusing as it is unbelievable.

Ayckbourn's exploration of how choice determines our lives takes a novel form in *Sisterly Feelings* (1979), a comedy written in "alternative scenes." In the beginning Ralph Matthews, an elderly physician, leads his family into the park where he proposed to his wife, whose funeral they have just attended. With him are his older daughter, Abigail, married to Patrick, and his younger daughter, Dorcas, who lives with Stafford. Both are attracted to Simon Grimshaw, recently returned from Africa extremely fit and attractive. Simon is the brother of Brenda, girlfriend of another Matthews sibling, Melvyn. As Ralph guides them uphill, we witness Abigail's frustration with Patrick when he leaves for a business meeting and watch Dorcas put up with the antisocial Stafford. At the end of the first scene the sisters are left with Simon; they have him flip a coin to decide who goes in the car and who walks back to town with him.

The coin toss determines which of Ayckbourn's alternative scenes will come next: one version depicts what happens if Abigail walks with Simon, the other if Dorcas accompanies him. In the first scenario, Abigail leaves Patrick and has an affair with Simon; in the other, Dorcas breaks with Stafford and has an affair with Simon. At the end of each version, the sister decides either to continue with Simon or to consider her former partner. What follows is determined by choice: there are again two different scenes, each predicated on what the sister decides. In the final, single scene, both sisters return to their respective mates, leaving Simon alone.

Sisterly Feelings implies that what happens to people is in part the result of what they choose to do under certain circumstances; it also, perhaps unintentionally, suggests that no matter what they choose, people end up with the lives they were meant to have. Thus, although Ayckbourn's portrait of fate through choices may be interpreted to mean that we are what we do, the final scene, which is always the same, feels almost deterministic. Perhaps aware that audiences might come away from this play with mixed emotions, Ayckbourn wrote *Intimate Exchanges* (1982), a series of alternative scenes that make up eight different plays, each with two endings. The whole work, which fills two thick volumes, explores the possibilities inherent in the lives of six characters: Toby, alcoholic headmaster of a small prep school; his bored wife, Celia; Miles, chair of the school's board of directors; his promiscuous wife, Rowena; Sylvie, who cleans for Toby and Celia; and Lionel, school groundskeeper. As in *Sisterly Feelings*, the characters' choices determine which scenes will be played. Two actors (a man and woman) play all the roles.

Both works had limited runs, for they were not easy to perform. Moreover, for spectators to comprehend fully what Ayckbourn was doing, they had to devote two or three evenings to each play. Critics appreciated Ayckbourn's ideas but protested that he was not breaking any new ground here, for his notion of "alternative scenes" had been used before. *Sisterly Feelings* and *Intimate Exchanges* were among his most interesting but least successful works.

In *Woman in Mind* (1985), Ayckbourn returns to the theme of the damaged wife and damaging family. Susan is married to Gerald, vicar in a small parish, and they live with Gerald's sister, Muriel, a widow incapable of doing anything correctly; their son, Rick, has joined a religious cult that forbids him to speak to them. As the play opens, Susan is returning to consciousness, having fainted in the garden. Bill Windsor, a physician who is on call while her regular doctor is away, passes by and resuscitates her. At first she cannot understand him, and as she revives she believes she is somewhere else and with other people. As Bill goes in to make her tea, imaginary characters enter: Andy, Susan's attentive husband; Tony, her charming brother; and Lucy, her endearing daughter. As she interacts with them and then with those from her actual life—the pompous Gerald and the reproachful Muriel—we understand why Susan hallucinates this dream family.

Susan's attacks recur as Gerald prepares for a visit from their son. Muriel's failed attempts to make coffee and omelettes draws Susan back to her kind, lively daydream characters. Yet when they too become demanding, Susan sees she is no better off with her imaginary family. Rick arrives, announces that he left the cult and is about to be married, and then admits that he and his new wife are going to the Far East to escape Gerald and Susan. Saddened, Susan blacks out again, awaking after midnight. From her conversation with Gerald, who begs her to come in from the garden, and with Rick, who tries to make her listen, we deduce that she in fact is responsible for several mean pranks in the house. Rick and Gerald go inside, and she remains, entrapped by her fantasy, caught in a twilight between consciousness and dream.

In *Woman in Mind*, Ayckbourn explores not just the bondage of marriage and the families that women must endure but also the images of womanhood they have internalized from a culture that demands such slavery. Susan may be, at least in part, the victim of a bad marriage, but she can imagine her escape only in images drawn from her cultural background, which, as she discovers, only lead her back to her immediate dilemma. Furthermore, although she wants to see herself as a good wife and mother, she has failed in major ways. Some of these we see firsthand: her unkindness to her son and his decision to leave suggest that she has driven him away. Yet she can no more admit to these faults than she can consciously take responsibility for the nasty pranks she commits at the end of the play. Susan is not so much passive as passive aggressive. Even victims, Ayckbourn implies, may become perpetrators of the very

things that oppress them. The West End run of this play, which received high praise, was long and profitable; *Woman in Mind* was a commercial and artistic success in Scarborough, London, and New York.

Ayckbourn again won critical accolades and large audiences with *Man of the Moment* (1988), which lampoons contemporary media hype of the supposedly private lives of public personalities. Seventeen years before the play begins, Vic Parks, now the host of several popular television programs, held up a bank. During the robbery he took a hostage, and Douglas Beechey, a mild-mannered bank clerk, intervened to take Vic's gun, which went off accidentally in the face of the hostage, Nerys. Vic went to prison. Later, however, he was interviewed by a young reporter, Jill Rillington, for the BBC. Radio and television appearances and best-selling books followed; through his TV shows, Vic became a celebrity. He married Trudy, and they had two children.

Act 1 opens in their Mediterranean vacation villa, where Vic is attended by servants and a nanny named Sharon, a young, chubby fan of his. Jill Rillington, who "discovered" Vic, has come to shoot her own show, *Their Paths Crossed*. She has set up a reunion between Vic and Douglas, the bank clerk, hoping for a dramatic confrontation. But as Jill awaits Douglas' arrival, we learn from what she tells Trudy and Vic's manager, Kenny, that Douglas is too agreeable, not bitter enough for tabloid TV. When he arrives, Jill tries to get him to admit to some feelings of anger over the fact that Vic, the villain in the crime, has succeeded while Douglas is forgotten. By Jill's standards Douglas is a failure: he happily runs a window-replacement business and has married Nerys, whose face Vic's bullet mutilated. Jill tries to convince Trudy that Vic should speak of his criminal past, but Trudy insists they have put all that behind them. Simultaneously, we glimpse the great Vic as a bully, bossing his wife and manager and humiliating Sharon. After an attempt at shooting the meeting scene (which already took place off camera), they all proceed inside.

Act 2 begins after the interview is over, with Jill lamenting that Douglas was disappointing. Vic, noticeably drunk, enters and verbally abuses Sharon. Douglas confronts him. Before their argument turns to a fight, Trudy enters. She has by now warmed to Douglas, for she sees that he is kind and has no desire to take advantage of them.

She breaks up the row by asking Douglas to walk her to the beach. That evening, when Trudy and Douglas return, he confides to her that he intervened in Vic's robbery because he adored Nerys, who refused to go out with him. After her face was disfigured, she lost interest in her other suitors and married him, although their marriage is not romantic. Touched, Trudy kisses him. Douglas leaves, and Trudy goes inside to discover Sharon ready to throw herself into the sea; she has longed for Vic in vain and suffered his nastiness too long. Trudy explains that Vic is so self-centered that no one can love him. Vic overhears. Trudy stands up to him, telling him how vile he has been to Sharon, who, now desperate, jumps into the pool, crying for help. As Vic smugly ignores Sharon's cries, Trudy goes to the door and shouts for Douglas.

When Douglas arrives, Trudy and Vic are arguing by the pool, and as Douglas tries to break them up he pushes Vic into the pool. Vic drowns as Sharon climbs out. To clear the nanny of possible charges, Trudy, Douglas, and Sharon, soon joined by Kenny, invent a story to explain what occurred. The story is played before us as a televised reenactment hosted by Jill. Vic dies a hero—supposedly trying to save Sharon—and although television loses a star, Jill lands the story of her career.

Man of the Moment focuses on acts of simulation, most notably in the character of Vic. The television celebrity is a total self-invention, amplified and promoted by the media. Vic's popular image is that of a felon who has turned his life around, but those who know him recognize that he is the same man he always was: a petty hustler who has managed to apply his criminal skills in his "rehabilitated" profession. Trudy has been bullied by her tyrant husband, and the happiness of their family has been built on precarious illusions, which are eventually swept away. Once more, Ayckbourn presents the cultural ideals of home and hearth as bogus.

In *Time of My Life* (1992), Ayckbourn examines the dissolution of the Strattons, a family that has achieved local prominence through ownership of a small factory. The play opens on Laura Stratton's fifty-fourth birthday: Gerry, her husband, and their sons, Glyn and Adam, are celebrating at their favorite restaurant. Glyn has recently reconciled with his wife, Stephanie, and Adam has brought his girlfriend, Maureen. We watch the party end: Maureen has drunk too much and runs for the la-

dies' room; Stephanie and Glyn leave, but not before Gerry makes Glyn promise to be faithful to her; Gerry and Laura drink into the night. As they argue, bits of the past and the future are enacted. We learn that Gerry will be killed in a car crash on the way home from this dinner but that Laura will survive. We watch as Adam's romance with Maureen fails because Adam cannot stand up to his mother. Despite his vow to Gerry, Glyn leaves his wife and moves in with a young woman. At first his abandonment overwhelms Stephanie, but eventually she recognizes that Laura has always dominated her sons. Although we know the future of this family, the play closes as they begin the fateful dinner that marks the last time they ever will come together.

Here, through the dislocation of time, Ayckbourn reveals the problems lurking behind the portrait of a happy family. As in *Woman in Mind*, spectators are asked to distance themselves from their own values and prejudices. None of the characters seems extraordinary or unusual; thus, the implication that marriage is an antiquated practice and that families no longer function as the basic unit of society applies not merely to these particular people but to the entire culture. The audience views the final scene in a context pointedly different from the way they viewed the first: The very same people who were so appealing and full of promise now appear doomed, not just because of who they are and what they do but because the culture at large does not provide the bases for a successful existence.

In *Time of My Life* the use of place and time is as significant as its themes. All the action occurs in the same restaurant: to contribute to the comedy, Ayckbourn has the staff of brothers from some unidentifiable foreign place all played by one actor. Amid the service and chatter, the dining room widens to represent the world. Within this one setting, episodes between characters take place without regard to chronological sequence. Although the themes in this play are hardly new to Ayckbourn, the method of delivery clearly is.

THE AYCKBOURN OEUVRE

THE themes explored in Ayckbourn's major plays permeate his work as a whole. His critique of marriage appears in his earliest efforts and continues into his scripts of the 1990s. As this theme deepened and developed he also showed increasing resourcefulness with regard to theatrical presentation. Rather than settling into a particular group of techniques, as some dramatists do once they have established themselves, Ayckbourn continued to experiment with various facets of playwriting and staging, with the result that his plays have never ceased to surprise and engage with audiences.

There are, predictably, few successful couples in Ayckbourn's plays. The significant exception is in *Joking Apart* (1978), which features a couple, Anthea and Richard, who left their spouses to live together. In this play we watch the couple and their friends change over the course of twelve years. Richard's business partner, Sven, sees that he has never amounted to much, not because Richard never gave him a chance but because he let Richard run their shop. Sven's wife, Olive, realizes that she has had to convince her husband of a self worth he never really had. Hugh, the local vicar, and his wife, Louise, despite their good intentions, are cursed by a brilliant son who despises them. Family friend Brian, who always believed he was in love with Anthea, emerges a lonely middle-aged man. Richard and Anthea, by contrast, are blessed with an atypically happy union. Unlike their friends and neighbors, the two have never tied the knot: truly happy couples, Ayckbourn implies, echoing the choice he made in his own private life, need no official certificate.

Yet Ayckbourn never entirely discounts the possibility of a productive match: In *Communicating Doors*, which opens in the year 2014, a call girl discovers that one of the doors in the hotel room to which she's been called actually leads into the past. Trapped in a dangerous situation in the present, she escapes to the year 1994 and interacts with people who had lived twenty years earlier. When she finally comes back to the future she finds her life has changed. Here, as with *Joking Apart*, we watch as characters change over time, but the science fiction in *Communicating Doors* allows female characters from twenty and forty years earlier to learn from one another's experiences and to anticipate and avoid mistakes, marital ones included. The implication is not that a good marriage is impossible but that, unless one can manage to address potential problems before they occur, a good marriage is improbable.

With this skepticism of wedlock comes Ayckbourn's nonjudgmental attitude toward the often adulterous consequences of an unsuccessful union. Such affairs are rarely portrayed as evil. In certain cases infidelity may be exploitative (as with the blackmailing Philip in *Relatively Speaking*), pathetic (compulsive Norman in *The Norman Conquests*), or neglectful (the philandering Geoff in *Absurd Person Singular*). Yet Ayckbourn's work suggests that there are worse things than a sexual affair, a notion that may be detected even in early plays. The dalliance of Fiona and Bob in *How the Other Half Loves* causes chaos within their marriages, but the basic instability of their marriages, not their tryst, is blamed; the faithful Detweilers are convinced that each has betrayed the other—an indication that their relationship, not the illicit act, causes their distrust.

If Ayckbourn's disapproval of marriage has led to his championship of women, his criticism of men has evolved from the same source. For example, Leonard in *Time and Time Again* and Norman in *The Norman Conquests* obsessively pursue women who ought to be unavailable to them: Leonard goes after his friend's fiancée and Norman chases his sisters-in-law. At first glance their unfulfilled longings seem to come from bad marriages, but eventually each man shows that what he really wants is power, not sex. Leonard is more interested in defeating his rival, Peter, than in winning Joan; Norman's constant seductiveness is his way of trying to make up for his sense of being a failure. Each is less interested in women than in his status among men.

Male attraction to power, as opposed to love, is perhaps clearest in *A Chorus of Disapproval* (1984), a comedy about an amateur operetta company's production of John Gay's *Beggar's Opera*. Guy Jones, a businessman whom the rest of the cast believe will give them important information about a land deal involving his corporation, manages to rise to the lead role in the show. Two unhappy married women in the cast pursue him with offers of sex, and he surrenders to their demands. In reality, both women not only seek his affections but, like their husbands, want to persuade him to supply them with inside information that will make them rich. Guy accepts their advances unquestioningly and then refuses to inform anyone when the deal falls through. He is convinced that, without doing anything to earn success, he deserves to be awarded the leading role, not only onstage but in life. He carries with him the same sense of masculine entitlement that we glimpse in Leonard and Norman and many other Ayckbourn males.

Moreover, the underlying similarities among Ayckbourn's male characters explode some of the myths surrounding masculinity. In many scripts, for example, we watch competing "types" of men, the most evident conflict pitting the neurotic intellectual against the robust athlete: Leonard versus Peter in *Time and Time Again,* Norman versus Tom in *The Norman Conquests,* the effete Stafford versus the rugged Simon in *Sisterly Feelings,* just to name a few. Yet whatever contrast Ayckbourn may draw—the bullying husband with the attentive stranger (in *Absent Friends* and *Season's Greetings*), the niggling perfectionist with the easygoing philanderer (in *Suburban Strains,* 1980), or the self-absorbed husband with the considerate mate (in *Woman in Mind*)—men always have control in their relationships with women. True, Karen, the zany protagonist in *The Revengers' Comedies,* manages to turn the tables on the males who have destroyed Henry's life, but she does so ultimately only to hold on to Henry. Only Stephanie, the wife who bravely reinvents herself after losing her husband in *Time of My Life,* manages to escape the traditional battle of the sexes in which she (by virtue of her sex) is fated to be the loser. And although some of Ayckbourn's male characters may not like marriage, they all seem to want its advantages. In Ayckbourn's world, marriage primarily benefits men and oppresses women.

In the first three decades of his playwriting Ayckbourn never traveled too far beyond the issues embedded in the conventional matrimonial institution. He seemed to believe that courtship and conjugal relations, and all the betrayals that come with them, sufficiently represent the human lives he portrayed. Few gays and lesbians featured in his casts: Kenny in *Man of the Moment* and Rick, a male-identified young woman in *Wildest Dreams,* are the two examples of nonheterosexuals. Ayckbourn's assumption, or perhaps the assumption that he assigned his audience, was that the world is, in very basic ways, heterosexual.

In later works, however, Ayckbourn integrated into his dramaturgy a critique of sexual identities. In *Henceforward . . . ,* set in a future London dominated by violent girl gangs, he presents in the character of the gender-confused adolescent daughter, Geain (pronounced "Jane"), a comic commentary of where modern ambiguities regarding sexuality may ultimately lead: Geain, the sweet little girl whom her father fondly remembers, now dresses like a boy and refers to herself as "he." And in *Body Language,* Ayckbourn actively attacks contemporary perceptions of sexuality. When the fashion model Angie and the obese reporter Jo exchange bodies, each comes to learn how men's objectification of women has shaped them. At first they are disappointed when the exchange cannot be reversed. Yet the two go on to write a book revealing all they grasped through this experience. Here, for the first time, Ayckbourn amusingly deconstructs those basic beliefs about gender that make his audiences who they are.

For all his discontent with the status quo, Ayckbourn is difficult to pigeonhole in traditional political terms. His cynicism about politics is clearest in *Ten Times Table,* in which a village's reenactment of a seventeenth-century massacre becomes a theatrical battle between Right and Left. While one side interprets the event as a proud victory for the local nobility, the other sees in it a protosocialist revolution. Both factions are satirized mercilessly, but we are left not with the Marxists but with the old lady whose common sense explains that there was no historical truth behind the reenacted "event." The massacre never took place. This final scene suggests that British common sense is his audience's best hope, a sentiment echoed in *Way Upstream,* in which a passive, mild-mannered Englishman is finally pushed to overthrow the cruel bully who has taken over the boat on which he and his wife are spending their vacation. We may also recall *Man of the Moment* and its pointed contrast between the flashy confidence man Vic and the simple, genuinely heroic Douglas. By lampooning the image of the overblown media figure, Ayckbourn suggests that the mob, manipulated by what it reads, hears, and watches, may in the end be misled. The trendy, Ayckbourn implies, is deceptive and must be distrusted, while the old, tried and true—the innocuous Douglas—is, in its humdrum banality, trustworthiness itself. Still, such a reading is further complicated by Ayckbourn's awareness that the media are the creation of a society dominated by power-hungry men. Vic's despicable treatment of the people around him indicates that what he really wants is control over others.

If, as in *Ten Times Table* and *Man of the Moment,* the past is a creation of the present, Ayckbourn's vision of a future based on our present promises to be even worse. His concern about the world to come is clear in his very early play *Standing Room Only*, a tale of overpopulation and traffic jams. The frightening landscape of a London tyrannized by marauding gangs in both *Communicating Doors* and *Henceforward . . .* warns that, as Noël Coward wrote, "There are bad times just around the corner." Only the symbiotic coupling in *Body Language* of Angie and Jo, who in coming to know their new selves come to know each other, offers a ray of hope. Still, Ayckbourn's point in all his futuristic works seems to be that if the mistakes we are now making can be averted, the bleakness of tomorrow might not be realized.

Such worthy themes are not, however, what makes Ayckbourn a genuinely significant playwright. As the ultrapolitical German playwright Bertolt Brecht cautioned, unless a play is first and foremost entertaining, no one will bother to listen to it. And as an entertainer, Ayckbourn excels.

Behind every Ayckbourn play lies a strong story. In fact, his work as a whole discloses a vital interest in storytelling, most obvious from two children's plays, *My Very Own Story* and *This Is Where We Came In,* in which a succession of storytellers compete to be *the* storyteller. In these plays Ayckbourn scrutinizes the very act of telling a story and explores the concept of how drama conveys narrative. Much effort is channeled into complicating, through restructuring, the way spectators construe the plot. By presenting scenes out of the time sequence in which they occur, Ayckbourn distances us from the belief that life is a simple, straightforward progression of events and places us in a position from which everything familiar suddenly looks very different.

In *How the Other Half Loves,* the unity of time is noticeably violated. The action occurs not in one place but two, in the Fosters' and the Phillipses' homes. During the dinner scene in which the Detweilers are entertained by both households, time is fractured; the play no longer represents events chronologically. A similar phenomenon occurs in *Time of My Life,* in which Ayckbourn defies the logical order of time by placing scenes nonchronologically, which in turn makes the audience convert the present into the past and the future into the present; fragments of the family's experience flash by, regardless of when they have (or will have) occurred. Ayckbourn thus challenges the Aristotelian notion that time orders what happens in a story: the lives of these people, he implies, cannot be ad-

equately understood through the usual linear sequence. What links events in these two nonlinear plays is the use of a single setting.

Yet the meaning of stage narrative, Ayckbourn implies, depends on the audience's perspective. In *The Norman Conquests,* narrative is contingent on physical situation, for each play locates characters in a separate place—dining room, living room, garden—while all of the action transpires over the same time period. The result is not simply a three-part reiteration of the same story but three very different stories. In the one-act play "Between Mouthfuls," from *Confusions,* point of view becomes crucial in the construction of narrative. Throughout the play a waiter shuttles between tables, hearing only bits of dinner conversation. The audience hears and sees only what he does, so the piecemeal story they glean is clearly different from the narrative the characters would tell.

Another way Ayckbourn incorporates the characters' subjective views into the narrative is to locate the story not in external action but in the interplay between fantasy and reality. In his sketch "Countdown" (from *Mixed Doubles*), there is little dialogue between the wife and husband, but through a series of monologues the two separately articulate their inner feelings, which contrast markedly with the few words they exchange. Ayckbourn presents not one story here but two, one the wife's, one the husband's, occurring simultaneously.

Even more pointedly, in *Woman in Mind* the story takes place sometimes in Susan's fantasies and sometimes in what we identify as the real world. Rather than show the story as it appears to "objective" characters such as Bill, Ayckbourn dramatizes what happens within Susan's mind: Bill's gibberish while Susan is regaining consciousness reflects the garbled way Susan hears him, not what he is actually saying. Her conversations with her fantasy family enact not a faithful version of reality but one that captures what transpires inside her head. As Susan drifts into her dream world, the audience separates from her viewpoint; we are able to comprehend that the violent pranks, about which she claims to know nothing, have actually been committed by her. *Woman in Mind* utilizes expressionistic techniques through which the playwright dramatizes what the central character feels.

Ayckbourn's most obvious experiments in narrative appear in plays with "alternative scenes." The two moments when more than one option is possible in *Sisterly Feelings* suggest how much may result from the choices one makes. The toss of a coin at the end of act 1, scene 1 is counterbalanced by a reasoned decision at the end of act 1, scene 2. Yet Ayckbourn hints that character is more important than chance or opportunity in determining what happens, because no matter what the coin indicates or what decision the sister makes, the play always ends with the same scene. Try as they may to change their futures, Abigail and Dorcas will not alter their final fates. This conclusion is contradicted in *Intimate Exchanges.* In the first scene, Celia decides whether or not to smoke a cigarette; this choice is followed by alternative scenes, each following the other through a series of choices. With an array of endings, conscious decisions by the characters propel the fates of all. Story is not a static progression of beginning, middle, and tidy ending; rather, narrative grows from who the characters are and what they elect to do.

Ayckbourn resurrects the "alternative scene" script in *Mr. A's Amazing Maze Plays.* Here, an audience of children vote on which scene should come next by determining which room Suzy should enter in Mr. Accousticus' labyrinthine mansion. The use of alternatives in this case proves highly appealing. Moreover, the young spectators do not have to come back to see other performances in order to appreciate the novelty of this approach. By this point in his career, however, Ayckbourn had begun looking at other ways to portray how a particular choice at a specific time has great resonance: the idea of revising the past, dramatized in *Communicating Doors,* is far more deft and practical.

Critics view Ayckbourn as a theatrical rather than a dramatic playwright because of his highly inventive use of spectacle: instead of presenting stunning visual effects, however, he often redefines how stage space is used. He is ingenious at employing setting as a means of connecting plot and time with character. In farce, an important role is played by the set, with its placement of entrances and exits and set pieces, props, and devices. The set determines what space is usable onstage and thus enables the physical and much of the verbal comedy to take place.

As noted above, the set in *How the Other Half Loves,* half of which depicts the Fosters' apartment and the other half the Phillipses', makes possible our ability to see the action taking place simultaneously in both homes. Thus we have an oppor-tunity to glimpse the impossible: two different dinners held on successive nights. Although the stage contains two different sets that overlap, the whole play requires that at least one be used and sometimes both. Moreover, even as the interconnection of these separate places permits the high comedy of two disastrous scenes, it also hints that while the two households seem distinct, an underlying similarity connects them. The set also comments on the play's title, the two halves being the Fosters' upper-middle-class flat and the Phillipses' lower-middle-class home. Even though each couple believes the other occupies a different status, Ayckbourn is reminding us that they are both middle class.

Ayckbourn's expertise in arranging the stage to show us action occurring in several places is also evident in *Bedroom Farce,* where he strings together three separate bedrooms, each in a different house. He does much the same in *Wildest Dreams,* in which Stanley's living room, Rick's basement, and Warren's attic are laid out before us. In *Taking Steps,* rooms on three different floors of the same house are placed on the same level. In other scripts Ayckbourn specifies multilevel settings. The children's play *Invisible Friends* calls for a first-floor sitting room, dining room, and kitchen, with a bedroom and hallway built above it. This house set and its appearance in the main character's fantasy unite the worlds of reality and dream. Another cutaway view, including rooms on both ground level and the second floor, forms the set of *A Small Family Business.* At the beginning, the house depicted belongs to Jack and Poppy, but the set gradually comes to represent the homes of their relatives. Later, the upstairs bedroom is located in Anita's house, with the kitchen in Desmond's and the sitting room in Jack's. Here the playwright suggests that although the people who live in these houses seem different, they are in reality the same: they all live in the same—indeed, the identical—environment, and the decision Jack reaches about the business is determined more by where he lives than by his morals.

Similarly, in *Things We Do for Love* Ayckbourn creates comedy through a cutaway view of a three-story apartment building. The lower floors, portraying the apartments of two different characters, are in full view; the third floor, representing another apartment, is placed so high that only a glimpse of the few inches above the floor are seen. The comedy comes not only from what the audience sees on lower floors but from what they imagine is happening in the highest, as clothes are tossed on the floor and bare feet are seen.

Often, Ayckbourn uses only a single set. *Time and Time Again* is set in a yard overlooking a cricket field. The garden set of *Woman in Mind* remains unchanged, like the garden in *Joking Apart* and the garage and garden in *Just Between Ourselves. Absent Friends* is fixed in a sitting room, as are *Season's Greetings* and *Henceforward . . . ; Sisterly Feelings* never moves from the park. The sets of these plays, like the restaurant of *Time of My Life,* give the stories unity of place and ambience.

Having developed his craft in an underfunded playhouse where the setup was in-the-round, Ayckbourn learned very early how to get by with no set at all. In *Mr. Whatnot,* his early children's piece, all props and set pieces are mimed: Whatnot himself rides in an invisible car, plays golf without clubs and balls, and visits a fabulous manor house, which is nothing more than an empty stage. The musical *Me, Myself, and I* (1980) requires only a table and some chairs; the characters' songs, dialogue, and actions create the bar in which the story takes place. In his two plays about storytelling, *This Is Where We Came In* and *My Very Own Story,* Ayckbourn specifies that all action take place on a bare stage. Spectators remain aware that what they are watching is a play taking place onstage; no attempt is made to disguise the experience or lend it the verisimilitude of real life. Of course, through the magic of narration, the audience manages to visit fields and forests, strange castles and villages. Still, the vehicle in which they travel is not theatrical illusion, which appeals to their eyes, but theatrical poetry, which appeals to their imaginations.

AYCKBOURN'S COMEDY

AYCKBOURN's talent for genuine comedy makes his work stand out from much of modern drama. Although his ideas are serious, he writes for a mainstream audience rather than for an intellectual elite in search of "significant" theater. Even as critics trivialize his comedic expertise, few have been able to identify exactly how he consistently manages to make audiences laugh. Ayckbourn's inventive use of theatricality is a primary ingredient, but his characters are a much more important source of mirth. The conventional wisdom about comic

characters is that they are not as profound as tragic ones. While many of the characters in Ayckbourn's broader comedies are superficial, most plays involve issues of personality and behavior and require rounded characters. At his best he offers characters who are fully developed and capable of change.

To be sure, in farces such as *Relatively Speaking* and *Taking Steps,* characterizations are sketchy. We feel some sympathy for the betrayed wife and the duped fiancé in *Relatively Speaking,* but they do not alter from who they were early in the play. Sheila outwits her husband but feels obliged to pretend she has a lover on the side in order to keep her husband in line. Similarly, with the well-plotted action of *Taking Steps,* anything more than broad characterizations would distract spectators from the physical comedy. If they felt profound pity for Roland, abandoned by his wife, spectators would not laugh. For farce, the dramatist relies on types: Roland, the insouciant upper-class squire always with a drink in his hand; Tristram, the befuddled but well-meaning law clerk; Kitty, the girl who can never make up her mind; and Leslie, the simple yet ruthlessly conniving yokel. Such plays are by necessity built on caricature and stock characters.

Still, Ayckbourn often veers from traditional formulas. Most plays, although amusing, conclude on a note of sadness: the frenzied hilarity of *Bedroom Farce,* for example, closes with Trevor and Susannah, the couple who have destroyed Saturday night for their friends, trying to resolve their anger but obviously failing. *Henceforward . . . ,* which initially holds out the hope that this future family can be reunited, leaves us with the protagonist, Jerome Watkins, alone in his besieged apartment, composing music that no one else will ever hear. Ayckbourn shrinks from resolving his plots cheerfully and unbelievably. He wants his plays to be funny but also to ring true. This contradiction allows him to create characters who, while inspiring us to laugh, grow throughout the play or at least reveal who they are inside. One such character is Leonard, of Ayckbourn's first "serious" comedy, *Time and Time Again,* which focuses on his attempts to improve his life. He is witty, and, unlike his brother-in-law, Graham, and Joan's fiancé, Peter, whom he befriends, Leonard holds out the promise of something exciting and attractive both for the audience and for Joan, who returns his hilarious declarations of love. Nonetheless, as the plot progresses, the play shows us Leonard's limitations. While his sister changes her life by rejecting her bullying husband, Leonard is at an impasse. Because he is unable and unwilling to break from his role as disaffected underdog, we regard him not with amusement but with pathos. If indeed we are still laughing at Leonard by the final curtain, we do so only because his behavior is so brilliantly self-defeating.

Ayckbourn also is adept at creating scripts that do not revolve around a single character. For example, Norman is not the central role in *The Norman Conquests* as Leonard is in *Time and Time Again*. Rather, Norman is a catalyst in the trilogy, propelling the action—a force that brings characters together and drives them apart. The characters in *The Norman Conquests* are fully drawn and three-dimensional. What gives the trilogy its humor is the way their complex personalities interact. Tom, the hesitant suitor, would not be amusing except for Annie, who is desperate to be courted. The contrast between them inspires us to laugh, as does that between the lackadaisical Reg and his proper wife, Sarah, or the overly passionate Norman and his matter-of-fact partner, Ruth. Thus, the characters, far more than the situations, are the sources of the ironic and embarrassingly familiar humor.

Like *The Norman Conquests*, comedies such as *Absent Friends, Bedroom Farce, Ten Times Table,* and *Joking Apart* involve ensemble casting. Such role distribution illustrates the influence of Scarborough and repertory theater, in which a troupe of players takes on roles in many different productions over a season. Even subsequent experiments such as *Sisterly Feelings* and *Intimate Exchanges* call for ensemble playing, as do *Season's Greetings, Way Upstream, A Chorus of Disapproval, A Small Family Business, Wildest Dreams,* and *Time of My Life.* With this kind of casting comes a parity of male and female actors: unlike the majority of playwrights writing for the modern stage, Ayckbourn almost always includes the same number of women as men.

Yet beyond theatrical and dramatic factors such as setting and characterization, Ayckbourn is master of that key component of comedy—timing. His scripts demonstrate a deft sense of pace and sequencing. Within a few minutes he is able to make the tempo of a scene race, slow down, and then speed up once more. Even Ayckbourn's minor works show this expert touch.

In *Invisible Friends,* for example, a comedy for children, Lucy Baines invents Zara, an imaginary playmate, to take the place of her parents and brother, who ignore her. One night Zara appears and assures Lucy that anything one believes in is real. The following morning, while Lucy is setting the table, Zara enters the dining room unseen and sits in one of the chairs. Lucy, turning, suddenly spies Zara and drops the silverware. As Lucy's parents chastise her, Zara mimics them, crying, "Clumsy!" Lucy immediately asks Zara, "What—?" as her parents, almost instantaneously, ask Lucy the same. Lucy crosses to Zara and very quietly inquires whether her parents can see her. Zara pops up, stands in front of Lucy's mother, and, gesturing madly, shouts, "Yoo-hoo!" Lucy's mother calmly places something on the table and exits. The next few lines between Lucy and Zara proceed in whispers; at the same time, Lucy's brother, Gary, comes downstairs, wearing Walkman earphones. Lucy's mother calls Gary and, unable to make him hear, insists that Lucy speak to him. Lucy screams at the top of her lungs that breakfast is ready, which makes her brother and father, in the next room watching television, jump.

To be sure, some of the laughter here originates in the presence of a character whom only one person onstage can see and hear—Noël Coward's *Blithe Spirit* makes use of the same device—and the audience is in on a joke. Yet beyond the comedy of the situation, Ayckbourn is orchestrating the scene from moment to moment in order to maximize its comedic effect. Before Zara makes her appearance, we watch Lucy mundanely set the table as the television blares a science lecture (about electrical conductors), which goes on for several minutes. In fact, Lucy and her father are oblivious, when the lecture suddenly ends, that Zara has turned it off. Thus, spectators see Zara before Lucy does and are able to anticipate the surprise Lucy will experience before it happens. Once it happens, of course, the moment hurries by: we hear the quick clatter of cutlery, a shout, and "What?" three times. A quiet moment follows, which in turn is shattered by Zara's unexpected gestures and screams. The momentum slows again as Zara and Lucy whisper, but even in this calm, the audience sees Gary descending the stairs and can anticipate the next interaction. Lucy's mother tries twice to call Gary, and her crescendo is heightened by Lucy's final roar, punctuated by a physical reaction from Gary and Lucy's father.

The flow of this scene onstage appears completely natural: the meticulous crafting of speech and silence, of tone and pace, is obscured by the audience's engagement through laughter. Much of the fun in Ayckbourn's plays, then, comes not from the playwright manipulating the audience but from allowing the audience to observe who the characters are. Rather than misleading spectators to arrive at false expectations, which are then shattered, Ayckbourn invites them to participate in discovering, and thus in creating, the comedy.

CONCLUSION

CRITICS often wonder how the commercially successful Ayckbourn will be remembered in the future. Will his name be heaped with those others whose efforts to amuse no longer do? Or will he be viewed as a significant writer whose work was greatly underestimated by his contemporaries? Although such concerns probably matter little to Ayckbourn himself, whose loyalty to popular stage comedy has made him scorn what critics call "serious drama," the collection of plays he has given us suggests that he is in fact a playwright of substance. There is in his work a growing sense of suffering that accompanies the laughter. The adolescent fantasy of *Invisible Friends* is made palatable by the slapstick just as Susan's pain in *Woman in Mind* is dramatized through the hilarious contradictions that materialize in her madness. The skeptics who forecast that Ayckbourn would never rise above deft farces cannot avoid the serious implications of his work in the 1990s.

SELECTED BIBLIOGRAPHY

I. PERFORMANCE HISTORY. *The Square Cat* by Roland Allen: Scarborough, 30 July 1959 (unpublished); *Love After All* by Roland Allen: Scarborough, 21 December 1959 (unpublished); *Follow the Lover* and *Double Hitch* by Roland Allen: Scarborough (amateur production), 1960; *Dad's Tale* by Roland Allen: Scarborough, 19 December 1960 (unpublished); *Standing Room Only* by Roland Allen: Scarborough, 13 July 1961 (unpublished); *Xmas v. Mastermind*: Stoke-on-Trent, 26 December 1962 (unpublished); *Mr. Whatnot*: Stoke-on-Trent, 12 November 1963; London, 6 August 1964; *Relatively Speaking,* originally performed as *Meet My Father*: Scarborough, 8 July 1964; then under its present title, London, 29 March 1967; *The Sparrow*: Scarborough, 10 July 1967 (unpublished); *Mixed Doubles,* including "Countdown" by Alan Ayckbourn, originally produced as *We Who Are About to Die . . . :* Hampstead, 6 February 1969; then under its present title, London, 9 April 1969; *How the Other Half Loves:* Scarborough, 31 July 1969; London, 5 August 1970; *The Story So Far:* Scarborough, 20 August 1970; revised as *Me Times Me Times Me* for 1970 pre-London tour; revised as *Family Circles:* Richmond, 1978 (unpublished).

Time and Time Again: Scarborough, 8 July 1971; London, 16 August 1972; *Ernie's Incredible Illucinations:* London, 17 September 1971; *Absurd Person Singular:* Scarborough, 26 June 1972; London, 4 July 1973; *The Norman Conquests* (*Table Manners, Living Together,* and *Round and Round the Garden*): Scarborough, 18 June, 25 June, and 9 July 1973; Greenwich, 9 May, 21 May, and 6 June 1974; London, 1 August 1974; *Service Not Included:* first aired on BBC 2, 20 May 1974 (unpublished); *Confusions,* ("Mother Figure," "Drinking Companion," "Between Mouthfuls," "Gosforth's Fête," and "A Talk in the Park"): Scarborough, 30 September 1974; London, 19 May 1976; *Absent Friends:* Scarborough, 17 June 1974; London, 23 July 1975; *Jeeves,* book and lyrics by Ayckbourn and music by Andrew Lloyd Webber: London, 22 April 1975; *Bedroom Farce:* Scarborough, 16 June 1975; London, 14 March 1977; *Just Between Ourselves:* Scarborough, 28 January 1976; London, 20 April 1977; *Ten Times Table:* Scarborough, 18 January 1977; London, 5 April 1978; *Joking Apart:* Scarborough, 11 January 1978; London, 7 March 1979; *Men on Women on Men:* Scarborough, 17 June 1978 (unpublished); *Sisterly Feelings:* Scarborough, 10–11 January 1979; London, 3 June 1980; *Taking Steps:* Scarborough, 27 September 1979; London, 2 September 1980.

Suburban Strains, book and lyrics by Alan Ayckbourn and music by Paul Todd: Scarborough, 20 January 1980; London, 2 February 1981. *Season's Greetings:* Scarborough, 4 September 1980; Greenwich, 14 March 1982; London, 29 March 1982; *First Course:* Scarborough, 8 July 1980; *Second Helpings:* Scarborough, 5 August 1980 (unpublished); *Me, Myself, and I:* Scarborough, 2 June, 8 July, and 9 July 1980; Richmond, 10 December 1982; *Way Upstream:* Scarborough, 2 October 1981; London, 18 August 1982; *Making Tracks,* skits and lyrics by Ayckbourn, music by Paul Todd: Scarborough, 6 December 1981; Greenwich, 14 March 1983; *Intimate Exchanges:* Scarborough, 3 June 1982; Greenwich, 11 June 1984; London, 10 August 1984; *A Trip to Scarborough,* adapted from Sheridan's play of the same name: Scarborough, 8 December 1982 (unpublished); *A Cut in the Rates:* aired on BBC-TV Schools, 21 January 1984; *Incidental Music,* skits and lyrics by Ayckbourn, music by Paul Todd: Scarborough, 12 January 1983; Richmond, 2 December 1983 (unpublished); *It Could Be Anyone of Us:* Scarborough,

5 October 1983 (unpublished); *The Seven Deadly Virtues,* skits and lyrics by Ayckbourn, music by Paul Todd: Scarborough, 21 January 1984 (unpublished).

A Chorus of Disapproval: Scarborough, 2 May 1984; London, 1 August 1985; *The Westwoods* ("His Side" and "Her Side"), book and lyrics by Ayckbourn, music by Paul Todd: Scarborough, 24 May 1984; London, 19 May 1987 (unpublished); *Woman in Mind:* Scarborough, 30 May 1985; London, 15 September 1986; *Boy Meets Girl* and *Girl Meets Boy,* book and lyrics by Ayckbourn, music by Paul Todd: Scarborough, 23 May and 25 May 1985 (unpublished); *Mere Soup Songs,* book and lyrics by Ayckbourn, music by Paul Todd: Scarborough, 22 May 1986; London, 13 December 1986 (unpublished); *Tons of Money,* based on the 1922 comedy by Will Evans and Valentine: London, 6 November 1986; *A Small Family Business:* London, 5 June 1987; *Hencefoward . . . :* Scarborough, 30 July 1987; London, 21 November 1988; *Man of the Moment:* Scarborough, 10 August 1988; London, 14 February, 1990; *Mr. A's Amazing Maze Plays:* Scarborough, 30 November 1988; London, 30 September 1989; *The Revengers' Comedies:* Scarborough, 13 June 1989; London, 16 October 1991 (Part I) and 17 October 1991 (Part II); *The Inside Outside Slide Show:* Scarborough, 22 July 1989 (unpublished); *Wolf at the Door,* adapted from *Les Corbeaux* by Henry Becque: Scarborough, 3 October 1989 (unpublished); *Invisible Friends:* Scarborough, 22 November 1989; London, 13 March 1991; *Body Language:* Scarborough, 4 February 1990; London, 1992 (unpublished). *This Is Where We Came In:* Scarborough, 4 August (Part I) and 11 August 1990 (Part II); *Callisto V:* Scarborough, 12 December 1990 (unpublished); *Wildest Dreams:* Scarborough, 6 May 1991; London, 14 December 1993; *My Very Own Story:* Scarborough, 10 August 1991; *Time of My Life:* Scarborough, 4 April 1992; *Dreams from a Summer House,* music by John Pattison: Scarborough, 1992. *Communicating Doors:* Scarborough, 2 February 1994; London, August 1995; *Things We Do For Love:* Scarborough, 29 April 1997; London, 3 March 1998; *Haunting Julia:* Scarborough, 13 May 1999 (unpublished).

II. PUBLISHED PLAYS. *Relatively Speaking* (London and New York, 1968); *Ernie's Incredible Illucinations* (London and New York, 1969); "Countdown," in *Mixed Doubles* (London, 1970); *How the Other Half Loves* (New York, 1971; London, 1972); *Time and Time Again* (London and New York, 1973); *Absurd Person Singular* (London and Garden City, N.Y., 1974); *Absent Friends* (London and New York, 1975); *A Chorus of Disapproval* (London and New York, 1975); *The Norman Conquests* (London and Garden City, N.Y., 1975); *Bedroom Farce* (London and New York, 1977); *Confusions* (London and New York, 1977); *Just Between Ourselves* (London and New York, 1978); *Joking Apart* (London and New York, 1979); *Ten Times Table* (London and New York, 1979).

Sisterly Feelings (London and New York, 1981); *Taking Steps* (London and New York, 1981); *Season's Greetings* (London and New York, 1982); *Suburban Strains* (London and New York, 1982); *Way Upstream* (London and New York, 1983); *Intimate Exchanges* (London and New York, 1985); *A Chorus of Disapproval* (London and Boston, 1986); *Woman in Mind* (London and Boston, 1986); *A Small Family Business* (London and Boston, 1987); *Henceforward . . .* (London and Boston, 1988); *Tons of Money* (London and New York, 1988); *Mr. A's Amazing Maze Plays* (London and Boston, 1989).

Man of the Moment (London and Boston, 1990); *Invisible Friends* (London and Boston, 1991); *The Revengers' Comedies* (London and Boston, 1991); *Mr. Whatnot* (London and New York, 1992); *Time of My Life* (London, 1993); *Wildest Dreams* (London and Boston, 1993); *This Is Where We Came In* (London and New York, 1995); *Communicating Doors* (London and Boston, 1995); *Things We Do for Love* (London and Boston, 1998).

III. BIOGRAPHIES AND CRITICAL STUDIES. John Elsom, *Post-War British Theatre* (London and Boston, 1976); Ian Watson, *Alan Ayckbourn: Bibliography, Biography, Playography: Theatre Checklist No. 21* (London, 1980); John Russell Taylor, "Art and Commerce: The New Drama in the West End Marketplace," in C. W. E. Bigsby, ed., *Contemporary English Drama* (New York, 1981); Elmer M. Blistein, "Alan Ayckbourn: A Few Jokes, Much Comedy," and Malcolm Page, "The Serious Side of Alan Ayckbourn," in *Modern Drama* 26 (March 1983); Sidney Howard White, *Alan Ayckbourn* (Boston, 1984); Bernard F. Dukore, "Craft, Character, Comedy: Ayckbourn's *Woman in Mind,*" in *Twentieth Century Literature* 32 (spring 1986); W. D. Howarth, "English Humour and French Comique? The Class of Anouilh and Ayckbourn," in *New Comparison* 3 (summer 1987); Richard Allen Cave, *New British Drama in Performance on the London Stage, 1970–1985* (New York, 1988); Albert E. Kalson, "On Stage, Off Stage, and Backstage with Alan Ayckbourn," in James Redmond, ed., *Farce* (Cambridge, England, 1988); Ian Watson, *Conversations with Ayckbourn,* 2d ed. (London, 1988); Bernard F. Dukore, "Alan Ayckbourn's Liza Doolittle," in *Modern Drama* 32 (September 1989); Malcolm Page, ed., *File on Ayckbourn* (London, 1989); Leslie Smith, *Modern British Farce: A Selective Study of British Farce from Piñero to the Present Day* (London and Totowa, N.J., 1989); Brian Stableford, "Henceforward: SF in the Theatre," in *New York Review of Science Fiction* 7 (March 1989).

Michael Billington, *Alan Ayckbourn,* 2d ed. (London and New York, 1990); Matt Wolf, "What Makes Ayckbourn Run?" in *American Theatre* 6 (January 1990); John L. DeGaetani, "Alan Ayckbourn," in his *Search for a Postmodern Theater: Interviews with Contemporary Playwrights* (New York, 1991); Bernard F. Dukore, ed., *Alan Ayckbourn: A Casebook* (New York, 1991); John L. DeGaetani, "Pirandello, Albee, and Ayckbourn: An Absurdist Tradition," in *PSA* 8 (1992); Albert E. Kalson, *Laughter in the Dark: The Plays of Alan Ayckbourn* (Rutherford, N.J., 1993); Gerhard Schulte, "Interview with Alan Ayckbourn," in *Theatre Topics* 3 (March 1993); Jonathan Romney, "Rules of the Game," in *Sight and Sound* 4 (September 1994); Colin Evans, "Intimate Exchanges: Resnais' Translation / Transformation of Ayckbourn in *Smoking / No Smoking*," in *Franco-British Studies* 19 (spring 1995); Hugh Rorrison, "Reception of and Critical Response to Botho Strauss and Alan Ayckbourn in Britain and Germany," in *History of European Ideas* 20 (January 1995); James Fisher, "Alan Ayckbourn," in William W. Demastes, ed., *British Playwrights, 1956–1995: A Research and Production Sourcebook* (Westport, Conn., 1996).

J. G. BALLARD

(1930–   )

Brian Stableford

J. G. BALLARD is the only British writer of his generation whose work is fully engaged with the central concerns and cultural dynamics of the second half of the twentieth century. Although his best-known novel, *Empire of the Sun* (1984), is set in the past—it is based on his own experiences of being interned by the Japanese during World War II—its story is told from a viewpoint that understands how drastically that war and its epoch-making conclusion changed the existential situation of humankind.

Ballard first made a reputation as a science fiction writer, but he differs from other writers to whom that label has been attached in being the only one who brings an authentic scientific detachment to his scrupulously methodical and clinically dispassionate narratives. He has always been an assiduous experimenter, in terms of the content of his works as well as their style. Although he never set out to be a prophet, he realized long before the great majority of his contemporaries that the Space Age, far from being a useful template for the mapping of future possibility, was a temporary madness that had become a thing of the past by the mid-1970s.

Ballard found his own profoundly disturbing template for futuristic speculation in those aspects of the present that he terms *The Atrocity Exhibition* in the title of his 1970 story collection. The template was further developed in his novel about the erotic potential of traffic accidents, *Crash* (1973), but his later work mellowed out considerably, as he appeared to realize that the amount of reality that his contemporaries could bear was less than he had supposed or thought good for them.

LIFE

JAMES Graham Ballard was born in Shanghai, China, on 15 November 1930. His father, also named James and a chemist in the textile industry, had been appointed managing director of the China Printing and Finishing Company the year before. Young Ballard's early upbringing was privileged, as befit the son of well-to-do British expatriates, but his situation began a slow deterioration a few days short of his seventh birthday, when invading Japanese troops captured Shanghai.

Although the invaders respected the privileges of Shanghai's International Settlement, the Ballard home on Amherst Avenue was outside its boundaries. The city became a virtual war zone, and the family was ultimately forced to move into the French sector of the settlement. After Pearl Harbor, when Japan became embroiled in World War II, the Ballards returned to Amherst Avenue for awhile, but they were interned early in 1943. Ballard lived with his parents and his sister, Margaret—then only five years old—in a single room in the Lunghua Civilian Assembly Centre for the next two and a half years.

It was in Lunghua that Ballard grew to adolescence, living on a daily ration of rice, congee, and sweet potatoes and attending a makeshift school. Although his parents found conditions very harsh, and Margaret nearly died of dysentery, Ballard was later to recall—usually without any manifest perplexity or shame—that he rather enjoyed life in Lunghua. The Japanese guards were friendly, at least until the war began to go badly, and the cosmopolitan mix of internees fascinated the boy, who previously had been sheltered from so many aspects of adult life by the zealous servants appointed to look after him.

Following his release from the internment camp Ballard spent several more months in Shanghai before being sent to England to attend Leys School in Cambridge. Always a voracious reader, he had been somewhat frustrated by the limited and rather haphazard stocks of reading matter that had been passed around the internment camp, and he was delighted by the fact that he now had access to the entire heritage of nineteenth- and twentieth-century literature. "In the next four of five years," he reported in an essay he contributed to Antonia Fraser's 1992 anthology *The Pleasure of Reading*, "I stopped reading only to go to the cinema" (*A User's Guide to the Millennium*, p. 181).

Ballard went on to King's College, Cambridge, to study medicine, with a view to becoming a psychiatrist, but he found the training uncongenial and left without a degree after two years. The experience left a deep impression on him, which mostly derived from his experience in the dissecting room. He found a particular fascination in the way in which a once-living body could be taken apart and separated into individual components, utterly transformed by exploration and reductive analysis.

Ballard's first published short story, "The Violent Noon" (1951), appeared in the Cambridge student magazine *Varsity*. After leaving the medical school he read English for a year in London but dropped out again and worked for brief periods as a copywriter and encyclopedia salesman while trying to sell short stories to literary magazines. He then volunteered for the Royal Air Force and became a trainee pilot; his lifelong fascination with flying had been abundantly fed during the war years, when he had watched American, Chinese, and Japanese warplanes in operation over Shanghai. He was posted to Moose Jaw, Saskatchewan, for basic training, and it was there that he first encountered the science fiction magazines that were to provide his first literary market. Unfortunately he found life in the RAF no more congenial than any of his earlier attempts to build a career. He wrote his first science fiction story, "Passport to Eternity," while he was still in Canada awaiting his discharge, but it would not be published until 1963.

When Ballard returned to England in 1955 he married Helen Mary Matthews and worked for awhile as a librarian before becoming a scriptwriter for a scientific film company. His son, James Christopher, was born in 1956, and the family settled in Chiswick in west London, although Ballard did not much like the environment. Having formed an impression of the capital from his parents' nostalgic reminiscences, he had been deeply disappointed to arrive in 1946 to find "a London that looked like Bucharest with a hang-over" (p. 185). After he had subjected the city to a severe new broom in his first novel, he told the readers of the British science fiction magazine *New Worlds* that "anyone wondering why I've chosen to destroy London quite so thoroughly should try living there for ten years" (profile in *New Worlds*, October 1961). In fact, he only lived there for five, until he moved to the small Thames Valley town of Shepperton in 1960. In the meantime, his family was augmented by two daughters: Fay, born in 1958, and Beatrice, born in 1959.

Ballard's first professional sales were made in 1956, to *New Worlds* and its sister publication, *Science-Fantasy*. Their editor, E. John Carnell, helped Ballard find work in the field of trade journals; he was briefly assistant editor of *The Baker* and eventually became the assistant editor of *Chemistry and Industry*—a post he held for more than three years. He continued to sell stories to Carnell, whose magazines remained his only market until 1962, when he achieved the crucial breakthrough that enabled him to concentrate entirely on his writing.

EARLY WORK: SCIENCE FICTION

IN a profile accompanying his first publication in *New Worlds*, Ballard revealed that his first novel had been written immediately after "The Violent Noon," but that it had been "a completely unreadable pastiche of *Finnegans Wake* and the *Adventures of Engelbrecht*." He was later to comment on more than one occasion that although *Ulysses* had made a deep impression on him in his teens, James Joyce had been a totally unsuitable model for his own work; it was not until he discovered surrealism that he found a philosophy and method more appropriate to his interests and ambitions. Ballard was, however, always more interested in surrealist art than literature. He was deeply intrigued by the way in which surrealist painters like Giorgio di Chirico, Salvador Dali, and Max Ernst seemed to fuse visual reality with the substance of dreams and nightmares, creating an alien but seamless whole.

Such imagery had a far more powerful influence on Ballard's literary work than the leading surrealist writers, who included André Breton, Alfred Jarry, and Guillaume Apollinaire. He was, however, prepared to borrow occasional inspiration from surrealist prose, as he did when he employed a modern version of Jarry's "The Crucifixion of Christ Considered as an Uphill Bicycle Race" as the final section of the most avant-garde of his books, *The Atrocity Exhibition* (1970), which is titled "The Assassination of John Fitzgerald Kennedy Considered as a Downhill Motor Race."

The 1956 *New Worlds* profile mentions a novel called *You and Me and the Continuum* as a work in progress, but it was not until 1966 that a short story of that title was published, subsequently to be incorporated into *The Atrocity Exhibition*. If the short story borrowed more than the title of the aborted novel, Ballard must have begun practicing exotic experiments in prose long before anyone was ready to publish them. One experimental work from the same period that did eventually see print was the prose collage "Project for a New Novel," written in 1958 and published in 1978.

Even Ballard's commercial work seemed rather outré to the readers of Carnell's science fiction magazines, who were used to straightforward action-adventure stories. His first story in *New Worlds*, "Escapement," details the existential crisis suffered by a man who finds himself living, over and over, the same interval of time, which is shrinking with every repetition. His debut in *Science-Fantasy*, "Prima Belladonna," was the first of what became a series of tales featuring exotic femme fatales, set in the louche artists' colony of Vermilion Sands. The enigmatic antiheroine of "Prima Belladonna" is Jane Ciracylides, whose disturbing presence has a remarkable effect on the musical flowers sold by the protagonist. These two stories were followed by "Build-Up" (1957; reprinted as "The Concentration City"), in which the world's population has increased to several trillion and the "free space" for which the young protagonist is drawn by his dreams to search can no longer be found. In "Manhole 69" (1957) the subjects of a sleep-deprivation experiment find their experience of quotidian reality becoming nightmarish as they descend into a quasi-catatonic withdrawal state.

Even in these early works one can see the emergence of the manner of presentation and set of concerns that were eventually to license the invention of the adjective "Ballardian." The three key elements of Ballardian work are a type of protagonist, a type of setting, and a narrative voice. The protagonist, who is always male, is passively detached and almost invariably haunted by dreams of a mysterious but not imaginary past. He usually falls prey to the psychological attraction of his dreams without ever being moved to urgent or constructive action. The setting may be a city or a wilderness—or, fairly frequently, a city that is returning to wilderness—but its fixed artifacts are almost invariably decaying. (Its swimming pools are always empty, or nearly so.) Its movable artifacts, especially those that ought to offer the possibility of rapid transit, are usually broken down and abandoned. If birds are not abundant their absence is usually conspicuous, and they will often turn up dead; like the lush vegetation that is ever apt to spring up abruptly, they offer ambiguous omens of new beginnings and terminal decay. The narrative voice is coolly clinical, even in first-person narrative, reporting without any considerable emotional involvement and no great sense of astonishment, although it is usually possessed of a quietly dignified awe and an itchy inquisitiveness.

Ballard must have been disappointed to find that the editor of the British science fiction magazines was the only man willing to entertain his intense existentialist nightmares and ironic decadent fantasies, and that Carnell was only interested in the more accessible examples. Such stories as "Track 12" (1958) and "Now, Zero" (1959) are casually quirky comedies slightly slanted to the marketplace, but Ballard's willingness to compromise was severely limited and he was later to recall that he collected a lot of rejection slips. Although he knew full well that the vast majority of magazine science fiction stories were tales of interplanetary adventure, Ballard could not bring himself to take such themes seriously. He wrote only two stories with an extraterrestrial setting: "The Waiting Grounds" (1959), which extrapolates existential angst to a cosmic timescale, thus adding an extra dimension to its alienating effect, and "The Time-Tombs" (1963), a delicate homage to Ray Bradbury.

The profile accompanying "The Waiting Grounds" summarized Ballard's attitude to science fiction at that time:

What particularly interests me about science fiction is the opportunity it gives for experimenting with scientific or psycho-literary ideas which have little or no connection with the world of fiction, such as, say, coded sleep or the time zone. . . . Just as psychologists are now building models of anxiety neuroses and withdrawal states in the form of verbal diagrams—translating scientific hypothesis into literary construction—so I see a good science fiction story [as] a model of some psychic image, the truth of which gives the story its merit.

In general, stories with interplanetary backgrounds show too little originality, too much self-imitation. More important, the characters seem to lack any sense of cosmic awe—spanning the whole of space and time without a glimmer of responsibility. . . . It's just this sense of cosmic responsibility, the attempt to grasp the moral dimensions of the universe, that I've tried to describe in "The Waiting Grounds."

(New Worlds, November 1959)

Ballard's fascination with the mysteries of "the time zone" were more elaborately displayed in the dystopian comedy "Chronopolis" (1960), about a future city from which tyrannical clocks have been banned, and "The Voices of Time" (1960; revised as "News from the Sun," 1982). In the latter piece, which became the most striking example of his concerns and literary method, signals from a distant galaxy have been intercepted by radio telescopes, but the only intelligence they contain is a countdown to the end of the universe. Adventures in genetic engineering offer glimpses of the possible evolution of life on earth, but the story's protagonists are consumed by their own existential crises, one of them sleeping increasingly longer hours while the other cannot sleep at all. Some of Carnell's readers complained bitterly about the story's gnomic imagery and sense of futility, but it caught the imagination of other writers, most notably Brian Aldiss and Michael Moorcock, who were anxious to break the pulpish mold in which science fiction had long been cast.

As science fiction expanded out of magazines into paperback books it began to offer new commercial possibilities to its writers. Ballard dashed off his first science fiction novel during a two-week vacation in 1961. He sold an abridged version to *New Worlds*, where it appeared as "Storm-Wind," and the full-length version, *The Wind from Nowhere*, to the U.S. paperback company Berkley for 1962 publication in the United States. Although the story uses multiple narrative viewpoints, its central figure is the immensely rich and powerful Hardoon, who responds to the advent of a world-scouring wind by constructing a gigantic pyramid in which he can maintain a luxurious haven of calm. The attempt is futile, and the mysterious wind does not begin to abate until it has toppled this final symbol of human hubris.

Superficially, *The Wind from Nowhere* is a disaster story of a kind that had amply demonstrated its

potential in the United Kingdom courtesy of works by John Wyndham and John Christopher, whose novels had acquired a measure of critical respectability as well as healthy sales. "Perhaps because of their climate," Ballard observed in the profile accompanying the *New Worlds* serialization, "English writers seem to have a virtual monopoly of the [cataclysmic story] genre, one or two of the contemporary ones producing almost nothing else." He stuck to the template himself for two more novels, but whereas Wyndham and Christopher had written grim survivalist tales in which the traditional English virtues of decency and industry eventually withstand all manner of trials, Ballard's accounts of environmental change took it for granted that resistance is useless. His stories accept as axiomatic that the sensible response to abrupt and irresistible environmental change is psychological adaptation, no matter how drastic.

Ballard was now hitting his stride as a professional writer. Carnell published six of his shorter pieces in addition to "Storm-Wind" in 1961, and his stories began to appear in the American science fiction magazines the following year. His delicate quasi-fabular account of "The Garden of Time" was in the *Magazine of Fantasy and Science Fiction*, and he had five stories in magazines edited by Cele Goldsmith, whose sympathy for stylish quirkiness allowed her to play a key role in the careers of such writers as Fritz Leiber and David Bunch—although Goldsmith, like Carnell, was prone to offer him "good" advice about those aspects of his work that he ought to set aside and replace with something more robust. By far the most important breakthrough was the sale of *The Wind from Nowhere* to Berkley, whose editor thought sufficiently highly of Ballard to publish three more of his books in the same year: two story collections and his second novel. These sales allowed Ballard to fulfill his long-held ambition to become a full-time writer, and he immediately set about the business of bending his work further toward his own agenda.

The "wind from nowhere" had relented at the end of his first novel, but there was no such easy let-off for the characters in his second one, *The Drowned World* (1962). As the book opens, the earth's mean surface temperature has risen dramatically and is still inexorably rising. Water released by the melting of the ice caps has inundated much of the land, and dense tropical jungle has spread rapidly through what were once the temperate zones, rendering them all but uninhabitable. The world is, in effect, undergoing a temporal retrogression that is restoring the environment of the Triassic period.

The story's protagonist is Robert Kerans, a biologist monitoring the changes from a research station in a submerged metropolis. The psychological effects of the world's transfiguration begin to manifest themselves as dreams in which Kerans sees a version of himself that is no longer human wandering in a primitive world dominated by a huge, fierce sun. These dreams, he concludes, are a kind of memory retained within the cellular heritage of mankind, now called forth again by the appropriate stimulus. They threaten—or promise—to free his nervous system from the domination of the recently evolved forebrain, restoring the innocent harmony of primeval proto-consciousness and archaic environment.

As the eventful but rather enervated story proceeds, Kerans watches his various eccentric neighbors trying to adapt in their own ways to the circumstances in which they find themselves, but he comes to understand that all their strategies are hopeless. Eventually he accepts the pull of destiny and sets off southward, submitting to a psychic devolution that strips away his humanity by degrees until he becomes "a second Adam searching for the forgotten paradises of the reborn sun" (London edition, p. 175).

Some American readers and critics protested the "downbeat" ending of *The Drowned World,* and Ballard's insistence that it was nothing of the sort was to them adding insult to injury. American editors such as John W. Campbell, Jr., and Donald A. Wollheim regarded science fiction as propaganda for the enabling power of science and technology, and they demanded active protagonists who would tackle problems decisively and triumph over all adversity. Subscribers to that ideology deemed Ballard's protagonists to be supinely passive in meekly adapting themselves to changing circumstances and considered their attitudes—which never aspired to anything more heroic than detached fascination—irrational as well as unconstructive.

Given the nature of his experiences in Shanghai, especially in Lunghua, the intellectual stances adopted by Ballard's characters are easy enough to understand, but it is also easy enough to understand why they struck more resonant chords in Britain than they did in the United States. Britain, like the rest of the world, has had to spend the greater part of the twentieth century meekly adapting to social, economic, and aesthetic imperatives forced upon it by the irresistible tide of American cultural imperialism. In Britain, *The Drowned World* and *The Four-Dimensional Nightmare*—a collection combining the best stories from his first three Berkley collections—were issued in hardcover by Victor Gollancz in 1963. *The Drowned World* was enthusiastically reviewed by Kingsley Amis, who had persuaded the aging Gollancz that he ought to issue *The Drowned World* in the science fiction line rather than packaging it as a literary novel. It went into a second printing a month after publication.

Ballard assembled a second collection for Gollancz, *The Terminal Beach* (1964), with five stories that he had been unable to sell to the magazines, including the title work. When Carnell heard the story would be thus employed, however, he rushed it into print in *New Worlds.* One of the others, "The Drowned Giant"—a brilliant quasi-Borgesian description of the dismantling of a giant corpse washed up on a beach, based on Ballard's experiences in the dissecting room at Cambridge—was reprinted the following year in *Playboy,* the highest-paying short-fiction market in the world.

On 18 March 1962 Ballard took part in a radio discussion on the BBC's Home Service channel chaired by Wilfred De'Ath, debating the significance of modern science fiction with John Wyndham, Kingsley Amis, Brian Aldiss, John Brunner, and Kenneth Bulmer. Ballard waxed lyrical on the need for science fiction writers to abandon tales of space travel and concentrate instead on the exploration of "inner space"—a case he had already made in an as-yet-unpublished essay that eventually appeared as a guest editorial in the May 1962 issue of *New Worlds.* It was here that he made the oft-quoted remark that "the only truly alien planet is Earth" and provided a definitive elaboration of the prospectus for the future evolution of the genre that he had laid out in 1959:

I'd like to see [science fiction] becoming abstract and "cool," inventing completely fresh situations and contexts that illustrate its theme obliquely. For example, instead of treating time like a sort of glorified scenic railway, I'd like to see it used for what it is, one of the perspectives of the personality, and the elaboration of such concepts as the time zone, deep time and archaeopsychic time. I'd like to see more psycho-literary ideas, more meta-biological and meta-chemical concepts, private time-systems, synthetic psychologies and space-times, more of the remote, sombre half-worlds one glimpses in the paintings of schizophrenics, all in all a complete speculative poetry and fantasy of science.

(*New Worlds*, May 1962)

This document became one of the central theses of the "new wave" of British science fiction for which *New Worlds* became the main vehicle when Michael Moorcock took over its editorship in 1964. "The Voices of Time" and *The Drowned World* were appointed as two of the key examples of new wave science fiction. Ballard's antipathy to space fiction became a significant bone of contention between supporters of the new wave and the traditionalists, and Ballard defended his argumentative ground with considerable vigor. The rocket scientists who had laid the groundwork for the endeavors of NASA had all taken their inspiration from science fiction, and the magazines had provided a hospitable refuge for such ardent propagandists for space travel as Willy Ley and Arthur C. Clarke; many contemporary science fiction writers, most of them American, felt that they had a moral duty to carry forward that inspirational and propagandist function. When Ballard wrote "Cage of Sand" (1962), the first of many near-future stories in which the U.S. space program has been abandoned as a brief folly of futile ambition, he knew that it would be regarded as a kind of intellectual treason within the science fiction community. As early as 1974 he began to rejoice in the casual observation that "as far as manned flights are concerned . . . the Space Age, far from lasting for hundreds if not thousands of years, is already over" (*A User's Guide to the Millennium*, p. 165). He continued to celebrate his foresight until 1988, when he was able to assemble a whole collection of his skeptical stories under the title *Memories of the Space Age*.

Ballard continued to publish short fiction prolifically during 1963 and the early months of 1964, but the flow dried up abruptly in the middle of that year. Just as his career was achieving a series of crucial breakthroughs, his life suffered a terrible setback with the sudden death of Helen Ballard, who contracted pneumonia while the family was on holiday in Spain. Ballard was left with three young children to bring up single-handed. That would in itself have affected his productivity, but the loss of his wife also had a profound effect on the nature and temper of his subsequent work. Although the account of the incident given in Ballard's quasi-autobiographical novel *The Kindness of Women* (1991) is carefully fictionalized, subsequent chapters of the novel presumably offer a genuine insight into the effect that the unexpected death had upon a man who was still laboring in the psychological shadow of his experiences in the Far East. The character of his work would have changed anyway as he repositioned himself within the literary marketplace, but the aftereffects of his wife's death undoubtedly helped to determine the direction and extent of that change.

In the summer of 1964, Ballard had already completed his third novel—or at least the version of it that was published as yet another original paperback by Berkley in the United States as *The Burning World*. He also had begun work on *The Crystal World* (1966), at least to the extent of producing the sequence that appeared as the short story "The Illuminated Man" in the May 1964 issue of the *Magazine of Fantasy and Science Fiction*. It is hardly surprising that the completed novel was markedly sketchier than its predecessor or that Ballard's work showed a sharp change in direction thereafter.

An extensively rewritten version of *The Burning World* appeared in the U.K. in 1965 from Jonathan Cape, one of the most prestigious British publishers of literary fiction. The new version was entitled *The Drought*. Here the pattern of physical change mapped out in *The Drowned World* is casually reversed. Earth's continents become vast deserts because industrial pollutants have produced a molecular film that covers the surface of the oceans, inhibiting evaporation. The concrete city-deserts are isolated, surrounded by expanses of hot sand, while the sea retreats from the land to expose a new wilderness of crystalline salt. Civilization shrivels, with uncheckable fires reducing forests and towns alike to white ash. Ransom, the novel's protagonist, is one of the stubborn few who are most reluctant to follow the seas. He watches the river on which his houseboat is moored dwindle away, leaving behind the dregs of the social and natural order.

Eventually Ransom and most of his remaining neighbors are driven to seek refuge in the "dune limbo" of the new seashore, where they take their allotted places in a repressive and rigidly stratified social order, the polity of which is dominated by the need to extract fresh water from the reluctant sea. In the final section of the story, however, he chooses to go inland again, to discover that the mad and monstrous city dwellers who were even more stubborn than he have contrived to keep themselves alive, following a way of life that is thoroughly nasty but nevertheless appropriate to the now-universal aridity—which is, of course, an aridity of the soul as well as of the land.

tive bias, its obsession with the subjective nature of existence, its real subject matter is the rationalisation of guilt and estrangement. Its elements are introspection, pessimism and sophistication. Yet if anything befits the twentieth century it is optimism, the iconography of mass-merchandising, and naïveté.

(*New Worlds*, February 1969)

"THE DEATH OF AFFECT"

BALLARD was not the only British science fiction writer to achieve a crossover to apparent respectability in the mid–1960s—nor was he the only one to make use of the opportunity to institute a new literary avant-garde that would import aspects of the science fiction lexicon of ideas into literary fiction—but he was the one best equipped to make use of the opportunity. Having ensconced himself at Cape, Ballard also formed an association with Martin Bax, the owner, publisher, and editor of the literary magazine *Ambit,* and became its prose editor. Most of the short stories Ballard produced during the 1970s appeared in *Ambit,* and in 1975 he also became a contributing editor to Emma Tennant's literary magazine *Bananas.*

The idea of postmodernism had yet to get off the ground in the late 1960s, but Ballard was already thinking along those lines. When Moorcock's *New Worlds,* having lurched toward extinction in a paperback-size format, was relaunched in 1967 with the aid of an Arts Council grant, which freed the magazine (at least for awhile) from the need to pay for its production costs through sales and advertising. Moorcock and his coterie could thus showcase that which they thought science fiction ought to become, without having to consider such "minor" details as whether there was an audience for it. In a notable article that passed itself off as a meditation on the surrealism of Salvador Dali, published in 1969, Ballard dismissed the idea that the attitudes and concerns of the "Modern Movement" were typical of the twentieth century.

On the contrary, it seems to me that the Modern Movement belongs to the nineteenth century, a reaction against the monolithic Philistine character of Victorianism, against the tyranny of the paterfamilias, secure in his financial and sexual authority, and against the massive constraints of bourgeois society. In no way does the Modern Movement have any bearing on the facts of the twentieth century, the first flight of the Wright brothers, the invention of the Pill, the social and sexual philosophy of the ejector seat. Apart from its marked retrospec-

At first glance, this may seem to constitute a renunciation of the outlook of Ballard's early novels. *The Drought* certainly seemed to most of its readers to be as introspective, pessimistic, and sophisticated as anything the Modern Movement had ever produced, and the same seemed to be true of such stories as "The Terminal Beach," whose protagonist strands himself in the derelict landscape of Eniwetok, an island formerly used as a base for H-bomb tests. It must be remembered, however, that Ballard had refused to concede *The Drowned World* was as downbeat as its detractors claimed. The detached attitudes of Kerans and Ransom do qualify as a kind of calculated naïveté whose open-mindedness is carefully contrasted with the "sophistication" of Hardoon's successors. This open-minded quality is more extravagantly developed and celebrated in *The Crystal World* (1966), in which the environmental "disaster" that begins to overtake the world is much more obviously represented as a surreal and perhaps hopeful metamorphosis.

In *The Crystal World* selected areas of the earth's surface are subjected to a strange process of crystallization as some mysterious substance is precipitated out of the ether. The first area to be affected is in Africa, where the novel's protagonist, Sanders, is the assistant director of a leper colony. Sanders is initially horrified when he finds his mistress and some of his patients joyfully accepting the process of crystallization into their own flesh, but he comes to realize soon enough that the lepers have found a better alternative to the kind of decay already consuming them. Eventually he accepts that no other destiny is appropriate even for healthy people. What seems to be happening is that time and space are becoming supersaturated with matter, and enclaves from which time has "evaporated" are being transformed by precipitation. Within these regions living things cannot continue to exist in the manner to which they have become accustomed, but once they have been transubstantiated they cannot die.

The Crystal World draws some inspiration from Graham Greene, a writer whose work Ballard admired greatly, although its scintillating account of the birth of a new light within the heart of darkness is a far cry from Greene's restless religious orthodoxy. The lush romanticism of the novel's imagery, tending toward an unrepentant gaudiness, is replicated in several near-contemporary short stories with a decadent flavor, many of them set in Vermilion Sands. Ballard had first returned to that setting in the beautifully melancholy "Studio 5, the Stars" (1961), but three new additions to the series, all possessed of a sharper sense of tragic irony, were published in 1967: "The Cloud-Sculptors of Coral-D," "Cry Hope, Cry Fury!," and "Venus Smiles." Other stories lavishly dressed with the same bitterly mournful romanticism are "Storm Bird, Storm Dreamer" (1966), "Tomorrow Is a Million Years" (1966), and "The Day of Forever" (1967). Published alongside these finely crafted and dreamlike stories were the first elements of *The Atrocity Exhibition,* a literary collage that attempted to carry forward the prospectus outlined in his 1969 attack on modernism with uncompromising resolution.

The pieces making up *The Atrocity Exhibition* seemed to many readers to be even less optimistic and naive than the catastrophe novels, but they certainly set out to tackle "the iconography of mass-merchandising," attempting to encapsulate and evaluate the key images and technologies of the twentieth century in a new way. They retained nothing of the dreamy and elegiac quality of the Vermilion Sands stories, parading instead a grimly uncompromising consciousness of the way in which all the world's tragedies had been packaged and transformed by the mass media and the fantasies of their avid audience.

The principal literary influence on the "condensed novels" making up *The Atrocity Exhibition* was William S. Burroughs, whose ruthlessly cynical view of the affectations of Americanized global culture Ballard extrapolated in a remarkable series of fragmented narratives. Ballard provided a schematic diagram of the method of these prose fancies in his article on Dali, which began by summing up the core of the artist's achievement in the following terms:

Dali's paintings constitute a body of prophecy about ourselves unequalled in accuracy since Freud's "Civilisation and Its Discontents." Voyeurism, self-disgust, biomorphic horror, the infantile basis of our dreams and longings—these diseases of the psyche which Dali rightly diagnosed have now culminated in the most sinister casualty of the century: the death of affect.

This demise of feeling and emotion has paved the way for our most real and tender pleasures—in the excitement of pain and mutilation; in sex as the perfect arena, like a culture-bed of sterile pus, for all the veronicas of our own perversions; in our moral freedom to pursue our own psychopathology as a game; and in our evergreater powers of abstraction—what our children have to fear is not the cars on the freeways of tomorrow but our own pleasure in calculating the parameters of their deaths.

(pp. 25–26)

The proposition that media consumers might appropriate and exploit the manufactured glamour of public figures and luxury consumer goods for erotic purposes seemed shocking to critics who protested against *The Atrocity Exhibition,* although it is arguable that their horrified attitude was based in willful blindness. The studious eroticization of images of Marilyn Monroe and Jackie Kennedy, the use of sexuality in the advertising of cars, and the erotic elements of fictional depictions of gunplay were already too obvious to carry any real shock value. In Europe, where the American content of the mass media had always seemed graphically alien, the grotesquerie of *The Atrocity Exhibition* seemed natural enough, if a trifle unhealthy in its preoccupations, but the view from within the great glamour factory of American culture was far more problematic. The novel was scheduled for U.S. publication in 1970 by Doubleday, but Nelson Doubleday ordered the print run to be destroyed a fortnight before publication when he learned that it contained a section entitled "Why I Want to Fuck Ronald Reagan." The next publisher who took it on, E. P. Dutton, had no objection to that ambition or its phrasing, but its directors were apparently dismayed by references to the controversial consumer advocate Ralph Nader. The book ultimately appeared in the United States in 1972 from Grove Press—publisher of William Burroughs, the Marquis de Sade, and other assorted erotica—as *Love and Napalm: Export U.S.A.* Burroughs provided a defensive preface for what he complimented as a "profound and disquieting book."

Ballard continued to pursue, in various ways, the implication that the image of the world collated and conveyed by the mass media qualifies as an "atrocity exhibition." He was particularly fascinated by the development of Anglo-American culture's love affair with the automobile and by the manner in which the landscapes of modern civilization were being transformed by the advent of motorways. In an article for the car magazine *Drive*, published in 1971, he observed that "the car crash is the most dramatic event in most people's lives" and suggested—following a speculative method established by the best-selling pop psychologist Eric Berne—that rather than being unfortunate accidents, crashes might be regarded as the real subconscious objective of fast drivers. "If we really feared the crash," he noted, "most of us would be unable to look at a car, let alone drive one."

In pursuit of this perverse insight, Ballard had already mounted, in 1970, an exhibition of crashed cars at the New Arts Laboratory in London. His first substantial TV appearance was in a twenty-minute film for the BBC entitled *Crash* (1971). The final product of the temporary preoccupation was the novel *Crash* (1973), which set out to explore the orgastic possibilities of reckless driving and crash-associated masochism.

Crash was the first novel that Ballard wrote in the first person—a device he took care to emphasize by giving the protagonist his own name. After being seriously injured in a car crash that results in a man's death, the narrator becomes intimately involved with the dead man's widow, Dr. Helen Remington, and the obsessive "hoodlum scientist" Vaughan, whose death is announced in the first sentence and described in more detail in the final chapter. The narrative's careful eroticization of every aspect of the car, and its careful equation of crashes and orgasms, is clinical rather than pornographic. The narrator maintains a dispassionate pose as he adds a careful psychoanalytic gloss to his account of the development of his new perversity, but it is obvious that his passive neutrality is a mask and that his recollections are charged with submerged excitement.

Cape's blurb writer described *Crash* as a "cautionary tale," but it is anything but alarmist in its import; it is disturbing not because it warns of dark things to come but because it insists that the psychopathology it describes is already established, although only a few pioneers have yet acknowledged and embraced it. The publication of the book in Britain and America did not give rise to any considerable furor, although a few critics took a strong dislike to the novel. It attracted a great deal more attention in France, where it achieved a remarkable succès d'estime and established Ballard's reputation as an important modern novelist. The fires of scandal were belatedly fanned a quarter of a century later, when David Cronenberg's relatively faithful but rather diffident 1996 movie version was initially denied a certificate by the British censors, but the protest soon petered out.

Although it carries forward the same fascination with the impact of cars and roads on modern life and modern relationships, the much more placid existentialist fable *Concrete Island* (1974) excited far less hostility than *Crash*. This novel and its immediate successor, *High-Rise* (1975), are curious "robinsonades" whose characters become castaways in the heart of urban civilization, always remaining within sight and earshot of the metropolitan hordes but isolated nevertheless. Unlike the most celebrated Crusoes of legend and literature, the hero of *Concrete Island* is so successful in making the best of his situation, stranded on a traffic island at a complex intersection, that he refuses the opportunity to leave when the flow of passing traffic finally relents. The high-rise apartment block in the latter novel succeeds so well in providing a comfortable microcosm in which its well-to-do residents can escape the stressful world of work that it swiftly becomes a private empire on course for independence—an empire that immediately begins to decay into violent anarchy and barbarism.

If *Concrete Island* is seen as Ballard's first extended version of Robinson Crusoe, then *High-Rise* was his first extended version of *The Lord of the Flies*, all the more shocking because it translocates the social decline of William Golding's novel from a remote island to suburbia, while taking it for granted that intellectually sophisticated adults are just as prone to revert to savagery as children who know no better. After the intensity and clinicality of *Crash*, however, both novels seem slightly tongue-in-cheek, as if neither narrative is able to take itself entirely seriously. Their return to the kind of matter-of-fact third-person narrative that Ballard had used in his earlier novels seems half-hearted, perhaps because their interest as psychological "case studies" is markedly reduced by their being set against relatively ordinary backgrounds. Even so, they continued the extended analysis of what he had called the "death of affect," present in all of Ballard's works of the early 1970s.

The death of affect, as Ballard conceives it, is a sterilization of the emotions, the chief corollary of which is moral anesthesia. He proposed in his fiction and nonfiction alike that this was a condition of the modern world and that its continuation into the future had to be taken for granted. *The Kindness of Women* freely admits, however, that some of Ballard's acquaintances were convinced that he was merely projecting onto the world a more personal emotional state, from which he might one day contrive a recovery. Either way, it is understandable that the greatest positive achievement available to the characters in the stories and novels Ballard produced in the early 1970s is a kind of ataraxia, a "calm of mind" rather different from the one Plato held up as an ideal. Only those who can live alongside all manner of horrors without being moved to fear or pity can operate within the world that is being born, and those who adapt most successfully to the coming era are those who can welcome the opportunities opened up by the separation of erotic experience from emotion and moral responsibility. His later deployments of this theme, however, became more heavily ironic, and most possess a certain dry humor that tacitly concedes that the announcement of the universal death of affect might have been a trifle premature.

The tongue-in-cheek element of such works as *High-Rise* was by no means unprecedented and might almost be regarded as a reversion to type. Although he rarely wrote outright comedies, Ballard's early short fiction had always displayed a sharp if somewhat mordant wit, which began to reappear in fuller measure in such satires as "The Greatest TV Show on Earth" (1972) and "The Life and Death of God" (1976). In "The Intensive Care Unit" (1977), the final work of the phase of his career begun by *The Atrocity Exhibition*, Ballard sarcastically adopts a quasi-anthropological pose to examine the awful fate of a family, living in a comprehensively privatized world, that unwisely decides to try to rediscover the lost joys of intimacy. Having taken this train of thought to this terminus, and being no longer able to take it seriously, Ballard had little alternative but to make another new beginning. Given that necessity and his earlier insistence that an authentic twentieth-century literature ought to be optimistic, it is not surprising that he began to consider the possibility that the future might yet be redeemed from awful aridity and the death of affect.

REDEMPTION AND EMPIRE OF THE SUN

BALLARD's redemption begins in *The Unlimited Dream Company* (1979), a messianic fantasy in which his hometown of Shepperton is exalted far above suburban mundanity. The novel's protagonist, Blake, crashes a stolen aircraft into the Thames at Shepperton. Although his dead body remains trapped in the cockpit he finds himself miraculously reincarnated on the river's bank. In the moment of his death he has glimpsed a number of people on the bank who are now appointed as his "family." These include Dr. Miriam St. Cloud, a young woman who has the care of three handicapped children. (In *The Kindness of Women* the narrator's wife is called Miriam.)

After making several unsuccessful attempts to leave the town, Blake is finally convinced by a series of visions that he has a mission to fulfill, which must be undertaken there and there alone with the aid of the healing powers with which he has been gifted. He must teach the people to fly so that they can transcend their earthly existence and achieve a mystical union with the vegetable and mineral worlds, dissolving themselves into eternity much as the chief characters eventually did in *The Crystal World*. Although the name of the central character is significant, the novel's theme is also strongly allied with the paintings of the defiantly eccentric Stanley Spencer, who lived in the Thames-side village of Cookham and delighted in using its mundane scenery as a backdrop for apocalyptic motifs and images of transcendence.

The Unlimited Dream Company is the first of Ballard's novels to feature a hero who is unreasonable in the sense specified by George Bernard Shaw's "maxims for revolutionaries." Instead of adapting himself to changes in the external world, Blake must force the world—or Shepperton, at least—to adapt to the opportunities provided by his own godlike status. Although the novel is not autobiographical in any strict sense, it is deeply personal; like *Crash* it is a first-person narrative. Although Blake is shot by the enigmatic funfair proprietor Stark and his mission is rejected by the wary citizens of Shepperton, he comes through his time of trial with flying colors, in more than one sense of the phrase. In the end Miriam precedes him into the next world, leaving him alone with his body still confined in his crashed plane, but he is not disheartened. "There I would rest," he announces, "certain now that one day Miriam would come for me" (p. 223).

The Unlimited Dream Company was followed by the lightheartedly satirical *Hello America* (1981), which describes the "rediscovery" in the twenty-second century of a largely abandoned America by an oddly assorted expedition from Europe. The apparatus of the twentieth-century mythologies that once ruled the world are here reduced to a series of shattered relics. The significantly named protagonist, Wayne, dreams of resurrecting America's technological optimism and returning its glamorous consumerism to operational status, but his quest is futile in a world that has at last outgrown such follies.

Although *Hello America* was not a seriously intended work—its production was prompted by a misguided suggestion by its publisher—in some important respects it is similar in spirit to its immediate predecessor, and it helped pave the way for Ballard's next new departure. His remark in the 1969 Dali article about "our moral freedom to pursue our own psychopathology as a game" had suggested that Ballard's extensive analysis of "the death of affect" might be regarded as a strategic self-indulgence, and once his fictions began to find scope for the redemption of the world it was probably inevitable that they would eventually begin to home in on their real target: Ballard's own seemingly atrophied emotions.

Although *Empire of the Sun* (1984) can certainly be categorized as an autobiographical novel in that it follows the exploits and adventures of a boy named Jim interned by the Japanese during World War II, it makes no bones about the fact that it is no mere documentary reconstruction. The narrative is carefully distanced from the authorial voice by virtue of being told in the third person, as if Ballard regarded his younger self as a mystery still in need of unraveling. Comparison of certain key incidents that are also mentioned in Ballard's nonfictional reminiscences—especially the attempted breakout and the incident in which Japanese soldiers murder a Chinese man at a railway station—suggests that the Jim of the novel is markedly more enterprising and more actively engaged in his experiences than the real Ballard ever contrived to be. Although the character is by no means sanitized, he is allowed to take on certain insights and responses of which Ballard himself was incapable in the 1940s. One of the differences between the story told in *Empire of the Sun* and Ballard's own

reminiscences of internment is that Jim actually witnesses the atmospheric aftereffects of the explosion of the atom bomb that destroyed Hiroshima, although he does not understand what it is. Here, as in several other instances, he benefits from his creator's hindsight, making a little more sense of what is happening to him than his real analogue was able to accomplish at the time.

Empire of the Sun was nominated for the Booker Prize and won both the *Guardian* fiction prize and the James Tait Black Memorial Prize. It became a best-seller in Britain and its celebrity was further enhanced when the film rights sold to Steven Spielberg, who produced and directed the movie. The enfant-terrible reputation won by *The Atrocity Exhibition* and *Crash* was set aside, at least for a while, on the grounds that Spielberg's endorsement was an ironclad guarantee of the new Ballard's suitability for children. Although the novel is markedly less sentimental than the film, which takes aboard Spielberg's constant preoccupation with the innocence and wonder of childhood, its portrayal of young Jim is far less clinically scarifying than the psychological dissections of the protagonists of Ballard's earlier novels. The narrative does recapitulate, to some extent, the tone and ambience of the early disaster novels, and it has obvious affinities with his tales of corrosive psychological confinement, but it is quite distinct from those earlier works. It does, however, cast some light on certain preoccupations of Ballard's early works that had seemed at the time to be strange and rather pointless. In *Empire of the Sun* the psychological significance and symbolism of empty swimming pools, dead birds, and abandoned military hardware is perfectly clear and straightforward; no one who has read the novel is likely to find such tales as "The Voices of Time" and "The Terminal Beach" as unrelentingly gnomic and bizarre as the unprepared English readers who first encountered them in the pages of *New Worlds*.

Empire of the Sun is unique among tales of Japanese internment camps—most of which are unremittingly grim and almost all of which embody an understandable but utterly conventional sense of outrage—by virtue of the eerily objective and accepting viewpoint that had long been Ballard's hallmark. What seems to the other characters in the novel, and also to the reader, to be a horribly unexpected and unmitigated catastrophe is to the adolescent Jim merely one more change in a routinely change-afflicted existence. The camp becomes his world, and the responses of the other prisoners—who cannot help but see their imprisonment as a cruel and intolerable subversion of the ordinary course of affairs—seem as unfathomable to Jim as any other adult behavior. It may be, however, that the more important acceptance is the narrative's concession that it is neither wrong nor unnatural for Jim to feel this way, and that the extent to which he is out of step with his fellow prisoners is not evidence of his being some kind of monster. The fact that Jim is allowed to do some of the things that Ballard apparently failed to do in similar circumstances might be regarded as a kind of self-indulgence, but the likelihood is that it is more akin to belated self-approval. *Empire of the Sun* was, in a sense, the novel that Ballard had avoided writing for forty years and that finally materialized as a redemptive reconstruction of his own memories: a calculated, if long-delayed, act of self-forgiveness.

Ballard followed *Empire of the Sun* with *The Day of Creation* (1987), a return to the Africa of *The Crystal World*, which is here more explicitly revealed as the symbolic continent of Joseph Conrad's *The Heart of Darkness*. The plot concerns the emergence of a new river whose seemingly miraculous flow begins after the uprooting of a tree at the end of the airstrip near Port-la-Nouvelle, a town in the border region between Chad and Sudan. The National Geographic Society registers it as the river Mallory, naming it after a doctor working in a local World Health Organization clinic. Mallory has dreamed repeatedly of a "third Nile," whose tributaries might bring new life to the desert sands of the Sahara, and he is quick to "buy" the spring from a local warlord, Captain Kagwa, while it is still a narrow and feeble steam.

As its flow increases, the river Mallory fills the dry basin of Lake Kotto and drowns Port-la-Nouvelle. Its advent has political repercussions, increasing the stakes in the festering conflict between Kagwa and his chief rival, General Harare. Following the suggestion that the river's true source is two hundred miles away in the Massif du Tondou, from which its waters have been liberated by a seismic event that has elevated the water table, Mallory sets off in the ferryboat *Salammbo* to follow the waters upstream. Alas, the new life to which the river has given birth begins to die almost immediately as the flow, having reached its maximum, begins to abate again. By the time Mallory and his companions reach the tantalizing source, nothing remains of the river's hope and promise but an exhausted expanse of primeval mud.

LATER NOVELS: "SOCIAL CRITIQUES"

BALLARD's ending for *The Day of Creation* had something in common with those of his early catastrophe novels, but the political allegory of the novel was much more elaborately developed than the psychological allegory, and the significance of the river's drying up was more general than personal. With the exception of *The Kindness of Women*, all of Ballard's subsequent novels can be interpreted as sarcastic sociopolitical allegories—in a 1996 interview Ballard classified them as "social critiques." Instead of regarding "the death of affect" as the central trend of modern society, these later novels suggest that the people of the modern world are "anesthetized" in a merely apathetic way, unprepared for change and challenge.

The novella *Running Wild* (1988) makes some slight pretence to be a mystery novel, although the only real mystery is why the narrator—a forensic psychiatrist—cannot persuade the Home Office that the obvious answer to the puzzle is true. In a small Thames-side enclave named Pangbourne Village—not the actual village of Pangbourne but an exclusive, fenced-off luxury estate designed to provide its wealthy middle-class professional inhabitants with peace of mind—every adult has been killed and all their children have disappeared. Even when one of the missing children turns up in a traumatized state, unable to explain what happened, no one but the psychiatrist and a lowly sergeant in the Thames Valley Police will accept that the only people who could have committed the crime are the children.

The reason for this refusal is that the children, never having been abused, have no motive; the narrator is the only one who can understand that they were not rebelling against hate and cruelty but its opposite: "a despotism of kindness. They killed to free themselves from a tyranny of love and care" (London edition, p. 39). By the time the story ends the Pangbourne children have branched out into political assassination, making an attempt on the life of the female prime minister, the "Mother of her nation." The narrator advances his supposedly expert opinion that many more violent anarchists will spring from the fertile breeding grounds of the protected estates of Europe and America.

Unlike *Empire of the Sun*, to which it is a sequel of sorts, *The Kindness of Women* is told in the first person. It deals with the substance of Ballard's life in England and has to struggle hard to overcome the handicap imposed by the fact that his life after leaving the internment camp could easily be seen as a long anticlimax. Because it deals with more recent events and with intimate relationships, it takes care to protect its characters by changing all their names, but it is not a roman à clef in the conventional sense. Although one could attempt to measure its accuracy by comparing the accounts of the characters with their real-life equivalents—thus, for instance, measuring the extent of the fictionalization of the late Dr. Christopher Evans as Richard Sutherland—this would not provide any real indication of the truthfulness of the story. Although the details of Miriam's death in the novel differ considerably from those of Helen Ballard's death, the differences would be insignificant if one could accept that the subsequent account of its effect on the narrator's state of mind were an accurate recapitulation of Ballard's actual experience.

There is, of course, a temptation to read the novel in exactly this way, as if all its differences from history were on a par with changing the names of the characters. It is, however, worth noting that there is a great deal of actuality that has been omitted from the novel, including the central enterprise of Ballard's career. Although it is mentioned on occasion that the narrator of *The Kindness of Women* is a writer, there is not a word about what he is writing or how he approaches his vocation. Given that it is so brutally frank in its descriptions of sexual relationships, the text hardly warrants description as "censored," but its careful omission of everything relating to the author's primary activity does not encourage the view that it offers a full picture of his mental life. However careful it might be as an exercise in psychosurgical dissection, its minute attentiveness to matters of urogenital detail cannot make up for the fact that the heart and guts are left to lie almost entirely unexamined.

Like *The Kindness of Women*, *Rushing to Paradise* (1994) seems at first glance to be a recapitulation of things surpassed, deftly recombining elements of *The Drowned World*, "The Terminal Beach," *High-Rise*, and *Empire of the Sun*. Its teenage protagonist, Neil Dempsey, falls under the spell of the curiously charismatic Dr. Barbara Rafferty, who continually trumpets the slogan "Save the Albatross" in her attempt to keep the French from using the Pacific island of Saint-Esprit as a nuclear test site. Using tactics borrowed from Greenpeace (whose *Rainbow Warrior* had been sunk by French agents in 1985) Dr. Barbara leads an ill-assorted crew of eco-warriors to the island, where they establish a sanctuary not merely for albatross but for any other endangered species the world cares to send.

Although *Rushing to Paradise* is a literal robinsonade, it is set in a world in which there are no more desert islands. Saint-Esprit receives far more visitors than the apartment block in *High-Rise*, and the passing traffic becomes so intense that Dr. Barbara becomes increasingly paranoid about the sanctity of her sanctuary. It is not isolation from the world that sends her little colony free-falling toward savagery but the desire to secure isolation and to establish a protected enclave where society can begin again from scratch. Neil retains his nonjudgmental attitude toward Dr. Barbara's tactics long after the reader has seen which way the wind is blowing, but in the end her methods become a little too much for him to stomach, especially when his crucial role in her grand plan seems about to be usurped by an even younger analogue, Nihal. Neil plays his part in bringing her experiment to an end, although he wonders at the end whether he and she might one day be able to start the whole thing over.

The political allegory at the heart of *Rushing to Paradise* is more conventional than that in *The Day of Creation* or *Running Wild*. Although the story is not a straightforward cautionary tale about the tendencies of charismatic leaders, Dr. Barbara is explicitly compared to the author of the Jonesville massacre, Jim Jones, who led 913 followers in a mass suicide in Guyana in 1978, and hers is a story of absolute corruption fostered by near-absolute power. Having been struck off the register of authorized physicians for practicing euthanasia a little too publicly, she proceeds by measured steps to the practice of callous mass murder—not for the sake of the albatross but for the sake of ill-formed utopian ideals that conceive of adult males as a plague without which the world would be far better off. The novel is wryly humorous without being outrightly comic or satirical, and it seems at times to be mocking notions that Ballard had formerly taken in deadly earnest—especially in "The Terminal Beach"—as well as various follies of contemporary history.

Like *Running Wild*, *Cocaine Nights* (1996) is thinly disguised as a murder mystery. The solution to the mystery is by no means as obvious, but it is related to the novel's real theme with similar obliquity. As in the earlier story, what is important is not who did the deed but why they (or anyone) should do such a thing. Whereas *Running Wild* was set in a custom-designed Thames Village, *Cocaine Nights* is set in Estrella de Mar, a retirement village on the Spanish Costa del Sol. The protagonist, Charles Prentice, is a travel writer to whom the idea of settlement is anathema; to him, the whole idea of Estrella de Mar seems strange, and this does not help his quest to understand why his brother Frank, the proprietor of the Club Nautico, has confessed to setting a fire that killed five people.

No one, including the policeman in charge of the case, believes that Frank is guilty, but Charles cannot identify anyone else who had a motive. While he continues his amateur investigation, convinced that Frank will eventually retract his absurd confession, he is continually sidetracked, tantalized, and attacked in the manner of the great tradition of amateur sleuthing, but he quickly becomes aware of the fact that the assumptions of that great tradition are irrelevant to his own situation. It becomes apparent that the key to the mystery is the tennis pro and one-man amateur crime wave Bobby Crawford, but the puzzle facing Charles is far deeper and more perverse than any mere matter of breaking Crawford's seemingly cast-iron alibi.

In the later phases of the plot Charles becomes Crawford's confidant and actually goes to work for him in applying the lessons learned in Estrella de Mar to the neighboring resort of Residencia Costasol. He hopes that by standing, as it were, in his brother's shoes, he will eventually come to understand how the Estrella de Mar tragedy unfolded. Inevitably, and ironically, he eventually comes to understand it far too well.

Like Pangbourne Village, Estrella de Mar is held up by its observers as a model for an emergent future: a future in which people will retire in their thirties, with half a century of idleness before them, a world no longer prey to wars and ideologies. The text suggests that the most urgent problem facing people in such a world would be a tendency to retreat into inactivity, to detach themselves entirely from society. The one character in *Cocaine Nights* who stands outside the processes of the plot is the psychiatrist Dr. Sanger; it is he who poses the rhetorical question of how people in that kind of world can be "energized" and united in a cause. Politics and religion, he suggests, are equally impotent, but there remains one thing that can generate a sense of community: crime. Having been told this on page 180, Charles spends the rest of the plot embodying the wisdom, helping Bobby Crawford in his criminal crusade to awaken the inhabitants of the Residencia Costasol from their torpor, progressing in measured steps from petty theft, drug-peddling, and trivial arson to the human sacrifices that will make the spiritual revivification of the resort irreversible.

LATER SHORT STORIES

By the time he wrote *Cocaine Nights*, Ballard's reputation as a writer of literary fiction was secure. When he first broke out of the science fiction ghetto there had seemed to be a possibility that the whole genre might be redeemed from all the prejudices that had accumulated while it was being marketed as the lowliest of the many garish brands of pulp fiction, but that did not happen. Despite the fact that the actual Space Age was over almost as soon as it had begun, the imagery of popular science fiction remained firmly committed to the imagery of futuristic space travel, which became even more absurd in the television shows and movies that displaced printed texts at the heart of the genre in the late 1970s. Ballard's escape from genre confinement was correlated with the careful, progressive de-emphasizing of the science fiction elements of his work, ultimately resulting in their extirpation from his longer works. In his short stories, however, he continued to play with science fiction imagery, albeit in a conscientiously skeptical fashion.

Although Michael Moorcock's several attempts to resurrect *New Worlds* never contrived to establish a viable audience, something of the spirit of that enterprise was inherited by *Interzone*, a magazine that borrowed its title from William Burroughs. Initially edited by a cumbersome collective, *Interzone* eventually came into the sole charge of David Pringle, a longtime Ballard fan and the author of an early monograph on his work, *Earth Is the Alien Planet* (1979). Pringle was eager to publish Ballard, and Ballard was prepared, on occasion, to oblige him—although when Pringle interviewed him in 1996 for a special issue celebrating his sixty-fifth birthday, Ballard lamented, somewhat disingenuously, that he had been forced to reduce his output of short stories drastically because there were no suitable markets left.

The longest of Ballard's *Interzone* stories is "Memories of the Space Age" (1982), a story so thoroughly Ballardian as almost to qualify as self-parody; it is set in a deserted Cape Kennedy where the only survivor of the last space mission—who thus qualifies as the only man to have committed murder in space—pilots an assortment of small planes, teasing and tempting the dream-stricken protagonist and the wife of his victim with his fanciful flights. "The Object of the Attack" (1984) is a more obviously ironic account of an assassination attempt that turns out to have been aimed not at the politicians and members of the royal family who were present but at a far more dangerous man: an astronaut turned religious mystic ambitious to become a charismatic leader. "The Man Who Walked on the Moon" (1985) is a reflective account of an impostor who obtains handouts from tourists in return for telling tales of his delusory but mythically charged career as an astronaut. "The Message from Mars" (1992) is yet another dissection of the hopelessness of dreams of space conquest.

Despite their preoccupation with the Space Age, these stories only qualify marginally as science fiction. Perhaps surprisingly, they are only marginal even to Ballard's notion of what science fiction ought to have become. His early insistence that science fiction would do better to devote itself to the exploration of inner space had been allowed to slide almost into oblivion. The one *Interzone* story that takes on such a task directly is "The Enormous Space" (1989), a painstaking reprise of a plot he had used several times in the first phase of his career, most notably in "The Overloaded Man" (1961). The formula is an account of a domestic experiment in which the protagonist carefully removes himself from the ever-present world by cultivating an altered state of consciousness. In this version, the central character converts the home from which his ex-wife has fled into a metaphorical desert island, analyzing the necessarily brief success of his project in exactly those terms:

In every way I am marooned, but a reductive Crusoe paring away exactly those elements of bourgeois life which the original Robinson so dutifully reconstituted. Crusoe wished to bring the Croydons of his own day to life again on his island. I want to expel them, and I find in their place a far richer realm formed from the elements of light, time and space.

(*War Fever*, p. 120)

Most of Ballard's subsequent contributions to *Interzone* were only qualified for inclusion there by their playful and quirky surrealism, and they fit in perfectly well with the stories he published elsewhere in the same period, which include the Borgesian "Report on an Unidentified Space Station" (1982) and the satires "The Secret History of World War 3" (1988), "Love in a Colder Climate" (1989), and "War Fever" (1989). These were collected in *War Fever* (1990), along with most of the *Interzone* stories and one story left over from an earlier phase of his career—the chilling fabular sardonic tale "The Air Disaster" (1975), one of the few stories Ballard ever equipped with a climactic twist.

Had he been so inclined, Ballard could have continued his explorations of inner space without risking stigmatization as a science fiction writer, and the fact that he virtually abandoned them in favor of idiosyncratic analyses of the world as it is has far more to do with his own personal development as a writer than with any determination to maintain the respectability of his reputation. In the end, inner space became almost as uninteresting to him as outer space, and his attention was entrapped by the world between. Although his social critiques remain distinctive, they remain social critiques, adrift in a vast crowd, whereas some of his earlier experiments took his pen into literary territory where, as the old joke has it, the hand of man had not previously set foot.

CONCLUSION

THANKS to the Spielberg film, *Empire of the Sun* now overshadows everything else that Ballard wrote. Not only is it his best-known work, but a case could certainly be made for its being his most engaging, or at least his most reader-friendly. Its autobiographical aspect adds an important extra dimension to the fascination with which the reader follows Jim's responses to the events that envelop him.

One could argue, however, that it is precisely the debt *Empire of the Sun* owes to memory and actuality that makes the book less striking as an instance of extraordinary creativity than some of its predecessors. Although *The Kindness of Women* slyly implies that *Crash* is a more autobiographical work than anyone without inside knowledge could have guessed, the embroideries of *Crash* are far more elaborate and at least a little more astonishing than those of *Empire of the Sun*. Although *The Crystal World* is probably slighter than it was intended to be, if it is considered as part of a collective with the two novels with which it forms a trilogy of sorts, *The Drowned World* and *The Drought*, the whole assemblage is remarkable indeed. No one had ever written anything like them before, and in association with "The Voices of Time" and "The Terminal Beach" they were the works that secured the coinage of the adjective "Ballardian" and established its exchange rate.

There is, therefore, some cause for regret in the fact that after *Empire of the Sun*, J. G. Ballard's work became gradually less Ballardian, and that those Ballardian elements it retained became less intense, more studied, and decidedly whimsical. On the other hand, there is certainly some cause for celebration in the fact that even *Cocaine Nights* is Ballardian enough to guarantee that few readers would misattribute it in a blind testing. Although it is a social critique set in the present and politely masquerades as a mystery story, its analysis of nascent social problems is highly unusual and its slyly and wryly proposed solution to those problems is even more unusual. The present in which it is set stands in for one of the many futures into which we seemed to be headed at the end of the twentieth century, and the mystery within its mystery is the unanswered question that has echoed throughout the disparate parts of Ballard's entire literary corpus. Exactly what, in the light of a scrupulously careful dissection of his actual and potential experience, should a man care about, if he can ever achieve the perversely difficult task of resetting himself to care at all?

SELECTED BIBLIOGRAPHY

I. COLLECTED SHORT STORIES. *The Voices of Time* (New York, 1962); *Billennium* (New York, 1962); *The Four-Di-*mensional Nightmare* (London, 1963); *Passport to Eternity* (New York, 1963); *The Terminal Beach* (London, 1964) and, with only a slight overlap in contents, *Terminal Beach* (New York, 1964); *The Impossible Man and Other Stories* (New York, 1966); *The Disaster Area* (London, 1967); *The Day of Forever* (London, 1967); *The Overloaded Man* (London, 1967); *Chronopolis, and Other Stories* (New York, 1971); *Vermilion Sands* (New York, 1971; London, 1973); *Low-Flying Aircraft, and Other Stories* (London, 1976); *The Best of J. G. Ballard* (London, 1977) and, with only a slight overlap in contents, *The Best Short Stories of J. G. Ballard* (New York, 1978); *Myths of the Near Future* (London, 1982); *News from the Sun* (London, 1982); *Memories of the Space Age* (Sauk City, Wis., 1988); *War Fever* (London, 1990; New York, 1991).

II. NOVELS. *The Wind from Nowhere* (New York, 1962); *The Drowned World* (New York, 1962; London, 1963); *The Burning World* (New York, 1964), rev. and expanded as *The Drought* (London, 1965); *The Crystal World* (London and New York, 1966); *The Atrocity Exhibition* (London, 1970), published in the U.S. as *Love and Napalm: Export USA* (New York, 1972); *Crash* (London and New York, 1973); *Concrete Island* (London and New York, 1974); *High-Rise* (London, 1975; New York, 1977); *The Unlimited Dream Company* (London and New York, 1979); *Hello America* (London, 1981; New York, 1989); *Empire of the Sun* (London and New York, 1984); *The Day of Creation* (London, 1987; New York, 1988); *Running Wild* (London, 1988; New York, 1989); *The Kindness of Women* (London and New York, 1991); *Rushing to Paradise* (London, 1994; New York, 1996); *Cocaine Nights* (London, 1996; Washington, D.C., 1998).

III. OTHER WORKS. Editors of *Re/Search*, *The Atrocity Exhibition*, annotated ed. (San Francisco, 1990); *A User's Guide to the Millennium* (London and New York, 1996).

IV. CRITICAL AND BIOGRAPHICAL STUDIES. James Goddard and David Pringle, eds., *J. G. Ballard, The First Twenty Years* (Hayes, Middlesex, England, 1976); David Pringle, *Earth Is the Alien Planet: J. G. Ballard's Four-Dimensional Nightmare* (San Bernardino, Calif., 1979); Andrea Juno and V. Vale, eds., *J. G. Ballard*, special issue of *Re/Search* 8/9 (San Francisco, 1984); Peter Brigg, *J. G. Ballard* (San Bernardino, Calif., 1985); Gregory Stephenson, *Out of the Night and Into the Dream: A Thematic Study of the Fiction of J. G. Ballard* (New York, 1991); Roger Luckhurst, *The Angle Between Two Walls: The Fiction of J. G. Ballard* (New York, 1997).

EAVAN BOLAND

(1944–   )

Karen Odden

EAVAN BOLAND'S FIRST four volumes of poetry, beginning with *New Territory* (1967), received a mixed response from critics: some thought she was a gifted but minor poet whose style was developing; some felt her first volume was a brilliant beginning but the other volumes were less impressive; some found her work stridently feminist; some found it antifeminist and overly concerned with domestic matters. This odd response stemmed from two sources: Boland was still finding her voice as a poet; and, because she was innovative in both her poetic forms and her topics, her reading public had to catch up with her. Since 1990, however, Boland has been hailed by many as the leading Irish woman poet of her generation, and in 1994 she was awarded a Lannan Foundation Award in Poetry.

Although Boland is best known for her poetry, she also has written the prose work *Object Lessons: The Life of the Woman and the Poet in Our Time* (1995). This lyrical and moving text is part memoir, part poetic manifesto. Expanded from her essays "The Woman, The Place, The Poet" (1990) and *A Kind of Scar* (1989), *Object Lessons* reflects the topics, projects, and concerns expressed again and again in the poems. She recovers for us her experiences of emigrating as a child from Ireland to London and the United States and of coming into being as a poet in today's Ireland, but she also lays out a philosophy of poetry that she developed over time.

Object Lessons should not be understood as some essential "truth" about Boland's past—indeed, the insistent repetitions and evocative language discourage us from accepting it as a transparent "story" of her life and urge us to read it as carefully as we read her poetry. Nor is Eavan Boland the author equivalent to the poetic narrator, despite a strong autobiographical component to her poems. Rather, *Object Lessons* is an important counterpart to her poetry. Just as her poems move back and forth between representing self and other, the domestic and the national, myth and real life, *Object Lessons* moves between memoir and manifesto, speaking at once *from* her own experience and *to* us about her own political, social, literary, and ideological concerns. For reasons that will be explored, this dualistic quality must be considered as constitutive—perhaps even a trademark—of Boland's work. One of her most important projects is to demonstrate that dualities and contradictions can and indeed should coexist; that splitting the world into rigid categories unfortunately often results in the establishment of one point of view and the silencing of the other.

EARLY YEARS: PORTRAIT OF THE POET AS A YOUNG WOMAN

EAVAN Boland was born on 24 September 1944, the youngest of five children of Frederick and Frances Kelly Boland. Eavan's father, she tells us, went to Clongowes—the same boarding school that James Joyce attended. Later he studied classics at Trinity College in Dublin and political science at Harvard University and the University of Chicago, after which he became a diplomat. Her mother was a painter.

The Bolands lived in Dublin until Eavan was five, when her father became ambassador to the Court of St. James's and the family relocated to London. Poems such as "The Game," "Irish Child in England," and "Fond Memory" provide a poignant picture of the disorientation and alienation Boland felt at finding herself in a new and much more formal house, a convent school in North London—where a teacher corrected her sternly for using the Irish contraction "amn't"—and a city full of yellow fog: "I was a child in a north-facing bedroom in / a strange country . . . I would get up and go to school in / the scalded light which fog leaves behind it; / and pray for the King in chapel and feel dumbly for / the archangels trapped in their granite hosannas" (*Outside History*, p. 25). About six years later her family relocated again, this time to New York City, where Boland lived until she was fourteen. As a young child in London she had had the disorienting experience of reading British books that confronted her with Irish stereotypes she could not recognize. But as a teenager in New York she began to read Irish poets such as Padraic Pearse; perhaps as a result, she began to have a certain self-consciousness about her own split national identity and to understand that writing from within Ireland and from without resulted in markedly different representations.

When Boland returned to Ireland after her time in London and New York City, she felt a sensation of not belonging; she had to get reacquainted with Ireland. She writes of this experience in "After a Childhood away from Ireland": "Coming home. / I had heard of this . . . / What I had lost / was not land / but the habit of land" (*Outside History*, p. 149). She spent time with her older sisters, who were still in Ireland; she attended boarding school, and she explored Dublin almost as a newcomer to its buildings and history. But as she began to reconstruct her life there, she realized that she was both Irish and not-Irish. As she put it in *Object Lessons*, "I was not the same as other Irish children. Like a daughter in a legend, I had been somewhere else" (p. 58). (We see some of these same struggles to bring together Irish heritage with a young woman's experience in America in Mary McCarthy's *Memories of a Catholic Girlhood*.) Boland finished school at age seventeen, and after a summer off she entered Trinity College. Living in an apartment near the center of Dublin, she participated in a literary circle that included gifted Irish poets such as Seamus Heaney, Derek Mahon, Michael Longley, Seamus Deane, Eiléan Ní Chuilleanáin, and Brendan Kennelly.

Boland published her first volume of poetry, *New Territory*, at age twenty-two. Most critics—and Boland herself—recognize that in this volume she was working firmly within the Anglo-Irish poetic tradition. She employs traditional literary forms and she addresses topics conventional to lyric poetry such as her coming into being as a poet, her relationship to the landscape, and the way myth and memory shape personal experience. (Those were the concerns of the Romantic poets such as Wordsworth.) Indeed, her poem "Yeats in Civil War" not only takes William Butler Yeats as the topic but follows in rhyme scheme and form Yeats's sonnet "Leda and the Swan." She writes about Ireland's myths and history in a series of poems including "After the Irish of Aodghan O'Rathaille," "The Flight of the Earls," "A Cynic at Kilmainham Jail," "Belfast vs. Dublin," and "The Winning of Etain." In this early volume she leans heavily on her Irish literary forefathers.

As she continued to read Irish poetry and write her own, however, she felt a sense of unease—a sense that she was writing poetry in a way that denied her feminine voice. She gradually saw the need for a new kind of poetry that had a feminine voice and expressed feminine concerns but wasn't so radically different that it would be ignored. The difficulty she faced in defining a new position within an established tradition was in some ways comparable to that faced by late-nineteenth-century Irish poets who wanted to forge a national poetic tradition that would differentiate itself from that of the English. One of the ways they did this was by resurrecting Gaelic myths and legends as the topics of their poetry. Two of the men who began what later became known as the Gaelic Revival were Standish James O'Grady (1846–1928), who retold in *Bardic Tales* the legends of the Red Branch and Cuchulain; and Yeats, who published *The Wanderings of Oisin and Other Poems* (1889), which drew its matter from Gaelic mythology. These men had both poetic forefathers and powerful male mythic figures upon whom they could draw to provide a ground for a new Irish poetry—a tradition that enabled them to authorize their own identity as Irish poets.

This option did not exist for Boland: she could not authorize her own *feminine* Irish literary identity by harking back to some previous tradition. As Virginia Woolf famously points out in *A Room of One's Own* (1929), women writers have had to face enormous odds. They often had no money of their own, no room of their own, and limited access to education; they often faced enormous prejudices against leaving the home and taking up professions. So the shelves where Woolf might have found women writers' books were virtually empty in comparison with shelves of male authors. Boland faced this same dilemma forty years later in Ireland, for she had almost no female Irish literary precursors. There were a few exceptions—the Gaelic poets Liadan of Cork and Eileen O'Leary (also known as Dark Eileen O'Connell) and nineteenth- and early twentieth-century poets such as Katharine Tynan, Emily Lawless, Lady Gregory, and Alice Milligan—but most have been all but forgotten. With so few literary foremothers, Boland wrestled with the difficulty of finding a feminine poetic voice within both a male literary tradition and an Irish culture that "kept those words [woman and poet] magnetically apart" ("Continuing the Encounter," p. 16). In *Object Lessons*, Boland writes that as she began her career as a poet, "one thing was lacking. . . . I wanted a story. I wanted to read or hear the narrative of someone else—a woman and a poet—who had gone here, and been there. . . . I remember thinking that it need not be perfect or important. Just there; just available. And I have remembered that" (p. xvi). We see this concern with trying to find a woman predecessor in her poem "The Rooms of Other Women Poets," which in title and theme echoes Woolf's work.

The second difficulty for Boland in finding her own Irish woman poet's voice was that the Irish literary tradition had long objectified women in poems, representing them as mythic figures or emblems for Ireland. In *Object Lessons* she quotes the literary historian Daniel Corkery's remark that "the vision the poet sees is always the spirit of Ireland as a majestic and radiant maiden" (p. 144). Women rarely figured in poems otherwise. Thus Boland had to labor to find a place for a real, ordinary woman's voice in a poem. She explains the dilemma of writing as a woman when women were so often represented as objects of a man's gaze and imagination rather than as subjects of their own experience:

I felt an estrangement. I had no words for it, and yet I felt it more and more. Put in the language of hindsight and rationalization, the crisis was this: However much my powers of expression made my mind as a human being the subject of the poem, my life as a woman remained obdurately the object of it. . . . I had written poems. Now I would have to enter them.

(*Object Lessons*, p. 28)

In other words, Boland was grappling with two questions simultaneously: Where does a woman poet fit within the literary tradition and where does a woman poet fit within her own poetry?

In the early 1970s she and her husband, the Irish novelist Kevin Casey, set up housekeeping in a suburb that she describes as a place where it

seemed "all the building would never be finished" ("Continuing," p. 15). The suburb became the place where she too began the ever-unfinished project of building a life as a woman, wife, poet, mother, and neighbor. She also wrote, and began earnestly to face the dilemma of the woman poet.

THE WOMAN / POET: NEGOTIATING A RELATIONSHIP TO THE MALE TRADITION

As a novice Irish woman poet Boland faced another problem: if she wrote in English, it could be said that she had adopted the language of her oppressors. However, while Boland frequently acknowledges the effects of English oppression of Ireland, she does not write in Irish, as does, for example, her contemporary Nuala Ní Dhomhnaill. One reason is that because she left Ireland young, Boland never learned Irish. Another is that, in her attempts to represent the life of the Irish woman, she recognizes that it is not only the English language but many sign systems—including those of Ireland—that prevent women from writing and are used to represent them as objects. That is, if Boland wrote in Irish, her poetry might be construed as solely concerned with the Irish experience of oppression by the English. This would be misleading, for she is also deeply interested in representing Irish women's experience of oppression by a male-dominated culture as well as the relationship between these two types of oppression. Precisely because Irish literature often conflates woman and nation, and shifts the suffering of the nation onto the figure of the woman, women's suffering tends to disappear. As Boland explains in *Object Lessons*, "all too often, when I was searching for such an inclusion [of a woman's story of pain in Irish literature], what I found was rhetoric of imagery which alienated me: a fusion of the national and the feminine which seemed to simplify both. It was not a comfortable realization" (p. 128). In order to disentangle the real woman from her role as national emblem, Boland would have to question the premises about women and Ireland that underpinned the existing male Irish poetic tradition. Like James Joyce, whom she admires for "breaking the traditional association of Ireland with ideas of womanhood and tragic motherhood" (p. 144), Boland resists these simplifications of women in order to write of real women whose participation in national history has been effaced.

Eavan Boland is certainly not the first woman to attempt to work within a predominantly male field while simultaneously trying to change it. She follows in the tradition of women writing within a masculine tradition, profession, or discipline—from physicians and scientists such as Elizabeth Blackwell and Marie Curie, who had to face sarcasm and the humiliation of being ignored or having their work attributed to men, to women writers such as the Brontë sisters, who used male or ambiguous pen names in order to have their work accepted.

However, the first half of the twentieth century saw the emergence of new ways of thinking and talking self-consciously about feminine experience, not only in the works of writers such as Woolf but in the research of psychoanalysts such as Karen Horney, Melanie Klein, and Joan Riviere. These women were trying to come to grips with women's ways of knowing the world around them, their own experience, and their own bodies; and they were constantly questioning the legitimacy of the stories that men use to represent feminine experience.

Boland's poems reflect projects similar to those of these earlier women. Like Horney, she acknowledges that the stories men tell about women have had material effects on women's abilities to conceive of their own power and sexuality; like Klein and Riviere, she recognizes the danger of "splitting" women (or any group) into binary oppositions such as virgin / whore or saint / victim. In her view, this "splitting" not only simplifies the complexity and mutability of real women's characters and experiences but also enables a point of view that considers ideal (or demonized) mythological Woman as an "object" whose identity is perceived only in relation to the male viewer rather than real women as "subjects" possessed of their own characteristics and experience. Boland employs the way of knowing called intersubjectivity—which, simply put, means that a person uses empathy in order to see her own point of view and simultaneously someone else's, rather than engaging in a power struggle over whose point of view is "right." This approach, which is flexible, even playful, offers an alternative to cycles of domination and submission, exclusion and revenge. Thus, Boland holds her own points of view, modes of experience, and representational strategies in her mind at the same time she holds those of the male literary canon. This enables her to rethink old stories and play with canonical forms. Her poetry often assumes that we know the canon, but it also urges us to recognize that it is both gendered and historically specific.

One of the techniques by which she negotiates a relationship to the male artistic tradition occurs in a group of what I will call "revisionist" poems. In these poems she refers to an ancient myth or a work by a man (either artist or poet) in which a woman is represented. She then revises the original representation of the woman in order to expose the masculine desires or modes of thinking that underpin the representation. She thus simultaneously upholds the canon and adds to it. Some poems relocate an ancient story into the domestic space; others change the meaning of a symbol or rewrite a myth; still others reframe a masculine representation to suggest the woman's point of view. For example, Boland rewrites John Keats's "Ode on a Grecian Urn" (1819) several times. In the poem "Object Lessons," she describes her husband's coffee mug, which has a "hunting scene on the side," in terms akin to those Keats uses for his Grecian urn. But in bringing the "Sylvan historian" (the urn) into the domestic space, questions of representation are given a peculiar twist:

> A wild rabbit.
> A thrush ready to sing.
> A lady smiling as the huntsman kissed her:
> the way land looks before disaster
> strikes or suffering
> becomes a habit
>
> was not a feature
> of the history we knew.
>
> (*Outside History*, p. 22)

Anyone familiar with Keats's poem will immediately recognize the similarity between the scene depicted on the side of the mug and the scene on the side of the urn. Keats too writes of a "bold lover" attempting to kiss a woman in a pastoral landscape. But there are several significant departures. First, Grecian urns such as Keats represents were used in formal ceremonies and as prizes; the coffee cup is ordinary, humble, and domestic. Second, the lover has kissed the maiden and she is "smiling"; Boland's revision turns the myth of the chaste woman fleeing a man's sexual desire on its head. And while Keats's poem ends with an encomium to "Beauty," which is frozen successfully by art at this moment in time, rendering the "flowery tale and legend" fixed and complete, Boland's poem ends with the coffee cup breaking.

> . . . the broken pieces of
> the sparrow hawk and the kisses of
> the huntsman . . . the thrush's never
> to-be-finished aria . . .
> on the floorboards you and I had sworn
> to sand down and seal
> with varnish.
>
> (p. 23)

This poem speaks of the impossibility of closure, of finishing; pieces are lost in the flooring because it is incomplete, and the sealing with varnish is an almost impossible project—perhaps one better left undone. If Keats's poem celebrates the permanence of artistic representations and the fleeting quality of human love, joy, and beauty, Boland's poem suggests that these ideas are incommensurate with "the history we know." For her, human love is enduring, but the permanence of art is problematic: the "Sylvan historian" that fixes a particular representation in time becomes an emblem for historians who believe they can "fix" one representation of events, make it seamless with varnish, and put it forth as the complete and "correct" one.

Similarly, Boland rewrites Greek myths in poems such as "Athene's Song" and a group of poems involving the mythic figure Daphne. According to different versions of the Greek legend, Daphne, a nymph whose name means "laurel," was either the daughter of a river god or a girl from Arcadia who loved to hunt. The god Apollo fell in love with Daphne, but she wanted to remain a virgin. He pursued her through the wood and nearly caught her, but she prayed to Gaea for help and was turned into a laurel tree. Apollo broke off a branch to wear on his head, and the laurel came to represent the prize for various victories. (See, for example, A. E. Housman's 1895 poem "To an Athlete Dying Young," which also transposes Greek mythic elements into a modern setting.)

The Daphne myth is powerful because it depicts both man's desire to "break" a woman and her inability to resist violence. It also suggests Daphne's fear of her own sexuality and the relationship among women, writing, and desire: women are transformed by masculine desire but they also could become the prize for men's poetry. Significantly, Yeats uses the Daphne myth in "A Prayer for My Daughter," in which he hopes she might live "like some green laurel / rooted in one dear perpetual place," suggesting a kind of perpetual virginity for her. Boland revises the myth in "'Daphne with Her Thighs in Bark' [Ezra Pound]." (The title comes from the first line of verse XII in Pound's "Hugh Selwyn Mauberley.") Boland has an ostensibly wiser Daphne speak to a woman: "Let her learn from me: / the opposite of passion / is not virtue / but routine" (*Outside History*, p. 128). Boland's revision of the myth (and of Yeats's hope for his daughter) makes feminine sexuality a powerful and positive force. For some feminists, the lines "His rough heat will keep you warm" and "I shall be here forever" come uncomfortably close to suggesting that a man's "heat" will keep a woman from becoming bored (p. 129). But more than that, it suggests that women must learn from other women—rather than from men—truths about feminine desire and its relationship to virtue. This poem undercuts the notion that a woman's "virtue" (or honor) depends upon her having no sexual desire—or at least not acting on it.

Another group of revisionist poems re-presents images originally created by a man in a way that makes clear that the emblematic "woman" is a product of a man's imagination. In "Degas's Laundresses" from *Night Feed* (1982), she describes the painting *Two Laundresses Ironing*. If we were to stand in front of the painting our gaze would approximate that of the male artist who depicts the washerwomen, and we too might see what she calls "roll-sleeved Aphrodites" laundering clothes. Boland's poem repositions us as viewers who see both the women *and* the painter, and it represents the women's experience in very different terms. These women are not "Aphrodites"; they are real, and they talk, work, and sweat. Boland's language reflects the difficulty and the physicality of the labor they perform: they work in "a linen pit of stitches," and the "pleasure of leisured women are sweated into the folds, the neat heaps of linen" (*An Origin Like Water*, p. 115). The subjects (the washerwomen) who are performing the "sweat[ing]" are effaced here, and the poem addresses them as "you" (lines 1 and 7) in order to imitate the point of view of the original painting. The way the women are figured by the male artist is emphasized finally by lines 17–18: "Your wrists basket your waist. / You round to the square weight." At this moment, just before the midpoint of the poem, the women's bodies are depicted as becoming like the round baskets in their environment. In the first half of the poem, however, the washerwomen have voices and talk among themselves: "Your chat's sabbatical" (although we don't hear what they say).

In the second half of the poem, however, the narrator steps inside the painting to talk with the women and the painter becomes visible. He has his own particular method of painting and his own agenda.

> Wait. There behind you.
> A man. There behind you.
> Whatever you do don't turn.
> Why is he watching you? . . .
>
> See he takes his ease
> staking his easel so,
> slowly sharpening charcoal,
> closing his eyes just so,
> slowly smiling as if
> so slowly he is
>
> unbandaging his mind.
> Surely a good laundress
> would understand its twists,
> its white turns,
> its blind designs—
>
> it's your winding sheet.

The repetition of the word "ease" within the phrase "staking his easel" suggests that his "ease" comes precisely from his position behind the easel, detached from the women. The second to last stanza of the poem suggests another difference: while the women must work hastily and "sweat," he works "slowly." And finally, it becomes clear that his point is not to represent these women as they are or even as he sees them—he is, after all, "closing his eyes just so"—but in a way that permits him to "unbandag[e] his [own] mind." In utilizing these women for his own purposes, he metaphorically kills them.

Other poems that address the representation of women by men include "Pose (After the Painting *Mrs. Badham* by Ingres)," "From the Painting *Back from Market* by Chardin," and "On Renoir's *The Grape-Pickers*." This is not to suggest that Boland believes Degas, Ingres, Chardin, or Renoir were malevolent artists, intent upon wiping out women's subjectivity; rather these poems suggest that in some representations of women, women's hard work and their voices are effaced in the service of artistic conventions or masculine desire. These poems suggest the importance of acknowledging the role of the painter in making the representation, for the painter always (however unconsciously) has a particular agenda in mind and does not—indeed cannot—paint a subject "as it really is," to borrow a phrase from Matthew Arnold. Representing the male artist in the poem has an effect similar to Jean Rhys's rewriting of *Jane Eyre* in *Wide Sargasso Sea* (1966). By telling the story from the madwoman Bertha Mason's point of view instead of Jane's, Rhys makes it impossible for us to reread Charlotte Brontë's novel without considering that there are two sides to every story. If we hear only one, we miss an important and meaningful perspective.

The difficulty of negotiating a position with respect to the male Irish literary tradition is a theme reflected in some of the poems of other Irish women writers of Boland's generation, including Eiléan Ní Chuilleanáin (1942–), Medbh McGuckian (1950–), and Nuala Ní Dhomhnaill (1952–). Like Boland, Ní Dhomhnaill (who writes her poetry in Irish) addresses the ways women are mythologized. Her poem "Parthenogenesis" describes a woman who swims in the sea: "supple, she struck out / with strength for the breaking waves." The woman is seduced by "a shadow, like a man's" and nearly succumbs to her "desire to escape to sea and shells . . . / the seaweed tresses where at last / her bones changed into coral / and time made atolls of her arms, / pearls of her eyes . . . / But stop!" Rather than remaining fixed, as a beautiful but inanimate object in the sea, she makes her way onto the beach and, after nearly dying, gives birth to a son. The Greek legend about a woman metamorphosed into a mermaid is transformed at the end of the poem into a Christian myth:

> But whoever she was I want to say
> that the fear she felt
> when the sea-shadow followed her
> is the same fear that vexed
> the young heart of the Virgin
> when she heard the angels' sweet bell
> and in her womb was made flesh
> by all accounts
> the Son of the Living God.
> (*Contemporary Irish Poetry*, pp. 437–439)

This poem, like many of Boland's, is to some extent about women poets. It suggests that men's "accounts" both define how women are perceived and permit men to ignore women's "fear" of being trapped as minor players in other peoples' stories. Like Boland, Ní Dhomhnaill recognizes the challenge of defining herself as a poet and rewriting the stories about women into stories belonging to women.

NEW TOPICS FOR POETRY

IN the previous section, the techniques by which Boland negotiates a position for a woman poet's voice within the male literary canon were explored. But once a woman finds a position from which to speak, what does she want to talk about? This is a question at the core of poetic ethics, and Boland makes it clear she wants to address it. In "The Journey," Boland rewrites Book VI of Virgil's *Aeneid* by providing Sappho as a guide to the underworld. This revision of the Greek story opens, however, with a plaint about the topics of poetry:

> . . . "there has never"
> I said "been a poem to an antibiotic
>
> . . .
>
> "or the devious Africa-seeking tern
> or the protein treasures of the sea bed.
> Depend on it, somewhere a poet is wasting
> his sweet uncluttered meters on the obvious
>
> "emblem instead of the real thing."
> (*Outside History*, p. 93)

Note that the poet who wastes "his" time writing about the "obvious emblem instead of the real thing" is male. Boland suggests that it is important to write about "real" life rather than rehashing uncomplicated legends; there are "real" topics that have not been covered and histories that have not yet been written. Not surprisingly, Boland proposes that these absent topics and histories are those that pertain to women.

Recovering an unwritten history is a powerful political agenda, and in this project Boland has Irish exemplars, one of whom she mentions in *Object Lessons*. In *The Hidden Ireland* (1924), Daniel Corkery explores the history and work of the eighteenth-century Gaelic poets. He opens his book with an introduction in which he discusses William E. H. Lecky's *History of England in the Eighteenth Century* (1878–1890). Lecky's book, he writes, will supplement Corkery's own, for

> [my] province is that side of Irish life, the Gaelic side, which to [Lecky] and his authorities was dark. He must have thought the Gaelic language a wayside *patois*, clearly not one of the permanent forces of the nation. . . . [Lecky] would have us consider as complete an analysis of Irish life in which [the soul of the Gael] is not referred to . . . of this literature, of these poets, Lecky knew nothing.
>
> (pp. 6–7)

Just as Corkery had to supply a missing "side" to Irish history, Boland believes she (and other women poets) must provide the missing stories of women in Irish literature.

Her strategy is not to further investigate legendary women such as Dark Rosaleen, the Old Woman of the Roads, and Cathleen Ní Houlihan; they already have been written about by men. Rather, she wants to recover history hitherto unrecorded and unrecognized: the story of the ordinary woman's life. In "It's a Woman's World" she writes: "as far as history goes / we were never / on the scene of the crime . . . we were gristing bread / or getting the recipe / for a good soup / to appetize / our gossip" (*An Origin Like Water*, p. 121). Here, "history" is literally "his story"; Boland wants to write a new kind of history (perhaps a "herstory") that incorporates ordinary women's stories into current histories in order that they might be more complete.

Boland recovers the unwritten woman's life and sets it forth as something both ordinary and vitally important. She proposes that the everyday events, ordinary objects, individual voices, and details of our lives are as important as—if not more important than—epic events such as wars, fabulous inventions, collective voices, and generalizations. She proposes the day-to-day experience of suburban women as a topic worthy of poetry. She writes of a trip with her husband, a tree in a garden, a chance meeting with a neighbor. By recovering what she calls these "snips and threads of an ordinary day," stories that formerly have been "outside history" (if "history" is the official record of the time) can begin to come inside.

While it is impossible to trace all the concerns in Boland's poetry, three of her important topics reflect her preoccupation with representing real women's lives. As a way to explore how all these topics come together, one might begin by examining an excerpt from the opening paragraphs of *Object Lessons*. The passage reflects her projects discussed in the first section of this essay: she resists general myths about women and binary oppositions, and she encourages empathy and intersubjectivity. From the first sentence, she regards the woman as an individual with whom "you" (the reader) can empathize, for both she and we "approach" the hospital. By describing the different routes to the hospital, she suggests multiple points of view, and the tropes are concentric rather than binary—that is, the events of which she speaks occur "in" days "of" a month (October), embedded "in" a year (1909), and the "hospital" is in the "center of the city":

In the early days of October, in the year 1909, a woman entered a Dublin hospital, near the center of the city. The building is still there. If you approach from the south, with the Dublin hills behind you, and look down a tunnel of grace made by the houses of Fitzwilliam and Merrion squares, your view will end abruptly in this: the National Maternity Hospital, red brick and out of character, blocking the vista. The rooms inside are functional and light-eating. They show no evidence of that zest for air and proportion which was the mask of an Augustan oppressor. . . . She may not have come that way. She might have traveled down the unglamorous back streets that lead more directly to the hospital. Fenian Street. Hogan Place. Past the mills. Past the Dodder River on its way to the Liffey. Up the slight gradient which would still, in that year, be cobbled. The prewinter chill, which can be felt on some October mornings, could have struck extra music out of the horses' hooves. . . . This is the way we make the past. . . . Giving eyesight and evidence to a woman we never knew and cannot now recover. . . . She was my grandmother.

(pp. 3–5)

This passage suggests three main topics for discussion. First, in stating that "we make the past," she identifies the need to explore the relationship between Irish history and its representation. In moving from the general and anonymous ("a woman" and "a hospital") to the particular ("the city" of Dublin) and then to the personal "you," she suggests that by disentangling an individual's story from general Irish history, we can obtain a better understanding of "real" history. Second, the hospital is an "object" that—because it is "still

there"—can connect us in some way to the past. Boland often uses an "ordinary" object that exists in both the present and the past to help her recover unwritten histories of women. Third, the hospital in which the woman will give birth is called first "a Dublin hospital" and then the "National Maternity Hospital." The name, like the concentric circles of time that begin the passage, points to a concern about the situation of the individual woman within a domestic (or, here, explicitly "maternal") space, which exists within local urban and national space.

HISTORY AND REPRESENTATION

THE relationship between Irish history and its representation, like that of any country (although perhaps even more so for a colony), is complicated by factors such as the sociopolitical position of the historian, the technologies available for writing and publishing, and the representational strategies available at a particular historical moment. Boland's work attempts to identify and avoid two of the dangers associated with the last these factors. The first is turning people into larger-than-life myths or ordering events into familiar plotlines. The second is erasing certain stories altogether. Although these may seem to be very different tendencies, they really are two sides of the same coin. Both work to elide the particulars of a history: they provide no account of individual people and the specific reasons these people take action, and they ignore the uniqueness of historical moments by making them seem like versions of stories we already know.

In *Object Lessons*, Boland recognizes the seductiveness of both of these options—to mythologize and to erase. When she writes of getting reacquainted with Ireland again as a teenager, she claims, "My years away had given me a crooked respect for episodes" (p. 62). It is precisely distance—a lack of familiarity—that makes us somewhat anxious to understand, and in our haste we may want to hear a story that has a fixed beginning and end and can fit into a nicely encapsulated "episode." Conversely, as a young poet she accepted the use of woman as an image in poetry and did not question the erasures required: "As I read the accepted masters of the tradition, it was all too easy to internalize a sense of power and control.

... Almost nowhere, at the beginning, did I see its exclusions. Nor did I want to. The exhilaration of language . . . is almost inseparable from its power. Later the suspect nature of the power would undermine the exhilaration" (pp. 26–27). The desire for episodes and acceptance of erasures reflect two deep psychic needs that are fairly universal: to make the unfamiliar familiar so that we can comfortably locate ourselves within our surroundings; and to ally ourselves with power so that we can feel a sense of autonomy. Neither impulse is inappropriate or harmful in and of itself—but as Boland began to discover, writing as an Irish woman poet necessitated finding a new relation between history and women so that their side of history could be recovered.

One way of resisting established history, which is usually constructed as events in time, is to consider history as events in *space*. In *Narratology* (2nd ed., 1997), the literary critic Mieke Bal writes about the representation of space and its relationship to memory and reconstructing history:

Memory is also the joint between time and space. Especially in stories set in former colonies, the memory evokes a past in which people were dislodged from their space by colonizers who occupied it, but also, a past in which they did not yield. Going back . . . to the time in which the place was a different kind of space is a way of countering the effects of coloniz[ation]. . . . Mastering, looking from above, dividing up and controlling is an approach to space that ignores time as well as the density of its lived-in quality. In opposition to such ways of seeing space, producing a landscape with a history is a way of spatializing memory that undoes the killing of space as lived.

(pp. 147–148)

Boland certainly recognizes the impact of the years of colonization on Ireland's self-image. But in order to avoid simplifying the story into a melodrama of a victimized Ireland overtaken by a ruthless, victorious England, Boland sometimes uses the Irish landscape as a way to re-member (literally, to reassemble) and dignify a history that exists independently of English versions of Irish history. She explores the way memory, space, and history are interconnected and posits an alternative to the linear historical narrative that marches through time. For example, in the opening passage of *Object Lessons*, the list of street names maps memory onto space. The landscape materializes (makes tangible) individuals or families of the past—with the name "Hogan"—as well as groups such as the Fenians, a military body said to have been exterminated by King Cairbre by the end of the third century, then reconstituted in the nineteenth century to promote Irish home rule. When memory is specialized it can become concentric and interrelated rather than linear, and the individual in the present landscape can have a personal response to a historical moment.

In "That the Science of Cartography Is Limited," which opens the volume *In a Time of Violence* (1994), Boland narrates that she and her husband go "to the borders of Connacht," where they see the remains of "a famine road." As in the opening passage of *Object Lessons*, time is organized concentrically, and an object in the landscape (here, the road) is used to connect past and present.

> I looked down at ivy and the scutch grass
> rough-cast stone had
> disappeared into as you told me
> in the second winter of their ordeal, in
>
> 1847, when the crop had failed twice,
> Relief Committees gave
> the starving Irish such roads to build.
>
> Where they died, there the road ended
>
> and ends still . . .
>
> (p. 7)

Despite the fact that the road is of "stone," it has nearly disappeared under the "ivy and the scutch grass." This disappearance in the landscape is a fairly obvious metaphor for the erasure of the painful history of the starving Irish who built this road. The ironic attitude toward the relief committees is heightened by positioning the word "gave" at the end of the line; the pause before the next line provides a moment when we might anticipate the phrase "the starving Irish some food" instead of "such roads to build." The "road" is therefore both the "gift" of the committees and the record of Irish deaths. If history is problematic because ugly truths can be erased, perhaps the landscape bears witness to cruelty in ways that other representations cannot.

After the poem moves back into the present tense, the narrator explores how maps fail to tell history:

. . . when I take down
the map of this island, it is never so
I can say here is
the masterful, the apt rendering of
the spherical as flat, nor
an ingenious design which persuades a curve
into a plane,
but to tell myself again that

the line which says woodland and cries hunger
and gives out among sweet pine and cypress,
and finds no horizon
will not be there.

(pp. 7–8)

Because her husband narrates to her the history of the road, this poem suggests that one person speaking to another is a far more reliable way to access histories than maps, which reduce historical moments to mere "lines." The map is a failure in one sense, for it does not "tell" her the history that lies behind the road. But because she has personally experienced the space where the road was, and because her husband has narrated the history to her, she can now "tell" herself that maps are inadequate ways to represent history and that there once *was* such a thing as a famine road.

In these lines she describes maps in geometric language ("spherical," "curve," "plane," "line") that contrasts with the natural language of the "fragrance of balsam, the gloom of cypresses" that opens the poem. She points out the false pride of inventors of maps who, through their "masterful" (note the gender inflection) "ingenuity," have silenced a story and replaced the "line" of the famine road with "lines" of longitude and latitude—lines that bring a false sense of order to the landscape instead of allowing the landscape to speak its "lines" for itself. Near the end of the poem, when she refers back to the "cypresses" in the third line, the poem itself becomes circular; poetically she offers an alternative to the "line" that cannot speak. In order to write history anew we need to place ourselves as individuals in historical moments other than our own, and one way of traveling through time is to travel *to* a space, which has sensual and emotional weight.

In "The Making of an Irish Goddess," Boland explores the way myths structure perceptions; here, even landscapes do not provide access to any sort of essential truth. We have already seen the way she revises the myth of Daphne. This poem describes Ceres (aka Demeter), the ancient goddess of earth and fertility, who in this version "went to hell / with no sense of time" to rescue her daughter, Persephone. Looking back at Ireland, Ceres saw only a homogeneous landscape, simple and unchanging:

the diligence of rivers always at one level,
wheat at one height,
leaves of a single color,
the same distance in the usual light;

a seasonless, unscarred earth.

(*Outside History*, p. 38)

Myths tell comfortable tales—of lands without change, with the rivers and the wheat "always at one level." Singleness, sameness, and usualness are comfortable fictions that conceal the complex truth of everyday experience. But later in the poem the narrator insists that the "real" Ireland has a very different story than that inscribed in myth, one that requires

an accurate inscription
of that agony:

the failed harvests,
the fields rotting to the horizon,
the children devoured by their mothers
whose souls, they would have said,
went straight to hell,
followed by their own.

(pp. 38–39)

The poem rewrites its earlier phrases depicting nature, exchanging the uniformity and stasis of "wheat at one height" for "fields" in the process of "rotting." But it also rewrites the myth into the history of real people: it is not Ceres, goddess of the earth, who goes down to hell but the children and mothers of Ireland who go through the hell of the famine. The poem describes mythmaking that would efface this history as a wound:

Myth is the wound we leave
in the time we have—

which in my case is this
March evening
at the foothills of the Dublin mountains,
across which the lights have changed all day,

holding up my hand
sickle-shaped, to my eyes
to pick out
my own daughter from
all the other children in the distance

(p. 39)

Like the opening of *Object Lessons,* this passage disentangles a particular and personal story of a woman (the narrator) from general history. The narrator locates herself precisely in time ("this / March evening") and space ("at the foothills of the Dublin mountains"); these specific details add to a feeling of realness and suggest her refusal to be mythologized into a homogeneous image of woman. She rewrites Ceres' vision of the unchanging landscape to describe her own vision: "the lights have changed all day." But like Ceres, she occupies a central position in her own story: she insistently repeats the possessive pronoun "my" to claim her moment in history, and she describes her hand as "sickle-shaped," suggesting an affinity with the goddess who governed the harvest. (The narrator may see her children as a different kind of harvest.) In describing the way she distinguishes her "own daughter from / all the other children in the distance," she suggests the parallel project of distinguishing her own story (or any individual history) from that of general history, which can be grasped only at a "distance." That is, specific lives—although they may be ordinary and domestic—must be seen up close. They are a means by which we can get at the truth of history and set aside the myth, which is like a "wound" that turns into a "scar." Boland's concern is that the myths about Ireland as a whole will efface the stories of individual Irish people.

Perhaps this is the reason she names one of her most poignant poems about Ireland "Mise Eire" ("I am Ireland"). Rather than remaining an emblem seen by others, the woman narrator ("Ireland") catalogs the stock elements and phrases used to talk about her history:

> . . . old dactyls,
> oaths made
> by the animal tallows
> of the candle—
>
> land of the Gulf Stream,
> the small farm,
> the scalded memory,
> the songs

> that bandage up the history,
> the words
> that make a rhythm of the crime

(*Outside History,* p. 78)

From the beginning of the poem she refuses to speak in the "old dactyls" that characterize bardic poetry. The word "dactyl" is the Greek word for "finger"; in poetry it is a metrical foot in which one stressed syllable is followed by two unstressed syllables (like a finger, with one long and two short digits). In refusing to speak in "dactyls," she claims she will refuse not only the bardic tradition but also the tendency to "point" at Ireland as an object rather than let it speak for itself as a subject "I." However, by using the two dactyls "memory" and "history" to end lines, she suggests that she cannot completely refuse existing notions of Irish memory and history.

In an attempt to replace this version of her "nation displaced" and recover the "crime" that "words" have concealed, she marshals individuals' histories, complete with tactile details: she describes a woman who is "a sloven's mix / of silk at the wrists" and another who wears a "gansy-coat / on board the *Mary Belle,* / in the huddling cold, / holding her half-dead baby to her" (pp. 78–79). At the end of the poem the woman on the boat is speaking in incoherent sounds that get stuck in her throat, an "immigrant / guttural with the vowels / of homesickness." The three dactyls ("immigrant," "guttural," and "homesickness") imply that the only available medium for expression is the language that already exists, while the moaned "vowels" gesture toward some experience that cannot be represented by the available language. Thus, language itself—like maps and myths—is inadequate for representing her experience.

The poem ends proclaiming the constant temptation we feel to use language to efface or scab over the wounds:

> a new language
> is a kind of scar
> and heals after a while
> into a passable imitation
> of what went before.

(p. 79)

The poem begs the question, To whom is this "imitation" "passable"? To the listeners who find

45

enough common ground between this language and their own to understand it? Or to the speaker, because she can make herself somewhat understood to the dominant culture? Either way, the poem reminds us that representation is always only "passable," incomplete and in some way inadequate.

SUBJECTS AND OBJECTS

By entitling her narrative *Object Lessons,* Boland suggests that she is open to learning from the "objects" in her environment. Refusing to take the position of sole and authoritative master of her own narrative, she views her experience of coming into being as a woman poet as unfinished, full of lessons that are sometimes forgotten and sometimes intuitively understood. Her mode of representing her life is circular rather than linear; she makes no pretense of writing a day-by-day or month-by-month account of her life. She includes other people's stories; she revisits an episode in her life, describing it differently each time; she discusses one location in a variety of ways. If her life is the "object" of her narrative, her poems similarly articulate the complexity and meaningfulness inherent in the activity of looking at objects.

Her poems defy attempts to hold a single, unified perspective and indeed even insist that this way of knowing is not only impossible but undesirable. For Boland, seeing and knowing an object requires that a subject look in two directions at once: at her own ideas and particular perspective as it is shaped by her gender, nationality, race, and so forth; and at the object of inquiry. Boland quotes Adrienne Rich, a poet she admires, on this point: "Until we can understand the assumptions in which we are drenched . . . we cannot know ourselves" or, as Boland suggests, our environment (*Object Lessons,* pp. 249–250). For Boland, this ability to move between perspectives, to occupy the position of observer and object simultaneously, is uniquely the province of the woman poet:

The woman poet is in that poignant place I spoke of, where the subject cannot forget her previous existence as an object. . . . [T]he poem she writes is likely to have a new dimension. . . . It is easy enough to see that her dual relation to the object she makes—as both creator and rescuer—shifts the balance of subject and object,

lessens the control and alters perspectives within the poem.

(*Object Lessons,* p. 233)

As we have seen, objects in the landscape become a means of accessing histories. In "That the Science of Cartography Is Limited," Boland uses a road that "still" exists in order to suggest the necessity for forming an empathic connection to the past. In *Object Lessons* she uses the hospital that is "still there" to recover an empathic connection to her grandmother but also to point out the meaning of there being multiple ways of getting to that hospital. Thus, two of the lessons that "objects" can teach are, first, the need to try to empathize with people of a different time in order to understand historical events and, second, the value of being able to see multiple points of view simultaneously.

Objects in the landscape are not the only means by which we can access histories of women. The "ordinary" objects in the domestic environment— a fan, a doll, a bowl, a bicycle, curtains, a photograph—always have stories attached to them if we are willing to look at them carefully. When reading Boland's poetry we often are required to enact the intersubjective viewing of objects because the language demands that we shift our perspective in the poem from one subject position to another. For example, "The Black Lace Fan My Mother Gave Me" opens with a series of sentences in which the pronouns keep changing their referents:

It was the first gift he ever gave her,
buying it for five francs in the Galeries
in prewar Paris. It was stifling.
A starless drought made the nights stormy.

They stayed in the city for the summer.
They met in cafés. She was always early.
He was late. That evening he was later.
They wrapped the fan. He looked at his watch.

She looked down the Boulevard des Capucines.
She ordered more coffee. She stood up.
The streets were emptying. The heat was killing.
She thought the distance smelled of rain and lightning.

(*Outside History,* p. 19)

The opening line seems so simple in its pronouns: "It" is the gift that "he" gives to "her"; there is an object (it) being transferred from an actor (he) to a recipient (she). But by line three, "it" has a new, vague antecedent—the weather or maybe the city or the café where she is sitting. This indeterminacy suggests a shift in perspective from the man (the "subject" of the first line) to the woman waiting for him in the café or perhaps to the people in Paris generally. Next, the pronoun "they" of lines 5 and 6, which refers to the man and woman, switches meaning in line 8 to refer to the salespeople at the store. Finally, "the distance smelled of rain and lightning" belongs to the woman's perspective, but "smelled" is a peculiar word: the "distance" smells of rain and lightning, but the woman is the one doing the "smelling." Subject and object have become mixed: the woman and her environment are intertwined.

Other elements of these lines point to a concern with perspective. "Prewar Paris" implies that the narrator is speaking from a position of "postwar Paris." The description of the man as "late" implies the woman's perspective, for she is kept waiting for him at cafés. "She was always early" implies the man's point of view—he finds her waiting for him. The parallel phrasing of "He looked at his watch. / She looked down the Boulevard des Capucines" almost suggests a pair of cameras, switching back and forth between the two people.

Just as multiple antecedents and parallel phrases suggest dual viewpoints, words can serve as bi-directional arrows. "Capucines" points in two directions, for it means both an order of nuns and a kind of nasturtium. A second way this poem plays with this binary opposition of "subject / object" is by introducing another binary—human / nature—and showing how the two terms begin to collapse into each other. In the following stanzas, the fan is described in ways that suggest it is both a highly crafted aesthetic object and also an "element" of nature:

> These are wild roses, appliquéd on silk by hand,
> darkly picked, stitched boldly, quickly.
> The rest is tortoiseshell and has the reticent,
> clear patience of its element. It is
>
> a worn-out underwater bullion and it keeps,
> even now, an inference of its violation.
> The lace is overcast as if the weather
> it opened for and offset had entered it.

As with the washerwomen, the "doer" of the labor is quite forthrightly erased out of this poem, and we are urged to ask, Whose "hand" is it? Who "appliquéd" and "picked" and "stitched"? How have these natural elements of tortoiseshell and roses been formed into an ornate fan? This erasure of the agent who does the work to make the mother's fan reflects Boland's concern with the way society refuses to recognize the value of women's work in the domestic sphere. The play on the words "bullion" and "overcast" affirms the integral relation between nature and the activities of human beings, perhaps particularly those of women. The word "bullion" refers to gold or silver metal in mass, as might be found in nature, but it is also defined as "lace, braid, or fringe of gold or silver threads." "Overcast" describes the weather but it can also refer either to a functional kind of sewing in which long stitches are used to prevent raveling or to decorative embroidery.

The final stanza suggests another relation between the handcrafted and the natural. The black-bird's wing is akin to the fan:

> the blackbird on this first sultry morning,
> in summer, finding buds, worms, fruit,
> feels the heat. Suddenly she puts out her wing—
> the whole, full, flirtatious span of it.

By drawing a parallel between a woman waving a black lace fan and a blackbird flirting by using its wing, the narrator suggests the affinity between human beings and nature. In his famous poem "The World Is Too Much with Us," William Wordsworth mourns that there is "little we see in Nature that is ours." Boland's poem suggests that "Nature" and "ours" are intertwined, perhaps more than we recognize.

While this poem is in part about how we should look at objects, it is also about the history that this small object carries with it: the story of two people in love in Paris, a man who tends to be late but is generous or likes to apologize with a gift; a woman who tends to be early, drinks coffee, and is acutely attuned to her environment; the repetitive ordinariness of afternoons in cafés; the calm that precedes war; the labor that crafts objects. The ordinary object in Boland's poetry becomes a tangible reminder of a moment in history—a moment that has meaning and can bind the history of an individual to the "official" history of nations.

THE WOMAN, THE DOMESTIC SPACE, AND THE NATION

As discussed previously in this essay, Boland is acutely aware of the problem that arises when a woman is used as an emblem in Ireland's "official" history: the woman becomes reduced to a body and her subjectivity is ignored. The problem is not merely aesthetic. Because no one (man or woman) can create a self-image in a vacuum, real women tend to think of themselves and their bodies in ways that accord at least in part with the ways society thinks about women. For most of us, our first "society" is our family; thus, a woman's idea of herself develops within both a domestic and a national space. Of course, considering the relationship between a woman's domestic space and her nation raises another set of questions: How is the family shaped by the nation, and how is the nation shaped by notions of family? Why is it that the nation is mythologized into a "mother country," but so many histories of Ireland omit the stories of the domestic sphere? These questions are potent ones and not easily answered.

In attempting to understand the way a woman's body is figured within these spaces, Boland examines the domestic space from different angles. Some poems work to undercut the myth that the domestic space is something sacred, a safe enclave that exists separately from the nation or society as a whole. She reveals the emotional trauma and violence that family members inflict upon one another (particularly upon women and children) and connects it to national identity and Ireland's violent history. Like some of Sylvia Plath's poems (such as "Daddy"), some of Boland's poems explore the dangers of familial relationships to a woman's body and identity. Another group of poems rescues the domestic space from its devalued status in the broader culture. Rather than treating the domestic as second in importance to national or political or economic concerns, she gives it dignity and accords respect to daily occurrences in the home. The domestic space is no longer a place of drudgery and unimportant daily routine but a place where families find love and where women can develop and ground their emotional and creative power. By extension, she asserts, domestic events are a topic worthy of poetry.

Many of Boland's poems fall into one of these groups, but the volume *In Her Own Image* (1980) takes as one of its central projects the exploration of the relationships among a woman, her domestic space, and her nation. The ten poems in this volume may be split into two groups of five. The first group concerns the violence that can be done to a woman's body and, through her body, to her very

conception of herself within the domestic space. The second group celebrates the power to be found in a woman's body. The title poem of *In Her Own Image* suggests the problematic relationship of a woman to her own body and to that of her daughter. The speaker of the poem is a woman who has just strangled her own child.

> She is not myself
> anymore she is not
> even in my sky
> anymore and I
> am not myself.
>
> I will not disfigure
> her pretty face.
> Let her wear amethyst thumbprints,
> a family heirloom,
> a sort of burial necklace
> (*An Origin Like Water*, p. 93)

The careful separation of "she" and "I" in these lines suggests that the woman's identity has been enmeshed with that of her daughter. It is unfixed, unstable; she confuses "self" and "other" precisely because she is not a separate subject. The woman's lack of identity, her tragic reliance on someone else to provide it for her, her inability to protect her daughter, and her fear that her daughter will inherit nothing but violence as "a family heirloom" lead her to perform the desperate act of murder.

We gain insight into why the woman has so little sense of self (and why she has killed her daughter) in the partner poem, "In His Own Image." While "In Her Own Image" explores the devastating effects of a woman's powerlessness and lack of identity, "In His Own Image" explores the causes of it: domestic captivity and physical cruelty. In this poem, the woman narrator inhabits a domestic space that does not reflect her identity in its entirety. Indeed, taken together, the two poems suggest that adequate mirroring is necessary to a person's development of identity. Someone (or society) must recognize and value a woman as she is. "In His Image" opens with a catalog of domestic objects that blend with her facial features in the distorted reflections that a "kettle" and "pan" provide:

> I was not myself, myself.
> The celery feathers,
> the bacon flitch,
> the cups deep on the shelf

and my cheek
coppered and shone
in the kettle's paunch,
my mouth
blubbed in the tin of the pan—
they were all I had to go on.

How could I go on
With such meager proofs of myself?
(*An Origin Like Water*, p. 94)

Because she has a fragile sense of self she cannot serve as her own mirror. Her identity remains unforged, and each day she diminishes "from the self I was last night." The turning point of the poem is the man's arrival on the scene. Here, as in some of Boland's poems in which it is made clear that the artist's vision shapes the woman, the man's "sculpting" of the woman reworks her:

And then he came home tight
. . .
   Now I see
that all I needed
was a hand
to mold my mouth
to scald my cheek
. . .
   He splits my lip with his fist,
shadows my eye with a blow,
knuckles my neck to its proper angle.
What a perfectionist!

His are sculptor's hands:
they summon
form from the void,
they bring
me to myself again.
I am a new woman.
(*An Origin Like Water*, pp. 94–95)

The stock phrase "bring me to myself," as if she were coming out of a fainting spell or a state of unconsciousness, has frightening implications: in order to recover the "myself" that she does not have in the first line, and in order to be brought back to life and consciousness, she must be beaten. Sadism is a form of recognition. The sobering realization of this poem is that, given that we all need recognition of some sort, perhaps there are far too few forms of valuation—particularly for housewives—through which a woman can gather a sense of self. This woman must take what recognition she can get, even if it destroys her body.

Boland does not suggest that a husband is the only one to damage a woman's body or self-image. In "Tirade for the Mimic Muse" she berates the male poets for creating a national "muse" who bears no resemblance to real women. In "Anorexic" she represents the pain women feel when forced to label their own desires as evil. ("My body is a witch," the narrator claims.) In "Mastectomy" it is the "specialist" and "the surgeon" who mutilate her body. The poem carries an insidious message—albeit not a particularly new one—that medical science has performed and legitimized the abuse and torture of women's bodies in the name of "curing" them. The poem also betrays what the speaker sees as the motive, both for the mutilation and the concealing of it under the guise of "care":

So they have taken off
what slaked them first,
what they have hated since:

blue-veined
white-domed
home

of wonder
and the wetness
of their dreams.
(*An Origin Like Water*, p. 99)

Because a woman's breast is both a maternal and a sexual organ, it reminds the man of his original powerlessness and vulnerability as well as his early attraction to her. Because feelings of vulnerability can be painful and because sexual desire for his mother is taboo, he cannot bear to look at the breast that reminds him of both feelings. In her essay "The Dread of Woman," Karen Horney discusses the fear men feel at the thought of women's power and their sexuality. Both Horney and Boland suggest that fear underlies the oppression of women.

The two "Image" poems suggest that violence is a family ritual, handed down from generation to generation. These poems and "Bright-Cut Irish Silver" begin to uncover the dramas of national identity within the domestic space. They suggest a continuum from family traumas and memories to national ones. In "Bright-Cut Irish Silver," a silver bowl becomes a crucible in which family history reproduces itself. The poem suggests that the Irish craft of cutting silver into a vase is a kind of scarring of the earth, a skill that is passed on by fathers to sons:

> I take it down
> from time to time, to feel
> the smooth path of silver meet the cicatrix of skill.
>
> These scars, I tell myself, are learned.
>
> This gift for wounding an artery of rock
> was passed on from father to son, to the father
> of the next son.
>
> Is an aptitude for injuring
> earth while inferring it in curves and surfaces.
> (*Outside History*, p. 29)

The language of the "scar" reappears from "Mise Eire," reminding us that putting things into a "new language" inevitably covers over a wound. Here, the national craft of silversmithing "injures" the earth under the guise of creating a fine piece of silver for the home. The injury done to the land in the name of a national craft is brought into the home, treasured, and passed on.

Some critics see a difficulty in reconciling Boland's feminist statements with the poems that focus on and even glorify the domestic. They have wondered if she means to suggest that the home is the proper place for women; that only there could they come to grips with their selves and their history. Other critics, including this writer, do not think that is the thrust of these domestic poems. As we have seen, far from glorifying the domestic space unreservedly, some of her most troubling and frightening poems are precisely about the danger of the domestic space.

However, the domestic space is indeed treasured and revalued in the series called "Domestic Interior" from *Night Feed* (1982). The title poem, the last in the series, is one of her most tender, and Boland dedicated it to her husband, Kevin Casey. Here the narrator valorizes domesticity as a privileged space in which occurs "a way of life / that is its own witness" (*An Origin Like Water*, pp. 150–151). In this domestic space there is a woman "who won't improve in the light," but although the husband's "convex . . . eye" can show "only this woman in her varnishes," the tradeoff is that the life they have crafted together is so well understood by both that there is no need to "witness" or "testify" to their experience. There is already a

"witness" to their way of life in the objects that represent the rituals they share:

> put the kettle on, shut the blind.
>
> Home is a sleeping child,
> an open mind
>
> and our effects,
> shrugged and settled
> in the sort of light
> jugs and kettles
> grow important by.
> (*Outside History*, p. 151)

The "jugs and kettles / grow important" because they emblematize the rituals between the woman and her husband: the closing of the day with a meal eaten together behind the blinds, with their sleeping child nearby, and minds that are open to each other. The domestic space is not a "woman's" space: it is shared equally. The "effects" are "ours"; and the "child" and "mind" are not assigned possessive pronouns—"my" and "your"—that might divide the parental and intellectual spheres between the wife and husband.

Although this domestic space is characterized by love, it is also the space in which the women can write her poetry. It is fitting, then, to conclude this essay with "The Women," in which Boland creates a narrator who moves between the roles of woman and poet. With marvelous excess, she crosses and recrosses boundaries that are intellectual, emotional, spatial, and temporal:

> This is the hour I love: the in-between
> neither here-nor-there hour of evening.
> The air is tea-colored in the garden.
> The briar rose is spilled crepe de Chine.
>
> This is the time I do my work best,
> going up the stairs in two minds,
> in two worlds, carrying cloth or glass,
> leaving something behind, bringing
> something with me I should have left behind.
>
> The hour of change, of metamorphosis,
> of shape-shifting instabilities.
> My time of sixth sense and second sight
> when in the words I choose, the lines I write,
> they rise like visions and appear to me:
>
> women of work, of leisure, of the night,
> in stove-colored silks, in lace, in nothing,
> with crewel needles, with books with wide-open legs,

who fled the hot breath of the god pursuing,
who ran from the split hoof and the thick
    lips
and fell and grieved and healed into myth,

into me in the evening at my desk . . .
The fission of music into syllabic heat . . .
         (*Outside History*, pp. 84–85)

Boland makes it clear that "woman" cannot be encompassed: no single woman can be an emblem for all women. Like the narrator's "sixth sense and second sight," which exceed the normal senses, women always exceed their representation. The parallel phrasing of "into myth" and "into me" suggests Boland's project throughout her work has been to write new—that is, plural—myths of "women." The poem suggests that her earliest struggles to write as both a woman and a poet helped her find a way to do it, for although the narrator of the poem is the one who writes, the women she seeks to represent also have the power to act. ("They rise like visions and appear to me," she writes, rather than "*I* see *them* rise like visions.") In the process of figuring these women who work and rest, desire and flee, run and fall, grieve and heal, Boland seems to have written herself into being as a woman poet who recognizes her own capacity for work and rest, grieving and healing.

SELECTED BIBLIOGRAPHY

I. VOLUMES OF POETRY. *New Territory* (London, 1967); *The War Horse: Poems* (London, 1975); *In Her Own Image* (Dublin, 1980); *Night Feed, Poems* (Dublin, London, and Boston, 1982); *The Journey and Other Poems* (Manchester and New York, 1987); *In a Time of Violence* (New York, 1994); *The Lost Land* (New York, 1998).

II. PROSE. "An Un-Romantic American," in *Parnassus* 14, no. 2 (1988); *A Kind of Scar: The Woman Poet in a National Tradition* (Dublin, 1989); "The Woman, the Place, the Poet," in *Georgia Review* 44 (spring 1990); "Truthful Tears," in *Parnassus* 16, no. 2 (1990); "The Serinette Principle: The Lyric in Contemporary Poetry," in *PN Review* 19 (March–April 1993); "Continuing the Encounter," in Eibhear Walsh, ed., *Ordinary People Dancing* (Cork, Ireland, 1993); "Compact and Compromise: Derek Mahon as a Young Poet," in *Irish University Review* 24 (spring–summer 1994); "Writing the Political Poem in Ireland," in *Southern Review* 31 (summer 1995); *Object Lessons: The Life of the Woman and the Poet in Our Time* (New York, 1995); "Letter to a Young Poet," in *American Poetry Review* 26 (May–June 1997).

III. ANTHOLOGIES. *Introducing Eavan Boland* (Princeton, N.J., 1981); *Outside History: Selected Poems 1980–1990* (New York, 1990); *An Origin Like Water: Collected Poems 1967–1987* (New York, 1996).

IV. INTERVIEWS. Amy Klauke, "An Interview with Eavan Boland," in *Northwest Review* 25, no. 1 (1987); Deborah Tall, "Q. & A. with Eavan Boland," in *Irish Literary Supplement* 7 (fall 1988); Marilyn Reizbaum, "An Interview with Eavan Boland," in *Contemporary Literature* (winter 1989); Nancy Means Wright and Dennis J. Hannan, "Q. & A. with Eavan Boland," in *Irish Literary Supplement* 10 (spring 1991); Deborah McWilliams Consalvo, "An Interview with Eavan Boland," in *Studies: An Irish Quarterly Review* 81 (spring 1992); Patty O'Connell, "An Interview with Eavan Boland," in *Poets and Writers* 22 (November–December 1994); Margaret Mills Harper, "Eavan Boland: An Interview," in *Five Points* 1 (winter 1997).

V. USEFUL TEXTS FOR READING EAVAN BOLAND. Jeffrey Gantz, trans. and ed., *Early Irish Myths and Sagas* (Harmondsworth, Middlesex, England, and New York, 1981); Daniel Corkery, *The Hidden Ireland* (1924; Dublin, 1986); Anthony Bradley, ed., *Contemporary Irish Poetry* (Berkeley, Calif., 1988).

VI. BIOGRAPHICAL AND CRITICAL STUDIES. Robert H. Henigan, "Contemporary Women Poets in Ireland," in *Concerning Poetry* 18, nos. 1–2 (1985); Sheila C. Conboy, " 'What You Have Seen Is Beyond Speech': Female Journeys in the Poetry of Eavan Boland and Eiléan Ní Chuilleanáin," in *Canadian Journal of Irish Studies* 16 (July 1990); Jody Allen-Randolph, "Ecriture Feminine and the Authorship of Self in Eavan Boland's *In Her Own Image*," in *Colby Quarterly* 27 (March 1991); Patricia L. Hagen and Thomas W. Zelman, " 'We Were Never on the Scene of the Crime': Eavan Boland's Repossession of History," in *Twentieth Century Literature* 37 (winter 1991); David Walker, "Improvising the Blackbird," in *Field: Contemporary Poetry and Poetics* 44 (spring 1991); Deborah McWilliams Consalvo, "In Common Usage: Eavan Boland's Poetic Voice," in *Eire Ireland: A Journal of Irish Studies* 28 (summer 1993); Ellen M. Mahon, "Eavan Boland's Journey with the Muse," in Deborah Fleming, ed., *Learning the Trade: Essays on W. B. Yeats and Contemporary Poetry* (West Cornwall, Conn., 1993); Deborah Sarbin, " 'Out of Myth into History': The Poetry of Eavan Boland and Eiléan Ní Chuilleanáin," in *Canadian Journal of Irish Studies* 19 (July 1993); Susan Brown, "A Victorian Sappho: Agency, Identity, and the Politics of Poetics," in *English Studies in Canada* 20 (June 1994); Jody Allen-Randolph, "Finding a Voice Where She Found a Vision," in *PN Review* 21 (September–October 1994); Kerry E. Robertson, "Anxiety, Influence, Tradition and Subversion in the Poetry of Eavan Boland," in *Colby Quarterly* 30 (December 1994); Ann Owens Weekes, " 'An Origin Like Water': The Poetry of Eavan Boland and Modernist Critiques of Irish Literature," in *Bucknell Review* 38, no. 1 (1994); M. Louise Cannon, "The Extraordinary Within the Ordinary: The Poetry of Eaven Boland and Nuala Ní Dhomhnaill," in *South Atlantic Review* 60 (May 1995); David G. Williams, "Responses to Elizabeth Bishop: Anne Stevenson, Eavan Boland and Jo Shapcott," in *English* 44 (fall 1995); Debrah Raschke, "Eavan Boland's *Outside History* and *In a Time of Violence:* Rescuing Women, the Concrete, and Other Things Physical from the Dung Heap," in *Colby Quarterly* 32 (June 1996); Jeanne Heuving, "Poetry in Our Political Lives," in *Contemporary Literature* 37 (summer 1996); Seija H. Paddon, "The Diversity of Performance / Performance as Diversity in the Poetry of Laura (Riding) Jackson and Eavan Boland," in *English Studies in Canada* 24 (December 1996).

ANITA DESAI

(1937–   )

A. Michael Matin

ONE OF THE preeminent contemporary Indian novelists, Anita Desai is doubly gifted with penetrating insight into the workings of the human psyche as well as an ability to craft prose so richly evocative that it often approaches the compact artistry of poetry. Her fiction, which inclines toward tragedy, is characterized by both stylistic and ideological eclecticism; she gracefully assimilates the techniques of a variety of literary modes, such as gothicism and expressionism, as well as the principles of disparate philosophies, ranging from Hinduism to existentialism. Although her primary interest is in sounding the depths of her characters' psyches, she is also a trenchant chronicler of the postcolonial experience in India, and particularly of the circumstances of Indian women. She is herself a product of extensive cultural cross-fertilization; although educated in English at a British missionary school, she was born to a Bengali father and a German mother and was raised speaking Hindi and German in a household located in Old Delhi, where her friends and neighbors were Hindus, Muslims, and Christians alike. Cosmopolitan both by upbringing and temperament, Desai celebrates what she terms in the 1996 essay "A Coat of Many Colors" India's "conglomerate culture"—its vast multiplicity of ethnicities, languages, and religions—and expresses utter contempt for "[t]hose purists who speak of the desirability of one language, one tradition, one culture" (p. 221). Her mistrust of chauvinism is based on a firsthand knowledge of its horrific potential; at the impressionable age of ten, she saw the fabric of that coat of many colors torn apart by the Hindu-Muslim violence that followed in the wake of the partition of British India into the separate nations of India and Pakistan. The tumultuous events of 1947—characterized in her novel *Where Shall We Go This Summer?* (1975) as "the stupefying bloodshed and violence that had erupted from the

dream of independence" (p. 91)—have provided one of the major, recurring themes of her fiction.

Desai has written nine novels, and it is this genre that best taps into her talents and predilections. But she has also made forays into a variety of other genres, having published short stories and children's fiction as well as numerous essays and reviews that have appeared in such periodicals as the *New Yorker, New Republic,* and *New York Review of Books.* Widespread recognition of her work came with her fifth novel, the highly lauded *Fire on the Mountain* (1977), which provided her with the first of the numerous honors that she has garnered. At the summit of her oeuvre stand three novels: *Clear Light of Day* (1980), *In Custody* (1984), and *Baumgartner's Bombay* (1988), the first two of which were shortlisted for Britain's Booker Prize. Her renown as one of the most highly esteemed of postcolonial writers is now firmly secure, but fame was a long time coming for her, a fact bound up with the precarious circumstances faced by post–1947 Indo-Anglian writers generally, especially women. As she has recalled,

When I was a young woman . . . in India, writing was a completely private and almost, I should say, a secret occupation. No one thought of me as a writer, and I barely thought of myself as a writer. It was simply something I went away and did in secret. I had no sense of community with other writers. . . . There were so few of us writing in English, and we were so scattered. . . . So I lived as a writer in complete isolation.

(Jussawalla interview, pp. 171–172)

Anglophone literature has been flourishing in India since the early 1980s—a sea change heralded, and to a large extent effected, by the publication of Salman Rushdie's *Midnight's Children* in 1980. Yet one can only understand the course of Desai's career—the halting, protracted development of her talents and the belated critical and public recognition of her accomplishments—if one recognizes

53

that her work has spanned the lean years of Indo-Anglian literature as well as the years of plenty.

LIFE AND CAREER

Anita Desai was born Anita Mazumdar on 24 June 1937 in Mussoorie, India. Her father was D. N. Mazumdar, a businessman from a village in an area of Bengal that is now part of Bangladesh; her mother was Toni Nime, a German who met Mazumdar while he was studying in Germany and who emigrated to India with him when he returned in the late 1920s. Desai recalls that her mother had "a European core . . . which protested against certain Indian things, which always maintained its independence and its separateness," and she identifies this fact as having had a profound influence on her own development. Even though she herself did not venture out of India until she was an adult and did not live outside of the country until she was nearly fifty, she has always felt her relationship to India to have been mediated by the sensibilities of her immigrant mother. "I am able to look at a country I know so intimately with a certain detachment, and that certainly comes from my mother," she has affirmed, maintaining that "I feel about India as an Indian, but I suppose I think about it as an outsider" (Bliss interview, p. 527).

Along with a brother and two sisters, Desai grew up in Old Delhi, in a home where the family spoke Hindi and German. It was not until she began attending the local elementary school, which was run by British missionaries, that she learned English, the language in which she has always written. By the age of seven she recognized that her vocation was to become a writer, and she began her publishing career two years later with a contribution to an American children's magazine. Such precociousness extended to her literary tastes as well; at the age of nine, she read Emily Brontë's *Wuthering Heights,* which "struck me with the force of a gale and I still vibrate to it" (Ram interview, p. 102). Although literature had a considerable effect on her early development, the truly transformative experience of her childhood came at the age of ten with India's independence from the British Empire and partition with Pakistan in August of 1947. The trauma of having her Muslim neighbors and schoolmates vanish overnight, in flight from Hindu violence and headed for the new border of Pakistan, was both intense and enduring, and a good deal of her career as a writer has been preoccupied with exploring these memories.

After attending Queen Mary's Secondary School, Desai went on to enroll in Miranda House, an elite college of Delhi University. While in college she befriended the writer Ruth Prawer Jhabvala, who was ten years her senior and, like her mother, a German immigrant to India who had married an Indian. She graduated with honors and a bachelor's degree in English literature in 1957, the same year that saw the publication of her first short story. She worked for a year in Calcutta before marrying Ashvin Desai, a business executive, in 1958. Except for her writing, she would not work again until the late 1980s, when she would begin a second career as a college professor in America. Instead, her energies were divided between her writing and the raising of their children, who by 1971 would number four: Rahul, Tani, Arjun, and Kiran. Her first novel, *Cry, the Peacock,* which tells the story of a mentally imbalanced young housewife, was published in 1963 and made immediately apparent her extraordinary abilities as a prose stylist. Although one might assume that her talents would lead her to write poetry (indeed, one often comes across arresting images in her fiction that one regrets finding buried within the pages of a novel), in fact this is no more the case for her than it was for the similarly gifted Virginia Woolf, perhaps her single most important literary influence.

The Desais resided in Calcutta from their marriage in 1958 until 1962, and they subsequently relocated several times within India—to Bombay, Chandigarh, Delhi, and Poona. Their years in Calcutta provided both the setting and the inspiration for her second novel, *Voices in the City* (1965), a story about several young adult siblings who move from a Himalayan village to that urban center. Like *Cry, the Peacock, Voices in the City* is a heavy, brooding novel populated by characters with tempestuous passions and a taste for melodrama. Although the melodramatic impulse has been tempered in her subsequent fiction, the fundamentally tragic vision has persisted, as have her formal techniques, which tend to hark back to earlier (chiefly European) literary movements and styles. Yet while Desai is fairly conservative in terms of the narrative modes upon which she draws, she is progressive socially and politically

and has been particularly engaged in illuminating the unique circumstances and challenges faced by postindependence Indian women. Indeed, her treatment of this subject merits comparison with the work of other postcolonial women writers of her generation who are more typically recognized as groundbreaking feminists, such as the Egyptian activist-novelist Nawal El Saadawi.

In 1965 Desai made her first trip out of India, visiting England, where she gathered observations that she would use in her next novel, *Bye-Bye, Blackbird* (1971), whose theme is the inhospitable treatment of Britons toward the post–World War II influx of immigrants from subcontinental Asia. She continued as a housewife, mother, and writer through the 1970s, during which time she experimented—during pauses between the periods of concentrated intensity of her novel writing—with shorter narrative forms, including short stories (collected in the 1978 volume *Games at Twilight and Other Stories*), children's stories, and brief novels. Her first book for children, *The Peacock Garden* (1974), tells the story of a family of Muslim peasants fleeing Hindu violence during the partition riots; she subsequently penned the fanciful and considerably lighter children's tale *Cat on a Houseboat* (1976). In 1975 Desai published the novel *Where Shall We Go This Summer?*, which focuses on the crisis of a middle-age housewife from Bombay who retreats from society—a theme she would revisit from a different generational standpoint in *Fire on the Mountain* (1977), a novel about a misanthropic great-grandmother who lives as a recluse in the Himalayas. Her first book to win critical and popular acclaim, *Fire on the Mountain* captured both the British Royal Society of Literature's Winifred Holtby Memorial Prize and the Indian National Academy of Letters (the Sahitya Akademi) Award.

Desai followed up the success of *Fire on the Mountain* with yet another quantum leap in *Clear Light of Day* (1980), a novel that skillfully imbricates familial and national stories by depicting a Delhi family whose dysfunctionality parallels that of the new nations of India and Pakistan. Shortlisted for the Booker Prize, *Clear Light of Day* is both her first great novel as well as the last work of an intensely introspective period of her fiction dealing with her childhood memories, which had begun six years earlier with *The Peacock Garden*. In 1982 she published *The Village by the Sea*, a story for adolescents that describes the tribulations of an Indian family who live in a traditional village that is destabilized by the effects of industrialization. It was awarded the *Guardian* Prize for Children's Fiction and would subsequently be adapted as a six-part miniseries by the BBC in 1992. Her next novel, *In Custody* (1984), is a comedy about the bumbling efforts of a college lecturer in Hindi to ally himself with a renowned Urdu poet. Desai herself subsequently coauthored a screenplay based on it for the Merchant-Ivory film adaptation, which was released in 1994.

She spent the 1986–1987 academic year in England as a visiting fellow at Cambridge University in what was the first extended period of time she resided outside of India. There she wrote her next novel, *Baumgartner's Bombay* (1988), which, centering on the life of a German Jew who emigrates to India in flight from the Nazis, enabled her for the first time to incorporate her mother's German heritage into her fiction. Desai's year in England gave her a taste for life outside of India, and in 1987 she moved to America, where, over the next several years, she was employed as a professor at the women's colleges Smith and Mount Holyoke. Since 1993 she has been a professor of creative writing at the Massachusetts Institute of Technology. Although she now resides in the United States, she unequivocally declares her home to be India and returns there frequently. Her relationship to the academy of which she is now a member is ambivalent. She appreciates the fact that her regular salary has kept her free from having to concern herself with the literary marketplace—something she has never paid much attention to, at any rate. Yet the experience of being a member of academe has evidently not mitigated her rather Manichean view of the differences between creative writers and critics. As she has said, "I keep miles away from critical theory, almost as if I fear it might have a negative effect on me. It seems to be so much the opposite of the creative impulse" (Pandit interview, p. 170). (Despite her claim, as a professor at one of the top research universities in the United States, she has clearly remained informed about developments in theory—if only through the process of osmosis.)

Desai has been the recipient of numerous accolades since 1990—among them the title of Padma Shri, awarded by the government of India in 1990, the New York Public Library's Literary Lion Award in 1993, and the Scottish Arts Council's Neil Gunn Award in 1994. Additionally, she is a

fellow of the Royal Society of Literature in London as well as an honorary member of the American Academy of Arts and Letters, and she has served on the Advisory Board for English of the National Academy of Letters in Delhi. In 1995 she published the novel *Journey to Ithaca,* which tells the story of non-Indians who seek spiritual fulfillment in Indian ashrams; it met with a mixed reception and, measured against its three superlative predecessors, does fall decidedly short. The youngest of her four children, her daughter Kiran, in 1998 published her own first novel, *Hullabaloo in the Guava Orchard,* which was well received, although Salman Rushdie's proclamation that "her arrival establishes the first dynasty of modern Indian fiction" (*New Yorker,* 23 June 1997, p. 61) is somewhat premature.

Desai's career must be viewed in the context of the vicissitudes of post–1947 Indo-Anglian literature generally. A perspicacious student herself of this history, she observes that, whereas Anglophone fiction in India had thrived in the hands of social reformers of the 1930s and 1940s such as Raja Rao and Mulk Raj Anand, after independence "Indian writer[s] seemed to lose a sense of purpose" and "in the Fifties and Sixties suffered from their sense of irrelevance and obscurity" (Introduction to *Midnight's Children,* pp. vii–viii). In an advanced state of atrophy during this period, English-language literature was put on a death watch in the anticipation that, with the ouster of the British, so, too, would the putatively deracinating language be expelled in favor of indigenous languages such as Hindi, Urdu, Tamil, and Bengali. "We thought we were a dying race, the ones who used English, that we were probably the last generation who would do their creative work in English. We were made to feel that we had no real position in the Indian world of writers," Desai recalls (Pandit interview, p. 162).

On this matter, Indian writers have wrestled with a dilemma faced by postcolonial writers generally: the vexed question of whose language to employ. The Kenyan novelist Ngũgĩ wa Thiong'o, one of the most eloquent and influential proponents of a return to indigenous languages (he himself has eschewed the use of English for his fiction in favor of Gikuyu), has asserted in *Decolonising the Mind: The Politics of Language in African Literature* that "language was the most important vehicle through which [imperial] power . . . held the soul prisoner. The bullet was the means of the physical subjugation. Language was the means of the spiritual subjugation" (London, 1986, p. 9). Presuppositions of this sort, Desai observes, largely guided the reception of the work of English-language Indian writers in the years after independence. "In India the English language had come to be considered a symbol of the shame of colonialism and the thwarting of national enterprise and creativity," she notes, maintaining that Anglophone writers such as herself were "stigmatized for writing in the language of their erstwhile rulers" (Introduction to *Midnight's Children,* pp. viii–ix).

Yet, as Raja Rao contends in the celebrated foreword to his 1938 novel about Gandhi's anti-British movement, *Kanthapura* (which Desai has adduced in justifying her own use of English), it is possible "to convey in a language that is not one's own the spirit that is one's own." And he consequently calls upon Indian writers to rework the English language in such a way as to create "a dialect which will some day prove to be as distinctive and colorful as the Irish or the American" (New York, p. vii). Rao's message of the liberative potential for English as a language of Indian literature appeared to have been relegated to the ash can of history for the several decades following independence, but in fact it was merely lying dormant. As Desai recalled in a 1990 interview, contrary to all expectations of the imminent demise of English-language literature in India, "What has happened in the last 10 years is exactly the opposite. Suddenly everybody is writing . . . in English . . . with tremendous confidence, a new confidence that I don't think we older writers had" (Pandit interview, p. 162). She explains the new willingness of Indian writers and readers to embrace English as largely a function of a generational shift: "In the 1980s, not only was there a new generation of readers who had never known colonial rule and had no need to question or to prove their Indian identity, but also of writers eager to take their place in the international mainstream" (Introduction to *Midnight's Children,* p. viii)—a process that none of the innumerable indigenous languages of India could have enabled.

While the use of the English language no longer poses a serious obstacle for Indian writers, another ideologically fraught issue persists—the question of what is to be admitted as authentically "postcolonial" work. One of Desai's early interviewers broached this subject by observing, "It is alleged that some . . . Indo-Anglian writers have nothing

peculiarly Indian to offer. Wherein lies the Indianness of your writings?" She bristled at the query. "It is very, very unfortunate that so much is talked of the 'Indianness' of Indo-Anglian writers," she acerbically retorted while averring, "If a writer is Indian and lives in India, his work will naturally be Indian" (Ram interview, pp. 102–103). The narrow criteria that have tended to be employed for making such determinations have led to a paradox in the reception of Desai's fiction: although she is held in the highest esteem as an *artist* (Rushdie, for example, reverently places her on a par with Jane Austen), there is relatively little scholarship on her work that treats it as specifically that of a *postcolonial* writer. And since many of the scholars whose work is engaged with contemporary Indian literature tend to select objects of study for their perceived postcolonial content, the consequence for Desai is that her work has remained decidedly undertreated. (Based on a glance at a bibliography of studies on Desai, one might get the impression that there has been copious scholarship devoted to her fiction, chiefly in the form of numerous monographs, but in fact the bulk of this work consists of unedifying graduate student theses published by Indian presses. These studies, for the most part, have been excluded from the Selected Bibliography at the end of this essay.)

There are some critical accounts that place Desai in a glowing light as a specifically Indian writer, such as Feroza Jussawalla and Reed Way Dasenbrock's characterization of her as "the first major novelist in English to emerge in India after independence" and a "pioneer in the exploration of feminist concerns in Indian literature" (pp. 157–158). Yet such pronouncements do not reflect the preponderance of critical estimations of her work. Likewise, while a modest number of scholarly articles have explored her fiction, and a handful of books have devoted chapters to her work—such as Richard Cronin's *Imagining India* (1989) and Fawzia Afzal-Khan's *Cultural Imperialism and the Indo-English Novel* (1993)—they are not nearly so plentiful as one would expect for a writer of her stature. Indeed, the more typical case is that of the arguably finest study of English-language literature by and about Indians, Sara Suleri's *The Rhetoric of English India* (1992), which devotes entire chapters to V. S. Naipaul and Rushdie yet does not mention Desai.

This state of affairs appears to be rooted in a perception of the Bengali-German hybrid Desai as an idiosyncratic rather than paradigmatic case, and hence she tends to be judged of neither great significance nor usefulness in the project of making broad claims about the Indian postcolonial condition. Further exacerbating the matter is the perception of her as Eurocentric (although less formidably so than Naipaul), and hence not altogether "Indian." To some extent the marginalizing effects of such perceptions have been counterbalanced by the mixed blessing of admitting her, on an honorary basis, to European canonicity; as Michael Parker and Roger Starkey observe in *Postcolonial Literatures,* insofar as her work has been valorized by critics and scholars, it has largely been through "tying the analyses of her novels to a canon of 'great [European] writers' " (p. 13). Yet while Desai, by her own admission, has been more influenced by European than by Indian literature, and while her tastes and standards of judgment—along with much of her heritage—do generally tend toward Europe, these facts have been subjected to specious interpretations. Her observation about the reception of the work of Jhabvala, her German-immigrant mentor, is elucidative in this context. She contends that Jhabvala's "success in reproducing Indian speech rhythms in English were ignored because she did not have the right credentials—she is not Indian" ("Indian Fiction Today," p. 212). One senses that Desai similarly feels her own marginalization by postcolonial critics and scholars to be largely a matter of the perceived dubiousness of her credentials.

A symptomatic example of how such perceptions of Desai have affected her representation in the criticism is that of the overview of her work by P. S. Chauhan in the *Encyclopedia of Post-Colonial Literatures in English* (1994), a widely used—and hence taste-making—reference source. Contending that Desai's fiction is characterized by a "western disdain for Indian social customs" (an inclination that is specifically imputed to the fact that "[h]er view of India is . . . Eurocentric"), Chauhan asserts that her fiction lacks "the warmth and compassion for the Indian humanity" that one finds in more authentically Indian writers. She is further charged with domesticating India for Western consumption by "interpreting to the west, in terms familiar to it, the Indian scene," and the essay concludes with the rather backhanded compliment that, despite her "limited range," her work will be of interest "if one is sensitive to lyrical expressions of transient emotions or to delicate hues

of an inner landscape" (London, pp. 353–354), which are clearly implied to be trivial concerns characteristic of bourgeois aesthetes. Such tendentious representations—based as they are on a narrow, exclusionary vision of what constitutes the postcolonial condition—are perhaps inevitable in an emergent field that has arisen to redress historical injustices (the analogy of the tendencies of early feminist or African-American literary studies is instructive here), and a deeper and more extensive engagement with Desai's work in the years to come will likely be a measure of the maturation and growing broad-mindedness of postcolonial studies as a scholarly discipline.

EARLY FICTION

Cry, the Peacock (1963), Desai's first novel, chronicles the morbid dread, descent into madness, and suicide of Maya, a young Delhi housewife who is trapped in a loveless, arranged marriage to the much older Gautama, a misogynistic lawyer. The Hardyesque tenor of the text—and of Desai's fiction generally—is established in the opening scene, with a grisly description of the rotting corpse of Maya's beloved dog. The death of her pet precipitates a series of reflections that circulate around a recently resurfaced childhood memory of having been taken by her ayah (Hindi for "nurse" or "nanny") to an astrologer who has mistily forecast a destiny worthy of Sophocles (indeed, the plot as a whole seems more appropriate to a classical tragedy than to a twentieth-century novel): four years after her marriage, either she or her husband would die by "unnatural causes" (p. 26). When Maya's father—who comes from "a family of Brahmins that for generations had lived their lives . . . according to the advice . . . of their horoscopes" (p. 65)—has learned of this event, he has torn up the prophecy, denounced the astrologer, fired the ayah, and prohibited the utterance of the word "fate" in his household.

Yet fate, of course, cannot be circumvented by such measures, and now, four years after Maya and Gautama's wedding, the repressed has returned, punctually and with a vengeance. Haunted by her memory of the grim prophecy, Maya becomes increasingly convinced of the inevitability of its fulfillment: "I knew the time had come. It was now to be either Gautama or I"

(p. 28), she believes, envisioning her marriage, in effect, as a duel to the death. With her mad obsession deepening, she ultimately lures Gautama up to the roof of their house and pushes him off, killing him. The trauma of this event having severed the vestiges of her connection with reality, she is taken to her father's home in Lucknow by her altruistic mother-in-law, who intends subsequently to commit her to a mental institution. Surrounded by the objects of her childhood, Maya assumes the identity suggested in her name—Sanskrit for "illusion"—by regressing into the role of a blissful little girl and gleefully romping around the home in which, spoiled by her doting father, she had narcissistically "lived as a toy princess in a toy world" (p. 77). In the text's final scene, perhaps registering a dawning lucidity, she cries out in horror and retreats to an upstairs balcony. In a melodramatic flourish, she and her mother-in-law—who, in a final act of selflessness, has attempted to rescue her—fall from the balcony together, presumably to their deaths.

A youthful book filled with rich imagery as well as the most extensive vocabulary of all of Desai's works, *Cry, the Peacock* is an impressive, if somewhat self-indulgent and overwritten, first novel. It is also the only one of her novels that is narrated in the first person (Maya is the voice of all but the first and last scenes). Desai has said that she learned from having written *Cry, the Peacock* that the first-person form "can be a very dangerous tool for a writer," as "[i]t tends to run away with one" (Bliss interview, p. 535), and in her subsequent fiction she would avoid it in favor of an almost exclusive use of indirect discourse. Associated with the novel's mode of narration is the fact that none of the supporting characters is accorded enough attention to command an actual subplot. It is, therefore, as Darshan Singh Maini has succinctly characterized it, "a splendid piece of writing, but not a great work of fiction" (p. 217). In a more mature phase, Desai would no doubt have linked Maya's protofeminist dissatisfaction with her arranged marriage to the comparable circumstances of Gautama's sister, who has come to Delhi to hire a lawyer so that she can obtain a divorce. But not yet having arrived at the position that her chief interest as a writer would be in depicting "the confrontation of the inner [mind] and the outer [world]" (Pandit interview, p. 166), Desai relegated the substance of her first novel to a largely unim-

peded transcript of the intrapsychic turmoil of its protagonist.

Maya's growing crisis is conveyed via two distinct semantic registers—theology (Hinduism) and psychology (Freudianism). Yet while Desai employs such terminology and categories of analysis in order to deepen the reader's sense of Maya's complexity, Gautama uses them for the contrary end of narrowly circumscribing his wife's sentiments and experiences within simplifying formulations. He complacently reduces the *Bhagavad Gita* to a series of didactic slogans for her to live by, and, with a "pontifical air," diagnoses her affliction: "If you knew your Freud it would all be very straightforward. . . . You have a very obvious father-obsession" (pp. 125–126). Further, not only does Gautama serve as an amateur theologian and psychoanalyst, but he is also a literary critic of sorts, and the pronouncements he makes in the latter role are not so readily dismissable. He berates Maya for using her "third-rate poetess's mind" (p. 98) to indulge in "melodrama" (p. 95), and, when he reads a letter from her estranged brother that sums up much of the plot of the novel that she narrates, he reacts with a "mocking, amused, objective smile," glibly terming it an "amusing . . . piece of fiction" and likening it to "a serialized romance in a woman's magazine" (p. 123). It is difficult to avoid the impression that Desai, either deliberately or subconsciously, registered in Gautama's contemptuous dissection of his wife's histrionics what must have been her worst fears about the potential critical reception of her own decidedly melodramatic first novel. She has affirmed that *Cry, the Peacock* represents "a stage of my work . . . that I have simply outgrown" (Ram interview, p. 97), and the textual evidence suggests that this process was already well under way before the novel was completed. For Gautama's intemperate criticisms of Maya appear, in effect, to constitute the displaced recriminations of Desai's own nascent critical sensibilities toward a work whose unchecked lyricism she is already developing beyond, even as she is writing in that mode. The harnessing of these solipsistic energies in the service of broader ends would be an important aspect of her maturation as a writer and one of the great strengths of her ensuing work.

Just such progress is becoming evident in her second novel, *Voices in the City* (1965), which explores some of the same doleful themes as *Cry, the Peacock*—unhappy marriages, frustrated artistic temperaments, existential ennui, suicidal despair—but enlists them in a more complex plot structure and situates them in a specific politico-historical context; set in the late 1950s, the novel depicts Indian society in transition a decade after independence from British rule. Each of the first three of the text's four sections is named after and focuses on one of three young adult siblings from a Himalayan village who, separately and for different reasons, have moved to Calcutta: Nirode, an aspiring playwright; Monisha, a dejected housewife; and Amla, a commercial artist. The brief final section is titled "Mother," and, although their mother, Otima, only appears at the very end, her influence—in keeping with the then-fashionable pop-psychology notion of Momism that evidently guides her depiction—is heavily felt throughout the work. The story begins with the twenty-four-year-old Nirode Ray having quit his menial job at a newspaper in order to establish a literary magazine. He abandons this project, in turn, in order to write a play, which he says—decadently revising the minimal requirements Virginia Woolf posits in *A Room of One's Own* for aspiring women writers—he can do successfully if he can secure "three drinks a night and a room of his own" (p. 11).

The experiences of a variety of Nirode's friends from the Calcutta artistic and business worlds comprise the bulk of the subplots: David Gunney, an amiable Irish ceramist whose cheery optimism contrasts with Nirode's brooding pessimism; "Professor" Bose, an author of children's literature; Dharma, a reclusive surrealistic painter; Sonny Ghosh, whose aristocratic family's fortunes have declined steeply since independence; and Jit Nair, who has abandoned his artistic aspirations in favor of a lucrative position with a British-owned company and is now guilt ridden over collaborating in neocolonial domination of India—the British "prosper while our country starves," he demurs while charging himself with being "an accomplice to their crime" (pp. 104–105). The novel's abbreviated second section consists of extracts from Monisha's diary and is the only portion of the text that is narrated in the first person. Having married the wealthy Jiban at the behest of her now deceased father, Monisha finds life with her new husband's family oppressive. Her situation worsens when her tyrannical mother-in-law discovers that she has surreptitiously used Jiban's money to pay hospital bills for Nirode, who, having neglected his body in pursuit of his art, has nearly died from dehydration and malnutrition. Section three begins with the arrival in Calcutta of Nirode and Monisha's younger sister, Amla, who has taken a job with an advertising firm. The subplots proliferate, but the main narrative thread remains the various experiences of the three siblings in the perilous city of Calcutta, which is personified as Kali, the Hindu goddess of destruction, whose role (she is worshipped as the Divine Mother) is figuratively conflated with that of Otima, the Ray matriarch. The novel climaxes in its final section with the suicide, by self-immolation, of the despairing Monisha, and it concludes with the arrival of Otima from her secluded home in the Himalayas in order to attend her daughter's funeral in "death's city, where funerals were processions that celebrated the city's chief deity, Kali" (p. 233).

Although not without visible seams and a certain degree of imbalance between its many parts, *Voices in the City* is considerably more ambitious and sophisticated than *Cry, the Peacock*. It is also Desai's most self-consciously existential novel, and, accordingly, it gets rather ponderous at times. Indeed, some of the ruminations of its characters sound like dialogue lifted from a Samuel Beckett play or voice-overs from an Ingmar Bergman film—for example, Monisha's vertiginous query, "What does it all mean? Why are lives such as these lived? At their conclusion, what solution, what truth falls into the waiting palm of one's hand, the still pit of one's heart?" (p. 121). Similarly, Nirode, who has been reading and extolling the works of the French philosopher Albert Camus, despairs over his sense that "[t]here was only this endless waiting, hollowed out by an intrinsic knowledge that there was nothing to wait for" (p. 64), and he makes the Sisyphean contention about his magazine that "I want it to fail—quickly. Then I want to see if I have the spirit to start moving again, towards my next failure" (p. 40). Such sentiments clearly reflect the preoccupations of Desai herself, who has acknowledged that she was profoundly affected by Camus and that in particular his novel *The Stranger* "influenced a great deal of my early writing" (Jussawalla interview, p. 170).

Of the various circumstances of postindependence India that the novel broaches, the one that it explores most deeply is incipient feminism. The Ray siblings' aunt, Lila Chatterjee, envisions the Indian "independence" movement in more than one respect: "We gave your generation your free-

dom," she says to Amla, while admonishing her to "take pride in your *independence*, in this wonderful liberty you have of choosing and undertaking a career" (Desai's emphasis, pp. 143, 146). Yet one ought not to assume that such claims are intended to be representative of an actual feminist movement. As Harveen Sachdeva Mann observes, historicizing the ostensible feminism of *Voices in the City* as specifically consisting of gestures of isolated recusancy, in fact the independence struggle in India (as elsewhere in the decolonizing world) "proved in many ways to be detrimental to the women's struggle," for "the glorification of indigenous traditions [that was] intended . . . to counteract colonial, racist denigration of the culture" actually tended to result in a rededication to "religiously and socially sanctioned patriarchal oppression" (pp. 157–158). Unless one recognizes this fact, one is liable to misunderstand the manner in which the other women in *Voices in the City* are represented; as Desai has remarked, the "younger generation of readers in India" has tended to take exception to her depictions of "helpless women, hopeless women" such as Monisha, yet, she points out, "the feminist movement in India . . . didn't even exist at the time I wrote that book" (Jussawalla interview, p. 166). Thus she defends her characterization of Monisha as a powerless victim—a virtual prisoner of traditional domesticity, nursing her "silent agony behind the barred windows of her house" (p. 189) and driven to suicide.

The tonal shift from the morose *Voices in the City* to Desai's next novel, the fairly upbeat *Bye-Bye, Blackbird* (1971), could hardly be more abrupt. The latter work is set in 1965 and takes as its subject the experiences of émigrés who have relocated from India to the capital city of the former British Empire. Twenty-two-year-old Dev has just arrived in London from Calcutta and is staying at the home of his friend Adit, who made that journey himself several years earlier and is now married to the Englishwoman Sarah. Much of the novel consists of a detailing of the myriad indignities to which subcontinental Asian immigrants are routinely subjected by xenophobic Britons. The contrasting attitudes of Dev and Adit on this matter are made clear early on, in their differing responses to being called "wogs": whereas Adit accepts such abuse with equanimity as the price of admission to the promised land, Dev responds with indignation, maintaining that "I wouldn't live in a country where I was insulted and unwanted" (p. 17).

The cast of supporting characters includes several other Indians and their English spouses, who comprise the majority of Adit and Sarah's small circle of friends (social opportunities in England for mixed-race couples being limited), as well as Emma Moffit, their eccentric English landlady, who, a caricatural antithesis to the novel's chauvinistic Britons, organizes an "India club" in order "to create a meeting-place where . . . great, wise [Indian] people can come and lecture to us lesser beings" (p. 43). The text, however, never strays far from its center—Dev, Adit, and Sarah's disparate experiences of England. The plot pivots around a trip taken by the three protagonists to the rural Hampshire home of Sarah's hidebound parents, who have been decidedly cool toward their daughter since her marriage to the Indian Adit. The effect of the English countryside on Dev is profoundly transformative: he is converted, overnight, from a resentful foreigner into an ardent Anglophile. Meanwhile, Adit's feelings have shifted in the opposite direction, and he returns to London with an acute "sensation of not belonging" in England and a "growing nostalgia" for India (pp. 181, 183). The outbreak of the brief 1965 war between India and Pakistan kindles Adit's patriotism and confirms his sense that he must return to India, and he and the now-pregnant Sarah decide to move to his family's home in Calcutta. An enamored Dev, well on the road to assimilation, elects to remain in Britain, thus completing their role reversal.

Whereas the chief flaws of both *Cry, the Peacock* and *Voices in the City* are consequences of an ambitious young writer's efforts to outstrip the development of her own skills (the former, attempting to delve too deep, becomes mired down in its narrator's fanciful ruminations, and the latter, stretching itself thin with subplots, tends to spin out of control), the shortcomings of *Bye-Bye, Blackbird* are of a different and less interesting sort. Its plot is so rigidly supervised and its characters so stereotypically "representative" as to be unconvincing, notwithstanding Desai's protestation that "practically everything in it is drawn directly from my experience of living with Indian immigrants in London" (Ram interview, p. 101) as to be unconvincing; the contrived symmetry of Dev and Adit's equal and opposite conversions is especially pedestrian. Yet while *Bye-Bye, Blackbird* is the least artistic and intuitive work of this most artistic and intuitive of novelists, it is, nonetheless, conceptually provocative, and this fact renders the book estimable in its own right, as opposed to its

being merely a precursor text for the later and more astute fictions about the experiences of subcontinental Asians in Britain by Hanif Kureishi—most notably, his fine screenplay for the film *My Beautiful Laundrette* (1985).

Gayatri Spivak has observed of India (whose borders were created by the spread of British imperial power) that it "is not really a place with which [one] can form a national identity because . . . [saying] 'India' is a bit like saying 'Europe' " (*The Post-Colonial Critic*, ed. Sarah Harasym, New York, 1990, p. 39). Desai makes much the same point when she remarks that "when one says 'India' no Indian really knows what you mean. It's just the opening to a hundred questions. Which region? . . . Which state? Which language? Which religion? . . . [E]ach little fragment has a culture which is so distinctly its own" ("The Other Voice" dialogue, p. 80). She illustrates this state of affairs in *Bye-Bye, Blackbird* by depicting ethnic and regional rivalries among her Indian characters, thereby undermining the presupposition of a homogeneous "Other" upon which British racism has been (and continues to be) premised. For example, the elitist Bengali Adit has nothing but disdain for what he views as the riffraff Punjabi Sikhs who work as manual laborers and live in the noisy, crowded apartment downstairs from him. And when the minor character Jasbir, who is himself from the Indian side of the Punjab, bitterly recalls having been termed a "bloody Pakistani" by an irate Briton (p. 26), it is unclear if the greater insult to him is being an object of British racism or being mistaken for a Pakistani.

What is most intriguing about *Bye-Bye, Blackbird* is its treatment of the cause implied to underlie the swift and irresistible transformation of Dev from Anglophobe to Anglophile. He arrives in England indulging grandiose fantasies of "showing these damn imperialists with their lost colonies complex that we are free people now, with our own personalities that this veneer of an English education has not obscured" (p. 123). (Although a Hindu, Dev has attended a Catholic school with an English literature–based curriculum, and he has gone on to take a bachelor's degree in English literature, thus paralleling the educational background of his missionary school–educated English-majoring author.) Yet he cannot sustain his resentment, and the reason for this inability, it becomes evident, is that his English-based education is not simply a "veneer." His frame of mind can only be properly understood in the context of the development of the British Indian educational system, which was founded upon the premise that the instilling of a reverence for English literature would render Indians more tractable to British rule; as Gauri Viswanathan observes in *Masks of Conquest: Literary Study and British Rule in India*, British administrators in India "discovered a[n] . . . ally in English literature to maintain control of their subjects under the guise of a liberal education" (New York, 1989, p. 85). It is specifically as a product of the remains of this imperial-era educational system that Dev finds himself fetishizing the land of Milton and Tennyson while recognizing that

so many people in his country . . . had been brought up on a language and literature completely alien to them, been fed it like a sweet in infancy, like a drug in youth, so that, before they realised it, they were addicts of it and their bodies were composed as much of its substance as of native blood.

(p. 122)

His cognizance of the ideological aims of this system, however, does not prevent him from succumbing to its effects.

While Desai aptly undermines the fantasy Dev entertains of gaining unconditional autonomy from his country's history of subjugation, in doing so she swings all the way in the opposite direction, virtually depriving him of agency and, in effect, suggesting that many postindependence Indian educational institutions serve as neocolonial hatcheries for Anglophiles. The model of postcolonial identity—and specifically of the relationship of the postcolonial subject to the culture of the erstwhile metropolitan center—with which she works is thus no more nuanced than that which informs Naipaul's much-decried novel *The Mimic Men* (1967) of several years earlier. It must be borne in mind, however, that when Desai was writing *Bye-Bye, Blackbird*, postcolonial studies did not yet exist as an academic discipline. Edward Said's landmark 1978 work *Orientalism*, taken by many to have inaugurated the field, was still seven years in the future, and since that time great strides have been made. If Desai had had at her disposal Homi Bhabha's theory of the hybridity of imperial cultures and the ambivalence of imperial authority (first developed in his seminal 1985 essay "Signs Taken for Wonders"), her characters would no doubt have been more intelligently devised, but she can hardly be faulted for not having arrived at

such insights on her own. In her fiction of the 1980s and 1990s, she would revisit the theme of postcolonial identities and treat it with markedly greater sophistication and suppleness.

MIDDLE-PERIOD FICTION

AFTER having completed *Bye-Bye, Blackbird*, Desai turned sharply inward, and the remainder of the 1970s constituted a deeply introspective period. It also was an experimental period for her in terms of genres, as she tried her hand at more compact narrative forms—short stories, brief novels, and children's stories—before returning to the extended novel form in the culminating text of this phase of her career, *Clear Light of Day*. Most of the fiction she published during this period draws heavily on her early memories, particularly those of the Hindu-Muslim violence associated with partition in 1947, which she has described as "the most traumatic event of my childhood" (Pandit interview, p. 153). (The Pakistani Bapsi Sidhwa witnessed these events as a child from the other side of the border and has also thematized them in her fiction, most notably in the poignant novel *Cracking India*.) Indeed, in much the same way that the American Civil War served for William Faulkner, so, too, for Desai has 1947 figured as an epochal event that shapes the destinies of her characters. For both writers, these cataclysms are the pivots around which national history rotates and are, accordingly, laden with mythlike symbolic freight.

The events of 1947 are briefly alluded to in *Bye-Bye, Blackbird*, when the outbreak of the 1965 India-Pakistan War reawakens the long-repressed memory for Adit "of Calcutta in 1947 when Muslims and Hindus . . . slaughter[ed] each other, burn[ed] each other's houses, rape[d] each other's wives and toss[ed] the children aside like broken twigs" (p. 197). What is relegated to an aside in that novel would become the focus of Desai's next work, the 1974 story *The Peacock Garden*, which is both substantive and realistic, despite the fact that it is written for young children. (In this respect, it differs from the cartoonlike children's tale she would publish two years later, *Cat on a Houseboat*, a story about a domestic cat named Papaya who spends a summer on a houseboat in Kashmir.) The first of her works to focus on non-middle-class protagonists (an experiment in class-bridging empathy to which she would return several years later in *The Village by the Sea,* a story for older children), *The Peacock Garden* details the plight of a peasant family of Muslim refugees who find themselves on the wrong side of the new border in the Punjab and must abandon their home as they flee from Hindu violence.

The tale centers on the experiences of a little girl named Zuni, who, along with her parents and elder sister, is escorted by Gopal, a Hindu family friend, to safety in a mosque, where they (unlike their Pakistan-bound neighbors) wait out the violence for several months before coming back to their ancestral home in what is now the nation of India. They return to the charred remains of their house and to the news that Gopal has been killed while attempting to defend their property from thieves. Happily, however, they learn that Ali, to whom Zuni's elder sister is betrothed, has made it safely across the border to Pakistan and is now returning so that they can be married. The family members begin to put their lives back together, but they now represent a tiny minority in their village—a fact made evident to Zuni when she returns to school and finds that "all the Muslim girls had gone and only the Hindu children were left" (p. 52). Desai has described her own experiences in Delhi of 1947 in similar terms: "The school I went to had been made up of 50 percent Muslim girls and perhaps 50 percent Hindu girls, and suddenly every Muslim girl in school had left" at the same time when "all of one's Muslim neighbors vanished" (Jussawalla interview, p. 161). Writing this heartfelt tale appears to have constituted an effort on her part to fill in this lacuna from her childhood by imagining what her vanished Muslim schoolmates may have experienced. Yet she did not write the story solely for her own personal ends: dedicated to her four children, it is also a didactic vehicle designed to ensure that this moment in India's history is neither forgotten nor minimized by subsequent generations.

The plot of the brief novel *Where Shall We Go This Summer?* (1975) also circulates around 1947, although independence and partition are not its focus. The first of the text's three parts is set in 1967 and describes the arrival of Sita, a housewife in her early forties, to the rustic island of Manori after a twenty-year absence. She has brought two of her four children, having abandoned the others along with her businessman-husband in their home in Bombay. In the third trimester of yet another preg-

nancy and convinced that the world is hopelessly marred by cruelty and violence, she has "refused to give birth to a child in a world not fit to receive [it]" (p. 139) and has fled to the island, which she recalls as a utopian refuge that she rather dizzily hopes will "hold her baby safely unborn, by magic" (p. 101). We learn why Sita's associations with this island are so powerful in the novel's second section, which takes us back to 1947, when she was brought there, along with her brother and sister, by her father, Babaji, a charismatic political figure who has been hailed as "the Second Gandhi" (p. 86).

Independence having been won, Babaji has retired from politics and has come to Manori in order to "put my social theories into practice" (p. 60). He subsequently assumes the role of a Prospero of sorts, transforming the island into an anti-industrial idyll and becoming a guru not only to the impressionable disciples he has imported (some of whom will later write hagiographies of him) but also to the benighted locals, who worship him as a benevolent miracle worker. (In fact, he is a fraud; in this "setting of ignorance and poverty and gullibility" [p. 75], he passes off the salubrious effects of modern agricultural methods and medicines for miracles and resorts to decidedly nonsupernatural means to cure attractive young wives afflicted with barrenness.) Babaji soon dies, and Sita is taken from the island to Bombay by her new husband, Raman, the son of one of his political colleagues. In the novel's final section, we return to 1967, and a disillusioned Sita to reality, as a reproachful Raman comes to Manori and reminds her of the responsibilities that she is shirking. Having come to the realization that her idealistic beliefs about the island are unfounded, she relents and returns to Bombay with him and the children so that they can resume their quotidian lives.

Sita's conviction that her choice is between beautiful illusion (the rustic island Manori) and ugly reality (the metropolis Bombay) is figured specifically as an aesthete's belief in the incompatibility of art and life. On this point, Desai's text follows the work that inspired it and that it parallels in a variety of respects—Virginia Woolf's 1927 novel. *To the Lighthouse,* which is similarly premised on the idea that the only refuge from the inexorable cruelty of life is in the relative (if not absolute) durability of art, a belief maintained by Woolf's alter ego, Lily Briscoe, who strives to "exchange . . . the fluidity of life for the concentration of painting"

(New York, p. 237). Sita makes clear her position on this matter during a quarrel with her eminently sensible husband when she discloses that the "one happy moment" (p. 145) she has experienced during their marriage was when she was moved by a fortuitous vision of two strangers, which effected an epiphany for her against whose bliss she has been measuring every subsequent moment of her life:

"I felt as if I were gazing at a painting, or seeing a vision. . . . They were like a work of art—so apart from the rest of us. They were not like us—they were inhuman, divine. . . . They were so white, so radiant, they made me see my own life like a shadow, absolutely flat, uncoloured."

(pp. 146–147)

Although Desai clearly has a measure of sympathy for Sita, as her own outlook tends to be consonant with that of her protagonist (the text's autobiographical overtones generally are unmistakable), ultimately her posture toward such a self-indulgent chasing of aesthetic dreams at the expense of familial responsibilities is one of condemnation. Indeed, the manner in which Sita's return to husband, children, and home is equated with a return to sanity renders the book (which notably bears a dedication to Desai's own husband, Ashvin) Desai's most resolute affirmation of her belief in the primacy of the nuclear family as well as her most transparently moralizing work excluding her children's fiction. The measure of Sita's new maturity—in contrast to her author's earlier and younger self-annihilating Chopinesque housewives, Maya in *Cry, the Peacock* and Monisha in *Voices in the City*—is her willingness to embrace her duties and to accept reality on its own nonnegotiable terms.

Like *Where Shall We Go This Summer?*, *Fire on the Mountain* (1977), is also a short novel whose focus is the desire of its protagonist to retreat from society into a tranquil idyll. Yet, unlike the middle-age Sita, the latter text's elderly Nanda Kaul has never shirked her family duties, either as wife, mother, or grandmother. Now a widowed great-grandmother, she has claimed her reward for a selfless life of service to others in the form of a retirement of solitude and has purchased a home in Kasauli, in the Himalayas, where, remote from the concerns of her family, she lives as a recluse. (Desai herself spent a summer of her childhood in Kasauli, and in other respects as well the story taps into her childhood memories.) The plot is structured around two infringements on Nanda's peace: first, she receives a letter from one of her daughters informing her of the imminent arrival of her great-granddaughter Raka; second, she receives a phone call from her childhood friend Ila Das, who says that she would like to visit her as well. She forestalls Ila's request but cannot decline to take in Raka, as marital problems between the child's parents have left her with nowhere else to be sent. When the dreaded little girl appears, in the second of the novel's three sections, she turns out, like Nanda, only to want to be left alone and to be allowed to play outside. For a while they live together like Trappist monks in placid, self-sufficient silence.

In spite of herself, Nanda soon develops an affection for Raka, yet her gestures of friendship are rebuffed by the child, who is as inscrutable as Herman Melville's Bartleby. (Although we are given some information about Raka's past, including the fact that she has been traumatized by her father's abuse of her mother, which we are led to believe may have driven her into her nearly autistic state, it is hardly enough to sketch a psychological profile.) The usually aloof Nanda is herself thus ironically reduced to the status of "a baby thwarted, wanting attention she did not get" (p. 101), thereby signaling her actual ambivalence over her life of solitude, which comes to the fore in the novel's climax. She even goes so far as to concoct exotic lies about their family's history in order to gain Raka's attention and contemplates willing her home, Carignano, to the child. In the novel's last section, Ila, a much-abused and pathetically inept creature, pays a brief visit to Nanda's home. A graceless, voluble social worker, she is antithetical to her host in every respect. The tale's contemplative tenor, along with Nanda's tranquil complacency, is destroyed in its final moments with a tumultuous finish. She receives a phone call from the police informing her that Ila has been raped and murdered after having left Carignano, and moments later, still reeling from this shocking news, she learns that the unsocialized pyromaniac Raka has ignited a forest fire around her home, the scope of whose damage we are left to imagine.

In terms of artistry, the compact, parable-like *Fire on the Mountain*—whose inspiration Desai has identified as Japanese poetry—represents a distinct advancement beyond her previous fiction. Acclaimed by critics and honored with prestigious awards both in India and Britain, it marks the boundary between her protracted apprenticeship and maturity as an artist. It is also her most concentrated treatment of the recurring theme in her fiction of the desire for solitude and the concomitant refusal of human community. (Desai appears to use this theme as a means of exploring her own sense of being torn between the conflicting exigencies of her family life and her artistic life; she has asserted that, for her, "[s]olitude and silence are [as] necessary for writing as they are for meditation" [Seguet interview, p. 46].) *Fire on the Mountain* is as brief as *Where Shall We Go This Summer?*, and it pursues similar themes and strives toward largely the same artistic ends. Further, both of these books serve as displaced outlets for the autobiographical reflections and introspections of their author, and both gather toward climaxes in which the protagonists' illusions are shattered. In these respects, as in others, they constitute companion texts. Yet whereas *Where Shall We Go This Summer?* remains sketchy and half-baked, *Fire on the Mountain* succeeds in being elliptical and richly suggestive. This difference is the measure of Desai's artistic development, and particularly of her newfound control over her material.

In the year after the appearance of *Fire on the Mountain*, Desai published *Games at Twilight and Other Stories* (1978). The volume consists of eleven short stories of varying quality, some of which had been published separately in Indian magazines in the preceding several years—for example, "Private Tuition by Mr. Bose" first appeared in 1970, "Surface Textures" in 1974, and "The Accompanist" in 1975. With the exception of the extended last tale, the engaging "Scholar and Gypsy," which focuses on visitors to India, the stories describe events from everyday life for various members of the Indian middle classes. Subjects range from children's games, to lessons in Sanskrit, to the desperate efforts of a painter to sell his work, to the marring of a wedding by catastrophe. The finest tale in the volume is the title work, "Games at Twilight." The other stories are for the most part of high quality if viewed as discrete episodes, and, as is the case with all of Desai's work, they are elegantly written, but they tend to feel like orphaned vignettes seeking homes in larger narrative structures. In fact, Desai, who has likened her writing method to the lengthy process of accretion by which an oyster transforms a grain of sand into a pearl, recognizes that her talents—unlike, for example, those of

Flannery O'Connor or William Trevor—require more sustained forms to be fully realized (the artistic success of the concise *Fire on the Mountain* remains an anomaly for her), and she has accordingly limited her experiments with this genre. As she has maintained, while explaining why she finds writing short stories dissatisfying, she prefers "the scope the novel gives you to ripen your ideas slowly and naturally" (Pandit interview, p. 159). This penchant is exemplified in the fate of the seventh story of *Games at Twilight*, "The Accompanist," about which she has said, "I kept thinking I hadn't fully developed it, there was still so much I wanted to say about it, so I wrote a whole novel on the same subject" (Jussawalla interview, p. 160). The result was the splendid 1984 work *In Custody*.

Desai's next novel, *Clear Light of Day* (1980), recounts the saga of the Das family, Hindus from Old Delhi. Structurally mimicking its chief intertext, T. S. Eliot's suite of poems *Four Quartets*, the novel is comprised of four sections; the first takes place in the present (the late 1960s or early 1970s), the second in 1947 and 1948, the third at several moments some years earlier still, and the last returns us to the present. The main characters are three of the four Das siblings: Bim, who is unmarried and teaches history at a women's college; her younger sister, Tara, who lives in America with her diplomat husband, Bakul, and their two teenage daughters; and their elder brother, Raja, who has given up his aspiration to become a poet and lives as a rich, fat businessman in Hyderabad with his Muslim-heiress wife, Benazir, and their five children. The story begins with Tara's visit to the now rundown family homestead in a suburb of Old Delhi, where Bim continues to live and to take care of their autistic younger brother, Baba. Tara has come to India to attend the wedding of Raja's eldest daughter, which event Bim is boycotting, having long been estranged from her once beloved brother.

In the novel's second section, we learn more about the family background that leads us to understand Bim's resentment toward Raja. It is 1947, and the stability of the Das family is shattered by a series of events that coincide with the forging of the Indian nation in the blood of Hindus and Muslims. The neglectful parents die in rapid succession—the mother of diabetes and the father in a car accident—and "Aunt" Mira (actually a widowed and impoverished cousin of the mother), who for years has served as a surrogate parent to the Das children, succumbs to alcoholism. Raja, who fancies himself a latter-day Byron and who has been inspired with a reverence for Islamic culture—Urdu poetry in particular—by their wealthy Muslim neighbor and landlord, Hyder Ali (Benazir's father), has dangerously announced his endorsement of the creation of a Muslim state to his Hindu classmates at college, some of whom are terrorists. Although the suburb-dwelling Das family members do not directly experience the violence of the city's partition riots, they keenly feel its effects, most notably in the fate of Hyder Ali's family, who are obliged to flee to Hyderabad. Shortly thereafter, Tara marries Bakul and departs, and Mira dies after suffering horribly with delirium tremens. Bim's sense of abandonment over her sister's defection is compounded by the conduct of Raja, who, after recovering from a bout of tuberculosis that has sidelined him during the partition violence, follows their displaced Muslim neighbors to Hyderabad where he marries Benazir and remains. Bim is thus left with sole responsibility for Baba, the family business, and the family home. The novel's third section takes us back to the formative childhood years of the Das siblings, deepening our sense of their lives together. We are returned to the present in the final section, which concludes with overtures of reconciliation toward Raja from Bim, who has experienced a moment of transcendence that enables her to overcome her festering resentments.

Intricately textured, psychologically penetrating, and flawlessly crafted, *Clear Light of Day* is Desai's most complex novel. In keeping with the proclivities of its characters, whose experiences tend to be mediated through art generally and poetry particularly, the text is replete with allusions to a wide range of Indian and British poets. The verse of T. S. Eliot plays an especially important role. Identifying "Eliot's concept of time" as "very Indian" (it is, in fact, directly traceable to his study of Hinduism and Buddhism), Desai cites his *Four Quartets* as having provided the inspiration for the novel's chronology (Bliss interview, p. 530). Indian narratives, she observes, tend to be premised on "a synchronic rather than a diachronic attitude" and on the concept of "time as a cycle, a wheel, ever turning, ever changing" rather than "as a sequence of events, beginning at the beginning and ending with a climax" ("Indian Fiction Today," p. 210). She also maintains that, by writing "a book that began at the end and tunneled its way back-

wards towards the beginning" (Bliss interview, p. 525), she endeavored "to construct a four-dimensional world" in which time has "as palpable an existence as the spatial world perceived by the five senses" (Srivastava interview, p. 224). Her practice of framing a delving into the past with bookend-like moments in the present is particularly suited to her inclinations as it renders the narrative process comparable to that of psychoanalysis. She had first experimented with this variation of the dual-chronology form in *Where Shall We Go This Summer?*, and her sense that this technique is particularly effective for her is suggested in the fact that she would return to it yet again to provide the organizing principle for the later novels *Baumgartner's Bombay* and *Journey to Ithaca*.

Clear Light of Day is not only Desai's most densely intertextual work, but, in its poignant depictions of the thwarted ambitions and arrested developments of women in an entrenched patriarchal culture, it is also her most deeply feminist work. As young children, the Das sisters gain insight into the arbitrary nature of male privilege; having cross-dressed in their brother Raja's clothing, "[s]uddenly they saw why they were so different from their brother, so inferior and negligible in comparison: it was because they did not wear trousers" (p. 132). Although Tara will relinquish this lesson by marrying at an early age the domineering, elder Bakul and embracing a life of traditional domesticity, the formidable Bim vows never to marry and will instead "earn my own living . . . and be independent" (p. 140). Rejecting the advances of her fatuous suitor, Dr. Biswas (who comes regularly to the Das home to treat Raja's tuberculosis and Mira's alcoholism), Bim puts herself through college and ultimately forges a career for herself as a teacher—a position that she uses as a platform for disseminating the message of education and economic independence for a new generation of Indian women: "I'm always trying to teach [my students] . . . to be different from what we were at their age—to be a new kind of woman," she says to Tara. Yet Bim's road to self-determination has been difficult, and she bears psychological scars from the struggle. She is particularly embittered by the disparity of opportunities between herself and Raja. It is as a matter of course that her brother has been sent to college, but as for herself, she recalls, "[f]or all father cared, I could have grown up illiterate—and *cooked* for my living, or *swept*. So I had to teach myself history, and teach myself to teach" (p. 155). The comparative rarity of Bim's achievement is suggested in the novel's depictions of less resourceful women. The industrious Misra sisters, Jaya and Sarla, who live next door, have been denied a proper education in favor of their profligate brothers who are "fat, lazy slobs drinking whisky . . . all day that their sisters have to pay for" (p. 32). (The situation replicates that described in *Fire on the Mountain* of the "clever, thrifty, hard-working" Ila Das and her sister, who benefit from none of the family fortune but whose "drunken, dissolute" brothers have all "been sent to foreign universities" [p. 123].) Yet as deplorable as such circumstances are, they pale in comparison to the egregious case of Mira, who, married at twelve and widowed at fifteen, has been grossly abused by her husband's family subsequent to his death.

The psychological portraits in *Clear Light of Day* are all the more compelling for the high degree of historical and political specificity with which they are sketched. In fact, the tumultuous national events of 1947 not only *coincide* with but are represented as *analogous* to the upheaval and fracturing of the Das nuclear family; the chief trope of the novel, in short, is a likening of the partitioning of the nation to the "partitioning" of the Das family. Not in the least recondite, the analogy is rendered explicit early in the text: Tara peruses a copy of "Sir Mortimer Wheeler's *Early India and Pakistan* and th[inks] how relevant such a title [i]s to the situation in their family, [given] their brother's marriage to [the Muslim] Hyder Ali's daughter" (p. 28); similarly, Bim, recalling the violent summer of 1947, muses, "*We* were anything but peaceful that summer" (p. 42). While both Das sisters are thus cognizant of these parallels, and while the reader is repeatedly steered in this direction as well, less clear is what is ultimately conveyed by the novel's insistent linkage of the story of the nation with the story of this particular family. Michael Gorra observes in *After Empire: Scott, Naipaul, Rushdie* (1997) that "[t]he degree to which historiographic metafiction maintains a tyrannical relation to its own characters . . . mark[s] a limitation in the great novels of our age," and he asserts that he is particularly "troubled that a book about the nightmare of history cannot make me care about the individual characters to whom that history happens" (Chicago, p. 147). The work to which he is referring is *Midnight's Children,* which takes the form of a mock-autobiography of the nation in which the life

of the protagonist-narrator, Saleem Sinai, is figured as a caricatural reduction of the history of postindependence India. A comparison of Rushdie's masterpiece with *Clear Light of Day* will illuminate some of the issues at stake in writing historical fiction.

Clear Light of Day and *Midnight's Children* were both published in 1980, and both are plotted around characters whose lives parallel the history of post-1947 India. Yet in their treatment of this history these novels part company, for, as Dieter Riemenschneider observes, in *Clear Light of Day* the stories of individuals and the story of the nation "are linked by coincidence rather than by the intrinsic logic we encounter in *Midnight's Children,*" as in the latter work "there is virtually no event which is not given an individual as well as an historical meaning" (pp. 189, 192). As Rushdie's Saleem remarks, thoroughly conscious of his own microcosmic status (a frame of mind that is in keeping with the postmodern self-referentiality of the work as a whole), he has "to bear the burden of history," as "I am the sum total of everything that went before me"; it has been his fate, he asserts in the novel's conclusion, "to forsake privacy and be sucked into the annihilating whirlpool of the multitudes" (New York, 1991, pp. 457, 552). As distinct from Rushdie's telepathically empowered midnight's children, the characters of *Clear Light of Day* live within the boundaries of intensely privatized, well-fortified egos and struggle mightily against the maelstrom of national history. (The force of this maelstrom is suggested in Arundhati Roy's 1997 novel, *The God of Small Things,* in which the Indian protagonist, Rahel, contemplates how in her country "personal turmoil [is] dropped by at the wayside shrine of the vast, violent, circling, driving, ridiculous, insane, unfeasible, public turmoil of [the] nation" [New York, 1997, p. 20].) Desai herself implies the fundamental difference between her fiction and Rushdie's when she rather sweepingly remarks in the 1989 essay "Indian Fiction Today" that, "from [the Nobel Prize–winning Bengali] Rabindranath Tagore . . . to Salman Rushdie," a prevailing tendency for "the Indian writer" is to use "characters, as he does features of the landscape, to represent wider truths. He does not see a character—or a tree, an ox, or a hill—as unique and particular; they merely symbolize the larger concepts that he regards as the only fit subjects for art" (pp. 208–209). She identifies herself as writing against the grain of this tendency. "I don't like to generalize about my characters; for me, they're individuals," she affirms while claiming that if she were to create characters who "are simply representatives" they would turn out as mere "cardboard creatures," as "posters rather than paintings" (Jussawalla interview, pp. 162, 167).

To observe this difference is not to suggest that one mode is superior to the other, but simply to identify the salient disparity of approach between—as well as the complementary strengths of—these two great writers. It is also to recognize that Desai's novel offers that which Gorra senses Rushdie's novel to lack; by keeping her work supple and suggestive rather than transparently allegorical, she skillfully balances our interest in the history that she recounts with our involvement in the specific individuals whom she portrays. Whereas Rushdie's Saleem finds himself to be "inextricably entwined with [his] world," as "the macrocosm of public affairs" demonstrates his "private existence . . . [to be] at one with history" (p. 286), by contrast, in the concluding scene of *Clear Light of Day*, Bim's cathartic release from the burden of her own resentments—her rapprochement with her "traitorous," Muslim-enamored brother Raja—is figured specifically as an extrication from the burden of being a symbolic receptacle for her nation's troubled history. Characteristically for Desai, this epiphany takes the form of a contemplative, aestheticized vision of harmonious multiculturalism: elicited at a gathering of Hindus by the singing of an Urdu poem written by the Muslim Muhammad Iqbal (Raja's favorite poet, he is regarded as the spiritual founder of Pakistan) whose words are filtered through the verse of the Christian T. S. Eliot, Bim's blissful sense of closure with which the novel finishes is in decided contrast to the fractious national story with which her life has coincided and intersected but to which it is not reducible.

LATER FICTION

OBSERVING that "every writer . . . tend[s] to use a handful of characters and a handful of themes over and over again," Desai maintains that "it is one's obsessions that one walks over and over, and [one] rarely feels one is finished" (Jussawalla interview, p. 177). This general principle is especially characteristic of her own fiction, which is marked by a

pronounced thematic continuity. Yet the deeply introspective *Clear Light of Day*, which she has described as "the most autobiographical of all my novels" and "the one in which I used the most of my childhood memories" (Pandit interview, p. 153), is singular among her works in that it appears to have effected a measure of closure not only for its protagonist but also for its author, thus enabling her to move on to new fictional terrain. Likening the act of writing to psychoanalysis, Desai notes that the process "clears up things and enables you to go beyond them or to integrate them in your mind," and she identifies the experience of writing *Clear Light of Day* as having been particularly efficacious for her in dealing with

the materials of my childhood, of infancy, of sisterhood, of motherhood, [which] I found I simply could not ignore. . . . I had to make some kind of order out of them. . . . I felt a great need to proceed with these ideas, to clear them before I could proceed to a more objective book. And, after having tidied away the subject of my childhood, I really was able to write books in a completely different tone.

(Seguet interview, p. 48)

Subsequent to *Clear Light of Day*, Desai's fiction thus became less personal and increasingly focused on characters, particularly men, whose experiences are remote from her own. The chief stylistic consequence of this broadening of scope was a shift of emphasis from interior monologue and indirect discourse to the less cerebral narrative mode of dialogue. This change, which she has termed a transition from "subjective" to "objective" writing, also made her fiction more suitable for film adaptation, and each of her next two works—*The Village by the Sea* and *In Custody*—would, in fact, be adapted for the screen, the former as a BBC miniseries and the latter as a feature film.

A novella for young people, *The Village by the Sea* (1982) tells the story of a family beset by misfortune in the traditional fishing village of Thul, on the west coast of India near Bombay. (Desai herself frequently holidayed in Thul while residing in Bombay, and in a prefatory note she avers that the tale "is based entirely on fact" [p. 6].) With the mother ill and bedridden and the father an unemployed, abusive alcoholic, the brunt of the family responsibilities devolve upon the elder children, the adolescents Lila and Hari, both of whom have stopped attending school in order to fulfill these duties and particularly to care for their two younger siblings. The family's hardships are compounded by imminent upheaval for the village as a whole: factories are going to be built in Thul that will extinguish the inhabitants' traditional way of life. Hari elects to relocate to nearby Bombay, where he earns money for his family and serves as an apprentice to Mr. Panwallah, an avuncular watch repairer. Meanwhile, in Thul, compassionate middle-class vacationers from Bombay take the ailing mother to a hospital, where she is diagnosed with anemia and tuberculosis. The news of her hospitalization jars her husband into reforming his dissolute ways. After a nine-month absence, Hari returns to Thul with new skills and new confidence; similarly, Lila has rapidly matured under the test of the responsibilities that have been thrust upon her. Soon thereafter, their mother returns from the hospital along with their now contrite and sober father. Hari plans to start a poultry farm and looks forward to opening a watch-mending shop in Thul, recognizing that, with the coming of the factories, so, too, will come customers. The tale ends happily, with familial reconciliation and a healthy embracing of the future.

Unlike Desai's other books for children, *The Peacock Garden* and *Cat on a Houseboat, The Village by the Sea* is not aimed at young children; indeed, one of its more impressive aspects is the facility with which Desai modulates her syntax, vocabulary, and story to suit a specifically adolescent readership. The tale is cast as a bildungsroman, and its rather dubious moral—framed in starkly Darwinian terms—is that one must accept progress and adapt accordingly. The point is articulated by the text's voice of wisdom and moral authority, Mr. Panwallah, himself a Parsi who has adapted to a society comprised mostly of people of other faiths: "Learn, learn, learn—so that you can grow and change," he counsels Hari, remarking that "if you want to survive, you will have to change" (p. 129). In some respects the novella is brutally realistic; we are presented with stark depictions of poverty, alcoholism, violence—even the grisly death of the family dog by poisoning at the hands of malevolent neighbors. Yet as the plot moves toward its conclusion, the sharp edge of reality is blunted as the facts, such as the swift resocialization of the father, are arranged with an increasingly improbable benevolence. Desai has acknowledged that, although the story is based on the experiences of a real family, "their lives didn't end as happily as

I made out in the book," and she points out that "I would have written it quite differently if I hadn't been writing it for children" (Bliss interview, p. 529).

The Village by the Sea was followed up by *In Custody* (1984), a novel whose protagonist is Deven Sharma, a mediocre, ineffectual, and overburdened man in his middle thirties who, in order to support his materialistic wife and young son, teaches Hindi at a college in the northern Indian village of Mirpore. The world is decidedly not Deven's oyster. Disdained and ill-treated by his students, his colleagues, and his family alike, he has only one source of solace: a pure love for Urdu poetry. The story begins with a request of Deven by his old school friend Murad, who edits a literary magazine, to conduct an interview with Nur Shahjehanabadi, the greatest living Urdu poet and Deven's hero since childhood. The starry-eyed devotee jumps at the opportunity. Yet what he discovers upon visiting Nur at the poet's home in Delhi is that his idol is, in fact, exceedingly human: he is immoderate with his food and liquor consumption, harassed by his wives (a Muslim, he has two), bestial in his personal habits, and has surrounded himself with an entourage of sycophantic, dissolute protégés who are more interested in raucous merrymaking than in the noble vocation of poetry. The visit ends catastrophically with the drunken Nur having vomited all over himself and the room of his shrewish younger wife, Imtiaz, and the "fallen hero" (p. 59) being scolded by her in abjectly humiliating terms. The sordid episode leaves Deven with "poetry for ever mixed with vomit in his mind" (p. 64).

Despite this abysmal encounter, Deven agrees, under pressure from Murad, to return to Nur's home in order to record the poet's recitations and perhaps even his memoirs. Yet two impediments stand in his way: Imtiaz will not consent, and he has no tape recorder. The former obstacle is overcome with the aid of the elder wife, Safiya, who (chiefly in order to spite Imtiaz) arranges for him to meet Nur surreptitiously for the recording sessions; the latter obstacle is dispensed with by Deven's colleague the Urdu professor Abid Siddiqui, who convinces administrators at their college to allocate funds for a tape recorder. The readily swindled Deven spends the money on an unreliable, secondhand machine, and, perplexed by modern technology, which is all rocket science to him, also hires a technician to work it. When he arrives for the first of the recording sessions, it turns out that Safiya has arranged for them to be held in a local brothel. In this squalid setting over the next several weeks Deven does his best to conduct the sessions in a professional manner, but he is thwarted at every turn and the result is a debacle: although we see flashes of the titan Nur's former greatness, he is more interested in procuring biryani and rum than in reciting poetry; the technician is uncooperative and incompetent; Nur's flattering disciples ensure that the atmosphere is kept boisterously nonconducive to serious purposes; and, after the several frustrating weeks of sessions are concluded, Deven inspects the tapes and finds them to be of such poor sound quality as to be useless. With nothing to show for his own good intentions and sincere efforts, or, more pressingly, for his college's expenditures, Deven foresees "an inquiry, an interrogation, exposure and blame" (p. 202) that will conclude with his censure and dismissal. The novel ends with him wistfully attempting to recapture his former reverence for Nur while contemplating his own imminent ruin.

A sharply incisive social comedy that occasionally veers into farce, *In Custody* is unlike anything else Desai has written. The timing is impeccable, and the undercutting of Deven's airy idealism is rendered with a particularly merciless proficiency. With this work, which has evoked comparisons to the fiction of R. K. Narayan, Desai vastly expands her repertoire of narrative options while at the same time disclosing hitherto unsuspected talents; indeed, prior to the publication of *In Custody* one would have been hard-pressed to produce credible evidence of the very existence of her sense of humor. The novel's lightness of tone, however, does not preclude it from taking on weighty themes. For example, it contains an acerbic critique of male-dominated Indian literary culture. Desai would remark in an interview several years later that, although there were "more openings for women writers" than in previous eras, such opportunities were still considerably fewer than for men (this disparity would, in fact, be diminished substantially in the 1990s), and that it remained the case that "few Indian women have the same training as men, and on the whole far less education" (Kenyon interview, p. 39). Clearly exemplifying these circumstances, Nur's younger wife, Imtiaz, a frustrated poet who lives in the shadow of her illustrious husband, mails copies of her poems to Deven along with a letter in which she dares him

to read them. "I am a woman and have had no education but what I have found and seized for myself," she writes, echoing Bim's proud claims in *Clear Light of Day* and maintaining that if he is reluctant to read her poems that is only because "they fill you with fear and insecurity . . . [and] threaten you with danger—danger that your superiority to women may become questionable." She particularly charges him with fearing that her work "might eclipse the verse of Nur Sahib and other male poets whom you revere" (p. 196). The pusillanimous manner in which Deven refuses this challenge is conveyed in intensely polemical terms:

Deven did not have the courage [to read her poems]. . . . He did not have the will or the wherewithal to deal with this new presence, one he had been happy to ignore earlier and relegate to the grotesque world of hysterics, termagants, viragos, the demented and the outcast. It was not for the timid and circumspect to enter that world on a mission of mercy or rescue. If he were to venture into it, what he learnt would destroy him as a moment of lucidity can destroy the merciful delusions of a madman. He could not allow that.

(p. 197)

Therefore, without so much as looking at them, he tears up her poems.

The chief theme of *In Custody*, however, is not the paucity of opportunities for aspiring women artists in India but rather the contest between the languages of India for dominance, and particularly the declining status of Urdu relative to Hindi. (Notably, the Merchant-Ivory film adaptation, for which Desai cowrote the screenplay, is in Urdu with English subtitles.) Indeed, in this novel Desai addresses the political aspects of language with a precision and depth that are unprecedented in her fiction. Whereas her naive protagonist Deven attempts to draw a cordon sanitaire around his beloved Urdu, having "always kept away from the political angle of languages" (p. 55), he finds that his idol, Nur (who scoffs when he sheepishly confesses that he teaches Hindi, not by choice but by necessity), views the matter in a resolutely political fashion: "How can there be Urdu poetry when there is no Urdu language left? It is dead, finished. The defeat of the Moghuls by the British threw a noose over its head, and the defeat of the British by the Hindi-wallahs tightened it" (p. 42), he bemoans. The Muslim Nur's sense of the antiquated and superseded status of his language in Hindu-dominated India is suggested in the home of the Urdu professor Abid; a descendent of a nawab (Urdu for "governor" or "prince"), Abid lives in an ancestral mansion whose dilapidated condition—it will actually be reduced by the end of the novel to "a heap of rubble from which dust rose like a ghost" (p. 198)—aptly symbolizes the increasingly precarious status of Urdu in modern India.

Desai's next novel, *Baumgartner's Bombay* (1988), her first to feature a non-Indian protagonist, recounts the tragic life and violent death of Hugo Baumgartner, a Jew who has emigrated to India in the late 1930s from Nazi Germany. The story begins in the late 1980s with the grisly scene of the murder of the elderly and impoverished Hugo at his squalid home in Bombay. The ensuing chapters alternate between scenes of his last hours and flashbacks that take us chronologically through his life. Born into a solidly middle-class German-Jewish family, Hugo has grown up in Berlin during the years of escalating anti-Semitism of the 1930s. His father is a prosperous furniture seller whose business declines as Berlin's wealthy Jews begin to shift their assets (and eventually themselves) out of an increasingly hostile Germany. After the trauma of *Kristallnacht* and an arrest by storm troopers who detain him for two weeks in Dachau, the father commits suicide, ironically by gassing himself in the family kitchen. With the Baumgartners' resources and safety eroding daily, the adolescent Hugo emigrates to Calcutta, where he works as an exporter of timber; his mother, however, refuses to go and remains in Berlin. In Calcutta, Hugo meets Lotte (then Lola), a German cabaret dancer who becomes a lifelong friend. When the war breaks out in 1939, his status as a Jewish refugee from Germany notwithstanding, he is incarcerated in a British detention camp along with other "enemy aliens" (p. 103).

Conditions in the camp are surprisingly cushy, and when Hugo is released at war's end six years later, he is delivered into the chaos and escalating violence of pre-partition Calcutta. Having lost touch with his mother years earlier, he is given a packet of postcards from her, the last one dated 1941, and he realizes that she has perished in the Holocaust. He subsequently seeks out his Muslim business partner from before the war, expecting to resume their work. But Habibullah, who has been harassed and threatened by Hindus, is emigrating to Dacca, in what will soon become part of East

Pakistan, and he advises Hugo to go to Bombay where it is relatively safe. (The parallels between the circumstances of Jews in Germany and Muslims in India during this period—loose though they may be—are clearly meant to be noted.) Once again a refugee, Hugo this time flees from riot-torn Calcutta to Bombay, where he stays for the remainder of his life. There he is reunited with his friend the chummy, gin-swilling Lotte. The mistake the eccentric Hugo makes that costs him his life is, characteristically, an act of kindness; a compulsive shelterer of stray cats, he likewise takes into his home a stray human, a young German drifter named Kurt who turns out to be a sociopath and a drug addict who stabs him to death. Fulfilling the pronouncement of its epigraph—"In my beginning is my end," again, from Eliot's *Four Quartets*—the novel ends where it begins, with the devastated Lotte's despair over the scene of Hugo's murder.

Whereas *In Custody*'s inept Deven is a wretched victim of circumstances, our sympathy for him is blunted by the comedic form through which his story is conveyed; he is thus thoroughly pathetic, but not particularly sympathetic. In contrast, the endearing Hugo Baumgartner, "a man without a family or a country" (p. 133), enlists our compassion unequivocally. His unenviable role as a kindhearted, lonely outsider is crystallized early in the novel: "Accepting—but not accepted; that was the story of his life. . . . In Germany he had been dark—his darkness had marked him the Jew, *der Jude*. In India he was fair—and that marked him the *firanghi* [Urdu for 'European foreigner']. In both lands, the unacceptable" (p. 20). What makes Hugo's story especially stirring is the elevation of his existential plight to a seemingly metaphysical level; the novel's supreme irony is that he has come to India specifically in order to be safe from death at the hands of Germans yet winds up brutally murdered by the Aryan Kurt—fate's hit man and a malevolent reincarnation of another mentally unstable, enlightenment-seeking hippie, the pesky freeloader Chid from Jhabvala's 1975 novel *Heat and Dust*. Observing the "historical logic" in having Hugo killed by a German (she had contemplated having him murdered by an Indian but found that scenario less effective), Desai remarks that "it is his history that he seemed to have escaped from that hunts him down and overcomes him" (Pandit interview, p. 165); in short, he meets "the kind of death which fate had devised for him"

(Jussawalla interview, p. 176). In this respect, the consummate victim Hugo is comparable to other of literary history's great sympathetic victims, such as Thomas Hardy's Tess, who is similarly hounded and ravaged by an inexorable fate. Further, the ironic repetitions of Hugo's life as an individual are paralleled by the novel's tragic envisioning of history generally as a recurring nightmare. Having fled the violence of Germany, he "felt himself [in India] overtaken by yet another war of yet another people. Done with the global war, the colonial war, only to be plunged into a religious war. Endless war. Eternal war" (p. 180).

Desai's fascination with the theme of cross-cultural migrancy has long been in evidence in her fiction, yet in no work does she depict India as a more concentrated meeting ground for myriad races, ethnicities, and languages than *Baumgartner's Bombay*, a novel that continues the explorations into colloquial and multilanguage writing that she had begun with *In Custody*. She has observed that "[i]n my earlier writing I tried to achieve a purity of language—the English language . . . —but increasingly I find myself concerned with amalgamating the languages of my childhood and the languages of India in my prose" (Bliss interview, p. 532), and, having completed *In Custody*, "I wondered if I could not push bilingualism still further, into trilingualism" ("A Coat of Many Colors," p. 229), which is precisely what she accomplished in *Baumgartner's Bombay* with the addition of German. Her sense of the bounty of narrative options that such a plurality of languages opens up is suggested in Hugo's appreciation of the wondrous linguistic abundance of India, where "[l]anguages sprouted around him like tropical foliage and he picked words from it without knowing if they were English or Hindi or Bengali" (p. 92).

For years Desai had been searching for a story that would enable her to tap into her mother's experiences as a German immigrant in India, and—inspired by an elderly Austrian Jew in Bombay—she hit upon Hugo's tale. Although her mother was not Jewish and left Germany in the late 1920s, before the rise of Nazism, the material for the scenes from Hugo's childhood is taken directly "from the stories my mother would tell me of her childhood in Berlin." It is also memories of her mother that render German for her "the language of infancy and affection. I find myself using it when talking to small children or animals" (Bliss

interview, pp. 526, 533). She poignantly conveys these associations in Lotte's anguished response to the death camp–written cards from Hugo's mother that she gathers from the scene of his murder, which are filled with German phrases such as "*Meine kleine Maus*" and other "baby-language" endearments: "All the marzipan, all the barley sugar, the chocolates and toffees of childhood descended on her with their soft, sticking, suffocating sweetness. . . . Sugary, treacly, warm, oozing love, childhood love, little mice and bunny rabbits of love—sweet, warm, choking, childish love. Lotte wept and drowned" (pp. 3–5).

One of only a handful of fulfilling relationships depicted in Desai's fiction, Hugo and Lotte's companionship is characterized by unqualified affection, mutual esteem, and physical intimacy. Yet the manner in which the physical aspect of their relationship is conveyed is ambiguous. Although they sleep together, it is not clear whether they have sex; and whether or not they do, Hugo's preference is "to sleep [with her] chastely . . . as if they were brother and sister" (p. 208). The point would not be remarkable if Desai's fiction generally were not curiously lacking in references to sex—not merely the physical act itself, but eroticism generally. What makes her negligence of this subject especially surprising is the fact that throughout her career as a writer she has been engaged with psychoanalysis and with depicting, often with painful specificity, the subterranean inclinations of her characters. As she herself has described her propensity for delving into the psyches of her characters, "I explore the inner reality, not the one tenth visible section of the iceberg" (Seguet interview, p. 43). Yet her actual engagement with the submerged, libidinal substance of the proverbial Freudian iceberg has been perplexingly minimal.

It may be tempting to assume that this state of affairs is simply a matter of her observance of the propriety (not to say prudery) characteristic of her class and her generation. But the example of a risqué moment from an early novel readily debunks any such presumption: in *Voices in the City*, openly wondering why manifestly unsuitable husbands tend to be chosen by Indian fathers for their daughters, her narrator iconoclastically speculates—apropos of the arranged marriage of Monisha that will lead to the young bride's suicide—"was it because fathers did, unconsciously, spite their daughters who were unavailable to them?" (p. 198). In fact, when one scours Desai's work for its rare allusions to eroticism, one finds that they tend to be consistent with the tenor of this caustic remark—for example, Babaji's sexual abuse of impressionable young women in *Where Shall We Go This Summer?* and the plight of the widowed child-bride Mira in *Clear Light of Day* who is spared sexual assault at the hands of her brothers-in-law only because of her own physical repugnance. The opposite of intimacy, sex in Desai's fiction is represented as that which men do to women—and to girls—against their will, the point evidently being to assail a traditional culture of unchecked male prerogative. One especially graphic scene, from *Fire on the Mountain,* epitomizes this tendency; note the effect created by the accumulation of reiterated terms, conveying the violence of the moment:

[I]t was Preet Singh, his lips *lifted back* from his teeth, his *eyes* blazing *down* at her in *rage,* in a passion of *rage.* She *lifted* her hands to *dislodge* his from her *throat* and she did *dislodge* them. They fell away, but only to tear at the cotton *scarf* that hung about his neck, only to wrap that about her *throat, tighter, tighter, tighter,* so that the last gasp *rattled inside* her, choked and *rattled* and was still. Her *eyes* still swivelled in their sockets, two alarmed marbles of black and white, and quickly he left the ends of the *scarf, tore* at her clothes, *tore* them off her, in long, screeching rips, till he came to her, to the dry, shrivelled, starved stick *inside* the wrappings, and *raped* her, pinned her *down into* the dust and the goat droppings, and *raped* her. *Crushed back, crushed down into* the earth, she lay *raped,* broken, still and finished.

(Matin's emphases, p. 143)

It is an eloquent fact that this horrific scene—the brutal rape and murder of the frail, elderly Ila Das by a man whom she, in her capacity as a social worker, has attempted to prevent from marrying off his child-daughter in exchange for property—constitutes the sole depiction anywhere in Desai's sizable oeuvre of a sexual act.

Whereas *Baumgartner's Bombay* is about a political refugee in India, *Journey to Ithaca* (1995) takes as its subject spiritual refugees in India. The first half of the text focuses on Matteo, an idealistic Italian, and his temperamental obverse, Sophie, a hard-bitten realist German. The countercultural pair marry in 1975 and immediately set off for India, chiefly in pursuit of Matteo's dream of enlightenment, which has been inspired by his reading of Hermann Hesse's *Journey to the East.* After some disillusioning guru-hopping, they arrive at an ashram in northern India that is led by a charismatic, elderly woman who calls herself "the Mother." Although the skeptical, earthbound Sophie remains unimpressed, Matteo is enthralled by what he finds to be the spiritually edifying environment, and they remain for several years, during which time they have two children, Giacomo and Isabel. Eventually Sophie leaves the ashram, taking the children with her, and returns to Europe. Yet, having grown increasingly jealous of the Mother for capturing the heart, if not the soul, of the ingenuous Matteo, she leaves the children with her husband's indulgent parents in Italy and, a trained investigative journalist, embarks on a quest of her own to unearth the enigmatic Mother's past. Most of the novel's second half consists of Sophie's retracing of the Mother's life, which is presented to us in the form of flashbacks to the early 1920s.

The Mother, it turns out, has been born Laila, a half-Egyptian and half-French girl who has grown up a Muslim in Cairo. Having come to Paris as a student, Laila becomes enamored of India after reading some books on the subject (one of many parallels between her story and Matteo's), and, an aspiring dancer, she runs off with a troupe of Indian dancers that is headed by Krishna, the star performer. After touring in Europe they go to the United States, where they are obliged to transform their spiritual dance into a vulgar, Orientalized spectacle for a philistine American public. Laila abandons the troupe in disgust and eventually makes her way to India. Having followed in Laila's footsteps over four continents, Sophie fills in the remainder of the story with the assistance of the now elderly Krishna, whom she has tracked down in Bombay and who presents her with a diary that Laila kept of her early experiences in India. It becomes apparent to Sophie that Laila's tale closely resembled Matteo's; she, too, came to India with great hopes and, after suffering a breakdown that drove her to the nadir of despondency, was propelled into what we are given to assume was a delusion of enlightenment. Having ascertained the truth about the Mother, Sophie returns to the ashram to learn that she has died of cancer and that a grief-stricken Matteo has left in search of the location where she is supposed to have had her revelatory vision. In keeping with the spirit of the novel's plot (unlike that of Homer's epic *The Odyssey,* to which its title alludes), there is no conclusion but rather a perpetuation of the journey as Sophie sets off in pursuit of Matteo.

It is perhaps inevitable that when a writer who has consistently been producing brilliant fiction publishes a work that is less than stellar the response of readers made avaricious with expectation will be primarily disappointed in the novel's shortcomings rather than satisfaction in what it does well; great writers in particular tend to inspire this sort of ingratitude. Such is the effect of *Journey to Ithaca*, a novel that not only thematizes roving aimlessness in the lives of its protagonists but also evidences this tendency in its structure. This flaw may have its origins in the risky method Desai employs for generating working drafts of her novels. "I start writing without having very much of a 'plot' in my mind or on paper—only a very hazy idea of what the pattern of the book is to be. But it seems to work itself out as I go along" (Ram interview, p. 101), she asserted early in her career and has since reaffirmed that she continues to use this approach. She has no doubt reaped benefits from creating according to the murky, inscrutable decrees of intuition, yet in *Journey to Ithaca* we see the pitfalls associated with this technique, as her usually dependable intuition appears to have led her astray. The text's structural flaws appear on two levels: both within the episodic depictions of the lives of the protagonists as well as in the paucity of connections established between the dual plots, which seem at times to be so disconnected as to constitute discrete narratives. In brief, it is a novel whose cumulative effect is only slightly greater than the sum of its parts.

Nonetheless, its shortcomings aside, *Journey to Ithaca* has much to recommend it. What the novel does particularly well is represent India as a site for the fetishistic fantasies of the disillusioned from elsewhere. This theme was first broached by Desai nearly a quarter of a century earlier, in *Bye-Bye, Blackbird*'s Indophilic Londoner, Emma Moffit. In *Journey to Ithaca*, however, she brings considerably more insight to the subject and treats it in much greater detail. "When will people from the West free themselves from Hollywood [accounts of India]?" (p. 36) a minor character muses, and his observation is followed up with a sardonic portrait of a country overrun by foreigners whose attempts at reverence stimulate only irreverence among those people whose spiritual lives they are striving to emulate: "All over India, in those years [the 1970s], ragged white mendicants in loose pyjamas and bandanas milled around ashrams and sadhus and yogis to the mirth and disbelief of Indians" (p.

59). Sophie views her husband's infatuation with the allure of the East with a similarly skeptical eye (the bulk of the narrative is refracted through her consciousness), noting that Westerners generally recount their allegedly religious experiences in India "with all the zeal . . . of shoppers in a market" (p. 62). Sophie's wry reduction of such aspirations to the status of materialistic fantasies is in keeping with the novel's ultimate irony: the fact that both Laila and Matteo envision India as a place of spiritual authenticity and as a refuge against a shallow culture of consumerism, yet neither of them recognizes that the specific accounts that have driven them there in search of "the mystery that is at the heart of India" (p. 57), and that have configured their idealistic imaginings, are themselves no more than exoticized fictions.

CONCLUSION

BOTH the trajectory of Desai's career and that of post-1947 English-language Indian literature are becoming increasingly visible, and when they are plotted against one another several conclusions suggest themselves. First, Desai's shifting fortunes as an author have largely mirrored those of this body of literature; having begun inauspiciously, both are now securely established. Second, her influence on younger writers has tended to be overlooked, a misapprehension in which she herself has been complicit by endorsing the prevalent view that casts Rushdie as the Zeus-like sole progenitor of an assemblage of literary Athenas: it was Rushdie's fiction that spawned "a whole generation of young writers," she has maintained (Pandit interview, p. 163). The current generation of young Indo-Anglian writers is, in fact, a many-parented entity and is not lacking in mothers as well as fathers; indeed, as Feroza Jussawalla has suggested, Desai herself may be viewed as having " 'mothered' the psychological novel in India" (p. 173), for filial resemblances to her fiction are abundantly evident in the work of many of the introspectively disposed writers who have risen to prominence in recent years. Third, her salutary effects on younger writers have been not only artistic, but also commercial; by fostering among readers and publishers a receptive climate for Indo-Anglian literature, she has materially enhanced the opportunities for talented younger writers such as Vikram Seth and Amitav Ghosh.

In the 1995 essay "Publishers, Agents, and Agendas," Desai recalls having completed her first novel, *Cry, the Peacock*, in 1960—three years before it would finally appear—and attempting to find a British publisher for it, yet,

[w]ith as great regularity as I sent out my manuscript, back came the rejection slips.

. . . Unfortunately I'd never heard at the time of such a thing as a literary agent. But persistence paid off—and what alternative did I have? There were perhaps three publishers of English in India then, and not one would risk publishing fiction by an unknown Indian novelist.

(p. 97)

An illuminating indication of the differences between the opportunities for writers of Desai's generation and those of younger writers today is the sharp disparity between the circumstances surrounding her efforts to secure a publisher for her first novel and those encountered by Arundhati Roy. Roy's submission of the manuscript of her 1997 tour de force, *The God of Small Things*, precipitated a bidding war among several major publishing houses, enabling her to negotiate a lucrative contract. Random House beautifully produced the novel and aggressively marketed and promoted it with the sort of hype normally associated with the release of a big-budget feature film, and it subsequently won the coveted Booker Prize. To observe these disparities is not to minimize Roy's skill or accomplishment, but simply to point out that she is not sui generis. On the contrary, the artistic and commercial success of *The God of Small Things* has a discernible prehistory that makes clear that such a phenomenon could not have occurred in the early 1960s, when Desai was beginning her career—in part for the same reasons that Virginia Woolf adduces in support of the contention that no woman could either have written so well or become so famous as Shakespeare in Elizabethan England. The literary marketplace is today fertile ground for Indian authors, men and women alike, who write in English. There is an abundance of eager and deep-pocketed publishers, a community of prestigious writers, a wide international reading public, and a scholarly niche that ensures the future of this body of literature in higher education. This propitious state of affairs is partly attributable to Desai, who steadfastly pursued her vocation under comparatively thankless circumstances. If one

wishes to gauge the true measure of her achievement, one must look beyond those books that bear her own name on the title page.

SELECTED BIBLIOGRAPHY

I. FICTION FOR ADULTS. *Cry, the Peacock* (London, 1963); *Voices in the City* (Delhi, 1965); *Bye-Bye, Blackbird* (Delhi, 1971, 1985); *Where Shall We Go This Summer?* (Delhi, 1975, 1982); *Fire on the Mountain* (New York, 1977); *Games at Twilight and Other Stories* (London, 1978); *Clear Light of Day* (London, 1980); *In Custody* (New York, 1984); *Baumgartner's Bombay* (London, 1988); *Journey to Ithaca* (New York, 1995).

II. FICTION FOR CHILDREN. *The Peacock Garden* (Bombay, 1974; London, 1979); *Cat on a Houseboat* (Delhi, 1976); *The Village by the Sea* (London, 1982).

III. ESSAYS AND BOOK INTRODUCTIONS. "The Indian Writer's Problems," in Ramesh K. Srivastava, ed., *Perspectives on Anita Desai* (Ghaziabad, 1984); Introduction to Rabindranath Tagore, *The Home and the World* (London, 1985); Introduction to Mitch Epstein, *In Pursuit of India* (New York, 1987); "Indian Fiction Today," in *Daedalus* 118 (fall 1989); "India: The Seed of Destruction," in *New York Review of Books* (27 June 1991); Introduction to Lady Mary Wortley Montagu, *Turkish Embassy Letters* (Athens, Ga., 1993); "Re-reading Tagore," in *Journal of Commonwealth Literature* 29, no. 1 (1994); "Bellow, the Rain King," in *Salmagundi* nos. 106–107 (spring-summer 1995); Introduction to Salman Rushdie, *Midnight's Children* (New York, 1995); "Publishers, Agents, and Agendas," in *Library Chronicle of the University of Texas at Austin* 25, no. 4 (1995); "A Coat of Many Colors," in Robert J. Baumgardner, ed., *South Asian English: Structure, Use, and Users* (Urbana, 1996).

IV. SCREENPLAY / FILM ADAPTATIONS. *The Village by the Sea* (a six-part miniseries adapted by the BBC, 1992); *In Custody*, screenplay by Desai and Shahrukh Husain (Merchant-Ivory, 1993).

V. INTERVIEWS. Atma Ram, "An Interview with Anita Desai," in *World Literature Written in English* 16 (1977); Ramesh K. Srivastava, "Anita Desai at Work: An Interview," in Ramesh K. Srivastava, ed., *Perspectives on Anita Desai* (Delhi, 1984); Jasbir Jain, in *Stairs to the Attic: The Novels of Anita Desai* (Jaipur, 1987); Pascale Seguet, "An Interview with Anita Desai," in *Commonwealth Essays and Studies* 10 (spring 1988); Corinne Demas Bliss, "Against the Current: An Interview with Anita Desai," in *Massachusetts Review* 29 (fall 1988); Florence Libert, "An Interview with Anita Desai," in *World Literature Written in English* 30 (spring 1990); Olga Kenyon, in *The Writer's Imagination: Interviews with Major International Women Novelists* (Bradford, England, 1992); Feroza Jussawalla, in Feroza Jussawalla and Reed Way Dasenbrock, eds., *Interviews with Writers of the Post-Colonial World* (Jackson, Miss., 1992); "The Other Voice: A Dialogue Between Anita Desai, Caryl Phillips, and Ilan Stavans," in *Transition* 64 (1994); Lalita Pandit, "A Sense of Detail and a Sense of Order," in Patrick Colm Hogan and Lalita Pandit, eds., *Literary India: Comparative Studies in Aesthetics, Colonialism, and Culture* (Albany, 1995).

VI. CRITICAL STUDIES. Darshan Singh Maini, "The Achievement of Anita Desai," in K. K. Sharma, *Indo-English Literature: A Collection of Critical Essays* (Ghaziabad, 1977); Ramesh K. Srivastava, ed., *Perspectives on Anita Desai* (Delhi, 1984); Jasbir Jain, *Stairs to the Attic* (Jaipur, 1987); Usha Bande, *The Novels of Anita Desai: A Study in Character and Conflict* (Delhi, 1988); Richard Cronin, "The Quiet and the Loud: Anita Desai's India," in *Imagining India* (Houndmills, Basingstoke, Hampshire, 1989); R. K. Dhawan, ed., *The Fiction of Anita Desai* (New Delhi, 1989); Alamgir Hashmi, "*Clear Light of Day* Between India and Pakistan," and Dieter Riemenschneider, "History and the Individual in Anita Desai's *Clear Light of Day* and Salman Rushdie's *Midnight's Children*," in Viney Kirpal, ed., *The New Indian Novel in English: A Study of the 1980s* (New Delhi, 1990); Mrinalini Solanki, *Anita Desai's Fiction: Patterns of Survival Strategies* (Delhi, 1992); Fawzia Afzal-Khan, *Cultural Imperialism and the Indo-English Novel: Genre and Ideology in R. K. Narayan, Anita Desai, Kamala Markandaya, and Salman Rushdie* (University Park, Penn., 1993); Geetha Ramanathan, "Sexual Violence / Textual Violence: Desai's *Fire on the Mountain* and Shirazi's *Javady Alley*," in *Modern Fiction Studies* 39 (spring 1993); S. Indira, *Anita Desai As an Artist: A Study in Image and Symbol* (Delhi, 1994); Indira Karamcheti, "The Geographics of Marginality: Place and Textuality in Simone Schwarz-Bart and Anita Desai," in Margaret R. Higonnet and Joan Templeton, eds., *Reconfigured Spheres: Feminist Explorations of Literary Space* (Amherst, 1994); Bettina L. Knapp, "*Fire on the Mountain*: A Rite of Exit," Harveen Sachdeva Mann, " 'Going in the Opposite Direction': Feminine Recusancy in Anita Desai's *Voices in the City*," and Judie Newman, "History and Letters: Anita Desai's *Baumgartner's Bombay*," in Michael Parker and Roger Starkey, eds., *Postcolonial Literatures: Achebe, Ngugi, Desai, Walcott* (New York, 1995); Pippa Brush, "German, Jew, Foreigner: The Immigrant Experience in Anita Desai's *Baumgartner's Bombay*," in *Critical Survey* 8, no. 3 (1996); Sandhyarani Dash, *Form and Vision in the Novels of Anita Desai* (New Delhi, 1996); Minoli Salgado, "When Seeing Is Not Believing: Epiphany in Anita Desai's *Games at Twilight*," in *Journal of Modern Literature* 20 (summer 1996); Sharad Srivastava, *The New Woman in Indian English Fiction: A Study of Kamala Markandaya, Anita Desai, Namita Gokhale, and Shobha De* (New Delhi, 1996); Katharine Capshaw Smith, "Narrating History: The Reality of the Internment Camps in Anita Desai's *Baumgartner's Bombay*," in *Ariel* 28 (April 1997); Tony Simoes Da Silva, "Whose Bombay Is It Anyway?: Anita Desai's *Baumgartner's Bombay*, in *Ariel* 28 (July 1997); Rajeswari Mohan, "The Forked Tongue of Lyric in Anita Desai's *Clear Light of Day*," in *Journal of Commonwealth Literature* 32, no. 1 (1997); Radha Chakravarty, "Figuring the Maternal: 'Freedom' and 'Responsibility' in Anita Desai's Novels," in *Ariel* 29 (April 1998).

RODDY DOYLE

(1958–   )

David Hawkes

IT IS DIFFICULT to consider Roddy Doyle's biography in isolation from his literary career, not only because he has generally been reticent about his private life but also because that life has been lived largely in the environment and among the people depicted in his fiction. Doyle was born on 8 May 1958, the second child of Rory Doyle, a printer, and Ida Bolger Doyle, a secretary. Growing up in the suburb of Kilbarrack on Dublin's unfashionable north side, he attended the local Christian Brothers' school before going on to University College, Dublin. After graduating he took a post teaching English and geography at the same school he had attended. He remained in this job for fourteen years and continued thereafter to live in north Dublin with his wife and two children. In the mid-1980s Doyle wrote his first novel, *The Commitments*, and after two years of unsuccessful attempts to find a publisher, he formed his own company, King Farouk Press, which put out an initial run of three thousand copies in 1987. The book's wit, veracity, and comfortable familiarity with popular culture made it an immediate underground success in Dublin, and the following year the London-based publisher Heinemann released a new edition throughout the United Kingdom.

The Commitments filled a yawning gap in the literary market. It was one of the first novels to seem at ease with the youth culture of the British Isles in the 1980s, and it addressed the tastes and concerns of Doyle's post–baby boom generation, which had achieved cultural awareness in the late 1970s and early 1980s. *The Commitments* tells the quintessential punk rock story—a group of unemployed youths attempts to escape poverty and boredom by forming a band—and it does so in a compelling and obviously authentic proletarian vernacular. It was an instant popular and critical success, and Doyle's reputation was firmly consolidated by the film version, directed by Alan Parker and released in 1991.

In the meantime Doyle continued writing about the experiences of the young urban Irish in two plays, *Brownbread* (1987) and *War* (1989), both of which enjoyed successful runs at Dublin's SFX Centre. Like *The Commitments* the plays are naturalistic representations of the charming, humorous side of working-class life. The major strength of Doyle's writing has always been his dialogue—his early novels, with their minimalist narrative voice and unforgettable turns of speech, read very much like play scripts or screenplays—and Dublin audiences relished hearing their own expressions and observing characters drawn from their own experiences. By the time his second novel, *The Snapper* (1990), was published, Doyle's reputation as an Irish man of letters was secure. This book made it clear that Doyle did not view his analysis of proletarian Dublin as a mere precursor of more refined literary concerns. *The Snapper*, like *The Commitments*, is set in "Barrytown" (a barely fictionalized Kilbarrack), and it, too, follows the fortunes of the Rabbittes, the likably feckless family introduced in his first novel.

Doyle's aim was clearly a protracted, microscopic study of a specific community. Through his narrow but intense focus on a particular locale, he attunes his readers so finely to the nuances and vagaries of his characters, to their mannerisms and habits of speech, that he is able to achieve a paradoxically universal perspective, so that the figures of his fiction seem to be at once representatives of a neighborhood and instances of ubiquitous human impulses and foibles. The main emphasis of *The Snapper* shifts away from Jimmy Rabbitte, the central character of *The Commitments*, toward his sister Sharon and especially to her relationship with the engagingly ineffectual patriarch, Jimmy Sr. The book's happy union of sharp humor and understated sentiment appealed equally to the public and the critics, and ensured the aesthetic and commercial success of the film version, directed by Stephen Frears and released in 1993.

In 1991, the same year as the release of the massively popular film of *The Commitments,* Doyle achieved one of the loftiest ambitions of the British literati when his third novel, *The Van,* was shortlisted for the Booker Prize. Featuring the Rabbittes once again, the novel deals with Jimmy Sr.'s entrepreneurial attempts to escape unemployment, which was running at almost 20 percent in Ireland at the time. *The Van* was thus topical and politically relevant in its subject matter while remaining essentially jovial in tone, and this once again proved a winning combination. However, some critics began to complain that Doyle's work was becoming rather formulaic and, more seriously, that he was offering a condescending and rose-tinted, sentimental picture of what one reviewer scornfully called "the happy poor."

There is some evidence that Doyle felt the weight of these criticisms: certainly his work took on much darker tones after *The Van.* In 1992 his first three novels were published as a single volume titled *The Barrytown Trilogy.* Doyle thus announced the fundamental kinship among these works and also, it is possible to see in retrospect, drew a symbolic line under the first phase of his career before embarking on a slightly different, less optimistic course. This new seriousness was soon rewarded when, for *Paddy Clarke Ha Ha Ha* (1993), Doyle was awarded the Booker Prize, the first Irish author to be so honored. Although the novel is set in the same working-class Dublin suburb as his earlier works, *Paddy Clarke* was a major departure for Doyle. Unlike *The Barrytown Trilogy* it is narrated by an identifiable, idiosyncratic character— the ten-year-old Paddy, whose anarchic adventures and troubled psychological development are followed with humor and sensitivity. It is an unflinching and troubling analysis of the youthful male psyche and evokes the dark side of the jolly, lighthearted world inhabited by Doyle's characters. The author's fourteen years of teaching experience clearly contributed an inexhaustible supply of anecdote and idiom to this text, and it therefore seems appropriate that he resigned from his teaching post to become a full-time writer on the day it was published.

Paddy Clarke is certainly humorous, but the childhood world it portrays is essentially cruel, harsh, and threatening. Doyle followed it up with a four-part drama written for television, *Family,* first broadcast in 1994. Half the adult population of Ireland watched, many in shock, as the hallowed institution of the Irish family was subjected to a ruthless and harrowing critique. The Spencers present a weary catalog of dysfunctionalities: incest, domestic violence, alcoholism, juvenile delinquency, adult criminality, and generalized despairing chaos are the stuff of their everyday existence. The program caused a furor in Ireland, where Doyle's withering depiction of the Irish male, in the person of the brutal Charlo Spencer, was the target of particular criticism. Doyle later spoke of listening to radio talk shows after *Family* was aired, and feeling convinced that he was about to be forced into exile. In fact, however, he had already done perfect justice to the optimistic elements of working-class life in the *The Barrytown Trilogy,* and it would have been unrealistic as well as insensitive to ignore the darker side of that culture. Indeed, Doyle commented that he envisaged the miserable Spencers living next door to the lovable Rabbittes. The truth is that over the course of a decade, Doyle constructed a well-rounded, inclusive, tolerant, and lovingly detailed portrait of his own community. It seems as misguided to castigate him for criticizing that community as it does to mock him for sentimentalizing it.

Just as his first three novels make up a single, extended narrative, so Doyle's next works can profitably be read as forming a unity. Paddy Clarke, whose troubling intimations of domestic violence gradually invade his childish view of the world, might be the offspring of the Spencers, whose disintegrating marriage was chronicled in *Family* and who also figure in Doyle's fourth novel, *The Woman Who Walked into Doors* (1996). The television drama ends with the drunken Charlo being beaten and expelled by his wife, Paula, and daughter, Nicola, after he has made an incestuous pass at the girl. The novel informs us of Charlo's ultimate, grisly fate before leading us through the story of Paula's life in a series of flashbacks interspersed with the painful and sensitive reflections of the thirty-nine-year-old woman. Doyle hinted in interviews that he foresaw a future for Paula in his fiction, and it appeared that his investigation into the north Dublin proletarian suburbs was by no means over. It seemed possible that he might move on to wider concerns, but some observers agreed it would be hard to criticize him if he chose to continue his protracted study of this community, having so completely mastered its vocabulary, ethos, and atmosphere. At the end of the 1990s the decision Doyle faced was whether to remain a locally oriented writer or, following the examples of James Joyce and Samuel Beckett, to use his observation of Dubliners as a foundation on which to construct a broader vision.

LITERARY AND CULTURAL CONTEXTS

DOYLE's fiction reflects the ambiguous, conflicted cultural position of Ireland itself. On the one hand his writing shows clear thematic and idiomatic kinship with his British contemporaries. The Dublin he portrays is saturated with British popular culture: his characters listen to British rock music, watch British television programs, and follow British soccer teams. Unlike other contemporary Irish novelists such as Robert McLiam Wilson, Doyle rarely addresses the political problems that beset Northern and Southern Ireland, and he told Charles Foran that, as he was growing up, "Boston was closer to me than Belfast" (p. 59). On the other hand there are elements in his writing that can be fully understood only in the context of the Irish tradition. Doyle's chronicles of the everyday lives of Dubliners, for example, naturally invite comparison with James Joyce. The provincial aspirations and limitations of the characters in Joyce's *Dubliners* anticipate the grandiose but doomed schemes of Jimmy Rabbitte Senior and Junior; the display of childish consciousness in the early pages of *A Portrait of the Artist as a Young Man* lies behind the figure of Paddy Clarke; and the unerring ear for working-class Dublin's verbal mannerisms that Joyce displays in *Ulysses* has clearly been inherited by the later writer. Doyle also shares with Joyce a specific concern with the Irish capital city, as opposed to the more rural and traditional areas to the south and west, as well as a deep suspicion of the kind of nationalism that finds inspiration in the Gaelic language and folk traditions of ancient Ireland. This suspicion divided Joyce from his overtly nationalistic contemporaries, such as W. B. Yeats, just as it separated Doyle from more politically active artists of the 1990s, such as Seamus Deane. Doyle's allegiances, it seems fair to say, are to a particular class and generation rather than to a nation.

Although the two could not be farther apart in subject matter, Doyle's sparse, dialogistic style betrays the influence of another Irish modernist exile, Samuel Beckett. Many of the exchanges between the Rabbittes recall the absurdist interchanges between Vladimir and Estragon, the main characters in Beckett's *Waiting for Godot.* Like Beckett, Doyle is determinedly minimalist and aphoristic in all his work. He generally eschews the perspective of the omniscient narrator, preferring to tell the story in the vernacular of his characters' idiosyncratic turns of phrase and colorful, obscenity-laced wit. As with Beckett there is virtually no visual description in Doyle's work, but this bareness does not seem to reflect the bleak, alienated condition of twentieth-century humanity so much as it indicates an easy familiarity with the environment in which the action occurs. Like many writers of his generation, Doyle transposes the formal techniques of literary modernism onto the homely, accessible material of popular genres such as soap opera and situation comedy. The result is a postmodern blend of high art and mass culture that has proved immensely successful by aesthetic and commercial criteria alike.

In fact, Doyle arguably is best considered as part of what we might call the postmodern generation of British novelists, whose formative experiences took place in the strife-ridden Thatcherite 1980s and who came into literary prominence in the following decade. In *After the Great Divide* (1986) the literary critic Andreas Huyssen argues that the postmodern sensibility of the late twentieth century is defined above all by the collapse of the traditional distinction between canonical art and popular culture, and the discovery of a rich, poetic vernacular in the speech of the underclass testifies to the perspicacity of this observation. The actor and dramatist Steven Berkoff anticipated many of the stylistic elements exploited by such writers in the colorful, obscene, working-class dialogue of plays such as *East, West* and *Greek.* Although their works are very different from Berkoff's, popular British novelists of the late 1990s such as James Kelman and Irvine Welsh developed his techniques in their brutal, surrealistic vignettes of the condition of the British underclass after fifteen years of Thatcherism. Doyle's work certainly partakes of this tradition, and it also reflects the tastes and concerns of a particular generation. Taking their common inspiration from the work of the slightly older Martin Amis, British novelists such as Nick Hornby, Jeanette Winterson, Will Self, and Alex Garland (all born between 1958 and 1970) won widespread popularity through their references to youth culture, punk music, feminism, unemployment, and similar concerns, which also animate the work of Doyle. The latter group of writers owes Doyle a particular debt, since *The Commitments* was arguably the first novel to announce the arrival of this generation as a viable and specific literary audience.

Doyle's formal technique might be described, using another postmodernist term, as a kind of "hyperrealism": he takes the characters, speech, and situations of everyday Dublin life and then pares away elements that are superfluous to a minimal but fast-paced plot and pithy, cutting one-liners. The characteristics of what Doyle has called "spare writing" can be deduced from two apparently contradictory descriptions he has given of his method. In one interview he sounds like a documentary observer, calling his work "a record of just how certain people in Dublin spoke. . . . I just write about people, generally they're from working-class backgrounds and I describe the worlds that they come from" (Cosgrove, p. 240). The statement is slightly disingenuous, however. The characters of Doyle's fiction are certainly drawn from real life but, like certain characters in the work of Martin Amis, they come across as exaggerated representations of particular types rather than as realistic characters in the traditional sense. Doyle says elsewhere, "I've never tried to just capture reality on paper. That would be tedious. So I speed things up. In other arts, exaggeration isn't a criticism. It is praise" (Foran, p. 60). Doyle's writing suggests that reality itself has become exaggerated, and by offering his readers a stylized, speeded-up impression of the world, he is, paradoxically, being true to its actual nature.

It is also worth considering Doyle's fiction as part of a "Celtic revival" that emerged in British culture in the 1990s and clearly reflected developments in British politics. In 1997 Scotland and Wales voted to set up their own national assemblies, which took over many aspects of government from the British Parliament in London. At the same time the hold of the British state over Northern Ireland was relaxed with the signing of a peace treaty that gave Dublin an increased role in the administration of the six northern counties. The deepening integration of Britain into the European Community was expected to further weaken the centralized British state, thus making obsolete the circumstances that kept British culture firmly ori-

ented around London for three hundred years. These political changes coincided with a resurgence of artistic projects made in and about the "Celtic fringe," such as Kevin Allen's film *Twin Town* (1997), which chronicles the South Wales underclass, and the novels of James Kelman, Jeff Torrington, and Irvine Welsh, which depict the underclass life of Glasgow and Edinburgh. Doyle's gritty Dublin realism is a contribution to this genre, although his style is ultimately too optimistic and good-humored to allow close comparison with the grim dystopias of Kelman and Welsh.

THE BARRYTOWN TRILOGY

THE best-known passage in Doyle's fiction comes from the scene in *The Commitments* in which Jimmy Rabbitte, who has just taken over the management of an amateurish band made up of three of his friends, announces to his charges that they will be performing soul music. The nonplussed musicians doubt their ability to master such an ostensibly alien genre, but Jimmy insists that soul music speaks the cross-cultural language of "sex an' politics" (p. 7):

—Yeah, politics. ——Not songs abou' Fianna fuckin' Fail or annythin' like tha'. Real politics. (They weren't with him.) —Where are yis from? (He answered the question himself.) —Dublin. (He asked another one.) —Wha' part o' Dublin? Barrytown. Wha' class are yis? Workin' class. Are yis proud of it? Yeah, yis are. (Then a practical question.) —Who buys the most records? The workin' class. Are yis with me? (Not really.) —Your music should be abou' where you're from an' the sort o' people yeh come from. ———Say it once, say it loud, I'm black an' I'm proud.

They looked at him.

—James Brown. Did yis know ———never mind. He sang tha'. ———An' he made a fuckin' bomb.

They were stunned by what came next.

—The Irish are the niggers of Europe, lads.

They nearly gasped: it was so true.

—An' Dubliners are the niggers of Ireland. The culchies have fuckin' everythin'. An' the northside Dubliners are the niggers o' Dublin. ———Say it loud, I'm black an' I'm proud.

(pp. 8–9)

Most of the major themes of Doyle's early work are contained in this passage. The aggressively urban, working-class standpoint from which Jimmy speaks is defined by its difference from the rural and Gaelic Ireland of traditional nationalism. The latter Ireland is represented here by the scornful reference to Eamon De Valera's "Fianna fuckin' Fail," which is explicitly denied the right to speak on "real politics." The reader might assume, judging from this speech, that Jimmy is rejecting Republican cultural nationalism in favor of a class-oriented, socialist agenda. But this is not the case: in a later speech, the left-wing parties are included among the political groups that are dismissed as irrelevant to the concerns of the people:

———Soul is the rhythm o' the people, Jimmy said again. —The Labor Party doesn't have soul. Fianna fuckin' Fail doesn't have soul. The Workers' Party ain't got soul. The Irish people ——— no. ———The Dublin people —fuck the rest o' them. ———The people o' Dublin, our people, remember need soul. We've got soul.

(p. 40)

Unlike many musical groups from similar backgrounds, the Commitments avoid overt politics altogether, performing only American soul standards. Jimmy, along with the group's trumpet player and elder statesman, Joey "the Lips" Fagan, preaches instead a politics of pleasure. In the following exchange Doyle coaxes the maximum of humor out of the cultural clash between Jimmy's sensualist radicalism and the parochial, Catholic conservatism of the group's other members:

—Imelda, said Jimmy. —You're a woman o' the world.
—Don't answer him, 'melda, said Bernie.
Jimmy went on. —You've had sexual intercert, haven't yeh? . . . —Did yeh enjoy it?
—It was alrigh', said Imelda.
More cheers and blushes.
—This lady is the queen of soul, said Joey The Lips.
—Wha' 're you the queen of? Imelda said back.
—Then you agree with us, Jimmy asked Imelda.
—It's oney music, said Imelda.
—No way, 'melda. Soul isn't only music. Soul—
—That's alrigh' for the blackies, Jimmy. —They've got bigger gooters than us. . . .
—The first side is sex, righ', said Jimmy. —An' the second one is ———REVOLUTION!
Cheers and clenched fists.
Jimmy went on.
—Soul is the politics o' the people. . . . —Our people.
———Soul is the rhythm o' sex. It's the rhythm o' the factory too. The workin' man's rhythm. Sex an' factory.
—Not the factory I'm in, said Natalie. —There isn't much rhythm in guttin' fish. . . .

———Politics. ———Party politics, said Jimmy,— means nothin' to the workin' people. Nothin'.
———Fuck all. Soul is the politics o' the people.
—Start talkin' abou' ridin' again, Jimmy. You're gettin' borin'.
—Politics ———ridin', said Jimmy. —It's the same thing.

(pp. 36–39)

Rabbitte and Fagan point out that oppressed social groups have frequently had recourse to a politics of the body, escaping from alienated or enforced labor through a retreat into sensuality. Their semicomic insistence on kinship with black Americans is based upon a shared sensibility, a common cultural awareness that comes with being perceived, and perceiving oneself, as marginalized by mainstream society. Rabbitte and his friends are marginal to Europe because they are Irish, marginal to traditional Ireland because they are Dubliners, and marginal to Dublin because they are proletarian. Such marginalized groups frequently channel their frustrated aspirations into vibrant and innovative forms of folk culture, most notably in the case of black Americans, and it is this that inspires Jimmy to insist that his band should follow their lead. A similar sense of "soul" as politics is expressed by Fagan, the novel's most memorable character, when he claims to have recently returned from the United States.

—The Lord told me to come home. Ed Winchell, a Baptist reverend on Lenox Avenue in Harlem, told me. But The Lord told him to tell me. He said he was watching something on TV about the feuding Brothers in Northern Ireland and The Lord told the Reverend Ed that the Irish Brothers had no soul, that they needed some soul. And pretty fucking quick! Ed told me to go back to Ireland and blow some soul into the Irish Brothers. The Brothers wouldn't be shooting the asses off each other if they had soul.

(pp. 25–26)

"Soul," in this book, functions as an alternative to the dogmatic political formations that have traditionally been the curse of Irish public life. The two authoritative characters, Rabbitte and Fagan, are distinguished from the others by their understanding of the concept of soul and more generally by their superior taste in popular music. Doyle anticipates an important theme of other writers of his generation when he records the subcultural status such knowledge bestows. (The encyclopedic, obsessive approach to popular music taken by Rabbitte and Fagan is satirized, for example, in Nick Hornby's *High Fidelity*, 1995.) The Commitments start to run into trouble when their guitarist develops overly sophisticated musical tastes, leading Fagan to pronounce sadly that "Dean is going to become a Jazz Purist" (p. 126). In his novel *Trainspotting* (1995), Irvine Welsh pays oblique tribute to Doyle's wit when the womanizing "Sick Boy" finesses his seduction technique by representing himself to potential conquests as "basically a jazz purist," to the scorn and disgust of his male friends.

The Commitments, then, is a novel about cultural syncretism—the process by which the values, symbols, and references of one marginalized subculture can become available for appropriation by another with which it appears to have little in common beyond the condition of marginality. This process is symbolized by the tendency of the band's singer, Deco Cuffe, to alter the words of soul standards in order to make them "more Dubliny" (p. 54). The group's most successful number is a version of James Brown's "Night Train" that replaces the original's catalog of great American cities with more local references:

Deco growled: —STARTIN' OFF IN CONNOLLY ——

The train in the hall stopped as they waited to hear what was going to follow that.
Deco was travelling north, by DART.
—MOVIN' ON OU' TO KILLESTER——
They laughed. This was great. They pushed up to the stage.
—HARMONSTOWN RAHENY——
They cheered.
—AN' DON'T FORGET KILBARRACK —THE HOME O' THE BLUES —
Dublin soul had been delivered.

(p. 105)

Unlike some contemporary rock-oriented novels, such as Hanif Kureishi's *The Buddha of Suburbia* (1990), in which the reader's credulity is strained when a central character suddenly achieves stardom, *The Commitments* is realistic enough to ensure that "Dublin soul" is stillborn. The band breaks up before releasing a record, and the book ends with Rabbitte and his friends plotting an alternative route to success, this time through the medium of "Dublin country":

——No fuckin' politics this time either. ——But, yeh know, Joey said when he left tha' he didn't think soul was righ' for Ireland. This stuff is though. You've got to remember tha' half the country is fuckin' farmers. This is the type o' stuff they all listen to. ——Only they listen to it at the wrong speed.

(p. 164)

We can discern here an allusion to the syncretic music of bands such as the Pogues—an English group descended from Irish emigrants—who achieved international success in the 1980s with an eclectic hybrid of traditional Irish folk music and fast-paced punk rock. The fusing of influences drawn from disparate cultures is a hallmark of today's popular music and is generally held to be a definitive characteristic of postmodern aesthetics. In *The Commitments*, Doyle produced a demotic, accessible reflection on this phenomenon.

The trilogy's second novel, *The Snapper*, takes up the theme of the increasing influence of popular culture and the mass media on a society that, by western European standards, remains deeply traditional. During the 1990s Ireland began to move away from its conservative, increasingly isolated attitudes toward issues such as contraception, divorce, and abortion, and Doyle records this shift in typically understated fashion. The novel's first scene is an interchange between two characters who feature very briefly in *The Commitments*— Jimmy Rabbitte's father, Jimmy Sr., and his twenty-year-old sister, Sharon. Sharon tells her father that she is pregnant and is pleasantly surprised to find that he does not fly into the rage she had anticipated. Instead, his reaction is described as a comical mixture of ingrained prejudice and a half-conscious attempt to move with the times:

Jimmy Sr now said something he'd heard a good few times on the telly.
—D'yeh want to keep it?
—Wha' d'yeh mean?
—D'yeh —d'yeh want to keep it, like?
—He wants to know if you want to have an abortion, said Veronica. —The eejit.
—I do not! Said Jimmy Sr.
This was true. He was sorry now he'd said it.
—There's no way I'd have an abortion, said Sharon.
—Good. You're right.
—Abortion's murder.
—It is, o' course.
Then he thought of something and he had to squirt his tea back into the cup. He could hear his heart. And feel it.

He looked at Sharon.
—He isn't a black, is he?

(p. 6)

Lines from television soap operas clash with residual old-fashioned attitudes in this subtle exchange. (A similar intrusion of popular culture into everyday life is registered when Sharon, inspired by the film *Letter to Brezhnev,* decides to claim that the father was a Spanish sailor on shore leave.) The characters often reflect on the shift in social attitudes they perceive taking place around them, and on which Sharon's pregnancy forces them to concentrate. At first, joy at what Jimmy Sr. insists is the "miracle" of new life displaces any lingering shame and guilt. Early in the story Sharon prays that her pregnancy is genuine: "She tried to remember the Hail Mary but she couldn't get past Hello Be Thy Name, and anyway, she didn't believe in it, not really; so she stopped trying to remember the rest of it. It was just something to do" (p. 26). This succinctly encapsulates the attitude of Doyle's major characters toward religion. Urban, working-class Ireland is not the priest-ridden, superstitious culture of racist mythology. A skeptical, robustly agnostic, and even anticlerical atmosphere prevails in Doyle's world, which recalls the situation in Britain far more closely than it does the traditional practices of rural Ireland.

It soon transpires that any social stigma attached to Sharon's pregnancy has to do not with the fact of illegitimate conception or premarital sex but with the identity of the baby's father. The "snapper" (the term is Dublin slang for "infant") turns out to be the product of a drunken one-night stand with the unattractive and middle-aged George Burgess, who, to add insult to injury, is the father of one of Sharon's close friends, Yvonne. It is Sharon's taste, not her morals, that leads to her censure by the community. In an ironic reversal of the traditional reaction of a young woman in her situation, Sharon is mortified when Burgess suddenly declares his undying love for her and offers to run away to London and find a job to support the child. Doyle's skillful, understated humor pervades this exchange, as Sharon refuses his advances:

—Is it because I'm older than yeh?
—It's because I hate the fuckin' sight of yeh.
—Oh. ——You're not just sayin' tha'?

(p. 129)

In the conservative, Catholic Ireland of stereotypical mythology, the taste in men of a pregnant, unmarried girl would not be the community's prime concern. But Doyle emphasizes that it is this aspect of the affair, rather than any moralistic censure, that leads Sharon to fear for her reputation. In the following passage she curses Burgess for revealing that he is the father:

The baby was nothing. It happened. It was alright. Barrytown was good that way. Nobody minded. Guess the daddy was a hobby. But now Burgess ——He'd cut her off from everything. She'd no friends now, and no places to go to. She couldn't even look at her family. God, she wanted to die; really she did.

(p. 119)

The social ostracism and family disgrace that once would have resulted from becoming pregnant out of wedlock are now nothing to fear: the ridicule and derision that come from sleeping with an older, ugly man seem far more threatening. This is true even for Sharon's father, whose most fervent hope is that she was telling the truth when she blamed her condition on an anonymous sailor:

Jimmy Sr stayed there, sitting in the kitchen. He was busy admitting something: he was ashamed of Sharon. That was the problem. He was sorry for her troubles; he loved her, he was positive he did, but he was ashamed of her. Burgess! Even if there WAS a Spanish sailor — Burgess! ———

(p. 147)

In fact it is Jimmy Sr. whose attitudes are most profoundly affected by his daughter's pregnancy. Doyle appears to be heralding here the emergence of the Irish New Man. Jimmy Sr. is mortified when he is discovered reading a book titled *Everywoman,* but his curiosity has been piqued, and he cannot resist questioning his daughter:

—I'd say Georgie Burgess was a dab hand at the oul' —wha' d'yeh macall it —the foreplay, wha'?
—Daddy!
—Sorry. Sorry, Sharon. It wasn't Burgess, I know. I just said it for a laugh. But —abou', yeh know, ridin' an' tha' —I thought it was just —D'yeh know wha' I mean?
—I think so.
—Jaysis, Sharon. I don't know —
—I'd better warn Mammy.

(pp. 171–172)

Jimmy Sr. regretfully recalls being in the pub when his own children were born and, to Sharon's alarm, volunteers to be present at the birth of his grandchild. He tenderly advises Sharon against drinking and recommends a careful diet, only to be told by the robust young woman, "Ah, feck off, Daddy. Cop on" (p. 200). The increased sensitivity of Jimmy Sr. compensates for the baby's illegitimacy, and it becomes clear that Doyle is suggesting that while its traditional form may be undergoing restructuring, the edifice of the Irish family is fundamentally sound. After an argument with her father, Sharon threatens to leave home, and Jimmy Sr.'s inarticulate, tearful apology catches the note struck by the book as a whole:

—I behaved like a bollix, I realize tha' now. —I didn't think you'd leave. Don't leave. We need you here. Your mammy —Your mammy's not always the best. Because of —Yeh know tha' yourself. I'm a fuckin' waster. Jimmy's worse . . . Poor Veronica. . . . Believe me, Sharon, we need you.

(p. 162)

The central message of *The Snapper* is that while the lives of Irish working people are not without difficulties, their innate resilience, and especially the fundamental strength of the family unit, is enough to see them through the various hardships they face. This message is reinforced by *The Van*, the final installment of *The Barrytown Trilogy*.

Doyle is careful to ensure a degree of continuity between the three novels. *The Snapper* ends with Sharon's determination to snub community opinion and purge her own feelings of disgust by defiantly naming her baby Georgina after George Burgess; *The Van*'s first scene introduces us to the toddler, now known simply as Gina. *The Van* is a significantly longer and more complex book than its predecessors, and it is also the most explicitly topical in its concerns. Jimmy Rabbitte Sr. now functions as a vehicle through which Doyle can examine the crisis in the traditional working-class notion of masculinity, brought on by the socioeconomic changes of the postmodern era. The book opens with Jimmy, unemployed and disconsolate, moping about the house and killing time in various unproductive activities. His role as breadwinner has been disrupted, and he consequently perceives a series of threats to his position as head of the family. Doyle conveys this process with great subtlety, never dwelling on it or even stating it outright, but allowing the reader to develop an understanding of the situation through a succession of small incidents. When his son Jimmy Jr.

gives him a small sum of money, Jimmy Sr. has to retire to the bedroom until his tears of rage and shame have passed. When his wife, Veronica, jokingly tells him he is "useless," he has a fleeting desire to kick her in the stomach. The connection between the father's economic impotence and the changes in the structure of family authority is illustrated with great pathos in the following scene:

—What abou' you? said Darren to his da. —Look at the state o' you.

Jimmy Sr looked at Darren. Darren was looking back at him, waiting for a reaction. Jimmy Sr wasn't going to take that from him, not for another couple of years.

He pointed his fork at Darren.

—Don't you forget who paid for tha' dinner in front of you, son, righ'.

—I know who paid for it, said Darren. —The state.

Jimmy Sr looked like he'd been told that someone had died.

(p. 102)

There are several hints at the serious consequences of Jimmy Sr.'s decline in authority, of which the most poignant are the references to another son, Leslie, who has run away from home and is now a petty criminal and delinquent somewhere in England. As the plot develops, Jimmy Sr. also begins to display the symptoms of a sexual midlife crisis. He lusts after his sons' girlfriends and his friend's wife and wistfully watches "young ones" pass in the street. To make matters worse, Jimmy's economic troubles are not shared by the community as a whole. Having been a plasterer, he is from that segment of semiskilled manual workers affected most devastatingly by the economic restructuring of the 1980s, a decade that brought unprecedented prosperity to more affluent sectors of society. Dublin is awash with expensive consumer goods, none of which Jimmy can afford, and as Christmas approaches, he meanders through his changing native city, feeling financially, sexually, and chronologically superfluous:

He went into town and wandered around. He hadn't done that in years. It had changed quite a lot; pubs he'd known and even streets were gone. It looked good though, he thought. He could tell you one thing: there was money in this town. . . . Young ones must have been earning real money these days as well; you could tell by the way they dressed. He'd sat on that stone bench with the two bronze oul' ones chin-wagging on it, beside the Halfpenny Bridge; he'd sat on the side of that one day and he'd counted fifty-four great-looking young ones going by in only a quarter of an hour; brilliant-looking women now, and all of them dressed beautifully, the height of style; they must have paid fortunes for the stuff they had on them; you could tell.

(pp. 68–69)

While Jimmy emblematically sits beside the bronze statue of "oul' ones," his wife is attending night school, his son Darren is set to become the first of the Rabbittes to go to university, and his daughter, Sharon, has a young daughter to care for. With no equivalent stimulus to divert him, Jimmy Sr.'s only recourse is to the bastion of traditional Irish masculinity, the pub. His drinking companions, Bimbo and Bertie, played minor roles in *The Snapper*, but in *The Van* they are fleshed out with skillful characterization, and the novel's most humorous interchanges are the deadpan jests and semiserious mockery that the men engage in over their pints.

Things begin to look up for Jimmy when Bimbo is laid off. At first he is just happy to have a companion for the lonely, empty afternoons, but when Bimbo uses his severance money to buy a fish-and-chips van, Jimmy sees an economic as well as a social opportunity. The two men go into business together, conquering their anxieties about doing what they consider to be women's work. Jimmy persuades Veronica to school him in the art of potato peeling and even to allow him to cook the family dinner for the first time ever. In this exchange Veronica and Bimbo's wife, Maggie, attempt to teach their husbands the rudiments of catering:

—Now, said Maggie. —What I thought we'd do tonight was finalise the menu.

—Wha' menu? said Bimbo.

—Yeah, said Jimmy Sr.

He was worried; he didn't want to be a fuckin' waiter. Bimbo nearly whispered over the table to Maggie.

—It's only a van.

Veronica started laughing, and Maggie did as well. Jimmy Sr wasn't sure what was happening, but he couldn't help thinking that he was being hijacked, himself and Bimbo.

—The menu, lads, said Maggie — a bit sarcastically, Jimmy Sr thought — is the list of things that the customer chooses from.

—Like on the wall behind the counter? said Jimmy Sr.

—Exactly, said Maggie.

Jimmy Sr nodded, like he'd known that all along; he was just checking.

(p. 135)

The two friends' enterprise is well timed: they open for business just as the Irish national football team's famous success in the 1990 World Cup is getting under way, and they sell enormous quantities of "dunphies and chips" to crowds of ecstatic fans. (A "dunphy," we are told, is Dublin slang for a sausage, after the soccer commentator Eamon Dunphy, who is widely considered a "prick.") Soon Sharon is brought in to help, and some of Doyle's funniest dialogue captures the chaos as the inexperienced trio tries to keep up with the demands of the drunken and ravenous horde:

—Wha' was tha'? he asked the young one.

—Curry chips, she said, raising her eyes to heaven.

—No curry chips, Jimmy Sr told her.

—Why not?

—Cos we're not fuckin' Chinese, said Jimmy Sr. —This is an Irish Chipper.

—That's stupih, said the young one.

—Next!

—Hang on, hang on! A large single an' – an' –

—Hurry —

—A spice-burger.

—A large an' a spice, Sharon, please!! Jimmy Sr roared over his shoulder. —Next. —You with the haircut there; wha' d'yeh want?

—World peace.

—You're barred. Next!

(pp. 168–169)

In the style of a classic morality tale, however, the economic success of Bimbo and Jimmy gradually leads to a breakdown in their friendship. This theme converges with the treatment of Jimmy's sexual insecurities in a climactic episode in which Jimmy persuades the happily married Bimbo to join him for a night of skirt chasing. As the evening wears on, Jimmy drunkenly expounds the stereotypical male view of women's traditional roles, which seems to offer him a sense of certainty amid his confusion. In his rambling, sexual and economic envy merge to revealing effect:

—Yeah, said Jimmy Sr. —Nine ou' o' ten women, if they had the choice between money an' looks, they'd go for the money.

—What abou' Maggie an' Veronica?

—Not women like Maggie an' Veronica, said Jimmy Sr. —I'm not talkin' abou' women like tha'. Ordinary women, if yeh known what I mean.

He waited for Bimbo to nod.

—I mean the kind o' women we saw in tha' place back there. Stylish an' glamorous —

—I think Maggie an' —

85

Jimmy Sr stopped him.

—I know wha' you're going to say, Bimbo. And I agree with yeh. They are as good lookin'. But they're not like those brassers back there, sure they're not?

—No, said Bimbo. —Not really.

—Thank God, wha', said Jimmy Sr. —Can yeh imagine lettin' any o' them floozies rear your kids?

(p. 258)

The simmering tension between the two men comes to a head when they attempt to chat up two women in a nightclub. Bimbo successfully "gets off" with one of the girls, and lets slip to her the true nature of their occupation. Jimmy, who has told his prospective conquest that they are "in catering," is mortified. When the woman rejects his advances, he blames his lack of success on Bimbo's indiscretion, and the night ends with the two men brawling in the club's bathroom. They patch up their friendship, but Bimbo takes the incident as an insult to his van, and shortly afterward he announces that instead of their dividing the profits equally, he will pay Jimmy a wage. Their relationship thus changes from a friendship into a contractual bargain between employer and employee. Jimmy takes every opportunity to remind Bimbo of this fact:

It was enjoyable enough in a sad sort of way, acting the prick.

—Will I turn on the gas?

—Wha' d'yeh mean? said Bimbo.

—Will I turn on the gas? said Jimmy Sr.

They'd just parked outside the Hikers and climbed into the back. It was a very stupid question.

—I don't get yeh, said Bimbo, although Jimmy Sr saw that he was beginning to smell a bit of a rat.

—D'yeh want me to turn on the gas? Jimmy Sr asked him.

—Wha' d'yeh need to ask me for? said Bimbo.

—Well, ——you're the boss —

—I'll turn it on meself!

He went too far sometimes, like asking Bimbo would he take the chips out of the fryer, would he put the chips into the fryer; he just fell into the habit of asking Bimbo's permission to do everything.

—You'll ask me can yeh wipe your arse next, said Bimbo once.

—No, I won't, said Jimmy Sr. —Me arse is me own.

It was at that moment – the way Bimbo had said it; the pretend annoyance in his voice – that Jimmy Sr realised that Bimbo was enjoying it, being the boss; like he was giving out to a thick lad, a thick kid he liked: he wasn't embarrassed any more.

(pp. 283–284)

In such passages Doyle records in miniature the social effects of Ireland's integration into the global economy. As throughout the Western world, traditional working-class jobs that fostered solidarity and patriarchal, cohesive communities were rapidly disappearing from Ireland during the 1980s. The kind of entrepreneurial, service-oriented business that Bimbo and Jimmy set up was precisely the kind of response to prevailing trends that Western governments urged on the working class. But economic restructuring on this scale brings with it major alterations in social customs and attitudes. In *The Van* Doyle indicates the corrosive effect of market-oriented relations of production on the ties of personal friendship and examines the decline in traditional male roles in working-class culture. These two themes converge in the figure of Jimmy Sr., as when he reflects on the causes behind his old friend's drastic transformation:

That wagon of a wife of his had ruined him. She'd taken her time doing it, but she'd done it. That was Jimmy Sr's theory anyway. There was no other way of explaining it.

—Look it, he told Bertie. —She was perfectly happy all those years when he was bringing home a wage.

—Si —, said Bertie in a way that told Jimmy Sr to keep talking.

—She was happy with tha' cos she thought tha' that was as much as she was gettin'. Does tha' make sense, Bertie?

—It does, si. She knew no better.

—Exactly. ——Now, but, now. Fuck me, she knows better now. There isn't enough cod in the fuckin' sea for her now. Or chips in the fuckin' ground; Jaysis.

—That's greed for yeh compadre.

—Who're yeh tellin'.

It was good talking to Bertie. It was great.

—It's her, said Jimmy Sr. —It's not really Bimbo at all.

—D'yeh think so? said Bertie.

—Ah yeah, said Jimmy Sr. —Def'ny.

(pp. 293–294)

Bimbo and Maggie prosper from the new social mobility, climbing from the working class into the middle class. As Jimmy sees it, this sparks an insatiable acquisitive urge in Bimbo that is undermining their personal friendship and transforming it into an unequal business partnership with Bimbo as capitalist and himself as exploited worker. Jimmy acts out the latter role with relish, demonstrating to Bimbo the altered nature of their relationship by insisting on tea breaks and even threatening to join a union. He consoles himself with the thought that the "mean, conniving, tight-arsed little cunt" (p. 294) that his friend has become is not the "real" Bimbo. We have already seen how Jimmy has been feeling emasculated by the combined forces of unemployment and middle age, so it seems natural when he blames Maggie for making Bimbo mercenary. The cutthroat competition of the marketplace is thus subliminally associated with the new self-assertion of women: both represent clear and present threats to the traditional, Irish masculine way of life, and, for Jimmy, the two developments become almost inseparable. Doyle makes something of a concession to the lighthearted tone of *The Barrytown Trilogy* by giving *The Van* a happy, almost sentimental ending: Bimbo and Jimmy, drunkenly reconciled, decide to "kill" the van by driving it into the sea. But the overall atmosphere of the book is significantly darker than those of its predecessors, and Doyle is clearly giving notice of the more serious concerns that will animate his later fiction.

DRAMA

DURING the late 1980s, while Doyle was writing *The Barrytown Trilogy*, he also scripted two plays, *Brownbread* and *War*. Also set in Barrytown, these can be read as supplements to the novels, adding local color, fleshing out Doyle's view of the neighborhood, and deepening our understanding of certain character types. In 1985, between struggles with early drafts of *The Commitments*, Doyle attended a rehearsal of a play titled *Wasters, the Passion Machine*, written by his friend Paul Mercier. In the introduction to the Penguin edition of his own two plays, Doyle recalls the performance in terms that are highly revealing of his artistic aims and inspirations:

For the first time in my life I saw characters I recognised, people I met every day, the language I heard every day. It was like watching an old cine-film; I could point out people I knew and remember them saying what they said. The way they dressed, walked, held their cans of lager—it was all very familiar. I'll never forget it.

(p. 1)

It is this combined effect of veracity and novelty that Doyle strives to achieve in his own work, especially in the plays he began to write in 1986 at the request of the company that had produced

Wasters. The plays, like the novels, attempt to offer a realistic account of the lives and speech of people who until very recently were rarely the subjects of serious literature.

Doyle's first play, *Brownbread* (1987), is somewhat far-fetched in its plot but uncompromisingly naturalistic in its characterization and dialogue. Like *The Commitments* the play describes an attempt by a gang of young Dubliners to break out of the boredom of their mundane, working-class existence. In this case, however, the young men take the less orthodox route of kidnapping a bishop. Martin Amis has spoken of the decline, in postmodern literature, of the concept of "motivation," which traditionally adds plausibility to the behavior of a fictional character. If the characters of literature seem increasingly lacking in motivation, Amis suggests, this is because many of the actions of real people no longer appear to be animated by any identifiable motive. In *Brownbread* the kidnappers' motivation is the central mystery, often alluded to but never resolved. At first the audience expects to be told exactly why the youths have abducted the bishop, but it becomes more and more clear that they themselves have no idea. Most of the play consists of a series of exchanges among the kidnappers, who are holed up in a terrace house, and various negotiators outside. During one such interchange one of the lads' fathers, Mr. Farrell, raises the obvious question:

FARRELL: Aidan, why are yeh doin' this?

JOHN (*to the lads*): We'll have to think o' somethin'.

FARRELL: Are yeh in the IRA, Aidan?

AO: No way. They're saps.

DONKEY: Ah here!

FARRELL: Or tha' other shower. The I.N.—yeh know. Whatever they fuckin' call themselves.

DONKEY *rolls up his sleeve and shows the tattoo he did on himself at the back of the class when he was in second year.*

DONKEY
(*pointing to the tattoo*): Eire nua. Eire bleedin' nua.

JOHN: You'd die for Ireland, wouldn't yeh?

DONKEY: I would in me brown.

AO (*to* MR FARRELL): No.

FARRELL: Well, why then?

AO (*after a pause*): Jobs.

DONKEY: Wha'!? I don't want a fuckin' job.

(pp. 20–21)

The most immediately plausible political explanations for the crime are thus rejected, and the impression is conveyed that the boys have acted out of an aimless, generalized sense of anomie and alienation. In a novel by the young Irish writer Colin Bateman, *Empire State* (1997), a very similar situation is described to great comic effect when the main character finds himself holding the president of the United States hostage on top of the Empire State Building. Asked by the negotiators why he is doing this, he replies, "For a bit of crack." The Americans panic, assuming that he is a crazed drug addict, but those characters with some fluency in Dublin argot recognize that "crack" is a term meaning "fun" or "a laugh." Much the same sense of aimless, undirected thrill seeking appears to lie behind the actions of *Brownbread*'s teenage kidnappers. About halfway through the play, it emerges that they do not even have a financial incentive. The boys reminisce about stealing apples as children:

BISHOP:	Is kidnapping me a bit like robbing apples?
AO (*not fully convinced*):	Yeah. Sort of.
DONKEY:	What's he on abou'?
BISHOP:	One thing puzzles me. —Why didn't you demand money, a ransom, in exchange for me?
DONKEY:	That's a fuckin' brilliant idea!
JOHN:	Jaysis, yeah! We never thought o' tha'.
DONKEY:	Better than fuckin' jobs annyway, wha'.

(p. 43)

It is this lack of motive, this impression of utter and complete indirection, that provides the play's humor, especially when it is contrasted with the highly organized but completely ineffectual ploys of the negotiators. It transpires that the bishop is an American citizen, and the U.S. government sends its troops into Barrytown to rescue him. But their use of force proves misguided, and negotiation fails, precisely because of the lads' lack of any purpose—they have no demands that the Americans can agree to meet. *Brownbread* squeezes as many laughs as possible out of this farcical situation, but the plot is ultimately too fantastic to suit the down-to-earth realism of Doyle's characters and dialogue. He achieves a more harmonious union between story line and mode of expression in his second play, *War*.

As Doyle reveals in his introduction, *War* is perhaps the most directly autobiographical and explicitly local of all his works: "*War* was inspired by a pile of pub quizzes I took part in, always on Monday night, in the Foxhound Inn, in Kilbarrack, and the Cedar Lounge, in Raheny" (p. 2). Longer and more subtle than *Brownbread*, *War* exhibits Doyle's rapidly developing eye for character and ear for dialogue. The action alternates between the quiz taking place in the Hiker's Rest (the same pub frequented by Jimmy Rabbitte and his friends in *The Barrytown Trilogy*) and the home of the Finnegan family in the days and hours leading up to the competition. Alternation between the public and private houses is used to show how the conflicts and problems of one realm of life get transposed into the other, so that George Finnegan's success or failure in the quiz directly affects his relationship with his wife, Briget. The play also features the Finnegans' teenage daughter, Yvonne, and thus the names of father and daughter anticipate those of George and Yvonne Burgess in *The Snapper*. In that book Yvonne angrily turns on Sharon Rabbitte when the latter announces that George is the father of her daughter, and in the play Yvonne Finnegan also stands up for her father, significantly declaring, "Daddy's great. All my friends think he's great" (p. 133). Bertie, Jimmy Sr.'s drinking companion from *The Barrytown Trilogy*, has an important role in *War*, and another character, Angela, seems to be a blueprint for Paula Spencer in *The Woman Who Walked into Doors*. It appears, then, that *War* provided Doyle with a kind of drawing board on which he could fashion and experiment with the kinds of characters who people his novels. The play's jokes also recall the humor of the novels: they are at once farcical, realistic, and indicative of the serious underlying dynamics of the relationships between the characters:

GEORGE:	Fuck the Beatles; I always said it.
BRIGET:	You always said Fuck somethin' anyway.
GEORGE	*is amused, but not sure what* BRIGET *is getting at.*
BRIGET:	You even said it when you asked me to marry yeh.
GEORGE:	I did not!
BRIGET:	You did so, George. I remember; God. You said, "Will yeh fuckin' marry me?"

(p. 205)

The absurd vision conjured up by George's lack of chivalry becomes less amusing when, later in the play, the situation in the family home turns ugly. Briget's outburst against her husband's continual put-downs indicates that, like Jimmy Rabbitte Sr., George Finnegan is translating his sense of vulnerability about his threatened masculine role into hostility toward his wife's social and professional aspirations. In one scene George flies into a jealous rage when Briget jokes with one of his friends:

BRIGET: It's always the same.
GEORGE: Shut up.
BRIGET: Always, it is. When I wanted tha' job. When—when I wanted to go to Liverpool with the girls. When I did tha' English night class. (*Triumphantly.*) An' I passed it, yeh bastard. Even when I just have a bit o' crack with someone else, yeh put me down.
GEORGE: Shut your fuckin' mouth, will yeh.
BRIGET: Always, yeh put me down. Yeh do, George. Even for laughin' at Tommy, because it wasn't you. Cos you're afraid I'll—

GEORGE *stands closer to* BRIGET, *over her. He clenches his fist and draws it back.*

GEORGE: Shut up!

(p. 191)

The crisis of masculinity, with its accompanying problems of insecurity, resentment, and domestic violence, is beginning to emerge as the dark underside of the happy Irish family portrayed in Doyle's early novels. George channels his aggression and energy—energy that, twenty or thirty years earlier, working-class men might have expended on their jobs—into the puerile competitiveness of Monday-night pub quizzes. The ferocious, cutthroat atmosphere at this event is comic in its extremity until, in the play's last line, we hear Briget, waiting for her husband's return, praying, "Please God, he didn't lose again. Please" (p. 215).

The sensitivity of moments like this is rather rare in Doyle's plays, which tend to accentuate the knockabout humor of his novels at the expense of their underlying sense of gravity. The stage directions for *War* are so lengthy that one gets the impression Doyle wished he were writing a novel, and there is one very long sequence of silent action for which the directions run more than four pages. Much of the most effective characterization is achieved in the stage directions rather than in the dialogue. For example, when we are told of Denis, the pompous quizmaster, that "He was the only person in Barrytown to vote for the Progressive

Democrats in the last election, although he accidentally spoiled his ballot paper" (p. 103), we are given an amusing insight into his personality that is not repeated in any of his own lines. Doyle appears to feel more at ease with screenplays for film or television, where the contributions of the director and cinematographer can supplement and develop the work of the writer, than with scripts for live drama. As two subsequent works confirm, however, Roddy Doyle's real forte is the novel.

PADDY CLARKE HA HA HA *AND* THE WOMAN WHO WALKED INTO DOORS

THE novelty of *Paddy Clarke*, Doyle's most accomplished work by the end of the 1990s, is due to the fact that the author's powers of minute observation and accurate mimicry are here turned upon the mysterious customs and mores of childhood. Doyle always treats Barrytown as a microcosmic, self-contained universe, and to ten-year-old Paddy, who narrates the story, that is precisely what it is. "We owned Barrytown," says Paddy of his gang, "the whole lot of it. It went on forever. It was a country" (p. 150). Nor is this impression undermined by our discovery, later in the book, that Barrytown contains exactly fifty-four houses. The childish viewpoint reveals, more clearly than the adult perspective of *The Barrytown Trilogy,* both the local idiosyncrasies and the universal experiences of the mythical Dublin suburb.

Paddy Clarke is more obviously autobiographical than the *Trilogy.* It is set in the 1960s, when Doyle himself was a child, and it succeeds in evoking the atmosphere of that decade through references to events like the Arab-Israeli war and personalities like George Best. However, the remarkable accuracy with which the novel captures the inner life of a ten-year-old seems less the product of memory than of the author's fourteen years as a schoolteacher. Certain of Paddy's most hilarious observations have about them the ring of actual, overheard conversations:

It was Monday; Henno was in charge of the yard, but he always stayed over at the far side watching whoever was playing handball. He was mad; if he'd come over to our side, the shed, he'd have caught loads of us in the act. If a teacher caught five fellas smoking or doing serious messing he got a bonus in his wages; that was what Fluke Cassidy said and his uncle was a teacher.

(p. 8)

The confused and contradictory, but winningly enthusiastic, tone of childhood anecdote is superbly rendered in Paddy's asides: "We saw mice. I never saw any, but I heard them. I said I saw them. Kevin saw loads of them. I saw a squashed rat" (p. 13). Doyle's choice of idiom and figure of speech is brilliantly attuned to the boy's range, as when Paddy remarks of a picture on his family's wall that "Jesus had his head tilted sideways, a bit like a kitten" (p. 38). As the story progresses, Paddy is gradually revealed as a particularly sensitive and intelligent boy. His speech begins to include adult-sounding phrases, often culled from his reading: "He'd lived under the shadow of the guillotine itself. . . . He found his sea legs almost immediately" (p. 47). Paddy absorbs stimuli from his social and intellectual environment with great intensity and vigor. When he encounters Richmal Compton's Just William books, a prewar series of novels describing the adventures of an upper-class English schoolboy, the working-class Irish lad gleefully adopts William's alien figures of speech:

I read William. I read them all. There were thirty-four of them. I owned eight of them. The others were in the library. William the Pirate was the best. I say! gasped William. I've never seen such a clever dog. I say! he gasped, he's splendid. Hi, Toby! Toby! Come here, old chap! Toby was nothing loth.

(p. 57)

Doyle does not flinch from describing the cruelty and sadism of boyhood, however, and the novel contains several excruciating scenes of beating and torture, mostly inflicted by Paddy upon his little brother, known as Sinbad. The author skillfully shows how Paddy genuinely believes that such exploits are carried out in fun. "Liam got serious, so we stopped" (p. 7), he remarks of one rough game, and on another occasion he says, "We threw stones at each other, to miss" (p. 15). The reader, of course, is well aware of the serious personal conflicts and resolutions worked out by young boys through what they think of as play, or "messing." *Paddy Clarke* thus provides an excellent example of the use of an "unreliable narrator"—a central figure whose recounting of the story reveals, unknown to himself, the skewed, partial nature of his own understanding of events.

Paddy's grasp of these childhood events is inevitably rather tenuous, for such events involve the very adult topics of domestic violence, separation, and divorce. The breakdown of his parents' marriage is conveyed with great subtlety, and Doyle is careful not to depart from Paddy's innocent perspective as he describes it. At first the boy notices that all is not well between his parents only when their arguments directly concern him, or when they do not react to his conversational gambits in the way he had anticipated:

—I want to be a missionary.
—Good boy, she said, but not the way I'd wanted. I wanted her to cry. I wanted my da to shake my hand. I told him when he got home from his work.
—I have a vocation, I said.
—No you don't, he said. —You're too young.
—I do, I said. —God has spoken to me.
It was all wrong.
He spoke to my ma.
—I told you, he said.
He sounded angry.
—Encouraging this rubbish, he said.
—I didn't encourage it, she said.
—Yes, you bloody did, he said.
She looked like she was making her mind up.
—You did!
He roared it.
She went out of the kitchen, beginning to run. She tried to undo the knot of her apron. He went after her. He looked different, like he'd been caught doing something. They left me alone. I didn't know what had happened. I didn't know what I'd done.

(p. 53)

There was a time when an announcement by a ten-year-old Irish boy that he felt a vocation to the priesthood would have been greeted by his parents with tears of delight and rejoicing. By the 1960s, however, the increasing secularization of Irish society meant that it merely provides the fuel for another of the increasingly frequent and serious arguments between the Clarkes. With great insight and economy of expression, Doyle traces the childish logic by which Paddy concludes that he is somehow to blame for the argument, and the reader is made to appreciate how a ten-year-old might easily reach that conclusion. Paddy's reaction to the situation is movingly contradictory. On the one hand the conflict makes him feel small and immature, reversing the power relations between himself and his brother, who is protected by his youth from a full understanding of the situation:

It was like he'd become me and I was him. I was going to wet the bed. . . . He'd found out; he'd found out. I'd wanted him to talk because I was scared. Pretending to be protecting him, I'd wanted him close to me, to share, to listen together; to stop it or run away. He knew: I was frightened and lonely, more than he was.

(p. 260)

After the way he has been brutalized by Paddy throughout the book, however, Sinbad is understandably inclined to withhold his sympathy. When his father eventually leaves home, Paddy is forced to grow up fast, and he slowly acquires a disturbingly adult mode of perception. On the penultimate page we discover the cruel significance of the novel's title as Paddy, now ostracized by his classmates, listens to them chant:

—Paddy Clarke—
Paddy Clarke—
Has no da.
Ha ha ha!
I didn't listen to them. They were only kids.

(p. 281)

This transition to maturity is confirmed in the last scene, when Mr. Clarke returns to the house with Christmas presents, to be greeted by Paddy as an equal:

He put out his hand for me to shake it.
—How are you?
His hand felt cold and big, dry and hard.
—Very well, thank you.

(p. 282)

Having broadened his range by writing from a child's perspective in *Paddy Clarke*, Doyle extended it further by adopting a female voice in *The Woman Who Walked into Doors* (1996). The narrator of this grim tale is Paula Spencer, who also appears as the battered and abused wife in Doyle's television series, *Family*. While the program is memorable mostly for the figure of her husband, the villainous Charlo, the novel involves a shift of emphasis from persecutor to victim. Unlike *Family*, the book offers the reader an understanding of how Paula came to be in her position. Charlo's main attraction for Paula, as she proudly admits at the novel's beginning, was sexual:

I swooned the first time I saw Charlo. I actually did. I didn't faint or fall on the floor but my legs went rubbery on me and I giggled. I suddenly knew that I had lungs

because they were empty and collapsing. . . . We'd been dancing together in a circle, our jackets and jumpers and bags on the floor in front of us, and I was sweating a bit. And I felt the sweat when I saw Charlo. This wasn't a crush—this wasn't David Cassidy or David Essex over there—it was sex. I wanted to go over there and bite him.

(p. 3)

Paula's reminiscences of the couple's teenage romance conjure up the 1970s in much the same way Paddy Clarke's narrative evokes the 1960s and *The Commitments* recalls the 1980s: through strategic references to popular culture. As in much postmodern fiction, Doyle's characters are partly defined through reference points in mass culture, and they tend to experience reality and interact with each other in ways that are colored by the media and entertainment industries. Paula and Charlo's first sexual encounter is marred for her by his failure to live up to the standards of gentility set by Robert Redford and Lee Majors, and Charlo's introduction to Paula's parents is carried out entirely through the medium of television:

—Sit yourselves down, said Daddy.
—We're watching Bob Monkhouse, said Mammy.
Charlo said nothing.
—D'you like Bob Monkhouse, Charles? said Daddy.
—He's alright, said Charlo.
—We like him.
—He's good guests, said Charlo.
I nearly fell off my chair. He was really trying.
—He does, said Daddy. —Sometimes.
Daddy looked at Charlo looking at the telly. . . . —Catweezil's on after this, said Daddy.—Although, God knows, the reception could be better. D'you like Catweezil, Charles?
—No, said Charlo. . . .
—We like it, said Daddy.
—It's a kid's programme, said Charlo.
—We like it.
—It's brutal.
—We like it.
There was nothing after that.

(pp. 117–118)

Twenty years later, Paula mentions that she watches *Coronation Street* for the sole purpose of having something to talk about with her fellow cleaners at work. Although she is a highly sympathetic character whose problems Doyle attributes to her environment rather than to any moral failings, Paula Spencer is also an example of the dangers of living life through the mass media. As she surveys the wreckage of her marriage and family, she consoles herself by thinking of the pop music she heard in the background as various tragedies and disasters befell her: "That's one thing about my life, it has a great soundtrack" (p. 94). The implication is that for many people the trauma of contemporary existence is such that they can get through life only by experiencing it as "hyperreality," as if it were a film with a "great soundtrack." It therefore seems morbidly appropriate that Paula discovers the manner of Charlo's death by watching the television news. The fact of its being televised makes it seem absurd, unreal, and consequently bearable. In this scene she breaks the news to her daughter, Nicola:

> —Shot, I said it again. —Can you believe it?
> We were still laughing. Denise closed the kitchen door so the kids outside couldn't hear us; it wouldn't have sounded proper. It was a bit indecent, laughing at the way your husband had got himself killed. We all had to wipe our eyes. I noticed that. Even Carmel.
> —The police, I told Nicola.
> She nodded.
> —We can watch it on the News, I said.
> Her forehead creased, the way it does.
> —Did they film it?
> —What? No, no. I meant just the news about it; it'll be on.
>
> (pp. 63–64)

Although it may bring comfort in moments of crisis, the fantasy diet of soap operas and pop music cannot compensate for the hopeless inadequacy of Charlo as husband and father. Once again, Doyle's major theme here is the crisis in working-class masculinity. Paula recalls her own father as distant but not cruel—"Fathers were different then" (pp. 46–47)—and when she picks up her children from school, she wryly notes the changes that the years have brought to the role of the Irish male:

> There are a few fathers there as well. They don't talk, not even to one another. They're embarrassed. No jobs to go to. Women's work. You'd feel sorry for them.
>
> (p. 96)

However, Doyle is too intelligent a writer to take the easy option of blaming Charlo's degeneracy entirely on the socioeconomic redundancy of working-class men. In a long, reflective passage near the end of the book, Paula considers the source of Charlo's rage and concludes that life is not, after all, as easily comprehended as the plot of a film:

> If he'd been a bit different he would have been great at something. . . . If he'd had the education. If he'd had other work when all the building around Dublin stopped and there was nothing left for him to do. He would have put that anger to use. He wouldn't have been wasted. . . . Charlo Spencer lost his job and started beating his wife. It's not as simple as that. He started robbing. He shot a woman and killed her. Because he didn't have a job, was rejected by society. It would be nice if it was that easy. If I could just think back and say Yes, that was how it was. Charlo Spencer lost his job and started beating his wife. I could rest if I believed that; I could rest. But I keep on thinking and I'll never come to a tidy ending. Every day. I think about it every minute. Why did he do it? No real answers come back, no big Aha.
>
> (pp. 191–192)

We have returned once again to the issue of motivation, and the disturbing question arises of whether there is any connection between the aimless, senseless, but infantile violence of Paddy Clarke and the aimless, senseless, and very adult violence of Charlo Spencer. Doyle deserves great admiration for the direction in which he has turned his career since 1993. The antics of the "happy poor" that fill his early work always had an edge to them; in his later writing Doyle shifts the emphasis to the depressing elements of working-class life, preserving his sense of humor but employing it to mine an increasingly black vein. For a writer who had established a comfortable and lucrative reputation at a very early stage in his career, this shift in emphasis was a bold and potentially risky step. The courage and integrity revealed by such a move bode well for Doyle's future artistic development.

POPULAR AND CRITICAL REACTION

THE book-buying public's reaction to Doyle's work was instant and unambiguous: at the turn of the twenty-first century he was one of the most popular serious novelists. *Paddy Clarke*, for example, sold many more copies than any other Booker Prize winner. Doyle's appeal was certainly augmented by the successful film versions of his trilogy, but these were not sufficient to explain his success. It seemed, rather, that like Martin Amis and Welsh, Doyle had transcended the gap between the popular and the canonical. People who read nothing else read *The Commitments* or Welsh's *Trainspotting* partly because of these books' literacy in rock music, soccer, and other forms of popular culture, but also because the authors had hit upon a style that was genuinely accessible without compromising aesthetic merit. In this broad appeal, as well as in his subject matter, Doyle was preeminently an artist of the postmodern era.

Doyle's first book was published in 1987, and a decade later there were no critical monographs devoted to his work, although Ulrike Paschel's *No Mean City?* (1998) deals with Doyle's portrayal of Dublin in some detail, placing it in the context of works by other young Irish novelists. What critical essays that did appear tended to take a "postcolonial" approach, focusing on the specifically Irish themes of the fiction and dwelling in particular on *The Commitments'* suggestive analogies between the sociocultural position of the Irish and that of African Americans. Essays by Lorraine Piroux and Lauren Onkey fall into this category. Other critics, such as Brian Cosgrove and M. Keith Booker, preferred to consider Doyle as a chronicler of Ireland's sudden and drastic transition from one of the poorest and most ideologically backward areas of Europe into the forward-looking "Celtic tiger." However, at the turn of the century it was far too soon to predict the kind of writer Roddy Doyle would turn out to be, and only a rash critic would attempt an overview of his career at this early stage. Doyle's swift development in the nine years between *The Commitments* and *The Woman Who Walked into Doors* gave every indication that his future progress would be every bit as rapid and profound.

SELECTED BIBLIOGRAPHY

I. Novels. *The Commitments* (London, 1987, 1988; New York, 1989); *The Snapper* (London, 1990; New York, 1992); *The Van* (London and New York, 1991); *The Barrytown Trilogy* (London and New York, 1992); *Paddy Clarke Ha Ha Ha* (London and New York, 1993); *The Woman Who Walked into Doors* (London and New York, 1996).

II. Dramas and Screenplays. *The Commitments*, with Dick Clement and Ian La Frenais (1991); *Brownbread and War* (London, 1992; New York, 1994); *The Snapper* (1993); *The Van* (1996).

III. Critical Studies and Interviews. Lauren Onkey, "Celtic Soul Brothers," in *Eire-Ireland* 28 (fall 1993); Charles Foran, "The Troubles of Roddy Doyle," in *Saturday Night* 111 (April 1996); Brian Cosgrove, "Roddy Doyle's Backward Look: Tradition and Modernity in *Paddy Clarke Ha Ha Ha*," in *Studies* 85 (fall 1996); M. Keith Booker, "Late Capitalism Comes to Dublin: American Popular Culture in the Novels of Roddy Doyle," in *Ariel* 28 (July 1997); Lorraine Piroux, " 'I'm Black an' I'm Proud': Reinventing Irishness in Roddy Doyle's *The Commitments*," in *College Literature* 25 (spring 1998); Ulrike Paschel, *No Mean City?: The Image of Dublin in the Novels of Dermot Bolger, Roddy Doyle, and Val Mulkerns* (New York, 1998).

PENELOPE FITZGERALD

(1916–   )

Karen Karbiener

PENELOPE FITZGERALD'S NINTH novel, *The Blue Flower* (1995), was cultivated with the wisdom and experience gathered over eight decades, but it took less than a year for the success of the book to bring Fitzgerald's literary career to full bloom. In 1997, the year *The Blue Flower* first appeared in an American edition, her collected works had sold fewer than 3,000 copies in the United States. In 1998 *The Blue Flower* went into its tenth U.S. printing, with 100,000 copies in circulation. Fitzgerald won the 1998 National Book Critics Circle fiction prize, the first time in the award's history that it was given to a non-American. She also held a prestigious post as judge on the panel for England's Booker Prize, which she had won in 1979. By 1999 all of her novels had become available in American editions, although Fitzgerald had waited about two decades for *The Bookshop* (1978) and *Human Voices* (1980) to be picked up by a stateside publisher.

All this recognition might seem the perfect culmination of a literary career for a writer in her eighties. But Fitzgerald only began writing when most people think about retiring, and she has shown no signs of putting down her pen. Perhaps she has felt obliged to make up for her first sixty years, which she spent doing almost everything but writing: she raised a family of three children, nursed a dying husband and beloved father, lived in a Thames houseboat and in an abandoned oyster warehouse, and worked as a journalist at the BBC and at odd jobs in various locales, from a bookshop on the East Anglian coast to a performing-arts school for children in London. When Fitzgerald finally embarked on a literary career in the 1970s, she had plenty of ideas for novels, nearly all of them inspired by her own life experiences.

Despite her successes, Fitzgerald has expressed some regrets concerning the way her career unfolded. "I have never been a young writer, and never belonged to a group, so really I have missed out," she admitted to Peter Lennon in 1998 (*Guard-*

ian, April 13). It is telling that the writers to whom she has been most often compared, Evelyn Waugh and P. G. Wodehouse, died before she even began writing. The careers that afford the best analogues to her own are perhaps those of Sebastian Faulks and Pat Barker, novelists who may not share Fitzgerald's status as octogenarian and grandmother but have likewise contributed to the new respectability of historical fiction.

"WE ARE A WRITING FAMILY"

THE important foreground to Fitzgerald's own literary life is her close relationship with the paternal side of her family. Her father and his brothers not only set respected precedents that greatly influenced her decision to take up writing, but they themselves also functioned as a subject for her second book, a biography titled *The Knox Brothers* (1977). The anecdotes about the brothers reveal her pride and affection for her father and uncles, as the style and tone of her writing demonstrate her intellectual inheritances from them.

Fitzgerald's father, Edmund George Valpy Knox, was the eldest and most long-lived of the four brothers. For nearly twenty-five years, "Evoe" served on the staff of *Punch,* an illustrated weekly comic periodical that was founded in 1841. Over the years the staff of *Punch* included such literary luminaries as William Makepeace Thackeray and Douglas Jerrold. Evoe, too, ensured his name in British literary history when he served as editor of the magazine from 1932 to 1940. A gifted wit and a master of understatement, Evoe helped shape Fitzgerald's trademark dry, spare humor. In an autobiographical sketch she recalls his preservation of his peculiar humor until the end: " 'One gets so little practice at this,' said my father gently when, in 1971, he lay dying" (Contemporary Authors Autobiography Series, vol. 10, p. 103).

Her uncles, too, are remembered for their intellectual yet playful banter. Dillwyn, called Dilly, was a brilliant Greek scholar who worked as a cryptographer during World War I and was also an extreme agnostic whose attitude was "always to reprove [God] for not existing." As Fitzgerald details in *The Knox Brothers,* Dilly made wry references to Jesus Christ as "that deluded individual, J.C."—humor that must have been more acerbic to the two brothers who were priests. But even Uncle Wilfred, the Anglo-Catholic priest, had a gift for sardonic wit: on one occasion, he informed his brothers that "no congregation ought to have to listen to a sermon for more than ten minutes, and any priest or minister who went on longer than that ought to have his income cut down proportionately every thirty seconds." The sharp wit of such aphorisms, and Wilfred's often expressed praise for spare, economical prose, were much admired by his niece.

Like so many of Fitzgerald's protagonists, the Knox brothers engaged in active intellectual struggles to establish meaning or order in the world. A precedent for such pursuits had been set by her father's father, the evangelic bishop of Manchester. Wilfred and the fourth brother, Ronnie, sought answers through spirituality as well, and both were ordained as priests. Dilly continued to question his faith in any system and denounced all religions. Evoe seemed to find some satisfaction through literature. The different paths the brothers ventured upon in the quest for "the truth" must have been bewildering for a young girl, but perhaps their various approaches and goals also helped Fitzgerald understand that there are no easy solutions and answers to life's questions; such a philosophy may account for her novels' frequent lack of closure.

Fitzgerald was gifted with the Knox family's natural intelligence, and she also was plagued with their common dilemma of how to balance it with a rich emotional life. Her difficulty in compromising one for the other is demonstrated best by her decision to embark on a serious literary career only after her children were grown and her husband's illness had passed. In *The Knox Brothers* she concludes a chapter on the religious uncertainties tormenting the four brothers by articulating the fundamental question asked by each of them: "God speaks to us through the intellect, and through the intellect we should direct our lives.

But if we are creatures of reason, what are we to do with our hearts?" Such broad epistemological questions also loom large for Fred Fairly and Friedrich von Hardenberg, the protagonists of *The Gate of Angels* (1990) and *The Blue Flower,* respectively.

Clearly, the paternal side of Fitzgerald's parentage influenced her decision to become a writer as well as her understanding of the value of understatement and wit in expression and her courage in the search for higher "truths." As for her mother's part in helping shape her life and career, Christine Hicks Knox is rarely mentioned by Fitzgerald or her biographers. Fitzgerald does relate that her mother came from a family "so musical that they could give an entire parish concert between them" (CAAS, p. 103)—although she is also quick to mention that she herself was not born with this gift.

The Feminist Companion to Literature in English describes Christine Hicks Knox as "a moderate suffragette," and this term may well apply to her daughter, at least as far as her writing is concerned. Although none of her female protagonists are crusaders for women's rights, they can be self-sufficient working women (Daisy in *Gate of Angels*), capable single parents (*Offshore's* Nenna), and powerful, authoritative figures (Freddie Wentworth of *At Freddie's* is a prime example). "I think women are stronger than men," she told Peter Lennon. "I make them stronger in my novels." Perhaps Christine stands as the silent inspiration behind these strong characterizations.

LIFE

In her sketch for the Contemporary Authors Autobiography Series, Fitzgerald writes, "I think that the best way to continue with these notes about my life would be to look back through the novels I have written" (CAAS, p. 104). The novels do indeed inform readers about Fitzgerald's various experiences, just as a sketch of Fitzgerald's life may assist in providing a more nuanced reading of her novels.

Penelope Fitzgerald, the second child of two, was born in Lincoln, England, on 17 December 1916. Young Penelope did have much in common with her older and wilder brother, Rawle, although he was to share in her destiny as a writer; after being held in a Japanese prisoner of war camp during World War II, Rawle became a journalist and a distinguished Far East correspondent.

Her father, who had returned from World War I with a wounded shoulder, struggled to keep his family comfortable on his *Punch* wages. "Making your living by being funny is always hard work, and, in the 1920s, not well paid," she writes (CAAS, p. 102). For a while Edmund Knox commuted to the *Punch* offices in London an hour each way from the village of Balcombe in Sussex, but in 1922, when he was asked to be the theater critic as well as the deputy assistant editor for *Punch,* the family moved to the city, settling in Hampstead. Fitzgerald remembers with fondness the years at 34 Well Walk, a location rendered poetic for her not only because John Keats had strolled under the lime trees of that street, but by the calls of the muffinmen during winter months, the scents of the lavender sellers in summertime, and the sight of the lamplighters who gave the streets a certain glow each night. Fitzgerald's growing interest in literature was encouraged by expeditions to the Poetry Bookshop in Bloomsbury—an important place in the history of British letters that encouraged young poets such as Charlotte Mew, and young readers such as Fitzgerald, by selling rhyme sheets—"a penny plain, twopence colored," writes Fitzgerald in her biography of Mew. "A whole generation learned to love poetry from these rhyme sheets" (*Charlotte Mew and Her Friends,* p. 142).

Fitzgerald's passion for books and reading brought her to Somerville College in Oxford, where she received first-class honors in English literature in 1939. She might have continued her studies there had not her love for learning come up against her patriotism. Within the year she took a job at Broadcasting House, headquarters of the wartime BBC. For six years Broadcasting House provided the British public with its sole source of news and wartime instruction. In her biographical sketch for CAAS she recalls the dramatic experience of living twenty-four hours a day in a building that looked like a great ship "with the best engineers in the world, and a crew varying between the intensely respectable and the barely sane. . . . At night with all its blazing portholes blacked out, it towered over a flotilla of taxis, each dropping off a spectator or two" (p. 104). She also admits to a love affair "with someone very much

older and more important, without the least glimmer of a hope of any return" (pp. 104–105).

Such dramatics would not last long with the subdued and level-headed Fitzgerald. "Certainly, towards the end of the war or just after it we all of us married, had children, and forgot why and even how we'd managed to love without return," she wrote (CAAS, p. 105). On 15 August 1953 she married Desmond Fitzgerald, whom she describes as an "Irish soldier" in the "travelling business."

With three children and very little money, the Fitzgeralds made do with some unusual living situations in their first twenty years of marriage. In the late 1950s they lived in a building that had once been an oyster warehouse, in the seaside town of Southwold. With the railway closed, the river silted up, and the car ferry ruined during the great floods of 1953, Southwold was cut off from public transport; without a car, the family found itself isolated from the world at large. *The Bookshop* was inspired by the insularity and gossipy nature of the town (renamed "Hardborough" by Fitzgerald) and her experiences working at its only bookstore. Returning to London in the early 1960s, the Fitzgeralds again found alternative living quarters, this time on a Thames houseboat docked on Chelsea Reach between the picturesque Battersea and Albert bridges. *Grace,* as the old barge was called, was connected to the wharf by gangplanks so unsteady that mail carriers and milkmen refused delivery, so once again the family found itself in the strange state of being isolated among strangers. *Grace* had never been fitted with an engine, so the belly of its hold served as ample living space, and the family learned to use lavatories only on falling tides and endure the bitter smell of tar-covered driftwood burning in the stove. As had been the case at Southwold, Fitzgerald's resourcefulness and humor served the family well, especially during potentially disastrous moments such as the two occasions when *Grace* sank. "We were taken off the first time by a kindly Swede in a dinghy," writes Fitzgerald, "and the second time by the river police in their patrol launch. Among our drenched and floating possessions I saw a bottle of champagne which had been intended for a party. I was glad to be able to retrieve the champagne so as to have something to give, in gratitude, to the police, who reminded me that they were not allowed to drink on duty, but agreed to put it aside for later" (CAAS, p. 107). The dedication in *Offshore,* Fitzgerald's novel about a houseboat community, reads "For Grace and all who sailed in her."

Home life was not the only source of inspiration for Fitzgerald's fiction. While her family lived on *Grace* she helped with expenses by teaching "a little arithmetic, a little spelling" at the Italia Conti Academy of Theatre Arts. Some of the challenges she faced here, dealing with children headed for careers in the entertainment industry, are included in her 1982 novel *At Freddie's*. Later, Fitzgerald worked part-time for Westminster Tutors, a tutorial college in London prepping students for admission to Oxford and Cambridge. Her dealings with university-age students helped her with the characterizations in *The Gate of Angels*, about life at the University of Cambridge. Several winter visits to Moscow inspired the setting of *The Beginning of Spring* (1988). Only for *The Blue Flower* has Fitzgerald turned to reading and research for inspiration.

Meanwhile, recognition of her literary achievements began to grow, at least in Britain. She won the 1979 Booker Prize for *Offshore* and has since been shortlisted for the prize on three other occasions. She also was shortlisted for the Whitbread and Sunday Express awards. Even so, her popularity remained limited and English until *The Blue Flower*. The success of this work can be attributed in part to the decision by her publisher, Houghton Mifflin, to use the novel as the flagship for a new paperback imprint, Mariner Books. As the *Guardian* reported on 26 March 1988, "an intensive marketing campaign secured high-profile reviews including the front cover of the *New York Review of Books*." It seems that Fitzgerald, who had railed against arts commercialism in such novels as *The Golden Child* (1977) and *At Freddie's*, neither welcomed nor was prepared for her new "pop" status. Upon winning the National Book Critics Circle fiction prize in 1998, Fitzgerald admitted to the *Guardian*, "To tell you the truth, I didn't really know about the award. My publishers entered it and I really didn't pay attention because I thought I had no chance of winning." She also did not write an acceptance speech.

Although the National Books Critics Circle prize is not a cash award, winning guarantees a writer massive publicity and increased sales due to its high-profile status. However, besides writing more articles for periodicals such as the *New York Times Book Review* and the *Times Literary Supplement*, she did not seem to have been greatly affected by fame and fortune. She continued to live in a flat in High-gate, North London, and to speak fondly of spending time with her grandchildren.

NONFICTION WRITING

"ONE should write biographies of people one likes, and novels about people one dislikes." This advice, offered by Fitzgerald's Uncle Ronnie in her family biography, *The Knox Brothers,* seems to have intrigued her; although her novels would not always follow Ronnie's formula, Fitzgerald's biographical writings do seem to reflect his philosophy. Writing as an independent scholar, Fitzgerald produced her nonfiction for her own intellectual and emotional satisfaction rather than for material reward, or for a community of like-minded thinkers. Her critical studies of writers and artists may not have brought her substantial royalties or a tenure-track position, but they do reflect her special interest in the late Victorian world of her parents.

Fitzgerald's curiosity concerning Victorian arts and letters is evident from the subject of her first book, *Edward Burne-Jones* (1975), a detailed investigation into the life of the pre-Raphaelite artist. After publishing *The Knox Brothers* in 1977, she edited and wrote an introduction to *The Novel on Blue Paper*, a previously unpublished work by Burne-Jones's close friend and fellow artist, William Morris. Fitzgerald's fascination with Victorian culture also brought her to the works of Margaret Oliphant, a prolific Scots writer specializing in domestic romances. The five-volume Chronicle of Carlingford series was published with Fitzgerald's introductions from 1986 to 1989. Her work on the republication of the out-of-print Carlingford series, like her involvement with the Morris text, demonstrate her interest not only in the writers but in making their works accessible to current readers; considering the delayed American publication of so many of her novels, it is understandable why accessibility was a particular concern for Fitzgerald.

In *Charlotte Mew and Her Friends* (1984), Fitzgerald shifts focus from the England of her father's youth to the London of her own girlhood. In the 1920s her family brought her along for browsings at Bloomsbury's Poetry Bookshop, to which the biography is dedicated. Fitzgerald may even have encountered Mew in the bookshop in the early

1920s, where the poet ventured, feeling welcome and for once not out of place. At the Poetry Bookshop, Mew's works were published, read, and sold on rhyme sheets "bought mostly for children"; one must wonder again if Fitzgerald had early appreciated the poet's economy of language and restraint of expression, perhaps later absorbing them into her own writing. A woman whose writing style distinguished her from contemporary Georgian writers, and whose lesbianism and ambiguous appearance ("neither quite boy nor quite girl," remarked an acquaintance) likewise positioned her outside polite society, Mew committed suicide just before turning sixty.

Mew, like Burne-Jones, would probably have resisted being the subject of a study. Lacking confidence and grace, she once answered the question "Are you Charlotte Mew?" with "I am sorry to say that I am." As for Burne-Jones, Fitzgerald herself notes in her foreword that he "regarded with gloomy distaste the prospect of becoming the subject of a biography." Yet a reader of her fiction knows that there is no subject Fitzgerald enjoys portraying more than an elusive or unwilling one. All of her writing, fictional or no, is an attempt to get a living, breathing person down on paper, complete with complexities and foibles, but without coming to simplistic conclusions or reaching for satisfying explanations of behavior. By documenting day-to-day realities—conversations, hesitations, food on plates, lighting in bedrooms—Fitzgerald hopes to bring out what she calls the "inner life" of individuals. And if she helps someone discover truths about real people, such as Burne-Jones or Mew, or fictional ones, such as Salvatore Rossi (*Innocence*, 1986) or Sophie von Kuhn (*The Blue Flower*), her writing accomplishes one of the noblest goals of any literary pursuit: to aid in self-discovery.

ASPECTS OF THE FITZGERALDIAN NOVEL

THE style and subjects of Fitzgerald's nonfiction writing helped prepare her for what she would attempt to render on the pages of her novels. But her more scholarly writings are clearly not what her writing career has been focused upon, especially in the 1990s. While she continued to utilize her academic style in articles and reviews, Fitzgerald spent most of her literary career refining and adding nuance to her fictional prose style. Several aspects of her novels are thus readily identifiable as "Fitzgeraldian," although one should keep in mind that over time her style changed greatly in some ways, and that her novels are often classified as "early" (in general, based more on her own experiences) and "later" (on the whole more complex and dramatic and set farther afield in terms of both time and place).

The most noticeable feature of her novels is their brevity. (*The Blue Flower,* which qualifies as one her longest, is just over 226 pages including the afterword.) Fitzgerald is a great admirer of economy and compression, explaining that "when I wrote my first novel, my publisher threw away the last eight chapters. He told me nobody wanted to read such long books. I have always stuck to that ever since" (*Guardian,* 26 March 1998). Her chapters also are quite short (*The Blue Flower* is comprised of fifty-five of them) and function more as a series of illuminations than as a means of relating a linear plot. Chapters avoid a strict sense of closure and also do not anticipate where the next one will begin. The effect is not unlike that of montage film-making—except, of course, the reader is able to pause and think during and after each scene.

The style of her prose complements the shape of her stories. Her compressed sentences, which often stand as paragraphs on their own, are rich with innuendo. What she omits is often more significant than what she actually says. Using natural speech rhythms and a simple vocabulary, Fitzgerald relays meaning through sharply juxtaposed images and digressions rather than through straightforward narrative. "You might say that Penelope Fitzgerald's novels are about subordinate clauses," wrote Richard Eder for the *New York Times* (5 May 1999). "A leading action, a statement, a mood are yanked from below like a fishing float and dart zigzag away." This buoyant quality is often mislabeled, to Fitzgerald's dismay, as "light" or "slight."

Plots are often unsensational and slender. As in Virginia Woolf's novels, essential relationships, pivotal incidents, and intense confrontations tend to happen offstage or to be rendered very concisely. Fitzgerald seems less interested in storytelling than in meditating on the human condition. What are the qualities that draw people together or apart? Why has bad always coexisted with good? How does one express the beauty of the common, the ugliness of conformity? Leaving ambiguities and questions unresolved at the end is another Fitzgeraldian hallmark; she forces no judgment upon her reader. As Fritz says in *The Blue Flower*, "if a story begins with a finding, it must end with a searching."

The lack of easy answers or resolved conflicts does not mean the novels qualify as amoral. Although she attempts to portray people and situations as complex and problematic, Fitzgerald does quietly celebrate those who exhibit the most traditional of English virtues: personal strength, courage, responsibility, decency, and honesty. One can appreciate A. S. Byatt's comparison of Fitzgerald with Jane Austen in this respect. If one admires Elizabeth Bennett's independence and pursuit of a higher emotional truthfulness, one must also credit Florence Green's desire for autonomy and self-preservation in *The Bookshop,* and Annie Asra's search for the "perfect chord" in *Human Voices.*

The tone of Fitzgerald's novels is not didactic or self-righteous. As if one eyebrow were perpetually raised, she imparts shrewd, unsentimental insight and dry wit. Her sympathy for her creations is always balanced by her straightforwardness and her awareness of human irony and division. Fitzgerald's search for the truth, her attempts to see into the life of the things, is thus not idealized or romanticized. As she has stated, "I have remained true to my deepest convictions—I mean to the courage of those who are born to be defeated, the weaknesses of the strong, and the tragedy of misunderstandings and missed opportunities which I have done my best to treat as comedy, for otherwise how can we manage to bear it?" (CAAS, p. 109).

EARLY NOVELS, 1977–1982

THE U.S. success of *The Blue Flower,* which spurred interest in and availability of her previous novels, meant that Fitzgerald's new American readership was being introduced to her writing very differently than her English readers had been. British fans could witness the changes and improvements in her writing over a span of twenty years, with novels appearing rather regularly every few years. Americans, however, had the advantage of directly juxtapositioning her early and later efforts, with the result that the differences in her content and style over time stood out all the more, in editions

that looked alike and showed no visible signs of age. American reviewers often took advantage of the foresight provided by her U.S. publishing history. For example, Richard Eder, who gave a glowing review of *The Blue Flower* in 1997 (*Los Angeles Times,* 13 April), was able to write of *Human Voices*'s first American edition: "As storytelling, the ending is patly contrived. Ms. Fitzgerald would [later] come to them better" (*New York Times,* 5 May 1999).

Eder is not alone in recognizing the limitations of Fitzgerald's earlier works in light of her later achievements. Although changes are apparent in all of her novels across her career, her first five are thought to possess a more confined scope and limited range of emotional portrayals than her last four. The early novels are all set in the England of Fitzgerald's own experience, in the present or the recent past. All offer criticism of institutions or communities in which a hierarchy of power and prestige is apparent: the British Museum, an insular East Anglian village, a houseboating community, the BBC, a performing arts school. Her stories focus on the complexities of the human condition and of relationships, and her plots would grow richer and more provocative with time; readers would have to wait for *Innocence* to see her first attempt to shock, or *The Blue Flower* to see how deftly she could portray an unorthodox tale of passion.

Fitzgerald claims that she wrote her first novel, *The Golden Child* (1977), to amuse her terminally ill husband, who died in 1976. But the motivation for writing a whodunit may have come from another important man in her life—her Uncle Ronnie, whose biography had been published by Fitzgerald that same year, and who wrote six detective stories himself. Reviewed with qualified favor by John Mellors in the *Spectator* (29 September 1977) and recognized as a "small, benign thriller" by Susannah Clapp in the *New Statesman* (7 October 1977), *The Golden Child* remains Fitzgerald's only venture in the genre of the mystery. Indeed, the style that would become readily identifiable as Fitzgeraldian—nonlinear, open-ended plot structure, a preference for showing instead of telling—does not work well within the typical jigsaw-puzzle structure of a detective novel. To readers who appreciate Fitzgerald's later adept use of understatement, the overinflated and sometimes unwieldy plot of *The Golden Child* indicates her discomfort with her choice of genre.

In 1971 and 1972 the enormously popular King Tut exhibit brought massive crowds—and profits—to the British Museum. Among those waiting on the long lines outside was Fitzgerald, who claims that she generated a story out of her suspicion that the exhibit's dim lights disguised a fake mummy. In *The Golden Child*, an unnamed London museum is host to a loan exhibition of the "Golden Treasure" of the Garamantes, an ancient North African civilization. But the artifacts are discovered to be counterfeit, and the museum's director, Sir John Allison, must decide how to maintain the museum's integrity: Should he conceal the great swindle of the modern replicas, or tell the truth and close down the exhibition?

The plot thickens when veteran archaeologist Sir William Simpkin is found murdered, his body pinned between steel shelves in the museum's library. The discoverer of the original "Golden Treasure," Simpkin is the only museum bureaucrat who is not motivated solely by self-interest. His death and the discovery of the fakes have the strongest effect on Waring Smith, a junior exhibition officer. Although at the outset Smith is preoccupied with commonplace thoughts about his marriage and his mortgage, he experiences a revelation of sorts when he is sent to Moscow by Sir John to verify the treasure's authenticity. When he sees spectators lined up to view the "embalmed head and hands, and the ghastly evening dress suit, of Lenin," Smith draws lines of comparison between the sensationalism of this scene and the crass commercialism of the phony "Golden Treasure" exhibit. He begins to wonder if his entire life has been controlled by such "shoddy undertakings." Is the whole world run by imposters and pretenders?

Fitzgerald offers her own wry answer to this when she pinpoints Sir William's murderer as the museum's director himself. As John Mellors writes in the *Listener* (23 November 1978), "Fitzgerald enjoys herself immensely destroying the credibility of the pompous and ambitious officials, whose voices betray 'the pride and bitter jealousy' that are 'the poetry of museum-keeping.'" *The Golden Child*, a twentieth-century novel of manners, is an obvious criticism of how institutional authority and personal power-seeking challenge the endurance of integrity and public responsibility. Clearly Fitzgerald is disturbed by the failure and hypocrisy of contemporary Britain's values and the bleak outlook for Western civilization as a whole. What happens when influence and power come into the hands of the foolish and the petty? *The Golden Child*, like *The Bookshop* and *At Freddie's*, explores this question.

What saves Fitzgerald from sounding preachy in this and later novels is her wry wit. The social satire of *The Golden Child* received praise from critics, who admired its parody of everything from the self-importance (and self-delusion) of scholars to the prefab essays schoolchildren plagiarize from museum bulletins. As is typical in Fitzgerald's writing, one detail goes a long way. When the reader is told, for example, that Smith and his wife "seriously decided that they should spend as little as possible on food, which, after all, was unimportant—you felt just the same afterwards whatever you ate" (p. 40), Fitzgerald offers wry commentary about their starved emotional life as well as their stale day-to-day existence.

Fitzgerald credits *The Bookshop* (1978) with being her first novel; "before that," she remarks, "I had only published a biography and a mystery story" (CAAS, p. 107). Critics, too, have cited the work as the first indication that Fitzgerald "was a novelist out of the ordinary (Francis King in the *Spectator*, 27 March 1982). The story was inspired by Fitzgerald's own experiences living and working in an East Anglian village when she was in her early forties. Her Southwold is *The Bookshop*'s Hardborough, a name that better captures the coldness and barrenness of the town's appearance and spirit. The time is the late 1950s, important in England's economic history as years of hardship and depression before the booming 1960s and in its literary history because of the appearance of the first British edition of Vladimir Nabokov's *Lolita*, in 1959.

Florence Green is the direct descendant of *The Golden Child*'s Waring Smith: a well-intentioned sort who is naive about the selfishness and blind ambition of others and destined to become enlightened the hard way. Green decides to do her part to revive Hardborough by opening up a bookshop. She chooses to use the decrepit Old House near the center of town, a building readily equipped with a bookshop's requisite shabby dignity, and even the occasional ghost. Florence becomes a local celebrity when she decides to stock *Lolita*—not for any crusading literary purposes but simply because she heard it was a "good book." When the delivery truck arrives, the townspeople cheer that "something new is coming to Hardborough."

Standing in the way of Green's success is yet another representative of a self-serving bureaucratic system such as was found in *The Golden Child.* This time, the officious and insular powers-that-be are represented by Mrs. Violet Gamart, self-proclaimed leader of Hardborough society. Resolved to turn Old House into a "centre for the arts" ("How can the arts have a centre?" asks Mr. Brundish, the village recluse), Gamart makes every effort to ruin Florence's business plans. Florence innocently suggests that their two concerns may be run out of the same building; when she is turned down, she begins to understand that Gamart is not as concerned with opening the centre as she is with triumphing in this situation. Ultimately the bookshop is closed down with the help of Gamart's nephew, a "brilliant, successful, and stupid young man" who helps pass a parliamentary bill making ancient buildings "subject to compulsory purchase even if . . . occupied at the moment" (p. 99). In the last sentence of the novel, Florence sits on a train to London, "her head bowed in shame, because the town in which she had lived for nearly ten years had not wanted a bookshop."

Whereas those who crave power and control seem to attain it in *The Golden Child* and *The Bookshop,* Fitzgerald's next novel suggests that no one has a firm hand on life's tiller. *Offshore* (1979) focuses on a community of barge dwellers living in the shadow of Battersea Bridge, who are "creatures neither of firm land nor water" (p. 10). Fitzgerald observed later that "it was a pity that the title was translated into various European languages with words meaning 'far away' or 'far from the shore,' which mean the exact opposite of what I intended. By 'offshore' I meant to suggest the boats at anchor, still in touch with the land, and also the emotional restlessness of my characters, halfway between the need for security and the doubtful attraction of danger. Their indecision is a kind of reflection of the rising and falling tide, which the craft at anchor must, of course, follow" (CAAS, p. 107).

Fitzgerald's model for the characterizations of torpor and inquietude in *Offshore* may well have been one of her favorite novelists, E. M. Forster. The unstable homosexual prostitute Maurice bears some similarity to Forster's semiautobiographical character of the same name. Questions plagued not only Maurice but Forster himself concerning the publication of his story: "Publishable, but worth it?" read a note found on the manuscript, about a Cambridge undergraduate coming to terms with his homosexuality. Fitzgerald's Maurice, like Forster and his Maurice, makes decisions to remain undecided. "When you can decide," insists Fitzgerald's Maurice, "you multiply the things you might have done and now never can."

The person to whom this comment is directed is Nenna James, the center of the story who nevertheless "lacks center" herself. After her husband had decided to stay in Central America for a job, Nenna had pooled her resources and bought a barge named *Grace,* upon which she and her two daughters now live. Why she chooses to live offshore is not explained, although the reader learns of the string of failures and disappointments that has been Nenna's onshore experience, from her frustrated musical ambitions to her unsuccessful marriage. Her move onto a houseboat represents her drift away from mainstream culture and her unwillingness to fit in. Even when her husband returns to London, he pointedly refuses to join his family in their unorthodox new lifestyle.

Nenna may have hoped to find a life in the margins, but even in this community, "overlooked by some very good houses," there is evidence of a social and economic hierarchy. Like Florence Green in *The Bookshop,* Nenna James finds herself in a social hierarchy but does not know quite where she fits into the scheme—or if she wants to. Maurice and other members of the community, like Willis, the sixty-five-year-old marine artist, are considered less respectable and are at the lower end of the power structure, while Richard Blake, an investment counselor who lives on the *Lord Jim,* is the undisputed leader of the community. Everything he touches is shipshape, or at least seems to be; evidence that the order and control in his life may be only an illusion resides in the quiet unhappiness of his wife, Laura, who reads *Country Life* and dreams of living onshore.

Some critics of Fitzgerald's early work have noted that her later novels seem more deserving of the Booker Prize than *Offshore.* But what is outstanding about the writing in this novel is Fitzgerald's ability to show instead of tell. Although aspects of this novel are obviously symbolic (the Thames, for example, both supports life and allows the residents to escape from it), Fitzgerald refrains from supplying easy and immediately gratifying answers to *Offshore's* most compelling questions. What went awry with Nenna's marriage? Why does she refuse to give up living on the barge? How will she be able to live anywhere else? And, most compellingly, does life really give us answers to such questions? Should fiction?

Of course, the danger of writing so subtly and elusively is that one is bound to be too subtle and elusive for some readers—and this is just the problem Fitzgerald encountered with the reception of her next book. She was disappointed by the criticism the novel received and offered a simple response. "The reviewers called [*Human Voices*] 'light,' and I suppose it is, although novelists never like to be called light. All I can say is that I never went far away from the truth. Broadcasting House in wartime was a life within a life" (CAAS, p. 105).

The headquarters of the BBC during the Blitz, the years in which Londoners and other British civilians were under attack by German aerial bombers, hardly sounds like the setting of a novel one could call "light." In later years Fitzgerald detailed her own experiences at Broadcasting House during the the 1940s and confirmed the high drama of that historic moment. Her years inside the BBC building were turbulent and exhausting, with every one of her senses on overload; Fitzgerald describes the continuous shrieking of alarm clocks marking the sleeping shifts in the concert hall–turned-dormitory; the piercing, acrid odor of the acetate-coated recordings; the chiaroscuro created by the stark overhead lights and the closed windows, which the younger workers were led to believe were to remain shut "until peace was declared" (CAAS, p. 104). But readers who expected such sensational descriptions in *Human Voices* would be disappointed. As the title of the novel suggests, Fitzgerald is once again more concerned with interior processes and the problems of being human than with depicting wartime operations and physical circumstances.

Human Voices documents a few months in the lives of two programming directors, the director of programme planning ("the DPP") and the director of recorded programming ("the RPD")—clearly, Fitzgerald has fun with the BBC's officious and impersonal use of initials. The latter, an eccentric, middle-aged man by the name of Sam Brooks, spends two weeks in the country taping something to be called "Lest We Forget Our Englishry." The recordings turn out to be nothing more than a church door opening and closing, as parishioners bring in their vegetable offerings to a harvest festival.

The egotistical Brooks thinks that the war is less important than the perfection of his recordings. His ego is fed by the power he exerts over the young female interns, most of whom leave after experiencing his sexual advances. The last of these assistants is Annie Asra, who speaks with the "scrupulously fair intonation" of the English Midlands, and represents the quest for fairness and truth—just as her father, a piano tuner, searched for "perfect chords." It is her truth-telling about Brooks's selfishness that brings them together: she is real music to his ears, after years of his immersion in recordings. The imperfection and authenticity of human voices may indeed "wake us, and we drown," as T. S. Eliot writes in the last line of "The Love Song of J. Alfred Prufrock." In Sam Brooks's case, he is brought out of an egotistical reverie and saved through Asra's truth-telling, a "baptism by fire."

The idiosyncratic voice of the novel itself—its resistance to telling a linear chronological narrative, its hesitations and ambiguities—is Fitzgerald's attempt to capture the human spirit of a voice on paper. As A. S. Byatt noted in the *Times Literary Supplement* (26 September 1980), "the scrappiness, the silences and absences, are essentially part of the theme and method of this novel." In the same review, however, Byatt added that she felt she wanted "to be told a little more, given a little more to go on." Richard Eder, writing for the *New York Times* (5 May 1999), also noted that *Human Voices* was "bumpy in places." Whether or not Fitzgerald included the "bumps" intentionally as representations of the fits and starts of a person's speech patterns, the sometimes difficult irregularities of the narrative may be part of the reason why *Human Voices* was the last of Fitzgerald's novels to be picked up by an American publisher.

In *At Freddie's* (1982), Fitzgerald returned to the setting that had brought her so much success in *Offshore:* London in the 1960s. Indeed, this novel is about the job Fitzgerald held at the same time she and her family lived on the barge that inspired her earlier novel. With some cutting and pasting, the Italia Conti Academy of Theatre Arts, where Fitzgerald taught basic reading and writing skills, becomes the Temple Stage School, dedicated to training children for juvenile roles in plays by William Shakespeare and the classics. Presiding over the school is Frieda Wentworth, or Freddie. A legendary figure in the theater world, she began her career working for Lilian Baylis at the Old Vic. Despite increasing pressure to change the curriculum and prepare children to act in television commercials, Freddie stands firm for the traditions of her school and the integrity of her craft.

At the beginning of the novel Freddie hires two young teachers. Hannah Graves is a young girl of twenty for whom "backstage was the enchantment." Pierce Carroll—the character who most resembles Fitzgerald herself—is hired by Freddie not on the grounds of his qualifications but because he will work for very low pay. Likable and honest, Pierce is not up to the task of teaching and controlling Freddie's fiercely competitive students. He does, however, feel a strong attachment to Hannah, to whom he eventually proposes in a straightforward, humble way; Hannah must then choose between the underachieving Pierce and another suitor, an actor by the name of Boney Lewis, who drowns in alcohol any realization that he is past his prime.

Freddie squares off against a formidable threat, a proposal for the creation of a National Junior Stage School, to be affiliated with the National Theatre and endowed with public funds. Launching an offensive through letters in the *Times,* she receives responses which are headed "At Freddies," and a visit from none other than Noël Coward. The surprise of the novel comes at the end, when the reader finds out that Freddie was interested in maintaining her own power more than the traditions of her craft: she decides that in the future she, too, will train her students for television commercials. Do materialism and self-aggrandizement ultimately triumph over art? Fitzgerald's last word on the subject is delivered in a powerful image as Freddie's most gifted pupil practices a leap for a performance of *King John* in the darkening schoolyard.

The commercialization of the arts in *The Golden Child,* the popularization of culture in Florence Green's bookshop, the insularity and exclusivity of communities in *Offshore,* the dehumanizing effect of institutions such as the BBC, and the mainstreaming of the performing arts in *At Freddie's*—such themes distinguish Fitzgerald as a critic of morals and society in the tradition of Austen, Waugh, and Wodehouse. Her recognition as a "thoroughly English writer" was considered positive by many British reviewers; Penelope Lively, writing in *Encounter* (June–July 1982), happily recognized in *At Freddie's* "all those English qualities of understatement and irony and lightness of

touch." American critics were not as enchanted. "*At Freddie's* is a hard book to dislike; it isn't a glitzy bid for easy sales, or an etiolated highbrow puzzle," wrote Roxana Robinson in the *New York Times Book Review* (8 September 1985). "It is well mannered, well-written, and instantly forgettable." Fitzgerald's themes were certainly universally important and applicable, but in order for her books to appeal to a wider audience, she would have to rethink the style and settings of her works.

LATER NOVELS

The gap of four years between the publication of *At Freddie's* and Fitzgerald's next novel, *Innocence* (1986), can in part be explained by the nonfiction writing projects she was absorbed with during this time period, including her work on Morris' *The Novel on Blue Paper* and Oliphant's Carlingford series, as well as her biography of Charlotte Mew. Whether *Innocence* emerged from the experience of living other people's lives or simply from this hiatus in what had become an ambitiously methodical novel-writing career, the book heralded a new age in Fitzgerald's writing and became the first of what would be described as her later novels.

The most apparent difference between the early and later works is that Fitzgerald abandoned the familiar English setting of her own experience and turned instead to foreign or unknown territory and to times past. "The temptation comes to take what seems almost like a vacation in another country and above all in another time," Fitzgerald notes (CAAS, p. 109). The next few novels would take her and her readers to Italy in the 1950s, Moscow in 1913, and an Edwardian Cambridge—an English scene she probably considered alien because of her strong ties with the competing university. Fitzgerald's habitual insight and authority seemed to carry over effortlessly into these more imagined, historically complicated settings.

While the stories may venture beyond her own experience, the themes remain Fitzgeraldian. The title "*Innocence,*" for example, might have suited any one of her other books. Not only do her novels revolve around the thoughts and decisions of a well-intentioned but naive person, but they also demonstrate Fitzgerald's fascination with the idea of innocence. Readers of her earlier novels were reminded again and again of the myriad forms innocence can take, and how innocence and righteousness do not necessarily go hand in hand. *Innocence* would be Fitzgerald's most dramatic restatement of these themes thus far in her career.

The plot of the novel revolves around two Florentine families: the aristocratic and ancient Ridolfi family and the working-class Rossis, whose tale begins in the formative years of Italian Marxism, the 1920s. The novel opens with an anecdote from the Ridolfi history dating back to the sixteenth century, when the family were midgets. When a daughter is born, also a midget, the parents make arrangements to protect their daughter's feelings by bringing another midget girl, a mute, to the villa as a companion for their daughter. But Gemma, the companion girl, begins to grow, and the Ridolfi parents find themselves caught in a bind. They do not wish to reveal to their daughter that they have deceived her concerning her normalcy, so they lead her to believe that Gemma is a "freak." After several weeks of praying for her companion, the daughter decides to protect Gemma from the knowledge of her status as "different." The young Ridolfi thus orders that Gemma's legs be cut off at the knees to give her a "normal" height and Gemma's eyeballs be taken out so that she cannot visually compare herself with others.

Neither Fitzgerald nor her characters ever spell out a moral to this story or explain its relationship to the central plot of *Innocence:* the troubled romance between Chiara, a descendant of the Ridolfi clan, and Salvatore Rossi, a peasant boy turned brilliant neurologist. Reconciling these disparate narratives is left to the reader—although Fitzgerald lets the initial tale resonate frequently over the course of the novel, most obviously through carefully chosen words. (Rossi, for example, complains that the controlling nature of his family and acquaintances has "cut down a grown man," and he views vinestocks as "massed rows of stunted patients.") But the anecdote does seem to speak of the harm and hurt that can be inflicted not only upon an innocent but by one considered innocent as well. The Ridolfi girl's "innocent" desire to protect her friend from judgment results in a horrible mutilation; Fitzgerald seems to suggest that the actions we undertake in order to "help" or "improve" loved ones are often mislabeled as "good intentions." The supposedly innocent wish to hide or eradicate differences instead of celebrating them can have cruel and horrible repercussions.

If the reader is supposed to draw parallels between the anecdote and the story of Salvatore and Chiara, Gemma and Chiara can both be considered innocents who are acted upon and manipulated by others. Chiara, the daughter of Giancarlo Ridolfi, is seventeen and just graduated from Holy Innocents convent school in England. She meets the young surgeon Salvatore Rossi at a concert, and there is instant passion between them. Chiara's schoolmate, Barney, tries to protect her friend from what looks like an ill-fated romance, and chides her for sleeping with the first man she met after leaving the convent.

Indeed, Salvatore, despite his brilliant career as a neurosurgeon, seems a poor choice for the sheltered, well-to-do Ridolfi girl. An avowed skeptic from his early years, Rossi resolved never to risk life, health, or freedom for the sake of principles, or to be emotionally dependent upon anyone. His parents—his mother a devout Catholic who had named Salvatore for the "Saviour," his father an equally devout communist—had unwittingly shown him the downside of forming strong attachments. Fleeing from the rural southern village of his heritage, Rossi fears the controlling power that others have wielded over his life. Throughout the novel Rossi seems unable to escape the feeling that his life is somehow false, and that who he now is, he has become without his consent or control.

After meeting Chiara, he is clearly obsessed with her, but he resolves not to act upon his feelings. Fitzgerald recounts in elaborate detail the buildup of passion and anxiety that precedes their meeting; when their affair finally begins, the reader hears about it through conversations between everyone but Salvatore and Chiara themselves. Despairing of ever living a life for himself, Salvatore concludes that suicide may be the way to cure his soul. Driving out to the Valsassina estate, the home of Chiara's cousin Cesare, Rossi sees the reclusive young vintner working carefully, as had generations before him. In response to Rossi's insistence that things cannot possibly continue as they are, Cesare responds: "We can go on exactly like this for the rest of our lives." Surprisingly, the story ends on a note of hope.

Reviewers seemed puzzled by Fitzgerald's decision to write about Italian aristocrats and Mediterranean passions, especially after a series of five books about English values on English soil. But other English writers have been known to fall under the spell of Italy—including E. M. Forster, whose novels Fitzgerald admired and taught to college-bound tutorial students. *Innocence* does indeed have direct parallels to some of Forster's work; like *A Room With a View,* the novel is about an experienced young man of humble origins who, amid lush and sensuous Italian settings, introduces a sheltered, well-to-do girl to the world of experience.

Fitzgerald's next book, *The Beginning of Spring* (1988), set in Moscow five years before the Revolution. Reviewers like Angela Huth in the *Sunday Telegraph* marveled at the courage of an English writer who dares "to enter Russian territory," and the book received enough praise to be shortlisted for the Booker Prize.

Pre-revolutionary Moscow provides a dramatic and colorful backdrop for the novel's action: "dear, slovenly mother Moscow, bemused with the bells of its four times forty churches, indifferently sheltering factories, whore houses and golden domes, impeded by Greeks and Persians and bewildered villagers and seminarists straying on to the tramlines, centered on its holy citadel" (p. 35). The reader is seduced by images of the literary city Leo Tolstoy evoked in his novels, as Tolstoy is himself evoked in *The Beginning of Spring.*

Despite its exotic locale, the story turns out to be familiar terrain for Fitzgerald: not only is it concerned with universal issues such as the human vulnerability to the tides of change, seen already in *Offshore* and *Human Voices,* but its protagonist is yet another outsider, like Florence Green in *The Bookshop.* Frank Reid is a second-generation English expatriate who is unsettled in virtually every aspect of his life. He has estranged relationships with his home country, his family, his employees, and his own religious beliefs. Abandoned by his wife for unknown reasons (later, he finds out she has run off with his accountant, a follower of Tolstoy), Reid makes a mistress of his children's young nanny. A half-hearted Anglican who claims he has faith but not beliefs, he turns to new sources—among them, Tolstoy—in search of spirituality and meaning. "One musn't encourage the survivals of the past," warns Reid's new accountant, who sees the business as an "undeclared war against every employee below the rank of cost accountant" (p. 116). Revolution is in the air, both on the streets and behind the closed doors of the Reid home at 22 Lipka Street.

Yet Reid is not simply adrift on a swelling sea of change. As its title suggests, this novel is not about helplessness or aimlessness but hope and regeneration—even if the reader must wait for the last sentence of the book for conclusive proof. Significantly, spring begins to stir in Fitzgerald's 1913 Moscow during Holy Week—and more than ever before in Fitzgerald's fiction, there are abundant references to metaphysics and spiritual matters. In his own soul-searching, Reid looks for new answers and finds them in Tolstoy. Showing a copy of *The Resurrection* to an employee, he says, "The resurrection, for those who understand how to change their lives, takes place on this earth."

Recognizing that everything that lives is holy is a theme in Fitzgerald's eighth novel, *The Gate of Angels* (1990), also shortlisted for the Booker Prize. As in previous novels, names are more than simple signifiers. If readers of *Offshore* found grace by the banks of the Thames, Fitzgerald's fans are let into the Gate of Angels in Cambridge; what's more, they are escorted down Jesus Lane and through Christ's Pieces and Bishop's Leaze. And although the landscape of East Anglia may seem less exotic than the vineyards of Italy or the streets of Moscow, the simple beauty of its pastoral scenes acquires a radiance of its own. The question remains, Will the rational creatures compelling the plot forward allow themselves to see it?

The Gate of Angels is set in 1912, around the fictional college of St. Angelicus at Cambridge University. The year is important in English history, because it is only two years before the beginning of World War I and marks the boundary between the Edwardian world and the modern era in Britain. Changes were imminent on British soil—not that one could tell at Angels (as the college is nick-named). Founded in the fifteenth century, the college has resisted change despite its dedication to science. Nowhere is this more evident than in the case of one of its leading physicists, Professor Flowerdew, who denies the existence of atoms and hence the research of Ernest Rutherford and C. T. R. Wilson, upon which modern physics is founded. Angels also has maintained certain clerical traditions dating from the Middle Ages, such as not permitting fellows to marry and not allowing "female animals capable of reproduction" upon college grounds. The state of the college is in limbo; indeed, Fitzgerald tells us that Angels "had no real existence at all, because its foundation had been confirmed by a pope, Benedict XIII, who after many years of ferocious argument had been declared not to be the Pope at all" (p. 17).

Just as Benedict XIII refused to admit defeat and spent the rest of his life holding papal court, Fred Fairly, a junior fellow at the college, also stubbornly holds on to what he believes is true and valid—in his case, Professor Flowerdew's empiricism, which denies belief in anything that the naked eye cannot see. Having decided to clear his mind "of any idea that could not be tested through physical experience," he tells his father, a rector, that he has decided to no longer be a Christian. The elder Fairly remains unfazed: "When you told me that you wanted to study Natural Sciences at university, which led, fortunately I suppose, to your present appointment, I took it for granted that you would sooner or later come to the conclusion that you had no further use for the soul" (p. 44).

If Fred admires Flowerdew, would it not make sense for him to be captivated by a Daisy Saunders? Raised by a single, working-class mother in South London, Daisy is also a rationalist of sorts. From early on, she realized that men in positions of power, especially her employers, would make unwelcome sexual advances on her; as a safeguard, she wears a wedding ring given to her by her Aunt Ellie. Knowing that unattached young women have to make their own way, she studies to become a nurse because she is interested in how the body works. Dismissed from a London hospital for violating professional bounds in helping a suicidal patient, Daisy travels to Cambridge to look for a job. Here Fred and Daisy's disparate worlds collide, when they are both injured in a bicycle accident involving a farmer's cart. As Salvatore immediately fell for Chiara in *Innocence*, so Fred is smitten with Daisy; and just as Rossi's own notions about the direction of his life interfered with his finding happiness in a relationship, Fairly, too, wonders about the repercussions of giving up his fellowship for Daisy's sake. Ultimately it would seem that rationality triumphs, and Fred and Daisy resolve never to meet again. But what is the reader to make of the wind, that correspondent breeze of the first lines that stirs up again in the last, when Fred and Daisy meet again by "chance"?

THE BLUE FLOWER

"Novels arise out of the shortcomings of history." This quotation by the German poet Novalis, from *Fragmente und Studien*, 1799–1800, confronts the reader from the dedication page of *The Blue Flower*, a novel about Novalis' life from 1790 to 1797. The reader is thus presented from the outset with a sort of ontological puzzle: to figure out not only how the quotation is to be understood but who is speaking and why. Is it the real Novalis, simply setting the stage for the story about him that follows (or precedes) him? Or is it Fitzgerald's Novalis, who, throughout *The Blue Flower*, recites passages from the writings of the real Novalis? The statement blurs the lines between art and life, preparing the reader for a narrative that constantly and imperceptibly shifts from telling stories to relaying histories. As she had creatively blended her experiences with her fictional creations in earlier novels, Fitzgerald now uses her imagination to pick up the slack of actual events.

Fitzgerald does let her reader know about her point of departure, however. "This novel is based on the life of Friedrich von Hardenberg (1772–1801) before he became famous under the name Novalis," she announces in the Author's Note. Fitzgerald spent two years in the London Library poring through the diaries and documents of von Hardenberg. Sprinkled with German words and expressions, the text assembles detailed descriptions of eighteenth-century Saxon landscapes and feasts, laundry days and holidays. On the last page of the American paperback edition, a photograph of von Hardenberg's gift of an engagement ring to Sophie von Kuhn is empirical evidence for the reader to contemplate. Significantly, the only other books in which Fitzgerald included illustrations were her biographies of Edward Burne-Jones and Charlotte Mew.

The novel covers the years in which Fritz (as Fitzgerald calls him) finishes his coursework in history, philosophy, and law at the universities of Jena, Leipzig, and Wittenberg and is then indentured to Kreisamtmann Coelestin Just. A local presiding magistrate and tax collector, Just is to train Fritz for a job in the Salt Mine Directorate, where Fritz's father also worked. The startlingly intelligent and poetically natured Fritz turns his attention to much more than his trade while studying under Just: when he is introduced to Rockenthiens, a former captain in the prince's army, he falls passionately in love with Rockenthiens' stepdaughter, the twelve-year-old Sophie.

In *The Bookshop*, Nabokov's *Lolita* was used by Fitzgerald and by the Hardborough residents as a source of inspiration and cultural rejuvenation; now Fitzgerald is up to the task of writing such a tale herself. Like Nabokov, Fitzgerald bases her story of a provocative and doomed romance between a thirteen-year-old girl and a man more than ten years her senior on real-life loves: whereas Nabokov uses the love affair between Edgar Allan Poe and his thirteen-year-old cousin Virginia, Fitzgerald bases her tale on Novalis' real love affair with an adolescent who died in her fifteenth year. The strange, complex relationship shimmers forth through small exchanges:

"In four years' time I don't know what I shall be."
"You mean, you don't know what you will become."
"I don't want to become."
"Perhaps you are right."
"I want to be, and not have to think about it."
"But you must remain a child."
"I am not a child now."

(p. 71)

As for the attraction Fritz feels for Sophie, no one can understand it except Fritz's brother Erasmus, who eventually falls for Sophie himself. Whereas others see just a noisy young girl with a yellowish complexion, Fritz envisions the rosy complexion of his "Philosophy," as he nicknames Sophie. For Fritz is the most thoroughly romantic character in the book, in addition to being its representative of German Romanticism. Intellectual and ideological, passionate and political, Fitzgerald's Fritz is ready and able to start a revolution.

Von Hardenberg does indeed turn out to be a revolutionary, not only in his own time but in Fitzgerald's, as critics offered almost unequivocal praise for his story. For the first time, Fitzgerald's talents had universal appeal, transcending previously unsurmountable boundaries of physical space and time. Reviewing *The Blue Flower* for the *Los Angeles Times* (13 April 1997), Richard Eder called Fitzgerald "the most cosmopolitan of English writers . . . like any excellent writer she creates a world, but like only a very few—Milan Kundera and Italo Calvino come to mind—she creates a metaphysics as well. In the *New York Times Book Review*, Michael Hofmann wrote that *The Blue Flower* was "as luminous and authentic a piece of imaginative writing . . . as George Buchner's 'Lenz,' Hugo von Hofmannsthal's 'Letter of Lord Chandos' or Thomas Mann's tiny story about Schiller, 'Weary Hour'—three of the great glories of German literature." Apparently, writing about

a great writer had put Fitzgerald in league with Novalis and his literary heirs.

"I WILL NOT SUBMIT"

WHILE instructing college-bound students at Westminster Tutors, Fitzgerald put her favorite writers to "the ultimate test of continual repetition," with some surprising results. As she told Peter Lennon in 1998, she found that works she had once admired, such as E. M. Forster's *Passage to India* and *Howards End*, did not improve and grow upon successive rereadings. In Fitzgerald's experience, the book that continued to reward student and teacher alike over time was James Joyce's *Portrait of the Artist as a Young Man*. Fitzgerald's *The Blue Flower* is in some ways comparable to Joyce's masterpiece. Both narratives describe the coming of age of artists at the outset of their careers, and neither text offers resolution or easy answers concerning their future accomplishments.

Like Joyce, Fitzgerald has never been a fan of decisive conclusions. One reason she often refuses to resolve her novels' events is that she seems intensely aware of pinning down the precise truth of a given situation. Her best novels possess a reflectiveness, an awareness of the contingency of the human condition, and a resistance to submit or to end.

As a subject for her own portrait, Fitzgerald herself deserves this same subtle treatment. To make any sort of conclusion about so unpremeditated, varied, and promising a career would sound as glib and assuming as the ranting of one of the villains in her early novels. But one can hope that she will continue to fulfill her destiny as an artist, and that her novels will also pass the test of time.

SELECTED BIBLIOGRAPHY

I. NOVELS. *The Golden Child* (London, 1977; New York, 1978); *The Bookshop* (London, 1978; Boston, 1997); *Offshore* (London, 1979; New York, 1987); *Human Voices* (London, 1980; Boston, 1999); *At Freddie's* (London, 1982; Boston, 1985); *Innocence* (London, 1986; New York, 1987); *The Beginning of Spring* (London, 1988; New York, 1989); *The Gate of Angels* (London, 1990; Garden City, N.Y., 1992); *The Blue Flower* (London, 1995; Boston, 1997).

II. LITERARY BIOGRAPHIES. *Edward Burne-Jones: A Biography* (London, 1975; rev. ed. 1997); *The Knox Brothers*

(London and New York, 1977); *Charlotte Mew and Her Friends* (London, 1984; Reading, Mass., 1988).

III. EDITED WORK. William Morris, *The Novel on Blue Paper*, edited and with an introductory essay by Fitzgerald (London and New York, 1982).

IV. INTRODUCTIONS. L. H. Myers, *The Root and the Flower* (Oxford, 1984); Margaret Oliphant, *The Rector and The Doctor's Family* (London and New York, 1986); *Salem Chapel* (London and New York, 1986); *The Perpetual Curate* (London and New York, 1987); *Miss Marjoribanks* (London, 1988; New York, 1989); and *Phoebe Junior* (London, 1988; New York, 1989).

V. AUTOBIOGRAPHICAL STUDY. "Penelope Fitzgerald," in Contemporary Authors Autobiography Series (CAAS), vol. 10 (Detroit, 1989).

VI. BIOGRAPHICAL STUDIES. Catherine Wells Cole, "Penelope Fitzgerald," in *Dictionary of Literary Biography*, vol. 14 (Detroit, 1982); Philip Harlan Christensen, "Penelope Fitzgerald," in *Dictionary of Literary Biography*, vol. 194 (Detroit, 1998).

VII. CRITICAL STUDIES. Bruce Bawer, "A Still, Small Voice: The Novels of Penelope Fitzgerald," in *New Criterion* (March 1992); Jean Sudrann, "'Magic or Miracles': The Fallen World of Penelope Fitzgerald's Novels," in Robert E. Hosmer Jr., ed., *Contemporary British Women Writers: Narrative Strategies* (New York, 1993).

VIII. ARTICLES AND REVIEWS. Guy Mannes-Abbott, "Angelic Voices: *The Blue Flower* by Penelope Fitzgerald," in *New Statesman and Society* (6 October 1995); Richard Eder, "Nouvelle Novalis: *The Blue Flower*," in *Los Angeles Times* (13 April 1997); Stuart Millar, "I'm a Literary Star, So No Ironing: At the Age of 82, Novelist Penelope Fitzgerald Keeps Her Cool After Scooping the Top US Book Award," in *Guardian* (25 March 1998); Peter Lennon, "Men Are Such Hopeless Creatures, Life's Just Too Much for Them: Penelope Fitzgerald Talks Men, Prizes, and Red-Hot Pokers with Peter Lennon," in *Guardian* (13 April 1998); Richard Eder, "Auditions for Hungry Muses at the House of Truth," in *New York Times* (5 May 1999).

BRIAN FRIEL

(1929–   )

Joseph Devlin

IN THE LATE twentieth century, Brian Friel was Ireland's most important living playwright and one of the most important dramatists of any nationality. The scope and achievement of his work is particularly remarkable considering the relatively constricted geographic context he chose for his plays. The rural area near Derry, Northern Ireland—comprising parts of the counties of Tyrone and especially Donegal in the Irish Republic—is to Friel's work what Yoknapatawpha County is to the work of William Faulkner, and as in Faulkner's work the exploration of a remote and seemingly unimportant place opens into limitless vistas of the human landscape. The conceptual center of this personal geography is an imaginary small town in Donegal called Ballybeg, a name that in the Irish language means literally "small town." Friel examines many different types of Ballybeg characters, even those who merely pass through on their way to somewhere else, thus presenting a varied and comprehensive portrait of life in this area and on this earth. Because of the depth and artistry of this portrait, Friel must be recognized as taking his place alongside the great twentieth-century Irish dramatists George Bernard Shaw, J. M. Synge, Sean O'Casey, and Samuel Beckett.

Friel's work, like that of Shaw, Synge, O'Casey, and Beckett, was shaped by the particular Ireland he experienced. Brian Patrick Friel was born into a Catholic family on 9 January 1929 in Killyclogher, near the town of Omagh in County Tyrone, in the newly created political entity known as Northern Ireland. His father, Patrick Friel, had moved there from Derry in order to teach school. His mother, Christina MacLoone, was from rural Donegal, across the border in the Republic of Ireland, and Brian spent many of his holidays there. In 1939, when Brian was ten years old, the family moved to Derry, and Patrick Friel took a job at the Long Tower School, which Brian attended. After Long Tower, Brian went to Saint Columb's College until

1945 and then enrolled at St. Patrick's College, Maynooth, the national seminary of the Irish Republic. Choosing not to enter the priesthood, and thoroughly disappointed by his experience at Maynooth, Friel decided to join the profession of his father and two sisters and enrolled at Saint Joseph's Teacher Training College in Belfast in 1949. He began teaching school in Derry in 1950. In 1955 he married Anne Morrison; they would have five children. Friel gave up teaching in 1960 in order to concentrate on writing—a risky decision at the time. In the late 1960s he moved from Derry to rural Donegal, which became his permanent home.

Although most of Friel's plays are set in Donegal, the Derry in which he spent so much of his life had a profound impact on his work. Like his father Friel was active in nationalist politics and chafed at the municipal control of Derry's Protestant Unionist minority, with its gross violations of the Catholic majority's civil rights. Although Friel later withdrew from active political involvement, he continued to view the partition of Ireland—the British-drawn border that created Northern Ireland in 1921—as foolish and unacceptable. Strangely enough, however, only four of his numerous plays appear to be motivated by nationalist concerns, and only two of these, *The Freedom of the City* and *Volunteers,* deal directly with the Troubles, as the conflict is known. Still, his difficulties as a Catholic in Unionist Northern Ireland influenced his work more subtly than through simple choice of plots and subject matter. Throughout the plays, regardless of the material chosen, Friel's characters are constantly forced to acknowledge and deal with unsolvable dilemmas and failure. Such an artistic vision could clearly have been developed partly in response to the frustration Friel said he felt "under the tight and immovable Unionist regime."

To explain Friel's artistic accomplishment solely in relation to his experience as a Northern Catholic would be reductive, however, and would require a willful ignorance of the many other themes and concerns treated in his plays. Another important issue is the controlling and constricting effect of the Catholic Church in Ireland. This issue ultimately may lead back to colonial concerns as well, as the devout Catholicism of rural Ireland is historically connected to the centuries-old struggle with Britain, in which faith became the key element of difference and hence of identity. Concerned with twentieth-century Catholicism in his works, Friel repeatedly suggests that the religion cannot give the support and solace that it claims to provide. The plays and stories are full of clerics who are either ineffectual or actively causing pain with their imposition of strict and often cruel social rules. Thus the spiritual expression of the people, which should provide relief from the frustrations and failures of a difficult life, actually becomes another force creating those frustrations and failures.

Along with their political and religious difficulties, Friel's characters are often the victims of economic failure and deprivation. Throughout most of Friel's life, the economies of Ireland and Northern Ireland provided little opportunity for the people, and the despair caused by this situation is everywhere evident in his writing. In *Philadelphia, Here I Come!*—Friel's first international success—the depressed economics of Ballybeg not only interfere with the protagonist's financial opportunities but also psychologically hinder his ability to take advantage of the personal opportunity to marry the woman he loves. It is this psychological effect that is most important for understanding Friel's drama. As with his depictions of characters dealing with political intransigence and religious rigidity, his portraits of people bearing with economic frustration are concerned less with the social phenomenon itself than with the damage it causes to individuals and the strategies by which they cope with their situations.

Political oppression, religious control, and economic deprivation are not the only obstacles blocking the happiness and contentment of Friel's characters. They also battle such personal tragedies as loneliness, physical and mental illness, and death. One of the subtle and yet striking aspects of Friel's drama is that the plays, like the characters, do not make a distinction between public and private pain: the beauty and tragedy of life are presented as a coherent artistic whole.

This discussion of the difficulty and despair at the core of so many of Friel's characters might lead one who has seen or read little of the work to conclude that the drama is unrelentingly sad and tragic, but the truth is far different. In response to the potential despair of their situations, these characters cope by creating a world of joy, humor, and movement, which the audience experiences as the primary texture of Friel's plays. One of the most important of these coping mechanisms involves the use of language and storytelling. It is possible to see these two elements as separate, and many studies of Friel's work have done so. Yet they can also be viewed as different ends of a single spectrum, for both are used to describe and control the nature of the characters' worlds. Friel's characters use language and stories to define, alter, and indeed escape from the inescapable reality with which they are faced. Whether the difficulty arises from a repressive governmental authority, religious authority, or economic situation, or from the personal dilemmas that all people face in life and that are exacerbated by the first three problems, the residents of Ballybeg and its environs respond with a torrent of words meant to drown out what is unacceptable or, failing that, to fool themselves into believing that it does not exist.

The most accomplished of these linguistic illusionists form a group of characters who share many of the same traits, and an understanding of these characters is central to any consideration of Friel's drama. They can be referred to as the "antic characters," borrowing the term from Hamlet's antic disposition, which one of these characters relates specifically to himself. They are improvisational artists who, in response to the pain and poverty of their existence, create a fabric of humor and story that comes alive for themselves and for the audience. This group includes Gar from *Philadelphia, Here I Come!*, Skinner from *The Freedom of the City*, and Keeney from *Volunteers*. Beyond these pure examples of the type, many of Friel's less histrionic characters engage in the same behavior from time to time. With the antic characters, however, this form of verbal and imaginative play, often arising in response to a childhood of misery and despair, has for them become a form of personal defense as well as their primary personal identity.

In addition to language and stories, Friel's characters often seek solace in music and dancing. At times these nonverbal forms of expression seem to come into play precisely at the moment when language fails. The conversations among the Mundy sisters in *Dancing at Lughnasa* can never bring the kind of physical and spiritual release they get from their wild and spontaneous dancing. The works of Chopin sound throughout *Aristocrats* as Claire escapes for a time from thoughts of her impending marriage of convenience into the beauty and expertise of her piano playing. As with the use of language and story, music and dancing not only fit the dramatic theme and arise naturally from the given characters but also contribute to the creation of an enjoyable and exciting theatrical experience. The audience's appreciation of Friel's works depends on its reaction to the new reality, verbal and nonverbal, created by his characters, and on its knowledge of the desperation out of which that reality springs.

SHORT STORIES

BRIAN Friel's literary career did not start with writing plays; his first published works were short stories. The first of these, "The Child," appeared in 1952 in *The Bell*, an important Irish literary magazine. In the following years he began publishing in high-profile American magazines, especially the *New Yorker*. Although Friel's talents and proclivities would eventually lead him away from the genre, his stories were very successful, and two collections, *The Saucer of Larks* (1962) and *The Gold in the Sea* (1966), were favorably reviewed in major U.S. publications. Some of the best stories from the two collections were later published in *Selected Stories* (1979) and *The Diviner* (1983). Despite their different titles, these two books include exactly the same stories. The only difference is that *The Diviner* has a very useful introduction by Seamus Deane, an important Irish literary critic and a friend of Friel's.

One of the most interesting aspects of Friel's work for *New Yorker* readers was the glimpse these stories afforded of a rural sporting culture unknown in most of the United States. "The Barney Game" presents a family drama of inheritance against the backdrop of greyhound racing, "The Widowhood System" discusses the love affair of a middle-aged pigeon racing enthusiast, and "The Ginger Hero" centers on cockfighting. However, these stories are far from being simple exercises in local color to please an American readership. Friel uses animal sports to illuminate and intensify the human drama with which they are intertwined.

The "game" of "The Barney Game" involves buttering up rich uncle Barney in hopes of inheriting his money. Barney's nephew Crispin exhibits strong ambivalence about playing this game, but by the end he is taut and alert, like the greyhounds that race after the hares and rip them to pieces. Through the inclusion of the blood sport of greyhound racing, the other meaning of the word "game" in the title becomes apparent, as do some disturbing parallels between human and animal psychology.

A similar but more lighthearted connection between animal and human occurs in "The Widowhood System." The title refers to an unusual strategy in pigeon racing that Harry Quinn believes will yield him a champion. Instead of racing a hen, whose instinct is to return to the nest, Harry races a cock, but first gets him sexually excited by a female. The sexual drive of the cock is supposed to bring him home quickly, but Harry's bird takes its time, and the widowhood system yields nothing but disappointment. Meanwhile, Harry is taking his time with his girlfriend, Judith, showing no great speed in coming to the nest. Unlike "The Barney Game," the parallel here does not make the protagonists appear animal-like. It actually seems to humanize them, as they engage in more "natural" behavior by the end of the story.

In "The Ginger Hero" the title character, a fighting cock, allows Friel to explore the nature of human characters through their behavior toward the bird. Ginger Hero proves himself a champion and continually wins money for his owners, Annie, Tom, and Billy. Eventually they bring him to a big-money match at the home of the aristocratic Captain Robson. The brutality of the cockfight, in which Ginger Hero is matched against a much larger bird, disturbs Annie and Tom, and they try to stop it. Billy, however, remains cold and calculating, his only emotional reactions relating to the question of winning or losing in the genteel surroundings that encourage his bloodthirsty yet bloodless attitude. The story thus presents a subtle examination of social class and personal loyalty that suggests some unpleasant things about human character and capitalist acumen.

"The Death of a Scientific Humanist" is an extremely funny tale that deals with the role of the Catholic Church in rural Ireland. The omnipresence of the Church becomes clear as the story opens with the dead body of a returned emigrant, Uncle Cormac, being watched over by nuns as the ten-year-old narrator and his mother say a rosary for him. Afterward the mother superior gives the narrator's mother, Cormac's twin sister, the disturbing news that he cannot be buried in consecrated ground. As he was dying Cormac refused last rites, telling the nun that he was a "scientific humanist" and then laughing in her face. But perhaps the most disturbing aspect of the situation to the good Catholics attending upon the mortal remains of Uncle Cormac is that he is smiling, "as if he were listening to an amusing story" (*The Gold in the Sea*, p. 55). Clearly a frightful and hideous death has not been visited upon the apostate in the way the nuns would expect. The callous fatuity of the Church's response to the unassimilable Uncle Cormac becomes clear in the discussion of his life abroad. When the mother superior finds out that Cormac's sister has not kept in touch with him, she says: "A pity. Your letters might have been lighthouses of hope in the pagan sea he was floundering in" (p. 58). But the satire in the story is not directed solely at Catholicism; the comical humanist funeral is performed by a debauched agnostic who recites verses more appropriate to a seduction than a burial. The reason such a person performs the service is that there is no provision for "scientific humanists" in this town. Everyone is either Catholic or Protestant, and the possibility of any other spiritual identity does not exist. Cormac is buried in the strip of land between the Protestant and Catholic sides of the cemetery, in an area where sheep graze. But the embrace of Catholicism, from which he fought so hard to disentangle himself, finally proves too much. Within twelve months the local canon has extended the Catholic portion of the cemetery by buying the strip of land where Cormac is buried, and thus he is brought back into the fold.

The thematic link between poverty and illusion that will later become important in Friel's plays is beautifully expressed in the stories "The Potato Gatherers" and "The Gold in the Sea." The two young brothers in "The Potato Gatherers" have skipped school in order to make some money for their family by gathering potatoes. Twelve-year-old Philly imagines all the wonderful things he is going to buy with this money, but his older brother, Joe, age thirteen, tells him that their mother will let them keep very little of it. This does not stifle Philly's imagination, however, and the story ironically juxtaposes his materialistic and movie-inspired fantasies with the pathetic reality of child labor. In the beginning the boys are in high spirits at the thought of skipping school, but by the end of the day their bodies are sore and their hands are shaking from the physical punishment of running after the tractor and stooping over for hours on end. The brutality of the situation is made especially apparent earlier in the story when Philly hears the school bell and, in his joyous celebration at not being there, nearly gets run over by the tractor. Thus Friel illustrates the boys' innocence and ignorance of their position at the very moment he emphasizes for the reader the viciousness of that position. The futility of the whole endeavor is reinforced as the story ends with a suggestion that the boys' father may have to pay a fine for keeping them out of school to work. Now it is the older brother's turn to take refuge in fantasy, and he solaces himself with the notion of buying red silk socks.

A similar examination of the relation between illusion and economic privation occurs in "The Gold in the Sea." The narrator of the story goes out on a fishing boat in the hopes of cashing in on the salmon run off the coast of Ballybeg. The gold of the title refers to the treasure lost when a World War I ship sank in those waters, as well as to the salmon from which the men convince themselves they will make a lot of money. The story plays upon the poignant irony that the mundane and seemingly achievable goal of catching a large number of fish proves just as unattainable as the fantastic notion of recovering the gold from the sunken ship. Both require resources that these men do not possess and cannot afford. The big boats with the expensive equipment get the salmon, and it turns out that a well-equipped Dutch salvage team has already taken the gold from the wreck. Thus the story illustrates one of the tragic realities of poverty everywhere: that in order to get the gold in the sea, you need to have a certain amount of gold already in hand. In response to this situation Old Con, the leader of the group, spins tall tales of wealth amid poverty, choosing not to tell the younger men that the treasure has been salvaged so that they will not lose that dream. Thus illusion proves the only alternative to despair. By the end of the story the young fisherman Philly, who had been attacking Con's storytelling while he still could believe that he would make a lot of money on the salmon, is willing to admit that, as Con says, the gold is still in the sea, just waiting to be hauled up.

Friel wrote many other excellent stories before turning to playwriting. "The Diviner" examines the cruelty of the rigid social morality of rural Ireland and suggests the clergy's obtuse involvement in this cruelty. "The Saucer of Larks" presents the conflict between efficiency and humaneness, suggesting that perhaps adoption of more effective and rigorous modes of behavior is not an unalloyed good. The great theme of necessity and illusion to which Friel devotes so much of his art receives a different emphasis in "The Illusionists." Here the economic necessity is present, but the main focus is the sense of personal and professional failure, and the illusions by which the two main characters hide this failure from themselves.

In addition to discussing the use of illusion by his characters in order to tolerate unacceptable realities, Friel's stories as a whole can be seen as enacting the same theme with regard to the border between Ireland and Northern Ireland. The stories take place in both Tyrone, Northern Ireland, and Donegal, Ireland, and the narratives and characters move back and forth as if these two counties were not in separate countries. Thus Friel shows that the narrative power of illusion, a deliberate disregard of external reality, can actually be a way toward creating a new reality, and indeed be an act of engagement rather than of escape.

EARLY PLAYS

WHILE teaching full-time in Derry and writing stories at night, Friel somehow managed to begin his career as a playwright. There was no theater to speak of in Derry, so he wrote radio plays. *A Sort of Freedom,* a dramatization of the contradictions and ultimate foolishness involved in extreme notions of personal freedom, was produced by the BBC Northern Ireland Home Service and broadcast on 16 January 1958. This was followed by *To This Hard House,* also broadcast in 1958, which

drew upon Friel's experience in education in its depiction of a teacher whose school is shut down because of falling enrollment. Friel's first stage play, *The Francophile,* was produced in August 1960 by the Group Theatre in Belfast. It was neither a financial nor an artistic success. He later rewrote it for radio as *A Doubtful Paradise,* which was broadcast in 1962. The Francophile of the original title is a postal worker whose romantic notions of French culture do tremendous damage to himself and his family. Friel's next play, *The Blind Mice,* was produced for the stage and radio in 1963, and provides an early example of the examination of the failings and frailty of the Catholic clergy. These first few attempts in the dramatic genre are generally considered apprentice pieces, and Friel chose not to have them published. They are important, however, for the way they point toward the theme of illusion that would come to provide so much of Friel's artistic impetus, and it may have been through these plays that he realized that drama provided the best opportunity for exploring this idea.

THE ENEMY WITHIN

FRIEL's first successful play left behind the contemporary world of his early attempts and dramatized an episode in the life of Saint Columba, patron saint of Derry, set in the year 587. The production of *The Enemy Within* by the Abbey Theatre in Dublin signaled a new step in Friel's career as a dramatist, and the play was eventually broadcast on BBC television in 1965. Although *The Enemy Within* premiered before *The Blind Mice* (on 6 August 1962), it had been written after, and shows marked development in Friel's dramatic style. The story is set in the monastic community that Columba has formed on the Scottish island of Iona. Despite the play's temporal and cultural remoteness, the setting comes to life through Friel's deft handling of the playful conversation of the monks. This monastic world of duty and affection is threatened, however, by Columba's connection to his home and family in Ulster. The life of his cousin Hugh is endangered by rivals, and the presence of the great priest Columba, founder of so many churches, would be a tremendous advantage to Hugh's side. Columba at first resists involvement in this violent squabble, but eventually his loyalty, and perhaps even his sense of excitement, causes him to leave the monastery to help his family. When he returns to Iona after the battle, Columba suggests that his cousin was never really in danger and describes the whole affair as just another bunch of dirty little murders. His disappointment in himself is compounded when he finds that Caornan, his closest friend, has died while he was away. In sorrow for his mistake, Columba asks for harsh penance, wishing once and for all to defeat the enemy within, to "crush this violent Adam into subjection" (p. 39).

Later, other members of his family, including his brother, come to the island with another problem and again ask him to lead them into battle. But this time Columba has the strength to refuse and is roundly cursed for it. The ambivalence toward his home that is at the center of Columba's struggle then becomes overt when he gives an impassioned speech in which he refers to Ireland as "damned" and claims that it wants to steal his soul. Immediately after this, however, his voice breaks and he speaks of "soft, green Ireland—beautiful, green Ireland" (p. 63). The play then ends with a brilliant coup de théâtre in which a young English monk who had been missing reappears, signaling a new beginning.

Although the extreme violence of the Troubles had not begun in 1962, when this play was written, the presentation of Ulster and Ireland as a place of discord and hatred, alternately loathed and loved, must be understood in relation to Friel's Derry. *The Enemy Within* cannot be taken as a straight allegory, but the emotions that inform the play have more to do with the twentieth century than the sixth. The joyful readmittance of an Englishman to the community, after strife has been rejected, is probably related to those emotions.

PHILADELPHIA, HERE I COME!

ALTHOUGH *The Enemy Within* was Friel's first successful play, it was the brilliant and dramatically innovative *Philadelphia, Here I Come!* that brought him to the attention of an international audience. Part of the reason for Friel's leap forward is the experience he had in 1963 during a visit of several months to Minneapolis, Minnesota. He had ar-

ranged to observe Sir Tyrone Guthrie's stage productions of *Hamlet* and *The Three Sisters*. This brief apprenticeship caused Friel to see the banality of much of his earlier dramatic work, and made him more aware of the need to entertain the audience— to allow them, in Guthrie's words, "to participate in lavish and luxurious goings-on!" (Maxwell, p. 62). It would seem strange, then, that Friel's next play would take him back to contemporary Ireland, to the nondescript small town of Ballybeg and the unremarkable house of a taciturn shopkeeper and his dissatisfied son. What Friel had discovered in Minneapolis, however, was that drama need not be gratuitously exotic in order to entertain. He had learned that the seemingly mundane could be made to feel exotic if handled properly. The particular method he evolved to bring about this "luxuriousness"—one that he may well have hit upon while watching the melancholy Hamlet crack joke after joke—is the antic character.

Philadelphia, Here I Come! premiered at the Gaiety Theatre in Dublin on 28 September 1964. It ran in New York for nine months at the Helen Hayes Theater and also was very successful in London. It is one of Friel's best-loved plays and has been revived many times. The main reason for this popularity is the protagonist of the work, Gar O'Donnell, a young man who is spending his last night in Ireland before emigrating to Philadelphia. Friel expresses Gar's anxiety and ambivalence about his life-changing decision to leave home by physically splitting the character in two. The Public Gar is the one whom all the other characters can see and speak with, and the Private Gar is played by another onstage actor of whom no one but the audience is aware. This technique of the split character had been done before, by Eugene O'Neill in *Strange Interlude,* but what is striking about Friel's play is the way the technique, character, and theme dovetail into a seamless and powerful dramatic presentation. In another innovative departure from his previous stage technique, Friel breaks up the linear chronology of action through flashbacks suggested by Gar's thoughts. Both of these nonrealistic techniques allow the playwright to express his character's inner psychological turmoil much more effectively than through a naturalistic presentation.

The antic aspect of Gar's character becomes apparent at the very beginning of the play, before his dual nature is revealed. He is singing "Philadelphia [California], Here I Come," the song that will provide an ironic refrain throughout the play, because it actually refers to someone coming back home, not traveling away for good. He grabs the old housekeeper, Madge, who serves as a kind of surrogate mother in this male household, and begins to waltz her around the room. He tells her that she dances like an angel, then jumps away from her and says, "Oh, but you'd give a fella bad thoughts very quick!" (*Selected Plays*, p. 29). What is particularly interesting about this opening is that Private Gar has not yet appeared. Gar is able to be himself around Madge, and his private self does not interfere or comment. Even though Private Gar will be present during other scenes with Madge, he hardly speaks unless his father comes up in the conversation.

The doubling of the character allows for the already antic nature of Gar to be fully acted out before the audience. A typical example of the "luxurious" fun this affords occurs during an exchange in which Private Gar interrogates Public Gar about his departure in the morning:

PRIVATE: You are full conscious of all the consequences of your decision?

PUBLIC: Yessir.

PRIVATE: Of leaving the country of your birth, the land of the curlew and the snipe, the Aran sweater and the Irish Sweepstakes?

PUBLIC (*with fitting hesitation*): I-I-I-I have considered all these, Sir.

PRIVATE: Of going to a profane, irreligious, pagan country of gross materialism?

PUBLIC: I am fully sensitive to this, Sir.

PRIVATE: Where the devil himself holds sway, and lust—abhorrent lust—is everywhere indulged in shamelessly?

PUBLIC: (*winks extravagantly and nudges an imaginary man beside him.*)

PUBLIC: Who are you tellin'?

(p. 32)

Throughout the play the two Gars keep up this sort of banter—joking, singing, and dancing their way through this difficult night.

In the course of the play, the likely cause of the manic intensity and divided nature of Gar's personality becomes apparent. The life he has been leading in Ballybeg is shown to be barren and emotionally stultifying. When his friends come by to wish him bon voyage, they act like typical con-fused, self-regarding adolescent males, with little understanding of the importance of this moment for Gar. The religious life of the community, personified onstage by the obtuse and tedious Canon Mick O'Byrne, has been useless to Gar, and Private Gar comments directly on Christianity's worthlessness, referring to it as "insane." The great love affair of Gar's life has proven similarly futile, and his sense of his own economic, and hence personal, unsuitability for his well-off fiancée causes him to drastically misplay the scene in which he is supposed to ask her father's blessing. Later, on the day of her wedding to a more economically suitable young man, Gar decides to go to America.

Gar's home life is no more fulfilling than these other relationships. Although Madge's affection provides solace from the barrenness of his world, she is not his mother. His mother died shortly after giving birth to him, and he has no brothers or sisters. He has been raised by his father, an emotionally distant man who feels sadness at his son's impending departure but never expresses it to him. Private Gar calls his father Screwballs, but this ridicule masks a desperate need for his affection. The effect of this sterile home life can be seen in an exchange between Public and Private Gar, in which the Mendelssohn Violin Concerto is on the record player as they talk about Gar's mother and her unhappiness after giving away her youth to marry a man twice her age.

PRIVATE: And he must have known, old Screwballs, he must have known, Madge says, for many a night he must have heard her crying herself to sleep . . . and maybe it was good of God to take her away three days after you were born. . . . (*Suddenly boisterous.*) Damn you, anyhow, for a bloody stupid bastard! It is now sixteen or seventeen years since I saw the Queen of France, then the Dauphiness, at Versailles! And to hell with that bloody mushy fiddler! (*Public goes to the record-player and sings boisterously as he goes.*)

PUBLIC: "Philadelphia, here I come—"

PRIVATE: Watch yourself, nut-head. If you let yourself slip that way, you might find that—

(pp. 37–38)

But Private Gar never finishes his thought. Public Gar takes Mendelssohn off the record player and puts on Ceilidhe Band music—"Something bloody animal! A bit of aul thumpety-thump!"—and starts dancing wildly around the room. In the midst of this action, Private Gar reveals something about the nature of Gar's divided character: "An' you jist keep atalkin' to you'self all the time, Mistah," he says, in a movie-cowboy accent that attempts to mask the seriousness of the statement, "'cos once you stop atalkin' to you'self ah reckon then you jist begin to think kinda crazy things" (p. 38). Thus the actual reason for the doubling becomes apparent. Private Gar may be the unspoken Gar, but he is not the inner Gar. The constant banter between Private and Public is in fact a means to avoid facing the inner Gar and dealing with the loneliness and pain of his existence.

THE LOVES OF CASS McGUIRE

For his next play Friel again chose a theatrical innovation suited to the particular character of the protagonist. In *The Loves of Cass McGuire,* the strong-willed title character addresses the audience directly and commandeers the stage in order to tell her story the way she wants. The play was first performed at the Helen Hayes Theater in New York on 6 October 1966, with Ruth Gordon playing the indomitable Cass. The action at first takes place in the elegant home of her wealthy brother Harry. Through a standard opening scene of exposition, the family speaks about Cass, the drunken ne'er-do-well, who has just come back to Ireland from New York, having lived there since she emigrated at a young age. Then Cass herself explodes onto the stage, destroying both the middle-class decorum of the home and the naturalistic suspension of disbelief of the bourgeois family drama. She shoos the other characters off and begins to tell the story her way. The family has put her into an old-age home because they cannot put up with her behavior, and the play revolves around Cass's learning to deal with her awful new life. In the old-age home she meets Trilbe and Mr. Ingram, two unhappy characters who have nonetheless learned to dream themselves into another, far happier world. By the end of the play Cass has learned this same trick and has escaped from the inescapable. However, the construction of the play makes this movement toward fantasy seem less an escape than a personal triumph.

LOVERS: WINNERS *AND* LOSERS

Friel's *Lovers* premiered 18 July 1967 at the Gate Theatre in Dublin. It is actually two short plays, *Winners* and *Losers.* The first of these titles is ironic, for the lovers "win" by drowning, thus escaping the tawdry and awful life the play has clearly signaled that they are in for. Mag has become pregnant, and Joe will have to quit his promising school career and work to support the new family. In the course of the play it becomes apparent that his anger and disappointment at the situation will never allow the two to be happy, even if they can rise above the squalid conditions they will be living in. As these realities are being intimated to the audience through the alternately playful and combative conversation of the characters, other realities are being communicated by two "Commentators," a man and woman sitting at the edge of the stage. They recount the events of the day—and the eventual deaths of Mag and Joe—in factual and dispassionate tones. Through this theatrical device Friel juxtaposes the fate of the lovers with their increasingly lively and joyful conversation, creating a poignant dramatic irony that simultaneously underscores both the joy and the sadness of life.

Losers is based on one of Friel's short stories, "The Highwayman and the Saint." It uses monologue and flashback to tell the story of Andy Tracey, his wife, and his invalid mother-in-law. The play shows the extreme piety of the old woman and her enforcement of her beliefs on Andy, as well as the subtle machinations that this piety does not seem to contradict. The play itself enacts these subtle machinations also, as the narrator Andy is ironically unaware of much that he describes to the audience.

CRYSTAL AND FOX

The staging technique of Friel's next work, *Crystal and Fox,* stays within the conventions of realistic presentation, but a metatheatrical element is added by the choice of theater as subject matter. The play, first performed at the Gaiety Theatre, Dublin, on 12 November 1968, presents the episodic dissolution of the old-style traveling theater or "fit-up" show of Fox Melarkey and his wife, Crystal. Friel would have seen these shows as a child, and the play opens with a performance in

Ballybeg. There have certainly been plays about the theater before, and they have exploited the life-as-stage analogy in clever ways. But Friel does something remarkably innovative with the staging of his theater play, all the while continuing to obey the laws of realism. Much critical attention has been paid to the "fourth wall" separating the stage and audience and to the experimental techniques meant to break through that barrier. In *Crystal and Fox*, Friel breaks through the "first wall," the one at the back of the stage. He turns the theater of this traveling show sideways, and his audience is presented with the dual reality of the stage-acting on the left and the "real" action backstage on the right. In this way the realism of the backstage goings-on is either heightened or undercut, depending on the level of awareness of the audience member. The metatheatricality of the situation is then suggested by comments like this from Fox: "All the hoors want is a happy ending" (p. 15). Fox will surely give them that happy ending, but Friel won't. As the play progresses, Fox subtly but deliberately alienates each member of his troupe, slowly dismantling the theater and divorcing himself from all human connection and responsibility. But when the final connection is cut—the connection with his wife, Crystal, which he had not been planning to sever—the emptiness that comes with total freedom becomes apparent.

THE MUNDY SCHEME

CONSIDERED one of Friel's worst plays, *The Mundy Scheme* was turned down by the Abbey Theatre, and although there have been suggestions that the political satire was too strong for them, it is more likely that the anemic ending was too weak for them. It was instead produced at the Olympia Theatre in Dublin, on 10 June 1969. The plot of the play is reasonably clever, although a bit slight. In response to political and economic chaos, the taoiseach (prime minister) introduces a scheme to turn the entire impoverished west of Ireland into a huge graveyard for rich foreigners. When the plan is adopted, however, what was supposed to be a life preserver for the country ends up being a luxury yacht for the taoiseach and his cronies as the land speculation begins. Although *The Mundy Scheme* is surely a lesser work, there are many ex-cellent touches, and at times Friel's talent almost makes the story believable.

THE GENTLE ISLAND

FRIEL'S next play, *The Gentle Island*, premiered at the Olympia Theatre on 30 November 1971. It tells the story of the depopulation of Inishkeen (Irish for "the gentle island") and the one family that stays behind. The modern decision to abandon several of the small islands off the west coast of Ireland involved important issues of culture and nationality, because the life led in the remote areas of the west, especially the islands, had been romanticized into a locus of national identity and heritage. Thus the opening scene of the play, showing the exodus of islanders passing by the one remaining family, taps into cultural memories and emotions that are important to the Irish audience. By the end of the play, however, Friel will have turned these emotions upside down and made the irony of the title apparent.

After the evacuation is complete, this lonely redoubt of the old Ireland is soon visited by emissaries of the new. Two tourists from Dublin, Shane and Peter, appear on the island and are warmly embraced by the lone family, the Sweeneys. The complete "otherness" personified by the visitors becomes clear when Sarah Sweeney mistakes them for Americans, suggesting that this new Ireland is an entirely different land from Inishkeen. That difference will later bring about the crisis of the play, because it turns out that the two visitors are gay, a reality that the gentle island cannot abide.

Shane, the younger of these two visitors, is another of Friel's antic characters. Growing up both gay and orphaned, he has learned to make his own reality out of his verbal creativity. His improvisation enlivens the play, yet when not clowning he is the most clear-sighted person on the island. Just as Shane alters and controls his world through verbal performance, so the Sweeneys and the island culture of which they are a remnant have been peopling their small world through language and stories. Manus, Sarah's father-in-law, tells Peter, "There's a name for every stone about here, sir, and a story, too" (p. 26). The particular stone being discussed is one of the Monks, a group of three rocks in the harbor about which the islanders have woven a tale of youthful escape to the mainland. The choice of this theme for the one story included in the play is not accidental, and the audience is led to surmise the longing and frustration behind much of the verbal brilliance, both on the island and in Shane's Dublin. In addition to the characters' public stories, there are private stories that the public versions mask, just as the name "gentle island," for the place and the play, masks the reality of Inishkeen. Old Manus is missing an arm, and he claims it was a mining accident in the outside world that took it. But eventually Sarah tells the true story, one of betrayal and violence, which occurred on the island itself.

One of these hidden stories involves the apparently unassimilable difference between the islanders' and the visitors' worlds, homosexuality. It turns out that Philly, Manus's son and Sarah's husband, is also gay. Thus Friel shows that the apparent dichotomy suggested earlier is false, and that the realities of the modern world are already present on the gentle island, albeit masked by language and culture. But the drive to keep that mask in place, motivated by cultural bias and Sarah's anger at discovering Shane and Philly together, proves stronger than any truth. Shane is brutally attacked and crippled for life, and he and Peter leave Inishkeen. Sarah then has Philly all to herself on the island. As long as they remain physically and culturally isolated, the sham marriage can continue— just as the more insular aspects of all rural Irish Catholic culture can continue, despite the modern world, only if the mask does not slip from the face of the gentle island of Ireland itself.

THE FREEDOM OF THE CITY

In writing his next play, Friel finally decided to speak out directly on the situation in Northern Ireland, specifically Derry. He had avoided the topic until then, insisting that he could not be objective enough about it to produce meaningful work. But history forced his hand, and the violent repression of the nonviolent Catholic civil rights movement, culminating in the Bloody Sunday massacre of thirteen unarmed protesters by the British military on 30 January 1972, became the basis for the fictitious massacre dramatized in *The Freedom of the City*. Just as Friel had feared, the play is not at all objective. It is, however, complex and powerful theater.

As with *Lovers,* Friel discards suspense in *The Freedom of the City* and chooses instead an elegiac mood. He does this by showing the dead bodies of three civil rights protesters at the beginning, thereby coloring all their conversations throughout the play with a sad dramatic irony, and symbolizing the brutal inevitability that controls the lives of people in their position. The three protesters—Lily, Michael, and Skinner—have been attacked and tear-gassed by British soldiers breaking up a banned protest march. They take refuge in the nearest open building, which unfortunately for them happens to be Derry's Guildhall, the seat of municipal government and the embodiment of everything they were marching against. The British soldiers discover their whereabouts and assume that this must be a terrorist takeover of the building, making wildly inaccurate and self-serving estimates of the number of "terrorists" involved. When they emerge from the building at the end of the play, the protesters will be shot on sight as a punitive measure against the movement.

The three protagonists are very believable as characters, but they are also types chosen and constructed by Friel in order to explore the issues involved. Lily is forty-three years old and the mother of eleven children. She is uneducated and desperately poor. In a way, she is the type of person for whom the play is written—aware of the unfairness of life but not yet conscious of how the world works, and how it does not work for people like her. Michael is the Boy Scout type: he believes that the system is basically good; it just needs to be fine-tuned as far as Catholic rights are concerned. The third protester, Skinner, scoffs at Michael's beliefs. One of Friel's most successful and compelling antic characters, he is shot while wearing the lord mayor's ornamental hat—dying, as he had lived, in "defensive flippancy" (*Selected Plays,* p. 150). He voices the play's concern that the movement can never be satisfied simply with equal rights for Catholics—that without some kind of strategy against poverty, having "the freedom of the city" is meaningless.

Contrasted with the human voices of the three people trapped in the Guildhall, Friel presents an array of official and quasi-official voices whose unfailingly inaccurate language comes to control reality itself. These scenes are intercut throughout the play, ignoring chronology and presenting a montage of voice and image. The most important of the official voices is the British judge who conducts the inquiry into the shooting. He is a stand-in for Judge Widgery, the real-life figure who presided over the exoneration of the British forces involved in Bloody Sunday. Friel's judge is made to deliver such deadpan lines as "This tribunal of inquiry, appointed by Her Majesty's Government, is in no sense a court of justice" (p. 109). His statement is proven more truthful than he knows when his avowedly "objective" view cannot admit the possibility that the three protesters were only running for their lives. This lack of objectivity is also signaled in the very sentence where the judge claims it, as he refers to the city as "Londonderry," a name that a clear majority of the citizens reject. At the end of the play, the judge announces his findings, which amount to a series of lies. The montage technique of the play allows Friel to juxtapose the shooting of the protesters with this pronouncement, suggesting that the condoning of official brutality amounts to a death sentence for the oppressed.

Friel is not interested, however, in presenting nationalist propaganda. The voice of the Irish balladeer, which turns the three protesters into heroes and eventually martyrs for Ireland's cause, is almost as inaccurate and damaging as the British voices. And although the nationalist priest at first seems heroic, risking his life in order to give last rites to the three, by the end of the play he is merely another of the voices of suppression, defending the economic status quo. The one voice seemingly unconnected to the situation, that of an American sociologist named Dodds, is often sympathetic and appears accurately to describe much of what is going on. However, his use of the word "orientate" suggests that Friel does not want him to be taken as his personal spokesman, and the unpleasant way that his theorizing about the culture of poverty is interrupted by the rumble of tanks suggests to the audience that this life on the bottom is not only learned, but also enforced.

One more group of quasi-official voices needs to be mentioned with regard to this play. *The Freedom of the City* premiered at the Abbey Theatre in Dublin on 20 February 1973 and at the Royal Court Theatre in London a week later. The London production and the later New York one were attacked violently by many critics who felt that Friel's political bias had interfered with his work. What they did not understand is that in attacking the play as a political statement, instead of reacting to it as a work of art, they were committing the very mistake that they were accusing Friel of.

VOLUNTEERS

THE exploration of issues relating to the renewed violence in Northern Ireland continues in *Volunteers,* which premiered at the Abbey Theatre on 5 March 1975. It tells the story of a group of Republican prisoners who have gone against the noncooperation rule of their fellow inmates in order to volunteer to help with an archaeological dig of an ancient Viking site. The topical resonance goes beyond the difficulties of the North, however, since the audience would recognize the situation as relating to the Wood Quay affair, in which an extremely important Viking site in Dublin was threatened by development, causing ongoing debates and protests about the recognition and preservation of the Irish past. One of the ironies of the play is that the inmate volunteers, particularly Butt, are more concerned with the preservation of the site than are the bourgeois academics and professionals in charge. This moral distinction is one of the most striking aspects of the work, and the self-righteous triviality of the authority figures is contrasted throughout with the loyalty and kindness of the volunteers. The play should not be read as supporting the violence of the Irish Republican Army, however: the volunteers' fellow Republican prisoners are presented as just another form of authority, who indeed are planning to kill the volunteers for going against orders to work on the dig.

In the play, the excavation of the Irish past begins with the title. The word "volunteers" has important historical meaning in Ireland, relating to those who engaged in violent resistance in prior struggles as well as the current one. This exploration of the history of violence continues with the Viking skeleton found in the site, a victim of murder or sacrifice who has been nicknamed Leif (an anagram for "life"). Friel borrows here a symbolic gesture from his fellow Northerner, the poet Seamus Heaney, whose poems about people found preserved in bogs have made the same metaphoric link between ancient violence and the current Troubles. The volunteers themselves make this connection, spinning stories around Leif that say much about their understanding of their own situation. The inmate most involved with this excavation of Leif as excavation of himself is Keeney, another of Friel's dazzling and doomed antic characters. The continual stream of humorous and brilliant improvisation that flows from him is occasionally punctuated by a seeming non sequitur, "Was Hamlet really mad?" (p. 21). The question goes to the heart of Friel's exploration of this antic disposition in all his plays. Does the "defensive flippancy" adopted as protection against the inescapable eventually become a form of madness? And is this madness actually necessary? The play itself asks these questions by presenting the same kind of black humor found throughout *Hamlet*. The constant clowning about death and dead bodies culminates at the end of the play with Butt's insistence that Keeney discuss some kind of strategy to deal with the inevitable attack on them when they get back to prison. Keeney's only response is to hold a mock funeral for Leif, vainly yet valiantly attempting to overcome through language and humor the greatest inevitability of all, death.

LIVING QUARTERS

THE first production of *Living Quarters* was at the Abbey Theatre on 24 March 1977. The action takes place in "the home, the house, the living-quarters of Commandant Frank Butler, OC of B Company of the 37th Battalion of the Permanent Defense Forces" of Ireland (*Selected Plays*, p. 177). The movement in this opening line of the play from the comfort and stability of the word "home" to the transitory sterility of "living-quarters" suggests one of the main reasons that things go terribly wrong for the Butler family. These living quarters are on the outskirts of Ballybeg, but the family is never really part of the town. Frank is attempting to create the home that has never been, coming back as a hero to his second wife, Anna, who is much younger than he. But the emptiness of her life alone in these "quarters" has proven too much, and while Frank was away, she became romantically involved with his son. The tragedy that ensues has happened long since, as has the entire action of the play. The family reunion presented is a composite memory, agreed upon by the characters and stage-managed by a figure known only as Sir. It is fitting that Friel decided to rewrite a Greek myth, Phaedra, for his modern exploration of the nature of fate. The central facts of the tragic episode that the characters will once again act out are written down in Sir's book, inescapable. Even though Father Tom Carty insists that he can be a helpful and caring spiritual adviser to the family during the reenactment, his actions on that fatal day forever identify him as an ineffectual drunk. By situating the fateful aspect of reality in the past, Friel leaves open the question of the future.

ARISTOCRATS

FRIEL's next play explores another segment of the society of Ballybeg, the declining aristocracy of Ballybeg Hall. *Aristocrats* premiered at the Abbey Theatre on 8 March 1979. It is partly based on one of Friel's stories, "Foundry House," which presents the disintegration of a genteel Catholic family and the reaction of one of their former dependents. In *Aristocrats* the character Eamon, one of the "common" people of Ballybeg who has married into the family, is much more disturbed by the abandonment of Ballybeg Hall than are the members of the O'Donnell family, who grew up there.

The play is strongly reminiscent of Anton Chekhov's *Cherry Orchard*, describing as it does the dissolution of a feckless aristocratic household and the eventual loss of the family estate. The only son of the O'Donnell family, Casimir, continually lies about the family's past, assuaging his sense of the inadequacy of the present by incessant invention. Much of the humor in the play comes from this new and different incarnation of the antic spirit, as when he describes impossible memories of visits by historical figures, such as W. B. Yeats "with those cold, cold eyes of his" (*Selected Plays*, p. 267). It is naturally Casimir who begins an imaginary croquet game on the site where real croquet formerly was played. Just as Chekhov's cherry orchard symbolizes the beauty and uselessness of the family and class presented in his play, so this imaginary game suggests the imaginary nature of the genteel status of Friel's aristocrats. The cherry orchard may be chopped down at the end of Chekhov's work, but at Ballybeg Hall it was gone before the play started and could only be temporarily reassembled by the power of imagination.

FAITH HEALER

FRIEL's *Faith Healer* was first produced at the Long-acre Theater in New York City on 5 April 1979. James Mason played Frank Hardy, the faith healer, and Donal Donnelly, who had played Private Gar in *Philadelphia, Here I Come!* and Keeney in *Volunteers*, played Teddy, Frank's manager. The run was very short, as was a later production in London, probably because of the uncompromising nature of the material. Although the play came very soon after *Aristocrats*, it displayed a radically different dramatic technique. *Aristocrats*, like *Cherry Orchard*, is an ensemble piece, with no one character dominating the action, although Casimir is the most intriguing of the group. But in *Faith Healer* the title character is clearly the center of the action, and ensemble playing is rejected completely. The play consists of four monologues delivered directly to the audience by the three characters— Frank; his common-law wife, Grace; and Teddy. Friel's fascination with the way people describe, alter, and control reality through their use of language and narrative is evident throughout the monologues, in which the characters present their individual and often contradictory versions of their life together.

These monologues tell the story of the trio's travels, mostly through Wales and Scotland, putting on faith-healing shows. Although usually nothing happens and Frank is presented partly as a mountebank, sometimes he is able to perform miraculous cures. The hit-or-miss nature of the miracles, and the way the pursuit of them continually damages Frank's life and those of his companions, has led critics to read the faith healing as a metaphor for art, and Friel has accepted this reading. The sacrificial, Christ-like nature of Friel's artist is enacted at the end of Frank's final monologue, although it has been discussed earlier in the play. Frank has come home to his native Ireland— to Ballybeg, in fact. And his failure to achieve the miraculous cure his people so desperately need leads to his own brutal death, a violent blood sacrifice that he strangely seems to welcome.

TRANSLATIONS

IN 1979 Friel and the actor Stephen Rea, who had played Eamon in *Aristocrats*, formed the Field Day Theatre Company in Derry. This organization would later expand its interests into many different aspects of literature and culture, drawing together an exceptional group of Northern writers, intellectuals, and literary critics. Its attitude was strongly nationalist, but like the Abbey Theatre earlier in the century, its main function was to examine the received ideas of all groups and to develop the possibility of a more meaningful Irish culture. The first production of this new company was Friel's *Translations*, on 23 September 1980. The place where Field Day staged *Translations* was none other than Derry's Guildhall, the building from which the three protesters in *The Freedom of the City* emerged to their deaths. The play was immediately hailed as a masterwork, and Irving Wardle of the *Times* wrote of the subsequent London production: "I have never been more certain of witnessing the premiere of a national classic" (14 May 1981).

The end of *Translations* is set in the familiar town of Ballybeg, but the play begins in a place called "Baile Beag"—the pre-Anglicized name of Ballybeg, with a different pronunciation. The distance between these two names is the central focus of the play, which dramatizes the Anglicizing of Gaelic culture in the early nineteenth century. The immediate agent of this Anglicization is the British army camped in the Irish-speaking town, engaged in mapping the area and translating place names into English equivalents. Another factor hastening the death of Gaelic in this colonized context is the question of economic opportunity. One of the characters, Maire, insists that she wants to learn English in order to prepare for her future, mentioning that the great Irish politician Daniel O'Connell has said that Gaelic is keeping the people back. But the most devastating impact on the native language in the west of Ireland comes from the national schools that Britain opens during this period and that teach only in English. The Irish readily accept this foreign educational system because their own is clearly inadequate. All of these factors are woven into Friel's play, much of which is set in a native "hedge school." These Irish schools had originally been outlawed; hence they were often held in places such as the shadows of hedges because property owners were in danger from the British if they allowed the schools indoors. By 1833, the time of the play, outright suppression is no longer a problem, but poverty, neglect, and previous oppression have taken their toll. In *Translations* the hedge school is held in a barn, and despite the intelligence and learning of the two teachers, the haphazard nature of this "system" is clearly detracting from the mission.

An important consideration to keep in mind is that the title of this play is not *Translation*, suggesting the single change from Irish to English, but *Translations*, suggesting a more varied exploration of different types of linguistic metamorphosis. The first of these translations involves the play as a whole. It is understood by the audience that most of the characters are speaking Irish, yet the play is in English, and hence a translation. Some of the characters, particularly the British soldiers, speak English, and this situation leads Friel to create a new dramatic technique, the dual-language device. Even though the actors on stage are all speaking English, the characters are known to be speaking two different languages, and hence they often do not understand one another. Thus this potential difficulty in the subject matter has been turned into a fascinating new aspect of the dramatic experience, and Friel exploits the situation in various and intriguing ways, especially in the love scene between Maire and the British soldier Yolland.

The translation or attempted translation of that love scene is important for understanding the play, as it suggests that not every translation is an act of aggression or erasure. A similar suggestion appears in the scene in which Yolland and the local interpreter, Owen, are trying to find suitable English equivalents for the place names of the Baile Beag area. They are laughing at confusion over Owen's name when Owen's brother Manus enters.

MANUS: What's the celebration?
OWEN: A christening!
YOLLAND: A baptism!
OWEN: A hundred christenings!
YOLLAND: A thousand baptisms! Welcome to Eden!
OWEN: Eden's right! We name a thing and—bang!—it leaps into existence!
YOLLAND: Each name a perfect equation with its roots.
OWEN: A perfect congruence with its reality. (*To* MANUS) Take a drink.
YOLLAND: Poteen—beautiful.
OWEN: Lying Anna's poteen.

(*Selected Plays*, p. 422)

The problem with the Eden analogy is that in Eden nothing had a name before. They are not in Eden; they are in Baile Beag, soon to be Ballybeg.

It is no coincidence that this enthusiastic outburst is fueled by alcohol from "lying" Anna. But the relationship between the two does suggest that translation can be a positive phenomenon, as does the love scene between Yolland and Maire. The real problem is not translation per se but enforced and involuntary translation. This will become abundantly clear at the end of the play when Yolland disappears and Captain Lancey, the leader of the British forces, destroys the countryside looking for him. In seeking to make the locals aware of his threats of reprisal, he issues an order to Owen that can be understood in relation to the whole nation of Ireland in the nineteenth century: "Translate" (p. 439).

RUSSIAN PLAYS

GIVEN Friel's heightened interest in issues of language and translation at this period in his career, it is fitting that his next work was a translation of Chekhov's *Three Sisters*, which had its premier on 8 September 1981 at the Guildhall in Derry, in a production by the Field Day Theatre Company. This was one of the plays Friel had watched Tyrone Guthrie put on in Minneapolis so many years before, and throughout Friel's career one can see a development toward a kind of plotless evocation of character that can only be called Chekhovian. Friel himself traced the origin of this development in literature to Chekhov's predecessor, Ivan Turgenev, and would later produce versions of two of the latter's works. *Fathers and Sons,* an adaptation of Turgenev's novel, was first produced at the National Theatre in London on 8 July 1987. And Friel's translation of Turgenev's play *A Month in the Country* premiered at the Gate Theatre in Dublin on 4 August 1992. Friel's versions are meant to make the artistic nuances of these Russian masters more understandable to an Irish audience than the available British and American translations.

THE COMMUNICATION CORD

AFTER Chekhov's *Three Sisters* Friel returned his focus to Ireland and Ballybeg in the most humorous of all his plays, *The Communication Cord,* which was first performed at the Guildhall on 21 September 1982. The exploration of language issues continues here; the protagonist, Tim Gallagher, is finishing his doctoral thesis in linguistics. The theories about communication that he explains to his friend Jack near the beginning of the play, involving direct and effective transfer of information through language, are hilariously exploded by the play's increasingly chaotic noncommunication. Tim is trying to fool his fiance's father into believing that he owns an authentic peasant cottage, and as this fiction becomes more and more difficult to maintain, Tim's lies become more and more absurd. The inadequacy of his positivist view of language is also suggested by the patriotic platitudes spoken about the cottage itself. Phrases such as "this is our first cathedral" are alternately sarcastic and sentimental, depending on the situation, and even become statements of erotic desire. The very elements of language upon which Tim focuses his thesis, "response cries" such as "Oh, my God," have no significance apart from the situation in which they are uttered. The realization that "it's the occasion that matters" (p. 85) and not the words themselves is also apparent from the title of the play. The "communication cord" refers both to the line of communication by which human beings are connected and the cord on a bus that one pulls when one wants to get off. The bell that sounds has no intrinsic meaning, but the situation ensures that the message will be understood.

MAKING HISTORY

QUESTIONS of the narrative construction of alternate realities, so central to Friel's work, were also important in late-twentieth-century academic debates about the nature of Irish history. Simplistic nationalist readings were attacked by revisionist historians intent on dismantling the unified story set forth. But when the dust settled, even though the narrative had become more complex and fascinating, British colonization and victimization remained the most salient feature of Irish history in the past few centuries. Friel's play *Making History*, first performed at the Guildhall on 20 September 1988, both enacts that revision into complexity and suggests that undeniable salience. It tells the story of the rebellion against British control by Hugh O'Neill, earl of Tyrone, and the catastrophic Battle of Kinsale (1601), in which Spanish aid proved in-

adequate, eventually forcing the famous "flight of the earls" to the Continent. This episode is particularly significant for Friel, and for Ireland, since O'Neill was the earl of Tyrone (Friel's original home) and the supplanting that followed the failed rebellion made Ulster into what it is today.

DANCING AT LUGHNASA

FRIEL'S next play, which returns to the twentieth century and Ballybeg, gave him another international hit. *Dancing at Lughnasa* premiered at the Abbey Theatre in Dublin on 24 April 1990 and went on to very successful runs in London and New York. The play is set in August 1936, during the time of the Festival of Lughnasa (LOO-na-sa) honoring the pagan god Lugh. The action takes place at the home of the five unmarried Mundy sisters, ages twenty-six through forty. The other occupants of the house are their brother Jack, a fifty-three-year-old priest who has just returned from spending his life as a missionary to a leper colony in Africa, and seven-year-old Michael, son of one of the sisters, who serves as narrator. Even though there is a seven-year-old as a character in the play, no child appears onstage. Michael remains invisible, and his lines are spoken by an actor representing the adult Michael. This striking innovation adds to the play in several ways. There is no need to use a child actor, who certainly would not have the expertise of an adult. The focus of the play remains firmly fixed on the ensemble of the five sisters and is not diverted by the presence of a child onstage. Last, the unrealistic presence of the adult Michael continually reminds the audience that this is all a memory, lending the elegiac tone that Friel had accomplished by other means in earlier plays.

The main issue in the play is the reduced circumstances, economic and social, of the Mundy family and the strategies by which they cope. Maggie Mundy is "the joker of the family" (p. 1) and Friel's first female antic character. Her humor helps to lighten the poverty and loneliness of the household, but the most effective renewal of spirit for these women comes from dancing to the old wireless set that Maggie has named Marconi. This dancing is wild and careless, contrasting strongly with the careful and measured behavior of the women at other times. Dancing is associated by the sisters with paganism and the god Lugh, after whom Maggie had originally wanted to name the radio. The redemptive and restorative possibilities in this unrestrained movement of the body—and, by implication, the mind—are not fully realizable in this Catholic household. But there are suggestions that this freedom is possible for the "people from the back hills" who still perform the pagan celebration of Lughnasa, and Father Jack describes such dancing as being a way of life for the Ugandan lepers to whom he has been ministering. Unaware of the incongruity and inappropriateness of talking about his participation in pagan rituals, the priest describes it this way:

That part of the ceremony is a real spectacle. We light fires round the periphery of the circle; and we paint our faces with coloured powders; and we sing local songs; and we drink palm wine. And then we dance—and dance—and dance—children, men, women, most of them lepers, many of them with misshapen limbs, with missing limbs—dancing, believe it or not, for days on end! It is the most wonderful sight you have ever seen! (*Laughs*) That palm wine! They dole it out in horns! You lose all sense of time . . . !

Oh, yes, the Ryangans are a remarkable people: there is no distinction between the religious and the secular in their culture. And of course their capacity for fun, for laughing, for practical jokes—they've such open hearts!
(p. 48)

Here is the solace of suffering that Friel suggests the Catholic religion is unable to provide. It is not accidental that Father Jack, almost the only likable priest in any of Friel's plays, has in fact long since ceased to be a Catholic priest. The real Catholic priest in the play, who never appears onstage, far from giving solace for the poverty and sadness of the household, adds to it considerably by firing Kate Mundy from her teaching job because of the scandal created by Jack's going native.

THE LONDON VERTIGO

FRIEL'S next play was an adaptation of *The True Born Irishman* by Charles Macklin, the original of which had premiered in Dublin in 1761. Macklin was a native Irish speaker and Catholic from Donegal who overcame the prejudices of his time by giving in to them. He learned English, moved to London, converted to Protestantism, and became a famous actor and playwright. The nature and success of this metamorphosis intrigued Friel, as did the play he chose to adapt, which deals with a similar metamorphosis. In *The London Vertigo* Nancy O'Doherty has traveled from Dublin to England and caught the London vertigo, a disease in which everything English becomes rare and exquisite and everything Irish becomes common and dull. The play presents the farcical strategy of her husband, Murrough, for bringing her to her senses. In adapting Macklin's play, Friel has reduced the number of characters and streamlined the action. He also has made liberal use of a dramatic technique more usually associated with earlier centuries than our own: the aside. Dialogue between characters is often interrupted by direct address to the audience, which allows for more complete characterization and greater humor through the disclosure of private thoughts. This technique is similar to all the other metatheatrical gestures in Friel's plays; it creates a kind of Brechtian alienation from the actual goings-on while also contributing to the complexity and economy of the work.

WONDERFUL TENNESSEE

ALTHOUGH Friel sets this play in the rural town of Ballybeg, his characters are from far more urban surroundings. As in the earlier *Communication Cord*, Ballybeg becomes a kind of Shakespearean green space in which the city characters can work through the complications of their lives before returning home. Unfortunately for Friel's characters, however, the twentieth-century world is not so easily sorted out. *Wonderful Tennessee* premiered at the Abbey Theatre in Dublin on 30 June 1993. It presents one of the most Beckett-like situations of any Friel play. The characters spend an evening and night at an abandoned pier waiting for the Godot-like Carlin to ferry them to Oileán Draoichta, the island of mystery. The occasion is a birthday party for Terry, husband of Berna, and they are joined by two other couples.

The play is full of mythological and literary references that lend various meanings to the waiting. The first of these is the ferryman Carlin, whose name is suspiciously like Charon, the figure from Greek mythology who takes souls across the River Styx to the underworld. Oddly enough, the minibus driver who brought the group to the pier is named Charlie, suggesting that they have already been ferried across one version of the Styx in coming to the seashore. Later in the play a story is told of a brutal murder, apparently a ritual sacrifice, of a boy on Oilean Draoichta. This incident takes on classical connotations involving Dionysian celebration, but the most immediate and cogent parallel for this group is the Christian myth that most have abandoned. Both of these religious traditions promise renewal following the sacrifice, and renewal is what all of these characters are desperately searching for.

As the play progresses, we learn that the three couples are either failures in life, trapped in unworkable marriages, or mentally or physically ill. The intense longing at the core of their private worlds is humorously suggested in the very first line of the play: "Help! We're lost" (p. 1). One of the ways the group passes the time is through singing and music. Before they even come on stage, the audience can hear "Happy Days Are Here Again" as the group rides up in the bus. This musicality continues through the play, and the songs almost always deal with themes of happiness. As the characters sing, it becomes apparent to the audience that they are desperately trying to convince the others or themselves that they are, in fact, happy. But the most dramatic instance of this use of music to express or mask the ineffable involves the terminally ill George, who provides accompaniment for the songs on his piano accordion. He was a professional musician, and now that he knows he is going to die, he plays continually. His wife, Trish, says that "he plays all day long. As if he were afraid to stop" (p. 15). Thus, through the character of George, the music in the play is associated with the myths of renewal and resurrection, and both are shown to be an expression of the longing at the center of Friel's world.

MOLLY SWEENEY

FOR *Molly Sweeney*, Friel chose to return to the monologue technique he had used in *Faith Healer*. This play is also about healing: Molly Sweeney has been blind from birth, and through numerous monologues by herself, her husband, Frank, and her doctor, Mr. Rice, the audience learns of the near-miraculous restoration of her eyesight. The play opened at the Gate Theatre in Dublin on 9 August 1994. In the title role was Catherine Byrne, who became Friel's favorite actress, starring in several of his plays.

Just as the story of the faith healer allegorizes artistic creation, so the medical and philosophical discussion of sight in *Molly Sweeney* explores the concept of knowledge. In embarking on this exploration, Friel has chosen to illustrate a fascinating and largely unknown phenomenon, that of a blind person learning to see. This is Frank's account of Dr. Rice's explanation of what will happen if the operations are successful and Molly becomes sighted:

The way he explained it was this. She knew dozens of flowers; not to see; not by sight. She knew them only if she could touch them because those tactile engrams were implanted in her brain since she was a child. But if she weren't allowed to touch, to smell, she wouldn't know one flower from another; she wouldn't know a flower from a football. How could she? . . . If you are blind you can learn to distinguish between a cube and a sphere just by touching them, by feeling them. Right? Right. Now, supposing your vision is suddenly restored, will you be able—by sight alone, without touching, without feeling—will you be able to tell which object is the cube and which the sphere?

(pp. 10–11)

But this learning is not an easy process, and after Molly's cure she is daunted by the new world she inhabits. She eventually develops a strange condition known as blindsight, in which she reacts as if sighted, avoiding obstacles in her way, but is unaware of being able to see anything. The new world into which she has been thrust has overwhelmed her, and rather than see everything, she sees nothing. The allegory of knowledge thus presented can be read in different ways—the movement from innocence into adult experience, the change from traditional viewpoints to modern or postmodern worldviews—but the play neither signals nor designates any of these. Perhaps this very act of allegorizing is comparable to the doctor's cure of Molly, a demonstration of intellectual skill that runs the risk of denying and discarding the very human tragedy at the heart of the story.

GIVE ME YOUR ANSWER, DO!

THE title of this play, which premiered at the Abbey Theatre on 12 March 1997, comes from the old song

"Daisy," but it also may refer to Friel's earlier *Philadelphia, Here I Come!*, in which Private Gar sings the same line to his father, comically expressing and at the same time distancing himself from his need for some sign of farewell. As in that play the characters here are waiting for an answer. The main question involves the novelist Tom Connolly's desperate need to find out whether David Knight, an agent for a university library in Texas, will buy his papers and thus restore Tom and his wife, Daisy, to financial solvency. By the end of the play, however, the situation is reversed, and it is David who desperately needs an answer. There are many other questions that require answers in the play, but the most poignant involves the couple's daughter Bridget. She is completely unaware of others and uncommunicative and lives in an institution. The play opens and closes with Tom visiting her and carrying on a one-sided conversation, asking questions that he then has to answer himself. These scenes clearly demonstrate the play's refusal to provide the answers for which its title calls. This indeterminacy is also highlighted by Daisy's comment about the selling of Tom's papers and the final assessment of his art: "there can be no verdicts, no answers" (p. 79).

CONCLUSION

THE need for answers, which never come, is at the heart of all of Brian Friel's work. Moments of apparent transcendence are always ambiguous; suggestions of personal fulfillment and happiness, always qualified. The words, stories, lies, humor, singing, dancing, and music that occur throughout his plays seem only to be attempts at filling this emptiness, avoiding the questions rather than answering them. But then, perhaps that is another kind of answer.

SELECTED BIBLIOGRAPHY

I. WORKS FOR THE STAGE. *Philadelphia, Here I Come!* (London, 1965); *The Loves of Cass McGuire* (London, 1966); *Lovers* (New York, 1967); *Crystal and Fox* (London, 1970); *Crystal and Fox and The Mundy Scheme* (New York, 1970); *The Gentle Island* (London, 1973); *The Freedom of the City* (London and New York, 1974); *Living Quarters* (Lon-

don, 1978); *Volunteers* (London, 1979); *Aristocrats* (Dublin and London, 1980); *Faith Healer* (London and New York, 1980); "American Welcome," in *Best Short Plays, 1981* (Radnor, Pa., 1981); *Anton Chekhov's Three Sisters: A Translation* (Dublin, 1981); *Translations* (London and New York, 1981); *The Communication Cord* (London, 1983); *Selected Plays* (London, 1984); *Fathers and Sons: After the Novel by Ivan Turgenev* (London, 1987); *Making History* (London, 1989); *Dancing at Lughnasa* (London, 1990); *The London Vertigo: Based on a Play, The True Born Irishman; or, The Irish Fine Lady by Charles Macklin* (Oldcastle, 1990); *A Month in the Country: After Turgenev* (Oldcastle, 1992); *Wonderful Tennessee* (Oldcastle, 1993); *Molly Sweeney* (Oldcastle and Harmondsworth, U.K., 1994); *Give Me Your Answer, Do!* (Oldcastle and Harmondsworth, U.K., 1997).

II. SHORT STORY COLLECTIONS. *The Saucer of Larks* (London and New York, 1962); *The Gold in the Sea* (London and New York, 1966); *Selected Stories* (Dublin, 1979); *The Diviner: The Best Stories of Brian Friel* (Dublin and London, 1983).

III. CRITICAL STUDIES. D.E.S. Maxwell, *Brian Friel* (Lewisburg, Pa., 1973); Elizabeth Hale Winkler, "Brian Friel's *The Freedom of the City*: Historical Actuality and Dramatic Imagination," in *Canadian Journal of Irish Studies* 7 (June 1981); Ruth Niel, "Digging into History: A Reading of Brian Friel's *Volunteers* and Seamus Heaney's 'Viking Dublin: Trial Pieces,'" in *Irish University Review* 16 (spring 1986); Edna Longley, "Poetry and Politics in Northern Ireland," in her *Poetry in the Wars* (Newark, Del., 1987); Ulf Dantanus, *Brian Friel: A Study* (London, 1988); George O'Brien, *Brian Friel* (Boston, 1990); Lionel Pilkington, "Language and Politics in Brian Friel's *Translations*," in *Irish University Review* 20 (autumn 1990); Richard Pine, *Brian Friel and Ireland's Drama* (London and New York, 1990); Wolfgang Zach, "Criticism, Theatre, and Politics: Brian Friel's *The Freedom of the City* and Its Early Reception," in Michael Kennelly, ed., *Irish Literature and Culture* (Savage, Md., 1992).

Terence Brown, "'Have We a Context?': Transition, Self, and Society in the Theatre of Brian Friel"; Sean Connolly, "Translating History: Brian Friel and the Irish Past"; Seamus Heaney, "For Liberation: Brian Friel and the Use of Memory"; Desmond Maxwell, "'Figures in a Peepshow': Friel and the Irish Dramatic Tradition"; and Fintan O'Toole, "Marking Time: From *Making History* to *Dancing at Lughnasa*," in Alan J. Peacock, ed., *The Achievement of Brian Friel* (Gerrard's Cross, 1993); Elmer Andrews, *The Art of Brian Friel: Neither Reality nor Dreams* (Houndsmills and London, 1995); C. C. Barfoot and Rias van den Doel, eds., *Ritual Remembering: History, Myth, and Politics in Irish Drama* (Amsterdam and Atlanta, 1995); Declan Kiberd, "Friel Translating" and "Translating Tradition," in his *Inventing Ireland* (Cambridge, Mass., 1995); George O'Brien, *Brian Friel: A Reference Guide, 1962–1992* (New York, 1995); Josephine Lee, "Linguistic Imperialism, the Early Abbey Theatre, and the *Translations* of Brian Friel," in J. Ellen Gainor, ed., *Imperialism and Theatre: Essays on World Theatre, Drama, and Performance* (London and New York, 1996); Maureen S. G. Hawkins, "Schizophrenia and the Politics of Experience in Three Plays of Brian Friel," in *Modern Drama* 39 (fall 1996).

Claire Gleitman, "Negotiating History, Negotiating Myth: Friel Among His Contemporaries"; Richard Kear-
ney, "Language Play: Brian Friel and Ireland's Verbal Theatre"; Declan Kiberd, "Brian Friel's *Faith Healer*"; F. C. McGrath, "Brian Friel and the Irish Art of Lying"; and George O'Brien, "*Volunteers:* Codes of Power, Modes of Resistance," in William Kerwin, ed., *Brian Friel: A Casebook* (New York and London, 1997); Shaun Richards, "Placed Identities for Placeless Times: Brian Friel and Post-Colonial Criticism," in *Irish University Review* 27 (spring/summer 1997).

WILSON HARRIS

(1921–   )

Vera M. Kutzinski

THEODORE WILSON HARRIS was born 24 March 1921 in New Amsterdam, a coastal city in the Berbice region of British Guiana (Guyana since 1966). Since 1945, when he published his first prose work, the short story "Tomorrow," in the inaugural issue of the Georgetown (British Guiana) journal *Kyk-over-Al*, Harris' literary output has been prodigious. As of 1998, he had published twenty novels, two collections of novellas, three volumes of poetry, a book of literary criticism, and four collections of essays and lectures. The first recipient of the Guyana Prize for Fiction (1985–1987), he has been called the most important writer of the second half of the twentieth century, and some regard him as a successor to Joseph Conrad, some even to William Blake. In astonishingly dense prose that recalls Joycean modernism on the one hand and the postmodernist work of Samuel Beckett and Gabriel García Márquez on the other, Harris conducts "experiments in literary form" that challenge readers to take seriously ways of thinking that are closer to associative imagination and intuition than to the linear logic and analytical reasoning that rationalism holds dear. Harris pushes language to its very limits by insisting that it can and must move beyond divisive binaries (such as self and other, colonizer and colonized) into an "art of compassion" capable of genuine change. Affirming one's humanity by denying another's is a form of intolerable conceptual violence that poses grave ethical problems which, according to Harris, postcolonial "protest realism" cannot address adequately.

Unlike other Caribbean writers of his generation, such as George Lamming, C. L. R. James, and Kamau Brathwaite, Harris has always kept aloof from militant racialist and nationalist politics. Profoundly concerned with the fate of humanity in a violent century, Harris' anti-apocalyptic literary and philosophical practice effectively carries the work of intellectual resistance to conquest and tyranny beyond vengeful oppositionality by reimagining human relations in nonviolent terms. "The nature of tradition," he writes, in "A Talk on the Subjective Imagination," "is . . . a ceaseless question about the nature of exploitation, self-exploitation, as well as the exploitation of others, the exploitation of one culture by another" (*Tradition*, p. 45). There is a palpable urgency to Harris' writing that is easy to understand in a time when ethnic cleansing and other forms of partisan violence, both conceptual *and* physical, ravage many parts of the world. These pressing problems, Harris cautions, cannot be overcome until and unless we choose to remember past injustices or traumas; his novels demonstrate that sources of regenerative morality reside miraculously and unexpectedly within "a universal plague of violence" at the end of the millennium (*Carnival*, p. 14).

Harris has traveled widely and taught at universities all over the world. His regular presence as visiting professor-cum-writer-in-residence at the University of Texas at Austin in the early 1980s inspired the establishment of the Wilson Harris Papers, an extensive manuscript collection, at the Harry Ransom Humanities Research Center in Austin. Smaller collections of Harris' manuscripts exist at the University of the West Indies in Kingston, Jamaica, which awarded Harris an honorary doctorate in 1984; at the University of Guyana; and at Indiana University in Bloomington.

LANDSCAPE AND PSYCHE: THE EARLY FICTION

"THE difficulty with Mr. Harris," ventured a reviewer in the London *Tribune* of 12 June 1970, "is not that he is obscure at all, but that our viewpoint is so much narrower than his." What partially accounts for Harris' "far viewing," as he himself calls it, is an intimacy with his landscapes and his view of history as human experiences inscribed onto the landscape. Harris maintains that landscape—be it the Guyanese rain forest or its counterpoint, the countryside around Chelmsford, Essex, Harris' residence since 1985—is not a "passive creature"; it has rhythms, dimensions, and complexities that address the senses and the unconscious in odd ways. Unlike V. S. Naipaul and others, Harris does not subscribe to beliefs in the New World's "historylessness" and Caribbean cultural destitution. For him landscape *is* history.

Harris' intense, detailed familiarity with his native South American landscape is the direct result of his career as a surveyor. After graduating from Queen's College at the University of Guyana in 1939, Harris studied land surveying and, in 1942, became assistant government surveyor. Promoted to government surveyor in 1944 and to senior surveyor in 1955, he led countless expeditions into Guyana's coastal areas and its interior, with its rivers and waterfalls, such as Kaieteur Falls, and mountains such as Roraima. The surveying trips Harris supervised between 1944 and 1953 resonate in the majority of his novels, most of which are at least partially set in Guyana and abound with local Amerindian myths and legends. Guyana, unlike the Caribbean islands, still has a large Amerindian population, a fact that informs what C. L. R. James once called "the continental perspective" that Harris adds to a conceptualization of the Caribbean. Especially notable in this regard are the seven novellas in *The Sleepers of Roraima* (1970) and *The Age of the Rainmakers* (1971).

Most immediately these expeditions affected the poetry of *Fetish* (1951), published under the pseudonym Kona Waruk, and of *Eternity to Season* (1954). In the epic poems of *Eternity to Season*, suggestively subtitled *Poems of Separation and Reunion*, Harris contrasts nature and history as his personae embark on a "tremendous voyage between two worlds" ("Behring Straits"). Metaphoric "voyage[s] in the straits of memory" (*Palace*, p. 62), characterized by an increasing overlap of the inner spaces of consciousness with the outer realms of the phenomenal world, come to define spiritual freedom in Harris' fiction. The Guyanese jungle is not only unclaimed economic and cultural territory but also a psychic hinterland populated by ghosts of the dead, be they African slaves, East In-

dian indentured laborers, or Amerindians. The Guyanese landscape of Harris' poetry and novels is painfully alive with traces of their historical experiences of exploitation, and so are the psyches of Harris' artistic personae.

Aspects of Harris' first major expedition into Guyana's interior in 1942, which moved up the Cuyuni River in the direction of Venezuela, are fictionalized in his first published novel, *Palace of the Peacock* (1960), which won the instant admiration of Charles Monteith, his first editor, and the loyalty of his publishers, Faber & Faber. (Of the novel manuscripts written prior to *Palace*, only a short excerpt has survived; it is titled "Banim Creek" and was printed in *Kyk* in 1954.) Considered Harris' masterpiece and translated into several languages, *Palace* opens *The Guyana Quartet*, which is completed by *The Far Journey of Oudin* (1961), *The Whole Armour* (1962), and *The Secret Ladder* (1963). Harris wrote *Palace* in 1959, the year after he resigned his position with the Guyanese government; was divorced from his wife, Cecily Carew; and, like so many other Caribbean writers, emigrated to the United Kingdom. On 2 April 1959 he married Margaret Burns Whitaker, a Scottish lyricist, librettist, and playwright whom he had met on an earlier visit to England.

Palace of the Peacock is a highly stylized symbolic journey into Guyana's interior that contains the seeds of Harris' entire literary oeuvre, most notably his use of African-Caribbean and Amerindian myth as intellectual and spiritual resources. The novel revolves around Donne, a modern-day Raleigh, whose relentless pursuit of elusive Amerindian laborers is figured as a quest for the same El Dorado that attracted earlier conquerors of the New World, including a host of scientific travelers in nineteenth-century British Guiana. Among the latter were Richard and Robert Schomburgk, two German explorers hired by the British Crown, which was interested in mapping its colony. Richard Schomburgk's *Travels in British Guiana, 1840–1844* (1922) and especially Robert Schomburgk's ethnographic romance *A Description of British Guyana* (1838) are accounts of the same territory traversed by Donne and his crew, in whom aspects of the Schomburgks and other early historical crews survive.

But El Dorado is an ambiguous trope in *Palace*; it not only stands for wealth and greed but also represents a mythic origin. As the tables are turned on the pursuers by the pursued and the crew members die one by one—as other explorers did before them—Donne's obsessive "hunt" changes conceptual direction and becomes a voyage of self-discovery in which the survivors confront the threat of extinction. Like the poems of *Eternity to Season* that wed timelessness to temporality, this fictional voyage draws heavily from Homer's *Odyssey*. That this epic, which Harris first read as a child with the help of his mother, was part of his legacy from his father no doubt contributed to the singular importance it has throughout Harris' writings. Theodore Wilson Harris, an affluent Guyanese insurance broker, died unexpectedly in 1923, leaving his two-year-old son to be raised by his mother, Millicent Josephine Glasford Harris. Millicent Harris, like most of Harris' characters of Amerindian, European, and African descent, moved herself and Wilson from New Amsterdam to the capital city of Georgetown, where she bought property. In addition to ample financial resources, her late husband's estate included a trunk filled with books, among them *The Odyssey*. In his 1992 autobiographical essay Harris repeatedly underscores the significance of this literary legacy. In addition to finding its way into his novels, where Homer's Greece is often linked with pre-Columbian civilizations, this paternal legacy inspired Harris to use Greek mythology in his poetry several decades before Derek Walcott wrote the acclaimed *Omeros*.

In his 1984 "Note on the Genesis of *The Guyana Quartet*," Harris advances the idea of "convertible images." Several such images are embedded in *Palace*'s opening paragraph. In this dreamed scene of murder, an unidentified horseman's "breakneck stride" prepares the metaphoric ground for rendering visible the sound of a sudden shot as a "stretched," "torn" rope "coiling" into the shape of a noose. With the figure of the noose appears the figure of an "executioner," whom the already "stiffened" "hanging man," almost an image sprung from a deck of tarot cards, acknowledges with a vexing salutary bow. In bowing to his executioner, the horseman establishes a firm symbolic bond between the two, subtly transforming what might appear as a random act of violence into a purposeful ritual slaying. The translation of shot into noose is as unexpected as the perception of the shot as coming from different places at once (it is "near and yet far"), an echolike simultaneity that

makes it impossible to establish direction (that is, agency and motive). We do not know for certain who fired the shot and for what reason, nor do we know who the dead horseman is. Only when the slain rider is later identified as Donne can we conjecture that the deed might have been an act of revenge committed by Mariella, his battered Amerindian mistress.

Along with eschewing any sense of objective reality, certainty, or truth, the language in *Palace* refuses to organize the novel's fictional world into rulers and ruled. Extreme versions of metaphor, figurative relations whose ground is ever shifting, complicate relations between characters, and between characters and external environment. The narrator, Dreamer, walks a fine line between states of sleeping and waking, between unconscious and conscious realities, a situation that calls into question any narrative authority with which we might invest him despite his partial blindness (one of his eyes has an incurable disease). Dreamer is but a partial narrator in a novel in which fragments of the crew's remembered lives, narrated in the third person, constantly interrupt and pull against the first-person narrator's perceptions—to the point of total disintegration. Tropes of blindness and insight, interiority and exteriority, locate areas of self-deception in all of the novel's male characters. Dreamer's interior, spiritual vision, a function of his worsening blindness, is oppressively "ruled" by Donne's hard, "clear" materialism, which threatens with extinction everything in his path: his Amerindian laborers, his mistress, his brother, and his crew.

As the novel progresses—or better, follows in a dead crew's footsteps—Donne's materialism becomes less and less coherent. It erodes to the point that Donne merges with Dreamer, thereby giving rise to a new first-person narrator in the novel's last two chapters. This narrative "I" is a composite of Donne and Dreamer in which binary oppositions—such as materialism and spiritualism—have been "healed." Such healing also reverses the seemingly unchangeable: when Donne climbs the cliffs above the waterfall and suddenly slips, he "gasped on the misty step and a noose fell around his neck from which he dangled until—after an eternity—he had regained a breathless footing. The shock made him dizzy—the mad thought he had been supported by death and nothingness" (p. 101). Donne's fall into the void represents an extreme disruption of his identity, the point at which he is forced to shed the mask of his self-sufficient individuality. His fall is also the point at which an instrument of death is converted into an instrument of salvation. The void—history's grave—is transfigured into a creative womb.

Palace's narrative, then, leads from self-division—that is, the division of an individual into self and other—to self-integration, or "person-hood." This self-integration takes place in a refurbished, but no less mythic, El Dorado. Through what he, drawing on Carl Jung, calls the "alchemical imagination," Harris empties the myth of the Golden Man of Donne's conquistadorial ambition and refills it with spiritual visions. According to the Gnostics, heretical early Christians who valued spiritual knowledge over faith, alchemy has seven stages, or initiations, represented in *Palace* by the seven days of the crew's journey, through which ordinary matter, known as *nigredo*, is transformed into *cauda pavonis*, a transcendental stage of being that Harris translates as "palace of the peacock." What connects alchemy to the myth of El Dorado is gold, believed to be the by-product of alchemy. The "melting gold" into which Donne dips his hand as he ascends the waterfall's cliffs is an image of self-deception that yields to the "golden sights" in the room of a Christ who is also a shaman. This figure reappears as Oudin in *The Far Journey of Oudin* and as Cristo in *The Whole Armour*.

Christian mythology abounds in Harris' novels, but it is always intertwined with the Caribbean vestiges of West African and Arawak fable and legend, the "rapport" of which he considers "part and parcel" of a West Indian imagination. In his Yeatsian forging of an intricate mythical scaffolding for his fictional world, Harris syncretizes European with native Arawak theology as his language works to reconcile the human with the divine. The flaming tree of life is a recurring image that brings into play resurrection stories from different cultures, from the Phoenix that rises from the ashes and Christ's ascension to the myth of flying Africans and the Arawak legend of the burning tree. Legend has it that during wartime the Arawaks, pursued by their enemies, the Caribs, fled to a tree that reached all the way into the heavens. When the Caribs set the tree on fire, the Arawaks burned to death and were transformed into the stars in the firmament. Harris gathers up these mythologies in the image of the peacock's tail, whose "eyes" are made from the splinters of the hard sun that represents Donne's rule.

I [Donne / Dreamer composite] saw the tree in the distance wave its arms and walk when I looked at it through the spiritual eye of the soul. First, it shed its leaves sudden and swift as if the gust of the wind that blew had ripped it almost bare. The bark and wood turned to lightning flesh and the sun which had been suspended from its head rippled and broke into stars that stood where the shattered leaves had been in the living wake of the storm. The enormous starry dress it now wore spread itself all around into a full majestic gown from which emerged the intimate column of a musing neck, face and hands, and the great tree of flesh and blood swirled into another stream that sparkled with divine feathers where the neck and the hands and the feet had been nailed.

(pp. 112–113)

As sound "redeems" vision, each twice-dead crew member is reborn as the act of listening that reconciles the human with the divine while the sensuous world merges with abstract spiritual concepts. The crew's second death repeats an earlier one, but with a significant difference: the second journey into the interior is a story of resurrection. Death is no longer an end but a second chance, a necessary transformation that makes it possible to "cancel" one's "fear of strangeness and catastrophe in a destitute world" (p. 116). In this sense *Palace* is an anti-apocalyptic revision of Joseph Conrad's *Heart of Darkness*, but unlike Kurtz, Donne finds spiritual fulfillment and self-knowledge, not "horror," in embracing otherness.

In Harris' novels, memory is not individual recollection but always includes traces of other presences; they are traces on the land of its "vanished" inhabitants, the Folk. Dreamer suspects that one has access to memories other than one's own, memories based on experiences one never had: "Could a memory spring from nowhere into one's belly and experience? I knew that if I was dreaming I could pinch myself and wake. But an undigested morsel of recollection erased all present waking sensation and evoked a future time, petrifying and painful, confused and unjust" (p. 48). Harris rather shockingly casts possible conversations between human persons and the "live fossils of another age" (p. 7) in terms of cannibalism, the consumption of human flesh that some chroniclers were eager to attribute to the Caribs to mark them as radically different from, and threatening to, Europeans. The most poignant of "live fossils" in *Palace* is the Carib bone flute: "The Carib flute was hollowed from the bone of an enemy in time of war. Flesh was plucked and consumed and in the process secrets were digested. Spectres arose from, or reposed in, the flute" (p. 9). Harris' version of the bone flute transfigures the terror of cannibalism—which, as in "Yurokon," from *The Sleepers of Roraima,* also connotes unchecked greed or lust for possession—into a covenant, a "mutual fortress of spirit between enemy and other" (p. 10) that becomes an "organ" of self-knowledge: knowing one's self means to consume and digest one's biases.

The curious mutuality Harris sees embedded in an ancient object such as the bone flute is an allegory of remaking instruments of war into instruments of salvation. The eye as "window" on the world from the novel's opening is also linked to the Carib bone flute in that the palace's "windows" are the holes through which the wind blows and makes music, the spiritual "music of the peacock" (p. 114). These "windows" represent frames of identity that have been hollowed out so that they can become vehicles for a new muse. Old myths thus become instruments capable of sounding a new music. The palace of the peacock is like the "living house" of *The Far Journey of Oudin* and the "ancestral house" in *The Whole Armour.* Unlike the ramshackle houses in Naipaul's *A House for Mr Biswas* (1961), Harris' perforated shells, or "crusts of bias," offer no protection to individuality.

The journey *Palace* undertakes, as it converts key images and reverses narratives of violence, domination, and greed, is a voyage that leads away from self-deception and from the complacencies that reside in "congealed meanings" toward the multiple uncertainties that come with the realization that we can always see only partial truths, even as we, like Harris' characters, undertake repeated quests for "impossible wholeness." In *The Secret Ladder,* another semiautobiographical journey upriver at the other end of the *Quartet,* Russell Fenwick, another surveyor, compares this approach to self-knowledge to his systematic gauging of the levels of the river. The benevolent Fenwick, outfitted with a dinghy named *Palace of the Peacock,* resembles Dreamer more than he does Donne. Donne's counterpart in *The Secret Ladder* is the Gorgon figure of the authoritarian Jordan, whom Fenwick beheads at the end. Yet Fenwick

shares with Donne a desire for "belonging" and, like him, eventually ascends toward the Folk, now represented by the black Merlin figure Poseidon, descendant of Guyanese Maroons whose land would be flooded as a result of the irrigation project that brings Fenwick and his crew into the interior. As in *Palace,* it is an "ascent" toward the Folk—that is, a shattering experience of the fear of extinction—that alerts Fenwick to his own guilt. He, too, is implicated in violence and terror beyond his control.

With *The Far Journey of Oudin* and *The Whole Armour,* we emerge temporarily from the thick of Guyana's rain-forested interior as the novels' settings change to savannas and coastal areas. These two novels' very different narratives make more accessible the complex union of opposites that joins Donne to Mariella. By the end of *Palace,* Mariella is no longer Donne's abused mistress, nor even the old Amerindian woman whom Donne presses into service as a guide. Rather, she appears to Donne more abstractly as a picture of a muse: a Madonna holding a child. This regenerative iconography recurs in *Far Journey,* where it is associated with Beti's future child. When Beti, another Mariella figure, becomes pregnant with Oudin's child, they become not only parents but also agents of spiritual rebirth, much as Bryant and Catalena do in *The Secret Ladder.* In *The Whole Armour,* where the symbol of the peacock metamorphoses into that of the tiger—Blake's "tyger" grafted onto the Guyanese jaguar—it is Cristo and Sharon who become "the first potential parents who can contain the ancestral house" (p. 110). But they can play this role only after they acknowledge that, appearances notwithstanding, "nobody innocent," as Abram puts it in a sentiment suggestive of George Lamming's *The Pleasures of Exile* (1960). So Cristo has to sacrifice himself to redeem the novel's community by accepting responsibility for a murder he did not commit. But redemption and community, in Harris, are never entirely and simply linked to procreation; children assure future community only to the extent that they share in a "compassionate alliance" between the living and the dead. An example is the myth of dead Osiris impregnating a living woman, which Harris uses in *Ascent to Omai* (1970) and in *The Carnival Trilogy* (1993).

The principle of compassionate alliance also explains why many of Harris' characters migrate between novels. This migration begins in *Heartland* (1964), a transitional novel whose tripartite structure echoes that of *The Secret Ladder,* when Zechariah Stevenson encounters three characters from *The Guyana Quartet:* Kaiser from *The Far Journey of Oudin,* and Da Silva da Silva and the Amerindian woman Petra, both from *Palace.* Da Silva, here a porknocker (a fortune hunter in the Guyanese forest), is Harris' first Virgilian guide to the interior purgatorial regions that Stevenson explores as he journeys toward an "identity of abandonment" analogous to Donne's self-surrendering fall at the end of *Palace.* This glimpse of Dante amid *Heartland's* life-in-death and death-in-life metaphors is a prologue of sorts to Harris' reworking of *The Divine Comedy's* allegorical structures in *The Carnival Trilogy.*

Heartland also anticipates Harris' late novels' metafictional strategies in imagining the writer as custodian and editor of a character's manuscripts. Whereas subsequent novels often name the editor as "W. H.," or even "Wilson Harris," *Heartland* proffers an unsigned postscript that tells of Stevenson's "bundle of scorched papers" recovered from a half-burned-down rest house (p. 93). These papers include three partially obliterated poems, all of them from Harris' *Eternity to Season,* through which the fiction identifies itself as emphatically and self-consciously reconstructive. As in *The Waiting Room,* where Harris also employs this device, a damaged text that survived a catastrophe, be it poem or logbook, offers unsuspected possibilities for fiction making: "This—while apparently depleting continuity—only served to enhance the essential composition of the manuscript that involved accidental deletions or deliberate erasures, reappraisals, marginal notes, dissociations of likely material (as well as associations of unlikely material) to confirm, and blend into, a natural medium of invocation in its own right" (*Waiting Room,* p. 10). While later novels abandon this particular representation of erasure, they do develop the idea of "translating" someone else's papers into a novel. In *Companions of the Day and Night* (1975) the term "papers" comes to include sculpture and painting.

NARRATIVE DRAMAS OF CONCEPTION

THE four novels in what Hena Maes-Jelinek, Harris' most prolific critic, regards as his second cycle—*The Eye of the Scarecrow* (1965), *The Waiting Room* (1967), *Tumatumari* (1968), and *Ascent to Omai* (1970)—represent an important point of departure from Harris' earlier writings. Characterized by increasingly abstract interiority, they begin where *Palace* leaves off, with the collapse of a character's individuality or "sovereign subjectivity." This point of radical disruption marks the beginning of a dialogue with a crumbling, chaotic past. "There are two kinds of relationships to the past," Harris points out in "A Talk on the Subjective Imagination," "one which *derives* from the past, and one which is profound *dialogue* with the past (one which asks impertinent questions of the past)" (*Tradition,* p. 45). Unlike *Palace,* whose visionary "eyes" inform its title, *The Eye* uncompromisingly eschews "the dead tide of self-indulgent realism" (p. 105), thereby making this relatively brief text one of Harris' most difficult novels. Conceding virtually nothing to a linear plotline, vestiges of which persist throughout *The Guyana Quartet,* most notably in *The Secret Ladder, Eye* bluntly rejects "false coherency."

What precariously holds together this text's "free construction of events" is not plot but "phenomenal associations" that emerge within the narrator N——'s journal and his letters to the engineer L——; their personalities increasingly overlap as the novel moves along. Much like Donne / Dreamer's recollections, N——'s quasi-Proustian remembrances of things past venture beyond the generic strictures of autobiographical and epistolary formats as they cross and recross the frontiers of the known world. For example, the entries in N——'s diary, which spans a symbolic nine months analogous to *Palace's* seven days, are written in Edinburgh and London in 1963 / 1964 but dated 1948, the year of the strike and violent riots that threatened to ruin British Guiana's economy. This historical datum, like the "crash" year 1929, to which some remembrances return in this and other novels, represents a catastrophic event whose disruptiveness stands for, and parallels, the evacuating of conventional memory, a strategy Harris uses frequently in his novels. As the novel's figure for self-deception or death-in-life, L——'s metamorphosis into a scarecrow, of which he himself is unaware, is closely connected to historical catastrophe.

It is in this "striking year of everyman's familiar obsession (1948 or 2048?)" that N—— and L—— "suddenly stumbled upon the faint but 'timeless' footprints of a *self-created* self—the stepfather for whom my mother wept (as if she has been weeping for *me* as well as for *him* all the time)" (*Eye*, p. 47). The abandoned woman—weeping Penelope—is an icon of grief that recurs in several of Harris' novels, from *Tumatumari* to *The Four Banks of the River of Space* (1990), always in connection with unexplained, seemingly accidental death of a lover or spouse. Prudence, in *Tumatumari*, loses not only her child but also, shortly after his stillbirth, her husband, Roi Solman, another surveyor, who is decapitated by the "sleeping rocks" in the rapids of Tumatumari. The novel's peculiar "drama of conception" (p. 41) unfolds as Prudence dreams of a head floating in the river Canje.

As in *The Eye*, where weeping Penelope first appears, this death evokes not only Harris' own near drowning accident but also the mysterious disappearance of his stepfather in 1929. Harry Reece was believed to have drowned in the Guyanese interior, and Millicent Harris was thus left a widow for the second time in six years. The cloak of autobiography, however, is rent as quickly as it is donned when N——— informs us that his actual father died "when I was less than a minute old" (p. 48). The biblical phrase *"In my father's house are many mansions,"* which rhythmically punctuates N———'s account of his voyage to the El Dorado of Raven's Head, testifies to the continued significance of lost fathers in Harris' fiction. In keeping with this, N———'s goal is to exonerate his father from charges of murder; his alleged victim is Hebra, sacred whore and another representative of the Folk.

What N——— finds in Raven's Head during the course of his "interior unpredictable dialogue" is a letter from one Idiot Nameless, who confesses to the murder as he testifies to "the continued erosion of self-made fortifications" and "the continuous and miraculous conception of 'living' and 'dead' nature, rehabilitation of the lost One, the unrealized One, the inarticulate One" (pp. 86, 108). Idiot Nameless, a trickster figure who reappears in the Mexico of *Companions*, is a radically strippeddown version of N———, who sheds layer after layer of his conventional personality until he achieves a state of namelessness, or "negative identity" (p. 101), that enables him to understand the deprivations suffered by the nameless Folk embodied in Hebra. Raven's Head (also Hebra's other name) stands at the provisional end of an impossible quest, where one question is always answered or complicated by another. Like the palace

of the peacock, Raven's Head represents an intellectual space and a spiritual condition "into which we are still to be born" (p. 107).

Extreme compression of language characterizes *The Waiting Room* no less than it does *The Eye*. Susan Forrestal, left totally blind after three eye operations, is the first major fictional role for the "character-mask" Penelope in Harris' novels. Susan's married lover disappears after a violent quarrel, and she eventually marries another man, but continues to be haunted by the one she loved before him. *The Waiting Room* also marks the debut of author / editor "W. H." as a fictional character who identifies himself as the recipient of "the disjointed diary of the Forrestals" after their untimely death in an explosion at their Edinburgh antiques store. "W. H." plays a similar role in *The Angel at the Gate* (1982), a fiction of "the traffic of many souls" that he fashions from the automatic writings of Mary Stella Holiday's therapy sessions with Father Marsden.

The Waiting Room, then, rests on a premise similar to that of *Heartland*: the reconstruction by "W. H." of the Forrestals' partially destroyed "log book." In this fictionalizing reconstruction, firstperson narrative yields to a third-person free indirect discourse that renders the increasingly complex relations between the author / editor and the novel's fluid consciousness contained in the antechamber of Susan's mind. As the logbook comes "to assume the symbolic proportions of a raft" (p. 61) floating across Susan's "sea of memory," the outlines of her husband and her former lover flow into one another: they are "fluid bodies akin to vortices of memory she had not fully anticipated" (p. 38). Susan's nameless lover is rendered as "he" in quotation marks "to emphasize that the lover in Susan's memory was indeed a sheer phenomenon of sensibility rather than identical character in the conventional sense" (p. 11). A similar triangulation occurs in the plot of *The Four Banks*, where the female protagonist, troubled by a dead husband, is actually named Penelope.

The Waiting Room's imagery of vessel, pilot, and crew, complete with masthead and siren song, continues Harris' Odyssean excursions as the space of the waiting room becomes *"the subterranean cave of Susan"* that represents "metamorphosis, endless creation" (p. 79). In the cave's changed, yet parallel, location of consciousness and geography, Susan is "translated" into an Amerindian woman whose husband, a fictional reincarnation of Susan's former lover, is struck by a poisonous snake; he is "punctured" as "he had once punctured her" (p. 58). Such reciprocal wounding across parallel universes characterizes "a species of fiction within whose mask one endured the essential phenomenon of crisis and translation" (p. 79). Harris later names this movement across parallel universes "quantum imagination."

According to Maes-Jelinek, the novel that comes closest to actualizing Harris' concept of narrative as dynamic structural design, *Ascent to Omai*, returns from female to male consciousness as its focus comes to rest on the ambiguously named Victor. Victor, a former child prodigy, searches for his father, Adam, a welder who recalls the patriarch Abram from *The Whole Armour* (1962). As he climbs over the Guyanese interior toward Omai, following in the footsteps of the shadowy figure of a ruined black porknocker who could be his lost father, Victor undergoes a sudden "Spider transubstantiation. Trickster transubstantiation" (p. 26). Having been bitten by a tarantula, he enters a "geography of delirium" akin to the state of namelessness. In the hallucinations that entangle him in an "ancient web, forbidden net, dangerous adventure—psyche of history, stigmata of the void" (p. 23), Victor (who is now also Anancy) recalls his father's trial forty years ago. After the death of his wife in childbirth, Adam is convicted of arson on the basis of circumstantial evidence and sentenced to seven years of hard labor; after his release he disappears. Doubts of his guilt remain, especially in the mind of the judge, who wonders repeatedly: "Why would Adam burn bed and board?" That same trial judge is now a ponderous passenger in the plane, a "limbo aircraft" (p. 48), that flies overhead and will crash into Mount Omai, chasm of memory and abyss of history, as in the "OH MY CHASM," a pun on "Omai Chasm," the title of the novel's first part.

The metaphor of the trial—both ordeal and self-judgment—appears in many Harris novels. Victor, much like Jonathan Weyl in *Carnival*, doubles as a judge as he emerges as one of Harris' figures of the artist. Judge's inquiry into Adam's sentence is also a probing into the potential of art to unsettle the victor / victim stasis in which son and father appear to be locked: "It's a question of the uncomfortable region one must approach time after time, again and again, down the ages shrouded by death in order to learn to bear by degrees what would otherwise be quite clearly . . . unbearable: the clas-

sical truths of courage and compassion which are the stuff, sometimes, of the greatest poetry" (p. 55).

Ascent includes a poem, presumably written under hypnosis by the illiterate Adam. It is Harris' own "Fetish," now described as "a rubbish heap of images" that is "invaluable" as "a new experimental source of wealth" (pp. 71–72). The poem functions as a microcosm of the novel in that it breaks the "tidiness" of self-indulgent rationalizations and, as Judge writes in his "novel-vision of history," "repudiate[s] the vicarious novel . . . where the writer, following a certain canon of clarity, claims to enter the most obscure and difficult terrain of experience without incurring a necessary burden of authenticity, obscurity or difficulty at the same time" (pp. 96–97). *Ascent* does incur these burdens or responsibilities. The final chapter, "Dance of the Stone," breathtakingly choreographs the novel's "rubbish heap of images" into a "dance" of seven "movements" by shuffling and reshuffling what appear to be random passages from earlier pages. These alternative sequences, which emphasize the necessary element of change in repetition, set Victor free from circular shelters, or prisons, such as his dead mother's petticoat, under which he hides whenever his father has sex with other women. From the narrative's dance emerges a new vision of Adam, one in which Victor beholds him fighting the blaze he had started. This image of "ultimate forgiveness" has "living spark[s]" that extend all the way from *Palace*'s tree of life in flames.

THE NOVEL AS INFINITE CANVAS

IN 1972, the year *Black Marsden* was published, Harris first taught at the University of Texas at Austin, to which he returned as visiting professor and writer-in-residence in 1980 and again in 1981–1982. From Austin he made several trips to Mexico, the setting of *Companions of the Day and Night*, a sequel to *Black Marsden* that he began to draft in 1972. In *Black Marsden*, Clive Goodrich, fatherless cosmopolite, patron of the arts, and editor of the Idiot Nameless Collection in *Companions*, "stumbles upon" Doctor Black Marsden, "Clown or Conjurer or Hypnotist Extraordinaire" (pp. 12–13), in the ruins of Dumferline Abbey and invites him to his Edinburgh home. With Marsden arrive a number of other artist characters—the seductive Jennifer Gorgon, the Jamaican Brown Knife, and the musician Harp—who are both Marsden's "agents" and aspects of Goodrich's own personality. The novel becomes an interior "*tabula rasa* comedy" as Goodrich participates in the lives of these eclipsed personae. The purpose of this comedy, or "reversible fiction," as it is called in *Carnival*, is twofold: first, to make Goodrich aware that the material generosity inscribed in his name does not assuage guilt, neither of individuals nor of nations; second, to sensitize him to the strange "others" inside himself and to possibilities for genuine community.

The shifting narrative modes, from Goodrich's first-person to a third-person narrator, support the novel's interplay between inner and outer landscapes. In the end Goodrich undertakes a visionary (or revisionary) journey to the state of "Namless," which is located in South America. Both his country of origin and an interior space, Namless stands as a warning that yesterday's victims may well become today's tyrants, whose revolutions only redistribute "fixtures of greed." Still wrestling with "other buried traumatic existences" (p. 94), Goodrich continues his travels into nam(e)lessness in *Companions,* where he agrees to "edit" Idiot Nameless' papers, paintings, and sculptures. Like N———in *The Eye,* the novel that first acquaints us with Idiot Nameless, Goodrich relives his life again and again, as if he were an Eliotic "ghost returning to the same place (which was always different), shoring up different ruins (which were always the same)" (*Eye,* p. 25).

Black Marsden, "Doctor of the soul," assumes different guises in several of Harris' novels. In *The Angel at the Gate* he is the psychiatrist Father Joseph Marsden; in *Da Silva da Silva's Cultivated Wilderness* (1977) and *The Tree of the Sun* (1978), he plays the role of Sir Giles Marsden-Prince, British ambassador to Brazil and adoptive father of Da Silva da Silva, the orphaned painter who bears the name of the Da Silva twins from *Palace.* Harris' idea of the novel as a painter's canvas finds its clearest articulation in these two novels, whose setting is the Holland Park area of London, where the Harrises themselves lived when they were first married. A passage from *The Secret Ladder* might well have served as an epigraph to both these novels: "The pure paint of love scarcely dries on a human canvas without a modicum of foreign dust entering and altering every subtle color and emotional tone, which affects the painter as well as the painted

property of life" (*Quartet*, p. 247). Such dust settles on the pages of all of Harris' novels.

In *Cultivated Wilderness,* as Da Silva paints into his own flesh "the mystery of the world's injustice," this dust takes the shape of the ghostly presences with whom "his void was instinct." It takes the forms, or sounds, of the "recurring voices" that afflict Da Silva, that "madman of a painter": "I hear them at the hearts of this great city, the regional accent of birds and bells, the voices of the past, the voices of the present" (pp. 10–11). These voices speak to him from the "canvases-within-canvases" that make up the paradise paintings Da Silva begins when his wife travels to Brazil to tend to her dying father. In the "wildernesse theatre" of his own mind and heart, Da Silva is intimately connected to two female muses, his wife, Jenine ("Jen") Gold, whose Peruvian family claims a distant cousinship to Paul Gauguin, and his model, Manya, a Brazilian who had come to England at the same time as Da Silva. Painting, for Da Silva, is a form of making love to his muses "through creatures that both blocked and reopened a territory of intercourse between species and species" (p. 16).

Whenever Da Silva paints, it is as if he were traveling on a ship with three decks represented by the intriguing diagram Harris includes in the novel. The ship's masthead, which is compared to a paintbrush, is an axis that runs through, or pierces, each deck, connecting the "Caribbean sun" (upper deck) to the "African sun" (middle deck) to "Canada's, Australia's, India's, Bangladesh's, New Zealand's Pacific sun" (lower deck). This arrangement helps the reader decode the figure of Legba Cuffey, another one of Da Silva's models, who combines the personality of a West African trickster ("god of the netted cross-roads") with that of Cuffy Ned, a black eighteenth-century Caribbean rebel, into a "cross-cultural deity" (p. 69). Anancy is the black youth with Legba's signature limp who in *An Angel at the Gate* is a close cousin to this and other trickster figures, such as Oudin and Idiot Nameless.

The Tree of the Sun begins where *Cultivated Wilderness* ends: with Jen's unexpected pregnancy after eight years of marriage, which becomes the subject of the "newborn canvas" Da Silva begins on the day that Jen conceives. This painting, pregnant with Da Silva's imagination in the same way that Jen's body is pregnant with their child, is significantly called *The Tree of the Sun,* a title that harks back to Arawak and Aztec myth. The painting's visible subject is the conquest of Mexico and the vanished Aztecs, a subject that relates to Jen's pregnancy through Da Silva's thoughts of her royal Inca lineage (he even considers replacing Montezuma with the Inca Atahualpa). The painting's pre-Columbian dead open the door to the book's other dead, former tenants of the house Da Silva and Jen now inhabit.

The quotation from Tennessee Williams that Harris uses as one of the epigraphs to Book Three of *The Eye* encapsulates the mysterious relationship that develops between the Da Silvas and Julia and Francis Cortez: "They are acquainted, / but they have forgotten the name of their acquaintance." As Da Silva and Jen read (and become editors of) Julia's concealed letters to Francis and Francis' secret novel about Julia, they find themselves gripped inexplicably by their parallel lives and passions, most notably by Julia's miscarriage and her illness (she died from cancer at the age of forty, in the room that is Da Silva's studio). As pages of writing become flesh, a new "transubstantial community" of oddly intimate strangers emerges from "trade winds of psyche" that blow across decades and centuries. Like the Da Silvas, Julia and Francis are racially mixed. Julia is a Creole from Zemi, a fictional West Indian sugar island where her British ancestor also fathered slave offspring. Her love affair with Da Silva, who "received her into his canvases as a woman receives a man" (p. 74), enables Julia to travel from her Holland Park apartment back to "Arawak Zemi-land." For her, as for most of Harris' characters, "home is always another journey" (p. 91). It is through Da Silva's paintings, which function as both ship and stage, that Julia and Francis are finally reunited in Zemi: "Francis lay in Julia's arms which were outstretched from the strangest living nothingness into the strangest living otherness" (p. 94).

In *Cultivated Wilderness* and especially in *The Tree*, Harris turns to painting and sculpture for a metalanguage in which the problems of defunct communities might be more adequately redressed. It is through a poetics of incompleteness derived mainly from sculpture (as early as the 1967 lecture "The Writer and Society") that, Harris claims, communion and community—what he calls "*coniunctio*" in the *Womb of Space* (1983)—become possible again as a "privileged rehearsal pointing to unsuspected facets and the reemergence of forgotten perspectives in the cross-cultural and the universal

imagination" (*Infinite Rehearsal*, p. vii). "Coniunctio," he adds in *The Radical Imagination* (1992), "has nothing to do with possession. It is a touching, but not a seizing" (p. 95). For Harris the idea of a "rehearsal," which first appears in *The Waiting Room*, is best expressed in the figure and event of carnival, a historically ambiguous but nonetheless exemplary Caribbean space characterized by creative disorder, or chaos. In Harris' fictions "the deep unconscious humor of carnival" articulates "life in its essential contradiction" (*Tradition*, p. 12). As a form of creative irony, humor provides complex alternatives to the ideological encrustations of conquest, in the West Indies and elsewhere.

WRITING OTHERWISE: THE LATE NOVELS

THE trilogy that consists of *Carnival* (1985), *The Infinite Rehearsal* (1987), and *The Four Banks of the River of Space* (1990) marks, according to Stephen Slemon, a new departure in allegorical writing, with the terms "carnival" and "rehearsal" self-consciously emphasizing the performative qualities of Harris' narrative. Harris' return to allegory responds to a need to alter the texture of the realist novel so as to release characters from ingrained, stereotypical patterns of thought and behavior. In his 1951 essay "Art and Criticism," Harris asked a question vital to his work: "Can the creative artist overcome the changeless spirit and mechanical institutions of his world ruthlessly enforced upon him?" (*Tradition*, p. 9). To answer this question and to achieve a greater density of texture within what he calls "prophetic allegory," Harris endeavors to revision Dante's *Divine Comedy* in such a way that Inferno, Purgatorio, and Paradiso are overlapping modes, not separate levels. In *The Carnival Trilogy* Harris' Dantesque protagonists move in and out of these modes, which represent relative states of consciousness and unconsciousness, led by guides from the realm of the dead. In this revisionary context Harris introduces the concept of reversibility. "A reversible fiction," Virgilian guide Everyman Masters explains to Jonathan Weyl, "unsettles false clarities . . . reopens the profoundest human involvements and perspectives to illumine a truth": that "Violence is *not* the cornerstone of a civilization" (p. 90; ellipsis in the original). The problem is not that violence is a cornerstone of European colonialism but, Harris believes, that later generations have become trapped in colonialism's ideological codes and fixtures, as if in unchanging tautologies. In *Carnival*, Harris calls this constraining pattern of historical succession "the law of the frame." The novel's most resonant example of "framing" is the case of the Amerindian man sentenced to death by the New Forest colonial regime for slaying his sick mother in accordance with his own society's laws.

Carnival, like most other Harris novels, is about freeing oneself from tragic blindness to historical and philosophical misconceptions. The novel is an extended dialogue between two Guyanese men "of indeterminate origin or pigmentation": Everyman Masters and his "foster-son" Jonathan Weyl, who is also Masters' would-be spiritual biographer; their friendship further develops the relationship between Sir Giles and Da Silva. Masters and Weyl leave Guyana for London in 1957, the year *Sputnik* became "the first rocket signalling the Inferno" (p. 11). The narrative proceeds episodically, like a series of theatrical "rehearsals," the first of which is Masters' second death. The novel's opening chapter, set in 1982 in Masters' Holland Park apartment, carefully stages the chance sexual encounter between Masters and a certain Jane Fisher on the eve of Masters' sixty-fifth birthday. After the woman leaves, Masters is stabbed to death, presumably by an intruder. But Masters' death, like that of the horseman in *Palace*, is more complicated, for Masters was stabbed once before, by another Jane Fisher with whom he had an affair in New Forest. Like Idiot Nameless in *Companions*, Masters becomes a Christ figure when he receives these wounds. Death's paradoxical repetition moves its second instance well beyond realism into the realm of ritual necessity where conventionally separate existences overlap. Jonathan learns to distinguish them as Masters the First, the Second, and so on in the biography he writes under the guidance of the "ghostly" Masters.

This biography, their joint book—which is, of course, *Carnival*—revisits and chronicles the different "stages" of Masters' first death. As the novel takes shape from remembered and imagined ("dreamed") conversations between Masters and Weyl, the latter confesses that

Soon I was to perceive in the complex loves and sorrows of Masters' life that I was as much a character (or character-mask) in Carnival as he was. Indeed in a real and unreal sense he and other character-masks were the joint authors of Carnival and I was their creation. They drew me to surrender myself to them. My hand was suffused as I wrote by their parallel hands.

(p. 31)

To write imaginatively, Weyl surrenders the course of his narrative to a host of unexpected presences, "refugee voices that W. H. heard in the sea," as they are called in *The Infinite Rehearsal* (p. 86). Metafictional meditations of this kind, on the part of narrators and characters alike, are much more common in the more abstract textual environment of Harris' later novels than in his earlier fiction.

Masters is not the only guide to rise out of the novel's uncolonized unconscious. *Carnival*'s female characters act, as they do in most of Harris' other novels, as figures of "involuntary divinity." They are "vessels" that mediate the passage of the male figures either through violence, as Jane Fisher does, or through artistic grace, as Alice Bartleby and Amaryllis do. In fact, Amaryllis, Jonathan's wife, has replaced Masters as Jonathan's guide by the end of the novel. Amaryllis' Catholicism enables Harris to connect spiritual with sexual ecstasy, and their marriage is often clad in splendid religious imagery, such as the glass cathedral in which they make love. The part of Catholicism that interests Harris is not its religious dogma, which he finds coercive, but its rich symbolism and the many possibilities for syncretic relations with aspects of other cultures, a practice with deep historical roots in the Caribbean and throughout the Americas. Harris was not brought up Catholic; in fact, Millicent Harris was a Congregationalist. But he attended Catholic schools in Georgetown while his mother was married to his stepfather, who was of mixed Portuguese descent and a staunch Catholic.

Also intriguing about the marriage between Jonathan and Amaryllis is that it allows *Carnival* to wear a heterosexual costume as a figure for spiritual wholeness. Underneath this costume, however, Harris' fiction reveals itself as profoundly hermaphroditic by calling attention to its characters' "latent homosexuality or latent bisexuality" (p. 88). Like Mr. Quabbas', Weyl's imaginative and erotic attachments are significantly dual: to Masters and to Amaryllis. What further complicates matters, signaling that creativity is by no means limited to procreation, is that Amaryllis does not bear a child of her own. Instead, the couple adopts Masters' purported offspring, the daughter that he, wearing the mask of Osiris, fathers with Jane Fisher the Second on the day of his death.

Carnival's use of gender and sexuality, along with race, as flexible, provisional constructs to be revised infinitely extends to the rest of the trilogy, most notably to *The Infinite Rehearsal*. During the first meeting of the Marlovian character Robin Redbreast Glass and the Tiresias figure Ghost, Glass initially hesitates to accept Ghost as a genderless persona, thereby highlighting the arbitrariness and the limitations of all essentialized distinctions:

Thus it was that I welcomed Ghost, conquistadorial and victimized Ghost (was (s)he male / female? I could not tell) when IT appeared on a beach in Old New Forest. . . . I decided to accept IT as male persona and trust that new fragile complications of divinity's blood would drive me to see the phenomenon I had encountered in the wholeness of a transformative light bearing on all genders, all animates and inanimates, all masks and vessels in which a spark of ultimate self-recognition flashed . . . faded . . . flashed again.

(pp. 1–2)

Although Glass's mirrorlike mind reflects Ghost as male, Robin does not erase Ghost's feminine aspects, notably the "long, rich plait of hair on the back of his neck. . . . It was so long and marvelous it could have been the wonderful text of a woman's hair through which to read the mysterious birth of spirit" (p. 2). Later in the novel this "wonderful text" of hair is transfigured into the "seamless robe of eternity" placed on the shoulders of Archbishop Emma, one of Harris' many Madonna figures.

At the end of *The Infinite Rehearsal*, Glass, having successfully deflected Doctor Faustus' and Billionaire Death's materialistic temptations, is finally "launched upon [his] voyage towards Emma" (p. 82) in a repetition of Donne's journey toward Mariella. As a gift to Emma, Robin carries with him a piece of the seamless garment that seems to belong to that moment of epiphany inside the palace of the peacock when Donne beholds a Madonna figure clad in an ancient, threadbare dress that is also her hair. The mysterious garment then stretches across the trilogy into the "loom and tapestry" of Penelope, the Queen of El Dorado in *The Four Banks*, who weaves a "tapestry of counterpoint, guilt and innocence, poverty and wealth" (*Four Banks*, p. 26). Weaving is also tied to the figure of the trickster Anancy and to imaginative writing as a "spider transubstantiation."

Glass concludes his narrative in *The Infinite Rehearsal* by turning another page in his fictional autobiography,

A blank page upon which I had not yet written. Whose hand would seek mine, whose mask become my age in the future? I saw a shadow upon the page, I saw an extension from Ghost. Spirit is one's ageless author, ageless character, in the ceaseless rehearsal, ceaseless performance of the play of truth. The fictionalization of the self in age and in youth is a multi-faceted caution of the universal imagination against the tyranny of hard, partial fact.

(p. 82)

Ghost's "shadow" acquires substance as the Postscript to *The Infinite Rehearsal*, dated A.D. 2025, in which he enjoins us, "Remember me, remember Ghost." Ghost's shadow on Glass's empty page alerts us to "parallel" writing, that is, writing by characters who inhabit different fictional universes and who catch occasional glimpses of each other. This kind of joint, multiple authorship is at the heart of what Harris calls "revisionary strategies," throughout this trilogy and elsewhere. In *The Infinite Rehearsal* Ghost patiently explains to Robin Glass and to the reader, "I say revisionary strategies to imply that as you write of other persons, of the dead or the unborn, bits of the world's turbulent, universal unconscious embed themselves in your book" (p. 46). In the novel's interior "intuitive theatre," author, narrator, and characters are all divinities in "animate costume." They are activated archetypes, or "character-masks," who, though they inhabit different times and universes, can encounter each other intuitively and imaginatively through the "world's unconscious."

The notion of "quantum reality," described by physicist Nick Herbert in one of the epigraphs to *The Four Banks*, elucidates this kind of time travel: "Quantum reality consists of simultaneous possibilities, a polyhistoric kind of being . . . incompatible with our . . . one-track minds. If these alternative (and parallel) universes are really real and we are barred from experiencing them only by a biological accident, perhaps we can extend our sense with a sort of 'quantum microscope'. . . ." Harris typically selects epigraphs after completing a novel, a procedure to which he refers in his preface to *The Four Banks* by mentioning that he received permission from the manuscript's author to "edit his book and add epigraphs." Epigraphs, in other words, are but some of the many voices that inhabit Harris' fiction, and it would be erroneous to read them as statements of influence in any linear sense.

These voices, like those of characters from inside the novels, "contest and validate" the writer's "discoveries." Since Harris' characters are never the author's "pawns," Robin Glass can be the signatory of an unusually testy and adversarial note at the opening of *The Infinite Rehearsal,* in which he complains that "W. H. has stolen a march on me and put his name to my fictional autobiography" (p. vii). The prefatory material we encounter regularly in Harris' later novels does not explain the fiction; rather, it offers another perspective on them, and it makes no difference if this perspective is attributed either to a fictional character or to Harris himself. His prefatory notes and introductions contribute to a formal procedure that may be called postmodern in its blurring of the boundaries between various genres, literary and nonliterary, which is analogous to Harris' blurring of genders and races. The genres whose epistemological status Harris' novels most typically unsettle are the travelogue (in *Palace*), biography (in *Carnival*), autobiography (in *Infinite Rehearsal*), and literary criticism (in *The Womb of Space*). Harris' self-titled autobiography, a collagic essay that incorporates examples of all these genres in excerpts from many of his novels, stands out as the most intense example of his use of generic boundaries as places of communication.

The Four Banks crosses a different kind of boundary by taking us into and across several dimensions of history and the human psyche. Geographical and metaphysical realities converge in the space and the figure of the Potaro River: "the river of the dead and the river of the living are one quantum stream possessed of four banks" (p. 44). *The Four Banks* is the "book of dreams" of Anselm, who, the preface informs us, gave his manuscript to Wilson Harris in December 1988, just before he disappeared in the Macusi heartland. There is no reason for us to expect to see Anselm again, except perhaps in another Harris novel. Like Harris, Anselm is Guyanese. Because he is also a veritable Renaissance man—engineer, painter, sculptor, architect, and composer—the novel's self-reflexive tropes are appropriately multiple. At the same time that it reaches into Da Silva's canvases, *The Four Banks* displays examples of "living sculpture" in one of the novel's several diagrams. It also ex-

plores "musical or antiphonal discourses" in which "the flute is akin to a spiral or a curious ladder that runs into space" (p. 43).

While all these are by now familiar figures for the imaginative eruption of memories *"within the person,"* they rarely cohabit any one Harris novel in such a visible fashion. To open other doors of association, Harris adds the technological media of film and photography, of which we catch a glimpse in *Black Marsden* when Black Marsden disguises himself as a camera. For Harris himself, as for *The Four Banks*'s first-person narrator, all these "memories" are activated by the countryside around Chelmsford, where Harris and his wife moved after they left London in the mid-1980s. It is the same landscape to which Ross and Penelope George, the British missionary couple on whom Anselm's narrative comes to focus, return in 1966 after their almost twenty-year stay in South America.

The Four Banks continues Harris' exploration of twentieth-century violence as trauma. Anselm's narrative, or play, opens in England with an unsettling encounter with Lucius Canaima, a killer whom he last saw on the banks of the Potaro River forty years earlier. The character mask Canaima is modeled on Kanaima, the evil spirit and god of retaliation in Arawak mythology. Canaima's conception goes back in the trilogy to the intruder who presumably kills Masters, an undeveloped character who drifts in and makes another cameo appearance as an escaped murderer who connives to join one of Masters' expeditions into the jungle. Canaima suggests that he is Anselm's guide, or mentor, by addressing him, "outrageously" and prophetically, as his "twin." Although Canaima's words, his metaphoric knife, make Anselm's "complacency . . . bleed as if [he] had received a wound" (p. 10), Anselm, unlike Masters, does not die from his wound. The wound does enable him, however, temporarily to don a "cloak of invisibility" for his Ulyssean "pilgrimage," or hunt, on the first bank of the river of space, where he comes upon Penelope and Ross. Ross initially mistakes him for Simon, Penelope's first husband, the prototypical epic lover and soldier. Simon, who died during World War II and recalls the ghost of Susan Forrestal's lover, haunts Penelope's memories until she imaginatively retraces her steps and frees herself from the "corpse of heroism" to which she had once been married.

A novel of disturbing confessions and "universal homecoming," *The Four Banks* is an ambitious mixture and reworking of "the great masks of legend and history," in which Dantesque allegory elegantly combines with epic, most notably with *The Odyssey* and *The Aeneid*. The purpose of these "translations" is for characters, several of whom are partial embodiments of Ulysses, to confront "great peril and strangest capacity for renewal" and, from this experience, to acquire "the strength to bear the full complication of relationships one had begun to unveil in ascending from bank to bank in the four banks of the river of space" (p. 141). Among such complications is Anselm's discovery that Canaima is none other than his half brother, forgotten and unwanted. Once Anselm no longer denies the wildness inside himself, his own "savage heart," Canaima vanishes. His disappearance near the end of the novel clears the path for a savior figure, Penelope's adopted black child, an embodiment of the "stranger" in herself. El Dorado's new "child-queen who might still breach an epic formula" (p. 160) and *The Four Banks* open yet another cycle of revisions.

The edited "Dream-book" *Resurrection at Sorrow Hill* (1993) returns to the site of Donne and his crew's epitaphs, their tombstones. First mentioned in *Palace* and revisited in *The Eye,* Sorrow Hill is "a place of myth" and of the "invention of truth." In *Resurrection* it is the location of an "asylum for the greats," run by Doctor Daemon. In residence are several patients: Hope, the dream book's author, and his six fellow inmates, who don the masks, among others, of Montezuma, Judas, Leonardo da Vinci, and Karl Marx. Returning in spirit to the Mexican settings of *Companions,* the novel takes abundant aesthetic and thematic cues from what Harris calls the "fossil womb" of pre-Columbian pottery and paintwork, adorned with faces that bear African, Greek, Semitic, Asian, and European features alongside representations of the Aztec god Quetzalcoatl, the plumed serpent. Hope, who does not narrate his own "process of therapy," closely resembles a character from an earlier novel, *Genesis of the Clowns* (1977). In that novel, set in 1974, first-person narrator Frank Wellington, a British land surveyor who lives in London after spending years in Guyana, receives an anonymous letter signed "Yours in hope," followed by his own initials, "F. W." The letter informs him that Hope, his old crew foreman and doppelgänger, killed another man in a quarrel over a woman and then committed suicide. *Resurrection* restages this bloody tale of jealousy that leads not to suicide but

to Hope's "acute breakdown." Although he believes that he is alive, Hope is also paradoxically convinced that he and his lover, Butterfly, were discovered, shot, and killed by Butterfly's enraged husband, Christopher D'eath, who now plays the part of Hope from *Genesis*. D'eath attempts to take his own life but survives. He is tried for murder and incarcerated in the old Mazaruni prison that later becomes an asylum. D'eath's ghost lingers in the six different cells he occupied during his prison term, and he visits with each cell's new resident.

Harris' longest novels, *Resurrection* and *Jonestown* (1996), address themes of revenge, violence, and extinction. At the same time they are novels about surviving catastrophe and overcoming trauma, about the mental processes involved in converting a legacy of violence into future creative energy. Even more so than *The Infinite Rehearsal,* which pinpoints 1986 as a year of terrifying catastrophe—Chernobyl, for one; the *Challenger* accident, for another—*Jonestown* concentrates on an earlier, even more terrifying historical event: the 1978 suicide / murder of close to one thousand members of the Peoples Temple who were forced, at gunpoint, to drink cyanide-laced fruit punch. *Jonestown*'s narrator, Francisco Bone, is a fictional survivor of this horrific Conradian nightmare, which took place at a remote location in the Guyana rain forest. The novel charts the nonlinear course of his gradual awakening from possibly self-induced partial amnesia during a seven-year self-confessional journey. Bone's goal, like Harris', is "to salvage a broken world and reclaim its bearing on a living future" (p. 112). The novel opens with Bone's letter to W. H., asking him to edit a "Dream-book" filled with specters of the Jonestown victims whose fate Bone connects to that of the unexplained fate of pre-Columbian peoples like the Maya. Bone meets his "oppositional twin" Deacon, one of Harris' orphans, in California, where both young men are on scholarship and where they fall under the spell of the charismatic Reverend Jonah (aka Jim) Jones. It is Deacon who shoots Jones before the latter can kill any survivors of the massacre, including Bone.

The ambiguous bond between Bone and Deacon is further cemented by Bone's love for Deacon's young wife, Marie, one of the novel's virgin figures; indeed, it is as if the savior child Marie bears were fathered by both men. Bone's journey, a figure for a consciousness that expands in the vessel of memory, ends up at Roraima, a sacred mountain located at the border of Guyana with Brazil and Venezuela. (It is also the charged setting of the novellas in *The Sleepers of Roraima*.) Legend has it that this mountain, "the soul of living landscapes," is the legendary El Dorado, the lost world that, since *Palace*, has served Harris as dual locus of human greed and possible spiritual salvation. At Roraima, Bone leaps into the void, the first of Harris' characters to do so on his own volition. But like Donne, whose fall is broken by the noose of salvation, Bone is caught by a spidery "net of music." This metaphor joins *Palace*'s fluted "organ of memory" in an intricate symphony of figuration whose eerie, often dissonant, sounds fill the echo chambers of all of Harris' novels.

ESSAYS AND CRITICISM

In his 1974 essay "The Muse of History," Derek Walcott defines mature literature as "the assimilation of the features of every ancestor." In his novels of "psychic reassembly" Wilson Harris goes well beyond assimilating the ancestral features of which Walcott speaks. Harris' writing reaches into the past and the future simultaneously, "gathering up all that had been experienced in every condition of existence," accumulating "apparently imperceptible change into true change, in which nothing was lost and everything possessed an inimitable difference akin to joy" (*Four Banks*, p. 51).

Although Harris rejects for himself the label of "theorist," the talks, lectures, essays, and interviews collected at the turn of the century in five volumes join his novels in elaborating a poetics of the imagination, or better, perhaps, of imaginative cross-cultural reassembly. The foundation for this poetics is Harris' sustained critique of realism, which began in 1952, in a *Kyk-over-Al* essay titled "Form and Realism in the West Indian Artist." ("Form and Realism," along with "Tradition and the West Indian Novel" and "The Writer and Society," two of the most remarkable early statements on Caribbean literature, is included in Harris' 1967 volume *Tradition, the Writer and Society*.) Harris has criticized the textual politics of realism throughout his literary career. Unlike György Lukács he does not see contemporary realism as a continuation of an earlier humanist revolt against imperialist economics; on the contrary, he regards realism, rationalism's literary offspring,

as central to any imperial ideology and as a troubling residue of imperialism's cultural politics. "So realism is authoritarian," he writes in *The Radical Imagination*, "in the sense that it has to stick to one frame. It cannot bring other texts into play. Realism has to work with one text. Very much like a journalistic text: one text, a single frame" (p. 26). Realism, in other words, equals dogmatism, in the Dickensian "novel of persuasion" and in any fiction that imposes a specific moral directive. In linking realism and imperialism, Harris' work anticipates that of postcolonial theorists such as Edward Said, James Clifford, and Homi Bhabha, who acknowledge that identity is not an "inert fact" and recognize that we–they distinctions, however useful they may be to national liberation movements, dangerously simplify the encounter between different cultures, traditions, and societies.

Harris' consistent effort to unravel the self-deception that resides in popular modes of literary representation such as realism has led him to lament the tendency among Caribbean writers of his generation to represent colonial relations in dogmatic narratives laced with revenge. Too many postcolonial writers, Harris cautions, devalue the imaginary in favor of ethnographical realism, and he warns repeatedly that "Political radicalism is merely a fashionable attitude unless it is accompanied by profound insights into the experimental nature of the arts and sciences" (*Tradition*, p. 46). Harris holds that imaginative writers have the moral responsibility to reveal to their readers areas of intellectual and emotional self-deception without resorting to political dogma and, implicitly, to violence. This belief leads him to seek alternatives to narrative domination in a "new density" of language. Realism, he asserts in "A Note on Zulfikar Ghose's 'Nature Strategies' " (1989), "negates the complexities of language" and thus denies "the unconscious as a complex vessel of evolutionary form" (p. 173). The opaque complexities of Harris' language are what many of his readers experience as an almost insurmountable difficulty. All of his novels have, at various times, been called at once brilliant and bewildering. One of the reasons why Harris' texts are so bewildering is that they go against the expectations that many readers have developed of contemporary texts, and of so-called postcolonial novels in particular. To a significant extent these expectations result from the desire for clear political messages and easy access to categories such as Otherness in the literary form of local cultural authenticity. Texts that systematically frustrate those expectations, even expose them as self-deceptions, still tend to be regarded with suspicion, especially when they endorse "universality," as Harris' novels do.

In Harris' writing opacity results when characters begin to acknowledge the existence of "inner problematic ties" to the rest of the world. These "ties" evoke a Jungian network that Harris terms the "world's unconscious." Eclipsed links to both the living and the dead complicate Harris' sense of individual identity to an unusual extent. V. S. Naipaul's *A House for Mr Biswas,* by contrast, struggles for a unified identity that would counteract the psychological disintegration that is part of colonialism's legacy; there is an acute need in that novel to protect Mr Biswas' self from further damage. Harris reverses this: instead of protecting the self in a house of fiction that functions as shell or fortress, he makes the self vulnerable to its own, and others', forgotten wounds. Unlike Naipaul, Harris is intent on exposing the self to "outrageous foreigners" within by restoring silent, and silenced, voices of others to the consciousness of a multidimensional being. In the essays in *Tradition,* he first distinguishes "the obscure human person" from "the ideology of the 'broken' individual" (pp. 27–28), "broken" because she / he is divided into self and other. Harris' novels seek to heal this modern self-division by exploring "a bridge across the divided conception of humanity" (p. 24).

The Womb of Space, subtitled *The Cross-Cultural Imagination,* draws further distinctions, specifically between cross-culturalism and various popular notions of multiculturalism and cultural pluralism, which celebrate diversity while emphasizing separateness. Harris' cross-culturalism, by contrast, refers to the ceaseless elaboration, or "unfinished genesis," of a gateway, or bridge, between humanity's collective unconscious and the miracle of a layered consciousness. The texts he sees involved in similar activities of cross-cultural "rapport" range from William Faulkner's *Intruder in the Dust* and Jean Rhys's *Wide Sargasso Sea* to Ralph Ellison's *Invisible Man* and Patrick White's *Voss.* This cross-culturalism is the "strange and subtle goal, melting pot," which Harris identifies, in *Tradition,* as

the mainstream (though unacknowledged) tradition in the Americas. And the significance of this is akin to the

European preoccupation with alchemy, with the growth of experimental science, the poetry of science as well as of explosive nature which is informed by a solution of images, agnostic humanity and essential beauty, rather than vested interest in a fixed assumption and classification of things.

(pp. 32–33)

Harris' writings, fictional and nonfictional, are truly remarkable in their scope and, even more important, in their willingness to perceive similar, parallel structures in the arts and the sciences. For Harris these structures significantly reside *within* the fabric of a language that gathers together in its fragile threads many different forms of natural, artistic, and scientific expression. Such language makes stones dance in the curvature of space, turns greenheart trees into "human timber," and represents the movement of waves as embroidery. It is a language, Harris trusts, that has at least a chance to lead readers from dread of other creatures to compassion for them.

SELECTED BIBLIOGRAPHY

I. Fiction and Poetry. *Fetish* (Georgetown, 1951); *The Well and the Land* (Georgetown, 1952); *Eternity to Season* (Georgetown, 1954; rev. ed., London, 1978); *Palace of the Peacock* (London, 1960); *The Far Journey of Oudin* (London, 1961); *The Whole Armour* (London, 1962); *The Secret Ladder* (London, 1963); *Heartland* (London, 1964); *The Eye of the Scarecrow* (London, 1965); *The Waiting Room* (London, 1967); *Tumatumari* (London, 1968); *Ascent to Omai* (London, 1970); *The Sleepers of Roraima: A Carib Trilogy* (London, 1970); *The Age of the Rainmakers* (London, 1971); *Black Marsden* (London, 1972); *Companions of the Day and Night* (London, 1975); *Da Silva da Silva's Cultivated Wilderness* and *Genesis of the Clowns* (London, 1977); *The Tree of the Sun* (London, 1978); *The Angel at the Gate* (London, 1982); *Carnival* (London, 1985); *The Guyana Quartet* (London, 1985); *The Infinite Rehearsal* (London, 1987); *The Four Banks of the River of Space* (London, 1990); *The Carnival Trilogy* (London, 1993); *Resurrection at Sorrow Hill* (London, 1993); *Jonestown* (London, 1996).

II. Essays. *Tradition, the Writer and Society: Critical Essays* (London, 1967); *Explorations: A Selection of Talks and Articles, 1966–1981,* ed. by Hena Maes-Jelinek (Mundelstrup, Denmark, 1981); *The Womb of Space: The Cross-Cultural Imagination* (Westport, Conn., 1983); "A Note on Zulfikar Ghose's 'Nature Strategies,' " in *Review of Contemporary Fiction* 9, no. 2 (1989); *The Radical Imagination:*

Lectures and Talks, ed. by Alan Riach and Mark Williams (Liège, Belgium, 1992); "Wilson Harris," in *Contemporary Authors Autobiography Series,* vol. 16 (Detroit, 1992); *Selected Essays of Wilson Harris,* ed. by Andrew Bundy (London, 1999).

III. CRITICAL STUDIES. Michael Gilkes, *Wilson Harris and the Caribbean Novel* (London, Port-of-Spain, Trinidad, and Kingston, Jamaica, 1975); Hena Maes-Jelinek, *Wilson Harris* (Boston, 1982); Sandra E. Drake, *Wilson Harris and the Modern Tradition: A New Architecture of the World* (Westport, Conn., 1986); Stephen Slemon, "Revisioning Allegory: Wilson Harris's *Carnival,*" in *Kunapipi* 8, no. 2 (1986); Michael Gilkes, ed., *The Literate Imagination: Essays on the Novels of Wilson Harris* (London, 1989); Hena Maes-Jelinek, ed., *Wilson Harris: The Uncompromising Imagination* (Mandelstrup, Denmark, and Sydney, 1991); Nathaniel Mackey, ed., "Wilson Harris," special issue of *Callaloo* 18, no. 1 (1995); Joyce Sparer Adler and David Madden, eds., "Wilson Harris and Alan Burns," special issue of *Review of Contemporary Fiction* 17, no. 2 (1997).

TONY HARRISON

(1937–)

Robert Squillace

TONY HARRISON MAY be the only important living poet who has never published a poem that does not rhyme. The importance of rhyme in Harrison's poetics is consonant with his fondness for puns; both devices involve a recognition of the double nature of words. In rhyme, words divided by meaning are unified by sound; in puns, a single sound stretches in two directions of meaning. Both of these devices also involve a third element thoroughly characteristic of Harrison's poetry: silence. No words bridge the gap between the dual meaning of a pun or the suggestive connection of a rhyme; through silence, rhymes and puns communicate more than they say. The divisions of Harrison's own life help explain both the centrality of division in his poetry and what he perceives as the necessity of silence in negotiating the gaps between what can be said.

Born on 30 April 1937 in Leeds, a metropolis of England's industrial North, Harrison reads his own childhood as a fall—perhaps fortunate, perhaps not—from the paradise of his family's love, brought about by eating of the fruit of the tree of knowledge. Although such memories of the Second World War as the rare public outpouring of unified joy at its end appear in Harrison's poetry, the seminal event of his early years was schismatic: in 1948 he won a scholarship to the elite Leeds Grammar School. In learning the languages of the classical world, Harrison lost the speech of his home (see, for instance, the sonnet "Wordlists" in "The School of Eloquence"); in subsequent years pursuing the life of a poet would further separate him from the world of his father, Harry, a baker, and his mother, Florence Horner Harrison, a housewife. In the Greco-Roman classics Harrison found not alienating elitism but mirrors of his own experience; he has never imagined any contradiction between a high regard for Greek and Latin literature and a low regard for the privilege of the moneyed classes. Rather, what Harrison chiefly held against the tuition of his youth was the assumption of his tutors that poetry—regardless of the language of its composition—was the private fiefdom of gentlefolk.

Still, the poet's education—he completed a B.A. in classics at Leeds University in 1958 and did some work toward a Ph.D.—barred his reentry to the world of his childhood with a flaming sword. In part he was not wanted, his poetic ambitions being distrusted as a betrayal of the traditional working-class value of self-disguising reticence; in part the artist's life of travel and opportunity simply gave him a frame of reference incommensurate with his family's. This division haunts his poetry; one might even understand his chief motive for writing at all as a fierce desire to undo that early separation, to write his way back to that lost world. His first response, however, was to get out: on 16 January 1960 Harrison married Rosemarie Crossfield Dietzsch, an artist, with whom he would have two children, and took up teaching fellowships in Nigeria (Ahmadu Bello University, 1962–1966) and Czechoslovakia (Charles University, 1966–1967). Stints at the universities of Newcastle and Durham and a traveling UNESCO fellowship would follow.

Although Harrison of necessity has accepted a number of such posts, he prefers to live by poetry itself, ill as it often pays. While poetry that pays may not quite restore Harrison to the artisan status that working-class audiences can respect, it may at least signify that someone is listening. To restore a public role to poetry has been a common dream of twentieth-century poets; like T. S. Eliot and W. H. Auden, Harrison has composed libretti and verse drama in the hope of being heard. After the publication in 1970 of *The Loiners,* his first full-length book of poetry (*Earthworks,* a pamphlet containing nine poems, had appeared in 1964), Harrison devoted a great deal of his energy for the balance of the decade to the stage, beginning with an extraordinarily successful translation of *The Misanthrope,* produced at the Old Vic in 1973. His first libretto, a translation of Bedrich Smetana's *The Bartered Bride* in which he managed the technically virtuosic feat of reproducing the precise number of syllables in every line of his English version as in the Czech original, debuted at the Metropolitan Opera in New York City in 1978; no more than a few years have since gone by without the appearance of some new libretto or verse play, whether translated or wholly original. Such work brought Harrison to the attention of the venerable film director George Cukor, among others; Harrison contributed lyrics to Cukor's film of Maurice Maeterlinck's *The Blue Bird,* which unfortunately proved to be an expensive flop.

The 1970s brought Harrison his first notable professional success, but they represented an even greater watershed decade in his personal life, setting the conditions under which his greatest poetry would be written. In particular the deaths of Harrison's mother and father affected his work, informing the twenty-six poems of the second and longest section of his continuing sonnet sequence "The School of Eloquence," portions of which appeared in 1978 (as *From "The School of Eloquence"*), 1981 (as *Continuous: 50 Sonnets from "The School of Eloquence"*), and 1984 / 1987 (expanded to sixty-seven pieces in the two editions of Harrison's *Selected Poems*). The shadow of oblivion begins to stalk Harrison's poetry after the death of his parents, which represents for the poet the death of a whole world now permanently inaccessible to him. In the last years of the decade, Harrison's first marriage ended; he soon began to keep company with Teresa Stratas, an internationally acclaimed soprano, who would become his second wife. Their love is palpable in all the happiest moments of his poetry in subsequent years.

Harrison achieved a considerably higher public profile in the 1980s. He continued to impress his peers in the narrow corridors of poetry, winning prizes for his poem "Timer" (1980) and his translation of *The Oresteia* (1981), serving as president of the Classical Association (1987–1988), and publishing the first and second editions of his *Selected Poems*. But the medium that most shaped the public consciousness of Harrison—at least in the United Kingdom—was television. Harrison's work for the BBC had already included the "mechanical pastoral" *Yan Tan Tethera,* a thoughtful and delightful children's musical drama titled *The Big H,* and a very well received modern English version of the York mystery cycle, *The Mysteries,* when a film of him reading his long poem "V." was broadcast in 1987. Given that the poem, which had been published to the usual praise from the usual people in 1985, employs the word "fuck" seventeen times (it concerns an imaginary encounter between the poet and a skinhead Leeds football supporter), the howling response of Tory politicians and religious figures seems unsurprising. Nevertheless, more Britons probably associate Harrison with the "V." controversy than with any of his myriad poems and plays.

In addition to bringing Harrison an ambiguous celebrity that he has regarded with a mixture of amusement at the ineptitude of his critics and concern over their impulse to silence him, the response to the broadcast of "V." suggested to him that television might provide a means to reach the sort of audiences poetry rarely visits. Over the next ten years Harrison would write and broadcast half a dozen film / poems while continuing to pursue his work in drama and translation; indeed, the only new lyrics he published in the 1990s were the two poems on the Gulf War contained in the pamphlet *A Cold Coming* (1991). While the broadcast of "V." was essentially a filmed reading, the film / poems attempt to combine the two media, which share a basic grammar of techniques for speaking through images. In fact the poetry itself is altered by the medium; Harrison speaks much more plainly in the film / poems and in his verse dramas than in his densely layered lyrics.

Tony Harrison's personal journey from being his block's one book-loving boy to his adult identity as one of the planet's few writers who composes virtually nothing that does not scan would be remarkable even if his poetry were not so fine. Like a compass he leaves one foot firmly planted in the Leeds of his youth while traversing the continents with the other, thus circumscribing in his poetry something as close to all the world as a poet can achieve.

THE LOINERS

SINCE he has never chosen to reprint the nine poems that compose the pamphlet *Earthworks* (1964), *The Loiners* can be regarded as Harrison's first collection of poetry. In this volume he opposes a grim frankness to the icons of propriety that he regards as oppressive in the areas of poetic diction and sexual reference. Despite the candid quality of its language, *The Loiners* contains the least personal poetry of Harrison's career; the poems have a slightly distant air, springing far more often from observation than from experience, which is rarely the case in his later work. Their blunt idiom also displays less of the colloquial flexibility of subsequent poems.

In "Thomas Campey and the Copernican System," with which Harrison began his *Selected Poems*, the title character becomes an emblem for the forgotten workers upon whom culture weighs in an entirely different fashion than it does on the brittle aesthetes of T. S. Eliot's early poems. Campey, handcart vendor of scrap paper, old clothing, and used books, has an understanding of the intellectual tradition he unwittingly helps to sustain that is extremely faulty: *"The earth turns round to face the sun in March, / He said, resigned, it's bound to cause a breeze."* Those charged with the necessary drudgery of materially maintaining a system that is far more than merely Copernican, the poem implies, have no access to its rewards. His years of book work have bent Campey's spine—physically, but also in signification of his mute acquiescence to his own exploitation—so that "every pound of this dead weight is pain / To Thomas Campey (Books)." In preserving the spines of the volumes he must sell, Campey has ruined his own. The books in Campey's cart, which include such potboilers as "Marie Corelli, Ouida and Hall Caine," are not only "dead weight" in that they perforce have value to him only as commodities; their conventional sentiments also stunt his imagination so that he can dream of deliverance only at the hand "of God as Queen Victoria." In the poem's final stanza Harrison sarcastically asks that Leeds thank royalty "For bringing Thomas from his world of dust / To dust, and leisure of the simplest kind." The systematic erasure of such figures as Campey is inscribed in language itself; a lexicon in which books represent "leisure" can accommodate no knowledge of the Thomas Campeys on whom the weight of others' leisure alights.

The major opposition that Harrison constructs in *The Loiners*, however, is between political repression and the open expression of individual sexual desire; indeed, he purposely confuses the issue of whether sexual repression serves the cause of the political variety or vice versa. In "Doodle Bugs," for example, the poet describes how a figure of conventional intellectual authority—a classics-teaching vicar—cannot help but notice how the boys in his charge alter their initially sexual doodles into the innocuous forms of bananas, eyeglasses, and so forth. What the vicar perhaps fails to note, given his character as an upholder of proprieties—presumably the shadow of his awareness is what forces the boys to disguise the nature of their drawings in the first place—is how essential it is that such desires escape from repression. In the poem's last two lines, Harrison avers that "adult exploration [is] the slow discovery / of cunt as coastline, then as continent."

Of course the transformation of women into landscapes and their implicit exclusion from a sort of "adult exploration" that is strictly masculine itself smacks of repression (although it also anticipates the collection's idea of colonization as sexual conquest, further developed in "The White Queen" and "The Songs of the PWD Man"); in any case Harrison became increasingly careful to avoid or qualify such identifications in subsequent work. A more cheerful assertion of subversive sexuality occurs in "The Bedbug." The title punningly refers both to a listening device planted in a bedroom (Harrison's year in Prague introduced him to a world of blatant invasion of privacy) and to the human pest monitoring the device. The poet instructs his invisible listener to do the impossible: distinguish the actual sounds of lovemaking from those produced purely for the sake of the supposedly secret microphone. The listener's presumable inability to make such a distinction suggests that sexual love establishes an interiority that no political oppression can penetrate; that is, what the lovers know cannot be understood from any exterior vantage point, and so cannot be controlled. Indeed, in *The Loiners* open expressions of sexual language are always subversive, regardless of what lies behind them.

"THE SCHOOL OF ELOQUENCE, ONE"

To enter the sonnet sequence of "The School of Eloquence," Harrison's masterwork, one must first pass, as it were, under the arches of three epigraphs, each of which identifies one of the three major elements of the work to follow: political resistance, poetic remembrance, and familial disturbance. The first epigraph rehearses an anecdote from E. P. Thompson's *The Making of the English Working Class;* the historian describes one of the final attempts of the London Corresponding Society—an organization founded by a London shoemaker to further the cause of working-class rights (including universal suffrage)—to continue its activities after government suppression in the wake of the French Revolution. Members apparently referred to the group under the code name "the School of Eloquence." The identity of political oppression with linguistic suppression is a central theme of Harrison's masterwork.

But, as the next epigraph suggests, Harrison's effort is less to speak for the classes to which he himself, as a successful poet leading the socially ambiguous life of an artist, no longer fully belongs, than to commemorate their separate struggles. Indeed, one might take the sixteen lines of Milton's "Ad Patrem" (To His Father) that Harrison quotes as his second epigraph to reveal the poetic credo of "The School of Eloquence." Milton's lines invoke the muse's aid in honoring his father so far as is possible by "vacuis . . . verbis" (empty words); thus Harrison's effort is to preserve what he may of the inarticulate lives of his closest relations and earliest companions while never forgetting the incapacity of his words either to render their experience fully or to compensate them for their suffering with the dubious gift of poetic immortality.

The third epigraph acts as the threshold of the sequence, consisting of a quatrain written by Harrison himself, a piece titled "Heredity." In these lines Harrison paradoxically claims that the origin of his poetic gift can be found in the incapacity for speech of his two uncles, "one a stammerer, the other dumb." In addition to proclaiming the sequence's foundation in Harrison's own life, the quatrain quietly introduces Harrison's characteristic theme of silence and naming. Poetry, for Harrison, resembles silence at least as closely as it resembles the confident attaching of names and labels by which ordinary speech proceeds; the point of contact between the profession he has chosen and the inarticulate careers of his immediate forebears is the struggle to bring into words what is essentially unwordable. This struggle encompasses not only the eternal lyric effort to make manifest in words the momentary, inarticulate insights that most resist speech in its dailiness and its mere practicality but also the political effort to articulate experiences systematically excluded

from the traditions of language (poetic and otherwise) in order to disempower whole classes and even whole peoples.

The first sonnet in the cycle, "On Not Being Milton," sounds the major themes of the first section of "The School of Eloquence" in an almost celebratory tone rarely found elsewhere in the work. The opening stanza does, however, contain an irony more typical of the sonnets. Harrison refers to the Miltonic epigraph as a *"Cahier d'un retour au pays natal";* the discrepancy between the poet's mastery of the French locution (the title of a work by Aimé Césaire) and his ostensible return to a birth country in which English itself had been a deeply problematic tongue for Harrison's people precisely mirrors the division between himself and the Leeds football hooligan that Harrison would later draw in "V." Harrison knows that if he is not Milton, neither is he the mute rustic of Gray's "Elegy" alluded to later in the poem; in fact the poem's title could as well refer to the earlier revolutionaries mentioned in the poem as to the poet himself.

But, uncharacteristically, the poem immediately veers away from the irony of Harrison's individual situation into an ecstatic recognition of the poetry in the compressed pronunciation and reticence of Northern speech, ultimately raising "Three cheers for mute ingloriousness." The glottal stops that mark the industrial Northern accent become signals of resistance, a refusal to share entirely a common tongue with the proprietors of "standard" English and so assent to their domination; "Leeds stress" falls on "the looms of owned language" like the Luddite hammers breaking apart the manufacturers' long-frame looms that siphoned away the livelihood of artisan weavers in the early nineteenth century. The sonnet itself, like all those in the work, breaks the frame of the conventional fourteen-line form, employing the highly unusual sixteen-line alternative developed by George Meredith. (The *Princeton Encyclopedia of Poetry and Poetics,* for example, questions whether poems in Meredith's format qualify as sonnets.) Further, Harrison's general refusal of the tonic couplet of the Shakespearean model gives his poems a far less settled, enclosed quality than traditional English sonnets.

But Harrison is always aware that words settle nothing; in the last stanzas of "On Not Being Milton," he recognizes the unity between the poet's effort to articulate the conditions of his inarticulation and the similar struggle of the linguistically disinherited. The sonnet ends by projecting a line into "the silence round all poetry" (line 14); a line, that is, set off by a stanza break from the rest of the poem, thus balancing the similarly lonely "Three cheers" of line 12. These words, attributed to Richard Tidd, who participated in a failed Cato Street conspiracy to assassinate the British cabinet in 1820, declare: *"Sir, I Ham a very Bad Hand at Righting"* (line 16). As with all poetry, the line derives its meaning from the unspoken conditions of its utterance, not from the mere denotations of its words. Tidd's misspelling of "am," in concert with his characterization of his penmanship as his "hand," suggests ham-handedness, the clumsiness with words that also informs the poem's terminal pun: Tidd cannot "right" because he cannot "write." But, at the same time, these inarticulate words *are* poetry. Thanks to Harrison's recognition of their metrical quality (he affirms in "Confessional Poetry" that everyone's speech, regardless of his or her fluency, "often scans"), they appear in a poem, and they communicate primarily by the silent suggestiveness that their literal meaning obscures. The poem confirms the idea that the condition of Harrison's mute and stammering uncles and his own penchant for expression in puns, rhyme, and poetic form might resemble each other almost hereditarily.

A more typically tart sonnet from the first section of "The School of Eloquence" is "National Trust." The poem begins with a sentence fragment, a scrap of speech only partially articulated: "Bottomless pits." An exemplum of the breach between the controllers of speech and the victims of silence follows: Harrison describes a convict lowered into a bottomless pit to settle a gentlemanly wager as to its depth; he returns so "dumb" that not even flogging will elicit a word. The terror of the pit, as the poem goes on to make clear, is the condition of wordlessness itself. To be void of language is to be effaced from history; the irony of the poem's title, developed in the third stanza, attacks the commemoration of a tin mine's pit shaft in Cornwall by the very scholarly institutions that effectively slew Cornish as a living tongue.

As always in the "School of Eloquence," Harrison shows a complicating self-consciousness in "National Trust" of his own poetic enterprise, his own effort to address the condition of silence in speech. The poem ends in a quatrain that first describes the descent of the voiceless—both the miners and all robbed of language—into the void as "go[ing] down in history"; the conventional phrase of remembrance is here transformed by the context into an index of oblivion. On the other hand, Harrison notes that the repressors of working-class speech have not "been brought to book"; in fact, "National Trust" both provides the indictment that law has failed to serve and records the experience of the class whose history has ordinarily been silenced, bringing them to book in a more positive sense. Finally, however, the poem's last two lines implicitly (wordlessly) acknowledge the limitation of this gesture of poetic remembrance. Harrison inscribes a Cornish proverb in his poem but must at once parenthetically identify it as Cornish and provide a translation: "the tongueless man gets his land took." The political ironies of the first section of "The School of Eloquence" are all the more pointed for their refusal to see poetic recognition as constituting a political solution.

"THE SCHOOL OF ELOQUENCE, TWO"

THE second section of "The School of Eloquence," an astonishing and heartbreaking sequence of twenty-six sonnets that sustains comparison with any such lyric gathering in English, begins with a pair of sonnets, collectively titled "Book Ends," that concern the sudden death of Harrison's mother, Florence. It is as if the event itself were so epochal that the original course of the sequence was diverted. Contemplation of Mrs. Harrison's loss involves no abandonment of the themes of language, oppression, and silence with which the first section deals; rather, it personalizes them so profoundly that the slightly theoretical air of some of the earlier poems utterly dissipates. Harrison involves himself thoroughly in the problem of fine language's falsification of both particular working-class and all human experience.

The opening lines of "Book Ends" find Harrison and his father using their mouths not to articulate their grief, which is unwordable in their lack of a shared language, but to eat together the last apple pie the poet's mother had baked before her sudden death. Their appearance of silent commonality, which reminds Harrison of his mother's characterization of the two as a pair of bookends, belies a deeper split; in fact only Florrie Harrison's belief in the resemblance of her husband and son had established any such likeness. They stand in different relations even to her; when Harrison reports of his father, "Your life's all shattered into smithereens," his use of second person leaves the implication that his own life, the life he has made through articulation rather than silence, remains intact, an idea confirmed in later sonnets.

But, the sonnet's closing line avers, more than youth and age distinguish the two Harrison men from one another, even in their common silence. Like any pair of bookends, they are separated by "books, books, books," the repetition of the word without a conjunction suggesting a shelf of volumes stretching an indefinite, indeterminable length. Harrison's possession of language renders even the quality of his silence incommensurate with his father's; the very existence of the poem testifies to a capacity for articulation not available to the old baker.

The control Harrison's poetic skill provides him, however, brings him into no closer a relationship with fundamental realities. The second sonnet in "Book Ends"—the bookend to the first piece, its opposite and equal—concerns the wording for Florence Harrison's headstone. Here the son's eloquence is no advantage, even though his father is so alienated from language that he fails to discern the absurdity of asking his son to find a briefer name for "'wife' in the inscription." The poet asserts, in the face of his father's scabrous incomprehension at his scholarly son's inability to pen an appropriate epitaph, that "I've got to find the right words on my own," but admits in the piece's final stanza that he cannot better his father's "misspelt, mawkish" lines, because he "can't squeeze more love into their stone." The use of the third-person pronoun "their" to characterize the headstone as belonging only to Harrison's mother and father implicitly excludes the poem's author from any share in the memorial. Indeed, the poetic declaration of intentions in line 13 is surrounded by the silence it cannot equal, set apart by spaces from either the preceding or the following stanza. That the significant opposition between the halves of the poem is never articulated but falls in the margin between them—this poetic pair of bookends separated by emptiness rather than books—also indicates the incapacity of words. Indeed, the end of any book is silence; in the context of this sonnet sequence, the title may both remind us that every book ends in silence and suggest that books (or poems) can achieve their ends only if they speak

through silence. Harrison does ultimately find "the right words"; not within the poem but in his composition of "Book Ends" itself, and not by exhaustively articulating the reality of his and his father's feelings toward each other and Florence Harrison but by gesturing with the greatest eloquence toward what cannot be said.

Throughout the second section of "The School of Eloquence," Harrison manages the hellishly difficult feat of making technical virtuosity serve the expression of deep feeling. "Turns" is a high point in this respect. The first of the turns on which the poem is constructed is a literal one: Harrison turns before a mirror, trying on his father's cap, which, his mother declares, suits him. Of course, to assume so personal an article of a parent's clothing is a way of trying on the parental identity for size; a hat, in particular, bears a metonymous association with the head, the locus of individuality. Similarly, Harrison's posture before a mirror indicates a conscious act of self-definition. But in the very moment of reporting it, Harrison recognizes the gesture's inadequacy, mocking himself in the sonnet's opening lines for assuming that "a bit of chequered cloth" can restore the working-class character that his education has wrung out of his speech and sensibility. That the barrier between Harrison and his father might be insuperable is further suggested by the form of the first stanza. It is cast as a sestet, with which English sonnets traditionally end; its closing couplet ironically reports the preference of Harrison's mother that her son declare his worth by dressing in the manner of the professional classes. Evidently the cap lends no air of class solidarity to the poet in her eyes, despite that form of headgear's long association with the working class.

But another turn or two follow the couplet—traditionally the last turn of thought in a sonnet—as Harrison again extends articulation into the silence that surrounds all speech. At the moment of his father's death, the cap metamorphoses into another misleading conventional signal; fallen beside the collapsed body, it falsifies its owner's working life by lying upside down in the attitude of the hat a beggar uses to collect coins. The cap's misarticulation of the father's life stands grimly, but honestly, unchallenged: "Death's reticence," writes Harrison, "crowns his life's." Via the selection of "crowns," Harrison implies both the real nobility of his father's unworded and unwordable life—the cap has been replaced by a crown—and the ironic continuity of the man's inability to explain himself in a world where language itself belongs to others. By contrast Harrison presents his own highly articulate "turns"—now in the sense of theatrical presentations; in particular the poetic performance of "Turns" itself—as busking a living from the very classes that excluded such as his father from power over words. The cap, symbolically, remains upside down, garnering through verbal chicanery the money that the father could earn only through physical labor.

And yet the poem virtuosically pulls off a final turn; Harrison pictures the money he earns by his writing as falling into "our cap." The plural possessive, which appears uniquely in the poem in these final words, suggests that a recognition of the worker's condition of dependence, whether the work involves words or dough, may at least partially elide the distance between father and son, between work and poetry.

Harrison further explores the power of poetry to restore lost connections—or, at least, to commemorate their loss—in "Background Material." The title of the poem, in concert with another opening sentence fragment—"My writing desk"—establishes a metonymic relationship between the objects on Harrison's desk and the origin of his poetry. In the opening stanzas, however, the title refers more literally to the backgrounds in a pair of photographs, each of which captures one of the poet's parents. Both pictures silently speak of absence, though in opposite ways. The snapshot of Harrison's late father was taken in a pub since demolished; although the poet still owns the place in which his mother was photographed, that continuity merely reinforces the fact of her absence from it. That each background is blurred further suggests the past's recession from present reality. Indeed, each photo commemorates a separate event, and neither shows the poet's parents together; now that they have died, their union is maintained only by their arbitrary inclusion in the same picture frame.

Or so it seems from the first two stanzas. Each photo, however, contains an equivalent flaw, a violation of the principles of good photographic form as telling as Harrison's own departures from poetic convention: each picture implies the presence of the photographer, Harrison himself. The point is not just that the dead remain united in the person of their offspring, their truest union, the fruit of their closest physical connection. In the photograph of his father, Harrison can make out an image of himself in "the gleam, the light" reflected in his father's eye; because, in references to the period not long before someone's conception, he or she is jocularly referred to as "just a gleam in his or her father's eye," the description harks back to the moment of the poet's origin. In the picture of the poet's mother with which it is paired, however, the past zooms breathtakingly into the present. Harrison finds his presence in the picture implied by a shadow, "as though just cast from where I write, / a shadow holding something to its eyes."

The man who held the camera and the man who sits writing the poem, the past and the present, collapse into one figure, one moment; as nebulous as Harrison's shadowy presence in the photo may be, the implicit access of emotion as he contemplates the shot is unmistakable. To write, or at least to write poetry, for Harrison involves the struggle to forge continuity and union; the poem, containing the two pictures of the dead as the frame itself does, discovers a moment of identity between mother and father, child and parents, past and present, that it cannot directly express in words, that must remain a shadowy implication like the poet's presence in the photographs. The poem ends the second section of "The School of Eloquence" (at least as presently constituted) with an intense gaze backward that typifies the method of the whole section.

"THE SCHOOL OF ELOQUENCE, THREE"

PERHAPS Harrison's subtlest and most powerful statement on the limits of articulation is the sonnet "Self Justification," which opens the third section of "The School of Eloquence," wherein the poet unites the incisive observation of the first section with the experiential specificity of the second. The poem's title pun uses the printer's sense of justification—adding spaces between words so all lines come out the same length—to refer equally to the process of justifying one's (poetic) lines and justifying one's life. In its opening stanzas the poem seems to offer a familiar reading of ambition as compensation for something absent, a theory that Harrison applies to his own poetry, to his daughter's track exploits—she was born with a damaged leg—and to his stammering Uncle Joe's brilliance as a compositor, by which he manipulated words with a fluency he could not approach in speech. The paper on which "I stammered my first poetry," Harrison reports, came free from his printer uncle.

The poem's final quatrain, however, suggests that poetry is born of its own impossibility. Harrison first notes the irony that his poems cannot speak to the audience from which they grow and to whom they are addressed; since language that is produced but not received is no language at all, Harrison finds "my would-be mobile tongue still tied." Then, in the poem's ravishing final lines, the poet faces the unwordability of the interior life that poetry struggles to express, envisioning "aggression, struggle, loss" as "blank printer's ems / by which all eloquence gets justified." The real, justified poetry, the lines imply, lies in the speechless heart toward which words can only gesture. Indeed, the space around the word "eloquence" speaks more eloquently than any of the poem's words; the absence of either the second modifying adjective or the pair of quotation marks one might expect to find surrounding the word "eloquence" alerts us to the inadequacy of both the term and the idea, except when it is justified by its evocation of what cannot be said.

The latest published poems in the "School of Eloquence" sequence foreshadow the more public concerns that Harrison would address in his increasingly public poetry of the 1980s. The last sonnets in "Art and Extinction," currently the work's last piece, explore a set of metaphors central to Harrison's work over the next decade. In particular he draws an extended parallel between the numerous species vanishing by either direct human exploitation or the destruction of their environments and the disappearance of poetic language and of all the languages of exterminated peoples, finally suggesting that all human language and human memory may be threatened by our species' ability to bring about its own extinction.

In the fourth poem of "Art and Extinction," for example, Harrison firmly places himself, in his character as poet, among the victims of imminent extinction. The poem's title, "Killing Time," describes both Harrison's activity while he awaits his flight at JFK International Airport—he peers into a vitrine of "death-protected creatures" that apparently are part of some sort of exhibit on endangered species, ironically preserved for view only by the fact of their being dead—and the present

era of mass extinction: a time of killing indeed. Not only do specimens of hawksbill turtle and margay cat look back at Harrison from inside the glass, so does his own reflection. Considering himself in this company, Harrison understands his poetic career both as a trophy for the rare few who can afford the art, much as leopard skin accessories declare their owner's wealth, and as a form of self-taxidermy.

These obdurate images are leavened by ambiguity; that the products culled from endangered species "cost the earth to buy" and that creatures "near extinction . . . grow in worth" suggests that the living animals—and, by extension, the rare remaining instances of living poetry, poetry that maintains a place in a community's life—have a value that transcends their market price. Harrison's description of himself in the poem's final line as "the poet preserved beneath deep permaverse" further indicates the distinction between art that is merely eternal and art that lives; Harrison's play on "permafrost," the climatic condition by which, the poem reports, mammoths have been well enough preserved to encourage possible cloning, suggests that an art kept intact only by the money of connoisseurs is as good as dead. It is not surprising how much energy Harrison has expended since the mid-1980s in an attempt to reestablish poetry as a public art.

In "Dark Times," the fifth poem of "Art and Extinction," Harrison uses the famous example of the adaptation of the peppered moth to the ecological changes caused by industrialization—the previously white-winged moth darkened so as to camouflage itself against the soot-blackened trunks of formerly white-boled trees—as an emblem of working-class retreat from self-expression into "the need for looking black." The poem, added to "The School of Eloquence" sequence between its appearance as *Continuous* in 1981 and the publication of Harrison's *Selected Poems* in 1984, anticipates the themes of "V.": to protect themselves in an atmosphere of oppression and violence, the unemployed children of miners and factory workers adopt the armor of black leather and self-denying aggression, just as the moths have survived through "dark times" by accommodating themselves to the darkness.

To read the violence of the urban dispossessed as the outcome of processes as impersonal in their operation as those of natural selection is, of course, a familiar tack; Harrison adds an original note by wondering, in the poem's last eight lines, whether the lessons of survival can ever be unlearned. In asking whether the moth can return to its original shade "to flutter white again above new Leeds," Harrison simultaneously questions the extent to which "Man's awakened consciousness" can reverse the damage of at least two hundred years of the depersonalization of working-class life, "where all of Nature perished." To broach such a question within the confines of a sixteen-line sonnet requires an abstraction of language at which many poets would balk; a phrase like "Man's awakened consciousness" offers little in the way of concrete imagery. But in his more public poetry of the 1980s and 1990s, Harrison has shown himself increasingly willing to trade the density—at times, even obscurity—of meaning that characterized his earlier work for a language of greater immediacy.

"V."

"V." is not only Tony Harrison's single most impressive poem, it is also the single poem that best represents the concerns and techniques of his entire body of work and the one that develops his characteristic insights to their farthest verge. That its necessary inclusion of very familiar obscenities with deep Anglo-Saxon roots qualified it for the predictable abuse of assorted prelates and busybodies when Harrison's reading was broadcast in 1987 (little protest marked its first printed appearance in 1984) suggests the ritualistic nature of such attacks. Even the most cursory reading of "V." reveals that it neither advocates the true obscenity of cruelty nor even argues the value of sexual license; Harrison uses obscenities at times for their value as plain, idiomatic words and at other times as part of an attempt to understand their more aggressive use. Indeed, a careful reading of the poem demonstrates its remarkable sensitivity to the most delicate nuances of meaning, the very opposite of the spirit of obscenity, which strips words of any meaningful relation to experience and transforms them into mere syllabified expressions of anger, hatred, or despair.

"V." unfolds as a series of minutely articulated tableaux, symbolic set pieces in which the poet struggles to understand the meaning(s) of a variety of divisions and unions. But every one of the poem's central images defeats unitary interpretation, from the title letter to the final expression of the interdependence of labor, excrement, and poetry. Further, the poet's express awareness of the indeterminacy of all his work's symbols transforms the poem into a passionate meditation on the linked political and personal significance of the irreducible multivalency of all the symbols by which we live.

The poem, composed in plainspoken quatrains, begins with Harrison meditating on the presumable site of his future grave, a family plot resting atop a worked-out coal seam on Beeston's Hill in Leeds. From this vantage point, he notes, "If buried ashes saw then I'd survey / the places I learned Latin, and learned Greek, / and left, the ground where Leeds United play" (V. and Other Poems, ll. 21–23). Going on to describe his final resting place—that is, symbolically, the point at which the career of his thought comes to rest, reaches final expression—Harrison perfectly balances images of union and division, of understanding and incomprehension. His work itself simultaneously unifies him with and divides him from his forebears, "butcher, publican and baker, now me, bard / adding poetry to their beef, beer and bread" (ll. 3–4); the locution "bard" alliteratively links Harrison's sort of labor with that of his ancestors, while the poetry he produces simultaneously contrasts with their more material products, a division reinforced by the discrepancy between the airier unvoiced initial *p* of "poetry" and the earthier voiced initial *b*s of the other three items.

Harrison brilliantly pursues the irony; at least, he wryly reports, he will have the company of "two peers" (l. 7), Wordsworth and Byron—in this case a maker of church organs and a tanner. They are at once the peers of Harrison in both their original and ultimate Leeds roots and his inverses, not being the poets their names more familiarly indicate nor "peers" in their capacity to lead the sort of life Harrison leads, which comprehends certain privileges and opportunities once reserved for gentlemen. The pit beneath the graveyard, meanwhile, serves as a reminder of the common material decay to which all flesh is subject. Harrison notes how "the distinguished dead" (l. 10) will one day tumble together in the empty galleries of the abandoned mine: an ultimate union of decomposition that ends the distinctions by which the living are differentiated one from another. In the opening stanzas of the poem, then, division is alienation, and union, understanding; simultaneously union is death, and division, a condition of life itself. Much of the rest of the poem is devoted to exploring these ambiguities.

The language of the graveyard consists of more than names and epitaphs; spray-painted on the most temptingly roomy headstones by Leeds United enthusiasts taking the shortcut through the cemetery are a number of four-letter words and, "more expansively, there's LEEDS v. / the opponent of last week, this week, or next" (ll. 49–50). Only the context and the subsequent rhyme with "curses" indicate that the "v" stands for "versus" (a pun, too, on "verses"); soon even these interpretive clues vanish. The phrase itself dwindles to a series of flying *V*s, misshapen from having been sprayed at a dead run. As Harrison remarks, the letter resembles the victory V he helped whitewash onto walls as a child during the Second World War, an act considered patriotism rather than vandalism. For the moment, however, he sidesteps such ambiguities and confidently declares that "These Vs are all the versuses of life" (l. 65), after which he enumerates all the internal and external conflicts that both bedevil and constitute life, from "LEEDS v. DERBY" (l. 66) to "male / female" (l. 74).

The especially violent incarnation of these conflicts in the present occupies the next segment of the poem, which was written during the N.U.M. (National Union of Mineworkers) strike of 1984. Harrison shoulders his own share of the responsibility for the decline of working-class England; whereas his father maintained the family plot by scrupulous weekly attention, he stops at the grave site only while hustling between other destinations, visits nearly as hurried as the hit-and-run attacks of the spray-painting Leeds supporters. Already a sort of identity between the poet and the vandal is established; when the poet finds the word "UNITED" (l. 84) spray-painted on his parents' stone, he makes the word his own, interpreting it as a reference to an eternal union of his parents (in the possibility of which he does not actually believe) and to his own hope for a healed nation. But such a reading only manifests Harrison's "power to master words," as the poem's epigraph puts it (quoting Arthur Scargill); the interpretation of the skinhead's symbol is simply a question, to paraphrase Lewis Carroll's Humpty-Dumpty, of who is to be master. Words under such circumstances communicate no commonality, produce no union; they only confirm divisions of power already extant.

Recognizing the one-sidedness of his first reading, Harrison embarks on a quest to understand what the skinhead meant by the word he sprayed. That the vandal felt the need of a personal emblem does not puzzle the poet; he notes that arms, cigarette, and liquor manufacturers—not to mention arms-bearing aristocrats—have long emblazoned their own names on billboards, on signs, and on coats of arms in far more genuinely obscene gestures than the dirty words of a football fan. But the appearance of racial insults and colloquialisms for excrement and women's genitals on tombstones puzzles Harrison more deeply. Then, in one of the poem's most startling moments, his speculation that a larger lamentation for mortality stands behind the words is interrupted by a foul-mouthed screed uttered by a " HARPoholic yob" (l. 328) from some hidden vantage point that Harrison cannot locate (the capitalization of both the skin's obscenities and of Harp, a brand of lager, reinforces the idea that many of the most truly obscene signs go unnoticed). Although the yobbo initially declares as the source of his rage the fact that the headstones of the dead attribute some meaningful occupation to their occupants, some evidence of a life lived, while his own perpetual subsistence on the dole hardly differs from death, his intentions in cemetery desecration prove surprisingly difficult to pin down. Harrison can find no way to argue him down from an aggression equally homicidal and suicidal, despite every attempt to find some fellow feeling on the basis of their similar childhoods.

But when Harrison does at last feel he has argued his foe—another versus—into a corner, the poem takes its most brilliantly illuminating turn. Aggravated by the hooligan's belligerent refusal to admit any commonality between them—and even more by his insistence that he needs no other form of expression than graveyard graffiti—Harrison administers what he thinks is a rhetorical coup de grace: " 'If you're so proud of it [the graffiti] then sign your name / when next you're full of HARP and armed with spray" (ll. 310–311). He is answered by a far greater assertion of union than he had bargained for: "He aerosoled his name, and it was mine" (l. 316). One realizes in a flash that, of course, all the yob's words are in fact Harrison's, their true author's; hence the figure's invisibility. The point is simultaneously linguistic and political. That Harrison cannot transcend his own interpretive consciousness to offer a definitive, objective account of the graffiti's meaning is partly the fault of language itself; the meaning of any symbol is irreducibly plural. The disputation between the poet and his opponent is in fact killingly inscribed within Harrison himself; indeed, it appears to be written into the nature of existence:

One half of me's alive but one half died
when the skin half sprayed my name among the dead.

Half versus half, the enemies within
the heart that can't be whole til they unite.
As I stoop to grab the crushed HARP lager tin
the day's already dusk, half dark, half light.

(ll. 319–324)

At the same time, far from repudiating the poem's political interests, the passage identifies—unifies—political and personal in a manner that makes a fuller life for such as the unemployed youth of Leeds all the more crucial: Harrison's internal rift can be healed only when the nation's has been. As long as others are left to decay by exclusion from any capacity to create meaning, Harrison's identification with them will divide his own energies between delicate articulation of the tenderest feelings and an obscure impulse to scrawl filthy words on tombstones. The "they" (l. 322) who must unite are at once the halves of Harrison's severed heart and the external forces that have pulled him apart. Oppression breeds anger and hatred even in those not directly oppressed.

When Harrison decamps from Leeds, the images of the graveyard follow. Indeed, the city is more funereal than the cemetery had been; on his bus journey back to the railway station through a Leeds he hardly recognizes (another of the poem's marvelous set pieces), Harrison contemplates the mystery of time's perpetual change from its most individual to its most general levels. He recognizes that the younger lads he has just heard humming "Here Comes the Bride" in the graveyard during a pickup soccer game—Harrison pauses to note the melody's source in *Lohengrin*, its escape into popular usage perhaps being an indication that art need not exclude anyone—may one day metamorphose into "skald [bard] or skin" and that the coal on which Leeds's former wealth rested is itself the product of 300 million years of decay. Paradoxically, the thought of the universality of decomposition, of beauty as the "brief flame" (l. 384)

released by life's transformation into waste and nothingness, allows the poem's fullest vision of union:

I hear like ghosts from all Leeds matches humming
with one concerted voice the bride, the bride
I feel united to, *my* bride is coming
into the bedroom, naked, to my side.

(ll. 405–408)

Only acknowledging the huge, impersonal forces upon which human life bobs along gives Harrison access to this personal moment of union that seems almost to exist outside of time in both its utter presence and its eternal repetition—"Leeds matches" can as well refer to millennia of weddings as decades of football.

Even this experience of beauty doesn't solve the quandary of the soccer hooligan, however; the last word he utters in the poem—after which Harrison explicitly identifies him as "my alter ego" (l. 413)—is a sarcastic *"Wanker!"* (l. 411). Like Malvolio he exits cursing. And yet, Harrison avers, "the skin's UNITED underwrites the poet" (l. 415). The masturbatory egoism implied by the hooligan's last word can be the beginning of love; the sensual experience of another sort of skin—the human body's—can be the origin of beauty. The epitaph Harrison provides for himself in the poem's last stanza—"V." ends precisely where it begins, with the poet contemplating what may remain of his grave site in a thousand years—confirms its suggestion of the union of poetry, waste, and silence while leaving all the piece's careful ambiguities intact:

Beneath your feet's a poet, then a pit.
Poetry supporter, if you're here to find
how poems can grow from (beat you to it!) SHIT
find the beef, the beer, the bread, then look behind.

(ll. 445–448)

The pit on which poetry rests is both the silence in which Harrison characteristically locates the truest eloquence and the emptiness into which all existence eventually sinks: death, the mother of beauty. That Harrison terms his putative interlocutor "poetry supporter" connects him or her with the soccer hooligan, the Leeds United supporter; poetry is not so far from the crudest self-assertion, nor is the crudest self-assertion so far from becoming poetry. Indeed, the "you" of the poem's penultimate line could equally refer to the reader or the yob.

The final two lines close the piece in the same multivalency with which it began. To understand how poems grow from excrement, we might consider the writing of poetry as a form of unemployment not far different from the hooligan's, a sort of waste product left over after the more practical work of material survival is finished (in the same manner by which beef and bread are transformed into excremental waste). Pursuing this reading, one might understand the poem's last word as a reference to our own behinds. Alternatively, one might hold that poetry grows from waste as the flame issues from coal, the essence of beauty released for a redeeming moment from its material prison; poetry stands "behind" the appearance of mundane production. One might also look behind the cemetery, at the divisions within Leeds during the coal strike of 1984 that provide the origins of the poem. Harrison scrupulously avoids privileging any one of these readings; for the language of poetry not to reiterate the oppressions of exclusionary speech, speech by and for a single class, it must acknowledge its own uncertainty: that "V." can mean united (see lines 432–433), that union can presuppose division.

RECENT LYRICS

HARRISON'S other lyrics of the 1980s and early 1990s, some of which are anthologized in his *Selected Poems* (1984) and the rest of which may be found either in *The Gaze of the Gorgon* (1992) or *V. and Other Poems* (1990), treat with beautiful lucidity such themes as the sanity of sensual happiness, the insanity of war, and the fragility of human love and memory in the powerful grip of time. Harrison speaks his plainest and most public, most universal English in these lyrics; there is considerably less echo than in his prior work of the specifically Northern tongue of the poet's earliest experience (although he hardly mimics the prevailing dialect of the ruling class; in "A Kumquat for John Keats," for example, he rhymes "saw" and "before"). With the exception of several of the war poems, these more recent lyrics—composed in longer, more meditative sentences—convey a much greater sense of spaciousness than one finds in "V." or "The School of Eloquence." While the less personal language of these poems is also less densely suggestive and offers less sense of unspoken depths filling the spaces between the lines than in, for instance, "The School of Eloquence," Harrison does achieve an accessibility that looks forward to the film / poems with which he has been largely occupied in the 1990s.

The world's sensual redemption provides the subject of both "A Kumquat for John Keats" and "The Pomegranates of Patmos," poems that make similar use of ripe, round fruit as an image for the pleasures of the flesh. By its mingled sweetness and sourness, the kumquat that Harrison consumes in answer to the burst grape of Keats's "Ode on Melancholy" becomes a symbol of the duality of bodily existence, source of pleasure and pain. Indeed, the poet cannot tell "if it's flesh or rind that's sweet," just as he finds it impossible to know if the sweetness of life originates in its proximity to death, or even where dying and living, like night and day, leave off from one another: the poem's final stanza remarks the identity between the creak of bedsprings under the percussion of sex and that of farmers' saws being sharpened. The poem itself is composed of rhyming couplets, an appropriate form for a piece about linked opposites. Moreover, Harrison enjambs the lines more frequently than in virtually any of his other poems, the thought continually bleeding across the boundaries of the pentameter in a manner far removed from the epigrammatic use the eighteenth century made of the couplet. Even the verse form suggests that the pain and pleasure of sensual existence are inextricably bound.

"The Pomegranates of Patmos," on the other hand, employs a comical three-beat dactylic line (deployed in rhyming quatrains) to ridicule those who would construe the ripe fruit of the world as an eschatological warning. Such joyless ascetics include Prochorus, an early Greek convert to Christianity who is also the brother of the poem's speaker, and President Ronald Reagan, for whom, the poem's epigraph implies, nuclear Armageddon evidently corresponds with a righteous scouring of the irreligious. The speaker prefers to envision the pomegranate as the flavorful emblem of the female labia, a life source he finds more worthy of worship. The poem provides an amusing answer to the more prudish critics of the "V." broadcast, but its target may be both too rhetorically defenseless and too strictly external for the satire to have much depth.

The finest meditative poems of this period, such as "Cypress and Cedar" and "The Mother of the Muses," dwell in the borderlands between the public and private worlds, moving with remarkable fluency from the minutest details of personal life to the most profound public concerns, from the simplest observations of public phenomena to the most complex dispatches from the mind's interior. In "Cypress and Cedar," Harrison introduces the title dichotomy with disarming casualness, recounting his visit to a Florida sawyer who works in both media, the fragrant cedar and the rank cypress. Much of the poem that follows takes the form of an explanation of the poet's purchase of one chair built from each wood for his cabin's porch.

As in "V." the central symbol soon proves to host a cluster of dualities; cedar is sex, poetry, pleasure, life, and union, while cypress is death, reality, necessity, extinction, and dissolution. In a sense they also represent the division of male and female in which life originates; Harrison is careful to note that each gender may inhabit either scent, but suggests that the mere opposition of the two odors symbolizes the difference that must precede union (as the two wood scents mingle on the cabin porch, so do the lives—sexual and otherwise—of the poet and his wife). In the coda to the piece, Harrison notes that the Vedic text he is annotating (with a cedar pencil) declares the world to have been shaped from a single tree, "but doesn't tell, / since for durability both do as well, / if the world he made was cypress wood; or cedar" (ll. 153–155). The poem thus ends with a wink, Harrison using the silence of the religious text to negate any assertion of the world's absolute character and so to indicate the eternal interdependence of all that the two forms of wood have stood for, an interdependence established by the poem's title, by the phonemic resemblance of the names of the two trees, and, of course, by the poet's choice to commemorate their union by his selection of porch furniture.

"The Mother of the Muses," Harrison's account of a Valentine's Day visit to his father-in-law, institutionalized with Alzheimer's, masterfully interweaves a surprising collection of elements—a Toronto blizzard, St. Valentine's Day lore, the firebombing of Dresden, the impoverished recollections of Alzheimer's patients, Harrison's own attempt to recall a slice of *Prometheus Bound* he once knew by heart (memory, of course, is the mother of the Muses)—into what is at once among his most harrowing and most hopeful poems. The failing memories of the Alzheimer's victims become a metaphor for the oblivion into which all experience slowly passes; not only does Harrison fail to recollect the scrap of Aeschylus he once knew so firmly, but he chooses a passage from a play that is itself a mere fragment of a two-thirds vanished trilogy. Even the recollection of horror— the poem includes an account of a keeper's intensely moving description of the suffering of the animals in the Dresden zoo on the night of the firebombing—is preferable to its erasure; Harrison acidly juxtaposes a passage on the reconstructed Dresden Opera House (a building that willfully represses any consciousness of the past) with a report on academic denials of the reality of the Holocaust.

The poem offers no easy vision of artistic permanence; Harrison never does recall more than two words from the Aeschylean lines (which concern the Promethean gift of writing, supposedly memory's divine crutch). But it does finally oppose an unspeakable ecstasy to the unspeakable oblivion of death; just as one of the Alzheimer's patients refers to a coffin as *that long thing where you lie* (*V. and Other Poems*, l. 94), so the poet refers to the bed he shares with his wife as "that long thing where we lay" (l. 272). Horror, as so often in Harrison's post-"V." lyrics, yields to celebration. In the last stanza of "The Mother of the Muses," Harrison recollects the old legend that birds choose their mates on St. Valentine's Day; after acknowledging that, for the birds of the Dresden zoo, this coupling meant only mutual incineration, the poet gazes into the obliterating snows for signs of life and sees "like words left for, or *by*, someone from Crete, / a bird's tracks, like blurred Greek, for Valentine's" (ll. 287–288). One should not suppose, of course, that the soul of Emmanuel Stratas has transmigrated; rather, the simile suggests that love's impulse to write itself into the landscape is as perpetual as death (the Greek words looking back immediately to the poet's father-in-law and ultimately to Aeschylus), and that the struggle toward articulation unifies all the living world. The titanic war of love and oblivion remains one of Harrison's chief themes in the film / poems to which he increasingly turned his attention in the 1990s.

War, as envisioned in Harrison's later lyrics, is no extension of political policy. Indeed, such poems as "Sonnets for August 1945," "The Act," and "A Cold Coming" focus almost entirely on the consequences of battle, remaining largely indifferent to either its immediate or its ultimate origins. The sonnet sequence evinces a mingled sense of horror and self-recognition at the poet's own youthful participation in the celebration of VJ-Day, the bonfires of which grotesquely mimic the disintegrating heat of the atomic bombs dropped on Hiroshima and Nagasaki. Harrison builds his personal experience, in which his only "sense of public joy" (*V. and Other Poems*, "The Morning After: I," l. 9) originated from the utter obliteration of thousands of fellow human beings, into an image of the human condition in the nuclear age. "The Act" records Harrison's ambivalence toward the swaggering, drunken soldiery he encounters on an early morning flight out of Newcastle. Ultimately he regards the revelers as victims—of poverty, of military discipline, of their own youthfully suppressed fears—and wishes them "pleasures with no rough strife, no iron gates, / and letter boxes wide enough for books" (*V. and Other Poems*, ll. 99–100). Still, even though both soldiers and poets use language for the inherent delight of its sounds—after noting one particularly filthy bit of alliteration (the old, native form of English verse), Harrison dubs the soldiers "my Ulster poet friends" (l. 98)—this poet harbors no illusion that his words can ever reach his putative audience. The poem may record the poet's understanding indulgence toward behavior he normally finds repugnant, but it establishes no contact; not a word of dialogue passes between the writer and the soldiers, the piece consisting entirely of overhead remarks and unexpressed thoughts.

"A Cold Coming," composed in rollicking tetrameter couplets, is the most striking of Harrison's war poems, managing to be simultaneously horrifying and funny in giving voice to a half-charred Iraqi corpse the poet encounters in a photograph, still sitting behind the wheel of his vehicle. The title itself alludes both to T. S. Eliot's poem on the journey of the Magi and to the semen frozen by three wise American marines as insurance against their possible deaths in the Gulf War. Harrison records (ostensibly on actual tape) the Iraqi soldier's half-amused response to the American precautions. In one sense this sperm-banking is ridiculous; it implicitly denies present danger by taking refuge in a vision of a future that can occur only if the soldiers aren't there to see it. But it is also an ominous exhibition of the same technologically advanced denial of life that made the war

itself a murderous rout. When the soldier expatiates on the macabre image of inseminating his wife in his present state of decomposition, Harrison begins to brood on the state of the eternally unborn millions potentially contained in a single soldier's ejaculant, wondering if such an indefinite delay of birth might be preferable to the violence and suffering of the current age.

Such is not the corpse's message, however; he demands that the poet "Lie that you saw me and I smiled / to see the [surviving American] soldier hug his child" (*The Gaze of the Gorgon*, ll. 137–138). Such a lie, the dead man hopes, will both excuse him from his own collaboration in Saddam Hussein's various atrocities and hasten the end of war itself. The ironies of this moment in the poem are beautifully complex. By asking that his lie be recorded, the soldier confirms its truth: if he cares enough about the hope of peace to falsify his feelings, then his essential feeling is in fact a hope for peace. At the same time Harrison undercuts this message by catching himself at his own game; when the corpse declares, "That's your job, poet, to pretend / I want my foe to be my friend" (ll. 153–154), one must also perceive that the entire conversation is Harrison's invention, constructed for the purpose of hastening the reign of peace. The poem ends with Harrison again meditating on the fate of the sperm banked against death in battle, now construing it as "Mankind on the rocks" (l. 176); it has come to represent the suspended future of genuine life that can be realized only should the human propensity toward destruction abate. Now, however, the voice is unambiguously Harrison's own; there is no indication that the wish for peace is anything more than a poet's hope (or fantasy).

The final stanza of the piece brilliantly encapsulates the poem's central tension between the desire to capture the voice of the other and the impossibility of doing so: "I went. I pressed REWIND and PLAY / and I heard the charred man say:" (ll. 183–184), followed by the white space of the unfilled balance of the page. One might, of course, read this uncompleted sentence as an instruction to return to the beginning of the Iraqi soldier's declamation, in which case the poet's words create only a self-contained, eternally repeating cycle of grief. One might also, however, read the blank space as the true silence in which the photograph is wrapped, an acknowledgment that the soldier's corpse in fact tells us nothing we can hear. In a militarized world, the poem perhaps suggests, even an interchange of human language between opposing sides becomes impossible.

TRANSLATIONS

No English poet of Harrison's status has done as many major translations since Pope. "Translation" is a problematic word to describe Harrison's enterprise, however, as he recognizes by citing, as the epigraph to his *Dramatic Verse 1973–1985,* Lion Feuchtwanger's "Adaptations," a poem that humorously denies the precedence of the original author; the only living mind at work is that of the "translator." Harrison invariably updates the context and / or the language of the works he adapts. His interest in translation, after all, is not historical but theatrical; it is less important to him that the piece introduce us to the world of its original author than that it comment meaningfully on the world into which the audience walks at the end of the performance.

The lyric poets Harrison has chosen to translate—Palladas and Martial—are both savage epigrammatists. Harrison's rendering of their work in *Palladas: Poems* (1975) and *U.S. Martial* (1981) retains this plainspokenness that borders on brutality in wonderfully musical colloquial English. In the case of Palladas, Harrison does unusually little surgery on his source; indeed, the value of this work of translation in disciplining the translator to a classical lucidity he has ever after observed in his own poetry is as great as the work's inherent value, which is sufficient in itself. The adaptations of Martial, undertaken while Harrison was staying at New York's Ansonia Hotel, are less successful. Harrison more greatly alters the context of these poems, casting them in contemporary America— the idiom, however, remaining largely English— but Martial's observations rarely seem trenchant in this setting, the social order of contemporary New York differing too greatly from that of imperial Rome.

Harrison's translations of Molière's *The Misanthrope* (1973) and Racine's *Phèdre* (*Phaedra Britannica,* 1975), composed in glittering couplets, retain the outlines of the original plots but transpose the action to De Gaulle's France and the India of the raj, respectively. Harrison uses this dislocation of context, a far less familiar technique in the early 1970s than it has since become, to transform the plays into palimpsests, the original context dimly visible through the foregrounded update. Whatever else they are about, dramas translated in this fashion are about the simultaneous unity and division of past and present. Paradoxically, the insubstantial theatrical moment—Harrison initially planned to have *The Trackers of Oxyrhyncus* (1990) performed only once, as were Greek tragedies and satyr plays—offers the surest link of then and now in its common immersion of people widely separated by history in the same emotion.

In his translations of *The Oresteia* (1981) and the York mystery cycle (*The Mysteries,* 1985), Harrison exercises what might be called an enlightened nativism. His involvement with the mystery plays— hardly the material one would expect him to find congenial—originated in a concern for the preservation of the specifically Northern character of their language. Harrison preserves this character (and the York plays of alliterative verse) while updating the vocabulary—the medieval manuscript's "This dede on-dergh we may noght drawe," for instance, becomes "This fastenin' up falls to us four" (*The Mysteries,* p. 134)—at the same time giving the verse a far smoother, more performable regularity of rhythm.

Harrison's conversion of Aeschylus into verse that observes the patterns of Anglo-Saxon alliterative meter is an even more technically virtuosic feat (Harrison worked on the translation for ten years). While perhaps this device draws too much attention to itself for one to focus entirely on the events of the play, the incantatory power Harrison achieves more than compensates for any such distraction. His metrical choice thrillingly conveys the tribal nature of the Oresteian world, stripping away any of the notions of classical loftiness audiences are apt to bring into the theater, reminding viewers that Aeschylus' play concerns a period he himself regarded as half-barbarous. Further, by superimposing the voice of early England onto the words of early Hellas, Harrison transforms the play into a universal statement on the process of state formation—which, Harrison subtly suggests, is a far more ambiguous process, equally repressive (particularly to women) as liberating, than the Aeschylean original might suggest.

One would surely choose other translations than Harrison's if one were interested in approaching the original text as closely as possible without learning the language in which it was written. But as contemporary poetry Harrison's dramatic translations are unequaled in their union of colloquial ease and rhetorical power.

ORIGINAL DRAMA, LIBRETTI, AND FILM / POEMS

To use the word "dramas" for Tony Harrison's original plays and libretti—*Bow Down* (1977), *Yan Tan Tethera* (1983), *The Big H* (1984), *Medea: A Sex-War Opera* (1985), *The Trackers of Oxyrhyncus* (1988; a largely original elaboration of the Sophoclean fragment *Ichneutae*, which means "the trackers"), *The Common Chorus* (1992; partially composed of translations of *Lysistrata* and *The Trojan Women*, but so significantly reworked by Harrison and with enough purely original material to fit more comfortably under the "Original Drama" rubric), *Square Rounds* (1992), and the still unpublished *The Kaisers of Carnuntum* (1995)—is misleading; one might better term them "theatrical presentations." Harrison shows little interest in developing convincing characters in these pieces, characters who seem driven by unspoken internal motives they might not themselves recognize or understand, nor does he structure his pieces around the unfolding and resolution of character conflicts. Rather, his theater pieces work in a lyrical fashion, developing a central theme by the concatenation of a series of related images and metaphors. Rather than a conflict of characters, the plays turn on the alternating unity and division of voices.

In *Square Rounds,* for example, Harrison presents a meditation on scientific magic through the metaphor of stage magic; scarves change color and characters emerge from boxes as different people than those who entered, reflecting the manner in which chemists and engineers convert one substance to another. The play's thesis—that all warfare is "chemical" warfare, representing a diversion of the naturally fertile properties of substances to destructive ends—unfolds, like "V.," as a series of tableaux that ultimately return to where they have begun. Early in the play we learn that the supply of human excrement, important as fertilizer, has been endangered by the invention of the water closet. It is replaced by artificially produced nitrates, which also increase the production of high explosives.

When the First World War breaks out, the technology of the Maxim gun—also a "chemical" weapon, the expanding gas from the ignition of one round feeding the next into place in order to obtain an extremely rapid rate of fire—yields to the invention of poison gas by Fritz Haber, who had earlier devised a way to derive ammonia from the air. Maxim and Haber work in a misguided attempt to shorten war and save lives by more efficient killing, but the genie of destruction cannot be controlled; the war drags on, Maxim suffers from emphysema, and Clara Haber (the inventor's wife) kills herself over her husband's willingness to aid the ferociously anti-Semitic kaiser. The piece ends where it had begun, at the magic box / water closet; a trio of Chinese men remind the audience that rocketry is very old and that the first "chemical" weapon was human excrement, a toxic substance when converted to a smoke bomb. Harrison's libretto for *Medea: A Sex-War Opera*, commissioned by the Metropolitan Opera but never performed because the music was never completed, works similarly, offering a brilliant gloss on the various legends of Jason and Medea.

In both his dramas and his film / poems, Harrison attempts a far more public poetry than in his lyrics; while the lyrics acknowledge the incapacity of words to name our profoundest realities truly, the film / poems—*Loving Memory* (1987), *The Blasphemers' Banquet* (1989), *The Gaze of the Gorgon* (1992), *A Maybe Day in Kazakhstan* (1994), and *The Shadow of Hiroshima* (1995)—offer much more confident generalizations. The focus of these works tends to be immediately political; Harrison seems less concerned with creating a sense of depth and complication than with reminding his audience as lucidly as possible of the costs of militarism and the infringement of intellectual freedom. *The Shadow of Hiroshima*, for instance, ends with a bald question that locates the significance of the piece squarely in the reaction of its viewers: "Pigeon / Peace-doves brawl and fight. / Is the world at peace tonight? / Or are we all like Shadow San / facing inferno with a fan?" (*The Shadow of Hiroshima and Other Film / Poems*, l. 17). Of course, evaluation of the film / poems on the basis of their texts alone—all that is readily available at the moment—is problematic. While the texts of such early works in the genre as *Loving Memory* can largely be read as independent poems, a later piece on the same themes of death and remembrance, *Black Daisies for the Bride* (1993), while not technically a film / poem because it incorporates music, depends as fully on image as on text.

CONCLUDING REMARKS

Harrison not only had established a body of work staggering in its volume, variety, and quality, but his productivity shows little sign of diminishing. He will undoubtedly continue his work in drama and television; his film/poems may one day be seen as the origin of a new genre. Although he has published few lyrics in the 1990s, the open-ended nature of "The School of Eloquence" promises a continuing augmentation of what already stands as one of the most impressive monuments of twentieth-century poetry in English. There seems little doubt that unless poetry should in the future once again become the private domain of a self-interested social elite, Tony Harrison will be regarded as one of the leading poets of the last twenty-five years of the twentieth century.

SELECTED BIBLIOGRAPHY

I. COLLECTED WORKS. *From "The School of Eloquence" and Other Poems* (London, 1978); *Selected Poems* (Harmondsworth, 1984; New York, 1987); *Dramatic Verse 1973–1985* (Newcastle, 1985); also published as *Theatre Works 1973–1985* (Harmondsworth, 1986); *V. and Other Poems* (New York, 1990); *Permanently Bard: Selected Poetry* (Newcastle, 1995); *The Shadow of Hiroshima and Other Film/Poems* (London, 1995); *Plays 3* (London, 1996).

II. SEPARATE WORKS. *Earthworks* (Leeds, 1964); *Aikin Mata: The Lysistrata of Aristophanes* (Ibadan, 1966), with James Simmons; *Newcastle Is Peru* (Newcastle, 1969, 1974); *The Loiners* (London, 1970); *Bow Down* (London, 1977); *Continuous: 50 Sonnets from "The School of Eloquence"* (London, 1981, 1987); *A Kumquat for John Keats* (Newcastle, 1981), *The Fire-Gap* (Newcastle, 1985); *V.* (Newcastle, 1985); *Ten Poems from "The School of Eloquence"* (London, 1987); *V.: New Edition with Press Articles* (Newcastle, 1989); *The Trackers of Oxyrhyncus* (London, 1990); *A Cold Coming: Gulf War Poems* (Newcastle, 1991); *The Common Chorus* (London, 1992); *The Gaze of the Gorgon* (Newcastle, 1992); *Square Rounds* (London, 1992); *Black Daisies for the Bride* (London, 1993); *Poetry or Bust* (Bradford, West Yorkshire, 1993).

III. TRANSLATIONS. *The Misanthrope* (London, 1973); *Palladas: Poems* (London, 1975); *Phaedra Britannica* (London, 1975); *The Passion* (London, 1977); *The Bartered Bride* (New York, 1978); *The Oresteia* (London, 1981); *U. S. Martial* (Newcastle, 1981); *The Mysteries* (London, 1985); *The Prince's Play* (London, 1996).

IV. BROADCASTS AND THEATRICAL PRODUCTIONS. *The Misanthrope* (London, 1973); *Phaedra Britannica* (London, 1975); *Bow Down* (London, 1977); *The Passion* (London, 1977); *The Bartered Bride* (New York, 1978); *Arctic Paradise* (BBC 2, 1981), published in Astley; *The Oresteia* (London, 1981; Channel Four, 1983); *The Big H* (BBC 2, 1984); *The Mysteries* (Channel Four, 1985–1986); *Yan Tan Tethera* (London, 1986; Channel Four, 1987); *Loving Memory* (BBC Bristol, 1987); *The Blasphemers' Banquet* (BBC 1, 1989); *The Trackers of Oxyrhyncus* (London and Delphi, 1990); *The Gaze of the Gorgon* (BBC 2, 1992); *Black Daisies for the Bride* (BBC 2, 1993); *Poetry or Bust* (Bradford, West Yorkshire, 1993); *A Maybe Day in Kazakhstan* (Channel 4, 1994); *The Kaisers of Carnuntum* (Vienna, 1995); *The Shadow of Hiroshima* (Channel Four, 1995).

V. BIBLIOGRAPHIES. No complete bibliographies of Tony Harrison exist; useful bibliographies can, however, be found in John R. Kaiser, *Tony Harrison: A Bibliography 1957–1987* (London, 1989); Neil Astley, ed., *Tony Harrison* (Newcastle, 1991); Joe Kelleher, *Tony Harrison* (Plymouth, 1996); and Sandie Byrne, ed., *Tony Harrison: Loiner* (Oxford, 1997).

VI. CRITICAL STUDIES. Alan Young, "Weeds and White Roses: The Poetry of Tony Harrison," in *Critical Quarterly* (spring–summer 1984); Helga Geyer-Ryan, "Heteroglossia in the Poetry of Bertolt Brecht and Tony Harrison," in *The Taming of the Text,* ed. by Willie van Peer (London, 1988); Michael Wood, "Classics and the Scarecrow," in *Parnassus* 14, no. 2 (1988); Bruce Woodcock, "Classical Vandalism: Tony Harrison's Invective," in *Critical Quarterly* (summer 1990); Neil Astley, ed., *Tony Harrison* (Newcastle, 1991); Rick Rylance, "Tony Harrison's Languages," in *Contemporary Poetry Meets Modern Theory,* ed. by Anthony Easthope and John Thomson (Toronto, 1991); Luke Spencer, *The Poetry of Tony Harrison* (London, 1994); Sean O'Brien, *The Deregulated Muse* (Newcastle, 1995); L. Peach, *Ancestral Lines: Cultural Identity in the Work of Six Contemporary Poets* (Bridgport, 1995); Joe Kelleher, *Tony Harrison* (Plymouth, 1996); Sandie Byrne, ed., *Tony Harrison: Loiner* (Oxford, 1997); Sandie Byrne, *H, v & O: The Poetry of Tony Harrison* (Manchester, 1998).

PATRICIA HIGHSMITH

(1921–1995)

Blythe Frank

PATRICIA HIGHSMITH, THE only child of Jay Bernard Plangman and Mary Coates, was born Mary Patricia Plangman on 19 January 1921 in Fort Worth, Texas. Her parents, both commercial artists, separated five months before she was born and eventually divorced for reasons Highsmith was never able to understand. Three years later her mother married Stanley Highsmith, an advertising illustrator. This marriage also was troubled, and Patricia often withdrew into herself to escape the constant bickering and strife. Highsmith was raised by her maternal grandmother in Texas during the first six years of her life and was devastated to leave her when the family moved to New York. As a young adult, Highsmith learned that her mother had tried to induce a miscarriage by drinking turpentine while pregnant with her. Highsmith would have no contact with her mother during the final twenty years of her life and explained in an interview why she couldn't love her: "First, because she made my childhood a little hell. Second, because she never loved anyone, neither my father, my stepfather, nor me" (Harrison, p. 1). Her biological parents' breakup and the absence of her father affected Highsmith greatly and came to have a bearing on the issues she dramatized in her work.

A precocious child who learned to read before kindergarten, Highsmith developed a taste for the morbid early on. Among her favorite books were a photographic study of the trenches in World War I and *The Human Mind* by Karl Menninger—case histories of the mentally disturbed. Highsmith explained in a 1988 interview with Joan Dupont, "I saw that the people looked outwardly normal, and I realized there could be such people around me." She wrote her first stories at age sixteen and continued to write during her years as an undergraduate at Barnard College, where she was the editor of the college literary magazine and was graduated in 1942. Her first professional writing job was inventing plots and dialogue for comic books "of the Superman and Batman variety to earn a living." While working on serious fiction in her spare time Highsmith held a variety of jobs, including writing television scripts for Alfred Hitchcock and working as a clerk in a department store, where she formulated the plot for *The Price of Salt*. She traveled extensively throughout the 1950s and moved to Europe for good in 1963. She set up residence in a small Suffolk village in England, using this as her home base as she traveled often to France and Switzerland.

Claiming that "art has little to do with morality, convention, or moralizing," Highsmith produced a steady stream of novels and short stories that were well received in Europe but drew little attention in the United States. She won many awards, including the British Crime Writers Association Silver Dagger in 1964, and she became an officier de l'Ordre des Arts et Lettres (France) in 1990. She died in Switzerland on 4 February 1995, after years of suffering from lung cancer and leukemia.

THE WORLD OF HIGHSMITH

PATRICIA Highsmith's work cannot be easily described as belonging to the genre of crime fiction or suspense fiction. Graham Greene called her "the poet of apprehension." Her stories are not so much "whodunits" as "whydunits." These are not the gore-filled tales one might find in a Stephen King or John Saul novel, nor are they the treasure hunts for clues found in an Agatha Christie mystery. Highsmith was initially surprised that her work was labeled suspense fiction; in her book *Plotting and Writing Suspense Fiction*, she wrote, "My first book, *Strangers on a Train*, was just 'a novel' to me when I wrote it, and yet, when it sold, was labeled 'suspense novel.' Thenceforth, I found myself in this category, which means also to find oneself fated to no more than three-inch-long reviews in the newspapers, squeezed in among good and bad books which get the same brief treatment" (p. 141).

Highsmith's writing style is straightforward, spare, and simple. She said of her work: "I like to be clear. I never think about being poetic or flashy" (Dupont interview). She uses words as tools to tell a story and does not waste time with metaphor or platitudes; instead, she pursues her deepest obsessions with subtlety and candor. Highsmith's fiction addresses the problems inherent in the banal routine of everyday modern life—a miasma through which her characters drift aimlessly.

Highsmith's entire body of fiction is a world riddled with doppelgängers, internment, and Kafkaesque alienation. Early novels and stories introduced certain elements that continued to surface throughout her work: the pairings of men complicit in a crime or murder, usually with homoerotic overtones; the marginalization of women and resistance to casting them in the "action" roles; the irrationality of her characters' actions and their subsequent absence of guilt; the way chance encounters inexorably change lives, primarily for the worse. The violence in Highsmith novels has more to do with the absurdity of human behavior than with calculated brutality. These are inherently modern works in that they are a direct reflection of a technological world that is progressively cutting off man from his fundamental humanity, including his sense of right and wrong.

Existentialism's insistence on the individual's freedom affects all of Highsmith's work. Even under extreme physical duress, one has a choice. Choice is necessary, yet it is rendered absurd by the irrational in human behavior and by inaction. Again and again, Highsmith's characters are given ample opportunity to make choices that will alter imminent outcomes, and they do not act. These characters show themselves to be isolated and self-obsessed errant existentialists. They undermine their will to power by making poor, rash decisions (or no decisions at all) and then wonder why their lives are spinning out of control. In the most frequently cited essay on Highsmith, Graham Greene said in his introduction to *Eleven:* "Her characters are irrational, and they leap to life in the very lack of reason; suddenly we realize how unbelievably rational most fictional characters are."

Highsmith's characters suffer from self-destructive vices: they smoke, drink profuse amounts of alcohol, and engage in few pleasurable activities. They are prisoners of habit—seldom does a page go by without a drink being poured or a cigarette lit. They are driven to consume out of a determined ennui, constantly seeking to fulfill their obsessive desires. Yet obsession has little to do with the pursuit of pleasure and results in fulfillment only of the drive itself. Highsmith spends considerable time focusing on the drives of her characters, drives that are fueled by uncontrolled emotion. In her interview with Joan Dupont, Highsmith said, "Emotion is worth more than intellect. To me, Francis Bacon paints the ultimate picture of what's going on in the world—mankind throwing up in a toilet with his naked derriere showing."

In 1948, after six rejections of her first novel, Highsmith accepted an offer from the author Truman Capote to stay at Yaddo, the writers' colony in upstate New York. It was here that she revised *Strangers on a Train,* and, shortly after its publication, Alfred Hitchcock bought the film and stage rights in perpetuity for $6,800, launching her career. (Upon her death, she left her entire estate of $6 million to Yaddo.)

Highsmith's best-known work is the tale of two strangers who meet on a train and jokingly agree to commit murders for each other. At the very core of the novel is one of Highsmith's prominent themes, that of the faux ami (false friend). Guy is a straightlaced young architect with a promising career, and Bruno is his antithesis: an unemployed drifter from a wealthy family who has nothing but time on his hands. Their lives intersect when Bruno realizes they both can profit from an exchange of favors—if Guy could be rid of his estranged wife, Miriam, he could marry his current sweetheart, and if Bruno could be rid of his father, he would inherit a vast sum of money. Like the majority of Highsmith's characters, Bruno and Guy are successful individuals in possession of the comforts and privileges of a middle- to upper-class lifestyle. Their normalcy is a reminder that criminal behavior does not belong to the fringes of society—in the first two decades of Highsmith's fiction, social and economic standing have no bearing on her characters' behavior.

Strangers is told in a limited third-person omniscient narrative, a technique to which Highsmith held throughout her writing career. The omniscient voice does not allow any possible psychological motivation behind her characters' actions to be stated explicitly. The reader must decide if the characters' actions arise from pure villainy or merely self-deception, while the plot races along without pause. Bruno's description of a robbery he committed shows no causal relationship between a profit motive and action. "I committed a robbery. . . . Not to get anything . . . I didn't want what I took. I especially took what I didn't want" (p. 53). Bruno, like most of Highsmith's characters, is out of touch with himself and does not know what he wants. The apparent straightforwardness of Highsmith's narrative is deceptive, for it is constantly undermined by her characters' inability to be self-analytical. Without the focus of motivated logic, the meaning of events must elude the reader.

Bruno, a psychotic, takes matters into his own hands and kills Guy's wife, expecting Guy to then fulfill his end of the bargain by murdering his father. Horrified and consumed by guilt, Guy refuses to carry out his end of the deal, and Bruno attempts to frame him for the murder already committed. The tension in the novel does not come from the expectation of a murder but rather from Guy's struggle to decide whether he will fulfill his end of the bargain. Bruno hounds Guy with letters and phone calls, appears at his home, and threatens to inform Guy's fiancée, Anne, of their agreement. Instead of going to the police or telling Anne the truth before he has committed any wrong, Guy does nothing. He is paralyzed by guilt.

The pairing of Bruno and Guy represents the different sides of one person, and Guy's ultimate decision to commit the murder is an attempt to rid himself of Bruno once and for all. Bruno escapes any formal punishment when, in a drunken stupor, he accidentally drowns, and now Guy carries the double burden of responsibility for the crimes as well as the knowledge of his own dark side awakened by Bruno. Following Dostoevsky's axiom of justice—that a guilty conscience seeks punishment in order to purge guilt from the body—Guy confesses the murders to Miriam's former lover and turns himself in to the police seeking punishment. The former lover's response to the confession is epitomal Highsmith: he couldn't care less. Highsmith's characters care only about themselves and have no moral compass, no inherent sense of justice.

Hitchcock immediately recognized the cinematic qualities of Highsmith's fiction. Along with his classic 1951 version, *Strangers on a Train* went on to be remade three times: by Robert Sparr in 1969 as *Once You Kiss a Stranger,* in 1996 by Tommy

Lee Wallace as *Once You Meet a Stranger,* and in 1987 by Danny DeVito in the dark comedy *Throw Momma from the Train.* Highsmith's attention to character and plot, combined with her streamlined dialogue, allows her fiction to be easily translated into film. The late 1990s saw a revival of interest in Highsmith's film adaptations; in 1998 the New York Museum of Modern Art, in conjunction with Yaddo, sponsored a nine-film series from the work of Patricia Highsmith, which was introduced by contemporary writers including Rick Moody, Romulus Linney, and Susan Cheever.

Highsmith's next work was a lesbian novel, *The Price of Salt* (1952), which she published under the pseudonym Claire Morgan. Because she was afraid of being labeled a lesbian writer, it wasn't until 1990, when the novel was published in the United Kingdom as *Carol,* that Highsmith openly acknowledged writing it. *The Price of Salt* is the first of two Highsmith novels (the other being *Edith's Diary*) that has a female protagonist. As she said in her interview with Joan Dupont, "I prefer to write about male characters because they are more interesting . . . women are tied to the home. Men can do more, jump over fences." Carol and Therese in *The Price of Salt* differ from Highsmith's traditional female characters in that they do not seek a conventional lifestyle that would bind them to the home. The pairing of these two women parallels the ill-matched male friendship in *Strangers on a Train* and is similarly symbolic of the narcissistic search for "the other half" of oneself. As Carol explains, "The rapport between two men or two women can be absolute and perfect, as it can never be between man and woman" (p. 246). This explains many of the failed heterosexual relationships in Highsmith's other novels, in which male and female characters searching for the "absolute and perfect" relationship encounter something shifting and uncertain.

The novel opens with both Carol and Therese in unhappy heterosexual relationships. Soon after meeting, they embark on a road trip across the United States, during which they fall in love. The book's love scenes are played out obliquely; the positive depictions of true intimacy and passion in *The Price of Salt* cannot be found anywhere else in Highsmith's body of work. Russell Harrison noted in his study of Highsmith that there is "an openness and vulnerability in Carol and Therese, and the convulsively cramped tension of [Highsmith's] other lovers is absent" (p. 104). They are tracked by a private investigator hired by Carol's husband, who is gathering incriminating evidence for a divorce, launching a cat-and-mouse pursuit. Through the gaze of the private investigator, we feel the condemning presence of the community at large, but such examination is not powerful enough to shatter the intimacy that these two women have found together.

The Price of Salt introduces Highsmith's recurring theme of the artist that discovers the possibility of self-transformation through creativity. Therese is a stage designer, and at the end of the novel, when the relationship appears to have ended, she turns to her art to restructure her broken world. Artistic creation is an affirmed value because it requires choice and selection; free will is valued as a means of creating a personal reality. Art allows Therese to transcend her conventional life and embrace a more subversive and ultimately more rewarding path. When she and Carol reconcile at the end of the novel, Therese has become the empowered half of the alliance.

The Blunderer, which appeared in 1954, was published in the United States as *Lament for a Lover* in 1956. This novel returns to the ill-matched friends pattern established in *Strangers on a Train,* as the protagonist, Walter Stackhouse, aligns himself with a sociopathic Eastern European, Melchior Kimmel. Kimmel is the first of several Eastern European characters who are depicted as economically deprived, emotionally unstable, and corrupt. Inspired by a newspaper clipping describing the unsolved murder of Kimmel's wife, Stackhouse fantasizes about killing his own sadistic wife. He keeps a scrapbook of clippings that allegorize his idea of mismatched relationships and the violence that erupts from them. Before he can carry out his plan to murder her, his wife, feeling depressed and rejected by him, commits suicide. She tries to frame her husband by making the suicide look like a murder, jumping from the cliff of a highway rest stop while her husband waits in the parking lot.

Stackhouse's fascination with mirroring Kimmel's actions is an existential search for identity. According to Jean-Paul Sartre, an individual has no innate characteristics. He is only what he chooses to be and wills himself to be; and it is only in relation to other people that an individual has a definite identity, not to himself alone. In order to recycle Kimmel's murder plot, Stackhouse needs to imitate his villainous characteristics. He visits Kimmel at the bookstore he owns in order to get a

firsthand impression of his murderer-ideal. Once they have met they become complicit in each other's crimes—if one is found out, both will be caught. The similarity between the two unsolved cases arouses suspicion in the police, who reopen Kimmel's case in order to solve the Stackhouse murder. Kimmel and Stackhouse endure a waiting game as each plots the other's murder.

Highsmith took the first of her many trips to Mexico in 1955 and while there wrote *The Talented Mr. Ripley* (1955), the first of a series that spanned her literary career and went on to win the Edgar Allan Poe Scroll from the Mystery Writers of America. Tom Ripley, a charming sociopath, was Highsmith's favorite character, one whom she felt "practically did the writing for her." Ripley was an immensely popular character in Europe; numerous *Ripley* novels have been made into films, including those by Claude Autant-Lara, Claude Miller, Claude Chabrol, Wim Wenders, and René Clement. Several reviewers have compared Ripley to André Gide's Lafcadio in *Les Caves du Vatican* (1914) and have accused Highsmith of authorial immorality because she confines the narrative point of view to Ripley alone, encouraging readers to identify with the "villain."

In *The Talented Mr. Ripley,*the traditional family structure is abandoned, and the young protagonists attempt to recreate a more idealized family unit outside the bonds of history or genetics. Tom was raised by a overbearing and controlling aunt after being orphaned at an early age. He ran away and at age twenty began a life of petty thievery and fraud that often made it necessary for him to adopt false identities to escape the police. Without parental role models, Tom quickly degenerated into criminality, but he wished for a group of peers he could claim as a surrogate family.

Dickie Greenleaf, the son of a wealthy New York businessman, left his family for a more fulfilling European life where he is free to pursue his painting without the criticisms of his father. Dickie has created a surrogate family in Italy that includes men and women his own age and eventually comes to include Tom Ripley. Dickie's father seeks out Tom in a New York City bar, and after discussing Dickie's extended absence proposes that Tom sail to Italy at his expense and convince Dickie to return home. Once in Italy, Tom and Dickie become fast friends, and Tom becomes so enamored with Dickie's more glamorous life that he stops pressuring him into going home. Falling victim to his own fantasy, Tom begins to mimic Dickie and insinuates himself not only into Dickie's house but into every aspect of his daily life. The friendship begins to wane when Dickie discovers Tom trying on his clothes and accessories: Dickie accuses Tom of being a homosexual, which Tom denies. They take one last trip together where Tom suddenly decides that the only thing to do is to brutally murder Dickie and assume his identity. This is the only way he can retain Dickie in his life and attenuate his fantasy.

René Clement's film version of this novel, *Purple Noon*, ends with Tom being caught and punished for Dickie's murder. In the novel, and in all subsequent Ripley novels, Tom remains free and harbors no guilt for the murders he commits. Highsmith claimed in a 1982 television interview that Ripley "kills when he absolutely has to and kills reluctantly." Highsmith had little respect for conventional mores, stating in *Plotting and Writing Suspense Fiction*: "The public by and large is not fond of criminals who go free at the end . . . a book is altogether more eligible for television and movie sales if the hero-criminal is caught, punished and made to feel awful at the end. . . . This goes against my grain, as I rather like criminals and find them extremely interesting, unless they are monotonously and stupidly brutal. . . . I find the public passion for justice quite boring and artificial, for neither life nor nature cares if justice is done or not" (pp. 50–51). Tom convinces himself of his innocence by pretending to be Dickie, with a clear conscience, one which does not bear the stain of murder.

In the next Ripley novels, Tom is married, living in the Paris suburbs, and embracing all the pleasures of domestic life surrounded by a constant peripheral current of "pesky" criminal business and an assumed identity. Tom and his wife, Héloïse, are childless and live in a large house, Belle Ombre, run by his maid, Madame Annette. Apart from that of the Sutherlands in *Found in the Street*, a later Highsmith novel, the Ripley marriage is the only functioning and peaceful union in Highsmith's mélange of loveless marriages, unrequited love, and bitter hatred. The fact that there are no children in the marriage is vital to its harmony. As Russell Harrison explains in his profile of Highsmith, "a child would unbalance the blissful but fragile ecology that is Ripley's Belle Ombre existence" (p. 28).

Throughout the series Ripley continues to embody a kind of free-flowing identity. He assumes the disguise of a dead painter in *Ripley Under Ground* (1970) in order to protect an art forgery scheme. In *Ripley's Game* (1974) he conceals his true identity from a picture framer with tuberculosis as a means of manipulating him to kill members of the Mafia. Ripley leads his victim to believe that his death is imminent; in exchange for the murders, his family will be taken care of financially. In *The Boy Who Followed Ripley* (1980) he instructs a young American runaway on how to conceal his identity in order to elude his family and a murder charge. Highsmith's final Ripley novel, *Ripley Under Water* (1991), completes the series, confirming that Ripley will receive no punishment for the crimes he has committed. In *Ripley Under Water*, Ripley is forced to confront his past when an American appears claiming to be Dickie Greenleaf. Hounded by this sadistic imposter, Ripley enters into a game of hunter and hunted in an attempt to discern how much of his past has been uncovered and what he can do to resubmerge his net of lies.

THE SURBURBAN EXPERIENCE: NO EXIT

DEEP Water (1957) is the first in Highsmith's series of studies of domestic life, which she portrays as one of the most harrowing of human experiences. The middle-class migration from the cities to the suburbs in the 1950s and 1960s was generated by the American dream that elevated the nuclear family to the status of a new Eden. *Deep Water*'s protagonist, Victor Van Allen, has married beneath him, and the profound differences between himself and his wife, Melinda, eventually destroy her self-esteem. Melinda engages in a series of extramarital affairs, flaunting them in front of Victor as means of retaliation for his contempt for her. Initially it is Victor who proposes that Melinda have the extramarital affairs, believing that as long as they are open with one another, this unconventional arrangement will suit him. Victor's sudden rage is provoked by his father's criticism that he is a weak man, and he reacts by killing several of Melinda's boyfriends. Victor claims he is not opposed to the affairs; what bothers him is Melinda's choice of "idiotic, spineless characters" (p. 40) and the fact that she broadcasts her infidelities all over town, thus marring Victor's reputation. His pretense of permissiveness collapses at the moment he realizes that he cannot control Melinda if there is no standard marital agreement or real respect between them. Victor eventually murders Melinda in a frenzy of wild passion, when he can no longer bear the pressure of emotional violence and insecurity in the domestic arena.

What compels Highsmith's characters to murder? Is madness or irrational behavior the result of an unhealthy environment? Or has the individual been marked for violent behavior in his genes, needing only the proper circumstances to bring it out? Highsmith's answer seems to lie somewhere between nature and nurture. The madness of modern life has a dehumanizing effect on individuals and they react in violent ways. Also, because Highsmith subscribes to the existentialist belief that each individual can construct his or her personal reality through choice, every person has the capacity for choosing *anything,* even murder. Several reviewers have commented on Highsmith's depiction of a desertlike, undifferentiated territory, one without values or moral landmarks, which produces great anxiety in her characters, and wherein any random act is possible. Terence Rafferty discusses a world where reliability has broken down and there is nothing solid to hold up Highsmith's characters.

A transitional novel, *A Game for the Living* (1958), begins to gravitate toward a more sociocultural perspective in a narrative that takes us again, like the Ripley novels, out of the United States. This is her only true whodunit, told from the perspective of an unreliable narrator, Theodore Schiebelhut, a German painter whose first-world consciousness clashes with that of third-world Mexico.

A beautiful young woman is found dead and viciously mutilated; the police eventually accuse Theodore and Ramón Otero, a professor and former lover of the deceased. Ramón has confessed to the murder as atonement for the illicit affair he was having with the victim. The police do not believe his confession and release him despite his insistence on his guilt. They understand that Ramón is a victim of an ingrained cultural and penitential guilt that drives him to seek punishment at all costs. Unlike Guy in *Strangers on a Train*, Ramón hasn't committed murder, but the psychological drive for atonement is the same.

The progress of the relationship between Theodore and Ramón is the most interesting aspect of the novel, as we see how they begin to affect one

another. As the friendship evolves, each learns from the other. Both Theodore and Ramón begin questioning their beliefs and how they color perceptions. Unlike most whodunits, no clues are introduced that would allow the reader to solve the crime. By the end we are so wrapped up in the relationship between Theodore and Ramón—especially in how their cultural differences affect their understanding of one another—that the crime itself has become peripheral. As Highsmith's work progresses from book to book, we see her growing proclivity for deemphasizing crime in the narrative and investigating human behavior and psychology instead.

This Sweet Sickness (1960) focuses on David Kelsey, a scientist living in semirural New York State, who constructs a fantasy world that he keeps secret from even his coworkers and closest friends. During the week Kelsey lives in a cheap boardinghouse, but on weekends he escapes to the house he shares with his true love, "Annabelle." Here he assumes another identity, that of "William Neumeister." Annabelle is a ghostly figure of his imagination, a love he lost years ago and who is now married and raising a child in Hartford, Connecticut. Kelsey's tangled identity is supported by lies he creates to maintain his (fictional) public persona. He tells his friends and coworkers that he visits his mother in a nursing home on weekends, even though his mother died several years before and, when she was alive, Kelsey had had an antagonistic relationship with her. Like the marital props that furnish his house, Kelsey is invested in appearances that have no truth behind them.

Kelsey rejects the real woman who is in love with him, Effie Brennen, opting for the controlled delusion of an imagined relationship. Unable to accept reality as it is, Kelsey's desire to appropriate his ideal, Annabelle, is so great that he kills her husband and blames it on his doppelgänger, William Neumeister. In an attempt to escape the police Kelsey disappears into New York City, where he disintegrates into a hallucinating psychotic state and eventually jumps from a window, believing that he sees Annabelle on the ground below him.

Marriage in *This Sweet Sickness* is a "redeeming" social event that Kelsey strives to obtain at any cost to himself and others. Yet the real marriages we see in the novel—Annabelle's as well as that of one of Kelsey's coworkers—are far from idyllic. Kelsey cheats on his wife, spending long periods of time away from the marital home, and Annabelle admits that she married for convenience and security, on the rebound from Kelsey. Characters are dissatisfied, and they yearn for other than what they have. This desire for the unknown makes them miserable. They are ultimately trapped, either in their fantasies or in a depleting reality.

Desire for the unknown also leads Robert Forester in *The Cry of the Owl* (1962) to a disturbing and unrequited end. Recently divorced, Forester lives alone in rural Pennsylvania and has begun spying on Jenny, a young woman, as she goes about her domestic duties. He imagines the normalcy of her life and takes comfort in this, but the illusion is shattered when he becomes involved with her in a direct way. Forester grew up in a dysfunctional home and was married to a possessive and manipulative alcoholic, Nickie. His only wish when he spies on Jenny, who is engaged to Greg, is to enjoy a vicarious domestic harmony. Appearances, however, are misleading, and no functional relationships exist in this novel.

A Highsmithian rule is "be careful what you wish for." Voyeurism is replaced by a reversed obsession when Jenny breaks off her engagement with Greg and falls in love with Forester. Jenny finds Forester exotic and dangerous, an escape from the mundanity of her secluded life. People are objectified in *The Cry of the Owl*: each character represents to the other the possibility of change; each acts as a screen upon which desire is projected. These characters want to possess one another and use one another as representatives of reality, actual or wished-for. Jenny wants Forester to love her for who she is rather than who he imagines her to be, Greg wants Jenny to consent to be his wife, and Forester, finally, just wants to be left alone.

In an attempt to frame Forester, Greg feigns his own death, a plan hatched by Forester's ex-wife, Nickie. In Greg's absence, however, the plot backfires. Jenny commits suicide, her hopes shattered when Forester rejects her romantically. The police discover that Greg is still alive when he murders Nickie in a rage over Jenny's death, yet the innocent Forester is nevertheless vilified by members of the community, who would rather believe the superficial appearance of the case than launch a full investigation of the facts.

The most important dimension of *The Cry of the Owl* is its hidden political agenda. Forester's persecution by his community is something like the McCarthy-era witch-hunts, where people were considered guilty merely by association. Forester's "prowling" at Jenny's house is interpreted by the public as a crime of seduction. It is assumed he is sleeping with Jenny when her car is found parked outside his house on several evenings, even though Forester has rejected her and she sleeps on the couch. And he is accused of murdering Greg before they have found a body. Although Forester is the most innocent character of the novel, he is punished for indulging in the satisfaction of his desire.

TROPES OF FOREIGN SPACES

THE *Two Faces of January* (1964) continues Highsmith's investigation of Americans abroad. Russell Harrison and Erlene Hubly have compared her exploration of rootlessness and dislocation to Henry James's interest in the experience of Americans in Europe. However, Highsmith takes it a step further as she explores the effect these states of being have on morality and personal ethics. Albert Camus's experience of the absurd as the inability to make rational decisions is provoked by the separation of man from all that was previously familiar to him. Without the moral landmarks a culture brings, decisions are based on nothing more than a singular and isolated view of reality. Rydal Keener and Chester MacFarland in *The Two Faces of January* are left without a moral compass, as they move in the fringes of a society to which they do not belong.

Set in Greece, *The Two Faces of January* revisits the theme of the symbiotic coupling of men who use one another to transform their personalities and lives. However, unlike many of Highsmith's novels, which fold the murder into the narrative, tucking it away into the obscure shadows of psychological drama, *The Two Faces of January* opens with the murder. When a Greek police officer comes to the hotel room of MacFarland, a con man, and his wife to arrest them for fraud, MacFarland shoots the officer and hides the corpse in a closet. Once the murder is out of the way, the real story is allowed to unfold. Rydal Keener, a young, married man wandering around Europe looking for direction in life, attaches himself to MacFarland, who bears a striking physical similarity to Keener's father, although his personality is clearly different. Whereas Keener's father was a resolutely moral man, MacFarland is a thief and forger. Keener's generosity to MacFarland is driven by a compulsion to resolve a long-estranged relationship with his recently deceased father.

Appearances are everything in *The Two Faces of January*. Initially Keener figures as a cultural compass for MacFarland, impersonating a knowledgeable tour guide. Keener procures new passports for MacFarland and his wife, translates newspapers, and explains how to travel among the Greek islands without being noticed. In return, MacFarland pays Keener a handsome sum of American money and allows him to flirt with his young wife.

Keener and MacFarland's tangled relationship evolves from a state of mutual dependence to a struggle that constantly promises violence but never delivers. Keener's initial munificence in protecting the MacFarlands soon changes to exploitation of the couple for money and sex. MacFarland desperately wants to extricate himself from Keener and decides the only option is to kill him. The personalities disintegrate into those of ruthless opportunists who will do anything to escape the police and each other. MacFarland's attempt on Keener's life results in the only true act of "brutality," Keener's accidental murder of MacFarland's young wife, which is dealt with in less than three sentences. Highsmith's flattening of her characters' psychological depth lessens the shock of any murder, because the reader has not had the opportunity to sympathize or bond with the victims. Nor does she allow rival emotions of disgust toward the killer—the murders are portrayed simply as acts necessary for survival.

Throughout the novel, Keener uses a journal to record and work out his insights. He ultimately comes to terms with the demons of his past and, through this investigation of his memory and perceptions, finds peace with his father.

Highsmith takes location as impetus for psychological tension one step further in *The Glass Cell* (1964) and shifts her focus away from psychopathology and into the realm of environmental causation. This takes place in an American prison. In *Plotting and Writing Suspense Fiction*, Highsmith wrote that her intention was to show "the deleterious effect of exposure to brutality in prison, and how this can lead to antisocial behavior after release" (pp. 104–105). She was inspired to write *The Glass Cell* after she received a fan letter from a convict and read a book about a man who became a morphine addict after being strung up by his thumbs in prison.

The novel chronicles the transformation of Philip Carter, an engineer, from a responsible, law-abiding citizen to a criminal who seeks nothing more than to survive in a corrupt society. Carter is so easygoing and trusting that he agrees to sign bogus receipts for deliveries of cement, bricks, and girders for a building project on which he is working. His boss pockets the money and Carter is unjustly accused, convicted, and sentenced to six years in prison. Once in jail he is forced to confront a world in which the corrupt rule and the innocent are punished for crimes they are unaware they have committed. Carter breaks one of the prison's unwritten rules while naively trying to help a fellow inmate, and he is sentenced to a dark dungeon cell for more than a week. There, he is strung up by his thumbs until they are permanently dislocated, and he is left crippled and in constant pain. He turns to morphine and quickly becomes an addict.

The turning point in the novel occurs when Carter murders a fellow inmate in retaliation for the murder of a friend. Carter is no longer the same trusting soul and realizes that he is capable of crime and violence. He puts this knowledge to use when he is released from jail, discovers his wife is having an affair, and subsequently murders her lover. Carter's character is so transformed that he is able to lie convincingly to the police, and they let him go. In a final epiphany he realizes that it was his ignorance that landed him in jail and that if he can accept that the world operates on an ethic of corruption, he will be able to survive and protect himself.

In *A Suspension of Mercy* (1965), published as *The Story-Teller* in the United States, we return to the theme of the artist who attempts to transform his reality through the prism of his imagination. An American residing outside London with his English wife, Sydney Bartleby is a novelist and struggling television writer. The novel opens without a hint of domestic strife. Sydney and his wife, Alicia, free to pursue their art and personal interests, live on Alicia's trust fund and have more time on their hands than may be good for them.

Suddenly the couple's marriage turns hostile for no apparent reason except perhaps boredom and superficial irritation. Sydney takes this opportunity to fictionalize a morbid outcome to their petty squabbles. Urging Alicia to spend some time away from home, Sydney writes his wife's death into a TV series with a hero known as "The Whip." Sydney takes the fiction one step closer to reality when he acts out the murder, burying a rolled-up carpet that holds the fictional corpse of his wife. This is witnessed by a neighbor, and the fantasy begins to turn real as the police are called in. Meanwhile, Alicia is hiding out in Brighton with a new lover and, ashamed to announce her infidelity even though her husband is being accused of murder, chooses not to let anyone know that she is still alive. The narrative now switches from the point of view of the charming protagonist, Sydney, and is shared equally among Sydney, Alicia, and her boyfriend. As Sydney loses control over his fictional narrative of "The Whip," Highsmith robs Sydney of his role as primary narrator of *A Suspension of Mercy*.

Alicia eventually changes her mind about turning herself in to the police, but before she can do it she falls off a cliff, and we are left to wonder whether she has committed suicide or been pushed over the edge by her boyfriend. Sydney murders the boyfriend by forcing him to take an overdose of secobarbitol and making it look like a suicide. Sydney fabricates a suicide note in which the boyfriend confesses to Alicia's "murder." Like Ripley, Sydney gets away with murder and suffers no guilt; in his mind the boyfriend's murder was a necessary measure to protect his innocence. Ultimately Sydney does succeed in rewriting his reality, as he successfully convinces others of his fictions. Beyond that, *A Suspension of Mercy* is notable for its focus on the people *around* a presumed murderer rather than on the murderer himself.

Those Who Walk Away (1967) again returns to the theme of two men caught in a strange and dangerous relationship, this time played out in the maze of Venice. An American painter, obsessed by the suicide of his only daughter, blames her husband of one year and begins stalking him through Venice with murder in mind. The young man, ambiguously guilt-ridden but feeling little sense of loss, at first goes into hiding and then turns on his tormentor. Both men are simultaneously the hunter and the hunted as they make several attempts on each other's lives.

However, missing from the novel is any ultimate act of violence. Instead, it is a study of unresolved and misunderstood emotions slowly going out of control. There is no resolution at the end of *Those Who Walk Away*, no explanation for the suicide, no

sense of the characters having learned something through the charting of their grief; instead, the conflict evanesces and all the characters go on with their lives as before. After the father attempts to kill his son-in-law, and the son-in-law goes into hiding for several weeks, it appears the father finally just gives up and leaves Venice.

The Tremor of Forgery (1969) was one of Highsmith's best-received novels. Like *The Two Faces of January*, it deals with Americans in a foreign environment and how dislocation affects their perceptions, behavior, and ethical systems. Setting her story in Tunisia around the time of the 1967 Arab-Israeli Six-Day War, Highsmith here shifts into a discussion of U.S. foreign relations and of political and social issues.

Howard Ingham, a writer from New York, has come to Tunisia to write a film script with a colleague, John Castlewood, who is scheduled to arrive in several days. While waiting for Castlewood, Ingham busies himself with the novel he is working on, also called *The Tremor of Forgery*. As the story progresses, the two novels, Highsmith's and Ingham's, interact to create parallel realities, each struggling to control the narrative.

The "forgery" of the title might best be understood in the context of Erlene Hubly's remark, in her biographical essay on Highsmith, that "a forger is both creator and criminal, one who forges, as in 'makes' something, but [also] one who forges, as in 'forgery,' the attempt to pass off that which is false for that which is real" (p. 122). Ingham refuses to identify himself with the lead character of his novel, a flawed and foolish man who finds it necessary to switch identities in order to survive. The longer Ingham spends in North Africa, the easier it is for him to realize how "forgery" of identity is better defined as mere flexibility, the ability to adapt to new situations.

Receiving word that Castlewood has committed suicide, Ingham remains in Tunisia alone and is plunged into a profound sense of disconnectedness with the United States and his native culture. His letters and phone calls to his fiancée in New York go unanswered. Feeling abandoned, he tries to immerse himself in his work until the fateful evening when someone breaks into his bungalow, and Ingham strikes the intruder with his typewriter in self-defense. We do not know who the intruder is, or if he is killed by the blow, and the crime is covered up by the hotel workers to avoid scandal. One suspects that a murder has taken place, but neither Ingham nor the reader knows the details of the event. Ingham struggles with whether or not to go to the police about the incident. He finds he cannot make up his mind and rationalizes his silence by postponing his guilt. He is slowly losing his grip on his identity and principles as he loses ties with his "civilized society" and immerses himself in Tunisian culture.

Ingham is befriended by Francis Adams, a right-wing archpatriot, and Anders Jensen, a Danish painter. Unlike Ingham, Adams and Jensen have little trouble knowing or expressing their opinions. Jensen attempts, unsuccessfully, to initiate a homosexual relationship with Ingham. But although Ingham fantasizes about sexual encounters with the Arab boys he does not act on his impulses. He is afraid that this kind of sexual experimentation could lead to a lowering of personal barriers that would result in deviant political and social behavior. Rejected by Ingham, Jensen invests his emotional life in his pet dog, Hasso. Shortly after the attack on Ingham's intruder, Hasso disappears and is presumed dead. When Hasso drags his weak, starving body back to Jensen's bungalow weeks later, he is, of course, unable to articulate what has happened to him. Jensen's attachment to Hasso is both parental and spousal, with the dog serving both as surrogate child and full-time companion. He is an emotional substitute for the biological child Jensen can never have and the role of lover that Ingham refuses to fill.

The Tremor of Forgery often has been compared with Gide's *The Immoralist* (1902), not only because of the question of sexual orientation but because of the most striking aspect of Highsmith's novel, its political ambivalence. All three of the protagonists exploit third-world natives in one respect or another: Jensen sexually exploits the young Arab boys, Adams treats the hotel workers like glorified slaves, and Howard believes Arabs' lives are worth less than Americans'. When Howard speculates about whether he killed an Arab named Abdullah that night in his bungalow, Jensen replies, "I hope you got him . . . I like to think you got him, because it makes up a little for my dog—just a little. However, Abdullah wasn't worth my dog" (p. 125).

Ina Pallat, Ingham's fiancée, flies to Tunisia, where Francis Adams tries to persuade her that Ingham is a murderer. Although nothing has been proven, the power of Adams' conviction persuades Ina of Ingham's guilt. She breaks off their engagement and returns to New York alone. *A Tremor of Forgery* ends with Ingham reconciling with his ex-wife, who has written him a provocative letter. By returning to this previously failed relationship, Ingham is attempting to efface history and the changes that have taken place within him. The final forgery is Ingham's self-deception.

YOU DON'T WANT TO GO HOME AGAIN

ALTHOUGH still living in Europe, in 1972 Highsmith returned to America in her fiction, focusing on the deterioration of the urban centers and society in general. Highsmith seldom made visits to the United States and collected most of her information about American culture through newspapers, television, books, and films. Her somewhat caricature portrayal of her homeland can at times be jarring and fantastic, but her literary lens managed to capture symbolic truths that resonate in the reader's mind. As she told Joan Dupont, she believed that living abroad had sharpened her perspective on her native country through the objective lens of geographical and cultural distance; "you see the class difference in America when you live in England." The grimness of her earlier portrayal of suburbia is exceeded only by her view of America's cities: any hope of a brighter existence beyond suburban domesticity is destroyed in the face of the teeming depravity of the urban centers.

A Dog's Ransom is set in New York City, an inferno filled with the dregs of humanity, an apocalyptic environ of madness. More than any other Highsmith novel, *A Dog's Ransom* investigates American social and economic conflicts but gives no satisfying solution.

Clarence Duhammel, a policeman (Highsmith's first and only protagonist in some way connected with detective work), is a naive and insecure man who is slowly stripped of everything he cares about in an environment indifferent to his suffering. He acts as a mediator for a society riven by class and ethnic hatred; his personality and his occupation allow him to move smoothly between villains and victims, trying to bridge an impossible gap.

Ed Reynolds' dog has been kidnapped from Riverside Park after his daughter was recently murdered. Clarence dedicates himself to solving the mystery and returning the animal safely to its owner. A sadistic Eastern European refugee, Kenneth Rowajinski, chooses the Reynolds' dog because he despises them for their wealth and status in society. Rowajinski has recently been abandoned by both his father and his girlfriend, and he wants to destroy the bonds that connect Reynolds to his beloved pet.

The relationship between Reynolds and Duhammel is marked by Duhammel's desperate desire to win Reynolds' approval and Reynolds' growing dislike of Duhammel's emotional fragility. Duhammel's frustration finally erupts when he murders the dognapper, and although Reynolds feels a vague sense of self-satisfied justice, he rejects Duhammel for his lack of self-constraint. Duhammel is finally murdered by a fellow police officer who resents his social ease with Reynolds. In this novel the institutions designed to protect the public cannot be relied upon to uphold either the law or a moral code. And Duhammel's mediation between warring factions of a divided community fails, for no reconciliation is achieved.

As in *A Tremor of Forgery,* Highsmith substitutes a pet for a child in the parent-child relationship, undermining the family structure by creating a genealogical dead end. Every creature Highsmith's characters endeavor to nurture is destroyed by the dangers of the city, most often by a maladjusted and unbalanced human being.

Highsmith's most famous female protagonist, Edith Howland, is the focus of one of her most ambitious works, *Edith's Diary* (1977). Published in the same year as *Little Tales of Misogyny,* a gallery of negative stereotypes about women, *Edith's Diary* gains some ground with feminists, although Highsmith plainly was not interested in being an advocate for the feminist movement. In *Plotting and Writing Suspense Fiction,* Highsmith wrote, "I prefer the point of view of the main character, written in the third-person singular, and I might add masculine, as I have a feeling which I suppose is quote unfounded that women are not as active as men, and not so daring. . . . I tend to think of women as being pushed by people and circumstances instead of pushing" (p. 88).

In this highly political novel, Highsmith attacks American culture, domestic family life, and the dream of the freestanding house as a sign of stability and security. The novel opens with Edith, her husband, and their young son moving from the city to a small town in Pennsylvania. However, just as in the streets of New York City or in foreign lands, Edith and her family gradually discover that they are not safe (from themselves or others) in their own home or in pastoral small-town America. The first sign that the environment is not as perfect as they imagined is Edith's desire to rewrite her reality in a diary. Edith takes further refuge in the fantasy world of her diary as, over time, the structure of her life falls apart: her husband, Brett, falls in love with a younger woman and divorces Edith; her emotionally disturbed son is unwilling to leave home and create an independent life for himself; and an elderly uncle's progressive illness begins to take over the household when he refuses to go to a nursing home. As the world around her changes, she becomes increasingly removed from it in order to maintain her sanity.

Edith's Diary portrays an America that is questioning its traditional political and moral ideology in the face of such events as McCarthyism, the Vietnam War, and Watergate. Highsmith's attempt to make sense of conflicting and confused ideas through Edith, although ambitious, was criticized by Michael Wood in the *New York Review of Books* as faulty in its desire to be a portrait of "Our Times." In response to her growing inability to maintain domestic structures in her life, Edith's political views become more conservative. Throughout the novel, she airs her radical political views in a self-published newspaper. Despite her trials, however, she never breaks down; she continues to pick up the pieces of her life as they fall around her. She takes a job instead of accepting money from Brett and continues to run the newspaper and her household. Brett calls in psychiatrists to assess Edith's state of mind, but her emotions never crack through to the surface. Brett and the doctors cannot convincingly pin any label of insanity on her, so he remains unable to rationalize his guilt for abandoning Edith and his family. At the end of the novel, Edith is left alone with her diary.

Edith's inability to confront her emotions, fears, and hopes signals something inherently wrong in her community at large. She cannot locate or maintain an intimate relationship with herself, her husband, or her son. Regardless of the imposed structure of the family unit, they are strangers who must each find a separate way to survive and create meaning in their lives. *Edith's Diary* preys on our most profound, modern fears of the meaninglessness of life and the inability to control the world around us. The modern world is a place where friends and family either abandon or burden us, where what we say is not necessarily what we mean, and where our dreams remain always in the realm of fantasy.

Despite the novel's implicit criticism of American society, many critics see *Edith's Diary* as a positive depiction of women, and it clearly surpasses Highsmith's view of women "as a bunch of pushovers" (*Plotting and Writing Suspense Fiction*). Highsmith's complaint that "I see them as whining, always *complaining* about something instead of doing something" is effaced as Edith achieves a limited agency through her imagination and especially through her writing. Like her diary, however, her achievements remain self-contained and suspect to others around her.

FINAL WORKS

HIGHSMITH's increasingly prominent political agenda crystallized in her final works. These are dedicated to exploring a corroding American society and expanding global community, focusing specifically on economic and social phenomena and the possibility of escape through expatriation. Character development and psychological profiles are diminished in Highsmith's final period as she streamlines her work to access crime, capitalism, Christian fundamentalism and right-wing politics, and homosexuality.

In *People Who Knock on the Door* (1983), Highsmith portrays right-wing political views as synonymous with crime. Although this is but one of several novels that investigate how a strict religious ideology can produce irrational and criminal behavior, unlike Highsmith's investigations into the mystery of seemingly puzzling criminal behavior, *People Who Knock on the Door* is simply plausible. A middle-class family in Indiana is torn apart after the father, Richard Alderman, becomes a born-again Christian and seeks to impose his new beliefs on his wife and two sons. Richard persuades his youngest son, Robbie, to unite with him against the elder son, who has helped his girlfriend obtain an abortion. Robbie takes his father's side, but he soon is forced to confront Richard's hypocrisy when he discovers that Richard has fathered an illegitimate child with a truck-stop waitress and ex-whore who depends on him for spiritual counsel. Robbie then murders his father, believing he must pay for his sins.

The protagonists in *People Who Knock on the Door* are all male, and the female characters are sketchy at best, but male characters are defined through their relationships to women, and the main thrust of action in the novel is because of or directly involved with the female characters. Although they are still in the background, women characters have an increasing presence in Highsmith's later fiction. The discourse of fundamentalism appropriates the father and son, filling them like empty receptacles. Arthur, the elder son, struggles to find meaning and begins to construct a personal code of ethics with which to chart his life. He refuses to subscribe to a grand, all-consuming narrative; he spends hours in the local library reading about different religious and ethical possibilities. Although he plays a minor role in *People Who Knock on the Door*, he is the only character to achieve a degree of self-knowledge, discovering that moral regeneration must be conducted on an individual basis, not administered by a larger governing force.

Found in the Street (1986), set in the same corrupt New York of *A Dog's Ransom*, is a drama of interlocking destinies that depicts the gay milieu of the 1980s. The atmosphere of unstable peril is established through a point of view that switches from one protagonist to the other as the novel progresses. *Found in the Street* begins from the perspective of Ralph Linderman, a lonely parking-garage guard, who finds a wallet in the gutter and returns it to its owner, Jack Sutherland. Once the wallet is returned to Jack the narration is given over to him and remains with him until the novel's end, when it switches back to Linderman. Linderman, having been abandoned by his wife and family, lives with his dog, named God (dog spelled backwards), and spends his time obsessing over Elsie, a young girl from the Midwest.

There are several positive portrayals of women in the novel, including Elsie and Sutherland's wife, Natalia, and an open rendering of homosexual relationships and the homosexual community. Family life, although not a perfect idyll, remains intact in the Sutherland household; unlike the Belle Ombre of the Ripley novels, Jack and Natalia's home in the West Village is not disturbed by the presence of their young child, Amelia. Traditional roles and habits are upended in *Found in the Street*. Sutherland assumes the more nurturing role with Amelia, while Natalia surrounds herself with homosexuals and lesbians even though she herself has subscribed to a traditional lifestyle. None of the characters maintains regular working hours, some characters do not work at all, and sleep deprivation seems inevitable in a novel where most of the scenes take place after midnight.

Puritanical and paranoid, Linderman is intent on protecting Elsie from the evils of the city, especially the sexual advances of men. Sutherland, a successful and educated artist, belongs to a different social milieu than Linderman, and had it not been for the wallet these two characters would surely never have met at all. Sutherland's privileged life has provided him with a freedom Linderman will never experience.

The apparently accidental intersection of their lives does not stop with the wallet. One night, trying to escape a sudden rain shower, Jack ducks into a coffee shop and meets Elsie. Sutherland feels a sexual ambivalence toward her, and beyond using her as a model for a few drawings, he does not make an attempt either to initiate an affair or to resolve his nebulous feelings. He does befriend her, however, and introduces her to Natalia. Soon after, Elsie and Natalia have a love affair. Sutherland accepts the affair just as he had accepted Natalia's close friendship with a gay man, a relationship that often took precedence over their marriage. Linderman does not know the nature of Elsie's relationship with the Sutherlands and repeatedly begs, then warns, Sutherland to stay away from her.

Elsie's career as a fashion model takes off, and she becomes the object of many people's affections, although sexually she obviously prefers the company of women. At this stage in her career Highsmith is not afraid to write about homosexual or lesbian relationships, but she still couches them in a semiconservative edifice. For example, the recurring and arguably main theme in *Found in the Street* is homosexuality, yet Highsmith chooses a heterosexual marriage as the axis of this novel. This is the simultaneous power and weakness of her narratives—situating the subversive within the realm of the conventional.

The first death in the novel, the suicide of Natalia's gay best friend, who has cancer, is registered almost as a footnote. When Elsie is murdered by the jealous girlfriend of one of Elsie's ex-lovers, everyone is stunned and shattered. Linderman and Sutherland accuse each other, and Linderman goes so far as to protest Sutherland's guilt to the police even after the real murderer has confessed. He does not want to believe that, despite his efforts to protect Elsie, he has failed to shield her from the dangers of the urban jungle.

All of the characters in *Found in the Street* feel a significant loss when Elsie dies, but they have trouble identifying exactly what that loss is. There is one moment at the end of the novel that borders on sentimentality but it evaporates at once, and we are left to accept unconditionally Sutherland's conclusion that "that's what this city has, what this city does" (p. 267).

Found in the Street probably is stylistically Highsmith's last novel. It attempts to reconcile her major themes, as if she had either exhausted many of her psychological explorations or grown tired of her chase to apprehend their meaning.

Highsmith's actual last novel, *Small g: A Summer Idyll* (1995), was published posthumously and is a great departure from her other works. The "Small g" is a Zurich café and the "g" refers to a designation in a tourist guidebook denoting a mixed crowd of homosexuals and straights. The novel embraces the global community of the 1990s, one that no longer interpreted homosexuality as divergent behavior. Set in neutral Switzerland, where anything goes and no one suffers for it, its protagonists, a man and a woman, indulge in a bohemian lifestyle that includes many casual and open relationships. The novel's tension derives from unreciprocated yearnings rather than from the guilt that plagues Highsmith's other characters. As a last novel, *Small g* is disappointing, despite its efforts to embrace tolerance and empathy. Highsmith readers prefer the more dangerous route.

SHORT STORIES

Highsmith published seven volumes of short stories, and within them is a great variety of style and subject matter. Many of her collections have a central theme that is apparent in their titles, such as *The Animal Lover's Book of Beastly Murder* (1975) and *Tales of Natural and Unnatural Catastrophes* (1987). Unlike her novels, Highsmith's short stories are less reminiscent of mainstream fiction, executed in highly stylized prose that at times is comparable to modernist writers such as Kay Boyle or Sherwood Anderson. For example, in the story "The Hand" (*Little Tales of Misogyny*), she writes:

A young man asked a father for his daughter's hand, and received it in a box—her left hand.

Father: "You asked for her hand and you have it. But it is my opinion that you wanted other things and took them."

Young man: "Whatever do you mean?"

Father: "Whatever do you think I mean? You cannot deny that I am more honorable than you, because you took something from my family without asking, whereas when you asked for my daughter's hand, I gave it."

(p. 1)

In Highsmith's stories, horror is shifted outside the human realm: animals often invoke the terror of and may be the culprit for horrific murders. Women protagonists are given a broader, though not necessarily positive, voice in Highsmith's short fiction, as in *Little Tales of Misogyny,* where, as mentioned earlier, her vignettes feature scathing female stereotypes.

Highsmith's short stories explore many of the themes found in her novels: fantasy versus reality, irrational anxiety and obsessive behavior, and the effects of changing socioeconomic conditions on Americans. Objects, such as the basket in "The Terrors of Basket Weaving," symbolize a world where the "other" plays a greater role in signifying reality than do human emotions. An ancient wicker basket evokes disturbing feelings of inadequacy and self-doubt in a young woman who does not want to face this reality; she destroys the basket in an effort to erase her fears.

Highsmith's first published piece of fiction, the short story "The Heroine," appeared in *Harper's Bazaar* in 1945. It is the tale of a young servant who sets her employer's house on fire so she will have the opportunity to rescue his family.

Horror creeps up on characters during the most mundane of moments. In "The Terrapin," young Victor recoils when he realizes that the turtle his mother brought home is to be cooked in a soup for the family to eat. In "Something the Cat Dragged In," a house cat disrupts a game of Scrabble when it drags in a piece of a human hand. And in "The Snail Watcher," as a man gazes admiringly on his beloved pet snails, they begin to multiply, then attack and kill him. Animals that ordinarily are considered tame harbor a vicious bestiality that can surface at any moment; these objects of Highsmith's characters' affections, like her human figures, are unreliable.

A recurrent theme in her collection *The Snail Watcher and Other Stories* is the desire for a fantasy to come true. In these stories the modest wishes of the characters—a letter from a lover, a long sought-after job, a new friend—are granted, but these successes are not what they seem. The love letter Don receives in "The Birds Poised to Fly" is perfect except for the fact that it is addressed to another man. Edith Beaufort in "The Empty Birdhouse" is finally able to convince her husband that she has seen something strange in their house, but her triumph is short-lived when the couple realizes that whatever strange beast inhabits their house is there to stay.

Highsmith's most interesting collection of short stories is *The Black House* (1981), which confronts the dangers of destroying people's personal myths. In "Old Folks at Home," a childless couple adopts an elderly husband and wife to fulfill an idealized notion of themselves as caregivers. Eventually, however, they decide the elderly couple is a nuisance, but the couple refuses to leave. In "A Clock Ticks at Christmas," a clock to which both a husband and wife attach passionate meaning disappears, ultimately destroying the marriage.

CONCLUSION

LIMITING Patricia Highsmith's work to the boundaries of the genre that inspired it would be erroneous; her fiction transcends normative limits and reaches for the unexplored fringes of human psychology and sociological inquiry. Throughout her writing career, Highsmith played with a variety of styles and attempted to break out of the genre of "suspense fiction," but she ultimately was unable to do so. Her American audience practically shunned her, but she was immensely popular in Europe, where book sales rocketed and film adaptations of her novels were commonplace. Her lack of readership in the United States may be due to the amorality in her work. Furthermore, the lack of resolution in Highsmith's work may be confusing to a culture that craves classification and closure.

To pin down what happens in a Highsmith novel is problematic, for almost nothing does. She does not fit into any genre of popular fiction that depends on conventions to guarantee a mechanical escapism. Highsmith's audience projected a generic reliability onto her writing that was not truly there. Even though she recycled themes with little modification throughout the body of her fiction, their persistence is not a formulaic device but the indication of a psychological and ideological dead end for both Highsmith and her characters.

Criticism on Patricia Highsmith is limited, but reviewers of her work seem to agree that the time to pay the most attention in her novels are the long stretches in which nothing seems to happen. Her attention to the mundane and the flat, opaque surfaces of modern life are not meant to distract the reader, but rather Highsmith exposes the very environmental causation for a frustration that erupts unexpectedly into violence. In her work, there is a constant stripping of identity and a capitalization on the emptiness inherent in modern life. Highsmith's "literary" success lies in her ability to fuse character and plot while rendering an obsessional, claustrophobic world that creates an apprehension that keeps her readers off guard. The element of surprise is removed from her work, as is judgment or justification. When her characters behave violently, like Tom Ripley, who kills in cold blood again and again, the flatness and banality of Highsmith's prose lessens the shock. There is no doubt that Highsmith's work is worthy of critical attention. She has constructed a world where the extraordinary is disguised by the ordinary, where literature is hidden behind the genre of crime fiction.

A biographical reading of Highsmith's work would explain many of her literary motifs. The absence of female protagonists could represent her rejection of her mother and her subsequent choice to identify herself with the male power structure. The lack of a cohesive, positive family structure could easily be paralleled with the unstable family life of her childhood. Her evasion of sexuality in her novels could signal her apprehension of revealing her own homosexuality, and her criticisms of American culture could have been an attempt to psychologically justify her expatriatism. Although Highsmith once said that she considered her work to be an argument with herself, to analyze her work biographically is something she would have despised. She distrusted writers who used their families as material for their work, telling Joan Dupont: "Some dramatic things happened in my family but I wouldn't dream of writing about them."

Highsmith wrote to explore the mysteries of human life. She was not invested in putting forth a political or aesthetic agenda in her writing. What is more important to look for in her fiction is what is missing from the text. Unlike most suspense fiction, there are no detectives, crimes go unsolved, and there is no hunt for truth. Her hero-villains live in a world exhausted of morality, reason, and cultural identification. Yet we like these characters and are fascinated by them, perhaps seeing glimmers of ourselves in them. Highsmith's fiction is a world immersed in apprehension—the apprehension of confronting everyday life. As Graham Greene said, "Apprehension nags at the nerves gently and inescapably. We have to learn to live with it."

SELECTED BIBLIOGRAPHY

I. NOVELS AND SHORT STORIES. *Strangers on a Train* (New York, 1950; Harmondsworth, Middlesex, 1974); *The Price of Salt* by "Claire Morgan" (New York, 1952; rev. ed. Tallahassee, Fla., 1991), published in U.K. as *Carol* by Patricia Highsmith (London, 1993); *The Blunderer* (New York, 1954; Feltham, Middlesex, 1978); published in U.S. as *Lament for a Lover* (New York, 1956); *The Talented Mr. Ripley* (New York, 1955; Harmondsworth, Middlesex, 1976); *Deep Water* (New York, 1957; Harmondsworth, Middlesex, 1974); *A Game for the Living* (New York, 1958; Feltham, Middlesex, 1978); *This Sweet Sickness* (New York, 1960; Harmondsworth, Middlesex, 1973); *The Cry of the Owl* (New York, 1962; Harmondsworth, Middlesex, 1973); *The Two Faces of January* (Garden City, N.Y., 1964; New York, 1988); *The Glass Cell* (Garden City, N.Y., 1964; Harmondsworth, Middlesex, 1973); *A Suspension of Mercy* (London, 1965; Harmondsworth, Middlesex, 1972); published in U.S. as *The Story-Teller* (Garden City, N.Y., 1967; Feltham, Middlesex, 1979); *Those Who Walk Away* (London, 1967; New York, 1988); *The Tremor of Forgery* (Garden City, N.Y., 1969; Feltham, Middlesex, 1978); *Ripley Under Ground* (Garden City, N.Y., 1970); *Eleven* (London, 1970; New York, 1989), published in U.S. as *The Snail Watcher and Other Stories* (Garden City, N.Y., 1970); *A Dog's Ransom* (New York, 1972; Harmondsworth, Middlesex, 1975); *Ripley's Game* (New York, 1974, 1993); *The Animal Lover's Book of Beastly Murder* (London, 1975; Harmondsworth, Middlesex, 1979); *Edith's Diary* (London and New York, 1977); *Little Tales of Misogyny* (London, 1977; New York, 1986); *Slowly, Slowly in the Wind* (London, 1979; New York, 1985); *The Boy Who Followed Ripley* (New York, 1980, 1993); *The Black House* (London, 1981; Harmondsworth, Middlesex, 1982); *People Who Knock on the Door* (London,

1983; Harmondsworth, Middlesex, 1984); *Mermaids on the Golf Course* (London, 1985; Harmondsworth, Middlesex, 1986); *Found in the Street* (London, 1986; New York, 1987); *Tales of Natural and Unnatural Catastrophes* (London, 1987; New York, 1989); *Ripley Under Water* (New York: Knopf, 1991); *Small g: A Summer Idyll* (London, 1995).

II. NONFICTION. *Plotting and Writing Suspense Fiction* (Boston, 1966).

III. INTERVIEWS, REVIEWS, AND CRITICAL STUDIES. Anthony Boucher, review of *Deep Water,* in *New York Times Book Review* (6 October 1957); Michael Wood, "A Heavy Legacy," in *New Statesman* 31 (May 1963); Thomas Sutcliffe, "Graphs of Innocence and Guilt," in *Times Literary Supplement* (2 October 1981); Erlene Hubly, "A Portrait of the Artist: The Novels of Patricia Highsmith," in *Clues* 5 (1984); Joan Dupont, "Criminal Pursuits," in *New York Times Magazine* (12 June 1988); Terrence Rafferty, "Fear and Trembling," in *New Yorker* (1 January 1988); Graham Greene, foreword to *Eleven,* by Patricia Highsmith (New York, 1989); Slavoj Zizek, *Looking Awry: An Introduction to Jacques Lacan Through Popular Culture* (Cambridge, Mass., 1991); Russell Harrison, *Patricia Highsmith* (New York, 1997).

GEOFFREY HILL

(1932–)

Tyrus Miller

I SAY IT is not faithless
to stand without faith, keeping open
vigil at the site

(Canaan, p. 9)

as actuated self-knowledge, a daily acknowledgement
of what is owed the dead.

(p. 63)

writes Geoffrey Hill in his poem "William Cobbett: In Absentia." These lines might stand as the motto of Hill's nearly fifty years as a writer, as the emblem of a poetry combining an intense religiosity and an equally intense suspicion of spiritual evasions and ruses, including those springing from religion itself. The "sites" at which his works stand vigil are those of historical suffering and loss: the remembered places of an English childhood in the late 1930s and during the war; the concentration camps that were opened when Hill was thirteen; the terrible religious persecutions and wars that gripped England and the Continent in the late sixteenth and the seventeenth centuries; the trenches winding through the mud of France and Belgium during World War I; the English cities ruined by the Nazi blitz early in World War II and the Allied incendiary bombardments of German cities that brought that war to its close. Hill is torn by his sense of the inadequacy, if not the outright duplicity, of poetic consolations in the face of such destruction, pain, and death. Yet he remains committed to his poetry's "vigil," seeking at once to commemorate those who have fallen to the violence of history and to keep vigilant against poetry's capacity to evade the fact of history's irreparableness. He finds moral predicament in the inertia of everyday usage and custom; attention, understanding, fidelity, and observance of nuance are invested with an according burden of moral difficulty. In a passage of his long poem *The Triumph of Love* (1998) he writes,

By understanding I understand diligence
and attention, appropriately understood

Yet the labor of poetry leads directly to quandaries of moral and aesthetic judgment, to problems of separating the seductive doubles of creative power from its elusive true forms.

In a 1971 essay on William Butler Yeats titled "'The Conscious Mind's Intelligible Structure': A Debate," Hill delineates a dichotomy within romanticism between its "false" and "true" masks. Through its adherence to "the finality of the useful," the false mask is lent its glitter by "the fecundity of money" (*Agenda,* p. 16) or its semblance of authority, which overrides more substantive moral considerations. This mask defines a realm of worldly action in which poetry fails to compete and falsifies itself in the attempt. The true mask, in contrast, is given shape by its bearer's fitting to a "grammar of assent," his adherence to a code more enduring and less pliant than himself, or alternatively by the difficult "syntax" of singular decision, the twisting byways of the individual grappling with reality in all its complex moral topography. Both pursuits have an apparent sublimity and a sort of aesthetic disinterestedness that led poet and insurance executive Wallace Stevens to venture in *The Necessary Angel* that "Money is a kind of poetry"; Stevens did not indicate whether he considered it a debased or an elevated kind. But Hill's scruples—and, it must be added, his professional track, far from the corporate world in which Stevens passed his working days—do not allow him the elder American's impassive broad-mindedness about this question. His is emphatically a poetry of judgment, ever seeking to drive the honed word between the false and true masks of creativity, between the expediencies of commerce and the rigors of moral decision.

GEOFFREY HILL

LIFE

HILL was born in Bromsgrove, Worcestershire, England, on 18 June 1932 and grew up in the neighboring village of Fairfield. His parents had received only a minimal formal education, both having left school at the age of thirteen. His father became village constable, and his mother's family was in the nail-making business. Hill attended the village school, then grammar school, and won a scholarship to Keble College, Oxford; he gained a First in English language and literature in 1953. He began his academic career the following year at the University of Leeds, and became professor of English there in 1976. In January 1981 he was named a fellow of Emmanuel College and University Lecturer in English at Cambridge University. In 1988 he moved to the United States to teach in the University Program at Boston University.

Hill published his first poems while a student at Oxford, including a Fantasy Press pamphlet of his work that appeared in the autumn of 1952. In 1959 he assembled his first book of poetry, *For the Unfallen: Poems, 1952–1958;* since then he has published three additional collections of individual lyrics, three book-length poems, a translation and adaptation of Henrik Ibsen's long narrative poem *Brand,* and two volumes of critical essays. An American edition of his first three volumes, titled *Somewhere Is Such a Kingdom: Poems, 1952–1971* and bearing an effusive introduction by the critic Harold Bloom, appeared in 1975. His *New and Collected Poems, 1952–1992* followed in 1994. In 1972 he became a fellow of the Royal Society of Literature, and he has been the recipient of numerous other literary honors, including the Hawthornden Prize (1969), the Heinemann Award (1972), and the Duff Cooper Memorial Prize (1979).

LYRIC COLLECTIONS

HILL's first book, *For the Unfallen,* is framed between two poems, "Genesis" and "To the (Supposed) Patron," which together betray a tension pervading the whole collection. They explore the fraught resemblance between the Creator and his doubles: on the one hand the visionary poet shaping words and meanings; on the other the rich man manipulating abstract values and their tokens. Although by no means an unequivocal affirmation of

heroic individual creation, "Genesis" seeks to project, if ultimately not to realize, the "true mask" of a syntax of struggle. At the opposite extreme "To the (Supposed) Patron" emphatically exposes the "false mask" in which any true visionary romanticism must confront its perverted doubles: those green-gold vistas fructified by money, and the aura of creative energy surrounding instrumental power, the starry-eyed awe of onlookers before the demiurge of the man who gets things done.

The book commences, appropriately, with "Genesis," a disenchanted bard's reworking of creation myth. In this five-part poem the poet speaks in the first person alternately as demiurge, witness, sovereign, and sacrificial victim of the created world. The first section presents the poet as a Blakean primitive whose words carry the force of storms and tides: "the waves flourished at my prayer, / The rivers spawned their sand" (p. 15). The next section, however, finds the poet shorn of his active power and compelled to witness the unintended outcome of the forces his creative word has unleashed, the blood law ruling the natural world and the instinctive violence of creature against creature:

> The second day I stood and saw
> The osprey plunge with triggered claw,
> Feathering blood along the shore
> To lay the living sinew bare.
>
> (p. 15)

In the third section a new phase of poetic creation emerges, the secondary fashioning of symbolic myths that supplant the direct efficacy of the earlier primary fabrication of the material world. Hill presents three such myths—the Leviathan, the albatross, and the phoenix—each at once broadly archetypal in character and yet specifiable with respect to points of reference in English literary history. Each represents an ascetic default from the tooth-and-talon power of the earlier state of nature in favor of a sublimated or artificial use of nature as a source of allegorical symbols.

Hill most obviously alludes in this verse to Thomas Hobbes's "artificial man," the Leviathan of the absolute sovereign, whose political body should encompass England's territory and keep vigilance over the surrounding seas:

> And I renounced, on the fourth day,
> This fierce and unregenerate clay,

> Building as a huge myth for man
> The watery Leviathan.
>
> (p. 16)

To depart from the horrors of faction and civil strife, the war of all against all, Hobbes's treatise argued, the individual Englishman must alienate his natural freedom, rooted in his natural instinct to survive, and accede to the collective will allegorically residing in the single person of the king. He must, in short, sacrifice his natural vitality in the interest of extending his life beyond its short span and its nasty, brutish quality in the state of nature.

A similar asceticism shades the other two literary myths. In Hill's lines the albatross, immortally brooding over the abyss of an empty sea, "scours" the "ashes" (p. 16) that float upon the water, as if Coleridge's ominous bird were trying futilely to read the traces left by the fiery wings of Milton's Satan over these same void expanses; immortality is won at the expense of homelessness and perpetual search. Similarly, Hill's "charmed phoenix," deathlessly perched "in the unwithering tree" (p. 16), ironically brings to mind the miraculous golden bird of William Butler Yeats's Byzantium poems, the aging poet's symbolic artifice of eternity set against the sensual music of embracing couples and salmon falls. While the classical phoenix was eternally renewed *through* death, the mechanical marvel of Yeats's poem collapses both moments into one: death-in-life and life-in-death meet in the goldsmith's bird of "changeless metal." All three myths have in common the diminishment of vital existence in the attempt, through political and artistic artifice, to evade death.

The fourth section admits this cost, and on "the fifth day" of creation the poet turns back to suffering vitality, to "flesh and blood and the blood's pain" (p. 16). The sixth day, the last day of creation before he may withdraw for Godlike rest, the poet surveys what his creating word has wrought. Everywhere he discovers the savage reality of blood and sacrifice, the very medium through which myth is perpetuated in the world:

> By blood we live, the hot, the cold,
> To ravage and redeem the world:
> There is no bloodless myth will hold.
>
> (p. 17)

Not even Christ's promise of salvation is exempt from the passage through mythic sacrifice, first in the crucifixion, then in the chain of persecutions, factionalism, and religious strife that Hobbes had hoped to quell through his second-order political myth, the allegorical Leviathan of the absolute state. At the poem's close the sobering question remains of what is left for poets to do: To prophesy the redemption or simply to bear witness, dismayed, to the seeming perpetuity of archaic violence?

At the outset, then, Hill responds to the mute demand of the *fallen* for recognition, the victims of the blood law coursing through history. His book title, however, is taken from his concluding poem, "To the (Supposed) Patron," which takes stock of unjustified happiness, the moral blitheness of those few who survive felicitously amid a general unhappiness:

> For the unfallen—the firstborn, or wise
> Councillor—prepared vistas extend
> As far as harvest; and idyllic death
> Where fish at dawn ignite the powdery lake.
>
> (p. 59)

At the opposite extreme of creation, in the charmed circle of the unfallen, a sheer fact, the fact of wealth, seems to fructify into value. With unsparing irony Hill sets out the predicament of poetry in a world of power and privilege, delivering in the end a disaffecting judgment:

> There is no substitute for a rich man.
> At his first entering a new province
> With new coin, music, the barest glancing
> Of steel or gold suffices. There are many
> Tremulous dreams secured under that head.
>
> (p. 59)

Judged on these terms of manifest potency and worldly efficacy, the poet cannot help but appear as the poor kin—if not, indeed, the fawning servant—of the wealthy patron.

The "true mask" of the poet, however, appears when he consciously adopts and intensifies to an extreme that impoverishment associated with loss, with useless sacrifice, with those fallen to the history that has cast the patron up, happily unscathed. Accordingly Hill maps a moral economy onto a figural and syntactical order. Figures of profit and utility, their syntax moving smoothly toward the gratifying end, are weighed in the moral balance against dead and broken things divested of use, with once-living bodies reduced to mere ashes and bones. This economic language appears most directly in "The Distant Fury of Battle," which catalogs a series of ways of coming to terms with the dead. Among the "pacts" (p. 27) forged to avoid confronting death is that of a ritualized dedication:

> Some keep to the arrangement of love
> (Or similar trust) under whose auspices move
>
> Most subjects, toward the profits of this
> Combine of doves and witnesses.
>
> (p. 27)

In the words "trust" and "combine," Hill's punning incongruously rhymes the arrangements made to commemorate the dead with corporate organizations forged to insulate companies against competitors and give them a free hand to pursue profits unrestrainedly. "Arrangements" refers at once to the social rituals by which we protect ourselves against loss and the syntactical forms with which we consign the "fallen" to a comfortable corner of our thoughts, the linguistic mechanisms that effortlessly combine "doves and witnesses" in figures for the heart's relief.

By contrast, drowning is Hill's privileged image of irredeemable loss and exit from the economies of use and compensation. The sea confounds the upward spiral of value that derives from the fecundity of money, drawing everything back into an unaltering cycle of submersion and return. "Water," Hill writes,

> Retains, still, what it might give
> As casually as it took away:
> Creatures passed through the wet sieve
> Without enrichment or decay.
>
> ("The White Ship," p. 41)

At its most intense the trope of drowning presses the line toward syntactical dissolution, with only the recurrent pattern of minimal rhymes holding together the discrete fragments adrift on the surface of the line. For example, the poem "Wreaths" begins: "Each day the tide withdraws; chills us; pastes / The sand with dead gulls, oranges, dead men" (p. 42). Such lines seek to offer an image not merely of the disordering force of the sea, but also of the poet's difficult moral choice to refuse the profit economy and to align himself with the syntax of loss and the detritus of history, a decision discernible in the syntax of the catalog.

Two other poems in *For the Unfallen* are notable for their juxtaposition of the figure of drowning as the ultimate loss with the figures of consolation that recuperate loss, compensating or even profiting from it. In the third poem of the sequence "Of Commerce and Society," subtitled "The Death of Shelley," the tortuous opening lines, which depict the sea-wracked body of the poet, slide neatly into the cliché image on the tomb and the clichéd phrasing of the line:

> Slime; the residues of refined tears;
> And, salt-bristled, blown on a drying sea,
> The sunned and risen faces,
>   There's Andromeda
> Depicted in relief, after the fashion.
>
> (p. 50)

"Picture of a Nativity," similarly, imagines Christ's incarnation as a sea change and plays off the violence of his passage through drowning with the proleptically elegiac figures of the angels in the picture. In these two poems Hill implicitly contrasts two relations of poetry to the dead: the elegiac falsification of the stone monument, with its consoling rigid syntax, and the sacrificial submission of the line to the syntax of drowning, which tears it to bits, fragmenting the line into discrete words and phrases. Only the latter realizes the "true mask" of romanticism, the face of an ultimate visionary impoverishment: Shelley's death mask and Christ's visage at the end of his passion.

In *King Log*, published in 1968, Hill intensifies his skeptical interrogation of the ruses and self-delusions by which elegiac ceremony is made to wring value out of loss. Penitentially targeting even his own capitulations to the "inertial drag of speech" (as he would put it in his essay "Redeeming the Time" in *The Lords of Limit*, 1984) and the consolations of rhetoric, Hill's irony often spills over into galled invective and self-mockery in *King Log*:

> Dry walls, and nettles battered by the dust,
> Odours from gathered water, muddled storm-clouds
> Disastrous over the manufactured West Riding.
>
> Mind—a fritter of excrement; step
> Aside, step aside, sir! Ah, but a priest
> In his prime watches where he goes. He goes
>
> To tender his confession. Forgiveness
> Journeys towards him like a brisk traveller

On the same road.
("Fantasia on 'Horbury,'" p. 45)

The opening lines, ponderously cranking the hurdy-gurdy of autumnal landscape description for elegiac effect, receive Hill's rude judgment in the second stanza: what a bunch of horseshit! The speaker's combination of high-toned absentmindedness ("step aside, sir!") and respectable caution ("a priest / In his prime watches where he goes") are strict correlates of his unashamed moral ease. The speaker, the nineteenth-century clergyman and hymn writer John Bacchus Dykes, traffics in atonement and absolution, as if getting to heaven were simply a matter of paying one's highway tolls and not stepping in anything nasty. Both Hill's own propensity for the quatrain stanza and the more general connection of elegiac poetry with music suggest that Dykes is a comic mask of the poet himself, his romantic indulgences satirized under the gaze of the more austere poet-judge; it is worth noting that Hill's next book, notably, was titled *Mercian Hymns* (1971), which further suggests this clerical persona might be understood as an unflattering self-identification.

If Pan's melodious lifting of the reeds into the wind after his unsuccessful grab at Syrinx and the lamentations of Orpheus at the death of Eurydice represent the two primal scenes of Western elegy, the transmutation of erotic loss and death into song, then Hill's consistent reference of his poetry to musical forms signals his troubled concern with this tradition. Along with "Fantasia on 'Horbury,'" the titles in *King Log* of "Locust Songs," "September Song," "Funeral Music," and "The Songbook of Sebastian Arrurruz" explicitly refer to music; several other poems present music or musical metaphors as a narcotic balm that dulls the perception of suffering. The opening poem of the collection, "Ovid in the Third Reich," provocatively pulls Ovid out of his troubled relation with Augustus and sets him in confrontation with Hitler. Raising the moral stakes of the poet's accommodation to dictatorial power, Hill foregrounds the bland "composure" this Germanic Ovid has achieved through his self-consoling metaphorical "composition." In the poet's homemade world victims, gods, and lovers are consigned to separate spheres, then "harmonized" in their poetic resonances:

I have learned one thing: not to look down
So much upon the damned. They, in their sphere,

Harmonize strangely with the divine
Love. I, in mine, celebrate the love-choir.
(p. 13)

A more positive, though still ambiguous, example is the second of Hill's "Soliloquies," in which the "old poet" (p. 43) speaks of trying to recapture his losses in the present. He uses the economic language of coinage and sale to characterize elegiac consolation, yet the very lines in which he expresses his desire for this poetic profit also, in their conditional mood and irony, confess to its impossibility:

If
I knew the exact coin for tribute,
Defeat might be bought, processional

Silence gesture its tokens of earth
At my mouth: as in the great death-songs
Of Propertius (although he died young).
(p. 43)

The longings of the old poet to recapture his losses as figures of elegy—coining tribute to them, buying their precious "defeat"—fix on the model of Sextus Propertius, considered one of the most refined Roman elegists. The old poet, however, ironically has missed his chance to be Propertius: he has lived too long for conviction. He must admit that Propertius' elegant "death-songs" now appear to him the lucubrations of a young man surprised by death and hence little touched by its daily presence in the "still-life" (p. 43) of old age. If the old poet achieves a poetic success in his soliloquy, it is not so much by measuring up to Propertius' example as in admitting his failure to do so: a stoical achievement of dwelling in loss, of accepting the necessary foundering of the desire to salvage a world out of time.

The sequences "Funeral Music," "Three Baroque Meditations," and "The Songbook of Sebastian Arrurruz" represent Hill's most extended and complex examination of the premises of elegiac compensation. They best illustrate his deft scattering of ironic sand in the rhetorical mechanisms of elegy, the elaborate technics of poetic consolation by which a raw material of ashes, bones, and ruined villages is transmuted into luxury goods of poetry and song.

The first of these three sequences focuses on historical violence, the War of the Roses, and its transfiguration into a monument for consumption by later generations. Throughout this sequence ceremonial pomp and callous violence are collusive as hanging judge and hooded executioner:

> The voice fragrant with mannered humility,
> With an equable contempt for this World,
> "In honorem Trinitatis". Crash. The head
> struck down into a meaty conduit of blood.
>
> (p. 25)

This hypocrisy extends to the perception of one's relation to the victims, who "dispose themselves to receive each / Pentecostal blow from axe or seraph" (p. 25). A similar and even more grotesque reversal of perspective occurs at the end of the fifth poem of the sequence, in which the tortured body puts on a show, generously contorting itself to delight the spectators. Hill conjoins the guilt of elegiac consolation with a spectrum of means by which the positive or negative substance of social acts is transformed into ritual and emptied of meaning. If the horror of torture can become a kind of theater, so can the virtues of justice, penitence, and mourning be supplanted by their mere symbols and ceremonies. It is from these representations, separated from the passions of the body, from the ardor of its efforts at virtue and the pain of its suffering, that we receive our primary knowledge of history, the monumental history that, as Walter Benjamin pointed out, is written by the "unfallen" at the expense of the defeated.

> not as we
> Desire life but as they would have us live,
> Set apart in timeless colloquy:
> So it is required; so we bear witness,
> Despite ourselves, to what is beyond us
>
> (p. 32)

Yet the completion of the monumental image handed down by history—being "without / Consequence when we vaunt and suffer" (p. 32)—is called to account by the dead speaker's plangent challenge, which disturbs the harmonic "resolution" of "Funeral Music" with a pathetic note of fear in the face of death:

> Then tell me, love,
> How that should comfort us—or anyone
> Dragged half-unnerved out of this worldly place,
> Crying to the end "I have not finished."
>
> (p. 32)

"Three Baroque Meditations" also revolves around rituals for assuaging loss. The term "baroque" signals Hill's use of a distancing persona for the sequence, and the general tone suggests ironic self-criticism: "I speak well of Death; / I confess to the priest in me" (p. 46). The second meditation offers another unpleasant aspect of the speaker (or perhaps another speaker representing that aspect): a kind of aesthetic delectation of the appurtenances of death. In the face of darkness and the night outside his room, the speaker is tempted to cry out, "Death! Death!" (p. 47). Unwilling to give himself over to the radical loss of self that is represented by the "Foxes and rain-sleeked stones and the dead" (p. 47) beyond the safety of his house, he nonetheless "spices" his life with the scent of death,

> Lifting the spicy lid of my tact
> To sniff at the myrrh. . . .
> In its impalpable bitterness.
>
> (p. 47)

The speaker is a connoisseur of cultivated melancholy; he takes his death in short draughts, piquant but without real risk. The third meditation, subtitled "The Dead Bride," presents the mourning poet-husband from the objectifying position of the dead. Through this unusual distancing device Hill presents the emotional gestures of elegy from the outside: "He weeps, / Solemnizing his loss" (p. 48). The dead bride betrays the elegist's ruse: she underscores the difference between mourning her and the reflexive sentiment of "solemnizing *his* loss"; the ostentatious displays of grief through which the poet appears to devote himself to the lost bride are but the final form of that self-involvement for which she hated him when she was alive.

"The Songbook of Sebastian Arrurruz" uses the fictive premise of a turn-of-the-century poet to explore the ambiguous faces of elegy. If "Funeral Music" highlighted the falsification of historical violence and "Three Baroque Meditations" focused on the psychological aspects of elegiac conceit, "The Songbook" explores the associations of elegy and eroticism. Sebastian's mannered stance of perpetual erotic torment, his glancing cynicism, and his self-conscious commingling of sensualized Catholicism and Catholicized sensuality certainly work to call his sincerity into question. So does his fictive name, identifying him with Saint Sebastian and the arrows that pierce his flesh, as well as, punningly, "error" and "ruse."

Sebastian indulges to a hyperbolic degree that transmutation of pain into song and those economic metaphors of elegiac compensation which had been the object of Hill's anger and mockery in other contexts. Similarly he is as self-involved as the poet of "The Dead Bride"; his own desire is the reflexive object of the play of erotic possession and loss:

> "One cannot lose what one has not possessed."
> So much for that abrasive gem.
> I can lose what I want. I want you.
>
> (p. 54)

Tonally, however, this sequence differs subtly from other poems in *King Log*. Hill's irony here is urbane and playful rather than scathing and judgmental. Sebastian's insincerity is theatrical; his words are intended for erotic enjoyment rather than moral suasion or political efficacy. Yet even so "Songbook" is not without moral ambiguity. The limits of the erotic are reached at the end of the sequence, with "A Letter from Armenia" and "A Song from Armenia" and with the two-part poem "To His Wife." The "Letter" and "Song" from Armenia show Sebastian indulging his aestheticism in the face of the Armenian genocide:

> I turn my mind
> towards delicate pillage, the provenance
> of shards glazed and unglazed, the three
> kinds of surviving grain. I hesitate amid
> circumstantial disasters. I gaze at the
> authentic dead.
> ("A Letter from Armenia," p. 60)

The second of the poems "To His Wife" reveals a similar aestheticism in his marriage, which Hill, like Søren Kierkegaard, views as an ethical relation of which Sebastian's aesthetic-erotic enjoyment is a betrayal:

> Scarcely speaking: it becomes as a
> Coolness between neighbors. . . .
> I wake . . .
> And enjoy abstinence in a vocation
> Of now-almost-meaningless despair.
> (p. 63)

In the opening poems of the sequence, Hill thus allows Sebastian a space of aesthetic play proper to the erotic. Yet he also suggests the potential for elegy to become a vehicle of sin when the aesthetic attitude is carried over into situations in which it occasions suffering or amounts to complicity with evil. Not in itself culpable, Sebastian's example

suggests, the aesthetic mind is nevertheless almost irresistibly tempted to trespass beyond its limits. His enjoyably intransitive speech becomes moral self-betrayal and sin when it serves to deflect the ethical demand for effective words and actions in the presence of suffering.

After the publication in 1971 of the book-length prose poem sequence *Mercian Hymns* (discussed below as a long poem), Hill returned to lyric verse in his 1978 volume *Tenebrae*. In this collection Hill's inclination toward the sequential poem is even more marked than in his earlier books: only five individual works of verse appear, along with the sequences "The Pentecost Castle," "Lachrimae," and "An Apology for the Revival of Christian Architecture in England," the eight-section title poem, and the paired "choral-preludes" based on poems by the German-Jewish-Romanian poet Paul Celan. This strong presence of the sequence form allows the book a considerable degree of compression and internal complexity, arguably bringing it closer to his book-length poems than to his other collections of lyric verse. Yet despite the reduction in *Tenebrae* to a small number of sequenced poems, the actual forms Hill uses are insistently lyrical, unlike the jagged prose forms of *Mercian Hymns*, the more discursively spacious quatrains of *The Mystery of the Charity of Charles Péguy* (1983), or the free odelike stanzas of *The Triumph of Love* (1998). Moreover, as the title suggests, the implicit model for the book is the sequence of matins and lauds sung during Holy Week as the candles are extinguished one by one; they commemorate the darkness at Christ's crucifixion. This title may also, however, once again nod toward the fractured lyric forms of Paul Celan, whose own poem titled "Tenebrae" (in *Poems of Paul Celan*, 1988) is a chilling fragment of antinomian liturgy:

> Handled already, Lord,
> clawed and clawing as though
> the body of each of us were
> your body, Lord.
>
> Pray, Lord,
> pray to us,
> we are near.
>
> (p. 113)

Celan stands behind Hill's book as the poet whose lifework, from his survival of the Holocaust and flight from Soviet-occupied Romania until his suicide in 1970 by drowning, was a protracted poetic recollection of the dead. The single exception the German-Jewish philosopher Theodor Adorno allowed when he made his famous remark that "Poetry after Auschwitz is a barbarity," Celan also serves Hill as the exemplary figure of unwavering vigil at the site of historical suffering.

"The Pentecost Castle," the fifteen-part sequence with which *Tenebrae* commences, utilizes a pared-down song form composed of twelve short lines in three stanzas; as the notes indicate, this sequence draws inspiration from a collection of Spanish poetry. The beauty and tension of the poem derive primarily from Hill's skillful use of repetitions and minimal variations:

> as he is dying
> I shall live
> in grief desiring
> still to grieve
>
> as he is living
> I shall die
> sick of forgiving
> such honesty
> (p. 14)

The simplified stanzaic form also allows Hill some of his most complex counterpointing of line and stanza breaks, syntax, and semantic ambiguities. Repeatedly forcing the reader to reframe expectations as the first eight lines progress, the fourth poem in the sequence evokes an intensely visual impression of the play of reflections in a church in which Mass is being said at dawn:

> At dawn the Mass
> burgeons from stone
> a Jesse tree
> of resurrection
>
> budding with candle
> flames the gold
> and the white wafers
> of the feast
> (p. 9)

Grammatical and syntactical uncertainties abound in these lines, in turn raising doubts about the appurtenances of the Mass to which they refer. The ambiguities simultaneously evoke a sense of participatory blurring of boundaries and provoke a series of suspicious double takes at things that are not what they seem at first glance.

Following immediately upon "The Pentecost Castle" is the elaborately wrought sonnet sequence "Lachrimae, or Seven Tears Figured in Seven Passionate Pavans." In this explicitly baroque title, alluding to John Dowland's 1604 song sequence of the same title, Hill implies a complex relation to the lyric form. The "tears" indicate both a religious poetry (as several of the poems confirm) and a poetry of emotional expression; "passionate" similarly alludes both to the passion of Christ and to the passions of love and sorrow. The epigraph, from *Marie Magdalens Funeral Teares* (1591) by the Jesuit martyr Robert Southwell, further establishes this conjunction of religious and secular significance in Hill's key terms: "Passions I allow, and loves I approve, onely / I would wishe that men would alter their object and better their intent" (p. 15). "Pavan" refers to a stately, slow dance introduced into England in the sixteenth century or to the music accompanying this dance. Thus Hill underscores both the artifice of this sequence of figured "tears" and the emphasis of the dynamic measure of dance, music, and "figuring" over discursive argument, narrative, or trope.

The first poem of the sequence, "Lachrimae Verae," addresses the "Crucified Lord" (p. 15) but also alludes to the poet himself. Hill makes covert reference to an idea discussed in his 1977 inaugural address at the University of Leeds, "Poetry as 'Menace' and 'Atonement,'" in which he stresses the etymological sense of atonement as reconciliation, divided things becoming "at one," and presents the integrity of poetic craft as the agent of this making whole. In a further act of self-reference, like Shakespeare asserting his "will" throughout the sonnets, Hill manages to inscribe his name into the image of a poetic Calvary: "You are the castaway of drowned remorse, / you are the world's atonement on the hill" (p. 15). Yet, as Christopher Ricks has remarked, such ostentatious artifice of "at-one-ment," the sonnet's punlike conjoining of the secular and sacred, of reference to Christ and self-reference, has an ironic effect: it highlights all the more the gap between the transcendent and the worldly that the poetic hyphen implied in "at-one-ment" pretended to span.

This paradoxical "hyphen" effect reaches its acme in the condensed language and imagery of quatrains of the fifth sonnet, "Pavana Dolorosa":

> Loves I allow and passions I approve:
> Ash-Wednesday feasts, ascetic opulence,

the wincing lute, so real in its pretence,
itself a passion amorous of love.

Self-wounding martyrdom, what joys you have,
true-torn among this fictive consonance,
music's creation of the moveless dance,
the decreation to which all must move.

(p. 19)

These lines pull out all the rhetorical stops, from the chiastic crossing of "love" and "passion" in the first and fourth lines, to the oxymoronic figures of "ascetic opulence," "real pretence," and "moveless dance," to the semantic shearing of the sign "tear" between its backward reference to joy (laughter and tears) and its forward reference to consonance (the whole and the "torn" piece). "True," in "true-torn," also splits its sense between two equally plausible readings: being "true" as figure, that is, being torn along the right line without straying or fraying, and being paradoxically torn into the order of truth, the immaterial and "decreated" figure, through participation in the aesthetic artifice of the dance, the fiction of consonance enacted by the music. Finally, Hill alludes to and reverses Tennyson's elegiac consolation in *In Memoriam*, in which a distant God is the measure to which all creation moves. The last lines, however, which suggest the interminableness of this pursuit of eternity within the apparent movement of poetry's measure, confirm the justice of Ricks's caveat: "I founder in desire for things unfound. / I stay amid the things that will not stay" (p. 19). The final sonnet, "Lachrimae Amantis" (a free translation, Hill notes, from Lope de Vega), similarly lingers on the pathos of living in the dream of expectation. Expectation, as Hill recognizes, can become a way of being "religiously secure" (p. 21) and hence an end in itself. Desire and expectation become precisely the spiritual ruse through which atonement is evaded, a mood in which the desired salvation will always be missed because its imminence eludes the one who waits for it:

So many nights the angel of my house
has fed such urgent comfort through a dream,
whispered "your lord is coming, he is close"

that I have drowsed half-faithful for a time
bathed in pure tones of promise and remorse:
"tomorrow I shall wake to welcome him."

(p. 21)

The closing line, overhearing the mind in the act of deluding itself, implies that the present becomes dreamlike and unreal when lived in a state of desire and expectation. Awaited in the arriving future, the saving event of the present *will have been* grasped perpetually too late.

The third major sequence of *Tenebrae*, "An Apology for the Revival of Christian Architecture in England," has a more fraught relation with the lyric genre than do the first two. Hill's sequence treats a nineteenth-century "dissociation of sensibility" in letters, emblematized by the gap between the authors of its two epigraphs: the poet and philosopher Samuel Taylor Coleridge, championing the "spiritual Platonic old England" and the novelist-politician Benjamin Disraeli, who represents the "New World" of industrial Britain. Although composed of thirteen largely orthodox Petrarchan sonnets—only the occasional slant rhymes depart from the strict scheme—the titles of the sequence and of the individual sonnets refer these lyrics to several other genres and media less clearly contiguous to lyric than was dance in "Lachrimae." "An Apology for the Revival of Christian Architecture in England" borrows its title from Augustus Welby Pugin's 1843 text, implying that the sequence is a kind of treatise with a discursive argument. Similarly, "Quaint Mazes" (sonnet 1) refers to Shakespearean comedy (the phrase is drawn from *A Midsummer Night's Dream*) and to ornamental gardening. "Who Are These Coming to the Sacrifice?" alludes to John Keats's romantic lyric "Ode on a Grecian Urn" but also remobilizes the gaps between spatial and temporal modes, verbal and visual art forms, religious practices and artistic artifacts that vexed Keats into thought. Three poems (sonnets 4–6) borrow the title "A Short History of British India," again tugging the poem between discourse and lyric expression. "Idylls of the King" (sonnet 11) suggests a relation to Tennyson's narrative long poem. And "The Eve of St. Mark" (sonnet 12) evokes a complex web of intertextual references, through Keats's fragmentary poem to the illustrated saint's life Bertha reads in that poem and to the Middle English poem incorporated into one of the illustrations and read by her.

The interference between the relatively pure and traditional form of the sonnet sequence and the titles' references to such disparate genres as treatise, novel, criticism, drama, narrative poem, hagiography, and history furnishes a textual correlate for the objective erosion of tradition. The "forms" of Platonic England, bound to enduring things of luxury and value, have detached themselves from their organic place in the ceremonies and rituals of class society, precisely as the things outlive the contexts in which they once played their role. At best they have become artifacts for connoisseurial appreciation; at worst they offer a profitable investment to those with money to spare for beauty:

> It stands, as though at ease with its own world,
> the mannerly extortions, languid praise,
> all that devotion long since bought and sold,
>
> the rooms of cedar and soft-thudding baize,
> tremulous boudoirs where the crystals kissed
> in cabinets of amethyst and frost.
>
> (p. 30)

In the end, however, Hill holds out a fragile dialectic of nostalgia, in which he admits that he seeks not so much to restore the past to its (perhaps mythic) wholeness as to grasp how its preciousness for him is conditioned precisely by its brokenness and ruin. He concludes with an image of the intense aura of sacredness with which the very movement of secularization has invested the remnants of premodern Catholic religious ceremony: "Touched by the cry of the iconoclast, / how the rose-window blossoms with the sun!" (p. 34). No longer able to persist in the light of the sacred (if that was ever possible), Hill recaptures it as a flash of radiation released from the fission of its remaining images at the hands of the icon smashers. Never had the images been so precious, he suggests, as at the moment of their shattering.

Hill's collection *Canaan*, published in 1997, is also his most extensive (with seventy-six pages it is nearly one-third as long as the *Collected Poems*) and his most explicitly public in its orientation. Its title refers England to the biblical lowlands by the sea occupied by the mercantile Canaanites, whose pursuit of commerce is presented by Hill as a constant temptation to the Israelites to abandon their difficult fidelity to their jealous God. Like biblical Israel in danger of losing its distinction and blending into pagan corruption, England, in Hill's view, is sacrificing its national integrity to the pursuit of trade, most recently in the move toward a federated Europe and common parliament. This reference to the European Union is most evident in the series "De Jure Belli ac Pacis," concerning the German anti-Nazi resistance and dedicated to the executed organizer Hans-Bernd von Haeften. The title

comes from the seventeenth-century natural law theorist Hugo Grotius, whose treatise on international law and the law of war bears this name. Addressing Von Haeften, Hill criticizes the Euro-liberal conclusions drawn from the resistance martyr's struggle against Nazi tyranny:

> Could none predict these haughty degradations
> as now your high-strung
>   martyred resistance serves
> to consecrate the liberties of Maastricht?
>
> (p. 30)

This same point is even more baldly put in the fourth poem of the sequence:

> In Plötzensee where you were hanged
>   they now hang
> tokens of reparation and in good faith
> compound with Cicero's maxims, Schiller's chant,
> your silenced verities.
>   To the high-minded
> base-metal forgers of this common Europe,
> community of parody, you stand ec-
> centric as a prophet.
>
> (p. 33)

The basic theme, the ease with which elegiac consolation slips into moral ease and a duplicitous assuaging of conscience, is long-standing in Hill's work; new are his directness of treatment and the pitch with which his poem attacks specific political happenstances.

Canaan has three poems titled "To the High Court of Parliament," two of which begin and end the book with laments for a free England self-betrayed by its politics. The opening poem gives a highly political turn to Hill's characteristic concern with the ceremonies and language of memorialization. His lines trope on the economic language of elegiac compensation and loss, turning his scorn on the technocratic and fiduciary betrayers of the national legacy:

> privatize to the dead
> her memory:
>   let her wounds weep
> into the lens of oblivion.
>
> (p. 1)

The series titled "Mysticism and Democracy," composed of five poems dispersed throughout the collection, provides the implicit counterpole to the corruption explored in the "Parliament" poems. Hill's title refers to a series of lectures at Harvard in 1930 and 1931 by Rufus M. Jones, titled "Mysticism and Democracy in the English Commonwealth." Examining the intense confluence of heterodox religious tendencies and revolutionary stirrings in seventeenth-century England, Jones argues that present-day loss of faith in modern democracy needs to take fresh inspiration from this period of its birth, "when a noble spiritual mysticism was one and inseparable with high-minded democracy" (*Mysticism and Democracy in the English Commonwealth*, 1932, p. xi). Despite his anger at the state of English politics, however, Hill is unable to affirm with conviction a reborn republic of virtue and mystical fervor. He is too aware of the intolerance and terror that have often followed from the political appeal to a spiritual measure, and he is admittedly in the world if not wholly of it:

> It is not wholly true
> that what the world commands is a lesser thing.
> Who shall restore the way, reclaim lost footage,
> achieve too late prescient telegraphy,
> take to themselves otherness of common woe,
> devotion bought from abeyance,
> > fortitude to be held
> at the mercy of door-chimes?
> > ("Mysticism and Democracy," p. 25)

Mystical democracy, whose dictates are received, telegraphically, from the distances of an inscrutable God, at best remains a trace, a faint pulse of divine power within the defective body of its worldly twin.

In the sequence "Psalms of Assize," Hill pushes this division between God and the world to the edge of a negative theology. The seven poems of the sequence are each prefaced by a quote from the Latin marginalia of John Colet, the early sixteenth-century dean of St. Paul's, to the *Epistolae* of the Italian humanist philosopher Marsilio Ficino. Hill's sequence passes first through Ficino's discussion of the goals and nature of the virtues and the "three guides of life." "Reason diligently. Gain wide experience. Gather authorities and take into account both past and present," writes Colet in his gloss (Jayne, p. 101). By the sixth and seventh poems, however, the inescapability of evil and the necessity of unknowing clearly surface in the quoted glosses from Colet, lending Hill's concluding poems their explicit note of mystical negativity.

Thus, under Colet's gloss on Ficino's letter on "the divine madness"—"There is no clearer image of divine wisdom available to man than his own unknowing" (p. 91)—Hill drives a wedge between an incomprehensible God and the wellsprings of democracy and of a civic poetry:

> we cannot know God
> > we cannot
> deny his sequestered
> power
> > in a marred nature
> if eloquent at all
> > it is
> with the inuring of scars
> and speechlessness
> it does not improve Sion
> it has no place
> > among psalms
> ("Psalms of Assize," p. 65)

The sequence's closing poem takes as its point of departure Ficino's letter discussing the proposition: "No one can completely eradicate evil and care" (Jayne, p. 126). Colet's gloss on this letter provides Hill's final epigraph: "Even if we master flesh and blood, the demons remain; we can never avoid them. Here, there, evil is always with us" (Jayne, p. 127). Although the title of the sequence, "Psalms of Assize," implies a scene of judgment and ordering, Hill's conclusion relinquishes judgment to God, of whose inscrutable will one discovers the image in a mystical unknowing, in the suspension of human judgment before God's higher necessity:

> O that nothing may touch
> this unapproachable
> levity of the creator
> conscience and guilt
> the formal alchemy
> not held to trial
> for what is beyond
> such mercurial reckoning
> its ultimate
> > cadence
> its fall impeccable
> the condign
> > salvation
> pure carnival in the spirit
> > (p. 66)

Hill thus reveals the mystical underpinnings of the vexed moral and political criticisms that so strongly mark his poetry in this volume. Hill's *Ca-*

naan ultimately weighs the political ends of temporal salvation against the mystical ends of eternal salvation. Although the latter remain unknowable and can offer no *positive* political ends, they do provide Hill a standard for discrediting any politics that betrays the mystically apprehended commonwealth that seventeenth-century rebels handed down in the tradition of English heterodoxy.

LONG POEMS

HILL's first book-length poem was his 1971 prose poem sequence *Mercian Hymns,* centered on the figure of King Offa (reigned 757–796). In this work, however, Offa is not simply a historical figure from the ancient past of Hill's native West Midlands but also the "presiding genius" of the place until at least the mid-twentieth century. Thus, it is possible for Offa to speak in Hill's poem of both "wergold" and "windshields" without contradiction. As king of Mercia and the sovereign figure of the poem, Offa can be understood as an allegory of the poetic authority that legitimates Hill's transgressions of chronology and narrative frame, as if the king's often dubious moral and political body were co-extensive with the ambiguous lexical body of the hymns that conjure him into modern life. This authority is aware of itself as an ambiguous mix of power to harm and to cure. Thus, in the eighth poem, "Offa's Leechdom" (referring to the antiquated sense of "leech" as "physician"), Offa declares himself to be king of Mercia, aware of the enemies around him and empowered to play the "leech" who will drain away their poisonous heresies and heal the land of its malaise:

Threatened by phone-calls at midnight, venomous letters, forewarned I have thwarted their imminent devices.

Today I name them; tomorrow I shall express the new law. I dedicate my awakening to this matter.
(unpaginated, VIII)

In an interview Hill has suggested his desire to conjoin historical and autobiographical reflection, the language of the poem itself serving as the medium in which this commingling may occur:

My feeling for Offa and Mercia can scarcely be disentangled from my mixed feelings for my own home country

of Worcestershire. . . . The murderous brutality of Offa as a political animal seems again an objective correlative for the ambiguities of English history in general, as a means of trying to encompass and accomodate [*sic*] the early humiliations and fears of one's own childhood and also one's discovery of the tyrannical streak in oneself as a child.
(Hart, pp. 163–164)

Put somewhat differently, we can see Hill as reaching through a child's playing out of historical roles as a way of gaining poetic access to that which is ambiguous both in the historical character and in the autobiographical self—a singular self that is nonetheless, through many layers of imaginative mediation, bound to the legendary past as its favorite son.

Hill has pointed to the Anglo-Saxon prose hymns presented in the many editions of *Sweet's Anglo-Saxon Reader* and to early Christian canticles and prose hymns in Latin as having suggested the book's title and offered a "precedent." Yet while Hill's prose invention in these texts is clearly not limited to imitation of past modes, he appears to have understated the degree to which they take their departure not just from the general form of the Old English works but also from their syntax and even at times their general situations. For example, a ninth-century Mercian text from the Vespasian Psalter takes as its premise David's recounting of his defeat of Goliath. It starts, however, with the young boy in his father's house among his brothers: "lytel ic wes betwih broedhur mine 7 iugra in huse feadur mines ic foedde scep feadur mines. . . . he drythen he alra geherde mec he sende engel his 7 nom mec of scepum feadur mines [small I was among my brothers, and grew up in my father's house, I fed my father's sheep. . . . God of all, he heard me, he sent his angel, and took me from my father's fold]" (Henry Sweet, *A Second Anglo-Saxon Reader,* 1978, p. 116). In *Mercian Hymns,* Hill's first-person passages, especially those spoken about boyhood, distinctly recall this Anglo-Saxon precursor:

I was invested in mother-earth, the crypt of roots and endings. Child's play. I abode there, bided my time:

(IV)

Similarly, analogous to the praises of God that are the dominant mode of the Anglo-Saxon hymns, the opening poem of Hill's sequence can be taken as an apostrophe enumerating the titles and virtues of his hero, King Offa:

> King of the perennial holly-groves, the riven sand-
> stone: overlord of the M5: architect of the his-
> toric rampart and ditch, the citadel at Tamworth,
> the summer hermitage in Holy Cross: guardian of
> the Welsh bridge and the Iron Bridge: contractor
> to the desirable new estates: saltmaster: money-
> changer: commissioner for oaths: martyrologist:
> friend of Charlemagne.
>
> (I)

Indeed, as Hill's list of titles reveals, this poem and the one that follows are called "The Naming of Offa," underscoring the poem's baptism of the king with a laudatory catalog of titles, the secular counterparts of those addressed to God in the Anglo-Saxon hymns of praise.

Hill moves freely between different voices and perspectives in the course of the poem, including the "I" associated with Offa or the twentieth-century "child-king" at play in historical roles, the "you" addressed in the songs of praise, the "we" of collective witness, and the "he" that is the object of narration. Just as "Offa" in the poem is "A name to conjure with" (II), so the pronouns are frameworks that are filled differently in the passage from the beginning to the end of the sequence, from the appearance to the disappearance of Offa from the West Midlands. The third poem ("The Crowning of Offa"), for example, suggests the association of this shifting pronoun reference with the political act of coronation:

> On the morning of the crowning we chorused our re-
> mission from school. It was like Easter: hankies
> and gift-mugs approved by his foreign gaze, the
> village-lintels curlered with paper flags.
>
> (III)

Accoutrements such as gift mugs and paper flags and the modern diction strongly hint that this scene can be dated to 12 May 1937, the coronation day of George VI. Hill's choice of this event is well considered. Within Hill's lifetime George was the "last king," and his coronation marks a convergence between the child's projection of himself into imaginary kingship and the English people's playing out of this fantasy on a collective scale. A contemporary commentary, from a Mass-Observation reporter's account of the Coronation Day events, took this playacting element to be the central motif of George's coronation: "The bus is an imitation Coronation coach—it appears and disappears—but the most important thing about it is that, as with the State Coach, its glamour is imaginary. The whole incident is a piece of make-believe such as children indulge in" (*May the Twelfth,* in Hynes, p. 285). In poetically overlaying the crownings of Offa and George, Hill reveals the loose but persistent structure of address and position, the ritualized relation of "he" and "we," that underlies English kingship, a "grammar" of rule that English kings from Offa to George have realized in ways appropriate to their times. It is in this bare grammar that the "tradition" of English monarchism lies; the particular idiom of monarchical power has ranged widely throughout English history, from the protopolitical founding violence of Offa's marking the boundary of his lands with his sword to the mass-media spectacle of George's Coronation Day.

Other poems in the sequence contrast the child's imaginative world with an implicit adult perspective. A particularly striking example is the twenty-second poem, "Offa's 'Second Defence of the English People,'" which presents the child's view of wartime radio listening and time in the bomb shelter:

> At home the curtains were drawn. The wireless boomed
> its commands. I loved the battle-anthems and the
> gregarious news.

> Then, in the earthy shelter, warmed by a blue-glassed
> storm-lantern, I huddled with stories of dragon-
> tailed airships and warriors who took wing im-
> mortal as phantoms.
>
> (XXII)

Hill offers here a self-reflexive myth of origin for himself as the poet of anachronistic legend and history, the characteristic mode of the *Mercian Hymns.* The history of England's resistance to foreign invaders links the ancient and modern scenes of war in a deeply felt relation to the land and its traditions. Yet at the same time the child's exultation and fantasy, fed by images of legendary tales read to pass the time in the shelter, transfigure the experience of the air war into a medieval fiction just as, once, brute and bloody medieval conquests were poetically transformed into fictions of warriors and dragons. In tracing out the "poetic" divergences of Offa from his unlovely historical image, Hill gains access to the ambiguity of his own birth as a poet and to the problematic nature of poetry's relation to history.

Hill's next long poem, *The Mystery of the Charity of Charles Péguy*, published in 1983, represents a significant shift from *Mercian Hymns* both formally and in the handling of the historical persona at its center. Formally it is composed of ten sections of between seven and twelve slant-rhyme quatrains in a jagged yet recognizably iambic meter; section 5 is exceptionally long, with eighteen quatrains. Unlike Offa, who is a kind of poetic schema for Hill's anachronistic rejoining of archaic past, recent past, and present, Péguy is a particular historical personage and fellow poet whom Hill elegizes and honors. In the brief essay appended to the poem, Hill concludes of his poem's subject: "Péguy, stubborn rancours and mishaps and all, is one of the great souls, one of the great prophetic intelligences, of our century. I offer *The Mystery of the Charity of Charles Péguy* as my homage to the triumph of his 'defeat'" (p. 36). One might say that whereas Offa provides Hill a vehicle for the poetic reimagination of the facts of history, both medieval and of Britain during World War II, Péguy confronts Hill with a complex historical *fact*, with which his poem seeks to come to adequate and just terms.

In his essay Hill remarks on the complicated character of Péguy; it is not hard to detect in his description more than a hint of psychologically discerning self-depiction as well: "A man of the most exact and exacting probity, accurate practicality, in personal and business relations, a meticulous reader of proof, he was at the same time moved by violent emotions and violently afflicted by mischance. Like others similarly wounded, he was perhaps smitten by the desirability of suffering" (p. 35). Hill further suggests a measure of self-portraiture as Péguy, when in the complaint that makes up the opening two quatrains of section 4, he incorporates the phrases from Auden ("the lords of limit") and Thomas Nashe ("the enemies countery") that would be the titles of his 1984 and 1991 collections of criticism:

> This world is different, belongs to them—
> the lords of limit and of contumely.
> It matters little whether you go tamely
> or with rage and defiance to your doom.
>
> This is your enemies' country which they took
> in the small hours an age before you woke,

went to the window, saw the mist-hewn statues of the lean kine emerge at dawn.

(p. 18)

In turn Hill used the fifth and sixth lines of this passage as his epigraph for his critical volume *The Enemy's Country: Word, Contexture, and Other Circumstances of Language* (1991).

Hill's poem commences with a dramatic gunshot: "Crack of a starting-pistol. Jean Jaurès / dies in a wine-puddle" (p. 13). He thus begins his homage at one of the most morally problematic moments of Péguy's career, the assassination of the great French socialist leader Jean Jaurès, his murderer possibly having been incited by Péguy's ringing denunciations of his former ally. Jaurès and Péguy had struggled together during the Dreyfus affair, in which a trumped-up charge of espionage against a Jewish member of the general staff of the French army led to a major crisis in French society and eventually brought the Socialist party to power. The practical policies of the governing socialists, however, and especially their campaign against the Catholic Church, led Péguy to break with his friend and to target some of his most virulent rhetoric against him. For example, Péguy christened Jaurès a "traitor in essence" and a "drum-major of capitulation" for his antinationalist, pacifist stance. Yet showing an extraordinary consistency and moral integrity in his justification for this position, Péguy argued against the socialists in power on the same grounds that he had cited when he took the risk of fighting with them in the name of justice for Dreyfus: that they, like those who had shrugged off the injustice against Dreyfus in the name of the greater good of the state, placed *temporal* salvation over *eternal* salvation. The mystique of socialism having been sullied by the pragmatic demands of governing, Péguy turned to a fervent mysticism of the *nation* and to such national-religious heroes as Jeanne d'Arc and Saint Louis as the true agents of collective redemption.

Péguy's early death makes any further development of this mystical patriotism speculative in his personal case, but not for his followers in a Europe moving incrementally toward fascism. Hill is no doubt correct in saying in his essay that "fascism, in whatever form, is a travesty of Péguy's true faith and position"; it is nonetheless a "travesty" that was carried out often in the thirty years that followed Péguy's death. In a 1932 encyclopedia article on the intellectual roots of fascism, for example, no less an authority than Benito Mussolini claimed Péguy as one of his inspirations. Likewise, the Péguy canon of national saints and the heroic poet and war victim himself provided a powerful font of religiously charged imagery for the Scouts de France, the Catholic youth movement that provided many of the Vichy regime's youth leaders, and a source of political inspiration for collaborationist writers such as Pierre Drieu La Rochelle. The historian Eugen Weber has well summed up the ideological lability of Péguy's legacy: "Would Péguy, the Christian patriot, have been in London with de Gaulle or in Vichy with Pétain? Both claimed him for their own, as they claimed God. And God could have been on the Right with either" (p. 206).

In placing the Jaurès episode at the head of his poem, Hill broods over the moral responsibility of the poet for his words in the context of action. This problem gets its most dramatic framing at the end of section 4 and the opening of section 5, in which Hill spills a sentence over the break between sections, testing the degree to which Péguy's culpability in Jaurès's death and his own early death at the First Battle of the Marne in September 1914 cancel an imbalance in the moral register:

> Jaurès was killed blindly, yet with reason:
> "let us have drums to beat down his great voice."
> So you spoke to the blood. So, you have risen
> above all that and fallen flat on your face
>
> 5
> among the beetroots, where we are constrained
> to leave you sleeping and to step aside
> from the fleshed bayonets, the fusillade
> of red-rimmed smoke like stubble being burned;
>
> to turn away and contemplate the working
> of the radical soul—instinct, intelligence,
> memory, call it what you will—waking
> into the foreboding of its inheritance,
>
> its landscape and inner domain; images
> of earth and grace.
>
> (pp. 19–20)

Hill seeks not to weigh abstract quantities of suffering caused and suffering endured by Péguy, but rather to ponder the writer's afterlife and judge the quality of mourning by those who survive Péguy, among whom the elegiac-eulogistic poet Hill takes his place. As in one of the poems in the *Mercian*

Hymns, in which the poet visits the site of Boethius's brutal execution under the Gothic cudgel, so in *The Mystery* he evokes the grotesque memorializing of the fallen hero Péguy as a tourist attraction:

> "'Sieurs-'dames, this is the wall
> where he leaned and rested, this is the well
>
> from which he drank." Péguy, you mock us now.
> History takes the measure of your brow
> in blank-eyed bronze, brave mediocre work
> of *Niclausse, sculpteur*, cornered in the park
>
> among the stout dogs and lame patriots
> and all those ghosts . . .
>
> (pp. 15–16)

Hill's attempt to win his way toward some more genuine way of remembering takes the reflexive path of Péguy's own litany for the fallen, "Heureux Ceux," with which *The Mystery* shares its quatrain stanza. Péguy's poem closes with these lines:

> Heureux ceux qui sonts morts, car ils sont retournés
> Dans la première argile et la première terre.
> Heureux ceux qui sont morts dans une juste guerre.
> Heureux les épis mûrs et les blés moissonnés.
>
> (*Basic Verities*, 1943, p. 276)

> Blessed are those who died, for they have returned
> Into primeval clay and primeval earth
> Blessed are those who died in a just war.
> Blessed is the wheat that is ripe and the wheat that is
> gathered in sheaves.
>
> (p. 277)

In the passage referring to this poem, Hill evokes a work of remembrance residing in the rituals of sheer persistence before time's oblivion, a dogged fidelity in the absence of external sanction for one's observances, a force of ceremony symbolized by the weak magnetism of Péguy's poem for readers long after its historical occasion has passed:

> We still dutifully read
>
> "heureux ceux qui sont morts." Drawn on the past
> these presences endure; they have not ceased
> to act, suffer, crouching into the hail
> like labourers of their own memorial
>
> or those who worship at its marble rote,
> their many names one name, the common "dur"

built into duration, the endurance of war;
blind Vigil herself, helpless and obdurate.

(pp. 26–27)

Hill ends his poem on a note of ambiguous triumph, which affirms this faithfulness in the face of contradictions of this latter-day saint, his worldly defeat, and his doubts about the power of the poetic word to redeem death. He affirms, on Péguy's authority, the emergence of modern poetry out of the very ambiguity of this primal scene and sets himself the task of reiterating it in an act of mournful homage to its cost and tainted glory.

Hill's 150-section book-length poem, *The Triumph of Love,* appeared in 1998, only one year after *Canaan.* The first and last sections are only a single line long, while the remaining sections range from very condensed passages of only a few lines to stanzas of thirty or more lines. The individual sections move freely between several different topics and tones, and follow one another more like a modernistic montage than an extended narrative or meditative poem of traditional stamp. The main unifying elements amid the plethora of learned allusion and serpentine argumentation are tropological and tonal: Hill's thematically self-conscious use of repetition and echo, and the insistent irony of his authorial persona—cranky, curt, self-deprecating, satirical, hectoring, and occasionally magisterial. Early in the poem Hill notes a rhetorical figure of oratorical doublespeak, drawn from the political grammar of reversible meanings:

"nation shall not lift up sword against nation"
or "nation shall rise up against nation" (a later
much-revised draft of the treaty). In either case
a telling figure out of rhetoric,
epanalepsis, the same word first and last.

(p. 4)

In an act of satirical mimicry, Hill adopts this trope in several stanzas of his poem and sets it up as the master figure of his poem as a whole. His poem begins with the line "Sun-blazed, over Romsley, a livid rain-scarp" (p. 1) and ends with a minimal variation, displacing the indefinite article in favor of an act of ostension, whether of a feature of landscape or of nothing other than the starting point of his poem: "Sun-blazed, over Romsley, *the* livid rain-scarp" (p. 82).

Similarly, the author makes frequent self-reference, regarding both the reactions of critics and readers to him and his practice of revision and correction of the text. Hill incorporates periodic interjections from irritated reviewers and readers: "Scab-picking old scab: why should we be salted / with the scurf of his sores?" (p. 17); "Rancorous, narcissistic old sod—what / makes him go on? We thought, hoped rather, / he might be dead. Too bad" (p. 20); "let him be touched / by his own angel, it will come to nothing: / born again, but still-born" (p. 46). There is also a running joke about Hill's fastidious revision and correction of proofs. A man who in his criticism has unearthed moral laxness in misused prepositions and typographical error discovers himself in mock-heroic battle against the legions of linguistic sin: "Not un-worded. Enworded" (p. 32); "Delete: sell myself; filched from. Inert: / tell myself; fetched from. For inert read insect" (p. 33); "Take out supposition. Insert suppository. / For definitely the right era, read: deaf in the right ear" (p. 54). More wounding, however, than this general background of randomly flying stones and arrows are the poet's better-targeted acts of exploratory surgery upon his own spiritual pretensions:

This is not Duino. I have found no sign
that you are visited by any angel
of suffering creation. Violent
sensitivity is not vision, nor is vision
itself order. You may be possessed
of neurasthenic intelligence as others
have been tormented by helpless self-
knowledge, though I doubt it. In any event
I would not parade comparisons.

(pp. 48–49)

Here a cutting intelligence speaks against a too facile adoption of Rilke's choice mannerisms, whose influence has proved so deleterious in shaping the angel-infested landscape of contemporary poetry; yet it is also a stern hiss of Hill's austere and skeptical religious conscience, denouncing the Rilkean temptation to seek personal salvation through poetic will.

Ultimately Hill pursues another poetic and spiritual end than Rilke. He seeks desperately to retrieve a moral voice for poetry, while recognizing the crepuscular state of that lodestar that guided Dante and Petrarch, and perhaps even, residually, Yeats and Ezra Pound: the "noble vernacular." Hill offers more a profession of faith and the recognition of a task than a determinate answer to the

questions he puts to the tradition of poetically refined vernacular speech:

> where is it?
> Where has it got us? Does it stop, in our case,
> with Dryden, or, perhaps,
> Milton's political sonnets?—the cherished stock
> hacked into ransom and ruin; the voices
> of distinction, far back, indistinct.
> Still, I'm convinced that shaping,
> voicing, are types of civic action.
>
> (p. 36)

Although the near repetition of the beginning line
indicates the arduous struggle required even to
win a minimum of determination ("a" changing to
"the"), Hill suggests that this persistence of poetry
against the wake of oblivion is its authentic task.
Near the end of the poem, Hill describes the Italian
Romantic poet Giacomo Leopardi pronouncing
somber words over the worn and faded letters of
the tomb of his sixteenth-century predecessor Tor-
quato Tasso: "a sad and angry consolation" (p. 82).
Successively Hill adopts this as his poem's true
conclusion, ironically qualified by the last two sections but by no means robbed of its final significance for the poem:

> what are poems for? They are to console us
> with their own gift, which is like perfect pitch.
> Let us commit that to our dust. What
> ought a poem to be? Answer, *a sad
> and angry consolation*. What is
> the poem? What figures? Say,
> *a sad and angry consolation*. That's
> beautiful. Once more? *A sad and angry
> consolation*.
>
> (p. 82)

TRANSLATION / ADAPTATION

ALTHOUGH the practice of imitation and use of authorial personae, including literary ones, had been
an element of Hill's poetry since the 1950s, several
poems in *Tenebrae* and a stage version of Henrik
Ibsen's long narrative poem *Brand* put translation
at the center of Hill's work of the later 1970s. The
sequence "Pentecost Castle" in *Tenebrae* was, as
Hill notes, indebted to J. M. Cohen's *Penguin Book
of Spanish Verse* (1956), and his "Two Chorale-
Preludes" represented partial translations, partial

rewritings of Paul Celan's "Eis, Eden" and "Kermorvan," from the 1963 collection *Die Niemandsrose* (No One's Rose). A comparison of the
translations of the first stanza of "Kermorvan" by
Michael Hamburger (in Paul Celan, *Poems of Paul
Celan*, 1988) and by Hill reveals the intuitive quality of Hill's adaptations even as they depart from
literal sense. Hamburger represents Celan's lines
with a reasonable degree of accuracy and even a
surface mimicry of some features of sound and
syntax:

> Du Tausendgüldenkraut-Sternchen
> du Erle, du Buche, du Farn:
> mit euch Nahen geh ich ins Ferne,—
> Wir gehen dir, Heimat, ins Garn.
>
> You tiny centaury star,
> you alder, beech and fern:
> with you near ones I make for afar,—
> to our homeland, snared, we return.
>
> (pp. 202–203)

In contrast, Hill's version in *Tenebrae* takes so many
liberties with literal sense that it is no longer in any
strict sense a "translation," but rather an "imitation" in the manner of Ezra Pound's and Robert
Lowell's rewritings of foreign poems:

> Centaury with your staunch bloom
> you there alder beech you fern,
> midsummer closeness my far home,
> fresh traces of lost origin.
>
> (p. 36)

Yet by comparison with Hamburger's rather flat-
footed literality, Hill achieves a richer and more
complex poetic weave out of Celan's material, in
places even capturing a finer sense of the lines than
the more semantically proximate translation. In
rendering the opening line, for instance, Hamburger has translated Celan's *Sternchen*, referring
to the starlike flower of the herb centaury, simply
as "tiny . . . star." Hill opts for a more radical envisioning of Celan's intention, splitting the image
between its sound correlate (*Sternchen* and
"staunch") and the literal sense of the "star" metaphor, the weed's "bloom." He compounds this
more complex treatment with implication of the
wild herb's sturdy vitality (its "staunchness"),
which makes it proliferate into an entangling snare
to trip up the one who returns; he also manages to
sound, faintly, the overtones that loyalty (being

"staunch" in one's faithfulness) had in Celan's life and poetry. Through such overdetermined, non-literal renderings Hill offers another sort of poetic fidelity than that demanded of a translator. Rather than recapitulating the literal sense of the original, he seeks to retrace the poetic procedures by which the original came into being, attaining to the allusive density of Celan's language and giving equivalent attention to its nuances.

The most extended example of this practice of translation and adaptation came in 1978 with Hill's theatrical version of Ibsen's poem *Brand*. Originally published in 1866, *Brand* dramatizes the struggle of the eponymous pastor-hero for salvation. His austere belief in the power of personal will to resist worldly temptation leads him, through the deaths of his mother, his son, and his wife, to the symbolical purity of the Ice Church at the top of a mountain. Yet his quest for purity proves both barren and fatal. Buried in an avalanche, he cannot hear the final pronouncement of the poem, as an anonymous voice states: "He is the God of Love" (p. 182). In a collaborative effort to prepare a version for performance by the National Theatre, Hill worked from Inga-Stina Ewbank's literal prose translation with glosses, cutting the poem down significantly and departing from the literal sense in favor of dramatic effectiveness.

Hill's main innovation was to adopt a freely syncopated shorter line of three or four beats, one that captures the compressed energy of Ibsen's Norwegian better than the iambic pentameter lines of James Kirkup and Christopher Fry's translation in *The Oxford Ibsen* (vol. 3, 1972). At the close of the first act, for example, Brand enumerates the three threats he must defeat to achieve his goal:

> det Lettsind som, med Krans af Løv,
> lar Legen gaa langs brattest Slug,—
> det Slappsind, som gaar Vejen sløv,
> fordi det saa er Skikk og Brug,—
> det Vildsind, som har slig en Flugt,
> at fast hvad ondt det ser, blir smukt?
> (Ibsen, *Samlede Verker*, vol. 5, pp. 201–202)

The Oxford translation renders this passage with accuracy at the expense of dissipating the lines' epigrammatic compactness:

> Is it
> That rashness of mind, garlanded in leaves and
> flowers,

> Dancing at the brink of the deepest abyss?
> Or that dullness of mind, plodding along
> Because that was the way it always went. . . .
> Or that madness of mind, so wild in its flight
> That all evil seems good!
>
> (p. 99)

Hill's version embroiders considerably on the original, expanding each pair of lines to three and even four; he also takes the capitalization of nouns as license to allegorize these pitfalls as three distinctly Bunyanesque "trolls":

> Feckless, with his garlands on,
> dances till he plunges down
> into the terrible abyss.
> Dullness mutters "thus and thus,"
> his catechism's sleepy rote,
> and treads the old, deep-trodden rut.
> Madness wanders from itself,
> half shadowing the other half;
> immortal longings gone astray,
> confusing darkness with the day.
> (*Brand: A Version for the Stage*, 1981, pp. 23–24)

Despite these departures from literal sense, Hill conveys the overall sense of the scene quite aptly; the impression of fidelity to the Norwegian original is notable. Syntactically and metrically, for example, Hill has managed to capture Ibsen's stark foregrounding of the three dangers—the strict succession of "*Lett*sind" to "*Slapp*sind" to "*Vild*sind"—by placing them in the initial position in each of the three lines that open the three parallel periods. In contrast the Oxford translation disperses these single terms into "rashness," "dullness," and "madness of mind," thereby losing the strongly reiterative force of "that" (*det*) through the use of "or" in the latter two clauses.

Throughout his adaptation Hill sensitively registers Ibsen's full range of diction, from base popular speech to high poetic sublimity, often playing these registers off against one another through the comical verbal duels of the high-minded Brand with such low cynics as the Mayor. His version retains its dramatic effectiveness over its full extent, which incorporates more than five thousand of Ibsen's original six thousand lines. Together, Hill's metrical sensitivity, his ear for linguistic nuance, and his ability to rise with the visionary flight of Ibsen's hero without betraying him to self-parody make Hill's *Brand*, in the words of his collaborator's preface, "an authentic imaginative creation by an English poet, conceived and executed in the spirit of Brand and Ibsen" (p. xxxv).

CRITICISM

HILL has published two volumes of critical essays, *The Lords of Limit: Essays on Literature and Ideas* (1984) and *The Enemy's Country: Words, Contexture, and Other Circumstances of Language* (1991). Although he has written numerous reviews and some occasional essays, these volumes represent Hill's most important work in the critical mode. With their density of reference and subtlety of argumentation, they stand in close continuity with Hill's richly allusive and compressed poetry; similar themes and even phrasings find their places in both his poetic and his critical writings. *The Lords of Limit* includes essays on the Jesuit poet and martyr Robert Southwell, on Ben Jonson's Roman plays, on Shakespeare's *Cymbeline*, on Jonathan Swift, on the nineteenth-century philosopher T. H. Green, and on the Fugitive poet and New Critic John Crowe Ransom. The four essays collected in *The Enemy's Country* focus especially on John Donne, Thomas Hobbes, Isaak Walton, John Dryden, and Ezra Pound.

Hill's typical handling of the critical essay defies easy paraphrase. Although his author persona claims in *The Triumph of Love* to be more attached to "The Scholastics" than "The New Science," this remark can be applied to Hill as the author of his critical prose only in a qualified sense. For there is little sign of the Scholastic passion for *logical* distinction. Instead, Hill worries a set of highly particular examples, focusing on fine points of diction and syntax and proliferating comparisons across the array of English literature and beyond, until inapparent moral and aesthetic distinctions emerge. Indeed, a generality one could safely venture about Hill's critical work is that he is fascinated by the situations of writing under constraint, in which moral and political distinctions are made under duress and hence often are occulted, muted, or displaced amid the figural web of a literary text or corpus. In turn, his critical method is to persist in the face of a work's indistinct or even indiscernible differences, probing and vexing its surface coherence until the composition's underlying structure of artistic and moral judgments offers itself for review. He is thus committed methodologically to an ultrafine empiricism, focused on single phrases, their context and historical variations. Yet the goal of this critical labor ultimately exceeds empiricism, as Hill seeks to discover in the nebula of inherited texts an enduring pattern of regularities in which time-bound, contingent speech acts of individuals are subsumed but not canceled. One might offer the Aristotelian-Scholastic term "topics" to describe these regularities, which for Hill emerge through particular interferences of text and context, hence also at the juncture of singular aesthetic and moral decisions.

Although this approach makes brief recapitulation of Hill's essays both difficult and inapt, it is possible to give an example of his points of departure and conclusion in order to suggest something of the paths he must travel before arriving at the place where judgment may be pronounced. In his essay "Dryden's Prize-Song," from *The Enemy's Country,* Hill considers Dryden's elegy "To the Memory of Mr. Oldham," dedicated to his fellow poet, friend, and sometimes rival John Oldham. Two propositions, though by no means appearing at the opening of Hill's essay, can be taken to mark his rhetorical entry point into the risky country of Dryden's poem. Both hinge on a hidden complexity masquerading as surface unity, on inapparent distinctions that are nevertheless decisive for the poem's meaning and true character. First, Hill states, "Sincerity is a complex, not a simple state" (p. 77). In claiming that Dryden's poem is "sincere," thus, one is irresistibly tempted to enclose the word in ironic scare quotes; yet the temptation, Hill suggests, lies not with the simple irony that "sincere" means "insincere," but rather that sincerity is different from and more difficult than one first thought. Second, like the Russian literary theorist Mikhail Bakhtin, Hill suggests that the apparent unity of texture that gives us the impression of a singular voice is a complex fabric that the critic must tease apart, to reveal its weave of voices and to show where they surface in the design and where they are covered up by other strands. "What we call the writer's 'distinctive voice,'" Hill writes, "is a registering of different voices" (p. 80).

These two premises are connected, for we take as a condition of ascribing sincerity to someone the distinction of personality that the singular voice conveys: a mere functionary can be honest or dishonest, helpful or unhelpful, efficient or inefficient, but to be sincere, one has to do more than actuate the rules of a system. Hill's interrogation of Dryden's poem considers the ambiguous mélange of circumstantial provocation and decorous magnanimity in the poet's response to his friend and competitor for the age's favor:

Dryden's contemporary, Samuel Butler, noted in his commonplace book that "Malice" has "Power . . . above all other Passions, to highten Wit and Fancy", adding that "Pangyriques" are "commonly as Dull as they are false." "To the Memory of Mr. Oldham" is a "pangyrique" which seeks to be lively and true and to associate with magnanimity those qualities of wit and fancy which Butler saw as the prerogative of malice. Dryden's strength and integrity manifest themselves in his running the difficult middle course between the impositions and implications of "Voulez-vous du public meriter les amours?" and "voudriez vous qu'il ne fut pas plus sçavant que moy, luy qui commande à trente legions?" One does not break decorum, or even syntax, in shifting from the *bienséance* of the first to the cynical stoicism of the second. Dryden does not break decorum either; for decorum becomes magnanimity, while magnanimity does not annul the force of his feelings.

(pp. 81– 82)

In Hill's reading, then, Dryden's "sincere" response to the provocation of Oldham and of his own unhappy circumstances is a perilous work of evading the spontaneous impulse, the superior energy, of responding with malice. And the magnanimity of Dryden's sincere evasion becomes the impetus to poetic wit and fancy, disturbing the dull generic weave of panegyric while complexly repairing the imperiled weft of decorum. The difficulty of granting Dryden his sincerity shows in the straining of Hill's own argument toward its painfully qualified conclusions; like its object Hill's text proceeds through a tissue of other voices, texts, quotes, unraveled and rewoven around the phrases of Dryden's urbanely gracious poem.

CONCLUSION

HILL's corpus of work up to 1997 has been surprisingly small, considering it represents four decades of writing and in light of Hill's emerging reputation as the most significant British poet of the postwar period. Far from being contradictory, however, his readers' sense of the quality and value of Hill's writing is inseparable from the evidence of its relative rarity. The 1994 *New and Collected Poems* revealed a poet who released a thin volume of densely wrought, highly compressed poems every five to ten years. The appearance of *Canaan* and *The Triumph of Love* in the short span of two years, however, alters this picture somewhat. Although still evidently the product of a powerfully controlling craft, they reveal a new discursive breadth and extensiveness in Hill's writing during the 1990s. Moreover, they suggest that this development has left its traces in both modes in which Hill has excelled in the past, the short lyric and the sequential long poem.

It is always risky to predict a writer's next step, and in *The Triumph of Love* Hill offers his muselike "vergine bella" somber recognition of his ripening mortality: "I have been working towards this for some time, / . . . I am not too far from the end" (p. 66). Hill may, however, be one of those rare poets—Yeats and Stevens would certainly be among them—who write much of their greatest work after the age of sixty. His two latest books will surely have to count among his most accomplished work. Thus his readers, desirous of more of his splendid and difficult poetry, must give the last word not to the poet persona but to the "copyeditor" of *The Triumph*, who provides an anxious qualification of the phrase "the end": "I am not too far from the end / [of the sequence—ED]" (p. 66).

SELECTED BIBLIOGRAPHY

I. COLLECTED POEMS. *Somewhere Is Such a Kingdom: Poems, 1952–1971* (Boston, 1975); *Collected Poems* (Harmondsworth, U.K., 1985); *New and Collected Poems, 1952–1992* (Boston, 1994).

II. SEPARATE WORKS OF POETRY. *For the Unfallen: Poems, 1952–1958* (London, 1959); *King Log* (London, 1968); *Mercian Hymns* (London, 1971); *Tenebrae* (London, 1978); *The Mystery of the Charity of Charles Péguy* (London, 1983); *Canaan* (Boston, 1997); *The Triumph of Love* (Boston, 1998).

III. TRANSLATION. Henrik Ibsen, *Brand: A Version for the Stage* (London, 1978; rev. ed. with restored passages, Minneapolis, Minn., 1981).

IV. LITERARY CRITICISM. *The Lords of Limit: Essays on Literature and Ideas* (New York, 1984); *The Enemy's Country: Words, Contexture, and Other Circumstances of Language* (Stanford, Calif., 1991).

V. UNCOLLECTED CRITICAL ESSAYS AND REVIEWS (SELECTED). "Letter from Oxford," in *London Magazine* 1 (May 1954); "The Poetry of Allen Tate," in *Geste* 3 (1958); "The Dream of Reason" (on William Empson), in *Essays in Criticism* 1 (1964); "'The Conscious Mind's Intelligible Structure': A Debate," in *Agenda* 9, no. 4–10, no. 1 (1971–

1972); "Gurney's 'Hobby,'" in *Essays in Criticism* 34 (April 1984); "Common Weal, Common Woe," in *Times Literary Supplement* (21–27 April 1989); "A Pharisee to Pharisees: Reflections of Vaughan's 'The Night,'" in *English* 38 (summer 1989).

VI. SOURCES AND OTHER WORKS RELEVANT TO HILL'S POETRY. Henrik Ibsen, *Brand*, in his *Samlede Verker*, vol. 5 (Oslo, 1928); Rufus M. Jones, *Mysticism and Democracy in the English Commonwealth* (Cambridge, Mass., 1932); Charles Péguy, *Basic Verities: Prose and Poetry*, trans. by Ann Green and Julian Green (New York, 1943); Charles Péguy, *Men and Saints: Prose and Poetry*, trans. by Ann Green and Julian Green (New York, 1943); Charles Péguy, *The Mystery of the Charity of Joan of Arc*, trans. by Julian Green (New York, 1950); Sears Jayne, *John Colet and Marsilio Ficino* (Oxford, 1963); Henrik Ibsen, *Brand*, in *The Oxford Ibsen*, vol. 3 (New York and London, 1972); Samuel Hynes, *The Auden Generation: Literature and Politics in England in the 1930s* (Princeton, 1976); Henry Sweet, *A Second Anglo-Saxon Reader*, 2d ed. (Oxford, 1978); Paul Celan, *Poems of Paul Celan*, trans. by Michael Hamburger (New York, 1988); Zeev Sternhell, *The Birth of Fascist Ideology: From Cultural Rebellion to Political Revolution* (Princeton, 1994); Eugen Weber, *The Hollow Years: France in the 1930s* (New York, 1994).

VII. SELECTED CRITICISM. "Geoffrey Hill Special Issue," *Agenda* 17 (spring 1979); Merle Brown, *Double Lyric: Divisiveness and Communal Creativity in Recent English Poetry* (New York, 1980); Charles Tomlinson, *The Sense of the Past: Three Twentieth-Century British Poets* (Liverpool, 1983); David Annwn, *Inhabited Voices: Myth and History in the Poetry of Geoffrey Hill, Seamus Heaney, and George Mackay Brown* (Frome, U.K., 1984); Christopher Ricks, *The Force of Poetry* (Oxford and New York, 1984); Peter Robinson, ed., *Geoffrey Hill: Essays on His Work* (Milton Keynes, U.K., and Philadelphia, 1985); Harold Bloom, ed., *Geoffrey Hill* (New York, 1986); Henry Hart, *The Poetry of Geoffrey Hill* (Carbondale, Ill., 1986); Vincent B. Sherry, *The Uncommon Tongue: The Poetry and Criticism of Geoffrey Hill* (Ann Arbor, Mich., 1987); E. M. Knottenbelt, *Passionate Intelligence: The Poetry of Geoffrey Hill* (Amsterdam and Atlanta, 1990); Eleanor Jane McNees, *Eucharistic Poetry: The Search for Presence in the Writings of John Donne, Gerard Manley Hopkins, Dylan Thomas, and Geoffrey Hill* (Lewisburg, Pa., 1992); Ralph Pordzik, *History as Poetry: Dichtung und Geschichte im Werk von Geoffrey Hill* (Essen, Germany, 1994).

ELIZABETH JENNINGS

(1926–   )

Angelyn Hays

ELIZABETH JENNINGS' OBSESSION with the linguistic nature of thought and the isolation of the individual resonates in fields like psychology, philosophy, and cognitive research. Jennings discovered poetry at age thirteen and has gone on to write thousands of poems and publish more than twenty books, including verse books for children. In her early seventies, she is still a prolific writer and composes several poems a week. She rarely revises beyond a few drafts and says her poems "come out very clean" (Gramang, p. 8). She is not as direct about her personal pain as Sylvia Plath or Anne Sexton, and she avoids overtly popular or political statements like those of Philip Larkin or Thom Gunn.

Jennings differs from most modern poets in that she takes Christianity, specifically Roman Catholicism, as her primary subject. For her, "poetry is not an exorcism but a sacrament, a sharing. However extreme her illness, poetry is a way back from the edge, not over it; [even] at her most disturbed she witnesses other people" (Schmidt, p. 802). Catholicism gave her a sense of personal stability and a mystical, cosmological worldview, but it also gave her an ongoing source of guilt and uncertainty. She also writes about friendship, relationships, places, and what artistic creation means to her. Her poems reveal an effort to engage poetry for personal emancipation and as a solace for loneliness.

Jennings first began to associate with other poets when she attended Oxford University in the late 1940s. These students and their acquaintances, later dubbed the "Movement," gave her an intellectual community. Although writers such as Kingsley Amis, Anthony Thwaite, Thom Gunn, Philip Larkin, and John Wain never officially formed a school, these writers were generous with their praise and attention to Jennings; Larkin corresponded with Jennings for many years. And while some Movement writers never met or discussed their methods with each other, their poetry does reveal a shared love of simplicity, musical meter, and comfortable diction. Jennings appropriates romantic, symbolist, and modernist poetics in ways that distinguish her work from that of her contemporaries.

EARLY LIFE

BORN on 18 July 1926 in Lincolnshire, England, Jennings moved to Oxford when she was six. Her mother, Jennings recalled, was "a woman of great natural wisdom" (autobiography, p. 14). Henry Cecil Jennings, her father, was a physician who became Oxford County's medical officer, and he earned an Oxford degree in geology while Elizabeth was growing up. Jennings recalls tramping around the countryside with her father and older sister looking for rock specimens and identifying geological formations.

Between the ages of six and eleven, Jennings and her sister attended a Catholic school. Her father had converted some years before she was born, and her parents zealously pursued their new faith. As a girl Elizabeth liked to stage her own performances of the Mass using her doll's oven as a tabernacle and a train on a string as a thurible. She recalled in a 1998 interview with Frances Welch, "We did the blessing of the sacraments, processions, [and] confession. One girl . . . was a Presbyterian. She was shocked and wouldn't play with me." As Jennings approached her fifties, more of her poems explores childhood. She retains vivid memories of her earliest years: her nanny, a bout with whooping cough, a fall down the nursery stairs. She admitted, "I'm accident prone. I always have been. . . . I remember another time I ran into a chair and had to get stitched up" (Welch interview).

Jennings described how she felt growing up: "I kept a neurotic hold on myself. I gave myself fearful indigestion. I remember once confessing that I'd pinched my sister and hearing a suppressed giggle [from the priest]. I was very shocked" (Crew review). She also recalled suffering as she grew up and admits, "I turned inward, and [I] was terribly self-conscious, full of religious doubts, and worrying about the meaning of everything. . . . I hated [Catholic school and] had all the makings of a juvenile delinquent—thieving, lying, stealing little bits of Hornsby trains." She further recalled: "My mother said I'd end up a murderer. I do get a feeling of being literally beside myself" (Crew review). After about four years her father took her out of the school and enrolled her in the Anglican Hyde School. Thanks to a good teacher, "I began to realize I was quite intelligent. This was a revelation" (autobiography, p. 16).

At the age of thirteen, Jennings discovered G. K. Chesterton's "Battle of Lepanto" in an English-class reading. She was instantly hooked and began reading Keats, Shelly, Browning, and Arnold. In *Let's Have Some Poetry!* (1960) she writes that discovering poetry was "an enlarging of the world which hitherto I had only known from maps" (p. 86). She turned to writing for "the curious mixture of excitement and exaltation which I had first experienced when I read Lepanto" (p. 86). Her uncle was a poet, and his example and encouragement were important to her.

Jennings had her first serious breakdown in her teens. "When I was fifteen, I thought the curse [menstruation] was a loss of innocence. Can you believe that?" (Davidson interview). She turned to reading and literature to ease her isolation. Her passion to learn about great poets shows not only her intellectual curiosity but also a determination to prepare herself through poetry for what she called in "Answers" (1955) the "Great conclusions coming near"[1] (p. 27). Her mother gave her T. S. Eliot's *The Four Quartets* (1943) for Christmas, when she was seventeen years old. She felt strongly drawn to his poetry and began to write. At first, her attempts to imitate Eliot caused her to write chaotic verse because she did not perceive Eliot's strict patterns, so she wrote a kind of free verse that she thought was like his poetry. She sent

her poems to literary magazines but later was glad editors had rejected this "twaddle" (Crew review). She was, however, encouraged by a handwritten rejection from the now-defunct *New English Weekly*, which said: "These poems show talent" (Bradley, p. 87). Jennings' childhood reading experiences were important to her later development, and she went on to write accessible books for children that show her high regard for young readers.

At the age of eighteen Jennings began studies at St. Anne's College, Oxford. Kingsley Amis, an early friend and admirer, recalls that in 1944, "it was hard to connect the poetry with the person. She seemed, on her bicycle and in her T-shirt, very advanced for those days. From her cheerful behavior and looks you might have thought she didn't have a care in the world. . . . But the face the writer shows is often not at all what they feel" (Blissett, p. 165). Around Oxford University, Jennings felt she had "found the most congenial kind of atmosphere in which a poet can write—friends who were themselves poets and who also seemed to be as interested in my work as they were in their own. I received ruthless criticism, certainly, but I always felt that the people who criticized my work really wanted me to write better, really believed in and cared about me" (p. 165).

Her first published poems appeared in the magazine *Oxford Poetry 1948* (1948), edited by Kingsley Amis and James Michie. Amis already held strong views on art, and he introduced Jennings to jazz. They spent hours together in record shops, but Amis never changed her preference for classical music. While her friends Amis and John Wain admired the eighteenth-century comic, episodic novels that inform some of their works, Jennings preferred more traditional expressions, although her view on what tradition included was expansive and somewhat unorthodox. As an editor, however, Amis wanted to publish hard, modern poems from cutting-edge poets, and he chose six of Jennings' poems for *Oxford Poetry 1948*. Amis recognized Jennings' emerging talent, however different their creative perspectives. The poets around Oxford in the late 1940s admired Jennings for her intelligence, formal dexterity, and insightful statements but not because they sought a sense of solidarity. Beyond their common grounding in T. S. Eliot, the other Movement poets took their bearing from William Empson, W. H. Auden, and John Betjeman. Jennings leaned more toward the crafted lyrics of Robert Graves and the allegorical,

---

[1]Poems quoted appear in Jennings's *Collected Poems, 1953–1985* (1986), except where otherwise indicated; page numbers refer to that edition.

Christian visions of Edwin Muir. Her stance is trusting: her poems are always open to vulnerability and tolerant of uncertainty. In "John of the Cross" (1961) she shares her belief that "the deep darkness had to be spoken of, / touched beyond reach of stars, entered without indications" (p. 57). Here, she recalls Rimbaud's self-contradictory declaration that he would "write of silence and of night, and note down the inexpressible."[2] In "Tribute" (1955), Jennings argues that "all the arts of mind and hand engage / To make the shadow tangible" (p. 24).

Another common factor among the other Movement poets was a rejection of neoromanticism. They were, for example, opposed to work in the neoromantic vein of Dylan Thomas. Jennings did not share their objections. She valued neoromantic directions and revered earlier poets such as Gerard Manley Hopkins and George Herbert. Jennings writes in "A Sonnet" (1972), "There are no categories for what I know" (p. 104). On her categorization as a Movement poet, she said the "two differences between me and my contemporaries were that I was a woman and a Roman Catholic, which meant that I wanted to write about subjects which were simply uninteresting to most poets; at least uninteresting to them in the way they were interesting to me" (Press interview). Jennings was "a more romantic, outgoing poet than" than the other Movement writers (Williams, p. 80). Her romantic influences and respect for tradition inform Jennings' search into the poet's identity and poetry's psychological function, but she would agree with novelist-philosopher Iris Murdoch's view that false dilemmas over tradition have left us "with far too shallow and flimsy a view of human personality." However different their respective worldviews, both women approached moral exploration by framing truth and fantasy, art and history. The individualist aesthetic Jennings inherited from Romantic symbolists and modern poetics conflicts with the attitudes of conformity and compliance that her religion demands. Her moral problems explore the intricate relation between creative art, ordinary human experience, and sublime states of mind.

In 1949 Jennings graduated with an M.A. degree in English from St. Anne's College. She had pre-

viously failed her advanced B.Litt. studies on Matthew Arnold. Her study sought to present Arnold as both a romantic and classical poet. About the time she graduated from St. Anne's College, Jennings fell in love with an older man, a former prisoner of war in the Far East. The couple became secretly engaged. Jennings recalled that her fiancé "went to see my father one Saturday afternoon when he was watching cricket in the park. I don't know what annoyed Father more—being interrupted at cricket or the man having bought a ring without his permission." She called off the engagement. "My father said afterward, 'It wouldn't have lasted six months,' and he was right. I was beginning to notice how vain the man was, always looking at himself in the mirror" (Crew review). Jennings never developed a lasting romantic attachment. She would admit in the late 1990s that "because of my beliefs, I've never had lovers. Not through lack of temptation. It sounds pious, but I don't think a bit of self control's a bad thing. I gave in to masses of other sins—judging and grudging. I'm acquisitive" (Crew review).

EARLY WORK

JENNINGS moved to London in 1949 and worked as a copywriter for an advertising agency. She later commented that the job made her writing style more relaxed and publishable. Her work absorbed some of Eliot's metaphysical strategies and his sharp eye for detail. She learned from Eliot, and later from Edwin Muir, to look for moral metaphors rooted in everyday life, but she discarded Eliot's multiple voices in favor of a singular, gentle, sane poetic persona. She feels that "[i]n Muir's vision, . . . man's struggle is cosmic and universal. In Eliot, it is personal, particular and expressed in the familiar terms of orthodox Western mystical experience. And Eliot makes it clear that the full vision is only to be attained in this life by the very few, by those who know that 'to be conscious is not to be in time.' For Muir, the vision is open to everyone, [and] is, furthermore, lived out in each individual life" (*Every Changing Shape*, p. 179).

After a face-to-face meeting with Eliot around 1950 in London, she wrote, "I really felt in the presence of greatness" (Gramang, p. 17). At the time, she had just begun to write *Every Changing Shape* (1960), a book on poetry and Christianity. She

[2]Translation of Rimbaud: "J'écrivais des silences, des nuits, je notais l'inexprimable." Quoted in Naomi Greene, *Antonin Artaud: Poet Without Words* (New York, 1970), p. 222.

wanted to write a series of essays on the influence of religion on great poets and on the influence of poetry on Christian mystics. Eliot helped her with the choice of authors. Jennings admired Eliot personally because, despite being a great poet, he was a "modest man" (Gramang, p. 17).

Edwin Muir's worldview deeply influenced many of Jennings' poetic beliefs. He was a traditionalist with a deeply held Christian vision of life. Muir's poetry uses allegory and parable to illustrate the divine at work in the life of every individual, and his position assumes sweeping universals about human nature. Muir's poetry often narrates acceptance after a period of suffering. He believed poetry and poets should constantly develop. More complex than Muir, Jennings learned from him how allegory and parable can be vehicles to a deeper level of experience, and he influenced her gentle, unhurried language.

In early 1950 Jennings' job at the advertising agency overwhelmed her writing career. After a stressful year trying to balance two careers, she went back to Oxford and took a librarian position at the Oxford City Library, where she would continue to work for the next eight years. Innocently highbrow, she once recommended Evelyn Waugh to a man who came in looking for "a good thriller" to read. Petite and already a recognized poet, she attracted male admirers to the library just so they could check out books from her. Jennings admits to flirtations at the library, but none of these interests ever developed into a more lasting attachment.

Her first book, *Poems* (1953), won an Arts Council prize in 1953. The volume was exceptional for being serious without being self-serious. In "Delay," Jennings works with one of her favorite themes: the complications of love.

> The radiance of that star that leans on me
> Was shining years ago. The light that now
> Glitters up there my eye may never see,
> And so the time lag teases me with how
>
> Love that loves now may not reach me until
> Its first desire is spent. The star's impulse
> Must wait for eyes to claim it beautiful
> And love arrived may find us somewhere else.
>
> (p. 15)

The poem employs the tentativeness and rationality found in most Movement writers. Her language is simple and spare, and her approach is commonplace and folkwise. The tone is wistful but accepting of love's injustice, and loneliness is seen as a natural, inevitable condition of nature. The physical properties of light reinforce the poem's matter-of-fact acceptance that leaves little room for questioning. We learn that separation disproves the old axiom that "absence makes the heart grow fonder." The regular stanzas and precise language enhance isolation's inevitable logic. Slant or half rhymes about the midline caesurae like "ago," "now," "star," "year," and "there" increase the first stanza's sonorous qualities. The pattern collapses in the first two lines of the last stanza but resumes with the slant rhymes "eyes" and "arrived." Her diction is exacting, yet the understatement of the final line conveys resignation without bitterness.

While working for the library during the 1950s, Jennings exchanged poems and discussed writing with many writers such as Paul West. She said West wrote "extremely vivid poems with quite a fresh approach to language" (autobiography, p. 94). Jennings praised the poetry of Dom Moraes as "extraordinarily well-made and mature" (autobiography, p. 94). A longtime friend, Peter Levi, a Jesuit poet, enthusiastically reviewed her books, and she in turn supported his work. For example, *The Animals' Arrival* (1969) is dedicated to Levi. In this book she writes about nightmares, love, getting old, and the seashore. Above all the poems reflect on death and religion. Jennings said she was "glad to meet these young men, see their work and feel their sympathy and friendship" (autobiography, p. 94). Michael Schmidt notes that Jennings "encouraged various near-contemporary poets, undergraduates at the time. The influence of her early poems can be felt in the apprentice work of Alan Brownjohn and of Anthony Thwaite" (Schmidt, pp. 346–347). Almost two decades later both of these poets jointly reviewed Jennings' *Collected Poems* (1967), calling her "one of the best living English poets under forty-five." The other poet they named was Philip Larkin. Jennings' propensity for engaging other poets included exchanging criticism, for which other writers praised and respected her. However different her worldview, she impressed these young writers. They formed a group around her and called themselves "Elizabethans"; among the group were John Wain and D. J. Wright. Jennings also discussed poetry with Anne Ridler and wrote the introduction to Ridler's first book of poetry, *Poems* (1953). She met and exchanged poems with Adrienne Rich, whose work she admired. She discussed her view of poetics as a sacred vocation with Kathleen Raine, observing that Raine's "ideas of God were rather different from mine as a Catholic" (autobiography, p. 13).

Many of her poems about other writers express the high value she places on their friendship. She believes that artists create an aesthetic order through their art that gives their lives a sense of purpose. One important consequence of Jennings' active intellectual life was her association with the painter-printer Oscar Mellor, who published *Poems* (1953) in his newly formed Fantasy Press series. Just after it was published, Jennings sent the book to Edwin Muir, and he "wrote back the kind of letter one only dreams of. He seemed to think quite highly of some of my poems and, as I admired his work very greatly, I was absolutely delighted" (autobiography, p. 76). While working at the library Jennings felt good about her life. "It was a relief neither to be obsessed by passion nor to be numbed by despair. . . . I think that the friendship and encouragement of so many contemporaries gave me immense hope and confidence" (autobiography, pp. 90–91).

Next to Larkin, Gunn, and John Holloway, all of whom have comparable, even amicable styles and content, Jennings might seem an odd intruder, at ease expressing strong emotions of loneliness and despair and deeply religious. Perhaps most widely known, Larkin's verse also represents many of the group's poetic conceits: wry, ironic, comfortably formal but self-distancing. All of the other major Movement writers went into higher education. These common features helped shape the popular image of a Movement writer. Blake Morrison observed that "by the middle of the 1950s the image of the typical Movement writer as a provincial lower-middle class, scholarship-winning, Oxford-educated university lecturer was firmly established, though it was apparent even then that there were certain incompatibilities between this image and the kind of work the Movement produced" (p. 56). Jennings' life and work also have surprising incongruities. For example, she was called the "bag lady of the sonnets" by the British press and admits that her epitaph may read: "She lived out of carrier bags" (Crew review). Yet her creative life spans broad intellectual resources, and her ambition might be described as an intent to revive mystical Catholicism through poetry in the late twentieth century.

Many critics viewed the Movement writers as the "coming" class and felt they represented shifts in the power and social structure in postwar Britain. Among them Jennings was the only woman, and a rare nonacademic, to appear in the influential 1956 anthology *New Lines*, edited by the poet Robert Conquest, and her aims set her apart from these contemporaries as starkly as differences in gender and background. Donald Hall devoted more pages to Jennings than to Robert Lowell or Philip Larkin in *New Poets of England and America* (1957). Jennings had clear talent and a voice so flexible that it seemed both wise and awed, matter-of-fact and ecstatic.

The other Movement poets emphasized a self-conscious awareness of language that Jennings took to a vulnerable extreme in her explorations of complex human relationships. Her predecessors in this endeavor include Rimbaud, perhaps the first great master of this poetics of fragmentation and innerness. Far from insisting on the essential ineffability of experience, as some writers have, Rimbaud thought it was possible to have truer and more vibrant levels of experience precisely through an "alchemy of the word." Jennings picks up this concept of a language-based inner life and employs communal themes and modes of expression to explore ethical questions from a Christian perspective.

Some of her poems comment on ideas expressed by other poets. These poems draw attention to her contemporaries' views and her predecessors' influence, and they reveal her concern with the poet's power. For example, Jennings refutes Anglican John Donne's 1624 meditation that contains the famous line "No man is an Island . . . never send to know for whom the bell tolls; It tolls for thee" in her poem "The Island" (1953):

> Each brings an island in his heart to square
> With what he finds, and all is something strange
> But most expected. In this innocent air
> Thoughts can assume a meaning, island strength
> Is outward, inward, each man measures it, . . .
>
> (p. 20)

The notion of a seamless community of mankind that Donne likens to the "main," or mainland, is redefined by Jennings as an individual's inner condition of isolation where one must make decisions in social circumstances, and every man is an "island" of ethical choices.

London reporters interviewed Jennings after she received the 1953 Arts Council prize, and this attention led to several opportunities. She was arguably the first of the Movement writers to establish a reputation as a poet. Both Amis and Wain had published novels by then, and Donald Davie's *Purity of Diction in English Verse* (1952) had received considerable critical attention, but Jennings was the Movement's first full-time poet. Tenaciously pursuing her writing career, Jennings felt that she should try to have at least one poem or book review appear every week in an important journal, and she nearly succeeded. She appeared often in *Time and Tide* and the *Spectator.* Stephen Spender requested her poems for his new magazine, *Encounter.* John Lehman's *New Soundings* radio program included a poem by Jennings in its first broadcast, and he published her poems in the *London Magazine* alongside Thom Gunn and T. S. Eliot, who wrote a special introduction for the first issue. In October 1954 J. D. Scot coined the term "The Movement" in a *Spectator* article to refer to a loosely knit group of writers. The label, however inappropriate, recognized among the talented "angry young men" of Oxford and Cambridge a petite, devout Catholic with her hair pulled back off her face in a sensible ponytail.

Her second book, *A Way of Looking* (1955), won the Somerset Maugham Award. Given to a poet less than thirty-five years old, it came with the stipulation that the winner would go abroad for three months. Jennings took a leave of absence from the library. "Italy held a strong attraction for her, [and] so did Italian literature" (Schmidt, p. 347). While in Rome for the first time, she wrote "Fountain" (1958). "It's lovely being a Catholic in Rome. I went up the holy stairs on my knees. It was very painful, but it's the greatest ever penance" (Crew review). The trip deepened Jennings' religious convictions, and it was during this period she developed her philosophy that art is a gesture and a sacrament. She came to see the power of God as revealed in the artistry of poets, sculptors, and painters, and her fascination with the lives of religious mystics intensified.

Jennings' friendship with Father Aelwin, her spiritual mentor, encouraged her to view poetry as a vocation and to think of poetry itself as a form of tribute or grace. She met Father Aelwin on one of her early trips to Italy while exploring the rich religious heritage of Rome. George Lakoff and Mark Johnson's work in cognitive philosophy, *Philosophy in the Flesh* (1999), recognizes how metaphors are foundational to our ability to think about morality, self, and mind. Jennings

uses poetry to discover the "truth, both in myself and in the world around me. . . . It is the creation of the world and also a way of knowledge" (Dickson interview). Her return to metaphors of mind, self, and ethics displays a personal obsession with loneliness and isolation, but it also shows her empathy with social concerns about how language constructs meaning and understanding between people.

Jennings often uses shadows to represent distance between individuals and ambiguity of meaning. Shadows appear in many poems over the course of her long career, but most appear in her first twelve books up to the early 1970s. In an early poem, "Afternoon in Florence," a shadow refuses to conform to an overwhelming light that "detains no prisoner here at all" (*Poems,* 1953, p. 17). Shadows are also signals for creative thought and the apprehension of knowledge. Her framing of shadows recalls the Latin roots of apprehension, a circumstance in which one both knows and fears.

Jennings' next collection, *A Sense of the World* (1958), begins with "The Child and the Shadow" and closes with a poem in which the last word is "shadow." "The Child and the Shadow" portrays a child's shadow as a toy but also as an adult means of denial and isolation. Yet the poem proposes faith in the unexplainable power of imagination and posits a hope for relief from isolation through creative expression. "Old Man" makes the shadow a measure of age, "what / His life has made of him his shadow shows" (p. 29). A poem with surreal elements, "The Shot" naturalizes shadows in the midst of violence:

> The bullet shot me and I lay
> So calm beneath the sun, the trees
> Shook out their shadows in the breeze
> Which carried half the sky away.
> (p. 36)

Jennings often compares making poems to the practice of prayer, and her writing strives for a spiritual stability, but prayer, confession, and poetry also risk shadows, risk naming desires. "A World of Light" (1961) highlights the tension between Jennings' creative life and her religious duties. She admits that:

> Yes when the dark withdrew I suffered light
> And saw the candles heave beneath the wax,
> I watched the shadows of my old self dwindle . . .
> (p. 53)

In "Rembrandt's Late Self-Portraits" (1975), she implicates herself when she declares, "To paint's to breathe, / And all the darknesses are dared" (p. 122). Her shadows are vigorous, creative, and threatening. As Schmidt correctly observed, "For the religious poet, crisis comes when grace recedes, as it does in Vaughan and Cowper, St. John of the Cross and Hart Crane, and from time to time, in Jennings: the anxiety of disconnection is potent and can be fatal" (p. 803). Shadows are one representation of Jennings' feeling of disconnection, but it is also in the isolation of the shadows that Jennings discovers powerful metaphors for her experiences.

"Notes from a Book of Hours" (1961) is possibly her most extensive treatment of shadows. A much longer poem than she usually produces, this work in four sections allegorically reveals her uneasy peace with the shadows of her thoughts. The speaker gathers the shadows in her "arms." Here, shadows can "take root" and "confuse." But Jennings goes on to explain that the confusion of shadows can be linguistically resolved by the words of religious observance, suggesting "that the liturgy is diffused / Theology" (p. 55–56). Her references to shadows decreased after "Notes from a Book of Hours" as she expanded into other explorations of mind and consciousness.

Critics such as Michael O'Neill (1986) have called Jennings' poetic choices in *Collected Poems* (1986) unfocused. O'Neill said that "her treatment of states of feeling avoids the particular detail one associates with the best confessional poetry; in its place she offers something more generalized." Thomas Kinsella, in a review of Jennings' *Recoveries* (1964), felt that she overworked minute details and that with her poems "we are left with a sort of poetry that stares in polite, over-explaining desire at its object" (Kinsella review). Nevertheless, says John Tagg (1992), "postmodern thought and postmodern art have thrown aside the security blankets of belief, the consoling myth" and have questioned "the adequacy of every discourse . . . to present the sublime fact that the unpresentable exists" (p. 159). What is extraordinary about Jennings is that from this shattered discourse, she insists on unity and grace. She reinforces her credibility with rational arguments even as she steadfastly believes in mystery. She presents her inquiries without grasping for heroics. In "Kings" (1955) she writes:

> Heros are nothing without worshiping,
> Will not diminish into lovers, friends.
> (p. 22)

She challenges authority with humanization and social connection, not rebellion. The voice of her persona speaks as much to herself as it does to her reader. For example, "The Enemies" (1955) posits an invasion by "strangers" that results in no "devastation" (p. 23). Yet an irrational fear grips the speaker, who suspects:

> Those strangers have set up their houses in minds
> I used to walk in. Better draw the blinds
> Even if the strangers haunt in my own house.
> (p. 23)

Fear of some subtler form of possession exists, as though through their presence alone the strangers have left behind their influence. The poem questions notions of self and ownership and confounds rational expectations.

Jennings' tenacious exploration of self, doubt, and isolation emerges in her refreshing language and engaging, accessible poetry. From her first books, the poems were brief (usually fewer than twenty-five lines) and plainly eloquent. She resists Latinate words or complex diction, and her poems are personal and immediate. In her poetry she assumes her relationship to the reader with personal pronouns like "I," "you," and "we." Poetic wit and lyrical innocence have characterized her poems throughout her career, though she did become dramatically more celebratory in her later works. Her moral metaphors explore the fractures and breakdowns of social concepts even as they argue for stability, tolerance, and growth, a position she assumes more often in poems published after 1975.

A Way of Looking (1955) takes the nature of individual consciousness and visual metaphors as Jennings' philosophical problem. Its poems are an effort to will herself into a relationship with the world in such a way as to explain her thoughts and inner life, as in "In the Night":

> All that I love is, like the night, outside,
> Good to be gazed at, looking as if it could
> With a simple gesture be brought inside my head
> Or in my heart. But my thoughts about it divide
> Me from my object. Now deep in my bed
> I turn and the world turns on the other side.
> (p. 26)

The gaze, as a physical act, separates her from the tangible experience of the night even as it makes her perception of it possible. For Jennings bodily senses can separate one from experience, and thoughts are seen as a more tangible connection to the world.

During the 1950s Jennings often spent her holidays abroad. "Italy was, to me, the great discovery," she writes, "a discovery of sun, sand, sea, architecture, and painting" (autobiography, p. 113). Her experiences in Italy deeply affected her and would continue to provide subjects for her poems. "I owe a tremendous debt to Somerset Maugham. His award not only meant the chance to visit and write about Italy, but it also meant, by some act of grace, a rediscovery of my faith, a knowledge of it and a freedom within it which I had never known before. My religion was meaning more . . . to me, and even though my fears and neurosis persisted, I found great peace and splendor in Rome" (autobiography, p. 113). Father Aelwin, whom she met about this time, guided and strengthened her intuitions about poetry and religion. Together they visited Ostia, "the ancient mosaiced city outside Rome, where St. Augustine had lived and where his mother, St. Monica, had died" (autobiography, p. 123). During the four months she spent in Italy in 1957, Jennings wrote, or conceived of, many of the poems that appeared in her next two books.

Jennings has called this period during the late 1950s the happiest time of her life. Captivated by everything she experienced, she was able to quiet her fretful inner self. She wrote "Fountain" quickly and "with a profound sense of excitement and concentration" (*Let's Have Some Poetry*, p. 86). A traditional icon, the fountain serves Jennings as a psychological water table that by consistently "Drawing the water down" (p. 43) relieves a high level of external stress. With this poem, she found the powerful themes that she could not express before she had gone to Italy. Of her attraction to art, including architecture, she would later say: "Art for me is that strength, that summoning fountain" (*Critical Quarterly*, p. 217). The poem symbolically addresses her sense of spiritual dislocation. The fountain embodies her poetic struggle as both a form of "elegance" and a "taming" of her inner conflicts. For Jennings the decorum and propriety required for creativity are analogous to the fountain's restraint of a "thousand flowering sprays" down to the "utter calm" (p. 43) of the fountain's pool.

Jennings uses precise observation and logical argument to take authoritarian possession of this symbol of "power and discipline" that she sees as controlling her imagination and mystical experiences. In the poem, the dramatic situation posits a conscientious mentor instructing an implied initiate. This strategy enables her to respond to and interpret the fountain. She can play both roles even as her presentation is coolly rational. The poem invites awareness of the "watcher" and the watched. Jennings tells the reader to "Stare at such prodigality and consider" (p. 43). The verbs "stare" and "consider" ask a reader to reach for concentration and interpretation. For many years "Fountain" was Jennings' favorite poem.

A Sense of the World also explores human conflict with God's will. "The Annunciation" opens with Mary's feelings of isolation when "nothing will ease the pain" (p. 45). Mary accepts her human child and survives the "great salvations [that] grip her side" (p. 46). The narrative suppresses images in favor of emotions. Yet, as philosopher Gaston Bachelard (1988) speculates, "if the initial image is well chosen, it stimulates a well-defined poetic dream, an imaginary life that will have real laws governing successive images, a truly vital telos" (p. 3). The angel's "shadow" or thought that has terrified Mary "has lifted." Mary's disorientation and fear dissipate as she looks at the room, but her newfound realizations have forever altered her perception of the ordinary objects she observes. The device invites a deeper understanding of Benjamin Fondane's remark in his *Faux traité d'esthétique* (Paris, 1938): "First of all, an object is not real, but [it is] *a good carrier* of what is real" (p. 90). Mary considers her future when she must go to "all men's eyes" (p. 46). She knows she will be an item of speculation on what is real and what is mystical, but for Mary it "is the human child she loves" (p. 46). "The Visitation" treats another segment of Mary's story. A visit by the angel who comes to Mary in "[the] uncalm moments" leads her to realize that "this was something she could share" (p. 46). Mary goes to her "cousin's house"

> And those two women in their quick embrace
> Gazed at each other with looks undisturbed
> By men or miracles
>
> (p. 47)

Father Aelwin encouraged Jennings to read Thomas Traherne's *Centuries of Meditations* (1908). Traherne immediately enchanted her, and she later wrote that he "was a man who was both a mystic and a poet, who found God *through* the natural world" (*Every Changing Shape*, p. 85). She noted that it is a sense of order, not undirected originality, that produces the extraordinary clarity of *Centuries*. This aesthetic would reinforce her use of commonplace observation, cliché, and sweeping moral metaphors. Jennings began composing essays on Traherne, T. S. Eliot, St. Teresa of Avila, Rilke, St. John of the Cross, and other poets and mystics who fit her thesis and supported her poetic vocation.

Jennings' fear and doubt subsided, and she gave up her position at the library in 1958. She took a job as an editor in London to support herself. She spent a busy year reading literary submissions for the publisher Chatto and Windus, living in a rented apartment over a convent where she "could get to Mass and communion each morning" (Davidson interview), and she traveled back to Oxford on weekends to work on *Every Changing Shape* (1961). She enjoyed the literary life in London this time, but "the old neuroses were beginning to arise again in a very ugly form" (autobiography, p. 142).

In October 1960 Jennings went back to Rome to renew her conversations with Father Aelwin. Upon returning to Oxford, she decided to quit her job and live on her writing, a bold act of faith that backfired when she "was suddenly beset with hideous religious doubts, with doubts about everything, including . . . God's existence" (autobiography, p. 142). Despite this profound crisis of faith, she continued to write poems and publish book reviews. She spent the rest of 1960 preparing her fourth book, *Song for a Birth or a Death* (1961).

In late 1960 Jennings left London for good, and while she had enjoyed working for Chatto and Windus, she felt her writing deserved her full attention. She took back to Oxford several freelance assignments, including the editing of an anthology and a commission to translate, with help, the sonnets of Michelangelo for the Folio Society. Not long after she moved back to Oxford, Jennings became ill with a stomach ailment that required surgery. She recovered and later collected the poems she wrote during her early illness in *Recoveries* (1964).

LATER WORKS

IN 1961, while Jennings stayed with a friend who was a Dominican priest, her depression returned and she was overcome by doubt and suicidal thoughts. She took an overdose of Nembutal, a powerful prescription drug that induces sleep. She later wrote that "a great darkness of spirit came over me and desperate things happened. . . . [It] seemed to me that to kill my fears, I must kill myself" (autobiography, p. 185). She recalls going to a film and "hot tears started rolling down my cheeks" (Crew review). She checked into a psychiatric hospital, but says, "I wasn't mad, until they gave me a drug I was allergic to and I hit the horrid sister on the jaw and jumped from bed to bed" (Crew review). After a brief hospital stay, Jennings underwent psychoanalysis for several years. She wrote about her depression in *The Mind Has Mountains* (1966). Even during this period of greatest turmoil, she continued to write poems, review books, and work on a critical survey of Christian poetry from the Anglo-Saxon era to the present time. After eleven years of effort, she published her prose collection on poetry and mysticism, *Every Changing Shape*, in 1961.

Mark Turner, in *Reading Minds* (1991), sketches "poetic thought and reason" as "overlapping spaces, contained within the larger space of everyday thought." In this model, "poetic thought is part of everyday thought; poetic language is part of everyday language" (p. 49). From these "conceptual patterns" arise metaphors that are more than simple clichés or folk expressions: these metaphors express the way we conceptualize ethical ideas. Ethical metaphors, like creative metaphors, are "far from being autonomous" (p. 49). These metaphors are "contingent at every point upon the unoriginal structures that inform" their meaning (p. 51). George Lakoff and Mark Johnson's *Philosophy in the Flesh* (1999) frames ethical metaphors as originating from common bodily experiences of well-being. These metaphors "are neither incidental, nor disposable; they are constitutive" (p. 339). Whatever energy Jennings loses with her generalizations and commonplace observations she makes up for in her vigorous and articulate pursuit of the ethical problems of intimate human relationships.

"Poem in Winter" (1955) explores the differences between adult and childhood reactions to a snowstorm. The children are free to play and look for "omens," but the adults must "stand behind a pane of glass / Untouched by it, and watch the children" (p. 21). The "glass" both facilitates and distorts perception. This perception is not the "wise illusion" of the children's watchfulness; rather, the window is a barrier to tangible experience and real hope. "In This Time" (1955) reinforces the idea that windows can deceive when they are "shuttered" against myths that could "revive by breathing on them" (p. 23). In "A Fear" (1958) the closed window is oppressive, and the speaker throws "the shutters back for air" only to meet "A face like mine still dream-bereft and white / And, like mine, shaken by a child's nightmare" (p. 39). Many other poems in *A Way of Looking* and *A Sense of the World* refine window metaphors even as they undercut the certainty of visual perception. A favorite metaphor, windows are imposed openings or opportunities that frame Jennings' awareness in "Song at the Beginning of Autumn" (1955):

> But I am carried back against
> My will into childhood where
> Autumn is bonfires, marbles, smoke;
> I lean against my window fenced
> From evocations in the air.
> When I said autumn, autumn broke.
>
> (p. 21)

Guilt and anticipation intersect with Jennings' metaphor of windows of perception and seasonal change. With the verbalization of "autumn," the anticipation of fall and the future causes the opposite reaction of thrusting the speaker back to childhood memories.

In her long poem "Sequence in Hospital" (1964) a window is at first a cheerful portal and could be a sign of pleasant associations as the "sun streams through the window" (p. 77) of the sick ward. Here, Jennings takes up the power of fear in a section titled "After an Operation":

> I learnt I was afraid,
> Not frightened in the way that I had been
> When wide awake and well, I simply mean
> Fear became absolute and I became
> Subject to it; it beckoned, I obeyed.
>
> (p. 77)

She says later in the poem that after she has recovered:

> fear can claim
> no general power. Yet I am not the same
>
> (p. 78)

The window, first a symbol of inviting light in the dark of the sick ward, is later recognizable as a barrier between those who are ill inside and those who are well outside the hospital. Lakoff and Johnson describe our concepts of inner life as hierarchal and state that "we experience ourselves as split" (p. 269). Jennings uses the window as a symbol of this split between person and self, persona and place. In another poem from the same collection, "A Depression" (1966), the "furious window shook / with violent storms" and serves as a boundary between a depressed woman and others who still "sensed the world" (p. 91). The depressed woman has "no power to share" (p. 91) this experience, and so she is cut off from everything. Her remission in the last half of the poem is certain in the present, but "will it last?" (p. 92). Jennings projects the depressive episode of this poem onto another woman, but its hesitancy sounds very much like Jennings' own uncertainty about cures. "Prisoner" (1975) makes another statement of perception understood through language:

> Feel up the walls, waters ooze. The cold
> Cranes down the spine. The wayward sky won't fit
> A window, a square, but a square equates itself
> With the eye in the brain, in the nervous system. All
> Which flesh becomes without food and a little water.
>
> (p. 134)

Here biology governs the "windows" of perception, and the thoughts of the brain are absolutely dependent on physical needs.

In early 1960 Jennings published a prose work for children called *Let's Have Some Poetry!* (1960) that is interesting reading for adults as well. Using personal anecdotes to show how she developed her talents, she details her method of writing poems and encourages everyone to write poetry. She says, "Poems, in fact, are rather like cakes; you can take them out of the oven when they are not properly cooked, when they are still heavy and soggy in the middle. It is also possible to leave an idea or an image too long in one's mind and imagination" (p. 87). To be able to write at any instant, Jennings always has a pencil and journal with her. Explaining how she works, she writes: "I have discarded work rather than re-written whole poems or parts of them. It is my belief that an early poem, if it has any value, should, when collected, be left as it is" (*Collected Poems*, p. 13). She calls her writing an emotional need. The deep satisfaction of writing a successful poem does not last very long for her. She wrote in "The State of Poetry" (1989) that she believes humility is necessary for her "restless energy" to return, and that a "deep self-knowledge and a sense of humor are . . . qualities necessary in a poet." *Every Changing Shape,* also published in 1960, takes its title from T. S. Eliot's poem "Portrait of a Lady." The book contains critical essays on St. Augustine, St. John of the Cross, Gerard Manley Hopkins, T. S. Eliot, and others.

Song for a Birth or a Death (1961) is a collection that goes fiercely to the point, as the book's title poem, about sex and violence, reveals:

> Last night I saw the savage world
> And heard the blood beat up the stair;
> The fox's bark, the owl's shrewd pounce,
> The crying creatures all were there,
> And men in bed with love and fear.
>
> The slit moon only emphasized
> How blood must flow and teeth must grip.
> What does the calm light understand,
> The light which draws the tide and ship
> And drags the owl upon its prey
> And human creatures lip to lip?
>
> Last night I watched how pleasure must
> Leap from disaster with its will:
> The fox's fear, the watch-dog's lust
> Know that all matings mean a kill:
> And human creatures kissed in trust
> Feel the blood throb to death until
>
> The seed is struck, the pleasure's done,
> The birds are thronging in the air;
> The moon gives way to widespread sun.
> Yes but the pain still crouches where
> The young fox and the child are trapped
> And cries of love are cries of fear.
>
> (p. 48)

The singsong rhythm recalls a nursery rhyme and understates the poem's brutality. In the third stanza pleasure "must" lead to "a kill" as though the outcome of love is inevitable. The "song" of the title may be as close as Jennings gets to satiric wit on a par with Larkin.

After Jennings was hospitalized for depression in 1961, she spent several years locked in a profoundly bitter, manipulative struggle with a psychoanalyst she later called the "Interrogator" in one of her poems. The experience left her "very anti-Freud" and opposed to the psychiatric profes-

sion generally. Over three decades later, she still referred to her analyst as "that psycho" (Crew review). According to Adam Phillips (1994), "there is, of course, no reason to think a psychologist's interpretation of a boxing match would be more necessarily revealing than a boxer's account of a psychoanalytic session" (p. 79). Jennings would later write "Freudish" in the margins of her draft poems, the connotation being clearly negative.

Jennings collected some of the poems she wrote during her psychoanalysis in *The Mind Has Mountains* (1966), deriving the book's title from the Gerard Manley Hopkins poem that begins "No worst, there is none. Pitched past pitch of grief," in which Hopkins echoes a line in Shakespeare's *King Lear*. She turned to Hopkins' sonnets of desolation, which speak of religious struggle and doubt, for the flavor she sought. Her collection reveals the sorrows and anxieties of the mental ward without developing a personal narrative. Jennings presents the hysterics of insanity in a calm tone, and while she may surprise, she never aims to shock or shame. A nurse is described in the poem "Night Sister" with sincere admiration; Jennings writes she "never met a calling quite so pure" (p. 88). She often sees other people as Christlike figures or teachers who embody morality. At the same time Jennings' sense of control rarely overworks this sense of awe, and the key to the nurse's piety is her "memory for everyone" (p. 88).

In "The Interrogator" Jennings abandons rhyme for repeated phrases: "He is always right" and "He can always find words" (p. 87). The device reinforces her sense of circular psychoanalytic reasoning and the client's helplessness against such entrenched beliefs. The poem evokes a catch-22 world in which the Interrogator is always right, and whatever the patient does is "just as he wishes" and confirms his opinions.

> And if you covered his mouth with your hand,
> Pinned him down to his smooth desk chair,
> You would be doing just what he wishes.
> His silence would prove he was right.
>
> (p. 88)

For Jennings aggression only confirms the pattern it seeks to upset, but her frustration with psychoanalysis is palatable.

Most of the poems in *The Mind Has Mountains* do not appear in Jennings' 1967, and 1986 collections of poems, a reflection, perhaps, of the involved critical debate over whether the poems are actually confessional. Jennings does not think they are confessional, and she points out that her poems are about other people and not herself. She does write about suicide, suffering, and madness, but she does not adopt a persona who is especially suicidal, in pain, or hysterical. While the flavor of her experiences is related, these poems do not divulge the details of her personal history. *The Mind Has Mountains* won a Richard Hilary Memorial in 1966.

Published the same year as *The Mind Has Mountains, The Secret Brother* (1966), a delightfully illustrated book, evokes the secret world of childhood. Jennings hoped to encourage children to enjoy poems. In a 1991 interview she described her childhood belief that she really had two siblings, one a real older sister, the other an imaginary brother she called Jack Baycock. "This is Freud, of course. Freud would go to town on that. Jack lived in the greenhouse. I used to have long conversations with him on my toy telephone. He materialized once, when I was seven. There was a ruggar match going on in the garden next door. A man was running with the ball. I knew it was Jack because he was doing well" (Crew review). The first poem of *The Secret Brother* (1966) describes this experience in slightly different terms:

> Jack lived in the greenhouse
> When I was six,
> With glass and tomato plants,
> Not slates and bricks.
> (*The Secret Brother*, pp. 1–2)

In the poem, Jack does not appear and the child of the poem loses Jack when

> He and his old mother
> Did a midnight flit.
> No one knew his number:
> I had altered it
>
> (pp. 1–2)

Drawing from her first seven books, Jennings published her first collection of poems in 1967. "To put together one's *Collected Poems* is a strange experience, it entails both a backward glance at all one has already written and also a forward look at what may be one's future verse. In both cases it is a revelation of mind and heart of the particular person" (*Poetry Society Bulletin*, 1961). During this period of reflection on her earlier life, Jennings wrote her autobiography. In this manuscript she reveals her early interest in the poet as subject and creates a sense of the inevitability of her own life as a poet. Jennings loses control of the materials, and the work suffers from evasive justifications and rational explanations. Poems she wrote twenty years later in *Extending the Territory* (1985) make a more controlled statement about some of these events and what she feels they mean. The autobiography was rejected for publication.

Jennings' first *Collected Poems* seemed to some to be a parting gesture of a poet lost to depression. Published when she was forty-one, the collection "reflect[s] . . . her development from an essentially thinking poet to a feeling and suffering poet," writes Michael Schmidt (p. 347). He goes on to say that "the disrupted style of her expressionist poems, gathered near the end of the [chronological] *Collected Poems,* where she abandoned metre, rhyme, and punctuation in favour of free association, are notable failures" (p. 349). Jennings seems to need traditional form to write successful poems. The heightening effect of plain rhymes and sensitive rhythms lends her subjects a sense of eloquent appropriateness. Although she continued to churn out thousands of poems and regularly publish prizewinning books, she largely fell from critical sight from the late 1960s until the mid-1980s. Interest in her work increased after *Collected Poems, 1953–1985* was published in 1986. (Many of her individual volumes are out of print.)

Jennings sometimes fears losing the ability to write poems. It is hard for her to endure periods when no poem appears, but "the perilous process of making a poem is [so] mysterious, exquisite and absorbing . . . that it more than compensates for the long dark periods when poetry seems to have dried up in one for ever" (*Poetry Book Society Bulletin*). In his review of *Tributes* (1989) for the *Spectator,* C. H. Sesson observes that "a number of poems—perhaps too many?—are concerned with the elusive business of writing poetry." Jennings' exploration of mind and creativity has dominated her work, and it shows in the number of poems that discuss the inner process of writing. However, Jennings' broad approach to explaining creativity makes evident her determination to divulge those elusive aspects of the imagination.

Around 1969 she met her future publisher, fellow poet Michael Schmidt. "We had awful wine once a week," Schmidt recalled. Jennings would be one of the first poets published by Schmidt's newly formed Carcanet Press. At the same time the press published two Nobel Prize– and four Pulitzer Prize–winning authors, including John Ashbery, and introduced the work of Vikram Synod, Jorie Graham, and Frank O'Hara for the first time in Britain. The press has made a sustained effort to support writing from Ireland, Scotland, Wales, and the United States, and in doing so placed Jennings' work in admirable, and competitive, intellectual company.

In the early 1970s Jennings' struggle with her psychoanalyst intensified. When she finally broke away from him, her sense of release led to a burst of poetry, and she began writing voluminously and somewhat indiscriminately. Schmidt said the poems in *Growing Points* (1975) were chosen from more than a thousand she submitted to him. In 1972 she was a nominee for poet laureate but did not win the honor. In 1974 she traveled to New York City, where she was a Guildersleeve Lecturer at Barnard College. New York left no impression on her comparable to her attraction to Rome and Italian culture.

CELEBRATORY WORKS

THE collection *Growing Points* signaled a new direction for Jennings. The poems display a substantial increase in her technical resources. Her work grew more confident, if somewhat more irregular. Schmidt commented that she achieves a graceful serenity that "in the course of her fifteen-year-long struggle with madness, would have seemed impossible. Here the old symbols, images and themes recur, but with different significance, . . . and often in the context of celebration" (p. 805). Jennings experimented with a longer line and tended toward a rhapsodic style, and a certain prolixity mars the work. "Elegy for W. H. Auden" begins with "Stones endure as your first and last things" (p. 125), but she loses her usually graceful diction in ornate language. Jennings said she learned from Auden the effectiveness of a "surprising adjective," and deeply admired his poetry. She met Auden when he was an old man, and she was deeply saddened by his death. The poem suffers from its awkward biographical content, and it seems to distance emotion and relationship rather than reveal them. The poem fails in ways her more metaphorical statements do not, such as in "Not Abstract." She observes that images are

where the river bends, where the bridges break,
Where the willow does not quite
Fall to the current—here is the place to stake
Your life in, . . .

(p. 132)

The joy of Jennings' new direction is tempered by her adult perspective. She still questions perfection, leaves room for the ineffable, and examines the inner life in terms of physical realities.

Jennings published the prose collection *Seven Men of Vision: An Appreciation* in 1976. These essays focus on seven visionary artists of the twentieth century: Yeats, D. H. Lawrence, St. John Perse, Lawrence Durell, David Jones, Antoine de St. Exupéry, and Boris Pasternak. She chose these writers because she saw them as "open[ing] up ways to the future: they are not static, all of them lead somewhere" (p. 241). She felt they were united by "hope, a rare quality nowadays—hope and a vivid, concrete awareness of our own world today" (p. 241). Although Jennings' criticism tends to interpret other writers in terms of how their work reinforces her own notions of poetic vocations, she is an attentive reader and presents logical, persuasive arguments to buttress her opinions.

Consequently I Rejoice (1977) takes its title from a line by T. S. Eliot: "Consequently I rejoice, having to construct something upon which to rejoice" (opposite title page). The collection includes a series on Christ's life, from Immaculate Conception ("Mary's Magnificat") to his suffering on the cross and resurrection ("Christ Surprised"). "Sufism" expresses themes common to both Christianity and Islam. Jennings compares writing poems to "Dervishing dances." Seeing the creator as part of creation, she writes: "Let the veil be stripped off, the Sufis say, let God / Step out of his own inventions" (p. 161). Jennings goes on to suggest we "take [the world] to us like lovers, embrace / the God we have summoned" (p. 161).

Her next children's book, *After the Ark* (1978), personifies animals who speak to humans about compassion. Jennings said: "I enjoyed writing [this book] so much. And I didn't think I was writing this for a child because I think if a poem is good enough for a grown-up it's good enough for a child" (Gramang, p. 5).

Her next two books, *Moments of Grace* (1980) and *Celebrations and Elegies* (1982), continue to investigate Jennings' ethical concerns and sense of personal isolation. In *Moments of Grace*, "Forgiveness" summarizes the relation between strong emotion and language:

> Anger, pity, always, most, forgive.
> It is the word which we surrender by,
> It is the language where we have to live.
> (p. 170)

After the publication of *Collected Poems, 1953–1985* in 1987, Peter Levi wrote: "having brooded over her [*Collected Poems*] for some months, I am sure [these poems are] the best she has ever written. She is one of the few masters" (p. 89). The volume won the W. H. Smith Literary Award in 1987.

Jennings' poetics of thought and creativity can be traced throughout her poetry in references to power and birds. Those of her poems that explore power reveal her complex relationship to authority, and they often intersect with images of birds, treated in a broad range of forms such as metaphor, allegory, literal subject, and parable. "The Bell Ringer" (1953) discusses the "bells" of a church as "Crowding the town together." The bell ringer does not consider the "lives of power" (p. 18) who might hear the church bells because:

> the sounds had left his hands to sing
> A meaning for each listening separately,
> A separate meaning for the single choice.
> (p. 18)

In the final stanza, the knowledge or awareness caused by the bells is described as if the air were "full of birds descending." In "Kings" (1955) a ruler's "power" comes from:

> how men bring
> Their thoughts to bear upon him, how their minds
> Construct the grandeur from the simple thing.
> (p. 22)

Jennings builds a concept of power through hierarchal relationships, but she releases no birds of imaginative power into this poem of unchecked authority. In "Absence" (1958) the birds have become "thoughtless" (p. 33), and this signals ongoing feelings of loss and nostalgia when the speaker visits a place she associates with an absent friend. "Rhetoric" (1975) argues against a notion of birds as the logicians' "Bright symbols" (p. 108). Jennings denies this abstraction, and she writes: "I have no need for birds to show my doubt" (p. 108).

She explores human powerlessness in "Thunder and a Boy" (1975). The terror of a violent storm leaves the group inside cowering, but

> Those birds escaping through showers show us
> They are more imperial than we are.
> (p. 112)

"Bird Study" (1975) makes a celebratory statement of the power of birds. The bird's power "of knowing when and where to strike" obsesses her

> with energy
> I can never touch. I am alive
> To what I only hear and see,
> The sweep, the sharp, the drive.
> (p. 114)

Jennings becomes defensive in "Creator in Vienna" (1975), in which she awkwardly derides Freud for

> leaping down our
> Apparently never-before-discovered minds, entering
> our dreams
> Telling us of love and power, . . .
> (p. 129)

"Song for the Swifts" (1977) takes the image of birds through several literary treatments. First, the birds "volley, parry, play with the new light" (p. 156). The second stanza is topological as the birds show the observer the "wind's weight" (p. 156), that is, its speed and direction. The third stanza toys with allegory and myth when the swifts become "Unthinkingly mating birds" (p. 157). In the fourth stanza the literal is combined with the philosophical metaphor:

> However dark our lands,
> Wisdom is in our bloodstream not in brain
> Alone and we take instinct on again
> Watching these birds and the soon-to-bear-fruit grain
> And what we never thought we could attain
> Falls, the uneaten apple, in our hands.
> (p. 157)

"Bird in the House" (1985) narrates a canary's death, refashioning the old superstition of a bird in the house as a bad omen or portent. The adult speaker instead rejoices that

> The yellow bird sings in my mind and I say
> that the child is callous but wise . . .
> (p. 186)

In a 1987 interview Jennings observed that poets are saner now, but duller than they used to be. She said she never felt discriminated against as a woman in literature but wondered "why critics are more malicious about poetry than about other books—maybe because so many manque poets write reviews" (Levi review). Her great unquenchable passion for more than fifty years has been another great English eccentric—Sir John Gielgud. The two corresponded for years but never met. Jennings does not hold back her enthusiasm for her stage idol. "I first saw him in Macbeth, when I was still in school. Then his Hamlet, his last Hamlet—one of the highlights of my life. I queued outside the stage door to get his autograph. Then his Lear. There has never been another actor to touch him. Olivier? You can stick Olivier . . . " (Dickson interview).

Jennings' way of life may seem out of step with modern beliefs, but she is uncompromising in defending her stance: "I've been waiting twenty years for a puritan revolution" (Dickson interview). Jennings may be socially conservative, but politically she is left of center. For example, she is comically disdainful of the Thatcher years. She admits she has composed limericks about Margaret Thatcher, but she has never written them down "for fear they will be used as evidence against me" (Crew review). She is primarily critical of the conservatives' treatment of the poor and homeless.

She published *In the Meantime* in 1996 and *Praises* in 1998. Jennings' freelance career has at times severely impoverished her. She has had to sell first editions of her own books and treasured gifts from colleagues to support herself. Throughout the 1980s and 1990s, she continued to publish reviews and criticism and edit major anthologies. From time to time, she made lecture and reading tours around Great Britain, and she continues to give poetry presentations at schools. She believes that "young minds see things in your poems you were not conscious of when you wrote them" (Gramang, p. 3). Her experience with young students of poetry is that teenagers "are most attentive, most intelligent, and most probing as askers of questions" (Orr, p. 94).

Although she is perhaps the most unglamorous poet of the late twentieth century, Elizabeth Jennings was awarded a C.B.E. (Commander of the British Empire) by Queen Elizabeth II in 1992. Jennings' bouts with depression and need for solitude have denied her the necessary instincts for self-promotion. She continues to churn out poems, many of which are still of the superior quality of her early work. Jennings believes that "poets are born, not made. They have a gift which demands to be obeyed" (Dickson interview). Jennings joins her passion for poetry and Catholicism to a Protestant work ethic. Max Davidson said in 1991 that what Jennings' work "lacks in virtuosity, it makes up for in grace of delivery, depth of feeling, and a kind of artistic integrity that is going out of fashion: big issues tackled head on, with no recourse to irony or post-modern tricks" (Crew review). Opinion of Jennings' work has varied, but she rarely fails to leave an impression.

In 1998 she published another children's book, *A Spell of Words*. She returned to exploring the magic of childhood experiences. The bulk of the collection consists of animal poems that explore nature allegory or dramatic monologues. Jennings is not an ecological or political writer, and she has never felt comfortable writing poems about popular issues and current events. She admits that good poems can be written about nuclear warfare and scientific experimentation, which have been topics for Conquest, Larkin, and other Movement writers. Yet she finds those subjects generally less compelling than the traditional poetic themes of love, death, and the self.

Asked in a 1993 interview when she last went to confession, Jennings replied: "I'm not going to say. Do you mind?" (Welch interview).

SELECTED BIBLIOGRAPHY

I. Autobiography. Four notebooks of autobiographical writings are in the Elizabeth Jennings Papers, Special Collections of the Morris Library, at the University of Delaware, Newark.

II. Poetry Volumes. *Poems* (Swinford, U.K., 1953); *A Way of Looking* (London and New York, 1955); *A Sense of the World* (London and New York, 1958); *Song for a Birth or a Death* (London and Philadelphia, 1961); *Recoveries* (London and Philadelphia, 1964); *The Mind Has Mountains* (London, 1966); *The Secret Brother, and Other Poems for Children* (London and New York, 1966); *Collected Poems of Elizabeth Jennings* (London and New York, 1967); *The Animals' Arrival* (London, 1969); *Lucidities* (London, 1970); *Relationships* (London, 1972); *Growing Points: New Poems* (Manchester, U.K., and Chester Springs, Pa., 1975); *Consequently I Rejoice* (Manchester, U.K., 1977); *After the Ark* (Oxford and New York, 1978); *Moments of Grace* (Manchester, U.K., 1979); *Selected Poems*

(Manchester, U.K., 1979); *Winter Wind* (Sindcot, Somerset, U.K., and Newark, Vt., 1979); *A Dream of Spring* (Stratford-on-Avon, 1980); *Celebrations and Elegies* (Manchester, U.K., 1982); *Extending the Territory* (Manchester, U.K., 1985); *Collected Poems, 1953–1985* (Manchester, U.K., 1986); *An Oxford Cycle* (Oxford, 1987); *Tributes* (Manchester, U.K., 1989); *Times and Seasons* (Manchester, U.K., 1992); *Familiar Spirits* (Manchester, U.K., 1994); *In the Meantime* (Manchester, U.K., 1996); *A Poet's Choice* (Manchester, U.K., 1996); *Praises* (Manchester, U.K., 1998); *A Spell of Words* (Manchester, U.K., 1998).

III. OTHER PUBLICATIONS. *The Batsford Book of Children's Verse* (London, 1958); *Let's Have Some Poetry!* (London, 1960); *An Anthology of Modern Verse, 1940–1960* (London, 1961); *Every Changing Shape* (London, 1961); *Poetry To-day, 1957–60* (London and New York, 1961); *Frost* (Edinburgh, 1964); *Christianity and Poetry* (London, 1965); translation of *The Sonnets of Michelangelo* (London, 1969); *A Choice of Christina Rosetti's Verse* (London, 1970); *Seven Men of Vision: An Appreciation* (London, 1976); *The Batsford Book of Religious Verse* (London, 1981); *In Praise of Our Lady* (London, 1982).

IV. SELECTED ARTICLES. "In Retrospect and Hope" and "The Future," in *Critical Quarterly* 11 (1969); "The State of Poetry," in *Agenda* 27, no. 3 (1989): 40–41.

V. INTERVIEWS AND REVIEWS. "Elizabeth Jennings," in *Poetry Society Bulletin*, no. 40 (1961); John Press, "The Making of the Movement," in *Spectator* (4 October 1963); Thomas Kinsella, "Recoveries," in *New York Times* (20 December 1964); Michael O'Neill, "Other Awareness," in *Times Literary Supplement* (28 November 1986); Peter Levi, "Otherwise Engaged," in *Spectator* (12 March 1987); C. H. Sesson, "How Spirit Speaks to Spirit," in *Spectator* (2 September 1989); E. Jane Dickson, "The Cafe Society of a B&B Poet," in *Daily Telegraph* (29 October 1991); Candida Crew, "Bag Lady of the Sonnets," in *Times Saturday Review* (23 November 1991); Max Davidson "Her Prize Money Is in the Bag," in *Daily Telegraph* (19 November 1997); Frances Welch, "Me and My God," in *Sunday Telegraph* (15 February 1998).

VI. CRITICAL STUDIES. Robert Conquest, ed., *New Lines* (London and New York, 1956); Donald Hall et al., eds., *New Poets of England and America* (New York, 1957); Anthony Thwaite, *Contemporary English Poetry: An Introduction* (London, 1959); John Wain, *Essays on Literature and Ideas* (London, 1963); Peter Orr, *The Poet Speaks: Interviews with Contemporary Poets Conducted by Hilary Morrish, Peter Orr, John Press, and Ian Scott-Kilvert* (London and New York, 1966); Julian Symons, "Clean and Clear," in *New Statesman* (13 October 1967); John Wain, *Letters to Five Artists: Poems* (New York and London, 1969); Margaret Byers, "A Cautious Vision: Recent British Poetry by Women," in *British Poetry Since 1960* (Oxford, 1972); John Wain, *A House for the Truth: Critical Essays* (New York, 1973); John Wain, *Professing Poetry* (London, 1977);

Michael Schmidt, *A Reader's Guide to Fifty Modern British Poets* (London, 1979).

Blake Morrison, *The Movement: English Poetry and Fiction of the 1950s* (Oxford and New York, 1980); Jonathan Culler, *On Deconstruction: Theory and Criticism After Structuralism* (Ithaca, N.Y., 1982); William Blissett, "Elizabeth Jennings," in *Dictionary of Literary Biography*, vol. 2, *Poets of Great Britain and Ireland, 1945–1960*, edited by Vincent B. Sherry, Jr. (Detroit, 1984); Martin Booth, *British Poetry: Driving Through the Barricades* (Boston and London, 1985); Jonathan Culler, "Changes in the Study of the Lyric," in *Lyric Poetry: Beyond New Criticism*, edited by Chaviv Hošek and Patricia Parker (Ithaca, N.Y., 1985); Edward Lucie-Smith, ed., "Introduction," in *British Poetry Since 1945* (Harmondsworth, U.K., 1985); Bruce K. Martin, *British Poetry Since 1939* (Boston, 1985); Erwin Sturzl, "Interview with Elizabeth Jennings," in *Acumen* 1 (April 1985); Peter Levi, "Elizabeth Jennings," in *Poetry Nation Review 53* 13, no. 3 (1986); John Williams, *Twentieth Century British Poetry: A Critical Introduction* (London, 1987); Ian Ousby, ed., *The Cambridge Guide to Literature in English* (New York, 1988); Sabine Foisner, "Elizabeth Jennings: 'Against the Dark,' " in *English Language and Literature: Positions and Dispositions* 16 (Salzburg, 1990); Jerry Bradley, *The Movement: British Poets of the 1950s* (New York, 1993); Gerlinde Gramang, *Elizabeth Jennings: An Appraisal of Her Life as a Poet, Her Approach to Her Work, and a Selection of the Major Themes of Her Poetry* (Lewiston, N.Y., 1995).

VII. PHILOSOPHICAL AND METAPHOR STUDIES. Iris Murdoch, "Against Dryness," in *Encounter* 16 (January 1961); Roger C. Schank and Robert P. Abelson, *Scripts, Plans, Goals, and Understanding: An Inquiry into Human Knowledge Structures* (Hillsdale, N.J., 1977); Carol Gilligan, *In a Different Voice: Psychological Theory and Women's Development* (Cambridge, Mass., 1982); R. Langacker, *Tense and Aspect: Between Semantics and Pragmatics* (Amsterdam, 1983); Gilles Fauconnier, *Mental Spaces: Aspects of Meaning Construction in Natural Language* (Cambridge, Mass., 1985); Roland Barthes, *The Responsibility of Forms: Critical Essays on Music, Art, and Representation*, translated by Richard Howard (New York, 1985); Mark Turner, *Death Is the Mother of Beauty: Mind, Metaphor, Criticism* (Chicago, 1987); Alfred R. Mele, *Irrationality: An Essay on Akrasia, Self-Deception, and Self-Control* (New York, 1987); George Lakoff, *Women, Fire, and Dangerous Things: What Categories Reveal About the Mind* (Chicago, 1987); Gaston Bachelard, *Air and Dreams: An Essay on the Imagination of Movement*, translation of *L'air et les songes: Essai sur l'imagination du mouvement* (1943) by Edith R. Farrell and C. Frederick Farrell (Dallas, 1988).

Eve Sweetser, *From Etymology to Pragmatics: Metaphorical and Cultural Aspects of Semantic Structure* (New York, 1990); Mark Turner, *Reading Minds: The Study of English in the Age of Cognitive Science* (Princeton, N.J.,

1991); Charlene Spretnak, *States of Grace: The Recovery of Meaning in the Postmodern Age* (San Francisco, 1991); Owen J. Flanagan, *Varieties of Moral Personality: Ethics and Psychological Realism* (Cambridge, Mass., 1991); John Tagg, *Grounds of Dispute: Art History, Cultural Politics, and the Discursive Field* (Houndmills, Basingstoke, Hampshire, 1992); Antonio Damasio, *Descartes' Error: Emotion, Reason and the Human Brain* (New York, 1994); Adam Phillips, *On Flirtation* (London, 1994); Paul M. Churchland, *The Engine of Reason, The Seat of the Soul: A Philosophical Journey into the Brain* (Cambridge, Mass., 1995); Adele E. Goldberg, *Conceptual Structure, Discourse, and Language* (Stanford, Calif., 1996); Marcus J. Borg, *The God We Never Knew: Beyond Dogmatic Religion to a More Contemporary Faith* (San Francisco, 1997); George Lakoff and Mark Johnson, *Philosophy in the Flesh: The Embodied Mind and Its Challenge in Western Thought* (New York, 1999).

RUTH PRAWER JHABVALA

(1927–   )

Radhika Jones

IN THE GROWING canon of international literature in English, Ruth Prawer Jhabvala cuts an impressive figure. Jhabvala's richly varied background—a German-Jewish émigré, she grew up in England, spent a quarter of a century in India, then moved to the United States—defies categorization along national or cultural lines; her range of forms, settings, and styles renders her equally elusive. Western critics have frequently compared her to that most English of English novelists, Jane Austen, or to Henry James and E. M. Forster, many of whose novels, not coincidentally, she has adapted for the screen. In her personal essay "Disinheritance" (1979), a lecture given upon receipt of the Neil Gunn International Fellowship, Jhabvala, cites George Eliot, Thomas Hardy, and Charles Dickens as her English inspirations; alongside them she adds some of their European counterparts—Marcel Proust, Leo Tolstoy, and Ivan Turgenev.

Yet Jhabvala's work is equally at home in the literary canon of Southeast Asia. In an issue of the *New Yorker* in 1997 devoted to Indian writers, Salman Rushdie, addressing that subject, placed her name between those of novelist Anita Desai and filmmaker, short story writer, and composer Satyajit Ray, both progenitors of the postcolonial Indian artistic community. Rushdie characterized Jhabvala's voice as that of the "rootless intellectual," and indeed, in a number of personal essays and statements, Jhabvala has willingly, even happily, described herself as rootless. In her fiction, whose settings and subjects span three continents, she has used her rootless voice and a dramatis personae of travelers and spiritual seekers to create a body of literature with a scope that ranges from the charmingly local to the casually worldly. In fact, it may be her characters very rootlessness that makes them so at home in the contemporary world.

LIFE

RUTH Prawer was born in Cologne, Germany, on 7 May 1927, the second child and only daughter in what she describes as a "well-integrated, solid, assimilated, German-Jewish family" ("Disinheritance," p. 5). It was a family, however, whose history was already marked by migration. Her parents were of East European origins: her father, Marcus, a lawyer, had fled his homeland of Poland for Germany during World War I to avoid military conscription; her mother, Eleonora, was born in Cologne to a German mother and a Russian father who was the cantor in Cologne's biggest synagogue. Jhabvala's "most basic childhood memory," as she recalls in "Disinheritance" (p. 5), is a picturesque family tableau dominated by the figures of her grandparents—grandmother at the piano, grandfather preparing to sing—in a heated room, the smell of tea cakes in the air, with aunts and uncles hovering around. The sense of stability implicit in this scene is one that Jhabvala would draw on decades later when describing the matriarchs and patriarchs of the European émigré families in her New York novels *In Search of Love and Beauty* (1983) and *Poet and Dancer* (1993), the strength of whose characters perfectly complements their heavy family furniture.

In the Germany of the 1930s, however, Adolf Hitler's rise to power ensured that such a tableau would become only a memory for Jewish families. Between 1933 and 1939 Jhabvala's grandparents died, and most of the aunts and uncles emigrated to other parts of Europe and the United States. In 1939 the Prawers took their son and daughter to England. Jhabvala speaks movingly in "Disinheritance" of those six years as the period from which that essay takes its theme and name.

I have slurred over the years 1933 to 1939, from when I was six to twelve. They should have been my most formative years; maybe they were, I don't know. Together with the early happy German-Jewish bourgeois family years—1927 to 1933—they should be that profound well of memory and experience (childhood and ancestral) from which as a writer I should have drawn. I never have. I've never written about those years. To tell you the truth, until today I've never even mentioned them. Never spoken about them to anyone. I don't know why not. I suppose they are the beginning of my disinheritance—the way they are for other writers of their inheritance.

(p. 6)

All of Jhabvala's father's relatives in Poland died in concentration camps during the war, and Marcus Prawer, overcome by the tragedy, ended his own life in 1948.

For Jhabvala, however, the decade following her emigration to England (1939–1949) was fruitful. It was then that she learned English and began to write in her adopted language. Even before the move, she had identified the writer's life as her destiny. "I was writing furiously all through my childhood" (p. 6), she says in "Disinheritance," and the fury continued throughout her school days in England as she produced prose fiction and plays "in a relentless stream" (p. 7), adapting easily both to writing in English and to writing about her new environs; she never wrote of the Germany she left behind. She immersed herself in the English classics—Dickens, Hardy, Eliot—and read James Joyce, James, Tolstoy, Fyodor Dostoevsky, Anton Chekhov: "This was the great gift, the inheritance, that England gave me: my education which became my tradition—the only tradition I had: that of European literature" (p. 7). Precious little of Jhabvala's mature fiction is set in England, however; her English training—elementary education at Hendon County School and university at Queen Mary College of London University from 1945 to 1951—supplied her with a literary tradition but did not bind her to England as subject. In 1949 she met an Indian architecture student named Cyrus Jhabvala at a party in London. Two years later, having completed her M.A. in English literature with a thesis titled "The Short Story in England, 1700–1750," she married him and, leaving her mother and brother behind, accompanied him to Delhi, where he was teaching architecture. She spent the next twenty-four years in India, during which time she launched both her career in fiction, culminating in the Booker Prize for *Heat and Dust* (1975), and her career in film, writing screenplays

for the filmmakers Ismail Merchant and James Ivory.

Having read Rudyard Kipling's *Kim* (1901) and Forster's *A Passage to India* (1924), Jhabvala considered herself familiar with India's literary landscape, but the actual landscape, so sublime in comparison with bleak, postwar England, amazed her. She describes her first ten years there as a protracted state of bliss; she was intoxicated by "the smells and sights and sounds of India—the mango and jasmine on hot nights—the rich spiced food—the vast sky—the sight of dawn and dusk—the birds flying about—the ruins—the music" ("Disinheritance," p. 8). Ever able to adapt to new homelands, Jhabvala, twenty-four years of age, sank into Indian life as deeply as she had once plunged into the imaginative world of English and European fiction. She and her husband and the three daughters born to them lived a "typical, middle-class Indian life" (Crane, 1992, p. 4); unlike some other European women in India—such expatriates as she would come to write about—she rarely socialized with Europeans. Cyrus Jhabvala's parents had both been involved in the struggle for India's independence from Britain, gained in 1947; it is almost as if Ruth Jhabvala, by her marriage, allied herself with that newly won independence and acted it out, distancing herself from her European ties and eventually becoming one of the forces that put the new India on the literary map. Her husband is of the Parsi community—itself a product of migration from Persia several centuries ago—a community that on the whole maintains a separate existence in India from its Hindu and Muslim compatriots. But through the couple's social life with Cyrus Jhabvala's colleagues and students, Ruth Jhabvala absorbed much information about other religious and social groups, especially the Hindu joint family, which would play a central role in her early Indian works. She began writing stories almost immediately upon arrival, stories peopled by her new countrymen and set in her new surroundings, and within two years she had completed her first manuscript, *To Whom She Will*.

EARLY INDIAN NOVELS

IT is easy to see why *To Whom She Will* (1955), published in America as *Amrita* in 1956, elicited enthusiastic comparisons to the work of Jane Austen. A sharply drawn, ironically narrated comedy of manners, the novel follows the trajectories toward marriage of a young man and woman foolishly attracted to one another, whose older relations steer them, not always gently, in more appropriate directions. Debts to Austen notwithstanding, Jhabvala's ability to weave the social and political realities of postcolonial India into the novel's plot development sets *To Whom She Will* apart as indubitably a product of India, unlike the book the author puts in the hands of her heroine.

It was a novel about India, written by an English lady: well-written too, Amrita could see that, all the proper accoutrements of style and sensibility, but Amrita could not understand why the lady had given Indian names to her characters.

(p. 220)

Amrita and her fellow characters could not have anything but Indian names, for the complex struggles posed by the novel between the young and the old, between modernity and tradition, represent the paradox of mid-twentieth-century India, a nation thousands of years old yet suddenly newly born.

The central narrative paradox concerns the two lovers. Amrita, a college-educated girl of twenty, comes from a westernized, well-to-do family. Hari is the elder son of a more traditional Punjabi Hindu family, one that was impoverished during Partition, when, because of their religion, they were forced, along with thousands of other families, to flee Pakistan. What makes the lovers' class-based conflict slightly more complicated than usual is that it cannot be resolved by Amrita raising Hari to her station—in the way that in Austen's *Pride and Prejudice,* Mr. Darcy's income raises Elizabeth Bennet to the level of social comfort we feel she deserves. While Hari would gladly move up the socioeconomic ladder, Amrita would rather move down to embrace what she feels are more authentically Indian customs. Fittingly for a comedy of manners, this discrepancy in their desires is first revealed at the dining table. Hari, who is used to eating with his hands, handles knife and fork awkwardly but would never dream of not using them for fear of appearing unmannered. Amrita, however, would rather he didn't use them at all, because she finds his "traditional, truly Indian ways" charming and assumes her familiarity with utensils will be one of many marks against her when she meets Hari's older sister.

"She may think I am very spoilt and westernized and affected; because my family have made me like that, I know it. I am afraid that your sister will despise that, and so she will not be able to like me. O Hari, often I worry about it, and then I am so grateful to you for not despising me for using knife and fork and speaking a lot in English and having been educated in a convent and at Lady Wilmot College."

Hari did not understand. The things for which she thanked him for not despising her were perhaps the things for which he loved and admired her most; and those for which he knew his sister would admire her the most. So, not understanding, he took refuge in murmuring, "My love for you is so great, surely it will break me."

(p. 24)

Their love is henceforth understood by the reader as a mutual misunderstanding; it grows not out of satisfaction with the other's merits but out of dissatisfaction with their own perceived shortcomings, all of which center on their respective social milieus.

This dissatisfaction is one of the major themes of the novel, for almost no one in it rests easily in his or her allotted place. Amrita's widowed mother, Radha, takes great pride in the memory of her husband, a supporter of Indian independence, but she must constantly reconcile this pride with the uncomfortable fact that idealistic crusaders tend to be poor, leaving their widows without motor cars. Krishna Sen Gupta, Radha's Bengali lodger and Amrita's eventual suitor, is still readjusting four years later to his native land after studying in England. His parents, like Amrita's father, had been imprisoned during the fight for India's independence, and he knows that however much he despises certain aspects of Indian life, he cannot abandon the nation they suffered to create. And Amrita's austere Aunt Tarla, surrounded by an opulence she does not notice, compensates for her wealth by standing on various committees to improve social welfare; her meetings are characterized by cries for "renewed effort," "duty and responsibility," and, above all, "Action!"—but the impassioned rhetoric is all too often undermined by unwelcome facts, as at Tarla's tea party early in the novel.

"Of course," said Tarla, in her best platform manner, "the greatest step forward was the abandonment of the idea of early marriage. We must be grateful that today Society is sufficiently advanced to think of women as something more than a mere marriageable commodity."

225

Dr. Mukherji made her second contribution to the conversation. "Last week," she said, "my sweeper's daughter was married. She is twelve."

(p. 32)

Tarla's claim is unfortunate not only because it draws an immediate refutation from the realist Dr. Mukherji but also because it turns our attention to Amrita, whose mother (Tarla's sister) most certainly thinks of her as a "marriageable commodity." These contradictions—between idealism and materialism, between the certainty of having "advanced" society and the coexisting certainty of stagnation—bring to the fore the question of social mobility, on the personal level, and society's mobility, on the collective level, in Jhabvala's Delhi.

The novel's American title, *Amrita*, underscores a reading of the book as a bildungsroman, a chronicle of Amrita's development from an infatuated young girl to a pragmatic woman whose choice of a life partner is clearly suitable from Radha's point of view and the reader's. But the original title of *To Whom She Will* gives us a different point of entry into Jhabvala's other early novels, touching on the theme of assimilation into a harmonious social fold with personal growth as a secondary part of the equation. The verse of the Vedic epic *Panchatantra* from which the line "To Whom She Will" derives, and which was used as an epigraph in the British edition, prescribes a moral code in which girls should be married off before puberty or run the risk of bringing shame to themselves and their families. Although Jhabvala could hardly be said to endorse such an extreme position, such critics as Haydn M. Williams accurately point out her tendency to write plots in which romantic love is subordinated to family order and social order; the Hindu joint family, in which extended families and in-laws often share one roof, acts as an emblem of the larger social system.

The conclusion of Jhabvala's second novel, *The Nature of Passion* (1956), reproduces this theme. In it Lalaji, a nouveau riche Hindu father—like Hari's family a refugee of Partition but a successful one—quickly arranges a marriage within his own community to protect his cherished daughter Nimmi from the scandal of having been seen with a Parsi boyfriend. The marriage Lalaji arranges is with the very boy to whom, by the end of the novel, Nimmi has independently found herself drawn. This neat resolution of romance and convenience is more suddenly imposed and less believable than in *To*

Whom She Will, and Nimmi's satisfied observation that "it was almost as good as having a proposal of marriage; almost as good as choosing one's own husband" (p. 188) only emphasizes to the reader that it was neither. Her lazy brother Viddi is also brought into the fold, convinced to join his father in the family business.

Yet the seemingly facile quality of this happy ending is undercut throughout by Lalaji's discomfort with his comfortable social position. From the first paragraph, which finds him sleeping outdoors rather than in his fashionable bedroom, with its "strange and unnecessary furniture" (p. 11), Jhabvala gives us a moving portrait of a well-meaning man who has made so much money that he has in effect become separated from the simpler lifestyle he loved. A permanent outcast from his ancestral home in the Punjab, Lalaji shares his feeling of displacement in Delhi with the anglicized Krishna Sen Gupta but also, significantly, with the many European characters of Jhabvala's subsequent early Indian novels.

Esmond in India (1957) is named for its hero, Esmond Stillwood, the first of these transplanted Europeans and by far the least likable. Esmond's profession produces the novel's central irony: he teaches courses on Indian culture to foreign women in India and is considered an expert on the local tourist attractions. By the time we learn how Esmond makes his living, however, we are already aware that he lacks the appreciation of Indian culture requisite to the trade. Gulab, his wife, sprays their apartment with DDT rather than let Esmond smell the Indian food she surreptitiously eats while he is away, and the servant, when addressed by his master in Hindustani, "wondered what the Sahib was saying; he could not even identify the language he was talking" (p. 33). As the novel progresses, we learn that Esmond's relationship to his adopted land and to his wife is characterized not only by false intimacy but by unmasked disgust bordering on violence. Although once charmed by Gulab's Indian ways, he now takes offense at her scent, her manners, her family, and what he calls her "babu English" (p. 38). Their hostile interactions indicate the most dire result of a clash of cultures, displacement. Neither spouse feels at home in the apartment—Gulab because of the alien, modern European furniture and Esmond because "she had succeeded somehow in superimposing her presence" on it (p. 39). The extremity with which Jhabvala presents this disastrous marriage of cultures, the psychological warfare the narrator depicts between the submissive Gulab and the dry, abusive Esmond, is nothing short of shocking. Esmond's viscerally negative reaction to India and things Indian acts as a warning that interaction between Westerners and Indians has as its potential a state of violence, of psychological and bodily harm. Esmond is best read as a hyperbolic prototype for the inflexible, incompatible European in India, a disruptive force in the Indian social fabric.

Esmond's sharply divided way of seeing the world draws attention to the significance of Jhabvala's use of setting throughout her work, especially in the context of the author's own eventual disillusionment with India. In her first novels, as critic Ralph Crane points out, Jhabvala's India is an idealized one; even when poverty is shown to exist, it tends not to intrude. Our sensory impressions from *To Whom She Will* and *The Nature of Passion* are primarily pleasant: sweet-smelling jasmine, aromatic cuisine, brightly colored saris and satins; even the fussy mothers and fathers have their children's best interests at heart. But as Jhabvala's own relationship with India became more conflicted—a relationship she outlines in her personal essay "Myself in India" (1966)—so does the Indian landscape she portrays. Esmond's discontent, though marked in the novel as a function of his churlish personality, foreshadows a negative India, of sweat and germs, heat and dust. Jhabvala's overarching theme of displacement requires that her depiction of place take on a meaning all its own; India unfolds in her oeuvre as a character in its own right and, more often than not, especially where Europeans are concerned, a source of conflict. The interior landscape is equally important. A household's material setting, always a clue to its inhabitants' social situation, holds the potential for enacting displacement. Lalaji's unfriendly bedroom suite and Gulab's stark, modern furniture draw our attention to how the characters fit their surroundings and to how those surroundings can render them strangers in their own land.

The hero of *The Householder* (1960), Prem, is a native of India but a stranger to Delhi and adulthood, and his struggle to adapt to the responsibilities of married life is the subject of the novel. A young Hindi instructor at a local college, Prem frets over anxieties that are highly personal—his unruly students, his unfamiliar new wife (with whom his marriage was arranged), his low salary, and his high rent—but they are also universal; they represent the difficulty of navigating the transition from dependence to independence. It is a transition that Prem is loath to make. Uncomfortable in his role as teacher, he waxes nostalgic about his carefree days as a student; uncomfortable in his role as husband, he longs for a visit from his indulgent mother so he can be treated as a son. This state of psychological anxiety is compounded by a corresponding anxiety about the body, specifically the sexual body.

In the novel's opening scene, Prem, on his way home from a lonely Sunday walk, buys a bag of nuts and raisins for his wife, Indu, but is so overcome by shyness at the thought of presenting her with it that he gobbles it down himself. Just two paragraphs later, we learn that Indu is expecting a child, but "her pregnancy was a terrible embarrassment for him. Now everybody would know what he did with her at night in the dark, as quickly and guiltily as he had eaten the nuts and raisins" (p. 8). The development of Prem's relationship with Indu from one of shyness and guilt, in which his desire to give is stifled by his inability to communicate, to one of mutual affection and sexual pleasure is fundamental to the novel's formula for maturation. Prem cannot consider himself a true "householder" (which, as critic Yasmine Gooneratne explains, is the second of four stages in life, according to the Hindu tradition) until he has come to terms with himself and Indu as sexual beings.

The Householder is typical of Jhabvala's early novels in that her ironic tone and comic voice turn many of its characters into caricatures. At a tea party hosted by Mr. Khanna, Prem's pompous superior, the stiffness of the ladies' posture creates a perfect backdrop for the stiffness of the host's conversation.

"Relaxation is necessary to the human mind as well as to the human body," said Mr. Khanna. "It is like a cool shower-bath we take on a hot day." Prem gave a polite laugh, but as no one else laughed, he realized that the remark had not been humorous. He brushed imaginary specks of dust from his knee. "Refreshed and revived," said the Principal, "we then resume our everyday duties with new vigour. I think we are all ready now for the tasty dishes which Mrs. Khanna has prepared."

Mrs. Khanna ceremoniously handed to each guest a quarter-plate of flowered English crocker. Everyone sat and held it and patiently waited.

(p. 73)

227

Indu provides comic relief by inserting pleasure into this awkward social milieu; when the sweet-meats come around she helps herself to a liberal plateful and digs in. "It was evident to Prem that Indu was by this time quite lost to her surroundings. She was continually biting, chewing, licking her fingers or flicking crumbs from her lips with her tongue. She seemed in a trance of enjoyment" (p. 74). Her behavior sends Prem into a state of panic, but her ability to transcend her surroundings illustrates the fundamental lesson Prem learns in the course of the novel: that the professional and financial problems plaguing him may never be resolved, but if he is to enjoy his life, he must rise above them when he can.

The other social gathering Prem attends in the novel is equally strained but this time for cross-cultural reasons. Befriended by a boisterous German called Hans who has come to India in search of spiritual fulfillment, Prem eagerly accepts his invitation to a party, but once there he finds himself mystified by the metaphysical rhetoric about his native land. Hans is the prototype, albeit crudely drawn, for the problematic figure of the spiritual seeker in India in Jhabvala's later books. His incessantly hyperbolic rhetoric and compulsion to interact with the natives—though never to listen to them—render his quest less than genuine, if not to Prem then to the reader. Significantly, however, Prem also comes off as pedantic: when Hans speaks of India's great soul, Prem replies by referring proudly to industrialization, steel plants, and the Five Year Plan. The contrast between Hans's assumption that Prem, by virtue of being an Indian, naturally possesses the ability to renounce the material world and the reality that Prem's concerns are overwhelmingly material represents a major tension in Jhabvala's work: whether India's fascinating spiritual tradition and its allure, especially to foreigners, can be reconciled with the material realities of the nation's present and the material problems of its native population.

LATER INDIAN NOVELS

IN 1960 Ruth Jhabvala paid her first visit to England since leaving it nearly a decade earlier, and when she came back, her vision of India had changed irrevocably. She had regained her European sensibility, she writes in "Disinheritance": "I

was no longer immersed in sensuous delight but had to struggle against all the things people do have to struggle against in India: the tide of poverty, disease and squalor rising all around; the heat—the frayed nerves; the strange, alien, often inexplicable, often maddening, Indian character" (p. 9). This description of India, far less conducive to the comic mode, colors all of Jhabvala's later Indian novels. Her new preoccupation with struggle as a way of life for both Indians and Europeans is perhaps nowhere more clearly articulated than in the title of her next novel, *Get Ready for Battle* (1962). Even the Hindu joint family, a reliable institution in her former work, has broken down in this novel; the party at the home of prosperous businessman Gulzari Lal in the opening scene is hosted by his mistress, Kusum, because Lal and his wife, Sarla Devi, have been separated for ten years.

Lal's estranged wife, a social activist, is the novel's link to Jhabvala's new India, and unlike Amrita's Aunt Tarla she is not all talk. Sarla Devi's work and her simple lifestyle bring the reader into direct contact with the poor and homeless who are the objects of her undivided attention. Instead of emanating from one character's consciousness, the squalor of India is now built into the narrative itself, as in this dispassionate rendering of a settlement Sarla Devi visits.

The colony was just off a busy main thoroughfare and she climbed down a bank by a railway bridge, into a kind of trough. Here there was a sea of huts, side by side, row upon row, tiny squat huts crowded one against the other. The colony was built out of the salvage that came floating down from a more prosperous world—rags and old bicycle tyres, battered tins and broken bricks. Walls were made of dried mud or of tattered matting, roofs were a patchwork of old tiles, rags and rusty sheets of tin held down at the corners by stones. Sarla Devi walked through the narrow lanes between the rows of huts. The earth was streaked with runnels of dirty water, vegetable waste and peels were trodden into the mud and scratched up again by mangy dogs and pigs and a few sick chickens.

(pp. 113–114)

Her presence in this landscape reminds us that Sarla Devi is always getting ready for battle. The end of the novel finds her in exactly the same place as the beginning, preparing to plunge yet again into what we are reasonably sure will be a fruitless struggle against the inexorable force of India's poverty. Jhabvala makes it difficult for us to sympathize fully with Sarla; her total absorption in social work leaves her blind to the interests of her son, Vishnu, who eagerly seeks her approval of his life choices but who does not share her priorities. Yet Sarla is a unique figure in the Jhabvala canon in that she is driven to action in the face of inevitable defeat and even, ironically, against her own spiritual desires. What she longs for is transcendence, but "all her life she had been tugged back by her compassion into a world where nothing could be accepted and everything had to be fought against. She was not even a good fighter, but still she felt she had to engage, like an enlisted soldier, and could not opt out" (p. 169).

The trio of European women at the center of Jhabvala's next Indian novel, *A Backward Place* (1965), cannot opt out of their connections with India either but for entirely different reasons. Etta, a native Hungarian, wants desperately to return to Europe—she even borrows the cry of Chekhov's three sisters: "Oh, to go to Moscow!"—but she cannot afford to leave. She follows Esmond's example of compensating for the outdoor scenery by turning her apartment into a continental oasis. Clarissa, originally from Britain, is sophisticated Etta's frumpy foil, clothed in ill-fitting, Indian peasant skirts; she was lured to India by its spiritual tradition, but her noisy enthusiasm masks a deep-seated loneliness. Judy, who of the three talks least about her relationship with India, is the one most intimately connected to it. Married to an Indian would-be actor, Bal, with whom she has two children, Judy has adapted quietly to Indian life. She speaks Hindustani fluently but with an accent, wears saris for convenience, and lives contentedly with her husband's family in a typical Indian neighborhood. But Judy's assimilation into Indian society has not erased her personality; rather, she is characterized by a self-assurance that sets her apart from the volatile Etta and the maladroit Clarissa.

Judy and Sudhir, a likable young intellectual reminiscent of *Amrita*'s Krishna Sen Gupta, work at the Cultural Dais, an organization for promoting international culture. The Dais provides a leitmotif of cultural mélange, culminating in a production of Ibsen's *A Doll's House* in Hindi at the end of the book. Jhabvala introduces the related subject of historical ties between East and West in India in this novel, foreshadowing, as Ralph Crane points out, the major role that British Raj society would play in *Heat and Dust* (Crane, 1992, p. 57). But here,

as in *Heat and Dust*, the institution of the Raj as an oppressive colonial system is meticulously separated from the issue of cross-cultural interactions on a personal level. Sudhir differentiates between the two after receiving a piece of unsolicited advice from Clarissa.

First he wanted to laugh. Then he wanted to be angry. He resented patronage of any sort, and to be patronized by a foreigner, a European, an Englishwoman of all people, was particularly distasteful. The hand laid on his shoulder seemed to him the pseudo-paternal hand of the British Raj, and his instinctive reaction was to want to shake it off as rudely and violently as possible. But then it struck him how foolish, how out of date this reaction of his was. There wasn't any British Raj any more, and here was only poor Clarissa, all on her own, who wanted nothing more than to have someone to talk to and who liked the company of young men. So he left her hand where it was, and he even bowed his head and looked thoughtful, to show how impressed he was by her words.

(pp. 123–124)

By placing the Raj in the historical past Sudhir remembers that it is he, not Clarissa, who holds the position of power in the present situation; by the end of the passage it is he who is patronizing her. Indeed, the vast differences among the three European women of *A Backward Place*—whose title represents only Etta's view of India—exist precisely to demonstrate the need to make such judgments on a personal basis. For Etta, India is backward, but for Judy it is home; for this reason, though they are both Europeans, they are also worlds apart.

In 1966 Jhabvala published an essay titled "Myself in India," a frank explication of the barriers she saw and set between herself and her adopted home. The significance of this essay for her fiction lies in its confession that the writer has effectively changed her subject. "I must admit that I am no longer interested in India," she writes. "What I am interested in now is myself in India" (*Out of India*, p. 13).

There is a cycle that Europeans—by Europeans I mean all Westerners, including Americans—tend to pass through. It goes like this: first stage, tremendous enthusiasm—everything Indian is marvelous; second stage, everything Indian not so marvelous; third stage, everything Indian abominable. For some people it ends there, for others the cycle renews itself and goes on. I have been through it so many times now that I think of myself as strapped to a wheel that goes round and round.

(p. 13)

The essay's pervasive imagery is of being separated yet simultaneously surrounded; Jhabvala stays in her room with the blinds drawn and the air conditioner on but the heat still bears down on her like a "physical oppression," and she knows herself "to be on the back of this great animal of poverty and backwardness" (pp. 19, 15). This, she admits, is the wrong way to live; she blames herself but leaves us with the knotty problem: "Should one want to try to become something other than what one is? I don't always say no to this question" (p. 21). To complicate matters, Jhabvala remarks at the end of the essay: "I also find it hard now to stand the European climate. I have got used to intense heat and seem to need it" (p. 21). The idea of studying selves in India not as cultural representatives but as individuals whose bonds with India are as conflicted as Jhabvala's own—who constantly question what it is they want to become—comes to the fore in the novels that followed this essay, *A New Dominion* (1972; U.S. title *Travelers*, 1973) and *Heat and Dust,* as the writer negotiates in fiction these issues of her last years of permanent residence in the subcontinent.

The primary "self" of the four main characters of *A New Dominion* is Lee, an English girl who is traveling around India "to lose herself in order—as she liked to put it—to find herself" (p. 2). The novel's divided structure—its many chapters are written as short vignettes, each focusing on one or more of the four main characters—allows Jhabvala to experiment with point of view, and Lee narrates some of her experiences in the first person. This is the first time the narrative "I" appears in one of Jhabvala's novels (it had already surfaced in her short stories); she does not use it frequently here but often enough to provide a vivid picture of Lee's interior landscape. Likewise, parts of the narrative of Raymond, the novel's other European, are in the first person, in letters he writes to his mother. Two Indians, Asha and Gopi, are the novel's other main characters. Asha, an older, wealthy woman of royal blood bored by her loveless life, enters into friendly competition with Raymond for the affection of Gopi, a young, middle-class student who thrives on their attention. Gopi, whose personal relations are marked chiefly by carelessness, resembles Hari of *To Whom She Will*; like Hari, he is

being pushed into an arranged marriage by his family but cannot bring himself to admit it to Asha for fear of losing her indulgent devotion.

Lee's spiritual quest leads her to an ashram outside of the holy city of Benares whose leader, Swamiji, then takes on a central role in the novel's tussle with religious belief. The character of the charismatic guru is a troublesome one for Jhabvala. As she explains in "Disinheritance," her skepticism of such holy men is counteracted by her desire to believe; she writes of the Indian swamis that she "loathed them. And yet at the same time always wishing: if only it could be.... I hated them for being what they were and not what they pretended to be, and what I wanted them to be" (p. 10). Likewise, of the Western girls who fell under their spells she writes: "I laughed at, even despised, them; but also envied them—for thinking they had found, or maybe—who am I to judge?—they had found, what I had longed to find" (pp. 10–11); and for much of the novel Lee finds herself caught in a comparable bind. She longs to emulate her fellow seekers Evie and Margaret, who have succeeded in prostrating themselves before Swamiji, but a mixture of pride and ambivalence, which we might interpret as self-preservation, prevents her from accepting their brand of peaceful submission. Jhabvala portrays Swamiji without much sympathy; his overt tactics of manipulation and sexual domination give the lie to his alleged spiritualism. Yet she cannot completely dismiss the potential value of the spiritual leader's role. She uses another guru figure in the novel, Asha's friend and spiritual guide Banubai, to disclose the irony inherent in the West's infatuation with finding such leaders.

For two hundred years you tried to make us believe that you are superior persons. But now the tables are turned. Now that your culture is bankrupt and your lives have become empty and meaningless, you are beginning to learn where truth has been hidden and stored away throughout the centuries. Even your scientists have learned this lesson.

(pp. 182–183)

Banubai ignores the possibility that the "truth" can be and is corrupted by India's own opportunists—the word "bankrupt" draws our attention to India's religion as a marketable commodity, and, indeed, Swamiji has plans to take his movement on a European fund-raising tour. But her outburst also serves as a reminder that for two hundred years the British in India had used their own methods of mental coercion. In the end, the narrative will not let us forget that, no matter what skeptics may think of Swamiji, Lee and her friends have sought him out of their own accord.

Near the end of the novel, witnessing the deterioration into illness of one of her ashram companions, Lee becomes preoccupied with "diseases that rot you away from within" (p. 189)—an ironic distortion of the inner purification sought at the ashram. This thematic movement inward toward the body's susceptibilities accompanies another new, outward focus in Jhabvala's use of setting: that of travel and movement. As Ralph Crane points out, *A New Dominion* opens with a travel scene that immediately distinguishes it from the domestic settings of the earlier novels; in fact, when the "family" of four characters eventually gathers at the only substantial home depicted in the book, Asha's father's "Retreat," they find that Asha's brother is preparing to sell the property to an Indian developer. Domestic instability would prove to be a hallmark of Jhabvala's New York novels, in which family units, unorthodox in a startling variety of ways, split themselves up over cities and continents just as their brownstone homes are split up into separate apartments. And all of these powerfully transformative elements—changes in the body, in the psyche, in the home, and in the landscape—converge in Jhabvala's acclaimed final novel of India, *Heat and Dust*, published in England in 1975 (U.S. edition, 1987).

Jhabvala's experimentation with shifting points of view in *A New Dominion* is refined in *Heat and Dust* into a meticulously crafted dual narrative structure linking a contemporary character's journey to India with a scandalous event that occurred fifty years earlier, during the colonial period. The lives of the present-day narrator (whose name we never learn) and her colonial-era counterpart, an Englishwoman named Olivia Rivers, are elegantly woven together in a series of pairings of place and circumstance. The narrator has come to India in part to explore its simpler lifestyle but also to "research" Olivia, who was the first wife of the narrator's grandfather Douglas before running off with an Indian prince, the nawab of Khatm, in 1923. The narrator's scholarly attitude—curious yet emotionally distant—toward Olivia (whose letters she carries) and toward India—as evidenced by her Hindi grammar and vocabulary books—lends her first-person account an authority that

Lee's commentary lacks. Above all, *Heat and Dust* is a superb example of Jhabvala's strengths of style and form: its structure proves integral to the plot by undermining the narrator's introductory claims that "this is not my story, it is Olivia's as far as I can follow it" (p. 2). The point is for the reader to recognize the similarities between their two interactions with India, so as to understand better the differences.

Olivia's separation from Indian society is partly due to her own tastes—her cool, European-furnished bungalow is nicknamed "The Oasis" by Harry, the nawab's English houseguest—but mostly it is institutional. The British civil servants around her live segregated lives and socialize with the nawab, the ruler of a neighboring state, generally as a group, expressing British solidarity. The young Olivia, however, is bored by the English matrons of her expatriate society and soon finds herself drawn into an intimate relationship with the charming nawab. The disastrous result is that she goes in too far, as Douglas's colleague Major Minnies puts it in his treatise on the effects of India on the English personality. Pregnant with a child whose paternity is in doubt, she arranges an Indian-style abortion and takes refuge from the scandal in the nawab's palace. She never returns to her husband or to England but disappears almost completely from public life in general, entering a purdahlike seclusion in the nawab's mountain retreat.

The narrator, too, has an intimate relationship with an Indian man—Inder Lal, with whose family she boards—but she incurs no accompanying scandal, because there is no longer a social apparatus to condemn her for going in too far. While Olivia bears certain resemblances to the European side of Jhabvala, shutting her doors and windows to keep out the heat and dust, the narrator embraces an Indian lifestyle with little restraint and little fanfare. She sleeps on a bedroll in Inder Lal's house, wears Indian clothes, and learns Hindi well enough to engage in meaningful conversation with the people around her. Although her perspective is realistically European—for example, she suggests psychiatric treatment for Inder Lal's wife, Ritu, who is subject to fits—she is aware that while she is getting used to Indian customs the Indians are also getting used to hers. Each of her interactions with Indians is marked by this consciousness of a reciprocal gaze—when Europe looks at India, India looks back. "I have already got used to being appraised," the narrator writes. "I suppose we must look strange to them, and what must also be strange is the way we are living among them—no longer apart, but eating their food and often wearing Indian clothes because they are cooler and cheaper." Later, she adds, "Although I'm now dressed like an Indian woman, the children are still running after me; but I don't mind too much as I'm sure they will soon get used to me" (pp. 8–9).

The narrator's adaptation to Indian life is accentuated by the number of foreigners she meets who have failed to adapt—who complain of dysentery, theft, jaundice, and general disillusionment. Their failure is personified in the character of Chid, an Englishman who has renounced his possessions to become a sadhu, or holy man. Although in his new spiritual state he claims to have no past, his Midlands accent gives his English origins away, and he writes home for money when his begging bowl is empty. Chid eventually succumbs to illness—"this climate does not suit you people too well" (p. 158), the doctor tells the narrator, when she takes Chid to the hospital. Disgusted with India, Chid returns to England, a parallel figure to Olivia's friend Harry, the nawab's guest, who leaves India in a similar state of mind at the end of the book. The doctor's warning, however, goes unheeded by the narrator—driven to know what could have made Olivia stay, she decides to do the same.

The awarding of the Booker Prize to *Heat and Dust* cemented Jhabvala's reputation in the West, but the novel met with a more negative reception in India. Some critics have attributed to the narrator's reflective tone an air of nostalgia for the Raj; others simply judged its description of heat, dust, and disease as an unfairly unfavorable portrait of India. From what we know of Jhabvala's ambivalence toward India, these criticisms seem incomplete. Indeed, many critics see in Jhabvala's work a response to the pessimistic ending of E. M. Forster's *A Passage to India*. Olivia's story is set in 1923, a year before the completion of Forster's novel, and her attraction to the glamorous nawab is an enactment of Adela Quested's desire to penetrate deeper into the "real" India, and Douglas Rivers and Ronny Heaslop stand together as stolid representatives of the British Raj. Nonetheless, the sentiment expressed in Forster's last paragraph—that East and West cannot yet meet as friends—is not the creed of *Heat and Dust*, particularly not for the narrator, whose interactions with India and Indians are marked by sincerity and success. And

unlike Jhabvala's other Western seekers in India, who go hoping to find self-awareness, the narrator has come to India to find not herself but Olivia: to connect with another. But in her retracing of Olivia's life she finds herself creating a new blueprint for her own.

NEW YORK NOVELS

IN 1975, Jhabvala left Delhi and moved to New York. She had lived in India long enough, she writes in "Disinheritance," and New York reminded her of Europe.

It is the most European city I can think of, with every kind of pocket of Europe inside it—German, Czech, Polish, Italian. . . . And literally I met the people who should have remained in my life—people I went to school with in Cologne, with exactly the same background as my own, same heritage, same parentage. Now here they were living in New York, as Americans, in old West Side apartments, with high ceilings and heavy furniture, just like the ones we grew up in in our Continental cities (as blissfully overheated as my grandparents' flat in Cologne), and with the delicatessen at the corner selling those very potato salads and pickled cucumbers and marinated herrings that our grandmothers used to make.

(p. 12)

If New York were only European, however, it would not be sufficient. The city also reminds her of India.

After India, can one ever really be satisfied with a country that is anything less than a continent? The way I usually put it is this: if you have for many years lived on a diet of hot spicy curries, how are you going to get used to boiled cabbage again? And as with one's sense of taste, so with all one's other senses and faculties, mental as well as physical.

(p. 14)

The novels Jhabvala has written since her move to New York reflect this combination of cultural appetites. Still attuned to the conflicts between East and West and the stresses of expatriation and acclimatization, she creates characters with mixed heritages and mixed feelings about them. Intercontinental travel replaces Indian tours, widening the novels' geographical range; their temporal scope widens too, so that where the Indian comic novels' action transpires over weeks or months, *Three Con-*

tinents spans two years, and *Shards of Memory,* with its two halves titled "Antecedents" and "Legacy," follows four generations. Embracing familiar themes, the New York novels shift the stage on which Jhabvala's characters perform from local to global, and the events they narrate range from comic to disquieting to tragic.

The title of *In Search of Love and Beauty* (1983), as Laurie Sucher rightly remarks, might apply to all of Jhabvala's novels (Sucher, p. 168); as such, it indicates a clear thematic continuity between the Indian and American works. Here the search centers around the charismatic figure of Leo Kellermann, an émigré from Western Europe whose theories of self-actualization attract a following so large that he eventually founds an institute, the Academy of Potential Development, in upstate New York. When he first arrives in Manhattan in the 1930s, he attracts the attention of a married woman named Louise, and the novel, narrated in flashbacks, tells the story of his decades' long relationship with her, her daughter, and her grandchildren.

In Search of Love and Beauty distinguishes itself from the Indian novels, however, in the way it overtly pulls together elements of Jhabvala's personal geography and history. Like Jhabvala's parents, Louise and her husband, Bruno, have emigrated from Germany. Their daughter, Marietta, entranced by Indian music and culture, spends much of her adult life traveling to India. But perhaps the most interesting episode from this point of view is the history of Marietta's adopted daughter, Natasha, "whose presence among them was a result of Marietta's search for identity; or rather, Marietta's rejection of her husband's identity" (p. 23).

Tim's family was as American as one could get—they had come, on his mother's side, from Scotland, on his father's from Ireland—and when, after less than a year of marriage, Marietta became disillusioned with Tim, this feeling extended itself to his family, and from them to their entire race and nation. Then she wanted to get back to her own roots, though she had to disentangle them first, since Louise, her mother, was a German Protestant, and Bruno, her father, a German Jew. Marietta decided on this latter part of her heritage: and when, in one of the spurts of energy with which she followed herself through, she decided to adopt a sister for Mark, she set about finding a one-hundred-percent-guaranteed Jewish child. This Natasha turned out to be.

(pp. 23–24)

Marietta's conflation of personal identity and heritage with "entire race and nation" places Jhabvala's own concerns with rootlessness and disinheritance, as well as her Jewish background, in the novel's spotlight. While Leo's philosophies focus on identity as existing in the future ("potential development"), there is, Jhabvala reminds us, an equally significant part of identity that is located in the past. Quests for identity, therefore, travel simultaneously backward and forward in time, a point made eloquently clear by the novel's mesmerizing use of flashbacks.

Three Continents (1987), a novel that follows wealthy twins Harriet and Michael Wishwell from their Long Island family estate, Propinquity, on their quest for spiritual fulfillment, also addresses issues of identity, but in this case there is little hope for development. Harriet, who narrates the novel, explains at the outset that, perhaps from having spent "some crucial years in the Middle East and then farther East," she and her brother have always felt a "restlessness, or dissatisfaction with what was supposed to be our heritage—that is, with America" (p. 11). Their remedy takes the shape of the Transcendental Internationalism movement, as embodied in a spiritual trio with mysterious Eastern origins, one of whom, Crishi, Michael had met while traveling in Delhi. Crishi, along with the rawul, ruler of a tiny Indian kingdom, and the exotic Rani, accepts Michael's invitation to Propinquity, and, once there, the three insinuate themselves into the twins' lives—taking over their property and their psyches in a cultural reversal, as Ralph Crane says, in which the East colonizes the West (Crane, 1992, p. 113). Although Harriet doubts their sincerity at first, she eventually becomes the Transcendental Internationalism movement's most devoted convert, entering into a strangely casual yet emotionally charged marriage with Crishi, who has also been Michael's lover.

Harriet and Michael accompany the trio to London and finally to India, where their association ends in tragedy. Crishi seduces Harriet into a state of complete sexual dependence. She rarely speaks of attempting to achieve any kind of transcendence—on the contrary, most of her time in London is spent by the telephone waiting for him to call. Although aware of his control over her, she is unable to acknowledge his faults and the corresponding faults of the movement. Her trajectory from the beginning of the book, which finds her shocked by her mother's and brother's desire to donate their home to the trio, to the end, when she willingly signs away her own substantial inheritance, is presented by Jhabvala not as development but as regression, an unnatural inversion of the bildungsroman. Harriet tells her own story, but her naivete reminds us that she has only the limited viewpoint of the disciple at her disposal, leaving no doubt that as her opinion of the movement grows more positive, Jhabvala's grows more negative. Laurie Sucher points out that the book was criticized by reviewers for this very reason—Harriet's narrative incompetence. On a structural level, the divergence between author and narrator, couched in the gradual revelation of Harriet's lack of intelligence and judgment, creates a distance between the reader and the novel that is profoundly disturbing. In the end, we are as disillusioned by Harriet as she ought to be by Crishi.

The plot of *Poet and Dancer* (1993) also revolves around a self-destructive relationship, this time between two cousins, Angel and Lara. Their first meeting, when Lara is seven and Angel eight, sets the tone for their future connection. Precociously aware of sexual pleasure, Lara shows Angel how to stimulate her, and uses her hand to stimulate Angel, but she stops as soon as she is satisfied, leaving Angel with a sense of overwhelming deprivation mixed with a physical and emotional dependence she cannot explain. When they are reunited as adults, Lara continues this domination; more glamorous and worldly than her cousin, she controls their relationship until it resembles an abusive marriage. Her doctor father is forever prescribing unnamed pills that Angel lovingly administers—presumably medication for psychological problems—but Angel remains stubbornly unwilling to consider Lara anything short of perfect. The reader waits in vain for the moment of disillusionment, but for Angel, as for Harriet, it never comes.

The novel's central concern with the harm one human being can inflict on another is chillingly expressed in the foreword, in which Jhabvala—explaining that Angel's mother has asked her to write the story of her daughter—interviews a waiter who had known the two girls during their youth.

I asked him about Angel and Lara. He still didn't have much to say about them—it was long ago, after all, and much had happened to him since. In the end I asked him outright if he thought that Lara had suffered from some form of schizophrenia or other severe personality disorder. He dismissed this quite contemptuously. "She wasn't mad," he said. "Just bad. People are, believe it or not," he added. "You can call it by all the fancy names you please, but that's what it is. There are good people trying to do all right, and there are bad ones that pull them down and win." I could see from the expression on his face that he was no longer answering my question, but speaking out of his own experience of living and working in the city.

(pp. 8–9)

His words touch on the novel's subplot as well, which involves an Indian family, Mrs. Arora and her son, Rohit, friends of Angel and her mother. The reason for their departure from India is revealed in the story of Rohit's brother Vikram, whose personal magnetism is a match for Lara's; he "had always had something irresistible about him, especially to his mother . . . but when Vikram grew older, he no longer wheedled, he demanded" (p. 142). Robbery and murder land him in prison, and after he dies there in a brawl the Aroras move abroad to escape the scandal. But as Rohit describes his mother's continuing devotion to Vikram, we are reminded of Angel's inexorable pull toward Lara, her desire to take care of her, and her ability to overlook all of Lara's wrongdoings if only she can be assured of her love. Lara and Vikram, though not religious figures, inspire in their relationships a deferential attitude reminiscent of Swamiji's followers in *A New Dominion*. Jhabvala makes the connection early in the novel, when the narrator notes that Lara is suspicious of the Aroras, "for she tended to associate all Indians with the manipulative holy men" whom her believing mother had taken her to as a child (p. 41). In *Poet and Dancer*, it is Lara herself who assumes the role of manipulative holy man, playing careless guru to Angel's careful disciple.

Shards of Memory (1995), like *In Search of Love and Beauty*, traces the effect of a spiritual movement over generations of its participants, eventually zeroing in on the great-grandson, Henry, who inherits the mantle of leadership from an Eastern guru called the Master. The novel is narrated chronologically; it begins with a first-person account, dictated into a tape recorder by Henry's grandmother, Baby.

I'm not really the right person to tell you anything because my thoughts—if I have any at all, my husband would have said—are not very orderly. If I tried to get things in order I would have to go back to my mother and the Kopf family, or my father and the Bilimorias. Kopf and Bilimoria: New York via nineteenth-century Germany and Bombay—here you can already see how mixed up everything is going to be, apart from the jumble inside my head.

(p. 10)

Baby's muddled rhetoric foreshadows the novel's complicated familial apparatus, in which, almost without exception, every set of parents amicably separates and every child is transplanted from home, usually crossing an ocean, and raised by grandparents or even great-grandparents. The contradiction here is clear: although family members abound as individuals, constantly appearing, interfering, and disappearing, the family is strikingly absent as an institution, with the result that it is never quite clear in any familial relationship where authority lies. Henry, as keeper of the Master's flame, takes it upon himself to restore order; indeed, it is he who puts all the relevant material together, for the second section of the narrative, after Baby's dictation, is "mostly based on Henry's research" (p . 41). But ironically, although Henry's ostensible mission is to sort out the Master's papers and journals, chronicling the leader's life and work, the novel that results—the novel we read— is a history less of the Master than of Henry's divided family and of Henry himself.

Shards of Memory reminds us of one of the most striking aspects of the New York novels as a group: the way in which they relentlessly attack the concept of family. In *Poet and Dancer,* for example, the family descends from stability to chaos. Angel's German grandparents, Siegfried and Anna, happily married with a daughter and a son, represent the perfect nuclear family. But Lara's entrance into Angel's world introduces familial pandemonium. She estranges Angel from her mother, initiates an affair with Angel's father (her aunt's ex-husband, who has his own wife and children), and eventually stakes her claim to the brownstone home in which Siegfried and Anna lived and Angel has spent her whole life. In *Three Continents* the family starts out on an unorthodox plane—Harriet and Michael live with their mother and her longtime lesbian companion, while their father contemplates remarriage with a considerably younger woman—but Crishi proves able to upset the one bond that still seems undissolvable, that between twin brother and sister. Not coincidentally, he also stakes a claim to their property. Jhabvala has trav-

eled a long way from her early portrayals of the Hindu joint family and its comical householders; in her later work, individuals exist without sanctuary. For them, as for her, the idealized family is chiefly a memory.

SHORT STORIES

JHABVALA began sending stories to the *New Yorker* and other magazines shortly after finishing her first few novels; by the time she left India, she had published three volumes—*Like Birds, Like Fishes and Other Stories* (1963); *A Stronger Climate: Nine Stories* (1968); *An Experience of India* (1971). *How I Became a Holy Mother and Other Stories* followed in 1976. In 1986 she published *Out of India,* selected stories from those volumes, with her essay "Myself in India" as its introduction; the *New York Times Book Review* selected it as one of the best books of the year. And in 1998, as a reflection of her now divided time between the United States and India, she published a collection, well received by the press, called *East into Upper East: Plain Tales from New York and New Delhi.* Where *Heat and Dust* speaks to Jhabvala's literary relationship with E. M. Forster, this latest title reminds us of another of her predecessors in the traditions of both the short story form and the Anglo-Indian subject: Rudyard Kipling, whose *Plain Tales from the Hills* propelled him to fame in 1888 and introduced English readers to the sublime landscape of India and the problems it poses for Western visitors.

Jhabvala does well to align herself with Kipling—his mastery of the short story form did much to establish the genre as a serious art, and she is an apt practitioner of that art. Her themes of displacement and searches for meaning, expressed so powerfully in her novels, are in fact peculiarly suited to the conventions of the short story, in which the requisite economy of language and detail allows the writer to hone in on an individual's struggle. Jhabvala does so in a number of ways, most noticeably by her use of point of view. While only one of her novels, *Three Continents,* is fully told in the first person, seven of the fifteen stories in *Out of India* make use of first-person narration, intimately involving the reader with a range of characters both Indian and European. We can place these characters along the continuum between self-awareness and self-deception—a continuum crucial to an understanding of Jhabvala's fiction—by what they reveal, what they conceal, and how they tell their stories.

The guileless Indian narrator of "My First Marriage," for example (*Out of India*, pp. 23–38), foreshadows Harriet Wishwell in her inability to be disillusioned. Now engaged to the same fiancé she had left to make her first marriage, the narrator recounts the story of her attachment to a man, "M," whose goal is to instruct in moral training; as it turns out, he is a bigamist with wanderlust who eventually disappears. Nevertheless, the narrator remains under the absent M's spell, chooses her words carefully to defend his actions, and considers herself, like his first wife, "as a candle burning for him with a humble flame" (p. 29). By contrast, the narrator of "The Man with the Dog" (*Out of India*, pp. 107–123) displays an admirable awareness of the paradoxical romantic position in which she finds herself. Also an Indian woman, this narrator is a widowed grandmother whose continuing affair with a Dutchman, Boekelman, enrages her family. With his meticulous grooming, his rolled-up English umbrella, and his European lady friends, Boekelman resembles Esmond Stillwood, a resemblance that is unfortunately borne out when, in a rage directed at a servant, he shouts in front of the narrator and her son that Indians are "Monkeys! Animals!" (p. 118). If this were a political story, Boekelman would have to go, but from the narrator's fondly phrased, minutely detailed descriptions of her lover—from his eau de cologne to his pampered dog—we know that it is a love story; although she understands rationally why her children despise him, still she cannot do without him. "It is a riddle," she says simply (p. 123), ending the story by cogently summing up the nature of passion.

Jhabvala's short stories also showcase her skill at creating a mood. The chilling subject matter of "Desecration" (*Out of India*, pp. 269–288) is emphasized by the voice of a disembodied narrator, distanced by perspective and time; in this story, Jhabvala relies on mood and setting to underscore tragedy. "It is more than ten years since Sofia committed suicide in the hotel room in Mohabbatpur," the story begins, casting a shadow over all that follows; the hotel is no longer there, nor the house where she and her wealthy husband, the raja sahib, had lived, and "now almost no one remembers the incident or the people involved in it" (p. 269). Sofia's doomed affair with Bakhtawar Singh, the lo-

cal chief of police, takes place in an atmosphere charged with unrest, anxiety, and violence: the dust storms in the barren terrain, "when the landscape all around was blotted out by a pall of desert dust" (p. 270); Sofia's tendency to nervous prostrations; and Singh's reputation as a "ruthless disciplinarian" (p. 272). The beginning of a later story, "Expiation," provides a similar atmosphere of foreboding. The narrator shivers outside prison gates on a cold winter's day waiting to claim the body of his youngest brother, who has been executed for kidnapping and killing a young boy. The narrator's conflicted emotions toward this favorite brother are represented in the words carved over the gates, which he cannot stop reading: "Hate the Sin but Not the Sinner" (*East into Upper East*, pp. 3–4).

The effective way in which Jhabvala begins these two stories with their conclusions demonstrates her unfailing attention to narrative structure. This attention is particularly important to the form of the short story, whose brevity precludes the more discursive rhetoric and looser form available to the novelist. "Desecration" communicates the horror of Sofia's suicide, all the more powerful for its absence, by transcending its own narrative time frame, using two episodes of displaced action as symbolic representations of events that do not occur within the bounds of the story. The first involves Sofia's and her lover Singh's first meeting, when she witnesses him beating one of his men and tells him afterward, "There is blood on your hand" (p. 275). These are the same words that could be said to him regarding her suicide, but the story ends before reaching that point; though ten years dead at the beginning of the story, she is alive at its conclusion, her suffering and her husband's suffering frozen in time. The second displacement occurs when Sofia, pleading on behalf of a servant her husband has decided to dismiss, throws herself at the raja sahib's feet and begs him in vain to forgive. The story's final paragraphs indicate that the raja sahib suspects his wife's infidelity, but because of his deafness to her earlier plea she is never brave enough to ask for forgiveness on her own behalf—instead, she "would have to go on bearing it by herself for as long as possible, though she was not sure how much longer that could be" (*Out of India*, p. 288).

Jhabvala plays with the reader's structural expectations in "A New Delhi Romance" (*East into Upper East*, pp. 91–114), whose title, indicating a single romantic plotline, masks the dual nature of the story, in which a blossoming romance withers while a withered love finds new life. The comic aspects of the latter temper the tragic aspects of the former, and both, ingeniously, center around a single bed. Indu, a woman who has married beneath her, lives apart from her husband in a small flat with her student son, Arun, who is in the habit of bringing his girlfriend, Dipti, home during the afternoons to the only bed in the house, his mother's. When a political scandal descends upon Dipti's household, it drives a wedge between the two young lovers, and eventually Dipti becomes engaged to another man. But at the same time, the reappearance of Arun's lively, sentimental father, Raju, reminds Indu of their passionate youth, and soon the older couple replaces the younger couple on the bed, a testimonial to Raju's faith in romance in the face of his son's bitter emotional defeat. The structure of this story, with its opposing romantic trajectories, allows it, too, to transcend the bounds of narrative time, for while Arun and Dipti find disappointment in their future, Raju and Indu find satisfaction in their past.

The common denominator among Jhabvala's dozens of short stories, however, may simply be the potency of her language:

Raju was nearly forty, he did not have an easy life—he told no one about the many shifts he had to resort to in Bombay, to keep himself going in between assignments, which often fell through, or were never paid for. Nevertheless, he had not changed from the time he had been a student in Delhi and used to creep up to the roof of Indu's parents' house. She often had to put her hand over his mouth to keep him from waking everyone up, for in his supreme happiness he could not refrain from singing out loud—he knew all the popular hits as well as more refined Urdu lyrics, and they all exactly expressed what he felt, about her, and the stars above them, and the white moonlight, and the scent of jasmine drenching the air around them.

(p. 112)

The length of the last sentence, the crescendo of the final clause, its accumulation of sensory impressions—sound, sight, scent—all give authenticity to Raju's emotion, transporting his past happiness into the present moment. Consequently they give authenticity to Jhabvala's story, whose resolution depends on the resurrection of that glorious moment on the roof.

FILMS

In a scene in the novel *The Householder*, Prem lectures his landlord's son on the importance of academics but meets with a decidedly negative response.

"I find studies very boring," Romesh said. "I like only pictures very much."
"What will you learn from going to pictures? This is only amusement for an idle hour."

(p. 39)

Given the disdain for the film industry Jhabvala expresses in this novel, it is ironic that James Ivory and Ismail Merchant called her, in 1961, to ask her to adapt it for the screen. She agreed, and the three have since collaborated on nearly twenty projects, resulting in—among other honors—Jhabvala's Academy Award for her adaptation of Forster's *A Room with a View*. In interviews Jhabvala has said definitively that involvement in films has affected her fiction technique. Critics such as Yasmine Gooneratne point to correspondences between the traveling Jhabvala did while researching and shooting films and her characters' increased travels around India; between the historical research Jhabvala did for films that draw on India's past and leaps in time in *Heat and Dust*; and between cinematic cuts and flashbacks and Jhabvala's own narrative cuts and flashbacks in such novels as *A New Dominion, Heat and Dust,* and *In Search of Love and Beauty*. There are also ways, conversely, in which writing for film draws on skills Jhabvala already possessed: her ear for speech patterns, for example, which is especially apparent in the early Indian novels and stories, in which she captures the inverted phrasing, idioms, and translated vernacular typical of Indian-English. More generally, Jhabvala's screenplays, in combination with Merchant-Ivory's attention to cultural and period detail, have resulted in a body of films that, as is often said, distance themselves from most mainstream productions by virtue of their literariness—a quality at least in part attributable to Jhabvala's literary touch.

Like *The Householder, Shakespeare Wallah* (1966), Jhabvala's first original screenplay, takes shots at the popular film industry; it also represents the decline of British influence in independent India. The Buckingham Players, a traveling troupe of actors performing Shakespeare in local Indian towns, find themselves playing to empty houses, their audiences lured away by the less erudite films of the prolific Indian cinema. Caught between these two worlds is Sanju (Shashi Kapoor), a wealthy young man who has an attachment to the glamorous film star Manjula (Madhur Jaffrey) but finds himself drawn to Lizzie Buckingham (Felicity Kendal), the daughter of the troupe's leaders, and to the Shakespearean tradition the Buckinghams represent. Lizzie has spent her whole life in India, but by the end of the film her parents decide "there's no future for her here, neither as an actress nor—just no future" (*Savages and Shakespeare Wallah*, 1973, p. 129); her relationship with Sanju ends, and she boards a boat for England. The Buckinghams' words clearly resonate with the end of the British Raj, and in this light, Lizzie's departure is an apt resolution. But the comically vain and vapid film star—"I am Manjula! When I come, hundreds, thousands follow me!" (p. 141)—speaks to Jhabvala's anxiety about the possibility of a homegrown cultural imperialism. In *Shakespeare Wallah*, British culture may be irrelevant, but Indian pop culture, albeit indigenous, poses a definitive threat to the cultivation of the mind.

Many of Jhabvala's screen adaptations have stemmed from her own literary tastes. In his book on Merchant-Ivory films, Robert Long writes that Jhabvala prompted James Ivory to read the novels of Henry James and Jean Rhys, leading to the productions of *The Europeans*, *The Bostonians*, and Rhys's *Quartet*. Future projects include *The Golden Bowl* (Long, pp. 112, 253). It was Ivory who suggested *A Room with a View*, and Jhabvala, with her talent for exploring personal relations in a lightly comic mode, proved well able to handle Forster, garnering an Academy Award for that screenplay and a nomination for her work on *Howards End*. She also earned praise for her adaptation of Kazuo Ishiguro's Booker Prize–winning novel *The Remains of the Day*.

But it is perhaps most instructive to consider Jhabvala's screen adaptation of her own novel *Heat and Dust* as an example of how her fiction complements her cinematic techniques, and vice versa. In the novel, transitions between past and present scenes focus on the narrator retracing, whether consciously or unconsciously, Olivia's footsteps. The homes of the old British civil lines have, fittingly, been converted into office spaces, giving the narrator the surreal opportunity to visit Olivia's home every time she posts her letters.

Towards evening I sometimes go to the post office which is situated in what used to be Olivia's breakfast room. If it is about the time when the offices close, I walk over to the Crawfords' house to wait for Inder Lal. Both houses—the Crawfords' and Olivia's—once so different in their interiors are now furnished with the same ramshackle office furniture, and also have the same red betel stains on their walls. Their gardens too are identical now—that is, they are no longer gardens but patches of open ground where the clerks congregate in the shade of whatever trees have been left. Peddlers have obtained licenses to sell peanuts and grams. There are rows of cycle stands with a cycle jammed into every notch.

(pp. 48–49)

This continuity of architectural forms—despite the buildings' changes in function—is Jhabvala's key strategy in recounting her parallel narratives, and it translates seamlessly into film. The film, which like the novel is narrated alternately in flashbacks and in the present, relies on constants of setting and space both to make visual connections between the narrator's story and Olivia's and to accentuate the radical changes that have taken place in the intervening fifty years. Jhabvala's crowning aesthetic achievement in *Heat and Dust*, both novel and film, is the weaving of Olivia's and the narrator's lives so that each one's story helps interpret the other's. Not coincidentally, the novel and the film share the same reciprocity.

CONCLUSION

There's a saying, and I can't (characteristically enough) remember whether it is a Jewish, or a Muslim, or a Hindu, or a Buddhist one: "It is forbidden to grow old." I take that to mean that one just has to go on—learning, being—throughout however many twenty-year stretches in however many different countries or places—actual physical ones or countries of the mind—to which one may be called.

("Disinheritance," p. 14)

Ruth Jhabvala is still being called to many countries. She divides her time between New York—where she lives in the same building as Merchant and Ivory—and New Delhi, where her husband, with whom she maintains a close relationship, still resides permanently. Her three children live in America, England, and India—in the same three continents of Jhabvala's novel of that name. Her personal geography has served literature well, from her novels of Delhi life, which speak from their local settings to the universality of the human condition, to her later explorations of personal quests across nations, drawn from the wider world of human experience. Out of her disinheritance, Ruth Jhabvala has created a body of work that is itself a legacy—one that, in accordance with her proverb, is unlikely to grow old.

SELECTED BIBLIOGRAPHY

I. NOVELS. *Amrita* (New York, 1989; orig. pub. *To Whom She Will*, London, 1955; *Amrita*, New York, 1956); *The Nature of Passion* (London, 1986; orig. pub. London, 1956); *Esmond in India* (New York, 1990; orig. pub. London, 1957); *The Householder* (London, 1985; orig. pub. London, 1960); *Get Ready for Battle* (London, 1978; orig. pub. London, 1962); *A Backward Place* (London, 1965); *Travelers* (New York, 1987; orig. pub. *A New Dominion*, London, 1972; *Travelers*, New York, 1973); *Heat and Dust* (New York, 1987; orig. pub. London, 1975); *In Search of Love and Beauty* (New York, 1992; orig. pub. London, 1983); *Three Continents* (New York, 1988; orig. pub. London, 1987); *Poet and Dancer* (New York, 1993); *Shards of Memory* (New York, 1995).

II. VOLUMES OF SHORT STORIES. *Like Birds, Like Fishes and Other Stories* (London, 1963); *A Stronger Climate: Nine Stories* (London, 1968); *An Experience of India* (London, 1971); *How I Became a Holy Mother and Other Stories* (London, 1976); *Out of India: Selected Stories* (London, 1986); *East into Upper East: Plain Tales from New York and New Delhi* (London and Washington, D.C., 1998).

III. PERSONAL ESSAYS. "Disinheritance," in *Blackwood's Magazine* (July 1979); "Myself in India" (as the introduction to *An Experience of India*, 1966; reprinted as introduction to *Out of India*, 1986).

IV. SCREENPLAYS. *The Householder* (based on her novel, 1963); *Shakespeare Wallah*, (with James Ivory, 1966; published in *Savages and Shakespeare Wallah*, London, 1973); *The Guru* (with Ivory, 1968); *Bombay Talkie* (with Ivory, 1970); *Autobiography of a Princess* (1975); *Roseland* (1977); *Hullabaloo over Georgie and Bonnie's Pictures* (for British television, 1978); *The Europeans* (with Ivory, based on the novel by Henry James, 1979); *Jane Austen in Manhattan* (1980); *Quartet* (with Ivory, based on the novel by Jean Rhys, 1981); *Heat and Dust* (based on her novel, 1983); *The Bostonians* (based on the novel by James, 1984); *A Room with a View* (based on the novel by E. M. Forster, 1986); *Madame Sousatzka* (with John Schlesinger, based on the novel by Bernice Rubens, 1988); *Mr. and Mrs. Bridge* (based on the novels *Mrs. Bridge* and *Mr. Bridge* by Evan S. Connell, 1990); *Howards End* (based on the novel by Forster, 1992); *The Remains of the Day* (based on the novel by Kazuo Ishiguro, 1993); *Jefferson in Paris* (1995); *Surviving Picasso* (based on the book *Picasso: Creator and Destroyer* by Arianna Stassinopoulos Huffington, 1996); *A Soldier's Daughter Never Cries* (based on the novel by Kaylie Jones, 1998).

V. CRITICAL STUDIES AND INTERVIEWS. Yasmine Gooneratne, *Silence, Exile and Cunning: The Fiction of Ruth Prawer Jhabvala* (New Delhi, 1983); Bernard Weinraub, "The Artistry of Ruth Prawer Jhabvala," interview in the *New York Times Magazine* (11 September 1983); David Rubin, "Ruth Jhabvala in India," in *Modern Fiction Studies* 30, no. 4 (winter 1984); Bruce Bawer, "Ruth Prawer Jhabvala," in *New Criterion* (December 1987); Laurie Sucher, *The Fiction of Ruth Prawer Jhabvala: The Politics of Passion* (New York, 1989); Ramlal G. Agarwal, *Ruth Prawer Jhabvala: A Study of Her Fiction* (New Delhi, 1990); Ralph J. Crane, editor of *Passages to Ruth Prawer Jhabvala*, collected essays (New Delhi, 1991), author of *Ruth Prawer Jhabvala* (New York, 1992); Jayanti Bailur, *Ruth Prawer Jhabvala: Fiction and Film* (New Delhi, 1992); Robert Emmet Long, *The Films of Merchant Ivory* (New York, 1997).

JAMES KELMAN

(1946–   )

Angus R. B. Cochran

SINCE THE EARLY 1980s James Kelman has been perhaps the most prominent figure in Scotland's literary revival. From the time his fiction first came to the attention of reviewers, he has been hailed as one of the most experimental postwar writers in the English language, due to his use of vernacular English and his working-class subjects. In an early statement prefacing his stories in *Three Glasgow Writers* (1976), Kelman announced the conditions of his work in a personal manifesto:

I was born and bred in Glasgow
I have lived most of my life in Glasgow
It is the place I know best
My language is English
I write
In my writings the accent is in Glasgow
I am always from Glasgow and I speak English always
Always with this Glasgow accent

This is right enough

(p. 51)

Drawing from his own roots to represent Glaswegian culture in his literature, Kelman declares that his allegiance is with the working classes, whose urban slang and Scots cadences he reproduces in his fiction. As an author he has invented an aesthetic form that counters the marginalization of the Scots within English literature. In Kelman's literature the working classes speak for themselves. Yet the twentieth-century desire to represent working-class culture and urban subjectivity from the inside has a long and storied past, and Kelman's creations build upon earlier models, particularly those offered by James Joyce's *Dubliners* (1914) and *Ulysses* (1922), by Samuel Beckett's painful monologues in *Three Novels* (1955–1956), and by Franz Kafka's sinister evocation of institutional power in *The Castle* (1926). Along with his peers Alasdair Gray, Tom Leonard, Liz Lochhead, and Jeff Torrington, and younger authors such as Irvine Walsh, Iain

Banks, A. J. Kennedy, and Duncan McLean, James Kelman is producing a portrait of contemporary urban Scotland that is free from condescension and cliché.

LIFE

BORN in Govan, a dockside district of Glasgow, on 9 June 1946, James Kelman grew up as one of five brothers in a family of modest means supported by his father, Ronald, a framemaker and picture restorer. Although not a very enthusiastic pupil, Kelman discovered reading early on, through the Elder Library in Govan. He told Anthony Quinn of the *Independent:* "There was no TV in those days, so I was exposed to books, as most working-class kids are, through the library. . . . The library is a place that's free to go to, it's warm, that's why working-class people use them" ("Category A Literature," p. 26). Early on, Kelman was drawn to American writers such as Louis L'Amour and Jack Kerouac, and in adulthood he read Katherine Anne Porter, William Carlos Williams, Charles Olson, and Robert Creeley. In fact, for a short time as a teenager, Kelman lived with his family in Los Angeles, where his father worked in a gallery. Kelman's attraction to American literature, he told the novelist Duncan McLean, was based in its realist evocation of working life:

The things I like to read about, and that I was interested in when I started to write, you know, like snooker, going to the dogs, standing in betting shops, eh, getting drunk . . . all these things weren't a part of literature, you know, apart from Russian, European and American literature. It didn't happen in English literature. In English literature the working class were always servants.

("James Kelman Interviewed," pp. 103–104, ellipses in the original)

As an autodidact, then, Kelman formed his taste for realism at a very early stage in his literary development.

Kelman left school at fifteen to begin an apprenticeship as a compositor, and after he returned from the United States, he took a job as a shoemaker in Govan. Thereafter, a number of laboring and semiskilled jobs took him the length of Britain, from Glasgow through Manchester down to London. In 1969, while in London, he married Marie Connors, a social worker. They returned to Glasgow, where he became a bus conductor. It was also in London that Kelman began to write, in the late 1960s. Back in Glasgow, in 1971, he joined a writers' group that was attended by Alasdair Gray, Liz Lochhead, Agnes Owens, and Tom Leonard, writers who are now internationally known but at the time were unpublished and struggling to reach an audience. The writers' group provided a forum for Kelman to workshop new writing, and it also revealed that he was not struggling alone to recast Scots fiction. More concretely, the group supplied the contact that led to the 1973 publication of his first collection of short stories, *An Old Pub Near the Angel*, by a small press in Maine. After the publication of this collection, Kelman had considerable success in placing short stories in literary magazines in Scotland and the United States and in anthologies of new Scottish writing.

In 1975 Kelman entered Strathclyde University in Glasgow to pursue a degree in philosophy and English literature. After two years, however, he found himself dissatisfied with the reading that was required of him, and he left without finishing his degree. He disclosed to Duncan McLean:

I didn't go to the uni. until I was 28 eh. I used just to write when I was on the broo and things like that. And I didn't really like literature at all. Or English literature. It's not even a question of it boring me, because I hated it, you know, I hated the class assumptions that were being made by anybody who was involved in English literature as I thought of it, and still think of it, to some extent.

("James Kelman Interviewed," p. 103)

This distrust of English literature stemmed from what Kelman perceived as the erasure of the working classes and minorities from its pages. For him, "the class assumptions" held by many English writers perpetuate an exclusive focus upon middle-class and aristocratic culture, as though these subjects were the only legitimate terrain for literary treatment. While Kelman may seem intemperate in his dismissal, his frustration is founded upon the belief that modern English literature is both formally unimaginative and socially constricting. His quarrel with many canonical English writers stems from the fact that they counterpoise culture and class; to be cultured in their terms, according to Kelman, is to be middle or upper class. By definition, being working class insulates one from the path to high culture—from private-school learning, from university training, from travel abroad—not because of one's abilities but because of one's accent and provincial attitudes.

Alternatively, for Kelman legitimate culture is to be found in the practice of everyday life. Thus, developing a voice in fiction does not consist of learning to mouth conventional wisdom from London and Oxbridge. Rather, literary achievement can be measured by the faithfulness with which a writer, drawing from a lifelong knowledge of a community, represents his or her own local culture. In 1994 Kelman underlined the importance of speaking from experience to Anthony Quinn:

I feel the business of finding a voice is something that should be examined more. For me the thing is to find the voice of your community, of your culture. Being from a marginalized culture [Scotland], it's straightforward for us, but in England the regional voice is the one that's consistently punished and negated. The obvious explanation for why English literature is so inadequate just now is because regional experience has not been allowed as the subject of literature.

("Category A Literature," p. 26)

Kelman chose, therefore, to abandon his studies in English literature in order to concentrate on producing his own form of fiction.

Kelman's first publishing success in Britain came in 1983, when Polygon, a student-owned imprint of Edinburgh University Press, published his collection of short stories *Not Not While the Giro and Other Stories* and offered a contract for his first novel, *The Busconductor Hines* (1984). Through the 1980s and 1990s, in quick succession, three novels, three compilations of short stories, a volume of plays, and an essay collection followed, to growing critical attention. Kelman's second novel, *A Chancer* (1985), was reviewed in most of the quality papers and literary reviews but reached only a limited audience. Two years later, however, when his second collection of short stories, *Greyhound for Breakfast*, captured the 1987 Cheltenham Prize, Kelman was firmly established as a major new force in contemporary British literature. Further cementing his reputation, his next novel, *A Disaffection* (1989), was short-listed for the Booker Prize and later went on to win the 1990 James Tait Black Memorial Prize. This success was followed by a collection of stories, *The Burn* (1991), and a controversial novel, *How Late It Was, How Late,* which won the Booker Prize in 1994. In 1998 Kelman published his most recent volume of stories, *The Good Times,* for which he was named joint winner of the Stakis Prize for Scottish Writer of the Year, along with the poet Edwin Morgan.

How Late It Was, How Late is Kelman's greatest literary achievement to date. Nevertheless, when the Booker Prize committee awarded Kelman the prize, the decision was met with considerable indignation in both England and Scotland. In the novel both the narrator and Sammy share a common form of Glasgow English, which is strewn with swear words, colloquial expressions, local slang, Scottish aphorisms, and country-and-western lyrics. The literary editor of the *Independent on Sunday* claimed that the novel contains over four thousand repetitions of "fuck." With some justification Kelman stated that his frequent adoption of the expletive simply mirrored working-class Glasgow street parlance. But many critics were discomforted by the relentless swearing, and some, such as Rabbi Julia Neuberger, a member of the prize committee, saw it as emblematic of Kelman's limitations as a novelist. In the *Times* Simon Jenkins declared, "Mr. Kelman is totally obsessed with the word [fuck]. He sometimes writes it over and over again when he cannot think of anything else with which to fill a line" ("An Expletive of a Winner," p. 20). In Scotland, Michael Kelly, the former Lord Provost of Glasgow, argued that Kelman was pandering to jaded metropolitan English tastes when he wrote in Glaswegian slang. Kelly told the *Times,* "It's the sort of language you hear every day from taxi drivers and plumbers. There's nothing innovative or different about it but down in London they say it's superb, unique expression" (Bowditch, "Glasgow Disowns Prize Novel," p. 2).

Kelman, of course, believes that he is working within a specific working-class, Glaswegian idiom and that bowdlerizing the language to suit middle-class readers would be self-censorship. When Duncan McLean asked him about expletives, Kelman responded:

I don't accept that it is swearing at all you see. How can you talk about it? "The use of the four-letter word"? That's not satisfactory. You actually have to be really specific and say "Let's have a discussion on the use of fuck and cunt and bastard and shite," because there's no way of really talking about them in any objective sense. Because it's *not* swearing. There are so many different parts of the argument, it's an argument about how language is used. . . . eh—fuck, cunt, bastard, and shite— they're part of language, and they have to be treated in the same way that the study of language treats other words.

("James Kelman Interviewed," pp. 109–110)

In 1994 Kelman told Anthony Quinn that the outcry over his use of coarse language hid a deeper and more insidious pressure: "When people talk about the so-called expletives they're not talking about the real issue, you know? The real issue is to do with suppression—the standard English literary voice won't allow it" ("Category A Literature," p. 26). Kelman suspects that the objections to his colloquial voice are rooted in the literary establishment's prejudices against the working classes and the Scots. As the *Guardian* reported, his acceptance speech at the Booker ceremony was a brief and eloquent reply to his detractors:

One of the few remaining freedoms we have is the blank page. No-one can prescribe how we should fill it. There are writers all over the world saying our culture is okay. It applies to places like Yorkshire and Cornwall as much as Scotland. Your own culture is valid. My culture and my language have the right to exist and no-one has the authority to dismiss that.

(Ellison, "Defiant Booker Winner Shrugs Off the Critics," p. 24)

All the time that he has been writing, Kelman has maintained an active connection with the working-class community he depicts. Just as his fiction affirms the place of everyday life in representation, so his public statements and advocacy demonstrate his concern for workers and their rights. As an activist Kelman became most vocal in 1990, when Glasgow was celebrating its status as European City of Culture. Much to the disgust of many Glaswegian writers and artists, the nominally left-leaning Glasgow District Council chose to mark the year by bringing to the city a succession of foreign celebrities and by making the centerpiece of the celebrations a multimedia exhibition called "Glasgow's Glasgow." To offer an alternative voice to the official pronouncements from the council, Kelman help set up "Workers' City," a collective of artists, writers, trades unionists, and teachers that met in Scotland's oldest pub, the Scotia. From the Scotia they offered a running commentary on the city council's expenditures and priorities during the yearlong festival. In return they were vilified by the Lord Provost and the council.

Throughout the 1990s Kelman continued his political work by campaigning for the compensation rights of victims of asbestosis in Clydeside and by supporting the struggle for Kurdish rights. He was a visiting professor at the University of Texas in Austin during the 1998–1999 academic year.

EARLY STORIES

IN the decade between 1973 and 1983, from the publication of *An Old Pub Near the Angel* to *Not Not While the Giro,* Kelman began to portray Glaswegian workers at home in the west of Scotland and in the south looking for work. Many of these tales are short vignettes that offer glimpses into daily life. When Kirsty McNeill asked Kelman, in the Scottish literary magazine *Chapman,* why he had "abandoned traditional narrative structure, with beginning, middle and end," he responded by noting that everyday life was interesting enough on its own terms to merit representation:

I think the most ordinary person's life is fairly dramatic; all you've got to do is follow some people around and look at their existence for 24 hours, and it will be horror. . . . The way that literature generally works in our society you never have to worry about these every [sic] routine horrors, the things that make up everyday reality for an enormous proportion of the population.

("Interview with James Kelman," p. 9)

Kelman intends, then, in his short stories to investigate the daily drama of working-class life. Beginning from this premise, *An Old Pub Near the Angel* represents Scots working-class characters struggling from one paycheck or social security payment to the next. The routine of this unemployed or underemployed existence consists of a succession of cups of tea at home, of trips to the "broo" (the unemployment office) for a payment and to the pub for a pint, of monotonous labor at work. Many of the stories, therefore, are little more than fragments built around a few hours or a single event experienced by a single character. "Abject Misery," for example, shows Charles, a twenty-three-year-old, deciding to look for a hotel restaurant that serves free meals to employees. It begins:

He was in his third month of poverty stricken freedom and fast losing most of his friends including the one commonly known as his best. It couldn't last much longer. He checked his pockets, again discovering that 1½ d. which had haunted him since Monday night. He also had the usual fruitless search for forgotten fags and butt ends. He couldn't understand how he'd managed to survive the past three days. One of these days he'd have to get a job. This no money was becoming a problem. How was one supposed to eat?

(p. 23)

The story ends inconclusively with the onset of rain and Charles nowhere near his destination. The depiction of Charles's impoverishment is complemented by a wry stream-of-consciousness narrative that reveals his craving for security. After he spots what he takes for a sixpence in the road, he thinks, "Still though imagine having lived on Britain's green and pleasant land for twenty three years and not a tosser to show for it, apart from the faithful 1½ d" (p. 25). Kelman's point is that large segments of the population exist at precisely this subsistence level, cut off from the affluence around them.

The thirteen stories in *Not Not While the Giro* strike a similar chord to the previous collection. "A Roll for Joe" describes a barroom encounter between the nameless narrator and a pub regular named Joe. The conversation itself accurately represents the aimlessness of barroom conversation, but it also masks deeper cultural tensions. As the narrator and Joe get increasingly drunk, they argue about the difference between their generations, until Joe notes ominously, "I mean we're quite enjoying the chat aren't we? But we could come to blows any minute. Let's face it" (p. 19). While Kelman disavows the necessity for fiction to hinge on unrealistically dramatic plot devices, the potential for violence in his fiction is a constant feature. Indeed, the title of the story insinuates that Joe is being set up as the victim of a mugging, for we learn that the narrator is discreetly communicating with another drinker, who does not speak. The story ends when Joe abruptly leaves the pub, followed by the silent drinker. "A Roll for Joe" highlights the drama that underlies the everyday rituals of working-class life.

The title story of the first collection, "An Old Pub Near the Angel," which Kelman reprinted in *Not Not While the Giro*, concerns Charles Donald, who has just received a large payment from the labor exchange in London, where he is living. Charles immediately goes for a couple of drinks and an early lunch in a nearby pub, where he contentedly checks the racing schedule. In general Kelman's characters cannot resist spending when they come into money, and Charles is no exception. He plans a wagering spree, thinking, "Nothing else could possibly do with all that back money lying about" (p. 60). This profligacy is perhaps understandable, considering the lack of prospects Kelman's characters have. Given a choice between saving his money, paying his back rent, or gambling, Charles's choice represents a rare opportunity to act in selecting his wagers. For all their seeming slightness, then, Kelman's early stories outline complicated cultural patterns in the attitudes and behavior they illustrate.

Between 1973 and the publication of *Not Not While the Giro* in 1983, individual stories by Kelman appeared with some regularity in anthologies and literary magazines, and many of these pieces, as well as some of the stories in *An Old Pub Near the Angel*, reappeared in slightly revised form in the 1983 collection. Again the scenes described by Kelman are largely working-class—boardinghouses, pubs, pool halls, tenements—but he broadens his terrain by examining the rhythms of the workplace. Predominantly, work in Kelman's writings is characterized by long stretches of boredom punctuated by moments of excruciating danger. In "The Bevel," for example, three laborers are employed to strip off the lining of a giant tank designed to hold chlorine. However, the scaffolding inside will not allow them access to a recess on one side of the tank. Mr. Williams, the foreman, rigs up an extension to the scaffolding and decides to demonstrate how his contraption will hold the combined weight of the workmen and their pneumatic hammer. During the demonstration the planks give way and Williams almost falls to the ground. The irony here, which is not missed by the workmen, is that for once it is not the workers who are endangered by their superiors but a foreman. Kelman's laborers are regularly expected to toil under conditions that middle-class employees would never dream of enduring. Much of the tension,

therefore, that builds in his representations of workplace culture is underlaid with the distressing possibility that someone is going to get hurt simply because management is cutting corners. In his interview with Duncan McLean, Kelman uses miners as an example to describe how he represents the dangers of physical labor:

Part of [the miners'] job is to take the sort of risks that nobody would take for less than say fifty grand if they were middle class. Or like my one page story "Acid," I mean I used to do that, I nearly lost my hand, I've got the scar here to prove it, blah blah. But it's something you do every day of the week, it's part of the job: it's very hard to get the drama of that, because the whole thing would seem to be a boring way of living indeed. . . .

In setting out the fact, you have to set out the danger, because the danger is inherent within the fact, you know.
("James Kelman Interviewed," p. 121)

For Kelman the dangers of factory labor are best exemplified through the facticity of the work itself. In "Acid," the story that Kelman refers to above, a single paragraph depicts the death of a workman who falls into a large vat of acid. Only one co-worker comes to the victim's aid: "In an instant this old fellow who was also the young man's father had clambered up and along the gangway carrying a big pole. Sorry Hughie, he said. And then ducked the young man below the surface. Obviously the old fellow had had to do this because only the head and shoulders—in fact, that which had been above the acid was all that remained of the young man" (p. 115). By concentrating on the social consequences of the accident, Kelman heightens the horror of the situation without overplaying its goriness.

Many of the other stories in *Not Not While the Giro* consider working-class domesticity and leisure rather than work. One of the best-modulated stories in the collection, "Remember Young Cecil," gradually takes the shape of a carefully laid-out oral history, as a snooker club member recollects the rise and fall of the club's best player in living memory. In "Nice to Be Nice" Kelman produces a tale about the dire conditions in a tenement: a single mother and her four children are soon to be evicted, and an unexpected tax refund of £42 is stolen by a young friend to wager on the dogs. Unlike the vast majority of Kelman's fiction, this story reproduces Glaswegian tonalities and slang through phonetic spelling. The story begins, for example, by relating the narrator's puzzlement:

Strange thing wis it stertit oan a Wedinsday, A mean nothin ever sterts oan a Wedinsday kis it's the day afore pey day an A'm ey skint. Mibby git a buckshee pint roon the *Anchor* bit that's aboot it. Anyway it wis eftir 9 an A wis thinking aboot gin hame kis a hidny a light whin Boab McCann threw us a dollar an A boat masel an auld Erchie a pint. The auld yin hid 2 boab ay his ain so A took it an won a couple a gemms a dominoes.

(p. 30)

Although the story imaginatively re-creates Glasgow speech, Kelman abandoned this form of narrative after reading the poetry of Tom Leonard, a contemporary Glaswegian poet. He explained to Duncan McLean, "I stopped writing phonetic transcriptions of dialect after that because he was obviously much better than me, and much more involved, in ways different from me" ("James Kelman Interviewed," p. 104).

In an early article on Kelman, the critic Craig Cairns pinpoints three areas in which Kelman's fiction has had the greatest effect: "the representation of working-class life, the treatment of 'voice,' and the construction of narrative" ("Resisting Arrest: James Kelman," p. 99). The title story in *Not Not While the Giro* exemplifies an early occasion in Kelman's career where all three elements in his writing coalesce. The story narrates the thoughts of a thirty-year-old, self-described "hopeless case" and "natural born beggar," as he contemplates everything from his hated neighbors to his nonexistent sex life to the timing of his next social security check (pp. 185, 190). While he lives in this state of suspended animation, his dream life is full of grandiose schemes for winning money and fame. Finally, the narrator realizes that money is not the problem: "Can I really say I enjoy life with money. When I have it I throw it away. Only relax when skint. When skint I am a hulk—husk. No sidesteps from the issue. I do not want money ergo I do not want to be happy. The current me is my heart's desire. Surely not. Yet it appears the case. I am always needing money and I am always getting rid of it" (p. 193). In the voice of the narrator, Kelman has found a perfect instrument with which to express the mixture of self-loathing, escapism, and vindictiveness that this life of paralyzing inactivity breeds. Clearly the narrator has a smattering of education, yet he has no use for learning except in exposing the banality of social relations and the

gathering pathology of his own psychological state. Because for many of Kelman's characters the future seems to have been excised, the present contains nothing but bitterness and parody.

LIFE ON THE BUSES

JAMES Kelman's first novel, *The Bus Conductor Hines* (1984), chronicles several weeks in the life of Robert (Rab) Hines, an on-and-off-again bus conductor who cannot decide whether he prefers to work or to collect unemployment insurance. In novelistic terms little conventional plotting occurs in the novel. At work Rab argues with his coworkers and frequently dodges his conducting duties; at home relations with his wife, Sandra, are strained due to the couple's cramped living conditions and lack of money. Rab shuttles back and forth to work, trying to decide how to reconcile his private and professional lives. The two incidents that punctuate the narrative are Sandra's leaving home after a quarrel and Rab's refusal to face a disciplinary hearing on his own time, which precipitates a labor stoppage at the bus depot. In the end, however, the long-term implications of these crises are left unresolved. Living in what is wryly described as "a no-bedroomed flat" in a tenement slated for demolition, trained in a job that will disappear with the advent of one-man buses, involved in a relationship with a tenuous future, Rab is poised on the brink of oblivion, whether he realizes it or not.

Kelman's realism is founded upon his evocation of daily life; no matter how slight or trivial individual events or statements may seem, in the economy of Kelman's fiction nothing is wasted. Kelman wrote in an assessment of South African writer Alex La Guma, "Realism is the term used to describe the 'detailing of day-to-day existence' and most writers who advocate social change are realists. . . . There is nothing more crucial, and potentially subversive, than gaining a full understanding of how the lives of ordinary people are lived from moment to moment." He concludes, "As long as art exists there are no areas of experience that have to remain inaccessible" (pp. 160–161). In his own attempt to illuminate the lives of working-class characters, Kelman concentrates on depicting how they experience the forces that structure their lives. Perhaps the most fundamental of these experiences in Kelman's fiction is the daily encounter with snobbery and hierarchy. In the bus terminal, for example, the supervisors always address Rab by his first name, while he calls them by their surnames. More insidiously, in Sandra and Rab's relationship class difference seems to underlie many of their personal problems. Rab's roots are solidly working-class, but Sandra comes from more middle-class folk. Although she understands and sympathizes with Rab's discontent working as a bus conductor, she urges him to keep his position and keeps looking for signs of ambition, hoping that one day he will be promoted to bus driver.

But Rab distrusts the bus drivers he works with, assuming, with some justification, that they are social climbers and are more interested in increasing their wage packets than objecting to layoffs. Although Rab sees the flaws in his own lassitude—"This fatalistic approach to life: no it is not so good" (p. 159), he acknowledges—he is either unwilling or unable to imagine himself as anything other than working-class Glaswegian. His characteristic response to the world is to assume a posture of incomprehension; repeatedly he thinks of life and thought as "a singular kettle of fish," an "astonishing bowl of parsnips," and "a very perplexing kettle of coconuts" (pp. 213, 214, 222). As a novel of working-class realism *The Busconductor Hines* documents the practical difficulties of eking out an existence from a dead-end job; but it deepens this picture of daily monotony by depicting the psychological effects, the paralysis and self-destructiveness, that grow out of habitually feeling helpless and disenfranchised.

Kelman's fiction demonstrates that he is as interested in exploring the psychological dimensions of working-class culture as he is in realistically representing its economic and laboring conditions. He told Maya Jaggi of the *Guardian*, "I write in the existentialist tradition: [I stand for] the validity of the individual perspective and perception" ("Speaking in Tongues," p. 30). But for Kelman, who aims to represent working-class interiority in all its complexity and contradiction, realism and existentialism mesh perfectly in the production of a narrative voice in the novel. Even with its third-person narration *The Busconductor Hines* is filtered through the perception of the protagonist; at times it even seems to slip into a voice that Rab impersonates, a voice that Edwin Morgan has labeled "jocular columnist" ("Glasgow Speech in Recent Scottish Literature," p. 397). Here, for instance, are some of the ups and downs of his job, narrated in a forbearing tone that is presumably Rab's own:

It has never been acutely necessary to think. Hines can board the bus and all will transpire. Nor does he have to explain to a driver how the bus is to be manoeuvred. Nor need he dash out into the street to pressgang pedestrians. Of its own accord comes everything. . . . But a driver can be new. The Newdriver is a problem. One should tread warily in gabbing to such a being lest a lapse in concentration causes the bus to crash. Hines seems to get more Newdrivers than is his fair share.

(p. 154)

After this philosophical consideration of bus conducting, an abrupt shift in style occurs, and we are immediately plunged into Rab's Glaswegian patter: "Fucking shite. But it's funny how he always seems to get lumbered with the cunts when Reilly's on the panel or whatever. They're all fucking idiots as well, this is the thing" (pp. 154–155). Representations of Rab's thinking swing between two poles, then—between the knowing patience of his introspective moods and the misanthropic ranting of his bitter moods. For a work designed to evoke everyday, working-class life, this innovative narration is particularly challenging, for it moves from the narrator's dispassion to Rab's moodiness with little warning. Peter Kravitz, an editor at Polygon Press, commented to Maya Jaggi, "Half the world wants to see Jim as a working-class writer using the words of men in the street, and the other half as an experimental modernist in the tradition of Kafka, Beckett and Joyce. Few are happy to see him as both, let alone as a humorous satirist. But he's all three" ("Speaking in Tongues," p. 27).

GAMBLING FOR A LIVING

KELMAN's second novel, *A Chancer* (1985), continues many of the themes from his earlier fiction while exploring new aspects of working-class culture. In this work Kelman takes gambling as the exemplary activity of everyday life for working people. The novel describes several months in the life of Tammas, a twenty-year-old habitual gambler, whose single-minded pursuit of betting is all-consuming. Nothing thrills Tammas so much as calculating odds, choosing horses and dogs to place bets on, and collecting his winnings. Like

Kelman's first novel, *A Chancer* contains little in the way of conventional plotting. In the course of the novel, Tammas quits his job, wins and loses large sums of money, plays half a game of soccer, acts as best man at his friend Rab's wedding, meets a group of gamblers who introduce him to casino life in Glasgow, initiates a relationship with a young single mother named Vi, and barely escapes a bar brawl. He is last seen hitchhiking down to London. The novel is in fact a picaresque tale in which gambling unifies the episodes that compose the narrative.

Much of the gambling description in the novel is autobiographical, as Kelman has readily admitted to Kirsty McNeill in an interview that discusses *A Chancer* at length: "I still gamble. . . . Gambling is good, it really is an escape. Leaves you *compos mentis* unlike drink or dope" ("Interview with James Kelman," p. 8). Kelman describes the gambling world as almost a secret society within working-class life: "It's just a different culture. Any subculture is. Something with luck and a game— i.e. not roulette—that produces a black economy. It's almost a Genet world, different value system altogether: murderer as hero, murderer as saint. And in order to grasp that you have to go through a transformation. Conventional values have to go altogether" ("Interview with James Kelman," p. 8).

For Kelman's middle-class readership, comprehending working-class culture already requires a transformation to recognize the complexity of the proletariat. However, Kelman asks even more of his readers with *A Chancer*, by focusing upon a subculture that many within the working class itself distrust. In the novel Tammas' friends are dismayed at the size of his wagers, and his brother-in-law is contemptuous of his irresponsibility. However, as escapism Tammas' wagering satisfies his desire to feel proficient or in control of some aspect of his life. The very act of gaming provides Tammas with the few moments of unmitigated happiness that he feels in the novel; his pleasure in spotting an undervalued dog in a particular race, in laying down a large bet at long odds, and in watching the dog come home first in the race instantly erases the losing card hands, fallen horses, and botched snooker games that precede the bet. Betting for Tammas only partly compensates for his lack of education and skills and for the social disconnection he feels, but it does provide a regular pattern in his otherwise haphazard existence; with money in his pocket, he always

knows what to do next. Ultimately this predictability may be more important to him than whether he loses or wins, since as long as he has money to bet, he is content.

In general *A Chancer* shares thematic concerns with much of Kelman's earlier work and even incorporates short stories that appeared in *Not Not While the Giro*. The opening scene, for example, where Tammas wins a lot of cash playing cards with his coworkers, develops "Double or Clear plus a Tenner," and a later incident when Tammas inadvertently sets fire to his sneaker at his job in a copper-wire factory builds on "The Chief Thing about This Game." One of the hallmarks of the novel, then, is its focus on external details and dialogue, a feature that renders Tammas relatively unself-conscious in his actions. By obscuring his protagonist's motives and desires from the reader, Kelman implies that because he is so young and unformed, Tammas can only partly understand and control his impulses. The only time the narrator comes close to dramatizing Tammas' thoughts is when he is betting, where distinctions between the narrator and the protagonist are hard to draw.

At the heart of *A Chancer* is the tension between the culture of betting and the working-class world. In Kelman's novel betting both mirrors and opposes the larger social form; its basis in chance mimics the contingency of manual labor, for example, and its hypermasculinity exaggerates working-class male culture. But fundamentally, despite the crowds, gambling is depicted as a solitary, competitive endeavor that starkly contrasts with the conviviality Tammas is offered but frequently declines at home and among his friends. Being a chancer (someone who lives by his wits), Tammas is essentially a loner whose social discomfort can be assuaged solely by retreating to the track or to the betting shop. Only Tammas' relationship with Vi seems to provide anything like the emotional charge that gambling does, and in the end he abandons even this tie. Although the time Vi and Tammas spend together is characterized by affection and caring, ultimately the gulf between them is too great. She is older and a mother and lives in fear of her violent, ex-con ex-husband; Tammas' capriciousness makes it seem improbable that he is ready to fulfill the roles of partner and stepfather. Kelman reveals to Kirsty McNeill, "[Tammas] is a reader, I think he's a trier. I mean I've got a lot of time for him, respect for him. He's the hero of the novel. He's trying hard in a world where things are very difficult. . . . He's a young man in a situation where he can't handle it" ("Interview with James Kelman," pp. 7–8). Kelman's achievement in this fine novel is to render sympathetically Tammas' flight from a future of factory labor into a virtual world of choice, expertise, and autonomy.

MIDDLE STORIES

AFTER the publication of *A Chancer,* Kelman returned to writing in the short-story format. From 1985 until 1994 only one novel—*A Disaffection*—appeared; two short-story collections—*Greyhound for Breakfast* and *The Burn*—and a lengthy contribution to the compilation *Lean Tales* complete his oeuvre from this period.

Lean Tales (1985) collects short stories from three Scots writers—James Kelman, Agnes Owens, and Alasdair Gray. Kelman's part is composed primarily of uncollected material that appeared in literary magazines; most of the stories predate or are contemporaneous with those from *Not Not While the Giro.* While detailing the lives of working people and the indigent, Kelman's stories here concentrate most fully on the plight of Scotsmen who have traveled south to London or to rural England or to the Channel Islands in search of work. Accordingly his characters cast off the anonymity they would have in Glasgow and become figures of attention for the English and French with whom they work. "Getting there" is told from the perspective of an itinerant Glaswegian who explains his journey with a terse "I had to vanish in England" (p. 53). The story ends with the traveler at his destination, sheltering, penniless, under a lean-to on a beach, waiting out the rain for a night. "Busted Scotch," the story from which the title of the American selection of Kelman's stories is taken, is less than two pages long. It describes the impatience of a Scottish worker waiting in a strip joint for a game of blackjack to commence. In the interim he watches a variety act performed by a "scotchman doing this harrylauder thing complete with kilt and trimmings." "A terrible disgrace," the narrator thinks:

Keep Right On To The End Of The Road he sang with four hundred and fifty males screaming Get Them Off Jock. Fine if I had been drunk and able to join in on the chants but as it was I was staying sober for the Brag ahead. Give the scotchman his due but—he stuck it out till the last and turning his back on them all he gave a big boo boopsidoo with the kilt pulled right up and flashing the Y-fronts. Big applause he got as well. The next act on was an Indian Squaw.

(p. 13)

In his sober state, the narrator recognizes that this performance is a travesty of his heritage, and he is also aware of the music-hall history that links Harry Lauder, the most famous Scottish vaudevillian, to the performer on stage in front of him. Yet his contempt is tempered by his admiration for the dancer's perseverance. For Kelman, the point is that for too long Scots audiences have indulged entertainers eager to profit from degraded images of their national culture. Kelman's own writing rebuts these traditional stereotypes by grounding his representation of Scottish identity in the struggles of everyday existence. Thus, "Busted Scotch" ends with the narrator losing a week's wages in the first hand of his first card game.

Greyhound for Breakfast (1987) marks a significant widening in the scope and concerns of Kelman's short fiction. The forty-seven pieces in the collection, which date from 1972 to 1987, range from short fragments, which communicate a moment or a feeling, to the long title story. Kelman continues to concentrate on unemployed and working-class Glaswegian characters, as in "Old Francis," which describes a confrontation in a park. Francis is accosted by three drunks, who initially ask for a cigarette but wind up offering him a drink of "sherry vindaloo" from the bottle they are sharing (p. 6). After Francis complains about one of the drunks' trousers, saying, "Your mate's trousers, they're fucking falling to bits. I mean look at his arse, his arse is fucking poking out!" (p. 4), the tension increases dramatically. The story ends with Francis fearing he is on the verge of taking a beating for his watch. Additionally, however, Kelman expands his repertoire of narrators and voices in this collection. Boys and adolescents come into focus in "Let that be a Lesson," where a couple finds their son and his friends gambling in his bedroom. "The wee boy that got killed" explores a fifteen-year-old's boredom and aggression at school, and "Sunday papers" humorously depicts a boy's attempt to do his big brother's paper route one Sunday, despite the fact that he can barely lift the load of newspapers he is supposed to deliver.

Kelman also begins to stage encounters between his working-class regulars and outsiders from other classes. In "Home for a couple of days," for example, the protagonist returns to Glasgow after working in London for three years, only to find that in a variety of subtle ways, he is no longer like his former mates; he can't drink as much as they can at lunch, he has a bank account, he has been employed for three years, and he is out of touch with Glasgow slang. For the first time one of Kelman's migrant Scots comes home and unexpectedly discovers that money has separated him from his roots. Another story, "In with the doctor," has a general practitioner confessing his unhappiness to a patient after he ascertains that the patient has read Kafka's story "The Country Doctor." But after the doctor implies that his patients do not understand him, the patient begins to resent his familiarity, telling him, "I think you're an elitist wee bastard" (p. 125).

The title piece, which is one of Kelman's best tales, returns to working-class themes in order to unravel the intricate emotional fabric that makes up family life in the tenements. In true Kelman fashion, the story traces the path of Ronnie, an unemployed Glaswegian, as he meanders around, visiting his mates at the local pub and reminiscing to himself about growing up and working in Glasgow. Unlike many of Kelman's naturalistic proletarian tales, however, the protagonist here frequently considers his own emotional state and tries to fathom how his actions reflect how he is feeling. Currently Ronnie feels depressed. His son has recently moved on very short notice to London, and Ronnie has just that day bought a greyhound for £80. Having nowhere to kennel the beast and no money to feed it, Ronnie is understandably reticent to return home to his wife, Babs, without an explanation for his purchase: "She was too good at arguing, Babs, too good at arguing. She was liable to make him totally speechless. This is because she was always right" (pp. 215–216). Ronnie tells his friends that he plans to race the greyhound, saying, "see if this fucking dog doesn't get me the holiday money I'll eat it for my fucking breakfast" (p. 210). But one of his mates dismisses its build as unsuitable for racing, and another cruelly suggests, "Your boy's fucked off to England and you've went out and bought a dog" (p. 211). As the evening wears on, Ronnie finally realizes, in a fit of resignation, that he has no excuse to offer Babs but that he needs to go home. The story ends with Ronnie's thoughts: "He would just tell Babs something or other, what the fuck he didn't know, it didn't fucking matter; what did it matter, it didn't fucking matter" (p. 230). For Kelman, this sense of resignation and bitterness characterizes working-class subjectivity.

His next collection, *The Burn* (1991), takes Kelman's short fiction in directions that show a deepening bleakness in his vision, coupled with a more explicit examination of cultural politics. A rare moment of self-reflection even intrudes in the comic "Naval History," when a pair of pretentious social climbers (who may be undercover policemen) ask their old friends, James, "Are ye no still writing your wee stories with a working-class theme?" The writer responds, "it's fucking realism I'm into as well if it makes any difference" (p. 95). In form the short stories collected in this volume are generally longer and less fragmentary than earlier compositions. In content they examine the forces that constitute social relations in working-class culture. The stories reveal how relationships and friendships are forged and broken through sexuality, education, class mobility, and economics. Because Kelman has focused his attention on relations between characters, his lengthy portraits of individual obsession and paranoia are rarer than in previous collections. In this collection personal alienation is frequently depicted as a response to past trauma, usually involving sexual abuse or bereavement. In "Pictures" the nameless protagonist sees a woman crying in the theater and thinks that it is the result of her seeing an act of oral sex simulated in the film: "Maybe this is why the woman was greeting [crying] along the row; maybe she once had this bad experience where she was forced into doing that very selfsame thing, years ago, when she was at a tender age, or else just it was totally against her wishes maybe" (p. 1). Later the protagonist confesses his guilt at having been forced in a public toilet to masturbate a stranger for loose change: "you were in cahoots with the guy, that was what it was, the bad fucking bit, you were in cahoots with him, it was like you had made a bargain, so that was that" (p. 11).

In the final story, "by the burn," told in Kelman's trademark free indirect style, we hear the thoughts of an unemployed man as he trudges through a bog and the rain to a job interview. With increasing clarity and grim humor, he realizes his disheveled state will not make a good impression, but he presses on, regardless. However, he recalls that he is near the spot where his daughter was killed by an unstable heap of sand: "Hiding out playing chases," he remembers. "Aye being warned to steer clear but in they went and then it collapsed on them, and it trapped them, all these tons of earth and they had all got suffocated. Aw dear. Aw dear" (p. 243). Instantly he is reduced to tears and longs for the comfort of his wife. Gathering himself, like the voice in Beckett's *The Unnamable,* the man thinks:

He was alone. He had to carry on now. He started walking, following the trail. One thing he did know but, see when he died, he was going to die of a heart attack, he was going to die of a heart attack and he was going to be alone, there wasnt going to be no cunt, no cunt, he was going to be fucking alone, that was the way he was going to die, he fucking knew it, it was a fucking racing certainty.

(p. 244)

Fundamentally Kelman's characters in *The Burn* seem, like those in his earlier work, to survive only through acts of will; here, however, the odds against them are not only general and class-related—poverty, joblessness, police violence—but also individual and particular—a death, a perversion, an infidelity.

As Kelman increases the complexity of his portraits of working-class life, he begins to consider Scotland as a separate cultural entity, distinct from England. Scottish workers may labor in the south and return alienated from their roots, as we have seen, but in *The Burn* Kelman also shows how English values threaten Scottish cultural identity. The exposition of this issue comes out most explicitly in "events in yer life," in which the protagonist, Derek, returns to Glasgow for his mother's funeral and meets his old art-school friend, Fin, who has quit his job in the Parks Department and militantly maintains a working-class lifestyle. Fin criticizes Derek's use of the term "Britain" to describe his country, saying that in Scotland nobody labors under the misapprehension that England and Scotland exist as a single nation in anything but name. When Derek asks Fin whether he is a nationalist, Fin replies, "Christ Derek that's hardly even a question nowadays I mean it's to what extent" (p. 222). Derek counters that the English would not even grasp what he meant by degrees of nationalism: "To them Scotland's nothing at all, it's just a part of England. No even a county man they think it's a sort of city.... Ye know they don't even

know geography. They've got this hazy view of the world. See a place like Inverness for instance, they think it's near Yorkshire. Next door to Crewe of somefuckingthing" (p. 222). The only time Derek feels he has anyone to talk to in England is when "ye bump into a black guy or something, maybe an Irishman" (p. 223). Kelman's recognition here is that the Scots, like Afro-Caribbeans and the Irish, are a minority population within British culture and that governmental neglect of Scotland is rooted deeply in English racist ignorance.

TEACHING THE FUTURE

KELMAN's return to novel writing was signaled in 1989 by *A Disaffection,* a study of class and pedagogy focused around the figure of Patrick Doyle, a single, twenty-nine-year-old teaching in a school in a poor part of Glasgow. After six years at the job, Patrick has lost confidence that his classroom time has any effect on his pupils other than to prepare them to be the next generation of the labor force. Predominantly, then, Patrick forgoes traditional forms of teaching and instead extemporizes in front of the class. On one occasion, for example, he mixes a short lecture on the Pythagoreans with an unorthodox class recitation: "Now then, I want you all to repeat after me: The present government, in suppressing the poor, is suppressing our parents.... We are being fenced in by the teachers ... at the behest of a dictatorship government ... in explicit simulation of our fucking parents the silly bastards" (pp. 24–25). At school his relations are strained. The headmaster informs him that his request to be transferred to a different school next term has been approved, even though Patrick cannot recall having asked to be moved and does not really want to leave his present school. Among the other teachers Patrick is truly interested only in Alison Houston, who is married and not especially responsive to his advances. After a couple of inconclusive meetings, she informs him, "I'm not going to have a relationship with ye" (p. 235). Overall, as the narrator concludes, using a Scots term for "flabbergasted," "[Patrick] has become scunnered by the carry on, that is all" (p. 88).

It is tempting to imagine that Patrick's response to his doubts and insufficiencies is a feeling of resignation or despair, and several times he does contemplate the subject of suicide, if not the act itself. Yet, as his fumbling overtures to Alison denote,

Patrick does desire an escape from his routine. In the novel this flight of fancy is accomplished through his learning to play a large pair of electrician's cardboard pipes that produce a range of low notes. In playing the pipes Patrick finds a creative, if unconventional, outlet for his self-expression. He even justifies his musical efforts from a historical perspective:

Once you had said pipe you had named the world. Consider the panpipes: they have been performed on by mankind since way back at the ancient of days. Aeons. At least six thousand years. And men have been playing the pipes. And here you have Patrick Doyle MA (Hons). What about a pair of fucking bagpipes! No, sarcasm doesni work. . . . And playing music has always been medicinal, psychotherapeutic.

(p. 82)

Playing the pipes frees Patrick from his professional self-loathing, his romantic failings, and his isolation. His idiosyncratic release is purely aesthetic, however. So, in some obscure, rudimentary fashion, because this is the story of Patrick's struggle to express himself, *A Disaffection* can be considered a *Künstlerroman,* a portrait of the artist as a young teacher, and conversely a portrait of the teacher as a young artist.

Throughout the novel the narrator doggedly observes Patrick's dilemma and notes his reactions to each new development. Yet the patience with which Patrick is developed in the novel is missing in Kelman's own comments about the protagonist he has created. In his interview with Kirsty McNeill, Kelman describes Patrick as "someone who thought there was a possibility of change from within the system—a mainstream socialist" ("Interview with James Kelman," p. 1). He continues:

Doyle is like a lot of people who come through university without any experience of working class jobs. They think and the educational process teaches them to think—that they can change the system from within. I think Doyle has only become aware of his own knowledge of the futility of things quite recently. He's led a fairly normal existence in the working-class-boy-goes-to-uni routine.

(p. 1)

Even though he tries to promote class-consciousness among his pupils, Patrick's pedagogical activism is hopeless, both because of its piecemeal quality and because of Patrick's own ambivalence. As Alison points out, if Patrick really feels that teaching is repressive and he is doing the state's work, then he should quit. However, when he tells his unemployed brother, Gavin, during a long afternoon drinking session, that he has decided to leave his job, Gavin furiously suggests that he is squandering his advantages: "That makes me really angry, so it does. He's a bloody teacher and he earns a bomb, a single man, he can do anyfucking-thing he likes. Anything; anything at all. So what does he do he wraps it! It makes me sick so it does" (p. 260). While the middle-class teacher agonizes over his scruples, his working-class brother tells him not to trifle with such niceties. In *A Disaffection* teaching indicates class mobility, but it also entails class alienation.

Formally *A Disaffection* returns to the mixture of third-person interior monologue and social observation that made up *The Busconductor Hines.* Patrick's ruminations are related in elaborate circumlocutions as he tries to correlate his knowledge of philosophy and history with his mystification at the world. This copious psychological narration is complemented with Kelman's spare, descriptive prose, which strips occasions down to their basic dimensions. Focusing exclusively on Patrick's thoughts and actions, the narrative becomes increasingly claustrophobic, a feeling exacerbated by all the allusions to Hamlet, which further underline Patrick's irresolution. Finally, however, Kelman's literary portrait escapes the stasis and self-consciousness of its protagonist through the sardonic humor that he and the narrator share. On one occasion, having just thrown up all over his trousers, Patrick connects his abject state with the city's, by imagining how else he might have come into this condition:

Hang on a minute. It is certainly true that the guy's wearing sick-stained trousers but this should hardly produce such inferences as: the fellow himself is responsible for it, the manner of it, these bottom sections, their current condition. He could easily have been strolling along the fucking road when up pops a sick dog, a drunken vagabond on all-fours. Anything. Anything's a possibility in this man's Glasgow.

(p. 212)

HOW LATE IT WAS, HOW LATE

THE next novel, *How Late It Was, How Late,* which appeared in 1994, begins with what is, for Kelman, an unusually dramatic premise. Sammy, an unemployed ex-con and petty thief, wakes up in a police cell after having been taken into custody for punching a policeman. That is about as much as he can reconstruct from the brief moments of lucidity in his otherwise blank recollection of a weekend binge with "the Leg," an associate with whom he was selling stolen leather jackets. Battered and bruised, he regains consciousness in the cell only to find that he has lost his sight. Unlike much of Kelman's earlier work, therefore, *How Late It Was, How Late* has at its core an acute problem that the protagonist has to face and surmount. The police release Sammy after a couple of days, and he finds himself groping his way home, without the familiar landmarks to guide him.

Ach it was hopeless. That was what ye felt. These bastards. What can ye do but. Except start again so he started again. That was what he did he started again. It's a game but so it is man life, fucking life I'm talking about, that's all ye can do man start again, turn ower a new leaf, a fresh start, another yin, ye just plough on, ye plough on, ye just fucking plough on, that's what ye do, that was what Sammy did, what else was there I mean fuck all, know what I'm saying, fuck all. Mind you it was a bit of a disaster, ye had to own up.

(pp. 36–37)

Over the course of the following week, Sammy begins to grow accustomed to his sight loss, but much of the time he simply sits in his flat, listening to his country-and-western tapes, trying to reconstruct events over the fateful week and wondering whether Helen, the woman he lives with, has left him for good.

The novel begins, therefore, with the aftermath of a violent encounter between Sammy and the authorities, signaling a desire by Kelman to examine the effects of institutional power upon individuals. However, as Sammy's ensuing Kafkaesque encounters with welfare agencies show, the state exercises power not only through violence. Despite the severity of his injuries, Sammy is reluctant to file a Dysfunctional Benefit, fearing retribution from the police. During Sammy's two interviews with the agencies, Kelman builds the drama of each occasion through the contrast in Sammy's and the bureaucrats' language; because they quite literally do not speak the same language, communication is often lost in a welter of technicalities. During the first interview at the fictional Department of Sight Loss, for example, Sammy tries to explain to the medical officer that he only wants to report his blindness, not pursue a claim against the police:

I mean that's all I'm doing, registering it here like I'm supposed to; I'm no being cheeky, if I'm entitled to benefit then I'm entitled to benefit. If I'm no I'm no. Know what I mean, that's all I'm saying.
Yes well the police department is empowered to restrain the customer Mister Samuels and certainly if the customer is then in receipt of a dysfunction, and this dysfunction is shown to be an effect of the restraints applied then the customer is entitled to submit an application to this department in respect of Dysfunctional Benefit and if it is approved then the benefit is awarded.

(pp. 104–105)

Between Sammy's wariness and the medical officer's measured official phrasing, the imbalance of power becomes excruciatingly apparent. If Sammy's report of his blindness is to be believed, then he must file a complaint, leaving him vulnerable to more police harassment.

With even greater force Sammy's powerlessness is underlined during his appointment with a doctor at the Health and Welfare office. The doctor examines Sammy and announces his finding: "Well Mister Samuels . . . in respect of the visual stimuli presented it would appear you were unable to respond" (p. 219). This observation is as much as he is willing to volunteer, and Sammy is scunnered:

So ye're no saying I'm blind?
It isnt for me to say.
Aye but you're a doctor.
Yes.
So ye can give an opinion?
Anyone can give an opinion.
Aye but to do with medical things.
Mister Samuels, I have people waiting to see me.
Christ sake!
I find your language offensive.
Do ye. Ah well fuck ye then. Fuck ye! Sammy crumpled the prescription and flung it at him: Stick that up yer fucking arse!

(p. 225)

Sammy is again outmaneuvered bureaucratically; his only response to the doctor's stonewalling is to attack his desk and throw his papers on the floor. Needless to say, after this confrontation Sammy gives up trying to have the state certify his condition, even after a client's advocate, Ally, volunteers to represent his case and shepherd it through the procedural hearings for him. But Sammy simply cannot bring himself to trust the man. Instead he decides to disappear to England, in an attempt to elude the police and begin again. After he spends an evening with his son Peter, Sammy packs a bag and hails a taxi. At the last "Sammy slung in the bag and stepped inside, then the door slammed shut and that was him, out of sight" (p. 374). Like *A Chancer,* the novel ends, with a departure to the south, and like the earlier novel it is an ending that offers little optimism about the future.

Although the narrative of *How Late It Was, How Late* resembles that of the earlier novels in combining a third-person description of Sammy's thoughts with a dispassionate account of his whereabouts and actions, the novel develops an innovative narrative style by collapsing the discursive distance between narrator and central character. In this novel, as opposed to virtually every other third-person novel, the narrator and Sammy share a single parlance and a single accent, both of which originate from the Glasgow streets. This style erases the conventional linguistic contrast between narrators who speak educated, grammatical English and characters who speak in slang or with an accent. For Kelman this standard relationship builds a hierarchy into fiction that is almost ethnographical in its imbalance; that is, implicitly, the educated narrator rises above the characters as he or she observes and describes their predicaments from what is presumed to be an unbiased perspective. This novelistic tradition, which Kelman identifies especially with English literary tradition, is fundamentally flawed because it privileges narrator over character and thus introduces a bias that has long gone unnoticed. Kelman tells Kirsty McNeill, "Getting rid of that standard third party narrative voice is getting rid of a whole value system," a system that he personifies through the narrator, whom he claims is invariably "economically secure, eats good food and plenty of it, is upper middle class, paternalist" ("Interview with James Kelman," pp. 4–5). Kelman purposely renounced this profile in *The Busconductor Hines, A Chancer,* and *A Disaffection* by reducing his narrators' role to a recitation of facts and thoughts. In *How Late It Was, How Late,* he take a different tack by fleshing out the narrative discourse into a voice independent of Sammy's but identical to it in class (in its accent) and bearing (in its usage).

In short the narrator of *How Late It Was, How Late* explicitly demonstrates a familiarity with Sammy's bureaucratic dilemma. In the logic of Kelman's novel, proper English usage is oppressive; it is after all the tongue of the functionaries—the doctors, policemen, and bureaucrats—who frustrate Sammy's claims. Here, the language of middle-class comfort is the language of working-class exploitation. Slang, vulgarity, a provincial accent, colloquialism, cliché—these are the markers of solidarity and sympathy that the narrator shows to Sammy. This respect even extends to a narrational reticence when Sammy is at his lowest, during his initial journey home from the police station:

Okay, cutting a long story short here cause Sammy's head was getting into a state and what was coming out wasnay always very good. The guy was fuckt I mean put it that way, he was fuckt, so there's nay sense prolonging it. If ye're wanting to play fair: alright? let it go, fucking let it go, just let it go, a wee bit of privacy, know what I'm talking about, ye give a guy a break, fuck sake, sometimes it's best just accepting that.

(p. 51)

After Sammy recovers and continues on his odyssey, the narrator is relieved that he is all right after all: "Ach he was making it, he was doing it his own way. Nay point pulling the plug on him after all. There was a wee bit of hallucinating going on but no that much, no when you come to consider it" (p. 51). Critics who complained about the torrent of swearing ironically failed to see that they were essentially weighing in on the side of those who would keep Sammy, and all that he represents, in his place, out of sight and out of literature. In Kelman's counternarrative silence and invisibility are the conditions destroyed by writing colloquially against the official story.

THE GOOD TIMES

In his most recent publication, a compilation of twenty short narratives titled *The Good Times* (1998), Kelman excavates further into working-class life. Moving away from the singular monologue of *How Late It Was, How Late,* he has increased the variety of voices heard in his new volume. Harking back to the dark, somber stories of *The Burn,* these new stories communicate a moodiness and truculence that belie the social rituals and conviviality that Kelman continues to depict. In earlier stories public occasions such as waiting in line at the unemployment office or standing around in the betting shop were excuses for conversation and commiseration. In *The Good Times* much of this sense of camaraderie is gone, replaced instead with suspicion. In "It happened to me once," as the narrator waits in a queue he is accosted by the man behind him, who shares an incoherent theory about cigarettes that burn forever. Afterward the narrator wonders why he is the target of such rants:

But how come it was me, it was aye me, I aye got fucking cornered by crackpots, it was like they followed me about, they waited there till I stepped out the close. Here he comes! I could imagine them nudging each other. Here he comes! probably they paid a couple of bob into a kitty. That was to get me. Else I was fucking raffled. Top prize. This morning's fucking halfwit. That was what I was, a fucking halfwit.

(p. 53)

Ever since the stories in *The Burn*, Kelman's characters have increasingly come to feel persecuted and panicky.

Even Kelman's favored venue for illustrating social life, the pub, becomes a site for deep-seated feelings of social isolation. "Every fucking time," for example, finds the narrator sitting with two former schoolmates, nursing a half-pint of lager and a dark rum while he waits for his wife to arrive. Although this is the narrator's regular pub, he dismisses the bartender as "a cheeky wee cunt" (p. 93) and despises the fact that his friends, who are brothers, still live at home with their mother. However, as usual with Kelman's tales, animosity toward others reveals a self-loathing that expresses itself obliquely as the story wears on. After gossiping about mutual friends and boxing, the narrator reminisces about his football-playing days at school, a story that he later regrets telling: "I just nodded; it was a time to drop out the conversation. I couldnay believe I had done so much yapping. Ye would have thought it was the highlight of my life the way I had been telling it. A game of football I played at 15 years of age, nearly thirty year ago. What a joke" (p. 109). Although the narrator discounts this game as his shining moment, the story insinuates that it was. One of the implications of the collection's title, then, as the story illustrates, is that the good times have by definition passed,

that from the perspective of the present, memory frequently recasts the past in a favorable light.

A further feature that *The Good Times* shares with *The Burn* is the greater role played by women. Kelman's writing has frequently been characterized as solely describing a male world, despite the presence of wives and girlfriends in his stories and novels. But it is not until *The Burn*, where ironically marriages and relationships are often broken or crumbling, that women become pivotal in Kelman's portraits of working-class life. In *The Good Times* women are not merely spoken for by their male partners but actually speak forcefully in their own interests. This new female voice occurs in "Oh my darling," a story set during a couple's Saturday afternoon shopping trip. When they stop for a coffee at a pretentious café, the husband grumbles about the "bourgeois bastards" and the snobby atmosphere (p. 86). The wife finally grows weary of her husband pointing out the obvious and chastises him for being "mean-minded"; she tells him, "Sometimes ye're stupid do ye know, ye make life so difficult for yerself" (p. 86, 87). So often in his fiction Kelman's men are limited in their thinking by their doctrinaire judgments about class, gender, age, and other social markers; in this story it takes a woman to arrest the process, even for a few minutes over a coffee. The feeling toward women that Kelman's male characters most frequently display is perplexity, as the narrator of "Constellation" confesses: "The thing was and there was nay doubt about it, women were different. Even the way they spoke was different" (p. 234). Asked about the women in Kelman's fiction by Maya Jaggi, Janice Galloway, another well-known Scots writer, responded, "Jim's writing in a male, not masculine, way, but there's a self-consciousness about his masculinity—that's the most you can do. The doings of women are mysterious to his characters, and that's honest" ("Speaking in Tongues," p. 30). For Kelman's male characters the irreducible difference between women and men must be carefully negotiated in bed and in conversation.

Stylistically *The Good Times* is the farthest Kelman has moved away from reconstructing working-class parlance. The stories here are still laced with the cadences and diction of Glaswegian English, but in their conversation and musing Kelman's characters in *The Good Times* speak a particularly mannered, idiosyncratic form of discourse. In part this change in usage stems from Kelman's increased emphasis on the intellectual accomplishments of his characters. Throughout his writing Kelman has always insisted that workers are also readers, that being working-class is not synonymous with being ignorant and uneducated. In *The Good Times* the learning that characters show seems far more academic and formal than previously was the case. In "Gardens go on forever," for instance, a young gardener spends his free time at work reading a German philosophical treatise on the nature of time. In the longest story of the collection, "Comic Cuts" (a piece derived from a radio drama of Kelman's called *The Art of the Big Bass Drum*), a discussion about the nature of aesthetics leads to an analysis of the politics of rock 'n' roll. A group of musicians gathers in a kitchen after the pubs close, to tell stories, drink, and wait (futilely) for a pot of soup to be ready. Gradually, however, they consider whether perfection is ever possible in rock music. The narrator argues that "the very notion of 'perfection,' the very notion, would itself be called into question," once one considered the social conditions that made the music possible: "Right ye are, that it just isnay possible to speak of perfection since the actual perception of it would perforce be filtered through the subject's knowledge that the person who wrote and perhaps even recorded the song originally was getting badly exploited by the white record companies" (p. 134). The narrator's language in "Comic Cuts" exemplifies the mixture of urban and sociological discourses that characterizes many of the extended monologues in these stories. To avoid simply reproducing, or parodying, his earlier, more recognizably working-class language, Kelman now mixes discursive forms in his fiction in a way that mirrors the hybridity of working-class culture at large, within postmodernity. As the narrator of "Comic Cuts" says, "My son it's not what ye know it's how, how ye know, the crux of the 21st century post-medieval intellectual position, as adopted by all religions and retail state-media outlets, let me tell ye boy this is the crux, thee crux, veritabeeleh" (p. 132).

PLAYS AND ESSAYS

IN addition to writing short stories and novels, Kelman has published a collection of plays and a volume of essays. The three plays in *Hardie and Baird and Other Plays* (1991) were written and staged between 1978 and 1990. In his foreword to the collection, Kelman argues vehemently for public funding for the arts, even though, he admits, "art and subversion are close allies" (p. 1). Public subsidies are necessary because art that attracts private, corporate sponsorship "will be decorative rather than challenging" (p. 3). Writers and artists who compete for private-sector arts subsidies, Kelman claims, "stop creating their own work. They no longer see what they do as an end in itself, they adopt the criteria of the 'market-place'; they begin producing what they think the customer wants" (p. 3). Having never been offered private funding for his productions, Kelman has predominantly staged his productions with experimental theater companies.

The first play in the compilation, a short three-act production titled *The Busker*, is adapted from "Old Holborn," a short story in *Lean Tales* describing the encounter between a street musician and a passerby who wants to help him earn more contributions by actively canvassing pedestrians walking past. The play builds on this premise by labeling the passerby "The Ponce," a slang term for a pimp, and by introducing a young woman whose attraction to the busker and the ponce is hard to fathom, particularly after she faints. Because so much of Kelman's short fiction is composed of dialogue rather than description, his plays seem to resemble his stories in their form, as well as in their inconclusive and open-ended nature.

In the second play, *In the Night,* a couple is awakened and dragged out of bed by three interrogators, who question them for hours about their politics, their sexuality, and their ethnicity. Near the end of the first act, the third interrogator concludes, "You are both subversive elements, you are radical left-wing communists. (*Couple smile.*) Loonies . . . ! (*Couple smile.*) Dont be humorous about it!" (p. 80). With *In the Night* Kelman stages an Orwellian drama that pits dissidents against state-security apparatuses charged with enforcing the values of the government and with rooting out competing lifestyles and beliefs.

In the third play, *Hardie and Baird: The Last Days,* Kelman looks back to a little-known weavers' uprising in Scotland in 1820 during which three weavers were executed and many others were transported abroad or imprisoned. The play depicts the final days in the lives of Andrew Hardie and John Baird, two leaders of the rebellion, who fought a company of government troops in the Battle of Bonnymuir. The play is set in the dungeons of Edinburgh and Stirling castles, where Hardie and Baird are being held and where they are visited repeatedly by three Presbyterian ministers. As they encourage the prisoners to accept God as a way to lessen the pain of their final days, Hardie becomes increasingly religious while Baird refuses either to believe or to talk to the clergymen. As an examination of political action and insurgency, the play explores the roles of conscience and friendship in the struggle for human rights and economic security.

In *Some Recent Attacks: Essays Cultural and Political* (1992) Kelman eloquently analyzes the social and literary conditions that govern how he writes and what he writes about. His essays on politics range from attacks on governmental neglect of victims of asbestosis to polemics against state-sponsored surveillance. He castigates the leftist Labour Party in Scotland for stifling true radical activism and for taking its working-class constituency for granted. Kelman also insists repeatedly that the parliamentary electoral process masks a permanent authority answerable to nobody except itself, and that correspondingly, Scotland has been treated as a colonial possession by English legislators.

In his literary essays Kelman continues to emphasize the material terms from which his own writing emerged. In "The Importance of Glasgow in My Work" he stresses that the impetus to write from his own class and voice came from the fact that nobody else was writing accurately about working-class culture:

Whenever I did find somebody from my own sort of background in English Literature there they were confined to the margins, kept in their place, stuck in the dialogue. You only ever saw them or heard them. You never got into their mind. You did find them in the narrative but from without, seldom from within. And when you did see them or hear them they never rang true, they were never like anybody I ever met in real life. None of the richness of character you'll find in any cultural setting, any cultural setting at all.

(pp. 81–82)

Kelman blames middle-class critics, reviewers, academics, and publishers for this absence: "The old story: the prime effect of censorship and suppression is silence" (p. 83). Conventionally, Kelman suggests elsewhere, there have been only two pos-

sibilities for underrepresented classes or races in English literature: invisibility or its opposite, stereotyping. In the essays "Artists and Value" and "English Literature and the Small Coterie," Kelman proposes that because minority populations have essentially been silenced by the literary establishment, the representation of "the other" occurs primarily by stereotyping. For Kelman stereotypes reveal not simply a failure of the artistic imagination but also, in their reductionist logic, a failure of literary technique: "When we perceive a member of a class we are not perceiving an individual human being, we are perceiving an idea, an abstract entity, a generality; it is a way of looking that by and large is the very opposite of art" ("Artists and Value," p. 11). Kelman's essays, which champion the rights of the downtrodden both in representation and in politics, offer a powerful corrective to those who like to consider literature and politics middle-class preserves.

CONCLUSION

As a working-class writer committed to representing his own class in fiction, James Kelman treads a fine line between speaking for working people and producing a unique form of literary expression. On the one hand his writing embraces realist conventions in depicting working-class culture authentically, and on the other it is highly experimental in its representation of individual psychology and perspective. Consistently, Kelman has established a successful balance between the social and aesthetic aspects of his literature. With each new novel and collection of short stories, he has extended his exploration of neglected areas of social experience in Scotland. Each time his narrative form draws from his earlier work, yet it also shows a developing awareness of the need to include an extended range of voices and perspectives in his class portraits. As Scotland develops into a more multicultural society, the challenge for Kelman will lie in depicting the personal pain and social contradictions that this transformation will inevitably occasion. Likewise, as the novelty of political devolution from England wears off in Scotland, and as the very existence of a "United Kingdom" is threatened, Kelman's fiction will have even greater scope for examining what it means to be Scottish and working class at the turn of the millennium. Referring to his own Gaelic- and English-speaking heritage and to his wife's Welsh, Irish, and Irish-Canadian roots, Kelman has noted: "All of these [cultural strands] are at play in my work, as filtered in through my own perspective, a perspective that, okay, is Glaswegian, but in these terms 'Glaswegian' is a late 20th century construct" (*Some Recent Attacks*, p. 84). As a means of filtering and distilling Scottish culture, Kelman's work plays a crucial role in examining the complexity of Scottish cultural identity.

SELECTED BIBLIOGRAPHY

I. COLLECTIONS OF STORIES. *An Old Pub Near the Angel* (Orono, Me., 1973); *Short Tales from the Nightshift* (Glasgow, 1978); *Not Not While the Giro and Other Stories* (Edinburgh, 1983); *Greyhound for Breakfast* (London and New York, 1987); *The Burn* (London, 1991); *Busted Scotch: Selected Stories* (New York, 1997); *The Good Times* (London, 1998; New York, 1999).

II. NOVELS. *The Busconductor Hines* (Edinburgh, 1984); *A Chancer* (Edinburgh, 1985); *A Disaffection* (London and New York, 1989); *How Late It Was, How Late* (London, 1994; New York, 1995).

III. PLAYS AND ESSAYS. *Hardie and Baird and Other Plays* (London, 1991); *Some Recent Attacks: Essays Cultural and Political* (Stirling, Scotland, 1992).

IV. CONTRIBUTIONS TO COLLECTIONS. *Three Glasgow Writers* (Glasgow, 1976), with Alex Hamilton and Tom Leonard; *Lean Tales* (London, 1985), with Alasdair Gray and Agnes Owens; "Foreword," in George E. Davie, ed., *The Scottish Enlightenment and Other Essays* (Edinburgh, 1991); "Alex La Guma (1925–1985)," in Murdo Macdonald, ed., *Nothing Is Altogether Trivial* (Edinburgh, 1995).

V. CRITICAL STUDIES AND INTERVIEWS. Edwin Morgan, "Glasgow Speech in Recent Scottish Literature," in J. Derrick Murison, ed., *Scotland and the Lowland Tongue* (Aberdeen, 1983); J. M. Hendry, *On James Kelman* (Edinburgh, 1989); H. Gustav Klaus, "James Kelman: A Voice from the Lower Depths of Thatcherite Britain," in *London Magazine* n.s. 29, no. 5–6 (1989); Kirsty McNeill, "Interview with James Kelman," in *Chapman* 57 (summer 1989); Ian Bell, "James Kelman," in *New Welsh Review* 3, no. 2 (1990); Gordon A. Craig, "Glesca Belongs to Me!" in *New York Review of Books*, 25 April 1991; Craig Cairns, "Resisting Arrest: James Kelman," in Gavin Wallace and Randall Stevenson, eds., *The Scottish Novel Since the Seventies: New Visions, Old Dreams* (Edinburgh, 1993); H. Gustav Klaus, "New Bearings in Scottish Writing: Alasdair Gray, Tom Leonard, James Kelman," in Hans Ulrich and Walter Gobel, eds., *Anglistentag 1992 Stuttgart: Proceedings* (Tübingen, 1993); Gillian Bowditch, "Glasgow Disowns Prize Novel," in *Times*, 13 October 1994; Mike Ellison, "Defiant Booker Winner Shrugs Off the Critics and Puts in a Word for Native Culture," in *Guardian*, 12 October 1994; Simon Jenkins, "An Expletive of a Winner," in *Times*, 15 October 1994; Marcello Mega, "Straight Talking Wins over the Critics," in *Scotsman*, 12 October 1994; Andrew O'Hagan, "The Paranoid Sublime: Review of *How Late It Was, How Late*," in *London Review of Books*, 26 May 1994; Anthony Quinn, "Category A Literature," in *Independent* (October 1994); Julia Llewellyn Smith, "The Prize Will Be Useful. I'm Skint," in *Times*, 13 October 1994.

James Ledbetter, "Making Booker: James Kelman Fucks with Literature," in *Voice Literary Supplement* (March 1995); Duncan McLean, "James Kelman Interviewed," in Murdo Macdonald, ed., *Nothing Is Altogether Trivial* (Edinburgh, 1995); Dorothy McMillan, "Constructed out of Bewilderment: Stories of Scotland," in Ian A. Bell, ed., *Peripheral Visions: Images of Nationhood in Contemporary British Fiction* (Cardiff, 1995); Roderick Watson, "Alien Voices from the Street: Demotic Modernism in Modern Scots Writing," in *Yearbook of English Studies* 25 (1995); Simon Baker, " 'Wee Stories with a Working-Class Theme': The Reimagining of Urban Realism in the Fiction of James Kelman," in Susanne Hagemann, ed., *Studies in Scottish Fiction: 1945 to the Present* (Frankfurt, 1996); Ian A. Bell, "Imagine Living There: Form and Ideology in Contemporary Scottish Fiction," in Susanne Hagemann, ed., *Studies in Scottish Fiction: 1945 to the Present* (Frankfurt, 1996); Roderick Watson, "The Rage of Caliban: The 'Unacceptable' Face and the 'Unspeakable' Voice in Contemporary Scottish Writing," in Horst W. Drescher and Susanne Hagemann, eds., *Scotland to Slovenia: European Identities and Transcultural Communication* (Frankfurt, 1996); Maya Jaggi, "Speaking in Tongues," in *Guardian Weekend*, 18 July 1998; Catherine Lockerbie, "Deep in the Heart of Kelman," in *Scotsman*, 18 July 1998.

THOMAS KINSELLA

(1928–   )

Susana Powell

THOMAS KINSELLA HAS been described by some critics as the leading living Irish poet, and second only to Yeats in modern Irish poetry. To others, his work is so obscure that it is incomprehensible.

The picture is more complex than either extreme suggests and is further complicated by Kinsella's dual audience. In Ireland his work can be considered the product of a long dual literary tradition. His translations from Irish into English have helped salvage many ancient manuscripts from anonymity. In the rest of the English-speaking world, where readers may miss many allusions to Eire's poetic and political past, the difficult work of interpretation may not always feel worth the effort.

Poetry is at once the most personal and the most public of literary expressions. On a personal level it may hit at the very heart of the reader's own experiences and perceptions. On a public level the oral expression of the poetic word may strike a national chord that places the poet in the highest echelons of a society which values it. Does an unreceptive public diminish a poet's work? How can such work be gauged? Is education failing if students can no longer make connections with their collective past?

These are questions that must be pondered to appreciate the work of Thomas Kinsella, whose life has taken him from the public sector of the civil servant to the halls of academe, and finally into that personal space of a poet within a family, within a country, a semirecluse absorbed by the art and nature that inspire him. The contradictions that mark the life and work of Kinsella can actually be seen to balance each other out in the kind of symmetry to which a poet aspires.

Born in 1928 to a working-class Catholic family in Dublin, Kinsella was married in 1955 to Eleanor Walsh, whose prosperous family came from the countryside of County Wexford. After having chosen the dull routine and stability of a life in the Irish civil service from 1946 to 1965, Kinsella was subsequently able to renounce that life and dedicate himself to poetry, thanks to the encouragement of his boss. Writing somewhat prosaic English verse while living in his native Ireland, Kinsella later explored his Irish roots and the Irish language, suffusing his verse with new and original cadences while living in voluntary exile in the United States. And then, after a successful public career as an American university professor and renowned Irish poet-scholar, Kinsella returned to Ireland in 1990, retiring to a private life of introspection.

Even his critical acclaim has been balanced by opposing views. Those who praise Kinsella's early work appreciate his technical mastery of poetic forms, while those who see more originality in his more obscure poetry laud his ability to rid himself of early influences. And while the issue of obscurity continues to plague his reputation as a major writer, Kinsella confesses he has no interest in poetry for entertainment but seeks a readership of shared commitment that will work to probe the mysteries of the universe in his work, as he has sought to mirror them in words and images.

EARLY WORKS: 1956–1962

WHAT is a poet? What is the poet's job? How does she or he do it? In his early works Kinsella provides characteristically contradictory views. In *Downstream* (1962) he is all humor, in bouncy rhyming couplets listing the expectations of a poet, tracing how mundane routine leads to poetic inspiration, but finally deriding his own muses: *"Helped along by blind Routine, / Futility flogs a tambourine . . ."* (*Collected Poems*, pp. 31–32).

In "Baggot Street Deserta" Kinsella considers the nature of poetry: it is a salve, but imagination arches over honest recollection and dreams fade to reality: "The goddess who had light for thighs / Grows feet of dung and takes to bed" (p. 14).

Although some critics suggest that Kinsella's early accessible poetry is easiest to comprehend and most praiseworthy, while his later work requires a readership trained in Jungian psychology, Taoism, and Irish myth, an examination of his first poems reveals that each collection is marked by a mixture of styles, foreshadowing future, more complex works.

At the beginning of his writing career, Kinsella published a slim volume of poetry every two years with Dolmen Press, an enterprise he helped establish. *Poems* (1956), *Another September* (1958), *Moralities* (1960), and *Downstream* (1962) comprise his poetic output while working in the Department of Finance in Dublin. Appropriately, since both his father and grandfather had worked for Guinness, Kinsella won the Guinness Poetry Award for *Another September*.

In the twenty-eight poems of this volume appear themes that recur throughout the oeuvre. There are poems that examine the personal, the natural (and sometimes national), and the literary. The personal poems come from experiences unique to Kinsella but recognizable by the reader: the love and pain of personal relationships. The natural poems stem from a perception of nature that arouses awe and circumspection, often linking a national past and present, which the reader can share, although it may elicit different reactions from different perspectives. The literary poems depend on a shared cultural background or on research by the reader. Like many young poets exploring their universe, Kinsella is preoccupied with death and the nature of poetry.

In "A Lady of Quality" Kinsella describes the dark, foreboding helplessness of a hospital room where his wife is trapped in illness, while he has one foot in her antiseptic world and the other in the doorway, ready to flee to the solace of penning poetry. While the meter and rhyming couplets lend reassurance, the sterility is frightening. We recognize and share his "tiny terrors" as the light of the room is contrasted to the dark of his fear:

> In hospital where windows meet
> . . .
> The air is like a laundered sheet,
> The world's a varnished picture.
> (*Collected Poems*, p. 8)

Likewise, the repetitious sadness of parting and awkward farewells are captured in the alliteration and rhyming couplet of "Tête à Tête": "Last time they spoke it was with fumbled feeling, / The station deafening, their voices failing" (p. 15).

Other poems in the collection recall the beauty of an Irish landscape marred by memories of the tyranny of English oppression. It is impossible to take a walk "In the Ringwood" or by "King John's Castle" without recalling the atrocities of occupation. History and geography converge in the poem "Lead," in which the discovery of two lead dice evoke a Roman past in which

> Flame-breathing Vulcan in a maker's rage
> Smelted and hammered on his smoking ledge
> A bit to bridle Chaos.
> (p. 23)

In the lush and lyrical title poem of the collection, "Another September," reminiscent of John Keats's "Ode to Autumn," Kinsella uses the traditional poetic devices of metaphor, simile, and personification to describe "Domestic Autumn, like an animal," rubbing its "kind hide" on the natives' furniture and home (p. 21).

Even in this first collection readers are assumed to have more than a general education. While any professor might be the subject of "Death and the Professor," and while "Thinking of Mr. D." remains powerful, without knowledge of the identity of Mr. D., some allusions must be understood in order to make sense of the poems. And while a general reader might be assumed to know Roman and Greek mythology, as well as Shakespeare and the Bible, Kinsella, like all high modernists, assumes knowledge of his own world (as with "Clarence Mangan," and Burke and Hare in "Baggot Street Deserta") that in fact may not be well known outside of Ireland or Irish scholarship.

Acutely aware of his artistic process, Kinsella revised his early poems meticulously and acknowledged that his goal was to "make real . . . the passing of time, the frightening exposure of relationships and feeling to erosion. An instinct which dramatizes events against such an alien background is both the source . . . and the reason for lack of public concern" ("Thomas Kinsella Writes . . . ," in *Poetry Book Society Bulletin* 17, March 1958, p. 1). In this statement he disavows responsibility for apathetic readers.

As a poet writing of his process, Kinsella expresses both frustration and inspiration. Poetry often pads and paces, like a "crippled leopard" in "Night Songs" (*Collected Poems*, p. 6) or a panther, while the poet is a mere recorder as "the ticking stars keep order" ("An Ancient Ballet," *Collected Poems*, p. 12). Sometimes inspiration appears in the form of an *aisling*, that mythical Irish spirit / dream woman who resembles "Hecate, the dark side of the White Goddess" (John Montague, in James Vinson, ed., *Contemporary Writers of the English Language: Contemporary Poets*, London, 1975).

Kinsella is ambivalent toward his muse, and he also treats Death in distinctly different modes. At times Death is the only equalizer, prowling and preying on all men, indiscriminate of virtue or vice, warrior or victim, as in "The Travelling Companion." In another poem, "Test Case," Man is the measure of all things, including Death, and the "heroic agenda" is blamed for being "full of frightening / Things to kill, or love, or level down" (*Collected Poems*, p. 4). But in "Pause en Route" the attitude is openly defiant: Death is a mere "final servant functioning." Death is only the conduit.

Moralities (1960) displays the architect in Kinsella. This slim volume of twenty poems is a quartet of "Faith," "Love," "Death," and "Song," with a prelude called "Moralities" and an "Interlude" in which form and function are meticulously matched. The prelude sets the scene, and the interlude takes time to lead the reader by the hand.

Kinsella's prelude evokes a medieval scene in which the performing arts confront the plastic arts. The facade of a church or cathedral, with its angelic and demonic carved bronze, stone, and stained-glass windows, is contrasted with a gaudy jester from a vagabond acting troupe. He carries props of hay, skin, and bone, and "Faith, Love, Death, Song, creep after him like flies" (*Collected Poems*, p. 25).

This eight-line stanza mirrors perfectly Kinsella's thoughts about the aspirations of the arts in contrast to the plodding abilities of the artisans with feet of clay, and he develops the concept in the quartets that follow.

Although Faith is the first allegory, in the first poem, "An Old Atheist Pauses by the Sea," the poet hints that the awesome erosion of the ocean will give humankind more pause to question atheism than organized religion, and in "A Pillar of the Community," the title referring to a statue on Merchants' Alley, it is Lucifer, the fallen angel, who inspires the inscription "Do good. / Some care and a simple faith will get you on" (p. 26).

Likewise, Love does not yield what we expect. Each of its four poems casts an unexpected shadow, whether it be from the martyred heroes of Irish history (in "Sisters") or the shredded expectations of a bird's nest, or, in the final poem's promise of an Easter garden, the final cutting couplet: "And now great ebb tides lift to the light of day / The sea-bed's briny chambers of decay" ("A Garden on the Point," p. 27).

In "Death," the third section of the quartet, Kinsella leads us through four contrasting aspects of Death, from "The Doldrums" of summer through a "Garden of Remembrance" to a memorial, "Sons of the Brave," and a nightmare, "Dead on Arrival." The glory of Death for a cause is deflated by imagery of pigs in a sty, while the taste of death's terror in dreams reminds us that sometimes we are the agents of our own destruction.

Finally, in "Song," Kinsella returns to the arts evoked in his prelude, as Reason and Passion clash in "Fire and Ice." Satyr and nymph, male and female, confront and conflict, but inevitably both must prevail for life to be sustained.

Thus, in miniature, Kinsella's predominant moods and modes are mapped for future reference in *Moralities*.

Downstream is the last of the early collections to escape censure from those critics who admired Kinsella's formal poetry. It is a natural link between the obvious and the obscure, opening with a parody of the public's expectations of a poet and continuing with familiar themes.

"The Laundress" contrasts male and female roles and foreshadows, both in its imagery and setting (Flanders, World War I), Muriel Rukeyser's powerful poem "Kathe Kollwitz," in which man is the sower of the seed, the seed itself, and the grim reaper, while woman nurtures, bears, and ultimately buries that seed.

The first hint of political and class issues appears in "Wedding Morning" and "A Portrait of the Engineer," which damn the rich for profiteering at the expense of the poor. They are followed by "Scylla and Charybdis" and "Dick King," which extol the virtues of the common man exemplified in Reynolds, a fishmonger; O'Neill, a greengrocer; and Dick King, a railway worker whose passion to save the Irish language inspired the young Kinsella.

Two more Death poems appear, "Death of a Tyrant" and "Old Harry." *Downstream* also includes longer narrative pieces: the title poem and "A Country Walk," in which the poet seeks solace in nature only to find at every turn a memory of Ireland bleeding at the hands of the invader, be it Norman or Briton. The tall chimneys of munitions factories recall Blake's hellish industrial landscapes and Dante's *Inferno*.

"Downstream" is an evening odyssey into night and nightmares. Drifting down the stream, Kinsella confronts ghosts of centuries of victims. Man is "swinish," demons are manlike in a landscape reminiscent of Hieronymus Bosch's Hell in the triptych *Garden of Earthly Delights*:

> Each night a fall
> Back to the evil dream where rodents ply,
> Man-rumped, sow-headed, busy with whip and maul
> . . .
> Among nude herds of the damned.
>
> (Collected Poems, p. 49)

In this journey that seems simultaneously literal and figurative, swift "phantoms of the overhanging sky" mingle with the "slow, downstreaming dead" (p. 51) as the poet and his partner search for safe landing. As Kinsella's career continued, there would be more nightmares and fewer landing places. "Chrysalides" and "Mirror in February," also in *Downstream*, have the thirty-four-year-old poet facing his mortality. In the former, he speaks of his "last free summer" and "youthful midnights" and accepts with resignation the image of what he sees as the middle-aged poet in "Mirror in February":

> Now plainly in the mirror of my soul
> I read that I have looked my last on youth
> And little more; for they are not made whole
> That reach the age of Christ.
>
> (p. 54)

TRANSITIONS (1963–1970)

IF it is the nature of the poet to explore uncharted territory, sometimes diving to dangerous depths to seek the unknown, then the reader must choose whether or not to take that plunge, an often risky business.

Kinsella's life and career, as well as his psychic quest, took a radical turn after the publication of

Downstream in 1962. Within the next five years this father of three and husband of an ai(s)ling wife won a scholarship to visit the United States, became a founding member of the now incorporated Dolmen Press in Dublin, and left his secure civil service job to accept a position as writer-in-residence and professor of English literature at Southern Illinois University. While these moves might indicate a new freedom and marks of respect and stability, the works that emerged from this period, *Wormwood* (1966) and *Nightwalker* (1967), indicate that Kinsella had chosen to make that plunge into the unknown. Some readers and critics would be left behind mourning the "old" Kinsella.

Wormwood signals not so much a radical departure from the early works as a decision to follow the darker path of introspection tentatively taken in the first decade of Kinsella's career as a poet. Prefaced by a quotation from the biblical book Revelation and a dedication to his "Beloved" that set the theme for the collection, *Wormwood* probes the nature of love and explores the relationship of life and death in both a personal and a cosmic sense.

Kinsella sees life as a series of disappointments and disillusionments, but the cycle of despair takes humanity through failure and bitterness to renewed innocence. The biblical reference is to a falling star that pollutes a third of earth's waters with bitterness but Kinsella holds that unless we embrace ordeals and drink our cup of bitterness to the dregs, no maturity or peace is possible. Life becomes, then, a series of trials and tribulations designed to test our stamina and "the restored necessity to learn" (p. 62).

The first, untitled poem in *Wormwood*, which serves as the prelude, presents a Beckettian tree in an Eliot Waste Land. Five rhyming couplets end with the question "What cannot rest till it is bare, / Though branches crack and fibres tear?" (p. 63).

This is followed immediately by the title poem of the collection, which describes another tree—this with twin trunks intertwined—and, in a dream, a flash of iron axing the core. With the biblical quotation having appeared just above, conventional images of the Tree of Knowledge, the Tree of Life, and the wooden crucifix of Christ immediately spring to mind. "Wormwood" is followed by "Mask of Love," and the proximity of the prelude to the Beloved and Ovid's mythical lovers growing together like a tree suggest more earthbound symbolism. As the ax seeks to sunder the twin trunks, so the relationship of the lovers is doomed to separation: they face one another across an abyss in a "nocturnal/ Suicidal dance" (p. 64).

Nor is the despair confined to conjugal relationships. In "The Secret Garden" the poet, having failed to stop thorny blackberry brambles from invading his lawn, rejoices in the dewdrops of his garden, the "pearl flesh" of his son, only to set the son free to experience his own life as "rasping boredom funnels into death!" (p. 65).

Kinsella recognizes domestic tranquillity in objects that order the chaos of emotion. In "First Light" a clean kitchen is "blank with marriage" after the lovers have "raved and wept" into the night. "Remembering Old Wars" recalls the "smell of decay" in lovemaking and dawn's renewal with a "savage smile." And in "Je t'adore" love is the "limiter" and the lovers are "propped above nothing" in one another's "iron arms" (pp. 65–66).

The merciless attack on Kinsella's own marriage continues in *Nightwalker and Other Poems* (1968) (which incorporates much of *Wormwood*), although the volume is dedicated to "Fair Eleanor. O Christ Thee Save." The union is not devoid of love. It is the nature of love to be devoid. In "Westland Row" Kinsella begs his "Daughterwife" to look *upon* him (not look *at* him), but they separate with neither gaze nor touch. And in "Before Sleep" again the ordered kitchen and the evening routine belie the nightly chaos, "All battered, scattered" as "love's detritus" is "swallowed into that insane / White roar" (*Collected Poems*, p. 72).

Death and disease, both medieval and modernist themes, are other preoccupations in this book. "Our Mother" and "Traveller" are hospital bound, and there are no fewer than five poems dedicated to the memory of the dead or aged: "The Shoals Returning," "Magnanimity," "The Poet O'Rahilly," "Homesick in Old Age," and "Death in Ilium," as well as "Office for the Dead" and "The Serving Maid," which deal with funerals and burial. Sir Thomas Browne is invoked.

Kinsella has moved into an acceptance of death as part of life. As nature regenerates itself through decay and decomposition, so the human life cycle should not end with death, which rather ought to be seen as a new beginning. The poet is paralyzed into stasis when confronted with pain and loss, but acceptance and understanding make life bearable.

The ebb and flow, rise and fall of the tide erode the flesh as they erode the shore, purifying "Blood washed white" (p. 57). And in noting a preying owl in "Traveller" and shrieking toads facing the harrow in "Folk Wisdom," the poet accepts that man, too, is able to find "a jewel / Made of pain in his hands" (*Nightwalker and Other Poems*, p. 17). In the grave William Butler Yeats grows whole and remote despite fangs tearing his corpse: "Dog faces in his bowels / Bitches at his face" ("Death in Ilium," p. 46).

As "Downstream" described a psychic journey enveloped in a physical environment, so "Nightwalker" is a walk both through Dublin and into the world of introspection prompted by physical clues, evoking Joyce, the "watcher in the tower." Recognizing that "The greater part must be content to be as though they had not been," the walker sets off groping for structure, mindful of madness, knowing "things seem and are not good" (*Collected Poems*, p. 76).

Whereas a traditional poet would glory at the beauty of the moon, Kinsella sees a "fat skull" hanging like a pendulum, a "mask of grey dismay." The moon is a moron, silent in the night, like the passive television viewers bathed in blue light whom he sees in window after window,

Faintly luminous, like grubs—abdominal
Body-juices and paper-thin shells, in their thousands
In the smashable wax, o moon!
(Nightwalker and Other Poems, p. 56)

Although this observation strengthens his view that humans make no impression on the universe, the walker does not exclude himself from the useless populace. He, too, will sleep and rise and work, and this inevitability gives rise to a rage about the "clear principles, with no fixed ideas" and the development "without principle, based on fixed ideas" that he observes in his daily routine (p. 57).

At the harbor mouth he sees the statue of Kathleen Ni Houlihan as an inverted Statue of Liberty. Instead of the inscription "Give me your poor," he suggests "Lend me your wealth, your cunning and your drive, / Your arrogant refuse. . . ." (p. 57), and then delivers a barrage of invective against Germans, specifically two young Germans he has met at work that day. Although the Irish government is encouraging German investment, Kinsella sees fat red faces and an oven door closing. Whether the oven is in the concentration camp or in the witch's kitchen, whether "Bruder und

Schwester" are the new young Nazis firing the oven or Hansel and Gretel, food for the oven, is left to the reader to decide.

Next comes a diatribe on the officials in the civil service, whose service to the community seems far from civil. Although he praises the early national figures, he finds current ministers smug and self-satisfied, which he emphasizes with internal rhymes: "the blood of enemies / And brothers dried on their hide long ago" (p. 57). And this thought leads Kinsella to a wedding photo with allusions completely incomprehensible to any reader not conversant with Irish politics from 1921 to 1927.[1]

In the final poems of the book, "Ritual of Departure" and "Phoenix Park," Thomas and Eleanor prepare to leave Ireland for the United States. On a final drive, visiting their old haunts and stopping at a pub for a drink, they say their good-byes, Eleanor with sadness, Thomas with anticipation. But under the surface their drink is the wormwood of the ordeal cup and the spirit of adventure is a hunger that, once sated, brings new hunger. "Our selves become our own best sacrifice" and "giving without tearing is not possible," which is why he repeats the invocation: "Fair Ellinor. O Christ thee save" (Collected Poems, p. 91).

TRANSLATIONS (1954–1955, 1968–1970, 1981)

KINSELLA is fiercely protective of the Irish language. He had completed several translations in 1954 and 1955, including the three "Translations from the Early Irish," published with some of his poetry in New York as Poems and Translations (1961), his first publication outside Ireland. "Thirty-Three Triads," "Faeth Fiadha: The Breastplate of Saint Patrick," and "Longes MACnUSNIG . . ." are "not literal [translations] but generally the deviations from the original are slight," states Kinsella in his introduction (Poems and Translations, p. 69).

The "Thirty-Three Triads" are quaint folk sayings from an ancient oral history, some practical, some philosophical, all compelling:

Three accomplishments well regarded in Ireland: a clever verse, music on the harp, the art of shaving faces.

(p. 70)

"Faeth Fiadha: The Breastplate of Saint. Patrick" is a hymn, a metaphorical armor "to guard the body and the soul from demons, desires and demented men." With six verses prefaced by "TODAY I PUT ON" and two by "I CALL THESE POWERS" and "I CALL CHRIST TODAY," the invocation ends with a Latin prayer, and is still used by the faithful. The most Irish and least Catholic of the verses evoke some of the natural forces used in Kinsella's poetry:

> TODAY I PUT ON
> The sinews of the sky
> suns' flames
> moon-shimmerings
> fires' astonishment
> the strike of lightning
> forces of the wind
> ocean's fissure
> ground that will not give
> solid rock.
>
> (p. 74)

"Longes MACnUSNIG: The Exile of the Sons of Usnech and The Exile of Fergus and The Death of the Sons of Usnech and of Deidre" is a long narrative with dialogue, in both verse and prose, from the twelfth-century Book of Leinster. But the language is from the oral history of the eighth century. Like Beowulf it tells of ancient kings, heroes, and legendary women renowned for their extremes of goodness and evil. Deidre, with her "downstreaming hair," is clearly a figure who captivated Kinsella and his fellow Irish. Cursed in her birth, her future is foreshadowed in an incident in which her "foster-father flayed" a calf; the slaughter attracted a raven that drank the spilled blood from the snow. Deidre says, "I could desire a man with those three colors: raven-black hair, the color of blood on his cheeks and a snow-bright body" (p. 79). In pursuing this desire she brings about the fall of the house of Usnech and her own suicide.

Kinsella's 1968 Guggenheim Fellowship enabled him to return to Ireland to work on his most ambitious translation, The Táin (pronounced "toyn"). When it was published in Dublin by Dolmen Press in 1969, it had features for which publications of Peppercanister Press, established by Kinsella in

---

[1] The politics of those years is admirably explained by Maurice Harmon, The Poetry of Thomas Kinsella: "With Darkness for a Nest," p. 64.

Dublin during the 1970s, became known: it was printed on high-quality paper, beautifully bound, and illustrated with original art. *The Táin* is illustrated by artist Louis Le Brocquy, and the black text is occasionally splashed with red. Copies of *The Táin* have become collectors' items, highly prized by libraries and housed in rare book collections.

The pleasure of reading evocative poetry while holding a lavishly illustrated book must be experienced. The reader's eyes and hands are feasted as he or she experiences the sensations of the art gallery and museum while absorbing the literal imagery. Le Brocquy's lavish brush drawings in printer's ink seem half Rorschach, half cave painting, clearly influenced by Japanese brush strokes. The overall impression is of entering an ancient culture replete with modern psychological inferences having universal cultural implications. The artist intended "shadows thrown by the text," and the drawings are such.

The Táin is a translation of the Irish epic *Táin Bó Cúailnge,* the Ulster cycle that is the oldest vernacular epic in Western literature. The saga seems set in the Iron Age civilization of Gaul and Britain, marked by a warrior culture of cattle raiding, chariot fighting, and beheadings. Although medieval manuscripts added Christian references, the barbaric world of *The Táin* clearly predates the fifth-century Irish conversion.

The Táin has seven tales of preparation (in which the reader learns what leads to the confrontation) in four sections, and the saga itself is in fourteen sections. The narrative acknowledges that many different versions exist. A reader not conversant with Celtic mythology has probably heard of the great hero Cuchulainn only through Frank McCourt's best-selling book *Angela's Ashes* (1996). But in Ireland this boy hero, the "Hound of Ulster," is the hero of every boy, being not only the great warrior but also the possessor of great moral virtues.

The epic mixes realism with folk tales and fantasy and has inconsistencies that are sometimes considered flaws by those who wrongly apply modern conventions. Kinsella points out in his translator's note that topography is an important feature of *The Táin* because the oral tradition incorporates geography as well as history. He also explains how earlier translations (for instance, by Lady Gregory) tastefully omitted aspects of human behavior and physicality then considered taboo for discussion but that play an important part

in the narrative: seduction, copulation, urination, incest, phallic prowess, impotence, and even the picking of vermin. These, Kinsella believed, were human touches necessary to hold an audience being regaled with impossible feats and supernatural powers.

The Táin is a quest saga, but not one in search of the esoteric Holy Grail. It arises from a quarrel between pig keepers and escalates to a royal couple's competitive pillow talk about the equality of the sexes and their comparative wealth. When the argument hangs in the balance because a druid bull has wandered into the wrong territory, all Ireland is engaged in the fierce cattle raid that ensues, bathing the countryside in the blood of thousands.

Aside from the powerful, sometimes brutal imagery of battles and beheadings, *The Táin* contains humorous and mundane incidents. When heroes are overexcited, they routinely burst their cushions, feathers flying as they jump for joy or flail in anger. Dialogue between nobles is often lofty but sometimes streetwise. "We needn't polish the knobs and knots in this," says Queen Medb, having failed to convince her rival to "lend" the bull: "It was well known, if it wasn't given freely, it would be taken by force. And taken it will be" (*The Tain*, p. 58).

The style of translation, matching the original, moves freely from prose narrative to lyric, and the reader can catch a glimpse of how ancient models influenced Kinsella's own poetic style in the use of alliteration, repetition, and staccato rhythm. The Brown Bull of Cuailnge is

> dark brown dire haughty with young health
> horrific overwhelming ferocious
> full of craft
> furious fiery flanks narrow
> brave brutal thick breasted
> curly browed head cocked high
> growling and eyes glaring
> tough maned neck thick and strong
> snorting mighty in muzzle and eye . . .
>
> (p. 49)

Some of the most compelling characters in the saga are women, always a match for their men, though often blamed as the root of all evil. Ailill, Medb's husband, tells Fergus, an Ulster hero:

> I know all
>   about queens and women
> I lay first fault

straight at women's
own sweet swellings
and loving lust . . .
(p. 105)

Although women always have their say, they do not always get their way. Cuchulainn kills his son, Connla, by the woman warrior Aife, from whom he has learned war craft, against the advice of his wife Emer.

Kinsella's *The Táin* became available to a larger public in 1970, when it was published in a less lavish edition by Oxford University Press. By the early 1980s university presses in America were also showing an interest in Kinsella's work, and his next major translation, *An Duanaire: An Irish Anthology, Poems of the Dispossessed, 1600–1900* (1981), was published by the University of Pennsylvania Press.

In that volume the selections of Seán Ó Tuama are on the left page in their original language, and Kinsella's translations are on the right. In his introduction Kinsella speaks of repossessing the Irish tradition lost during the "troubled centuries from the collapse of the old Gaelic order to the emergence of English as the dominant vernacular" (*An Duanaire,* p. vii), from the 1600s to the time of the Great Famine in the mid-1800s.

Although Ó Tuama's selections and Kinsella's translations were critically acclaimed, Kinsella was criticized for ignoring other translators' versions of some of the poems by those who felt indebted to Yeats and Lady Gregory for the Irish Revival, and for whom those versions were already part of the Irish literary heritage.

This volume is a good introduction to the history and geography of Ireland, providing illustrations and photographs that illuminate the poems as well as the conditions under which they were written. Kinsella would continue to examine the dual tradition of Irish literature, the ancient Gaelic and the modern English, which has been called both the curse and the blessing of Irish writers.

PEPPERCANISTER POEMS 1–7 (1972–1978)

WITH Kinsella's move to Temple University in Philadelphia as professor of English in 1970, and his second Guggenheim Fellowship for research in Ireland in 1971, the poet and his family began a

twenty-year, transatlantic nomadic life beneficial to both continents. In Dublin, Kinsella set up the Peppercanister Press, which would be a conduit for "pamphlets" produced under his scrutiny. In Philadelphia he established an Irish Studies program with a Dublin campus. Both projects were still functioning at the end of the twentieth century, although Kinsella had retired in 1990.

Kinsella's departure from Ireland also marked a departure for some of his readers and critics. While previously it had been useful to know Irish history and mythology to fully appreciate his poetry, hints in Kinsella's work during this transitional period indicate a growing need for a deeper exploration into the poet's subconscious and a leap of faith for both poet and reader. *Notes from the Land of the Dead* represents such a leap.

Published as *Notes from the Land of the Dead and Other Poems* (1973) in the United States by Knopf and as *New Poems* (1973) in Ireland by Dolmen Press, this collection of poems is rooted in childhood experiences. Although "Land of the Dead" is the Celtic name for the province of Munster, mundane references take on psychic significance. The descent into the underworld is terrifying but strangely renewing. There are "Dark nutrient waves," "albumen bodies," and "red protein eyes." Although the naked ancient women with "Nothingness silted under their things / and over their limp talons" (p. 97) terrify him, he nevertheless returns from this journey with hope:

But perhaps
you won't believe a word of this.
Yet by the five wounds of Christ
I struggled toward, by the five digits
of this raised hand, by this key
they hold now, glowing, and reach out with
to touch . . . you shall have . . .

—what shall we not begin
to have on the
count of
O
(*Notes from the Land of the Dead and
Other Poems,* p. 6).

After that egg-shaped cipher, we enter the next segment of the volume: "an egg of being."

The egg is Thomas; the poems in this segment are family portraits and well-remembered incidents. In "Hen Woman," for example, he marvels at the miracle of an egg being laid while a beetle rolls a ball of dung: life and death, food and excrement, in the eternal cycle. Although the slippery egg falls out of her hands and smashes, the Hen Woman laughs: "There's plenty more where that came from!" (*Collected Poems*, p. 100).

In the next poem, "A Hand of Solo," Kinsella uses the red heart and black spade of a present passion to slip into the memory of a childhood game played by adults. He watches

Red deuce. Two hearts. Blood-clean, Still.

Black flash. Jack Rat grins.
She drops down. Silent. Face disk blank. Queen.
(p. 101)

The images are from Celtic myths, and the style is similarly staccato. The reverie is broken as Thomas is sent with a penny to his grandmother's shop. Literally, he is given a pomegranate for his penny, but under the surface lurk the excitement and danger of the crone figure hugging the child and tempting him with seeds of seduction and fertility: she, old and withered; he, too young to activate the symbolism. He remembers being hugged to her apron pocket, and the smell of her "stale abyss" (p. 102).

In "Survivor," from the second segment, "a single drop," stasis and nihilism reduce his verse to minimalism. He ends the poem: "Hair. Claws. Grey. / Naked. Wretch. Wither" (p. 116).

In a stark Beckettian landscape inhabited by decaying hags, Kinsella seems to be aiming for the ultimate reduction of monosyllabic utterances, heading for eventual silence. The next poems, "At the Crossroads" and "Sacrifice," echo the primeval "Flux of forms" (p. 117) in which all are predator or prey and the moon is an evil force presiding over ancient rituals. But Kinsella returns to present passion and ends with a line reminiscent of Yeats: "My heart is in your hands: mind it well" (p. 119).

The third and last segment, "nightnothing," reflects on the poet's inward journey of "Memoirs, maggots." In "Ely Place" a concrete memory, "In Mortuary Lane a gull / cried on one of the Hospital gutters," evokes a bare fifteen minutes of "empty understanding" (pp. 126–127), while a pastoral purity of snow in "The Liffey Hill" is soon dirtied and soured by the smell of wet wool. "Good Night" drags us from normality to nightmare. Eventually, Kinsella tells us in "Death Bed," personal loss is irreconcilable with cosmic cycles.

Although Kinsella already had connections with Dolmen Press, which collaborated with Oxford University Press in publishing his poems and translations, in 1972 he inaugurated his own press, Peppercanister, named for the architectural design of St. Stephen's Church, across the Grand Canal from Kinsella's Dublin home. Through Peppercanister, Kinsella was able to publish timely pamphlets in response to national disasters, such as the 30 January 1972 Bloody Sunday massacre of civil rights activists in Derry, Northern Ireland; the death of Irish composer and patriot Seán Ó Riada; and the tenth anniversary of the assassination of U.S. President John F. Kennedy.

Peppercanister 1, *Butcher's Dozen* (1972), plays on the English expression "baker's dozen," meaning thirteen, and is subtitled "A Lesson for the Octave of Widgery." Widgery was the lord chief justice who headed the tribunal of eight that exculpated the British army for the Derry massacre. The poem was read aloud during the first anniversary vigil and is in angry rhyming couplets that are entirely appropriate to the occasion although outside Kinsella's poetic style of the early 1970s. Paraphrasing the witches in *Macbeth* and speaking in the voices of the thirteen dead, the poem is a powerful and effective cry against injustice.

Peppercanister 2, *A Selected Life* (1972), and Peppercanister 3, *Vertical Man: Sequel to* A Selected Life (1973), are both tributes to Ó Riada, whose death provoked a national day of mourning in Ireland. Kinsella remembers him alive, "thin / as a beast of prey," drumming as he "struck the skin cruelly / with his nails" (p. 143).

In *The Good Fight* (1973), Peppercanister 4, Kinsella mourns Kennedy and posits Lee Harvey Oswald as the predator preying on the prince. This tribute is perhaps the most dated of the three, because Kennedy is elevated above human status, but at the time it was probably a moving eulogy.

Peppercanisters 1–4 were published by Dolmen in 1979 under the title *Fifteen Dead*, referring to all those honored by the poems. Peppercanister numbers 5 through 7 also were published separately in their original versions and as an anthology, *One and Other Poems*, in 1979. It is important to note that the quality deckled paper and lavish line drawings by Anne Yeats add much to the joy of reading *One* in the original 1974 Peppercanister edition. The snake, which is the dominant symbol of this collection of poems, is shown in word and sketch as a coiled serpent, phallic and erect, as well as female, with wide-open mouth, fangs exposed.

In "Up and Awake," the poet is a snake in his dream, vividly catching his prey. When he wakes, he makes practical associations with the imagery. "The Entire Fabric," also in *One and Other Poems*, is a parody of the poet, and the self-consciousness of the artist, through a theatrical performance harking back to the *Moralities* prelude.

But perhaps the most compelling poem in the collection *One*, and one of Kinsella's most evocative ever, is "Finistère." "Finistère" literally means Land's End, which is paradoxical for a beginning poem. But Finistère is a well-known Irish place-name, being hourly repeated on BBC weather forecasts from the inception of radio.

Marked by a cipher "I," which might mean "One" or might be the first-person narrator in the persona of the first Irish poet, Amergin, the poem describes the journey of the first inhabitants of Ireland, analogous with the psychic journey of present Irish.

The style combines Kinsella's newly coined sparse form with the patterns of the ancient Irish that he translated in *The Táin*. These include short lines, parallel structures, and no punctuation, which together promote a fast-flowing pace:

> —Ill wind end well
> mild mother
> on wild water pour peace
> (p. 169)

Next follows a series of rhetorical questions posed as riddles and full of emblems from the Irish sagas and, finally, in "The Oldest Place," the Ireland after Eden:

> We would need to dislodge
> the flesh itself, to dislodge that
> —shrivel back to the first drop
> and be spat back shivering into
> the dark beyond our first father
> (p. 171)

The end of *One* is a return to "38 Phoenix Street" and childhood memories: of staying at a neighbor's house, where a detached Sacred Heart picture terrified the young Thomas, and the "hisshorror" fear of snake strike evoked for him

the Medusa hag *cailleach* who still presides over the harvest and influences rituals of Halloween.[2]

Another highly praised poem in *One* is "His Father's Hands," in which Kinsella's father honors his grandfather. Where female ancestors have been feared and derided, here are loving details of the men's interaction in the tool shed, cobbling shoes and playing the fiddle.

Peppercannister 6 is *A Technical Supplement* (1976). This is not, despite the title, an explanation of Kinsella's techniques, but a series of poems borrowing its inspiration from eighteenth-century France. The preface is a 1758 letter from Denis Diderot to Voltaire expressing his fatigue and depression because the artist seemingly has no impact on improving the world. Then follow twenty-four poems with illustrations from Diderot's *Encyclopedia*, completed in 1772.

Critical interpretations of this collection differ. Some say that Kinsella was emerging from the darkness of his Jungian phase into the Enlightenment that Diderot represents. Others believe Kinsella is writing a parody of Diderot's text.

Kinsella opens the collection of the untitled twenty-four poems in a volume of unnumbered pages with the invitation "let us see how the whole thing / works" (*Collected Poems*, p. 184). In the next two poems he deconstructs the human anatomy and examines a corpse decomposing. Following the third poem is an illustration from Diderot's *Encyclopedia* of Laocoön struggling with one of the sea serpents that will kill him.

The next three poems deal with knives: a surgeon's scalpel, a dagger, and butchers' knives in a slaughterhouse. The cutting of skin and the gushing of blood are described in detail. In Swift's slaughterhouse in Chicago, the setting of the sixth poem, Kinsella describes with nauseating detail the killing of cattle, sheep, and pigs.

He then shifts quickly to "play-blood," questioning the ethical implications of a writer's probing with a pen, another kind of killing. Poems 8 and 9 discourse on "a living thing swallowing another" (p. 189) and aquarium tanks where fish swim to the "music of slaughter" (p. 190). This poem is followed by a Diderot illustration of an anatomical dissection of a human head.

[2]See Brian John, *Reading the Ground: The Poetry of Thomas Kinsella*, p. 177.

In poem 14 torture precedes beauty: "a dish of ripe eyes" is pressed into "a sheet of brilliant color" (p. 194). This is followed by another *Encyclopedia* illustration, a hand with a chisel, and then poem 15, in which the poet imagines stabbing his female muse.

Inevitably the progression leads to death, through age and loneliness (poem 20). The wasted energy in poem 21 is illustrated by a brain surgeon with an awl, and poem 22 describes surgery as the splitting of mirror images. In poem 23 the blade of pain splits the body, so that "the knifed nous" (p. 201) may taste reality, suffer, eat, yield, fail, anticipate and *not* do all these. The final poem depicts a fall from dream and reality with no feeling: "twinned, glaring and glowing" (p. 201).

In this treatise of twinning, doubling, mirror images, and the cutting and dividing that accompany them, Kinsella is continuing his examination of the numerological concept of "0," the woman / emerging self; "1," the man / discovering self; and the additions and multiplications to reach the perfect quincunx or cosmic center of the number 5.

This concept is further developed in Peppercanister 7, *Song of the Night and Other Poems* (1978). Changing form as well as tone, it consists of a prelude and five longer poems, each subdivided. Although critics persist in ascribing Kinsella's imagery to Jungian psychology, the poet's first reference to Jung is in his first poem here, "C. G. Jung's First Years." In the first part Kinsella's previous memories of his grandmother are linked to Jung's memories: "A nurse's intimate warm ear / far in the past; the sallow loin of her throat . . . " (*Collected Poems*, p. 203). But, like Jung, Kinsella acknowledges that black and white must coexist for natural harmony. This idea is not, of course, unique to Jung, but part of the ancient Asian philosophy of yin and yang. "Dark waters churn amongst us / and whiten against troublesome obstacle" (p. 203), says Kinsella. In this case young awakening male sexuality is opposed to old (too old) female sexuality.

The second part of the poem addresses another taboo topic: the corporeal aspect of Jesus. The young Jung recalls being terrified and confused by a man in seemingly female robes—a Jesuit priest, "witchbat" (p. 204). He has a vision of Jesus eating the dead, which Kinsella transposes into a young Catholic's experience of First Communion:

> Since when I have eaten Jesus . . .
> And stepped onto the path
>
> . . .
>
> And have assumed the throne.
> (p. 204)

In eating Jesus the poet becomes Jesus, experiencing the stretching of the crucifixion as well as the ascension to the heavenly throne.

In "Song of the Night," the final poem, Kinsella the exile drifts between Ireland and America in his consciousness as he did physically for so many years. Pointing the way for new moods characterized by Gustav Mahler's music, Kinsella takes as his symbol the curlew, whose plaintive cry reminds the poet of the bird as messenger of Hecate and his muse. The tension between light and dark, movement and stillness, action and stasis, male and female is finally accepted as the way to wholeness.

PEPPERCANISTER POEMS 8–12 (1978–1988)

ALTHOUGH it would be another decade before Kinsella anthologies appeared (*Blood and Family*, 1988; *Selected Poems, 1962–1989*, 1989), he continued to write one or two Peppercanister pamphlets every two years. *The Messenger* (Peppercanister 8, 1978) was written in memory of his father, John Paul Kinsella, who died in 1976. Whereas *Song of the Night* had been illustrated with the "witchbat," *The Messenger* features the coiled snake form familiar from ancient Lindisfarne manuscripts. The poem dwells on the goodness of common men, his father among them.

Although the snake is phallic and masculine virtues are praised, the circular feminine symbols also abound:

> Goodness is where you find it.
> Abnormal.
> A pearl.
> A milkblue
> blind orb.
> (*Collected Poems*, p. 222)

Perhaps one of the most openly autobiographical segments of all his work, *The Messenger* acknowledges Kinsella's patrilineal emergence "up from the bloodied slime," but as always "filth" and "muck" (*The Messenger*, p. 15) have a positive, nourishing connotation as well as carrying their more derogatory meanings.

The boy John is a bicycle messenger, with a Post Office bike but no uniform "and a clean pair of heels" (*The Messenger*, p. 18). Mercury, messenger of the gods, had winged heels, and Lucifer bruised the heels of man, but John "followed . . . the wings / down at heel" (*The Messenger*, p. 10).

Kinsella praises his father as a union leader, and sees a hammer raised at the workbench as the Marxist symbol. He remembers him walking out of Mass when the priest directed the congregation how to vote: an ordinary hero, but a hero nonetheless. Even the moment of his own conception is mentioned as a celebration of nature, as a dragonfly quivers on his mother.

Songs of the Psyche (Peppercanister 9, 1985) is the longest, most complex, and most obscure segment of the *Blood and Family* anthology. Returning to former poems and preoccupations, Kinsella places demands on the reader, who is challenged to recall the elliptical forms of multiplicity that, like the illustration of a glass ornament on the title page, radiate from a dark center.

Divided into four sections—"Settings," "Invocation," "Songs," and "Notes"—the collection revisits Kinsella's childhood and chief themes. We return to classrooms, streets, and homes, finding the boy Thomas alone and introspective:

> The taste
> of ink off
> the nib shrank your
> mouth
> (*Collected Poems*, p. 231)

The invocation is "Judge not. / But judge" (p. 233).

The man turns inward, musing on the monsters outside and the monster within, eating and being eaten.

In Song 8 familiar images such as the twisted tree of lovers reappear, as do multicolored flowers symbolic of the stages in relationships:

> gold for the first blaze,
> red for the rough response,
> dark blue for misunderstanding,
> jet black for rue
> (pp. 236–237)

In Kinsella's verse, images in nature that appear serene on the surface always have an underside of cruelty or cannibalism. Even as he dandles his daughter on his knee, the poet has thoughts of letting her fall. But there is humor, too. In Song 13, after a long treatise on creation myths that explain life, culminating in Prometheus and Christ, Kinsella characteristically ends:

> Unless the thing were to be based
> on sexuality
> or power.
> (p. 240)

Thus he bursts the reader's ideological bubble as well as his own.

In the last section, "Notes," Kinsella returns to the strong negative forces of female sexuality. In "A New Beginning" God himself, starting "out of the *ache* / of *I am*," gives birth to creation over the "mothering pit" (pp. 240–241), and in "Talent and Friendship" the *sheela-na-gig* Irish fertility icon opens her lower lips, "a still youthful witch" (p. 243).

The last three poems are "Self-Scrutiny," "Self-Release," and "Self-Renewal." In the writing of words, Kinsella acknowledges his responsibility for the "thunderdrive to Hell" (*Blood and Family*, p. 37), for which he will pay dearly, as he likens the agony of thought made word to the crucifixion of Christ and foreshadows the death of John Scotus Eriugena, stabbed by his students' pens.

The title page of *Her Vertical Smile* (Peppercanister 10, 1985) features a design from an early fifteenth-century Irish astronomical tract showing the sun and Earth of equal size, with Earth throwing its vertical shadow above and among the stars. Music, predominantly German, wafts through this volume, with strains of Gustav Mahler echoing through the pages and notes from Richard Strauss's *Der Rosenkavalier* opening the prelude. Like the smell of madeleines jolting Marcel Proust's memory, the sound of music evokes romantic memories in Kinsella. But as the "father" dominated *The Messenger*, so father figures are the central focus of *Her Vertical Smile*, and the female figure is as often Mother Earth as woman.

In "Overture," the first of the five poems in *Her Vertical Smile*, Kinsella celebrates the Irish composer Seán Ó Riada and Mahler. But the beauty and order of music glide into military marches and massacres in which dead bodies are seen in photographs posing like family groups.

The "Intermezzo" is in the form of a letter from Thomas Mann to the German poet Richard Dehmel in which he glorifies the German cause in World War I, followed by Kinsella's reflection back to Mahler and metal instruments turning to weapons of destruction. Kinsella ends on a humorous note in "Coda":

> I lift my
> baton and my
> trousers fall.
> (*Collected Poems*, p. 260)

Out of Ireland (Peppercanister 11, 1987) is one of Kinsella's most pleasingly constructed slim volumes and the first (perhaps after urging from readers and scholars) to include notes, called "precedents," that explain the poet's intent and inspiration. With an "Entrance" and "Exit" and five poems forming the perfect quincunx, "Out of Ireland" both reverts to past writing and expands the celebration of forefathers to ancient Irish figures. One of them, John Scotus Eriugena, a ninth-century scholar, is featured on the title page.

In "Harmonies," Kinsella parodies Giraldus Cambrensis, a twelfth-century Welsh scholar whose criticism of Ireland extended to all but its polyphonic music. In "The Furnace" he glorifies the refiner's fire that melts all creativity into a molten liquid that flows back through the centuries, linking all scholars, artists, and lovers.

"The Dance" celebrates a Dionysian Ó Riada, and "The Land of Loss" returns to Eriugena, who died at his students' hands:

> They stabbed him
> with their pens
> because he made them think.
> (*Collected Poems*, p. 266)

"Exit" links all these threads as the dead call out *Tabhair dom do lamh*, "Give me your hand," in a dance of death that provokes the poet to reach for his pen "in the goat-grey light" (p. 267).

In the last volume comprising *Blood and Family*, *St. Catherine's Clock* (Peppercanister 12, 1987), the poet reverts to earlier techniques as he surveys a Dublin street scene from one to three o'clock in the morning. Brian John, in *Reading the Ground: The Poetry of Thomas Kinsella* (p. 244), states that he chose "Reading the Ground" for the title of his book because the Irish concept of reading the ground incorporates the ancient notion of seeing all Irish history and culture through geography. Thus, place is much more than landscape.

St. Catherine's Church provides the backdrop for historical events that are the subject of Kinsella's poems in this volume. And while a clock is round, and the usual association with St. Catherine is the wheel on which she was tortured, the frontispiece illustration shows only the hands of the clock, spiked like the nib of a pen from which a single drop of blood falls. Thus, male and female symbols characteristically clash and merge.

In the four one o'clock poems, Kinsella envisions a drug addict injecting himself, the execution of the nationalist hero Robert Emmet from an 1803 engraving by George Cruikshank, and the legendary Irish hag "Centre, barefoot / bowed in aged rags to the earth" (*Collected Poems*, p. 271) in a 1792 streetscape by James Malton. By evoking Cruikshank, an English caricature artist, and Malton, an Irish lithographer, Kinsella the artist is alluding to the artists' perspectives. In "1938" he alludes to his own, returning to numerous aunts and to his grandmother's sweets shop featured in earlier poems. In boyish cruelty and sexual awakening, he poses himself as part of the Dublin picture:

> I have struggled, hand
> over hand,
> in the savage dance
>
> . . . eating and eaten.
> (p. 276)

Kinsella continues this reminiscence into the second hour, into Thomas Street, remembering his origins and the trickle of blood from the scaffold. As "a tooth on the big measuring wheel" of the clock (p. 281), which also recalls the torture wheel, moves to 3 A.M., he sees in "1740" the figure of literary forefather Jonathan Swift

> reading the ground
> all dressed up
> in black, like a madwoman.
> (p. 281)

"Reading the ground," seeing history through the earth on which the events took place, is thus established as a central metaphor in Kinsella's poetry.

PEPPERCANISTERS 13–19 (1988–1997)

IN the late 1980s and the 1990s Kinsella's writings included Peppercanisters 13 through 17, collected in the anthology *From Centre City* (1994); *The Dual Tradition* (1995), a prose piece that examines Irish literature in English and the vernacular; and *The Pen Shop* (1997). *From Centre City* is comprised of *One Fond Embrace* (1988), *Personal Places*, (1990), *Poems from Centre City* (1990), *Madonna and Other Poems* (1991), and *Open Court* (1991).

Lest we assume that *One Fond Embrace* (Peppercanister 13, 1988) is a love poem, the Dürer-like cover engraving shows the Last Supper, with Christ being kissed by Judas Iscariot. The theme is betrayal.

Kinsella returns to Dublin, falling in love again with his birthplace but still finding much fault in the city, the city fathers, and his own circle of friends. Seeing corruption everywhere ("Dirty money gives dirty access"), he despairs: "And I want to throw my pen down / And I want to throw my self down" (*Collected Poems*, p. 285). Instead, he embraces the imperfections of the city and invites his friends, in a parody of the Last Supper, "Take one another / and eat" (p. 286).

In the second person Kinsella addresses thirteen individuals, whom he admits in the foreword are real but "redistributed so as to make them unrecognisable." He scathingly criticizes them and injects cruel humor: "But give us a kiss" (p. 289) "as I have loved the lot of you" (p. 291). His solution to the Irish problem is to dig a mile-wide channel along the border, with open season on both sides.

In a complete departure from the illustrative designs on previous Peppercanister pamphlets, *Personal Places* (Peppercanister 14, 1990) features cupid lips on candy stripes. The image refers to "Dura Mater," the second poem in the first section of the collection, evoking Kinsella's mother, both living and dead. The living woman is painted with cosmetics, her pursed mouth "a Cupid's Bow puckered" (*Collected Poems*, p. 300), she offers a formal kiss to her son. This kiss is returned on the cold forehead of the dead mother: "Dura Mater.

Finished." Revising this poem for *Collected Poems*, Kinsella removed "Finished," softening the harsh memory of the unloving and unlovable mother and the reaction of the unforgiving son.

Personal Places, however, does have a more forgiving tone than *One Fond Embrace*, despite calling Dublin "Grossness uprisen, / Godforsaken" (*Collected Poems*, p. 294). As the Kinsella family prepares to move to the country, it recalls other departures.

In the final section Kinsella returns to fellow poets Austin Clarke, Yeats, Lady Gregory, and Egan O'Rathaille; "Brothers in the Craft" are evoked and revered as Kinsella recalls his younger self, respectfully reading and translating their work, breathing in the essences of Ireland through their inspiration.

Poems from Centre City (Peppercanister 15, 1990) also pays tribute to literary forefathers; the first poem, "A Portrait of the Artist," recalls James Joyce's *Portrait of the Artist as a Young Man* (1916), and the last is dedicated "To the Memory of W. H. Auden."

Extolling the "good old days" with memories of solid old-timers like O'Keeffe the drayman (reminiscent of Kinsella's father), the poet continues to deride contemporary institutions and administrators, whether Catholic or Protestant. Neighbors are named, while some allusions are left to the imagination of the reader. In "Household Spirits," for example, the "cannibal committee" (*Collected Poems*, p. 308) might be carvings in the wood of the house but actually refers to aboriginal paintings inside the house, which only an insider would know.

References are also made to places familiar from earlier poems: Baggot Street, the peppercanister church, and places along the Grand Canal. Themes of darkness and light, lost and found are explored, but with less vigor and originality than in earlier poems.

At the beginning of *Madonna and Other Poems* (Peppercanister 16, 1991), Kinsella seems to be reluctantly renouncing a relationship with a younger woman, and at the end he is preoccupied with a mother figure. But as in all his poems, the female figure doubles as muse, the female creative spirit who both inspires and betrays him. As always, physical love is linked to both food and excrement: theirs is a "urinary privacy" (*Collected Poems*, p. 317).

In "Madonna" he makes tea; in "Morning Coffee" there is a hint of attempted suicide, strengthened by the following poem, "Visiting Hour," in which a hallucinating poet sees his mother: "One thin hand out, denying," "taking refreshment at my well of illness" (p. 322), while tempting him with her lace-stockinged thighs. In the final poem, "At the Head Table," she reappears with "A smile, dry and lipless" as they toast "the Father" (p. 325).

The seventeenth Peppercanister, *Open Court*, also published in 1991, contains the long narrative title poem and five short poems. "Open Court" skips along in rhyming couplets, belittling the Irish literary establishment as a group of poets including "ruined" Arnold and Auden and Wilde, Anonymous (probably Patrick Kavanagh), and an "ageing author . . . of vague renown" (*Collected Poems*, p. 328) with a female student, who may be Kinsella with his "Madonna." None escapes ignominy as they all espouse their literary theories while getting blind drunk in a pub from which they are finally ejected at closing time.

The next poem, "Dream," is more like a Hieronymus Bosch nightmare, with grotesque man-eating creatures inhabiting a Beckettian landscape. The last four short poems, however, anticipate leaving the "hissing assemblies" of the city (p. 335) for the pastoral peace of the countryside, which is what Kinsella was about to do in his move to County Wicklow.

Since Kinsella's retirement in 1990, three books of his have been published: *The Dual Tradition: An Essay on Poetry and Politics in Ireland* (1995), *Collected Poems, 1956–1994* (1996), and Peppercanister 19, *The Pen Shop* (1997).

The Dual Tradition is a prose essay on poetry and politics in Ireland from the fifth century to the present. It is a compilation and development of ideas previously expressed in lectures, prefaces, and articles about the native Irish and the English literary heritage of modern Irish writers.

In five chronological chapters Kinsella traces the Irish literary heritage from pre-Christian through colonial times to the twentieth century, with sections on Yeats, Joyce, Austin Clarke, Kavanagh, Beckett, and Irish publishers. The last chapter is devoted to the politics of the dual tradition.

Pointing out that "power politics and Irish literature lie close together" (*The Dual Tradition*, p. 3), Kinsella traces the downward spiral of the Irish poet from privileged position to voice of the dispossessed. While acknowledging the importance of the work of Yeats and Lady Gregory in restoring early Irish literature to a higher plane at the beginning of the twentieth century, he also identifies their attitude as unwittingly condescending. Irish literary figures familiar throughout Kinsella's poetry, such as Aogán O'Rathaille, Jonathan Swift, Clarence Mangan, Thomas Davis, and Sir Samuel Ferguson, are placed in historical context, making this a useful book to read before embarking on Kinsella's poetry. Stressing the ambiguity of a changing Ireland, Kinsella uses poignant and pertinent quotations, such as the question posed by Swift: "Am I a free man in England, and do I become a slave in six hours by crossing the channel?" (p. 35).

Using Yeats and Joyce as models, Kinsella makes an important distinction between modern Irish poets who address the majority, a responsive audience, and whose aim is communication through known tradition (Yeats), and those whose route is exploration (Joyce). Although Kinsella does not state it openly, his reader knows from other sources that he has mostly followed the path of the exiles Joyce and Beckett.

Much of what Kinsella says about the poetry of Austin Clarke seems to apply to his own work: "a constant test of discrimination and patience," "legitimate obscurity," "poems accumulate and illuminate one another," and the need for an "energetic" reader (pp. 94–95). On the controversial topic of accessibility, Kinsella has said: "I require a reader to complete the act of communication. I don't want to entertain" (Badin, p. 198).

Writing of Beckett, Kinsella seems to suggest the reasons for his own self-imposed exile: "It is the act of uprooting that matters, linguistic as well as physical; with the uprooted psyche, wherever it finds itself, adopting itself as its own subject matter" (*The Dual Tradition*, p. 106). He cites not only Beckett but also Joyce and others suffering from the dilemma of choosing English or Irish publishers, or from being spurned by both. In this, too, we see the importance of Kinsella's own choices in the development of Dolmen Press and Peppercanister, leading eventually to copublication in Ireland, England, and the United States.

Finally, Kinsella upbraids even pro-Irish critics such as Hugh Kenner for playing into Irish stereotypes, in what he calls the perpetuation of the "Stage Irish." Even in phrases intended as compliments, the assumption of Irish wit, charm, and decency are problematic, always separating Catholic and Protestant, landed gentry and dispossessed. Kinsella sees a complex blend of alienation and divided loyalty, a confusion of identities straddling colonizer and colonized: "It is one of the findings of Ireland's dual tradition that an empire is a passing thing but that a colony is not" (p. 111).

The last poetry anthology after *Poems from Centre City* (Peppercanisters 13–17, 1994) was *Collected Poems, 1956–1994* (1996). Most, but not all, of Kinsella's poetry of the stipulated years is included in the latter volume. It is interesting to note in passing which of his poems Kinsella selected to represent his work in his 1986 anthology, *The New Oxford Book of Irish Verse*. "A Hand of Solo," "Ancestor," "Tear," and "Wyncote, Pennsylvania: A Gloss" are all from *New Poems, 1973* (1973) and *Notes from the Land of the Dead and Other Poems* of the same year. Ignoring twelve years of new work, Kinsella presents three poems evoking childhood and family in Ireland and one reflective poem written in exile.

The slimmest volume of Kinsella's poetry is Peppercanister 19, *The Pen Shop* (1997). In what we now recognize as his characteristic style, a short prologue is followed by two longer poems, "To the Coffee Shop" and "To the Pen Shop," on unnumbered pages, with subdivisions marked by asterisks.

The first two lines of the prologue seem like a dedication: "Under my signature, a final kiss. / In fading ink. With added emphasis." But the last eight lines proclaim the end of a relationship, emphasizing not love but finality. The poet then leaves a high-vaulted room with a sagging Promethean statue, passing through revolving doors into the Dublin streets, passing more statues (mostly of statesmen), bridges, and urban architecture, to a coffee shop attended by women waiting on men.

Two references are made to the "family queen." As the poet wanders past the river, "dirty and disturbed . . . with a smell of country and family," he prays: "Family queen, / accept him, fumbling at your flank." Sitting at the coffee table, lifting the "coarse cup" as he takes two pills, he toasts "the family queen." With references to family and the physical presence of a woman, the "family queen" might be the wife betrayed by the relationship with the woman abandoned in the prologue. But the invocation beside the river suggests a wider symbolism, with the plea for acceptance applying to both wife and country.

There is also ambiguity in the "black draft" that "entered the system direct, / foreign and clay sharp." This may be black coffee or, since glasses are clinked, Guinness, which should not be "foreign" to a native son. Knowing the poet's penchant for intertextuality and anticipating the next section, "To the Pen Shop," the "black draft" may also be the ink sucked from the nib by the boy Thomas, a taste both "foreign" and "clay sharp."

In "To the Pen Shop" the poet again wanders through the city, but the statues are now those of writers and the location the castle, the college, and "places / beyond your terminus." He invokes the poets of the western shore, the southern counties "Wicklow; / Wexford, and the company of women; Finisterre," and we recall the bleak world of his earlier poem of that name.

Finally, dreaming "Beyond Liverpool, rising out of Europe; . . . rising beyond Jerusalem," he enters the pen shop to find the same ancient salesman as the one who served him as a child selling his "best black refills."

It is tempting to read this extended poem as a synthesis of Kinsella's work. The wandering poet is infused with the black liquid of love (inspiration), of coffee (stimulation), of ale (consolation), and of ink (creation). But we have learned that Kinsella's poetry is dense not with obscurity but with a richness awaiting the patience, diligence, and energy of the reader. A simplistic analysis will not suffice.

It should not be assumed that no more work will flow from Thomas Kinsella's pen or that Kinsella's readership will not grow in direct proportion to his challenge for us to "read the ground" and to move, if we move, like water, whether we live and read in or out of Ireland.

SELECTED BIBLIOGRAPHY

I. COLLECTED WORKS (POETRY). *Nightwalker and Other Poems* (Dublin, 1968); *Notes from the Land of the Dead and Other Poems* (New York, 1973); *Selected Poems, 1956–1968* (Dublin, 1973); *One and Other Poems* (New York, 1979); *Peppercanister Poems, 1972–1978* (Winston-Salem, N.C., 1979); *Poems, 1956–1973* (Winston-Salem, N.C., 1979); *Blood and Family* (Oxford, 1988); *Selected Poems, 1962–1989* (Helsinki, 1989); *Poems from Centre City* (Oxford, 1994); *Collected Poems, 1956–1994* (Oxford, 1996).

II. INDIVIDUAL WORKS (POETRY). *Poems* (Dublin, 1956); *Another September* (Dublin, 1958); *Moralities* (Dublin, 1960); *Poems and Translations* (New York, 1961); *Downstream* (Dublin, 1962); *Wormwood* (Dublin, 1966); *Tear* (Cambridge, Mass., 1969); *Butcher's Dozen* (Dublin,

1972); *Finisterre* (Dublin, 1972); *Notes from the Land of the Dead* (Dublin, 1972); *A Selected Life* (Dublin, 1972); *The Good Fight: A Poem for the Tenth Anniversary of the Death of John F. Kennedy* (Dublin, 1973); *New Poems, 1973* (Dublin, 1973); *Vertical Man: A Sequel to* A Selected Life (Dublin, 1973); *One* (Dublin, 1974); *A Technical Supplement* (Dublin, 1976); *The Messenger* (1978); *Song of the Night and Other Poems* (Dublin, 1978); *Fifteen Dead* (1979); *Her Vertical Smile* (1985); *Songs of the Psyche* (Dublin, 1985); *Out of Ireland* (Dublin, 1987); *St. Catherine's Clock* (Dublin, 1987); *One Fond Embrace* (Dublin, 1988); *Personal Places* (Dublin, 1990); *Poems from Centre City* (Dublin, 1990); *Madonna and Other Poems* (Dublin, 1991); *Open Court* (Dublin, 1991); *The Pen Shop* (Dublin, 1997).

III. Translations. *The Táin* (Dublin, 1969); *An Duanaire: An Irish Anthology, Poems of the Dispossessed, 1600–1900*, ed. by Seán Ó Tuama (Philadelphia, 1981).

IV. Anthologies Edited. *Selected Poems of Austin Clarke* (Dublin, 1976); *The New Oxford Book of Irish Verse* (Oxford, 1986).

V. Essay and Commentary. *The Dual Tradition: An Essay on Poetry and Politics in Ireland* (Dublin, 1975).

VI. Critical Studies. Maurice Harmon, *The Poetry of Thomas Kinsella: "With Darkness for a Nest"* (Dublin, 1974); Robert F. Garratt, "Poetry at Mid-century: Thomas Kinsella," in his *Modern Irish Poetry: Traditions and Continuity from Yeats to Heaney* (Berkeley, Calif., 1986); Maurice Harmon, " 'Move, if You Move, Like Water': The Poetry of Thomas Kinsella, 1972–1988," in Elmer Andrews, ed., *Contemporary Irish Poetry: A Collection of Critical Essays* (London, 1992); Thomas H. Jackson, *The Whole Matter: The Poetic Evolution of Thomas Kinsella* (Syracuse, N.Y., 1995); Brian John, *Reading the Ground: The Poetry of Thomas Kinsella* (Washington, D.C., 1996).

MEDBH McGUCKIAN

(1950–   )

Clair Wills

MEDBH MCGUCKIAN IS one of the most enigmatic and controversial of contemporary poets. She is the foremost woman poet to have emerged in the North of Ireland since the 1960s and the first to be published by a mainstream poetry press. She was born Maeve McCaughan in Belfast on 12 August 1950, the third of six children. The family lived in the Newington District in North Belfast, a small area populated by Roman Catholics that forms an interface with the Protestant Tiger's Bay area and was therefore fraught with sectarian tension throughout McGuckian's childhood. Her mother had worked in the post office before her marriage but gave up her job to look after her children. Her father was a teacher, the vice principal of the local Holy Family Primary School, which McGuckian attended before completing her secondary education at the Dominican convent in Fort William.

In 1968 McGuckian went to Queen's University, Belfast, to read English, staying on after she graduated with a B.A. degree to complete an M.A. degree and a Diploma in Education. In 1974 she began work as an English teacher, first returning to the Dominican convent, and subsequently teaching at St. Patrick's College, Knock, in East Belfast. In 1977 she married John McGuckian, also a teacher. They had four children. It was around the time of the birth of her first child in 1980 that McGuckian's poetry began to win public notice. She won the National Poetry Prize for Britain in 1979, and her first volume, *The Flower Master* (1982), was published by Oxford University Press. McGuckian continued to work as a schoolteacher, writing poetry in her spare time, until the birth of her third child in 1985. Since then she has been a full-time writer. At the end of the twentieth century she had published six volumes of poetry and won further poetry prizes and awards, including the Rooney Prize in Ireland, the Cheltenham Award, the Bass Ireland Award for Literature, and the American Ireland Fund Literary Award. In

1986 she became the first woman poet-in-residence at Queen's University, Belfast; she has also been writer-in-residence at the University of Ulster, Coleraine (1994–1997), and in 1991 she was visiting fellow at the University of California, Berkeley.

Despite this acclaim, there is little consensus regarding the nature and meaning of her poetry, or on how to read it. McGuckian's style is unmistakable; she writes intricate, obliquely autobiographical poems thick with sensuous imagery and an often complex private symbolism. Her poems are dense with emblems of flowers, planets, weather systems, houses, and the human body, as well as references to poetic antecedents and to violence and religion. Her meanings can be hard to disentangle as her verses are cut across by sudden, incongruous images that often develop in unpredictable ways, as in these opening lines from the title poem of *Venus and the Rain*, published in 1984:

> White on white, I can never be viewed
> Against a heavy sky—my gibbous voice
> Passes from leaf to leaf, retelling the story
> Of its own provocative fractures, till
> Their facing coasts might almost fill each other
> And they ask me in reply if I've
> Decided to stop making diamonds.
>
> (p. 31)

We can detect in this stanza a number of characteristic aspects of McGuckian's style, notably her habitual use of the first person, the lyric "I," which is defined in relation to a "they," and later an "us" and a "her." But it is hard to say to whom or to what these pronouns refer. The poem seems to be set out as a riddle. Is it a description of the planet Venus, passing behind rain-soaked trees? Of a woman telling the story of the wounds of childbirth ("provocative fractures") through the leaves of a book? Certainly the lines suggest a need for healing, a curing of the split between "facing coasts," an image that inevitably suggests the shores of Britain and Ireland. The indeterminacy of the speaking voice in McGuckian's poetry is thus related to other stylistic characteristics: syntactical ellipses, discontinuities of sense, sudden changes of grammatical subject and tense, unlikely juxtapositions. Despite the richness of this imagery, there is something curiously abstract about these lines from "Venus and the Rain," as ideas and emotions are embodied in images that are then referred to other images in a seemingly endless movement. Undoubtedly there are dangers with this kind of poetic style, the most pressing being that the reader may find it hard to engage with the fluid movement of the verse. But against this difficulty we need to consider the high degree of imaginative freedom McGuckian's poetry contains. The seeming randomness of thoughts and images masks a complex layering of meaning, which keeps unfolding in this richly suggestive, powerful verse.

Certainly it can be hard to find a way in to McGuckian's poetry, and its difficulties account in part for the divergence of critical views on her work. While many admire the dense texture of her poetry, the shifting kaleidoscope of image and voice, others confess to bafflement. McGuckian has been criticized for "rhetorical posturing," for writing "mannered" or "whimsical" poetry—for, in sum, failing to make sense. Feminist literary critics are among the most vocal of her defenders. Their argument is that McGuckian's style is an intrinsic part of her attempt to explore feminine experience, and that since such experience has been largely excluded from the dominant male poetic tradition, it is not surprising that she has had to forge a new language. This defense of McGuckian as creating a new feminine language is not tantamount to the claim that every poem works, and it does not make the deciphering of the poetry any easier. However, such critics claim that if we are to understand the idiosyncrasies of a poet who is widely acknowledged as brilliant and original, and yet is often experienced as baffling, we would do best to start with the assumption that she is writing as a woman about women's experience.

The feminine nature of McGuckian's concerns is indeed central to an understanding of her poetry and has been encouraged by the poet herself, who tends to explain her work in terms of the themes of pregnancy and childbirth, and the process of self-definition of the woman, as writer and mother. Such themes are particularly strong in her early work; she explores the contours of domesticity and familial relationships and sexuality and eroticism in *The Flower Master* and the experience and psychological effects of childbirth in *Venus and the Rain.*

Despite the intimate subject matter, it would be a mistake to regard this poetry as primarily autobiographical or confessional. Although personal experience lies behind McGuckian's writing, her work is in no sense a revelation of the personal. Her poetry is not the disclosure of what is usually kept secret or private in the individual's life. While female experience is at the center of its concerns, these concerns remain veiled, oblique, hidden behind a multitude of conflicting images, literary allusions, and social and political references. Far from writing, as some feminist poets have done, in order to make publicly accessible experiences that have been hidden or hushed up, McGuckian has made the remarkable suggestion that she writes poetry in order *not* to express herself in ways that can be understood. In a 1995 interview with Nuala Ní Dhomhnaill in the *Southern Review,* she said: "I began to write poetry so that nobody would read it. Nobody. Even the ones who read it would not understand it, and certainly no other poet would understand it" (p. 590). Far from being open, her work seems to be almost hermetically closed. Put another way, McGuckian is concerned with the ways in which poetic language can give shape and form to experience by transmuting it into ritual, with its own obscure significance. Significantly, in a 1994 interview with Kimberly S. Bohman in the *Irish Review,* she compared the practice of writing poetry to the habit of the confessional:

I love the feeling of control over my life that [poetry] gives me. Instead of events just passing you, for me it's in amber. Poetry is about desire, maybe it's sublimating desire, but I think desire is at the heart of it. If I didn't express those desires and exorcise them, I think it would be very unhealthy for me—to keep it bottled up. I guess I feel pretty guilty about all these inner yearnings and so I had to write them—like a confession. I think that my Catholicism is very deeply embedded in me and that the poems are confessions of . . . sins of thought.

(p. 96)

Here McGuckian suggests that her poetry effects a form of release analogous to that offered by the emotionally charged rituals of Catholicism—indeed, that it directly replaces religious practice.

It would be hard in the late twentieth century to imagine a less theoretically respectable view of poetry, that it is therapy for subversive emotions. Yet McGuckian's sense that the constraints of ritual and form offer a way of controlling emotion while allowing it to be expressed is a fundamental tenet of post-Romantic aesthetics. McGuckian's analogy with the confessional is not about emotional outpouring; she suggests that the alleviation of distress comes not through open, unrestrained expression but through articulation within a particular, strictly codified structure. The poems are intimate yet reserved; the self that is offered up to be understood is veiled by language as much as revealed. Notwithstanding its lyric charge, therefore, this poetry undermines a fundamental principle of traditional lyric poetry. The poems are engaged in self-definition, but it is not a self-definition that offers an obvious focus of identification for the reader. Hence, while feminist advocates of McGuckian's work are not entirely wrong about its preoccupations, it is misleading to think of her as shaping expressions of feminine experience whose transparency makes them sharable. Rather than offering the possibility of self-understanding to the reader, the poems highlight the need for investigation and interpretation. But at the same time they render it all but impossible, for the distance between writer and reader is compounded by countless divisions within the lyric voice itself. The poetry's constantly shifting pronouns chart the fluidity of a body parceled out between male and female, inside and outside, mother and child, individual and nation.

As McGuckian suggests in referring to the confessional, the influence of Catholicism on her work is strong. Her family were practicing Catholics: her father was active in the Charity of St. Vincent de Paul, but she has also spoken of the inspirational effect on her of her devout grandmother, with whom she spent a great deal of time as a child. She seems to have occupied herself as a child in, among other things, preparing for the priesthood, and she registers the shock and disillusionment she experienced when she realized that was not possible because of her sex. As she has said in the 1995 conversation with Dhomhnaill, eventually poetry took the place of the priesthood as a goal:

I remember going to a poetry reading in Belfast, I was about sixteen, and around that time—1966—Heaney's *Death of a Naturalist* came out, and I was amazed that somebody from Derry could be an acclaimed poet. The poetry reading was like a secret society meeting—no other woman in the room—and I remember this feeling of "I am here," like going to Mass. I decided that the second-best thing to becoming a priest would be to become a poet. This is something I can do even though it's nearly as difficult, but it is not actually unlawful. So it was only when I went to Queen's and Heaney was teaching there—in my final year, '72, I had him in a seminar, and he was just a wonderful mediatrix.

(pp. 591–592)

As McGuckian's frustrated desire to become a priest might suggest, the tension between longing, including sexual longing, and the conventions of the family and the religious community are a veiled subject of McGuckian's early work. Particularly in her first two volumes, McGuckian explores a girl's growing awareness of her sexuality, the experience of marriage and motherhood, and the puritanism of much Catholic doctrine. More generally she is interested in how to practice "liberation" within the constraints of tradition, a preoccupation that is also evident in her innovations, which reveal a deep awareness of and commitment to the European literary tradition. This conception of tradition, and even of the constraints of inherited ritual, as something that enables "liberation" rather than merely embodying the dead weight of the past is another feature of McGuckian's poetry, one hard to reconcile with the straightforwardly feminist interpretation of her work. Since the death of McGuckian's father in 1992, religion as a pervasive aspect of identity has become an ever more explicit theme within her poetry. As with her earlier work, it is the relationship between bodily submission and spiritual freedom that particularly interests her. And in her later work, a sense of poetry as an alternative to religious devotion is at its most explicit. In *Shelmalier* (1998), for example, the poems often seem analogous to prayers, as the themes of hope and freedom are explored through use of the full panoply of Catholic symbolism. The book is full of images of crosses and crucifixion, saints, and the language and gestures of the Mass.

But McGuckian's anecdote about the poetry reading also points to another fundamental influence on her work: the Northern Irish poetry renaissance that began in the 1960s in Belfast.

McGuckian went to Queen's to study English in 1968, where she met acclaimed figures of the Belfast "Group" including poets such as Seamus Heaney, Michael Longley, and Derek Mahon. As important as the atmosphere associated with the older writers, however, were McGuckian's relationships with the other young aspiring poets among her fellow students, including Paul Muldoon, Ciaran Carson, and Frank Ormsby. This cultural context raises the question of whether there is a political aspect to her work. How far should she be read as responding to the Troubles in Northern Ireland? This controversy has dogged Northern Irish poets since the Troubles flared up again in the late 1960s; the question of how far poetry can be "responsible" for or make "redress" to the political situation without inhibiting imaginative freedom has, at different times, been a central theme in the work of Seamus Heaney, Paul Muldoon, and others. Yet unlike poets such as Heaney, Carson, and Muldoon, McGuckian's poetry has rarely been discussed in relation to the political situation in the North of Ireland. Indeed, an anthology of poetry edited by Frank Ormsby devoted to the poetry of the Troubles, *Rage for Order: Poetry of the Northern Ireland Troubles* (1992), explicitly excludes McGuckian's work on the grounds that any reference to the Troubles is unconscious.

This exclusion betrays an exceedingly one-sided reading of her work, for McGuckian has long explained certain poems as responding to the Troubles. For example, "Dovecote" (from *The Flower Master*) is an early poem that draws an (albeit concealed) analogy between the isolation and sacrifice of the hunger strikers and the swelling and contraction of the body in pregnancy and childbirth. More generally, throughout McGuckian's work images of plantation signal a concern with Ulster's past and possible future, in that they allude to settlement of the province by Protestants from Scotland and England. Admittedly, these references are veiled, but as her work develops, any attempt to understand it without reference to the Troubles seems increasing misguided. In her later books, *Captain Lavender* (1994) and *Shelmalier* (1998), McGuckian makes more and more explicit references to war, political prisoners, and a history of violence and insurrection. *Shelmalier* even includes a preface in which McGuckian explains her preoccupation with the 1998 bicentenary of the United Irishman rebellion as an analogue for the contemporary situation in Northern Ireland. Like the allusions to the rituals of the Mass, and to Catholic devotions, references to the Troubles and to the history of violence in Ireland have become more and more explicit in her work.

EARLY POETRY: THE FLOWER MASTER *AND* VENUS AND THE RAIN

UNLIKE other poets in the Belfast circle during the late 1960s and 1970s, such as Paul Muldoon and Ciaran Carson, who published young, McGuckian wrote privately for a long time. The Irish-language poet Nuala Ní Dhomhnaill has described this trajectory as typical for women poets in Ireland at the time, due partly to the requirements of family life, a lack of confidence, and fear of a critical reception skewed by male bias. In McGuckian's case it was marriage and approaching motherhood that spurred her on to publication, as she explains in her 1995 dialogue with Nuala Ní Dhomhnaill:

MMcG: Others are being published now, but I was the only one who managed to bypass the early pamphlet stage. The bypassing was amazing. When I married I knew it was now or never and that what I had to do was to win a competition. I hate competitions and judging things . . . I did it so clinically. I sent away for the previous year's winners and saw that they liked narrative poems of about forty lines—it had to be substantial and to flitter about the place. I wrote three poems in this style and submitted them under a pseudonym, and I won.

NNíD: Why a pseudonym? Was it male or female?

MMcG: It was female—Jean Fisher. But they assumed that I was a male pretending to be a woman. They couldn't believe I was six months pregnant when they came over with their cameras. The big thing about it was that a well-known literary figure came second to me, and they rearranged the prize money so that I got less and he got more. I didn't care. I was pregnant, and I had won this. But the *TLS [Times Literary Supplement]* cared. They created a huge fuss for weeks, wanting to know whether my prize money was cut from £1,000 to £500 because I was Irish, or Catholic, or a woman, or unknown. And then British publishers began writing to me—Faber wrote, and Charles Monteith was on the phone—and I ended up getting published with Oxford.

NNɪD: Do you think it had to be short-circuited like that?

MMcG: There was no other way. I would still not have a book out. I would still be sitting there with my Emily Dickinson tome.

(pp. 592–593)

In 1979 "The Flitting" won first prize in the National Poetry Competition organized by the Poetry Society of Great Britain. Immediately after winning the prize a pamphlet titled *Portrait of Joanna* (1980) was published by Ulsterman Publications, in Belfast. In 1980 McGuckian received an Eric Gregory Award; she was later included in Faber's *Poetry Introduction* (1982) and the *Penguin Anthology of Contemporary British Poets,* edited by Blake Morrison and Andrew Motion. In 1982 her first full-length collection, *The Flower Master,* was published by Oxford University Press. It won both the Rooney Prize in 1982 and the Alice Hunt Bartlett Award in 1983.

Much of *The Flower Master* has to do with the growth from childhood through adolescence to womanhood, and the consequences of moving from one family into another as a wife and mother. The poems consider how to create new forms of continuity and inheritance, and how tradition can be both preserved and renewed. One of the most immediately striking aspects of this volume is its shy eroticism. The voice of the poems is both sensuous and beguiling; poems such as "Tulips" and "Gentians" and "The Flower Master" itself obliquely explore the language of touch and response with the utmost delicacy. At the same time these are startling poems of everyday life, describing chopping an onion, or preparing for school exams. In 1993 a revised edition, *The Flower Master and Other Poems,* was published by Ireland's Gallery Press; it includes about a dozen poems absent from the Oxford University Press edition, poems that allow the reader to chart even more clearly the development from a burgeoning adolescent sexuality to loss of virginity and the mature woman's "thickening" dreams. The additional poems also reveal McGuckian's early fascination with the relationship between desire and control, as in these lines from "Smoke," the first poem in the new edition:

They set the whins on fire along the road.
I wonder what controls it, can the wind hold
That snake of orange motion to the hills,
Away from the houses?

They seem so sure what they can do.
I am unable even
To contain myself, I run
Till the fawn smoke settles on the earth.

(p. 11)

As the title of the volume suggests, McGuckian takes the traditionally feminine "language of flowers" and masculinizes it, describing it in terms of "mastery." This crossover is indicative of the central concern of the volume, a concern with the relation between natural processes of growth and change on the one hand and artifice and design on the other. The success of a garden can be seen as depending on the integration of the two, and McGuckian makes clear that her own poetic "seed-work" is as much a matter of contrivance and planning as of spontaneous organic processes. In "The Seed-Picture" McGuckian portrays her artwork as a joining of disparate elements, a process that she relates to the traditional feminine arts:

Was it such self-indulgence to enclose her
In the border of a grandmother's sampler,
Bonding all the seeds in one continuous skin . . . ?

(p. 28)

Clearly, McGuckian's exploration of the interplay of nature and artifice is a way of approaching the fundamental axis of the book: the relationship between historical containment and the liberation that may flow from it. Accepting the restraints inherent in the traditional feminine roles of girl, wife, mother, and grandmother (like acknowledging the restraints of poetic form) may open up spaces of freedom, bring a form of release. But it is important to note that this freedom is not understood in terms of the exercise of power within a distinct feminine sphere. On the contrary, as the poem "Slips" suggests, maternal and (through them) familial relationships are shifting and elusive, associated with violence, loss, and discontinuity:

The studied poverty of a moon roof,
The earthenware of dairies cooled by apple trees,
The apple tree that makes the whitest wash . . .

But I forget names, remembering them wrongly
Where they touch upon another name,
A town in France like a woman's Christian name.

My childhood is preserved as a nation's history,
My favourite fairytales the shells
Leased by the hermit crab.

I see my grandmother's death as a piece of ice,
My mother's slimness restored to her,
My own key slotted in your door—

Tricks you might guess from this unfastened button,
A pen mislaid, a word misread,
My hair coming down in the middle of a conversation.

(p. 21)

The poem presents a series of innocent and not so innocent "mistakes." It begins with an idealized image of a simple rural home; the speaker's memory is not pure but a studied and overlaid romantic creation. (It is even infected with the language of soap-powder advertisements!) It is perhaps this misremembering that links her personal history to that of the nation, since both are composed of fairy tales, tales of nonbelonging, stolen homes. Her fairy tales are those that tell her she belongs to the idyllic vision of the first stanza. But nation and individual have more in common than faulty memory. The nation also invents a personal past; Irish history not only has the same structure but the same content as her memories of childhood, a mythic celebration of an idyllic agrarian existence. McGuckian links this type of memory slippage with Freudian slips, slipping on ice, the slippage of a baby out of the mother's body, with each slip revealing the arbitrariness of women's lives, in which they move from home to home, taking possession by being the ones possessed. The implication is perhaps that this history will be misremembered in its turn, and another fairy tale of possession overlaid on the real events of their lives.

But what is the difference between slips and tricks? The poem turns on the inability to distinguish accident from design, and also on the intertwining of apparent subordination and the achievement of authority. In one sense, the poem suggests, women enter where they do not belong ("My own key slotted in your door"); their apparent slips are designed to allure those in command, to engage by means of the half-seen, by covering rather than revealing. In one sense the key in the door is a mistake, or perhaps a sign of belonging to another. But in another sense, it can be seen as an act of taking possession of the house, just as what seems like a flirtatious accident could be seen as an expression of erotic power. As we have known since Freud, slips ("A pen mislaid, a word misread") can have a purpose. At work here is a

type of lateral logic, the opposite of clarity and openness, which the poem itself exemplifies. If the poem is about the woman's oblique, "accidental" path toward the achievement of authority, it is also about the way in which the constant slippages of poetic language offer an escape route from the burdens and responsibilities of the definitive statement. Meaning can be veiled yet still remain potent, and it is impossible to tell whether the unfolding of a life, like the pattern of a poem, is a matter of accident or of design.

At the same time, throughout the volume McGuckian implies the need to take possession of houses and land in order to establish a sense of place and identity, and she repeatedly suggests that bearing children is one way of gaining authority. In "The Soil Map" and "The Heiress" the metaphor of possession is obliquely politicized. "The Heiress," for example, alludes to the story of Mary, Queen of Scots (a Catholic), for whom bearing a son (who became King James VI of Scotland, and eventually King James I of England) meant deferred power:

But I am lighter of a son, through my slashed
Sleeves the inner sleeves of purple keep remembering
The moment exactly, remembering the birth
Of an heiress means the gobbling of land.

(p. 57)

So the image of possession in McGuckian's work is familial and sexual but also fraught with historical and political overtones. At a fundamental level references to possession conjure the dispossession of Catholics during the seventeenth-century plantation of Ulster (begun by James I). The associated image of children as seeds, an image she will pursue in a later volume, *On Ballycastle Beach* (1988), continues this ambiguity. Indeed, this movement and interplay between the intimate sphere and the public sphere is typical of McGuckian's use of metaphor and symbol.

McGuckian's second volume of poetry, *Venus and the Rain* (1984), was published only two years after *The Flower Master*, and it furthers many of the themes and the style of the first book. But this book is more concerned with its own creation, as McGuckian meditates on the relation between poetic inspiration and the experience of pregnancy and childbirth. Again themes of motherhood, sexuality, domesticity, and the role of the poet predominate, but in general the poems betray a darker, more violent mood. In this book more than ever, motherhood is a state not of wholeness but of disruption and sacrifice. The reasons for this are in part biographical. Shortly after the birth of her first child in 1980, McGuckian experienced a severe psychotic breakdown and was hospitalized for a time. In the 1995 conversation with Nuala Ní Dhomhnaill, she described this experience as both brutal and intense:

Everything exploded and erupted: my relationship with my father and mother, my husband, and with the Church . . . my unresolved moral thing with sexuality. For six weeks I didn't sleep, and my whole body seemed to be weeping with liquid from every orifice. The whole body was just seared and opened and the mind was as well.

(p. 595)

Venus and the Rain can in part be understood as the healing of these wounds. As has been suggested here of the title poem, it is concerned with how "retelling the story of its own provocative fractures" may bring a form of release. At the same time McGuckian writes of the experience of childbirth itself as a kind of initiation, an entry into new knowledge that has affinities with Romantic revelation and poetry's vatic role: "I realised I had some kind of message to hand on and that I was in some degree a priest, from having been through this awful sacrificial thing" (p. 596).

In keeping with the idea of secret knowledge, a coded, symbolic system runs through many of the poems. The focus is on the self in relation to others, as the poems play with seemingly abstract notions of distance, proximity, influence, dependence, and self-sufficiency. These are imaged above all in terms of the planetary system. Just as she had used the "language of flowers" in *The Flower Master*, here McGuckian takes another traditional image of femininity, that of the goddess Venus, and places it in a new context, that of the planet itself. In "Venus and the Sun," for example, McGuckian explores the symbiotic relationship between Venus and her master, the sun:

> The scented flames of the sun throw me,
> Telling me how to move—I tell them
> How to bend the light of shifting stars:
> I order their curved wash so the moon
> Will not escape, so rocks and seas
> Will stretch their elbows under her.
>
> (p. 9)

As so often in McGuckian's poetry the tension or dynamism here springs from the speaker's resistance to doing what she is told. She is always moving elsewhere, and as readers we are plunged into a game of hide-and-seek, a search for formal definition that is constantly escaping: "I am the sun's toy—because I go against / The grain I feel the brush of my authority . . ." (p. 9).

Throughout *Venus and the Rain*, McGuckian describes the relationship between husband and wife, mother and child, woman and poet, as a dance of independence and influence. Nothing has identity on its own. It is not just relationships between people that bend and alter according to force and pressure but the relationship between aspects of the psyche, in particular the masculine and feminine aspects of the woman poet. In one sense, McGuckian suggests, poetic creation can be understood as procreation. Just as the woman has to open herself to the male in order to become impregnated, so the poem cannot emerge without exposure to what is other. Inspiration consists precisely of such openness. But at the same time gestation, whether physical or poetic, requires a certain withdrawal and self-enclosure. Isolation and connection are both aspects of the poetic process.

Venus and the Rain also continues McGuckian's concern with domesticity and the image of the house. The analogy between the house and the woman's body is a traditional one, and unsurprisingly, a preoccupation with this analogy persists throughout her work. But in this volume her concern is also more specifically with the Victorian house in which she lives, in an area of Belfast originally built for wealthy Protestants but now inhabited mostly by Catholic families. Poems such as "To the Nightingale," "Isba Song," and "For the Previous Owner" use the fabric of the house and garden as an image for the relationship between husband and wife, or as an image of poetic creativity. But McGuckian is also interested in the house as a repository of history. In "Sabbath Park," for example, she imagines an alliance between herself and a Victorian lady of the house. The house itself seems to act as her muse and inspiration:

> I feel the swaggering beginnings
> Of a new poem flaring up, because the house
> Is dragging me into its age, the malady

Of fireplaces crammed with flowers, even
On a golden winter Sunday.

(p. 54)

ON BALLYCASTLE BEACH *AND* MARCONI'S COTTAGE

THROUGHOUT the 1980s McGuckian's poetry increased in difficulty, certainly in comparison to the relatively straightforward lyrics of *The Flower Master*. The difficulty of interpretation is in large part a consequence of McGuckian's increasing use of allusion to, and quotation from, other writers. Volumes subsequent to *Venus and the Rain* maintain, for the most part, a loose symbolic or metaphorical system, but this is now derived less from observation than from McGuckian's own readings in poetry, literary history, and literary biography. In both *On Ballycastle Beach* (1988) and *Marconi's Cottage* (1992), McGuckian alludes to a diverse community of European Romantic and modernist poets. In addition to Yeatsian echoes, the poetry nods toward Robert Frost; the English Romantic poets Coleridge, Byron, and Shelley; and European poets including Rainer Maria Rilke, Marina Tsvetaeva, Anna Akhmatova, Boris Pasternak, and Osip Mandelstam. As she says in "Balakhana" in *On Ballycastle Beach:*

> The door I found
> So difficult to close let in my first
> European feeling.
>
> (rev. ed. 1993; p. 36)

At one level we could understand this as a desire on McGuckian's part to move outside an exclusive emphasis on Irish history and literature, and she suggests as much in her 1995 interview with Dhomhnaill:

My main interest at the minute is the Russian poets, because of my living through this particular revolution, if it is a revolution. It's heart-rending what we go through, and it's been so wearing in the last phase of this past twenty years. It's been a daily grind of death around you and the Russians have been my solution; I just hang on to their love for each other—this little nest of four Russians [Akhmatova, Mandelstam, Pasternak, Tsvetaeva], where wonderfully there are two women who seem to be the source of it all. Those figures have become of

mythic proportion to me, and there's Rilke, and they take me out of the local violence and into Europe.

(p. 605)

Of course, the invocation of Europe has special connotations in Ireland, which are evident, for example, in the political discourse surrounding the Irish Republic's membership in the European Union. To speak of Europe is to bypass, in a kind of geographical ellipsis, the relation (traditionally one of subordination) to the powerful neighboring island of Great Britain, which lies between Ireland and the European mainland. Here, as elsewhere in McGuckian's work, what seems like a matter of poetic allegiances in fact carries an implicit political charge.

The idea of Europe is fundamental to *On Ballycastle Beach*, a volume that is also concerned with familial tradition and in particular the relationship between father and daughter. The volume is divided into two parts, the first preoccupied with the characteristics of sea and sky, the second with the contrasting themes of mobility and travel (by sea and by air) and territoriality or groundedness. The beach of the title might be thought of as an in-between place: unstable, not securely part of the land, open to sea and sky, but not outside the territory either. The volume seems to pose the question of how to make this edge a meaningful place, a question that takes on all sorts of political dimensions in the book.

Ballycastle is on the far north coast of Ireland, and it has personal significance for McGuckian because it is the place from which her father originated. But as other poems in the book remind us, the far north coast of Ireland also has political significance. In "The Bird Auction," for example, McGuckian refers to the Flight of the Earls, an event that has long been held as a symbol of crushed hopes for Irish Catholic independence. Four years after the defeat of the rebellion led by Hugh O'Neill, earl of Tyrone, in 1603, the defeated Catholic earls left Ireland for France, forfeiting large tracts of land in Ulster to the crown. These lands were later given to Scottish Presbyterians by King James I in what became known as the Ulster Plantation. Obliquely referring to the many Irish poets who have left for England or America, McGuckian rejects exile, suggesting instead that for the woman poet rootedness and growth are the only viable solutions. "For a Young Matron" draws a distinction between an aeroplane and a womb (a characteristic disjuncture, since the comparison is such an unlikely one):

> An aeroplane unlike
> A womb claims its space
> And takes it with it.
> It says, Once it wasn't like this.
>
> But wood grows
> Like the heart worn thin
> Within us, or the original
> Spirit of October.
>
> (rev. ed. 1993, p. 38)

Throughout the volume the language of seeds and growth—a growth that is only possible through fixity, through sinking roots in the earth—vies with that of ships and planes. In a development of her early poem "The Seed Picture," McGuckian seems to be suggesting the need for a new "plantation," a new commitment to place. But characteristically, the poetry also blurs the distinction between the fixed and the mobile.

One example of this blurring is the analogy McGuckian draws between the female body and vessels such as ships and planes. An oblique narrative progresses through the two halves of the book. It charts the course of a woman-ship; the first poem evokes "ships and their wind-blown ways," and these often indirect and unpredictable ways are followed throughout the sequence until the ship sails "in to harbour" in the title poem at the end of the book.

> If I found you wandering round the edge
> Of a French-born sea, when children
> Should be taken in by their parents,
> I would read these words to you,
> Like a ship coming in to harbour,
> As meaningless and full of meaning
> As the homeless flow of life
> From room to homesick room.
>
> (rev ed. 1993; p. 61)

Here the words "homeless" and "homesick" suggest that what is at issue is a longing for a return, a reclamation of the land. McGuckian has said of the poem "On Ballycastle Beach" that it was written for her father, who, as mentioned, comes from that part of County Antrim, but who has been displaced and urbanized through his move to Belfast. There may be an ironic reference in the poem to Yeats's play *On Baile's Strand*. It is on the beach that

the seemingly childless Cuchulain unwittingly kills his own son who has sailed to Ireland, thereby ensuring that his inheritance will be broken up. In contrast, in McGuckian's poem it is the daughter who arrives (from a "French-born" sea, that is, from the land to which the earls fled) to reclaim her father's inheritance. Again it is through the domestic, familial relation, but this time as a child rather than as a parent, that McGuckian will sow the seeds of a new plantation.

One poem that offers an insight into McGuckian's analogy between children and a new future for Northern Ireland is "A Dream in Three Colours." The title at first suggests the Irish tricolor (green, white, and gold), but the words of the Irish language exist in "scattered rooms," "like pearls that have lost their clasp." The language has no "hold" and it appears that the child's dream will be shattered by introduction into the syntax of the English language, symbolized by the three colors red, white, and blue:

> Far more raw than the spring night
> Which shook you out of its sleeve,
>
> Your first winter sheds for you
> Its strongest blue, its deepest white,
> Its reddest silk lapel you can let go
> Or hold, whichever you love best.
>
> (rev. ed. 1993, p. 42)

The child will learn an "alien" mother tongue, and thereby experience a separation by implication greater than the separation from the mother's body at birth. And yet the final lines do not suggest an unquenchable nostalgia for the lost Irish language, but rather that the child retains an element of choice in relation to his mother tongue. Even if the language of the tricolor has lost its hold, the child can choose whether or not to reject the Union Jack. McGuckian implies here that we are not bound by the past, that the preservation of identity does not necessarily depend on clinging to particular symbols of belonging. There can be other, unforeseeable developments.

Here, McGuckian seems at her most political, speaking the language of flags and national tongues, yet as has been suggested, the seeds of these images themselves come from European literature. Many of the poems in this and subsequent volumes are formed from quotations from literary essays and biographies. For example, "The Dream-

Language of Fergus," a poem whose title leads us to expect lines about McGuckian's third son, is a palimpsest of quotations from Osip Mandelstam's essay "Conversation about Dante." McGuckian herself has suggested that the Russian poets are important to her because of a parallel with the political situation in Northern Ireland, and in particular, as "A Dream in Three Colours" suggests, because they articulate a similar experience of violence and dislocation:

The experience of the community in the North of Ireland since 1969, while the emigration was not of the same kind or under the same pressures, nevertheless in its relentlessness, its day to day despair, has influenced the artists affected by it in many of the ways that 1917 shaped [Marina] Tsvetaeva. One bereavement Marina with her trilingual upbringing did not suffer was the substitution of a people's language, literature, culture and religion by those of the colonising neighbours—so deeply destructive a displacement, we are scarcely aware of the damage.

(Murphy, "You Took Away My Biography")

McGuckian's increasing reliance on precursor texts has caused some controversy. As Shane Murphy suggests, when a poem is created almost entirely of unacknowledged "borrowings" from other texts, questions of originality inevitably arise. Murphy analyzes two poems in detail: "Harem Trousers," from *On Ballycastle Beach,* and a later poem, "The Aisling Hat," from *Captain Lavender.* He shows how both are palimpsests of Russian texts, essays by Tsvetaeva and Mandelstam, respectively. Yet he goes on to demonstrate the ways in which McGuckian transforms and renews her source texts by restitching them into a new context. In the case of "Harem Trousers," the words are twisted to become a celebration of the Irish language poet Nuala Ní Dhomhnaill, and in "The Aisling Hat," Mandelstam's words are woven into an elegy for McGuckian's father:

The palimpsestic texts of Medbh McGuckian are also storehouses, made up of personal memories, anecdotes, political reflections and, crucially, a multitude of literary allusions, quotations and references. Indeed . . . the layered subtexts and varied entrance points offered by her word-hoard enable her conversations to be held simultaneously with a pantheon of exemplary writers, as well as the reader of her own poems.

For the publication of her fourth volume McGuckian left Oxford University Press; *Marconi's Cottage* was published in 1992 by Gallery Press in Ireland and Bloodaxe Books in England. It was Poetry Ireland Choice in 1992. The volume continues and deepens McGuckian's engagement with Russian literature and can be roughly divided into three parts. An initial sequence of poems focuses on the conflict between motherhood and artistic creativity, the claims of differing types of fertility. This is followed by a sequence celebrating the birth of a daughter, and then by a series of uplifting poems asserting the productivity of both types of creation and affirming a creative dialogue between the poetic and the quotidian.

Each part is underpinned once more by literary references and allusions, which McGuckian reworks into a shaping, plastic symbolism. There are references to the Irish poet Patrick Kavanagh, Virginia Woolf, and Sylvia Plath as well as extended meditations on Mandelstam's poem "Silentium" and Rilke's "Requiem for a Friend." Rilke seems to be important partly because of his own ambiguous sexual upbringing (his mother dressed him in skirts and called him Sophie until he was two), and partly because of his sympathy with women artists, "handicapped" by their femininity. "Requiem" was written in memory of the artist Paula Modersohn Becker, who died in childbirth. In "Visiting Rainer Maria" and "To Call Paula Paul," McGuckian explores the feminine and masculine elements within the psyche of poet and mother.

In the volume McGuckian also continues to pursue her fascination with Ballycastle and the north Antrim coast. Marconi's cottage itself is located near the village of Ballycastle. In the two-room rudimentary structure purchased by McGuckian, Marconi experimented with sending radio waves to Rathlin Island in the North Channel during 1898. Marconi's harnessing of electromagnetic waves perhaps suggests a means of communicating between the principles of masculinity and femininity, as also between body and spirit, and from soul to soul. To some extent the wave theory is offered ironically as a kind of technological advance on Tsvetaeva's "lyrical wires," through which, while in Germany, she dreamed of communicating with Pasternak in Russia. Many of the poems in *Marconi's Cottage* are concerned with the possibility of dreams and intuitive understanding between women. One of the striking departures for McGuckian in this book is the prevalence of female addressees—fetus, daughter, mother, and other writers; besides Plath and Woolf, she invokes Emily Brontë and Tsvetaeva.

Like *On Ballycastle Beach,* much of the symbolism of *Marconi's Cottage* is again concerned with images of seas and houses, or containing vessels. The title poem, in which the poet addresses the cottage, suggests a desire to find a balance between the order and shaping power of buildings, and the fluidity of the sea:

> Small and watchful as a lighthouse,
> A pure clear place of no particular childhood,
> It is as if the sea had spoken in you
> And then the words had dried.
>
> (p. 103)

The mention of the lighthouse inevitably recalls Virginia Woolf's search for a balance between the opposing forces of masculine and feminine creativity in *To the Lighthouse* (1927). McGuckian's cottage suggests that oppositions between nature and culture, house and sea, order and chaos are never stable. The house, a place of meaning, both forms and is formed from the inchoate disorder of the waves. And in a related vein the poem itself seeks a point of equilibrium between the architecture of the stanzas and the fluidity of thought and imagination contained in them. This achievement of a "dry" but fluid poetic wave (like the radio wave) recalls McGuckian's attempt to control the relation between the sun and rain in *Venus and the Rain.* It has been suggested that, in *Venus and the Rain,* McGuckian employs a procreative analogy for artistic creation, which casts poetic inspiration as masculine. But, in fact, such a description, while not simply inaccurate, cannot do justice to the shifting, androgynous play with gender that typifies her work. Thus, in *Marconi's Cottage,* the cottage (in one sense a feminine "house") exemplifies the masculine "architecture" of the poem, while the sea—here cast in the inspirational role—appears as feminine. In a similar way, images such as that of "seed" switch between masculine and feminine roles from poem to poem, and even within the same poem.

Marconi's Cottage includes some of McGuckian's most lyrical work to date; this lyricism is evidenced in particular in those poems celebrating the birth of her daughter, such as "Breaking the Blue":

> Deluged with the dustless air, unspeaking likeness:
> You, who were the spaces between words in the act of
>   reading,
> A colour sewn on to colour, break the blue.
>
> (p. 84)

Here McGuckian's habit of representing tangible objects such as people and places as elemental and relational is at its most successful. In these lines the unborn child is a palpable absence, an absence that gives meaning to that which surrounds it. Throughout McGuckian's work it is this ability to offer images from everyday experience, such as the substance of the atmosphere, or the tangibility of sound, that is her real gift. Despite the intense literariness of many of these poems, the feel of the volume as a whole is lighter than *On Ballycastle Beach.* Although allusive and demanding, the poems are less syntactically complex, and McGuckian experiments with a wider variety of verse forms and framing narratives, such as the fairy tale and the dream vision. Furthermore, the literariness of these poems never becomes purely self-enclosed and self-referential. McGuckian displays an impressive ability to weave back and forth between the realm of letters and the conflicts and dilemmas of everyday life, bringing the two together in an integrated vision.

CAPTAIN LAVENDER

IN the early 1990s the political situation in Northern Ireland began to shift, after decades of seemingly intractable conflict. In 1994 the IRA declared a cease-fire, opening a space for negotiations. The cease-fire broke down after eighteen months but was eventually restored, a development that led, after the election of a new Labour government in Britain, to the brokering of a political settlement between Unionists and Nationalists, the Good Friday Agreement of 1998.

McGuckian's fifth book, *Captain Lavender* (1994), responds indirectly to the new political prospects these developments opened up. Once more McGuckian approaches public issues through explorations of personal relationships, and in particular the relationship between femininity and masculinity both within and between individuals. Again, familial relations are central to the volume but here the family dynamic centers on men. The book is an extended elegy for her father, and in the interview in 1994 with Kimberly Bohman, McGuckian spoke of her wish to renew his life through poetry:

Sometimes what was happening outside gave me a metaphor. Like when I tried to deal with my father's death. It wasn't a war-death, it was a normal-death, but I treated it as a war-death. I address him as if he is a political prisoner. It eased it. But it was a metaphor to help me deal with something I couldn't deal with. . . . He was born in 1919, and he died in 1992, and his whole life he was a second-class citizen. . . . He didn't really live I don't think, and it [the poem] gives him an energy. By holding on to him, I give him the life he denied himself.

(p. 100)

So far from articulating the conventional worry that as a poet she may derive aesthetic profit from his death, here McGuckian states simply her hope that the father will profit from her poetry. Born in the Civil War, he died during the Troubles in Northern Ireland, so that his whole life was, quite literally, bounded by struggles over nationality and citizenship. McGuckian implies that the lack of political redress for her father's "second-class" citizenship (and that of his entire generation) was keenly felt, and that poetry may be able to seek this redress on another plane. Poetic metaphor becomes a way of reimagining his life and his social standing. Given that his life was bounded by war, McGuckian responds by giving him military honors. Yet she does this in a characteristically witty and ambivalent way: if the "flower master" was a way of masculinizing traditionally feminine arts, the name Captain Lavender in turn feminizes the military role. McGuckian repeatedly describes her father in feminine terms: he has a "womb already primed" ("Black Virgin," p. 56); he is "in danger of becoming a poetess" ("Elegy for an Irish Speaker," p. 42). This feminization vies with an exaggerated strength and physicality: in "The Aisling Hat" she portrays him in Homeric terms, so far from a second-class citizen that here he has grandiose, epic proportions:

Even your least movement was connected
with the very composition of the soil,
you lived and died according to its laws.

Your Promethean head radiated
ash-blue quartz, your blue-black hair
some feathered, Paleolithic arrowhead,

set off the bold strokes of your ungainly
arms, created for handshakes, sliding
like the knight's move, to the side.

(pp. 44–45)

As John Kerrigan has pointed out in a review of *Captain Lavender* in the *London Review of Books*, the title of this poem shows McGuckian "trying a genre on for size" (p. 26), in a witty interpretation of the adage that "if the cap fits, wear it." The cap or hat in this case is the Aisling, a genre popular with nationalist poets throughout the nineteenth century. It usually presents a vision of Ireland as a beautiful and radiant maiden, exhorting her young men to fight for her liberation. McGuckian's exaggerated conceit, however, suggests instead the possibility of poetic liberation through the death of the father, who is represented as harnessing powerful natural energies: "his denial / of history's death, by the birth of his storm" (p. 45).

Throughout *Captain Lavender*, McGuckian's sense of her father's imprisonment within life, and her desire to acknowledge the war situation of both his life and death through envisioning him as a soldier, is linked to images of Northern Irish political prisoners. While writing the book McGuckian was involved in creative writing workshops with prisoners in The Maze, the notorious prison in Northern Ireland where both Loyalist and Nationalist offenders were held. Many of them were serving life sentences for terrorist crimes. As in the following lines from "White Windsor Soap," her father and the prisoners become metaphors for one other:

In the hospital robe of your Catholic eyes,
their bars painted prison-issue blue,
like a submarine, I have been entirely released . . .

(p. 81)

Physical entrapment may take place within a sick body, or a prison regime. And in a similar way, imaginative and physical release complement and balance each other through the volume. The verse, as in "The Over Mother," articulates a strong consciousness of the daughter's poetic responsibility:

I keep seeing birds
that could be you when you stretch out
like a syllable and look to me
as if I could give you wings.

(p. 64)

Birds, flight, and song are central images throughout this volume, representing the possibility of escape from many kinds of confinement and constraint through the power of imagination. (There are possibly echoes here too of Yeats's "Sailing to Byzantium," where the old man, the poet, imagines himself perfected in death as a golden bird.) The title poem presents an image of night flight, guided by the otherworldly presence of the dead father as "Captain Lavender":

> Sperm names, ovum names, push inside
> each other. We are half-taught
> our real names, from other lives.
>
> Emphasize your eyes. Be my flare-
> path, my uncold begetter,
> my air-minded bird-sense.
>
> (p. 76)

McGuckian's thought here is not simply the familiar one—that the injustices of history (whether personal or national) may be redressed or healed in poetry. She is also suggesting that poetry learns from the reality of these losses and sufferings, indeed, that it is created out of the attempt to deal with loss, and in the very awareness that loss is, in a fundamental sense, irredeemable. There is, in fact, a story behind "Captain Lavender" that bears this reading out. It concerns one woman, Beryl Markham, whose husband was killed on a solo flight from London to Nova Scotia in the 1930s; in order to come to terms with his death, Markham repeated the dangerous solo journey herself, so that her flight could be guided and defined by his. For both poet and pilot the dead man acts as a metaphysical guide. In one of McGuckian's typical gender inversions, he is a muse figure for the woman left behind.

This story touches one of the central paradoxes of McGuckian's work, which we have already encountered: freedom's need for constraint. Just as a bird's flight is regulated by its homing instinct, which directs the paths of its flight, so consolation is not simply a matter of emotional release but is achieved through the constraints of poetic form. In the final two stanzas of "Waxwing Winter," this process is imaged in terms of an imprisoned bird:

> It bathes in smoke and windswept flight.
> If it is found towards the end of the day
> you must put its wing out of action
> until it is healed or free
> of flesh in a fume-cupboard.

> Its heat is what for us would be fever:
> if you use the fingers of one hand
> to form a "cage," can you hear
> through the leaf litter and imagined open space
> the light-proof birdsong
> as the bird itself might hear it?
>
> (p. 65)

In keeping with McGuckian's comments about her father's life sentence as a second-class citizen in Northern Ireland, this poem equates death with liberation. To be healed is to be free of flesh (that is, a skeleton). But, as the line break insists, it is also to be simply free. The last stanza suggests that it is as impossible to tell sickness from health as to distinguish inside from outside, the state of being caged from that of being free. Like the poem itself, the cage is created by hand, and inside it is open space and song. This image conjures the many different sorts of metaphysical freedom that are held captive, yet somehow also sustained, by physical constraints: the soul in the body, the prisoner in the jail, the lyric transcendence in the strict lineation of words on the page.

McGuckian's work is clearly committed to an idea of metaphysical release through poetry, to the possibility of healing through poetic form. Yet, as has been suggested, it would be a mistake to associate this stance with the adoption of a conventional lyric voice, and with ideas of balance and integration. Rather, healing seems to depend on dislocation. As the lines from "Waxwing Winter" imply, there is a need first to break in order to heal ("you must put its wing out of action"). Just as a bird needs to be away from home in order to activate the homing instinct, so poetry requires estrangement and dislocation. Throughout *Captain Lavender*, McGuckian stresses the importance of strangeness, of the fact that one town is not another town, that North is not South, that Britain is not Ireland, that this world is not the other; all are "as gracefully apart / as a calvary from a crib" ("Lines for Thanksgiving," p. 13). Such distances both require and admit the mediation of speech and language. At times McGuckian comes close to suggesting the need for the conflict within Northern Ireland, in order to facilitate language:

> Until we remembered that to speak
> is to be forever on the road,
> listening for the foreigner's footstep.
> ("The Aisling Hat," p. 47)

But a crude political reading does not do justice to the depth of McGuckian's meditation on language and the intimacy of its relation to the self. The foreigner here is not only the British presence in Ireland, but the other in general, including us, her readers:

> Most foreign and cherished reader,
> I cannot live without
> your trans-sense language,
> the living furrow of your spoken words
> that plough up time.
> ("Elegy for an Irish Speaker," p. 43)

For McGuckian, poetry is clearly a regenerative force, but it is one "at home" with homelessness, with the losses, discontinuities, and disjunctures that are its defining concern.

SHELMALIER

Even accomplished readers, prepared for the syntactical complexity and literary allusiveness of McGuckian's poetry, may find themselves daunted by her sixth volume, *Shelmalier* (1998). The poems have all the shifting images, bizarre trains of thought, and conceptual leaps characteristic of her style. Perhaps more than in any of her previous work, the reader experiences the difficulty of making connections in McGuckian's poetry. *Shelmalier* relies too on "precursor" texts, but rather than literary essays and biographies, the texts that McGuckian engages with here are the various histories of the United Irishmen rebellion of 1798. The book was published during the 1998 bicentenary of the failed attempt by both Protestant and Catholic Irishmen to proclaim an independent Irish Republic, modeled on the American and French revolutions. The rebellion, whose centers were in Ulster and in county Wexford, was put down by the British with vastly disproportionate casualties on the Irish side.

Shelmalier emphasizes the bloody nature of the conflict, in which rebels were executed or massacred in the field. It is full of images of ghosts, of the dead and dying, of war, battle, courthouse, and prison. The book is divided into five sections: in the first, the ghosts of the past call to the poet to remember and celebrate the past; the second part expresses the hopes kindled by the rising itself; the third revolves around the devastation of battle and punishment, in particular the gibbet; the fourth is full of images of imprisonment; and the final section offers hope for the future. But the central image throughout the volume is the tree. At once gibbet, cross, and tree of liberty, the tree represents both terrible violence and the possibility of redemption. McGuckian's Catholic sensibility returns in force in the pervasive religious symbolism of the volume, but strikingly, the Christian iconography is used to join Protestant and Catholic rather than, as so often, to divide them. The focus on the physical suffering of the crucifixion is usually taken to be distinctively Catholic. But in *Shelmalier* the crucifixion provides an encompassing image of death and resurrection. This inclusiveness is further enhanced by a typical gender twist, as McGuckian highlights the way in which the vulnerability and passivity of the crucified Christ disrupts preconceptions of masculinity. "The Feminine Christs," the final poem in the first section, dwells on the helplessness and powerlessness of the dead. But this powerlessness also has its own persistence and endurance: "their dreams churn in the midyears / from century to century . . ." (p. 34).

The title of the volume itself is a conundrum. The word derives from a name for an Irish clan in Wexford, the síol malure, a people who were wiped out by repeated English incursions into the country. It was anglicized as the name of a barony in Wexford during the Ordnance Survey of Ireland in the early nineteenth century. The name appears in two well-known nineteenth-century ballads commemorating 1798. In a ballad celebrating the actions of the warrior-priest Father John Murphy, it is the name of the place in Wexford where the rebels gathered before their successful attack on Wexford Town. In the other ballad it is a term for a member of the peasant insurgency. ("What's the news, what's the news, O my bold Shelmalier?") There were, apparently, Shelmaliers on both sides, both yeomen and peasantry, and it may be this ambiguity, as much as anything else, that draws McGuckian to the name. In either case the term is firmly associated with the rebellion in Wexford, in the Irish Republic. Thus, in another inclusive gesture, McGuckian links north and south, the present Troubles and the past, by appropriating the term "shelmalier." A true healing of Ireland's divisions, she implies, will come only with the remembrance of shared moments in history, and not simply from a future of increasing commercial and economic union.

Like Tom Paulin in his 1983 volume *Liberty Tree*, McGuckian's imagination is caught by the confluence of Presbyterian and Catholic in the rebellion, although the poetry itself could not be further from Paulin's blend of toughness and clarity. But it would be a mistake to read the book as a celebration of violence against the English; instead it is the ideals of liberty and common cause that seem to fire McGuckian's imagination. She admits in the preface to the volume that the poems are a result of her own process of discovery, particularly of the sacrifices made for liberty by well-born Protestant gentlemen, such as Theobald Wolfe Tone, Lord Edward Fitzgerald, and later, Robert Emmet. "The theme is less the experienced despair of a noble struggle brutally quenched than the dawn of my own enlightenment after a medieval ignorance, my being suddenly able to welcome into consciousness figures of an integrity I had never learnt to be proud of" (author's note to *Shelmalier*, p. 13).

In the background of the poems lie texts and speeches, biographies of the leaders of the 1798 rebellion, and letters and memoirs such as the memoirs of Wolfe Tone. McGuckian also includes material relating to other rebellions, such as Robert Emmet's speech in the dock after he was sentenced to death for leading the rebellion of 1803. This speech is referred to in the title poem, and 1803 forms another link in a historical chain that runs through the book, to the 1848 rebellion, the 1916 rising, and even the hunger strikes of the early 1980s. Underlining this sense of the continuity of struggle, the epigraph to the volume quotes another Protestant Unitedman, James Hope, who suggests an inexorable movement towards liberation: "Physical force may prevail for a time . . . but there is music in the sound of moral force which will be heard like the sound of the cuckoo. The bird lays its eggs, and leaves them for a time; but it will come again and hatch them in due course, and the song will return with the season (p. 12).

Thus, in a more clearly political key, *Shelmalier* continues McGuckian's meditation on the intertwining of liberation and tradition. In her preface to the volume she elaborates on the key notion of recurrence and regeneration. "I found that what I had written in the form of epitaph and commemoration or address for the present-day disturbances in the North fitted like an egg into its shell that previous whirlwind moment when, unbeliev-ably, hope and history did in fact rhyme" (p. 13). Her poetic song is offered as a continuation of earlier moments, with the hope that the current moment will herald the emergence of a new political dispensation. McGuckian is undoubtedly responding here to the paramilitary cease-fires and movements toward peace that shaped the politics of Northern Ireland in the 1990s. In "The Feastday of Peace," McGuckian is called by the dead, who offer a form of orientation to the poet:

> Deep in time's turnings
> and the overcrowded soil,
> too familiar to be seen,
> the long, long dead
> steer with their warmed breath
> my unislanded dreams.
>
> (p. 23)

Of course, McGuckian's preoccupation with the interlacing of history and the present, and with the revitalizing relation to tradition, courts the danger of inertia, of becoming stuck in an idealization of lost heroic moments. But just as damaging, of course, would be a naive notion of progress, one that lost touch with what is valuable in the past. McGuckian's complex imagery reveals her sensitivity to these twin perils, as she seeks to retrieve the special lessons of the alliance between Catholic and Protestant, between North and South. Against the stereotyped association of Catholicism and nationalism, *Shelmalier* recalls the many Presbyterian young men who died for Ireland.

The volume's sense of historical continuity ("Your eighteenth-century fingers spice the soil / with blood and bone" ["Cleaning Out the Workhouse," p. 30]) is underpinned by McGuckian's reflection on the turning of centuries. *Shelmalier* is, in one sense, a millennial work, located "where the decade / hinges into the visible century" ("Cornet Love," p. 57). But here 1998 looks back not only to 1798 but also to another fin de siècle, that of the 1890s. In one sense, this historical reference is a continuation of her interest in Victoriana. Significantly, the two *Shelmalier* ballads are Victorian creations, not contemporary with the uprising. And this historical "double exposure" is emphasized by the painting on the front cover of the book, which is a late-nineteenth-century scene of a woman tending a wounded poacher. (Again, it is the wounded, feminine aspect of masculinity in which McGuckian is interested.) In a further reflection of this sense of multiple historical levels, McGuckian can also be seen as rewriting the response of W. B. Yeats and his friend, Maud Gonne, a political activist, to 1798. But whereas the Yeatsian image was straightforwardly heroic, McGuckian's strategies of "feminization," her stress on suffering and vulnerability, while not denying the heroism, introduce another dimension.

These complexities are not easy to grasp; undeniably, the movement of thought in *Shelmalier* often seems capricious and obscure. Some poems read rather like word pictures, reminiscent of Gertrude Stein; they seem not to convey any identifiable meaning. Yet McGuckian's work does not fit comfortably within a theory of the poetic avant-garde, with its stress on depersonalization and the disruption of representation. The Romantic inspiration of her poetry is too evident, as is her claiming of a certain vatic role. Along with the difficulty of the poems in *Shelmalier,* however, goes a surprising return to conventional forms. While some poems in the book read almost like prose poems, despite their lineation, in others McGuckian experiments with rhyme, including the sonnet form, and even rhyming couplets, as in the introductory poem, "Script for an Unchanging Voice":

The leaves are tongues whose years of blood are
   locked
in the wrong house, time feels unclocked

or has been dead too long by now to cast
its freshly slaughtered shadow from the past . . .
                (p. 16)

The suggestion here is that things are caught in a pattern and cannot move on. The neatness and closure of rhyme seems linked with the impossibility of a future; rhyme is chilling, a harbinger of war. Yet, as usual, this is only one side of the story. Other poems in the book suggest that estrangement can be overcome through rhyme. The title poem, for example, a sonnet and an elegy for McGuckian's father, ends: "This great estrangement has the destination of a rhyme. / The trees of his heart breathe regular in my dream" (p. 75).

As in *Captain Lavender,* McGuckian is convinced of the need for difference in order for there to be rapprochement, separation in order for there to be joining. Estrangement gives definition to the two communities in Northern Ireland, a definition

that is essential to any interdependence, as these lines from "The Spirit Dolls" suggest:

They substract us as matter from their lives—
spice-merchants, tanners, coopers, weavers,
wine-merchants, innkeepers, florists, casual
   mercenaries.
They made themselves up as they went along,
their cross-streets linked in city wards,
the Parish of Hospital, in the Diocese of Emily.

Authentic children of the Covenant, my anti-family,
my anti-home, my counter-home, residence
is being conferred on them, a homely dress
that they have donned, as insiders' outsiders,
as a new us and an old them, in the scoured pot
of our acid, indigestible, please-and-thank-you army.
                (p. 38)

The relational sense of identity that McGuckian expresses here is essential to her work at every level. Within the nation, within the family, between genders, and within the psyche itself, apparently opposing or conflicting elements are constantly blending and sliding into one another. This is a complex and demanding vision. To grapple with the remarkable poetic style, at once fluid and full of startling transitions, which McGuckian has forged to articulate it, is both a challenging and rewarding experience.

SELECTED BIBLIOGRAPHY

I. CHIEF WORKS. *Portrait of Joanna* (Belfast, U.K., 1980); *The Flower Master* (Oxford, 1982); *Venus and the Rain* (Oxford, 1984); *On Ballycastle Beach* (Oxford and Winston-Salem, N.C, 1988; rev. ed. Oldcastle, County Meath, Ireland, 1993); *Two Women, Two Shores,* with Nuala Archer (Baltimore and Galway, Ireland, 1989); *Marconi's Cottage* (Dublin and Winston-Salem, N.C., 1992); *The Flower Master and Other Poems* (Oldcastle, County Meath, Ireland, 1993); *Captain Lavender* (Oldcastle, County Meath, Ireland, 1994); *Shelmalier* (Oldcastle, County Meath, Ireland, 1998).

II. INTERVIEWS AND ESSAYS. Rebecca E. Wilson, ed., "Medbh McGuckian," in Rebecca E. Wilson, ed., *Sleeping with Monsters: Conversations with Scottish and Irish Women Poets* (Edinburgh, 1990); Medbh McGuckian, "How Precious Also Are *Thy* Thoughts unto Me," *Common Knowledge* 2 (spring 1993); Kimberly S. Bohman, "Surfacing: An Interview with Medbh McGuckian," *Irish Review* 15 (autumn / winter 1994); Medbh McGuckian and Nuala Ní Dhomhnaill, "Comhrá [Conversation], with a foreword and afterword by Laura O'Connor," *Southern Review* 31 (July 1995); John Kerrigan, "Belonging," in *London Review of Books* 14 (18 July 1996).

III. BIOGRAPHY AND CRITICISM. Michael Allen, "The Poetry of Medbh McGuckian," in Elmer Andrews, ed., *Contemporary Irish Poetry: A Collection of Critical Essays* (London, 1992); Thomas Docherty, "Initiations, Tempers, Seductions: Postmodern McGuckian," in Neil Corcoran, ed., *The Chosen Ground: Essays on the Contemporary Poetry of Northern Ireland* (Brigend, U.K., 1992); Peggy O'Brien, "Medbh McGuckian," in *Colby Quarterly* 28 (December 1993); Clair Wills, *Improprieties: Politics and Sexuality in Northern Irish Poetry* (Oxford and New York, 1993); Patricia Boyle Haberstroh, *Women Creating Women: Contemporary Irish Women Poets* (Dublin and Syracuse, N.Y., 1996); Shane Murphy, "Obliquity in the Poetry of Paul Muldoon and Medbh McGuckian, in *Eire-Ireland* 31, no. 3–4 (1996); Shane Murphy, "You Took Away My Biography: The Poetry of Medbh McGuckian," in *Irish University Review* (spring-summer 1998).

A. A. MILNE

(1882–1956)

Lisa Hermine Makman

A. A. MILNE HAS been loved and lauded as a writer for children since the 1920s, when he first created stories featuring the benevolent but bumbling toy bear Winnie-the-Pooh. Generations of children have come to know Pooh and his fellow denizens of the Hundred Acre Wood: timid Piglet, pompous Owl, imperious Rabbit, cheerless Eeyore, spirited Tigger, motherly Kanga, and imprudent Baby Roo. These figures, with their characteristic attributes, have become part of a potent mythology known throughout the world. In the global commercial idiom of the late twentieth century they came to adorn myriad merchandise: children's clothing and linens, mugs and magnets, games and toys. At the same time, Milne's Pooh books, translated into dozens of languages, continued to be praised as masterpieces of children's literature.

Milne joined the ranks of the classical children's writers with the publication of his four famous children's books, all of which were immediate hits: *When We Were Very Young* (1924), *Winnie-the-Pooh* (1926), *Now We are Six* (1927), and *The House at Pooh Corner* (1928). Late-twentieth-century critics hailed him as the last figure in a great tradition of children's literature, part of a canon that includes the Victorian writers Edward Lear, Lewis Carroll, and George Macdonald and the Edwardian writers Frances Hodgson Burnett, Beatrix Potter, J. M. Barrie, Edith Nesbit, and Kenneth Grahame. These authors produced their works in England and America between the 1860s and World War I (1914–1918), an epoch during which the social roles played by children and the symbolic values ascribed to childhood shifted dramatically. During this period, as legislation in Britain increasingly limited child labor and enforced school attendance, a carefree, labor-free childhood came to be understood as a fundamental right of all children, regardless of their social class. Moreover, childhood became an increasingly popular locus for fantasies about leisure and freedom. The canonical children's writers participated in this cultural trend in two key ways. First, they introduced elements of fantasy, magic, and play into children's literature, which previously had been predominantly didactic. Second, they described childhood in spatial terms, as a protected place for unrestricted play, detached from the sober grown-up world. This view of childhood as an Arcadian space for playful recreation is epitomized in Milne's Pooh books. Critics such as Humphrey Carpenter and Jackie Wullschläger have discussed the Arcadian strain in Milne's work. They have claimed that Milne marks the end of an Arcadian tradition in children's literature.

In his works for children Milne was highly influenced by his predecessors. Like Lear and Carroll, he revels in wordplay and nonsense. Like Potter and Grahame, he innovates the genre of the animal tale. Like Barrie and Macdonald, he invents an idyllic world that works according to its own logic, its own laws. Strikingly, however, Milne's Hundred Acre Wood, unlike forerunners such as Carroll's Wonderland and Barrie's Never Land, is hermetic, protected from the adult realm of commerce, politics, violence, sexuality, and work. There is no money and there are no weapons in Pooh's world; the animals neither don clothes nor drive cars. The wood holds no tangible danger. Rather, it is a world free from fears and anxieties, except perhaps for those of the fainthearted Piglet, which are always revealed to be unfounded. Whereas Potter's Peter Rabbit is menaced by Mr. McGregor and Barrie's Peter Pan is imperiled by pirates, Milne's characters remain secure.

The safe haven Milne imagines in his children's fiction is just the sort of place craved by his British contemporaries of the 1920s. The safety and freedom of movement granted by the Hundred Acre Wood reflects the desires of an increasingly insular Britain, a Britain in decline as a military, industrial, and imperial force. Although Milne was a child at the height of the Victorian age, he began his life as a writer during the Edwardian period. He composed his fantasies about Pooh in a swiftly changing twentieth-century world in which social norms were in rapid flux and perceptions of space and time were being altered by new inventions such as the airplane, automobile, telegraph, and telephone. Edwardian writing in general expresses a yearning for escape and diversion. The First World War, a conflict of unprecedented violence, only amplified this British predilection. Many of Milne's works for adults, like his works for children, requited this lust for escapist pleasure. They commonly represent life as a stable and comprehensible pleasure ground of class privilege in which witty, attractive characters engage in sparkling dialogue. An awareness of the possibility of loss rarely penetrates these protected spheres. The style and content of Milne's writing remained predominantly Edwardian in flavor throughout his life: while his style is lighter and more clipped than that of the ponderous Victorians, his work looks back longingly toward the knowable world of the nineteenth century. After the 1920s, when such sprightly work became less fashionable, the audience for Milne's adult writings dwindled. Demand for his children's books, however, remained high. Increasingly, the light and nostalgic writing at which Milne excelled was accepted only in works for children.

Milne complained frequently and bitterly that he was not just a children's writer. Before he began to write for children he was best known for his essays and plays. He first gained recognition as a writer before the First World War, composing weekly sketches for the popular periodical *Punch*. Just prior to and during his wartime military service he began to direct his attention to writing drama, and in the 1920s many of his plays achieved tremendous success on the stages of Britain and America. Throughout Milne's career, his English successes would be repeated on the other side of the Atlantic. Although Milne thrived as a playwright and was for a brief period one of the most prominent and best-paid dramatists in England, he never focused exclusively on the stage. Priding himself on his versatility, he experimented with a broad range of genres, publishing novels, poetry, short stories, political tracts, a mystery, and an autobiography. Although at least initially popular with his adult audiences, Milne was from the start somewhat unpopular with the critics, who in-

creasingly groused that his writing was trivial and sentimental. After he achieved fame and fortune for his children's works, reviewers harped on what they deemed the "childish" quality of his writing. Milne's bitterness about these criticisms lasted until the end of his life.

Like his friend and mentor J. M. Barrie, who also achieved success both as a playwright and as a children's author, Milne frequently was judged to be too "whimsical." He came to abhor this word, so often applied to himself and to his writing, and to detest its connotations of sentimentality. Nevertheless, throughout his life his writing was to be marked by a persistent and characteristic wistfulness. Milne's only child, Christopher, model for the legendary character Christopher Robin, writes of his father, "for as long as I knew him [nostalgia] was the only emotion that he seemed to delight in both feeling and showing" (Christopher Milne, p. 146). For A. A. Milne, nostalgia signified both an imaginary era of stability antedating the changeful culture of early-twentieth-century Britain and the experience of his own contented childhood at the apex of the Victorian age.

EARLY LIFE

ALAN Alexander Milne was born on 18 January 1882 at Henley House in Hampstead, London. He was the third and youngest son of John Vine Milne and Maria Milne, upwardly mobile teachers who had met as faculty members at schools in Shropshire. At the time of Alan's birth John Milne was proprietor and headmaster of Henley House, a private school for middle-class boys whose parents could not afford the elite public schools.

Henley House consisted of two buildings: the Milnes' home and the schoolhouse. Thus Alan grew up with both his immediate family—which included two brothers, Barrie and Ken—and an extended "family" of dozens of schoolboy siblings. Although Alan was never close to his eldest brother, Barrie, he adored Ken, who was only sixteen months older than he and who became a lifelong friend. As children the two younger brothers were as inseparable as the characters Piglet and Pooh; Milne writes of himself and Ken, "Save for the fact that he hated cheese, we shared equally all belief, all knowledge, all ambition, all hope, and all fear" (*Autobiography*, p. 19).

According to Milne family lore, Alan learned to read before he was three. At the age of six he began a dazzling career as a student at Henley House. A singularly industrious schoolboy, he excelled in most subjects, especially mathematics—which he loved at least in part because his father taught the class—and the natural sciences, an interest aroused in part by his science master at the school, H. G. Wells, who not too many years later would become a prominent writer of science books, novels, and science fiction. Years later, when Alan began his own career as a writer, Wells would offer him both friendship and encouragement.

At age eleven Milne became the youngest student ever granted a scholarship to the prestigious Westminster School. Although Alan's interest in writing was well established by the time he finished his schooling at Westminster, he entered Trinity College at Cambridge in 1900 with a mathematics scholarship. There he continued halfheartedly to pursue his education and wholeheartedly to pursue his writing. At the university he published humorous poetry and articles in the undergraduate magazine *The Granta,* which was often called "the Cambridge *Punch.*" In 1902 he was named editor of *The Granta* and wrote prolifically, developing his light and witty signature style and dreaming that he would someday write for the true *Punch* in London.

A PUNCH *HUMORIST*

IN 1903, after graduating from Cambridge with a mathematics degree, Milne moved to London to launch his professional life as a writer. Soon after his arrival he made his first sale, "The Rape of the Sherlock," a parody of Arthur Conan Doyle's Sherlock Holmes stories, which *Vanity Fair* accepted for fifteen shillings after *Punch* had rejected it. That same year *Punch* published one of Milne's poems, and by 1905 the magazine was printing his poetry and prose regularly. From 1906 until 1914, Milne served as an assistant editor of *Punch,* and throughout that period he made weekly contributions to the magazine, generating a stream of essays, sketches, and reviews.

He had developed a reputation as a writer of what he himself dubbed "light articles," usually personal essays or short scenes peppered with witty, offhand dialogue. The substance of these essays and sketches sprang from his own life experience. A garden party, a pantomime, a shopping expedition—anything could serve as food for Milne's humor, which resides in his wry, digressive style. For example, after describing a mishap that occurred during a cricket match, he stops himself before relating another: "Once when—But no, on second thoughts, I sha'n't tell you that story. You would say it was a lie—as indeed it is" (*The Day's Play,* p. 19). These light pieces and their comic mode reflect the gay mood in England in the years before the war. They were energetically praised by critics as "a new kind of nonsense" (noted in Thwaite, p. 114) and compared to the works of Lewis Carroll.

Essay and sketch writing would continue to play an important role for Milne, whose first and last books were collections of such works. Most of his books of essays were published at the beginning of his career, in the period before Pooh first appeared. The first of these collections was *Lovers in London* (1905), a group of twenty-four sketches, all of which had originally appeared in *The Saint James Gazette.* These meandering pieces describe the London outings of an English gentleman and his American sweetheart, whose expeditions lead to their engagement. Milne writes of the book, "I took an imaginary girl to the Zoo, to the Tower, to Earl's Court, whence we proceeded together into print" (*Autobiography,* p. 202). The narrator here, as in most of Milne's essays, is modeled on himself. He typically cultivates a picture of himself as a playful and foppish good sport, the sort of chap one would like to invite for a weekend in the country. In fact, Milne did receive numerous invitations to the country homes of the wealthy, places that provided the backdrop for many of his pieces.

While Milne was a proponent of escapism in his life and in his writing, he held a fixed belief that one could not escape from oneself. Of his own process of essay and sketch composition he wrote, "One had supposed that one was saying something true about gold-fish or walking-sticks or bandstands, whereas actually it was the gold-fish and the walking-stick and the bandstands which were saying something true about oneself" (*By Way of Introduction,* p. 4). Like Michel de Montaigne, inventor of the essay genre, Milne believed that all essays disclose and illuminate the self. The title of any book of essays, Milne confessed, should be "Myself." Although he never followed this suggestion, the titles of his early collections of essays point to his focus on the playful and light side of life: *The Day's Play* (1910), *The Holiday Round* (1912), *Once a Week* (1914), and *The Sunny Side* (1921), four volumes that eventually were combined in a single book nostalgically entitled *Those Were the Days* (1929).

Lovers in London was promptly and unanimously panned by the critics. Embarrassed by the book, Milne later bought back the rights to prevent it from being reprinted. He would later refer to his second book, *The Day's Play*, a collection of essays from *Punch*, as if it were his first. *The Day's Play*, the title of which parodies Rudyard Kipling's title *The Day's Work*, is emblematic of Milne's writing before the war. At the time Milne wrote his early essays, the meaning of "play" was in flux. Victorian convictions about the inherently moral value of work, particularly for young people, were being questioned. Play was increasingly valorized as the legitimate activity of the young and the objective of adult life. Values associated with play—spontaneity, passion, and group participation—were increasingly encouraged in adults. Milne's characters exemplify the new model for middle-class adulthood that emerged with the development of mass consumer culture: an adult might rightfully remain a Peter Pan, a child for life, and it was acceptable for play to be one's principal concern and primary activity. The characters Milne introduced in his sketches, particularly a group of young people he christened the "Rabbits," are emblematic of this new understanding of leisure time as the domain within which one's "true" identity becomes manifest.

Levity was the hallmark of Milne's writing and the source of his popularity, which by 1910 was remarkable. Writing in 1939, Milne elucidates his understanding of levity and of himself in the prewar context: "You can't be light and gay and offhand and casual and charming in print unless you are continually reassured that you are being some of these things" (*Autobiography*, p. 240). His light pieces were consistently popular, and he had many imitators. Nevertheless, Milne's father and Owen Seaman, his editor at *Punch*, encouraged him to engage in more serious writing, to take off "the mask of levity," a criticism he later repudiated:

Levity was no mask put on for the occasion. The world was not then the damnable world which it is today; it was a world in which imaginative youth could be happy without feeling ashamed of its happiness. I was very young, very light-hearted, confident of myself, confident of the future. I loved my work; I loved not working; I loved the long week-ends with the delightful people of other people's delightful houses. I loved being in love, and being out of love and free again to fall in love. I loved feeling rich again, and having no responsibilities, but only the privileges of a benevolent uncle. I loved hearing that some Great man, full of serious purpose, had loved my last article.

(*Autobiography*, p. 234)

The First World War lessened, although only slightly, the giddiness of Milne's writing. He turned to literary criticism and wrote with great sensitivity about, among others, his heros Saki, J. M. Barrie, and Kenneth Grahame. Overall, his essays became less trivial, more rigorous, and more focused after his stint as a soldier.

A WAR AND A WIFE

IN 1913, just before the Great War, Milne married Dorothy de Selincourt, goddaughter of Owen Seaman. Like the heroines in Milne's sketches and dramas, Daphne, as she was called by her friends, was a pert and witty conversationalist. More important to Milne, she was a terrific audience. She laughed readily at his jokes; "she had (it is now clear) the most perfect sense of humour in the world" (*Autobiography*, p. 243). For the remainder of his life Milne would depend on Daphne for her laughter and encouragement, even though the two were incompatible in other ways.

Shortly after the marriage Milne promised his new wife that he would one day take her godfather's position, becoming the senior editor of *Punch*. However, as soon as war was declared in 1914, he abandoned the magazine in order to enlist in the army, despite his long-held pacifist beliefs. Trained as a signal officer, Milne was at first stationed close to home and far from combat, on the Isle of Wight. Soon after he arrived Daphne joined him, and together they organized entertainment for the troops and their families. To this end Milne wrote a skit for children that he eventually spun into an amusing novel-length fairy tale, *Once on a Time*. Determined not to allow the war to stay his development as a writer, he wrote two of his first comedies during this period, *Wurzel-Flummery* (1917) and *Belinda, An April Folly* (1918), both of which introduce themes that recur in Milne's later plays.

In *Wurzel-Flummery* a wealthy man leaves his riches to a pair of enemies—politicians from opposing parties—contingent on their taking the absurd name Wurzel-Flummery. At first the two haughtily refuse the offer, but by the end of the play they have changed their names. Here Milne satirizes the pride of allegedly great men and pokes fun at his society's commercialism. *Belinda*, like *Wurzel-Flummery,* is a farce. In it, a coquettish middle-age woman energetically flirts with two men, a poet and a statistician, until her long-lost husband appears on the scene to reclaim her. Belinda's marriage is saved and a new match is made as her daughter and the poet fall in love.

Eventually Milne saw combat, spending four months on the battlefields of the Somme. Invalided home with trench fever in November 1916, he was set to work in the War Office. Only months after his return to England, he began to see his plays performed. J. M. Barrie chose *Wurzel-Flummery* to accompany two one-acts of his own for a triple bill, and the trio of plays opened in London in the spring of 1917. *Belinda* was performed the following year, with Irene Vanbrugh, one of London's best-known actresses, in the title role. Among its admirers was Bernard Shaw, who called the character Belinda "a minx" (Thwaite, pp. 186–187). When the reviews came in Milne rejoiced because one critic had compared his farce to Oscar Wilde's *The Importance of Being Earnest,* the play he claimed he would most like to have written.

During the war Milne made a single attempt to write directly about the impact of the fighting, a one-act play called *The Boy Comes Home,* which is striking in part because of its seriousness. In the play a young man named Phillip returns from the war and entreats his profiteering uncle to pass on the money Phillip's father bequeathed to him while he was away fighting. When the uncle withholds this promised money, the boy becomes enraged and threatens to kill him. The older man finally gives in, and the boy suddenly becomes calm, as if nothing unusual had transpired. Like *The Camberley Triangle* (1919), *The Boy Comes Home* expresses animosity toward those men who did not fight. In his fiction Milne would rarely again write about war and when he did it was never with great success.

DRAWING-ROOM DRAMAS OF A FAMILY MAN

DURING and after the war Milne cheerfully produced escapist entertainment of the sort that would later be found in Hollywood films and television sitcoms. The postwar British public embraced these diversions. Milne's plays were so popular that many films, both silents and talkies, were adapted from them. Even the drama critics—most of whom complained that Milne's characters lacked depth—applauded the author's imagination and wit. In his plays Milne introduces fascinating and sometimes fantastical situations, but the characters that populate his stage are rarely as riveting as the predicaments in which they find themselves. His heroines are usually the most clearly delineated of his characters, but even they commonly fall into one of several types: devoted wives, cigarette-smoking modern girls, mysterious vixens, or women who are smotheringly maternal. Nevertheless, Milne's female characters, like Belinda, often steal the show.

Some of Milne's most successful works during this period center around marriage and family life, including *Mr. Pim Passes By* (1921), *The Great Broxopp* (1921), *The Truth About Blayds* (1921), *The Dover Road* (1922), and *Michael and Mary* (1929). Milne's own life during the 1920s was focused on domestic concerns; as he writes in his memoir, "In August [1920] my collaborator produced a more personal work" (p. 278). That collaborative "work" was the child Christopher Robin, whose presence in the Milne home would revive for his father pleasant memories of childhood and inspire him to produce works for children.

Not long before Christopher's birth, Milne had his first major stage success. *Mr. Pim Passes By* opened in London in January 1920, with Irene Vanbrugh again playing the lead. The show was an immediate hit, although it was criticized for being too whimsical, the complaint that would echo throughout Milne's career. Combining a pair of themes that would remain central in Milne's work, marriage and illusion, the story focuses on the unusual marital struggles of an unlikely couple, George Marden, a strict traditionalist, and his wife, Olivia, a modern woman who embraces novelty and longs for excitement. *Mr. Pim* ran in London for more than one hundred performances and promptly opened in New York. When Milne published an adaptation of the play as a novel the same year, that too was a great success.

Critics often complained that Milne's plots were unrealistic and his characters improbable. Milne, in turn, expressed his disdain for strict realism and professed his love of fancy. He was intent on enchanting the workaday world. In *By Way of Introduction* he asserts that a work of art should be "literally 'too good to be true.' That is why we shall never see Turner's sunsets in this world, or meet Mr. Micawber. We only wish we could" (p. 26). Milne stressed that fantasy should play a role in art because wishing has a role in life. Many of his plays contain fairy-tale elements or take the form of fanciful folk stories, and some of these can be enjoyed by both children and adults. Even before he introduced Pooh to his readers, Milne brought magic and romance into the mundane modern world.

FAIRY TALES

MANY of Milnes's most critically acclaimed and best-selling works are plays and stories that contain elements of the fairy tale. Such works bring his theme of the power of illusion into a mythical setting.

The plot of his popular one-act play *Portrait of a Gentleman in Slippers* (1926) is pared down to a parable, which appropriately takes place in the storybook world of "once upon a time." We meet the play's hero, King Hilary XXIV, on the eve of his marriage to the princess Amaril, whom he has not seen since they played together as children. Just before the wedding an anonymous guest delivers a proper fairy-tale gift: a magical mirror that reveals the true self buried beneath one's everyday facade. Gazing into this looking glass Hilary is forced to confront the unlovely truth about himself: the perfect monarch that his public perceives in him is vastly different from the grotesque image the mirror exposes. Once he discovers that he is cruel, cowardly, vain, and cunning, he must figure out what to do with this knowledge. *Portrait of a Gentleman in Slippers* focuses on the moral dilemma thrust upon someone who has seen through illusion. King Hilary's people need to maintain their deluded vision of their ruler. The monarch's betrothed, on the other hand, only loves him once he allows her to peer into the glass and to recognize in him all his imperfections, which turn out to be precisely the same faults for which she loved him

when they were children. Clearly Hilary's secret is safe with his bride. Acquainted with the Great Man's secret nature, the queen will preserve his pristine image for the public.

Human attachment to illusion is again the theme of *The Ivory Door* (1929), one of Milne's best-liked plays. *The Ivory Door* also takes place in the realm of "once upon a time" and features a young king whose marriage is imminent. In a brief prologue Milne introduces the hero, Perivale, as a child engaging in playful conversation with his father. Perivale expresses curiosity about a mysterious door in the castle—notorious throughout the land—beyond which, it is believed, lie demons and certain death. According to legend Perivale's great-grandfather walked through the door and was never seen again. Although the king warns his son to avoid the door, he hints at the unreliability of conventional wisdom: "You will find that people say many things which are not true; particularly about kings" (Tucker, p. 115). Such untruths generate the play's main action, which begins fifteen years later when Perivale decides to walk through the door on the eve of his marriage. He discovers that there is nothing behind the door but a long, dark passage leading outside the castle, and he soon realizes that danger lies not behind the door but in front of it, in the fantasy life of the kingdom's subjects.

Upon Perivale's reappearance, his people, clinging to the legend, condemn their king as an imposter sent by the devils that lurk behind the door. They insist he must prove his identity by demonstrating his talents, as their king was the greatest warrior, the greatest poet, and the greatest intellect in the kingdom. He scoffs at these requirements, remembering his father's warning. When his bride arrives and the people tell her what has happened, she decides to walk through the door to find out what had happened to him. When she returns she too is decried as a fake. They compare her to her portrait and find that she is not nearly as beautiful as the painting, which, of course, presents an idealized image. The people would rather lose their king and queen than their legend, and Perivale would rather lose his kingdom than his life. To escape execution he and his consort play along with the superstitious people; they confess that they are in fact demons and retreat to the door. As Perivale and his bride step over the threshold he says, "It is Life, not Death, which waits behind the Door for us" (p. 177), implying that the life of a monarch is no life at all. As in *Portrait of a Gentleman in Slippers*, the royal couple can see beyond illusions; they know the truth about the door and the truth about one another. Throughout the play the romanticism of the people serves as a foil for the king's irony. While Milne privileges the prince's ironic, truthful perspective, he does not condemn the people for their need to preserve their romantic illusions.

POEMS FOR CHILDREN

IN 1923, on a family vacation in Wales when Christopher Robin was three years old, Milne "wasted a morning" writing a funny and fanciful poem called "Vespers." He presented the poem to his wife "as one might give a photograph or a valentine" (*Autobiography*, p. 279), and soon afterward Daphne submitted it to *Vanity Fair* for publication. The poem was a big hit, and Milne's name and his works for children henceforth would be inextricably linked. Upon the success of this first rhyme Milne quickly generated a slew of new poems, which were published together in *When We Were Very Young* in 1924. The book was in high demand from the start. In a single day the first edition of 5,040 copies sold out. In the first year, more than fifty editions were printed, and the book has been in print ever since.

The popularity of *When We Were Very Young* was founded on both the playful quality of Milne's verse and the talents of the book's illustrator, Ernest H. Shepard, who was able to match Milne's vision of boyhood fantasy and play in his famously pretty images. About Milne's poems most critics agree with the author himself, who wrote that "whatever else they lack, the verses are technically good" (*Autobiography*, p. 282). The poems' rhythms and rhymes are playful, varied, and often innovative. Devices such as capitalization, parentheses, and italics add to the poems' complexity and appeal. Milne's tone, form, and rhyme schemes are to a great extent novel. His tone is typically sweeter than that of poets such as Edward Lear and Hilaire Belloc and more biting than that of Christina Rossetti. In the tone and patterning of the verses he owes most to Lewis Carroll's nonsense rhymes, Robert Louis Stevenson's *Child's Garden of Verses*, and traditional nursery verse such as the Mother Goose rhymes.

With his works for children, Milne finds a place in which to revive the aimless play of the characters from his early *Punch* sketches in a postwar context. Like his work for *Punch*, the writing for children is filled with satire. Many early critics failed to see the ironic humor in his work, chiding him for perpetuating Victorian idealizations of childhood. On close scrutiny Milne's works for children discredit the attacks against him, which were usually accusations of sentimentality. In his autobiography he defends himself, making reference to William Wordsworth's illustrious "Intimations of Immortality." He writes,

The beauty of childhood seems in some way to transcend the body. Heaven, that is, really does appear to lie about the child in its infancy, as it does not lie about even the most attractive kitten. But with this outstanding physical quality, there is a natural lack of moral quality, which expresses itself, as Nature always insists on expressing herself, in an egotism entirely ruthless.

(p. 283)

Here Milne attacks the Romantic view of childhood by claiming that the child's physical beauty masks something more sinister. Echoing his idol J. M. Barrie, Milne emphasizes the selfishness and heartlessness of children, which he contends constitute the truth about them.

Milne points to his poems "Disobedience" and "Vespers" in *When We Were Very Young* to exemplify the "ruthlessness" and the "egotism" of children in his work. In "Disobedience," a young boy with an impressive name, "James James Morrison Morrison Weatherby George Dupree," issues a warning to his mother: "You must never go down to the end of town, / if you don't go down with me" (p. 30). When she disobeys she disappears forever, and the child's response is simply to instruct his "Other relations / Not to go blaming *him*" (p. 32). In his discussion of the poem Milne focuses on the coldness of the child, but James is an unusual Milne protagonist. Milne's fictive children are generally neither so detached nor so unkind. Their predominant quality is playfulness.

"Vespers" presents a milder portrait of childhood than "Disobedience." Milne pokes fun at conventional fantasies about the goodness of children as he gently mocks the tradition of the child's nightly recitation of prayers. He begins by generating an expectation of a portrait of the cloying, good-natured child: "*Little Boy kneels at the foot of the bed, / Droops on the little hands little gold head. / Hush! Hush! Whisper who dares! / Christopher Robin is saying his prayers"* (p. 99). The reverence and piety in this scene are ruses. Using irony Milne shows that appearances can be deceptive. He continues, italicizing the child's spoken lines, as he had italicized the entire first stanza: *"God bless Mummy.* I know that's right. / Wasn't it fun in the bath tonight? / The cold's so cold, and the hot's so hot. / Oh! *God bless Daddy*—I quite forgot" (p. 99).

Many of Milne's children's poems suggest the arbitrary and aimless nature of child's play. "Spring Morning" begins with a child's question, "Where am I going?" The boy goes on to describe the aimlessness of birds and clouds and ends with the lines "What does it matter where people go? . . . Anywhere, anywhere. *I* don't know" (p. 36). Wherever the child goes in Milne's poems, he is having fun. In many verses, anticipating experiments by modernist poets like e. e. cummings, Milne captures the movements of aimless play in the pattern his poetry makes on the printed page. In "Busy," Milne evokes the child's playful experimentation with identities, creating a sense of playful physical motion. While sometimes the boy-narrator imagines himself in conventional social roles, as a postman, a doctor, or a nanny, he intermittently becomes more excited and more inventive. The form of Milne's poem reflects the increased wildness of the play:

> I think I am an Elephant,
> Behind another Elephant
> Behind another Elephant who isn't really there. . . .
> > SO
> > > *Round* about
> > > And *round* about
> > > And *round* about and *round* about
> > > And *round* about
> > > And *round* about
> > I go.

With italics and the patterning of lines Milne captures the speed of the child's movement as he whirls around "the table in the nursery." The stanzas are punctuated with the refrain, "I'm feeling rather funny and I don't know *what* I am—" (p. 9). Milne produces an impression of dizziness and exuberance as well as freedom from constraint.

Milne's conflation of imaginative freedom and child's play reflects early-twentieth-century understandings of children's psychological development. At the time Milne wrote, many child psychologists and educators like Maria Montessori

and John Dewey were studying and theorizing about child's play, which was increasingly deemed an essential part of the child's education and development. These thinkers generally described play as the natural activity of the child and defined it as a spontaneous and noninstrumental endeavor. Child's play was commonly associated with freedom and set up in contrast to work.

For Milne, as for Dewey, freedom from economic pressure is a precondition of play. Milne's poems depict a wealthy childhood that reflects the actual conditions of Christopher Robin's upbringing. The playing child is a wealthy child, and his affluence ensures a safe arena for his free play. Although money has no practical application in the poems, it can be put to fantastical use by children and may project a vague sense of power. The child of "In the Fashion" proposes that if he had sixpence he would buy a tail, something that in the context of the poem is clearly desirable although its immediate application is unclear. In "Sand-Between-the-Toes," Christopher Robin, equipped with sixpence, walks to the beach, where his money is worthless, and clutches his coin like a talisman. In "Market Square" money is ultimately replaced by a more potent supplement. Over the course of the poem the child-narrator makes a series of trips to the market with ever larger sums of money, but he is unable to find a vendor who can sell him what he wants to buy: "a little brown rabbit." Finally he goes to the market square with "nuffin'" and only then does he find what he desires: "But I walked on the common, / The old-gold common . . . / *And I saw little rabbits* / *'Most everywhere!"* (p. 28). The common is the only sort of "gold" that can "purchase" rabbits, whereas sixpence is utterly useless. The blending of natural setting (the common) with images associated with wealth (gold) points to an idea implicit in many works for children. The protected space of childhood so often envisioned by writers as an Arcadia is premised on the presence of riches.

Many of the poems in *When We Were Very Young* take place in an urban setting, but in *Now We Are Six* (1927), Milne's last volume of verse for children, nature seems the "natural" habitat of the child, and freedom is linked to nature. Milne associates the wealth of the child's imagination with the bounty of nature. In "Cherry Stones," after the narrator enumerates various possible people he might be, identities he might possess, he exclaims, "Oh, there's such a lot of things to do and such a lot to be / That there's always lots of cherries on my little cherry-tree" (p. 21). Bountiful nature here is equated with the abundance of resources within the playful self.

The children who inhabit *Now We are Six* are notably more mature than those in *When We Were Very Young*. In the later work, although the child still plays by himself, he more frequently seeks the companionship of other children as well as imaginary friends. Moreover, the exclusion of adults from the child's imaginative world is made more explicit here than it was in the earlier volume. In "Solitude," the narrator finds a "house . . . Where nobody ever says 'No'; / Where no one says anything—so / There is no one but me" (p. 3). At the same time Milne intimates older children's increasing curiosity about that world and their broadening understanding of it. In "Explained," Elizabeth Ann asks "how God began," and in "Wind on the Hill," the nameless narrator asks where the wind comes from. Grown-ups, it seems, are ill equipped to answer such questions, but children are ever better equipped to figure things out on their own or with the help of a friend. "The Friend" begins: "There are lots and lots of people who are always asking things, / Like Dates and Pounds-and-ounces and the names of funny Kings." The pressure on the child to get the answer right is eliminated by the presence of "the friend," Winnie-the-Pooh, who guesses the answer to such questions: "And then it doesn't matter what the answer ought to be, / 'Cos if he's right, I'm Right, and if he's wrong, it isn't Me" (p. 63).

As he would later do in his final Pooh book, Milne hints in *Now We Are Six* that the child is growing up and that the time for playing must come to an end. In "Forgotten," a group of toys abandoned in a nursery imagine that their master is lost and will not come back. The tone here is slightly melancholy and somewhat foreboding. In the final stanza, however, the missing child's activities are finally disclosed—he has not disappeared but merely played all day and then gone to bed. In the last lines of the volume's final poem, "The End," Milne dispels the fear of growing up with a line that conjures Barrie's character Peter Pan: "But now I am Six, I'm as clever as clever / So I think I'll be six now for ever and ever" (p. 101). The child here refuses to grow up. But Milne's readers by this time had already been introduced to "children" who would never grow up—the animals in Pooh's forest.

WINNIE-THE-POOH

IN August 1921, on his first birthday, Milnes's son Christopher Robin received as a gift a stuffed bear from Harrods, which soon became a favorite toy. Originally dubbed "Edward Bear," this simple plaything would within a half-decade become known to countless readers as Winnie-the-Pooh. Milne improvised the first Pooh tale (chapter one of *Winnie-the-Pooh*) as a bedtime story for his son. He only jotted down this episode when the *Evening News* requested a piece for children from him. The story appeared on Christmas Eve, 1925, and a reading of the story was broadcast on Christmas day. Within a year Milne had published his first book of Pooh stories. Like his books of poems, it was an instant best-seller, immediately labeled a classic. Before too long Milne had composed enough stories for a second volume. Eagerly anticipated by thousands of fans, *The House at Pooh Corner* met with as much success as its predecessor.

There have been many stories explaining the origin of Pooh's name, most spun by Milne himself. "Winnie" was assuredly the title of a real black bear Christopher liked to visit at the London Zoo, but the source of the name "Pooh" remains somewhat obscure. Indeed, the problem of the bear's name becomes a thematic issue in the beginning of the first book. After "Edward Bear" appears on the first page of *Winnie-the-Pooh*, Milne introduces him for the first time by his more innovative appellation. In a direct address to the reader, the narrator announces,

> . . . here he is . . . ready to be introduced to you. Winnie-the-Pooh.
>
> When I first heard his name, I said, just as you are going to say, "But I thought he was a boy?"
>
> "So did I," said Christopher Robin.
>
> "Then you can't call him Winnie?"
>
> "I don't."
>
> "But you said—"
>
> "He's Winnie-ther-Pooh. Don't you know what 'ther' means?"
>
> "Ah, yes, now I do," I said quickly; and I hope you do too, because it is all the explanation you are going to get.
>
> (pp. 3–4)

Even before he begins to tell his story, Milne inducts the reader into the child's perceived world. The boy's logic may be satirized here, but it is accepted as tenable. His carelessly invented nonsense word determines his bear's name and gender. After Pooh's name has been accounted for with this pseudo-explanation, Christopher Robin requests a story from his father—the narrator—indicating that Winnie-the-Pooh would like to hear a tale about himself, "because he's *that* sort of Bear" (p. 4). By displacing the boy's childish egotism onto the toy, Milne hints at what is to come in the stories he will tell. Pooh and the other animals will play the parts of children, and Christopher Robin will play the part of a powerful agent—a parent or god—among his toys.

The Pooh books were recognized as classics in part because they fit into an established tradition of children's literature, a set of books that pictured the world of childhood as a changeless place, insular and idyllic. Milne's Hundred Acre Wood was familiar to readers already acquainted with Barrie's *Peter Pan* and Kenneth Grahame's *Wind in the Willows*. These readers came to expect the world depicted in a children's book to have the feeling of a desert island. While as a child Milne relished stories of actual desert islands, such as J. D. Weiss's *Swiss Family Robinson* (1848) and Captain Frederick Marryat's *Masterman Ready* (1857), in his essay "The Robinson Tradition" he criticizes the authors of these stories for admitting moralism and parental authority onto the remote isles they depict. A proper island adventure, Milne asserted, should exclude reality. He writes, "a desert-island is a child's escape from real life and its many lessons. Ask yourself why you longed for a desert-island when you were young, and you will find the answer to be that you did what you liked there, ate what you liked and carried through your own adventures" (*If I May,* pp. 24–25). In his Pooh books Milne creates the desert island of his dreams, one that shuns "real life and its many lessons," even more than those imagined in previous children's classics.

The Hundred Acre Wood resembles a desert island settled by a circle of friends. Like Kenneth Grahame's magical group of creatures by the River, and like the real Henley House community in which young Alan Milne lived, Milne's society of toys stands for a society of boys. The "boys" are free to carry through with their own adventures, exploits that are playful and aimless, as meandering as Milne's early *Punch* sketches. Milne's narratives reflect the nature of the adventures they depict. They are episodic; rather than tracing a linear development they present a series of discrete capers, each of which stands on its own. Despite the haphazard nature of the animals' play, the stories tend to take a familiar shape, in which characters come together, join in adventures, and, in the end, go home.

Home is a solitary place. The only veritable parent in the stories is the only real female—motherly Kanga, whose maternal attentions are restricted to her offspring, Roo. The presence of this mother-and-child relationship points to the absence in the wood of romantic couplings and marriage, central themes in Milne's works for adults but aspects of reality that are refused by Milne's desert-island world.

In the Hundred Acre Wood there are no families and thus no punitive parents. Excluding the scene of storytelling that frames the tales, there is not even a distant grown-up world on the outskirts of the animal realm as there is in *Wind in the Willows*. The only authority on Pooh's "island" is the child Christopher Robin, whose human failings Milne loves to emphasize. The child is positioned as a god but has the frailties of a boy. He is offhand rather than masterful both in his speech and in his actions; repeatedly Milne describes him as feeling "careless" or speaking "carelessly." He can boldly command an expedition to the North Pole, but he holds an absurd belief that the pole he seeks is a literal pole—a sort of stick. And yet for the animals the boy is a wise master who can arbitrate all disagreements, answer all questions, and settle all perplexity.

Although he is a peripheral character in most of the stories, Christopher Robin, a benign and magnanimous ruler, sets the moral tone in the wood. His kindness and his ability to soothe the other characters is apparent in many of the tales. For example, when Pooh foolishly follows his own tracks in the snow round and round a tree, believing he is trailing a pack of possibly hazardous "Woozles," Christopher Robin, who watches the bear's antics from a perch in the tree, assuages Pooh's wounded pride once the bear discovers his mistake:

"I see now," said Winnie-the-Pooh.

"I have been Foolish and Deluded," said he, "and I am a Bear of No Brain at All."

"You're the Best Bear in All the World," said Christopher Robin soothingly.

"Am I?" said Pooh hopefully. And then he brightened up suddenly.

(p. 43)

Christopher Robin's love for the animals creates a pervasive atmosphere of kindness in the forest. Thoughtfulness and compassion are the qualities most highly valued in the Hundred Acre Wood. Pooh is the character who embodies these qualities.

The bear is not only the kindest friend but also the most imaginative playmate. In the first Pooh story the bear demonstrates his inventiveness by concocting a creative scheme to pilfer honey from some bees. He borrows a balloon from the trusty Christopher Robin, and then, after blackening himself by rolling in mud, he hangs on to the balloon, which lifts him up to the bees' nest. Once aloft, he nervously asks Christopher Robin what he looks like.

> "You look like a Bear holding on to a balloon," [Christopher Robin] said.
> "Not," said Pooh anxiously, "—not like a small black cloud in a blue sky?"
> "Not very much."
>
> (p. 14)

Despite this discouragement Pooh goes on to persuade the boy to participate in his charade by parading beneath him with an umbrella, muttering "Tut-tut, it looks like rain" (p. 15). Unfortunately the bees are too shrewd to fall for this ruse and Pooh never gets his paws on their honey. Here as elsewhere in the Pooh stories, Christopher Robin is for the most part an amused onlooker, a realist foil to the idealistic Pooh.

Pooh's opposition to realism is connected to his ontological status—he is not "real." Besides marriage, one key reality that Milne purges from his wood is that of flesh and blood. Except for Christopher, Owl, and Rabbit, the major characters in the stories are stuffed animals modeled on toys in the Milne nursery—a fact that perpetually reminds the reader that the story world is a fantasy. Shepard's illustrations contribute to this effect by differentiating between the inanimate animals, which he draws to look like toys, and the forest, which he depicts naturalistically.

The elevation of the toy in Milne's work is historically significant. During Milne's lifetime, as children lost their earning power they came to be viewed as expenses—part of the world of consumption rather than production. More and more they were perceived as toylike objects for whom to buy. Born in the era of the toy-child, Milne's toy-characters play the role of children in the stories.

Whereas live animals and nature had been associated with the child throughout most of the age of classical children's literature, Milne linked artificiality to childhood. Although the Pooh stories recall earlier tales that portray anthropomorphized animals in nature, Milne transformed the traditional talking-animal parable. Unlike the heroes of Joel Chandler Harris or Beatrix Potter, Milne's animals are not tricksters. They do not need to be "tricky" for they do not know Darwin's struggle for survival. In the Hundred Acre Wood there are plentiful resources for all, and the most dangerous-seeming animal, Tigger, is of all the characters the most childish; what is more, he eats only extract of malt. Unlike the stuffed-animal hero of Milne's only prominent predecessor, Margery Williams Bianco's *Velveteen Rabbit* (1922), who longs to be "real," Milne's characters are content with their status. Because they are not real they need not face dangers and, more importantly, need never grow up.

Although the toy animals have no real bodies, they have very real desires. Like Lewis Carroll's Alice, Winnie-the-Pooh cannot quite regulate his cravings. His unwieldy appetite repeatedly gets him into trouble. In the second episode in *Winnie-the-Pooh,* on a visit to Rabbit's house, Pooh devours so much honey that he gets stuck in Rabbit's front door as he attempts to leave. Christopher Robin rescues Pooh from this jam. He prescribes no eating for a week and reads "a Sustaining Book, such as would help and comfort a Wedged Bear in Great Tightness" to distract his friend from his hunger (p. 30). Although Pooh's hunger sometimes gets him into trouble it inevitably brings him home. In his house, the clock is stuck at five minutes to eleven, so, according to the bear's logic, it is always "time for a little smackerel of something" (*The House at Pooh Corner,* p. 5). Pooh is a bear who lives in the moment and that moment is usually snack time.

Milne presents Pooh's play as a mode of heroism, thus slyly mocking the heroism of typical English adventure stories—the heroism of empire. The objective of Pooh and the others is neither conquest nor gain; rather, like the Boy Scouts—an invention of Milne's era—they undertake sundry adventures that instill group spirit and build character. If their adventures have a purpose, that purpose is shown to be absurd. During Christopher Robin's journey to find the North Pole, Pooh wins credit for discovering the "pole," a long stick that he grabs in order to draw Roo out of a stream into which he has fallen. Pooh's heroism is recognized by the forest community, especially by Christopher Robin, who holds a party in his honor at the end of Milne's first volume of Pooh stories and knights him at the conclusion of the second.

Various aspects of Pooh's stouthearted character are illuminated through their contrast to qualities held by other key figures in the stories. The brooding and solitary nature of the donkey Eeyore, for instance, points to Pooh's energetic optimism and sociability. Milne introduces Eeyore, the only lonely figure in the books, as a contemplative pessimist: "The Old Grey Donkey, Eeyore, stood by himself in a thistly corner of the forest, his front feet well apart, his head on one side, and thought about things. Sometimes he thought sadly to himself, 'Why?' and sometimes he thought, 'Wherefore?' and sometimes he thought, 'Inasmuch as which?' " (*Winnie-the-Pooh*, pp. 44–45). Eeyore, who invites discomfort—both emotional and physical—into his life, highlights the comfort of the community the others experience. Furthermore, the presence of this gloomy soul provides opportunities for the other characters to do good deeds, thus further affirming their sense of community. On one occasion Pooh comes upon Eeyore and by chance discovers that it is the donkey's birthday and no one has taken notice. Pooh runs off to rally the others to tend to their friend. After he fetches a large pot of honey from his house generously selected as a birthday gift, he eats the contents on his return trip to Eeyore's corner of the wood. Piglet, who decides to bring Eeyore a balloon, slips and falls on his present. Nevertheless, the two gifts—an empty pot and a deflated balloon—suit Eeyore.

In another episode, Pooh, again by chance, notices that Eeyore's tail is missing, and, observing the despair of the donkey, he gallantly vows to find it. The bear eventually discovers the tail, which Owl has been using for a bellpull:

"Owl," said Pooh solemnly, "You made a mistake. Somebody did want [the tail]."

"Who?"

"Eeyore. My dear friend Eeyore. He was—he was fond of it."

"Fond of it?"

"Attached to it," said Winnie-the-Pooh sadly.

(p. 54)

Pooh's punning and understatement in this last line are emblematic of his use of language. Although he is unable to understand Eeyore's irony, Owl's sophisticated language, and Rabbit's grandiloquent babbling, Pooh has a playful relationship to language that distinguishes him from the other characters, and Milne connects the bear's particular use of language to his kindness and heroism. Pooh often misunderstands the "difficult" words he hears, usually those uttered by the pompous Owl. When Owl begins to tell Pooh of the "customary procedure in such cases [as when one loses a tail]," Pooh, his imagination partly driven by appetite, hears "Crustimoney Proseedcake" (p. 50). This misunderstanding highlights Owl's obtuseness and pedantry; although the bird has a fancy term to describe what to do to find the missing tail, he himself only contributes to the problem. Milne, like Pooh, uses language in a fanciful manner. His pleasure in wordplay and nonsense is evident throughout the Pooh books. For example, he capitalizes expressions such as "Noise of Sadness and Despair" and "Bear of Little Brain." These capitalizations poke fun at grown-up catchphrases and grown-up self-importance, just as Pooh's misapprehensions parody Owl's pedantry, albeit unintentionally.

Milne links Pooh's peculiar use of language to his lack of "Brain." Pedantic Owl and Rabbit are the most "brainy" and, aside from Kanga, are the most grown-up characters in the wood. Rabbit says to Owl, "you and I have brains. The others have fluff. If there's any thinking to be done in this Forest—and when I say thinking I mean *thinking*—you and I must do it" (*The House at Pooh Corner*, p. 78). However, this trumpeted possession of "Brain" limits imaginative abilities; thinking gets in the way of playing and thus of participating in the community. Owl poses as a wise creature, and yet he spells his name "WOL" and is unable to answer the other characters' earnest queries when they come to him expecting wisdom. He always makes mistakes, as evidenced when he takes Eeyore's tail for a bellpull. Moreover, he often misses out on the adventures of the others.

Pooh is a romantic figure: the wise fool. He comes across wisdom in a haphazard manner, usually through sudden inspiration. Pooh's playful use of language is matched by a playful use of objects, and this ability enables him to outthink Owl and even Christopher Robin. When the entire wood becomes flooded, creative thinking helps

Pooh make boats out of common household objects, a plugged-up honey jar and an upturned umbrella. During another natural disaster, when Owl's house is toppled and turned upside down by a "Blusterous" wind, Pooh, Piglet, and Owl are trapped inside the wreckage until the bear conceives of the mail slot as an escape route for Piglet.

Inspiration also leads Pooh to compose fanciful poems he calls "hums." For example, as he climbs a tree to reach the beehive, he sings a "complaining song":

It's a very funny thought that, if Bears were Bees,
They'd build their nests at the *bottom* of trees.
And that being so (if Bees were Bears),
We shouldn't have to climb up all these stairs.

(p. 8)

Pooh, with his inversions of bees and bears, is reminiscent of Carroll's Alice, who confuses bats and cats. In this scene, as he ascends the tree, Pooh's thoughts wander aimlessly, and the result of that wandering is the poem. In another episode, the bear reveals his random method of composition: "I shall sing that first line twice, and perhaps if I sing it very quickly, I shall find myself singing the third and fourth lines before I have time to think of them, and that will be a Good Song" (*Winnie-the-Pooh*, pp. 110–111). The lack of intentionality, Pooh predicts, will make his verse worthy.

Milne contrasts Pooh's creative wisdom with Rabbit's "Brain." In *House at Pooh Corner*, when Rabbit overhears Pooh singing a freshly composed song, he asks,

"Did you make that song up?"

"Well, I sort of made it up," said Pooh. "It isn't Brain," he went on humbly, "because You Know Why, Rabbit; but it comes to me sometimes."

"Ah!" said Rabbit, who never let things come to him but always went and fetched them.

(p. 83)

While the arrogant and "captainish" Rabbit loves to plan and plot, humble Pooh can only ponder the present. However, whereas Rabbit's schemes tend to be unsuccessful, Pooh's inspired ideas are usually effective. Rabbit is the least humane character in Milne's wood, and he is the creature least like Pooh. Despite his troop of "friends and relations" he is the most antisocial animal in the forest. He concocts hostile plots against animals new to the wood—Kanga, Roo, and Tigger—and these schemes, which backfire, are the only actions in the Pooh stories that elicit punishments.

Just as J. M. Barrie's Lost Boys shoot down Wendy when she first appears in Never Land, so Rabbit plots to chase away Kanga and her babe as soon as they arrive in the forest. Marshaling the gullible Piglet and Pooh for this purge, Rabbit warns them that a Kanga "is one of the Fiercer Animals." Milne quickly ironizes this characterization by displaying Kanga in her habitual motherly mode, repeatedly saying, "Roo, dear, just one more jump and then we must go home" (*Winnie-the-Pooh*, p. 99). Clearly she is neither fierce nor a strict disciplinarian. Rabbit comes up with a plan to steal Baby Roo and leave Piglet in his place. When Kanga discovers she has been duped, she turns the tables on Piglet. When the confused pig tries to explain that he is not her child, she ignores him, scrubbing him clean and feeding him unpleasant medicine.

The wily Rabbit also masterminds a plan to get rid of Tigger, and once again he enlists Pooh and Piglet to help him. They will walk with Tigger in the forest and then, when he bounces ahead, they will hide, leaving him confused and alone, far from home. But again in this adventure the tables are turned. While the abandoned Tigger easily finds his way back home, the others are lost. Ultimately Pooh and Piglet go in one direction and Rabbit in another; Rabbit, who insists on trying to find the way home, remains lost until Tigger rescues him. Pooh, no longer harassed by Rabbit's constant chatter, is free to find his way using his sense of smell—his longing for the honey pot will move him in the right direction. Thus Pooh's insatiable hunger is an integral part of his wisdom, leading him to solutions despite his seeming naïveté and, more importantly, leading him home.

FAREWELL TO POOH

THE young boyhood of Milne's son Christopher had inspired the production of the Pooh stories, and as that stage of Christopher's life came to an end, so did the Pooh stories. In 1929 Christopher left for boarding school, and he could no longer serve as a symbol for Milne's own childhood. Moreover, Milne himself was outgrowing his identity as a writer for children. He begins his second and final volume of Pooh stories, *The House at Pooh Corner,* with a "Contradiction," which, he explains, is Owl's term for "the opposite of an Introduction." Milne clarifies, "An Introduction is to introduce people, but Christopher Robin and his friends, who have already been introduced to you, are now going to say Good-bye." School lessons, it appears, have displaced storytelling, and Pooh's adventures are to be relegated to the land of dreams. But farewells to childhood are deferred in this book as they were in *Now We Are Six.* Milne concludes his preface, "it isn't really Good-bye, because the Forest will always be there . . . and anybody who is friendly with Bears can find it." Nevertheless, despite this seeming reprieve for childhood fantasy and for Pooh and the rest, the faintly despondent tone in Milne's preface permeates much of the volume.

The "House" in the title of Milne's second Pooh volume points to its central theme. Whereas *Winnie-the-Pooh* begins with a comforting frame tale that situates Christopher Robin with his father at home, *The House at Pooh Corner* begins with a blizzard in which Eeyore has stood homeless alone in the cold, letting snow amass on his back. Palpable threats haunt these stories, and the lurking fear is not of bodily harm—after all, these are toys—but of the loss of home and the loss of Christopher Robin, who provides a broader-scale shelter for the animals. Whereas in *Winnie-the-Pooh* nature was tame, in the later volume the weather waxes wild and causes problems. On a "Blusterous day" the wind knocks down Owl's house; during a great deluge, Piglet, "entirely surrounded by water," needs to be rescued; after freezing in a snowstorm, Eeyore determines that he needs the protection of a house.

Milne, who had always been an advocate of "escapist" literature, understood that escapist children's literature is about both running away from home and the security of home. Imaginative escape is contingent on the presence of a secure home. Each of the characters in the Pooh stories except for the very young (that is, Roo and Tigger) must have his or her own home; every animal deserves a private space. Shepard depicts the animals' homes from the outside as shacks or, more often, as trees with doors, but within the portals of these places are cozy, middle-class sitting rooms depicted naturalistically. Milne stresses that his characters treasure these snug houses. At the start

of one adventure, Pooh, pointing to the importance of homes, solemnly reminds Piglet that each creature in the wood possesses his own house except for "poor Eeyore," who has "nothing." In contrast to this "nothing," a home is everything. Piglet assents, and they trudge off to build the donkey a shelter.

Ironically, Piglet himself will later be left homeless, due to Eeyore's carelessness. After Owl's tree house is blown down in the wind, Eeyore, eager to help the homeless Owl, discovers Piglet's lodging and, believing it to be abandoned, offers it to the bird. At this point Piglet does a "Noble Thing"; instead of laying claim to his property, he gives up his home for a needy fellow creature. Christopher Robin, who, of course, comprehends Piglet's generosity, asks him meaningfully, "What would you do if your house was blown down?" Pooh answers lovingly for his friend, "He'd come and live with me." Thus, with the end of the stories, as homes become less dependable, friendship becomes more so.

As friendship among the animals becomes stronger, however, the animals' ties to Christopher Robin weaken. Although the characters still look to the boy for reassurance, they sense that his days with them are numbered. As soon as they discover that he is being educated every morning, they comprehend that lessons will take him away from them: "Christopher Robin was going away. Nobody knew why he was going; nobody knew where he was going; indeed, nobody even knew why he knew that Christopher Robin was going away. But somehow or other everybody in the forest felt that it was happening at last" (p. 162). The attitude of the animals and the melancholic tone of the writing here are reminiscent of the poem "Forgotten." However, while in "Forgotten" the toys in the nursery are mistaken about their boy, here Pooh and the other toys are right on target.

At the end of the book the animals gather to say good-bye to Christopher Robin and to give him a farewell poem. But when they approach him, none of them is able to utter parting words. Eeyore tries: "We've come to say—to give you . . . but we've all—because we've heard, I mean we all know. . . ." (p. 169). But, flustered, the donkey fails to speak his feelings, and he and the other animals slowly wander away. Pooh is the only creature who remains with Christopher Robin in this scene, so he and the boy take off together for a final romp.

Now it is the child's turn to defer a farewell. He says,

"Pooh, *whatever* happens, you *will* understand, won't you?"
"Understand what?"
"Oh, nothing."

(p. 179)

Finally it is Milne's turn to avoid the inevitable, and he concludes his work as follows, echoing the last stanza of the poem "The End": "So [Pooh and Christopher Robin] went off together. But wherever they go, and whatever happens to them on the way, in that enchanted place on the top of the Forest, a little boy and his Bear will always be playing" (p. 180).

LIFE AFTER POOH

IN 1929, shortly after *The House at Pooh Corner* appeared, Milne suffered two losses, one great and one small: his beloved brother Ken died of tuberculosis and Christopher Robin went off to boarding school. For more than two decades, memories of childhood and youth had fueled Milne's writing both for children and for adults. With these two departures his principal links to his childhood were severed, and he would write no more children's books.

Milne left the literary world of London to spend most of his time in the countryside. He wrote few plays after the 1920s, and in the early 1930s he turned to other forms of writing; in the last twenty-five years of his life he published several novels and a quantity of short stories. The stories were published in a broad assortment of magazines, such as *Ellery Queen Mystery Magazine, Colliers,* and *Good Housekeeping,* and were collected in two volumes, *Birthday Party* (1948) and *A Table Near the Band* (1950). The work Milne produced from the 1930s until the end of his life never approached the success of his earlier writings. The tastes of audiences and critics had evidently turned from escapist fare toward more realist works. In *Year In, Year Out* (1952), Milne bitterly asks "why drink and fornication should seem to bring the realist closer to real life than, say, golf and gardening" (pp. 138–139). His writing was considered unfashionable, in part because it was neither deeply psychological in its themes nor experimental in its

forms. Milne still focused on Edwardian motifs and wrote with Edwardian attention to diverting description and dialogue.

In his satirical short story "A Rattling Good Yarn," Milne wreaks revenge on his critics and simultaneously attacks the writings of modernists such as Gertrude Stein and e. e. cummings, works that he found inscrutable. The hero of Milne's tale is a popular writer of adventure novels who uses the pseudonym Michael Hartigan. Milne valorizes Hartigan for his bluntness: "He had no illusions about himself" (*A Table Near the Band,* p. 135). The story begins when a young aspiring writer whose given name is Michael Hartigan visits the famous author to lay claim to his title: "I'm going to be a writer," he says, "and how can I write when you've bagged my name?" (p. 138). Hartigan ridicules the boy, who clearly does have illusions about his prospects as a writer, and advises him to "bag" someone else's name. The boy, who eventually takes the name Gryce, craves revenge. He later fails as a writer and becomes a critic, starting an "advanced literary monthly" called "Asymptote." Clearly Gryce, a malignant and bitter man, has found his calling: "At last he had a platform from which he could get back at the world. Everything and everybody that he hated could be dragged in somewhere, and held up to contempt. Most of all . . . the man who had robbed him of his birthright: Michael Hartigan" (p. 144).

Here Milne paints an unlovely portrait of the abusive critic. Although Gryce attempts to ruin Hartigan, the clever writer gets the better of him in the end, and Milne too has a chance to turn the tables on his disparaging critics. Through the figure of Gryce, an advocate of new literary forms, Milne attacks critics and the modernist writings they praised. Above all, Gryce champions *Metronomic Beat,* a novel by J. Frisby Withers, whose work Milne describes with caustic wit: "To the old-fashioned reader they suggested an almost illegible, much corrected, first pencil draft, which had been pulled together with a '*stet* everything,' and handed over to a typist whose six easy lessons had not taken her up to capital letters and punctuation marks. The result was chaos and old night, but very impressive" (p. 146). In another short story, "Spring Song," Milne once again mocks the modernist aesthetic. One of his characters, a supercilious poet, has produced a work in praise of his beloved, a department-store saleswoman: "steam hammers like white thoughts clanking / as once

(once) / 'as once' in Nanking / once in months the visceral bull . . . pulsing and repulsing equal and opposite / Ice" (*Birthday Party*, p. 229). Ironically, the object of the poet's affection cares more about his salary than about the quality or profundity of his verse.

The bitterness and satirical edge in "A Rattling Good Yarn" and "Spring Song" are not unusual in Milne's later work. Although critics still charged Milne with sentimentality, his writing had become much darker, particularly his representations of romance and marriage. In Milne's literary works of the 1930s and after, female characters seem increasingly impenetrable and marriages increasingly problematic. The novel *Two People* (1931) tells the story of a writer, Reginald Wellard, whose sudden fame brings trouble to his marriage. In the wake of his unforeseen success, Wellard and his strikingly beautiful wife, Sylvia, move from the countryside to London, where they flit around in literary circles and become distant from each other; disappointed and unhappy, they finally move back to the country, where once again they find contentment. The novel, which has focused on Wellard's turbulent feelings for his wife, concludes with the following tribute to her magnetism: Wellard says, "I know so little about you, Sylvia. I know nothing about you. I'm not sure that I want to know. It's part of your beauty that you're so unknown to me" (p. 313). More than a decade later Milne wrote another novel that featured a mysterious and attractive woman and focused on the problematic aspects of romantic relationships, *Chloe Marr* (1946), his most ambitious novel. Here the intelligent and attractive title character is presented through the eyes of her myriad admirers, whom she easily seduces. Like Sylvia, Chloe is an enigma to the men who worship her. At the unsatisfactory denouement of the novel, Chloe dies in a plane crash, her own thoughts never disclosed.

Born a generation after the first practitioners of detective fiction, Milne was a fan of mysteries, especially those of his eminent predecessors Arthur Conan Doyle and Wilkie Collins. Milne loved games, mathematical problems, and crossword puzzles, and for him mysteries granted the same pleasure as such amusements. His first sale as a writer, as mentioned earlier, was a parody of Conan Doyle, and he wrote mysteries throughout his career. A number of the short stories Milne published in the last two decades of his life were mysteries.

Milne's most successful contribution to the mystery genre was *The Red House Mystery* (1922), which received critical acclaim just before Agatha Christie published her first detective novel, *The Mysterious Affair at Styles*. Milne's work was an early contribution to the country-house-mystery subgenre that Christie later made popular. In such stories guests are spending time at a country manor; when a corpse suddenly appears, all the guests become suspects; Milne's play *The Perfect Alibi* (1920) also follows this pattern. In *The Red House Mystery* the action begins when an amateur detective, Antony Gillingham, arrives at the country house of Mark Ablett, just after a shot is fired that kills Ablett's brother. When the body is discovered Ablett is nowhere to be found, and suspicion thus rests on him. The plot turns on a case of mistaken identity—that of the corpse, which Gillingham ultimately deduces must be that of Mark Ablett himself, not of his brother. Gillingham and his friend Bill Beverley, a guest at Ablett's home, play Holmes and Watson and eventually solve the crime. Although there is little action and little suspense in the novel, the plot is tightly structured and the dialogue amusing. The setting and conversation are reminiscent of Milne's early sketches. He depicts a life of leisure—of card games, amateur plays, tennis matches, and playful conversation. Most of the dialogue is between Gillingham, a Holmes-like polymath, and Bill, an amiable blunderer, whose lumbering intelligence and periodic exclamations of "Bother!" render him more like Pooh than like Watson. The tone of their conversation is often wryly ironic.

Although Milne wrote only one other full-length mystery, *Four Day's Wonder* (1933), he skillfully engaged the conventions of detective fiction in many of his plays and stories. Like *The Red House Mystery*, Milne's detective stories often have an ironic cast. Sometimes, they are playfully self-reflexive, as when the central characters themselves are readers or writers of detective fiction. For example, when the curtain is raised on the first scene in *The Perfect Alibi*, Susan is reading a detective story. Milne's device—bringing the production and consumption of detective stories into the plot of the mystery—increases the artificially and absurdity of the tales. In his detective fiction, as in his plays and children's stories, Milne strove for humor and artificiality, for these qualities furthered his "escapist" project. At the end of his life, in *Year In, Year Out* (1952), Milne asserts that "there is no need to be ashamed of the detective story which is so exciting 'it is impossible to put down.' . . . Sometimes I think wistfully of a world in which the conventional literary values are transposed; a world in which romance is rated over realism, and comedy above tragedy" (p. 138). In such a utopia, detective fiction would be treasured, and so would the rest of Milne's work.

MILNE'S LEGACY

WHEN A. A. Milne died in 1956, only his children's books remained in print. As a writer for adults he had been virtually forgotten. In the decades since Milne's death, however, the animals from the Hundred Acre Wood have become the common property of children all over the world. They are international stars, and the greatest contributor to their celebrity is also the greatest contributor to their commercialization—the Walt Disney Company. Disney bought the rights to the characters in 1961. In 1965, almost ten years after Milne's death, the company released the animated children's film *Winnie-the-Pooh and the Honey Tree,* an adaptation of Milne's Pooh stories, and in 1974 a sequel, *Winnie-the-Pooh and Tigger Too,* appeared. Although the movies include many of the original plots, and although the cartoon images bear a close resemblance to Shepard's drawings, the film is far more Disney than Milne. There are many concrete changes: new characters have been introduced and clothing added. The most significant change, however, is in the overall tone. The Hundred Acre Wood is no longer the peaceful place for play that Milne originally envisioned. Instead, the animals work and perform chores; they are plagued by real-world anxieties and fears. Since the release of the first film Disney has produced countless spin-offs—television programs, books, and other products from which the company has reaped immense profits.

Besides these Disney versions, there have been countless other tributes to the influence of Milne's Pooh books. One of the earliest and most erudite is *Winnie ille Pu* (1960), a Latin translation of *Winnie-the-Pooh* that became an international best-seller; indeed, it was the first foreign-language best-seller in America. One of the most clever homages to Milne's stories is *The Pooh Perplex: A Freshman Casebook* (1963), Frederick C. Crews's

burlesque of the literary criticism of his day. Crews's book not only parodies critical methodologies but pokes fun at the Pooh stories themselves, which are scrutinized by imaginary critics. The book includes twelve satirical essays representing an array of critical styles by invented authors with amusing names such as Karl Anschauung, M.D., a Freudian critic, who writes "A. A. Milne's Honey-Balloon-Pit-Gun-Tail Bathtubcomplex"; Martin Tempralis, a Marxist critic, who writes "A Bourgeois Writer's Proletarian Fable"; and P. R. Honeycomb, a poet, who writes "The Theory and Practice of Bardic Verse: Notations on the Hums of Pooh." Crews's essays, which demonstrate an intimate knowledge of the Pooh stories, had the unfortunate effect of discouraging scholars from examining Milne's children's books. As the critic Alison Lurie has noted, *The Pooh Perplex* led to the great scarcity of Pooh criticism.

In the more recent best-sellers *The Tao of Pooh* (1982) and *The Te of Piglet* (1992), Benjamin Hoff employs Milne's characters and Shepard's pictures to elucidate Taoist teachings. Hoff fuses excerpts from the Pooh books with new dialogues between his narrator and the characters. For Hoff, the character Pooh embodies qualities exalted by Taoist philosophy, such as equanimity, simplicity, and an ability to accept the world on its own terms. All in all, Pooh is shown to illustrate the principle of "p'u, the uncarved block": "From the state of the Uncarved Block comes the ability to enjoy the simple and quiet, the natural and the plain. Along with that comes the ability to do things spontaneously and have them work" (p. 21). In *The Te of Piglet,* Piglet is shown to embody another Taoist precept, the principle of *te,* virtue. Although Hoff's depictions of the individual characters resemble Milne's, in a crucial way these works differ from the originals: Hoff takes a story that is definitively *not* part of the didactic tradition of children's literature and transforms it into a teaching tool that elucidates and promotes a particular system of belief.

Over the years Pooh and his friends have been appropriated and transformed in innumerable ways. Even during Milne's lifetime, the characters had moved off the page and into the commercial marketplace. Pooh became a lucrative business, and decades later images of Milne's animals were still a common sight, emblazoned on sweatshirts, dishes, knapsacks, and flags hung from homes. In fact, sales of Pooh products have far outstripped sales of Milne's books. Milne's characters have entered into both our visual and our verbal language. Hundreds of websites have been devoted to Pooh and his cohorts, and popular songwriters, politicians, and parents alike have made references to Milne's characters. Not only in "that enchanted place on the top of the forest" but on the World Wide Web and throughout the contemporary world, "a little boy and his bear will always be playing."

SELECTED BIBLIOGRAPHY

I. PLAYS. *First Plays* (London, 1919); *Second Plays* (London, 1921); *Three Plays* (London, 1922); *Four Plays: To Have the Honour; Ariadne, or Business First; Portrait of a Gentleman in Slippers; Success* (London, 1926); *The Princess and the Woodcutter*, in John Hampden, ed., *Eight Modern Plays* (London, 1927); *Toad of Toad Hall* (London and New York, 1929); *Michael and Mary* (London, 1930); *Four Plays: Michael and Mary, To Meet the Prince, The Perfect Alibi, Portrait of a Gentleman in Slippers* (London and New York, 1932); *The Ivory Door*, in Samuel Marion Tucker, ed., *Modern Plays* (New York, 1932); *Other People's Lives or They Don't Mean Any Harm* (London, 1935); *More Plays* (London, 1935); *Miss Elizabeth Bennet* (London, 1936); *Four Plays: To Have the Honour, Belinda, The Dover Road, Mr. Pim Passes By* (Harmondsworth, 1939); *The General Takes Off His Helmet: A Note From an Earlier War* (London, 1939); *Sarah Simple* (London, 1939); *The Ugly Duckling* (London, 1941); *Before the Flood* (London and New York, 1951).

II. ESSAYS, SKETCHES, AND AUTOBIOGRAPHICAL WORKS. *The Day's Play* (London, 1910); *The Holiday Round* (London, 1912); *Once A Week* (London, 1914); *Happy Days* (London and New York, 1915); *Not That it Matters* (London, 1919); *If I May* (London, 1920); *The Sunny Side* (London, 1921); *The Ascent of Man* (London, 1928); *Those Were the Days* (London and New York, 1929); *By Way of Introduction* (London, 1929); *Peace With Honour* (London and New York, 1934); *It's Too Late Now: The Autobiography of a Writer* (New York and London, 1939); *War With Honour* (London, 1940); *War Aims Unlimited* (London, 1941); *The Pocket Milne* (New York, 1941); *Year In, Year Out* (London, 1952).

III. NOVELS AND STORIES. *Lovers in London* (London, 1905); *Mr. Pim* (London, 1921); *The Red House Mystery* (London, 1922); *The Secret and Other Stories* (London, 1929); *Two People* (London and New York, 1931); *Four Days' Wonder* (London and New York, 1933); *Chloe Marr* (London, 1946); *Birthday Party and Other Stories* (London and New York, 1948); *A Table Near the Band* (London, 1950).

IV. POETRY. *For the Luncheon Interval: Cricket and Other Verses* (London, 1925); *Behind the Lines* (London and New York, 1940); *The Norman Church* (London, 1948).

VI. WORKS FOR CHILDREN. *Once on a Time* (London, 1917); *When We Were Very Young* (London, 1924); *A Gallery of Children* (London, 1925); *Winnie-the-Pooh* (London, 1926); *Now We Are Six* (London, 1927); *The House at Pooh Corner* (London, 1928).

VII. CRITICAL AND BIOGRAPHICAL STUDIES. Thomas Burnett Swann, *A. A. Milne* (New York, 1971); Alison Lurie, "Back to Pooh Corner," in Francelia Butler, ed., *Great Excluded: Children's Literature* (New Haven, Conn., 1972); Christopher Milne, *The Enchanted Places* (New York, 1974); Christopher Milne, *The Path Through the Trees* (London and New York, 1979); Tori Haring-Smith, *A. A. Milne: A Critical Biography* (New York, 1982); Humphrey Carpenter, *Secret Gardens: A Study of the Golden Age of Children's Literature* (London and Boston, 1985); Ann Thwaite, *A. A. Milne: His Life* (London and Boston, 1990); Paul T. Connolly, *Winnie-the-Pooh and The House at Pooh Corner: Recovering Arcadia* (New York, 1995); Jackie Wullschläger, *Inventing Wonderland: The Lives and Fantasies of Lewis Carroll, Edward Lear, J. M. Barrie, Kenneth Grahame, and A. A. Milne* (London, 1995).

VII. SPIN-OFFS. Alexander Lenard, *Winnie-ille-Pu* (New York, 1960); Frederick C. Crews, *The Pooh Perplex: A Freshman Casebook* (New York, 1963); Benjamin Hoff, *The Tao of Poo* (New York, 1982); Benjamin Hoff, *The Te of Piglet* (New York, 1992).

RICHARD MURPHY

(1927–   )

Benjamin La Farge

RICHARD MURPHY HAS been called a "poet of two traditions," a poet whose deepest loyalties, both literary and personal, are divided between his English and his Irish heritage. He himself has spoken of reconciling "a division" in his mind "between an almost entirely English education, an English mind and Irish feeling" (Harmon, *Richard Murphy: Poet of Two Traditions*, p. 8). Although he is widely acknowledged as one of the major Irish poets living today, he is something of an odd man out among them. Unlike Seamus Heaney, Thomas Kinsella, Michael Longley, Derek Mahon, John Montague, and Paul Muldoon—all, except Kinsella, from Northern Ireland—Murphy comes from a family with a tradition of military and civil service in the British Empire.

Readers who expect an Irish poet to sound like William Butler Yeats should be forewarned that Murphy has none of his predecessor's visionary idealism; his art is reticent in feeling and earthbound in subject, grounded in history rather than myth. His poems are often characterized as "objective" in their precision, yet all of them, even the most seemingly objective, have what Dennis O'Driscoll, one of his more astute critics, has called "a personal significance which makes them, quite literally, 'objective correlatives' of the poet's emotions" ("The Poetry of Richard Murphy," p. 72). Murphy has been both admired and disparaged for his patrician detachment, yet many of his most successful poems demonstrate a remarkable empathy for the lonely and the outcast—people living in isolation like the philosopher Ludwig Wittgenstein, Irish fishermen on the Connemara coast, and "tinkers," as the itinerant poor were called in Ireland. Although he is a patrician by birth and a cosmopolitan by education and upbringing, he has led the life of a displaced person.

Murphy is a master of versification, frequently experimenting with different kinds of meter. Most of the longer poems in his first three books—such

as "The Woman of the House," "The Cleggan Disaster," "The God Who Eats Corn"—are in decasyllabic meters (ten syllables per line); some of the shorter poems and even one long one—such as "Girl at the Seaside," "The Last Galway Hooker," and "Years Later"—are in accentual meters (the number of stresses per line). Many of the new poems in his fourth book, *High Island: New and Selected Poems* (1974), and many of those in his sixth book, *The Mirror Wall* (1989), are in free verse, whereas the fifty sonnets in his fifth book, *The Price of Stone* (1985), are in strict pentameters. All of his poems are carefully located in the places he has lived in, and it is sometimes difficult to understand their imagery and subject matter without having some knowledge of their physical setting and their relevance to his life. Yet although they are rooted in biography and history, they are not bound by them; often their subject matter, whether person, place, or event, is best understood as metaphor.

LIFE AND EDUCATION

MURPHY's life has been a rather mobile one. Born in County Mayo on 6 August 1927, he grew up traveling back and forth between Ireland, England, Ceylon (now Sri Lanka), the Bahamas, Crete, and most recently South Africa. Since the mid-1970s he also has spent time in the United States, where he has earned his living by teaching at universities and colleges.

Both of Murphy's grandfathers were Protestant clergymen, but his father's family was not many generations removed from a rural Catholic past:

My father's father came out of the dark poverty of rural Ireland where nothing was written down—it was handed down in oral tradition. I don't know at what period his father or grandfather became Protestants, but I suspect, because there is no record of it, that during

313

one of the many famines one of them couldn't afford to get to America or Liverpool and became a Protestant, as vast numbers did in the 19th century in order to survive—it was one of the ways of surviving.

(Brophy, "Richard Murphy: Poet of Nostalgia or *Pietas?*," p. 50)

On his mother's side Murphy's family was of the Protestant Ascendancy—the descendants of English "planters" who had colonized Ireland by settling on large estates from which they governed for more than three centuries following the successive conquests of Ireland under Queen Elizabeth I, Oliver Cromwell, and King William of Orange. This was the class that Yeats, himself an Anglo-Irishman, venerated in the dramatist Lady Augusta Gregory and her son Major Robert Gregory, whom he commemorated in "An Irish Airman Foresees His Death." Murphy was born in the west wing of Milford House, his maternal grandfather's home in County Mayo—on the border of County Galway, he says, explaining that their postal address was in the latter. The house and its grounds seem to have been a decaying version of Yeats's idealized "Ancestral Houses," the first part of his poem "Meditations in Time of Civil War." In describing his grandparents' quarters in "The Pleasure Ground," a revealing essay about the two happy childhood years he spent on their estate, Murphy recalls these relics of the family's colonial and Ascendancy past: "a Turkish rifle [his grandfather] picked up on the beach at Gallipoli. Battle-axes hung on hooks, and the stairs were decorated with prints of the fighting in Rangoon. . . . Black Labrador dogs jumped up on you in the pitch-dark flagged and slippery corridors" ("The Pleasure Ground," p. 237).

Shortly after his birth Murphy was taken to Ceylon, where his father, William Lindsay Murphy, was serving in the English colonial administration. The boy was brought back to Ireland in 1929 for two years, then from 1932 to 1934 was again in Ceylon, when his father was the mayor of Colombo. Throughout his first eight years Murphy was cared for by a British nanny, who appears in one of the earliest poems he wrote about Ceylon. From 1934 to 1937 he attended Baymount Preparatory School, a Protestant boarding school in Clontarf, a suburb of Dublin. From there he was sent to the Choir School in Canterbury, where he spent three years singing the Anglican liturgy in the famous cathedral. This immersion in music and in the language of the Book of Common Prayer and the King James Bible was, Murphy says, the most formative influence on his development as a poet. In 1940, following the German invasion of France and the English evacuation from Dunkirk, he returned to Milford House with his mother, Elizabeth Mary Ormsby Murphy, and two older and two younger siblings, living this time in the east wing, which had been the servants' quarters. Here the children were educated by two private tutors, one of them a woman named Sally Stokes, a childhood friend of C. S. Lewis. This was a happy time for Murphy, as he suggests in the following passage:

My mother devoted herself to restoring this pleasure ground. It had been in her family since the victories of King William of Orange, and the first thing she did was to knock a huge stretch of the wall which had formerly imprisoned the servants, so that our house lay open to the garden. It was looking on to this pleasure ground, or sitting in the shade of the copper beech, that we did our lessons.

(p. 237)

His mother wanted Murphy to be a diplomat, but the lessons he learned in that garden were "not the right training for a civil service career. We were much too wild. Our life went from one extreme to another, from discipline to anarchy" (p. 237). Perhaps the most enduring lesson he learned there was not in the garden itself but in the surrounding countryside, where he first encountered the Irish poor—those who were "truly Irish," unlike his brother and himself:

It was a desperately poor part of the country. Huddled among boulders were those whose ancestors had lost the pitiless struggle for the land which ours had won. The planters of our pleasure ground had acquired an estate of 70,000 acres, which famine, revolution and liberalism had cut down to its present size of 300 acres. But these people lived on five or only two-and-a-half-acre holdings, and we loved them better than our relations, or the children of the rectory parties we had to attend. They were truly Irish, and that is what my brother and I wanted to be.

(p. 237)

To the two boys the "truly Irish" seemed "sharper, freer, more cunning. . . . Stones, salmonfalls, rain-clouds and drownings had entered and shaped their minds. . . . They seemed most mysterious and imaginative to us" (p. 237). But it was their manners and their speech that attracted young Murphy most of all—a poignant confession coming from a man who, to this day, speaks with an English accent and has the manners of the class in which he was raised. What moved and attracted him was their authenticity, their Irishness; and his affection for those qualities has remained with him ever since. The longing to be like someone less fortunate than oneself is common among those born to privilege, and in Murphy's case some such ambivalence about his privileged childhood and especially about his family's colonial connections—some underlying sense of guilt or self-blame—can be detected in many of his poems. This blissful period of his life came to an end when he received a scholarship to the Kings School, Canterbury. At Milford, Murphy writes, his grandmother was still "mistress of a beautiful disorder . . . but the discipline of the garden had died":

> The spirit that I was looking for in the yew-berry, the fig, and the beech-tree had withdrawn—that spirit which had once made poetry and music and painting, even mathematics, an effortless delight. There was no masculine energy in the place, to mend walls, plant new trees, sow and cultivate and labour, and I felt lost, and guilty.
>
> (p. 240)

The ambiguity in those last few words—did Murphy feel guilty for abandoning the garden in its ruined condition, or guilty for having enjoyed such privilege, and lost without it?—reminds us once again of his divided heritage. Both meanings seem equally present. It is not too much to say, given the evidence in many of his poems, that Murphy spent years trying to rediscover elsewhere that idyllic pleasure ground which for a while he thought he had found in the sea, and that he was always thereafter driven by a need to atone for the guilt he felt on leaving it behind, and perhaps also for having enjoyed its possession. At the time he wrote the essay, in 1963, he was living in County Galway, on the Connemara Peninsula. He concludes with a rhapsodic passage:

> So I went back to that older, earlier pleasure ground in the treeless hills, on the sea's edge, and rediscovered Connemara. There at the age of nineteen I abandoned myself to mountains, lakes and waterfalls; I rolled naked in snow, and stretched without clothes on the cold ground on summer nights. I wanted to write poetry, and believed that some day, like the ripening of the figs, I should taste that fruit and it would not be poison. . . .

As I grew older the garden grew wilder, losing its form as trees were felled, and its spirit as the old people died and the young left the country; so I searched more and more into the origins of that garden till I found them finally in the sea.

(p. 240)

Murphy and one of his brothers were sent to the Kings School because his father did not wish the boys to remain in Ireland, which was neutral during the war. The school had been evacuated to the Carlyon Bay Hotel in Cornwall. From there he was sent to Wellington College in Berkshire, a boarding school with military traditions, where he spent two unhappy years (1943–1944). In rebelling against the military ethos there, he began his lifelong commitment to pacificism; thanks to one teacher who took him in hand, he also discovered his love of poetry in the sonnets of Shakespeare:

> It was the fear of death during the war that started me writing poetry at the age of sixteen, as I heard the first German rockets landing on England. I had been reading Shakespeare's sonnets, and dared to imagine myself leaving in poetry a record, not immortal, but perhaps outlasting the war, of my love for Ireland, where I could not go; for my mother who was in Bermuda. . . . I became a pacifist at a school which was founded to commemorate the Iron Duke of Wellington.
>
> ("Address to the International Writers' Conference," p. 100)

In 1944 Murphy won a scholarship to Magdalen College, Oxford. One of his tutors there was C. S. Lewis, whom Murphy honors in "Oxford Staircase," a sonnet in his fifth book, *The Price of Stone*. With another tutor he read Anglo-Saxon, which has had an enduring effect on his poetic style that is especially evident in his fondness for obscure and archaic words, such as "wambling," "scurvy," "whaleroads," and "jooking" in the opening stanza of "Stormpetrel," in *High Island* (1974):

> Gipsy of the sea
> In winter wambling over scurvy whaleroads,
> Jooking in the wake of ships,
> A sailor hooks you
> And carves his girl's name on your beak.

In 1946 Murphy dropped out of Oxford for one term, renting a cottage at Lecknavarna, a wild mountain place between a waterfall and a lake, where he began to write poetry. His grandmother persuaded him to return, and he received his B.A. with honors, together with an M.A, in 1948.

After graduation Murphy moved frequently from one occupation to another, including aide-de-camp to his father, who was then in his last year as governor of the Bahamas (1948–1949); a position with Lloyds of London (1949–1950); night watchman on a salmon river in Ireland (1952); director of the English School in Canea, Crete (1953–1954); student at the Sorbonne, where he met his future wife, Patricia Avis (1954); sheep farmer with his wife in County Wicklow (1956–1957); and owner and skipper of a Galway "hooker," one of two old sailing boats by which he made a living from 1959 to 1963. He and Patricia were married in May 1955, and their daughter, Emily, was born a year later. Emily was raised a Catholic, a symbolic choice on Murphy's part implying rejection of his Protestant upbringing. In 1959 the couple were divorced. Patricia Avis has written a novel, *Playing the Harlot, or Mostly Coffee* (1996), a roman-à-clef about her life in which one of the lovers of the protagonist, Mary, is a man named Martin Freemantle, who is based on Murphy. Murphy is also the father of a natural son, William, born in 1982. A year after his divorce, Murphy moved to Inishbofin, an island off the Connemara coast. There he met Tony White, an actor who was in retreat from the London stage. When Murphy bought the *Ave Maria*, the boat he was later to celebrate in "The Last Galway Hooker," Tony White helped him rebuild it. White died in 1976, and the poems his death inspired are among the most moving in *The Price of Stone*.

Since the late 1960s Murphy has made several attempts to help "tinker" children and Sri Lankan orphans. In 1966, in Connemara, he taught a "tinker" boy to read and write, until the boy ran off. "The Reading Lesson," in *High Island*, re-creates this experience. In 1972 Murphy obtained the release of two "tinker" boys from an industrial school (the subject of the sonnet "Letterfrack Industrial School," in *The Price of Stone*) and their five sisters from an orphanage, reuniting them with their parents; he also purchased and refurbished an old stone house for the family near his own house in Cleggan. In 1985, after visiting Sri Lanka several times, he became the legal guardian of three Sri Lankan boys whom he had found in a Methodist orphanage in Colombo, and brought them home to Knockbrack, his house in the hills south of Dublin. Three years later, following a massacre of Sri Lankan students, he brought two more Sri Lankan boys to Ireland. Murphy's effort to help these boys suggests that he was following the ex-

ample of his mother, who had been awarded the M.B.E. (Member of the British Empire) for her social work during a malaria epidemic in Ceylon, and who with his father had started and run a school for the children of farmworkers in Rhodesia.

Since the publication of *The Battle of Aughrim* and *The God Who Eats Corn* in 1968, Murphy has held a succession of teaching positions, including Compton Lecturer in Poetry at the University of Hull (1969); O'Connor Professor of Literature at Colgate University (1971); visiting professor of poetry at Bard College (1972, 1974); at Princeton University (1974–1975); at the Writers Workshop, University of Iowa (1976–1977); and at Syracuse University (1977–1978). Since then he has been a distinguished visiting poet at Catholic University of America (1983), at Pacific Lutheran University (1985), at Wichita State University (1987), and at the University of Tulsa (1992–1998).

Murphy is a fellow of the Royal Society of Literature and of the Aosdána in Ireland. His awards and honors include the A. E. Memorial Award for Poetry (1951), the Guinness Award (1962), and the Arts Council of Great Britain Award (1967, 1975).

LITERARY INFLUENCES AND AFFINITIES

MURPHY's boyhood experiences of singing the liturgy at Canterbury and discovering Shakespeare's sonnets at Wellington were invaluable. Among Irish poets, Yeats has been his single greatest influence, an influence from which he has worked hard to wean himself. Murphy does not idealize the Anglo-Irish Ascendancy, as Yeats did, and his view of the Irish past is historical rather than mythopoetic, but some of Yeats's later poems—such as "In Memory of Eva Gore-Booth and Con Markiewicz," "Coole Park, 1929," "Coole Park and Ballylee, 1931"—can be felt as presences in some of Murphy's work. (Appropriately, the Abbey Theatre in Dublin commissioned him to write additions to Yeats's version of Sophocles' *King Oedipus* for the 1973 production of that play, directed by Michael Cacoyannis.) Murphy has a fondness for some of Louis MacNeice's poems, and for Patrick Kavanagh's work, which he honored when he reviewed Kavanagh's *Collected Poems* in 1965 for the *New York Times Book Review*. Murphy has been on friendly terms with Heaney, Kinsella, and others among his Irish contemporaries. In 1976 he wrote an admiring review of Seamus Heaney's volume *North,* the book that secured Heaney's reputation. Among English poets of the modern period, Thomas Hardy looms large, and Gerard Manley Hopkins' invention of sprung rhythm may have inspired Murphy's own metrical experiments. What Murphy especially values in Hardy is his skill at compressing narrative into short lyrical form. With Hardy, as with Hopkins, he shares a penchant for unfamiliar and archaic words, as in the stanza from "Stormpetrel" quoted above.

Two other poets he admires are John Betjeman and Philip Larkin. In a 1975 review of Larkin's book *High Windows,* Murphy commends Larkin in terms that might also apply to his own work. Larkin's "admirers . . . , feel that he writes with more precision than any other living poet about real people in real places; they can quote him, because his mastery of rhyme and meter enables him to write memorably" ("The Art of Debunkery," p. 87). In 1955, shortly before Larkin became famous, Murphy read a selection he made of poems by Larkin, Theodore Roethke, and Vantentin Iremonger on the BBC.

Among his English contemporaries, Murphy was on very close terms with Ted Hughes and Sylvia Plath, whom he met in 1962. They both encouraged him to write dramatic monologues. In 1965, two years after Plath's suicide, Hughes came with Assia Guttman to live for a time in Connemara, and there, in the winter of 1966, Murphy and Hughes, who was beginning to write his *Crow* poems, met regularly. Murphy has said that he wrote some of the best parts of "The Battle of Aughrim" under the stimulus of Hughes's personality and conversation. (In 1970 he and Hughes made a joint reading tour of the United States.)

THE ARCHEOLOGY OF LOVE *AND* SAILING TO AN ISLAND

MURPHY's poems are invariably meticulous in construction, and many are characterized by an emotional reticence as well, sometimes giving an impression of austerity. Yet the reticence is a mask, often concealing strong emotions, and a wary reader soon learns to regard the poem's surface as a sign of something deeper that is not being overtly expressed. Typically a Murphy poem is a careful evocation of a person, place, or event re-created through memory, and undoubtedly this is why some have seen him as a poet of nostalgia. By 1955, when his first book, *The Archeology of Love,* came out, Murphy had already published thirty-two poems in various journals. The book is very much the work of a young man in despair, as Dennis O'Driscoll suggested years later when he wrote that it "contains a reference to death on almost every page" ("The Poetry of Richard Murphy," p. 70). Murphy now dismisses the book, yet he salvaged several of the poems in it for his next collection.

Sailing to an Island (1963), the book that brought Murphy recognition as a promising young poet, represents a considerable advance in the range and skill of his art. The sixteen poems collected here are divided into three parts; the poems he revised and carried over from the first volume are in the second and third parts. Some of these are death-obsessed; in others Murphy is clearly trying to purge the past. All but one are rather short. "Auction," the first, commemorates the loss of much-loved possessions from the family home—among them his "great-aunt's chair" and the "yew-hedges / House-high, where / The dead made marriages." It ends with a forlorn question:

> With what shall I buy
> From time's auctioneers
> This old property
> Before it disappears?

In the earlier version the poet, after asking, "With what shall I buy. . . . This property?" answers the question: "Poor words I'll offer." In either version the poem may be read as Murphy's farewell to the pleasure garden of his childhood. The poem that follows this one, "Epitaph on a Fir-Tree," confirms the impression of a young Murphy purging himself of his privileged past, since the tree in question is part of a large estate being auctioned off. The fifth and sixth stanzas of this eight-stanza poem sound a note of relief as the speaker, recognizing that the colonial past is irretrievable, welcomes the sun back into the house, metaphorically suggesting a more open receptiveness to the world outside:

> We think no more of granite steps and pews,
> Or an officer patched with a crude trepan
> Who fought in Rangoon for these quiet acres.

Axes and saws now convert the evergreen
Imperial shadows into deal boards,
And let the sun enter our house again.

Following these two elegiac poems are three short ones carried over from the first volume. The first, "Girl at the Seaside," is a dramatic monologue in five highly compressed, four-line stanzas, each line of which receives two or three stresses. In the first stanza the girl, leaning "on a lighthouse rock / Where the seagowns flow," reveals a mind troubled by memories of the past when she observes, "A trawler slips from the dock / Sailing years ago." In the second stanza the imagery turns surreal and even mythical, blurring reality as she tells us: "Wine, tobacco and seamen / Cloud the green air, / A head of snakes in the rain / Talks away desire." In the third stanza she confesses, "I analyse misery / Till mass bells peal." In the fifth and final stanza she is on the verge of suicide:

I've argued myself here
To the blue cliff-tops:
I'll drop through the sea-air
Till everything stops.

Here "tops / stops" echoes and completes the sense of something hard and conclusive suggested by the "rock / dock" rhyme in the first stanza. The occasion for this poem was a 1954 trip that Murphy and Patricia Avis made to Brittany. They were in a poor state of mind, he says, and Patricia came close to suicide.

The other two shorter poems, also from the first volume, are "To a Cretan Monk in Thanks for a Flask of Wine" and "The Netting," which had been the title poem of that volume under its original name, *The Archeology of Love.*" It was Theodore Roethke, visiting Inishbofin with his wife in 1960, who persuaded Murphy to change the title. The poem, one of his most elusive, is an extended metaphor in which the poet, addressing an unnamed other, expresses his gratitude to that person for having "netted this night / From the sea a vase." Later in the poem the vase is identified as the poet's own "heart" and the net as the other's "grace." The person addressed was Patricia Avis, and Murphy intends to restore "The Netting" to its original title in a volume of his collected poems that he hopes to bring out in the future.

The last of the early poems that should be mentioned is "The Philosopher and the Birds." In 1951, when he returned to Connemara, Murphy rented the same house in Rosroe where the philosopher Ludwig Wittgenstein had lived in 1949. The poem, subtitled "In Memory of Wittgenstein at Rosroe," shows Murphy exploring a different mode from the five shorter poems discussed above. In nine stanzas of three lines each, with roughly four stresses per stanza, it celebrates the great philosopher's success at breaking out of the prison of language:

He broke prisons, beginning with words,
And at last tamed, by talking, wild birds.

Through accident of place, now by belief
I follow his love which bird-handled thoughts
To grasp growth's terror or death's leaf.

Yet the poem ends ironically, for though the great man "becomes worlds / where thoughts are wings," yet "at Rosroe hordes / Of village cats have massacred his birds." The lines metaphorically underscore the gap between intellectual achievement and the world's indifference or hostility, signified by the village cats.

A companion piece to that poem (not from the first volume) is "The Poet on the Island," dedicated to Theodore Roethke. Of interest here is the metaphor of poems as orphans, suggesting a deep connection between Murphy's view of his own work and his sympathy for dispossessed children:

To be loved by the people, he, a stranger,
    hummed

In the herring-store on Sunday crammed with
    drunks
Ballads of bawdry with a speakeasy stress.
Yet lonely they left him, "one of the Yanks."

The children understood. This was not
    madness.
How many orphans had he fathered in words
Robust and cunning, but never heartless.

Sailing to an Island was a success, running to three hardcover editions before it was brought out in paperback. Perhaps the secret of its success lies in three long narrative poems, all concerned with sailing and the sea, and "The Woman of the House," a portrait of Murphy's grandmother Lucy Mary Ormsby (1873–1958), "whose home was in the west of Ireland," as the subtitle tells us. This latter poem, one of his most memorable, announces its intention from the first stanza:

On a patrician evening in Ireland
I was born in the guest-room: she delivered me.
May I deliver her from the cold hand
Where now she lies, with a brief elegy?

Murphy praises her for her compassion toward the poor, those "truly Irish" he had first encountered on the pleasure ground of her estate:

Mistress of mossy acres and unpaid rent,
She crossed the walls on foot to feed the sick:
Though frugal cousins frowned on all she spent
People had faith in her healing talent.

She bandaged the wounds that poverty caused
In the house that famine labourers built, . . .

Yet his view of her is not sentimental; after she lost her mind and had to be "removed / To hospital to die there, certified," she withdrew, becoming hostile:

"I don't know who you are, but you've kind eyes.
My children are abroad and I'm alone.
They left me in this gaol. You all tell lies.
You're not my people. My people have gone."

Near the end of the twenty-six-stanza poem, Murphy compares her ironically with the ancient Irish poets who lived and wrote among the poor:

The bards in their beds once beat out ballads
Under leaky thatch listening to sea-birds,
But she in the long ascendancy of rain
Served biscuits on a tray with ginger wine.

The ironic pun on "ascendancy," although implicitly judgmental, is fraught with affectionate sorrow, as Murphy makes clear in the very last line of the poem: "Only to think of her, now warms my mind." The meter is decasyllabic, sometimes loosely counted, although it may also be scanned as accentual, with roughly five stresses per line. The critic Hilary Corke, reviewing the poem in *London Magazine* (7 April 1960), objected to the absence of a strict iambic pentameter; this set off a minor controversy, conducted by letter, in the *Times Literary Supplement*.

First broadcast on the BBC's Third Programme, the poem was published shortly thereafter in 1959, the same year that the American poet Robert Lowell's *Life Studies* came out. In that book Lowell began to write portraits of writers he had known and of some of his own relatives. Murphy's poems

about Wittgenstein and Roethke do not in any way resemble Lowell's portraits of Ford Madox Ford and Delmore Schwartz, nor does "Woman of the House" resemble Lowell's portraits of his grandparents or other relatives. Nevertheless, Murphy and Lowell simultaneously produced memorable poems in a vein that no one else was exploring at the time. The coincidence may not seem so remarkable, however, if one considers that both are patrician poets who feel connected to the past through family lineage.

Of the three long sea poems that open *Sailing to an Island*, the title poem is metrically notable for its use of irregular decasyllabic lines in stanzas of irregular length. The narrative describes an unsuccessful attempt by Murphy and his brother to sail to Clare, a remote island. The boat is an old one, in poor condition, and everyone on board is aware that it was the boat "that belched its crew / Dead on the shingle in the Cleggan disaster," a famous shipwreck years before. As the seas grow rough, Murphy's language takes on a figurative precision:

Now she dips, and the sail hits the water.
She luffs to a squall; is struck; and shudders.
Someone is shouting. The boom, weak as scissors,
Has snapped. The boatman is praying.
Orders thunder and canvas cannonades.

The second of the long narrative poems, "The Last Galway Hooker," describes in loving detail the history of an old fishing boat, called a hooker in the vernacular, that Murphy restored. The act of restoration and the poem itself may be understood as a metaphorical recovery of Murphy's Irishness. Also of interest is the "Metrical Note," placed at the start of this poem (but not reprinted in later versions), in which Murphy explains, "The typical line has four stresses (though not of equal emphasis) which fall usually into two groups of two stresses each." The division of each line into halves with two stresses each is reminiscent of the Anglo-Saxon meters he first encountered at Oxford.

"The Cleggan Disaster," the third of the long sea narratives, describes a famous shipwreck that occurred "off the west coast of Ireland in 1927." That was the year of Murphy's birth, a coincidence that suggests the depth of his identification with "the truly Irish" after he had put his childhood pleasure ground behind him. The hero of the poem is based on a real man named Pat Concannon, who survived the disaster, in which four other boats were lost and sixteen men from one village and nine from another drowned. What makes the poem memorable is not the action, even though Concannon saved the boat by his heroic feat and lost his sight in the process; the action in fact is almost drowned in the descriptive language. It is Murphy's figurative decoration of the event that transforms it, as in the following passage:

The wind began to play, like country fiddlers
In a crowded room, with nailed boots stamping
On the stone cottage floor, raising white ashes.
The sea became a dance. He staggered to the floor
As the music unleashed him, spun in a circle.
Now he was dancing round the siege of Death:
Now he was Death, they were dancing round
    him,
White robed dancers with crowns and clubs . . .

The narrative is followed by an epilogue, "Years Later," which won the 1962 Guinness Poetry Award at Cheltenham, England. This poem is an elegy in five stanzas of eight lines each, with three stresses to each line. Each stanza begins with a rhetorical question: "Whose is that hulk on the shingle / The boatwright's son repairs . . . ?; Where are the red-haired women / Chattering along the piers . . . ?; Where are the barefoot children / With brown toes in the ashes . . . ?; Where are the dances in houses / With porter and cakes in the room . . . ?; Why does she stand at the curtains / Combing her seal-grey hair . . . ?" The repetition achieves a powerful keening effect, and in its rhetorical evocation of the loss and grief common to Irish fishing towns along the Atlantic coast, the poem is certainly one of the least reticent of Murphy's earlier works.

Much as "The Cleggan Disaster" has been admired, it is not an easy poem to enter, and the surface density of its language may remind a reader of Hopkins' "The Wreck of the *Deutschland*." Indeed, like Hopkins' poem, which also commemorates a tragic shipwreck, Murphy's may be the kind of poem that is more honored than loved. In his seminal essay on Murphy, however, Seamus Heaney confessed that his judgment of the poem had undergone a change: "I used to think that the loving art bestowed on the texture of the thing impeded the story, that the poet was needlessly working a tapestry, where what was required was something more like a newsreel, but my sense of the poem has changed" ("Poetry of Richard Murphy," p. 24). Now Heaney had come to feel "that

the loaded, encrusted, stained-glass richness of 'The Cleggan Disaster' serves, in Yeats's words, 'to prolong the moment of contemplation,' and that Murphy's gift is not for the dramatic but for the picturesque—in the sense that 'The Eve of St Agnes' is picturesque" (p. 24). Heaney has put his finger on a quality in the narrative poems that no one else has addressed. The poem in question is aptly described as picturesque, and the comparison to Keats's ballad is also apt, suggesting as it does that the pleasure given by this kind of narrative is the pleasure of its highly decorative surface—the "loaded, encrusted, stained-glass richness" that both conceals and embodies the story.

Heaney's change of opinion about this poem touches on a problem that had troubled Murphy years before in an essay he wrote for the *Listener* in 1951, "Why Has Narrative Poetry Failed?" The two principal reasons why narrative poetry has come to be "discarded as impure," he argues, are, first, the increasing isolation of the individual, which "took from him the sense of having a place in a settled order," and, second, "the disintegration of the world of ideas and common religious assumptions on which a great deal of narrative poetry" had depended. *Paradise Lost,* once the "great model for narrative poetry in English," can no longer be taken seriously as "a justification of the ways of God to man," he says, because "We no longer think and feel and write and criticise within a framework of revealed truth." As a consequence the poet is "thrown back on his own experience. . . . One result of this change was the loss of the sense of action and time" (p. 227). Having made this argument, however, Murphy thinks he sees in myth a solution to the dilemma for modern poets. "The most moving moments in modern verse," he argues, are "in some way associated with myths or legends" (p. 227), and by way of proof he points to passages in T. S. Eliot's *The Wasteland* ("Tiresias, the typist and the clerk"), to Eliot's "The Journey of the Magi," to Ezra Pound's *Cantos* ("particularly the Homeric opening"), and to Edwin Muir's "The Labyrinth." Nevertheless, he acknowledges a difference in the way myth can be used today:

The poet's mind has become the stage on which the action takes place, and the myth is treated as an indication or reflection of the state of that mind. The narrative poet appeals now to his own experience of the subject . . . and not to a common belief about what things are or what they might become.

(p. 227)

Murphy's faith in the poetic possibilities of myth has not been borne out by the poetry written since the late 1940s. Even in his own narrative poems he has made no overt use of myth, nor can they be said to have achieved any mythical moments like those he mentions in Eliot, Pound, and Muir. Perhaps a number of them do invest the characters and events they describe with a legendary aura—there is something almost legendary about Concannon's heroic survival in "The Cleggan Disaster"—but Murphy's characteristic view is historical and biographical rather than mythical or even legendary. On the other hand, his concept of the poet's mind as "the stage on which the action takes place" is revealing. For if, as Heaney suggested, Murphy's narrative poems are dramatically sluggish, it is surely because their primary concern is not the action they describe but the mind of the poet in a state of "prolonged contemplation" of that action. At the same time, in all of his narrative verse Murphy has always been preoccupied with the historical truth and the physical actuality of the person or events being contemplated. Invariably the subject of his verse is something real, however distanced. Historical and physical reality are nowhere more evident than in the two ambitious long poems that comprise *The Battle of Aughrim*.

THE BATTLE OF AUGHRIM *AND* HIGH ISLAND

MURPHY's *The Battle of Aughrim* is more openly political, and his *High Island* more personal, than his earlier volumes. In the first of these, his anti-Ascendancy sympathies for the "truly Irish" are made clear. A seldom-mentioned poem in *Sailing to an Island*, "Droit de Seigneur: 1820," points in the direction Murphy was to take in *The Battle of Aughrim*. The ironic title, from the French, literally meaning "right of the lord," refers to the practice among the pre-Revolutionary French nobility of asserting their right to sleep with a servant's or peasant's wife on her wedding night. In the opening stanza a clergyman—implicitly Protestant—is reading a newspaper while famine is spreading among the peasantry outside. At the end of the second stanza he is "the master" leading a few sol-

diers as they hunt down "the Ribbonmen," a secret band of Irish Catholics who from 1820 to 1870 refused "to pay tithes or rent to the landlord." The clergyman's soldiers ambush "a wedding from the next parish," all of whom escape "except a young simpleton" whom they march to Galway, where he will be executed. This is the first poem in which Murphy vents his outrage over injustices committed under Ascendancy rule, and it may be seen as a trial run for *The Battle of Aughrim* (1968).

Perhaps the most distinguishing feature of the "The Battle of Aughrim," which took Murphy six years to write, is its narrative form, a succession of short poems in different modes—narrative, dramatic, lyrical—and different meters. The poem as a whole is divided into four sections—"Now," "Before," "During," and "After"—each containing a varying number of poems: nine in the first, ten in the second, six in the third, and five in the fourth. The strategy of shifting rapidly from the present to the past and from one scene or point of view to another allows Murphy to represent many different participants, from the leading generals to the lowest peasants; it also makes the experience of reading the poem highly dramatic, because with each poem we see the event from a different perspective. The poem is filled with the kind of antique words that Hardy loved to use; in the first stanza alone, for instance, we encounter "eskar ridge" (Irish for a gravel ridge) and "the rector's glebe" (land given to a Church of Ireland clergyman). The word "Aughrim" itself is Irish for "horse-ridge."

Murphy has given an account of his intentions in writing "The Battle of Aughrim" that helps to explain his seeming objectivity in telling the story from all points of view:

I was trying to get clear a division in my mind between England and Ireland—between an almost entirely English education, an English mind and Irish feeling. I tried to reconcile these two by focussing on the battle (in which my ancestors fought on both sides), finding out all I could, what it was really about and what people thought it was about; putting in different points of view, the errors and atrocities of which myths are made, and drawing up an evaluation of what the religious conflict meant: what it meant in the past and how the past is still influencing us.

(Harmon, *Richard Murphy: Poet of Two Traditions*, p. 8)

Despite its unfamiliar subject, the poem is not difficult to understand, because Murphy provides a brief headnote explaining the historical background. The importance of this battle, which took place in 1691 between an Irish army, fighting for the Catholic interests of the exiled James II, and an English army of mercenary troops fighting for the Protestant interests of the planters in the name of the English king and queen, William and Mary, was that its outcome, the English victory, decided who was to control Ireland for the next 231 years.

The first section, "Now," provides an overview of the battle and its legacy today, and the first poem in it begins with a rhetorical question:

> Who owns the land where musket-balls are buried
> In blackthorn roots on the eskar, the drained bogs
> Where sheep browse, and credal war miscarried?
> Names in the rival churches are written on
>   plaques.

The question would have been meaningless to the Irish poor, for whom the concept of owning land meant nothing. Yet it is by no means insensitive of Murphy to ask it, since it can also be read as meaning "Who has the right to this land?," to which the implicit answer would be the landless poor, "the truly Irish." The tragic outcome of this "credal war" (between the Catholic and Protestant creeds), we are told, is still visible in the "plaques" commemorating the dead in their rival churches. From there on, although he maintains his objective strategy, Murphy's political sympathies emerge with increasing clarity. We begin to be aware of this in the next poem, in which an old Catholic woman, reading a history of the war, is reminded how she (a personification of all Irish peasant women before her) "starved to feed" her absentee landlord with the rent she paid, and thinks:

> Aughrim's great disaster
> Made him two hundred years my penal master.

Soon she is so aroused that she "takes up tongs" to strike the poet for the "crop of calf-bound wrongs" her people have suffered. At the end she brings him a china dish with a picture of the slain U.S. President John F. Kennedy on it, an emblem of another Irish victim of Protestant hostility. This poem is followed by "Orange March," an account of the annual parade of Ulster militants in Northern Ireland that celebrates the Williamite victory:

> In bowler hats and Sunday suits,
> Orange sashes, polished boots,
> Atavistic trainbands come
> To blow the fife and beat the drum.

> Apprentices uplift their banner
> True blue-dyed with "No Surrender!"
> Claiming Aughrim as if they'd won
> Last year, not 1691.

In "Historical Society," the fifth poem of "Now," Murphy introduces himself as a physical presence in the poem by describing a modern symposium he attended on the battle. In the seventh poem, "Inheritance," he describes a "kinsman" of his who bulldozes the trees on "a Cromwellian demesne" he has inherited (Murphy's "pleasure ground"):

> No tree can survive his chainsaw:
> Hewing is part of the land reclamation scheme.

> He's auctioned grandfather's Gallipoli sword
> And bought a milking machine.

In case the reader mistakes the "scheme" for a good one, Murphy condemns the kinsman, whose justification for covering "his pig-sty roof" with slate from an abandoned church steeple was "Better a goat's hoof in the aisle / Than rosary beads or electric guitars." In "Christening," the next poem, Murphy describes his own Church of Ireland baptism in language that makes unmistakable the guilt he feels about his Anglo-Irish heritage: "Two clergy christen me," he says, adding with rueful irony: "I'm saved from Rome."

Yet for all the anti-Ascendancy feeling, Murphy is careful to be evenhanded. In the following section, "Before," he allows the French general St. Ruth, speaking through a translator, to address the army in a prose poem that is taken almost verbatim from an early history of the battle written by a Protestant clergyman. St. Ruth comes off as boastful and self-important, and the words he speaks to his Catholic troops, for all their sincerity, betray a conventional Catholic view of the Protestant as heretic:

> You are not Mercinary Souldiers, you do not fight for your Pay, but for your Lives, your Wives, your Children, your Liberties, your Country, your Estates; and to restore the most Pious of Kings to his Throne: But above all for the propagation of the Holy Faith, and the subversion of Heresie.

In the same evenhanded vein Murphy contrasts a cynical soldier (presumably on the Protestant side) who says, "Who cares which foreign king / Governs, we'll still fork dung," with a professional (presumably Catholic), who quotes his tentmate as boasting, "he'll hack / From a shorn heretic a pair of testicles." Likewise he gives us a planter who prays, "May the God of battle / Give us this day our land / And the papists be trampled," then follows this with "Rapparees," a poem about the Irish guerrillas, armed with pikes, who hid in the streams like otters.

In the fourth section, "After," two of the most affecting poems are "The Wolfhound," in which a faithful hound guards the corpse of its master on the battlefield, and "Patrick Sarsfield's Portrait," which honors Murphy's Catholic ancestor in decasyllabic stanzas of four lines. In the last poem of this section, "Battle Hill Revisited," Murphy describes "strangers"—apparently American tourists of Irish descent—who drive up from Shannon airport:

> They know by instinct the sheepwalk
> As it was before the great hunger and the exodus:
>
> Also this cool creek of traitors.
> They have come here to seek out ancestors.

Murphy was acutely aware of the problems inherent in writing such a poem:

> I think the dangers with writing a historical poem are in being dogmatic, and in being political. . . . In "The Battle of Aughrim," for example, I was harsher, I think, on the Protestant side because I was reared on that side and because I was living at the time in a small fishing village on the west coast of Ireland with Catholic friends.
> ("The Use of History in Poetry," p. 21)

Undeterred by such considerations at the time, however, Murphy extended his political concerns into his next poem, "The God Who Eats Corn," which is both a portrait of his father and a meditation on the colonization of Africa. First published in 1964, and then brought out in book form in 1968 as a companion piece to the "The Battle of Aughrim," it is dedicated to his father, who in 1950, after retiring as governor of the Bahamas, had settled on virgin land in Southern Rhodesia (now Zimbabwe), "where he established a farm and later a school for African children." In certain respects it is reminiscent of "The Woman of the House," but it differs from that earlier poem in being both more

ambitious and more explicitly political. In forty-one stanzas of four lines each, divided into six parts with a varying number of stanzas in each part, it is also much longer. Once again the meter is decasyllabic, sometimes loosely counted. There are delayed rhymes in almost every stanza, most of them slant rhymes, as in "out / hut" and "pile / pole," or "clinics / chickens" and "flower / roar." (Murphy is fond of these and skilled in using them.)

Like the earlier portrait of his grandmother, this portrait expresses a deep affection for his father, but here his filial affections are complicated by a filial criticism implied in numerous anticolonial passages. Throughout the poem one feels a tension between them. Even the title subtly forewarns the reader; Murphy appends a footnote explaining that, since "there was no word in the language of the Matabele to describe the white man who came to settle in central Africa," the people called him by this epithet, which means "that although he had god-like powers, he had to eat, and to die" (p. 64). The tension is made explicit in the first section of seven stanzas, when Murphy tells us that his father, in true colonial fashion, always "asks his visitors to plant a tree," so that his garden is filled with trees, each one labeled, given by various British dignitaries:

> . . . a chairman of mines
> Gave this copper beech, that silver oak
> Was trowelled by a Governor: great names
> Written on tags, Llewellin and Tredgold.

His son defiantly plants a "native candelabra" that had been "Perched on an ant-hill" through "years of drought." The act of planting a native tree is clearly a declaration of Murphy's political sympathy for the Africans, who were soon to rise against colonial rule. In the third section we are given a brief history of how the whites settled this region, starting with Livingstone, whose "prayer"—"To do some good for this poor Africa"—was not shared by Cecil Rhodes, the "Founder" and "childless millionaire" whose "dream" inspired the pioneers to come looking for "gold and diamonds":

> In dusty dorps they slept with slave-girls,
> On farms they divided the royal herd.
> In stifling mine-shafts the disarmed warriors
> Were flogged to work, their grazing grounds
> wired.

323

So now at white homesteads, the coffee
    steams
On creepered verandahs. Racial partners
Do not mix in wedlock sons and daughters.
The white man rides: the black man is his
    horse.

To each black, his ten acres for millet;
To each white, his three thousand of grass.
The gospel of peace preached from the
    pulpit;
From the hungry fields the gospel of force.

Although he honors his father for starting a school, described in the fourth section, and for having helped to build a high dam, Murphy depicts him, in the fifth section, with "His scholar's head, disguised in a bush hat," standing "Tall in his garden, shaded and brick-walled," where he "upholds the manners of a lost empire." In the sixth and final section we are given images of the destructive aftermath of colonial rule: "the old mopani forest is felled" and "Pyres kindle under *Pax Britannica*" while his father, well-intentioned but unaware, "stays to build a club-room for the school."

Understandably, when Murphy showed him the poem (which had taken him four months to write), his father was displeased: "I think the trouble with the poem is that you don't love Africa." Murphy comments:

He was right. My father was a kind man, and he didn't want to cripple me with parental criticism: but nor was he prepared to disguise his dislike of the attitude he perceived in the poem's author, a son who had developed in ways he had never really understood or imagined. . . . I defended myself by saying:

"The poem was written by someone who doesn't love Africa about his father who does: and perhaps the irony of this may increase the interest." I had perceived the poem as a portrait of a good man behaving as well as possible in a bad situation not of his own making.

("On Writing 'The God Who Eats Corn,'" p. 106)

High Island. New and Selected Poems (1974) represents a shift away from history and toward personal experience. The book is divided into four parts, including fourteen of the sixteen poems from *Sailing to an Island*, all of "The Battle of Aughrim" and "The God Who Eats Corn," plus twenty-five "New Poems." The book is named for the island off the Connemara coast that Murphy purchased in 1969. The new poems may be divided into clusters according to their subject matter:

those concerned with High Island itself; with the birds he observes on the island; with house building and love; with "tinkers" and others on the mainland; and with childhood experiences in Ceylon.

Some of the best poems are evocations of mating and sexual longing, as in "Seals at High Island," where Murphy, standing on "a cliff-top, trying not to move," observes "A dappled grey bull and a brindled cow" copulating "in the green water of a cove." It is the delicate balance between the poet's respect and his empathy for the mating mammals that gives this poem its force. After "the great bull withdraws his rod" and "the cow ripples ashore to feed her calf," a rival male attacks "the tired triumphant god, / They rear their heads above the boiling surf, / Their terrible jaws open, jetting blood." In the last stanza the poem achieves what Seamus Heaney, in his 1977 essay, called "a music of sea and sex and sorrow, moving like a long swell" ("Poetry of Richard Murphy," p. 29):

At nightfall they haul out, and mourn the
    drowned,
Playing to the sea sadly their last quartet,
An improvised requiem that ravishes
Reason, while ripping scale up like a net:
Brings pity trembling down the rocky spine
Of headlands, till the bitter ocean's tongue
Swells in their cove, and smothers their
    sweet song.

Clearly the sorrow that resonates throughout this poem is an echo of the poet's own longing, and this is also true of several other of the "New Poems." Characteristically Murphy is alone, an outsider looking on, but it is his empathy for what he sees and hears that makes the best of these poems memorable. The tone of sorrow is less detached and more intimate in the five bird poems, in four of which he addresses a bird (a corncrake, a stormpetrel) in affectionate and sometimes even bantering language, using the second-person singular, as in "Song for a Corncrake:"

Why weave rhetoric on your voice's loom,
Shuttling at the bottom of my garden
In meadowsweet and broom? . . .

Why draft an epic on a myth of doom
In staunchly nailed iambics
Launched nightly near my room?
Since all you need to say is *crex*
Give us lyrics,
Little bridegroom.

The note of longing becomes more intense in "Nocturne," a free-verse poem without punctuation:

> Wings beating on stone
> Quick vibration of notes throats tongues
> Under silverweed calling and calling
>
> Come back come back
> I'm here here here
> This burrow this wall this hole

After this it is no surprise that "Sunup," printed on the facing page, is an explicit love poem, addressed to someone who has left the speaker for a new lover:

> The sun kisses my eyes open:
> Another day of wanting you.
> I'd like to kiss your eyes again,
> No comfort now in being alone.
>
> Is she delighting you in bed
> In her caravan on a cutaway road?
> Does the sun give you the same kiss
> To wake you, with her at your side?

The confessional candor of this is exceptional, but elsewhere in this collection there are seven free-verse poems about "tinkers" in which Murphy explores sexual molestation and other problems. Although his handling of free verse in most of these poems is not entirely confident, he uses it to brilliant effect in "Pat Cloherty's Version of *The Maisie*." This poem is devoid of figurative description as Cloherty tells the story of a shipwreck, and his account draws to a climax in these laconic stanzas:

> The woman came up from the forecastle
>   she came up alone on deck
>   and a great wave cast her out on shore
>
> And another heave came while she drowned
>   and put her on her knees
>   like a person'd be in prayer
>
> That's the way the people found her
>   and the sea never came in
>   near that mark no more

Murphy's ear for free verse is pitch-perfect in this poem, possibly because he is hearing the voice of a real man as he writes; and it anticipates his masterful use of it in his later book, *The Mirror Wall* (1989). Yet in "The Reading Lesson," perhaps the most successful of all the "New Poems," he reverts to loosely counted decasyllabic meter. The poem is about his own frustrated attempt to teach a "tinker" boy how to read and write:

> Fourteen years old, learning the alphabet,
> He finds letters harder to catch than hares
> Without a greyhound. . . .
> He's caught in a trap, until I let him go . . .

When the poet asks him, "Don't you want to learn to read?" the boy replies with unregenerate pessimism, "I'll be the same man whatever I do." Two stanzas later, when he defiantly announces he will not read any more, the poet, wondering whether to give up, thinks how his "hands, long-fingered as a Celtic scribe's, / Will grow callous, gathering sticks or scrap; / Exploring pockets of the horny drunk / Loiterers at the fairs, giving them lice." He concludes:

> If books resembled roads, he'd quickly read:
> But they're small farms to him, fenced by the
>   page,
> Ploughed into lines, with letters drilled like oats:
> A field of tasks he'll always be outside.
> If words were bank-notes, he would filch a wad;
> If they were pheasants, they'd be in his pot
> For breakfast, or if wrens he'd make them king.

This poem, built on a tension between the poet's desire to teach the boy and his simultaneous empathy for the boy's resistance, suggests a larger question: Can learning be of any help to those who cannot imagine how it could be?

One of the four free-verse poems about his memories of childhood in Ceylon, "Coppersmith" (a kind of bird), is a parable of the young Murphy's awakening as a poet:

> Where I stood and listened to the tiny
>   hammer-stroke
> Of the crimson coppersmith perched above my
>   head,
> His *took took took*
> And his *tonk tonk tonk*
> Were spoken in a language I never understood:
> And there I began to repeat
> Out loud to myself an English word such as
>   *beat beat beat*.

THE PRICE OF STONE

ALL of the poems in *High Island* are included in the first three sections of Murphy's *The Price of Stone* (1985), but it is the twenty-one poems in the fourth section and the fifty sonnets in the fifth that mark this volume as the crowning achievement of his career thus far. All of the poems in the fourth section, "Care," celebrate ways of caring, from three or four elegiac poems about his friend Tony White, who died unexpectedly in 1976, to "Visiting Hour," in which Murphy pays a call on another poet in the hospital. Perhaps the most revealing is a short aphoristic poem, "Moonshine," concerning an inner conflict between the two things he cares about most, love and work. In four terse stanzas of four lines each, it begins:

> To think
> I must be alone:
> To love
> We must be together.

and ends:

> Alone I love
> To think of us together:
> Together I think
> I'd love to be alone.

Also revealing are four poems in which Murphy blames himself for his obsession with building houses at the expense of his work and his friendships. (Murphy had restored an abandoned hut on High Island in 1971 and built a stone hexagonal studio on Omey Island in 1974 and a stone house in Cleggan as well.) In "Stone Mania," comprising twenty-four lines of long two-line clauses with five to six stresses in the first line and three to four in the second, he castigates himself:

> How much it hurts me to tidy up when all my
>   papers are heaped on the desk in a three-
>   month mess, . . .
> How much it hurts to see the destruction that all
>   good building, even the best, must cause, . . .
> How much it hurts me to have neglected all this
>   summer the friends whom I might have
>   seen, . . .

The poem "Amsterdam," ostensibly about a Dutch miser, may be considered indirectly confessional because it comes after "Elixir," in which Murphy, speaking in the third-person singular, censures someone as obsessive as himself:

> Turning a life's work into stocks and shares
> Converted him to shirk the tears and shocks
> Of love, rid of laborious household cares
> And freed him to buy sex on piers and docks.

Immediately preceding this is "Arsonist," whose third-person protagonist "drifts alone / On the soundwaves of his vacant house." But "All he can feel / Is a dying to get rid of it," and the poem ends with a two-stanza fantasy of burning the house down in a "blaze" that would look "spontaneous and elemental."

Two love poems in the confessional mode prepare us for the obliquely autobiographical sonnets to come. In the first of these, "A Nest in a Wall," Murphy addresses a lover of indeterminate gender:

> Smoky as peat your lank hair on my pillow
> Burns like a tinker's fire in a mossy ditch.
> Before I suffocate, let me slowly suck
> From your mouth a tincture of mountain ash . . .

The last line, "Make your nest of moss like a wren in my skull," confirms the suggestion, made by the imagery throughout, that Murphy is speaking to one of "the truly Irish." In "Displaced Person" he addresses a woman he had once loved with this confession:

> Those years ago, when I made love to you,
> With fears I was afraid you knew,
> To grow strong I'd pretend to be
> A boy I'd loved, loving yourself as me.

In "Morning Call" the poet is awakened by "two beautiful teenage girls from a tribe of tinkers" who have been out all night on a spree and are afraid to go home. In three stanzas with seven long lines of six stresses each, they appear

> Lovely as seals wet from fishing, hauled out on a
>   rock
> To dry their dark brown fur glinting with scales
>   of salmon
> When the spring tide ebbs. This is their
>   everlasting day
> Of being young. They bring to my room the sea's
>   iodine odour
> On a breeze of voices ruffling my calm as they
>   comb their long
> Hair tangled as weed in a rockpool beginning to
>   settle clear.

The sympathetic analogy of girls with seals underscores Murphy's perception of the "truly Irish" as being closer to nature. "Care" is a narrative in eleven stanzas of three decasyllabic lines each. The story, told in loving detail, describes a goat that Murphy and some local children took care of until it was carelessly fed a poisonous sprig of yew, and died. Affecting on its own simple terms, the poem may also be read as a parable of nurturing.

"The Price of Stone" is a sequence of fifty autobiographical sonnets that is certainly Murphy's masterpiece and quite possibly, as more and more readers are coming to feel, one of the great sonnet cycles in the English language. In his 1977 essay Seamus Heaney characterized Murphy's verse as "moving in a restricted space"—an observation some have since disputed. Yet if there was ever any truth in it, this sonnet sequence might seem to prove it so. Its underlying premise is the analogy, repeatedly made by Murphy (and before him by Wordsworth), between a building and sonnet. In May 1984 the Australian Broadcasting Commission in Sydney recorded Murphy (in a Dublin studio) reading the cycle in four twenty-five-minute programs; the recordings, together with his introductory comments on each of the sonnets, are of great value in explaining their imagery. (The transcript, revised by Murphy, is available to scholars at the University of Tulsa, in Oklahoma, which holds the poet's archive.)

At a time when few poets writing in English have cared to offer sonnets to their public, Murphy has chosen to frame his *apologia pro vita sua* in this conventional form, but he has used it in a most unconventional manner. All but one of its poems ("Natural Son") are built on the improbable conceit of a building, monument, or habitable structure speaking directly to the poet in the second-person singular. This was the same conceit used by the anonymous Anglo-Saxon author of *The Dream of the Rood*, Murphy now says, although he claims he did not remember this while he was writing the sequence. The very absurdity of the conceit releases the poet from his habitual reticence, allowing him to speak more confessionally than he would normally do; and the oblique perspective of each building endows the poems with great power. Murphy handles the iambic pentameter with consummate skill, frequently using substitute feet and enjambment to vary the insistent effect of the five-foot line. The cycle as a whole is an autobiographical confession, and many of its poems are loosely clustered according to subject or theme—scorn for the Ascendancy mixed with affection and scorn for his patrician family, sexual ambivalence, his feelings about the places where he was educated, self-reproach for his compulsion to build and then leave houses, and sympathy for the "truly Irish."

The first nine sonnets are spoken by buildings in the vicinity of Dublin, including "Knockbrack," where he lived for many years. "Folly," the first of these, sets the tone by introducing the themes of political scorn and sexual ambivalence. The edifice is an architectural folly, built in the nineteenth century by an Ascendancy lord "to relieve the poor / With heavy work lifting my spire, and the rich / With light step ascending my gazebo stair . . . ":

> My form is epicene: male when the gold
> Seed of the sun comes melting through my skin
> Of old grey stucco: female when the mould
> Of moonlight makes my witch-pap cone obscene.

Phallic and castration images recur throughout the cycle, and in two of the Dublin poems they are associated with monuments honoring the British military heroes Nelson and Wellington. (The monument to Nelson was blown up by Irish extremists in 1966.) In both of these, the concluding couplets seem to suggest that Murphy, masking himself as a monument, is speaking about his own purpose in writing the cycle:

> Dismasted and dismissed, without much choice,
> Having lost my touch, I'll raise my chiselled
>   voice.
>
> ("Nelson's Pillar")

> My sole point in this evergreen oak
>   aisle
> Is to maintain a clean laconic style.
> ("Wellington Testimonial")

Sexual ambivalence is acknowledged in "Portico," which tells us that " . . . solitary shadows of men cruise / My concrete cloister, ghosts questing blood," and describes itself in language that reflects Murphy's love of unfamiliar words:

> I perch on rocks by the cineritious sea
> Fossilized in decay: no painted porch
> For a stoic mind, no shore temple of Shiva,
> But a new kind of succursal, deviate church.

The theme is repeated in "Gym," where "Nude club members, immune from women, bask / In tableaux mixed with musak, cocaine, jism . . . ," and again in "Convenience" (the British term for a public toilet), which reminds the poet how he came there as a young man, and puns on the words for earthquake as a metaphor of the fear, excitement, and shame he felt:

> Your profane oracle, I speak through a crack
> In a mental block, going far back to the year
> You stood here, epicentred on the shock
> Of gross accusation, quaking at words like queer.

Murphy's ambivalence about his Anglo-Irish family—affection for place mixed with self-reproach and scorn for patrician reserve—can be heard in several sonnets that speak to him from Milford, the pleasure ground of his youth where his grandparents lived. In his introduction to "Family Seat" for the Australian Broadcasting Commission, Murphy says: "I'm not sure how this happens, but I know that by letting the Big House of my mother's five maiden aunts and bachelor uncle in County Mayo speak about its family problem of preferring things to people, I can say something difficult to say about myself":

> Clouds make me look as though I disapprove
> Of everyone. You know that grim, grey face
> Of limestone cut by famine workmen. Love
> Is never allowed to show it rules the place.

Murphy's great-grandfather on his father's side, his namesake who was known to be a stern disciplinarian, had lifted himself from poverty by teaching, and "Carlow Village Schoolhouse" compares him to the poet:

> Much as you need a sonnet house to save
> Your muse, while sifting through foetid pits
> Of blighted roots, he needed my firm, grave
> Façade, to be freed from bog-dens and sod-huts.

> Such symmetry he gained from me, you got
> By birth, given his names. . . .

"Birth Place" (Milford, his grandparents' house) speaks to Murphy about his own birth in a voice of tender irony:

> I'd been expecting death by absentee
> Owner's decay, or fire from a rebel match.
> Too many old relations I'd seen die
> In the same bedroom made me scared to watch.

> Between her cries, I heard carts trundling books
> Gone mouldy to a bonfire in the yard.

And in "Milford: East Wing," the house speaks with ironic humor in praising the family's generosity to the poor:

> No judder shook my back door's ease of pulling
> Lame ducks in; tinkers with babies, diseased
>   and poor,
> For a bite to eat; mockery of the cook killing
> A rat with a poker on the foul scullery floor.

In "Suntrap" the house reminds Murphy of one happy wartime year when his favorite tutor, Sally Stokes, introduced him to "knight-errant books" and his childhood pleasure ground became a "Bower of Bliss, painlessly scanned," an allusion to Spenser's *Faerie Queene.* The boarding schools he attended as a boy speak to him in five sonnets, including "Baymount," "Choir School," and "Carlyon Bay Hotel." In "Canterbury Cathedral," where he sang while attending the choir school there, the great edifice reminds him of his poetic debt:

> What building tuned your ear for poetry? Mine,
> You remember, trained your childhood voice
>   that filled
> My quire with a sharp sound. You poured in
>   my fine
> Keyed vaults the grains of song my stonework
>   milled.

And "Wellington College" reminds him of another debt:

> Fear makes you lock out more than you include
> By tackling my red brick with Shakespeare's form
> Of love poem, barracked here and ridiculed
> By hearty boys, drilled to my square-toed norm.

There are a number of poems in which some of the buildings Murphy lived in or visited on the west coast of Ireland speak—including the wild place he briefly left Oxford to stay in ("Lecknavarna"); the house where Wittgenstein had lived at Rosroe ("Killary Hostel"); the cottage he lived in as a night watchman on a salmon river ("Waterkeeper's Bothy"); the hut he rebuilt on High Island ("Miner's Hut"); the stone studio he built on Omey Island ("Hexagon"); the house he rebuilt in Cleggan ("New Forge"); the bar that he and Tony White frequented in Cleggan ("Pier Bar"); and "Tony White's Cottage."

In several of these sonnets Murphy blames himself for his compulsion to leave a house he has built or rebuilt. His self-reproach is most acute in "Roof-Tree" (a metonym for the house itself), in which the house blames the poet for rebuilding it when he should have been caring for his wife and their newborn daughter:

> After you brought her home with your first child
> How did you celebrate? Not with a poem
> She might have loved, but orders to rebuild
> The house. Men tore me open, room by room.
>
> To renovate my structure, which survives,
> You flawed the tenderest movement of three lives.

Closely related to the theme of self-blame are a number of sympathetic sonnets about "tinker" dwellings: "Horse-Drawn Caravan," "Old Dispensary," "Chalet," and "Wattle Tent." Tucked among these, significantly, is "Prison," which speaks to him in accusatory tones about his visit to the "tinker" boy he had once tried to teach, now serving time: " . . . You knew / His touching thievery often gave you life." Murphy's introductory commentary on "Wattle Tent" for his Australian broadcast is invaluable in helping us understand his guilt-ridden feelings about the "tinkers":

Camping in tents of calico stretched over bent poles . . . outside the demesne walls of places like Milford, the tinkers who used to be tinsmiths going from farm to farm selling cans and begging and stealing in my youth, are still the outcasts of society in Ireland. But so in another sense are we who used to live inside those walls. Descended from evicted tenants, wandering scholars and bards, and from hordes of nomadic beggars on the roads in the past, the tinkers have their own language: not Romany but "cant" or "shelta"—a garbling of Irish words for their own protection. Very few tinkers could read or write until recently. Their preliteracy is part of their fascination in the eyes of some one enslaved to a literate muse.

The cycle ends with three poems of atonement—the first one honoring the ruins of an ancient Franciscan "Friary" ("Each time you breathe my name . . . / Young leaf-growth rustles in the druid wood"); the second, a "Beehive Cell," originally built for hermits on High Island, where, according to local legend, at the time of the Great Famine, a fisherman's wife gave birth without assistance; and the third, "Natural Son," in which Murphy, lovingly attending his son's birth, speaks in his own voice for the first time and once more celebrates the analogy between the "restricted space" of house and sonnet underlying the entire cycle:

> Before the spectacled professor snipped
> The cord, I heard your birth-cry flood the ward,
> And lowered your mother's tortured head, and
>   wept.
> The house you'd left would need to be
>   restored.

THE MIRROR WALL

THE *Mirror Wall* (1989), Murphy's sixth and most recent book of verse, is a radical departure from everything he had written before. As he explains in the preface, he spent "much of [his] happy childhood in Ceylon," which had become Sri Lanka when he returned "after a gap of fifty years." It was then that he visited a rock fortress called Sigiriya, in the central province, and saw the astonishing frescoes painted on rock above a path leading up to the fortress. The frescoes depict women, bare-breasted and bejeweled, whose identity and significance are a mystery, although it seems likely they represent the "cloud nymphs" of Kuvera, the Hindu god of wealth who lived on Mount Kailasa in the Himalayas. Twenty of these, painted near the end of the fifth century, have survived—four of them reproduced in color photographs for this volume.

Beneath the frescoes is a plaster or "mirror" wall on which are inscribed 685 songs composed by nobles, merchants, Buddhist monks, and travelers (including women), who came from all over Sri Lanka and southern India to see the paintings. The songs—written in Old Sinhala, the ancient Sinhalese language, during the eighth, ninth, and tenth centuries—were transcribed and translated into English by a Sri Lankan scholar named Senarat Paranavitana, who first published them under the title *Sigiri Graffiti* in 1956 (reprinted by the Sri Lankan Government Press in 1983). These and the frescoes above them were the inspiration for Murphy's book of seventy-seven poems.

The original poems are in a traditional syllabic meter that Murphy says he has tried to replicate in a few of his adaptations. While all of his poems are derived from the originals, he has rendered most of them either in free verse or in a syllabic meter of his own devising. The order in which they appear is open-ended, without any division into time frames; each poem represents a different person's view, and for this reason the scheme as a whole is somewhat reminiscent of the *The Battle of Aughrim*. The overall effect, however, is joyful and comic—more like a miniature version of *The Canterbury Tales* than anything else—since all of the original songs, whether written out of sexual appreciation or moral disapproval, represent the voices of people from different backgrounds who once looked on these painted images. Typical are the following three verses, the first of which offers the male point of view:

> Women like you enable people
> To say just what they think:
> At Sigiri
> You compelled my hair to bristle,
> My whole body rose up thrilled.

A disapproving monk, who may be admonishing himself as much as subsequent visitors, commands: "No, don't look at her! / Let's go away. / The golden figures / With wet-nurse breasts / Should be hacked off." By contrast, another speaker announces, "As a woman I'll gladly / sing for these women / who are unable to speak," and mocks the male viewers by saying: "You bulls come to Sigiri / and toss off little lovesongs / making a big hullabaloo."

But in the following verses, also adapted from the original, Murphy seems to speak for himself as well as everyone else who has laid eyes upon the figures:

> Becoming attached
>   to one of these colourful
> Wallflower girls
>   who have such fetching eyes,
>
> Is like being stitched
>   into the body of a poem
> With a gaping wound
>   that won't heal in your mind.

Readers wishing to appreciate Murphy's achievement as a poet soon come to realize that his work derives from a complex, personal relationship to British colonialism in its declining years. The formative experiences of his childhood and youth took place in Ceylon and in English schools, as well as on the pleasure ground at Milford House. In the most memorable of his poems—the poems that have brought him growing recognition

as one of the major Irish poets of our time—he pays homage to the memory of those experiences, to the tragic history of Anglo-Irish rule, and to the precolonial art of Sri Lanka.

SELECTED BIBLIOGRAPHY

I. POETRY. *The Archeology of Love: Poems* (Glenageary, 1955); *Sailing to an Island: A Poem* (Dublin, 1955), thirty-five numbered copies; *The Woman of the House: An Elegy* (Dublin, 1959); *The Last Galway Hooker* (Dublin, 1961); *Sailing to an Island* (London, 1963; New York, 1964); *The Battle of Aughrim* and *The God Who Eats Corn* (London and New York; 1968); *High Island* (London, 1974); *High Island. New and Selected Poems* (New York and London, 1974); *The Price of Stone* (London, 1985); *The Price of Stone & Earlier Poems* (Winston-Salem, N.C., 1985); *The Mirror Wall* (Newcastle upon Tyne and Winston-Salem, N.C., 1989); *New Selected Poems* (London, 1989).

II. RECORDINGS. *The Battle of Aughrim* (London, 1969), recording (Claddagh Records) of the first broadcast on the BBC Third Programme, August 1968—read by Cyril Cusack, C. Day Lewis, Ted Hughes, Margaret Robertson, and Niall Toibin, music composed by Sean O'Riada; *The Price of Stone*, three programs recorded in May 1984 at Windmill Lane Studios in Dublin for the Australian Broadcasting Commission—read by Murphy, who gives a brief introduction for each sonnet, and directed by Dennis O'Driscoll.

III. CRITICISM AND REVIEWS. "Before Yeats," in *Times Literary Supplement*, 13 April 1951, review of Geoffrey Taylor, ed., *Irish Poets of the Nineteenth Century*; "A Story-Teller in Verse," in *The Spectator*, 4 May 1951, review of Robert Frost, *Collected Poems*; "Why Has Narrative Poetry Failed?" in *The Listener*, 9 September 1951; "Appreciation of Milton," in *Times Literary Supplement*, 15 May 1953, review of S. Ernest Sprott, *Milton's Act of Prosody*; "The Art of the Translator," in *The Spectator*, 18 September 1953, review of D. D. Paige, ed., *The Translations of Ezra Pound*; "Donne and Milton," in *The Spectator*, 20 March 1953, review of Helen Gardner, ed., *John Donne: The Divine Poems*, and vol. 1 of Helen Darbishire, ed., *The Poetical Works of John Milton*; "The Music of Poetry," in *The Spectator*, 13 February 1953, review of Wallace Stevens, *Selected Poems*; "Three Modern Poets" [Theodore Roethke, Philip Larkin, Valentin Iremonger], in *The Listener*, 9 September 1955; "The Muse in Chains," in *Times Literary Supplement*, 17 June 1960, letter in the metrics controversy over "The Woman of the House"; "The Pleasure Ground," in *Writers on Themselves* (London, 1964), first printed in *The Listener*, 15 August 1963; "New Beauty for Old Clay," in *New York Times Book Review*, 23 March 1965, review of Patrick Kavanagh, *Collected Poems*; "The Art of Debunkery," in *New York Review of*

Books, 15 May 1975, review of Philip Larkin, *High Windows*, repr. in *The Snow Path: Tracks 10* (Dublin, 1994); "The Irish Situation," in *New York Review of Books*, 17 April 1975, letter replying to Donald Davie's review of *High Island* (12 April); "Poetry and Terror," in *New York Review of Books*, 30 September 1976, review of Seamus Heaney, *North*; "To Celebrate Existence," in *Hibernia*, 17 December 1976, review of Ted Hughes, *Season Songs*; "The Use of History in Poetry," in Audrey S. Eyler and Robert F. Garratt, eds., *The Uses of the Past: Essays on Irish Culture* (Newark, Del., 1988); "Address to the International Writers' Conference in Dublin, 20 June 1991," repr. in *The Snow Path: Tracks 10* (Dublin, 1994); "On Writing 'The God Who Eats Corn,'" in *The Snow Path: Tracks 10* (Dublin, 1994).

IV. BIOGRAPHIES AND INTERVIEWS. Isabel Healy, "In Cleggan, Co. Galway, Isabel Healy Met . . . / Richard Murphy: A Poet in a Pink Granite House," in the *Irish Press*, 3 November 1971, interview; John Boland, "Relating to Our Past," in *Irish Press*, 7 June 1973, interview following Abbey Theatre production of Yeats's *King Oedipus* with Murphy's additions to the text; Rebecca Shull, "Rebecca Shull Talks to the Poet Richard Murphy About His Recently Completed Additions to the W. B. Yeats Version of Sophocles' 'King Oedipus' for the Abbey Theatre, and About His Own Background," in *Irish Times*, 17 May 1973, interview; Elgy Gillespie, "Richard Murphy upon Omey," in *Irish Times*, 21 November 1975, interview; Cormac MacConnell, "A Poet on His Own Island: Annalist of the Galway Hooker," in the *Irish Press*, 22 January 1976; Maurice Harmon, "Biographical Note on Richard Murphy," in *Irish University Review* 7 (spring 1977).

V. CRITICAL STUDIES. Hilary Corke, "Is Metre a Dirty Word? and Other Observations on the Present State of Poetry," in *London Magazine*, 7 April 1960; Edna Longley, "Searching the Darkness: Richard Murphy, Thomas Kinsella, John Montague and James Simmons," in Douglas Dunn, ed., *Two Decades of Irish Writing: A Critical Survey* (Cheadle Hulme, 1975); Maurice Harmon, "Introduction: The Poet and His Background," in *Irish University Review* 7 (spring 1977), repr. in Maurice Harmon, ed., *Richard Murphy: Poet of Two Traditions*; Seamus Heaney, "The Poetry of Richard Murphy," in *Irish University Review* 7 (spring 1977), repr. in Maurice Harmon, ed., *Richard Murphy: Poet of Two Traditions*; Michael Herity, "The High Island Hermitage," in *Irish University Review* 7 (spring 1977), repr. in Maurice Harmon, ed., *Richard Murphy: Poet of Two Traditions*; J. G. Simms, "The Battle of Aughrim: History and Poetry," in *Irish University Review* 7 (spring 1977), repr. in Maurice Harmon, ed., *Richard Murphy: Poet of Two Traditions*; Anthony Whilde, "A Note on the Storm Petrel and Corncrake," in *Irish University Review* 7 (spring 1977), repr. in Maurice Harmon, ed., *Richard Murphy: Poet of Two Traditions*; Jonathan Williams, "A Glossary to *The Battle of Aughrim* and *The God Who Eats Corn*," in *Irish University Review* 7 (spring 1977), repr. in Maurice Harmon, ed., *Richard Murphy: Poet of Two Traditions*; Mary Fitzgerald, "A Richard Murphy Bibliography," in Maurice Harmon, ed., *Richard Murphy: Poet of Two Traditions*; Maurice Harmon, "Beginning with Words," in Maurice Harmon, ed., *Richard Murphy: Poet of Two Traditions*; Maurice Harmon, ed., *Richard Murphy: Poet of Two Traditions* (Dublin, 1978); Dennis O'Driscoll, "The Poetry of Richard Murphy," in *Poetry Australia* (Wollongong, NSW, 1979).

Mark Kilroy, "Richard Murphy's Connemara Locale," in *âEire-Ireland* 15, no. 3 (1980); Neal Bowers, "Richard Murphy: The Landscape of the Mind," in *Journal of Irish Literature* 11 (September 1982); James L. Lafferty, "Perceptions of Roots: The Historical Dichotomy of Ireland as Reflected in Richard Murphy's *The Battle of Aughrim* and John Montague's *The Rough Field*," in Heinz Kosok, ed., *Studies in Anglo-Irish Literature* (Bonn, 1982); James D. Brophy, "Richard Murphy: Poet of Nostalgia or *Pietas?*" in James D. Brophy and Raymond J. Porter, eds., *Contemporary Irish Writing* (Boston, 1983); Terence Brown, "Poets and Patrimony: Richard Murphy and James Simmons," in Gerald Dawe and Edna Longley, eds., *Across a Roaring Hill: The Protestant Imagination in Modern Ireland* (Belfast and Dover, N.H., 1985); Joseph Sendry, "The Poet as Builder: Richard Murphy's *The Price of Stone*," in *Irish University Review* 15 (spring 1985); Joseph Swann, "The Historian, the Critic and the Poet: A Reading of Richard Murphy's Poetry and Some Questions of Theory," in *Canadian Journal of Irish Studies* 16 (July 1990); Rand Brandes, "Drafting *The Price of Stone*: Richard Murphy's Manuscripts for 'Beehive Cell,'" in *The Snow Path: Tracks 10* (Dublin, 1994); Terence Dewsnap, "Richard Murphy's *Apologia: The Price of Stone*," in *Canadian Journal of Irish Studies* 22 (July 1996).

EDNA O'BRIEN

(1932–   )

Laura Engel

MOST ARTICLES ABOUT Edna O'Brien open with a lengthy description of her, much like the beginning of a novel that features O'Brien herself as the tortured, beautiful, and brilliant heroine. In an article for the *Washington Post* (8 April 1987), Mary Battiata wrote, "In the rosy gloom of a local lunchroom she sat looking much like one of her characters: worldly, recklessly romantic, and despite a long absence from County Clare, wearing her Irishness like a French perfume" (p. C1). Five years later the critic Megan Tresidder echoed the sentiment in a piece for the *Sunday Telegraph* (13 September 1992): "It is a dull overcast morning in Chelsea but Edna O'Brien is dressed as if for evening cocktails in a satiny shirt and a long sheath of printed velvet, clinched with a large silver buckle. Her shoes are purple suede" (p. 103).

O'Brien's reputation as a theatrical and controversial figure is a legacy that has followed her from the publication of her first book, *The Country Girls* (1960), a novel that was banned in her native Ireland because of its frank depiction of young women and the issues that confront them in their search for independent identities. A prolific writer, O'Brien has written more than twenty books, including novels, story collections, plays, screenplays, and a memoir. In all of her work O'Brien has remained interested in one subject above all: the loves, triumphs, and struggles of passionate women. But her methodology, as well as her range of contexts, situations, and characters, has evolved. In her later work O'Brien focuses less on the psyches of her heroines than on the inner workings of the culture that shaped them—specifically, the complex and dynamic heritage of Ireland.

O'Brien was born on 15 December 1932 in Taumgraney, County Clare, a rural town in western Ireland. Although she left Ireland in 1946 and has lived in London ever since, it is Ireland—its landscape, people, literature, religion, political struggles, folklore, and mystery—that forms the backdrop of her writing. Most of her heroines struggle with O'Brien's own conflict of living in two worlds: the "old" world of Ireland, with its repressive traditions and unhappy memories, and the "new" world of England, full of possibility and the potential for tragedy. The Ireland that O'Brien describes in her fiction offers few possibilities for modern women, yet it is Irish traditions and the minute details of everyday Irish country life that animate her novels and allow the full emergence of her gifts as a writer. Like her hero, James Joyce, and one of her favorite authors, Anton Chekhov, O'Brien is at her best when she is writing about day-to-day life, conveying the emotion of just one moment, or describing the atmosphere of a specific community. In a *New York Times* (12 March 1989) interview with Richard B. Woodward, O'Brien explained: "Ireland is the most rich, unescapable land. That's not a sentimentality. Imagine a brand that's put on a beast. America is a transient land. I read the plays by Sam Shepard or Raymond Carver's stories. They're not stamped by their country, they're trying to put their stamp on the country" (section 6, p. 42).

For O'Brien, the stamps on her work are related to her unhappy childhood. Her father, Michael O'Brien, was an irresponsible man who drank too much. Her mother, Lena, suffered silently while trying to raise her four children. O'Brien's parents reappear as characters in her fiction, where the heroine is always searching for adventure with a sense of guilt and betrayal, tormented by the belief that she is too excessive or not grateful for what she has. In many of O'Brien's stories, the heroine is plagued with the guilt of separating from a miserable, dangerous father. And O'Brien might have been thinking of her own mother in her description of Cait's mother at the beginning of *The Country Girls*: "She was waving. In her brown dress she looked sad; the farther I went, the sadder she looked. Like a sparrow in the snow, brown and anxious and lonesome" (*The Country Girls Trilogy and Epilogue*, 1986, p. 9). In her interview with Woodward, O'Brien described clearing out her mother's things after she had died and finding a defaced copy of *The Country Girls* hidden under a pillow. "The dedication page had been pulled out. She had gone through the book with black ink and a pen. She had effaced every outspoken word. She must have thought it was so awful. I wanted her to appear from the dead and confront me, I was that angry" (p. 42). Such complicated relationships between mothers and daughters are a central theme in much of O'Brien's work.

In her early childhood O'Brien was rarely exposed to literature. She explained in a *New York Times* interview with the author Philip Roth that the only books in her house were "prayer books, cookery books and blood stock reports" (cited in Woodward interview, p. 42). From 1936 to 1941 she attended the National School in Scariff, where her claim to fame was a botched performance of *Our Lady of Fatima* in the school play. At age twelve she was sent to the Convent of Mercy at Loughrea, County Galway, where she excelled as a student. (In many of O'Brien's narratives, convent school is the place where her heroines discover their aptitude and appetite for learning.) In 1946, after finishing high school, O'Brien left County Clare for Dublin, where she worked in a chemist's shop while studying to be a pharmacist. She submitted her first stories to the *Irish Press* in 1948. In 1952, despite the disapproval of her parents, she eloped with Ernest Gébler, an older writer, and moved with him to the country. She had two sons, Carlos and Sacha. The marriage dissolved in 1964.

By then O'Brien had moved to London, where she began working as a manuscript reader. The details of her relationship and breakup with her difficult husband are chronicled in *The Lonely Girl* (1962) and *Girls in Their Married Bliss* (1964), and the recurrent figure of an older, overbearing husband appears both in her short fiction and subsequent novels. While living in London and raising her children O'Brien published on average one novel or collection of short stories every two years. During this period she also adapted her novel *Zee & Company* (1971) into a screenplay, which was made into a movie (entitled *X, Y, and Zee*) starring Elizabeth Taylor, and wrote *Virginia*, a play about the life of Virginia Woolf that was staged in 1980 by the Stratford Shakespeare Festival in Ontario, Canada. Farrar, Straus and Giroux began publishing O'Brien's novels in the late 1980s, and she became a frequent contributor to the *New Yorker*. In the late 1990s she was living several months each year in New York City, teaching a course in creative writing at New York University, and also spending time in Ireland researching two novels, both of which concerned controversial issues of contemporary Irish politics.

Views of O'Brien's fiction have ranged from outraged criticism—for her frank depiction of women's desires, her politics, and from feminists, for ostensibly making her heroines passive victims—to adoration from fellow writers and students of literature who find O'Brien's prose stunning and her subjects haunting. She is often compared with Virginia Woolf and Colette. Others group her with Irish writers such as Oscar Wilde, W. B. Yeats, James Joyce, Sean O'Casey, and Samuel Beckett; like these authors, she left Ireland and wrote most of her work abroad. O'Brien cites Ernest Hemingway, Albert Camus, and William Faulkner as major influences on her work. She also shares a similar literary stage with contemporary British women writers including Margaret Drabble, Anita Brookner, and A. S. Byatt. Even though some of these writers have a more academic background than O'Brien (particularly Byatt), their work similarly concerns literary women who came of age in the 1960s and their struggle to define themselves as separate from their male counterparts. Dermot Bolger included O'Brien in his anthology, *The Vintage Book of Contemporary Irish Fiction* (1994); he sees O'Brien as part of an important second generation of Irish writers who came after pioneers such as Joyce and Beckett. According to Bolger, O'Brien and others paved the way for an emerging generation of Irish talents such as Patrick McCabe, Colm Toibin, and Anne Enright. In his introduction to the anthology Bolger explains that the connection among the writers in the book is their "sense of being engaged with understanding both their own and their parents' past" (p. xvi). This is exactly what O'Brien set out to do with her debut novel, and it is a subject with which she has been concerned ever since.

EARLY WORK: THE COUNTRY GIRLS TRILOGY

THREE decades after its publication, *The Country Girls* remains O'Brien's most famous novel. It tells the story of Cait, a dreamy, awkward redhead who struggles to find her own voice, and Baba, her more savvy, wisecracking counterpart, and loosely follows events in O'Brien's early life. Written in three weeks, the narrative has a breathless quality that O'Brien would later describe to Mary Battiata as "bloated, high flown and foolish really. I was so in love with writing that I didn't care, as long as I could keep on with it" (p. C1). Although the novel is clearly the work of a young writer, O'Brien immediately establishes her gift for description, her feel for the nuances of feelings and gestures, her ability to capture the tactile qualities of a landscape, and her indebtedness to a rich heritage of Irish literature and folklore. The landscape of her birthplace is as much a character in this novel as Cait and Baba. As the story unfolds, the wildness of the countryside is reflected in the character of Cait, who knows, despite the teachings of her family, church, and school, that there is something greater and far more exciting in the world outside the confines of her small town.

The novel begins with the image of Cait waking up, literally and figuratively: "I wakened quickly and sat up in bed abruptly. It is only when I am anxious that I waken easily and for a minute I did not know why my heart was beating faster than usual. Then I remembered. The old reason. He had not come home" (*The Country Girls Trilogy and Epilogue*, p. 3).

This opening could be an introduction to many of her subsequent heroines, all of whom find themselves waiting for their lives to happen, their thoughts distracted by a "he": a male figure who is coming, leaving, or just hovering. The "he" figure in this instance is Cait's father, who has been out on another drinking binge and has not returned. (In later novels, the men will be reckless lovers, angry ex-husbands, or misguided sons.)

As Cait gets out of bed she begins her narrative journey with the everyday details of country life. Here O'Brien echoes Joyce with the clarity and precision of specifics : the smell of frying bacon, the lawn "speckled with daisies that were fast asleep," "haloes of water" (p. 3) around the forget-me-nots. Soon we are introduced to Cait's mother, whose "blue eyes were small and sore. She hadn't slept" (p. 5). We also meet Hickey, the faithful farmhand: "His teeth were green, and the last thing at night he did his water in a peach tin that he kept under his bed" (p. 4). The family, we discover, lives in fear of the unpredictable father. Cait in fact is terrified that she will meet him on the road on her way to school. When Jack Holland, a friendly neighbor, sees her walking, he notes her father's overnight absence. She replies that things are well, "remembering Mama's maxim 'weep and you weep alone.'" The importance of suffering in isolation is a notion that Cait will always keep with her.

In contrast to the bleak position of her family, the majority of Cait's fantasy life centers on her fascination with a wealthy older man whom she nicknames Mr. Gentleman. She describes him as "a beautiful man who lived in the white house on the hill" (p. 12). Later he will become her first lover. Cait's other main preoccupation is Baba, her sometime nemesis and closest friend. O'Brien reveals how Cait sees herself through descriptions of how she compares with the stylish Baba: "I was wrapping myself up in the cloakroom when Baba came out. She said 'Cheerio' to Miss Moriarity. She was Miss Moriarity's pet, even though she was the school dunce. She wore a white cardigan like a cloak over her shoulders so that the sleeves dangled down idly. She was full of herself" (p. 19). Despite Baba's constant refrain that Cait is "right looking eejit," the two have an unspoken attachment to one another, a closeness that proves crucial to Cait when her mother dies unexpectedly in a boating accident.

O'Brien's matter-of-fact description of what Cait knows about her mother's death marks the beginning of Cait's discovery of a rich inner life. She sees that her only connection to her mother will be in her own thoughts:

They give me pills all that day, and Martha . . . painted her nails and polished them with a little buffer. . . . The phone rang sometime after lunch and Martha kept saying, 'Yes, I'll tell her' and 'Too bad' and 'Well I suppose that's that,' and then she came up and told me that they had dragged the great Shannon lake but they hadn't found them; she didn't say that they had given up, but I knew they had, and I knew that Mama would never have a grave for me to put flowers on. Somehow she was more dead than anyone I had ever heard of.
(pp. 44–45)

Her mother's death will continue to haunt her throughout the novel. In Cait's later life, her search for a parental figure becomes confused with her desire for a lover; both of her significant relationships are with older men. She begins an innocent affair with Mr. Gentleman, who takes her on day trips in his car and tells her, "You're the sweetest thing that ever happened to me" (p. 56). Naïve Cait falls in love with him: "My soul was alive; enchantment; something I had never known before. It was the happiest day of my whole life" (p. 56).

Cait continues to see Mr. Gentleman while she is living with Baba and her parents. Soon, however, the girls are sent to a dark and gloomy convent school. School establishes Cait as a student; she excels in reading and writing and she gets great pleasure out of her teacher's interest in her talents. After leaving the convent the two settle in Dublin, where Cait gets a job in a grocery store while Baba plots to secure them party invitations and dates with men who have money. Cait describes how she and Baba look in their new stage of independence: "Baba was small and thin, with her hair cut short like a boy's and little tempting curls falling onto her forehead. She was neat looking, and any man could lift her up in his arms and carry her off. But I was tall and gawky, with a bewildered look, and a mass of bewildered auburn hair" (p. 121).

Cait's idea that she is too gawky and awkward to be carried off reinforces the notion that she still believes that a man will rescue her and that she will not be a complete person until the "he" arrives. Fortunately, Mr. Gentleman finds Cait in Dublin. She has her first sexual experience with him in the living room of the boardinghouse where she and Baba live. This undoubtedly is one of the scenes that made the book so scandalous to certain Irish audiences. Mr. Gentleman, a married man, asks Cait to take off all of her clothes so that he can see all of her body. He then does the same. Cait laughs, explaining that "he was not half so distinguished out of his coal-black suit and stiff white shirt" (p. 164).

Soon after, Mr. Gentleman promises to take Cait away on a trip. She packs her things, hoping that she will be escaping with him to another life, but predictably she waits for hours at the train station. He never arrives. Instead she receives a telegram: "Everything gone wrong. Threats from your father. My wife has another nervous breakdown. Regret enforced silence. Must not see you" (p. 175). Like the death of her mother, Mr. Gentleman's disappearance marks another turning point in Cait's story. The end of *The Country Girls* echoes the beginning; Cait has experienced an awakening and is left waiting for another mysterious man to arrive and rescue her.

The Lonely Girls, O'Brien's next novel in the trilogy, begins with Cait reading F. Scott Fitzgerald's *Tender Is the Night.* She describes it as "a beautiful book, but sad . . . , I skipped half the words in my anxiety to read it quickly, because I wanted to know if the man would leave the woman or not. All the nicest men were in books—the strange, complex, romantic men, the ones I admired most" (*The Country Girls Trilogy and Epilogue,* p. 179). In this second installment of the lives of Cait and Baba, Cait's search for her own identity is still tied to her search for a man, but also to her love for reading and her literary fantasy of who the perfect man might be. Mr. Gentleman is gone, but into his place steps a new figure, Eugene Gaillard, an older filmmaker whom Cait and Baba meet at a magazine party. One can imagine that the character of Eugene is modeled on O'Brien's husband, Ernest Gébler, who was an older, accomplished writer when they first met.

From the outset Eugene sees Cait as a cute and innocent country bumpkin. Cait imagines that he is something fascinating and new. She explains, "I felt suddenly at home with him—I don't know why. He wasn't like anyone I knew; his face was long and had a gray color. It reminded me of a saint's face carved out of gray stone which I saw in the church every Sunday" (p. 185). Eugene and Cait begin a relationship even though they are clearly from different worlds. He brings her to his house in the country where she reads books from his extensive library collection and tries to avoid confrontations with his surly housemaid, Anna. Cait becomes more and more enthralled with Eugene and tries to impress him with newfound words. One day she tells him, "You have a look of mystique on your face." Eugene is not impressed. "His pale expression fell to pieces, and he hollered with laughter and asked where I had picked up such a word. I realized that it must have been the wrong word, but I had read it in some book and liked its sound." Eugene replies, "Dear girl, you'll have to give up reading books" (p. 222). The poignancy of the moment lies in the fact that while Cait thinks that she has made an embarrassing mistake, she is simply trying out words so that she can formulate her own language and write her own story, a process O'Brien herself is clearly engaged in as she writes these early novels.

Cait's past and present come into conflict again when her father arrives unexpectedly in Dublin and forces her to come home with him. Cait is miserable at home, yet she feels she must stay with her family because of an aunt who now lives with her father. O'Brien's description of Cait's aunt's history resembles an Irish ballad or folktale: "She had had her own sorrows. Her young love had been shot one morning on the Bridge of Killaloe, during the time of the Black and Tans. She had remained loyal to her murdered love and kept a picture of him in a gold locket on her neck" (p. 255). Although critics might see this moment as a self-conscious Irish flourish, it is one of the few places in the text where Cait acknowledges that she is tied to a political history and a past full of controversy and sacrifice, particularly among women. That Cait, and by extension O'Brien, is somewhat detached from politics at this point in her story signifies that she has not yet found her identity. Ultimately, however, she will come to understand that only by leaving Ireland and what it represents has she been able to discover what her heritage means to her. O'Brien's development as a writer has followed a similar path.

Despite warnings from the village doctor and priest that she must leave Eugene or be forever disgraced, Cait manages to escape back to Dublin with the help of an old family friend. Her decision to leave her family again is a decision to embrace a new life with Eugene. Unfortunately, she effectively moves from one domineering male presence to another. To make matters worse, her father does not give up easily. He arrives at Eugene's country home with a posse of Cait's unruly cousins to collect his daughter. In a hilarious scene, her relatives storm the house while she hides under the bed. Eugene barely escapes being shot, but he manages to convince her father that she has no intention of returning home.

At first Cait is happy with Eugene, but she quickly discovers that his cruelty is more powerful than her father's. She finds out that he has an ex-wife and daughter in America who still want to be in his life. She finds pieces of his past around the house—letters, toys, jewelry—that indicate she is just a guest, an unwelcome intruder in Eugene's world. In another plot twist, Baba arrives from Dublin and announces that she may be pregnant. Eugene offers to let her live with them. Although this development provides O'Brien with a narrative direction, she once again switches gears, and Baba's news turns out to be a false alarm.

Ultimately, Cait is unable to get along with Eugene, and the two girls sail off to London to begin a new chapter of their lives. Cait gets a job in a delicatessen and goes to London University at night. She comes to terms with the failure of her relationship and discovers once again that she is a natural student. In the end it may be literature and writing that save her. "Even Baba notices that I'm changing, and she says if I don't give up this learning at night, I'll end up as a right drip, wearing flat shoes and glasses. What Baba doesn't know is that I'm finding my feet, and when I'm able to talk I imagine that I won't be so alone, but maybe that too is an improbable dream" (p. 377).

Girls in Their Married Bliss, the third installment in the trilogy, begins with Baba's voice, which is jarring to the reader who is used to Cait's (whose name is now always spelled Kate). The novel alternates between Kate's and Baba's perspectives, a more sophisticated narrative technique for more sophisticated characters. Perhaps the use of Baba as a narrator is also O'Brien's way of distancing her readers from young Cait (a version of O'Brien's former self), whose voice has disappeared with her newfound maturity.

From the outset Baba's voice sounds almost like a parody of the Baba that has been represented in the previous novels: her language is deliberately crude, her tone irreverent and hip. On the first page she gives us the background for the novel: "We weren't here a year when she remet a crank called Eugene Gaillard whom she'd known in Ireland. They took up their old refrain, fell in love, or thought they did, and lost no time making puke out of it" (*The Country Girls Trilogy and Epilogue,* p. 381). Although Baba's sarcasm is an interesting contrast to Kate's more literary sensibility, her character seems strangely out of place when compared to the women characters in the two previous volumes. In fact, Baba's voice anticipates the more liberated heroines of O'Brien's next novels.

Baba is now married to Frank, a boring rich man who has given her everything she wants except a loving relationship. Kate has had a son with Eugene named Cash, who seems to be the only thing that is keeping her unhappy marriage together. The scenes with Cash introduce another important theme in O'Brien's work, a mother's unconditional love for her son—a bond that is very different from what the author sees as the fraught and complex relationship between mother and daughter. The novel begins with Eugene's discovery that Kate is having an affair. He sues her for divorce, and she goes to Baba for help. Eugene takes up with another woman and tries to take Cash away from her. Kate begins to lose her sense of reality and has a nervous breakdown on the street, the first sign that she may not be able to survive her choices. She describes her state of mind using images from her past: "To her there was something disastrous about losing grip on oneself, like a dead woman she'd seen once on the road with her clothes above her knees and one shoe a bog of blood" (p. 458). The memory of a dead woman in a "bog of blood" reminds the reader of the country landscape of Kate's childhood. Now in London, Kate is alone and vulnerable. She is exposed, like the woman in the road, and part of her has been cast aside.

Eventually, Eugene gains custody of Cash. Kate has herself sterilized and moves in with Baba. Without children, Baba and Kate are able to return to a childlike existence all their own. As Baba explains, "They would have each other, chats, their moments of recklessness; they could moan over plans that they'd both stopped believing in, long ago" (p. 507). The novel ends with a hope that maybe together Kate and Baba can salvage their lives and gain some strength from each other. Yet somehow Baba knows that part of Kate is already gone: "She was looking at someone of whom too much had been cut away, some important region that they both knew nothing about" (p. 508).

When the three novels were rereleased in 1986 as *The Country Girls Trilogy and Epilogue*, the epilogue finishes the story. In the new ending written from Baba's point of view, Kate commits suicide by slashing her wrists while Baba is left to make sense of the failures in her own life. In this version it is Baba's materialism that saves her while art, books, and romance fail to save her friend. Kate dies because she cannot learn to trust or like herself; she continues to believe that others will save her, as if she were a character in a novel. It is Baba's realism, her lack of education and sentiment, that keep her intact, a depressing implication for the possibilities for literary women. O'Brien finishes the epilogue with Baba's thoughts about Kate's son. The starkness of Baba's voice is poignant here, as if O'Brien has finally come to terms with her character: "I'm praying that her son won't interrogate me, because there are some things in this world that you cannot ask, and oh, Agnus Dei, there are some things in this world you cannot answer" (p. 532). The silences expressed here, of what is unspoken and unsaid, will continue to haunt O'Brien's heroines for years to come.

MIDDLE YEARS

AFTER *The Country Girls* and its two sequels, from 1965 to 1988 O'Brien wrote many novels, several volumes of short stories, a memoir, a play, and a screenplay. She introduced a new type of modern heroine, one who is featured in many of the novels in this period, and she continued to write about Irish girls and women, returning to many of the themes that she introduced in her first three novels. At this stage in her career, O'Brien garnered both positive and negative critical attention. While the author John Updike described her novel *Night* (1972) as a "beautiful and brilliant book," the critic Anatole Broyard wrote of her novel *Johnny I Hardly Knew You* (1977): "I hardly knew him either and I see no reason to regret his demise" (both cited in Haberstroh, p. 578). Her book *Mother Ireland* (1976) prompted the critic Denis Donoghue to offer: "Edna O'Brien, a famous and popular novelist, goes back to Ireland for a spell, a touch of nostalgia, a bit of grousing" (cited in Woodward's *New York Times* interview, p. 42).

Despite some lesser works, O'Brien developed important themes and narrative techniques in some of the novels written in the late 1960s and early 1970s that resurface in her subsequent work. A good example is her book *A Pagan Place* (1970), which takes place in the rural west of Ireland. The novel is about a young girl who, like Cait, is coming to terms with her sexuality. She has an affair with the village priest who eventually abandons her, and in order to redeem herself she joins a convent of nuns who wish to save the world. She leaves home without seeing her mother; she only hears a "howl" that will follow her for the rest of her life. Themes of hidden knowledge, abandonment, and betrayal operate on many levels in this novel and will continue to reappear as important issues in O'Brien's later work. As in *A Pagan Place*, many of O'Brien's narratives emphasize the idea that Irish mothers lead their daughters to believe in traditions that do not work in the modern world. Girls are unprepared for the power of sexuality and for the choices that they are often forced to make between their own bodies and their sense of religious piety and family honor.

A Pagan Place is told in the voice of an outside narrator. In an interview, O'Brien explained why she used this narrative technique: "I felt that in every person there are two selves: I suppose they would be called the ego and the alter ego. And then there's almost a kind of negative state where things happen to you and you're not really realizing that they're happening" (Haberstroh, p. 577). What is interesting and relevant about this technique is that it allows O'Brien to explore the split between mind and body common to the women of her narrative world, who are taught not to own their bodies and not to acknowledge either the pleasure or pain that can result from a sexual experience.

During this period O'Brien also wrote a series of novels that featured a new kind of heroine, a woman living in London who is trying to figure out how to survive on her own. The character is either divorced or just extricating herself from a relationship, and she will try anything, including various sexual encounters, experimentation with drugs, and travel to distant places to make up for the loss she has suffered. Each of these characters is haunted by a past that is more conventional than her present life, and her attempts to be unconventional only make matters worse. There is no sense of closure at the end of these stories. The heroine takes readers on a psychological journey, but we don't arrive anywhere. Like Kate in *Girls in Their Married Bliss*, these women are exiles, trying to recreate a sense of home they have left behind.

O'Brien's "modern" heroines are featured in the novels *August Is a Wicked Month* (1965), *Casualties of Peace* (1966), and *Johnny I Hardly Knew You*, which were anthologized together as *The Edna O'Brien Reader* in 1994. In an introduction to the collection O'Brien explains, "I wrote these novels . . . at a time when I was particularly concerned with the fate of women. These concerns and (sometimes) furies still preoccupy me but with a different perspective—as I change, the work imperceptibly changes" (p. ix). In these books, which variously concern the death of a son, murder of a lover, and mourning for a lost relationship, passion equals destruction, death, and loss of self for the narrator. The heroines try desperately to "find themselves" but seem forever lost in their desire to be rescued. In response, perhaps, to some criticism of these works, in the introduction O'Brien adds, "I have been accused, often by women, of depicting victims, and indeed I would be the first to agree that my heroines are not blithe spirits, but neither are they victims. It is too simplified a label" (p. x).

During this period O'Brien also developed her gift for writing short stories, many of which are collected in *A Fanatic Heart* (1984). The title is borrowed from a stanza of Yeats's "Remorse for Intemperate Speech," which beautifully encompasses many of O'Brien's central themes: the scars of exile and betrayal and the ever-present power of motherhood:

> Out of Ireland have we come
> Great hatred, little room,
> Maimed us at the start.
> I carry from my mother's womb
> A fanatic heart.

A Fanatic Heart includes selections from *Returning* (1981), *The Love Object* (1968), *A Scandalous Woman* (1974), *A Rose in the Heart* (1979), and uncollected stories from 1979 to 1981, some of which originally appeared in the *New Yorker*.

In his introduction to the book Philip Roth praises O'Brien's careful use of language: "The sensibility is on two levels and shuttles back and forth, combining the innocence of childhood with the scars of maturity. It is what gives these stories their wounded vigor. The words themselves are chiseled. The welter of emotion is rendered so sparsely that the effect is merciless, like an autopsy" (p. viii). Indeed, many of these stories focus on children reconciling themselves to the mistakes of their parents, or on adult women who often have made disastrous choices. These themes are linked by O'Brien's attention to details, her rendering of a particular landscape, the descriptions of Irish village life, the eccentric figures of the present along with the ghostly legends of the past, and the longings of girls and women to imagine themselves into lives with possibilities.

It is possible to read the collection as a kind of novel with different characters inhabiting the same world. The narrator often is an adult who has left the country life of her childhood and is now trying to understand what the past has meant to her and why it stays with her. The narrator of "The Connor Girls," a woman who has left the small Irish town of her youth, tells the story of Amy Connor, one of the daughters of a wealthy, mysterious Protestant family that lives down the road. The narrator remembers Amy's beauty: "Her skin was soft and her brown eyes had caught the reflection of her orange neck scarf and gave her a warm theatrical glow" (p. 9). Despite her advantages the lovely Amy was disgraced by her doomed love affair with a Catholic bank clerk. The narrator recalls that Amy was devastated and rumored to be out of her mind. Years later, when the narrator returns home with her Protestant husband, she sees Miss Amy, who "showed no signs of her past despair." Amy offers a sweet to the son of the narrator, whose husband rudely makes the child give back the candy. In that moment the narrator sees "that by choosing [her husband's] world I had said good-bye to my own and to those in it. By such choices we gradually become exiles, until at last we are quite alone" (p. 16). Amy's story thus provides the narrator with a way to describe her own choices.

Other stories, such as "Sister Imelda," "The Doll," and "Irish Revel," are coming-of-age tales in which the narrator learns something about herself through unusual circumstances and relationships. The protagonist in "Irish Revel" thinks she has been invited to an elaborate party by a wealthier neighbor but discovers that she has been asked only to help with the preparations and serving the guests. In "Sister Imelda" a young girl forms an intense friendship with one of the nuns at her convent school, a relationship that ends when she discovers boys and the outside world. "The Doll," by contrast, is about a perverse teacher who steals the narrator's special doll. Her mother tells her that the teacher was "probably teasing" and that she would return the doll in a day or so, but the narrator knows better. She describes trying to see the doll through the teacher's window: "Passing by their window, I would look in. I could not see her because the china cabinet was in a corner, but I knew where she was, as the maid Lizzie told me. I would press my forehead to the window and call to the doll and say that I was thinking of her and that rescue was being hatched" (p. 51). Years later the narrator returns to the village for a funeral. The teacher is gone, but the "confiscated doll," now "gray and moldy," is still in the same cabinet. The narrator chides herself for caring so much about the doll and for letting the crime go unpunished. She sees that she has escaped her past but must continue to escape every time she returns home.

Several of the stories feature accomplished adult heroines who are also discovering hidden sides of themselves. In "The Plan," the narrator describes her intention to confront her lover at a party where he will be with his wife. Here O'Brien displays her talent as a dramatist, for the story reads like an extended monologue. As the protagonist describes the details of her ill-fated love affair, she tries to anticipate what will happen when she sees her lover and his wife together. The "plan" is to pretend to befriend the wife. The narrator explains: "I shall join the group that his wife is in. I know that she will want to talk to me. I know that she will detach herself from the others and veer toward me, that she will talk about everything under the sun" (p. 451). With all of this new information the heroine is sure that she can control her lover. Her last words are: "I scarcely know what will happen. All I know is that I cannot endure it alone, and as they have become a part of my life I shall become a part of theirs; our lives, you see, are intertwined, and if they destroy me they cannot hope to be spared" (p. 452). O'Brien's familiar themes of tortured romance and male cruelty are here given a twist with her presentation of a character like Lady Macbeth, a heroine as frightening as she is seductive. Even though she relies on desperate tactics, she takes matters into her own hands.

In "A Rose in the Heart of New York," a daughter tells the story of her relationship with her mother, whom she adored as a child but could not communicate with as an adult. The story begins with a graphic scene of the daughter's difficult birth. Even though the mother wasn't interested in her at first, the two soon become inseparable. Eventually the daughter grows up and moves away from home. She becomes more estranged from her mother, who seems to be living in a different world. When she attempts to get closer to her mother by taking her on a vacation, the results are disastrous. The two women have nothing in common, and all the daughter's attempts at reconciliation are thwarted by the mother's inflexibility. After the mother dies the daughter finds an envelope addressed to her. Inside the envelope she finds money and trinkets but no letter. She imagines what her mother might have written had she left her daughter a note, "words such as 'Buy yourself a jacket' or 'Have a night out' or 'Don't spend this on the masses.' She wanted something, some communiqué. But there was no such thing" (p. 404). Without any words to guide her, the daughter is left to make sense of her feelings: "A new wall had arisen, stronger and sturdier than before. Their life together and all those exchanges were like so many spilt feelings and she looked to see some sign, or hear some murmur. Instead a silence filled the room and there was a vaster silence beyond as if the house itself had died or had been carefully put down to sleep" (p. 404). O'Brien ends this story as she ends others in the collection, refusing to provide simple answers to any of the questions she poses. Instead, she leaves her protagonist in a moment of suspended silence: the character has realized something, but it is an uneasy emotion that gives no sense of closure.

Although her novel *The High Road* (1988), about a woman who travels to the Mediterranean, was not critically successful, her short-story collection *Lantern Slides* (1990) was very well received and earned her a Los Angeles Times Book Review Prize for Fiction. Her reputation in the United States was growing, but, as Woodward explains, she was recognized only in select circles (Woodward, p. 42).

Her next book, *Time and Tide* (1992), reworks many of the issues left unresolved at the end of *The Country Girls Trilogy*. After revising the ending of the last volume and doing away with the character of Kate, O'Brien has seemingly recast her in a different form to continue her narrative in *Time and Tide*. At the opening of the novel, the narrator, Nell, realizes that her marriage is falling apart. Like Kate's experiences with Eugene, Nell discovers that her husband is cruel and patronizing. She leaves him and assumes the task of raising her two young sons alone. Much of the novel details Nell's struggle to rediscover herself and at the same time remain a good mother to her children. As they grow older and go away to school, Nell begins to lose herself in an ill-conceived love affair. One of her sons also becomes lost in a world of drugs, and Nell is powerless to save him. He eventually drowns in a terrible accident. In the end Nell finds that in coming to terms with her son's death she makes peace with her own failures. In her subsequent work O'Brien would become less focused on retelling versions of her own history and more concerned with the way that many stories connect to shape versions of a collective history.

LATER WORK: HOUSE OF SPLENDID ISOLATION *AND* DOWN BY THE RIVER

O'BRIEN's novel *House of Splendid Isolation* (1994), about an Irish widow's unexpected and moving relationship with an Irish Republican Army terrorist, marked a new period in her work. Unlike *Time and Tide*, which received mixed reviews, the next novel was well received on both sides of the Atlantic and won her new respect from many Irish

readers. The *Irish Voice* hailed the book as "a brave and important work . . . convincing psychological mystery. . . . A resounding work that is virtually unique." The *Irish Times* called it "a kind of tour de force, a brilliant experiment in political fiction."

O'Brien's accomplishment here is her presentation of many sides of the political situation in contemporary Ireland. There is no escape for anyone in the story, regardless of political affiliation, because in O'Brien's world everyone shares a history, whether or not they acknowledge its power and even if they do everything to avoid its tenacious grasp. The title introduces a central paradox of the book: a house, a place traditionally associated with warmth, domesticity, and protection, is instead portrayed as a place of "splendid isolation." The book is divided into sections that are like beautifully interwoven short stories. With this novel O'Brien found a way to combine her greatest skills in both short and long fiction. She begins and ends the novel with sections entitled "The Child," a device that gives the book a historical framework, as if the anonymous narrator is somehow inextricably related to the people and events in the story.

The book opens with an image of the house: "History is everywhere. It seeps into the soil, the subsoil. Like rain, or hail, or snow, or blood. A house remembers. An outhouse remembers. A people ruminate. The tale differs with the teller" (p. 1). As in a Greek tragedy, O'Brien reveals everything and nothing at the beginning of the novel. The story will be about memories and blood, about what people remember and what they choose to forget. It is also clear at the outset that O'Brien is experimenting with a crisper language. Her sentences are shorter and more deliberate. The effect is similar to that of clever editing in a movie: O'Brien rapidly cuts from one scene to the next, using flashbacks and other cinematic techniques to fill in the details of the characters' histories.

We meet McGreevy, an accomplished IRA operative, as he is escaping from the police. O'Brien's description of his hiding place introduces the powerful resonances of the Irish landscape for all of the characters. McGreevy is "scarcely breathing, curled up inside the hollow of a tree once struck by lightning; cradle and coffin, foetus and corpse" (p. 7). The image of a tree struck by lightning, holding the past, present, and future for its occupant, is a metaphor for Ireland's divided identity. O'Brien constantly reminds her readers that what gives birth to us may also destroy us. The idea of destruction relates to the larger political context of the story, but as we read further we discover that destructive forces are also operating on a more insidious level, within the average Irish family.

The scene with McGreevy is followed by a scene with Rory (the detective out to catch McGreevy) at home with his wife and children. The tension in the household is clear as Rory tries to avoid his wife's attempts to talk to him. Rory, the man who is supposed to be the "good" person, is happiest when he is shooting deer, something that his wife cannot understand. In contrast to the thrill Rory gets from conquering an animal, McGreevy interrupts his escape to help a cow give birth to a calf that is trapped inside her. Thus, O'Brien emphasizes the unexplained ironies of each man's character. With McGreevy and Rory, O'Brien creates new kinds of male characters. These men are not nearly as complex as the main heroine, Josie, but they are more sympathetic than the one-dimensional lovers and angry ex-husbands of her earlier work.

At the end of the first chapter we are introduced to Josie, an old woman at home with her nurse. For readers to understand Josie's importance to the story we must first hear about her past. Josie's arrival at the house of splendid isolation, her unhappy marriage, and her coming of age are detailed in a chapter that is in itself a beautifully crafted narrative that begins like a nineteenth-century novel: "Long ago she had come as a bride, a bride with a loose fox collar over her velvet outfit. . . . Her husband shouted, took the reins, and steered them around to the second lot of gates, the imposing silver gates which led to the front of the house and which were ceremoniously opened" (p. 29).

The silver gates open onto Josie's new life with her husband, James, a wealthy farmer. She soon learns that although the house is majestic and she has her own servants, her husband is cruel and unforgiving. As usual, O'Brien describes Josie's state of mind using images of the landscape. On a boat ride with her husband, Josie observes: "The water was so still that it looked like glass, with here and there bubbles on it, as if spat on. She kept seeing herself in it, her face all distorted" (p. 31). As Josie feels increasingly trapped, James becomes more menacing. In an attempt to taunt her, he tells a crude story about the mating habits of the female mayfly, who lays eggs until she dies and "makes the play and does all the tricks." Josie asks, "Do the males die too?" (p. 37).

Like many of O'Brien's heroines, Josie realizes that she has no choice but to succumb to her husband. She describes her life with him as an endless waiting game: waiting for him to come home drunk, waiting for him not to come home at all, waiting for her own life to begin. "Everything seemed to be in waiting: the dead animals, the trees, the fields, and the mountains all suspended in an eerie, breezeless stiffness" (p. 45). In time Josie becomes pregnant. She is desperate to get rid of her unborn child. She describes how the baby "cried inside the walls of her womb. It was more like a banshee than a child. She prayed that she would lose it, that its crying meant it did not want to live" (p. 49). She loses her child (we aren't told how) and this loss turns out to be a blessing because James's drinking becomes so much of a problem that he is sent away to a monastery for a short time to recuperate. Yet in other ways, Josie's inability to have children only enhances her sense of isolation. The death of her child foreshadows the many losses yet to come in her life.

In another self-fulfilling prophecy, Josie inadvertently causes her husband's death. James decides to harbor a fugitive on the run from the police. In a fit of anger Josie slips a note under the police sergeant's door, describing the man's whereabouts. When the police come at night to find him in the fields around the house, they shoot the drunken James by mistake. Josie's account of the events reads like a detailed confession:

How was she to know where it would end? How was she to know that her husband would go up that night under the cover of darkness, or that the Guards would be waiting, or that her husband would be drunk, or that in the brawl, fire would be exchanged and her husband fatally wounded? Yes, the dark threads of history looping back and forth and catching her and people like her in their grip, like snares.

(p. 58)

James's death is one of the threads of history that will eventually connect Josie's past to McGreevy's; she too has committed a crime, a kind of murder. She has secrets that make her morally "suspect." For Josie and "the people like her"—those who are not even directly involved in the fighting—there is no escape. They are snared in a situation that was not of their making. The images of threads, webs, loops, and snares all suggest that there is a collective weaving of history going on at many levels.

In the next section of the novel, entitled "Captivity," we are back in the present and Josie is once again an elderly woman. Ironically, as if she were rewriting the previous section of the novel, Josie here recalls some very sympathetic details about her relationship with James. She explains that although they were at odds in the beginning of the marriage, as time went on and James became more vulnerable, the two experienced a connection to one another. Here, O'Brien suggests that not only does the story differ with the teller, but that the teller's story can differ depending on her age and perspective. Josie's revisions are like the threads of history, always looping back and forth, stories enmeshed without a clear beginning, middle, and end. The metaphor of history as a web of interlocking narratives is thus mirrored in O'Brien's own narrative structure.

Although the reader is ready for the two protagonists to meet at this point in the novel, McGreevy's entrance into the house is still very disturbing:

What it took was the turning of the wooden knob, two, three swivels, then a wrench because of its loose threading, the door itself swinging back and forth quietly but with a livid glee, then a face hooded, eyeballs prominent, eyes like grit, and a voice reasoned telling her not to move and not to scream, saying it several times. He lowers his gun when he sees that the only thing confronting him is an elderly woman in a four-poster bed, clutching the strings of her bedjacket.

(pp. 65–66)

O'Brien creates quick, precise images in this passage, mirroring the way memory works. Pieces of events come back to Josie in flashes, yet the reader experiences them in the present tense, just as he or she might have lived the story. Once McGreevy is convinced that Josie's house is isolated enough he takes up residence, and the two begin an uneasy existence together. McGreevy reveals that he found out about Josie and her house through one of her old servants who was also a member of "the organization." He recalls a story that the servant told him about Josie's affair with the village priest. This is a piece of Josie's personal history that O'Brien has not touched on, so it is an interesting twist when McGreevy has more information about Josie than the reader. O'Brien further complicates the authority of her narrator by switching at moments from an outside perspective to Josie's diary and McGreevy's letter to Josie, which he writes in order to justify his presence in her house. As the novel progresses these layers of voices will uncover more layers of secrets.

At first McGreevy and Josie cautiously avoid one another and communicate only when necessary. Josie feels displaced and nervous; she "walks through her several rooms in order to confirm them as hers" (p. 76). Eventually they begin to have tense conversations in which she challenges his position. She says, "If women ran your organisation there would be no shooting . . . no bombs" (p. 82). When McGreevy retorts that there have been many women involved, Josie shoots back, "Then they're not mothers." McGreevy replies, "How would you know whether they're mothers or not?"

Through their back-and-forth commentary, O'Brien gets at questions of Irish politics at the same moment she is developing a relationship between the two characters. Josie writes in her diary: "The saddest bit is that we're the same stock, the same faith, we speak the same tongue and yet we don't. Language to each of us is a Braille that the other cannot know" (p. 93). As Josie feels more sympathy for McGreevy she begins to share things with him. At one point she gives him a tackle box that belonged to her husband:

"I'll tell you what. . . . It's more a thing for a man than a woman," she says, and thrusts the tin into his hands with something akin to joy. So long since she has given anyone anything, since she has had the opportunity to. He says she will miss it, surely. She insists. Everything happens then; his eyes grateful and shy, like magnets brushed with gold, and something soft and yielding in his bearing, as if drenched in moonlight.

(p. 99)

Just as McGreevy is beginning to reveal hidden aspects of himself, O'Brien reminds the reader that people are still looking for him and they are closing in fast. Time is running out. Josie explains, "I can't go back and I can't go forward" (p. 123). In the next section, entitled "Love Affair," she will go back one last time to tell us the story of her passionate love affair with the priest, her greatest sin and her deepest joy. Interspersed with her story are vignettes in which McGreevy thinks of his love for his wife, who, like Josie's husband, is also dead. O'Brien suggests that their love for others is what ultimately connects them in their depth of feeling.

In the final section, "Last Days," the novel progresses quickly toward tragedy. Rory tracks

McGreevy to Josie's house. She lies for McGreevy to buy some time, but the police can see that she "knows too much." In her last hours Josie leaves a note to be "opened after my death" in which she confesses to aborting her child, another acknowledged sin that brings her closer to McGreevy. When the guards storm the house it is Josie who dies and McGreevy who lives. She saves him in a way that she could not save her own child. As the police are closing in she thinks to herself: "He must be taken alive. His life has many chapters to it and many evolutions. They do not know that. But she knows it, because she knows him" (p. 221).

The "child" ends the novel, again speaking in the first person. Is the child O'Brien herself, speaking about her own history? Or is the child Josie's unborn infant? Whoever she is, she has no certain answers except to say that the land will still be there. "History has proved that." It is the inhabitants who will have to make peace with themselves and each other. "To go in, within, is the bloodiest journey of all. Inside, you get to know—that the same blood and the same tears drop from the enemy as from the self" (p. 232).

O'Brien again takes on politically sensitive subject matter with *Down by the River* (1997), the story of a young Irish girl who is raped by her father and tries to obtain a legal abortion in England while angry groups of lawyers and activists try to prevent her from getting rid of her baby. The plot is based on the 1992 case of a teenage rape victim in Ireland, whose struggle to get a legal abortion in England created a storm of controversy that reached both sides of the Atlantic and ultimately resulted in a national referendum on abortion law. The book took three years to write and O'Brien spent time in Ireland gathering information, interviewing barristers, and attending antiabortion rallies.

Reaction to the novel was mixed. Although some critics praised O'Brien's daring, her "devouring eye for detail," and her "blend of insight, intellect and poetry," others criticized what they thought of as her newfound political interests as well as her obsessive emphasis on particular images and themes. In a 1996 interview with Denis Staunton (*Observer*, p. 18), O'Brien said of her detractors, "Perhaps my fiction is too naked for them. They like less piercing stuff, less disturbing. That may be why they still bypass me." O'Brien's sympathies in *House of Splendid Isolation* were multilayered, but here there is no question whose side she

is on, and no question that many of the issues she tackled in the 1960s with *The Country Girls* were alive and well in Ireland thirty years later.

Readers familiar with O'Brien's work may have a sense of déjà vu with *Down by the River,* but although we have met versions of some of the characters before, seen some of the images, and witnessed some of the events, we have never seen them in this context. O'Brien uses an outside narrator to tell Mary's story. (Later in the novel she will offer us sections of Mary's diary.) As in *House of Splendid Isolation,* O'Brien's use of an outside narrator reminds the reader that this story reaches beyond Mary's individual experience, for it is also the story of many other Irish women of the past and the present. In this way O'Brien continues to write a version of Irish history.

O'Brien begins the novel as she often does, with a description of the landscape. This time it is near the place where the act of incest occurs: "The road silent, somnolent yet with a speech of its own, speaking back to them, father and child, through trappings of sun and fretted verdure, speaking of old mutinies and a fresh crime mounting in the blood" (p. 1). Setting the tone for the rest of the story, O'Brien alternates between prose and poetic and precise descriptions of what Mary is feeling when her father touches her:

In the instance of his doing it, she thought she had always known that it would happen, or that it had happened, this, a re-enactment of a petrified time. To impede him she stood up and made fidgety bustly movements, remarking that they had better be getting back. . . . Darkness then, a weight of darkness except for one splotch of sunlight on his shoulder and all of the differing motions, of water, of earth, of body, moving as one, on a windless day.

(pp. 3–4)

After it is over Mary tells herself, "It does not hurt if you say it does not hurt," even though she knows that nothing is "ever the same again" and "there is no one that she can ask" to help her. The opening ends with an image of the barristers, the lawmakers in the city with their coifed wigs, "their juniors a few paces behind them laden with briefs and ledgers. . . . Men of principle who know nothing of the road or the road's soggy secret will one day be called to adjudicate upon it, for all is always known, nothing is secret, all is known and scriven upon the tablet of time" (pp. 5–6). The juxtaposition of the "civilized" enclosed chambers of the court with the barbaric wildness of the country underscores the idea that the two worlds have no common ground, and that the novel will take us into the realm of the "soggy road" with images we will not forget.

In some ways Mary's life is similar to the childhood of Cait (heroine of *The Country Girls*). She lives in a small rural village on a farm with her angry alcoholic father and loving but powerless mother, although Mary has the additional burden of not being able to tell her secret. She is sure that everyone "knows already," and everything around her seems to remind her of her father's brutality. The sight of two horses mating in a field makes her cry. She is sure that the image of Our Lady on her wall is mocking her, and she cannot suppress her wish to run and continue running.

Interspersed with Mary's thoughts are scenes of village antiabortion activists. The leader, Roisin (a name tellingly close to "poison"), shows the other women two pictures, one of a "contented baby, curled up in a womb" and another of a "torn baby, its body mangled, pools of black blood in the crevices and in the empty crater of its head" (p. 16). When one member of the group brings up the question of unwanted pregnancy due to scandal, rape, or incest, another member suggests that girls who undergo such trauma have a hormone that stops them from wanting to drown themselves— "It's medically proven," she says.

Soon after the rape, Mary asks to be sent away to school at a convent. Her experience there is a lovely respite from her life at home: "She shone at lessons and when a nun praised her she blushed" (p. 33). For a time it seems that Mary has escaped her father, but her mother becomes ill with cancer and she is called home. As elsewhere in O'Brien's fiction, when her mother dies the heroine realizes that there was much left unsaid and that her mother is still in some ways alive: "Mary let out a little shriek when she saw her mother's expression, a more alive than dead determining in it. There was a snarl at the corner of her mouth, her upper lip raised in a helpless and grotesque curl" (p. 56).

Left at home alone with her father, Mary witnesses another side of him when he helps a horse give birth. As in *House of Splendid Isolation,* in which the terrorist McGreevy assists in the delivery of a calf, this moment of unexpected tenderness helps to make the brutal male figure more human. Mary sees her father in a different way after this birth: "The absolute and instantaneous rapport with the animal, so tender and true such as he had never shown her or her mother or possibly anyone. She thinks then that if she could be a child, maybe if she can be truly a child and make her needs known, he can feel as a father" (p. 63).

Unlike McGreevy, however, who becomes more sympathetic as the novel progresses, Mary's father is redeemed only in fleeting moments—and not because of his own actions but because of the way Mary sees him and wishes he could be. She soon realizes she was mistaken in thinking that her father's kindness to animals would translate to her, and she escapes to the city. Just when the reader thinks she will be safe, the police arrive and drag her back to her father. In a horrifying scene, Mary tells her father that she is pregnant, and he tries to give her an abortion with a broom handle. She lies to get him to stop, telling him that it is working. She then attempts to drown herself in the river, but she is rescued by Betty, a neighbor walking her dog.

Eventually Betty becomes Mary's savior, taking her to England so she can have a legal abortion. But in their rush to leave, Betty leaves evidence behind detailing their whereabouts, and the police catch up with them. At this point the case becomes a national scandal. Mary is sent to live with her cousin Veronica, who is instructed to watch her and care for her until the baby comes. Meanwhile everyone is talking about Mary, on the streets, in the papers, and on radio talk shows. Here the focus of the novel moves outward, as the narrative centers less on Mary's point of view and more on the arguments about her. One caller to the radio show remarks, "I think the poor kid is a human football" (p. 187).

In the end Mary's lawyers force a confession out of Mary's father, who finally gives his "permission" for the case to go to trial. Before a verdict can be decided, Mary has a sudden and bloody miscarriage, which occurs a few pages after a violent description of her father's suicide. Although there is no legal justice for Mary, she does receive a kind of natural justice. The novel ends with Mary's voice—"a great crimson quiver of sound going up, up to the skies" (p. 265)—and with the suggestion that she has somehow reconnected with her damaged self, which now has the chance to heal.

CONCLUSION

IF there is one common quality in Edna O'Brien's work it is the passion she brings to whatever issue she is grappling with. Whether she is writing about love, betrayal, history, or politics, her keen sensitivity to language allows her to construct vibrant, memorable images along with a nuanced, emotional landscape for her heroines. At the end of the 1990s she was said to be working on several projects, including a novel about a murder in Ireland and a screenplay about Yeats's muse, Maud Gonne. Yet despite her numerous publications, her considerable critical acclaim, and her heartfelt interest in her native country, O'Brien was still often put in the position of defending herself. "I'm tired of being told that I don't know anything about Ireland," she explained to Helen Meany of the *Irish Times*. "That is not to say that it's the same as yours or some other writer's" (p. 12). O'Brien's Ireland is a changing Ireland, and as she herself has progressed as an author, so too have her characters. In many ways O'Brien has already achieved what she set out to do as a country girl: to revise the formula for the Irish heroine. She no longer waits for the "he" but instead writes her own script, without a final act. In O'Brien's words, "Some writers know the end when they start. I'm interested in the journey" (Rourke interview, *Los Angeles Times*, pt. E, p. 1).

SELECTED BIBLIOGRAPHY

I. NOVELS. *The Country Girls* (London and New York, 1960); *The Lonely Girl* (London and New York, 1962); *Girls in Their Married Bliss* (London, 1964; New York, 1968); *August Is a Wicked Month* (London and New York, 1965); *Casualties of Peace* (London, 1966; New York, 1967); *The Love Object* (London, 1968; New York, 1969); *A Pagan Place* (London and New York, 1970); *Zee & Co.: A Novel* (London, 1971); *Night* (London, 1972; New York, 1973); *Johnny I Hardly Knew You* (London, 1977), republished as *I Hardly Knew You* (Garden City, N.Y., 1978); *The High Road* (New York and London, 1988); *Time and Tide* (New York, 1992); *House of Splendid Isolation* (New York, 1994); *Down by the River* (New York, 1997).

II. OTHER WORKS / COLLECTIONS. *A Scandalous Woman: Stories* (London and New York, 1974); *Mother Ireland* (London and New York, 1976); *Seven Novels and Other Short Stories* (London, 1978); *Mrs. Reinhardt and Other Stories* (London, 1978), republished as *A Rose in the Heart* (Garden City, N.Y., 1979); *Virginia: A Play* (London and New York, 1981; rev. ed. San Diego, 1985); *Returning: Tales* (London, 1982; New York, 1983); *A Fanatic Heart: Selected Stories* (New York, 1984); *The Country Girls Trilogy and Epilogue* (New York, 1986); *Lantern Slides: Stories* (New York and London, 1990); *An Edna O'Brien Reader* (New York, 1994).

III. CRITICAL STUDIES. Lotus Snow, " 'That Trenchant Childhood Route'? Quest in Edna O'Brien's Novels," in *Eire-Ireland: A Journal of Irish Studies* 14, no. 1 (1979); Patricia Boyle Haberstroh, "Edna O'Brien," in Jay L. Halio, ed., *Dictionary of Literary Biography*, vol. 14, pt. 2, *British Novelists since 1960* (Detroit, 1982–1983); David Herman, "Textual You and Double Deixis in Edna O'Brien's *A Pagan Place*," in *Style* 28 (fall 1994); Michael Patrick Gillespie, "(S)he Was Too Scrupulous Always: Edna O'Brien and the Comic Tradition," in Theresa O'Connor, ed., *The Comic Tradition in Irish Women Writers* (Gainesville, Fla., 1996); Frances M. Malpezzi, "Consuming Love: Edna O'Brien's 'A Rose in the Heart of New York,' " in *Studies in Short Fiction* 33 (summer 1996).

IV. REVIEWS AND INTERVIEWS. Mary Battiata, "Edna O'Brien's Toil of the Heart," in *Washington Post* (8 April 1987); Richard B. Woodward, "Edna O'Brien: Reveling in Heartbreak," in *New York Times* (12 March 1989); Mary Rourke, "Spellbinder," in *Los Angeles Times* (17 June 1992); Megan Tresidder, "Sweet Prose from Bitter Experience," in *Sunday Telegraph* (13 September 1992); Terry Coleman, "Sins and Lovers," in *Guardian* (31 March 1994); James Clarity, "At Lunch With: Edna O'Brien," in *New York Times* (30 August 1995); Denis Staunton, "Edna O'Brien, Sexual Revolutionary," in *Observer* (4 August 1996); Helen Meany, "Bravo, Edna," in *Irish Times* (24 August 1996).

BEN OKRI

(1959–   )

Gabriel Brownstein

BEN OKRI WROTE his first novel, *Flowers and Shadows* (1980), when he was nineteen. He won England's prestigious Booker Prize in 1991, when he was in his early thirties. In the six years after winning the Booker Prize, he published three novels, a volume of poetry, and two collections of essays.

Okri, a Nigerian living in England, is as ambitious as he is prolific. An experimental writer who seeks to abandon conventional European notions of plot and character, he uses lavish language to create nightmarish worlds in which the realities of African slum life are presented as phantasmagorias of horror. His characters and narrators accept the miraculous with the same complacency that they accept the depredations of ghetto life. The mythic, the dreamed, and the experienced are equally valid and present in Okri's world. A child views his father's violent outbursts with the same distanced fascination with which he regards a sudden rainstorm, an awful vision come to life from a dream, or a political rally that turns suddenly to riot.

Okri's writing, he insists, is not surrealist; rather, it is "a realism with many more dimensions" than conventional Western naturalism offers (Ross, p. 338). For Okri conventional realism is insufficient to describe the complexities of African life; he must seek other orders of representation to characterize and portray the world in which he grew up:

If my characters are going to be set in Nigeria and I am going to write about them truthfully, I've got several different options. First, I've got the option of naturalism, which means I write about them from the viewpoint that only what I see is what exists. Secondly, I have got the mythic dimension, which is a very important part of our world view. It's not separable from anything else. Third, I've got all the different dimensions of our world view plus naturalism. So what seems like surrealism or fantastic writing actually is not fantastic writing, it's simply writing about the place in the tone and spirit of the place. . . . All I'm trying to do is write about the world from the world view of that place so that it is true to the characters.

(Ross, p. 337)

Okri did not begin writing with this multidimensional outlook. His early novels could be described as conventionally naturalistic; from one book to the next, however, he has sought to explore ever more "dimensions" of the real, to demonstrate, as he says, that from the African point of view the mythic is not easily separable from the experienced. Thus far Okri's work has been marked by a clear trajectory: a move from naturalism in his first two books, *Flowers and Shadows* (1980) and *The Landscapes Within* (1981); to what might be called magic realism in his two collections of stories, *Incidents at the Shrine* (1986) and *Stars of the New Curfew* (1988), and also in the Booker Prize–winning *The Famished Road* (1991); to fairy tale, pure and simple, in *Astonishing the Gods* (1995). One can see the writer's work as a continuous project, in which Okri consistently seeks a "true" way of representing Africa.

This project is terribly audacious, and Okri reinvents himself constantly, with varying degrees of success. When he succeeds in drawing on traditional African mythologies and narrative forms that meld the real and the fantastic, the resultant work is remarkably original, powerful, and compelling. When Okri fails, his metaphors split the mythic from the natural, and the work lacks cohesion and drive.

Okri wrote his first two novels—*Flowers and Shadows* and *The Landscapes Within*—before he was twenty-one. Both books are studies of sensitive young men on the cusp of adulthood. In each book a crisis forces the protagonist to come in contact with the seamier side of slum life. The novels are remarkable for their cool portraits of a wild, impoverished city. Jane Bryce remarked in regard to *Flowers and Shadows*, "Okri spares us no detail of the smells, the jostling for buses, the excreta in the gutters, the clamour of the maimed, begging for coins" (p. 1047). Against this superreal backdrop Okri poses dreamy characters. Jeffia Okwe, the hero of *Flowers and Shadows*, tends to ask himself questions like "What happens when people die?" and "What makes people cry in their sleep?" (p. 169). Omovo, the young painter who is the hero of *The Landscapes Within*, is given to pronouncements such as "An African Mona Lisa would have nothing to smile about. Nothing" (p. 24).

Okri's first two books investigate the "dimensions" of the young protagonists' psychologies and the squalor of the world around them. But these novels are juvenilia that display great but undisciplined talent. In 1996 Okri himself wrote of *The Landscapes Within*, "The many things I wanted to accomplish were too ambitious for my craft at that time" (*Dangerous Love*, p. 325). It is in his two volumes of short fiction, *Incidents at the Shrine* and *Stars of the New Curfew*—published after his second novel and before his third—that Okri began to discover a way of writing very much his own. In these books he juxtaposes his fierce reportage of slum life with striking dreamlike images drawn from Nigerian mythologies. Here we begin to see "dimensions of realism" that lie beyond naturalism or psychological realism.

In many of these short, potent tales, Okri's characters leave cities haunted by terror, poverty, and filth, and in the African countryside discover strange spirit worlds, places where medicine men cut open their patients' bodies and draw forth rusted steel trash, and where deformed ghosts stroll casually out of houses built in trees. These are the works for which Okri first garnered great acclaim. In 1987 he was awarded the Commonwealth Writers' Prize for Africa and the *Paris Review*'s Aga Khan Prize.

He followed these collections with his greatest work, *The Famished Road* (1991). Here Okri's melding of the real and the magical finds its highest development. The long novel tells the tale of an *abiku*, a spirit child whose mind straddles the physical world and the netherworld. In place of a conventional linear plot, Okri builds his work in cyclical, almost musical patterns; conflicts and events repeat themselves, almost like choruses or refrains in a song. Over and over again the protagonist, Azaro (whose name is a corruption of Lazaro, or Lazarus), is tempted by death and then returns to life. The characters in this book—

Azaro's careworn mother; his father, an ex-boxer; and a local bar owner named Madame Koto—seem like figures in a pageant, more iconic than psychologically dense: they are blazingly present on the page, yet their interior worlds are curiously flat and unstudied. Okri gives his readers a wild dreamscape—the novel as conceived of by a Yoruba Hieronymus Bosch.

It is here, in *The Famished Road*, that Okri comes closest to his "realism with more dimensions," and it is in this book that his large ambitions are to a large degree fulfilled. Henry Louis Gates, Jr., wrote of *The Famished Road*:

The book's publication may well prove as significant for the evolution of the post-modern African novel as [Chinua] Achebe's *Things Fall Apart* was for the beginning of the tradition [of the black African novel in English] itself, or as Gabriel García Márquez's *One Hundred Years of Solitude* was for the novel in Latin America. . . . [Okri] has ushered the African novel into its own postmodern era through a compelling extension of traditional oral forms that uncover the future in the past.

(p. 20)

In Gates's view Okri is a revolutionary, reclaiming the African novel in English for Africa, removing it from the shadow of European tradition. K. Anthony Appiah, too, saw *The Famished Road* as without precedent in the black African novel in English: "Until now work of this rhetorical complexity has largely been found in Africa in Francophone fiction" ("Spiritual Realism," p. 147).

However, it is important to note that even those critics who viewed the book most favorably noted some weaknesses in Okri's writing, weaknesses that tend to come to the fore in the work he has produced since *The Famished Road*. Appiah pointed to Okri's penchant for "lush excess" ("Spiritual Realism," p. 147), and even Gates felt the novel suffered from "a tendency . . . to *name* the terms of its allegory" (p. 20). Looking over his career after *The Famished Road*, one sees Okri falling prey to these weaknesses. Too often in his work after *The Famished Road*, the superlush and allegorical dream imagery lacks rigor or concision, leading Appiah (for one) to wish for a great editor for Okri: "a Maxwell Perkins or two to leaven the emerging Pan-African literary culture" ("Azaro and the Spirits," p. 5).

Songs of Enchantment (1993), a sequel to *The Famished Road* that picks up exactly where the earlier work left off, has moments of great power and vivid imagery, but it does not seem to be either a book of its own or a significant extension of the themes of *The Famished Road*. Indeed, both Appiah, reviewing the book in the *Washington Post,* and Michael Gorra, reviewing it in the *New York Times Book Review*, asked virtually the same question of the book's unformed excesses: the former wondered if that book's scenes were "a collection of excerpts from the earlier book" (p. 5), and the latter asked if they were "outtakes from a single enormously long manuscript, one whose best pages became *The Famished Road*" (p. 24). There were critics who admired the book, but even they seemed to see it as a revisiting rather than a reinvigoration of the world of *The Famished Road*.

Okri followed *Songs of Enchantment* with collections of poetry and essays, then *Dangerous Love* (1996), a close revision of *The Landscapes Within*, and *Astonishing the Gods* (1995), a mystical novella that marks an experimental move away from both Western novelistic convention and African narrative form. This allegory—an earnest tale of an invisible man who visits an invisible city and there sees unicorns, angels, broken-winged doves, and beautiful princesses—begins as a parable of identity in postcolonial Africa and ends as a sermon on self-fulfillment. Alev Adil, writing in the *Times Literary Supplement*, noted that, "While [*The Famished Road*] could broadly be described as a work of magic realism, *Astonishing the Gods* has abandoned reality altogether." He continued, "Those seeking to read invisibility as a metaphor for textual (and therefore political) absence from literate culture will not be rewarded" (p. 123). Probably it is best to view this book as an experiment gone awry: the work of a young writer straining to reinvent himself.

Okri's project, after all, is stunningly ambitious—he seeks to reinvent the novel in English, and make it work for another culture, another way of seeing: to retool a European form and a European language, and to discover in them something genuinely African. In his best work he discovers metaphors that cleave the mythic to the real and is able, without the use of conventionally dramatic plot or psychological characters, to build readable, inventive fictions. In those books Okri's sometimes dreamy and imagistic prose carries real power. Moreover, the novels themselves are important not only in their own brutal clarity; they also seem breakthroughs in the history of black African novels written in English.

Okri's work is a high-wire act. When he succeeds, one can only marvel at his grace, daring, and accomplishment; when he fails—well, one wishes he were working with a safety net.

LIFE

BEN Okri is hesitant to talk about his early life. "I'd rather leave that for the complex manipulations of memory that only fiction can provide" (Wilkinson, p. 77). Still, a fair amount is known about him.

He was born 15 March 1959 in Minna, Nigeria, to Grace and Silver Oghekeneshineke Loloje Okri. His family is of the Urhobo ethnic group. At the time of Okri's birth, his father was a clerk for Nigerian Railways; after Nigerian independence in 1960, Silver Okri left for England to study for a law degree. In 1962 Ben joined his parents. There young Okri studied at John Donne Elementary School in the Peckham section of London, while his father studied and simultaneously worked in a Camberwell launderette, earning some money to support the family. In 1966 Ben had to leave England with his mother. During the Nigerian civil war of 1967–1971, he was moved to a small village away from the fray, but he did not entirely escape the conflict. "My education took place simultaneously with my relations being killed," he said in a 1986 interview, "and friends who one day got up in class and went out to fight the war" (Shakespeare, p. 23). He studied at schools in Ibadan and Ikenne before attending Urhobo College at Warri for secondary education. He says he studied to be a doctor or a chemist. He was perhaps the youngest boy in his class when he completed his secondary education in 1972. Thereafter he moved to Lagos to study for advanced levels and a degree in journalism but was disappointed when he was not accepted into any of Nigeria's universities.

Okri first began to think of himself as a writer in those years after secondary school. "I wrote as a way of waiting," he says. "I wrote stories and poems. I wrote a play and a novel. I got a job in a paint company, and in 1976 I had my first article published which was about the failure of rent tribunals in the ghetto" (Wilkinson, p. 78). In 1976, when he was sixteen, his father returned from England, bringing with him a large library of classics which his son read; these volumes helped form a good part of Okri's literary imagination. In a 1991 interview Okri was precise in locating the instant he came to his vocation:

Things had taken a tumble in our lives. We were living in the ghetto in Lagos with my dad, and there were many kids. On a particular day, everyone else was out, and it rained. I was in the living room alone. I think it was because it was the first time in a long, long time that I was actually alone in the house, and I knew the rain would keep the others from getting home, that I took out a piece of paper and drew what was on the mantelpiece and wrote a poem. I looked at the drawing and I looked at the poem. The drawing was not particularly good and the poem was tolerable. It was a simple decision after that. I just knew that writing was where my own river flowed more naturally.

(Ross, p. 338)

Okri continued writing during those very frustrating years in Lagos. While he worked as a clerk in the factory, he also worked as a journalist and wrote stories and poems. It was during these years that he completed his first novel, *Flowers and Shadows*, which was published in 1980.

Although Okri is the child of a fairly middle-class Nigerian family, and though he has spent most of his life in England, his work has focused for the most part on the lives of the very poor. In a 1986 interview he explained his fascination with ghetto dwellers: "The ghetto was the place I've felt most at home because the terms on which everyone lives are so transparent. . . . There was an extraordinary vibrancy there, an imaginative life. When you are that poor, all you've got left is your belief in the imagination" (Shakespeare, p. 23). But Okri left the ghetto, left Nigeria, and went to England when he was twenty. In 1978 he enrolled at the University of Essex, where he received a B.A. in comparative literature. After finishing his studies, he suffered a period of bitter poverty and homelessness. He slept in subway tunnels in London—despite the publication of his two novels. He characterizes his years after university as a time of experimentation when he put aside the novel and focused on short fiction. During these years Okri was the poetry editor of *West Africa* magazine, in which he published a few poems and short stories; he also published book reviews and articles in the *New Statesman* and worked for the BBC World Service. It did not take long for him to achieve professional success. In 1984 he was awarded a British Arts Council grant. In 1987, after the publication of *Incidents at the Shrine,* he was awarded the Com-

monwealth Writers Prize for Africa and the *Paris Review*'s Aga Khan Prize. *The Famished Road* came out in 1991 and Okri won the Booker Prize for that year. His career then changed considerably. In October 1991, less than ten years after sleeping in the streets, he was appointed a visiting fellow at Trinity College, Cambridge.

It is a seeming contradiction: a Cambridge don who says he is most at home in the Lagos ghetto. But it is that contradiction that is resolved in Okri's work and that has made Okri's work possible. His origins in Africa and his distance from his homeland are perhaps equally important. Okri sees his stories as profoundly African, even an extension of African tradition, and yet he sees his place in England as central to his ability to produce those fictions. He says of his work's roots in African narrative:

We are a people who are massaged by fictions; we grow up in a sea of narratives and myths, the perpetual invention of stories. When I was growing up, you sat with your age mates in the evenings and the elders would come out and tell you stories, if you asked them. . . . The storytelling that was part of my growing up is not something that has to be drawn attention to; it was there just like the lizards and the sun and the moon. Nobody would extricate the midges of England as being an influence on a writer who grew up in England.

(Ross, p. 339)

And he puts his relation to England as follows:

The main attraction of England is that it gives you distance and perspective. In Nigeria you could write a novel of the street without ever going into a room. In London . . . it's cool, quiet, ingrown. But Africa is the only place I really want to write about. It's a gift to a writer. . . . You can't write about it with a logical mind. You have to suspend judgement and education and see it afresh.

(Shakespeare, p. 23)

If Nigerian streets and skies are swimming with the stuff of stories, Okri's writing is a reworking of that stuff—distillations produced at a distance and not necessarily bottled at the source. Okri is not shy about this: at the end of each of his novels, he writes the date and place in which he finished the work: *The Landscapes Within* is marked "London, March, 1980," and *Songs of Enchantment* ends with the words, "March 1992; London—Trinity College, Cambridge." With these quick postscripts Okri in effect announces that his work is a mediated vision of the land it portrays. Moreover, as Henry Louis Gates, Jr., points out, a good deal of Okri's mythic sources are drawn from his studies and not his origins. Gates argues that since Okri is of Urhobo descent, his "sense of the Yoruba tradition . . . is derived from his reading its literature and was not simply gained (as some anthropologists still fancy about "third world" authors) at his mother's knee" (p. 3). Again, this is not something Okri hides—the literary allusions are overt in his work. The title of *The Famished Road* is drawn from a Wole Soyinka poem, "Death in the Dawn," and the mythic figure of the *abiku*—so central to *The Famished Road*—appears famously in another Soyinka poem, "Abiku." Indeed, the greatness and, as Gates would have it, the "post-modern" quality of Okri's work lie in part in the author's ability to synthesize sources. Whatever Okri says about his relation to Africa, a few things are clear: a book like *The Famished Road* does not exist as do the African lizards and the sun and the moon; it is something African, but man-made—manufactured in the United Kingdom.

For K. Anthony Appiah it is precisely Okri's distance from Africa and his position as an African writer living in England that allow him to produce work of striking originality:

Though [Okri] lives and writes in London, he has chosen to speak as an African writer (which, as someone born in Nigeria in 1959, he is surely entitled to do). This choice is what gains him the license *outside* Africa to invent—from the resources of Nigerian folklore and the English language and his own wide reading and ample imagination—a language and a universe of his own.

("Spiritual Realism," p. 147)

Appiah goes still further with this, pointing out that Okri's great success with *The Famished Road* began not in Africa but in England and America, where reviewers were in the habit of "explicitly connecting Okri with postcolonial Latin America, another place where Otherness has lowered our barriers to 'disorders' of language and the imagination" (p. 147). And, Appiah muses further, "It will be interesting to see how this novel finds readers at home [in Africa]" (p. 147). The argument works as follows: Okri, by positioning himself as an African writer in England, has granted himself license to draw broadly from an entire continent's literature and has garnered for himself an audience that will see him as an authority on that continent's mythology.

One could argue that Okri, who has seen the highs and lows of English and Nigerian life, is no longer of either culture but has perched himself above the two, and that this high perch has allowed him the freedom to draw from various sources, African and English, and the freedom to reinvent those sources. It is not his Europeanness or Africanness alone that gives power to Okri's fiction but his straddling of two worlds.

IT'S NOT UNNATURAL TO SEE SPIRITS

GABRIEL García Márquez, the great South American magic-realist writer, famously said that his surrealism mirrored the reality of Latin America. One might expect that Ben Okri—who wants his surrealistic writings to capture the essence of his continent—would find literary fellowship in the words of Márquez. However, Okri is impatient with any comparisons with Márquez. In a 1991 interview he said:

The difference is this: the Latin American writers—let's be quite honest—are largely European Latin American writers. Their writing has, as it were, come through the journey of symbolism, surrealism, and then come right around to the reality of that particular place. That's very different from what I'm saying. Whereas in Gabriel Garcia Marquez's *One Hundred Years of Solitude* there's a scene in which the woman flies, in my book you'd have an effect where the kid sees spirits. If you accept the basic premise that this kid is an *abiku*, a spirit child, it's not unnatural that he would see spirits. If all the characters were to see spirits, that would be pushing it a bit, as far as Western thinking is concerned. But from this kid's point of view, it's completely natural. That is different. I'm looking at the world in *The Famished Road* from the inside of the African world view, but without its being codified as such. This is just the way the world is seen: the dead are not really dead, the ancestors are still part of the living community . . . and so on.

(Ross, pp. 337–338)

It may seem like foolish hubris for a young writer like Okri to compare the native authenticity of his own work with the native authenticity of the work of a whole continent's worth of writers, or to compare himself favorably with one of the world's most praised writers; but it is probably best not to judge Okri on those terms, and to view his words not as a critique of the work of any South American writers but, rather, as a declaration of his goals as a writer.

What Okri is striving for in his work is pure expression of the experience of the land from which he comes—and he sees his work as a continuous development of that project. "Running through all my books," Okri says, "is a quite logical progression. I've been exploring a set of questions, and they're quite apparent; I've just gone deeper and deeper because the older you get, the more you see and the more difficult it is to transform that seeing into fiction" (Ross, p. 338). The questions that Okri has been asking are both technical and thematic. The first set of questions, the technical, seems largely to have to do with the relation of the mythic, the historical, and the real—that is, the grand questions a writer might pose when figuring how best to represent the spirit and the tone of Africa, questions that resolve themselves in Okri's shifts from naturalism to magic realism to allegorical fairy tale. The second set of questions, the thematic, seems to go hand in hand with the first. It is as though the characters in Okri's fictions are all on quests parallel to the writer's—they seek to extricate themselves from, and integrate themselves into, their worlds; they want to find out who they really are, and to glimpse the truth about the world around them.

The key to Okri's success in navigating these questions and in sorting through the "dimensions" of his world has been his success in finding metaphors that help him to peel back layers of his "realism." In Okri's universe there seem to be worlds rising within, behind, and beneath the present, palpable world. His universe is layered so that the profound lies just beneath the surface of the observable. This layering is present in all of Okri's work, from his earliest, most conventional novels to his most recent fabulous work. In both *Flowers and Shadows* and *The Landscapes Within* Okri establishes this layering most obviously by contrasting the psychological worlds of his protagonists—one the son of a man who runs a paint factory, the other a young painter living in a Lagos slum—with the harsh worlds around them. Symbolically, however, he establishes the layering by considering the various roles of paint: paint as a house painter's tool that conceals what lies beneath it, and paint as an artist's medium that reveals private visions.

In *Flowers and Shadows,* Jeffia Okwe's father, Jonan Okwe, is the corrupt owner of a paint company, and as Jonan loses his power, the smooth surface of Jeffia's world flakes off like so much cheap, corruptly made paint. In *The Landscapes Within* the metaphoric value of paint is inverted; Omovo uses paint artistically, to represent the corruption of the world. His great work is a snot-green scumscape whose seemingly two-dimensional surface hints at depths that neither Omovo nor his good friend, Keme, can sound. Omovo and Keme discuss the work and explicitly point to its layered meanings:

"Hey, Omovo, what's that painting really?"

"Keme, I don't know. A scum-scape, though I think it is something much more. What do you think?"

"It is disturbing. It's a commentary on our damned society, isn't it? We are all on a drift, a scummy drift, isn't that what you're trying to suggest?"

"Keme, you know better than that. You can read into it what you like."

(p. 48)

In the stories in *Incidents at the Shrine* and *Stars of the New Curfew,* there are a number of ways in which Okri hints at the sedimentary layering of his "dimensions" of the real. "In the City of Red Dust" (in *Stars*), Okri follows the lives of two drunkards who sell their blood for money, and with the cash buy cheap liquor to drink: they take the good from within themselves and replace it with poison. The title of the story refers to ashy dust that coats the entire city these men live in; by the layers of dust the men can read the age of buildings and, sometimes, the history of the world around them. In "A Hidden History" (in *Incidents*), a neighborhood becomes a garbage dump, and one ghostly narrator resides within, exploring the geological layers of filth and the record of the ruin that befell the district. Always Okri seems to be excavating, digging through the visible to discover what lies within, looking at the outside of a body and thinking about what goes on inside it. His physical metaphors enforce his larger project.

The brilliance of *The Famished Road* lies in part in Okri's breaking the pattern of simple layering of real upon unreal, or juxtaposing real and unreal, but instead intertwining the two—so that the world, as Okri would have it, exists in many "dimensions" simultaneously. In *The Famished Road* the miraculous does not lie beneath the ordinary, or apart from it. What might be considered, from a Western reader's point of view, to be most ordinary may in fact be the seat of magic for Azaro, and what might seem ordinary to Azaro may seem miraculous to the Western reader. Here he describes his first encounter with a white man:

After a long period of wandering [through the forest] I burst into a world I had no idea existed before. . . . In one of the tents swung an illuminated bulb. One of the boys stole into the tent with the sole purpose of blowing out the light. Before he could succeed a worker came in, saw him, and chased him out. We waited for the man to do something wonderful with the illumination of the bulb. But instead of doing anything he shut the entrance to the tent. . . . The tent entrance flapped open. And while we were looking, we saw the man come out again. His color had changed. We could not believe our own eyes. He was now a curious cream colour with blotches of pink. . . . His hair was like straw, like bright tassels of corn.

(p. 277)

Here the world is not so much layered as protean. The basic rules of perception shift. What is real seems magical and what is magical seems real. Okri describes the book's metaphorical structure thus: "The novel moves towards infinity, basically" (Wilkinson, p. 83).

This movement toward infinity carries with it real dangers. *The Famished Road* is grounded in metaphorical consistency and powered by ancient mythologies synthesized through Okri's imagination. But in the works that follow, Okri seems to lose some of that grounding—in both African myth and African reality—and he loses the focus and consistency that he seems to have discovered in his short stories.

In *Songs of Enchantment* and *Astonishing the Gods,* Okri once again seems to be layering his worlds, but here the layers seem too deep to fathom—Okri seeks to evoke a level of meaning that lies beneath words. Both *Songs of Enchantment* and *Astonishing the Gods* end with extended, unquoted, prophetic pronouncements. These hint at great profundity but specify little. Here is the beginning of the penultimate chapter of *Songs of Enchantment,* a description of a speech by Azaro's father:

He talked about the continents of our hidden possibilities, about the parts of us facing inwards in the direction of infinity, and about how we should bring those realms into our visible world and so create a kingdom of serenity and beauty on earth. He spoke for a long time about the intimations that had come to him when he was blind and when he was unconscious on the floor of the forest. I partly understood him to be conjecturing about the dreams of the dead and the unborn; but he declared over

and over again that the most astonishing lives we lead are the lives beyond the mirror.

(p. 289)

In *Astonishing the Gods* Okri's fascination with the obscure deepens. At the end of this book, prophecies are again hinted at, unquoted, but here their incomprehensibility is made explicit, and that incomprehensibility seems to be their primary value. In the passage below, Okri's unnamed narrator absorbs the unspeakable wisdom of invisible sages:

He listened to the resonant speeches from the platform and realized that he couldn't understand what was being said. He noticed however that the uttered words transformed the air.
The first master of the long table spoke slowly, and his words induced a great calm over the hall. A wind of peace blew over from the words, spreading warmth and extending the spaces. Soon the hall seemed very vast. The words began to resonate from the magical frescoes.

(p. 137)

We never find out what the man says.

The virtue of wordlessness is something Okri often extols in his more recent writings. In *A Way of Being Free,* his 1997 collection of essays, he writes: "When narrative fiction has entered us, it no longer exists as words" (p. 49), and "Yes, the highest things are beyond words" (p. 89). He explains: "I think we need more of the wordless in our lives. We need more stillness, more of a sense of wonder, a feeling for the mysteries of life. We need more love, more silence, more deep listening, more deep giving" (p. 90). This quest for wordlessness, for a layer of storytelling that exists below (or maybe above) the mere verbal, has led Okri to write two very dreamy novels.

In these two books the incomprehensible words are the most precious. Okri seems to be attempting to peel back language as if it were a coat of bad paint, and to find something profound lying beneath words. But this might not be possible in a novel—after all, the way to see what's under written words is to erase them, and once they're erased, there's no novel left.

FLOWERS AND SHADOWS *AND* THE LANDSCAPES WITHIN

BEN Okri was twenty-one when he wrote *The Landscapes Within,* and younger still when he wrote

Flowers and Shadows. The books have the ambition and scope only a young writer would dare: the plots hurtle mercilessly along, gathering more sub-plots than any one narrative can handle, and characters and events are often lost in Okri's headlong dashes through Lagos' city life. The writer has astounding talent, yet he doesn't always seem to know where to direct it. Okri himself wrote of the second novel: "I poured my heart into the book; but the heart alone isn't enough, in art as well as in life" (*Dangerous Love*, p. 325). As with so much juvenilia, the books are at least as interesting for the ways in which they foreshadow Okri's future achievements as they are in themselves. In them Okri describes the ordinary horrors of Lagos life with the same clarity that he later used to describe ghosts and ghouls.

In *Flowers and Shadows* the plot is propelled as a series of coincidences. Jeffia Okwe meets his father's ex-mistress after he finds the woman's dog being tortured in the street by bored children; later he finds a man lying by a road—one of his father's business partners, beaten nearly to death by his father's thugs. Cynthia, the nurse who attends to this beaten man when he is brought to a clinic, becomes Jeffia's love interest, but there are complications; her father is one of Jeffia's father's former business partners, and his life has been ruined by Jeffia's father. Eventually Jeffia's uncle, Sowho, appears—another man bearing a grudge against Jeffia's father, Jonan—and the confrontation between Sowho and Jonan leads to violence and to the death of both men. In the meantime Jeffia's best friend dies, Jeffia has several harsh encounters with the law, and Jeffia, who has just finished secondary school, worries about whether he will have a future as a schoolteacher. As the events of the novel pile one atop the other, the son discovers more and more of his father's villainy, and his father's world slowly comes crashing down. In the end Jeffia quite happily renounces his father's ill-gotten money and the buffer it has placed between his life and the life of the city around him.

The Landscapes Within bears many similarities to *Flowers and Shadows*. Omovo, like Jeffia, lives in his family home, and he, too, has a domineering, violent father. Like Jeffia, Omovo is a lover, and his love is forbidden: Jeffia's, because Cynthia, his girlfriend, is the daughter of his father's enemy; Omovo's, because Ifeyinwa, his lover, is married. But whereas Jeffia's father owns a paint factory, Omovo works at a chemical factory and, in his pri-

vate time, uses paint to create art. The crucial difference, in terms of setting, is that Omovo lives in the kind of slum in which *Flowers and Shadows* ends. Indeed, in the last few chapters of *Flowers and Shadows*, Jeffia stares at a pool of scum similar to the one that entrances Omovo at the opening of *The Landscapes Within*:

I walked past the stagnant pool of greenish water that had refused to dry up even in the terrible heat of the dry season. A woman with nothing on the upper part of her body but a piece of cloth covering her fallen breasts walked in front of me carrying a small pot. She poured her baby's excreta into the stagnant greenish water. I avoided a filthy dog that was licking someone's excreta at the corner of the scum.

(p. 205)

This seems very much the same puddle that Omovo, in *The Landscapes Within*, converts into art:

He had walked round the large greenish scum near their house a thousand times. He had smelt its warm stale nauseous damp stench and had stared at it as though hidden in its greenish surface lay the answer to some perennial riddle. He was also uncertain and a little afraid of those unchartable things that had happened within him, those obscure and foul correlatives that had been released and which stood there on the canvas—snot-colored, vicious, unsettling.

(p. 35)

In comparing these two passages, the reader can see another crucial difference between the first novel and the second, a difference crucial in the development of Okri's career—the marked influence of James Joyce. *The Landscapes Within* has as its epigraphs quotations from Joyce and from Chinua Achebe, and if the clear-eyed realism is reminiscent of Achebe's early work, the influence of Joyce is evident in the focus on interior life, the mix of the low-down and the high-flown. Okri even borrows famously Joycean vocabulary. If in *Ulysses* Joyce has a "snot-green sea," here Okri has a "snot-colored" scum.

The Landscapes Within is eventful, but far more static than *Flowers and Shadows*. In this book Okri is almost obsessively concerned with Omovo's awareness, and a number of sentences contain the phrase "he was aware": "He was aware that he had created something on the canvas that wasn't there before" (p. 38), or "He was dimly aware of himself walking back to his room" (p. 151), or "He was aware that he wanted to paint something deep and painful" (p. 206). This book is about Omovo's coming to consciousness, and what he becomes aware of—generally speaking—is the absolute horror of the world around him. All the events of the novel lead to violence and failure. His affair with Ifeyinwa ends with the two of them receiving violent beatings and then moving apart; he hangs his scumscape painting in a gallery, and it is confiscated by government thugs; he takes a walk in the park with his friend, and they discover the defiled corpse of a girl.

In this book, as in *Flowers and Shadows*, Okri offers a relentlessly grim vision of his city, but it is not until his collections of stories that he endows his grim vision with hints of magic and surrealism.

INCIDENTS AT THE SHRINE *AND* STARS OF THE NEW CURFEW

THE stories in *Incidents at the Shrine* and *Stars of the New Curfew* are the work of a more disciplined, mature, and focused writer than Okri's early novels. John Melmoth, comparing Okri's short stories with his early novels, wrote: "With them [the stories] Okri has found a voice and established a style of his own" (p. 863). In Okri's first two books one often feels the youth of the writer in the sentimentality of theme and the ramblings of the narrative, but in the two collections one finds oneself in the hands of a competent and mature craftsman. Gone are the overt musings on the nature of life, as in Omovo's "The sky has no meaning. The meaning is hidden inside me—as are many other mad things" (*Landscapes*, p. 164). Gone also are the effete young protagonists. Instead Okri focuses on the world that so upset those dreamy young men—the impoverished, bedraggled, African landscape—and he describes his characters' psychologies not with interior monologues but with rough imagery drawn from myths and dreams.

The short story, as a form, plays to Okri's strength as a writer and insulates him against his weaknesses. He does not have the time to go in for the "lush excess" that Appiah said his work suffered from, or to indulge his "tendency . . . to *name* the terms of its allegory" that Gates indicated. It is bracing to open *Incidents at the Shrine* right after reading *The Landscapes Within*. If, in Okri's earlier

novel, one sensed a tentative writerly presence— an author not quite capable of taming his talents or taking their measure—in his first collection of stories one knows, right from the first page of the first story, "Laughter Beneath the Bridge," that one is in the hands of a master storyteller:

Those were long days as we lay pressed to the prickly grass waiting for the bombs to fall. The civil war broke out before mid-term and the boarding school emptied fast. Teachers disappeared; the English headmaster was rumored to have flown home; and the entire kitchen staff fled before the first planes went past over-head. At the earliest sign of trouble in the country parents appeared and secreted away their children. Three of us were left behind. We all hoped someone would turn up to collect us.

(p. 1)

Gone is the sensationalism of the earlier work; the narrator here is an unsentimental child, with none of the preciousness that marked Jeffia and Omovo. What is more, Okri discovers magic in the horror, and does so without reaching for the patently marvelous or absurd. In the world of this child, everything seems to happen passively and irrationally. People appear and disappear. Bombs fall. Parents secret away their children.

Vultures showed up in the sky. They circled the school campus for a few days and then settled on the watch-night's shed. In the evenings we watched as some religious maniacs roamed the empty school compound screaming about the end of the world and then as a wild bunch of people from the city scattered through searching for those of a rebel tribe. They broke down doors and they looted the chapel of its icons, statuaries and velvet drapes; they took the large vivid painting of the agony of Christ. In the morning, we saw the Irish priest riding furiously away from town on his Raleigh bicycle.

(p. 1)

With the Irish and the English flying and riding away, Africa comes and reclaims the ground on which they have built their European monuments. Ghosts and lizards invade the school's chapel. Were it not for the laconic, child's-eye view of the prose, one could read the above passages as something out of Joseph Conrad—dark forces of the jungle conquering the civilized world. But Okri's language does not allow for Manichaean division between civilization and wilderness: the rebels, the vultures, the English, the bombs, the ghosts, and the lizards—all discrete forces, none more remarkable or upsetting than any of the others.

In *Incidents at the Shrine* the fragmentation of the world is made whole by the writer's sturdy sentences. In the title story, for example, a man with two names, Anderson and Ofuegbu, loses his job as a messenger for a museum and leaves the city, heading back to his village of origin. There he is subject to ritual purifications, described as follows:

The Image-maker proceeded with the extraction of impurities from Anderson's body. He rubbed herbal juices into Anderson's shoulder. He bit into the flesh and pulled out a rusted little padlock which he spat into an enamel bowl. He inspected the padlock. After he had washed out his mouth, he bit into Anderson's shoulder again and pulled out a crooked needle. He continued to do this till he had pulled out a piece of broken glass, a twisted nail, a cowrie, and a small key. There was some agitation as to whether the key would fit the padlock, but it didn't.

(p. 63)

The images may be wild here, but the prose is rock steady. No matter what the miracles Okri puts forward in these stories, they seem as real—or even more real—than the ordinary, "naturalistic" world around them.

The careful surrealism of *Incidents at the Shrine* is quite impressive in itself, but in comparison seems like a set of warm-ups for the more strenuous magic Okri practices in *Stars of the New Curfew*. In the second collection the structures of Okri's stories become less conventional and seemingly more African. In these stories events unravel not in a clear, causal narrative line—from a crisis to a climax and then to a resolution—rather, they progress as if moving down a list, one miracle after another, the miracles becoming stranger, the world moving slowly away from the overtly naturalistic.

"Worlds That Flourish" begins in a relatively ordinary, realistic setting. A narrator whose wife has died loses his job. He goes home and is accused by his neighbor of walking around without eyes—he doesn't really notice that a war is on. Awful things happen to him: his house is robbed and he is arrested along with the burglars. When, finally, the arresting soldiers release him, the narrator drives around a deserted city, hopelessly searching for a job, and then heads into the wilderness. All of this is set out blandly, the man describing the disasters as if they weren't quite happening to him. He drives through rain, his car hits a goat, he is attacked by a mob, his car crashes, and suddenly the world becomes transformed:

When I was out of the wreckage I saw that the car had run into a large anthill. There were ants everywhere. I pushed on through the rain. I couldn't find the road. I went into the forest. I passed rocks flowering with lichen. I moved under the endless lattice of the branches. Thorns of the forest cut into me. I didn't bleed.

(p. 25)

He is dead—or has entered the land of the dead—but doesn't know it. He enters a town of ghosts that he describes in the same flat sentences: "Some of the people came out of tree-trunks. Some had wings, but they couldn't fly. After a while I got used to the strangeness of the people. I ceased to really notice their three legs and elongated necks" (p. 28). Incidents pile one on another, spiraling out of the naturalistic world and, quite gracefully, into the mythological. There is no plot conflict but rather a lifting of the layers of civil life: wife, job, home, city, car, rationality leave the narrator one by one until he is in a waking dream world.

The title story follows a similar, seemingly absurdist logic, but again is told in even, measured tones. It begins with a narrator haunted by nightmares; he is a salesman of sham cures, "medicines" that more often cause diseases than heal them: "It turned out the medicines I sold for getting rid of worms were so powerful that a child had practically excreted its own intestines" (p. 88). He calls himself a "salesman of nightmares" (p. 96), and after the selling of one of his most powerful remedies leads to a horrific bus accident, the shaken, nightmare-haunted narrator flees the city for the town where he grew up. There he runs into old school acquaintances who reminisce about events that seem to have come out of nightmare—the night, for example, the narrator was tied to a pole and had oranges thrown at him by a mob. While in the town he suffers fantastic visions, perhaps hallucinations:

I saw the secrets of the town dancing in the street: young men with diseases that melted in their faces, beautiful young girls with snakes coming out of their ears. I saw skeletons dancing with fat women. I passed the town's graveyard and saw the dead rising and screaming for children. . . . Nightmares, riding on two-headed dogs, their faces worm-eaten, rampaged through the town destroying cars and buildings.

(p. 129)

Soon ordinary life begins to take on the quality of his dreams. The narrator witnesses a grand rally that takes place in an open-air pavilion. A crowd of people is boxed into a small space; money is dumped on them from above.

The helicopter hovered over us. Then a door opened and bags of coins were emptied over us. No one moved for a while. It rained coins through the silence. We watched the silvery fall, bright in the coloured spotlights trained on the helicopter. The coins poured on us, an amazing event. The silvery sparkles floated down through the air like tangible stars. It was when the coins fell on us, hitting us, hitting our heads, our faces, that we began to scramble.

(p. 138)

The narrator's bad dreams become his universe. He says at the end, "I had begun to see our lives as a bit of a nightmare" (p. 144). In the best of these stories, the world spins out of control, but the narrative never does. Okri is distanced and precise in his writing; the images are forceful, and effectively reimagine a brutal world.

THE FAMISHED ROAD *AND* SONGS OF ENCHANTMENT

THE *Famished Road* marks Okri's most successful and complex intermingling of worlds—magical and real, African and European—and yet, in the *Times Literary Supplement,* Charles Johnson ended a generally laudatory review of the book with the following assessment: "At 500 pages, [*The Famished Road*] is too long, and it is padded out with descriptive passages that slow it down. . . . Ben Okri is, if not yet a careful craftsman, a gifted poet of the African experience. . . . With a bit more control, he is destined to produce a very good book indeed" (p. 22). And one can see where Johnson's argument comes from. At times *The Famished Road* does seem to ramble. The book has no central narrative tension; the hero has no discernible goal; there is very little in the way of psychological exploration or character development; and, at the end of the book, nobody learns anything and nothing is resolved. *The Famished Road* is loose-limbed and wild, but—and this is where many readers would disagree with Johnson—the book's rambling quality may have less to do with a lack of craft on Okri's part and more to do with the sheer degree of difficulty of his task.

The novel succeeds against all odds. It is a miracle that a book like this holds together at all. And when one compares it with Okri's later work, *Songs of Enchantment* and *Astonishing the Gods*—both of which at times exceed the poetic inventiveness of *The Famished Road,* but neither of which matches its coherence or readability—one can see just how well crafted *The Famished Road* is. In his masterwork Okri flies off into a world of wild fancy, but that fancy is grounded in solid narrative terms. *The Famished Road* offers its readers an otherworldly narrative point of view, but that view is—in the book's terms—absolutely consistent. And although the events of *The Famished Road* unfold in a seemingly random way, they retain an underlying order. This book is not just the accomplishment of an exotic, associative imagination; it is the work of a writer who, after four books of studious apprenticeship, brings his vision to its fulfillment.

The Famished Road lives simultaneously in the spirit world and the natural world because Azaro does. And if the plot of the novel does not move in a straight line, it follows a discernible pattern. *The Famished Road* is built around a series of events that repeat themselves: Azaro goes into the woods and faces death; he returns to Madame Koto's bar and sees spirits; he goes home, where his father gets into a terrible fight; his mother then has to deal with the consequences, which usually have to do with debt and threats of eviction; then Azaro again heads off into the woods, where he sees figures that tempt him back into the world of the spirits. In this novel Okri takes the order he had practiced in the stories in *Stars of the New Curfew* and inverts it. Instead of beginning in a solid, naturalistic world and then spiraling out into a world of myth and magic, he begins in a magical world, then spins in circles in and out of the world in which we ordinarily live.

In the hands of a less careful craftsman, the distinction between the solid world and the spirit world could become cluttered, but in *The Famished Road* that distinction remains clear. In the early pages of the novel Okri evokes the spirit world vividly, and so distinctly from the world introduced in later pages that one cannot forget it.

In that land of beginnings spirits mingled with the unborn. We could assume numerous forms. Many of us were birds. We knew no boundaries. There was much feasting, playing, and sorrowing. We feasted much because of the beautiful terrors of eternity. We played much because we were free. And we sorrowed much because there were always those amongst us who had just returned from the land of the Living.

(p. 3)

Despite the apparent vagueness and generality, the passage evokes a particular place and the voice of a particular storyteller. The clipped sentences are in a child's voice, and the netherworld has a weird clarity—it is a world of sorrowing birds. One reads passages like these and does not forget—three hundred pages later, at a political rally gone awry—that one is looking at the world through the eyes of a boy who is from someplace very strange.

Okri's high craft is apparent not only in the way he separates the mystical from the real but also in the way he interweaves the two. Here is a simple paragraph in which the boy narrator sees some photographs of his family celebrating:

When I looked closer at the pictures we all seemed strange. The pictures were grained, there were dots over our faces, smudges everywhere. Dad looked as if he had a patch over one eye, Mum was blurred in both eyes, the children were like squirrels, and I resembled a rabbit. We all looked like celebrating refugees. We were cramped, and hungry, and our eyes were fixed. The room appeared to be constructed out of garbage and together we seemed a people who had never known happiness. Those of us that smiled had our faces contorted into grimaces, like people who had been defeated but who smile when a camera is trained on them.

(p. 91)

In this short passage Okri takes a two-dimensional, naturalistic representation and turns it into a source of revelation—it is not a family photograph that Azaro sees but a metaphor, a group of refugee squirrels and rabbits grimacing sadly in a garbage heap. In *The Famished Road* Okri takes the careful reportage of his first two novels and filters it through the eyes of a character from the spirit world of his stories.

We see the awful realities of Okri's Nigerian slum, but the spirit child endows even the grimmest awfulness with a sense of strange transformations. In the passage below, Azaro accidentally stumbles upon his father at work:

And then I saw Dad among the load-carriers. He looked completely different. His hair was white and his face was mask-like with ingrained cement. He was almost naked except for a very disgusting pair of tattered shorts which I had never seen before. They loaded two bags of salt on his head and he cried "GOD SAVE ME!" and he wobbled and the bag on top fell into the lorry. The men loading him insulted his ancestry.

(p. 148)

Unfortunately there are few so carefully written passages in *Songs of Enchantment*, the sequel to *The Famished Road*. Indeed, perhaps the high craftsmanship of the first book is best seen when contrasted with the effusive, undisciplined sequel. K. Anthony Appiah wrote:

In the reviews of *The Famished Road* (including my own) there was an occasional acknowledgment that the book had its longueurs. While most of its episodes had a liveliness that kept one reading, they rarely seemed to advance a new idea. . . . I remember wishing that some editor had had the time and (more importantly) the will to urge Okri to condense his work: Diffused over 500 pages, even writing this powerful begins to pall. . . . Okri's new book, *Songs of Enchantment*, suggests these thoughts were ungenerous. Looking back now, I am sure that *The Famished Road* was disciplined by an editorial intelligence. For *Songs of Enchantment* contains nearly 300 more pages of the same story, taking it up exactly where the novel left off; 300 pages that might well have been left in the first volume without wise editorial intervention.

("Azaro and the Spirits," p. 5)

While Appiah's particular surmise—that an outside voice gave discipline and shape to Okri's masterwork—might be unfair to the author, Appiah's criticism does point to the gap between the first novel's clarity and the second's relative muddiness. This is not to say that *Songs of Enchantment* has nothing to recommend it: there are some gorgeous passages, terrific flights of mad language, and wonderfully horrible visions—but here the work feels undisciplined.

Songs of Enchantment begins with a lyricism similar to that of *The Famished Road*, but the perspective is imprecise and the effect is flat. The book's first two sentences run as follows: "We didn't see the mountains ahead of us. We didn't see how they were always ahead, always calling us, always reminding us that there are more things to be done, dreams to be realized, joys to be re-discovered, promises made before birth to be fulfilled, beauty to be incarnated, and love to be embodied" (p. 3). The "we" in *The Famished Road*'s opening refers to Azaro—as yet unborn and unnamed—and the rest of his spirit kindred. The place described is specific—a spirit world. The "we" in *Songs of Enchantment* is less specific, and so is the place. One assumes the "we" refers to Azaro and his family, but perhaps it includes the people in the town in which he lives, maybe even the people of his nation. The laundry list of things-to-be-done is so imprecise—these tasks would be there for the doing in fifth-century Rome or in the South Bronx circa 1957. The rambling sentences belong to no one's voice—certainly not a child's—but to a voice of a poetical and omniscient narrator who seems to intervene unannounced between Azaro and the reader. Where the opening of *The Famished Road* might at first blush seem obscure, it is grounded in a particular fictional place and vision; the opening of *Songs of Enchantment* is obscure, and the book remains so.

Songs of Enchantment involves essentially the same dramatis personae but the presentation of characters is far less consistent. Azaro's previously stolid mother becomes a dancer in a bar; Madame Koto, the bar owner, becomes a cross between a crime boss and a magician; his father, the mad boxer, becomes a prophet. The world seems to reinvent itself on every page. "The world has changed," says Azaro on page 24; on page 67, "When strange times are coming the world takes on aspects of a dream"; then, ten pages later, Azaro's father exults, "My wife has changed!" And, chapter 23 begins: "Everything was changing, the face of the world seemed an endless series of masks, and we did not know what to believe" (p. 171). This constant reinvention wears the reader down and seems less like magic than inconsistency. As the reinvention gets more fevered, the effects become duller. When Azaro's great epiphany comes at the end of *Songs of Enchantment*, the book argues for wild magic but never quite brings it home:

I watched the glorious stream of hierophants and invisible masters with their caravans of eternal delights, their floating pyramids of wisdom, their palaces of joy, their windows of infinity, their mirrors of lovely visions, their dragons of justice, their lions of the divine, their unicorns of mystery, their crowns of love-won illumination, their diamond scepters and golden staffs, their hieratic standards and their shining thyrsi of magic ecstacy.
(p. 295)

The excessive vocabulary and redundant listing seem less like the voice of the careful spirit child

and more like the words of an author intoxicated by his own musings.

In many ways the failure of the sequel marks the triumph of the original. *The Famished Road* is, as Gates points out, a great invention, something new. The invention is the result of a good deal of labor—four books in which Okri consciously blended the prose styles of Joyce and Achebe, in which he developed stern sentences with which to describe fantastic worlds, in which he carefully grafted myth to horror. *Songs of Enchantment* is written without the same vigor.

RECENT WORK

THE period since *The Famished Road* has been, for Okri, a time of great experiment. Along with *Songs of Enchantment*, the sequel to *The Famished Road*, he has released *Dangerous Love*, a revision of *The Landscapes Within*; one collection of poetry, *An African Elegy*; two collections of essays, *Birds of Heaven* (1996) and *A Way of Being Free* (1997); and a mystical short novel, *Astonishing the Gods*.

Okri's poetry is clearly the work of a novelist. Okri allows himself to be more didactic than he does in his fiction, and perhaps more forthrightly outraged. In "Lament of the Images," for example, he rips into those who pillaged Africa of its treasures and art:

They took the painted bones
The stools of molten kings
The sacred bronze leopards
The images charged with blood
And they burned what
They could not
Understand.
(p. 9)

And in the following lines from "To an English Friend in Africa," he offers advice on how to live life:

Fear not, but be full of light and love;
Fear not, but be alert and receptive;
Fear not, but act decisively when you should;
Fear not, but know when to stop;
Fear not, for you are loved by me;
Fear not, for death is not the real terror,
But life—magically—is.
(p. 83)

359

While in fiction Okri is often oblique and ambiguous, in poetry he tends toward the direct and pedantic.

Okri's essays are similarly marked by a tendency toward pontification. For example, in a numbered set of aphorisms and fragments that Okri published in both *Birds of Heaven* and *A Way of Being Free,* he writes: "81. The higher the artist, the fewer the gestures" (*A Way of Being Free,* p. 124), "86. The infinite life of a beautiful story" (p. 125), and "100. Ah, the sweet suffering of creativity" (p. 125). At times Okri speaks of art and of love with a kind of religious fervor. In "Beyond Words," which appeared in both *Birds of Heaven* and *A Way of Being Free,* he writes:

All art is a prayer for spiritual strength. If we could be pure dancers in spirit we would never be afraid to love, and we would love with strength and wisdom. We would not be afraid of speech, and we would be serene with silence. We would live beyond words, among the highest things. We wouldn't need words. Our smile, our silences would be sufficient. Our creations and the beauty of our functions would be enough. Our giving would be our perpetual gift.

(*A Way of Being Free,* pp. 93–94)

In 1996, the same year as *Birds of Heaven,* Okri published *Dangerous Love,* a reworking of *The Landscapes Within,* which was then out of print. In an author's note appended to *Dangerous Love,* he explained the project as follows:

I came to see [*The Landscapes Within*] as the key to much of my past work, and perhaps also to my future, and became sure that it would not let me go until I had at least tried to redeem it. Many years past before I took up the raw material again and from that grew this new work. *Dangerous Love* is the fruit of much restlessness.

(p. 325)

But Okri seems to be slightly disingenuous here. *Dangerous Love* is, for 250 or so pages, a serious revision of the earlier novel, hewing close to its events, characters, chapter structure, and even dialogue. In *Dangerous Love* Okri tames some of the excesses but does not reinvent the central plot, images, or ideas of the earlier novel. Most of the revision remains quite close to the early material. Here, for example, is a passage from page 217 of *The Landscapes Within,* the opening of the seventh chapter of book 3:

The air was suddenly heavy with the miasma of pail toilet clearing lorries. Then he saw the imposing, slouching figures. Their faces were swathed in cloth giving them an eerie, impersonal, ritualistic quality. They passed by carrying over-loaded pails from the various compounds, staggering but not falling, buckling under the ridiculous weights, moving with a certain ritualistic grace. The place stank unbelievably. Everybody around hurried and fled and covered their noses and averted their eyes and tried to think of other things. Little bits of faeces had slithered down the sides of the pails on to the ground and had taken their places beside the accumulating and endless debris. There were no flies around.

And here is page 216 of *Dangerous Love,* the same event recounted in the opening of a chapter similarly situated in the novel's third book:

As he turned into a street the air suddenly was pungent with nightsoil smells. Then, like figures emerging from the semi-darkness of a curious nightmare, he saw them. Buckling under the weights of brimming nightsoil buckets, their faces swathed with cloths, ritualistic in their impersonality, the nightsoil men came towards him. They staggered to the waiting lorries, rested a while, went into the various compounds light and came out again weighted.

The place stank. People fled from them. People hurried. They ran, covering their noses, averting their eyes. The nightsoil men moved clumsily, their knees trembling, their backs arched. They grunted. The buckets they carried were often too full and things slithered down and took their place amongst the accumulated rubbish on the streets. There were no flies around.

Throughout the novel the methods remain the same: Okri sharpens diction, extends a paragraph here, cuts one there. In the earlier novel Omovo, the hero, speaks in Standard English while many of those around him speak in a kind of pidgin; in the later work everyone speaks Standard English. The last of the novel's four books, titled "Fragments" in *The Landscapes Within,* is the only one that has been deeply reimagined—but even here the new work is not clearly an improvement over the old. While perhaps some of the language is sharper, the very looseness of the earlier work was part of its strength and beauty. There is, of course, great historical precedent for this sort of revision: Henry James revisited old work, as did Flannery O'Connor, as did Raymond Carver. And it is hard to know precisely what drove Okri to this revision: the motives of a writer are never quite clear to a critic or a reader.

Although he has released several books since *The Famished Road,* *Astonishing the Gods* is the only wholly original book-length work of fiction that

Okri has published since his masterwork; that is to say, the novella is neither a revision of nor a sequel to an earlier work. In this book, about an unnamed hero's spiritual journey through an invisible city, the sermonizing tone of Okri's poetry and essays enters into his fiction writing. The Eden that Okri's hero visits—replete with angels and unicorns—is at a far remove from the grit and dirt Okri explored in his earlier work. The roots of the mystical novella seem to lie not in African or Christian mythologies, nor in any kind of realism, but rather in Western contemporary new age and spiritual movements. Throughout, Okri seems to view art—including his own novel—as a cure for unnamed ills.

The masters of the land believed that sickness should be cured before it became sickness. The healthy were therefore presumed sick. Healing was always needed, and was considered a necessary part of daily life. Healing was always accompanied by the gentlest music. When healing was required the sick ones lingered in the presence of great paintings, and sat in wards where masterpieces of healing composition played just below the level of hearing. Outdoor activity, sculpting, story-telling, poetry, and laughter were the most preferred forms of treatment. Contemplation of the sea and of the people's origins and of their destiny was considered the greatest cure for sickness before it became sickness.

The inhabitants of that land, who were the hardest workers in the universe, were seldom ill. When they were ill at all, it was in order to regenerate their dreams and visions.

(pp. 69–70)

Astonishing the Gods did receive some positive notice—it was called "a modern classic" in the *London Evening Standard*—but it also received rough treatment. "The trouble with Okri's castles in the air," wrote Alev Adil in the *Times Literary Supplement*, "is that he writes the air well but he doesn't seem moved to write the castles" (p. 23). And David Buckley, writing in the *Observer,* was still less generous: "Ben Okri goes full diddley for myth and magic in *Astonishing the Gods* and comes badly unstuck" (p. 19). To be fair, *Astonishing the Gods* is in many ways Okri's bravest book to date. It takes real daring to put forward earnestly a book that strives for genuine wisdom and that offers it in the form of aphorisms like "You can only receive what you already have"; Okri must have known he was opening himself up to mockery.

Ben Okri's story thus far is of a remarkably serious young writer who, early in his career, succeeded brilliantly, both in the terms of his own project and in garnering the praise of the world. After his early success he has wavered somewhat, producing work that does not always rise near the level of quality of his best writing. However, Okri is still quite a young writer, and the period of experimentation that followed his moment of great success may yet lead him into new triumphs.

SELECTED BIBLIOGRAPHY

I. COLLECTED WORKS. *Incidents at the Shrine* (London, 1986; Boston, 1987); *Stars of the New Curfew* (London, 1988; New York, 1989); *An African Elegy* (London, 1992); *Birds of Heaven* (London, 1996); *A Way of Being Free* (London, 1997).

II. NOVELS. *Flowers and Shadows* (London, 1980); *The Landscapes Within* (Harlow, U.K., 1981); *The Famished Road* (London, 1991; New York, 1992); *Songs of Enchantment* (London, 1993); *Astonishing the Gods* (London, 1995); *Dangerous Love* (London, 1996).

III. UNCOLLECTED WORKS. "I Came on Stage," in *West Africa* (29 July 1980), a poem; "Fear of Flying," in *West Africa* (3 November 1980), an essay; "In Another Country," in *West Africa* (20 April 1981), a story; "For Julie," in *West Africa* (9 November 1981), a poem; "Journeys Through the Imagination," in *West Africa* (14 February 1983), an essay; "Fires New Time Are Always Small Enough," in *West Africa* (25 April 1983), a story; "How Reality Overwhelms Good Fiction," in *Guardian* (Manchester) (26 September 1985), an essay; "Newton Enigmas," in *Times of London* (4 July 1992), a poem; "A Prayer from the Living," in *New York Times* (29 January 1993), a story; "A Song for Rwanda," in *Independent* (1 October 1994), a poem.

IV. INTERVIEWS. Nicolas Shakespeare, "Fantasies Born in the Ghetto," in *Times of London* (24 July 1986); Kate Muir, "An Author in Search of Humility," in *Times of London* (25 October 1991); Jonathan Green, "Ben Okri Reflects on a Year as the Miss World of Bookdom," in *Times of London* (13 October 1992); Jane Wilkinson, "Ben Okri," in Jane Wilkinson, ed., *Talking with African Writers* (London, 1992); Hunter Davies, "Ben Okri's Green-apple, Left-handed Sort of Day," in *Independent* (23 March 1993); Philip Howard, "There Is Wonder Here," in *Times of London* (13 October 1993); Jean Ross, "CA Interview," in *Contemporary Authors*, vol. 138 (Detroit, 1993).

V. REVIEWS AND CRITICAL STUDIES. Jane Bryce, "Out of the Earth," in *Times Literary Supplement* (19 September 1980); Biodun Jeyifo, "The Voice of a Lost Generation: The Novels of Ben Okri," in *Guardian* (Lagos) (12 July

1986); John Melmoth, "From Ghetto to Badland," in *Times Literary Supplement* (8 August 1986); Abioseh Michael Porter, "Ben Okri's *Landscapes Within:* A Metaphor for Personal and National Development," in *World Literature Written in English* 28 (fall 1988); Michiko Kakutani, "Brave New Africa Born of Nightmare," in *New York Times* (28 July 1989); Alan Ryan, "Ben Okri's Modern Fetishes," in *Washington Post* (7 August 1989); Charles Johnson, "Fighting the Spirits," in *Times Literary Supplement* (19 April 1991); K. Anthony Appiah, "Spiritual Realism," in *Nation* (3–10 August 1992); Giles Foden, "Speaking for Africa," in *Times Literary Supplement* (17 April 1992); Henry Louis Gates, Jr., "Between the Living and the Unborn," in *New York Times Book Review* (28 June 1992); Adewale Maja-Pearce, *A Mask Dancing: Nigerian Novelists of the Eighties* (London, 1992); K. Anthony Appiah, "Azaro and the Spirits," in *Washington Post* (3 October 1993); Michael Gorra, "The Spirit Who Came to Stay," in *New York Times Book Review* (10 October 1993); Alev Adil, "More Narnian Than Olympian," in *Times Literary Supplement* (10 March 1995); David Buckley, "Full Diddley Delirium," in *Observer* (16 April 1995).

JOE ORTON

(1933–1967)

H. Martin Puchner

WHEN JOE ORTON died at the age of thirty-four, he was just beginning to establish himself as one of Britain's new voices in the theater. Only two of his full-length plays and a few shorter ones had been produced on the stage; one of them, *Loot,* had earned him an *Evening Standard* Drama Award for the best play of 1966, an alleged £100,000 in film rights, and international fame. Three years of moderate recognition and one year of success came to an abrupt end when, on 9 August 1967, Kenneth Halliwell, his lover of fifteen years, killed Joe Orton with a hammer and himself with an overdose of Nembutal. Since then, Orton's increasing fame and the publication of his earlier plays, novels, and diary have been inextricably linked to a fascination with his life. Twenty years after his death, his biography, written by John Lahr, was turned into a feature film with a cast including Vanessa Redgrave and Wallace Shawn. By the time Simon Moss's *Cock-Ups,* a play that uses characters and dialogue fragments from Orton's major plays as well as events from his dramatic life, premiered in Edinburgh in 1981, Orton had become a celebrity. It was one of many plays devoted to a theatrical celebration of this playwright, who had become an icon of the "New Wave" of English theater as well as of the increasingly visible gay culture. *Time Out* described Moss's play as a "gloriously farcical investigation of the circumstances of Orton's death . . . in Ortonesque manner," thus testifying to the fact that Orton had been turned into a tragic hero for gay liberation. "Ortonesque" had become the name for a particularly dark type of comic farce. With only a handful of plays, Orton had managed to create a new art of comedy.

The stylization of Orton's life had begun years before his death, promoted primarily by Orton himself. One of the first steps in this direction, recommended by his savvy agent, Peggy Ramsay, was to give up his real name, John Kingsley Orton—"too close to John Osborne"—for the simple (and demonstrably working-class) Joe Orton. It was also at the insistence of Peggy Ramsay that he started writing his posthumously published diary, a text that contributed significantly to turning his life into a lifestyle. Not only in his diary but in other private and public statements Orton presented himself as genuinely working-class, emphatically gay, openly promiscuous, and radically subversive. His self-consciously conceived diary and the exposure of both his social background and his sexual orientation affiliated him with two models: the French playwright Jean Genet, who had combined a working-class image with a homosexual identity in his fictional diary, *The Thief's Journal;* and Oscar Wilde, with his notorious nonconformism and his well-made comedies. Orton's affinity with the latter prompted the label, coined by a London reviewer, "Oscar Wilde of the welfare-state gentility." From Genet, Orton inherited an intriguing mixture of aestheticization and the gutter, and from Oscar Wilde, subversive wit and artful dialogue. Equally important, however, is the fact that Orton shares with these two figures the active mingling of their personal life and work. All three stylized themselves, and were in turn stylized, as gay icons. What Orton himself did to the presentation of his own life and what other people did to his biography have thus inevitably become major components in discussions of his oeuvre.

This mixture of Orton's achievement as a writer and the fascination with his life has ensured that most of his writings are now in print, including his only film script, *Up Against It;* his early novel *Head to Toe;* his diaries; and, since 1998, juvenilia, including the novels *Between Us Girls, The Boy Hairdresser,* and *Lord Cucumber* and the early, as yet unperformed, plays *Fred and Madge* and *The Visitor.*

JOE Orton was born 1 January 1933 in Saffron Lane Estates, a working-class development in Leicester, to which he used to refer, not unproudly, as the "gutter." His mother, Elsie Orton, was a machinist in a hosiery factory; his father, William, always frail, worked in the footwear industry before he became a gardener for the city of Leicester. This was the milieu that Orton would describe and satirize in his plays *The Good and Faithful Servant* and *Entertaining Mr. Sloane,* except that these plays turn the complete repression of sexuality at the Ortons', which John Lahr describes in his biography, into celebrations of promiscuity. Elsie Orton liked to live beyond her means and instilled in her eldest son the ambition to escape the limitations of his parents. When Joe failed the eleven-plus exams, she used her savings to send him to the private Clark's College, where he had to suffer through a practical and commercially oriented curriculum. After graduating he failed to pursue a career that would satisfy his mother's ambitions and instead held a succession of temporary jobs, without apparent goal or orientation, dreading the dullness of everyday work.

What had begun to capture Orton's imagination, however, was the theater. In 1949 he joined the Leicester Dramatic Society and made his acting debut in *Richard III,* playing the small parts of Dorset and a messenger. At the Dramatic Society he first heard about the Royal Academy of Dramatic Art (RADA), where he eventually enrolled in 1951. It was an unlikely place for Orton to end up, but he had found a goal for his ambition. In preparation he joined two more amateur dramatic societies, the Bats Players and the Vaughan Players, and appeared in a number of productions, including Maurice Maeterlinck's *The Blue Bird,* with moderate success. He also began to take private elocution lessons and applied to RADA, despite the discreet discouragement of his teacher, Madame Ada Rothery. Orton auditioned successfully with a piece from *Peter Pan* and began the three-year program in 1951. His career in acting, however, was short-lived. After graduating in 1953, he worked as assistant stage manager for one summer but became critical of the routine of repertory work. When he returned to London, he was determined to become a writer. This decision was influenced in large part by another disillusioned RADA graduate, Kenneth

Halliwell, who had initiated him into the world of writing.

Orton and Halliwell had become roommates and lovers within a month of their arrival at RADA. Halliwell, seven years Orton's senior, dominated the first phase of his literary career. Between 1951 and 1956 they collaborated under the guidance of the already ambitious Halliwell and produced a number of novels, among them *The Silver Bucket* (1953), *The Last Days of Sodom* (1955), and *The Mechanical Womb* (1955), and *The Boy Hairdresser* (1956), a satire in blank verse that they later turned into a novel. Although they were encouraged by Charles Monteith, an editor with Faber and Faber, none of these works was published. Dominated by an artificial and stilted classicist wit and a tendency toward provocative social satire, they violated both the aesthetic and the cultural sensitivities of the literary establishment. *The Last Days of Sodom,* for example, which transposes the biblical city into modern times, delights in descriptions of homosexual practice and satirizes "unnatural" heterosexuality. *The Mechanical Womb* is a parodic science fiction novel that is less interested in the coherence of plot or character than in the invention of different species of mutants and robots. *The Silver Bucket* describes the adventures of a young girl expelled from her native village for an unnamed offense. These works were written primarily under the influence of Ronald Firbank, whose mannered satire, homosexual leaning, and witty dialogue—in the tradition of William Congreve, Richard Sheridan, and Wilde—became the model for Orton's first literary phase.

Even though these collaborative works were ultimately failures, Orton later used them as reservoirs of characters, just as he retained something of their satirical style, provocative plots, and overt homosexual allusions. And while Orton ultimately abandoned his early classicist diction, his later works are still dominated by the juxtaposition of crudity and artificially elevated speech that dominates these early works. Most important, however, these novels, like his later works, can be described as parodies of existing genres: *The Mechanical Womb* is a parody of science fiction; *The Last Days of Sodom,* of social critique; and *The Silver Bucket,* of nineteenth-century melodrama. The pleasure of parody, too, was something Halliwell and Orton had learned from Ronald Firbank, who satirized everything from symbolism, in his play *The Mauve Tower,* and Wilde's aestheticism, in *A*

Disciple from the Country, to the comedy of manners, in *The Princess Zoubaroff.* Through these collaborations Halliwell not only introduced Orton to Firbank but also intensified his studies of Greek tragedy, Elizabethan drama, and Restoration comedy, all of which shaped Orton's later work to a considerable degree.

During this period Orton increasingly gained literary and intellectual independence from his lover, who had so far been his most important teacher and inspiration. The two writers were living in a small studio apartment and worked occasional odd jobs in order to finance their ascetic, literary life. It was this secluded life at the fringes of London, in the small studio with a collage by Halliwell covering a whole wall, that became an icon for the plays and films that turned Orton into a romantic, nonconformist critic of the establishment. After years of unsuccessful novel writing in the studio that bound them so closely together, they decided to end their literary collaboration in 1956. Halliwell continued his literary endeavors with a new novel, *Priapus in the Shrubbery,* in the same Firbankian style. In contrast, the first novel written by Orton alone, *Between Us Girls* (1957), shows that he was beginning to experiment, adapting the stilted dialogue of Firbank to a more contemporary diction. The form Orton employed is that of a diary, in which Susan Hope, an aspiring young actress, records her adventures, which lead from a strip club in London to a bordello in Mexico and eventually to stardom in Hollywood. The plot resembles that of a modernized picaresque novel: the protagonist's episodic life is dominated by chance encounters, misunderstandings, and complications that do not seem to leave any traces on the character of the protagonist, except, perhaps, for a growing pragmatism.

Unlike the bildungsroman, in which every seemingly random experience finally adds up to the formation of the protagonist, the adventurers of the picaresque novel seem strangely detached from the catastrophes and triumphs of their turbulent life. Voltaire's *Candide* is one model for Susan Hope's adventures, a female picaresque in which even the most cruel disasters fail to change the heroine's Leibnizian conviction that she lives in the best of all possible worlds. Even though Susan Hope does not explicitly subscribe to this piece of Baroque philosophy, she maintains a naively uncritical view of the world at large, and takes both blows and successes with the same fundamental

and unchanging indifference; true to her name, she will never give up her hope. Susan Hope participates in a show at a strip club whose main attraction is the surprise evoked when Countess Sirie von Blumenghast is suddenly revealed naked, having been clandestinely undressed while playing the piano, a stunt that Susan Hope simply "adores" for its originality. The pianist at the show arranges a gig for her in Mexico that threatens to turn into a veritable nightmare: Susan finds herself abducted and forced into a guarded brothel in Mexico. But in good picaresque manner, just when the situation seems most hopeless, an old pursuer of hers turns up at the brothel, frees her heroically, and brings her to Hollywood, where miraculously she makes it big in the musical *The Divine Marquisé,* as little shocked by her sudden success as by her previous disasters. It is precisely this refusal of the characters to be impressed by their experiences, to learn and to improve, that continues to characterize Orton's later work.

Between Us Girls, which was finally published in 1998, is a transitional work for Orton: he applies everything he learned from Firbank, Restoration comedy, and Wilde to this modern picaresque story. The language is contemporary and colloquial, but it is not naturalist. The descriptions Susan Hope uses in her diary are a parodic stylization of teenager camp—the silly mannerisms, little jealousies, vague hopes, and general naïveté of a group of young girls dreaming about success in acting while being forced to take jobs in stores, in revue shows, and even in strip bars. It is a world as limited and closed as, for example, the clique of British expatriates in Firbank's *The Princess Zoubaroff,* transposed into a more contemporary, but equally stilted, language; as driven by gossip as the plays of Congreve, Sheridan, or Wilde; and as dominated by careful observation of social interaction and the ruthless and socially disguised hunt for the best husband as Jane Austen's novels. Besides being a modern version of a girlish picaresque, *Between Us Girls* is a teenager comedy of manners, a Jane Austen rendering of twentieth-century adolescence.

Orton returned to the picaresque in a later novel, *The Vision of Gombold Proval,* which was posthumously published as *Head to Toe* (1971). In it characters and acquaintances keep reappearing, with little motivation or plausibility; friends are separated and reunited randomly. The world that Gombold enters, we don't know how, is as strange as it could be; the figures he encounters are enigmatic, deceptive, dangerous, and grotesque. Gombold gets lost repeatedly and is finally taken hostage by a gigantic female, who puts him up in a woman's chamber, forcing him to dress in women's clothes and to perform all the duties of a housewife. In this intensely unstable world Gombold rarely stays in the same place for long; almost everyone—his gigantic wife / husband, his prison friend, his rebel comrades—keeps reappearing, remembering old entanglements without, for the most part, holding grudges against one another. During his travels Gombold shoots a female prime minister, who had established an Amazon world in which only women hold public offices, is put into prison, escapes, and gets involved in a savage war. What is most striking about this novel is that Gombold's adventures are set on a gigantic body. His journey literally takes him from the body's head to its toe, via some of its more interesting parts. As Rabelais had done in *Gargantua* and *Pantagruel* and as Jonathan Swift had done in *Gulliver's Travels*, Orton uses the magnified body as an object of laughter; *The Vision of Gombold Proval* looks at the body so closely that it loses all integrity. In addition Orton satirizes a long tradition of political allegory: where Shakespeare's *Coriolanus* and Thomas Hobbes's *Leviathan* had used the body as a figure for the state, Orton employs it merely to describe a war between the right and the left buttocks. Orton would never use such an extended bodily allegory again, but he reused many plot elements from *The Vision of Gombold Proval* in his film script *Up Against It*. And most of his later plays rely on the crude laughter evoked by the body in parts, as theorized by Bakhtin.

Orton continued to experiment with genre and style when *Between Us Girls* and *The Vision of Gombold Proval* failed to be published. And for the first time he turned to the dramatic form, bringing together his experience in the theater and his literary efforts. His literary experiments in the picaresque could not serve as direct models for the theater, because the picaresque, with its bifurcating plots, numerous characters, and rapid changes of scene, does not fit the narrow confines of drama. Instead, Orton began to explore the limits of the theater and of the dramatic form. *Fred and Madge* (1959), like *Between Us Girls,* was published only in 1998 and so far has been virtually ignored by critics. It describes the dull and repetitive routine of everyday life, but not in a comical fashion (as in some of

Orton's later plays); rather, he uses a technique that is indebted to the modernist tradition. The play opens with a scene in which Fred and Madge, in order to break the monotony of everyday life, are entertaining such thoughts as getting bats as pets. Both the monotony and their desperate attempts to escape it are grotesquely exaggerated, as is the language in which they converse. Strange objects, such as large bathtubs and umbrellas, appear and disappear without sufficient motivation, and the dialogue is dominated by sudden interventions, non sequiturs, and constant switches of style:

MADGE: I can't seem to get her to stop the habit of dusting when she's excited.
QUEENIE: She's highly strung, that's what it is.
MADGE: She's had a nasty cold.
MADGE: Look at her now—brushing the steps. I'm thinking of having her trained.
MADGE: She's got it in her, I'm sure. (*Pause.*) I gave you a ring last night, weren't you in?
QUEENIE: It was you, was it? I heard the phone go about eight. We were watching the re-makes of those detergent adverts.

(pp. 12–13)

Not only do these characters possess strange habits—dusting when excited or watching remakes of detergent ads—but they live in a world in which such habits appear customary. This detachment of the characters from their environment, the ways in which they keep their poker faces throughout any number of absurd events, seemingly unmoved by an incomprehensible and chaotic world, are defining features of Orton's developed art of farce; they are also the only aspect of his picaresque novels that Orton could reuse in these plays. From the point of view of the theater, this degree of detachment and the arbitrary nature of events place this play more directly in the tradition of the theater of the absurd, with its scenes of grotesque domesticity, counterlogical language, and unmotivated events. *Fred and Madge* was significant for Orton because it allowed him to transpose his novelistic satire into a theatrical form. The shortest route from the picaresque novel to drama led Orton to a new kind of absurdist farce.

To this kind of modernist farce Orton added an element of theatrical self-reflexivity, taken from such plays as Luigi Pirandello's *Six Characters in Search of an Author. Fred and Madge* presents an absurdist take on the domestic drawing-room drama, but with the added turn that it satirizes the daily routine of the theater itself. The stage manager comes and goes, actors are replaced, and we constantly drift in and out of the actual plot. The play thus mocks the dull, everyday existence not only of a couple but of the theater, which had driven Orton away from the stage after a summer job at the Ipswitch Repertory Theatre. In good modernist fashion, the whole process of production is represented on stage, interrupts the play, and becomes part of the action itself. The subjects of this play are, therefore, the margins of the theater, the backstage, the side entrance, the prompter, and the actors; theatrical illusion is thus made impossible and the audience is confronted with the dull drama behind the scenes. *Fred and Madge* testifies to the fact that the avant-garde tradition is one of the sources from which Orton's later farces would derive their irreverent attitude toward realist conventions, motivations of character, and consistency of dialogue. It is the play in which Orton allowed himself the highest degree of formal freedom, and his experiments here with the limits of theater would become fruitful for his later, and more famous, farces.

Orton's next play, *The Visitor* (1961), also virtually unknown and not published until 1998, folds the more overtly absurdist elements of *Fred and Madge* into a more realist setting: a retirement home in which a resident awaits a visitor. This setting, however, is realist only in order to develop a farcical plot all the more successfully. The dying old man in the ward, the bickering of the nurses, the inappropriate remarks of his daughter, the debates about the cleanliness of other inhabitants, all make a nursing-home comedy out of the characters' tragic loneliness. For the first time Orton superimposes realism onto the most outrageous plots and comments, a style that characterizes all of his successful plays. With *The Visitor* Orton received, for the first time, positive responses from both the Royal Court Theatre and the BBC, even though both institutions ultimately rejected the play. These responses may very well have influenced his decision to continue embedding farcical and absurdist elements in a naturalistic frame, a structure that appears in all of his mature work.

In 1963 Orton at last achieved some public recognition for his work. *The Boy Hairdresser* (later retitled *The Ruffian on the Stair*), his dramatic adaptation of one of the early novels he had written with Halliwell, was accepted by the BBC Third Programme and broadcast on 31 August 1964. Encouraged by this success, Orton began to work on a new drama conceived exclusively for the stage, *Entertaining Mr. Sloane.* He sent the piece to the powerful literary agent Margaret Ramsay, who convinced Michael Codron to produce the play almost immediately. This success marked the beginning of a period of intense dramatic production that continued for the final four years of Orton's life. By June 1964 he had completed the television drama *The Good and Faithful Servant,* and four months later another stage play, *Loot.* The first production of *Loot* was a failure, but Orton nonetheless continued writing, finishing a new play, *The Erpingham Camp,* in September 1965. Shortly afterward, while *Entertaining Mr. Sloane* was playing on Broadway, *Loot* was revived, this time bringing Orton national and international recognition. In the same year, 1966, Orton wrote another television play, *Funeral Games,* and began his last, and best, play, *What the Butler Saw.* After these three years of intense dramatic production, the year 1967 finally brought Orton the success he had always hoped for. *Loot* won the *Evening Standard* Award and the *Plays and Players* Award for Best Play of 1966, and Orton was able to sell its film rights. He was also contracted to write the script for what would have been the third Beatles film. In the same year *The Good and Faithful Servant* was broadcast for the first time, and his early television plays, *The Ruffian on the Stair* and *The Erpingham Camp,* were performed at the Royal Court Theatre on a double bill titled *Crimes of Passion.* This period of productivity and success was brought to an abrupt end by Orton's violent death on 9 August 1967.

THE ORTON DIARIES

Most of the plays and studies about Orton devote a great deal of energy to psychological speculations about his relationship with Halliwell. At the heart of these speculations is Orton's diary, which he began more than half a year before his death, in December of 1966. This diary traces the tensions that emerged, predictably enough, between Orton and Halliwell as Orton became increasingly successful and the balance of power in the relationship began to shift: whereas Orton had once typed Halliwell's manuscripts, Halliwell now took calls from Orton's agents, producers, and actors. Almost as detached from the content of his diary as his characters are from their environments, Orton records these growing tensions without hesitation, and he records them knowing that Kenneth would read his diary. Eventually, the diary became Halliwell's suicide note:

If you read his diary all will be explained.

K.H.

P.S. Especially the latter part

(*The Orton Diaries,* p. 1)

A crucial document in Orton's biography, the diary has also become one of his posthumous literary successes. Orton had experimented with the form of the diary between the ages of fourteen and eighteen, and again in *Between Us Girls;* the so-called *Orton Diaries* are his final version of the diary as a literary genre. In an emotionally distanced manner he records not only the increasing tensions between himself and Halliwell in their claustrophobic studio but also the lifestyle of gay "mod" London in the mid-1960s. Entries about the current productions and rehearsals of his plays alternate with sudden visits to dark bathrooms, the stages for homosexual orgies. Besides public bathrooms, parks and private apartments are the frequent sites of such transient sexual encounters. The most celebrated parts of the diary, however, deal with an extended visit to Tangier, the preferred holiday resort for gay men. In these Orton records the flocks of underage Algerians swarming around the pale British couple, turning the town into a *locus amoenus* with merry threesomes, shared lovers, and conspicuous consumption of hashish cakes, of which Orton becomes a veritable master cook. Orton shows no concern for the sexual and economic exploitation in which the sex tourism of Tangier is implicated, but instead celebrates the place and the young boys as instances of a countercultural freedom. He considers the existing laws against homosexual contact with minors as instruments of a repressive and repressed society.

In these pages Orton is indebted to the novels of Jean Genet, to whose diary, *The Thief's Journal,* Orton's own diary seems, at times, to aspire. Orton reflects explicitly on his relation to Genet at the beginning of the diary. In a longer passage he observes: "A combination of elegance and crudity is always ridiculous. . . . I had the idea that the play I intend to write is set in prison, *Where Love Lies Bleeding,* should be, in the main, a satire on Genet

. . ." (p. 70). And indeed Orton uses the same combination of "elegance and crudity" he admires in the French playwright in his own journal as he alternates between elaborate and witty observations about the theater world and sudden scenes of bathroom sex.

The diary thus serves as a valuable cultural document of "mod" London; in it Orton not only provides insightful comments on his plays and his career but experiments with the dramatic style he is concurrently developing in his comic farces. His almost instinctive tendency toward satire and parody, which is central to his entire oeuvre, appears even in the lines written about Genet. He did not plan to write in the style of Genet but to write a "satire on Genet," a plan that conflicts, as Orton indicates in the following sentences, with a previous plan to write the work as a "parody on Brecht" (p. 71), as if he could not conceive of a literary predecessor without immediately falling into parody. But whether parody or not, Orton's farcical style permeates his diary, even—and especially—when it is concerned with moments of personal tragedy. Orton always presents himself as an Ortonesque character and his world as an Ortonesque world.

One extreme instance of this self-stylization occurs when Orton has to visit Leicester for his mother's funeral in December 1966. The only thing he records of this sad event is that her displayed corpse looks "fat, old and dead" (p. 42). The entry the next day describes his having casual sex with a man he picks up somewhere close to home, and records laconically, "He had a very tight arse. A Catholic upbringing, I expect" (p. 45)—a line one could find in almost any of his plays. As if the comments about this dead mother and the juxtaposed sex were not enough to prove that he lives in a grotesquely Ortonesque world, we read that Orton finds his dead mother's false teeth and keeps them in order to "amaze the cast of *Loot*" (p. 44), a play that takes place around a dead and dismembered body. No moment of compassion, and no expected reaction to his mother's death, but rather a combination of detached observation, anonymous sex, and laconic remarks about "Catholic upbringing" characterizes the entries. Indeed, the entry five days later records that he confronts the actor playing Hal with his dead mother's teeth—"Here, I thought you'd like the originals." In response to the actor's shocked reaction, Orton complains, "'You see,' I said, 'it's obvious that you're not thinking of the events of the play in terms of reality, if a thing affects you like that'" (p. 47). Orton presents this scene as a lesson: even though the plot and dialogue of *Loot* may strike everyone, including the actors, as utterly improbable, artificial, and purely farcical, it nevertheless has to be taken "in terms of reality." Behind this macabre joke stands the claim, upon which Orton kept insisting, that in fact his farces were lifted from his life, and that even the most grotesque and farcical of his comedies are realist in essence.

But the *Orton Diaries* cannot be taken at face value. Because the project of the diary was undertaken as a publishing idea, the diaries are not written in a private voice—Orton in dialogue with himself—but are written as much for the public as are his plays. What the diaries show, however, is that Orton systematically tried to see and to present his life in a farcical light. In entries such as those cited above, he selects and presents events of his life in order to align them with the tone and manner of his plays. His life may be more farcical than the shocked actor knows, but this is true in part because he deliberately transforms his life into a comic spectacle with all the ingredients of his plays presented as a combination of crudity and elegance à la Genet.

PRACTICAL JOKES

ORTON'S taste for practical jokes had surfaced years before in two separate instances that are symptomatic of his tendency to turn his life into a farcical play. In 1962, during their most isolated and frustrating time, Orton and Halliwell began to deface books in their local library by gluing pieces of writing and pictures to their opening pages. These acts of vandalism were undertaken not for the purpose of destruction but for their amusement: they secretly watched the readers in the library react to these unexpected jokes and mild obscenities. At a time when he had no hope of having his writing published or performed, Orton turned the library into a kind of theater. Eventually a library employee tracked them down, and Orton and Halliwell had to spend half a year in prison. But Orton's imprisonment came in handy for his own mythmaking. This short time in prison brought him, in his own eyes, closer to the jailbird Genet; and once famous, Orton occasionally mentioned his time in prison to foster his image as an outcast.

The second series of practical jokes was more playfully transgressive than the first. Orton invented the persona Edna Welthorpe, in whose name he sent series of letters. Edna would respond, for example, to a letter questioning her alleged request for seventy-eight admission tickets for the International Trade Fashion Fair, or ask a perplexed Rev. G. W. Sterry for permission to use his Heath Street Baptist Church hall for a theater performance. Later, she sent letters to the editors of various newspapers complaining about the loose morals of that new playwright, Joe Orton, and his play *Entertaining Mr. Sloane:* "Sir . . . I myself was nauseated by this endless parade of mental and physical perversion. And to be told that such a disgusting piece of filth now passes for humour!" (*Orton Diaries*, p. 281). Orton used Edna from 1958 until his death, taking pleasure in the confused, defensive, and awkward responses of the victims of the attacks, and he frequently sought to prolong these correspondences as long as possible.

Both the defacements of library books and the interventions of Edna Welthorpe testify to Orton's pose as a trickster and to his pleasure in impersonation. With Edna's letters to the editor, Orton also made explicit the kind of audience reaction that was implied in his texts. His plays require an audience that is ready to be shocked by crude farce and moral satire, not one that would respond by raising eyebrows at Orton's unmotivated one-liners. With Edna Welthrope, Orton, perhaps unwittingly, invented a character who not only plays tricks on innocent victims and satirizes the conservative press but acts as an ideal spectator of his plays.

UP AGAINST IT

ONE of Orton's last projects, begun in January 1967, was a film script for the Beatles, titled *Up Against It*. Although the move of *Loot* to the West End and the *Evening Standard* Drama Award had brought him great success, the orbit of the Beatles was an altogether different thing. Orton's visit to the Beatles is among the culturally most interesting entries in his diary. Orton not only records their conversation about mushrooms, LSD, and tattoos but looks at everything in terms of a play. Fascinated with the first "real" butler he encounters there, he writes, "The crusted old retainer—looking too much like a butler to be a good casting—busied himself in the corner" (p. 74). Although Orton did remark on the fact that the Beatles' mustaches made them look like "anarchists in the early years of the century" (p. 74), he was always skeptical as to whether the Beatles' pop image could be made to work together with his anarchic farces, and *Up Against It* does not try to reconcile their image and his style. Rather, it represents Orton's most explicit attempt to combine his early picaresque style with his newly found farcical voice. It was in film, not in the theater, that his picaresque plot structures and their proliferating scenes could be accommodated; and the flexibility of film made it the ideal medium for Orton to incorporate his older, novelistic material.

Up Against It uses extensive material from Orton's novel *The Vision of Gombold Proval*. But where the novel has one protagonist, the film script has two: McTurk and Christopher Low are the red thread through the adventurous and confusing plot. The two are expelled from their city, for various sexual and anarchic offenses, and go on to survive a series of random episodes. Some figures and scenes are taken straight out of the novel—most important, the scenes resembling the classical gender-reversal comedy, with acts of cross-dressing and inverted gender roles. The two protagonists become part of a male rebel force that will kill the female prime minister of this all-female republic, an event that is also a parody of John F. Kennedy's assassination. As in *The Vision of Gombold Proval*, McTurk, the assassin, ends up in prison and escapes through the sewers with the help of an inmate, Jack Ramsay. No action seems to have proportional consequences, and the outcome of each episode is as unpredictable as it is improbable. What Orton gives up is the bodily allegory of *The Vision of Gombold Proval*; the adventures no longer take place on a gigantic body but in seemingly unconnected places. What he adds is the quick, farcical dialogue that he had learned by writing his successful plays, from *Entertaining Mr. Sloane* to *What the Butler Saw*: the single lines and the quick, unexpected repartees, motivated only by their witty effect and not by their context. When at one point McTurk encounters Jack Ramsay's father, he asks him, "Aren't you Jack Ramsay's father?" Ramsay's father replies, "I was before the war. I don't know who I am now" (p. 58).

As always in Orton, the laughter evoked by such replies has its grotesque and violent side; the father is not consciously witty but pitiable. The stage direction describes him as "white-faced and shaken. Blood pours down his ragged tunic" (p. 58), and his lack of memory is an effect of a severe wound. The film script is a tour de force from the picaresque to melodrama, from farce to tragicomedy. This rapid succession of modes and styles reaches a climax when the script dives into an outright parody of romanticism. Scene 121 is described in the following words: "A Garden. Moonlight. Dark leaves. Roses. A nightingale. Faintly blown by the wind comes the sound of a waltz. McTurk walks with Rowena under a rose arbor" (p. 64). Orton was proud of this dig at romanticism and comments on it in his diary with great satisfaction. Eventually McTurk, Low, and Ramsay are all married to Miss Drumgoole, the woman because of whom McTurk and Low were expelled from their native town.

When confronted with this final scene, the Beatles' agent complained that "the boys" would find themselves in bed not only with one woman but with one another. Walter Shenson, the producer of the first two Beatles films, had always been skeptical about the project. Orton records a conversation that testifies to these tensions: "He [Shenson] was most concerned to impress upon me that 'the boys' shouldn't be made to do anything in the film that would reflect badly upon them. . . . I hadn't the heart to tell him that the boys, in my script, have all been caught *in flagrante*, become involved in dubious political activity, dressed as women, committed murder, been put in prison and committed adultery" (*Orton Diaries*, p. 83). These differences proved to be ultimately unbridgeable. Rather than attempting to adapt his script to the Beatles' public image, Orton tried to sell the script to someone else, unsuccessfully.

INFLUENCES ON ORTON'S WORK

ORTON'S mature oeuvre, the texts to which he owes his recognition as a writer and dramatist, consists of seven plays written, and at times heavily revised, between 1963 and 1967: *The Ruffian on the Stair, Entertaining Mr. Sloane, The Good* and Faithful Servant, Loot, The Erpingham Camp, Funeral Games, and What the Butler Saw. Only three of them—Entertaining Mr. Sloane, Loot, and What the Butler Saw—were originally written for the stage; the others were either radio or television plays that Orton rewrote for the theater. In order to assess their contribution to the contemporary drama, they must be considered in three different contexts: the history of comedy from Aristophanes through the Restoration period to the aestheticism at the turn of the century; the avant-garde theater, including the theater of the absurd, tragicomedy, and surrealist farce; and the New Wave British dramatists, such as John Osborne, Harold Pinter, and John Arden, as well as their predecessor Arnold Wesker. To these three traditions Orton adds his own particular twist, which can be described as his parodic imagination.

What is most important to Orton in the history of comedy is the comedy of manners, which exposes social absurdities by pushing them to an extreme. Screens and closet doors that conceal moral and sexual hypocrisy are forced open, inviting gossip, scandal, and intrigue. Socially scripted behavior and modes of interaction are pushed toward moments of crisis through the confrontation of character stereotypes: Molière's imagined invalid, his misanthrope, and his imposter are only a few examples of such types that verge on moral allegories. In the British tradition the comedy of manners adds to this structure an emphasis on wit, usually expressed in quick observations and the art of repartee. Restoration comedy, which proved particularly important for Orton, derives its humor from both the confrontation of various types and the wit with which some of these types express themselves. Laughing at characters and their limitations, the Restoration audience laughed with these characters as well, appreciating their mastery of verbal wit. Wit is presented as a value in these plays, and witty characters are the true heroes of comic dialogue, even if they are so morally corrupt that they must finally be excluded from the play's happy ending.

Orton does not have such scruples. For him, exposing what Molière had called "social absurdities" no longer requires something like Tartuffe's public exposure or a critique of the school for scandal. His endings can be more ambiguous, more ironic, or more grotesque. Orton is not so much concerned with assuring the distance of comedy from tragedy; in fact he remarks in his diary on the proximity of his farces to tragedy. In some cases this means that he reworks material from Greek tragedies—for example, The Erpingham Camp is a farcical version of the Bacchae. While Orton's plays do not follow the endings of classical comedy, they nonetheless rely on some of its plot elements, such as complicated intrigues and escalating levels of deceit and conspiracy that are brought to climactic confrontations. What Orton also takes from the comedy of manners is an extensive use of its character types. He lifts some of them directly from classical comedy—the imposter, the hypocritical priest, the naive, good-hearted victim—but adds newer ones, such as the corrupt police detective and the confused psychiatrist. And as in the comedy of manners, the comic situation arises out of the confrontation of these narrowly confined types.

What differentiates Orton's plays from Restoration comedy and its nineteenth-century inheritors is the disparity between characters and dialogue. This is partially due to the fact that Orton's plays are not set in the aristocratic circles of the comedy of manners but in the working-class or lower-middle-class circles of social or naturalist drama. Despite this difference Orton insists on endowing his characters with a debased version of Restoration wit, often sacrificing the verisimilitude of his dialogue to it. While for some critics this combination of lower social class and wit is an artificial yoking of opposites, for others it constitutes a crucial element of Orton's revision of the traditional genre conventions of comedy. Most convincingly Martin Esslin describes Orton's work as a "comedy of (ill) manners." Orton characters are not ashamed of their bad, working-class manners, and at the same time they are endowed with a fast dialogue that seems to aspire, albeit unsuccessfully, to Congreve's or Sheridan's repartee. The humorous one-liners are not just the low end of Restoration wit; often they come out involuntarily and are therefore less the product of the characters' presence of mind than of the author's. Whereas in the comedy of manners, we usually laugh with the witty characters, in Orton's plays we more often than not have to admire Orton's crooked wit while laughing with him at the ill manners of his characters, who are the victims of language and not its masters.

This forced alliance of artificial wit and low characters mutates the comedy of manners to a considerable extent; it marks, as well, the transformation of comedy and farce through the historical avant-garde and the theater of the absurd. The particular form of farce that developed around the turn of the twentieth century emerges from the appropriation, by the established drama, of elements of popular puppet theater. Such plays as Alfred Jarry's *Ubu Roi* and Federico Garcia Lorca's puppet farces exploit the extreme violence that characterizes puppet plays, such as Punch and Judy, for the use of the theater at large. Like puppets, bodies are frequently dismembered and killed, evoking shrill laughter rather than horror or compassion. These presurrealist plays are followed by the violent performances of futurists and dadaists, leading ultimately to the theater of the absurd. What the theater of the absurd has retained from the avant-garde tradition of farce is a fundamental disrespect for the integrity of the human body and a detachment of characters from moral concerns. Death, destruction, and dismemberment—dead bodies, glass eyes falling out of corpses, and casual murders—are common elements in Orton's plays. Considered by themselves, they amount to a repertoire of violence befitting not a comedy but a revenge tragedy, a genre for which Orton repeatedly expressed an affinity. However, in the hands of the avant-garde and of Orton, these elements, no longer part of systematic and tragic violence done to the human body, generate carnivalesque laughter directed toward the body's lack of integrity. Even though none of Orton's plays, with the notable exception of *Fred and Madge,* are directly part of the historical avant-garde, his farces would not have been possible without the avant-garde and the theater of the absurd.

Another way in which the theater of the absurd, and in particular the works of Samuel Beckett, influenced Orton is through his place in the New Wave British theater. Orton was something of a latecomer in this group; its most important figures—Wesker, Osborne, and Pinter—had their debut successes years before *Loot,* or even *Entertaining Mr. Sloane,* appeared on stage. In his *Chicken Soup with Barley* (1959), Arnold Wesker was primarily concerned with a social and socialist critique, with the representation of a revolution and its adversaries. Partially following Bertolt Brecht's epic theater, Wesker expressed explicit political partisanship, which he combined with a naturalist investment in the determining force of social and material conditions. Even though Orton's plays do not reproduce those of the engaged playwright

Wesker, they share his social critique and potentially anarchic attitude. Orton's *The Good and Faithful Servant,* for example, criticizes the dehumanizing nature of industrial labor and the cynically exploitive attitude of those possessing the means of production. Orton and Wesker therefore share not only the milieu in which their plays are set but also a commitment to social critique from the point of view of the working class.

John Osborne's breakthrough success, *Look Back in Anger* (1956), also looks at the world from the point of view of the disenfranchised, but in a less naturalist manner than Wesker. Violence, here, is enacted not by the police and the establishment but by the inhabitants of confined, domestic spaces, and not with stones or clubs but with manipulations of language. The careful and subtle construction of nuanced dialogue is something Osborne shares with Harold Pinter, the most influential of the New Wave dramatists. His eminence, first achieved in 1958 with *The Birthday Party,* exerts an almost threatening influence on Orton's *Entertaining Mr. Sloane,* which borrows its architecture and even fragments of its dialogue. Pinter's "comedies of menace" evoke the kind of menace emanating not only from physical violence, as in Orton or Wesker, but also, as in Osborne, from the repressed tensions between domestic characters. Nevertheless, some of Orton's plays—*Entertaining Mr. Sloane, The Ruffian on the Stair,* and *Funeral Games*—are indebted to Pinter's scenes of domestic violence. The first two, in particular, are set in enclosed spaces that are shaken up by violent acts of intrusion. Pinter's shadow looms so large over these plays that Orton went out of his way to establish his distance, even to the point of claiming that it was he who had influenced Pinter's work. In his *Diaries* Orton records a conversation in which he asserted that Pinter's *"The Homecoming* couldn't have been written without *Sloane"* (p. 238). It was perhaps because Orton was the youngest of the New Wave dramatists that he found himself in a struggle of influence with them.

Orton's strategy for responding to the traditions of history of comedy, avant-garde farce, and contemporary British theater, and for dealing with their domineering impact on his own work, is parody. If Orton ever mastered the art of drama, he mastered it as the art of parody. Stunned by Genet's writing, he reacted by planning a parody of Genet; encountering Brecht or Wesker, he planned a parody of the political theater. Furthermore, Orton had parodied the diary form in *Between Us Girls,* the picaresque novel in *The Vision of Gombold Proval,* and science fiction in *The Mechanical Womb.* Similarly, he would claim that his drawing room plays are not imitations of Pinter and Osborne but parodies. Each of Orton's late plays must be read and viewed as a parody, and the differences between them are due to the particular genres and styles he parodies in them.

THE RUFFIAN ON THE STAIR

ORTON's first performed play, *The Ruffian on the Stair* (1964), confronts the dilemma of imitation and parody most urgently. In the opening scene a couple, Joyce and Mike, are chatting over breakfast. As soon as Mike leaves, another man, Wilson, appears, in the mistaken belief that there is a room to rent. Exploiting Joyce's halfhearted hospitality, he refuses to take no for an answer and forces his way into her home. This exposition resembles that of Pinter's *The Room,* which begins with a similar misunderstanding and subsequent intrusion. In *The Room,* as in related plays by Pinter such as *The Birthday Party* and *The Caretaker,* an initial violation leads to more and more oppressive acts of direct and indirect violence while the motives and the history of the intruders remain hidden; the plays thus stage an increasingly claustrophobic and enigmatic oppressiveness with sudden eruptions of violence. In *The Birthday Party* one inhabitant of a house is brutally abducted, and in *The Room* the same kind of violence is directed toward another resident, who is eventually killed. Whereas in Pinter these culminating moments of violence are used sparingly, after careful buildups through dialogue, Orton's *The Ruffian on the Stair* does not obey such well-made schemes. The violence of the intruder appears in the first moment, and thus seems more spontaneous and arbitrary than the action of Pinter's enigmatic, but determined, characters. Orton simply takes the figure of Pinter's intruder as a given, as something that can be almost carelessly taken for granted, in order to people his own plays. His energy is directed not at creating original characters but at perverting those he finds in his predecessors.

The Ruffian on the Stair begins to revolt more openly against Pinter when the violence, with

which Pinter always ends, does not lead to the expected catastrophe. The returning husband does not pay attention to Joyce's report about the violent intruder, not even when Wilson repeats his clandestine intrusions several times. When finally, in the fourth scene, Joyce manages to confront Wilson with Mike, Mike not only fails to throw Wilson out of the house but instantly befriends him because of their shared Irish ancestry. As the conversation wanders even more astray, from Wilson's mother to the pope, the oppressive atmosphere of the previous three scenes is completely forgotten. Here, too, Orton is not concerned with the credibility of dialogue and situation, only with its farcical effects. In the final scene the intruder does not perform the long-expected sexual assault; he pretends to be intimate with Joyce, as a provocative joke directed at Mike. He has Mike find him with his pants unzipped, embracing Joyce. Even though Joyce, by now used to the intruder's abrupt behavior, laconically recommends, "Put your clothes on. Don't be so silly" (*Complete Plays,* p. 60), Wilson insists on performing his show. This unmotivated joke goes wrong when Mike breaks into the room and fires, without a word, first at the goldfish in the corner and then at Wilson, who is mortally wounded but still capable of uttering: "He took it serious. How charming" (*Complete Plays,* p. 60).

In contrast to Pinter, Orton's characters do not notice the contradictions inherent in the situations they are in, and they do not react to them in predictable ways. Whereas Pinter's characters get caught up in gripping and oppressive dialogues, Orton's conversations never stay focused and keep getting sidetracked by trivialities and details. Intrusion as a practical joke; culminating violence as misunderstanding; and a continual disproportion between cause and effect, situation and behavior, character and dialogue—these are the techniques with which Orton undermines the Pinter play and through which his passion for parody turns Pinter's threatening shadow into farce.

ENTERTAINING MR. SLOANE

EVEN though Orton was able to add his own edge to Pinter's comedy of menace by turning menace into farce, this did not mean that he was capable of easily giving up the model he was parodying. His next play, *Entertaining Mr. Sloane,* begins with a similarly Pinteresque situation. The stage direction reads, "A room. Evening" (*Complete Plays*, p. 65) and the opening dialogue again is about a room to rent. Now, however, the landlady, Kath, is determined to exploit her new tenant, Mr. Sloane, for her pleasure; and the inhabitants of this home are not a married couple but Kath and her frail, though imposing, father, Kemp. At first it seems as if Kemp and Kath's brother, Ed, are going to intervene in the ensuing affair between Kath and Mr. Sloane. This predictable plot, however, is perverted and parodied as soon as it is begun. Through a first coincidence it turns out that Mr. Sloane killed his former boss; but no one, besides Kemp, who discovers the identity of Sloane, takes any interest in this circumstance, because by the time the murder is revealed en passant, the power relations have shifted considerably. Now both Kath and Ed have taken advantage of Mr. Sloane, Kath as landlord and lover, and Ed as employer, mate, and lover. No one is taken aback when Mr. Sloane kills the only person who could spoil their fun, the siblings' father, Kemp. And by now the audience should not be very much surprised that Mr. Sloane's second murder is as of little consequence as his first one. The third act is devoted to devising ways of concealing the murder, for both siblings are ready to accept the sacrifice of their father as the price of their pleasure. The final arrangement between the two to share Mr. Sloane equally, each enjoying him for half a year, takes place, not uncharacteristically for Orton, in front of their father's corpse.

Orton's version of Pinteresque violence is as macabre as it is farcical. The characters are driven by their desires to such an extent that they have a hard time keeping up even a minimum of decorum. In pursuit of their passions, they are detached from their environment and their own interiority. The characters' artificial dialogue is grafted onto a farcical parody of any kind of expected plot. What promises to become either a melodramatic family struggle among father, brother, and sister or a detective story leading to the discovery of the murder, or even an attempt to reform Mr. Sloane into someone capable of holding a steady job under Ed's guidance, instead turns out to be nothing but a set of traps the characters have laid for one another. The only thing that counts is the satisfaction of desire, and to desire everything will be subjected. Ed says, "You're had him six months; I'll have him the next six" (p. 148). The reality of this desire, whether it is heterosexual or homosexual, is presented not as subversive but as a matter of fact. It is perhaps in this casual representation of desire that Orton's plays, even as they are constructed, artificial, and derivative of the material they parody, seem to gather their own momentum, if not their own language.

THE GOOD AND FAITHFUL SERVANT

WITH his next play, *The Good and Faithful Servant* (1967), Orton is able, for the first time, to leave behind the enclosed rooms and their intruders, operating instead with a new set of figures, problems, and constellations. The domestic scene is opened onto the world of industrial labor and pensions, of capitalist production and exploitation. Having worked his way through Pinter, Orton now tackles Wesker's combination of social drama and melodrama. Again he uses a given material and structure only to scavenge from it what he can use to put together his patchwork of farce and parody. Buchanan, an industrial worker, is supposed to be honored by his firm on the day of his retirement. One of the rewards is an electric toaster, which breaks the first time it is used. But while the plot is threatening to take a turn that would classify it as a social critique of the heartless capitalist system, Buchanan, by coincidence, encounters the secret love of his youth. What is even more surprising is that he has been working in the same firm with her, without knowing it. Eugene Ionesco's *The Bald Soprano*, with its couple who discover by coincidence that they have been living together, comes to mind here. What we see at work in these scenes is the plot structure that defines melodrama, what Eric Bentley has called the long arm of coincidence. Although the firm is not impressed by Buchanan's discovery—"Have you been feeding false information into our computers?" (*Complete Plays*, p. 159)—this coincidence nevertheless makes the social critique of the play more melodramatic.

Needless to say, in Orton's hands melodrama is even more parodied than the social and naturalist plot of alienated industrial labor. In the last analysis, however, this engaged plot does not altogether lose its critical impact, for parody, too, and not just naturalism, can have the subversive effect of unmasking social hypocrisy. The play, for all its farce, is therefore Orton's most socially engaged statement in the theater. Whereas in most of his other plays the characters' detachment from their environment and their language is in the service of parody for its own sake, here parody acquires a certain political depth. The characters' emotional detachment satisfies farce's demand that they retain their poker faces no matter what, but here it appears as an extreme kind of apathy that might be the consequence of industrial labor. The detachment of farce thus becomes the alienation of capitalism. *The Good and Faithful Servant* remains true to Orton's parodic style, but it also is capable of sustaining a critical impetus that is indebted to more than just a farcical unsettling of conventions and expectations. In this play farce and social drama thus form a curious, but effective, symbiosis.

LOOT

ORTON's next play, *Loot* (1965), prefaced with a passage from Shaw's *Misalliance,* promises a similar kind of farcical social critique, directed, this time, at the police. "Anarchism is a game at which the police can beat you" (*Complete Plays*, p. 193) is the line from Shaw, and anarchism certainly characterizes the mode of the play. The police, however, are not the only object of parody, nor the only agent of anarchy. Everyone is engaged in different, barely concealed, plots and plans that keep going wrong, thus necessitating more intrigues and schemes to contain them. Fay, a nurse who has taken care of the late Mrs. McLeavy, tries to seduce the recent widower; his son Hal, who has robbed a bank with the help of his mate Dennis, tries to get away from home; and Dennis, in turn, woos Fay. All of this happens around, in front of, and on top of the coffin in which Mrs. McLeavy is being displayed before she is taken to her final resting place.

But this is just the beginning of the play's systematic irreverence. When Detective Truscott, a truly overdone parody of Sherlock Holmes, begins investigating the bank robbery, Dennis and Hal decide that the stolen money is no longer safe in a locked wardrobe and proceed to hide it in the coffin, putting the corpse in the wardrobe. As always in farce, such measures never go undetected, and Fay discovers the whole matter all too soon. Since the course of events is dictated not by probability but by the emotionally disengaged scheming of its agents, Fay soon becomes part of the conspiracy and is enlisted to take the corpse out of the wardrobe again, in order to place it in a mattress cover tied with strips of cloth. The corpse will continue to wander around, for the rest of the play, in its newly acquired role as a wrapped sewing dummy. The three conspirators and the parodic detective continue their dance around the dead body, to the increasing horror of McLeavy, who is the helpless witness to this madness and the only character to retain a minimum of common sense while intrigue and irreverence are evolving around him. This, too, is a frequent structure of farce, which needs a hapless victim to celebrate the play's anarchy all the more. McLeavy's traces of common sense are necessary to throw into relief the absurdity of the rest of *Loot*'s world.

What *Loot* stages in this confrontation of farcical detachment and the mourning McLeavy is a parody of the comedy of manners. The play finds its voice not in the programmatic anarchy of events, which it shares with any other farce, but in the conflict, typical of the comedy of manners, between intrigue and the necessity of keeping one's face. While the traditional comedy gradually exposes the characters who cling all the more desperately to their social masks, in *Loot* these characters hardly bother to conceal their ulterior motives, such as hiding stolen money or marrying a rich widower. Only the presence of Detective Truscott makes them worry about their deeds at all. But even in front of Truscott, they cannot maintain their faces and good manners for long. The final blow to manners comes when the detective no longer even pretends to embody law and order but reveals himself to be as corrupt and anarchic as the play has promised all along. At the end Truscott joins the conspirators, McLeavy is outwitted by the anarchists, and the comedy of manners has been successfully perverted to a comedy of ill manners.

THE ERPINGHAM CAMP

IN his next play Orton directs his parodic energy to tragedy, for *The Erpingham Camp* (1966) is a parody of Euripides' *Bacchae.* Along with the early *Fred and Madge,* this play is more directly concerned with theatricality than any other of Orton's farces. As in *Fred and Madge* a stage manager, who is a typically ill-mannered Ortonesque character, without any sense of decorum or taste, plays a central role. As organizer for the evening entertainment at Erpingham's holiday camp, this stage manager, Redcoat Riley, insults the audience to such a degree that it eventually revolts and starts attacking the camp's management in an ecstatic frenzy that resembles that of the Bacchae. For all its parodic quality this play perhaps entertains the fantasy that an Ortonesque character on a stage might in fact trigger anarchy and incite a bourgeois audience to acts of bacchic destruction. Two figures try to contain this eruption: Erpingham himself, who keenly observes, "This whole episode has been fermented by a handful of intellectuals" (*Complete Plays,* p. 308), and therefore believes himself to be capable of controlling the frenzy, and the Padre, who, like Erpingham, overestimates his authority and the authority of the Catholic Church.

Catholicism is the most frequent object of Orton's farcical satire. Henri Bergson, in his pivotal study on comedy and laughter, identifies the external imitation of religious practices as one of the central techniques of comedy. Orton uses this technique frequently and without hesitation. He does not always attack institutions of actual power and oppression, but uses mock figures from the popular tradition of satire, whether they be part of the establishment or just common objects of comedy. Orton, for all his posing as an underprivileged revolutionary, directs his farcical critique at those social groups and institutions that have always been the object of British comedy: Catholics, the Irish, and the police. What drives his parodies is not primarily social commitment but the necessity to produce readily identifiable characters whose typified representation he can easily turn into parodies. Not the critical effects of his plays, but their satirical technique, is thus at the center of their inception.

The Erpingham Camp derives its power from the fact that tragedy and farce are more alike than farce and classical comedy. What farce and tragedy share is their violence and will to destruction, and this play uses violence freely. At the end of the play, Erpingham, having been severely beaten, falls through the floor of his office and lands among dancers on the ballroom floor, leaving the place in blood. Because it parodies tragedy and not the comedy of manners, this play can unfold its

farcical crudity most ruthlessly. The detachment of the characters from their language and their environment is not in the service of effecting a debased but artificial wit, as in so many other Orton plays, but rather exposes the violence such emotional detachment produces. Erpingham and the Padre in particular have to pay for their blindness, their naive belief in their own authority, and their ignorance of the anarchic, bacchic forces that are unleashed against them. This play, more than any other, shows what it means to be a farcical character, and it shows that farcical characters only barely survive when they are threatened by tragic endings.

FUNERAL GAMES

WITH his next play, *Funeral Games* (1968), Orton again changes the direction of parody. The dramatic genre *Funeral Games* parodies is less clearly defined than in Orton's other plays: it retains elements of a comedy of intrigue, such as blackmail and adultery; it presents a perverted detective story; and it stages a revenge plot with violent dismemberment of human bodies. This mixture of elements is intensified by the fact that speech, character, expected emotion, and scenic situation are not coordinated with each other, and the disjunctions between them are more extreme than in any of Orton's other farces. If there is something in this play that holds together the different generic elements, it is the extreme to which its characters show a lack of emotion, retain their poker faces even in the most ghastly of situations, and remain trapped in their blindness and the brutal ways in which they pursue their goals.

While *Funeral Games* does not quite know exactly what it is trying to satirize in terms of genre, it knows all the better what kind of figures it is dragging into its farce: as in *Loot* it most severely ridicules the institutions of religion. This time McCorquodale, a defrocked priest who murdered his wife, and Pringle, a founder of a vaguely defined hedonistic sect under a religious cover, who is concerned with his wife's supposed infidelity, are the agents of religious hypocrisy. In order to save himself from the embarrassment of cuckoldry, Pringle spreads the rumor that he has killed his wife and proves it by circulating a hand from McCorquodale's murdered wife, in the fashion of such plays as Shakespeare's *Titus Andronicus*. Pringle's self-destructive desire to save face goes so far that he allows himself to be arrested for the alleged murder of his wife at the end of the play. His last words show that not even the most outrageous hypocrisy will keep him from producing religious platitudes: "Let us go to prison. Some angel will release us from our place of confinement" (*Complete Plays*, p. 360). Like *Loot*, *Funeral Games* tries to shock the audience not only with its irreverent use of corpses but also, and more importantly, with the failure of its characters to be shocked at all. These characters pursue their bizarre individual trajectories with radical determination and without concern for the consequences of their actions. At the same time they are engaged in a dialogue that is so artificial and so geared toward blunt comic effects that it leaves them as ill defined as the wooden puppets in a Punch and Judy show. *Funeral Games* is perhaps Orton's most radical, but not his most convincing, experiment in combining a macabre revenge plot with parodies of priests and artificial farce.

WHAT THE BUTLER SAW

ORTON's last play, *What the Butler Saw* (1967), which he never saw performed, is arguably his best. The artificial one-liners are more tightly connected to their speakers; the characters, more individualized; and the farcical energy of the play, more channeled. The sense that the characters are more integrated into their environment might have to do with the fact that their excesses take place in a lunatic asylum, and the absurd madness of two psychiatric experts, Dr. Prentice and Dr. Rance, seems perhaps more promising as a farcical setup than as priestly hypocrisy. Compared with Orton's other plays, *What the Butler Saw* is less a parody of an existing genre than a combination of comedy and farce, with undressing and cross-dressing, intrigue and desire, sadomasochist interludes, increasing complications, and a final confrontation. The play is prefaced with a quote from *The Revenger's Tragedy*, but it retains fewer elements of a revenge tragedy than either *Funeral Games* or *Loot*. Even though the characters leave the stage "weary, bleeding, drugged and drunk" (*Complete Plays*, p. 448), they are nevertheless alive at the end and thus have managed to avoid an-

other Dionysian tragedy. While the play ends almost a tragedy, it begins in good comic fashion. Dr. Prentice tries to seduce his new secretary, Geraldine, under the guise of a medical exam that requires undressing: "And kindly remove your stockings. I wish to see what effect your stepmother's death had upon your legs" (p. 366). By the end of the play, everyone else not only has undressed, but also is wearing someone else's clothes. While Dr. Prentice conceals his desires behind a medical facade, Dr. Rance appears as a disinterested, professional observer. However, he not only accepts Dr. Prentice's absurd diagnoses but imposes a new, and even more absurd, one onto the hapless Geraldine, who is thus violated by male desire and psychiatry at the same time. Dr. Rance is the parody of a *raisonneur*, the supposedly disinterested analyst of the play, whose maxim, "No madman ever accepts madness. Only the sane do that" (p. 415), is true particularly in that it applies to his own blindness. Otherwise, every other bit of his analysis is as wrong as could be.

As in comedy or in comic opera, the confusions and complications ensuing from Dr. Prentice's heavy-handed seduction plot draw more and more characters into their vortex, including, once more, a representative of the police, Sergeant Match. Topic and structure are more directly indebted to classical comedy, especially to the open sexuality of Aristophanes and Plautus, and for this reason *What the Butler Saw*, while still bearing Orton's signature, is his most classical comedy or comic farce. The play is driven less by the project of parodying a whole genre than by an interest in a particular constellation of figures: the two psychiatrists, Dr. Prentice's wife, the sergeant, and Geraldine. The artificial wit does not appear as arbitrary as in some other plays, because it is grounded in a specific discourse, psychiatry, and in the doctor-patient relation. *What the Butler Saw* can therefore be called Orton's first mature work, if maturity is a category appropriate to his art of parody. With this last play Orton has not given up parody, but he has found ways to integrate it more tightly with dramatic and generic structures, with character and dialogue. *What the Butler Saw* uses many elements of previous plays, such as the long arm of melodramatic coincidence, when Geraldine and Nick Beckett turn out to be Mrs. Prentice's children, whom she had given up for adoption. The proof is the two pieces of a brooch—Mrs. Prentice had pinned one piece on each child; they appear in the final act, just at the moment when the play threatens to turn into a nightmare. This parodic appearance of melodrama infuses the final scene with enough sentiment to counterbalance the farcical detachment of the characters. In *What the Butler Saw* Orton has finally found the right proportion of violence, intrigue, parody, tragedy, and melodrama to create a coherent play—his masterwork.

Orton's collected works, from his picaresque novels and experimental plays to his successful dramatic pieces, form an unusual trajectory in the evolution of a parodic style that combines extreme farce and crude wit to mold a new kind of comedy that we now refer to by the adjective "Ortonesque." However, from the perspective of his last and best play, *What the Butler Saw,* all the others might be considered important and skillful studies in the art of parody, but mere preparations for a new chapter in the history of farce. That Orton had only begun this chapter is one of the tragedies of his untimely death.

SELECTED BIBLIOGRAPHY

I. PLAYS. *Entertaining Mr. Sloane* (London, 1964; New York, 1965); *Crimes of Passion: The Ruffian on the Stair and The Erpingham Camp* (London, 1967); *Loot* (London and New York, 1967); *What the Butler Saw* (London and New York, 1969); *Funeral Games and The Good and Faithful Servant* (London, 1970); *Joe Orton: The Complete Plays* (London, 1976; New York, 1977); *The Boy Hairdresser and Lord Cucumber* (London, 1998); *Fred and Madge and The Visitor* (London, 1998).

II. OTHER WRITINGS. *Head to Toe* (London, 1971), a novel; *Up Against It* (New York, 1979); *The Orton Diaries: Including the Correspondence of Edna Welthorpe and Others,* ed. by John Lahr (London, 1986); *Between Us Girls* (London, 1998), a novel.

III. BIOGRAPHICAL WORKS. K. Fraser, "Joe Orton: His Brief Career," *Modern Drama* 14 (1971); John Lahr, *Prick Up Your Ears: The Biography of Joe Orton* (New York, 1978); Simon Moss, *Cock-Ups* (London, 1984).

IV. CRITICAL STUDIES. John Russell Taylor, *The Second Wave: New British Drama for the Seventies* (New York, 1971); Manfred Draudt, "Comic, Tragic, or Absurd? On Some Parallels Between the Farces of Joe Orton and Seventeenth-Century Tragedy: *Loot, Hamlet, Revenger's Tragedy,*" *English Studies* 59, no. 3 (1978); Simon Shepherd, "Edna's Last Stand, or Joe Orton's Dialectic of Entertainment," *Renaissance & Modern Studies* 22 (1978); Mary I. Camus, "Farce and Verbal Style in the Plays of Joe Orton," *Journal of Popular Culture* 13 (1980); Martin Esslin, "Joe Orton: The Comedy of (Ill) Manners," in *Contemporary English Drama,* ed. by C. W. E. Bigsby (London and New York, 1981); C. W. E. Bigsby, *Joe Orton* (London, 1982); Michael Beehler, "Joe Orton and the Heterogeneity of the Book," *Sub-stance* 33, no. 341 (1982); Maurice Charney, *Joe Orton* (London, 1984); Randall S. Nakayama, "Domesticating Mr. Orton," *Theatre Journal* 45, no. 2 (May 1993); Goran Nieragden, "Comedy and Menace: A Grecian Look at the Dialogue in Joe Orton's *Loot,*" *Germanisch-Romanische Monatsschrift* 44, no. 1 (1994); Francesca Coppa, "Coming Out in the Room: Joe Orton's Epigrammatic Re / Vision of Harold Pinter's Menace," *Modern Drama* 40, no. 1 (1997); Grant Stirling, "Ortonesque / Carnivalesque: The Grotesque Realism of Joe Orton," *Journal of Dramatic Theory and Criticism* 11, no. 2 (1997).

CARYL PHILLIPS

(1958–   )

Louise Yelin

CARYL PHILLIPS WAS born on the Caribbean island of St. Kitts, grew up in England, and now divides his time among New York, London, and the Caribbean. He began publishing novels in Britain (his work has been translated into many languages); his early books are set in the Caribbean; and he was inspired to become a writer in the United States when he read Richard Wright's *Native Son* (1940) and Ralph Ellison's *Invisible Man* (1952). Much of Phillips' work explores what it means to be black and English or, more generally, a black European. He rejects the exclusionary notions of British identity promoted by Enoch Powell and, later, Margaret Thatcher. Thus his career as a British writer needs to be placed in a transatlantic, transnational, cosmopolitan, postcolonial context that expands traditional notions of Britishness.

The global context of Phillips' work governs the settings and subject matter of his novels: exile and displacement in and around what sociologist Paul Gilroy identifies as the "black Atlantic." Equally important is Phillips' probing of the relationship of history and memory, his recovery of voices muted and experiences rendered invisible in archives that preserve the records of what he calls European tribalism—that is, racism in the many and diverse forms it takes in the modern and postmodern world.

Phillips' fiction attempts to reconstruct or imagine the lives of those marooned, to use a word that recurs throughout his work, in Europe, in Africa, in the Caribbean, in the United States, in history itself. His project of reconstruction is not a quest for authenticity, but rather an acknowledgment and adumbration of cultural difference. He carries out this project through postmodern narrative strategies of irony and quotation, and—in the voices and perspectives of the women, often but not always white women, who are among the most powerfully realized characters in his fiction— through writing across differences of race, place, gender, and generation. The female protagonists with whom he clearly identifies offer a vantage point, an outsider's perspective, that is not his own. Similarly, he invents his own fictional universe by composing his novels out of intertextual allusions that critically mark, and thereby revise, precursor texts ranging from the canonical to the obscure. Phillips' poetics of difference produces a literary enterprise at once suspicious of naive notions of identity and respectful of historical specificity and otherness.

Phillips is also a prolific writer of plays, film and television scripts, essays, and literary journalism. His work reflects a consistent point of view, that of a cosmopolitan black intellectual at home everywhere and nowhere, one for whom exile and diaspora have made possible a remarkable body of work.

LIFE

PHILLIPS was born in St. Kitts, in the British West Indies, on 13 March 1958. Three months later his parents migrated to Leeds in northern England. As a child Phillips lived in a series of predominantly white, working-class neighborhoods. At school there was little or no discussion of the accomplishments of black people, and the writings of black authors were not studied. The political climate he inhabited was punctuated by such well-known expressions of British racism as the 1968 address in which Enoch Powell warned that the growth of Britain's black population would flood the nation, and the 1979 election campaign speech in which Margaret Thatcher claimed that England was in danger of being "swamped" by its enemies. Thus, Phillips observes, he "grew up riddled with the cultural confusions of being black and British . . . at the older end of a generation who eventually found their communal voice in the Notting Hill riots in 1976" (*The European Tribe*, p. 2).

After secondary school Phillips entered Queens College, Oxford University, where he earned his B.A. degree in English literature with honors in 1979. At Oxford he played several sports and was centrally involved in the drama society, for which he directed plays by Shakespeare, Ibsen, Tennessee Williams, and Harold Pinter. While searching for plays to direct and books to read, he found nothing about the experience of blacks who, like himself, had grown up in Britain. After his second year at Oxford, Phillips traveled to the United States; the examples of Wright and Ellison and the absence of a comparable literature in Britain gave him the impetus to become a writer.

After Oxford, Phillips lived in Edinburgh, Scotland, where he began writings plays and scripts. He subsequently returned to London. Three of his plays were produced during the early 1980s: *Strange Fruit* (1980) in Sheffield; *Where There Is Darkness* (1982) in London; and *The Shelter* (1983) in London. During this period Phillips also wrote numerous television scripts and *The Wasted Years* (1984), which won the BBC Giles Cooper Award for best radio play of 1984. He also wrote the screenplay for the film *Playing Away,* which appeared in 1986. In 1983 Phillips took a "sabbatical from Mrs. Thatcher's Britain" ("Living and Writing in the Caribbean," p. 47) and returned to the Caribbean for the first time since he had left as an infant. He arrived as St. Kitts and Nevis were becoming an independent nation. His experiences in St. Kitts appear, transformed, in his first two novels, *The Final Passage* (1985), which was awarded the Malcolm X Prize for Literature, and *A State of Independence* (1986). He did not settle in the Caribbean, however; while he was completing *A State of Independence,* he undertook the travels around Europe that form the basis of *The European Tribe* (1987), which brought him the Martin Luther King Memorial Prize. For several years thereafter Phillips divided his time between London and the Caribbean. Since his appointment as visiting writer (1990–1992) and writer-in-residence (1992–1998) at Amherst College, he has lived mainly in New York City and London.

In the late 1980s and into the 1990s, Phillips continued writing fiction while teaching at Amherst, and reading from his work and lecturing throughout the world. *Higher Ground* (1989) was followed by *Cambridge* (1991), for which he was named London (Sunday) *Times* Young Writer of the Year; *Crossing the River* (1993), which was short-listed for the 1993 Booker Prize and won the James Tait Black Memorial Prize in 1994; and *The Nature of Blood* (1997). In 1998 he became professor of English and Henry R. Luce Professor of Migration and Social Order at Barnard College in New York City. As part of the Luce professorship, he has organized the Barnard College Forum on Migration, a series of lectures to be given over several years. Phillips' interest in the topic also led him to edit *Extravagant Strangers: A Literature of Belonging* (1997), a collection of essays by British writers—ranging from Olaudah Equiano and William Makepeace Thackeray to Doris Lessing and Timothy Mo—who became British by migrating to Britain. Throughout this period Phillips has also written numerous essays and reviews; his nonfiction reflects not only his breadth of knowledge but also his active involvement in a worldwide community of writers.

EARLY NOVELS: ATLANTIC CROSSINGS

PHILLIPS observes that he writes about the Caribbean because it "contains Europe and Africa, as I do. . . . It is where Africa met Europe on somebody else's soil" (Swift, "Caryl Phillips Interviewed," p. 102). His first two novels, *The Final Passage* and *A State of Independence,* explore the aftereffects of this meeting between Africa and Europe. Set on both sides of the Atlantic, they focus on the postwar migration from the Caribbean to Britain. They situate this migration in the larger histories of decolonization and displacement that define the second half of the twentieth century. In presenting the Caribbean as at once a point of departure, a destination, and a locale traversed in a global circulation of people, goods, and culture, Phillips explores the ways in which those who leave and return define themselves: not by where they were born or where they happen to be living, but rather by the journeying back and forth that underlies their nomadic identities.

THE FINAL PASSAGE, 1985 / 1958: MODERNISM WITH A DIFFERENCE

THE *Final Passage* is a novel about migration from the Caribbean to Britain. In the course of the narrative, Leila and Michael Preston, a young married couple with an infant son, Calvin, leave the place where they were born and grew up and journey to England. Seeking opportunities lacking on the "small proud island, overburdened with vegetation and complacency . . . [that] had been [their] home" (p. 20), they follow Leila's mother, who has gone to London for medical treatment. In London, Michael and Leila are thwarted by poverty and racism, including discrimination in housing and employment. Within a few months Leila's mother dies, and Michael drifts away from Leila. In fact, they have been alienated from one another since the outset of their relationship. Both before and after their marriage, Michael is involved with a woman named Beverley. In England, repeating a pattern established at "home," he spends more and more time away from Leila and Calvin and takes up with other women. Leila finds a job but, pregnant again, she is unable to work. The novel ends with her decision to return to the "small island she had left behind" (p. 203).

In *The Final Passage* Phillips tells the story of the first generation to leave the Caribbean and migrate to Britain in significant numbers, a postwar generation to which his own parents belong. In this he recalls such novels as George Lamming's *The Emigrants* (1954) and Samuel Selvon's *Lonely Londoners* (1956). Leila is born "the day war was declared in Europe" (p. 126); she is nineteen years old when she goes to England in 1958, the year Phillips was born and, three months later, he and his parents left St. Kitts. Leila is placed in a particular historical moment. Among the events that defined this moment were eruptions of violence against black West Indian immigrants in the London district of Notting Hill and in the city of Nottingham in the north, and an election campaign punctuated by a slogan, scrawled on billboards, that Leila notices as she enters London for the first time: "IF YOU WANT A NIGGER NEIGHBOUR VOTE LABOUR" (p. 122).

Written from the vantage point of the 1980s, *The Final Passage* not only recalls but also revises postwar narratives of immigration. Phillips complicates the polarities Caribbean-Britain and home-exile. "Home," reminiscent of St. Kitts, is an unnamed, unidentified island with a specific political and economic landscape, one that recurs in Phillips' second novel, *A State of Independence,* and in some of the later ones. This landscape is bounded by the principal city, Baytown, the small town of Sandy Bay, and the tiny village of St. Patrick's, where Leila grows up. Emigration to Britain is not a trajectory with one point of departure and one destination, but rather defines a segment of a global scene in which the United States looms large as a place where many go to make their fortunes.

Phillips eschews "realism," in particular, the accumulation of telling detail that, from the nineteenth century on, has filled out British novels with explicitly social themes. Instead, he presents characters through their observations, memories, and reflections. He also rejects a linear chronology of departure, journey, and arrival, a chronology that represents migration as a version of progress or, conversely, of decline and fall. Instead, his narrative moves back and forth through time and space. In the first section, "The End," Leila is waiting to board the ship that will take her and Michael to England. The second, "Home," returns to the year that precedes their departure. The third, "England," describes the period just after they arrive in London. Their journey across the ocean is recounted in the fourth, "The Passage." And their experience in London is resumed in the fifth section, "Winter," which describes Leila's mother's death, Michael's abandonment of her, and her decision to return home.

The novel is introduced by an epigraph from T. S. Eliot's *Little Gidding* (1942):

> A people without history
> Is not redeemed from time, for history is a pattern
> Of timeless moments. So, while the light fails
> On a winter's afternoon, in a secluded chapel
> History is now and England.
>
> (n.p.)

The epigraph also signals Phillips' polyglot, postcolonial frame of reference, echoing anthropologist Eric Wolf's use of its opening phrase in *Europe and the People Without History* (1982) to refer to the non-Western people, peasants, laborers, and immigrants, among others, omitted from traditional accounts of Western modernization. Under the sign of Eliot, an American who became an English writer, Phillips addresses the issue of British identity and raises questions that recur throughout his work. He asks, that is, whether "the people without history"—black immigrants and their children from the Caribbean and, by extension, from British colonies and former colonies in South Asia and Africa—can take title to the history that is "England" and claim English, or British, nationality.

The invocation of Eliot marks Phillips' affiliation with a high modernism not usually associated with British social novels, with narratives of immigration, or with the writings of British people of color, all of which are often treated—that is, misread—as authentic accounts of unmediated experience. Phillips' rupture of linear chronology, his "breaking the sequence," as Virginia Woolf puts it in *A Room of One's Own* (1929), fragments a conventional narrative that moves from colonial beginnings to metropolitan ends. The fourth section, "The Passage," mimics a conventional tale of departure, journey, and arrival, but, set in the middle of the novel, this story is relegated to a subordinate role in a larger narrative. A romance plot moving from courtship to marriage is evoked but derailed because Michael is not committed to Leila and Leila is emotionally withdrawn, passive, and disconnected. Thus, Phillips suggests, the new beginning of immigration, like the marriage that constitutes the denouement of romance, may be a dead end.

In articulating experimental form with subject matter usually identified with the social novel, *The Final Passage* exemplifies modernism with a difference. Phillips dissects the dominant—metropolitan—culture not, as Eliot does, through the tired voices of Tiresias and Prufrock, but rather from perspectives absent from or muted in the literary canon whose fragments are shored up in *The Waste Land* (1922). *The Final Passage* has an omniscient, impersonal, third-person narrator, but the most prominent point of view in the novel is that of Leila, the first of Phillips' female protagonists—others include Emily in *Cambridge* (1991), Irene in *Higher Ground* (1989), Joyce in *Crossing the River* (1993), and Eva in *The Nature of Blood*—who offer privileged angles of vision on the events they experience and, in some cases, recount. In writing from a woman's vantage point or in a woman's voice, Phillips undermines essentialist notions of gender and, for that matter, of race.

Leila's outlook, unlike that of some of her successors, is unremittingly negative. Yet her negativity is not simply a function of temperament, psychology, or her relationship with Michael; it also reflects the annihilating experience of racism, as when, looking for a flat to rent, she is assaulted by signs that read " 'No coloureds,' 'No vacancies,' 'No children' " (p. 155). Negation also enables her to come to terms with the strangeness of metropolitan London through an implied comparison with the familiar scenes she has left behind:

There were no green mountains, there were no colourful women with baskets on their heads selling peanuts or bananas or mangoes, there were no trees, no white houses on the hills, no hills, no wooden houses by the shoreline, and the sea was not blue and there was no beach, and there were no clouds, just one big cloud, and they had arrived.

(p. 142)

By describing the metropolitan scene from the perspective of a remembered colonial landscape, Leila's rhetoric of negation enunciates a postcolonial understanding of Britain, one elaborated in a black British culture in which Phillips himself plays a prominent role.

The Final Passage offers little substantial alternative to Leila's pervasive negativity. Millie and Bradeth, friends of Leila and Michael who remain on the island when Leila and Michael leave and grow closer to each other as Leila and Michael become estranged, function chiefly as foils for the main characters. Michael, the other character whose point of view is presented in the novel, also confronts a world in which whites are dominant, and blacks, subordinate. He is struck, before he leaves the island, by the "defeated faces that lined these streets" (p. 98). A friend warns him about the difficulties of life in England, yet urges him to leave: "You must be careful in England. Concentrate. . . . For a West Indian boy like you just being there is an education, for you going see what England do for sheself and what she did do for you and me here and everyone else on this island and all the other islands. It's a college for the West Indian" (p. 101). In London this warning is underscored by a West Indian coworker named Edwin:

They treat us worse than their dogs. The women expect you to do tricks with your biceps and sing calypso, or to drop down on one knee and pretend you're Paul Robeson or somebody. . . . You going to behave like a kettle for without knowing it you going to boil. It's how the white man in this country kills off the coloured man. He makes you heat up and blow yourself away.

(p. 168)

The racism that Edwin sketches so vividly is not monolithic: Leila is befriended by a white neighbor named Mary, yet Mary's friendship alone cannot salve Leila's experience of alienation and displacement.

The conflict between Leila and Michael is not resolved in the novel. Leila is suspended between England and the island "home" to which she intends to return. That return is realized in Phillips' second novel, *A State of Independence,* a text that, like its predecessor, asks whether those who traverse the Atlantic are at home on either side of the ocean.

A STATE OF INDEPENDENCE: *RETURN TO THE NATIVE LAND*

A State of Independence (1986) belongs to a genre that might be called the narrative of return. The protagonist, Bertram Francis, has lived in England for twenty years. The novel describes his return to the island of his birth at the moment of its emancipation from British colonial rule. Like Aimé Césaire's 1939 *Cahier d'un retour au pays natal* (Notebook of a Return to My Native Land), *A State of Independence* delineates the political and cultural geography of the Caribbean. Like Nadine Gordimer's *A Guest of Honour* (1970), it scrutinizes the politics that follow in the wake of decolonization. Like Jamaica Kincaid's *A Small Place* (1988) and Michelle Cliff's *No Telephone to Heaven* (1987), it explores the consequences of colonial and neocolonial exploitation of land and people alike. All these texts frame their inquiries into colonialism and its aftermath from the vantage points of protagonists returning to colonial or formerly colonial locations they left years before; in the process they call into question the very notion of emancipation. But unlike Kincaid, Cliff, Gordimer, and Césaire, Phillips conducts his investigation from the perspective of a character whose banality makes him an exemplar of the dubious state of independence reflected in the events described.

Published not long after St. Kitts and Nevis attained full independence from Great Britain in 1983, *A State of Independence* questions both key terms in its title. The novel asks whether, in a global order dominated by the United States, a small Caribbean island with a population of thirty-five thousand can exist as an independent nation-state. In fact it explores several different notions of independence, but rejects them all as inadequate, ineffective, or otherwise untenable in the Caribbean location it describes.

Soon after Bertram arrives on the island, he remarks, "The only way the black man is going to progress in the world is to set up his own shops and his own businesses independent of the white man" (p. 51). But the ostensible independence of black shop owners is compromised, if not foreclosed altogether, by their struggle to make a living. Visiting Baytown, Bertram remembers what he learned in the colonial school he attended: "Like most Caribbean towns, it was originally part slave-market and part harbour . . . [and] designed to facilitate the importation of Africans and the exportation of sugar" (p. 57). Slavery gave way to economic exploitation, which is now followed, in turn, by the freedom whose limits are manifest in the naming of "Independence-ville," a temporary shantytown (p. 58). Later, Patsy, the woman Bertram left behind when he went to England and the novel's most reliable observer of the political scene, tells him, "Nothing in this place ever truly falls into the past. It's all here in the present for we too small a country to have a past" (p. 142). Patsy's remark, which is echoed by Kincaid in *A Small Place,* is amplified at the end of the novel in Bertram's vision of the "abandoned and crumbling sugar mills, modest, almost discreet reminders of a troubled and bloody history, . . . [soon] to be converted into centrepieces for hotel complexes" (p. 157). Pointing to what has been or is about to be obliterated or transformed into monuments of tourism, Phillips insists on the importance of historical memory.

The history of deprivation, violence, and loss leads not to emancipation but rather, as Bertram discovers in his encounters with an old friend and rival, Jackson Clayton, to new—neocolonial—forms of political, economic, and cultural subjection. Jackson's career illustrates the history of black politics on the island. When Bertram goes to England on scholarship, Jackson remains behind. In the 1960s he refashions himself as Jackson X. Now, about to become a minister in the government of the new nation, he tells Bertram, "You English West Indians should just come back here to retire and sit in the sun. Don't waste your time trying to get into the fabric of the society for you're made of the wrong material for the modern Caribbean" (p. 136). What Jackson has in mind, however, is not "independence," but a relationship with the United States: "We living State-side now. We living under the eagle" (p. 112). Jackson's politics of expediency, or his tilt toward the United States, is not simply an expression of a personal lust for wealth and power. Many of the characters in the novel share his sentiments, most notably a young man resonantly named Livingstone who works at the Royal Hotel, where foreign delegates to the independence celebration are staying. Livingstone tells Bertram that he looks toward the "New York Yankees, Washington Redskins, Michael Jackson" (p. 103). American influence is reflected not only in the neocolonial kitsch of the Royal Hotel and similar landmarks of the emerging order but also, at the very end of the novel, in the advent of American cable television.

A State of Independence suggests that nationhood marks not a break with, but a repetition of, the colonial past. At the same time it undermines the oppositions between departure and return, home and exile, Caribbean and Britain that structure the myths of decolonizing nations. These binaries are decentered in Phillips' next book, an account of the wanderings around Europe that occupied him while he was completing work on its predecessors.

THE EUROPEAN TRIBE: *"OF AND NOT OF"*

In *The European Tribe* (1987) Phillips takes off in new directions. In genre he moves from fiction to nonfiction; in setting, from Britain and the Caribbean to Europe and North Africa. Yet in addressing questions of exile, nomadism, and displacement, this book elaborates the concerns of his first two novels and anticipates the scope of the later ones. Combining reportage, memoir, and travel writing, *The European Tribe* offers an ethnography of Europe, taking its place alongside such differently constructed ethnographies as James Clifford's *The Predicament of Culture* (1988) and Wolf's *Europe and the People Without History*. At the same time *The European Tribe* is an autoethnography, an examination of Phillips' own cultural identity as a black European. In this respect it can be read in conjunction with such essays as Salman Rushdie's "Imaginary Homelands" (1982) and Hanif Kureishi's "The Rainbow Sign" (1986), and the theoretical discussions of Homi Bhabha in "Dissemination" and other essays collected in *The Location of Culture* (1994).

Phillips was prompted to write *The European Tribe* by a series of circumstances. His immediate motivation was a desire, after living in and writing about the Caribbean, where he "felt like a transplanted tree that had failed to take root in foreign soil," to travel around "a Europe that I [felt] both of and not of" (pp. 9, xiii). Intertwined with his exploration of Europe, or Europeanness, and the related issue of British identity, is an affirmation of the role of American culture, and especially black American literature, in his development as a writer. It was in the United States that he became "conscious of [the] desire to write" when he discovered the work of Richard Wright, Ralph Ellison, and James Baldwin: "If I was going to continue to live in Britain, how was I to reconcile the contradiction of feeling British, while being constantly told . . . that I did not belong. . . . I knew now I would have to explore the European Academy that had shaped my mind" (p. 9).

In chapters that track, roughly, from south to north, *The European Tribe* scrutinizes several varieties of "rampant tribalism": "intolerance towards outsiders, . . . immigrants, seasonal workers, political refugees, or nationals of a different skin colour or faith, . . . [a] deeply ingrained racism" (p. xii). At the same time it presents an increasingly homogenized, transnational European culture that reflects the legacy of the colonial past, the hegemony of the North (and West) over the South, a range of responses to American dominance, and the influence of economic and political globalization. Phillips' tour begins just outside Europe, in Morocco, where the image of Casablanca, produced by the Hollywood film and reproduced by "the tentacles of media colonization" (p. 10), collides with the reality of widespread poverty, itself an expression of neocolonial dependency on multinational corporations. In Gibraltar, a "finger" pointing from Spain to Africa, Phillips finds a heterogeneous culture dominated by British elements—colonial rulers, neocolonial tourists. Here most people look and sound British even though the "ethnic Gibraltarean" is, at least theoretically, a "mixture of Jewish, Genoese, Maltese, Arab, British, and Spanish and speaks Yanito, a Hispanicized version of the English language" (p. 23). Phillips' "pagan Spain"—the phrase comes from Richard Wright—is a nation whose complex history is visualized in the dark skin of a boy of Jewish, Gypsy, Moorish, Arab, and European ancestry. Once "pagan" denoted Moorish and Arab civilization; now it refers to the situation of the Costa del Sol, conquered, or colonized, by commercialization that transforms ancient cities into "resorts" for British settlers and tourists.

The most powerful part of *The European Tribe* is the middle section, in which places are associated with persons—James Baldwin, Othello, and Anne Frank—who differently embody the effects of "tribalism." Phillips visits Baldwin at his home in St. Paul de Vence in the South of France. The older writer "kindle[s] the imagination" and graciously welcomes the aspiring young writer. But Baldwin seems lonely, isolated in the "child's paradise" behind "tall iron gates separating [him] from the outside world" and in a village where the only other black inhabitant is his personal assistant (pp. 39, 41). A similar loneliness besets the subject of the next piece, "A Black European Success." This rereading of Shakespeare's *Othello* places Othello in Renaissance Venice, a city that "both enslaved the black and ridiculed the Jew" (p. 45). "A man of action, not a thinker," Othello is an "alien, socially and culturally." Taken up by the Venetian nobility because he is a brilliant soldier, he experiences "bitter lack of respect . . . as a man." "The most famous of all the black European successes" (pp. 46–47) prefigures later instances of the type in his estrangement from his culture of origin and from the European society that exploits his talent. From Othello, Phillips turns to the Venetian ghetto, which occasions a reflection on the anti-Semitism that represents Jews as "Europe's niggers" and an attempt to understand the "virulent anti-Semitism that seems to permeate much black thought," especially in the United States (p. 53).

In Paris, geographically on the way from Venice to Amsterdam, Phillips encounters government officials who lament the growing number of immigrants, black and otherwise; the increasing strength of Jean-Marie Le Pen's National Front; and a culture that, like British culture, "combines racialism with an admiration for semi-chic black fashions in music" (p. 63). But Paris is a detour from the representation of the devastating effects of racism and anti-Semitism portrayed in the figures of Othello and Anne Frank. Like the other places Phillips visits, the Netherlands is a nation of contrasts: during the Nazi occupation a brave resistance movement versus large numbers of collaborators; now liberal policies versus racist neofascism in the anti-immigration Centrum Party; the numerous black Dutch prostitutes and drug addicts versus the black Dutch woman who greets him at Anne Frank House, which he visits in homage to the writer of the diary whose "clarity of expression, . . . humility and courage make it one of the most important books of the century" (p. 68). In connecting slavery and the Holocaust as expressions, and blacks and Jews as victims, of European tribalism, *The European Tribe* anticipates Phillips' next novel, *Higher Ground* (1989), and his most ambitious work, *The Nature of Blood* (1997), which revisits Othello and Anne Frank as they are sketched in this text.

In the chapters of *The European Tribe* that follow, Phillips describes his travels in Northern Ireland, Germany, Poland, Norway, and the Soviet Union. In these places black immigrants experience racist antagonism and, worse, violence. "Guest workers" in Germany—Turks, mainly—have no civil rights, cannot vote, are ineligible for social security: that is, they have no official existence. Neither the Soviet bloc nor Scandinavia is a refuge from tribalism. In Poland, Phillips causes confusion when he says that he is British. But he appreciates the Western freedom not to conform when a Polish friend, a writer, describes the censorship that makes Poland like a part of the Third World. Phillips arrives in Norway as Bishop Desmond Tutu is about to be awarded the Nobel Peace Prize. He finds, yet again, hostility toward immigrants and, in a Trinidadian woman who neglects her children and drinks to assuage her loneliness, another avatar of the black European marooned, like Baldwin in France or Othello in Venice.

The last chapter, "The European Tribe," returns to a British society trying to come to terms with postimperial decline. European nations, once vying for dominance as they scrambled for colonial possessions, are now "trying to forge unity through trade" (p. 121). Yet, Phillips remarks, Europeans—white Europeans—lack a "cogent sense of history" (p. 121). Historical amnesia effaces the role played by black people in producing "Europe." Recovering cultural memories lost or buried, Phillips writes as a black European, "culturally of the west, . . . an inextricable part of this small continent" (pp. 128–129). It is this position that his later work explores.

GENEALOGIES OF THE PRESENT, 1989–1993

In his novels published in the late 1980s and early 1990s, Phillips extends his range both formally and thematically. Unlike *The Final Passage* and *A State of Independence,* which are set in the recent past or in the present, *Higher Ground* (1989), *Cambridge* (1991), and *Crossing the River* (1993) are historical novels. They reach back to the slave trade on the west coast of Africa in the late eighteenth century, plantation slavery in the British West Indies on the eve of abolition, the United States in the era of the Fugitive Slave Act and just after the Civil War, World War II in the north of England, the Holocaust, and the 1960s in the American South. In the classical historical novel either the relationship of past and present is traced through a linear, chronological plot, or the past is used as a metaphor for the present. Phillips' historical novels counterpose narratives set in the past and the present. "Subverting received history," as Phillips puts it ("Of This Time, of That Place," p. 157), and engaging writer and readers alike in an imaginative reconstruction of historical memory, these novels undertake a genealogy of the present.

Phillips has observed that the novel is a "democratic medium" (Swift, "Caryl Phillips Interviewed," p. 98). In displacing the omniscient narrator of his first two novels, he decenters narrative authority and democratizes his text. In *Higher Ground, Cambridge,* and *Crossing the River,* different times and places are refracted through the experiences of particular individuals recounted, for the most part, in the first person; in each novel several discrete narratives are juxtaposed. The different vantage points, the distinct historical and geographical locations in which the narratives unfold, conflict with and at the same time correct each other. The diverse narratives, some couched in interior monologues like those that make up Virginia Woolf's *The Waves* (1931), or fragmented voices like those in *The Waste Land,* uneasily occupy the same textual space. Their fragile coexistence, the reverberations from one to the other, evoke the desire for connection and powerfully represent an absence or lack, connections missed or never attempted. At the same time, in Phillips' audacious narration across differences of race, place, and gender, these novels enact connections apparently foreclosed in the narratives themselves.

HIGHER GROUND: *THE MEANING OF SURVIVAL*

IN *Higher Ground* there are three narratives, each focusing on one protagonist. The first, "Heart-land," is a monologue, in the present tense, of an African man who facilitates the slave trade by collaborating with British authorities. The second, "Cargo Rap," consists of letters written in prison in 1967 and 1968 by Rudy Williams, a black nationalist convicted of robbery. The third, "Higher Ground," alternates between the first and third persons in telling the story of Irene, a Jewish refugee in England after World War II. Each of these narratives is a window on a particular history; in each protagonist the capacity for love is atrophied, deformed, crushed. All three stories raise questions about what it means to survive catastrophe and trauma.

"Heartland" illustrates the consequences of acquiescing in injustice. The unnamed African narrator is caught between British slave traders and colonial officials, and the village society he left behind when he was captured and sold to a factor who taught him to read and write so he could assist in keeping records of the traffic in human flesh. Compelled to satisfy the competing demands of the liberal, naive Governor, the brutal deputy, Price, and the soldiers who man the fort where captured Africans are imprisoned before they are sent to the Americas, the narrator is a translator, a cultural interpreter who mediates between the British authorities and the villagers who now regard him as an enemy. He procures a native girl for Price, who brutalizes her. Later he is drawn to the girl, who is banished from the community because she is "ruined"; he admits that he has "forfeited the right to the emotion of love" (pp. 40, 46). The soul-killing quality of slavery is conveyed in his deadpan recital of what he euphemistically calls "trading equipment": "whips, flails, yokes, branding-irons, metal masks" (p. 15).

The narrator's self-justification has a resonance beyond his own situation; it is part of the tissue of cross-references that link the novel's three sections. He makes no profit for himself: "I merely survive, and if survival is a crime, then I am guilty" (p. 24). Now, however, he is no longer valued; an interpreter is not necessary because "trading" has given way to sheer capture. Replaced by Price's "new 'linguist,'" then chained in the dungeon with others, he joins the "hitherto baffling rebellious music" (p. 59) that voices the slaves' resistance. After the Middle Passage he "feigns ignorance" (p. 60) of the language of the auctioneer. His reflections on language hark back to Caliban in Shakespeare's *The Tempest*:

> You taught me language, and my profit on't
> Is, I know how to curse. The red plague rid you
> For learning me your language!
>
> (Act 1, scene 2)

and look forward to the title character in *Cambridge*. Phillips forces us to confront the narrator's complicity in the treatment of human beings as "cargo." At the same time he shows us that slavery and the slave trade are not monolithic, unchanging institutions, but have a history through which we can glimpse possibilities of resistance.

If the narrator of "Heartland" is co-opted by whites, Rudy Williams, the epistolary narrator of the second section, "Cargo Rap," wants nothing to do with whites. Like George Jackson, author of *Soledad Brother* (1970), and Eldridge Cleaver, author of *Soul on Ice* (1968), Rudy begins as a petty criminal and is radicalized in prison. He witnesses the important events of the late 1960s—the war in Vietnam, the assassinations of Martin Luther King and Robert F. Kennedy—from his prison cell. As a strategy for survival, Rudy's black nationalism is as ineffective as the African's collusion with slave traders. And it has similar consequences. Rudy writes, looking back to the African and ahead to Irene in the next section, "I have no emotional attachments to anything or anybody. Love is an emotion that I have learned to eradicate" (p. 68). Perhaps for this reason, those to whom he writes are unresponsive. He is intolerant of weakness, which, replicating sexist platitudes, he identifies with femininity. He cannot sustain the ascetic regime he sets for himself. When he is placed in solitary confinement, harassed, and degraded by the guards, his self-discipline collapses; eventually he sinks into delusion, imagining that he is a slave on a plantation.

Rudy's sense that he is a prisoner of the capitalist system is not altogether inaccurate. And he does manage to educate himself while he is in jail, writing letters about such heroes of the African diaspora as Crispus Attucks, Paul Robeson, Harriet Tubman, and Marcus Garvey. But he lacks what the narrator of "Heartland" achieves, an understanding of the intricacies of culture. Tone-deaf, he misrepresents Louis Armstrong as an "African [who] begins to play the fool for the white man, unthinkingly parodying himself and his people in the most grotesque and demeaning caricatures" (p. 135). Rudy's incomprehension of irony or mimicry—what Henry Louis Gates, Jr., calls "signifying"—makes his own hectoring, arrogant "cargo rap" all the more ironic.

Irene, the protagonist of "Higher Ground," the third section of the novel, is caught between the pain of remembering and the pain of forgetting. Her story suggests that the suppression of the painful past is one cause of the "memory-haemorrhage" (p. 180) that engulfs her. Identifying herself as a writer of "unanswered letters" (p. 217), she recalls both Rudy and the African, whose attempts at communication also are thwarted. She also prefigures Eva Stern in *The Nature of Blood*.

Irene, born Irina, grows up in eastern Europe, her adolescence prematurely and brutally ended by the Nazi threat. After her sister is beaten in the street, her parents arrange for her to go to England, alone, as part of a *kindertransport*. In Liverpool she finds a job in a factory, but, cut off from her family, she is unable to connect with her coworkers. Her passivity is a symptom of the emotional deadness that afflicts Rudy and the African. She submits to the attentions of a man named Reg; eventually she "surrender[s] to this man who was the least-worst of those she had known, and the first who had ever shown any interest in her body" (p. 188). The rupturing of her life is suggested in her reflection immediately afterward: " It was not so much that she felt like a woman, it was just that she no longer felt like a child" (p. 190). Later she and Reg separate. She attempts suicide and spends time in an asylum, where she is given shock treatments. In another of the novel's powerful echoes, the "iron handcuff around her head" (p. 201) recalls the neck chains and metal masks of the slaves in the African dungeon. Now, working in a library, she meets a West Indian named Louis. But, subjected to racist slurs, he decides, like Leila in *The Final Passage*, to go home. Louis' kindness cannot heal Irene's wounds; the aborted relationship between them is yet another instance of connection evoked but not achieved. Like Rudy, Irene cannot maintain her sanity. At the end of the novel, she is waiting to be returned to the asylum and, in its final sentence, is reciting the Sh'ma, the holiest prayer in the Jewish religion.

Unanswered letters, human cargo, and the apparatus of slavery and shock treatment link the three parts of *Higher Ground*. These links point to connections missed between the three main characters and also, within the three narratives, between Louis and Irene, Rudy and his family, the African and the young girl in whose "ruin" he is complicit. Like *Higher Ground*, Phillips's next novel centers on characters who do not connect with each other and whose failed connection has implications beyond the historical moment in which they live.

CAMBRIDGE: *BROKEN HISTORIES*

IN *Cambridge* Phillips once again juxtaposes several narratives. Unlike the three parts of *Higher Ground*, however, the narratives in *Cambridge* present different versions of the same events, commenting on and, as Paul Sharrad points out, contradicting each other ("Speaking the Unspeakable," p. 203). The protagonists and principal narrators are Emily Cartwright, an Englishwoman who travels to her father's plantation in the Caribbean on the eve of the marriage he has arranged for her with an unappealing, elderly widower, and Cambridge, a slave on the plantation, who kills a brutal overseer and is hanged. The narratives of Emily and Cambridge are followed by a third account, which describes the killing and its aftermath as they might be represented in plantation records, court documents, the local press, and island lore.

If *Higher Ground*'s "Cargo Rap" recalls and reworks the prison writings of Cleaver and Jackson, *Cambridge* alludes, among other texts, to the journal of a Scotswoman who traveled to the Caribbean, on which Emily's narrative is loosely based, and the abolitionist poem "The Dying Slave" (1773) and *The Interesting Life of Olaudah Equiano or Gustavus Vassa, the African* (1792), prototypes for the experiences of Cambridge (Swift, "Caryl Phillips Interviewed," p. 97; Sharrad, "Speaking the Unspeakable," pp. 211–212; see also O'Callahan, "Historical Fiction and Fictional History"). *Cambridge* also refers to the nineteenth-century British novel in general, as well as to particular examples of the genre. The situation in *Cambridge*—a plantation in the Caribbean at a moment of crisis in the political economy of slavery—evokes that in Jane Austen's *Mansfield Park* (1814), in which Sir Thomas Bertram's family in England depends on his plantation in Antigua. Phillips' naming of Emily and the man that she is supposed to marry (but does not), Thomas Lockwood, recalls the author

and quintessentially unreliable narrator of Emily Brontë's *Wuthering Heights* (1847). (Hawthorn cottage, where Emily takes refuge at the end of the novel, is almost an anagram for Haworth, where the Brontës lived.)

Emily is a remarkably sympathetic character, perhaps the most compelling of Phillips' female protagonists in her attempt, however unsuccessful, to resist the patriarchal gender constraints represented most prominently by the father to whom she writes. Yet, unable to transcend her situation, she vacillates between one view of slavery and another. At one point she says that she intends to lecture about "this tired system" (p. 86) when she returns to England, but she repeatedly lapses into unthinking rationalizations of slavery and uncritically parrots its apologists. Her lurching from one set of beliefs to another is a sign not simply of bad faith but also of her vulnerability to male power, in England and the Caribbean alike.

Emily's journey across the Atlantic, on a ship that she describes as a "chaotic world of men and freight" (p. 7), is a paradigmatic instance of the voyage that turns Europeans into Americans. Her experience at once resembles and differs from that of Cambridge, who, in Phillips' sly underscoring of the importance of the journey in which Africans are transformed into Americans, undergoes the Middle Passage twice. Once she is on the island, Emily relates her observations in the conventional manner of (European) travel writing. Unlike *The Final Passage*'s Leila, for whom the Caribbean is the constant against which England is measured, Emily assimilates the island landscape to an English scene, likening the "infamous sugar canes" with "young shoots [that] billowed in the cooling breeze" to "fields of green barley." At the same time she presents the island through the commonplace of the "tropical paradise" (p. 18). Through Emily's eyes we observe plantation life. In describing the slaves she zigzags from one set of clichés to another: "that the black is addicted to theft and deceit"; that the "negro village" is so "picturesque a scene" (pp. 39, 42). And she shows us a professional class made up of functionaries—doctors, managers, clergymen—dependent on, and therefore subservient to, the plantocrats.

Emily arrives at a moment when Mr. Wilson, a relatively benevolent overseer, has been replaced by the brutal Mr. Brown. The change in regime is linked to a crisis in the economy of slavery and to abolitionist activity in both the Caribbean and England. Initially Emily is repelled by Brown, but she later succumbs to his influence and, under his tutelage, tours the island and visits the city of Baytown. She is particularly offended by the *"amours,"* as she puts it (p. 75), of Brown and Christiania, a slave who practices obeah. When, in retaliation, Christiania threatens Emily, Cambridge is sent to stand by Emily's door and protect her. In what might be the most poignant moment in the novel, Emily initiates a conversation by asking him about his Bible reading, but when he in turn inquires about her family and her attitudes toward slavery, she retreats. Not long afterward Brown is killed by the *"intelligent* negro with whom he waged a constant war" (p. 128), as Emily describes Cambridge. We read in Cambridge's narrative and in the epilogue that Emily is pregnant; after she delivers a stillborn child, she goes mad. The last word she utters, and the novel's final word, is "Stella" (p. 184), the name of the slave who befriends her, instructs her about the customs of plantation life, and tends to her throughout her troubles.

Cambridge's narrative supplies what Emily leaves unsaid. It takes the form of a confession. Like *The History of Mary Prince*, a slave narrative published in England in 1831, it is retrospectively shaped by the subject's conversion and by the Christian notion of a fortunate fall. Unlike Emily, who has a lively voice, Cambridge, who adopts the homiletic style of Evangelical Christianity, is often stodgy, even plodding, in his recitation of a "history . . . truly broken" (p. 137).

Cambridge has little knowledge of his early life. The story proper begins with the Middle Passage, that is, at a point when his original identity, if not his name, Olumide, is already lost to memory. Inverting the commonplaces of colonial discourse, he notes that "native conversation was forbidden," that the "English talk" of his captors "resembled . . . the manic chatter of baboons," and that he "wondered . . . if [the white men] . . . were not truly intent upon cooking and eating us" (p. 135). He arrives in Carolina and is immediately taken to England on the way he is given a new name, Thomas. In London he survives by demonstrating, or pretending, that "my sole pleasure . . . derived from the great privilege of being able to serve [my master]" (p. 142). He marries a fellow servant and, under her influence, becomes a Christian and, after his master's death, an itinerant preacher and abolitionist orator. Renamed again—he is now called David Henderson—he rejoices: "Truly I was now

an Englishman, albeit a little smudgy of complexion!" (p. 147).

Cambridge's assumption of Englishness is premature, however; as the excess of names suggests, his identity is repeatedly put into question. After his beloved wife dies, a missionary society sends him to Africa to convert the heathen. When he is once again enslaved, this time by the ship's captain, he protests, "That I, a virtual Englishman, was to be treated as base African cargo, caused me such hurtful pain as I was barely able to endure" (p. 156). Bought at auction by Mr. Wilson and renamed Cambridge—soon he will be known as Hercules because of his strength—he becomes "manifestly a West Indian slave" (p. 159). On the plantation he befriends a young girl who becomes his wife; despite the fact that she practices obeah, he attempts to convert her and, in imitation of his masters, gives her a new name, Christiania. Cambridge regards Christiania as a victim of Brown's lust and, echoing Toni Morrison's *Beloved* (1987), sees her reversion to dirt eating as a *"sickness* brought on by Mr. Brown's hunger" (p. 163). He is sent to protect Emily but says, "the Englishwoman did not concern me" (p. 164). His lack of interest in her deflates the myth, a staple of British colonial attitudes from *The Tempest* onward, that white women are the object of black men's desire. He tries to talk about his wife to Brown, "as one man to another" (p. 166); when Brown strikes him, he resists, killing Brown and then praying for forgiveness.

While the narratives of Emily and Cambridge supplement each other, the third part of the novel, which omits the motives and feelings they detail, presents a particularly truncated version of the events they describe. Stella and Christiania, who are crucial even if muted in the narratives of Emily and Cambridge, are silenced and invisible in this account. In the conspicuous absence of these black women from a story in which they play significant parts, Phillips points to crucial gaps in the official record of plantation slavery. He cautions us not to draw conclusions about what is excluded from the archive. At the same time he rereads and rewrites the history of the Caribbean in the era of slavery, urging us to attend closely to what might have been ignored or misinterpreted in the past.

Cambridge represents Caribbean colonial—and, by extension, postcolonial—culture as the result of a process of "creolization" that transforms black and white alike. Emily herself describes the "seasoning" of Africans and, after the slave trade is made illegal, the emergence of "creole" slaves. Like their white counterparts, black creoles are those "deemed to have safely entered this new tropical life" (p. 38). Emily also highlights two different relationships between colonial and metropolitan cultures. On the one hand the colonial culture, particularly the culture of the colonizers, is a parodic imitation, a pastiche of the excesses in the metropolitan "original." Thus, in Baytown, the "spirit of ostentation enjoyed full play" (p. 102). On the other hand colonial culture, particularly the culture of the colonized, in its mimicking of metropolitan models, opens a space for resistance.

Emily does not know how to interpret the song of a free black cobbler, yet her confused account offers a glimpse of the cobbler's self-fashioning creativity:

He sang a tune in a minor key which Mr. Brown identified as negro music, but which to my ear seemed a corrupt version of an old Welsh air. . . . On observing us the black rolled up his eyes until only the whites were visible, and then, . . . he prostrated himself before us in a gesture of base supplication. . . . Most of the sooty tribe have embraced dully a belief in their own degradation and inferiority, and clearly this is the greatest impediment to their making progress. . . . However, truly I was unsure, in the case of this *sambo*, whether or not he was making sport of us, for I detected about his free person touches of wit which he appeared to be only partly concealing, but to what purpose I could not fathom.

(p. 105)

Emily's incomprehension is only partial. She hears the cobbler's song as a corruption of a Welsh, not even an English, air, but she senses that the wit that baffles her is somehow a sign of his freedom. Her discomfort is intensified a moment later when she observes the "proceedings of a slave-court" (p. 105). She notes with unwitting irony that "A formal system of law whereby any offender, irrespective of colour or quality, is meted out just punishment, seems not to have taken hold on this island" (p. 107). Through Emily's fragmentary account Phillips winks at his readers, showing us what Emily misses.

Emily and Cambridge cannot acknowledge what they might have in common. (Nor, for that matter, can either see what Emily might have in common with Christiania or Cambridge with Brown.) Phillips observes that Emily grows (Swift, "Caryl Phillips Interviewed," p. 99), yet she

never recognizes Cambridge as an equal—as he puts it, "man to man." In Emily's vulnerability "to the prejudices which despise my sex" (p. 113) and Cambridge's uneasy assumption of English identity, Phillips not only represents the early-nineteenth-century Caribbean but also addresses the late-twentieth-century British context, in which Cambridge's predicament is echoed in that of blacks—descendants of those Emily identifies as creoles—born in England but excluded by restrictive, racist notions of Englishness.

CROSSING THE RIVER: *DIASPORIC IMAGININGS*

PHILLIPS continues the genealogical investigations of his previous two novels in *Crossing the River*. Like *Higher Ground*, *Crossing the River* juxtaposes discrete narratives whose protagonists occupy different times and places. The characters in *Crossing the River*, however, unlike those in *Higher Ground*, are related to each other by ties of filiation. As in *Cambridge*, the narratives in *Crossing the River* not only complete but also interrupt each other. Taken together, they outline a history of the African diaspora from the 1750s to World War II and beyond.

Crossing the River begins and ends with the reflections of an African father: "A desperate foolishness. The crops failed. I sold my children. I remember . . . I soiled my hands with cold goods in exchange for their warm flesh. A shameful intercourse. . . . And soon after, the chorus of a common memory began to haunt me" (p. 1). These children are the progenitors of characters who participate in a "many-tongued chorus" (p. 1) and, later in the novel, realize possibilities latent in their ancestors or prototypes: Nash Williams, a former slave who goes to West Africa in the 1830s to establish missionary settlements; Martha Randolph, who escaped from slavery and now, in the immediate postemancipation era, journeys westward from Kansas to Colorado with black pioneers; and Travis, an American GI stationed in the north of England during World War II.

Nash's story, which occupies the first section of the novel, "The Pagan Coast," is told in his letters to his former master, Edward Williams, in the letters of others, and by an omniscient narrator. The second section, "West," tells Martha's story in the first and third persons. Travis appears in the fourth section of the novel, "Somewhere in England." He is displaced, however, as a narrator and barely speaks at all. He is seen in the first-person narrative of Joyce, a young, white British woman who falls in love with him, marries him, and bears his child, a son named Greer. At the end of the novel, when the old father sums up, he names Joyce as his daughter. Thus Phillips undermines the conventional notions of lineage, family, and race—that is, identity—implicit in the prologue, substituting a secular structure that emphasizes choice, or vocation, for a structure of inherited filiation in which individual will plays little or no part.

Inserted into the "many-tongued chorus" is the third section of the novel, the ledger and letters of James Hamilton, captain of a slave ship sailing the west coast of Africa in the 1750s. (Hamilton buys the three children sold by the narrator of the prologue and epilogue; fragments of Hamilton's account of the transaction are interspersed in those parts of the book.) Hamilton is a willing, even eager, agent of historical catastrophe. A brutal master not only to the slaves in the hold but also to the sailors who serve under him, he meticulously enumerates the punishments he metes out. But his letters represent him as a tender and faithful husband who eschews the sexual escapades common among men of his class. Hamilton's story at once disrupts and makes possible the other stories the novel tells. Yet its power is defused because it is contained, confined, embedded in the narratives of the " diasporan souls" descended from the frame narrator, those who "arrived on the far bank of the river, loved" (p. 237).

If *Crossing the River* invites us to see the resilience of slaves and their descendants, it recalls *A State of Independence* in cautioning about naive notions of "emancipation." Nash Williams' tale is a story of "devolution." Initially he intends to establish a Christian mission, but his religion cannot "take root" (p. 62) in Africa. Next he tries to found a school; he decides, later, to start a farm. The "final Nash Williams settlement" is just a collection of grass huts, "brown cones" (pp. 68–69) in which men, women, and children live "alongside hog, goat, and fowl" (p. 66). Reversing what he has learned from Edward Williams (although not, perhaps, Edward's example), Nash becomes a polygamist. His refrain, "Father, why have you forsaken me?" echoes in the next narrative as well. Martha tells of different kinds of loss. Taken to Kansas by her new masters after her daughter is sold away from her, she escapes and ends up running a res-

taurant and working as a laundress. She finds fulfillment with a black cowboy named Chester, but emancipation cannot save him from being murdered by whites. Martha joins a black exodus heading west, following a friend to California and harboring the hope of finding her daughter there. But, old and ill, she dies en route.

The most powerful part of *Crossing the River* is "Somewhere in England." Like Graham Swift's *Last Orders* (1996), "Somewhere in England," set in the "home front" in the north of England, represents World War II as the crucible of contemporary British identity. As in *Last Orders* and *The Final Passage,* which scramble chronology, Phillips tells Joyce's story in brief segments that move back and forth between 1939 and 1943, with flashbacks to 1936 and 1937 and flash-forwards to 1945 and, briefly, to 1963. In Joyce's story, and in the novel that it concludes, reciprocal transracial desire represents utopian possibility. We first meet Joyce with Len, whom she marries to get away from her mother. A con man, Len is later imprisoned for petty black marketeering during the war. Travis represents a new beginning for Joyce, but he is killed in the war, and soon afterward Joyce is persuaded to give up her son for adoption. In this she echoes the act of the African father who sells his children. But unlike the African, she is reunited with her child; she meets Greer briefly in 1963, in an episode that functions as an epilogue to this section of the novel.

Greer, like Hortense, the black daughter of a white mother in Mike Leigh's film *Secrets and Lies* (1996), evokes a past that has been, but will not remain, buried. Exemplary "diasporan soul," Greer recalls the colonial history encompassing slavery and its aftermath with which contemporary Britain must now come to terms. Unearthing the history of European racism is one aspect of Phillips' genealogy of the present. He expands this project in his most recent novel, *The Nature of Blood.*

THE NATURE OF BLOOD: *MAROONED IN EUROPE*

LIKE its immediate predecessors, *The Nature of Blood* (1997) explores the relationship of history and memory, and, in excavating the past, attempts a genealogy of the present. It is also, as the title suggests, a meditation on the meanings of "blood," that is, of identity, violence, and mortality. As in *Higher Ground* and *Crossing the River,* Phillips juxtaposes discrete narratives about disparate groups of characters in different times and places. Among these characters are Eva Stern, a German Jewish girl who survives the Holocaust but kills herself not long after the war; her Uncle Stephan, a Zionist instrumental in founding the State of Israel; a group of fifteenth-century Jews in Portobuffole, in the Venetian Republic; and Othello, portrayed, as in *The European Tribe,* as a military hero isolated in Venice. Like many of Phillips' protagonists, the characters in *The Nature of Blood* are marooned in circumstances that they can neither escape nor transcend. In telling their stories Phillips once again shows us possibilities of resistance occluded in or otherwise lost to the conventional historical record.

In Phillips' earlier books slavery—plantation slavery in the Americas—is either part of the novel's represented world or is visible in its effects. In *The Nature of Blood,* however, plantation slavery is not explicitly referred to. Rather, it is represented obliquely through the story of Othello, who reminds us that he was once a slave (p. 107). The main focus in *The Nature of Blood* is on another expression of European tribalism, the anti-Semitism manifest in the persecution of the Jews of Portobuffole and, writ large, in the Holocaust. Yet the connections made—through reverberations comprising, as in *Higher Ground, Cambridge,* and *Crossing the River,* a tissue of cross-references—associate the Holocaust and slavery as defining events of modernity and as catastrophes that, in their traumatic effects, ineluctably divide subjects from their histories and thus from themselves.

The Nature of Blood is formally the most difficult of Phillips' novels. The narrative is fragmented, and the different stories are not parceled out in clearly marked sections or chapters; rather, they flow into each other, sometimes interrupted by the interpolated utterances of unidentified, apparently omniscient voices. The social and emotional isolation of Eva and Othello marks their narratives, offered mainly as interior monologues in which bits of remembered dialogue are contained. Although Eva and Othello occupy distinct narrative and historical realms, they are linked, implicitly, through the European tribalism of which both are victims, and through the Jews of Portobuffole, who, like Othello, are exploited by the ruling elite of Venice. Moreover, as in *Higher Ground* and *Crossing the River,* connections foreclosed within the

novel by the separation of the discrete narratives are set in motion textually through words, phrases, and situations that echo from one narrative to another. In representing the particularity of each character's experience, Phillips insists that readers acknowledge difference. At the same time, in inviting us to uncover links among the narratives, he asks us to reach across difference and to find connections in history itself. Thus, *The Nature of Blood* realizes tendencies inchoate or potential in *Higher Ground.*

The Nature of Blood is framed by the experiences of Stephan Stern in a refugee camp in Cyprus just after the war and in Israel in the present. Stephan is presented as a bearer of historical memory and of connections across time and place. He remembers what might otherwise be lost, the stories of his brother's family. His words, "I remember" (p. 10), are echoed by Othello, "I remembered" (p. 121). As the Nazis threaten, Stephan dedicates himself to Zionism, leaving behind his wife and daughter, who emigrate to America, and his brother Ernst (Eva's father), who remains in Europe. At the end of the novel, as an old man, Stephan is drawn to a young Ethiopian woman. Alienated from the culture of her immigrant parents and the object of discrimination by eastern Europeans still dominant in Israel, this black Jew represents a new generation of Israelis and also harks back to Stephan's niece Eva. In her situation Phillips calls into question racialist constructions of "blood": identity, ethnicity, nationality.

Eva's story is told in a fragmented narrative that reflects her psychological disintegration. (It also recalls Anne Frank's *The Diary of a Young Girl* [1952]. Phillips explains, in "On *The Nature of Blood* and the Ghost of Anne Frank," that he has long been haunted by Anne Frank; in inventing Eva, who survives the camps but cannot survive the liberation, he imagines an alternate destiny for Anne herself.) Eva moves back and forth in time from the liberation of the camp and her experiences after the war to what would be, in normal times, the ordinary events of adolescence. Details of family life are overwhelmed by their incorporation in a larger history of nightmare and rupture. Eva's father can no longer practice medicine; Eva is beaten in the street; she and her sister cannot attend school; Jews, young and old, wander the city in search of scraps of food. As she puts it, reflecting on the fact that the Sterns are forced to leave the comfortable home where she has grown up, "In time, there would be no evidence that any of us had ever lived here. We never existed" (p. 71).

The surreal quality of Eva's narrative is reminiscent of that of Kazuo Ishiguro's *The Unconsoled* (1995). In Ishiguro's novel, however, the uncanny logic of events is apparently unmotivated. Here it is an expression of a history that is specified and, therefore, commemorated. But at the same time, through a chain of associations, Eva's story evokes other histories as well. Eva says that the shooting of those who do not comply with the Nazis' demand that they leave all their property behind produces a "river of blood flowing across the platform" (p. 162). Her words here allude to the 1968 speech—recalled in popular memory as the "River of Blood" speech—in which Enoch Powell, ideologue of British racism, decries the growing black population of Britain by warning that "like the Romans I seem to see 'the River Tiber foaming with much blood.' "

"Appalled," after the arrival of British soldiers, by the realization that she is "comfortable being confined" (p. 22), Eva cannot experience even the nominal freedom promised by the end of the war. Having lost mother, father, and sister, she is all but lost herself. Her isolation in a solipsistic world of memories reaches back to Irene in *Higher Ground* and looks toward Othello in *The Nature of Blood*. Befriended by a British soldier, Eva follows him to England. There she kills herself; in a psychologist's clinical discussion of the suicide and acknowledgment that, at the time, little was known about the guilt experienced by survivors, Phillips points to the ineffable character of trauma and catastrophe, and the inadequacy of interpretive protocols conventionally marshaled to explain them.

Eva's fractured narrative is intercut with the story of Servadio, Moses, and Giacobbe, Jews put to death in Portobuffole for the murder of a young Christian boy. It is claimed that these men slaughtered the boy so they could use his blood in the preparation of Passover matzo; confessions wrested out of them by torture are crucial in their conviction of a crime for which there is little or no evidence against them. The story of these three men is set in a larger history of Portobuffole and Venice. Having fled persecution in Germany, the Jews are now caught between a Venetian state that needs their services as bankers and a local populace that makes them convenient scapegoats in this and other situations requiring the assigning of blame.

The Jews of Portobuffole, marooned in the Venetian Republic, also forge a connection to Othello, who is literally and figuratively central to *The Nature of Blood*. Othello resembles many of Phillips' earlier protagonists. Like his prototype in *The European Tribe*, this Othello is a "foreigner" who has "moved from the edge of the world to the centre. . . . A man born of royal blood, a mighty warrior, yet a man who, at one time, could view himself only as a poor slave, had been summoned to serve this state; to lead the Venetian army; to stand at the very centre of the empire" (p. 107). Othello is not comfortable in his new surroundings. The marriage to Desdemona that will take him "to the heart of the society" (p. 144) might be a compensation for his feeling of estrangement.

Othello's story is especially powerful because much of it is told in his own voice. Like Cambridge he narrates a story of self-division. His marriage to Desdemona "did indeed mark me off from my past" (p. 146). Like Eva's father, Ernst, he marries a woman whose family thinks him unworthy of her, and like Stephan Stern and Cambridge, he leaves behind a wife and child who symbolize the life from which he is irreparably severed (pp. 107, 134). And, like Cambridge, Othello has a stilted style, a plodding tone, which suggests that he has internalized the Venetians' view of his inferiority and has not acquired "fluency" in Venetian language and customs. Othello wanders through the ghetto; his inability to understand why the Jews "should choose to live in this manner" (p. 130) recalls Emily's observations of the slaves on her father's plantation. Perhaps most poignantly, Othello is the object of an anonymous voice that, echoing Rudy in *Higher Ground*, dismisses him as an Uncle Tom, "Fighting the white man's war for him / Wide-receiver in the Venetian army / The Republic's grinning Satchmo" (p. 180). Although this attack might contain a grain of truth, it is as distant as Shakespeare's play from the portrait we glean from Othello's own monologue.

In placing Othello at the very center of *The Nature of Blood*, Phillips presents his story as a suppressed narrative that makes possible the other histories the novel recounts. He shows, too, how Europe depends on those it excludes or rejects even when, or especially when, they are forgotten or misremembered. Thus, Phillips reiterates the crucial importance of historical memory and of the genealogical recovery of experiences lost, buried, or otherwise forgotten. The uncanny echoes that link Othello and Anne Frank and connect Phillips' two Othellos have a slightly different valence. These echoes invoke the importance of narration across race and place in an era when heterogeneous identities forged by histories of exile, migration, and nomadism are more common than those implicit in such traditional categories as "European," "British," "Jewish," and "black."

WORK IN PROGRESS

PHILLIPS' projects in the late 1990s reflected the range of his interests. An edited anthology of writing about tennis, *The Right Set,* was to be published in 1999 in London and New York. He continued as editor of the Faber Caribbean Series, consisting of original works and classic texts produced—in the four languages of the area—in the Caribbean and its diaspora. He was writing a screenplay for a film based on V. S. Naipaul's first novel, *The Mystic Masseur* (1957), and was commissioned by the Royal National Theatre to write a play based on Selvon's *Lonely Londoners.* Another of his plays was scheduled to be produced in New York in 1999. Phillips awaited publication in the *New Yorker* of an article on the death of Motown singer Marvin Gaye, part of a longer work on African-American fathers and sons. Finally, he was working on a nonfiction book about the cities of Charleston, South Carolina; Elmina, on the west coast of Africa; and Liverpool, England—three corners of the transatlantic slave trade. Phillips has produced, to date, an impressive body of work, one that not only promises much in the future but also is contributing to the invigoration of contemporary British culture and, in the process, redefining the geography of Britishness itself.

SELECTED BIBLIOGRAPHY

I. FICTION. *The Final Passage* (London and Boston, 1985); *A State of Independence* (London and New York, 1986); *Higher Ground* (London and New York, 1989); *Cambridge* (London, 1991; New York, 1992); *Crossing the River* (London, 1993; New York, 1994); *The Nature of Blood* (London and New York, 1997).

II. NONFICTION. *The European Tribe* (London and New York, 1987); *Extravagant Strangers: A Literature of Belonging* (London, 1997; New York, 1999).

III. PLAYS AND SCRIPTS. *Strange Fruit* (London, 1981); *Where There Is Darkness* (London, 1982); *The Shelter* (London, 1984); *The Wasted Years,* in *Best Radio Plays of 1984* (London, 1985); *Playing Away* (London and New York, 1987).

IV. SELECTED ARTICLES AND ESSAYS. "Othello's Real Tragedy," in *Guardian* (7 February 1987); "'A Good Man and an Honest Writer': Caryl Phillips Pays Tribute to James Baldwin," in *Race Today* 18 (January 1988); "Living and Writing in the Caribbean: An Experiment," in *Kunapipi* II, no. 2 (1989), repr. in Gordon Collier, ed., *Us / 2Them: Translation, Transcription, and Identity in Postcolonial Literary Cultures* (Amsterdam and Atlanta, 1992); "On *The Nature of Blood* and the Ghost of Anne Frank," *CommonQuest* 3 (summer 1998).

V. SELECTED CRITICISM AND INTERVIEWS. Kay Saunders, "Caryl Phillips: An Interview," in *Kunapipi* 9, no. 1 (1987); C. Rosalind Bell, "Worlds Within: An Interview with Caryl Phillips," in *Callaloo: A Journal of African-American and African Arts and Letters* 14 (summer 1991); Charles P. Sarvan and Hasan Marhama, "The Fictional Works of Caryl Phillips: An Introduction," in *World Literature Today* 65 (winter 1991); Graham Swift, "Caryl Phillips Interviewed by Graham Swift," *Kunapipi* 13, no. 3 (1991); Benedicte Ledent, "Voyages into Otherness: Cambridge and Lucy," in *Kunapipi* 14, no. 2 (1992); Evelyn O'Callahan, "Historical Fiction and Fictional History: Caryl Phillips's *Cambridge*," in *Journal of Commonwealth Literature* 29, no. 2 (1993); Carol Margaret Davison "Crisscrossing the River: An Interview with Caryl Phillips," in *ARIEL: A Review of International English Literature* 25 (October 1994); Hank Okazaki, "Dis / Location and 'Connectedness' in Caryl Phillips," in *Journal of West Indian Literature* 6 (May 1994); Paul Sharrad, "Speaking the Unspeakable: London, Cambridge, and the Caribbean," in Chris Tiffin and Alan Lawson, eds., *De-scribing Empire: Post-colonialism and Textuality* (London and New York, 1994); Benedicte Ledent, "Overlapping Territories, Intertwined Histories: Crossculturality in Caryl Phillips's *Crossing the River*," in *Journal of Commonwealth Literature* 30, no. 1 (1995); Jenny Sharpe, "Of This Time, of That Place: A Conversation with Caryl Phillips," in *Transition: An International Review* 5 (winter 1995); Frank Birbalsingh, "Caryl Phillips: The Legacy of Othello, part (1)," and "Caryl Phillips: The Legacy of Othello, part (2)," in Frank Birbalsingh, ed., *Frontiers of Caribbean Literature in English* (London, 1996); Louise Yelin, "An Interview with Caryl Phillips," in *Culturefront* (summer 1998).

WILL SELF

(1961–   )

Maura Spiegel

"BRAINY" IS A word Martin Amis has used to characterize Will Self's fiction, and as one of Self's characters remarks about himself, he certainly "has the gift of gab." His ductile prose interweaves up-to-the-minute street slang and a profusion of five-dollar words. He is a daring verbal trickster, a dark satirist who writes at times as if he were performing high-wire stunts, juggling five tropes while riding a unicycle, building a riveting fifty-page story, like a house of cards, around a frail conceit. He has said that he writes because he is afraid he cannot write, and indeed his work has a hyperactive charge to it, an urgent unrelentingness that is oddly touching. His energized prose seems to demonstrate, but never fully annotate, the vulnerability of an exceedingly vivid and cerebral imagination that has given up seeking relief in quiescence and has acceded to its own fervid impulses. Alternately, Self's verbal restlessness seems to be that of a writer who could write (or talk) his way out of anything and who thus appears at times distrustful of his gift, expressing the self-doubt, even moral scruple, of the successful flimflammer.

Self acknowledges a profusion of influences, from Jonathan Swift to William Burroughs and J. G. Ballard, and he writes lovingly of comic writers like Woody Allen and Joseph Heller, but he is also very much the younger sibling to post-realist writers like Martin Amis and Salman Rushdie. His ironical moods can swing between a Heller-like haplessness before criminally irrational social forces to a Ballard-like sullen self-relinquishment to erotic torment. He can also alternate between a *Twilight Zone* take on the overlooked weirdness of ordinary daily disruptions in ontological regularity and a Gogolian agreeableness before the truly weird, a delight in the mundanity of delusion. He is a creator of parallel worlds (a phrase he uses to describe his work), meaning both *any* fictive construct and the uncanny topologies he specializes in.

William Self was born in London in 1961. His father, Peter Self (the name Self derives from the Norse "Sewelf," seawolf), was a professor of political science and his mother, Elaine Rosenbloom Self, originally from New York City, worked in publishing and in child welfare; their marriage ended in divorce. Self's adolescence was more than ordinarily turbulent. By his own account, he was diagnosed by turns as neurotic "with schizoid tendencies," depressive, manic-depressive, suicidal, alcoholic, and drug-addicted. A "hard-core" heroin addict for almost eight years, Self underwent rehabilitation in the mid-1980s (Heller, "Self-Examination"). He attended Oxford University intermittently between 1979 and 1992, ultimately receiving a master's degree with honors. In June 1990 he married Kate Chancellor, and they had two daughters, Alexis and Madeleine, before the marriage ended in divorce. He is now married to Deborah Orr, a journalist for the *Guardian,* and they have a son named Ivan.

Before launching his literary career, Self supported himself with various jobs, including that of garbage collector. Beginning in the late 1980s, he contributed cartoons to periodicals including *New Statesman* and *City Limits* and articles and reviews to *Esquire, Harper's,* and the *Independent.* He wrote a column called "Malespeak" in the magazine *She,* a restaurant column in the *Observer,* and in the late 1990s was writing a weekly column of cultural criticism for the *London Times.* In 1991 Self burst upon the literary scene with the publication of his first book of short stories, *The Quantity Theory of Insanity: Together with Five Supporting Propositions,* which was short-listed for the John Llewellyn Rhys Prize, and he has published a new book every year since then. In 1992 he won the Geoffrey Faber Memorial Prize, and in 1993 he was named by *Granta* as one of the twenty best young British writers.

Will Self occupies a highly visible role in the contemporary British literary scene, where his outspoken positions on illegal drugs (he has described himself as a "recreational user"), along with his generalized and strategic irreverence, has earned him the seemingly permanent characterization of one of the bad boys of English letters. He enjoyed and suffered considerable notoriety in the mid-1990s to late 1990s, appearing frequently on television, and finding himself at the center of a tabloid scandal in April 1997 after being fired by the *Observer* for allegedly shooting heroin in the bathroom of John Majors' campaign airplane while on assignment for the paper. Of his public persona Self observed on a television show in August 1998, it is "useful to operate behind a kind of bowdlerized version of oneself . . . to have this odd Golem wandering around that people think is me."

In essays and interviews Self often refers in passing to the fact that he is half Jewish and half American. These personal themes have not fully emerged in his fiction, except perhaps in his distinctive ease of allusion to, and interjections of, American Jewish humor.

MY IDEA OF FUN: A CAUTIONARY TALE

IN *My Idea of Fun*, Self's first novel, he opens his bag of postmodern narrative tricks to explore the unlikely postmodern subject of evil. The narrator, Ian Wharton, is the Devil's disciple (or one of them). Ian's dreary seaside childhood and adolescence, which at times call up dark scenes from Roald Dahl, are punctuated by visits from Mr. Broadhurst, a reclusive, ominous retiree who takes up seasonal residence in the shabby genteel trailer park that Ian's mother owns and manages. Broadhurst, an oedipal figure for Ian, whose father has abandoned the family, acquaints the boy with many arcane forms of knowledge, from Cabala to Feng shui. Gradually we absorb the fact that Mr. Broadhurst is indeed the Devil himself. Ian's first real sortie into the dark side occurs in exchange for Broadhurst using his black arts to clear up Ian's adolescent acne. Over the course of his youth and early manhood, Ian is exposed to (and implicated in) Broadhurst's diabolical deeds, eventually discovering and refining his own wicked idea of fun.

Even before Mr. Broadhurst's appearance, Ian is marked in childhood by an uncanny "eidetic" gift,

the ability to call up visual memories with remarkable accuracy and to manipulate the images at will. "I can summon up faces from my yesteryears and hold a technician's blowtorch to their cheeks. And then, once the skin has started to pullulate, I can yank it away again and count the blisters, one by one, large and small. I can even dig into them and savour the precise whisper of their several crepitations" (p. 16). Ian's "gift," which may have initially drawn the Evil One's attention to him, is honed and sharpened in training sessions with Mr. Broadhurst. Ian's natural or unnatural capacity, a form of overactive imagination, appears to be, for Self, a version of the artist's mark of Cain, not unimplicated in the production of the narrative we are reading, itself a devilish bit of handiwork.

One of several conceits around which this novel is organized is formulating a devil-for-the-nineties. What is evil's most concentrated form these days? What is Beelzebub up to now? Would he wear a red suit and tail? Horns and hoofs? No; he is a fat businessman, a supercapitalist who buys souls not in exchange for knowledge or artistic genius but for class mobility, for a piece of the deregulated, post-Thatcher pie. Ian's mother apparently hands over her unpromising little boy to the mysterious and omnipotent Mr. Broadhurst in exchange for the transformation of her dreary coastline trailer park into a swank holiday resort—and for a secure perch in the "English social funfair." As her son reports, she evolves from "the young trollop I remembered to the middle-aged reader of Trollope she had always wanted to be" (p. 135).

Self's Angel of Darkness is a man of many miens, but all of them fat. Self links this demon to a humorous host of famous fat men, the "great fatties of all time," some of whom are named: Nero; Falstaff; Fatty Arbuckle; Casper Gutman, the aesthete-villain played by Sydney Greenstreet in *The Maltese Falcon* (1941); and the Fat Controller, an *apparently* benign figure from the children's book and television series *Thomas the Tank Engine*. Other famous fat men are subtly and mischievously invoked; at various times Broadhurst calls to mind W. C. Fields (in his contempt for small children), Alfred Hitchcock (in his inimitable habit of making unexpected cameos in Ian's consciousness), Beau Brummell (with his vanity and dandy attire), Willy Wonka (as Ian's guide through a hellish version of the chocolate factory), the Monopoly Man, and the more generalized anticapitalist trope of the cigar-chomping "fat cat."

Evil is motivated here, it seems, by nothing more profound than the Evil One's own particular "idea of fun," a joyless, not especially inspired malevolence, as in Broadhurst's pinprick poisoning of a woman who insults him in a restaurant. The search for fun, however, is not undertaken by the Tempter alone; the perversities of pleasure seeking emerge as one of many ways in which the average contemporary person strikes his or her bargain with the devil. Indeed, pleasure, Self suggests, has had a diminishing return of late; the pursuit of fun has become more arduous, decadent, and specialized (if not expensive) as the Devil has done his work in robbing contemporary culture of innocent avenues to pleasure. Ian observes:

No, no, there's no fun any more, just my idea of it. Mine and his, his and mine.
    We're like coke heads or chronic masturbators, aren't we? Attempting to crank the last iota of abandonment out of an intrinsically empty and mechanical experience. We push the plunger home, we abrade the clitoris, we yank the penis and we feel nothing. Not exactly nothing, worse than nothing, we feel a flicker or a prickle, the sensual equivalent of a retinal after-image. That's our fun now, not fun itself, only a tired allusion to it. . . . Have we fallen from grace? Is that it? Have we lost our collective innocence? Sometimes it seems that way, doesn't it? We feel like we've been thrust into, deflowered by the smirking brutal world. But on the other hand it also feels as if we were the defilers.

(p. 163)

But there are many ways to fall under the Devil's sway in our world. As Ian matures, he announces his career ambition; he is interested in "products," in "how you persuade people to buy this sort of thing rather than that sort of thing" (p. 81). Studying business at Sussex University, Ian remarks, "Although we were sneered at by the arts and humanities students, those of us who were doing business studies felt, quite reasonably, that we were closer to the spirit of the age than the old hippies of the faculty" (p. 93). Here again we sense the Devil's handiwork.

Ian's business studies are supplemented by Mr. Broadhurst, now making himself known as Mr. Samuel Northcliffe, international financier, "a member of syndicates involved in leveraged buyouts, a prominent Lloyd's underwriter, a consultant for this corporation and an adviser to that emirate" (p. 148). (The name Northcliffe is perhaps borrowed from the early twentieth-century newspaper mogul known as "the father of the English popular press," including the tabloid.) Visiting him at the university, Northcliffe takes Ian on an "eidetic journey" to teach him the history of a specific product, a skill that will help him, Northcliffe explains, to assess the market demand for a particular product by "instantly unpack[ing] the portfolio of its genesis" (p. 117). Together they travel through time and space (a pedagogical technique that recalls Merlyn's methods of instructing the Wart in *The Sword in the Stone*, 1939) to discover the history of one particular name-brand product that Ian happens to be wearing, his upscale, 100 percent Egyptian cotton mid-thigh-length boxer shorts.

In one of the novel's most winning set pieces, Ian and his fiendish mentor travel first to Egypt, to the cotton fields where the cotton for Ian's shorts is "distributed over a half-acre of plants" (p. 110). Half-starved workers develop an equivalent of repetitive stress syndrome in their painstaking plucking and twisting of the white "fibrous globs." Following the product to its first point of exchange, Northcliffe informs Ian that the cotton pickers must accept the dealer's paltry price if the workers are to have "any hope of paying off their lengthening tab at the provisioners and if—haha, a'haha—they want their thin children to live to grow thinner!" (pp. 111–112). They continue on their journey with the cotton, through its processing (where the fingers of children are frequently mangled) to shipment to England. There the goods are received in South London by an importer, who then haggles with a youngish man who runs a sweatshop in Clapton. There the imported goods are inspected by a fashion designer, and then they are off to the retail outlet on the King's Road, where the proprietor emerges from his stylish shop to be informed by the designer that the boxer shorts can be turned out at the sweatshop for less than 50 pence (80 cents) a unit. Here is laid bare the ugly material and economic basis of our consumer culture. In participating in its logic, in the everyday activity of shopping, we are all occupied, Self suggests, with the Devil's work.

Before leaving the university, Ian determines to seal his self-making as a "smartly turned-out, bright and efficient young executive" by rendering himself "generic" (p. 124), a move that involves two important steps: ridding himself of the Arch Fiend, and entering psychotherapy. He considers the possibility that Mr. Broadhurst / Northcliffe is merely an extended delusion, linked somehow to the fact of his father's unexplained disappearance in his childhood, to the "lack of a proper role model" (p. 125). He commences treatment with Dr. Heironymous Gyggle, and manages to recast the avatar of Evil into a symptom of his neurosis. Ian begins to live "as others did, blithely and unconsciously" (p. 140). His career takes off; he makes his way up the corporate ladder as a marketing consultant, until one day, out of the blue, Northcliffe is back, tempting him away from his "suburbs of maturity" (p. 164).

In the chapters that follow, no longer narrated by Ian but told in the third person, we discover along with Ian that Dr. Gyggle, Ian's psychoanalytic savior, is in fact in league with Broadhurst / Northcliffe. We learn that Northcliffe's business interests include a new "banking product" to which Ian has been assigned. Indeed, we see that like the figure of the Fat Controller on the storybook Island of Sodor, Mr. Northcliffe controls "all the automata on the island of Britain, all those machines that bask in the dream that they have a soul. I am also the Great White Spirit that resides in the fifth dimension, everything is connected to my fingertips—by wires" (p. 75).

Recalling Burroughs' Dr. Benway, Dr. Gyggle runs an addiction-rehabilitation center; his patients, six junkies, are not in fact being rehabilitated but are part of an experiment conducted by the doctor. Indeed, the drug therapy that Gyggle recommends for Ian becomes the chemical agent of his psychic and moral undoing, as he is chemically transported from Dr. Gyggle's heroin rehab center straight into the bowels of his own personal hell. "The Land of Children's Jokes" is a "garish room full of clashing primary colours" (p. 184) furnished with giant toadstools instead of chairs where sadistic children's jokes are embodied: a baby sits in the corner chewing razor blades, an armless, legless man bobs up and down in a swimming pool. Here Ian confronts his nemeses, Northcliffe and Gyggle, and his pact with Evil is sealed as he is forced to take another "eidetic journey" to the site of a monstrous crime he has apparently committed. In exchange for his eternal soul, Northcliffe gives Ian a wife and finally allows him to achieve the full genitality he has denied him in classic oedipal fashion.

In the penultimate scene of the novel, Northcliffe makes an appearance at Gyggle's rehab center, now inhabited by junkies *and* the nightmarish characters from Ian's private hell. Northcliffe makes the mistake of trying to intimidate a tough black junkie named Mandingo. Self clearly amuses himself with the idea that the only character tougher than the Devil himself is an insulted black junkie; Mandingo pulls out a switchblade and calmly informs His Satanic Majesty that he's "gonna have to fucking cut" (p. 302) him—with apparently fatal results.

In the novel's epilogue we find ourselves in New York City. Ian, now the father of a son, is taking the child to the Oyster Bar in Grand Central Station to celebrate the boy's birthday. The novel's closure evokes the kind of horror film where you are led to believe that the monster or malignant force has been eradicated once and for all, only to discover that in another place, an unsuspecting place, the Evil One is present and about to start the whole nightmare going again. The little boy turns out to be our friend Northcliffe—in miniature, apparently reborn through Ian's wife.

My Idea of Fun is a novel infused with high and low cultural references to stories of pacts with the Devil, and it perhaps owes a special debt to the Rolling Stones song "Sympathy for the Devil," itself inspired by Mikhail Bulgakov's novel *The Master and Margarita* (1967). Self has written of his novel that it "is an attempt to examine what is happening to the belief systems of individuals in an age when our relentless practice of applied psychology has kicked the legs out from under our social ethic. . . . The really secret cult in our culture is the one we all belong to" (*Junk Mail*, 1995, p. 221).

GREAT APES

THE premise of *Great Apes*, an extended satire, is that one morning, following a particularly indulgent night of drugs, drinking, and sex, Simon Dykes, a fairly well-known London artist, wakes up to discover that he has become a chimpanzee. But unlike in Kafka's ur-metamorphosis, in this story our hero is not alone in his transformation; the world is now entirely populated by chimpanzees, and apparently always has been. Humans, an endangered and less intelligent species, are living mostly in Africa, at zoos and in laboratories where they are subjected to hotly protested experimentation. Much of the novel's humor emerges from the transposition of mundane human behavior to the apes, who inhabit a world exactly like ours, down to name brands and television shows.

The chimp world of *Great Apes* does differ from our own in certain distinctive species behaviors. Notably, the chimps maintain their social hierarchy by a simple system of physical dominance whereby the dominant alpha male (the attending physician, for example) will strike and beat his inferiors (residents and other underlings, for example) whenever his dominance is threatened. In addition, inferior chimps show deference to the dominant male by "presenting" their rear ends to be patted, kissed, or otherwise admired, and by a profuse rhetoric of subservience. (Politeness generally calls for some admiration between equals of one another's nether parts.) These patterns, Self suggests, are really quite close to our own, except that we are just slightly less overt about them.

Much is made in the novel of chimp sexual practices. (The novel provides an engaging quick course in primate behavior.) The chimps do not practice monogamy, but rather form natal groups that remain intact for the purposes of child rearing. These temporary families by no means remain insular, as adults take multiple mates and in fact engage in repeated (and very swift) sexual relations at any time, in any place where a female is in estrus, including on the London Tube or while waiting for a table at a restaurant. And since chimps routinely copulate with their offspring, Self advances the conceit that one female, Jane Bowen, finds herself medically denoted an "abused infant" because her father neglected to have sexual relations with her.

Self has even found a chimpanzee analogue to the barbarous stupidity of racism. In this ape world, bigotry is displayed by the chimps toward their close relations (members of the same genus), the bonobo, found only in the Congo. Conveniently for Self, these primates are born with black faces, while the chimpanzee starts life with a white face. Primatologists tell us that the bonobo is distinguished from the chimp by its lithe, upright form and nattier hairstyle. In Self's London we find bonobos trading drugs, waiting tables, and generally experiencing economic and social exclusion. On the theme of racial and species "othering," the liberal-minded character of Dr. Zack Busner considers,

He had never imagined the relation between the chimpanzee and the human to have so many submerged implications. Western civilization, it was true, had projected itself toward divinity on the up-escalator of the Chain of Being. And like Disraeli, everyone wanted to be on the side of the angels. For white-muzzled chimpanzees to be approaching perfection, bogeychimps were needed, distressed versions of the other. It was easy to see how the bonobo, with its disturbing grace and upright gait, had fulfilled this role; but Busner now realised that in the shadow of the bonobo was a more unsettling, more bestial "other"—the human.

(p. 273)

In our travels through this chimp-inhabited London, we are taken to a chic club where chimps network and sniff cocaine, and to a posh art opening of Simon's paintings where, except for an episode of mass copulation, the scene is entirely familiar. Self has great fun doing a send-up of the oblique system for establishing pecking order in the art world. These "artistic" characters do not practice the more conventional forms of domination and subservience that pertain in the broader chimp culture; they do not "present" their rear ends to the dominant males, who are commonly identified by a combination of physical strength, money, or professional prestige. In the art world, talent and cultural capital are the currency, so these art-world characters establish dominance by arcane codes of stylish dress and snobbish behavior, a hierarchy that Self portrays as equally codified and ruthless.

Plot features of the novel are relatively unimportant; Self is more interested in presenting a coherent and resonant parallel world than in event or characterization. Upon awakening into this new dispensation, Simon Dykes (a character who appears in several of Self's short stories) is quickly hospitalized as delusional and dangerous. His girlfriend, Sarah, now, of course, a chimpanzee, terrifies and disgusts him, as do his doctors, one of whom calls in Dr. Busner, well-known clinical psychologist and former television personality who has gained renown for his unorthodox thinking and methods, "inherited . . . from the antipsychiatrists of the sixties" (p. 127). Intrigued by the coherence of Simon's delusion, Busner accepts the case, and most of the novel is taken up with Dr. Busner's patient, "chimpmane" therapeutic treatment of Simon, as he urges him toward acceptance of his "chimpunity."

Along the way we observe a series of petty professional rivalries, as a cabal of psychiatrists seeks to retire Busner from his alpha position. Into these subplots Self weaves an elaborate intertext with

399

other of his fictions, so that this chimp-dominated parallel world takes on the added dimension of referencing the parallel worlds of his fiction. Characters such as Zack Busner, Jane Bowen, Anthony Bohm, Colin Weeks, and Jean Dykes (Simon's first wife) and their two children are familiar from Self's short stories; in *Great Apes* they and their stories resurface, except that now they have become chimpanzees.

Gradually it emerges that in order to release himself from his delusion that he is human, Simon must first come to terms with one specific chimera, that he has a human son by the name of Simon, Jr. Fearful that this human child has become a zoo animal or, worse, subject to experimentation, Simon sets out to find the boy. His visit to the human house at the zoo is a marvelous study in estrangement:

> The first thing that Simon noticed about the humans was their buttocks. They were obscenely null and ludicrously curvaceous, more like blanched beach balls than body parts. . . . Simon concentrated, trying to discern the physiognomy of a man, but couldn't really perceive it. It certainly had something that might be a nasal bridge—at any rate a fleshy proboscis; and also a flat area above its eye sockets, rather than a pronounced ridge. This either made the beast's eyes appear more prominent—or else they were in reality; at any rate they blearied at Simon, blue, protuberant, and utterly without the least flicker of rationality, or self-awareness.
>
> (pp. 247–248)

Simon's quest for his human son takes him finally to a human preserve in Africa run by a fanatical animal-rights activist. It appears that Simon's actual relation to the boy was as his "sponsor" in a program organized by Lifewatch whereby chimps could "adopt" or pay the upkeep of individual humans. When Simon finally locates the boy, now named "Biggles" (the name of the RAF pilot hero of Captain W. E. Johns's imperialist adventure stories for English schoolboys, published from the 1930s to the 1960s), Simon

> stared for a long time into the brutish muzzle of the human infant, who stared back at him, his white-pigmented eyes glazed and turned in on themselves. Simon took in the bare little visage, the undershot jaw and slightly goofy teeth, then he turned on all four of his heels, vocalized "H'hooo," and gestured to the rest of the patrol, "Well, that's that then," and they headed back to the camp.
>
> (p. 403)

The novel ends with the eerie sound, the yowl and yammer, the "meaningless vocalization" of the humans echoing through the equatorial night, and it sounds like: "Fuuuuuckooooffff-Fuuuuuuckoooofff-Fuccckooooofff" (p. 404). Simon is cured.

THE QUANTITY THEORY OF INSANITY

THE six stories presented in *The Quantity Theory of Insanity* (1991) share a preoccupation with distinctly contemporary forms of wigging out, losing balance, or slipping just slightly out of synch. The worlds they evoke are sometimes very different from one to the next, but each is almost uncannily current, giving readers the sense that they are receiving news from the front. Each of the stories is organized around a kind of "What if?" ideation, a cerebral disjuncture that might occur to one in a state of altered consciousness or inebriation. Self's idiosyncratic formulations are realized with stunning vividness and remarkable verbal flare.

The opening tale, "The North London Book of the Dead," recalls Gogol's masterpiece, "The Nose" (1836), in its perfect tonal modulations. Our narrator recounts the recent death of his mother: "Cancer tore through her body as if it were late for an important meeting with a lot of other successful diseases" (p. 1). He describes her cremation, a period of depression following her death, and a series of dreams he has about her in which she makes random appearances, uninvited, to dinner parties and other gatherings. He describes the jarring work of going through her papers, taking care of the necessary business. After about six months, the dreams recede, but soon he begins to see likenesses of her on the street. Eventually he stops seeing these "fake mothers," and seems to have come to terms with the loss, "her absence no longer gnawed at me like a rat at a length of flex. I was over it" (p. 5).

Then comes the Gogolian turn as the narrator informs us with some alarm that on a "drizzly, bleak Tuesday afternoon," walking down toward Crouch End, he sees Mother. "She was wearing a sort of bluish, tweedish long jacket and black slacks and carrying a Barnes & Noble book bag, as well as a large handbag from Waitrose" (p. 5). The absurdist strategy of placing syntactical emphasis on the details of her attire sets the tone for the rest of the story. The narrator approaches Mother, who "looked me up and down to see how I was weighing in for the fight with life. Then she gestured at the shop window she'd been looking into. 'Can you believe the prices they're charging for this crap. . . . '" (pp. 5–6). When the narrator confronts her with, "But Mother, what are you doing in Crouch End? You're dead," she responds indignantly, "Of course I'm dead, dummy, whaddya think I've been doing for the last ten months? Cruising the Caribbean?" (p. 6). Soon the narrator visits her in the basement flat where she is quietly and modestly residing. The narrator questions her about the cremation, "But Mother, what about that performance at Golders Green. Weren't you in the coffin?" She responds, "All right I'll admit it, that part of it is a bit obscure. One minute I was in the hospital—feeling like shit, incidentally—the next I was in Crouch End and some estate agents were showing me around the flat" (p. 8).

Self's conceit, that the dead simply relocate to another part of London (with the added salvo that "When you've been dead for a few years you're encouraged to move to the provinces" [p. 11]) is worked delightfully in this oddball confection. What makes this conceit so resonant? Is it that it seems a kind of literalization of a Dickensian trope? In any case, we feel that a new page has been inscribed in the great annals of London's literary portraits, and that a bold entrance has been made onto the literary landscape.

"Ward 9" is a harrowing story, narrated by Misha, of a young artist who takes a job as an art therapist in a psychiatric inpatient unit and then loses his sanity. The story opens with the laughter of a madman, not an inpatient in the hospital, but a derelict in the park whom Misha passes each morning. Clearly, madness is neither contained nor containable. On his first day of work Misha has some initial difficulty distinguishing the patients on the ward from the medical staff, and Self's portraits of the patients are acute and unsparing. As the narrator begins to sink into madness, it is revealed that the patients are in fact close relations to the doctors, often their offspring. "We are all family here, Misha" (p. 66), explains Dr. Busner (a figure who will appear in a number of Self's stories), "You had a choice, Misha. On Ward 9 you could have been therapist or patient; it seems that you have decided to become a patient" (p. 67). These phrases suggest to the reader a host of conventional propositions, that is, that the inmates are saner than the doctors, or that the mad are treating the mad, that shrinks make patients of their children, that *all* parents make patients of their children, that our therapeutic culture makes patients of all of us (and makes children of all of us), that institutions reproduce themselves *ad infinitum.* Yet Self manages to spin these familiar ideas into a rich pattern, so that the story exceeds its conceptual bounds.

"Understanding the Ur-Bororo" is a hilarious story narrated by a young man about his mentor, an anthropologist named Janner who studies an obscure Amazonian tribe called the Ur-Bororo. The narrator is Marlow to Janner's Kurtz in this story which seems at moments a pastiche of Joseph Conrad's *Heart of Darkness* (1899). After many years with no news of his mentor, the narrator, now a secondary school physical education teacher, fortuitously rediscovers Janner and invites him to dinner. Here the story turns to Janner's description of his fieldwork experiences with the Ur-Bororo, a tribe, it turns out, whose distinctive feature is that it is excruciatingly boring—not only to the anthropologist but to its own members. The Ur-Bororo wear no ornament, no body or facial tattooing, no lip plugs or breech clouts; they produce no decorative ceramics. Janner explains that they refer to themselves as, in translation, "The People Who You Wouldn't Like to be Cornered by at a Party" (p. 82).

Self's description of these people (who bear in some respects a telling likeness to a certain class of English citizenry) is rendered in plausible anthropological terminology:

every word in the Ur-Bororo language has a number of different inflections to express kinds of boredom, or emotional states associated with boredom, such as apathy, ennui, lassitude, enervation, depression, indifference, tedium, and so on. . . . the Ur-Bororo regard most of what they do as a waste of time. In fact the expression that roughly corresponds to "now" in Ur-Bororo is "waste of time."

(p. 83)

Self's detailed account of this unaccountable tribe includes descriptions of their gods, who are believed to "lay about, bloated on sofas, sleeping off a carbohydrate binge" (p. 84). The humor here is often generated by the contrast between the solemn professional discourse and its ludicrous content, by the un-Kurtzian discovery, not of darkness, but of ennui, and we enjoy the fact that these far-off, boring lives are certainly reiterated in that of the physical education teacher and his family, if not in English culture as a whole.

In the title story, "The Quantity Theory of Insanity," we reencounter Dr. Busner, now the originator of a radical academic theory enjoying considerable vogue. His "quantity theory of insanity" proposes that in any given group (be it a family, organization, workplace, or nation) only a certain quantity of sanity is available, so that if one member of the group experiences relief from his or her psychic turmoil, it is a statistical certainty that another member of that group will succumb to some kind of mental breakdown. The story explores this premise with great inventiveness, proposing not only that this discovery will be put to the service of class domination but also of family warfare; we observe an upper-class mother undergoing "quantity theory therapy," ruthlessly obtaining her own sanity at the cost of her son's. This story has a number of connections with "Ward 9," besides the presence of Dr. Busner, who narrates it with a distinctly lunatic verve. The idea that theories of madness and therapeutic techniques in fact assist people into a state of mental derangement and help to keep them there is familiar from the prior story, as is the idea of the family as a private system in which madness circulates.

The final two stories, "Mono-Cellular" and "Waiting," provide rather grim portraits of sidelined males. In "Mono-Cellular," the obsessive-compulsive narrator is waiting throughout the story for a call from a business partner that never comes. The reader slowly recognizes—while the narrator struggles not to—that his new partner has set him up to take the rap for an embezzlement scheme. In "Waiting" we find a comic variation on the midlife crisis in the story of Jim, a man so aggrieved by all forms of waiting (traffic jams, elevators, and so on) that he gives up his normal life and family to join a subversive cult that, he explains, "exist[s] at the precise juncture between the imminent and the immanent" (p. 190), and which looks to the outside observer very much like a motorcycle gang. Its leader, Carlos, possesses a preternatural talent for avoiding traffic jams and for making good time across London, even during rush hour. These final stories are less engaging than the others but convey Self's utter commitment to the fictive worlds and premises he devises.

GREY AREA

THE nine stories in *Grey Area* (1994) extend over a wider thematic and narrative range than those collected in *The Quantity Theory of Insanity.* Self's many worlds have expanded, sometimes even to include our own. In "Incubus, or the Impossibility of Self-Determination as to Desire," Self gives us, perhaps for the first time, a portrait of a fully recognizable world of relative normalcy. Into the domestic life of an aging philosophy professor married to a beautiful, smart, and caustic wife comes a frumpy female graduate student hired to assist her mentor. Moving uncharacteristically among its characters' consciousness, Self's narrator gives us glimpses of ordinary yearnings and disappointments, but these feelings are so fully located in the precise logic of his characterizations that there is ultimately nothing ordinary about them. Following an alcohol-saturated dinner party, the professor wanders drunkenly into the graduate student's bedroom and makes passionate love to her. The next morning the young woman, faced with the awkward necessity of going down to breakfast, soon discovers that her mentor remembers nothing of the previous night's events. Self's treatment of the cultural milieu of the household and of the blistering strains of marital life are piercing and knowing.

The collection's opening story, "Between the Conceits," is an almost indescribably novel invention. It presents a narrator who, like Dostoyevsky's Underground Man, addresses us, within the limits of a single sentence, with a mixture of bungled intimacy and excessive, contrived formality, balancing anxiously on the psychic seesaw of self-aggrandizement and self-abasement. The "conceit" of the story is that along with seven assorted other characters—who by their descriptions sound like a roster of half-mad dole recipients—the narrator controls, by an unspecified method of telepathy, certain daily behaviors of the London populace. These behaviors include saying good morning, receiving junk mail, giving bad birthday presents, blowing air kisses, making throat-cutting gestures, not returning phone calls, and writing groveling letters, and are monitored and controlled like chess pieces by the eight, each of them controlling a percentage of the population. Our narrator explains:

Pah! I make more such calculations in an hour than Kasparov does in a year. I stretch, then relax—and 35,665 white-collar workers leave their houses a teensy bit early for work. This means that 6,014 of them will feel dyspeptic during the journey because they've missed their second piece of toast, or bowl of Fruit 'n' Fibre. From which it follows that 2,982 of them will be testy throughout the morning; and therefore 312 of them will say the wrong thing, leading to dismissal; hence one of these 312 will lose the balance of reason and commit an apparently random and motiveless murder on the way home.

(pp. 9–10)

While Dostoyevsky's Underground Man is preoccupied with the question of "primary causes," our narrator seems to have found the prime mover, and it is himself, along with his seven cohorts. In this grandiose inversion of paranoia, and in the marvelous catalog of petty narcissistic injuries, we find a brilliant analysis of the preoccupations of the contemporary underground man.

"Chest" is a dark fantasy set in an imagined "middle England" where, due to persistent airborne chemical poisoning, the population suffers from a range of debilitating and ultimately fatal lung diseases. As in much science fiction, this premise is not directly stated or commented on; it is simply the way things are now. An underground market in precious inhalers, oxygen cylinders, nebulizers, and various drugs that assist breathing allows for some mobility in the predominantly housebound and dying populace. Only the very rich are adequately equipped with sophisticated chemical masks.

The dying England that Self portrays is peculiarly genteel and not, as one might expect under such conditions, engaged in a ruthless fight for survival, and it is inflected with a conventional, if not exactly familiar, Christian religiosity. And it is a world without irony. The story narrates the last days of Simon-Arthur Dykes's life. (Simon Dykes is a character who appears repeatedly in Self's short stories and in his novel *Great Apes*; in this story names mysteriously include a patronymic.) Simon-Arthur is an artist who devotes himself to making icons that "featured all the correct elements of traditional icons, but the Trinity and the saints depicted were drawn not from life, nor imagination, but from the sort of photographs of public personages that are printed in the newspapers" (p. 143). Unlike comparable work of artists in our own world, these pieces are void of irony. Simon's works are in great demand; nevertheless,

as Simon's wife explains, "Simon-Arthur doesn't sell his. He paints them for the greater glory of our Savior, for no other client" (p. 143).

Out on an evening walk, Simon-Arthur encounters his chemical-masked lord of the manor and his hunting party; they are in pursuit of a pheasant, but before being shot, the bird keels over and dies of a hideous, burgeoning cancer. The story ends—after Simon-Arthur's death—with the landlord considering how he might provide oxygen masks for his remaining pheasants. This is a story so viscerally realized, with ample descriptions of bilious fog, varicolored mucus, sputum, and all manner of mucilaginous ooze, that the reader is likely to find himself gasping for air.

"A Short History of the English Novel" and "The End of the Relationship" both work with gimmicky premises that remind us of Self's brief career as a cartoonist. The former presents us with two youngish, stylish, literary-publishing types, disputing, over lunch, the issue of contemporary literary production and whether or not literature holds a central place in contemporary English culture. As their afternoon together progresses, from restaurant to coffeehouse they discover that every waiter they encounter is writing a novel; in fact, the story will insist, *all* waiters write novels. This hyperbolic "gag" points to a mixed blessing in the current vitality of English letters; Self suggests that a world of novelists is not devoutly to be wished for. "The End of the Relationship" presents the travails of an "emotional Typhoid Mary" (p. 285), a young woman who experiences the unaccountable effect of destroying every romantic relationship she comes near. In the single day the story narrates, the day she finds her own romance has come to an end, she wanders about town, visits a friend, takes a cab ride, and finally ends up seeing her psychotherapist. With each encounter a relationship comes crashing down: her friend's marriage, the cab driver's marriage, her therapist's marriage. Self ends the story with the therapist terminating her relationship with her patient, a clueless carrier of emotional dissension.

The story "Scale," broken into short sections and lacking narrative momentum, gains force by an extended troping on the idea of scale. It offers itself to be read as a miniature key to Self's mythology, or perhaps a satirical critique of his own life and career, as it isolates and treats a number of central preoccupations and themes that run through his works. "Scale" is narrated by a dispossessed intellectual junkie whose wife has taken the kids and left; whose marginal existence is punctuated by efforts to refine a legal kaolin and morphine compound into an illegal granulated, injectable form of morphine known as "Scale"; and by a deep engrossment with all things pertaining to superhighways. Notably, our self-destructive narrator is exceedingly prolific. He is working on a mystery titled "Murder on the Median Strip," is the proud originator of a lyric subgenre called "Motorway Verse," and has produced a volume titled "A History of the English Motorway Service Centre." (The mystery of why there are "no services" on the M40 recurs throughout the story.)

These subjects—innovative writing, self-stimulus, dissociation, self-marginalization, and self-destruction—are rich veins in Self's work, as are superhighways. Not unlike his narrator, Self has confessed a fascination with superhighways, with an eager nod to J. G. Ballard. Self is drawn, one suspects, to their topological and tropological potential; while they seem to emblematize for him the contemporary landscape and our remote relationship to it, he also sees them as in some ways "under-imagined," as we have yet to acknowledge their imprinting on our psyches, the states of dissociation they induce, and their centrality in our everyday lives. In "Scale" the narrator informs us that "since the universal introduction of electric cars with a maximum speed of 15 mph, the glamour of motorway driving seems entirely lost" (p. 122). He considers how future archaeologists will interpret the grassed-over superhighway system and the language of road signs. Will they mystify, like the ruins at Avebury? Will their symbolic weight finally be realized?

Of the narrator's efforts to write fiction, a reader comments to him that perhaps Self means to be reflexive of his own work:

You can have a limited success, chipping away like this at the edges of society, chiselling off microscopic fragments of observation. But really important writing provides some sense of the relation between individual psychology and social change, of the scale of things in general.

(p. 103)

In this arguably representative story, Self offers marginality as a gauge of "things in general"; his narrator concludes, "It may be said of me that I have lost my sense of scale, but never that I have lost my sense of proportion" (p. 123).

COCK AND BULL

Of *Cock and Bull* (1992) Self has remarked, "it is an elaborate joke about the failure of narrative" (*Junk Mail*, p. 381), and that he wrote the stories to voice his "anger at the way gender-based sexuality is so predetermined, the way we fit into our sex roles as surely as if we had cut them off the back of a cereal packet and pasted them onto ourselves" (Heller, p. 127).

"Cock: A Novelette" is a framed narrative, a story told to our narrator by "a slightly faggoty, fussy middle-aged don" (p. 15) who corners the narrator on a train. The story, conveyed in a flat and matter-of-fact style, is intermittently interrupted by the increasingly hostile conversation between the two men in the train compartment. The don details the story of Carol, an unexceptional "lower middle class" provincial university student, "lithe, and pretty in the mean-featured English provincial way" (p. 8), who falls into a dreary marriage with Dan from the slim incitement that he occasioned her first orgasm, a feat he is never able to duplicate. Carol and Dan move to a two-bedroom maisonette in North London; Dan works and goes to the pub each night; Carol stays home, finding herself "with lovely, indolent time on her hands" (p. 11). Dan's habitual boozing reduces his propensity to "climb on board" (p. 10), as he calls it, and Carol learns to pleasure herself from a description she's read in a pornographic novel. "This, then, was the pattern that they established," the narrator explains. "Dan went out drinking, and Carol, as soon as he was out of the way, treated herself to a really big wank" (p. 28).

One day, while pursuing her ritual, Carol discovers something new, "a tiny nodule, a little gristly frond of flesh . . . a minature volcanic column of tissue, sinew, blood and vessel" (p. 32). Carol's growing anxieties about this budding member are temporarily sidelined by events in the household, as Dan decides to stop drinking with the aid of a fanatical mentor from Alcoholics Anonymous who invades their homelife with military and religious zeal, spouting empathy and drinking endless cups of instant coffee. Carol's relative complaisance is finally shattered one morning when she opens her jeans to discover that the "frond" is now big enough to be "taken out." As "it" grows, Carol, we learn, is subtly changing, becoming "more aggressive"; she decides to learn to drive, and begins stopping into pubs for a pint and a greasy lunch.

Soon, in her afternoon masturbatory rituals, she explores the new possibilities of her now fully functioning penis.

Meanwhile, back in the train compartment, the conversations between the two men are growing increasingly bizarre. The storyteller grows more belligerent toward his homophobic listener; he insists that his story has "no lurking, shadowy narrator" (p. 83), that it is the unmediated "truth." He says:

"Hold up! I sense something, my laddie. I sense that as I describe the glories of the newest member you are . . . placing different interpretations on what I am saying. . . . Well educated are we? . . . I hope you aren't deriving any signifiers or symbols from Carol's penis. I hope you aren't undertaking some convoluted analysis of this story in your sick sheeny mind."

(p. 105)

In his rantings, he draws analogies between the "tale" and the phallic "tail."

Back in Carol and Dan's living room, Carol takes the occasion of their anniversary dinner to tempt Dan back to his alcoholic dependency. Groping and drunk, Dan stumbles and hits his head, falling unconscious on the floor. Then follows a most uncommon formulation: "He barely noticed when she turned him over. But he did notice when she entered him" (p. 126). The story-within-the-story ends with a description of Carol's brutal rape and murder of Dan. Carol, of course, is never suspected, since Dan has apparently been raped by a man.

The final pages of "Cock" recount the rape of the listener by the knife-wielding storyteller in the train compartment. The narrating listener closes his portion of the story by explaining that he did not report the rape to the police because he was certain that they would not take the charge seriously, "They would shake their jug heads as they listened to how the don seduced me, bamboozled me" (p. 144). "Cock" closes with the intrusion of a new and unidentified voice. (Is it the fiction police?) "Now quite honestly, sonny . . . what do you expect if you wander out into the fictional night alone. . . . But really, luvvie—come on. This is what you get if you sit there like a prat, listening to a load of cock . . . and bull" (pp. 144–145).

This gender-bending narrative builds in a Nabokovian false bottom. The story likens the dynamics between male (aggressive) and female (passive) to that between the storyteller and his audience; and like the switch that takes place in Carol's story, Self suggests, there is a fluidity in the power dynamic between teller and tale, a dynamic that can transform the pleasure giver to sadist in the flash of a knife.

"Bull: A Farce" is a far less harrowing story, narrated in a lighter, more jovial tone. Perhaps there is something intrinsically less ominous for Self about a man finding himself doubly equipped than a woman in that condition. Like "Cock," "Bull" presents two stories together, this time within one narrative that traces the actions of two men: J. Bull, a hearty, football-playing journalist who "awoke one morning to find that while he had slept he had acquired another primary sexual characteristic: to wit, a vagina" (p. 149); and Dr. Alan Margoulies, married with a young child, a conscientious physician whose one moral flaw is his unchecked philandering. "A little devil sat on Alan's left shoulder, a little angel on his right. On the right-hand shoulder of the little devil sat a littler angel; and on the left-hand shoulder a little devil. It was the same for the first angel, and so on, and so on" (p. 218).

Upon discovering his mysterious "wound"—located behind his right knee—Bull takes himself to see Dr. Margoulies, who, in an effort to protect his patient, does not tell Bull what he has there behind his knee; he cleans and bandages the "wound" and sends him home. But Margoulies finds that he can't get this virginal member out of his mind, and he decides to pay Bull a house call, and thus begins an affair between the men. It doesn't take very long, however, for Margoulies to lose interest in this fling, and Bull is left with wretched (and implicitly feminine) feelings of abandonment. Margoulies returns to the bosom of his family while Bull, discovering that he is pregnant, contemplates suicide. The story ends with an epilogue stating that Bull does not commit suicide but goes to San Francisco to have his baby, and then settles in Cardiff, where he has "become entirely accepted," as has his "large and darkly handsome son Kenneth" (p. 310).

As in "Cock," the appearance of the new organ carries with it a host of what Self appears to deem secondary sexual characteristics, the most prominent of which is Bull's new sense of "vulnerability," a trait that endears him to the reader. Indeed, Bull, unlike Carol, settles happily into his ambiguous sexual identity (he runs a sporting goods and memorabilia shop), his life distinctly improved by this added organ.

THE SWEET SMELL OF PSYCHOSIS

THE *Sweet Smell of Psychosis* (1996) is more accurately described as a long short story than a novella. This satire, published in a handsome edition with comically sinister illustrations by Martin Rowson, takes us into the bowels of the lush, cocaine-saturated London club scene of the media elite. It centers on an inconspicuous, listings magazine writer, Richard Hermes, and a high-profile television personality, known only as "Bell," who specializes in scandal, power, and glib malevolence. Richard engages in a largely one-sided battle with Bell for possession of the "nubile" siren Ursula Bentley and, in modified form, for his own soul. Bell is "kingpin, a grand panjandrum" (p. 15) of the Sealink Club; surrounded by a clique of sycophantic acolytes, he controls the local flow of cocaine, sex, and professional advancement. Another Tempter in the tradition of Broadhurst / Northcliffe in *My Idea of Fun*, Bell was "capable of seducing those who attempted to evade him" (p. 18), and his favorite enterprise is to seek out "some long-established relationship—marriage, cohabitation, or a clandestine affair, even—and interpose his dissolutive bulk between the pair-bonding, unsticking the accretions of years, experiences, children . . . even love" (p. 19). Young Richard does not stand much of a chance, but his desperate, *really* desperate lust for Ursula keeps him in the game, as he tags along in the fast-lane debauchery of Bell and his clique.

Ursula is portrayed throughout the story as a figure out of a noir film: "Ursula Bentley leant against the banisters, a Venus in spangles, trails of her long, dark brown hair twining around her upper body, forming a growing bodice" (p. 64). The question of whose side she is really on—that of darkness or light—remains suspended for Richard, although the serpent imagery here gives the reader a clue. The story's climax occurs just as Richard has resolved to abandon the clique and to quit London for a homey Christmas with his family, "but before he did so he would make one last assault on Mount Ursula" (p. 78). He calls her for a date, and for the first time she agrees to see him alone; after dinner they return to her place. Rich-

ard is surprised to learn that she lives modestly in a cramped flat, that she is not rich, a circumstance that augurs well for her turning out to be a "good girl" after all. Things develop as in one of Richard's dreams; she is all compliance, "There was no fumbling, no awkwardness as his hands roamed over her." Then, "She simply sat upright, crossed her arms in front of her, and pulled the dress over her head" (p. 85). But things are not what they seem, and Richard's dream date turns into a nightmare as Ursula's glorious body is transformed into that of Bell. "Richard couldn't understand why it was that he could hear what Bell was saying, because his own screams bounced and whined around the room. 'It's good to have you on board,' said the big man; 'I thought you were never really going to join—become one of us'" (p. 89).

In this cautionary tale, Bell and Ursula are perhaps meant to embody the media, with its hidden psychic systems of control; you think you know what is seducing you, but you do not. In addition, in this story Self's distinct uneasiness about sex itself is vividly revealed; the sexual act seems to strike him as a kind of preposterous activity from which his characters can find themselves quite suddenly estranged. In his conversation with Martin Amis in *Junk Mail*, Self quotes the aphorism, "God created sex in order to humiliate man, by forcing him to adopt ridiculous postures" (p. 392).

JUNK MAIL

JUNK *Mail* (1995), a collection of Self's journalistic writing and cartoons, is divided into sections titled "On Drugs," "On Other Things," "Book Reviews," "Features," "Profiles," and "Conversations." A lively and entertaining, if uneven, smorgasbord, it offers, in the subjects and writers he interests himself in, a discursive gloss of Self's fiction.

The fifteen short pieces that fall under the heading "On Drugs" range widely, from four pieces on William Burroughs to a vivid portrait of a London crack house, and from an irate response to the failed legislative effort to legalize marijuana in England to a review of Richard Price's novel *Clockers* (1992). From these refracted polemics the reader gleans that while generally in favor of drugs, Self is quite opposed to addiction, and he writes movingly about an experimental rehabilitation program he visits in a prison in Surrey. Self finds much to regret in the pronouncements of some drug proponents:

Aldous Huxley, that veteran psychedelic experimenter, once said of his younger and more turbulent acolyte, Timothy Leary, "If only Tim weren't such a silly ass." This could usefully serve as blanket condemnation for most of the philosophically inclined figures who owe their mindset . . . to the cultural revolutions of the 1960s.

(p. 18)

Self seems inclined to replace a "pathological" use of drugs (including alcohol) with their "ritualized" employment:

Young people should be educated to use drugs in a meaningful way. Our culture should have its own defined initiation ceremonies involving the use of drugs, just as other cultures do, and these rituals should be socially approved. . . . I believe there is more genuine 'spirituality' in most acid-house raves than you'll find in a pub.

(p. 32)

In "On Other Things" Self offers a bouquet of humorous pieces on such subjects as television, flying in first class, superhighways, and "slacking," and he is thoroughly comfortable and at ease in this genre. His essay "Slack Attack," perhaps the funniest of the group, although terrifically knowing on the subject, reminds us that these pieces that appear almost effortless are indeed works of invention, because Self's astonishing creative output makes it clear that he is anything but a slacker. Self reviews books by Joseph Heller, Woody Allen, and Adam Phillips, and his "Features" include a humorous, probing essay on the "state of English culture," and one on cryonics, detailing a visit he paid to the Alcor Life Extension Foundation in Riverside, California. We are treated to profiles of Thomas Szasz, the "anti-psychiatrist" who bears some relation to his fictional figure Dr. Busner; Damien Hirst; Martin Amis; and Bret Easton Ellis. The book finishes with two long, transcribed conversations, one with J. G. Ballard, and the other with Martin Amis, and indeed these truly are conversations, not interviews, in which Self and his work are as much the subject as are his interlocutors.

CONCLUSION

SELF has emerged as a distinctive voice in English fiction, though also one with many links to his contemporaries. Like Martin Amis, Self has profited from what Amis terms "the promiscuity of verbal . . . registers" (*Junk Mail,* p. 394) in the American language. Like many of his contemporaries, Self sees his work as a deliberate turn from the psychological realism of the nineteenth-century English novel. "[Milan] Kundera's point," Self has remarked, is "that people do construct elaborate motifs to grace their lives, to explain their lives to themselves. Perhaps in the nineteenth century people were much happier to do that, they had a sense that it was legitimate. Perhaps we don't feel that way anymore?" (*Junk Mail,* p. 381). Indeed, Self's rendering of character often appears more semiological than psychological, as he often will suggest character by a description of the specific name brands the character prefers or by where he or she purchases home furnishings.

Self's London, where most of his fiction is set, is a place where class plays almost no role, where money and celebrity rule, as Empire is still on the decline while the economy is on the incline. It is a city thoroughly saturated with things American, from films and television shows to crack cocaine. But Self's London is also a kind of conceptual playground:

I can draw an A-Z of my London. A schizophrenic once knocked on my door in Shepherd's Bush and said, "Can you drive me to Leytonstone and give me £17.37", and I did. As we were driving to Leytonstone he was ranting, completely incoherent. And I said, "Look, you're mad. I want to check in the A-Z exactly where you want me to take you before I go further." And he said: "But you and I know that the A-Z is a plan of what's going to be built." That's how I conceive my London.

(p. 390)

Self's favored targets of satire are academia, psychology, the fashionable art world, and all vested interests and systems of control, including, one might argue, fiction itself. His readers have good reason to anticipate what his next targets might be.

SELECTED BIBLIOGRAPHY

I. FICTION. *The Quantity Theory of Insanity: Together with Five Supporting Propositions* (London, 1991; New

York, 1995); *Cock and Bull* (London, 1992; New York, 1993); *My Idea of Fun: A Cautionary Tale* (London, 1993; New York, 1994); *Grey Area and Other Stories* (London, 1994; New York, 1997); *The Sweet Smell of Psychosis* (London, 1996); *Great Apes* (London and New York, 1997); *Tough, Tough Toys for Tough, Tough Boys* (New York, 1999).

II. Nonfiction. *Junk Mail* (London, 1995); articles, reviews and cartoons in *City Limits, Esquire, Guardian, Harper's, Independent, London Times, New Statesman, Observer, She.*

III. Critical Studies and Interviews. Nick Hornby, "Mad About Insanity," in *Times Literary Supplement* (20 December 1991); Mark Marvel, "Five Fantastic First Novels," in *Interview* (May 1993); Zoë Heller, "Self Examination," in *Vanity Fair* (June 1993); Phil Baker, "Tutorials from Hell: *My Idea of Fun,*" in *Times Literary Supplement* (10 September 1993); Will Blythe, "Self Loathing: *My Idea of Fun,*" in *Esquire* (April 1994); Craig Seligman, "Buster Keaton in Hell," in *New Yorker* (11 April 1994); George Stade, "The Yum-Yum Man," in *New York Times Book Review* (24 April 1994); Will Eaves, "Beaconsfield Philosophers," in *Times Literary Supplement* (18 November 1994); Will Eaves, "Speeding Offences," in *Times Literary Supplement* (5 January 1996); Walter Kirn, "The Bodily-Fluid Bard," in *New York* (18 March 1996); Anna Henchman, "Will Self: An Enfant Terrible Comes of Age," in *Publishers Weekly* (8 September 1997); David Thomas, dir., "Will Self," on *The South Bank Show,* ITV (August 1998).

ALAN SILLITOE

(1928–)

John L. Tucker

NOVELIST, SHORT-STORY WRITER, playwright, essayist, poet, author of more than fifty separately published works, Alan Sillitoe is best known for two early fictions about life in the industrial North Midlands, *Saturday Night and Sunday Morning* (1958) and "The Loneliness of the Long-Distance Runner" (1959). Harshly realistic and violently opposed to the British class system, these works quickly won popular and critical recognition; both were made into successful movies. The author's working-class background and his lack of a university education accredited him in the public eye as a representative of the laboring poor.

Sillitoe's reception makes a revealing chapter in the history of British culture and class consciousness and accounts for much of the academic interest in his career. The critics Eugene F. Quirk, Stanley Atherton, Allen R. Penner, Ronald D. Vaverka, and Peter Hitchcock have drawn attention to the ways in which British cultural institutions, criticized from within and without after World War II, helped to deflect political antagonism by packaging and promoting representations of working-class life, notably in the theater, which welcomed oppositional writers such as John Osborne (*Look Back in Anger*, 1956), Brendan Behan (*The Quare Fellow*, 1956), and Shelagh Delaney (*A Taste of Honey*, 1959), and also in the traditionally conservative realm of the novel. A late arrival, Sillitoe was quickly tagged as one of the "Angry Young Men," a heterogeneous group of writers including Kingsley Amis (*Lucky Jim*, 1953), John Wain (*Hurry on Down*, 1953), and John Braine (*Room at the Top*, 1957), whose common cause was contempt for the status quo. Sillitoe dismisses the "Angry" label as a publicity trick, a "total misnomer . . . a journalistic catch-phrase" (Halperin, p. 182). In fact, much of his early work seems more radical than that of his contemporaries, many of whose plots end in compromise. By comparison, Sillitoe's first characters see themselves as resis-

tance fighters, enrolled from birth in an unrelenting class war. They also are victims of that war, isolated by poverty, illiteracy, and an ingrained tradition of pessimism. These portraits are frankly autobiographical: Sillitoe's first protagonist, Arthur Seaton, shares the author's initials and works at a machinist's job as the author did before joining the Royal Air Force; many details of the Seatons' family life match recollections in Sillitoe's published memoirs.

Sillitoe's early life was not one likely to nurture an artist. Had it not been for World War II and its aftermath, the class war might have silenced the author, despite his early love for storytelling. He needed the distance of military service, followed by an enforced convalescence from tuberculosis, before he could commit himself to writing. When he began to describe the world of his upbringing he was no longer part of it. Turning it into fiction meant imaginatively reliving the struggles and confinement of class, and with the success of his first works he also faced the classic dilemma of the regional writer: the possibility of being defined and even imprisoned by his frame of reference. Branching out, he began to articulate the politics his first characters might have come to had they known more of the world. In the process his work became more polemical and somewhat less three-dimensional; witness the belligerence of *The Rats and Other Poems* (1960), the pro-Soviet enthusiasm of *Road to Volgograd* (1964), and the Maoist pronouncements of *The Death of William Posters* (1965) and *A Tree on Fire* (1967). By the early 1970s Sillitoe could be seen as preaching "violent social rebellion" (Penner, p. 22).

Sillitoe moved away from socialist propaganda when he saw how the Soviet Communist Party treated dissident writers and Jews; by the mid-1970s he was becoming interested in Zionism. Other, more complex tendencies latent in his writing emerged and flourished in the 1970s and 1980s.

His chief concern had always been the damage done to marriage, family life, work, and community relations by narrow expectations, and he continued to address this issue throughout his career, never losing his oppositional spirit but saving it several times from political and literary oversimplification. To trace this process through the whole body of Sillitoe's work would require a book in itself; the present essay confines itself to a selection of Sillitoe's longer fiction and his poetry.

LIFE AND CAREER

BORN 4 March 1928 in Nottingham, Sillitoe was in many respects a child of the Great Depression. His male forebears on both sides of the family were laborers and small artisans. His mother, Sylvina, was the daughter of a village blacksmith; Alan's father, Christopher Sillitoe, an illiterate tannery worker, was an upholsterer's son. Christopher Sillitoe lost his job in 1934; until World War II began in 1939 the family survived on welfare and the five children ate their dinners at a community kitchen. Fascinated by history and maps, the young Alan did well in local schools and began teaching himself French at the age of ten. In the British educational system of the period, the university-bound elite were selected by examination at the ages of eleven and twelve. Sillitoe's schooling had not prepared him for the examination; he failed twice and wound up in the industrial curriculum. At age fourteen he left school and went to work, first at the Raleigh Bicycle factory, then at a plywood factory, then as a capstan lathe operator for a small machine shop. At age seventeen he joined the Air Training Corps. He was called up in 1946, trained as a radio operator, and served two years in Malaya. Sent back to England in 1948, he was found to have tuberculosis and spent sixteen months recovering in an Air Force sanatorium, where he read voraciously, mostly classical literature and the works of novelists ranging from Henry Fielding to Albert Camus, and began to write poetry and fiction. Discharged at the end of 1949, he went back to Nottingham, determined to become a writer.

In 1952 he went abroad with his future wife, the poet Ruth Fainlight (they were married in 1959 and have two children, David Nimrod and Susan). In the 1950s Sillitoe and Fainlight lived in France, moved to Spain, and then settled on Majorca,

where the poet Robert Graves encouraged Sillitoe to begin *Saturday Night and Sunday Morning*. Published in 1958, it won the London Authors' Club prize. Sillitoe returned to England and lived in London while finishing "The Loneliness of the Long-Distance Runner," which appeared as the title story of his first collection in 1959 and won the Hawthornden Prize in 1959. The following year saw the publication of *The Rats and Other Poems*; a new novel, *The General*; and the release of the movie version of *Saturday Night and Sunday Morning*, starring Albert Finney as Arthur Seaton. Sillitoe continued the story of the Seaton family in 1961 with *Key to the Door*, whose main character, Arthur's older brother Brian, relives some of the author's own experiences, including his tour of duty in Malaya. In 1961 Sillitoe also published his second collection of short stories and wrote a screenplay based on "The Loneliness of the Long-Distance Runner." The film, featuring Tom Courtenay and Sir Michael Redgrave, appeared the following year.

Success brought opportunities for travel, gratifying one of Sillitoe's ruling passions. In 1962 he visited Morocco, where he began planning the William Posters trilogy (*The Death of William Posters*, 1965; *A Tree on Fire*, 1967; and *The Flame of Life*, 1974). In 1963 he made his first trip to the Soviet Union and recorded his impressions as *Road to Volgograd* (1964), a travel memoir. During the 1960s Sillitoe expanded his literary range, publishing a third volume of poetry in 1964 and two more in 1968. The first of his children's books appeared in 1967 and a third short-story collection, *Guzman Go Home and Other Stories*, in 1968. At decade's end he bought a house in Kent and began spending part of each winter abroad, in Spain or the south of France.

Since 1970 Sillitoe's career has alternated between experimentation and retrospection, striking out in new directions and then returning to reimagine his origins. Within the Nottingham frame of reference he has written fiction mainly in two modes, one serious and realistic, the other comic and escapist, a variation on the traditional picaresque. The latter mode won him new popularity in 1970 with *A Start in Life*, the first of his two Michael Cullen novels. He returned to the serious vein for *The Widower's Son* (1976) and *The Storyteller* (1979). The 1970s also saw two quite different experiments, the anti-utopian fantasy *Travels in Nihilon* (1971) and a meditation, partly biographical and partly fictional, called *Raw Material* (1972). Two more short-story collections also appeared, along with five volumes of his own poetry, two more to which he contributed, one volume of essays, and three short plays on political themes (*The Slot Machine, The Interview,* and *Pit Strike,* published together in 1978). In 1974 Sillitoe visited Israel for the first time; the experience helped to shape the developing interest in Zionism that would inform *Israel: Poems on a Hebrew Theme* (1981) and the novel *Her Victory* (1982). Also in 1974 he gained recognition as a travel writer by being elected a fellow of the Royal Geographic Society.

In the 1980s and 1990s Sillitoe often revisited familiar territory: *Down from the Hill* (1984) and *Out of the Whirlpool* (1987) return to the realism of his early Nottingham stories; *Life Goes On* (1985) gives Michael Cullen a second picaresque outing; and Brian Seaton reappears in *The Open Door* (1988), a long-delayed sequel. *Snowstop* (1993) is a picaresque tale of characters stranded at an inn. But there were also some new departures, such as a neocolonial adventure fantasy, *The Lost Flying Boat* (1983), and *Last Loves* (1989), which combines a plotline that suggests retrospect (three English tourists revisiting their past in Malaya) with innovative technique. *Leonard's War: A Love Story* (1991) uses a similar combination, interweaving the collapse of a marriage with headline news of the Second World War. Another change of focus distinguishes *Her Victory* (1982), where the point of view is most often that of the character Pam, an abused woman who leaves her husband to strike out on her own. *The Broken Chariot* (1998) reimagines elements of Sillitoe's own career as a working-class writer, but his fictional representative in this novel has a split personality and finally has to choose between his assumed identity as a Nottingham factory worker and his real origin as the well-educated son of a career army officer. During this period Sillitoe also published four new volumes of poetry and two more memoirs (in 1995 and 1997). Entering his seventh decade, Alan Sillitoe was still a resourceful and versatile writer.

SILLITOE AND THE TRADITION OF WORKING-CLASS WRITING

IN the mid-nineteenth century, concern for the lives of the working poor began to register in En-

glish fiction in an outpouring of social-problem novels. Some, like Thomas Martin Wheeler's *Sunshine and Shadow* (1849–1850) and Ernest Jones's *De Brassier: A Democratic Romance* (1850–1851), were inspired by Chartism, a political movement of the late 1830s and 1840s seeking improved conditions for the lower classes. As works of art these novels tend to be conventional, imitating the approved drawing-room style of the day. More interesting and enduring are the novels of the period by middle-class writers: Charles Dickens's *Oliver Twist* (1837–1838), *Dombey and Son* (1846–1848), *Bleak House* (1852–1853), and *Hard Times* (1854); Charles Kingsley's *Yeast* (1848) and *Alton Locke* (1850); Elizabeth Gaskell's *North and South* (1855); Benjamin Disraeli's *Coningsby* (1844) and *Sybil* (1845); and George Eliot's *Felix Holt the Radical* (1866). Realism, which chooses ordinary people for its subjects and gives them probable, believable experiences, opened the novel to voices that were closer than ever before to those of the actual poor. Generally speaking, however, these novels seek to appease social conflict, and they accomplish this not by encouraging the expression of a working-class identity but by inviting dissidents and outsiders to find a home within the moral system and culture of the middle class.

The inequities produced by industrialization continued unabated through the nineteenth century, and in the late 1880s and 1890s working people began to organize for self-defense, joining trade unions and initiating what was to become the Labour Party. The new oppositional mood was reflected in the next wave of socially conscious fiction, naturalist writing, which began in England with George Gissing (*Workers in the Dawn,* 1880; *Demos,* 1886; *New Grub Street,* 1891), George Moore (*Esther Waters,* 1894), Arnold Bennett (*A Man from the North,* 1898; *The Old Wives' Tale,* 1908), and Arthur Morrison (*A Child of the Jago,* 1896). These writers were influenced by French novelists, especially Victor Hugo (*Les Misérables,* 1862) and the naturalist Emile Zola (*Les Rougon-Macquart,* 1871–1893). Sillitoe recalls that *Les Misérables* had a powerful impact on him in childhood: "Something spoke to me in that book about the condition of my existence" (Rothschild, p. 131). Naturalist fiction exposed class conflict, which shapes and overwhelms individual lives, as the product of a diseased social system in need of drastic reform. In the first decade of the twentieth century some writers openly agitated for a new socialist order.

One who influenced Sillitoe significantly was Robert Tressell [Robert Noonan] whose novel *The Ragged Trousered Philanthropists* (published posthumously in 1914) was circulated by English strikers during the Depression as propaganda for their cause; given a copy during his military service in Malaya, Sillitoe was told "it was the book that won the 1945 election for Labour" (Hitchcock, p. 19). Sillitoe wrote the introduction for a paperback edition in 1965.

Perhaps the most important early twentieth-century working-class writer to influence Sillitoe was D. H. Lawrence. Like Sillitoe he was born in Nottinghamshire; his father was a miner, and some of his most moving fiction describes the work and family life of miners. Mary Eagleton and David Pierce see him as a pioneer in English literature: "It is not really until D. H. Lawrence that one finds in the novel an expression of a working-class culture, of the day-to-day life-style, feelings, tensions, aspirations of the majority of the population. It is obviously crucial that Lawrence was himself born into that class and experienced from the inside all that he writes about" (p. 14). The Lawrence novel that mattered most to Sillitoe as a young writer was *The Rainbow* (1915): "It was a revelation to me to read a book that was about places I knew. It suddenly occurred to me that I could write about my own life rather than write adventure stories that were impossibly romantic and had nothing to do with life as I knew it" (Rothschild, p. 131).

Sillitoe valued not only Lawrence's fidelity to the social scene but his psychological depth: "After all he was a novelist and this is what one is finally judged by in the end—not whether your picture of a certain topographical area is accurate, but whether the picture of yourself is accurate and the people who are in a sort of spin-off situation from that are accurate" (Halperin, p. 178). Many of Sillitoe's characters, notably the Seatons, can be understood as "in a sort of spin-off situation" from their author—not autobiographical duplicates, but variations on a personal theme. Sillitoe's work also echoes Lawrence's in its close attention to the intimate life of working-class families, where privacy is scarce and communication often almost wordless. Commenting on this theme in Lawrence, Raymond Williams emphasizes "the sense of quick close relationship, which came to matter more than anything else. This was the positive result of life of the family in a small house, where there were no such devices of separation of children and parents as the sending-away to school, or the handing-over to servants, or the relegation to nursery or playroom" (*Culture and Society, 1780–1950*, quoted in Atkins, p. 23).

Between the wars the most admired strain in English fiction was modernist experimentalism, led by James Joyce and Virginia Woolf, who, although sympathetic to working people, are not primarily concerned with questions of social justice. Working-class novelists did publish during the same period, notably Lewis Crassic Gibbon (*A Scots Quair*, 1932–1934) and Lewis Jones (*Cwmardy*, 1937), but the working-class novel as a genre was categorically dismissed by the influential critic William Empson, whose celebrated 1935 study *Some Versions of Pastoral* in part argued that proletarian literature could never rise above the level of propaganda. Sillitoe's judgment of working-class novels of this same time is similarly harsh, although it is not extended to proletarian literature generally and singles out one 1930s proletarian novel for praise: "The whole proletarian movement in literature before the war or between the wars really failed—with the possible exception of Walter Greenwood's *Love on the Dole* [1933], which was a good book."

Some more recent critics have agreed; Pamela Fox cites Roy Johnson, who, in her words, "denies the very existence of a proletarian literary culture, citing . . . the absence of an independent, greater working-class culture from which it would arise and the failure of working-class novelists to challenge the bourgeois values laden within the novel form" (p. 59). A leading school of British Marxist cultural history takes the opposite view, however, led by Richard Hoggart, Raymond Williams, and E. P. Thompson.

THEMES: REINVENTING PICARESQUE IN A WORLD OF WAR

THE word "picaresque" has been used so often to describe Sillitoe's fiction that there is some danger of obscuring its significance. Readers tend to associate it with an eighteenth-century mood of bawdy licentiousness, in the manner of Fielding's *Jonathan Wild* (1743) or *Tom Jones* (1749). Sillitoe himself is fond of such associations because they can be used to supply a historical background for modern anti-establishment politics. In Sillitoe's estimation, "The generous and lecherous spirit of the eighteenth century, crushed for more than a hundred years by the descending death-trap ceiling of tight-arsed Victorian hypocrisy and repression is at last trying to break free" (*Raw Material,* p. 176). Some such rebellion has been discerned in Sillitoe's fiction from the beginning. Reviewing *Saturday Night and Sunday Morning* for the *New Yorker,* Anthony West praised the book for showing "the true robust and earthy quality characteristic of English working-class life" (5 September 1959). In a similar vein, John W. Aldridge finds it "comforting" that "the grand old roistering 'low life' tradition of Fielding and Dickens . . . is not yet dead" (p. 240). Stanley S. Atherton recalls that Sillitoe's picaresque *A Start in Life* (1970) "disarmed" critics who had expressed "reservations about Sillitoe's departure from the working-class milieu he had depicted so admirably in earlier fiction" (p. 38). Some of these critics welcome the picaresque as a safe entertainment for middle-class readers, and the practitioner as one who is, as Aldridge approvingly observes, "basically content to keep the working man in his place" (p. 240). To be so misunderstood must gall a committed writer like Sillitoe, whose long engagement with the picaresque has deliberately exposed its seductions.

Picaresque is an open-ended form, a series of loosely connected adventures limited only by imagination and demand. The hero is usually "a rascal of low degree engaged in menial tasks and making his living more through his wits than his industry" (Harmon and Holman, p. 389). Originally a popular entertainment, picaresque quickly became a model for satire produced by middle-class writers. A famous case is that most enduring and subversive English example of the genre, Daniel Defoe's *Moll Flanders* (1722). Through theft and prostitution, Moll pursues the dominant values of her culture: self-determination, security, and respectability. Moll shows the compatibility of these values with a life of crime, thus turning the tables on the respectable voyeurs who, presumably, made up a large part of Defoe's audience. The book is brilliant satire, but it also shows how the authentic street tale can be co-opted by the middle class.

For D. M. Roskies, this instability is characteristic of pastoral, the general category within which he locates working-class or "proletarian" literature, following William Empson's influential study. Roskies sees Sillitoe's "refusal of pastoral simplesse" as the product of a writer who, anxious to resist "the conventionalizing force of literary precedent," invents "an art which transgresses, in a calculated and technically unusual way, the limits of pastoral convention" (p. 171). Extending Roskies' argument, we might say that by writing not only about but also for the working class Sillitoe turns the picaresque away from pastoral. "Though proletarian novelists are read mostly by a middle-class audience," Sillitoe wrote in 1959, "they should make themselves readable by the people they grew up with—not necessarily an impediment to good writing" ("Proletarian Novelists," quoted in Hitchcock, p. 62). Nonetheless, perhaps it is the consciousness of speaking to two different audiences that makes Sillitoe's practice as a comic writer appear inconsistent. In the William Posters trilogy one main character condemns the picaresque as a danger to the working class (an evasion, a false promise of escape from repression) while another appears to be enacting it. *Saturday Night and Sunday Morning* and "The Loneliness of the Long-Distance Runner" offer no respite from the class war, yet both are often read as rogue-tales. Hailed as picaresques in the classic manner, the Michael Cullen novels of 1970 and 1985 are better seen as cynical send-ups of the very book trade that promoted them.

Because the episodic, never-finished rogue's tale has always been a staple of popular entertainment, its attractions for a politically committed writer may outweigh its dangers. To write such a work is to ally oneself with an underground literature, the transient, often anonymous storytelling of the streets that inspired and shaped mainstream novels from Cervantes and Defoe to Dickens. Picaresque is the novel's poor relation and alter ego—the perfect form for an outsider like Sillitoe. But it is susceptible to takeover by the dominant culture ever alert for new entertainments, new drugs, new commodities. Sillitoe's best solution to this dilemma has been to saturate his picaresques with a contrary theme: war.

By his own account, Sillitoe has always been "fascinated" by war (Halperin, p. 187). His personal experience of combat was limited (he left Malaya just as the communist insurgency began), but he studied military history and acquired a detailed knowledge of both world wars. Some of the most memorable passages in his fictions are battlefield scenes, as vivid and harrowing as anything in contemporary literature—accounts of desert warfare in *The Death of William Posters* and *A Tree on Fire*, artillery operations before Dunkirk in *The Widower's Son*, the Malay jungle ambush in *Last Loves*. But the defining war in Sillitoe's work is the one his father's generation faced, the "Great War" of 1914–1918. Sillitoe has rarely focused on it directly (an exception is "The Sniper," collected in *The Second Chance and Other Stories*, 1981). More typically the Great War is a background reference to some psychological maiming, as in the story "Uncle Ernest" (*The Loneliness of the Long-Distance Runner*, 1959) and *The Widower's Son*. But the influence of the Great War pervades Sillitoe's work, most noticeably at the level of language. World War I catchphrases such as "over the top" and "no-man's-land" occur throughout Sillitoe's work, with disturbing implications. In this respect Sillitoe reads like an illustration of Paul Fussell's thesis in *The Great War and Modern Memory* (1975), which shows how in the twentieth century the horror of mass destruction first imprinted itself on western consciousness.

For Sillitoe, the Great War represents primal violence, inescapable and deeply threatening. He gets closest to confronting its meaning in his autobiographical meditation *Raw Material*, ten chapters of which focus on the Battle of the Somme (1916), and in particular on the Gommecourt salient, where two battalions of Sherwood Foresters, largely conscripts from Sillitoe's home district of Nottingham, were wiped out in a diversionary attack planned with criminal ineptitude and disregard for life by the British high command. Sillitoe's outrage is twofold. Speaking almost as a professional officer might, he indicts the British staff for wasting in ten minutes its most skilled and spirited troops. Worse, he believes that the disaster served the interests of the British ruling class, "those five percent, who owned ninety-five percent of the country's wealth" (p. 108), whose hegemony would have been threatened had those same troops returned to agitate for reform. Death took the best of England's educated working class, Sillitoe writes, "intelligent, technically minded, literate, men of a sensibility whose loss sent England into a long decline . . . thrown away with prodigal distaste because they were coming to the point of stepping into their own birthright" (p. 113). In his view the Somme "finished Britain as a world power, and as a country fit for any hero to live in" (p. 108).

Sillitoe's anger is clear, but there is also some ambivalence about war and about national pride. Both would seem utterly discredited and demystified by the evidence he presents; still, he wants to preserve the concept of the "hero." To be sure, he uses the word unconventionally. He awards it, for example, to the two hundred fifty British soldiers who were "murdered by their own firing-squads" for refusing to fight (p. 101) but not to those who went over the top willingly, exhausted from lack of sleep, deluded by the belief that the old class system would be done away with when they returned—despite his sorrow over their deaths.

Nor does Sillitoe use the word "hero" to describe his uncle Edgar, whose story *Raw Material* also tells. Collapsed between the lines, afraid to return to his own side unwounded and without a rifle, trapped, literally and figuratively, in no-man's-land, Edgar never truly returns home: after the war, he drinks, loses his business, survives on piecework, and is finally killed by a bus. (A fictional version of his solitary life is told in "Uncle Ernest.") For a counterexample Sillitoe points to his uncle Frederick, whom the author calls a "hero of humanity" for his refusal to go to war (p. 125). An artist and lace-designer but also a cantankerous solitary, he "left his wife after twenty years of marriage to devote himself to art and freedom" (p. 153). The question posed by Sillitoe's definition of "hero," then, is whether a hero has anything definite to do in the modern world, whether his life can be anything better than evasion.

In *Raw Material* Sillitoe sums up the problem with a list of made-up casualties of the Somme, men who might have served had England not imagined war as a sport. The names, suitably gazetted, in fact constitute a roster of England's most famous outlaws and rebels: "L/Cpl John Cade, Pte Robert Hood Pte, Edward Ludd, Sgt William Posters, Cpt George Swing, Pte Richard Turpin, Cpl Walter Tyler" (p. 105). Robert Hood is, of course, the famous Robin. The other names may be less familiar: Jack Cade, who led a rebellion in 1450 against King Henry VI; Ned Ludd, the hero, probably imaginary, of English craftsmen who rioted against the use of machines in the textile industry, 1811–1816; Captain Swing, another imaginary leader, in whose name southern English farm laborers rioted in 1830, protesting low wages; Dick Turpin (1705–1739), a cattle thief, smuggler, and highwayman, romanticized in Harrison Ains-

414

worth's *Rockwood* (1839); Wat Tyler, the martyred leader of the Peasants' Revolt of 1381. (For the significance of William Posters, see the discussion below of Sillitoe's William Posters trilogy.) The list is deliberately ambiguous because these are precisely the sort of heroes about whom one never knows "whether they were killed, wounded, or simply missing" (p. 105). In literary terms, they represent the picaresque. These outlaws are all violent men and soldiers, but not the kind who inherit the kingdom. "Their demise was not reported in *The Times*," Sillitoe observes, "though in their disappearance they were not divided" (p. 105)—an ironic play on David's eulogy for Saul and Jonathan (II Samuel 1:23). The outlaws sum up Sillitoe's mixed feelings about the Great War, which was fought without them, to England's lasting sorrow, but which they never would have joined in the first place.

All of Sillitoe's stories eventually intersect with his understanding of war as the fundamental condition of modern life. As Vera Seaton says, reading the headlines on the eve of World War II, "There'll be no peace in *our* time," to which her husband responds, "No, . . . nor in any other bloody time, either" (*Key to the Door*, p. 151). His characters live in violence at every level of consciousness, from their awareness of geopolitics to their personal concerns. The question they face, and that each Sillitoe work raises anew, is how to live under this violent dispensation. On this question Sillitoe's fiction splits into three kinds of plots, the tragedies, escapes, and hybrid forms—dark comedies and grim tales with happy endings. *Her Victory* is one of the latter—the story of a brutally abused wife who runs away, attempts suicide, nearly murders her husband when he pursues her, and then finds happiness with a sailor who nurses her back to life. At the novel's end he has left her temporarily to make a home for them in Israel, having discovered in himself a buried Judaism. *Her Victory* is a brilliant study of violence and self-destruction, hardly a picaresque in any of the usual senses yet veering toward it by virtue of its avoidance of realistic closure.

The Widower's Son (1976), perhaps the finest novel of Sillitoe's middle period, follows a similar path. Here again two different plots appear to collide. The first charts the upward mobility of career officer William Scorton, whose success is made possible by the devoted, narrow-minded attention of his father, a former coal miner who finished twenty-four years in the army as a sergeant. After World War II, William has the misfortune to fall in love with and marry a brigadier's daughter who does not love him. Their marriage begins to dissolve almost at once, initiating the second, tragic plot. Childless, they remain locked together for years, their very sexuality having become a battlefield. The climax of their struggle, recounted in chapter 19, is one of Sillitoe's most moving achievements, a long scene of quarrel and lovemaking enacted by both participants entirely in the language of military maneuvers. The mutual destruction is complete—there seems to be nothing left but suicide. But in the end William's old servant saves his life, the seemingly doomed couple manages a divorce, and William finally escapes his father's well-meant but deadly influence by beginning a new life as a teacher.

In these plots Sillitoe experiments with the idea that violence can be cleansing if you survive it. The hope is understandable, because it is in a sense the story of Sillitoe's own life; he retells it several times, notably in the Brian Seaton novels, *Key to the Door* and *The Open Door*, where once again there is tension between realistic accounts of working-class hell and the hopeful possibility of a way out. But Sillitoe is not always so optimistic. One early novel, *The General* (1960), invents a fantasy world in which two global superpowers duel across a no-man's-land using World War I tactics. Into this nightmare killing zone stumbles an entire symphony orchestra; sent to entertain the troops on one side, they are captured by the other and held pending execution. They escape, thanks in part to a remarkable performance they put on for their captors, and partly to the irresolution of the general who has captured them. Despite their escape, the ending is a bitter one, for the general's inability to kill them dooms him with his own superiors, and the musicians have lost all faith in their own civilization for having put them thus at risk.

Sillitoe returns to this tragic mode in *Last Loves*, the story of two older men, George and Bernard, who revisit the site of their military service in Malaya forty years earlier. The trip is a sixtieth birthday present to Bernard from his wife, who also has arranged for George, recently divorced, to go along. On arrival the two men befriend Gloria, an English tourist in her thirties whose father had spent his civil service career as a prison administrator in Malaya. George and Gloria fall in love; Bernard gets a "Dear John" letter from his wife, revealing that the trip had been part of her plan to leave him. Crushed, he goes for a walk in the same jungle where forty years before he and George had chased communist insurgents. As the worried lovers try to track him, George feels the onset of what proves to be a fatal heart attack. The novel ends with Gloria and Bernard flying home to England, sitting together but separated by grief, anger, and guilt.

SATURDAY NIGHT AND SUNDAY MORNING

Set in Nottingham in the early 1950s, Sillitoe's first published novel covers a year and a half in the life of Arthur Seaton. The character is age twenty-three when the book begins, and his main interests are women, booze, and outsmarting the world. "Once a rebel, always a rebel," he says of himself (p. 220); critics have seen him as a modern picaro, reviving "the rogue-hero tradition in English fiction" (Penner, p. 75). Arthur's wits are sharp enough, but unlike the classic picaro, he has to live by industry: he is a machinist in a bicycle factory. He knows that working-class life is a closed circuit, its monotony punctuated once a week by the spirit of carnival. It is all Arthur can do to survive; his sardonic motto, "It's a hard life if you don't weaken," bears witness to the trap in which he finds himself. His one advantage is a mental dexterity related to his machinecraft: sharply observant, he is good at calculating just how far he can go within a given set of tolerances. At work, for example, he could easily step up production but the firm would retaliate by lowering his piece rate. Arthur handles the situation by working fast in the morning so he can daydream in the afternoon. Rather than fight or quit, he carves out a little latitude for himself within the system. His strategy works, but at the cost of some isolation for which he compensates by involving himself in a series of love affairs, first with Brenda, the wife of his coworker Jack, then later with Brenda's sister Winnie, also married, then with a younger girl, Doreen. The crisis comes after Arthur is beaten up by two soldiers, one of them Winnie's jealous husband. Shaken, Arthur decides to settle down with Doreen, but as the novel ends the ingrained carnival pattern of his mind appears to be threatening their marriage.

This pattern, in place in the early pages of the novel, is summed up in the description of Saturday night as "a violent preamble to a prostrate Sabbath" (p. 4). Arthur's preamble is violent enough: in the opening scene he wins a drinking contest at the White Horse Club, falls down a flight of stairs, vomits on two patrons, and staggers back to Brenda's house. The sprees continue through twelve of the novel's sixteen chapters—a year of Saturday nights—not, however, without disturbing indicators of stress and of a Sunday of reckoning on the horizon.

Outbreaks of aggression reinforce the sense of a subliminal crescendo. Leading Brenda to a tryst in the woods, Arthur suspects that she would betray him as easily as she does her husband. He knows that he is squeezing her wrist too hard, "but it did not occur to him to relax his hold. . . . there was something about her and the whole situation that made him want to hurt her" (p. 49). In chapter 7, after being warned about Winnie's husband, Bill, Arthur goes drinking, picks a fight, watches a bereaved drunk break the window of an undertaker's shop, nearly gets hit by a drunken driver, threatens the offender, and upends his car. Chapter 9 describes another binge, this time during Arthur's summertime military service. In Chapter 11 Arthur barely escapes the enraged Bill; in the next chapter, Bill catches up.

The sense of impending crisis is punctuated with scenes of fun but even the jokes are mixed with threat, as in chapter 8, where Arthur gets even with a neighborhood gossip by plinking at her with an air rifle. Once again farce prepares the way for a deeper level of violence: chapter 9 describes Arthur's fortnight at a military training camp where the weapons are deadly:

When it was not his turn at the sandbags he loved to stand and listen to the total bursting of bullets from the dozen guns firing, hearing the lifting and falling of sound, the absolutely untameable rhythms that ripped the air open with untrammelled joy.

(p. 148)

The patternless sound of gunfire makes violence seems abstract—almost purified—but the phrase about the air ripped open recalls the underlying urge to harm. The window-breaking scene in chapter 7 conveys the same anarchic mixture of feelings.

Why there should be so much menace in Arthur's world is not immediately apparent. With the war over, jobs are available and recreation and some luxuries are within reach: a foreman at the factory can afford a secondhand car. Home can be comfortable: the Seatons' Monday-morning kitchen looks "warm and cheerful" with a "bright fire . . . in the modernised grate" (p. 20). But prewar poverty has left scars. Arthur has a vivid sense of how his parents struggled "all the years before the war on the dole, five kids, and the big miserying that went with no money and no way of getting any" (p. 22). Against that background the new glamour seems unreal. The Seatons' television set, for example, "a glossy panelled box," looks to Arthur "like something plundered from a space-ship" (p. 22). Uneasiness underlies Arthur's teasing of his father about going blind from nightly telly watching. There are new anxieties, too, such as inflation and the threat of nuclear war, which make saving money a "mug's game, since the value of it got less and less and in any case you never knew when the Yanks were going to do something daft like dropping the H-bomb on Moscow" (p. 23). Fears like these flicker through Arthur's mind, giving his characteristic jauntiness an undercurrent of gallows humor: "War was a marvellous thing in some ways, when you thought about how happy it had made so many people in England" (p. 22). Situated between a grim past and an uncertain future, Arthur does his best to live in the moment. The exact degree of his disconnection from conventional British history is made clear in a tart and funny scene in chapter 10. Chatting up Doreen in a pub called the Horse and Groom, Arthur shows off his knowledge of *Henry the Fifth* (he means Laurence Olivier's 1944 film of the Shakespeare play); he singles out "that long speech he does on his hoss before the fight" (the king's "band of brothers" speech: *Henry V,* IV. iii. 20–67), some of which Arthur can recall:

"Can you say it, then?"
Some of it. Certain phrases came in the king's loud voice, but he could not speak them. For any man this day that shed his blood with me shall be my brother . . . shall in their flowing cups be freshly remembered . . . his passport shall be made and crowns for convoy put into his purse . . . I would not die . . . old men forget . . . that fought with us upon St. Crispin's day. . . . His fingers forgot the jar handle for a moment, and he stood up as if to hear better once more the destructive flight of arrows at Agincourt, the noise of two hosts destroying each other in colourful slaughter, risking an arm and a leg for promises of loot and fire.
"I've forgot it. It's too long. But if you want it I'll copy it from our Sam's book."

"No, don't take all that trouble. I think Laurence Olivier's a good actor, don't you? He's handsome. He reminds me of a lad I once knew, who worked in our office."

(p. 162)

Even jumbled and misquoted, Shakespeare's cadences have the power to cut through the barroom buzz. The moment may recall passages in T. S. Eliot's poem *The Waste Land* (1922), which made literary history by rendering modern consciousness as distracted conversation intermingled with garbled fragments from old literary masterpieces. However, Eliot uses the technique to mourn the loss of high culture; Sillitoe uses it to expose the use of high culture as polite mystification. Sillitoe's target here is not Arthur but the culture hero Laurence Olivier, whose famous colorful, realistic location shots may have been in Sillitoe's mind as tending to sentimentalize war ("colourful slaughter"), which Shakespeare himself did not. In any case, patriotic appeals are lost on Arthur. What brings him to his feet is not who won but the violent excitement of mutual destruction.

Arthur's disaffection has roots in the class history of World War II. His cousins were deserters in that war, and Arthur recalls one of them explaining why. Before the war, with his family on the dole, the cousin had been given three years' juvenile detention for stealing food. " 'Do yer think I'm going ter fight for them bastards, do yer?' " (p. 139). Arthur's memories of the homefront conflict with the newsreel images many readers will remember: "Churchill spoke after the nine o'clock news and told you what you were fighting for, as if it mattered" (p. 139). As Arthur sees it, the only enemies are those who send other people out to die:

When I'm on my fifteen-days' training and I lay on my guts behind a sandbag shooting at a target board I know whose faces I've got in my sights every time the new rifle cracks off. Yes. The bastards that put the gun in my hands.

(p. 141)

Despite appearances, this is not a revolutionary's point of view. Arthur understands and sympathizes with his father, his cousins, his long-suffering aunt Ada, even with working people he sees only at training camp. But organized solidarity has no place in his life. He tells Jack he doesn't believe in sharing the wealth; his dream is to win a lottery or football pool and keep it all for himself and his family. It is not only the warmonger Arthur hates but anyone with a hand in his pocket. Politics are meaningless in "the common battleground of the jungle" (p. 194). Even the distinction between peace and war disappears: "In the army it was: 'F——— you, Jack, I'm all right.' Out of the army it was: 'Every man for himself.' It amounted to the same thing" (p. 140). Arthur knows that life is solitary, manageable only "if you don't weaken."

Even Arthur's affairs with women are not as free as he imagines them to be. Loving Brenda means going out the front door when Jack comes in the back, a series of close shaves demanding perfect timing and wry acceptance of the status quo. For Arthur, Brenda, and Winnie occasional happiness is what life has to offer. So completely does Arthur take the situation for granted that he feels little embarrassment chatting with Jack at work. Love is essential to his well-being, but it has to be illicit, peripheral:

It's a hard life if you don't weaken, so you grab like owt to earn a few quid, to take Brenda boozing and back to bed, or to the footpaths and woods up Strelley, passing the big council estate where Margaret my sister has a house and three kids from her useless husband, taking Brenda by all that to a broken-down shepherd's cottage that I've known since I was a kid and laying her on the straw and both of us so loving to each other that we can hardly wait.

(pp. 34–35)

A makeshift shelter on the margins of an equally makeshift community represents a fitting emblem for Arthur's inner life: passion juxtaposed with isolation. Arthur and Brenda have their moments, but they cannot stand up to a crisis together. When Brenda gets pregnant Arthur cannot understand her distress. Bitterly, she insists on ending the pregnancy. In Chapter 6, with Arthur and a neighbor standing by, she tries a method of abortion that Arthur has heard of: gin and a hot bath. By the time Jack comes home, Brenda is past caring and out goes Arthur. Later that evening Arthur is also past caring: "he could hardly remember Brenda, thinking that perhaps he had dreamed about her sometime, but nothing more" (p. 100). Going to bed that night with Brenda's sister, Arthur cheerfully peels off his socks, as if he had done with grief and rage.

In picaresque, abortion is a common but incidental occurrence; here, as Peter Hitchcock says, it

is a "central" event. Eagleton and Pierce observe (pp. 131–132), and Hitchcock agrees, that abortion is a politically significant theme for postwar working-class novels, including Shelagh Delaney's *A Taste of Honey* and John Braine's *Room at the Top*, an occasion for class solidarity and "community response" (Hitchcock, pp. 71f, 117). A more complicated reading develops if one observes that in this novel every movement toward community meets a countermovement. The pattern begins in chapter 5, when Arthur goes to his aunt Ada for the abortion recipe and won't admit that he himself is the father. Later that evening Arthur and his cousin Bert help a drunk on the street, and their friendly gesture turns abruptly hostile. They see him safely stowed, but Bert steals his wallet, as empty as the man's life: "nothing in it except a tiny newspaper clipping cut neatly from the 'situations vacant' column, which Arthur screwed up and sent rolling over the cobblestones into the gutter" (p. 86). Where there might have been sympathy (the Seatons know something about searching for work), there are only silent gestures and mixed feelings: contempt, disappointment, a sense of futility. Chapter 6 follows immediately, presenting Brenda in the bath. Here, instead of intimacy or a sense of joint purpose there is only bickering and disconnection, with an exhausted and helpless Arthur fading in and out of the nightmarish scene:

He watched Brenda's face disintegrating, her features mixing beneath the fire of hot gin and a sea of water. . . . He felt drunk, though he had taken no more than a sip of the gin. Sometimes he was part of the scene, sitting among the two women, warmed by the fire, choked by the steaming bath; then he was looking down on it, like watching the telly with no part in what he was seeing.

(p. 90)

The failure of community here is brilliantly defined. Whereas the picaro is conventionally a loner, these three are alone together. That Brenda did in fact "bring it off" is barely mentioned in a later aside.

Inner and outer violence converge after the beating in chapter 12. Although not badly hurt, Arthur is shocked into a new awareness of mortality: "he knew for the first time in his life that there never had been any such thing as safety" (p. 197). The spree, eleven chapters long, turns into a Sabbath insidiously "prostrate" in unexpected ways. Courting Doreen for the "sweetness in it," Arthur admits to himself that he is no longer "pursuing his rebellion against the rules of love or distilling them with rules of war" (p. 221). An outing with Doreen ends with both of them staring down into a canal and Arthur thinking that "you were dragged down sooner or later whether you liked it or not" (p. 225). After they decide to marry, their lovemaking takes on deadly overtones, and conversation between them stops:

Arthur held her murderously tight, as if to vanquish her spirit even in the first short contest. But she responded to him, as if she would break him first. . . . He spoke to her softly, and she nodded her head to his words without knowing what they meant. Neither did Arthur know what he was saying: both transmission and reception were drowned, and they broke through to the opened furrows of the earth.

(p. 234)

With such a mood hanging over Arthur's marriage, it is not surprising that we see him one last Sunday morning in spring, fishing alone in the canal. He catches and releases a fish, seeming to recognize an emblem of himself on the hook, then settles down to the necessarily merciless hunt. Still cocky, he hopes that marriage will be a new adventure and that he can still make the world take notice, but he knows that he has taken life's bait.

"THE LONELINESS OF THE LONG-DISTANCE RUNNER"

SILLITOE's second early success is a long story or novella in three parts, told by Smith, a seventeen-year-old Nottingham delinquent who gets arrested for theft and is sent to Borstal (juvenile prison), where the "governor" tries to rehabilitate him by turning him into a cross-country athlete. Smith likes running—it gives him space and time to think—but not if it means performing in the governor's circus. In the main event of the season he takes a comfortable lead, but near the finish line he pulls up and stands still, deliberately losing the race in plain view of the grandstand. Smith gets six months' punishment duty for his defiance. After his release he becomes a professional thief; Borstal has prepared him for a career after all.

Below the narrative surface there are other stories and glimpses of a more complex plot. Part 1 consists of Smith's thoughts during a typical early-morning workout, a five-mile run through the wintry landscape of the Borstal estate. Little of Smith's attention is on the running. Like Arthur Seaton working at his lathe in *Saturday Night and Sunday Morning*, Smith runs automatically, pouring his energy into thought, analyzing the class system and resolving never to collaborate with it. Part 2 is a flashback, recalling Smith's homelife, crime, and arrest. The loneliness here is mostly unconscious: Smith seems at home in the context of family and neighborhood, although shadowed by the recent death of his father and driven by aimless consumerism. Part 3 recounts the race and Smith's continuing train of thought, which culminates in the forcible return of a painful image: his sick father dying in an upstairs room alone, the boy finding him in the blood of a final hemorrhage. In retrospect his father's blood can be seen trickling through the story, seeping in part 2 into the rug that Smith's mother throws out and replaces with a new one bought with her husband's death benefits, contributing secretly to Smith's waking nightmare in part 1 about being the "last man" on earth. Under Smith's brash talk of telly, adverts, cops and robbers, loot, and spending lies this death. It is why Smith will not race to win: he knows his life is "on the run," with no prize ahead other than whatever thinking he can do along the way.

Refusing to finish is one sign of the picaresque novel, and like many of Sillitoe's protagonists, Smith is often said to belong to that tradition. It is a tale about cunning, after all, and part of its aim is to expose the fraud in conventional morality. The governor makes a good target, inviting Smith to "play ball" and work hard, while his own "lily-white workless hands" are preoccupied with the *Daily Telegraph* (pp. 9–10). But whereas the classic picaro has little inner depth and does not change, Smith is changing as we read, visibly coming to a new understanding of himself and the life ahead of him. He has inherited a static situation, an eternal war between "them" and "us," "In-laws" against "Out-laws," but his relationship to this situation is dynamic. He comes to unexpected insights, such as this rejection of the master-slave dialectic:

By Christ, I'd rather be like I am—always on the run and breaking into shops for a packet of fags and a jar of jam—than have the whip-hand over somebody else and be dead from the toe nails up. By God, to say that last sentence has needed a few hundred miles of long-distance running. I could no more have said that at first than I could have took a million pound note from my back pocket.

(p. 14)

In a less imaginative writer, Arthur's critique of power and privilege might read simply as a propaganda, but Sillitoe renders Arthur's insight as a discovery, a process driven by questions and sudden upsurges of memory.

We know from the start of part 3 that Smith plans to lose the race, but this ensuing narrative is still a tense, emotional drama that unfolds as he explores the meaning and implications of his decision. He starts off mulling over the governor's suggestion, made just before the race, that winning might put the "lad" in the position to turn professional.

[It] wasn't until he'd said this that I realized it might be possible to do such a thing, run for money, trot for wages on piece work at a bob a puff rising bit by bit to a guinea a gasp and retiring through old age at thirty-two because of lace-curtain lungs, a football heart, and legs like varicose beanstalks. But I'd have a wife and car and get my grinning long-distance clock in the papers and have a smashing secretary to answer piles of letters sent by tarts who'd mob me when they saw who I was as I pushed my way into Woolworth's for a packet of razor blades and a cup of tea. It was something to think about all right. . . .

(p. 39)

As an estimate of an English runner's prospects in the 1950s this is not unrealistically grim. What lifts this passage to the level of brilliant satire is that it proceeds from a working-class understanding of quid pro quo, a point of view utterly outside the governor's frame of reference. One can see the distance between the two men as Smith translates "run for money" into "trot for wages"; from there the idea shifts into high gear and races though its implications, with Smith envisioning the professional athlete's life all the way through to its apotheosis in Woolworth's. This is an impressive performance for a seventeen-year-old, wickedly exact ("wife and car"), and he is obviously enjoying it. It also marks a significant advance from the prostrate telly-worshiping described in part 2. For Smith has seen illness and death already, most bitterly in the case of his father, who worked in a factory, was betrayed by his wife, got throat cancer, refused hospital treatment, was reduced to "skin and stick," and died an "Out-law death" that left his body looking "like a skinned rabbit" (p. 50).

Pieces of this subterranean, primordial plot have been surfacing in Smith's mind as he runs. The running makes it possible for him to take in all that his father was. Although his father's story is not the cause of Smith's decision to lose the race, the father's and son's stories ultimately lend each other dignity: "By God I'll stick this out like my dad stuck out his pain" (p. 51).

One might compare Sillitoe's choices in writing this story to the ones that faced Mark Twain as he tested the limits of picaresque in *Huckleberry Finn* (1884). The life of Twain's novel is the Mississippi, offering Huck and Jim a chance at freedom while at the same time carrying them South toward trouble. Twain struggled against the tragic implications of his own plot; finally, he had to bring Tom Sawyer back into the story to rescue Jim, turning the novel's ending into a parody of the conventional boy's adventure story. Sillitoe faces a similar problem on a smaller scale: Smith's life is on the run but there is nowhere to go. To solve this dilemma Sillitoe makes the running itself transparent, a lens through which we see Smith coming of age. Smith may become a rogue after all, living in infinitely extendable installments, as does Michael Cullen, the conventional hero of *A Start in Life* and *Life Goes On.* Sillitoe prevents us from witnessing that outcome in this story, although the threat of it is never far away. Smith himself distrusts closure in fiction, describing the books he has read in Borstal as "useless . . . because all of them ended on a winning post and didn't teach me a thing" (p. 54). Fiction keeps repackaging what Virginia Woolf rejected as "the narrow plot of acquisitiveness and desire" (Fox, p. 25) based on the desirability of getting somewhere, or someone; such fiction belongs to "them," the "In-laws."

Sillitoe's desire to sidestep the usual business of books appears in the tongue-in-cheek coda of the story. Smith plans to entrust his story to one of "us":

I'm going to give this story to a pal of mine and tell him that if I do get captured again by the coppers he can try and get it put into a book or something, because I'd like to see the governor's face when he reads it, if he does, which I don't suppose he will; even if he did read it though I don't think he'd know what it was all about. And if I don't get caught the bloke I give this story to will never give me away; he's lived in our terrace for as long as I can remember, and he's my pal. That I do know.

(p. 54)

Smith cannot compromise his Out-law status by turning author; he needs an intermediary "pal" to help him repackage his life, to translate it into the only weapon that has a chance of getting through the In-laws' defenses, "a book or something." But Smith's dilemma is that if the book represents him truly, the In-law reader will find it incomprehensible and the weapon will have no impact. The joke here is double-edged: Sillitoe is poking fun at conventional readers and also admitting that as a self-conscious representative of the working class, he would like both to have his cake and publish it.

This political dilemma is built into the story from the beginning. In part 1, Smith addresses the reader as a member of the enemy camp, one of "them":

And there *are* thousands of them, all over the poxeating country, in shops, offices, railway stations, cars, houses, pubs—In-law blokes like you and them, all on the watch for Out-law blokes like me and us—and waiting to 'phone for the coppers as soon as we make a false move.
(p. 10)

Evidently Sillitoe sees himself as a borderline figure, native to the Out-law community but with access to In-law infrastructure. Under the kidding is some real anxiety about the difficulty of being a working-class writer: Sillitoe's last gesture in this story is to locate himself wishfully back in Nottingham.

THE WILLIAM POSTERS TRILOGY

IN his first two fictions, Sillitoe fenced with the picaresque; by the mid-1960s he was trying to dismantle it, for political, artistic, and psychological reasons. A fictional recasting of his situation at the time appears in Sillitoe's most recent novel, *The Broken Chariot* (1998), about the rise of a working-class novelist who is, interestingly, a fraud with a split personality: born Herbert Thurgarton-Strang, an army officer's son with professional prospects, he runs away from boarding school, lands in Nottingham, where he takes the name Bert Gedling, camouflages himself with the local accent, and becomes a machinist. After a stint in the army as an enlisted man, he returns to Nottingham and begins to write, trying, he says, "to do something that hasn't been done before: which is to write about people who work in factories. Do it properly,

though, from the inside" (p. 163). Writing is also his best hope of building a third, integrated self, "not turning into a Bert or a Herbert, rather someone a little of both but unique to neither" (p. 192). But he has to manage this new metamorphosis carefully, with one eye on his career: his publishers are delighted with him as Bert, a lout with an unaccountable (and profitable) gift; they expect him to "keep on churning out the same old thing" (p. 274). *The Other Side of the Tracks*, his second novel, does not come quite so easily as the first. In the end, threatened with exposure and wanting to marry his middle-class girlfriend, Herbert decides to dispense with Bert altogether.

Of course, this story is not Sillitoe's autobiography, but a re-imagining of some of its elements with the class antagonism of the 1960s muted now by distance and hindsight. Still, Herbert's struggle with Bert recalls (no doubt deliberately) Sillitoe's long duel with "William Posters," the picaresque shadow-character who haunts *The Death of William Posters* (1965), *A Tree on Fire* (1967), and *The Flame of Life* (1974).

The name "William Posters" comes from a Nottingham joke, a play on the ubiquitous urban sign that warns against unauthorized advertisements: "Bill Posters Will Be Prosecuted." In the Nottingham pubs the locals joked about who "Bill Posters" might be, giving shadowy birth to an imaginary Out-law who stood for Nottingham's resentment of the Establishment. Sillitoe took to him as a figure of the long-distance runner on the loose, a Nottingham Robin Hood cherished by the poor, "who keep his furtive ever-enduring figure alive as it flits at dusk or dawn down slum streets from one harbouring district to another. . . . Everyone knows Bill Posters is one of us" (*The Death of William Posters*, p. 18). These are the reflections of Sillitoe's character Frank Dawley, a Nottingham machinist fed up with work and married life who tries to break away but finds England itself a trap, "as if 'Bill Posters will be prosecuted' were written on every blade of grass and white sea wave and he was William himself on the run even beyond cities" (p. 16).

After some wandering Frank spends the winter with Pat Shipley, a nurse, in a Lincolnshire village, where he also gets to know an eccentric local artist named Albert Handley. After a fight with Pat's ex-husband, Frank moves out. Part 2 opens in London, where Frank has found temporary work. At an exhibition of Handley's paintings Frank meets

Myra, a dissatisfied, married suburbanite who is taking courses at the London School of Economics. They survive a murderous automobile attack by Myra's husband. With Myra pregnant, the lovers go abroad together—first to Spain then Tangiers, where Shelley Jones, an American, invites Frank to join him running guns to the FLN, the Algerian guerrillas fighting for independence from France. Frank wants to exchange his Bill Posters life for one of committed action; the lovers separate and Frank and Shelley deliver the guns. After taking part in an ambush, Frank decides to join the freedom fighters and forces Shelley to go with him. As the novel ends, Frank is hoping that the desert will finish off William Posters for good; in the sequels, however, it appears that that Frank's alter ego is not so easy to kill.

Like many Sillitoe novels, *The Death of William Posters* is a set of variations based on the theme of escape, which is announced at the start with Frank Dawley crisscrossing "tiny" England; later he is eager to take Myra and get "off this island." The motif of lovers voyaging abroad to escape restrictive, provincial British life doubtless owes something to Sillitoe's own expatriate experiences; the theme recurs in several of his fictions, notably "Guzman, Go Home" and *Her Victory.*

In Sillitoe's works escape is not always life-affirming—it sometimes has suicidal overtones, especially where automobiles are involved. Frank and his rivals Keith and George (Pat Shipley's ex and Myra's husband, respectively) are all shown driving compulsively to escape private demons; in *A Tree on Fire* Albert Handley's teenage daughter Mandy is so obsessed with driving that she spends weeks on the M1 motorway and at home refuses to get out of her car. Images of the car as a weapon and highways as theaters of murderous or suicidal warfare occur in a number of Sillitoe's works, including *Her Victory* and the Michael Cullen novels. This theme is so insistent that it tends to erase differences of personality, gender, and class. Frank, Keith, George, Tom, Pam: these monosyllabic names are attached to people who hail from different social strata, but they behave so similarly in escape mode that they begin to look like faces of one character. They experience auto accidents, pregnancy (as another kind of "accident"), fistfights, marital violence, and the discovery that love exhausts the lovers. Marriage is represented as a trap; it can precipitate escape, usually a violent process, or it can turn into an equally violent

prison. The image of a cornered husband smashing wedding gifts occurs in Sillitoe's autobiographical meditation *Raw Material* and reappears in *Her Victory;* traces of it can be seen in the ongoing struggle between Albert Handley and his wife, Enid. In Sillitoe's works violence is never far away, exposing the coercive nature of social institutions.

Although Bill Posters is a hero to the working class, as a picaro he is ultimately also their betrayer because he will not stand and fight. Yet without him Frank would have no story at all, as he recognizes: "In some big way Bill Posters had also been responsible for his exploding out of life so far, leaving wife, home, job, kids, and Nottingham's fair city where he had been born bred and spiritually nullified" (p. 16). Still, Frank knows that Posters has no future. He is the long-distance runner at large, "ever-enduring" but marginalized, seen only at dusk and dawn, restricted to the slums, contained in one "harbouring district" or another (p. 18). The Bill Posters ethos of evasion finally seems to Frank to be nothing but collaboration with the status quo, an insidious acceptance of failure. To kill him Frank must finish with the picaresque, which means leaving England and its myths about Christ and Robin Hood. Hence the novel's two-part structure: the first is episodic and apparently aimless, the second seeks a trajectory. Changes in tone accompany this shift of direction; the first part tends toward satire and surrealism, the second toward romantic lyricism. In effect, then, this novel changes genres in midstream, and although the effort is deliberate, the results are disorganized, as though the author were not in full control of the project. The ideological and artistic burden is on the second part, and here the plot gives out. Although part 2 has one sharply realized scene (the desert ambush, Frank's baptism of fire) the plot itself lacks closure. "To be continued" is the signature of picaresque: Is Frank's jump into the desert only another episode? Or is it that the territory now in view is too fully occupied already by the literary predecessors that this novel goes out of its way to evoke—Lord Byron, Joseph Conrad, T. E. Lawrence, Ernest Hemingway, Albert Camus, and William S. Burroughs? (Frank reads Burroughs' *Naked Lunch* at Pat's house and says he admires "the writing.")

The only point at which this novel goes off the map is in part 1, chapter 8, which describes Frank's first visit to the Albert Handley household. Frank is powerfully moved by a painting of Handley's called "Christ the Lincolnshire Poacher." He then experiences a series of dreamlike encounters. He stumbles into a darkened room and finds a bald man in a suit, sweating, shaking, sending Morse code by wireless, who points a gun at Frank and yells at him to get out. In the next room Frank discovers two young men planning a war game on a large-scale ordnance map. Moments later seventeen-year-old Mandy drags him into her bed, then asks for money. Frank stumbles downstairs; revisiting Handley's painting he finds it changed, the Christ metamorphosed to "my old friend William Posters, not dead yet, but surely dying, hanging as a warning for all to see" (p. 119). These surreal juxtapositions and disjunctions convey Frank's experience of being assaulted and challenged at his most instinctive levels of consciousness and identity. The result is memorable; it is the only part of this novel anthologized in the Sillitoe collection *Every Day of the Week* (1987). The experiment remains an orphan, however. Sillitoe evidently dislikes surrealism—in *Raw Material* he calls it one of the "lifeboats" of sinking bourgeois culture (p. 184)—so perhaps it was intended here as a satire, a takeoff in the style of Dylan Thomas' "Adventures in the Skin Trade" (1955), another modern incarnation of the picaresque.

Having rejected all these options, *The Death of William Posters* reaches an impasse, represented in the plot as a rupture between Frank and Myra. "Love's not much more than a holiday in life," says Frank. "The most important thing is work— to do something that means something" (p. 236). In Granada, Myra feels that the arrival of their baby will be a "rebirth towards a life that would be hers only" (p. 268). For his part, Frank is "exhausted, in all things nearing the rock-bottom of his heart" (p. 271). Sitting by the harbor as if at "the world's edge," he sees their journey as a necessary emptying to prepare for new relations based on a new world order:

The end had been reached, not the end of love, but the beginning of something else in which the sort of love he had always known about and felt as fully as anyone was to be discarded as a fraud and a trick, the stone tied about a corpse to make it sink. To cut it loose would enable a man and a woman to live in equality, with regard and respect for each other's purpose in the world. Mutual destruction had to cease.

(p. 268)

However admirable the thought, this is manifesto, not narrative, announcing what it cannot dramatize: "The old idea of love is sliding away from the fingertips of the new man," thinks Frank, replacing himself with an abstraction (p. 272). The speaker of a manifesto is a convenience, not a character with a life of his own. Now that Frank no longer believes in "the inner life . . . that the society he'd been brought up in told him existed" (p. 271), there is no more story to tell. The novel has consumed itself.

In *A Tree on Fire* (1967), the second installment of the trilogy, Albert Handley emerges as a major character; this five-part novel spends as much time on him in England as on Frank in Algeria. The novel moves back and forth between the battlefield, the studio, and the family ménage. The tree of the title is at once Handley's art, the moribund society that his brother John wants to burn, and the stubborn natural resistance that Frank observes in Algeria, where a tree has been napalmed by the French and torched by the FLN, "yet an anemic green shoot always grew from part of the shattered base" (p. 148). It is an uneasy book, memorable for its battle scenes and the especially effective accounts of Frank's long delirium on a march, a mixture of fear, exhaustion, and exaltation.

However, the tendency toward manifesto is even more pronounced in this volume than in its predecessor. The narrative is frequently interrupted by political tracts: passages from Shelley Jones's copy of Mao, FLN leaflets on the nature of guerrilla warfare, extracts from John Handley's diary. This effort to downplay the author's controlling presence in favor of a multivocal, self-critical text can be compared to the leftist films that Jean-Luc Godard was making in the same period, such as *La Chinoise* (1967), in which members of a small urban commune of students and teachers quote at length from Mao's *Red Book*.

A Tree on Fire also experiments, perhaps less successfully, with shifts of tone. Some of the Handley scenes are farcical, but conventionally so, in contrast to the vivid writing of Frank's Algerian ordeal. Handley's angry, perceptive wife, Enid, their five variously disaffected children, and Handley's eccentric brother John—all at war with repressive local officials and gentry—make up a singular family of ill-assorted originals, but Handley himself is a wenching, truth-telling maverick altogether too reminiscent of the painter Gully Jimson in Joyce Cary's *The Horse's Mouth* (1944). Moreover,

423

the odd-lot family at war with the local officialdom and establishment is itself a stock property—see H. E. Bates's *The Darling Buds of May* (1958). Such figures and associations seem unfortunate in *A Tree on Fire* because their comedic tradition is essentially conservative, based on acceptance of class distinctions. As if to insist that these shifts of tone are deliberate, Sillitoe recycles parts of a crucial chapter from the previous volume, describing Frank Dawley's first visit to the Handleys (see above): what was disturbingly real in that context returns here as threadbare slapstick.

Karl Marx regarded parody as the doom of bourgeois culture; his well-known formula predicts a degenerating cycle: first time tragedy, second time farce. Whatever the political point, it is perilous for an author to parody himself. Sillitoe pays the price in *The Flame of Life* (1974), the last installment of the William Posters trilogy. He seems to admit in the novel's half-apologetic preface that he found it difficult to finish the project. His solution is no solution, an aimless, circular plot, involving the coming to England of Shelley Jones's Spanish girlfriend, bringing with her a trunk full of Shelley's revolutionary musings, supposedly of great value to the Handley commune. She also wants to shoot Frank Dawley, whom she blames for Shelley's death in Algeria (described in *A Tree on Fire*). The shooting is artificially delayed by various subplots involving the increasingly disaffected Handley children and the coming apart (again) of Handley's marriage (his wife's departure with a teenage pot smuggler is one of the novel's more embarrassing inventions). In effect, nothing happens; the novel succumbs to picaresque in its weakest form.

POETRY

FICTION brought Sillitoe recognition and success, but his first art was poetry, and he continued to practice it for more than forty years, producing thirteen independent volumes. His *Collected Poems* (1993) selects and revises from *The Rats and Other Poems* (1960); *A Falling Out of Love and Other Poems* (1964); *Love in the Environs of Voronezh and Other Poems* (1968); *Storm and Other Poems* (1974); *Snow on the North Side of Lucifer* (1979); *Sun Before Departure* (1984); *Tides and Stone Walls* (1986), and adds twenty-one new poems written from 1986 to 1990.

At the beginning of the 1990s Sillitoe commented that he saw himself as "primarily a poet," and observed that he used poetry "to express emotions that can't be expressed in any other medium" (Sadler, p. 899). A few years later he went further, claiming that the novelist and the poet in him were "two entities" almost like "two different people," the aims of poetry coming from "an elevation of the psyche that the novel can know nothing about" (*Collected Poems*, p. 1). This is a late formulation. The early, Marxist Sillitoe might have found it difficult to justify the idea of poetry reaching higher elevations that those of plain narrative. Some of Sillitoe's early poetry does make an effort to speak the common language of revolution, as for example in "The Rats," a vision of a totalitarian future and a call to resistance, written in the same period as *Saturday Night and Sunday Morning*:

> Under your feet spring
> The Rat-State Sapper Brigade:
> Do not let their forces overwhelm you
> Rather go insane before they
> Force you to their ranks
> Or kill you.
> (*Collected Poems*, p. 31)

Thirty years later Sillitoe wrote, "The sentiments deployed in *The Rats* bled into the views of the hero of my first novel, but from that point on, poetry and fiction came out of totally different territories" (p. 2). In fact, the two genres were diverging from the outset: the speaker of "The Rats" is no Arthur Seaton but a poet who has read T. S. Eliot ("The wasteland was my library and college"), whose language, resonant with prayer book and hymnal rhythms, still remembers the sacramental words of Christian hope: "A meal of pure white bread is bad / When given to a dog the dog goes mad. / The bread of life is of a different grain / It feeds the body wholemeal and the brain" (pp. 38, 40).

Through the 1960s Sillitoe's poetry tended to turn inward, charting private losses in *A Falling Out of Love and Other Poems*, and retaining a private, meditative tone even when registering the tragedies of global war, as in "Love in the Environs of Voronezh," an understated lament for the Russian poet Osip Mandelstam (exiled to Voronezh by Stalin from 1934 to 1937) and hence, by extension, for all the waste of war and ideology: "There's no returning to the heart: / The dead to the environs go / Away from resurrected stone" (p. 98). In "The

Poet," written in the same period, Sillitoe imagines himself living and writing on a bridge between two warring nations, fed and cajoled by both sides, promising propaganda to both, maintaining his vigor and independence at the cost of staying put: "But he owns and dominates his bridge. / It is his bread and soul and only song— / And if the people do not like it, they can cut him free" (p. 96).

Further stages of a spiritual journey can be traced in *Snow on the North Side of Lucifer* (1979), a cycle of poems on the problem of evil that questions and re-imagines the Manichean tradition of dueling powers of light and darkness, and in the Jerusalem poems from *Sun Before Departure* (1984) that record Sillitoe's deepening response to Zionism. Between these peak experiences Sillitoe also continued to write short, modest lyric poems about daily experiences—the seasons, repairing and pruning, the rhythms of work—good-humored poems that seem, especially the later ones, to define an older man's understanding that he has survived the violence within and without that might have killed him over and over.

Sillitoe has produced a significant body of work, and yet his poetry is still not widely read. Most chronologically arranged anthologies pass him by in favor of the better-known postwar poets Philip Larkin, Donald Davie, Geoffrey Hill, Ted Hughes, and Charles Tomlinson. Issue-oriented anthologies tend to include one or two of his early "angry" poems, ignoring the later, more personal investigations of power and loss, which Martin Booth thinks qualify him as "one of the most important love poets of the post–D.H. Lawrence era" (p. 217). Sillitoe's poetry is not easy to categorize. Like his "Movement" contemporaries, he sometimes exhibits a demythologizing, antiromantic streak, but he has never stopped searching for a renovating presence in the world and in the creative act. Geoff Sadler thinks he brought a "new and challenging voice to the poetry of the last three decades, and is destined to remain a significant figure in the immediate future" (p. 900). So why is Sillitoe's poetry so little known? Booth blames the narrow conventions of the book trade, claiming that Sillitoe's publishers made little effort to use his prestige as a novelist to help advertise his poetry. Booth also suggests that Sillitoe's reputation for independence has cost him: "Sillitoe is a major poet, yet because he is an outsider, one who has been seen to steer his own path, he has been unjustly ignored. Had his work appeared in, for example, the Pen-

guin Modern Poets series, then his reputation as a poet would be justifiably much larger" (p. 217).

CONCLUSION

AT the end of the 1990s Alan Sillitoe's work had not been accorded the mainstream attention it deserved. Not all of his fiction lives up to the promise of his famous first successes, but the novels that do, especially *The Widower's Son, Her Victory,* and *Last Loves,* take considerable risks by breaking new ground while at the same time reminding us of their links to the Nottingham of his early stories. Perhaps most impressive is the way Sillitoe's political commitment has matured along with his craft. Everything he writes bears witness to the violence and suffering of our culture. The complexity of his thought comes from an understanding of violence as an inescapable medium and signature of growth. "Fundamentally," he has observed, "there's no growth without great pain. It always take some kind of crisis for a human being to move into a new dimension of awareness" (Rothschild, p. 139). Sillitoe's best work does not simply accept or glorify this essentially tragic conception of life but opens itself to violence in order to understand it. The result is a text at war with conventional expectations, always remarkably and disturbingly engaged, at ground level, with crucial realms of modern experience.

SELECTED BIBLIOGRAPHY

I. BIBLIOGRAPHY. David Gerard, *Alan Sillitoe* (London, 1988).

II. COLLECTED WORKS. *A Sillitoe Selection* (London, 1968); *Mountains and Caverns: Selected Essays* (London, 1975); *Every Day of the Week: An Alan Sillitoe Reader* (London, 1987); *Collected Poems* (London, 1993); *Collected Stories* (London, 1995).

III. POETRY. *Without Beer or Bread* (London, 1957); *The Rats and Other Poems* (London, 1960); *A Falling Out of Love and Other Poems* (London, 1964); *Shaman and Other Poems* (London, 1968); *Love in the Environs of Voronezh and Other Poems* (London, 1968); *Poems by Ruth Fainlight, Ted Hughes, Alan Sillitoe* (contributor; London, 1971); *Canto Two of the Rats* (London, 1973); *Storm and Other Poems* (London, 1974); *Barbarians and Other Poems* (London, 1974); *Words Broadsheet Nineteen* (with Ruth Fainlight; Bramley, Surrey, 1975); *Day-Dream Communique*

(Knotting, Bedfordshire, 1977); *Snow on the North Side of Lucifer* (London, 1979); *More Lucifer* (Knotting, Bedfordshire, 1980); *Israel: Poems on a Hebrew Theme* (London, 1981); *Sun Before Departure* (London, 1984); *Tides and Stone Walls* (London, 1986).

IV. NOVELS. *Saturday Night and Sunday Morning* (London, 1958; rev. ed. New York, 1968); *The General* (London, 1960); *Key to the Door* (London, 1961); *The Death of William Posters* (London, 1965); *A Tree on Fire* (London, 1967); *A Start in Life* (London, 1970); *Travels in Nihilon* (London, 1971); *The Flame of Life* (London, 1974); *The Widower's Son* (London, 1976); *The Storyteller* (London, 1979); *Her Victory* (London, 1982); *The Lost Flying Boat* (London, 1983); *Down from the Hill* (London, 1984); *Life Goes On* (London, 1985); *Out of the Whirlpool* (London, 1987); *The Open Door* (London, 1988); *Last Loves* (London, 1989); *Leonard's War: A Love Story* (London, 1991); *Snowstop* (London, 1993); *The Broken Chariot* (London, 1998).

V. SHORT STORIES. *The Loneliness of the Long-Distance Runner* (London, 1959); *The Ragman's Daughter and Other Stories* (London, 1961); *Guzman Go Home and Other Stories* (London, 1968); *Men, Women and Children* (London, 1973); *Down to the Bone* (Exeter, 1976); *The Second Chance and Other Stories* (London, 1981).

VI. PLAYS. *Saturday Night and Sunday Morning* (London, 1964); *Citizens Are Soldiers* (with Ruth Fainlight, adapted from Lope de Vega, *Fuente ovejuna*: first performed London, 1967); *Three Plays: The Slot Machine, The Interview, Pit Strike* (London, 1978).

VII. SCREENPLAYS. *Saturday Night and Sunday Morning* (Woodfall Films, 1960); *The Loneliness of the Long-Distance Runner* (Woodfall Films, 1962); *Counterpoint* (based on his novel *The General*: Universal Films, 1968); *The Ragman's Daughter* (TCP / Penelope Films, 1972).

VIII. CHILDREN'S BOOKS. *The City Adventures of Marmalade Jim* (London, 1967); *Big John and the Stars* (London, 1977); *The Incredible Fencing Fleas* (London, 1978); *Marmalade Jim on the Farm* (London, 1979); *Marmalade Jim and the Fox* (London, 1985).

IX. TRAVEL. *Road to Volgograd* (London, 1964); *The Saxon Shore Way* (with Fay Gidden, London, 1983); *Nottinghamshire* (London, 1987); *The Far Side of the Street* (London, 1990); *Leading the Blind: Century of Guide Book Travel, 1815–1914* (London, 1995).

X. AUTOBIOGRAPHY. *Raw Material* (London, 1972); *Life Without Armour* (London, 1995); *Alligator Playground Stories* (London, 1997).

XI. INTERVIEWS. John Halperin, "Interview with Alan Sillitoe," in *Modern Fiction Studies* 25 (1979); Joyce Rothschild, "The Growth of a Writer: An Interview with Alan Sillitoe," in *Southern Humanities Review* 20 (spring 1986).

XII. BIOGRAPHICAL AND CRITICAL STUDIES. John W. Aldridge, "Alan Sillitoe: The Poor Man's Bore," in *Time to Murder and Create: The Contemporary Novel in Crisis* (New York, 1966); Allen Richard Penner, *Alan Sillitoe* (New York, 1972); Eugene F. Quirk, "Social Class as Audience: Sillitoe's Story and Screenplay 'The Loneliness of the Long-Distance Runner,' " in *Mid-Hudson Language Studies* 1 (1978); Ronald D. Vaverka, *Commitment as Art: A Marxist Critique of a Selection of Alan Sillitoe's Political Fiction* (Stockholm, 1978); Stanley S. Atherton, *Alan Sillitoe: A Critical Assessment* (London, 1979); D. M. Roskies, "Alan Sillitoe's Anti-Pastoral," in *Journal of Narrative Technique* 9 (fall 1980); David Craig, "The Roots of Sillitoe's Fiction," in Jeremy Hawthorn, ed., *The British Working-Class Novel in the Twentieth Century* (London, 1984); Martin Booth, *British Poetry, 1964 to 1984* (London, 1985); H. M. Daleski, "Alan Sillitoe: The Novelist as Map-Maker," in Hedwig Bock and Albert Wertheim, eds., *Essays on the Contemporary British Novel* (Munich, 1986); Peter Hitchcock, *Working-Class Fiction in Theory and Practice: A Reading of Alan Sillitoe* (Ann Arbor, 1989); Geoff Sadler, "Alan Sillitoe," in *Contemporary Poets*, 5th ed., ed. by Tracy Chevalier (Chicago and London, 1991); William Hutchings, "Proletarian Byronism: Alan Sillitoe and the Romantic Tradition," in Allan Chavkin, ed., *English Romanticism and Modern Fiction* (New York, 1993).

XIII. CULTURAL STUDIES AND FURTHER READING. Richard Hoggart, *The Uses of Literacy* (London, 1957); Raymond Williams, *Culture and Society* (London, 1958); E. P. Thompson, *The Making of the English Working Class* (New York, 1966); P. J. Keating, *The Working Classes in Victorian Fiction* (London, 1971); Paul Fussell, *The Great War and Modern Memory* (New York, 1975); Roy Johnson, "The Proletarian Novel," in *Literature and History*, no. 2 (October 1975); John Atkins, *Six Novelists Look at Society* (London, 1977); Mary Eagleton and David Pierce, *Attitudes to Class in the English Novel from Walter Scott to David Storey* (London, 1979); Dale Salwak, *John Wain* (Boston, 1981); Gustav H. Klaus, ed., *The Socialist Novel in Britain* (Brighton, 1982); Gayatri Spivak, "Subaltern Studies: Deconstructing Historiography," in her *In Other Worlds: Essays in Cultural Politics* (New York, 1987); Brian Finney, *The Inner I: British Literary Autobiography of the Twentieth Century* (Oxford, 1985); M. M. Bakhtin, *The Dialogic Imagination*, ed. by Michael Holquist and trans. by Caryl Emerson and Michael Holquist (Austin, 1986); Pamela Fox, *Class Fictions: Shame and Resistance in the British Working-Class Novel, 1890–1945* (Durham, N.C., and London, 1994); William Harmon and C. Hugh Holman, eds., *A Handbook to Literature*, 7th ed. (New York, 1996).

GRAHAM SWIFT

(1949–   )

Gita May

GRAHAM COLIN SWIFT was born on 4 May 1949 in London, where he still lives and works. His father, Lionel Allan Stanley Swift, was a civil servant who served as a naval pilot in World War II; his mother, Sheila Irene Bourne Swift, stayed in London through the Blitz. Even though Swift did not experience the war personally, his fiction frequently refers to it while dealing with historical events and their impact on people, both collectively and privately. History, especially war, intertwined with mundane daily concerns is always a theme in his novels.

Swift attended Dulwich College (1960–1967) and obtained a B.A. and an M.A. from Queen's College, Cambridge University (1970, 1975). He also attended York University (1970–1973). After completing his education he worked as a part-time teacher of English at colleges in London (1974–1983). He had begun writing in his teens but decided to become a full-time author only in 1983, after the successful publication of *Waterland*, which was short-listed for the prestigious Booker McConnell Prize and won the *Guardian* Fiction Prize (1983), the Winifred Holtby Memorial Prize (1984), and the Italian Premio Grinzane Cavour (1987).

Swift, who is unmarried, has been living with the same woman for at least two decades. They have no children. An enthusiastic fisherman, he edited with David Profumo an anthology of fishing in literature from antiquity to the later twentieth century, titled *The Magic Wheel* (1985).

A superb storyteller, Swift knows how to use all the possibilities of the first-person narrative, with all the immediacy and spontaneity that this form entails. The constant subjective flow and ebb of sensations and emotions, and the ever present and intrusive recollections of past experiences, inform the narrator's story. Swift's intricate and boldly experimental narrative style, his skillful conjoining and juxtaposing of past and present in a seamless and highly suggestive narrative, his piercing insights into the complexities and ambiguities of family relationships and baffling contradictions of human behavior, and his uncanny ability to weave family sagas into the larger canvas of national history make him one of the most important novelists of the postmodernist era. He has been compared to James Joyce in the way he is able to unlock the poetry within the existence of quite ordinary people trying as best they can to cope with overwhelming events and to make some sense of their lives.

THE SWEET-SHOP OWNER

SWIFT's first published novel, *The Sweet-Shop Owner* (1980), is an engrossing chronicle of a middle-class British family presented through the flashbacks of Willy Chapman, an earnest, hard-working shopkeeper. The time frame of the novel is the last day of Willy's life, between the moment he wakes up at 4:30 in the morning, on a Friday in June 1974, and 7:30 in the evening of the same day, when he draws his last breath. Through bouts of angina relentlessly pressing on his chest, he relives in dreamlike sequences bits and pieces of the events, both big and small, of his existence.

In school sports, especially in distance running, in which he excelled, it looked as though Willy might become a serious contender on the world stage: "How brave, how solitary. The eternal athlete, the eternal champion, running into his future" (p. 195). At competitions his parents, smartly dressed for the occasion, were among the spectators, shouting themselves hoarse as they urged their son to take the lead:

There would be cries of delight as they watched him breast the finishing tape; frenzied clapping and self-important smiles as they watched him walk up to take the 440 Trophy, the Mile Cup, the *Victor Ludorum*. The

father would light a cigar. Honour to the family. Rejoicing in the home that night.

(p. 197)

But Willy's glory days were soon over. He did not
get to serve on the front line in World War II because of a stupid accident:

He had lost his balance on a pair of ladders, fallen off
and damaged his back. They wouldn't take him for a
soldier. He wouldn't have the opportunity, as they put
it, to "see action." Such a strange phrase and such an
odd notion—as if there were no action besides wars.

(p. 56)

As a result Willy's military service is of the most
humiliating kind. His limp becomes the butt of
cruel jokes in the barracks and mess halls:

He didn't mind the orders, the regimentation. He was a
performer, wasn't he? Give him the uniform, tell him
what to do, he'd do it. And it was easy to pretend to be
a soldier. To salute, to obey, to clomp one's black heels,
even with a limp, over the wooden barrack-hut floor.

(p. 58)

When Irene Harrison enters Willy's life, it is love
at first sight, at least for him. The Harrisons are
financially well off and socially well connected.
Willy and Irene are married, and her family money
sets him up in a sweets shop. For Willy, who had
been a printer's assistant, this is a significant step
up the social ladder. And for his parents this is a
cause for great rejoicing, for they had "lived to see
their son come into money and marry a beautiful
woman" (p. 46).

But a dark cloud hovers over the marriage. At
the age of fourteen Irene had been raped by a family friend. This violent act had caused a breakdown
from which she eventually recovered. But it left her
emotionally fragile, sexually frigid, and unable or
unwilling to be sexually intimate. She repeatedly
thwarts her husband's sexual advances: " 'Willy,'
she said, stopping him. He was poised and trembling, ready to take his gift. 'Willy, I'm sorry. I'm
not—all I should be. Do you forgive me?' And
what should he have done? Protested, demanded
explanations?" (p. 30). Irene eventually yields to
him, and a child, Dorothy (Dorry), is born. This
happy event brings about a brief rapprochement
between Irene and Willy, but soon thereafter Irene
takes refuge in a state of psychosomatic asthma
and invalidism:

No, she did not get better. How many more visits to
Doctor Cunningham? Though he never spoke again,
true to her command, to that suave-voiced man with his
files and sheets of notes. Nor was he asked. She made
sure of that. "They can do nothing, Willy.". . . In between her attacks her breath wheezed continuously, her
voice fluttered and rattled. . . . And that face slowly being worn away; the cheeks hollow and drained from
sleeplessness, the mouth stretched from the effort of
breathing. Only the eyes remained, ashy-blue and
steady, as if they watched in some mirror the dismantling of her other features and approved the process.

(p. 127)

As the offspring of this unlikely, ill-matched union, Dorothy grows up with bitter resentments
against both her parents, whom she judges harshly
and unfairly. She sees their marriage as one of convenience, her mother as a heartless and manipulative woman, and her father as his wife's
weak-willed slave. Willy realizes, too late, that he
has failed to communicate with his daughter on
the deepest level: "If the word love is never spoken, does it mean there isn't any love?" (p. 116).
The dying Willy's lingering hope that his daughter
will relent and return to him with greater understanding and compassion remains unfulfilled.
Ironically, he dies on her twenty-fifth birthday.

In his first novel Swift experimented successfully with the confessional, autobiographical
form and with a new kind of intertwining of
intimate, personal, and national history. The
world of small shopkeepers and the misunderstandings and ambiguities of family relationships
are probed through a narrative technique consisting of successive visual descriptions and
dialogues. Through the innermost hopes and frustrations of the dying Willy Chapman, the English
middle-class mentality of the mid-twentieth century is evoked with uncanny sensitivity and insight, but also with a sometimes cruel acuteness.

Willy Chapman as the quintessential loser is of
course not a new character in fiction. In many ways
he is a postmodern kind of Romantic unheroic
hero whose youthful dreams of transcendent
achievements are quickly crushed by personal circumstances. That he is desperately trying to make
sense of his life as it is ebbing away from him
makes his story especially compelling.

Past and present are interwoven through a back-
and-forth technique that superimposes scenes, dialogues, and images unfolding in the dying man's
feverish consciousness without the benefit of the

usual narrative transitions. But history is always there, if only in the background and in fleeting but suggestive references to such events as the Battle of Britain, the bombing of London, and the austere postwar years.

Willy Chapman is not the traditional narrator of the confessional, autobiographical novel, relating his life's story to a captivated and sympathetic listener or reader. On his deathbed he has little control over the memories that press upon his consciousness. Furthermore, he will not be given the time and opportunity to benefit from whatever self-knowledge and moral insight such a retrospective journey usually provides. For him it is too late. But this lends the autobiographical form a special kind of psychological realism, urgency, and poignancy.

SHUTTLECOCK

SWIFT's second book, *Shuttlecock* (1981), is a mystery novel as well as a psychological thriller that operates on several levels: it delves into the complex workings of personal and professional relationships, into humanity's relation to nature (including animals), into the ambiguous and frequently contradictory nature of love and family loyalty, into those unfathomable qualities that constitute moral and physical courage, and especially into the dangers involved in seeking a deeper knowledge of human beings and of life itself.

Once more we have a first-person narration. But this time it assumes the more direct and confessional mode of a diary inspired by the narrator's gnawing sense of guilt and unworthiness, and by his unrelenting need to look into the dark, hidden corners of his past. Prentis is the diarist and narrator, and for him writing, especially attempting to probe the inner recesses of his self, constitutes a novel, disquieting experience that he approaches in the most tentative terms:

And isn't it possible that this whole voluntary confession (I never dreamed I would be setting down things like this) is inspired by some upsurge of guilt where guilt should not apply, and that I over-sensitively exaggerate what I suppose to be shamefulness of my proclivities? What is healthy and normal in this sphere, after all?

(p. 75)

The initial impulse to write his confession had begun with the gnawing memory of how as a young boy he had manhandled, and at times even tortured, Sammy, a pet hamster he had received as a birthday gift:

It is over twenty years since my tenth birthday, since my hamster came to live in our house, but today I remembered it as if it still existed. I remembered its blond fur, its pink nose, its jet-black eyes which seemed, under certain circumstances, to be about to spill, like drops of ink, from its head.

(p. 5)

Prentis is a senior clerk in the crimes division of the London Police Department. His department, located in drab, subterranean offices near Charing Cross, has little to do with the usual day-to-day police activities. Its business, rather, is to deal with unsolved cases and, in the official phrase, with "dead crimes" (p. 15). Prentis considers himself an archivist rather than a policeman. Much of the information stored in the files of the department is of a highly sensitive, even inflammatory nature:

What then is the object of our department? You will be surprised—the police are no fools. They know that every scrap of information is worth preserving. If in every hundred files only one contains a fact that may be useful in future, then it is worth keeping a hundred files.

(p. 15)

As the son (and only child) of a World War II hero, Prentis is tormented by a feeling of inferiority and inadequacy. His father had been a handsome, successful, happily married, highly regarded, and socially well-connected engineer. Prentis keeps reading and rereading a memoir his father published about his World War II experiences, *Shuttlecock: The Story of a Secret Agent:* " 'Shuttlecock' was Dad's code-name during his final operations in France" (p. 49). The book, which enjoyed some success upon its publication in the mid-1950s, relates in vivid and compelling detail the story of Prentis' father having been dropped into France during the German occupation: he had been captured, stripped naked, repeatedly interrogated and tortured as an enemy agent in the cellars of a chateau, and somehow managed to escape just in time to meet the Allied liberating forces in 1944. Prentis keeps asking himself what such a terrible experience must have really been like, and finds it hard to reconcile the smooth, highly readable narrative with the horror of what took place in the Kafkaesque world of his father's cell. He is intrigued by the fact that the scenes of torture are always described in the scantiest detail, then reaches the understandable explanation that the human mind is blissfully forgetful about dreadful experiences.

Now, however, as a result of a stroke or mental breakdown, which suddenly occurred a year after his wife's unexpected death, and which the doctors have never clearly diagnosed, Prentis' father is deprived of the power of speech and faculties, and has been reduced to living in a home for the aged, insane, and disabled. Prentis dutifully visits him twice a week, spending many hours in the company of the mute old man, trying to decipher the mystery behind the still handsome but blank face and expressionless eyes, and observing the frequently perplexing behavior of the other residents of the home.

Prentis' own family life is far from harmonious. In the vain hope of recapturing the simple, spontaneous sexual pleasures he had enjoyed in the early years of his marriage to Marian, a slim, attractive, former physiotherapist with a pliable, docile character, as well as in what he calls a quest for "enlightenment," Prentis repeatedly subjects her to strenuous, contorted bedroom gymnastics. His discontent is heightened by the sullen attitude of his two rebellious and disrespectful sons, Martin and Peter, who spend all their free time in front of the television set, watching such mindless programs as *The Bionic Man* and hardly paying attention to their father when he comes home after an exhausting and frustrating day at the office.

A constant war of nerves pits Prentis against his family, whom he suspects of conspiring against him. There are tense scenes during which he senses that his authority is being directly tested and challenged by his elder son, Martin, with the secret encouragement of Marian and Peter. One such confrontation takes place after the boys have been deprived of their favorite pastime and Prentis discovers that a copy of his father's book, inscribed to him, has disappeared. That Martin silently and stoically withstands the physical punishment meted out to him by his enraged father arouses the latter's secret admiration and envy. In Martin, Prentis recognizes the moral courage and steadfastness that he is convinced he himself sorely lacks:

But I knew we weren't talking about just the television. I looked into his face. His cheeks were bright pink from the slapping he'd had. I thought of the cunning with which he must have planned this little operation, and the guile and resolution with which he had carried it out. Those glances out of the window; the readiness to go hungry, to provoke and endure punishment. He was brave, he was resourceful, all right. He was his grandfather's grandson. His eyes bored into me. How much did he understand?

(p. 84)

In his job Prentis has a difficult, frustrating relationship with his superior, Quinn, who treats him in an authoritarian, condescending way that only aggravates Prentis' anxieties and insecurities. Quinn entrusts Prentis with puzzling, apparently disparate assignments, repeatedly prodding him to see connections that he fails to detect. Prentis wonders if Quinn, like his sons, is testing his will and mettle, and suspects that some of the documents in the files he is asked to investigate and correlate are missing, perhaps stolen or hidden by his boss. He furtively engages in a secret investigation of his own that enables him to discover that there is a connection, after all, between the documents, and that his father may somehow be involved. But he is at a loss to pinpoint the nature of this connection. In the meantime Quinn continues his cat-and-mouse game with his subordinate after casually mentioning that he will soon be retiring and that Prentis will be his successor.

Eventually Quinn invites Prentis to his home, where he lives with three Siamese cats, and reveals to him that the missing documents indeed concern his father. They offer fairly convincing proof that, far from having been the peerless hero portrayed in *Shuttlecock*, he had broken down under torture, had betrayed other secret agents in his network, and, as a reward for his cooperation, had been allowed to escape. After several drinks Quinn confesses that he himself had been a coward during the Normandy invasion. Prentis turns down Quinn's offer to let him see the files in question, and, by mutual agreement, they are burned in the garden incinerator:

He flicked alight the cigarette lighter. Before setting the flame to the file he pulled out some of the documents and spread them loosely to help them burn. The papers blackened, curled and flared up. I thought of funeral pyres. I thought: they can arrest us for this.

(p. 200)

Now Prentis will never know the truth about his father's role in the war. But he prefers it that way, for, as he puts it in rather banal, clichéd terms, "What people don't know can't hurt them" (p. 212). In his heart, however, Prentis is convinced of the truth of those terrible allegations, and the likelihood that his father had been a coward and a traitor has a liberating effect on him. He still dutifully visits him twice a week and is determined never to pose those questions that might at one and the same time restore and destroy his father. But he has stopped reading *Shuttlecock* and, for the first time in his life, experiences a sense of release and freedom.

Quinn retires and Prentis is duly promoted. He inherits his boss's high-perched office, which enables him to observe his underlings through a glass partition, and he, too, will play mind games with his immediate subordinate. But his harrowing experience has taught him that all human beings are vulnerable and fallible, and this painfully acquired understanding makes him a gentler, more loving husband and a better father. Family harmony is restored, and on a bright summer Sunday, Prentis decides to forgo his visit to his father in order to take his family on an outing to Camber Sands, a beach on the English Channel that is still littered with World War II matériel. While their sons frolic in the sea, Prentis and Marian forget their bedroom sexual gymnastics and in the dunes make happily spontaneous love that is reminiscent of their early married life.

The novel ends on a tentatively positive, lyrical note of joyous affirmation of the perpetually renewed value of the simple, sensual pleasures of life and of the healing power of nature, with a final tribute to Sammy, the hamster who was the hapless victim of young Prentis' cruel love as well as the initial cause of his slow, painful, and at times nightmarish quest for enlightenment and self-knowledge.

At the core of the novel the reader is confronted with the perpetual conflict between the human need for truth and the more powerful drive for dominance. *Shuttlecock* is a fundamentally pessimistic work, because it makes quite clear that the strongest human impulse is a ruthless quest for power. It shows individuals relentlessly seeking, by any means available, to assert and maintain authority and control over others, be it the Nazis brutally humiliating and torturing their prisoners in occupied France or, on a far smaller scale, the young Prentis tormenting his hamster. At the center is Prentis the guilt-ridden narrator, paranoid

and secretly motivated by the need to demolish the image of his father as wartime hero in order to achieve a measure of self-respect and self-confidence, all the while trying to cope with his boss Quinn's disconcerting cat-and-mouse games and involved in a war of nerves with his passively resisting wife and two rebellious sons.

In this second novel Swift reveals that he has found a powerful, original way of using the first-person narrative in order to probe the darker corners of the human soul through juxtaposing individual memories against the cataclysmic events of twentieth-century history.

LEARNING TO SWIM AND OTHER STORIES

SWIFT's collection of short stories, *Learning to Swim and Other Stories,* appeared in Britain in 1982 and was generally well received by critics. When the collection appeared in the United States in 1985, however, the reception was much less favorable.

The story that gives its title to the collection is essentially the tale of a failed marriage. Its main protagonist is Mrs. Singleton (no first name given), who "had three times thought of leaving her husband" (p. 9). The first time they were students just graduated and not yet married. They were on a charter flight coming back from a holiday in Greece:

> They had rucksacks and faded jeans. In Greece they had stayed part of the time by a beach on an island. The island was dry and rocky with great grey and vermilion coloured rocks and when you lay on the beach it seemed that you too became a hot, basking rock.
>
> (p. 9)

On the plane she sensed that he had not enjoyed the holiday and thought she ought not to marry him. Nevertheless she did so, a year later. Mr. Singleton was a civil engineer and soon became a junior partner in a firm with a growing reputation. The couple moved into a large house with a garden and spent weekends in country hotels, and Mrs. Singleton enjoyed the comforts and material advantages that money provides. But her husband became increasingly withdrawn and uncommunicative. This was the second time she thought she should break off with him, because he seemed more attached to his bridges and tunnels than to her. But once more she failed to act on this impulse.

The third time it occurred to Mrs. Singleton that lovemaking had become a rare occurrence in their marriage. Then she unexpectedly became pregnant.

Mr. Singleton also had considered leaving his wife, first after a symphony concert, when he felt that her insistence on his becoming conversant with classical music and great books was meant to humiliate him. At school Mr. Singleton had been an excellent swimmer, breaking many records and winning numerous prizes. He felt that "swimming vindicated him" (p. 14). His accomplishments as a swimmer somehow excused his poor performance in such academic subjects as physics. But out of practical considerations he dropped swimming from his program and at the university concentrated on engineering. Yet "[s]ometimes he went for a dip in the university pool and swam slowly up and down amongst practising members of the university team" (p. 16). Later Mr. Singleton not only has frequent dreams about swimming, but also when he made love to his wife, "her body got in the way; he wanted to swim through her" (p. 16). The problem with Mr. Singleton is that he "did not know what fear was; the same as he did not know what fun was" (p. 27).

When Mrs. Singleton becomes pregnant, she thinks she has gained the upper hand with her husband: "He was excluded from the little circle of herself and her womb" (p. 21). Ironically, their son Paul is terrified of water, despite his father's repeated inducements:

Paul Singleton hated water. He hated it in his mouth and in his eyes. He hated the chlorine smell of the swimming baths, the wet, slippery tiles, the echoing whoops and screams.

(p. 27)

When Paul decides to overcome his water phobia, instead of swimming toward his father, who is urging him on from a beach in Cornwall, he kicks and strikes away from the shore, "half in panic, half in pride, away from his father, . . . in this strange new element that seemed all his own" (p. 28).

The message seems fairly clear: Paul, the offspring of an unhappy and ill-matched couple, will somehow manage to escape and to make it on his own in the world. Related in the rather detached voice of a third-person narrator, which establishes distance from the main characters and events, "Learning to Swim" is a minimalist short story that condenses the tale of a bad marriage into its bare, almost abstract, essentials.

"Hoffmeier's Antelope," narrated in the first person, focuses on Uncle Walter, a typically English idiosyncratic character. He is the deputy keeper of one of the mammal houses at the zoo of the town of Finchley, where he lives, and considers himself a lover of animals and of nature. Uncle Walter becomes particularly attached to the last known pair of a fictional species of antelope, named after the German-born zoologist who had identified the species and had been forced to leave his country in the 1930s. The pair of antelopes refuse to mate, and Uncle Walter's role, like that of any zookeeper, is to coax the animals to copulate, for he is determined that there will be an offspring of these rare creatures. He develops a paranoiac belief that the world is maliciously bent on destroying the Hoffmeier's antelope. At the same time the narrator is privy to a disquieting confession. In thirty years of marriage, his uncle has never been able to approach his wife, Mary, "without qualms" about what he calls her "secret regions" (p. 38).

"Gabor," also related in the first person, is a tale, both touching and humorous, of a refugee from Budapest in 1957. Gabor is a lanky, dark-haired boy who is welcomed into the family of the narrator, who at first does not take kindly to this intruder: "Though he was not a proper adoption and was to be with us at first only on what authorities called a 'trial basis,' I was envious of him as a substitute child" (p. 46). The initially hostile feelings toward the stranger eventually change into an acceptance and understanding of Gabor's plight, and a friendship ensues:

I took Gabor up on the train to London Bridge. . . . We had fun. We rode on the Underground and on the top decks of buses. In the City and around St. Paul's there were bomb-sites with willow-herb sprouting in the rubble. We bought ice-creams at the Tower and took each other's photo in Trafalgar Square. We watched Life Guards riding like toys down the Mall.

(p. 53)

When, upon his return from this excursion, Gabor is questioned about his experience, his enthusiastic response, in broken English, is "I like London. Iss full history. Iss full history" (p. 53).

In "The Son" the narrator is a Greek restaurant owner in London who is trying his best to cope with a burdensome World War II legacy: "What do you do when your country is in ruins, when a war's robbed you of a father, then a mother, and of a nice future all lined up for you in the family business?" (p. 125). His transplantation to London has not been an easy one, and he laments: "Yes, I want sunshine. I'm Greek. What am I doing in the Caledonian Road? I should be sitting in one of the big, noisy cafés on Stadiou or Ermou, clicking my beads and reading *To Vima*" (p. 125). His first endeavor, to find a wife, was realized in the person of Anna. He has never been able to bring himself to tell his son, Adoni, that he was adopted after his natural parents were killed in the war.

The story focuses on the narrator's ambiguous relation to his wife and to his son, as well as on the problem of selfhood and truth. At the end of the story the question is left unanswered: "Tell me, who are we? What's important, what isn't? Is it better to live in ignorance?" (p. 135). In the background, as in so much of Swift's work, looms the long shadow of World War II. Once more we are shown how irrevocably history intrudes into the lives of individuals.

The last story in the collection, "The Watch," differs markedly in both content and tone from the others. It is a dramatic fantasy with whimsical fairy-tale overtones about the inescapability of time and the stranglehold ancestors have on their descendants. The narrator, Adam Krepski, prefaces his story with this question: "Tell me, what is more magical, more sinister, more malign yet consoling, more expressive of the constancy—and fickleness—of fate than a clock?" (p. 158). Adam Krepski belongs to a family of clockmakers who, several generations earlier, had fled to England from the Polish city of Lublin in order to escape political turmoil. These were not ordinary craftsmen working in dim workshops but rather "sorcerers, men of mission" (p. 159).

On a September day in 1809, in Lublin, Adam Krepski's great-grandfather, Stanislaw, made the kind of breakthrough "which to the clockmaker is as the elixir to the alchemist" (p. 160). He invented a magic clock that not only required no winding but also seemed to confer upon anyone having access to it some measure of immortality. Time, for example, seemed to stand still for its creator, for after having established himself in London, he died at the age of 133, not of old age but as a result of being struck by a horse-drawn omnibus. Other members of the family who came into contact with the watch benefited from a similar reprieve from

mortality. These men had a strong misogynist bent and disdained women and "the breeding instinct" (p. 162). Looked upon as little more than property, the wives they chose were carefully kept apart from "the masculine mysteries of clock-making" (p. 162). What puzzles the narrator is the awesome loneliness that these Methuselahs must have experienced, having remained the sole survivors of their generations.

Adam Krepski's father was the rebel of the family; he vociferously refused to become a clock-maker. In 1910, at the age of fifteen, he escaped from landlocked Lublin and ran away to sea, eventually took up with the widow of a music-hall manager, impregnated her, and married her: "Thus I arrived on the scene" (p. 166). When in 1914 his father took once more to the sea, this time in the service of his country, a German shell sent him and the other members of the ship's crew to the bottom. Thus, by an ironic twist of fate, Adam Krepski could connect with the Napoleonic era through his great-grandfather, but had no memory of his father or, indeed, of his mother, who died of a combination of grief and influenza six months after learning of her husband's demise.

The magical watch comes into Adam Krepski's possession on the wedding anniversary of his marriage to Deborah, a primary school teacher: "Deborah and I waged war. We bickered, we quarrelled, we made threats" (p. 173). When, after four years of this tumultuous relationship, Deborah was told about the magical watch, she promptly left her spouse, she refused to coexist another hour with someone who had an "indefinite lease on life" (p. 173). Adam Krepski was thus left alone to support his 162-year-old grandfather. With his small savings he rented a cottage in Sussex and brought his reluctant grandfather there. But the latter, defying, or perhaps inviting, the wrath of the skies, braved a terrific storm and was struck down by lightning:

One of the trees had been split and felled by a scimitar of lightning. Grandfather lay lifeless beside its twisted wreckage, an anguished grimace frozen on his face. And in his waistcoat, beneath his sodden coat and jacket, the Great Watch, its tiny, perfect, mechanical brain ignorant of storms, of drama, of human catastrophe, still ticked indifferently.

(p. 179)

Adam Krepski, the lone surviving member of his family, the last of the Krepskis, is strongly tempted to throw away the magical watch but decides to keep it. It seems to have lost its spell, however, for he dies of natural causes at the relatively young age (in Krepski terms) of sixty-three.

The promise of immortality embodied in the magical watch has turned out to be a curse after all, a theme frequently encountered in the allegorical, fairy-tale genre to which this story belongs, a genre in which magic, charms, and spells are major ingredients. Swift succeeds in modernizing it through a compelling autobiographical narrative and a subtle interpretation of human motivation and psychology.

Learning to Swim and Other Stories, like Swift's novels, deals with the emotional stresses of family life and with individuals facing an existential crisis. These terse and pithy tales also exemplify his concern with showing how the past constantly impinges on and shapes the present.

WATERLAND

WATERLAND, Swift's third novel, was published in 1983 and established him as a major writer. Larger, bolder, and more ambitious in scope than his preceding novels, it was also his first work to appear in America (in 1983). Critics on both sides of the Atlantic greeted it with enthusiasm, and it was promptly nominated for the Booker McConnell Prize. Its plot is complex and weaves backward and forward in time. Furthermore, *Waterland* involves such dark themes as murder, abortion, and suicide, and it combines elements of the Gothic tale and the mystery story with disquisitions on such topics as love, sex, and the meaning of history for both families and individuals.

The story is related in the first person by Tom Crick, an English history teacher in his mid-fifties who has been forced into early retirement primarily because, in reaction to his students' contemptuous rejection of history as a valid discipline and their callow belief that only the present matters, he has abandoned the official curriculum in order to offer highly personal and intimate reminiscences about his own childhood and adolescence. Instead of lecturing about the French Revolution, for instance, he prefers telling his students, in a kind of stream-of-consciousness monologue that moves backward and forward in time, about his family history and about his personal experience as a child in the Fen country.

The Fens, the haunting setting of *Waterland,* is a low-lying region of eastern England, a marshland formed by silt over the centuries. It is evoked as a kind of mysterious, almost magical, place removed from the bustle of the modern world:

The silt accumulated, salt-marsh plants took hold, then other plants. And with the plants began the formation of peat. And peat is the second vital constituent of the Fens and the source of their remarkable fertility. Once it supported great forests which collapsed and sank when climatic changes caused water to re-immerse the region. Today, it forms the rich, black beet-and-potato-bearing soil which is second to none in the country.

(pp. 7–8)

The epigraph to the book, "Ours was the marsh country," from Dickens' *Great Expectations,* reinforces the message. From the outset Swift depicts, through strongly suggestive strokes, the peculiar character of the Fen country, with its broad sweeps of land and water merging under a low horizon. That its inhabitants, who live in a symbiotic relationship with nature and are frequently eccentric loners, are unpredictable and excessive in their behavior should therefore come as no surprise.

Waterland unfolds a dramatic event: on a July morning in 1943, the narrator, then an adolescent living in the cottage of his father, Henry Crick, a lockkeeper, discovers a dead body in the River Leem:

It bobbed gently. It swivelled and rocked in the eddies, face down, arms held out, bent at the elbow, in the position of someone quietly, pronely asleep.

(p. 22)

The body turns out to be that of one of Tom's friends, Freddie Parr, a garrulous, irrepressible fellow who frequently got drunk on whiskey stolen from his father.

Tom's mother had died while he was still very young, so he lives with his father, who is very good at storytelling, and his older half brother, Dick, who is mentally retarded. Dick can speak only in baby language, but he is capable of remarkable feats of dexterity and his physical strength is awesome. He feels much more at ease with machines than with people, and he is so fond of his motorbike that, for company and solace, he talks to it "more than he talks to any living thing" (p. 33).

His mental shortcomings had led his parents to curtail his education drastically:

Dick lacks, indeed, certain accomplishments which even the mechanically-minded find useful. Dick cannot read or write. He is not even good at putting a spoken sentence together. He has received a rudimentary schooling at the village school. . . . To the younger son was given the privileged role of the bright schoolboy of whom much was expected and who was therefore to be protected from all things menial.

(pp. 31–32)

Freddie Parr's heavy corpse is pulled out of the water, and a big gash on his temple rules out either a suicide or an accidental death. Freddie must have been murdered and thrown into the river. The entire experience, especially when Tom's father tries in vain to revive Freddie by giving him artificial respiration, is a terrifying one for the young boy, who has never seen a dead body before:

Thus I see us, grouped silently on the concrete tow-path, while Dad labours to refute reality, labours against the law of nature, that a dead thing does not live again; and larks twitter in the buttery haze of the morning sky, and the sun, shining along the Leem, catches the yellow-brick frontage of our cottage.

(p. 27)

Tom is obsessed with the mystery of Freddie's violent death. Freddie, when he was about the same age as Tom, had lived less than a mile away from the Crick cottage. Who could have been the murderer, and what might have been the motive for the crime? The mystery posed by this death constitutes the leitmotiv and unifying thread of the novel.

Meanwhile Tom is not only experiencing such sensual pleasures as swimming in the River Leem but also, and more important, is discovering the thrilling ecstasies of sex through secret trysts with Mary Metcalf, a farmer's daughter, who will eventually become his wife. Mary's father, Harold, is a well-to-to, ambitious, hardheaded farmer whose wife had died in the second year of their marriage, while giving birth to Mary. He dotes on his only child and sends her to an exclusive Roman Catholic school for girls.

Undoubtedly what initially draws the two young people together is the fact that both have no mother and both attend good schools above their station in life: Mary, the St. Gunnhilda Convent School, and Tom, the Gildsey Grammar School for Boys, where he is beginning to immerse himself in the history books that will determine his eventual choice of a career.

But an even more powerful impulse brings Tom and Mary into daily secret and feverish contact: an overwhelming, irresistible, mutual desire for sexual exploration and gratification. Their frantic meetings are described in memorable scenes that are almost comical in their graphically provocative detail. The fifteen-year-old Mary discovers she is pregnant when "her menstrual cycle, of which she was so proud, and so secretive, stopped cycling" (p. 224). So, since Tom and Mary love each other, why not get married?

It means we'll have to tell the world, that's all, and face the music. And then get married. It happens all the time. It's an old, old story.

(p. 227)

But Mary has other plans, and she tells Tom, "I know what I'm going to do" (p. 228). And what she does is horrific. She attempts to abort her child by jumping repeatedly from a five-foot windmill emplacement. Tom tries in vain to stop her:

And she jumps again, ignoring me, as if in serious practice for something, swinging her arms, screwing her eyes resolutely; as if she's not going to be deterred, as if this jumping's more important than anything else. And lands, in that abrupt, staggering fashion, then sinks onto her haunches.

(p. 252)

As a result Mary will not be able to conceive again. She becomes the dutiful wife of Tom and gives in to mysticism. In a fit of delusion brought about by her frustrated maternal instinct, she kidnaps a child, a reckless act that causes her to be arrested and eventually committed to a mental institution. It also contributes to her husband's dismissal from his job.

Tom Crick shares his students' doubts about history and the ways in which it tends to be mythicized, especially under the impact of nationalism and patriotism. But while recognizing the dubious nature of officially recorded history, especially as it is taught in schools and universities, he acknowledges history's impact on the present. Anniversaries and commemorations perpetuate certain historical events for obvious political and nationalistic reasons. Thus it is that the French national celebration of the fall of the Bastille on 14 July seems somewhat ironical when one considers what really took place:

Let us not overestimate the actual character or the actual achievements of the Fall of the Bastille. Seven prisoners released (that was all the fortress contained): two madmen, four forgers and a hapless roué. Seven heads—the governor and six of the defending garrison—paraded on pikes. Two hundred or so of the besiegers killed or wounded. The stones of the Bastille itself, a mountain of rubble, carried away by professional contractors and disposed of at a tidy profit.

(p. 155)

Thus Tom ends up agreeing with his students that the history taught in textbooks is bunk: "Hey, this is good. This is juicy. Forget the Bastille. Forget the March of History" (p. 167). And he therefore wants to encourage his pupils to question what they are taught in their history classes:

Children, don't stop asking why. Don't cease your Why Sir? Why Sir? Though it gets more difficult the more you ask it, though it gets more inexplicable, more painful, and the answer never seems to come any nearer, don't try to escape this question Why.

(p. 113)

As a history teacher Tom had used stories in order to make his subject more meaningful. But as a disaffected and disenchanted teacher he rejects the optimistic and all too facile belief in progress, subscribing instead to the more pessimistic and disabused view that history is cyclical and repeats itself. In other words, children "grow up pretty quickly to be like their parents, to make the same mistakes as their parents, . . . the same old things will repeat themselves" (p. 208).

Amid such disquisitions the narrative sequences keep going back to Tom's dramatic discovery of Freddie Parr's corpse. The mystery of Freddie's death is eventually unraveled as a result of Tom's quiet but persistent detective work. He is horrified to identify his brother Dick as the killer. Both Dick and Freddie Parr had solicited Mary's sexual favors, and in order to protect Tom, she had intimated that Freddie was her lover. Dick, the "potato-head" and "numbskull," reacted to this false statement with a fit of jealous rage that resulted in his murderous attack on Freddie. When confronted with the truth by his brother, he commits suicide. Mary's sexuality, as the focus of male desire, plays a crucial part in causing the tragic deaths of Freddie Parr and Dick Crick.

Waterland is a provocative novel, experimentally bold and passionately intense in the ways it deals with the loss of innocence and with the inescapability and inscrutability of the past. Its finely detailed first-person account by a history teacher who tries to come to terms with his past, with his marital difficulties, and with his failed career is storytelling at its most intriguing and compelling:

What do you think all my sounding off is about, and what do you think all these stories are for which I've been telling as a finale to my teaching career. . . . It helps to drive out fear. I don't care what you call it—explaining, evading the facts, making up meanings, taking a larger view, putting things into perspective, dodging the here and now, education, history, fairy-tales—it helps to eliminate fear.

(p. 208)

By rejecting the chronological narrative sequence, Swift made a significant contribution to the possibilities, as well as the means and methods, of postmodern fictional autobiography. In this he exemplifies the suspicion that a continuous, sequential, and chronological narrative tends, by its very nature, to falsify autobiographical truth. Furthermore, Tom does not relate his story from the vantage point of someone who views his life from a distance and who has acquired a sense of equanimity. He writes from the midst of his personal and professional disaster.

By harking back to the stark landscape and sturdy people of his youth, Tom hopes to uncover the reasons why things went wrong for his family, for himself and his relationship with Mary, and for his career as a teacher. History and storytelling are inextricably intertwined in *Waterland*, and Tom's sharing of the story of his life and his innermost thoughts with his callow, skeptical students is done in the hope of imparting to them a new, more meaningful, and authentic concept of history. Swift's rejection of conventional autobiographical narrative and the way in which it romanticizes or sentimentalizes the chaos and terror of lived experience represents writing from within at its best.

The critical success of *Waterland* prompted an outstanding adaptation for film by Peter Prince, directed by Stephen Gyllenhaal and released in 1992, in which Tom Crick is powerfully played by the renowned British actor Jeremy Irons. The film version generally remains remarkably faithful to the novel. It captures in stunning and memorable images the austere beauty of the Fens; it depicts in dramatic scenes, monologues, and dialogues Tom Crick's personal and professional difficulties; and by a skillful use of flashbacks it follows Swift's bold narrative technique, which ignores chronology and sequential storytelling in favor of shifting back and forth between past and present.

OUT OF THIS WORLD

Out of This World, Swift's next novel after *Waterland,* appeared in 1988. Comparisons between the two works were inevitable, and while *Out of This World* did not achieve the great critical success of *Waterland,* it was generally acknowledged as an example of Swift's demonstrated mastery of the art of the novel and as an affirmation of his reputation as a major talent of his generation.

The two main protagonists in the novel are the noted photojournalist Harry Beech, a widower, and his estranged daughter, Sophie. There has been no communication between father and daughter for ten years, ever since Harry's father, Robert Beech, a World War I hero and arms manufacturer, was killed in a car booby-trapped with a bomb by IRA terrorists, and Sophie was outraged to see Harry taking photographs of this horrific scene moments after the explosion. She looks upon such single-minded dedication to one's profession as monstrous. Furthermore, she had been raised by her grandfather after her mother died in a plane crash when Sophie was only five years old, and she had long harbored feelings of resentment toward her absentee father, always on far-flung photographic assignments. She had dearly loved her affectionate and generous grandfather, who had taken over her father's role. Thanks to him, her childhood had been a pampered and privileged one while her father was becoming a stranger to her.

Harry, now in his sixties, has given up photojournalism but not photography. He has grown more reflective about the circumstances and motives that propelled him into his demanding and frequently dangerous profession. He also relives some of the scenes, mostly dreadful ones of war and violence, he has witnessed and photographed over the decades: "If you're in the thing it's terrible, but there aren't any questions, you do what you have to do and you don't even have time to look" (p. 49). Besides, "the whole world is waiting just to get turned into film" (p. 13), and "seeing is believing and certain things must be seen to have been done. Without the camera the world might start to disbelieve" (p. 107). Harry also indulges in melancholy reminiscences about his own lonely childhood (his mother had died in childbirth) and about his beautiful Greek wife, Anna, who died tragically and prematurely in a plane crash on Mount Olympus while on her way to visit an ailing uncle.

Sophie is now married to the easygoing, good-natured Joe Carmichael, a travel agent she met on a trip to Greece. She is the mother of twin boys, Tim and Paul, and leads a comfortable life in New York. She has grown to appreciate the hard beauty of this city, but she is seething with feelings of anger and restlessness, and she recklessly indulges in a succession of fleeting adulterous affairs. Tormented by guilt over her promiscuity, which her husband does not suspect, and needing to gain insight into her torment, Sophie becomes the patient of an expensive Park Avenue psychiatrist, Dr. Klein. During the sessions with her analyst, Sophie conjures up nostalgic images of the happy times in her life, as a cherished and spoiled little girl and later, in the hedonistic 1960s, as a carefree young tourist in Greece, enamored with its people, its traditions, and its perpetual sunshine.

When Harry decides to marry a young woman in her twenties, he writes to his daughter, after much hesitation, in order to reestablish contact and to seek her consent. The letter has an unexpected effect on Sophie. She emerges from her embittered frame of mind and determines, on the spur of the moment, to go to England. The novel ends on a positive and hopeful note as an excited Sophie, sitting in the plane with her two boys, explains to them the marvels of modern air travel:

We're travelling in one direction but the sun is travelling in another. And the sun is moving slower than we are. Don't you think that's wonderful? To be moving faster than the sun? Of course, it's not that the sun is *really* moving. The sun isn't really going anywhere. It's that the earth— It's—

(pp. 201–202)

As in his previous novels, Swift deals in *Out of This World* with such basic, human, and compelling concerns as family, mortality, and history, both national and individual. Since the main focus here is the troubled relationship between father and daughter, he has devised two alternating narratives that complement and sometimes contradict one another: one by Harry, in the form of an interior monologue, and the other by Sophie, mainly in free-association monologues during her sessions with Dr. Klein, who as a faithful practitioner of Freudian analysis is careful to make his patient do all the self-revealing talking. The language of the book is therefore couched mainly in a two-voice monologue that allows the protagonists to give full expression to their innermost thoughts and feelings. There is an implied dialogue between the two monologues, and the reader becomes privy not only to both versions of the estrangement between father and daughter but also to a more profound generation gap in the way each of them experiences and interprets life.

But probably more important than the plot itself is the masterful way in which Swift intertwines personal and collective history and manages to contextualize the individual stories of a father and daughter, with their sometimes petty resentments and guilts, within the larger framework of the turbulent and frequently tragic saga of the twentieth century. Events of historical import are encapsulated in brief but arresting descriptions and in striking images evoking wars and revolutions, royal marriages and coronations, freshly liberated concentration camps and the Nuremberg trials, the protest movements during the Vietnam War and the missions to the moon. Swift's dense, rich prose succeeds in rendering the texture and actuality of these events as they etched themselves into the consciousness of a perceptive eyewitness. There is a strong emphasis on the visual, as befits a century increasingly in the thrall of photographic journalism and media reporting. For instance Harry, as a fledgling news photographer, had been assigned to cover the 1946 Nuremberg trials of Nazi criminals:

I was looking, as my employers were looking, as the whole world was looking, for monsters. Goering, Hess, Keitel, von Ribbentrop. . . . Capture in their faces the obscenity of their crimes, capture in their eyes the death of millions, capture in the furrows of their brows the enormity of their guilt. . . .

But I didn't find monsters. I found this collection of dull, nondescript, headphoned men, thin and pale from months in prison, with the faces of people in waiting rooms or people co-opted into some tedious, routine task. Only Goering rose—if this is the right phrase—to

the occasion, and with a smart line in sarcasm and courtroom repartee, played the part of stage villain.

(p. 101)

Swift is equally adept at capturing the intimate, private experiences of his characters, and he also knows how to evoke the fragile hopes and aspirations of ordinary people. Some of the most affecting pages of the novel describe the typically English lower-middle-class background of Joe Carmichael, his modest beginnings in Tottenham, north London, and the sad story of his "mum and dad," whose cherished dream of a secure, happy old age is thwarted by illness and death (pp. 153–156).

EVER AFTER

EVER After appeared in 1992 and, like *Out of This World*, was sometimes unfavorably and unfairly compared with *Waterland*. It nevertheless won the French Prix du Meilleur Livre Etranger. In it Swift resorts to an autobiographical first-person narrative in order to deal, once more, with some of the major themes of his fiction: the difficulties of family relationships, love and sexuality in all their carnality and spirituality, and especially death:

Death! Death! You think it is elsewhere, but it is suddenly all around you, like a mist, a tide. It springs up like overnight mushrooms, it descends like the ghostly parachutes of secret agents, slipping behind enemy lines.

(p. 207)

The narrator, Bill Unwin, is a fifty-two-year-old don, a childless widower who has recently recovered from a nearly fatal heart attack and is pondering the meaning of his existence. His reflections and reminiscences feel like memoirs from beyond the grave, so to speak, as he tells his reader: "These are, I should warn you, the words of a dead man" (p. 3). His near fatal experience has endowed him with a sense of personal and ironical detachment but also with a sense of renewal: "One of the disquieting thoughts that beset me in this curious post-mortal condition of mine is that everything might be beginning again. This *is* my second life, my reincarnation" (p. 87). At the same time, however, Bill is motivated by an urgent and irrepressible need to uncover the truth about himself and about the people who have been the closest to him, notably his mother, Sylvia Jane Unwin; his father, Philip Alexander Unwin; his stepfather, Sam Ellison; and his wife, Ruth Vaughan.

Bill Unwin was born in December 1936, "in the very week that a King of England gave up his crown in order to marry the woman he loved" (p. 63)—a reference to Edward VIII's decision to forsake the throne in order to marry Wallis Warfield Simpson. To Bill this coincidence seemed to be an omen. Romantic, triumphant, transcendent love would be the primary force governing his own life. Like Edward VIII, better known as the duke of Windsor, he, too, would sacrifice everything for love. Bill would forsake his budding career as an academic, a lecturer in English literature at the University of London with a possible future as a professor, in order to devote himself completely to being the manager of his wife's career. She was a famous actress who started out as a chorus girl, rose to being a nightclub performer, and eventually achieved celebrity and stardom. Love prompted Bill to become his wife's manager, literary consultant on Elizabethan and Jacobean plays, and essentially her husband and "stage-cuckold" (p. 121); Ruth Vaughan was inconstant and promiscuous. Bill came to bitter conclusions about love: "Romantic love. A made-up thing. A concoction of the poets. Jack shall have Jill. *Amor vincit omnia*" (p. 121).

In his self-exploratory quest Bill constantly identifies himself with Hamlet:

Fifty-two, you will say, is a little old to be playing Hamlet, but the fads of adolescence die hard. . . . I was for many years, for the best years of my life, a happy man. Yes, a happy man. But perhaps the pensive prince was always there, lurking in some morbid toy-box, a foil to the brightness of my days. And when the lights suddenly went out, less than two years ago, he popped up again with a vengeance—vengeance being another of his preoccupations.

(p. 7)

Bill's perceived affinity with Hamlet is reinforced by his mother's adulterous affair with Sam Ellison, an American from Cleveland, Ohio, and founder of Ellison Plastics, to whom Bill consistently refers as the Claudius to his Hamlet. Bill is convinced that the premature and somewhat mysterious death of his father, a colonel who in 1946 committed suicide in Paris while in the diplomatic service, was caused by the discovery of his wife's infidelity.

Bill spent the earliest and happiest years of his life in Paris with his beautiful, hedonistic mother and distant father. He accompanied his mother on shopping sprees in luxury boutiques and immersed himself in silks and perfumes. From his mother Bill learned to see the world "as a scintillating shopwindow" and was initiated into the delights of "ogling and coveting," of spending money "to buy hats, necklaces, gloves, shoes, dresses, cakes" (p. 18). It hardly occurred to him then that "this same Paris which we came to in November 1945 had been occupied not so long ago by Hitler's soldiery and that our very apartment in the rue de Bellechasse, in the heart of the ministerial quarter, had perhaps been the temporary home—as it was our temporary home—of some official of the Reich" (p. 16).

The ironical twist in the novel is that Sam Ellison was not after all the Claudius to Bill's Hamlet. After persistent inquiries Bill finds out that his father's suicide had not been for the reasons he had suspected. Philip Unwin had been involved in liaison activities connected with the development of atomic weapons, but compelling reasons of moral conscience had led to a painful and insoluble conflict with his professional duties. The only way out of this impasse was suicide. For reasons of national security, the "romantic" explanation for his death had been promoted, and Bill's mother had cooperated by going along with an explanation that "served very fortuitously the interests of secrecy" (p. 205). So this father, whom Bill had so long venerated and cherished as a heroic victim, was after all only "a reluctant, a regretful, a squeamish spy" (p. 205).

In *Ever After* Swift paints several psychologically compelling portraits. There is, of course, Bill Unwin, the disillusioned, melancholy romantic, dreamer, and lover who has learned some hard lessons from life, notably that reality and personal fantasy hardly ever coincide, and who returns to the comforting world of books and scholarship after his wife's death. Sylvia Jane Unwin, Bill's glamorous, sophisticated, fun-loving mother, embodies Parisian elegance, style, and refined epicureanism. Ruth Vaughan, Bill's ambitious and unfaithful wife, is the consummate actress who projects the perfect illusion of naturalness in life and on the stage. Less convincing is the somewhat caricatured portrait of Sam Ellison, the ostentatious, blustery

American businessman. Overall, however, *Ever After* demonstrates Swift's uncanny ability to probe the complexities of the human psyche and his deftness as a storyteller who by means of a first-person narrative knows how to capture and retain the reader's interest.

LAST ORDERS

SWIFT'S *Last Orders*, published in 1996, also has unfairly been compared with *Waterland*. It is an original, powerful work that goes farther than any of Swift's previous novels in exploring the narrative possibilities of the dialogue form.

On the surface *Last Orders* tells a fairly simple, straightforward story. Three older working-class men and drinking buddies from Bermondsey, a working-class district in south London, travel in a rented Mercedes to the seaside resort of Margate in order to dispose of the ashes of Jack Arthur Dodds, a butcher by trade and a wartime comrade, in accordance with his last wishes. In this pilgrimage they are joined by Jack's adopted son, Vince.

Dealing with old-timers allows Swift to make a number of references to World War II and to such terrible events as the bombing of London, which had orphaned young Vincent. More than in any other novel by Swift, the emphasis is on human frailty and mortality. With the exception of Vincent, the characters are men in their late sixties and early seventies who have temporarily given up their everyday activities in order to perform a solemn ritual, the last rite of passage of their old friend. In the process they are led to contemplate their own impending demise and to take stock of their life experiences. But the seriousness of the occasion does not change long-entrenched habits, ingrained foibles, and trivial concerns. Nor does it overcome the primordial urge to endure and to pursue the quest for those comforting little pleasures and satisfactions that make life worth living.

Last Orders is probably Swift's most tightly structured and focused work. The novel does not have a principal character or single narrator; the story is told in a succession of first-person voices: notably by Ray, the office worker who is lucky at betting on horses; by Vic, the undertaker; by Lenny, who had to give up his ambition of becoming a boxer; and by Vince, a car dealer. The individual personality of each man is brought into strong re-

lief as he recounts his life; his experiences with war, love, and family; and his relationship with Jack, who was about to retire and move to a bungalow in Margate when he was stricken with stomach cancer.

Swift meets the challenge of painting a completely authentic and convincing picture of a specific English class and urban locale. For instance a number of scenes are set in the familiar and homely setting of a neighborhood pub, the Coach, which is the favorite meeting place of the friends. The opening scene, which takes place there, is described by Ray:

> It aint like your regular sort of day.
> Bernie pulls me a pint and puts it in front of me. He looks at me, puzzled, with his loose, doggy face but he can tell I don't want no chit-chat. That's why I'm here, five minutes after opening, for a little silent pow-wow with a pint glass. He can see the black tie, though it's four days since the funeral. I hand him a fiver and he takes it to the till and brings back my change. He puts the coins, extra gently, eyeing me, on the bar beside my pint.
> "Won't be the same, will it?" he says, shaking his head and looking a little way along the bar, like at unoccupied space. "Won't be the same."
> I say, "You aint seen the last of him yet."
> He says, "You what?"
> I sip the froth off my beer. "I said you aint seen the last of him yet."
> He frowns, scratching his cheek, looking at me. "Course, Ray," he says and moves off down the bar.
> I never meant to make no joke of it.
>
> (p. 1)

Throughout the novel Swift allows his characters to speak in their own words, in the colorful, lower-class colloquialisms of south London. Since the narrators have little formal education, they are necessarily limited in their intellectual and cultural references, and their dialogues and interior monologues are consistently rendered in an earthy, pungent English that, with its phrasing and rhythms, can express a rich gamut of thoughts and emotions, from the quotidian and jocular to the introspective and the subliminally lyrical and poetic.

This technique of effacing the omniscient authorial voice in favor of dialogues and monologues endows Swift's characters with a stark kind of psychological realism reinforced by the unspoken epic drama, even the austere grandeur, conveyed by their unpretentious and simple dignity and humanity. *Last Orders* is a bold and successful experiment in renewing the age-old theme of the fragility of the human condition as it is experienced and expressed by ordinary, aging Londoners facing and coming to terms with the basic truths of their lives during a funeral pilgrimage. And, as always with Swift, individual narratives are embedded within the larger canvas of some of the cataclysmic historical events of the twentieth century.

CONCLUSION

THE great success of *Waterland* has all too frequently caused critics to judge Swift's subsequent fiction in light of that novel. To focus on *Waterland* at the expense of his other works is to make a premature and all too facile judgment of his important contribution as one of the outstanding writers of his generation.

Since his first novel, *The Sweet-Shop Owner,* Swift has single-mindedly continued to explore the themes and narrative techniques that have established his reputation as a powerful chronicler of characters deeply affected in some way by the great events of the twentieth century. His deft intertwining of private and public history within one narrative singles him out as an author with a keen awareness of what it means to have lived in an age of social, political, and scientific upheavals. At the same time Swift has brilliantly pursued his profound interest in the first-person retrospective and confessional mode as a means of revealing the complexities of individual psychological motivation and truth. Furthermore, as a child of post–World War II England, Swift is young enough to meet our expectations of future great achievements in a literary genre to which he has been so consistently, passionately, and uncompromisingly dedicated.

SELECTED BIBLIOGRAPHY

I. NOVELS. *The Sweet-Shop Owner* (London, 1980; New York, 1985); *Shuttlecock* (London, 1981); *Waterland* (London and New York, 1983); *Out of this World* (London, 1988); *Ever After* (London, 1992); *Last Orders* (London, 1996).

II. SHORT STORIES. *Learning to Swim and Other Stories* (London, 1982; New York, 1985).

III. OTHER WORK. *The Magic Wheel,* ed. with David Profumo (London, 1985), an anthology.

IV. CRITICAL STUDIES. Ivan Del Janik, "History and the 'Here and Now': The Novels of Graham Swift," in *Twentieth-Century Literature* 35 (Spring, 1989); Marc Porée, "Différences et répétition dans *Waterland* de Graham Swift," in *Tropismes,* série no. 4 (1989); Catherine Bernard, "Les Années quatre-vingt: Vers une autre alchimie romanesque," in *Caliban* 27 (1990); George P. Landow, "History, His Story, and Stories in Graham Swift's *Waterland,*" in *Studies in the Literary Imagination* 23 (fall 1990); Catherine Bernard, "*Waterland:* Lire et délire," in *Arts, littératures et civilisations du monde anglophone* 1 (1991); Sylvain Floch, "Sous la Voie lactée: Mythes féminins du cosmos et de l'histoire dans *Waterland* de Graham Swift," in *Arts littératures et civilisations du monde anglophone* 1 (1991); David Leon Higdon, "Unconfessed Confessions: The Narrators of Graham Swift and Julian Barnes," in James Acheson, ed., *The British and Irish Novel Since 1960* (New York, 1991), and "Double Closures in Postmodern British Fiction: The Example of Graham Swift," in *Critical Survey* 3, no. 1 (1991); Marc Porée, "La Voix et le débit. *Waterland,*" in *Arts, littératures et civilisations du monde anglophone* 1 (1991);

Bernard Richards, "Graham Swift and the Fens: A Study in Inter-Textuality," in *Etudes britanniques contemporaines* 0 (April 1992); John Schad, "The End of the End of History: Graham Swift's *Waterland,*" in *Modern Fiction Studies* 38 (winter 1992); Catherine Bernard, "Dismembering / Remembering Mimesis: Martin Amis, Graham Swift," in Theo d'Haen and Johannes Willem Bertens, eds., *British Postmodern Fiction* (Amsterdam, 1993); Ronald Shusterman, "Fragmentation et montage en littérature: L'exemple de Graham Swift," in Bertrand Rouge, ed., *Actes du Second Colloque du Cicada* (Pau, 1993); Ernst van Alphen, "The Performativity of Histories: Graham Swift's 'Waterland' as a Theory of History," in Mieke Bal, Inge E. Boer, and Jonathan Culler, eds., *The Point of Theory: Practice of Culture Analysis* (New York, 1994); Lailla Germanos-Thomas, "Historicité et métafiction dans *Ever After* de Graham Swift," in Max Duperray, ed., *Historicité et métafiction dans le roman contemporain des Iles Britanniques* (Aix-en-Provence, 1994); Richard Todd, "Narrative Trickery and Performative Historiography: Fictional Representation of National Identity in Graham Swift, Peter Carey, and Mordecai Richler," in Lois Parkinson Zamora and Wendy B. Faris, eds., *Magic Realism* (Durham, N.C., 1995); Peter Widdowson, "Newstories: Fiction, History and the Modern World," in *Critical Survey* 7, no. 1 (1995).

Pamela Cooper, "Imperial Topographies: The Spaces of History in *Waterland,*" in *Modern Fiction Studies* 42 (summer 1996); Sean P. Murphy, "In the Middle of Nowhere: The Interpellative Force of Experimental Narrative Structure in Graham Swift's *Waterland,*" in *Studies in the Humanities* 23 (June 1996); Bertrand Westphal, "Le

Complexe de Scheherazade: Temps et histoire chez Graham Swift," in *Etudes anglaises* 49 (January–March 1996); Heinz Antor, "Graham Swift, the Novelist," in *Anglistik* 8 (September 1997); Geoffrey Lord, "Mystery and History, Discovery and Recovery in Thomas Pynchon's *The Crying of Lot 49* and Graham Swift's *Waterland*," in *Neophilologus* 81 (January 1997).

V. Reviews. Frank Rudman, review of *The Sweet-Shop Owner*, in *The Spectator* (26 April 1980); John Mellors, review of *Shuttlecock*, in *London Magazine* (November 1981); Bryn Caless, review of *Learning to Swim and Other Stories*, in *British Book News* (December 1982); Sally Emerson, review of *Waterland*, in *Illustrated London News* (November 1983); Hugh Hebert, review of *Waterland*, in *Guardian* (1 October 1983); Michael Gorra, review of *Waterland*, in *The Nation* (31 March 1984); William H. Pritchard, review of *Waterland*, in *New York Times Book Review* (25 March 1984); Michael Gorra, review of *Learning to Swim and Other Stories*, in *New York Times Book Review* (23 June 1985); Jonathan Penner, review of *Learning to Swim and Other Stories*, in *The Washington Post Book World* (15 April 1985).

VI. Interviews. John Kenny Crane, "Interview with Graham Swift," in *Cimarron Review* (July 1988); Marc Porée, "Entretien avec Graham Swift," in *La Quinzaine littéraire* (1–15 April 1993); Bettina Gossmann, "Graham Swift in Interview on *Last Orders*," in *Anglistik* 8 (September 1997).

MASTER INDEX

it is over twenty years since my tenth birthday, since my [daughter] came to live in our house, but today I remembered it as if it still existed. I remembered its blind [...] its pink nose [...] its black eyes which seemed, under [...] [...] to be about to spill, like drops of ink, from its head.

(p. 3)

Prentis is a senior clerk in the crimes division of the London Police Department. His department, located in dank, subterranean offices near Charing Cross, has little to do with the usual day-to-day police activities. Its business, rather, is to deal with unsolved cases and, in the official phrase, with "failed crimes" (p. 15). Prentis considers himself an archivist rather than a policeman. Much of the information stored in the files of the department is of a highly sensitive, even inflammatory nature:

What is the object of our department? You will be informed—the police are no fools. They know that every scrap of information is worth preserving. If in every hundred files only one contains a fact that may be useful in future, then it is worth keeping a hundred files . . .

(p. 20)

As the son (and only child) of a World War II hero, Prentis is tormented by a feeling of inferiority and inadequacy. His father had been a handsome, successful, happily married, highly regarded, and socially well-connected engineer. Prentis keeps reading and rereading a memoir his father published about his World War II experiences, entitled *Shuttlecock: The Story of a Secret Agent*. ("Shuttlecock was his father's code name during his final operations in France" [p. 49]). The book, which enjoyed some success upon its publication in the mid-1950s, relates in vivid and compelling detail the story of [Prentis's] father having been dropped into France during the German occupation, he had been captured [...] tortured repeatedly, interrogated and [...] as a secret agent in the cellars of a chateau, and somehow managed to escape just in time to meet the Allied liberating forces in 1944. Prentis often asks himself what such a terrible experience must have really been like, and finds it hard to reconcile the so-well, highly readable narrative with the horror of what took place in the Kafka-

The following index covers the entire British Writers series through Supplement V. All references include volume numbers in boldface Roman numerals followed by page numbers within that volume. Subjects of articles are indicated by boldface type.

Boy in the Bush, The (Lawrence), **VII:** 114

Boy: Tales of Childhood (Dahl), **Supp. IV:** 204, 205, 206, 208, 225

Boy Who Followed Ripley, The (Highsmith), **Supp. V:** 171

"Boy Who Talked with Animals, The" (Dahl), **Supp. IV:** 223, 224

Boy with a Cart, The; Cuthman, Saint of Sussex (Fry), **Supp. III:** 191, 194, 195, 196

Boyd, H. S., **IV:** 312

Boyer, Abel, **II:** 352

Boyle, Robert, **III:** 23, 95

"Boys' Weeklies" (Orwell), **Supp. III:** 107

Bradbrook, M. C., **I:** xi, 292, 329; **II:** 42, 78; **VII:** xiii–xiv, xxxvii, 234

Bradbury, Ray, **III:** 341

Bradbury, Malcolm, **Supp. IV:** 303, 365

Braddon, Mary Elizabeth, **V:** 327

Bradley, A. C., **IV:** 106, 123, 216, 235, 236

Bradley, F. H., **V:** xxi, 212, 217

Bradley, Henry, **VI:** 76

Brady, F., **III:** 249

Braine, John, **Supp. IV:** 238

Brand (Hill), **Supp. V:** 199, 200–201

Brander, Laurence, **IV:** xxiv; **VII:** xxii

Branwell Brontë (Gerin), **V:** 153

Branwell's Blackwood's (periodical), **V:** 109, 123

Branwell's Young Men's (periodical), see Branwell's Blackwood's

Brass Butterfly, The (Golding), **Supp. I:** 65, 75

Brassneck (Hare and Brenton), **Supp. IV:** 281, 282, 283, 284–285, 289

Brave New World (Huxley), **III:** 341; **VII:** xviii, 200, 204

Brave New World Revisited (Huxley), **VII:** 207

"Bravest Boat, The" (Lowry), **Supp. III:** 281

Brawne, Fanny, **IV:** 211, 216–220, 222, 226, 234

Bray, Charles, **V:** 188

Bray, William, **II:** 275, 276, 286

Brazil (Gilliam), **Supp. IV:** 442, 455

"Bréagh San Réilg, La" (Behan), **Supp. II:** 73

"Break My Heart" (Golding), **Supp. I:** 79

"Break of Day in the Trenches" (Rosenberg), **VI:** 433, 434

"Breaking Ground" (Gunn), **Supp. IV:** 271

"Breaking the Blue" (McGuckian), **Supp. V:** 287

Breath (Beckett), **Supp. I:** 60

Brecht, Bertolt, **II:** 359; **IV:** 183; **VI:** 109, 123; **Supp. II:** 23, 25, 28; **Supp. IV:** 82, 87, 180, 194, 198, 281, 298

"Bredon Hill" (Housman), **VI:** 158

Brendan (O'Connor), **Supp. II:** 63, 76

Brendan Behan's Island (Behan), **Supp. II:** 64, 66, 71, 73, 75

Brendan Behan's New York (Behan), **Supp. II:** 75

Brennoralt (Suckling), see Discontented Colonel, The

Brenton, Howard, **Supp. IV:** 281, 283, 284, 285

Brethren, The (Haggard), **Supp. III:** 214

Brett, Raymond Laurence, **IV:** x, xi, xxiv, 57

Bricks to Babel (Koestler), **Supp. I:** 37

Bridal of Triermain, The (Scott), **IV:** 38

"Bride and Groom" (Hughes), **Supp. I:** 356

Bride of Abydos, The (Byron), **IV:** xvii, 172, 174–175, 192

Bride of Frankenstein (film), **III:** 342

Bride of Lammermoor, The (Scott), **IV:** xviii, 30, 36, 39

"Bride's Prelude, The" (Rossetti), **V:** 239, 240

Brideshead Revisited (Waugh), **VII:** xx–xxi, 290, 299–300; **Supp. IV:** 287

"Bridge, The" (Thomas), **Supp. III:** 401

"Bridge for the Living" (Larkin), **Supp. I:** 284

"Bridge of Sighs, The" (Hood), **IV:** 252, 261, 264–265

Bridges, Robert, **II:** 160; **V:** xx, 205, 362–368, 370–372, 374, 376–381; **VI:** xv, **71–83,** 203

Brief History of Moscovia . . . , A (Milton), **II:** 176

Brief Lives (Aubrey), **I:** 260

Brief Lives (Brookner), **Supp. IV:** 131–133

Brief Notes upon a Late Sermon . . . (Milton), **II:** 176

Briefing for a Descent into Hell (Lessing), **Supp. I:** 248–249

Bright, A. H., **I:** 3

"Bright-Cut Irish Silver" (Boland), **Supp. V:** 49–50

Bright Day (Priestley), **VII:** 209, 218–219

"Bright Star!" (Keats), **IV:** 221

Brighton Rock (Greene), **Supp. I:** 2, 3, **7–9,** 11, 19

Bring Larks and Heroes (Keneally), **Supp. IV:** 345, 347, 348–350

"Bringing to Light" (Gunn), **Supp. IV:** 269–270

Brinkmanship of Galahad Threepwood, The (Wodehouse), see Galahad at Blandings

Brissenden, R. F., **III:** 86n

Bristow Merchant, The (Dekker and Ford), **II:** 89, 100

Britain and West Africa (Cary), **VII:** 186

Britannia (periodical), **V:** 144

Britannia (Thomson), **Supp. III:** 409, 411, 420

Britannia Rediviva: A Poem on the Birth of the Prince (Dryden), **II:** 304

"Britannia Victrix" (Bridges), **VI:** 81

"British Church, The" (Herbert), **I:** 189

British Dramatists (Greene), **Supp. I:** 6, 11

British History in the Nineteenth Century (Trevelyan), **VI:** 390

British Magazine (periodical), **III:** 149, 179, 188

British Museum Is Falling Down, The (Lodge), **Supp. IV:** 363, 365, 367, 369–370, 371

British Women Go to War (Priestley), **VII:** 212

Briton (Smollett), **III:** 149

Brittain, Vera, **II:** 246

Britten, Benjamin, **Supp. IV:** 424

"Broad Church, The" (Stephen), **V:** 283

Broadbent, J. B., **II:** 102, 116

Broadcast Talks (Lewis), **Supp. III:** 248

Broken Chariot, The (Sillitoe), **Supp. V:** 411, 421

Broken Cistern, The (Dobrée), **V:** 221, 234

Broken Heart, The (Ford), **II:** 89, 92, 93–98, 99, 100

"Broken Wings, The" (James), **VI:** 69

Brome, Richard, **II:** 87

Brontë, Anne, **IV:** 30; **V:** xviii, xx, xxi, 105, 106, 108, 110, 112–119, 122, 126, **128–130,** 131, 132, **134–135, 140–141, 145, 150, 153; Supp. III:** 195; **Supp. IV:** 239

Brontë, Branwell, **V:** xvii, 13, 105, 106, 108–112, 117–119, 121–124, 126, 130, 131, 135, 141, 145, 150, 153

Brontë, Charlotte, **III:** 338, 344, 345; **IV:** 30, 106, 120; **V:** xvii, xx–xxii, 3, 13–14, 20, 68, 105–107, **108–112,** 113–118, **119–126,** 127, 129, 130–140, 144, 145–150, 152, 286; **Supp. III:** 144, 146; **Supp. IV:** 146, 471

Brontë, Emily, **III:** 333, 338, 344, 345; **IV:** ix, xvii, xx–xxi, 13, 14, 105, 106, 108, 110, **112–117,** 118, 122, 130, 131, **132–135, 141–145,** 147, 150, 152–153, 254; **Supp. III:** 144; **Supp. IV:** 462, 513

Brontë, Patrick, **V:** 105–108, 109, 122, 146, 151

Brontë Poems (ed. Benson), **V:** 133, 151

Brontë Story, The: A Reconsideration of Mrs. Gaskell's "Life of Charlotte Brontë" (Lane), **V:** 13n, 16

Brontës, The, Their Lives, Friendships and Correspondence (ed. Wise and Symington), **V:** 117, 118, 151

Brontës of Haworth, The (Fry), **Supp. III:** 195

French Eton, A (Arnold), **V:** 206, 216
"French Flu, The" (Koestler), **Supp. I:** 35
French Gardiner, The: Instructing How to Cultivate All Sorts of Fruit-Trees . . . (tr. Evelyn), **II:** 287
French Lieutenant's Woman, The (Fowles), **Supp. I:** 291, **300–303**
French Lyrics (Swinburne), **V:** 333
French Poets and Novelists (James), **VI:** 67
French Revolution, The (Blake), **III:** 307
French Revolution, The (Carlyle), **IV:** xii, xix, 240, 243, 245, 249, 250
Frenchman's Creek (du Maurier), **Supp. III:** 144
Frere, John Hookham, **IV:** 182–183
Freud, Sigmund, **Supp. IV:** 6, 87, 331, 481, 482, 488, 489, 493
"Freya of the Seven Isles" (Conrad), **VI:** 148
Friar Bacon and Friar Bungay (Greene), **II:** 3
Friar's Tale, The (Chaucer), **I:** 30
"Friary" (Murphy), **Supp. V:** 329
"Friday; or, The Dirge" (Gay), **III:** 56
Friedman, A., **III:** 178, 190
Friel, Brian, **Supp. V: 111–129**
Friend (periodical), **IV:** 50, 55, 56
"Friend, The" (Milne), **Supp. V:** 303
Friend from England, A (Brookner), **Supp. IV:** 129–130
"Friendly Epistle to Mrs. Fry, A" (Hood), **IV:** 257, 267
Friendly Tree, The (Day Lewis), **Supp. III:** 118, 130–131
Friends and Relations (Bowen), **Supp. II:** 84, **86–87**
"Friends of the Friends, The" (James), **VI:** 69
Friendship's Garland (Arnold), **V:** 206, 213n, 215, 216
Fringe of Leaves, A (White), **Supp. I:** 132, 147–148
Frog He Would A-Fishing Go, A (Potter), **Supp. III:** 298
Frog Prince and Other Poems (Smith), **Supp. II:** 463
Froissart, Jean, **I:** 21
Frolic and the Gentle, The (Ward), **IV:** 86
"From a Brother's Standpoint" (Beerbohm), **Supp. II:** 53–54
From a View to a Death (Powell), **VII:** 345, 353
From Centre City (Kinsella), **Supp. V:** 272
From Feathers to Iron (Day Lewis), **Supp. III:** 118, 122, 123–124
From Man to Man (Schreiner), **Supp. II:** 439, 440, 441, 442, **450–452**
"From My Diary. July 1914" (Owen), **VI:** 446
"From Sorrow Sorrow Yet Is Born" (Tennyson), **IV:** 329

From the Four Winds (Galsworthy), **VI:** 276
"From the Frontier of Writing" (Heaney), **Supp. II:** 280
"From the Greek" (Landor), **IV:** 98
"From the Night of Forebeing" (Thompson), **V:** 443, 448
"From the Painting Back from Market by Chardin" (Boland), **Supp. V:** 40
From "The School of Eloquence" (Harrison), **Supp. V:** 150
"From the Wave" (Gunn), **Supp. IV:** 267
"From Tuscan cam my ladies worthi race" (Surrey), **I:** 114
Frost, Robert, **VI:** 424; **Supp. III:** 394–395; **Supp. IV:** 413, 420, 423, 480, 487
"Frost at Midnight" (Coleridge), **IV:** 41, 44, 55
Frost in the Flower, The (O'Casey), **VII:** 12
Froude, James Anthony, **IV:** 238, 240, 250, 324; **V:** 278, 287
Frozen Deep, The (Collins), **V:** 42
"Fruit" (Betjeman), **VII:** 373
Fry, Christopher, **IV:** 318; **Supp. III:** **191–210**
Fry, Roger, **VII:** xii, 34
Fuentes, Carlos, **Supp. IV:** 116, 440
Fugitive, The (Galsworthy), **VI:** 283
Fugitive Pieces (Byron), **IV:** 192
Fulbecke, William, **I:** 218
Fulford, William, **VI:** 167
Full Moon (Wodehouse), **Supp. III:** 459
"Full Moon and Little Frieda" (Hughes), **Supp. I:** 349–350
Full Moon in March, A (Yeats), **VI:** 222
Fuller, Roy, **VII:** 422, 428–431
Fuller, Thomas, **I:** 178; **II:** 45
Fumed Oak (Coward), **Supp. II:** 153
Fumifugium; or, The Inconvenience of Aer and Smoak . . . (Evelyn), **II:** 287
"Function of Criticism at the Present Time, The" (Arnold), **V:** 204–205, 212, 213
Funeral, The (Steele), **II:** 359
Funeral Games (Orton), **Supp. V:** 367, 372, 376–377
"Funeral Music" (Hill), **Supp. V:** 187–188
"Funeral of Youth, The: Threnody" (Brooke), **Supp. III:** 55
"Funeral Poem Upon the Death of . . . Sir Francis Vere, A," **II:** 37, 41
Furbank, P. N., **VI:** 397; **Supp. II:** 109, 119
Furetière, Antoine, **II:** 354
"Furnace, The" (Kinsella), **Supp. V:** 271
Furness, H. H., **I:** 326
Furnivall, F. J., **VI:** 102

Fussell, Paul, **Supp. IV:** 22, 57
"Fust and His Friends" (Browning), **IV:** 366
"Futility" (Owen), **VI:** 453, 455
"Future, The" (Arnold), **V:** 210
Future in America, The: A Search After Reality (Wells), **VI:** 244
"Futurity" (Browning), **IV:** 313
Fyvel, T. R., **VII:** 284

G. (Berger), **Supp. IV:** 79, 85–88, 94
G. B. Shaw (Chesterton), **VI:** 130
G. M. Trevelyan (Moorman), **VI:** 396
"Gabor" (Swift), **Supp. V:** 432
"Gabrielle de Bergerac" (James), **VI:** 67, 69
Gadfly, The (Voynich), **VI:** 107
Gager, William, **I:** 193
Galahad at Blandings (Wodehouse), **Supp. III:** 460
Galile (Brecht), **IV:** 182
Galland, Antoine, **III:** 327
Gallathea (Lyly), **I:** 200–202
"Gallery, The" (Marvell), **II:** 211
Galsworthy, Ada, **VI:** 271, 272, 273, 274, 282
Galsworthy, John, **V:** xxii, 270n; **VI:** ix, xiii, 133, 260, **269–291; VII:** xii, xiv; **Supp. I:** 163; **Supp. IV:** 229
Galsworthy the Man (Sauter), **VI:** 284
Galt, John, **IV:** 35
"Game, The" (Boland), **Supp. V:** 35
Game, The (Byatt), **Supp. IV:** 139, 141, 143–145, 154
Game at Chess, A (Middleton), **II:** 1, 2, 3, **18–21**
Game for the Living, A (Highsmith), **Supp. V:** 172
Game of Cricket, A (Ayckbourn), **Supp. V:** 3
Game of Logic, The (Carroll), **V:** 273
"Games at Twilight" (Desai), **Supp. V:** 65
Games at Twilight and Other Stories (Desai), **Supp. V:** 55, 65
Gandhi (film), **Supp. IV:** 455
Gandhi, Indira, **Supp. IV:** 165, 231
"Ganymede" (du Maurier), **Supp. III:** 135, 148
Gaol Gate, The (Gregory), **VI:** 315
García Márquez, Gabriel, **Supp. IV:** 93, 116, 440, 441, 454, 558
"Garden, The" (Cowley), **II:** 194
"Garden, The" (Marvell), **II:** 208, 210, 211, 212, 213–214; **Supp. IV:** 271
"Garden in September, The" (Bridges), **VI:** 78
Garden of Cyrus, The (Browne), **II:** 148, **150–153**, 154, 155, 156
"Garden of Eros, The" (Wilde), **V:** 401, 402
"Garden of Proserpine, The" (Swinburne), **V:** 320, 321
"Garden of Remembrance" (Kinsella), **Supp. V:** 261